ANSON'S
LAW OF CONTRACT

ANSON'S
LAW OF CONTRACT

32nd Edition

SIR JACK BEATSON

DCL, LLD, FBA

Formerly a Lord Justice of Appeal and Rouse Ball Professor of English Law, University of Cambridge

JOHN CARTWRIGHT

BCL, MA

Emeritus Professor of the Law of Contract, University of Oxford

PAUL S DAVIES

PhD, MA

Professor of Commercial Law, University College London

OXFORD
UNIVERSITY PRESS

OXFORD
UNIVERSITY PRESS

Great Clarendon Street, Oxford, OX2 6DP,
United Kingdom

Oxford University Press is a department of the University of Oxford.
It furthers the University's objective of excellence in research, scholarship,
and education by publishing worldwide. Oxford is a registered trade mark of
Oxford University Press in the UK and in certain other countries.

Twenty-ninth Edition 2010
Thirtieth Edition 2016
Thirty-first Edition 2020

Published in the United States of America by Oxford University Press
546 Fifth Avenue, New York, NY 10036, United States of America

British Library Cataloguing in Publication Data
Data available

Library of Congress Control Number: 2026935917

ISBN 9780198994992

Printed in the UK by Bell & Bain Ltd., Glasgow

The manufacturer's authorized representative in the EU for product safety is
Oxford University Press España S.A. of Parque Empresarial San Fernando de Henares,
Avenida de Castilla, 2 – 28830 Madrid (www.oup.es/en or product.safety@oup.com).
OUP España S.A. also acts as importer into Spain of products made by the manufacturer.

FSC www.fsc.org MIX Paper | Supporting responsible forestry FSC® C007785

PREFACE

It is over five years since the last edition of this book. In June 2020, after its completion but shortly before publication, Andrew Burrows, who has been one of its two predominant writers since the 29th edition in 2010, and was a pleasure to work with, became a justice of the UK Supreme Court. When OUP contacted us to discuss a new edition of Anson he understandably decided to stand down. The two of us were delighted that Paul Davies, who has made significant contributions to the subject and will take up the Downing Professorship of the Laws of England at Cambridge this autumn, accepted our invitation to join the team.

JB and JC

Our intention continues to be to reflect Sir William Anson's approach to provide a clear statement of the basic principles 'which govern the contractual obligation from its beginning to its end', illustrating 'general rules by the most recent or striking decision', and doing so 'in such a way as might best induce the student to refer to cases and to acquire the habit of going to original authorities instead of taking rules on trust'.[1]

The courts and the legislature have been active since the last edition. New material has been added to every chapter. The new legislative material in this edition principally constitutes reform of provisions of EU-derived law which were retained and assimilated into UK domestic law after withdrawal from the EU, in particular the Digital Markets, Competition and Consumers Act 2024, replacing (inter alia) the Consumer Protection from Unfair Trading Regulations 2008 (consumer rights of redress for misleading actions and aggressive practices). Again, however, the major changes have been as a result of the activity of the courts. The new decisions we discuss or refer to include 31 by the Supreme Court, 14 by the Privy Council, 49 by the Court of Appeal, and over 30 by the High Court. These are greater numbers than in the last two editions and the large number of new Privy Council decisions in this period shows the significance of its contribution to contract law.

We note in particular changes to the chapters on terms of the contract, duress and undue influence, damages, and third parties. The matters discussed include approaches to construction and implication, consideration of the extent to which good faith should have a role in English contract law, the difficulties in mounting a contractual claim for an account of profits and the status of the decision in *Attorney General v Blake*, 2000. There are also recent examples of the more flexible approach taken to enable compensatory damages to be more accurately calculated, and the trend to uphold all but the most extreme liquidated damages clauses as genuine pre-estimates of loss rather than penalty clauses. The Supreme Court and Privy Council cases on these topics include *Triple Point Technology Inc v PTT Public Co Ltd*, 2021 (interpretation of exemption clauses); *Barton v Morris*, 2023 (implied terms and failure of basis); *King Crude Carriers SA v Ridgebury*

[1] Preface to 6th edition (1891).

November LLC, 2025 (rejecting the approach of the House of Lords in *Mackay v Dick*,1881); *Times Travel (UK) Ltd v Pakistan International Airlines Corp*, 2021 ('lawful act' duress); *Law Debenture Trust Corp plc v Ukraine*, 2023 (duress, and the approach to good faith). They also include *One Savings Bank plc v Waller-Edwards*, 2025 (third-party misrepresentation and undue influence); *Sharp Corporation v Viterra BV*, 2024 (mitigation); *Primeo Fund v Bank of Bermuda (Cayman) Ltd*, 2023 (role of contributory negligence in contract) and *Secretary of State for the Department of Environment, Food and Rural Affairs v Public and Commercial Services Union*, 2024 (the first decision of the Supreme Court on the Contracts (Rights of Third Parties) Act 1999).

Other Supreme Court and Privy Council cases since the last edition include *National Union of Rail, Maritime and Transport Workers v Tyne and Wear Passenger Transport Executive*, 2024 (rectification); *Grondona v Stoffel & Co*, 2020, and *Henderson v Dorset Healthcare University NHS Foundation Trust*, 2020 (illegality); *Peninsula Securities Ltd v Dunnes Stores (Bangor) Ltd*, 2020, and *Harcus Sinclair LLP v Your Lawyers Ltd*, 2021 (restraint of trade); *Cobalt Data Centre 2 LLP v Revenue and Customs Commissioners*, 2024 (discharge by agreement: variation or rescission); *RTI Ltd v MUR Shipping BV*, 2024 (discharge by frustration and force majeure clauses); *Delta Petroleum (Caribbean) Ltd v British Virgin Islands Electricity Corp*, 2020 (affirmation); and *Ramsbury Properties Ltd v Ocean View Construction Ltd*, 2024 (repudiatory breach of lease).

We have again sought to refer to all significant decisions in the Court of Appeal and the High Court, but here single out only *IGE USA Investments Ltd v Revenue and Customs Commissioners*, 2021, and *MDW Holdings Ltd v Norvill*, 2022. The first deals with the application of the statutory limitation period in tort of deceit to a claim for equitable rescission. The second provides guidance on the use of hindsight in the context of claims for breach of warranty.

The initial drafting of each chapter was undertaken by either John Cartwright or Paul Davies. As in the last edition, Jack Beatson acted as general editor and is immensely grateful to them for doing all the heavy lifting. The three of us each read, commented on and discussed all chapters so that the final result remains a collaborative joint enterprise in the sense that term is used in the criminal law.

We are very grateful to our publishers' production team for their courteous, patient and efficient assistance. We are also very grateful to friends, colleagues and students for assistance, and for comments on the contents of the last edition. The law is stated as at 31 October 2025 but it has been possible to include some material since that date.

April 2026 JB, JC and PSD

OUTLINE CONTENTS

PART 5 REMEDIES FOR BREACH OF CONTRACT

PART 6 LIMITS OF THE CONTRACTUAL OBLIGATION

DETAILED CONTENTS

PART 1 FORMATION OF CONTRACT

PART 2 CONTENTS OF THE CONTRACT

PART 3 FACTORS TENDING TO DEFEAT CONTRACTUAL LIABILITY

PART 5 REMEDIES FOR BREACH OF CONTRACT

TABLE OF STATUTES

TABLE OF STATUTORY INSTRUMENTS

TABLE OF INTERNATIONAL RULES AND CONVENTIONS, EUROPEAN UNION AND OTHER NATIONAL LEGISLATION, AND RESTATEMENTS

TABLE OF CASES

(*Pages on which the facts of a case are given are printed in* **bold** *type*)

SOME ABBREVIATIONS USED IN REFERENCE

The Table of Cases contains the English Report references for cases reported in the Nominate Reports

Reports (except the Law Reports, 1865–date: see below, p xcii)

A & E	Adolphus & Ellis	QB	1834–1840
ALJR	Australian Law Journal Reports	Australia	1927–date
Aleyn	Aleyn	KB	1646–1648
All ER	All England Reports	All	1936–date
All ER (Comm)	All England Reports (Commercial Cases)	All	1998–date
ALR	Australian Law Reports	Australia	1973–date
Amb	Ambler	Ch	1737–1783
B & Ad	Barnewall & Adolphus	KB	1830–1834
B & Ald	Barnewall & Alderson	KB	1817–1822
B & C	Barnewall & Cresswell	KB	1822–1830
B & P	Bosanquet & Puller	CP	1796–1804
B & S	Best & Smith	QB	1861–1869
BCLC	Butterworths Company Law Cases	All	1983–date
Beav	Beavan	Rolls Court	1838–1866
Bing	Bingham	CP	1822–1834
Bing NC	Bingham, New Cases	CP	1834–1840
BLR	Building Law Reports	All	1976–date
Brown PC	Brown, Parliamentary Cases	HL	1701–1800
Bulst	Bulstrode	KB	1609–1626
Burr	Burrow	KB	1756–1772
C & M	Crompton & Meeson	Exch	1832–1834
C & P	Carrington & Payne	Nisi Prius	1823–1841
CB	Common Bench	CP	1845–1856
CBNS	Common Bench, New Series	CP	1856–1865
CLC	CCH Commercial Law Cases	All	1994–date
CLR	Commonwealth Law Reports	Australia	1903–date
CLYB	Current Law Year Book	All	1947–date
Cab & El	Cababé & Ellis	QB	1882–1885
Camp	Campbell	Nisi Prius	1807–1816

Cl & Fin	Clark & Finnelly	HL	1831–1846
Co Rep	Coke	KB	1572–1616
Com Cas	Commercial Cases	All	1895–1941
Con LR	Construction Law Reports	All	1985–date
Cowp	Cowper	KB	1774–1778
Cox	Cox's Equity	Ch	1783–1796
Cro Eliz	Croke, of the reign of Elizabeth	CP, QB	1582–1603
Cro Jac	Croke, of the reign of James	CP, KB	1603–1625
Dalison	Dalison	CP	1546–1574
DLR	Dominion Law Reports	Canada	1912–date
De G & J	De Gex & Jones	Ch	1857–1859
De G & Sm	De Gex & Smale	Ch	1846–1852
De GF & J	De Gex, Fisher & Jones	Ch	1859–1862
De GJ & S	De Gex, Jones & Smith	Ch	1862–1865
De GM & G	De Gex, Macnaghten & Gordon	Ch	1851–1857
Doug	Douglas	KB	1778–1781
Dr & Sm	Drewry & Smale	V-C	1860–1865
Drew	Drewry	V-C	1852–1859
E & B	Ellis & Blackburn	QB	1852–1858
E & E	Ellis & Ellis	QB	1858–1861
EB & E	Ellis, Blackburn & Ellis	QB	1858
EMLR	Entertainment & Media Law Reports	All	1993–date
ECR	European Court Reports	EEC and EU	1954–date
East	East's Term Reports	KB	1800–1812
Eden	Eden	Ch	1757–1766
Esp	Espinasse	Nisi Prius	1856–1857
EG	Estates Gazette	All	1858–date
EGLR	Estates Gazette Law Reports	All	1975–date
Exch	Exchequer Reports	Exch	1862–1865
FLR	Family Law Reports	All	1980–date
F & F	Foster & Finlason	Nisi Prius	1856–1867
H & C	Hurlstone & Coltman	Exch	1862–1866
H & N	Hurlstone & Norman	Exch	1856–1862
H Bl	Henry Blackstone	CP, Exch	1788–1796
HLC	House of Lords Cases	HL	1847–1866
Hare	Hare	V-C	1841–1853
Hob	Hobart	KB	1603–1625

ICR	Industrial Cases Reports	All	1972–date
IRLR	Industrial Relations Law Reports	All	1972–date
Ir Rep	Irish Reports	Ireland	1838–date
Ir Rep CL	Irish Reports, Common Law	Ir QB	1866–1878
J & W	Jacob & Walker	Ch	1819–1821
JP	Justice of the Peace and Local Government Review	All	1837–date
K & J	Kay & Johnson	V-C	1854–1858
Keen	Keen	Rolls Court	1836–1838
LGR	Local Government Reports	All	1903–date
LJ CP	Law Journal, Common Pleas	CP	
LJ Ch	Law Journal, Chancery	Ch	
LJ Ex	Law Journal, Exchequer	Exch	1832–1949
LJ QB	Law Journal, Queen's Bench	QB	
LT	Law Times Reports	All	1859–1947
Lev	Levinz	KB, CP	1660–1697
Ll LR	Lloyd's List Law Reports	All	1919–1950
Lloyd's Rep	Lloyd's (List) Law Reports	All	1951–date
M & G	Manning & Granger	CP	1840–1844
M & S	Maule & Selwyn	KB	1813–1817
M & W	Meeson & Welsby	Exch	1836–1847
Mod	Modern Reports	All	1669–1755
My & K	Mylne & Keen	Ch	1832–1835
NZLR	New Zealand Law Reports	NZ	1883–date
Noy	Noy	KB	1559–1649
P & CR	Property, Planning and Compensation Reports	All	1950–date
Peake	Peake	Nisi Prius	1790–1812
Peere Wms	Peere Williams	Ch	1695–1735
Ph	Phillips	Ch	1841–1849
QB	Queen's Bench Reports	QB	1841–1852
RPC	Reports of Patent Cases	Pat Cas	1884–date
Russ	Russell	Ch	1823–1829
SC	Session Cases	Scotland	1906–date
SCR	Canada Supreme Court Reports	Canada	1876–date
Salk	Salkeld	All	1689–1712
Sid	Siderfin	All	1657–1670
Sim	Simons	V-C	1826–1849

SLR	Singapore Law Reports	Singapore	1992–date
Sm & G	Smale & Giffard	V-C	1852–1857
Stra	Strange	All	1716–1749
Swan	Swanston	Ch	1818–1819
TLR	Times Law Reports	All	1884–1952
Taunt	Taunton	CP	1807–1819
Term R	Term Reports	KB	1785–1800
Ventr	Ventris	All	1668–1691
Ves Jun	Vesey Junior	Ch	1789–1817
Ves Sen	Vesey Senior	Ch	1746–1755
WR	Weekly Reporter	All	1853–1906
Wilmot	Wilmot	All	1757–1770
Wils	Wilson	KB, CP	1742–1774
Y & C Ex	Younge & Collyer (Exchequer)	Exch	1834–1842
YB	Year Books (with regnal year)		

Law Reports, 1865–date

LR CP	Common Pleas	1865–1875
LR Ch App	Chancery Appeals	
LR Eq	Equity Cases	
LR Ex	Exchequer	
LR HL	House of Lords, English and Irish Appeals	
LR PC	Privy Council Appeals	
LR QB	Queen's Bench	
LR Sc App	Scottish Appeals	
CPD	Common Pleas Division	1875–1880
Ex D	Exchequer Division	
App Cas	Appeals Cases	1875–1890
Ch D	Chancery Division	
PD	Probate Division	
QBD	Queen's Bench Division	
AC	Appeal Cases	1891–date
Ch	Chancery Division	
KB or QB	King's (Queen's) Bench Division	
P	Probate Division	1891–1971
Fam	Family Division	1972–date
WLR	Weekly Law Reports	1953–date

Neutral Citations

EWCA Civ	England & Wales Court of Appeal, Civil	2000–date
UKHL	United Kingdom, House of Lords	1996–2009
UKPC	United Kingdom, Privy Council	2001–date
UKSC	United Kingdom, Supreme Court	2009–date

Periodicals

ALJ	Australian Law Journal
CLJ	Cambridge Law Journal
CLY	Current Law Yearbook
Can Bar Rev	Canadian Bar Review
Const LJ	Construction Law Journal
Conv (NS)	Conveyancer and Property Lawyer (New Series)
Harv LR	Harvard Law Review
ICLQ	International and Comparative Law Quarterly
JALT	Journal of the Association of Law Teachers
JBL	Journal of Business Law
JCL	Journal of Contract Law
LMCLQ	Lloyd's Maritime and Commercial Law Quarterly
LQR	Law Quarterly Review
LS	Legal Studies
MLR	Modern Law Review
OJLS	Oxford Journal of Legal Studies
RLR	Restitution Law Review
SALJ	South African Law Journal
SJ	Solicitors' Journal

Other abbreviations

ALI	American Law Institute
CISG	United Nations (Vienna) Convention on Contracts for the International Sale of Goods
CMA	Competition and Markets Authority
CP	Consultation Paper
CPR	Civil Procedure Rules
FCA	Financial Conduct Authority
FSA	Financial Services Authority
OFT	Office of Fair Trading
TEU	Treaty on European Union
TFEU	Treaty on the Functioning of the European Union
WP	Working Paper

1

INTRODUCTION

The principles of the English law of contract are almost entirely the creation of the English Courts; until recently, the legislature has played a relatively small part in their development. They are mostly also a development of the last 200 years, for contract law is the child of commerce and has grown with the growth of Britain from a mainly agricultural into a mainly commercial and industrial nation. Blackstone's *Commentaries on the Laws of England*, which were first published in 1756, devoted 380 pages to the law of real property, and only 28 to contract. The industrial revolution, however, brought about a fundamental change in the structure of the British economy. Land was no longer the primary source of wealth. Mills, mines, and factories sprang up and raw materials were manufactured into products for sale in the markets of the world. The capital required for these enterprises was beyond the capacity of most private individuals and it was raised by public subscriptions for shares in joint stock companies or by loans from banks and other financial institutions. The growth of international trade further led to the creation of international commodity, shipping, insurance, and money markets, many of which were centred on London. All of these commercial developments depended—and still do depend—for their successful operation upon contract.

This chapter considers briefly: first, the nature and function of contract; secondly, the history of contractual obligations in English law; thirdly, the European and international influences to which the English law of contract has been exposed, particularly during the last 40 years; fourthly, the content of the contract law as set out in this book which is concerned with the 'general principles' of contract rather than the detailed rules applicable to different types of contracts; finally, the location of contract as part of the law of obligations and its relation to other parts of the law of obligations, tort and restitution of an unjust enrichment, and to property law.

1. THE NATURE AND FUNCTION OF CONTRACT

(a) PROMISE OR AGREEMENT

The law of contract may be provisionally described as that branch of the law which determines the circumstances in which a promise shall be legally binding on the person making it. Section 1 of the American Law Institute's *Restatement, Contracts (2d)*[1] gives the following definition:

A contract is a promise or a set of promises for the breach of which the law gives a remedy, or the performance of which the law in some way recognizes as a duty.

This definition is broadly acceptable, provided that it is realized that, in law, a promise may be constituted by an assurance that a thing *has been* or *is* (eg that the engine of a car has been recently overhauled or is now in good mechanical condition) as well as that a thing *will be*, and provided that it is also appreciated that most, but not all, contracts take the form of an agreement by which each party agrees to accept the promise or promises of the other in return for the promise or promises made by itself.[2]

(b) FUNCTIONS OF CONTRACT

The above definition is, however, very much a lawyer's definition and gives little indication of the nature of contract, and still less of its function. Most readers will have some general notion of what a contract is. Indeed, they will enter into a contract very frequently, in some cases almost every day, for example, a contract of carriage (travel by bus or train), or a contract for the sale of goods (the purchase of groceries), or for the supply of services (a haircut), or one involving both sale and the supply of services (having a meal at a restaurant). But the law set out in the following pages of this book is law which is mostly derived not from such simple consumer transactions, but from commercial transactions between business people and companies. Commercial transactions involve the exchange of land, goods, or services for money. This exchange is generally not immediate, as in a supermarket, but is to take place in the future. Contract has an important function of securing that the expectations created by a promise of future performance are fulfilled, or that compensation will be paid for its breach.

Take the example of the construction of an office building. The developer must first purchase the site. This will often be done with money borrowed from a bank, the developer promising to repay the loan with interest at some future date. It must then engage an architect to design the building, engineers to design the structural, electrical, and other components of the building, a quantity surveyor to draw up bills of quantities of work and materials that will be required, and a solicitor to do the legal work connected with the development. The building work will be put out to tender and the successful tenderer will be awarded the contract as main contractor. The main contractor will often subcontract parts of the work to other contractors. It may be that the developer will market the office space while the building is still under construction

[1] See below, p 22, n 122.

[2] Agreement is unnecessary for the enforcement of a promise in a deed (below, p 33). It is therefore sometimes characterized as a unilateral act, binding by virtue of the formality and not as contract, but this book includes it in the general definition of contract because it is a promise binding in law; see also Supply of Goods and Services Act 1982, s 1(2)(d); Consumer Rights Act 2015, s 3(3)(d). Agreement is perhaps not an altogether appropriate description of a unilateral contract, on which see below, pp 32–3, 40, 55–6.

and would-be occupants will agree to take a tenancy once it is completed. All of these relationships will depend on the promise of the participating parties that they will carry out their obligations in the future, whether these consist in the payment of money, or otherwise, and that they will be legally bound to their promised performance. No doubt, normally, each participant will duly fulfil its promise without the need for any intervention, or threatened intervention, by the law.[3] But the recipient of the promise (the 'promisee') is in the last resort able to rely upon the law to reinforce by appropriate sanctions the promise of performance. By entering into a contract, the promisee is able to have recourse to those sanctions.

Another important function of contract is a constitutive one: to facilitate forward planning of the transaction and to make provision for future contingencies.[4] The more complex the transaction, the greater the need for such planning and the more detailed the provisions that are likely to be made. First, and most obviously, a contract will normally establish the value of the exchange, that is, how much is to be paid for the land, goods, or services to be provided. In the above example, the developer will need to measure the likely cost of the development against anticipated revenue. While this may largely be a matter of estimate, the developer will seek, so far as is practicable, to establish by contract the value of items that make up that cost, for instance, the interest to be paid for the loan and the price to be paid to the main contractor.

Secondly, the contract will establish the respective responsibilities of the parties and the standard of performance to be expected of them. A building contract will incorporate the specifications for the work, sorting out what is to be done, the nature and quality of the materials to be used, and the date for completion of the work. It will provide for stage payments to be made by the developer. The respective responsibilities of the developer, architect, engineers, quantity surveyor, contractor, and subcontractors will also be established by contracts.

Thirdly, the contract enables the economic risks involved in the transaction to be allocated in advance between the parties. A building contract may provide, for example, for an increase in the price in the event of an increase in the cost of labour or materials to the contractor, and who is to bear the risk of strikes, bad weather, or fire. The party affected by the risk may then be able to cover it by insurance.

Finally, the contract may provide for what is to happen if things go wrong. Suppose that the contractor fails to remedy defects when required to do so by the architect, or that the developer fails to pay for work which is certified to have been done. The contract can provide for payment in advance,[5] and can determine whether the party not in default is entitled to terminate the contract and on what terms.[6] The contract may also provide for payment by the contractor of a specified sum by way of 'liquidated damages'[7] in the event of delay in completion beyond the date fixed.

Contract is, in effect, the instrument by which the separate and conflicting interests of the participants can be reconciled and brought to a common goal.[8] The importance

[3] Macaulay (1963) 28 American Sociological Review 55. [4] *Ibid.* [5] See below, pp 592, 610.
[6] See below, pp 150, 534. [7] See below, p 583. [8] See Gurvitch, *Sociology of Law* (1942).

accorded by English law to the planning function is shown by its preference for rules that provide certainty, particularly in commercial contracts where speed and certainty have been said to be of paramount importance.[9]

(c) FREEDOM OF CONTRACT

Contract has a significant role in any economic system. The issue is the extent to which the law does, or should, assume that parties enjoy freedom of economic decision when entering into contracts. The concept of freedom of contract has two meanings. The first is the freedom of a party to choose to enter into a contract on whatever terms it may consider advantageous to its interests, or to choose not to. Contractual obligation is thereby attributed to the will of the parties. This was one of the cornerstones of nineteenth-century *laissez-faire* economics.[10] Adam Smith in his *Wealth of Nations*, published in 1776, offered the first systematic account of economic affairs, championing the cause of freedom of trade against the economic protectionism current at that time, and freedom of contract was taken up as an ideal into classical economic theory.

When, therefore, in 1861, Sir Henry Maine wrote his *Ancient Law*, he postulated that the movement of progressive societies had hitherto been a *movement* from status (with its entrenched protection of privilege by legal and social restrictions) to contract. He considered this movement to be not only desirable, but inevitable. 'Imperative Law', he said,[11] has 'abandoned the largest part of the field which it once occupied, and [has] left men to settle rules of conduct for themselves with a liberty never allowed to them till recently'.

But freedom of contract also referred to the idea that as a general rule there should be no liability without consent embodied in a valid contract. This second and negative aspect of freedom of contract was influential in narrowing the scope of those parts of the law of obligations which deal with liability imposed by law: tort and restitution of an unjust enrichment.[12]

Today the position is seen differently. Freedom of contract is generally regarded as a reasonable social ideal only to the extent that equality of bargaining power between contracting parties can be assumed, and no injury is done to the economic interests of the community at large. In the more complicated social and industrial conditions of modern society it has ceased to have much idealistic attraction except, perhaps, to the proponents of a completely free market economy, who have advanced it in recent years in a modern and sophisticated way, some using the tools of micro-economic analysis.[13] But whatever its status may be as an ideal, the concept of freedom of contract has suffered severe inroads as the result of developments in modern social life and policy.

[9] See below, pp 34–5, 62, 155–6, 160, 525.

[10] See Atiyah, *The Rise and Fall of Freedom of Contract* (1979); Cornish, Banks, Mitchell, Mitchell, and Probert, *Law and Society in England, 1750–1950* (2nd edn, 2019) 194–7.

[11] *Ancient Law* (1861) ch ix, p 305.

[12] Below, pp 17–8.

[13] eg Posner, *Economic Analysis of Law* (9th edn, 2014) ch 4. Fried, *Contract as Promise* (2nd edn, 2015) provides a non-economic approach.

(i) Statutory restrictions

In the first place, statute law today interferes at numerous points with inroads into the freedom of the parties to make what contract they like. The relations between employers and employees, for example, have been regulated by statutes[14] designed to provide protection for employees, including rights relating to redundancy and against unfair dismissal, and to know their terms of service. The public has been protected against economic pressure by such measures as the Rent Acts,[15] the Consumer Credit Act 1974,[16] the Unfair Contract Terms Act 1977,[17] the Consumer Rights Act 2015,[18] and other similar enactments. These legislative provisions will override any contrary terms which the parties may make for themselves. Freedom of contract is also affected by statutorily imposed terms which set the 'default' rule for both consumer and non-consumer contracts, although this can sometimes be varied by the parties in non-consumer contracts.[19] Further, legislation[20] has been enacted to promote competition in industry and to safeguard the interests of consumers, and the Financial Services and Markets Act 2000 (amended by the Financial Services Act 2012) and the Financial Services and Markets Act 2023 contain provisions to safeguard the interests of investors.

There are also wide-ranging restrictions in the Equality Act 2010 on discrimination on such grounds as disability, race, religion, sex, and age in the provision of goods, facilities, and services, and in the selection of employees and in the terms upon which they are employed. These are a significant departure from the general freedom at common law to refuse to contract.[21] Although they primarily give rise to compensation orders, these statutory provisions can exceptionally lead to specific relief.[22] The prohibition on discrimination in the provision of goods, facilities, and services applies where the provision is made to the public or a section of the public.[23]

(ii) Standard form contracts: contracts of adhesion

Most contracts are not the result of individual negotiation. An employee's contract of employment, for example, will often be determined by a collective agreement made between trade unions and employers. Standard form contracts are also frequently used, even between businesses. These lay down the terms on which the supplier is prepared to

[14] Now the Employment Rights Act 1996, amended from time to time.

[15] In particular the Rent Act 1977, the Housing Act 1988, and the Renters' Rights Act 2025 (providing security of tenure and rent control for private residential lettings), the Housing Acts 1980 and 1985 (public sector tenants), and the Landlord and Tenant Acts 1985 and 1987 (landlords' duties of information and implied terms as to condition of premises and repair, and tenants' right to buy).

[16] Below, p 237 (as amended by the Consumer Credit Act 2006).

[17] Below, p 212.

[18] In particular, Part 2: below, p 227.

[19] eg Consumer Right Act 2015, ss 9–17, 34–37, 41, 49–52, below, p 189 (consumer contracts); Sale of Goods Act 1979, ss 12–15, below, p 182; Supply of Goods and Services Act 1982, ss 2–5, 7–10, 13–15 (non-consumer contracts).

[20] Fair Trading Act 1973 (now repealed); Restrictive Trade Practices Act 1976 (now repealed); Competition Act 1998; Enterprise Act 2002; Enterprise and Regulatory Reform Act 2013; Digital Markets, Competition and Consumers Act 2024.

[21] *Timothy v Simpson* (1834) 6 C & P 499. Cf *Constantine v Imperial Hotels Ltd* [1944] AC 693.

[22] Equality Act 2010, s 124.

[23] *Ibid*, ss 29, 31(2).

do business, or they embody or incorporate by reference the terms of a trade association. The freedom of the parties to negotiate is limited by such standard form contracts. Although a party, often a consumer, is free to decide not to deal with a particular retailer and to negotiate prices, delivery dates, and so on, in many areas similar terms will be offered by other retailers so that the individual has either to accept the terms laid down in their totality, or go without. Since, however, it is not feasible to go without many such goods or services, the individual is effectively compelled to adhere to those terms.[24] In certain types of standard form contracts, however, particularly between commercial parties (such as a contract for the charter of a ship, or for the construction of a building), the standard form is often extensively modified or supplemented by other terms appropriate to the particular transaction.

(iii) 'Compulsory' transactions

In the case of utilities such as water or electricity, which are in effect necessities of modern life, but the supplier is a monopoly or near monopoly, there may be a legal compulsion to supply, at least, domestic consumers. Under the legislation regulating such utilities, including electricity and gas where it is now possible to choose an alternative supplier, there is a duty to supply those who wish to be supplied,[25] there are certain prohibitions on undue preference and undue discrimination,[26] and a statutory regulator is given power to control prices and other terms of supply. This may be the modern equivalent of the common law duty on common innkeepers and common carriers to serve all comers on a reasonable basis,[27] probably because of their monopoly or near-monopoly position. These common law doctrines have not, however, been developed: the field has been left to the anti-discrimination legislation, and legislation for the control of monopolies and restrictive trade practices, and for regulating utilities. Where there is a statutory obligation to supply and no or little power to negotiate about the incidents of the relationship, the Courts may regard its compulsory nature as incompatible with its being contractual.[28]

(iv) Implied terms and the standard of 'reasonableness'

Finally, the negative aspect of freedom of contract, that there should be no liability without consent embodied in a valid contract, sits uneasily with the practice of implication of terms into the contract, and the use of the standard of 'reasonableness'

[24] Hence standard form contracts are sometimes referred to as contracts of adhesion, following the French (*contrat d'adhésion*): Saleilles, *De la Déclaration de la Volonté* (1901) 229.

[25] Gas Act 1986, s 10 (substituted by Gas Act 1995); Electricity Act 1989, s 16 (substituted by Utilities Act 2000). See also Water Industry Act 1991, s 37.

[26] Gas Act 1986, s 9(2) (substituted by Gas Act 1995); Water Industry Act 1991, s 2(3)(b) (substituted by Water Act 2003); see also Telecommunications Act 1984, ss 3, 8(1)(d), and Electricity Act 1989, ss 3(2), 18(4) (now repealed).

[27] *Clarke v West Ham Corp* [1909] 2 KB 858, 879–82. Note that almost all carriers contract out of their common law liability.

[28] *Norweb plc v Dixon* [1995] 1 WLR 636; *Read v Croydon Corp* [1938] 4 All ER 631.

as a way of dealing with gaps in the contractual language.[29] Terms are implied not only under statute, but also at common law. Although the basis of such implication is said to be 'necessity'[30] or in the case of custom 'presumed consent',[31] in many cases this is rather artificial, and in truth in many standard transactions the implied terms are the legal incidents of the transaction,[32] from which the parties are, subject to statute, often free to deviate although in practice many parties will simply be bound by those implied terms without seeking to negotiate otherwise. Freedom of contract is also difficult to reconcile with the adoption of the 'objective theory' which provides, in essence, that a person (A), whose conduct is such that the other party reasonably believes that A has assented to the terms of a contract, will be bound no matter what A's real intention is.[33] This rule can lead to the imposition of non-consensual obligations, since what creates the obligation is not consent in fact but acting as if consent is being given.

(v) Summary

In many areas of contract, freedom of contract in the classical sense is manifestly lacking. But English law and English judges still to a great extent proceed on the assumption that the parties are free to choose whether or not they will enter into a contract and on what terms. As recently as 2024, in the Supreme Court, Lord Hamblen and Lord Burrows observed:[34]

> The principle of freedom of contract is fundamental to the English law of contract. One aspect of that principle is that (subject to where the consent of a party is impaired by factors such as mistake, misrepresentation, duress, undue influence, or incapacity) parties are generally free to contract on whatever terms they choose. As Lord Diplock put it in *Photo Production Ltd v Securicor Transport Ltd*:[35] 'A basic principle of the common law of contract . . . is that parties to a contract are free to determine for themselves what primary obligations they will accept.' And in the words of Lord Toulson JSC in *Prime Sight Ltd v Lavarello*:[36] 'Parties are ordinarily free to contract on whatever terms they choose and the court's role is to enforce them.'

It may be objected that the general principles of contract law therefore present an inadequate, if not distorted, picture of modern economic life. This may be so, but it is nevertheless the case that the law does still rest on the assumption of freedom of choice, and where a relationship is entered into in which there is no choice, a Court may hold that it is not contractual.[37]

[29] eg *Tillmanns & Co v SS Knutsford Ltd* [1908] AC 406; *Abu Dhabi National Tanker Co v Product Star Shipping Co Ltd (No 2)* [1993] 1 Lloyd's Rep 397, 404.

[30] *Liverpool City Council v Irwin* [1977] AC 239, 254. See below, p 176.

[31] *Produce Brokers Co Ltd v Olympia Oil & Cake Co Ltd* [1916] 1 AC 314, 324. See below, p 178.

[32] *Mears v Safecar Security Ltd* [1983] QB 54, 78.

[33] Below, pp 34, 276–7.

[34] *RTI Ltd v MUR Shipping BV* [2024] UKSC 18, [2025] AC 675 at [41].

[35] [1980] AC 827, 848.

[36] [2013] UKPC 22, [2014] AC 436 at [47].

[37] Above, p 6.

(d) SANCTITY OF CONTRACTS

Closely associated with the concept of freedom of contract is another principle, the sanctity of contracts.[38] Business people in particular are concerned to ensure that the parties to a contract keep to their bargain and that as few avenues as possible should be afforded for escape from contractual obligations. In general, English law is reluctant to admit excuses for non-performance. But the Draconian requirements of commercial convenience have to be reconciled with the moral qualifications introduced by the need to discourage the grosser forms of unfair dealing. Thus the common law, and even more so equity, have admitted defences based on fraud, misrepresentation, mistake, duress (including economic duress), and undue influence, and endeavoured to curb the economic exploitation (in particular) of employees by the doctrine of restraint of trade. Although there is no general principle of 'inequality of bargaining power',[39] Courts take account of such inequality in interpreting the contract and in applying these doctrines. Additionally, statutory protection overrides unfair terms in certain types of contracts, for instance those made between consumers and businesses, and between employees and employers. It should not be imagined, however, that contractual obligations can be repudiated by one party merely because that party was in the weaker bargaining position. In the 'rough and tumble' of commercial relationships, various types of pressure are frequently brought to bear and terms may be imposed which are, objectively, harsh; but the contract will still bind.

Further, the law will not permit a person of full age and understanding who failed to read the contract, or to appreciate its full import and effect, to escape from the contract. It will not rewrite a contract for the parties or imply additional provisions merely because it would be reasonable so to do. And it will, in general, give effect to a written contract in accordance with its recorded terms, and not admit evidence to show that one party intended them to be construed in a different way from that which they actually express.[40]

In certain situations, however, the law will pronounce that the parties are relieved from performance of their obligations by reason of a change of circumstances occurring after the contract was made. But this principle—'frustration of the contract'[41]—is very limited in scope. It does not apply merely because a subsequent event changes the financial equilibrium of the transaction and forces a party who expected to make a profit from the transaction into a position of loss. The event must be of such a serious and fundamental character that to enforce the contract in the changed circumstances would be to enforce a radically different contract from the one which the parties made.

(e) THE INTEREST PROTECTED BY CONTRACT

The entering into of a contract creates an interest in each party that the contract will be performed.[42] The obligation may be strict, for example a seller's undertaking that it has good title to the goods sold, or it may be qualified, for example to use reasonable

[38] See Hughes Parry, *The Sanctity of Contracts in English Law* (1959), and below, p 17.

[39] *National Westminster Bank plc v Morgan* [1985] AC 686, 708; *Times Travel (UK) Ltd v Pakistan International Airlines Corp* [2021] UKSC 40, [2023] AC 101 at [26]; below, pp 411–2.

[40] Below, pp 164–5, 172, 192.

[41] See below, Chapter 14.

[42] See Fuller and Perdue (1936–37) 46 Yale LJ 52, 573; Atiyah (1978) 94 LQR 193; Taylor (1982) 45 MLR 139; Burrows (1983) 99 LQR 217; Friedmann (1995) 111 LQR 628; Coote [1997] CLJ 537.

care, as is the case in many aspects of contracts for services by professionals such as lawyers or surveyors. If one party fails, in whole or in part, to perform the obligations undertaken in the contract, the other party, whose economic, physical, and, in some cases, psychological interests will be affected, will be entitled to redress. But what form will that redress take?

Where the breach of contract consists of a failure to pay money, whether for goods bought and delivered or for services rendered, the redress for breach will often take the form of (direct) specific enforcement of the contract by an action (in debt) for the sum due.[43] Where the breach consists of the failure to render a non-monetary performance, for example, a seller's failure to deliver goods to a buyer, in some cases the injured party will also be entitled to (direct) specific performance of the other party's obligation. Normally, however, the redress will not take the form of specific performance of the contract, but will consist of monetary compensation.[44] How is that compensation to be assessed?

The object of compensatory damages in contract is to put the injured party, from the position it is now in after the breach, into the position it would have been in had the contract been duly performed. The injured party is entitled to protection of its interest in the performance of the contract. Suppose, for example,[45] a port authority by contract promises a car ferry operator that it will allow it to use the port facilities for car ferry operations during the coming year, but in breach of that contract repudiates the contract almost immediately after it is made. The wasted expenses sustained by the ferry operator may be no more than (say) the trifling expense of having prepared draft timetables of ship movements for the contract period. But it will nevertheless be entitled to be compensated in damages for the profit which it would have made on the car ferry operations during the year in question. Compensation assessed on this basis is, in effect, a substitute for the performance of the other party's obligation, whether by the payment of a debt that has accrued due[46] or by the rendering of other forms of performance.[47] This protection of the 'expectation' or 'performance' interest (these two terms are synonymous) is not peculiar to the English law of contract. It is a consequence of contract in all developed legal systems. Even if the contract is wholly executory, that is to say, nothing has been done by either party under it at the time of its breach, damages for lost performance will be recoverable.[48]

It has sometimes been suggested that, as an alternative to the expectation or performance interest, compensation in contract protects the claimant's 'reliance' and 'restitution' interests.[49] This is misleading. While reliance damages can be awarded for breach of contract, they are best viewed as an alternative way of protecting the claimant's expectation interest and are not protecting a separate reliance interest.[50] Again, restitution of money paid or the value of services rendered can be awarded where a contract has been discharged for breach or frustration or where a contract is ineffective, as well as in situations far removed from a contractual context. But that

[43] Below, p 591.
[44] Below, pp 545–6.
[45] See *Thoresen Car Ferries Ltd v Weymouth Portland BC* [1972] 2 Lloyd's Rep 614.
[46] Below, p 591.
[47] Below, p 594.
[48] But see the criticisms by Atiyah (1978) 94 LQR 193, and in *The Rise and Fall of Freedom of Contract* (1979).
[49] Fuller and Perdue (1936–37) 46 Yale LJ 52, 573.
[50] See below, p 555.

restitution is for the independent cause of action of unjust enrichment at the claimant's expense and is not a remedy *for* breach of contract.[51] In *Attorney-General v Blake*[52] the House of Lords held that an account of profits can be awarded, as an alternative to compensatory damages, for breach of contract to remove profits made by the contract-breaker. However, this remains an exceptional and very rare remedy.[53]

2. THE HISTORY OF CONTRACTUAL OBLIGATIONS IN ENGLISH LAW

The modern law of contract contains much which can properly be explained (if at all) only in the light of its history. Hence, even in a book which aims only at stating the principles of the modern law, it is desirable to summarize how that law developed. The law has not been moulded by any process of analysis and elucidation of the essential nature of a contract. Indeed, the very idea of enforcing promises or agreements as such, which seems most natural to us, may not be an early one in the history of any legal system. We shall find the key to the story by examining the conditions which the Courts have attached at different stages to the actions which they were willing to admit for the enforcement of the kind of rights which we now regard as contractual. The story can here be given only in the barest outline,[54] and it should be understood that there are some points in it which remain obscure or controversial.

(a) THE EARLY ACTIONS

(i) 'Wager of law'

Actions in what we call contract and tort were at first within the jurisdiction of local and manorial courts. The action would commonly end in a general denial of liability, upon which the defendant would 'wage his law', that is, undertake to come at the next court day and swear to this denial in the presence of neighbours (their number specified by the Court) who would then swear to their belief in this oath. If on the day all the oaths were made correctly, the defendant won. The efficacy of this depended partly on the fear of damnation for perjury, and partly upon standing among the neighbours (the city of London, for example, which lived by the credit of its citizens, set particular store by this mode of proof). This social sanction would be lost as lawsuits were diverted from the local setting into royal courts in Westminster.

[51] See below, p 606.

[52] [2001] 1 AC 268. See below, pp 616–7.

[53] *Morris-Garner v One Step (Support) Ltd* [2018] UKSC 20, [2019] AC 649 at [35], [82], [95]. See below, p 618.

[54] For fuller treatment, see Atiyah, *The Rise and Fall of Freedom of Contract* (1979); Baker, *An Introduction to English Legal History* (5th edn, 2019) 338–85; Baker and Milsom, *Sources of English Legal History: Private Law to 1750* (2nd edn, 2010) 231–337, 399–554; Cornish, Banks, Mitchell, Mitchell, and Probert, *Law and Society in England, 1750–1950* (2nd edn, 2019) 194–220; Milsom, *Historical Foundations of the Common Law* (2nd edn, 1981) 243–360; Simpson, *A History of the Common Law of Contract* (1975); Stoljar, *A History of Contract at Common Law* (1975).

(ii) Trespass

In the field of tort, for which the very rough medieval equivalent is 'trespass', a case would come to a royal court only if there was some royal interest, normally a 'breach of the king's peace'. That allegation had two other effects. It precluded the defendant from answering by wager of law and required the case to go to a jury. And as between the main royal courts, it gave jurisdiction to the King's Bench concurrently with the Common Pleas. The allegation itself became increasingly fictionalized in the early fourteenth century; and around the middle of the century the Chancery began to make writs of trespass returnable into royal courts with no mention of the king's peace. This was the effective beginning of 'actions on the case'; and logically plaintiffs should not have been able to sue in the King's Bench, and defendants should have been permitted to wage their law. But on both points logic was overruled. All actions of trespass and case could go to either of the royal courts, and all went to jury trial; and this was a cause of developments to which we shall come, by which remedies in contract came to be sought by actions in tort.

In the field of contract, jurisdiction as between local and royal courts came to depend upon the amount at stake. From a beginning in the thirteenth century, originally concerned only with the recovery of debts, a general jurisdictional barrier developed at 40 shillings, then a sum so large that very few transactions of ordinary people would reach it. But the amount was never altered, so that a period of rapid inflation in the sixteenth century brought transactions of falling real value to Westminster, and therefore to the modes of proof in use there. In particular, since there had been no equivalent of the king's peace to affect proof as well as jurisdiction, wager of law was often available; but those who swore to the defendant would be not neighbours but persons hired in Westminster. In the old contract actions, therefore, the focus of attention for lawyers and litigants was not some substantive law of contract but modes of proof.

(iii) Covenant

The word 'covenant' (*conventio*, agreement) is the nearest medieval equivalent to our 'contract'. But even in local courts an action for money due under a contract would be called not covenant but debt (or detinue if the action was for a specific chattel lent or bought, for example), so that actions called covenant mainly concern breaches of agreement for services like building or for sales or leases of land. The primary claim was for performance, and in royal courts the action was begun by a writ, known (from its opening word) as a *praecipe* writ,[55] ordering the defendant to keep the agreement; but judgments ceased to order specific performance and damages were awarded instead. Some think that the plaintiff would have to have done his part of the bargain, but we are not informed about the early requirements; and in the royal courts the question was suppressed by a new requirement about proof. Early in the fourteenth century it became settled that the plaintiff was not entitled to an answer unless he could produce a document under the defendant's seal (in illiterate times the equivalent of a signature)

[55] Baker, *Introduction to English Legal History* (5th edn, 2019) 65–6.

setting out the terms of the agreement. Soon after this the action of covenant fell out of use, not because of this requirement but because the kind of sealed document to which we are about to turn proved more effective. But covenant retained a negative importance: parties might contract for the building of a house, for example, not thinking of royal courts or sealing wax, and find the natural remedy barred.

(iv) Debt

Any claim for a fixed sum of money or a fixed quantity of fungible goods would in the royal court be made by the *praecipe* writ of debt. At first even a claim for specific goods would be made by the same writ, so that one who borrowed money and a book was seen to owe the book in the same way that the money was owed; but the separation of detinue need not be discussed here. In royal as in local courts, the defendant could normally answer by wager of law; and one lending a large sum or selling goods for a large price might take precautions, and this led to a separation between two principal uses to which the single writ of debt might be put.

(a) Debt on an Obligation. The simplest precaution for, say, a lender was to require the borrower to execute a document under seal, a bond. This was evidence not of a promise to pay but of indebtedness itself, and it was conclusive. The defendant could not deny that the debt was owed, though he could deny that the deed was his (non est factum).[56] But that was a risky issue to take: it went to a jury, who would compare seals etc; and if they found against the defendant he would go to prison. At law the defendant could not even say that payment had been made; and though he eventually got equitable protection from the Chancery in this situation, that was only after a long struggle between the competing goods of general certainty and individual justice.

But bonds were put to wider uses than ensuring that a lender or a seller would get the money that was due. One hiring a builder to build a house, for example, would take from him a bond by which the builder would acknowledge that he owed the customer an essentially penal sum, which bond would be void if conditions (written sometimes on the back of the bond, sometimes in a separate indenture) were satisfied; and those conditions specified the site, dimensions, materials, completion date, etc of the house. If the customer sued it would be on the bond for the penalty, and the builder could of course plead that he had satisfied the conditions. Conversely, the builder would take a bond from the customer, commonly for double the agreed price, to be void if the agreed price was duly paid. Such conditional bonds became the principal vehicle for large transactions; and they continued to be so until the Chancery began to relieve against penalties and until *assumpsit*[57] provided a simpler mechanism.

(b) Debt on a Covenant. A sealed document was never required in debt as it was in covenant. The lender could always sue for the repayment of the money lent, the seller for the price, and the builder or other provider of services for the agreed payment. But

[56] For the defence of *non est factum* in the modern law, see below, p 282.

[57] Below, p 13.

normally this was only possible when the plaintiff had done his part of the bargain, when the defendant had his *quid pro quo*. And the medieval word 'contract' did not have its modern meaning: it meant precisely the obligation 'contracted' by a debtor who had received his *quid pro quo*. But much of the reality is hidden by the defendant's usual denial by wager of law—not a denial of any specific facts but just that he owed. And the availability of wager had a further consequence. Only the debtor himself could swear that he did not owe: even if the debt had been publicly incurred it might have been privately paid. So the executor of a dead debtor could not wage law, and it was held by a perverse logic that the executor could not be sued. But that applied only to debt on a contract: the executor could be sued if the plaintiff had a bond which would anyway exclude wager.

The combined effect of these actions may be described in terms of an agreement to build a house. Well-advised parties would set it up by conditional bonds, so that the party alleged to be in breach would be sued in debt for the penalty and could plead that the conditions had been satisfied. If the agreement was informally made, the builder who had built could sue in debt for the price (normally answerable by wager of law). But the customer could not bring covenant if the builder did not build, because he had no document under seal; and probably he could not even bring debt to recover any money he had paid. This inequity played its part in the rise of *assumpsit*, where the writ asserted that the defendant had 'undertaken' (*assumpsit*) to do something; but it is important not to suppose that from the beginning lawyers saw that *assumpsit* was to become a general contractual remedy.

(b) *ASSUMPSIT*

(i) Misfeasance

Among the tort actions which came to royal courts when the need to allege a breach of the king's peace was dropped were some in which there was a contractual background to the wrong. In 1348 a ferry-man was sued: he had undertaken to ferry a horse across the Humber, but so mismanaged it that the horse was drowned.[58] Its owner sued in tort, and the defendant (knowing there was no sealed document) argued that the proper action would be covenant. The action was held to be rightly brought in tort: the plaintiff complained of the killing of his horse, not the failure to transport it; and such claims for 'misfeasance' regularly succeeded.

(ii) Nonfeasance

There was more difficulty if the defendant had made an undertaking but done nothing in the matter at all: this was clearly 'covenant' rather than 'trespass'. Many attempts to get 'trespass' remedies were made, mostly in situations in which performance of the *praecipe* order in covenant would be impossible (eg the date by which the house was to be built has passed) or would be no sufficient remedy (eg timbers have rotted because

[58] *Bukton v Tounesende, The Humber Ferry Case* (1348), translated in Baker and Milsom, above, n 54, 399.

the roof was not mended as promised). These would have been arguments for not suing in covenant even if the builder or roof-mender had made their promises under seal; and this may have been among the reasons why customers set up their agreements by conditional bonds in which the penalty would cover any consequential damage as well as the value of the performance. And one must remember that all these early attempts to use *assumpsit* for a nonfeasance were by plaintiffs who had omitted the proper formalities. Perhaps they were caught out by the only transaction of a lifetime large enough to come to a royal court. But their hard cases seemed to a judge in 1425 to threaten bad law: 'if this action [against one who had not built a mill as promised] should be maintained . . . then a man would have an action of trespass for every broken covenant in the world'.[59]

He was to be proved a prophet: but his logic was hard to overcome and we cannot be sure how and when it happened. A stage seems to be marked by a case of 1442 in which the defendant agreed to sell and convey land to the plaintiff from whom she took money. But she actually conveyed to a third party; and the plaintiff sued in tort for a deceit.[60] The agreement was made in London about land outside the city. If the land had been inside the city, the action would have been brought in city courts under the custom of London by which (a) actions in covenant did not require a document under seal, (b) the normal remedy in covenant was an order for performance, and (c) one who had put it out of his power to perform would be sued in deceit and imprisoned until he made fine with the city and repaid the money to his claimant. In London therefore the plaintiff's action would not have been a dodge to get round the absence of a sealed document but the natural remedy, essentially in rescission. In Westminster the logic got the plaintiff a remedy: but the Court could not order imprisonment (and therefore repayment of the money) but only damages.

This looked like enforcement rather than rescission, and the king's courts were left with a distinction without a real difference: the disappointed buyer who had paid for the land could get damages if his seller had conveyed to a third party, but not otherwise. Many approaches were tried; and around 1500 it begins to appear that nonfeasance was becoming remediable, at first only when the claimant had actually paid or there was some other detrimental reliance (and at any period one who has suffered no damage would normally prefer to hire somebody else rather than sue). Mutual promises do not become actionable until later in the century, by equally obscure stages; and the underlying illogicality is increasingly masked by elaborate and unreal allegations of deceit.

(iii) *Assumpsit* for money

From the use of *assumpsit* in lieu of covenant (where the absence of a sealed document might leave a plaintiff entirely without remedy) we turn to its use in lieu of debt (where the plaintiff always had a remedy, but might be faced by wager of law). But again one

[59] *Watkins' (or Wykes') Case* (1425) translated in Baker and Milsom, above, n 54, 425, 427 (Martin J).

[60] *Shepton v Dogge (Nos 1 and 2)* (1442), translated in Baker and Milsom, above, n 54, 433–8.

must not think that the end was aimed at from the beginning. The beginning is early in the sixteenth century in cases involving not money but fungible goods: a brewer contracts to buy malt or barley, and when it is not delivered has either to buy at a much higher price or to let his brewery go off stream.[61] The substantial claim goes not to the goods themselves but to the damage flowing from reliance upon the promise to deliver them; and this may be reflected in the language of deceit. When money is involved the reliance claim seems first to have appeared in situations involving third parties. Seller sells to Buyer in reliance upon the promise of a third party to pay if Buyer does not. It is Buyer who got the *quid pro quo* and contracted the debt; and any liability of the third party must be on the basis of reliance.[62]

One must not assume that the first use of the same logic as between two parties was intended as a conscious circumvention of debt. Debtor owes Creditor, and when pressed promises to pay the amount at a specified future date. Relying upon this promise, Creditor makes other bargains with third parties. When Debtor does not pay Creditor, Creditor cannot pay the third parties; and, particularly if he is a merchant, this failure so damages his own credit that he is ruined. This consequential damage is the gist of this action, not the original debt, which is not in principle even claimed. But jurors would include the amount of the debt in their assessment of damages; and such actions soon came to be used to recover debts but exclude wager of law.

Since debt was in the exclusive jurisdiction of the Common Pleas, it was the King's Bench that led in this development and an unseemly difference of practice arose. On the general issue of '*Non assumpsit*', where the defendant denied the undertaking, the Common Pleas would direct the jury that if they were to find for the plaintiff they must find both that the defendant was *indebitatus* (indebted) and that he made an express promise to pay the debt, the King's Bench that they need find only the indebtedness (because every debtor could be presumed to promise to pay: every contract executory imports in itself an *assumpsit*). But since the issue would be tried at *nisi prius*,[63] the judge actually directing the jury might not come from the Court in which the action had been begun. It seems clear that in *Slade's Case* the judges at *nisi prius* made a conscious effort to have the matter resolved. The jury was induced to bring in a special verdict that the debt was owed but that there was no subsequent promise to pay it. This was reported to the King's Bench, in which the action had been started; and instead of giving judgment that Court referred it to the Court of Exchequer Chamber, not really a Court but an informal conference of all the judges. That body was unable to agree; the King's Bench gave judgment for the plaintiff in accordance with their own practice; and this result was unwillingly accepted by the Common Pleas.[64]

Various consequences followed. Since the *indebitatus assumpsit* action was formally for reliance damage and not the debt, it now had to be made clear that the debt itself was recoverable as well as any damage, that the actions were alternative, and that the

[61] eg see the cases in Baker and Milsom, above, n 54, 448 and 452.
[62] Such cases are cited by Baker and Milsom, above, n 54, 454–6.
[63] Baker, *Introduction to English Legal History* (5th edn, 2019) 23–5.
[64] (1602) 4 Co Rep 91a.

one barred the other. And since formally the reliance damage flowed entirely from the promise to pay the debt, there was no logical need to specify how the debt had arisen; and so a defendant in the *indebitatus* action might not know the actual case he was to answer. The Courts therefore required minimum particulars to be given; and a series of 'common counts' developed stating that the debt was for goods sold and delivered, for work and materials, and so on. More importantly *Slade's Case* marked the effective end of wager of law; and it was necessary to make explicit the important consequence that executors could now be sued for simple contract debts. Nor was the ending of wager unequivocally beneficial: it turned out that jury trial could be manipulated by fraudulent plaintiffs; and in 1677 the Statute of Frauds provided that in certain situations action could be brought only if there was some written evidence signed by the defendant.[65]

With the important exception of agreements supported by sealed documents, in which covenant or debt still could and had to be brought, all contract litigation after *Slade's Case* was brought in *assumpsit*; and it was from this that the modern law of contract developed. It is indeed a general law of contract rather than a law about particular contracts as in Rome.[66] But its beginnings in tort, which remained obvious in the persistent language of deceit until the nineteenth century, inhibited the development of a satisfactory theoretical structure. Instead we have the 'doctrine' of consideration.[67] There has been much speculation about its 'origin', on the basis that it must have developed from some earlier phenomenon. Consideration as detriment to the claimant looks much like the damage he suffered when the case was put in terms of deceit or reliance, and this provides some explanation of the uselessness of past consideration and of the rule that consideration must move from the claimant. Consideration as benefit to the defendant looks much like the *quid pro quo* of debt; and it must be remembered that after *Slade's Case* the debt and therefore the *quid pro quo* was the only issue in *indebitatus*. Other origins have been suggested, such as the canonist idea of *causa* which indeed played some part in the Chancery. But the reality seems to be that sixteenth-century pleadings used the word to mean the reason for which the promise was given, and judges then and later decided which of these were a sufficient basis for legal action. If so, consideration is not so much a 'doctrine' as a considerable body of the substantive rules of contract.

[65] The long title of the Statute of Frauds is 'for prevention of many fraudulent Practices which are commonly endeavoured to be upheld by perjury and subornation of perjury'. In the modern law, only s 4 remains: see below, p 83.

[66] In Roman law, a promise or agreement was given legal recognition and enforcement as a contract only if it fell within one of a number of particular types for which an action was provided (such as sale, hire, partnership, mandate, loan of a fungible, loan for use, or a unilateral promise made and accepted in a formal oral exchange between the parties): Nicholas, *Introduction to Roman Law* (1975) 165–7. Modern European civil law systems retain the Roman law legacy of a strong doctrine of particular contracts which have special regulation in their Codes but have also, unlike ancient Roman law, added a general law of contract: see, eg, Bell, Boyron, and Whittaker, *Principles of French Law* (2nd edn, 2008) 297–8.

[67] For consideration in the modern law, see below, Chapter 4.

(c) SUBSEQUENT DEVELOPMENTS

There has been much later development, too detailed and perhaps too little explored by historians, to consider in this summary. Lord Mansfield in the eighteenth century and Lord Denning in the twentieth sought to rationalize consideration, but the substantive changes needed were too obtrusive. The English promissory estoppel,[68] for example, is a pale shadow of the American, perhaps because the lesser weight given in the USA to deeds left more obvious injustice if promisees sought to escape liability by reliance on the gratuitous nature of their promises. The American reliance basis for remedy, essentially as alternative to consideration, is also a reminder of the mongrel nature of the common law of contract.

The law started with covenant (or contract) as something essentially different from trespass (or tort). That difference was the continuing obstacle in the rise of *assumpsit*; and its overcoming introduced continuing confusion. It was nineteenth-century judges and writers, including Anson, who sought to restore contract law as a thing in itself: rules mostly about the formation of binding agreements, with ancillary rules about the damages recoverable for breach.[69] The impulse may have been partly juristic, partly due to commercial demands for certainty and for more sophisticated rules to deal adequately with the expansion of trade and commerce that resulted from the industrial revolution. Consideration (or a deed) is then represented as something like offer and acceptance: one of the requirements for formation. But it sprang from a law about tort, about damage suffered by the claimant at the end of the story rather than about the beginning of a binding relationship between the parties. Like many mongrels the result may not be elegant; but it is strong.

(i) The nineteenth century

We have noted that the concepts of freedom of contract and sanctity of contract were at their strongest during the nineteenth century. In 1875 Sir George Jessel MR stated:[70]

> if there is one thing which more than another public policy requires it is that men of full age and competent understanding shall have the utmost liberty of contracting, and that their contracts when entered into freely and voluntarily shall be held sacred and shall be enforced by Courts of justice.

This was said to have led to the reduction of supervision over the contractual terms to a bare minimum[71] and the deprivation of the tools available for such control of much of their effectiveness. The doctrine of consideration acquired a predominantly formal meaning, although it was on occasion used to invalidate unfair agreements.[72] A substantial part of the law of contract was attributed to the parties' agreement, and the role of equity, with its discretionary remedies, and its ability to avoid common law rules, was less central.

[68] Below, p 121.

[69] See Simpson (1975) 91 LQR 247.

[70] *Printing & Numerical Registering Co v Sampson* (1875) LR 19 Eq 462, 465.

[71] Atiyah, *The Rise and Fall of Freedom of Contract* (1979). But cf Simpson (1979) 46 U Chi L Rev 533; Barton (1987) 103 LQR 118.

[72] *Stilk v Myrick* (1809) 2 Camp 317; 6 Esp 129, below, pp 111–5.

At the same time, non-contractual liability was kept within narrow boundaries. As regards liability to make restitution of an unjust enrichment (then known as quasi-contract), Bowen LJ's famous statement that '[l]iabilities are not to be forced upon people behind their backs'[73] was profoundly influential. Indeed, Lord Sumner and Sir William Holdsworth argued that all such claims were founded upon an implied contract.[74] If there could not be a contract, there could not be an implied contract; there was no independent non-contractual claim. Tort liability was restricted by what was later called the 'privity of contract' fallacy, that duties which originated in a contract were confined to the parties.[75] It was also mainly concerned with the protection of proprietary interests and with providing a remedy for certain categories of physical injury. Although a number of economic torts were developed, notably deceit, injurious falsehood, inducement of breach of contract, and conspiracy, they required wilful misconduct. There was no liability for pure economic loss which was inflicted negligently.

(ii) The twentieth century

The twentieth century saw some reshaping of contract law accompanied by an expansion of non-contractual obligations in tort and restitution of unjust enrichment. In tort the recognition of liability for negligent misrepresentation causing purely economic loss was of particular significance. There was also some dilution of formal requirements and increased regard is given to considerations of substantive fairness. The erosion of the doctrine of consideration in the context of contract re-negotiation, and its partial replacement by rules of equitable estoppel[76] and economic duress is perhaps the most prominent example, but there are others, including an approach to discharge of contract, whether by breach or frustration, that gives greater emphasis to the consequences of an event than to the, often fictional, intentions of the parties.[77] The evolution of new doctrines and approaches has been gradual, and there have been exceptions and inconsistencies. For instance, when, in 1976, economic duress was first recognized as a factor vitiating contract, its theoretical basis was said to be 'coercion of the will', that is, absence of consent. But this was rejected in less than a decade,[78] whereas in the case of frustration, first recognized in 1863, it took almost 100 years for the Courts to turn away from regarding implied contract as the basis of that doctrine.[79]

(iii) Legislation

The last 150 years have also seen a rapid growth in the importance of statute law. There were great codifying Acts of the nineteenth century for particular types of contract, such as the Bills of Exchange Act 1882 and the Sale of Goods Act 1893. We have noted the considerable, and increasing, amount of regulatory legislation, which is designed to protect certain classes of the community or to implement government policy. A number of reforming

73 *Falcke v Scottish Imperial Insurance Co* (1886) 34 Ch 234, 248.

74 *Sinclair v Brougham* [1914] AC 398, 452 (overruled by *Westdeutsche Landesbank Girozentrale v Islington LBC* [1996] AC 669); Holdsworth (1939) 55 LQR 37. Cf Lord Wright [1938] CLJ 305, 312 ff.

75 *Winterbottom v Wright* (1842) 10 M & W 109.

76 Below, p 121.

77 Below, pp 494, 531–2.

78 Below, p 381.

79 Below, pp 491–2.

statutes, such as the Law Reform (Frustrated Contracts) Act 1943, the Misrepresentation Act 1967, the Civil Liability (Contribution) Act 1978, the Minors' Contracts Act 1987, and the Contracts (Rights of Third Parties) Act 1999, were passed to remedy defects or to make good particular deficiencies in the common law. Very significant legislative intervention has been aimed at the protection of consumers, most recently the Consumer Rights Act 2015 and the Digital Markets, Competition and Consumers Act 2024. However, despite all these developments, the English law of contract remains predominantly judge-made law.[80]

(iv) Codification

In 1965, the Law Commission of England and Wales and the Scottish Law Commission announced their intention to codify the English and Scots law of contract.[81] The code as originally envisaged was to be a uniform body of law applying throughout England and Scotland, and it was to embody amendments to the existing law of both countries. Subsequently, however, the Scottish Law Commission withdrew from this enterprise. In 1973, therefore, the Law Commission decided to suspend its work on a contract code.[82] Since then it has examined particular areas of the law of contract, and has either recommended reform, such as in the case of exemption clauses,[83] contribution,[84] minors' contracts,[85] implied terms as to quality in the sale of goods,[86] formalities and covenants of title in the sale of land,[87] contributory negligence as a defence in contract,[88] contracts for the benefit of third parties,[89] unfair contract terms,[90] consumer remedies for faulty goods,[91] insurance contract law,[92] consumer redress for misleading and aggressive practices,[93] electronic execution of documents and deeds,[94] and transfer of ownership in consumer sales contracts,[95] or has concluded that no legislation is necessary, as in the case of the parol evidence rule,[96] illegal contracts,[97] and 'smart' contracts.[98] It seems

[80] Cf Arvind and Steele (eds), *Contract Law and the Legislature* (2022).

[81] Diamond (1968) 31 MLR 361. The Indian Contract Act 1872 codified (with some variations) the general English law of contract for use in the Indian sub-continent.

[82] The draft as it stood when the project was abandoned has since been published: McGregor, *The Contract Code Drawn Up on Behalf of the Law Commission* (1993).

[83] Law Com No 69 (1975), implemented by the Unfair Contract Terms Act 1977, below, p 212.

[84] Law Com No 79 (1977), implemented by the Civil Liability (Contribution) Act 1978.

[85] Law Com No 134 (1984), implemented by the Minors' Contracts Act 1987, below, p 267.

[86] Law Com No 160 (1987), implemented by the Sale and Supply of Goods Act 1994.

[87] Law Com No 164 (1987) and Law Com No 199 (1991), implemented respectively by the Law of Property (Miscellaneous Provisions) Acts 1989 and 1994.

[88] Law Com No 219 (1993), rejected by the Government.

[89] Law Com No 242 (1996), implemented by the Contracts (Rights of Third Parties) Act 1999, below, p 639.

[90] Law Com No 292 (2005) and Law Commission, *Unfair Terms in Consumer Contracts: Advice to the Department for Business, Innovation and Skills* (2013), partly implemented in Part 2 of the Consumer Rights Act 2015, below, p 226.

[91] Law Com No 317 (2009), implemented in Part 1 of the Consumer Rights Act 2015, below, p 520.

[92] Law Com No 319 (2009), implemented by the Consumer Insurance (Disclosure and Representations) Act 2012, below, p 364; Law Com No 353 (2014), implemented by the Insurance Act 2015, below, p 364.

[93] Law Com No 332 (2012), implemented by the Consumer Protection (Amendment) Regulations 2014 (now replaced by the Digital Markets, Competition and Consumers Act 2024), below, p 358.

[94] Law Com No 386 (2019).

[95] Law Com No 398 (2021).

[96] Law Com No 154 (1986), below, pp 148–9.

[97] Law Com No 320 (2010).

[98] Law Com No 401 (2021).

unlikely that the codification project will be revived.[99] In contrast, there has recently been published *A Restatement of the English Law of Contract*[100] by Burrows assisted by an advisory group of academics, judges, and practitioners.

(v) Extra-judicial controls on contract

The law of contract as presented in this book is that applied by the English Courts. It comprises common law and legislation. However, it is important to realize that, in practice, there are controls on contracts other than through the Courts. Arbitration is the most obvious example although, if English law applies to the dispute, arbitrators will seek to apply the law of contract as presented in this book in the same way as a judge would do. The Competition and Markets Authority and other regulators have an important role in, for example, controlling unfair terms not only by occasionally bringing actions in the courts but also by enforcing them administratively and much more commonly, by informally negotiating with businesses and seeking undertakings from them.[101] The Financial Ombudsman has wide powers to make awards, enforceable in the courts, without being bound to apply the strict rules of contract law.[102] Finally one should bear in mind the increasing encouragement to parties to mediate because it is seen as a relatively inexpensive and quick way of resolving disputes without going to court.[103]

3. EUROPEAN AND INTERNATIONAL INFLUENCES

The United Kingdom was a Member State of the European Union[104] from 1973 to 2020.[105] Throughout that period the English law of contract was exposed to the influence of the EU and, through the EU, the predominantly civilian systems of its Members, because of the perceived importance of the harmonization of contract law in the development of the single market. The most significant initiatives affecting contract

[99] Between 2010 and 2018 the Scottish Law Commission undertook a general review of Scots contract law in the light of international comparators, especially the *Draft Common Frame of Reference* (see below, pp 21–2). The Commission did not revive the 1965 codification project, but recommended reforms of the law on formation of contract and remedies for breach of contract: Scots Law Com No 252 (2018), implemented by the Contract (Formation and Remedies) (Scotland) Act 2026.

[100] 1st edn 2016; 2nd edn 2020.

[101] Taking over powers formerly exercised by the Office of Fair Trading; see below, p 227.

[102] See Financial Services and Markets Act 2000, Part XVI and Sched 17. For discussion, see Smith, *Atiyah's Introduction to the Law of Contract* (6th edn, 2005) 250–1, 330–1.

[103] Courts now commonly stay proceedings to allow for mediation and there may be cost penalties for a party that refuses to go to mediation. Directive 2013/11/EU on alternative dispute resolution for consumer disputes was implemented in the UK by SI 2015 No 542 (amended by SI 2015 Nos 1392 and 1972), and replaced by the Digital Markets, Competition and Consumers Act 2024, Part 4, Ch 4 with effect from 6 April 2026.

[104] Originally the European Economic Community (EEC), then (from 1993) the European Community (EC). The EU replaced the EC under the Treaty of Lisbon from 1 December 2009.

[105] The UK withdrew from the EU on 31 January 2020, followed by an implementation period of the withdrawal agreement which ended on 31 December 2020: European Union (Withdrawal) Act 2018, s 20(1) as amended ('exit day'); European Union (Withdrawal Agreement) Act 2020, s 39(1) ('IP completion day').

law were the Directives on Unfair Terms in Consumer Contracts,[106] Consumer Sales,[107] Unfair Commercial Practices,[108] and Consumer Rights,[109] and those which seek to ensure that there is no discrimination in tendering procedures for major contracts for public works, supplies, and services.[110] Much of the EU-derived domestic law as it stood at the end of 2020 (such as Directives that had already been implemented) continued to have effect as 'retained' EU law,[111] although in 2023 Parliament revoked a number of provisions deriving from EU law and 'assimilated' the remaining retained EU law into domestic law.[112] Further legislation is already removing a significant number of legislative provisions which derive from EU law,[113] although the implementation of changes will take time. It remains to be seen how closely English law continues to be aligned to EU law in the longer term.

Over the last 40 years there has also been a movement to develop common principles of European contract law which has resulted in a significant body of academic research comparing the national systems of contract law, and making proposals for possible harmonization.[114] Those who favour this argue that there are many benefits to be derived from a formulation of principles of contract law within Europe. These include the facilitation of cross-border trade, the strengthening of the European single market, the provision of an infrastructure for European Union laws governing contract and of

[106] Council Directive 93/13/EEC, implemented first by Unfair Terms in Consumer Contracts Regulations in 1994 (SI 1994 No 3159), then 1999 (SI 1999 No 2083), and now by Part 2 of the Consumer Rights Act 2015, below, p 227.

[107] Directive 99/44/EC, implemented first by the Sale and Supply of Goods to Consumers Regulations 2002 (SI 2002 No 3045), amending the Sale of Goods Act 1979 and the Supply of Goods and Services Act 1982, and now by the Consumer Rights Act 2015, below, pp 520–1, 596. See also the Package Travel and Linked Arrangements Regulations 2018 (SI 2018 No 634), implementing Directive (EU) 2015/2302, below, pp 236, 375, 658 and the Timeshare, Holiday Products, Resale and Exchange Contracts Regulations 2010 (SI 2010 No 2960), implementing Directive 2008/122/EC.

[108] Directive 2005/29/EC, implemented by, inter alia, the Consumer Protection from Unfair Trading Regulations 2008 (SI 2008 No 1277) and amended by SI 2014 No 870 to provide consumers' private rights of redress for misleading and aggressive commercial practices. The 2008 Regulations have now been replaced by the Digital Markets, Competition and Consumers Act 2024: below, p 358.

[109] Directive 2001/83/EU, implemented by the Consumer Contracts (Information, Cancellation and Additional Charges) Regulations 2013 (SI 2013 No 3134).

[110] Directive 2014/23/EU, implemented by the Concession Contracts Regulations 2016 (SI 2016 No 273), Directive 2014/24/EU, implemented by the Public Contracts Regulations 2015 (SI 2015 No 102), and Directive 2014/25/EU, implemented by the Utilities Contracts Regulations 2016 (SI 2016 No 274). The 2015 and 2016 Regulations have now been replaced by the Procurement Act 2023.

[111] European Union (Withdrawal) Act 2018, ss 2, 3, amended by the European Union (Withdrawal Agreement) Act 2020. Many statutory instruments were made under s 8 of the 2018 Act to amend (after the implementation period completion day) existing primary or secondary legislation to take into account withdrawal from the EU.

[112] Retained EU Law (Revocation and Reform) Act 2023, ss 1–2, 5. Ss 3 and 4 abolished the application of the principle of supremacy of EU law, and removed from domestic law the general principles of EU law, insofar as they had been retained in relation to the law enacted before the end of 2020.

[113] See, eg, Digital Markets, Competition and Consumers Act 2024, below, p 358.

[114] See in particular Lando and Beale, *Principles of European Contract Law Parts I and II* (2000); Lando, Clive, Prüm, and Zimmermann, *Principles of European Contract Law Part III* (2003); Research Group on the Existing EC Private Law (Acquis Group), *Principles of the Existing EC Contract Law (Acquis Principles), Contract I: Precontractual Obligations, Conclusion of Contract, Unfair Terms* (2007); von Bar and Clive (eds), *Principles, Definitions and Model Rules of European Private Law: Draft Common Frame of Reference (DCFR)* (2009).

guidelines for national courts and legislatures, and the construction of a bridge between common law and civil law systems. Following the publication in 2000 of the *Principles of European Contract Law Parts I and II* by the (independent) Commission on European Contract Law,[115] the European Commission produced an Action Plan designed to increase the coherence of the EC *acquis* (existing law) in the area of contract law, to promote the elaboration of EU-wide general contract terms, and to examine whether there should be an 'optional instrument' which contracting parties could choose as their governing terms.[116] The movement towards the drafting of a new instrument to give effect to these aspirations initially gained significant momentum but did not attract sufficient support and the proposal was withdrawn at the end of 2014. It appears that the idea of a new European Contract Code[117] is no longer on the horizon.

There are wider international initiatives, such as the UNIDROIT Principles of International Commercial Contracts (1994; the current edition is 2016), the United Nations (Vienna) Convention on Contracts for the International Sale of Goods (the CISG) (1980), and growing numbers of international standard form contracts. The UK has not ratified the CISG because of a perception by some that English contract law is more sophisticated, and fear that uncertainty would result from the broadly formulated provisions of the Convention,[118] and the Government stated most recently in 2020 that it had no current plans to ratify the Convention.[119] Furthermore, the provisions of the European Convention for the Protection of Human Rights, in particular the right to a fair trial under Article 6 and to the protection of property under Article 1 of the First Protocol to the Convention also have an impact on English contract law as a result of the Human Rights Act 1998.[120]

While this book is concerned with English law, the approach of other European systems is mentioned where, as in the case of the use by the Consumer Rights Act 2015 of the civilian concept of good faith, these are now directly germane to English law.[121] There are also brief references to European principles and international conventions, as well as to other approaches and developments in common law countries, including the American Law Institute's *Restatement, Contracts (2d)*,[122] where these might be helpful in giving a comparative perspective to problems faced by English law.

[115] Above, n 114. For the origin, composition, and sponsorship of the Commission, see Lando and Beale, *Principles of European Contract Law Parts I and II*, xi–xvi.

[116] Communication from the Commission to the European Parliament and the Council: a more coherent European contract law; an action plan: COM(2003) 68 final (12.2.2003), following Communication from the Commission to the Council and the European Parliament on European Contract Law COM(2001) 398 final (11.07.2001).

[117] Resolution of the European Parliament 26 June 1989 [1989] OJ C158/400; COM(2001) 398 final (11.07.2001), paras 61–9.

[118] Hobhouse (1990) 106 LQR 530. Cf Steyn, in Birks (ed), *The Frontiers of Liability* (vol II, 1994) 11; Nicholas (1989) 105 LQR 201, 240–3.

[119] Written answer in the House of Commons by the Department for International Trade (20 November 2020).

[120] *Wilson v First County Trust Ltd (No 2)* [2003] UKHL 40, [2004] 1 AC 816; *Shanshal v Al Kishtaini* [2001] EWCA Civ 264, [2001] 2 All ER (Comm) 601.

[121] Below, pp 233–4.

[122] The ALI Restatement is not a binding legislative text, but a very influential and 'acute interpretation of American case law': Winfield (1929) 11 J Comp Leg 179, 189 (on the first edition).

4. THE CONTENT OF CONTRACT LAW

(a) A LAW OF CONTRACT OR OF CONTRACTS

The increasingly complex social and commercial relationships of the twentieth century produced a situation where it is too simple to say that there is a law of contract rather than of contracts. Particular principles and rules of law are applicable, sometimes as the result of statutory definition, to contracts of sale of goods, sale and lease of land, insurance, carriage of goods by sea, employment, and consumer contracts, which are peculiar to those contracts. In the past, a number of commercial contexts, such as shipping, insurance, and construction, have been particularly influential in the development of contract law. Some have suggested that they have been disproportionately influential. Whatever the influence of particular contexts, however, apart from statutory intervention the ideology of the common law of contract remains that of a single body of general principles of contract law which apply, with or without modification, across the range of such contracts. It is those general principles of contract law that this book seeks to expound.

The contract law contained in this book follows, for the most part, the subject-matter established by Sir William Anson in his *Principles of the English Law of Contract and of Agency in its Relation to Contract*. It deals with the Formation of Contract, the Contents of the Contract, Performance and Discharge, Remedies for Breach of Contract, and the Limits of the Contractual Obligation (including Agency). It also deals with those factors which tend to vitiate a contract, such as incapacity, mistake, misrepresentation, duress and undue influence, and illegality. A word must be said at the outset about these.

(b) EFFECT OF VITIATING FACTORS

Not all the factors that vitiate a contract are uniform in effect. Some of them may render a contract void, others voidable, while others still may make the contract unenforceable at the suit of one or other of the parties. These terms (void, voidable, and unenforceable) therefore denote different degrees of ineffectiveness, and they are in constant use in the law of contract. They are, however, not infrequently used with insufficient precision,[123] and even the same term may have a different meaning in different situations.

(i) Void contracts

In the case of a void contract, for example, the basic position is that such a contract is simply one which the law holds to be no contract at all, a nullity from the beginning. The parties would be in the same position as they would have been had the contract never been made. No property would pass under such a contract; so, for example, a

[123] See Turpin (1955) 72 SALJ 58; Honoré (1958) 75 SALJ 32. The effect of illegality on the enforceability of a contract is dealt with in Chapter 11. In that context the Courts have tended to use the terms 'void' and 'unenforceable' interchangeably, although 'unenforceable' is the modern preferred terminology: *Hawkins v Abarbanel Ltd* [2025] UKPC 58, [2026] 1 WLR 115 at [38].

third party who purchased goods which had been the subject of a void contract would acquire no title to the goods.[124] Conversely, money due to be paid, or in fact paid, in pursuance of a void contract would not be payable, or could be recovered from the person to whom it had been paid.[125] This is the meaning of 'void' where a contract is said to be void for mistake.

(ii) Voidable contracts

A voidable contract is a contract which one of the parties has the option to rescind or affirm. If the choice is to affirm the contract, or if the right to rescind is lost for some other legal reason (such as delay), the party who had the option to rescind will be bound by the contract; otherwise that party is entitled to have the contract set aside. Nevertheless, the contract is not a nullity from the beginning. Until it is rescinded, it is valid and binding. A third party who in good faith purchases goods which had been the subject of a voidable contract, without notice of that prior defect, acquires a good title to the goods.[126]

(iii) Unenforceable contracts

An unenforceable contract is one which is good in substance although, by reason of some defect, one or both of the parties cannot be sued on it. A contract may be good, but incapable of enforcement because it is not evidenced by writing as required by statute.[127] But, in some cases, the defect is curable: the subsequent execution of a written memorandum may satisfy the requirements of the law and render the contract enforceable, but it is never in the power of either party to avoid the transaction. The contract itself is unimpeachable, but it cannot be directly enforced in court.

5. CONTRACT AS PART OF THE LAW OF OBLIGATIONS

The law of obligations has traditionally been divided into contractual obligations, which are voluntarily undertaken and owed to a specific person or persons, and obligations in tort, which are primarily based on the wrongful infliction of harm to certain protected interests, primarily imposed by the law, and typically owed to a wider class of persons.[128] More recently it has been accepted that there is a third category, restitutionary obligations, primarily based on the unjust enrichment of the defendant at the claimant's expense,[129] such as where the claimant has mistakenly paid the defendant

[124] *Cundy v Lindsay* (1878) 3 App Cas 459, below, p 294.

[125] *Couturier v Hastie* (1856) 5 HLC 673, below, p 308; *Westdeutsche Landesbank Girozentrale v Islington LBC* [1996] AC 669.

[126] Sale of Goods Act 1979, s 23; *Car and Universal Finance Co Ltd v Caldwell* [1965] 1 QB 525, below, p 336.

[127] Below, p 83 (contract of guarantee).

[128] Winfield, *Province of the Law of Tort* (1931) 380; Cane, *The Anatomy of Tort Law* (1997).

[129] *Lipkin Gorman v Karpnale Ltd* [1991] 2 AC 548; *Kleinwort Benson Ltd v Glasgow City Council* [1999] 1 AC 153. See Burrows, *A Restatement of the English Law of Unjust Enrichment* (2012).

money or discharged the defendant's debt. Contractual liability, reflecting the constitutive function of contract,[130] is generally for failing to make things better (by not rendering the expected performance), liability in tort is generally for action (as opposed to omission) making things worse, and liability in unjust enrichment is generally for unjustly receiving the benefit of the claimant's money or work. It accordingly follows that it is a defence to a claim for restitution of an unjust enrichment that the defendant has changed its position, for example by incurring expenditure in reliance on a payment received from the claimant, so as to make it inequitable to order that the money be repaid.[131]

Although this tripartite division is a useful starting point, it is a rationalization of a less tidy common law, as the summary of the history of contract above indicates. The recent expansion of all these types of obligation also increases the occasions on which the different categories will overlap and it has been argued that the division made between duties which are voluntarily assumed and duties which are imposed by law is an oversimplification.[132] Moreover, care must be taken not to reverse the contractual allocation of risks by non-contractual actions.[133]

(a) CONCURRENCE OF CLAIMS IN CONTRACT AND TORT

Although the Court may decline to find a duty in tort where the parties are in a contractual relationship,[134] or may hold that a term of a contract has excluded or limited what would otherwise be a tortious duty, pre-contractual events, such as misrepresentation, may give rise to an action in tort.[135] Additionally, it is clear that in many cases, exemplified by negligent failure by professionals, such as solicitors and surveyors, to carry out their undertakings to their clients, a defendant may be liable to the same claimant both in contract and in tort.[136] Indeed, the fact that tort liability in these contexts may be grounded in an 'assumption of responsibility',[137] means that a negligent breach of contract may often give rise to claims in both contract and tort.[138] Where this is so, the claimant 'can advance his claim, as he wishes, either in contract or in tort, and no doubt he will . . . advance the claim on the basis which is most advantageous to him'.[139] The practical differences between contract and tort include, for example, the measure of

130 Above, p 3.

131 *Lipkin Gorman v Karpnale Ltd* [1991] 2 AC 548, 579–80.

132 Atiyah (1978) 94 LQR 193, 223. Cf Burrows (1983) 99 LQR 217.

133 eg *Marc Rich & Co AG v Bishop Rock Marine Co Ltd* [1996] AC 211, and see below, p 666.

134 *Tai Hing Cotton Mill v Liu Chong Hing Bank* [1986] AC 80, 107; *Greater Nottingham Co-operative Society v Cementation Piling and Foundations Ltd* [1989] QB 1.

135 *Hedley Byrne & Co Ltd v Heller & Partners Ltd* [1964] AC 465, below, p 349.

136 *Midland Bank Trust Co Ltd v Hett, Stubbs and Kemp* [1979] Ch 384; *Henderson v Merrett Syndicates Ltd* [1995] 2 AC 145. Cf *Williams v Natural Life Health Foods* [1998] 1 WLR 830.

137 Cf *Customs and Excise Commissioners v Barclays Bank plc* [2006] UKHL 28, [2007] 1 AC 181.

138 Cf *White v Jones* [1995] 2 AC 207, below, p 644, where the tort claim was available to a third party to the contract.

139 *Coupland v Arabian Gulf Oil Co* [1983] 1 WLR 1136, 1153 (Robert Goff LJ). See also Lord Goff's speech in the leading case of *Henderson v Merrett Syndicates* [1995] 2 AC 145, 193–4.

recovery,[140] the period of limitation,[141] the relevance of the claimant's contributory fault (it is generally irrelevant in contract but relevant in tort),[142] and assignability, since only a contractual claim can generally be assigned.

(b) CONTRACT AND UNJUST ENRICHMENT

Historically, the effect of the implied term theory[143] was that contract was thought in effect to have swallowed up restitution of an unjust enrichment. While it is now clear that the two are independent of each other and that 'implied contract' is a fictional explanation for restitution of an unjust enrichment,[144] it is in the context of money having been paid and services having been rendered under ineffective contracts and contracts discharged by breach or by frustration that many claims in unjust enrichment are made.[145] Sometimes it can be difficult to distinguish the enforcement of a contract or promise from the restitution of an unjust enrichment, as where one person has 'freely accepted' or 'acquiesced' in services rendered by the other.[146] Where there is a contract and it makes provision for repayment or recompense—or, indeed, that there should be no payment in the circumstances that have arisen—there will be no claim for restitution of an unjust enrichment.[147] Where, however, it does not, a claim may lie, and, for example, in the case of a contract discharged for breach, the innocent party's claim for restitution of an unjust enrichment may be greater than the contractual claim for damages.[148] We shall also see that a remedy for restitution of an unjust enrichment may be available in respect of work done by one party during pre-contractual negotiations which do not ripen into a contract.[149]

The restitution of an unjust enrichment, independent from contract, is significantly different from an account of profits, given as a remedy *for* breach of contract. The basis of such a restitutionary remedy is the contract and not an independent cause of action in unjust enrichment. Traditionally, such a restitutionary remedy, while available for civil wrongs, such as breach of fiduciary duty and some torts, was not available for breach of contract. But that was departed from by the House of Lords in *Attorney-General v Blake*[150] in which it was accepted that, in exceptional circumstances, an account of profits can be awarded for breach of contract.

[140] Below, pp 330 and 567–9 (remoteness of damage).

[141] *Henderson v Merrett Syndicates Ltd* [1995] 2 AC 145, 185.

[142] Below, p 577.

[143] Above, n 74.

[144] *Westdeutsche Landesbank Girozentrale v Islington London BC* [1996] AC 669; *Haugesund Kommune v Depfa ACS Bank* [2010] EWCA Civ 579, [2012] QB 549.

[145] Below, pp 254, 261, 507, 607–16.

[146] See Beatson, *The Use and Abuse of Unjust Enrichment* (1991) ch 2.

[147] *Pan Ocean Shipping Co Ltd v Creditcorp Ltd* [1994] 1 WLR 161; *Barton v Morris* [2023] UKSC 3, [2023] AC 684.

[148] Below, p 615.

[149] Below, pp 44, 66.

[150] [2001] 1 AC 268. See above, p 9; below, pp 616–8.

6. CONTRACT AND PROPERTY

The law of obligations must be distinguished from the law of property which essentially governs the acquisition and content of the rights persons have in things, which may be land or moveables. In a wider sense, the law of property deals with all assets, including intangibles such as a debt, shares in a company, a beneficiary's right under a trust, or a patent.[151] Whereas a person's property right in a thing is generally valid against the whole world, the rights under the law of obligations, including contract, are personal and valid only against a specific person or persons. Property rights may be *protected* by the law of tort, as where the use and enjoyment of land is protected by the torts of trespass and nuisance, and the right to possession of goods is protected by the tort of conversion. Property rights may be *transferred* by contract, as where A sells goods to B, and the property passes under section 18 of the Sale of Goods Act 1979, but they may also be transferred in other ways, for example by delivery with the requisite intention, as where a gift is made. Property can pass under voidable and unenforceable contracts as well as valid ones, but not normally under void contracts.[152] Where property has so passed (whether under the contract or by delivery), B may in turn resell the goods and pass the property in them to C, even though B may not have paid A, or may have committed some other breach of contract, but an unpaid seller in possession of goods has the power to dispose of them in certain cases.[153] Where property has not passed to B, B is only able to confer a contractual right to the goods upon C. The position of a person who only has a contractual right to a thing is less secure than that of a person who has a property right since contractual rights may generally only be enforced against the other party to the contract (in our example, B) whereas property rights are generally enforceable against all persons. C would therefore only be able to enforce a contractual right against B, and not against A, or anyone who acquires the goods from A. There is, however, a tendency to reduce the discrepancy between the two and in certain circumstances contractual rights will be protected against third parties.[154]

[151] Lawson and Rudden, *The Law of Property* (3rd edn, 2002) ch 2.

[152] Above, pp 23–4.

[153] See Sale of Goods Act 1979, ss 39(1)(c), 48(3)–(4).

[154] eg *Lumley v Gye* (1853) 3 E and B 216, below, p 671.

PART 1

FORMATION OF CONTRACT

2

THE AGREEMENT

A contract consists of an actionable promise or promises. Every such promise involves at least two parties, a promisor and a promisee, and an outward expression of common intention as to the declaration or assurance contained in the promise.

This outward expression of a common intention normally takes the form of an agreement.[1] In most cases, therefore, it will be necessary to ascertain at the outset whether or not an agreement has been concluded.

This chapter considers the establishing of an agreement by offer and acceptance; uncertain and incomplete agreements; and the intention to create legal relations.

1. ESTABLISHING AN AGREEMENT

The fact that an agreement has been reached will sometimes be self-evident, since the agreement will be set out in a document signed or initialled by both parties.[2] But where there is no such document, it may be more difficult to discover whether the parties have agreed. The alleged agreement may, in whole or in part, have been concluded by word of mouth or by conduct. Difficulties of proof will then arise and the resultant questions of fact will have to be determined by the trial judge from the evidence given by the parties and their witnesses. We are not here concerned with difficulties of proof, but rather with problems that occur even where there is no dispute as to what the parties said or did. Such problems are not infrequent in practice, especially when the fact of agreement has to be elicited from an exchange of letters or text messages, for example. As Lord Clarke observed in *RTS Flexible Systems Ltd v Molkerei Alois Müller GmbH & Co KG (UK Production)*:[3]

> Whether there is a binding contract between the parties and, if so, upon what terms depends upon what they have agreed. It depends not upon their subjective state of mind, but upon a consideration of what was communicated between them by words or conduct, and whether that leads objectively to a conclusion that they intended to create legal relations and had agreed upon all the terms which they regarded or the law requires as essential for the formation of legally binding relations. Even if certain terms of economic or other significance to the

[1] See above, p 2.

[2] Although as a general rule English law has no requirements of writing or other form: see below, Chapter 3.

[3] [2010] UKSC 14, [2010] 1 WLR 753 at [45].

parties have not been finalised, an objective appraisal of their words and conduct may lead to the conclusion that they did not intend agreement of such terms to be a pre-condition to a concluded and legally binding agreement.

(a) OFFER AND ACCEPTANCE

To determine whether an agreement has actually been concluded, it is normally necessary to inquire whether in the negotiations which have taken place between the parties there has been a definite offer by one party, and an equally definite acceptance of that offer by the other. If, for instance, A and B have agreed that A shall purchase from B a car for £10,000, we can trace the process to a moment at which B must have said to A, in effect, 'Will you give me £10,000 for my car?', and A has replied, 'I will'; or at which A has said to B, 'Will you let me have the car for £10,000?', and B has said, 'I will'. Where a contract is alleged to have been made by an exchange of correspondence between the parties in which the successive communications other than the first are in reply to one another, the Court should look at the correspondence to see whether there is an offer by one party and an acceptance by the other party.[4]

It would be a mistake to think that all contracts can easily be analysed through the lens of offer and acceptance. Difficult cases include the acceptance by two parties of terms suggested by a third, and multiparty agreements.[5] The analysis is, however, a working method which, more often than not, enables us to ascertain whether a contract has in truth been concluded, and as such should be retained.

(i) Offer and acceptance in unilateral and bilateral contracts

The process of 'offer and acceptance' may take place in one of two main ways:

(1) In the offer of a promise for an act:[6] as when a person offers a reward for a certain act, which may be accepted by carrying out that act.

Illustration: A, who has lost her dog, offers by advertisement a reward of £25 to anyone who will bring the dog safely home: a promise is offered in return for an act. When B, knowing of the reward, brings the dog safely home, the act is done and A is bound to pay the reward.

(2) In the offer of a promise for a promise: when the offer is accepted by the giving of the promise, the contract consists of an outstanding obligation on both sides.

Illustration: C offers to pay D a certain sum of money if D will promise to dig C's garden for him within a certain time. When D makes the promise asked for, he accepts the promise offered, and both parties are bound: one to do the work, the other to allow the first to do it and to pay for it.

[4] *Gibson v Manchester City Council* [1979] 1 WLR 294, 297 (Lord Diplock); *Global Asset Capital Inc v Aabar Block SARL* [2017] EWCA Civ 37, [2017] 4 WLR 163. Cf *Port Sudan Cotton Co v Govindaswamy Chettiar & Sons* [1977] 2 Lloyd's Rep 5.

[5] *Clarke v Earl of Dunraven, The Satanita* [1897] AC 59, below, pp 33–4.

[6] Or forbearance. See also below, p 106.

Case (1) differs from (2) in an important respect. In (1), it is performance on one side which makes obligatory the promise of the other; the outstanding obligation is all on one side. Such a contract is termed 'unilateral'[7] as only one person is bound.[8] In (2), however, each party is obliged to some act or forbearance which, at the time of entering into the contract, is in the future; there is an outstanding obligation on each side. This is known as a 'bilateral' contract, and each party is both a promisor and a promisee. It is reasonable to presume in cases of doubt that a bilateral, rather than a unilateral contract has been concluded. So if G says to H: 'If you will let me have that table you are making, when it is finished, I will give you £25 for it', and H replies 'All right', there is a bilateral contract and H is bound to deliver the table.[9]

(ii) Promises in deeds

In one exceptional situation, however, it is clear that a contract can come into existence without any need for an 'offer and acceptance'. This is the case of a promise in a deed. For example, if a wealthy person, by a document executed as a deed, promises to pay a college £100,000 in order to establish a scholarship, the promise is binding without any need for an acceptance or even knowledge of the promise by the person to whom the promise is made.[10]

(iii) Inferences from conduct

The description which has been given of the possible forms of offer and acceptance shows that conduct may take the place of written or spoken words either in the offer or in the acceptance.[11] An agreement may also be inferred from conduct alone; the intention of the parties is a matter of inference from their conduct, and the inference is more or less easily drawn according to the circumstances of the case.[12] In day-to-day contracts such inferences are frequent. For example, a person who boards a bus or who hires a taxi thereby undertakes to pay the fare to his destination even though he makes no express promise to do so.[13] Again, a person who puts a coin in an automatic machine thereby enters into a contract with the supplier although no words have been exchanged on either side.

Sometimes the inference from conduct is not so clear, because the contract has assumed a less simple form. If more than two parties are involved, it may not be particularly helpful to look for a definite offer and acceptance. In *Clarke v Earl of Dunraven, The Satanita*:[14]

[7] *GN Ry v Witham* (1873) LR 9 CP 16, 19; *New Zealand Shipping Co Ltd v AM Satterthwaite & Co Ltd* [1975] AC 154, 167–8, 171, 177; *Soulsbury v Soulsbury* [2007] EWCA Civ 969, [2008] Fam 1.

[8] See also below, p 55.

[9] ALI *Restatement, Contracts (2d)* para 31.

[10] Although he cannot be compelled to accept the benefit: *Townson v Tickel* (1819) 3 B & Ald 31. On deeds, see generally below, pp 80–2.

[11] Save in the most exceptional circumstances an offer or acceptance cannot be inferred from inactivity; on acceptance by silence, see below, pp 50–2.

[12] Cited with approval in *Wright & Co Ltd v Maunder* [1962] NZLR 355, 358.

[13] See *Wilkie v London Passenger Transport Board* [1947] 1 All ER 258. See also *Steven v Bromley & Son* [1919] 2 KB 722; *Sullivan v Constable* (1932) 48 TLR 369.

[14] [1897] AC 59.

The owners of two yachts, the *Satanita* and the *Valkyrie*, entered them in a club regatta. The rules of the regatta bound competitors to make good any damage caused by fouling. While preparing for the start of a race, the *Satanita* fouled and sank the *Valkyrie*.

Although the immediate relationship of each owner was not with the other, but with the secretary of the yacht club, it was held that a contract existed between them, and that the owner of the *Valkyrie* could recover damages. Lord Herschell said:[15]

The effect of their entering for the race and undertaking to be bound by these rules to the knowledge of each other, is sufficient, where those rules indicate a liability on the part of the one to the other, to create a contractual obligation to discharge that liability.

Perhaps, on entering the race, each person made an offer to any subsequent entrants and accepted the offer already made by any previous entrants. But fitting the case within an orthodox analysis of offer and acceptance is not easy. Similarly, in the case of a company or other corporate entity there will, for certain purposes, be a contract both between the entity and its members and between each of the members themselves.[16]

(b) THE TEST OF INTENTION

In common with most European legal systems, the test of a person's intention is not a subjective, but an objective one.[17] The intention which the law will attribute to a person is always that which that person's conduct bears when reasonably construed by a person in the position of the offeree, and not necessarily that which was present in the offeror's own mind. Thus a person may be held to have made an offer although not appreciating that one was being made[18] or not realizing that the terms of the offer embodied a mistake, as where a rent of £65,000 was mistakenly proposed by a landlord instead of £126,000.[19] If a person's words or conduct, when reasonably construed, amount to an offer or to an offer on particular terms, that person will be held to have made that offer provided that the offeree neither knew nor could reasonably have known of the misunderstanding at the time the offer was accepted. The same objective approach applies to an acceptance. Although the approach is objective, the intentions

[15] *Ibid*, 63.

[16] *Rayfield v Hands* [1960] Ch 1 (company); Companies Act 2006, s 33; *JH Rayner (Mincing Lane) Ltd v Department of Trade and Industry* [1989] Ch 72, 190, [1990] 2 AC 413, 515 (international organization whose members were states).

[17] An exception is French law: see Lando and Beale, *Principles of European Contract Law Parts I and II* (2000) 145–6.

[18] *Upton-on-Severn RDC v Powell* [1942] 1 All ER 220. But there the liability (to pay for the provision of fire-fighting services) is perhaps (see *William Lacey (Hounslow) Ltd v Davis* [1957] 1 WLR 932, 938) best regarded as non-contractual restitution for the value of the services rendered rather than being contractual because neither party believed it was entering into a contract: the fire brigade rendering the services (the 'offeree') believed it was under a duty to provide the service without charge. Cf *Henkel v Pape* (1870) LR 6 Ex 7.

[19] *Centrovincial Estates plc v Merchant Investors Assurance Co Ltd* [1983] Com LR 158. See also *Moran v University College Salford (No 2)*, The Times, 23 November 1993 (mistaken unconditional offer of university place); *OT Africa Line Ltd v Vickers plc* [1996] 1 Lloyd's Rep 700 (payment of £150,000 mistakenly offered instead of $150,000). See also below, pp 272–4.

of the parties are not entirely irrelevant so that a contract cannot be formed which is in accordance with the intention of neither party.[20] It has been stated that 'the judicial task is not to discover the actual intentions of each party; it is to decide what each was reasonably entitled to conclude from the attitude of the other'.[21]

2. THE OFFER

An offer is an intimation, by words or conduct, of a willingness to enter into a legally binding contract, and which in its terms expressly or impliedly indicates that it is to become binding on the offeror as soon as it has been accepted by an act, forbearance, or return promise on the part of the person to whom it is addressed.

(a) OFFERS AND INVITATIONS TO TREAT

It is sometimes difficult to distinguish statements of intention which cannot, and are not intended to, result in any binding obligation from offers which admit of acceptance, and so become binding promises. A person advertises goods for sale in a newspaper, or announces that they will be sold by tender or by auction; a shopkeeper displays goods in a shop window at a certain price; or a bus company advertises that it will carry passengers from A to Z and will reach Z and other intermediate stops at certain times. In such cases it may be asked whether the statement or act made is an offer capable of acceptance or merely an invitation to make offers. A statement or act of this nature, if it is not intended to be binding but contemplates that further negotiations will take place, is known as an 'invitation to treat'.

Since the classification of any particular act or statement as an offer or an invitation to treat depends on intention to be bound rather than upon any *a priori* principle of law, it is not easy to reconcile all the cases or their reasoning. Where the intention is unclear, the Court will take account of the surrounding circumstances and consequences of holding an act or statement to be an offer as well as what is in fact said.

A statement of fact made merely to supply information cannot be treated as an offer, so cannot be accepted to create a valid contract. In *Harvey v Facey*:[22]

[20] Cf *Upton-on-Severn RDC v Powell* [1942] 1 All ER 220, above, n 18; *Furness Withy (Australia) Pty Ltd v Metal Distributors (UK) Ltd* [1990] 1 Lloyd's Rep 236, 243; *Williston on Contracts* (4th edn, 1991) para 6.58. On the merits and demerits of this 'detached objectivity', see Howarth (1984) 100 LQR 265; Vorster (1987) 104 LQR 274.

[21] *Gloag on Contract* (2nd edn, 1929) 7; approved by Lord Reid in *McCutcheon v David Macbrayne Ltd* [1964] 1 WLR 125, 128. See also *Paal Wilson & Co A/S v Partenreederei Hannah Blumenthal* [1983] 1 AC 854, 924 (Lord Brightman); *ibid*, 914 (Lord Brandon) and cf *ibid*, 916 (Lord Diplock); *Edmonds v Lawson* [2000] QB 501. See generally Spencer [1973] CLJ 104, 106–13; Cartwright, *Unequal Bargaining* (1991) 5–24. On the objective test generally, see below, pp 272–9.

[22] [1893] AC 552. See also *Schuldenfrei v Hilton (IT)* [1999] STC 821, 831, 833.

A telegraphed to B 'Will you sell us Bumper Hall Pen? Telegraph lowest cash price, answer paid.' B replied by telegram, 'Lowest price for Bumper Hall Pen £900.' A telegraphed, 'We agree to buy Bumper Hall Pen for £900 asked by you.' Bumper Hall Pen was a plot of land, and A claimed that this exchange of telegrams constituted a valid offer and acceptance.

The Judicial Committee of the Privy Council pointed out that A's first telegram asked two questions, (1) as to the willingness of B to sell, and (2) as to the lowest price; and that the word 'telegraph' in it was addressed to the second question only. It was held that no contract had been made, that B in stating the lowest price for the property was not making an offer but supplying information, that A's second telegram was an offer by him—not the less so because he called it an acceptance—and that this offer had never been accepted by B.

In *Gibson v Manchester City Council*:[23]

The city council adopted a policy of selling council houses to its tenants. Gibson, on a printed form supplied by the council, applied for details of the price of the council house he was renting and mortgage terms. The council replied, 'The corporation *may be prepared to sell* the house to you at the purchase price of . . . £2,180.'[24] Gibson thereupon completed and sent off the application form to purchase the house.

The House of Lords held that there was no contract because the council's letter was not an offer to sell (it was merely an invitation to treat). The words italicized were fatal to regarding the letter as an offer.

(i) Advertisements and displays of goods for sale

Generally speaking advertisements in newspapers or periodicals that the advertiser has goods for sale are not offers.[25] Neither are catalogues or price lists.[26] Again, a display of goods marked at a certain price by a shopkeeper in a shop window[27] does not bind the shopkeeper to sell at that price or to sell at all. The display is merely an invitation to treat; it is for the customer to offer to buy the goods, and, subject to anti-discrimination legislation,[28] the shopkeeper may choose either to accept or to refuse the offer. One reason given for this conclusion is that otherwise the advertiser, catalogue publisher, and shopkeeper would be obliged to sell to every person who accepted such an 'offer', even where supplies had run out. In the case of displays on shelves in a self-service shop, which are also generally invitations to treat, it is said that if the display were an offer, once an article was selected and placed in the receptacle, the customer would have

[23] [1979] 1 WLR 294.

[24] Author's emphasis.

[25] *Partridge v Crittenden* [1968] 1 WLR 1204 (advertisement of 'Bramblefinch cocks and hens' for sale). The position is the same in Germany but not in France: Lando and Beale, *Principles of European Contract Law Parts I and II* (2000) 162. But advertisements of a *unilateral* contract are offers: *Carlill v Carbolic Smoke Ball Co Ltd* [1893] 2 QB 49, below, p 41; *Bowerman v ABTA* [1995] 145 NLJR 1815; the 'reward' cases, below, pp 52–3.

[26] *Grainger & Son v Gough* [1896] AC 325 (bookseller's catalogue with prices); *Seacarriers A/S v Aoteraroa International Ltd* [1985] 2 Lloyd's Rep 419 (quotation of freight rates).

[27] *Timothy v Simpson* (1834) 6 C & P 499 (below, n 31); *Fisher v Bell* [1961] 1 QB 394 (on which, see now, Restriction of Offensive Weapons Act 1961, s 1); *Esso Petroleum Ltd v Commissioners of Customs and Excise* [1976] 1 WLR 1 (indication of price at which petrol to be sold at attended service station not an offer).

[28] Above, p 5.

no right to change his mind.[29] Another reason given is that if a display was an offer a shopkeeper might be forced to contract with his worst enemy: a 'shop is a place for bargains, not for compulsory sales'[30] but this is less convincing in the light of modern regulation of trading practices, for example the prohibition of discrimination on grounds such as disability, race, religion, sex, and age,[31] and the statutory protection of consumers.[32] Where the display clearly states that the goods will be sold to a person who pays the required price it is, however, likely to be held to be an offer. For example, a notice stating 'We will beat any TV HiFi and Video price by £20 on the spot' was held to be 'a continuing offer' and the shop manager was criminally liable for a misleading indication as to the price at which goods may be available.[33]

(ii) Transactions by machine

Different considerations apply where the transaction is effected through a machine,[34] such as where the display is on a vending machine. In such cases the display is likely to be an offer. In *Re Charge Card Services*[35] an open offer to sell at pump prices was held to have been accepted by a motorist putting petrol in the tank.

(iii) Tenders

An announcement inviting tenders is not normally an offer; unless accompanied by words indicating that the highest or the lowest tender will be accepted,[36] it is a mere attempt to ascertain whether an acceptable offer can be obtained.[37] Where there is no offer to contract with the highest or lowest bidder, there may nevertheless be an offer to consider all conforming tenders, especially if the invitation to tender prescribes a clear, orderly, and familiar procedure. For instance, a local authority was held liable for breach of contract when it did not consider a tender submitted before the deadline due to its failure to check its letterbox.[38]

[29] *Pharmaceutical Society of Great Britain v Boots Cash Chemists (Southern) Ltd* [1952] 2 QB 795, aff'd [1953] 1 QB 401, criticized by Unger (1953) 16 MLR 369. Note (i) the context was whether the display constituted an unlawful 'sale' of drugs unsupervised by a registered pharmacist under the Pharmacy and Poisons Act 1933, s 18(1), and (ii) in the USA it has been held that there is no acceptance until the goods are presented at the checkout: *Lasky v Economic Stores* 5 NE 2d 305 (1946).

[30] Winfield (1939) 55 LQR 499, 518. See *Said v Butt* [1920] 3 KB 497 (theatre manager refused entry to critic who had got someone else to buy a ticket for him to a first night performance).

[31] Equality Act 2010, above, p 5. See also *Quinn v Williams Furniture* [1981] ICR 328; *Gill v El Vino* [1983] QB 425. Cf *Timothy v Simpson* (1834) 6 C & P 499 (a person who went into a shop was asked to pay 7/6d although item was marked at 5/11d and the shop assistant said 'don't let him have it, he's only a Jew. Turn him out').

[32] Below, n 33.

[33] *Warwickshire CC v Johnson* [1993] 1 All ER 299, 302.

[34] *Thornton v Shoe Lane Parking Ltd* [1971] 2 QB 163, 169 (machine controlling entry to car park); *National Car Parks Ltd v HMRC* [2019] EWCA Civ 854, [2019] 3 All ER 590 (analysis of offer and acceptance in relation to a parking ticket machine that does not give change).

[35] [1989] Ch 497, 512. See also *Chapelton v Barry UDC* [1940] 1 KB 532 (display of deckchairs for hire an offer). On non-self service petrol sales, see above, n 27.

[36] *Harvela Investments Ltd v Royal Trust of Canada (CI) Ltd* [1986] AC 207.

[37] *Spencer v Harding* (1870) LR 5 CP 561. Contrast *GN Ry v Witham* (1873) LR 9 CP 16; *Percival Ltd v LCC Asylums etc Committee* (1918) 87 LJ KB 677.

[38] *Blackpool and Fylde Aero Club Ltd v Blackpool BC* [1990] 1 WLR 1195. See below, p 533 on the remedy for breach of this obligation.

Difficulties can arise where, in response to an invitation to tender, a party makes a bid which can only be quantified by reference to other bids. Such 'referential bids' were considered in *Harvela Investments Ltd v Royal Trust Co of Canada Ltd*:[39]

The Royal Trust Company of Canada invited bids for shares in a company and promised to sell to the highest bidder. Harvela Investments Ltd bid \$2.175 million. Sir Leonard bid \$2.1 million, or \$101,000 in excess of the next highest bid. The Royal Trust Company thought that this was a valid acceptance, but the House of Lords disagreed.

If everyone made a bid which could only be quantified by reference to other bids then it would be impossible to determine which was the highest. If a referential bid were effective, a buyer who made a fixed bid would invariably lose out. The result might be different if the invitor made it clear that referential bids were welcome, although in *Harvela* Lord Templeman thought that in such circumstances each bidder would need to specify a maximum sum it was prepared to bid: for example, '\$2.1 million, or \$101,000 in excess of the next highest bid, *up to a maximum of \$2.5 million*'. This makes clear that bidder's 'best bid', eliminating any danger of the bids escalating without end. Nor would other bidders be deprived of any chance of success: this might be achieved by simply bidding over \$2.5 million.

(iv) Auctions

Where goods are put up for sale by auction upon an advertised condition that the sale shall be 'without reserve' the auctioneer thereby indicates to prospective buyers that the bid of the highest *bona fide* bidder will be accepted, and that the goods will not at any stage be withdrawn, even if a reserve price has not yet been reached. An auctioneer who does so withdraw the goods is said to be liable for breach of contract with such a bidder. In *Warlow v Harrison*:[40]

An auctioneer advertised a brown mare for sale by auction 'without reserve'. The owner's name was not disclosed. The claimant bid 60 guineas; the owner bid 61 guineas, and the auctioneer knocked down the mare to him. The claimant, as the highest *bona fide* bidder, sought damages from the auctioneer.

A majority of the Court of Exchequer Chamber considered that the auctioneer was liable on a contract that the auction sale was to be 'without reserve'.[41] Certainly there was no contract of sale. A bid at an auction is only an offer which can be retracted at any time before it is accepted by the auctioneer by the fall of the hammer,[42] and an

[39] [1986] AC 207.

[40] (1858–59) 1 E & E 295, 309; *Johnston v Boyes* [1899] 2 Ch 73. Contrast *Fenwick v Macdonald, Fraser & Co Ltd* (1904) 6 F 850 (Scotland). By the Sale of Goods Act 1979, s 57(4) the seller is now precluded without notification from the bidding himself or employing anyone to bid for him, and any sale contravening this rule may be treated as fraudulent by the buyer.

[41] The minority held that the auctioneer would be liable for breach of warranty of authority: see below, pp 711–2. In fact, a new trial was ordered but never took place.

[42] *Payne v Cave* (1789) 3 Term R 148. See now Sale of Goods Act 1979, s 57(2). See further *Harris v Nickerson* (1873) LR 8 QB 286 (auctioneer not liable upon a contract to indemnify those who have incurred expense in order to attend the sale).

advertisement that goods will be auctioned on a certain day is a mere invitation to treat which does not bind the auctioneer to sell the goods. Accordingly, where an auctioneer withdraws the goods prematurely, refusing to knock them down to the highest bidder, there can be no possible action on any *contract of sale* because none has yet come into existence.[43]

However, the Court's conclusion that the claimant in *Warlow v Harrison* was not suing upon a contract of sale but on a different, collateral contract between the auctioneer and the highest *bona fide* bidder that the sale of the mare be 'without reserve',[44] which was broken when a bid was made by or on behalf of the owner, has been criticized.[45] First, if an advertisement that an auction sale will be held is merely an invitation to treat, how can a stipulation contained in it that the sale will be 'without reserve' be an offer? Secondly, if a bid may be retracted, or outbid, at any time before it is accepted, how can it be said that it is certain who is the highest bidder? Thirdly, what is the consideration for the promise, since the promisee is not bound to purchase but may withdraw the bid at any time?

The answer to this last question is that the bidder provides consideration by bidding and being exposed to the risk that the bid would be accepted by the auctioneer. This is perhaps a little artificial, but this unilateral contract analysis[46] accords with the modern approach to similar situations.[47] It was applied in *Barry v Davies*,[48] effectively ending the controversy over *Warlow v Harrison*:

Customs and Excise put up for sale by auction two new engine analyser machines. Each could be obtained from the manufacturers for £14,521 but they were being sold without a reserve price. After the auctioneer failed to obtain bids of £5,000 and £3,000, the claimant bid £200 for each machine. The auctioneer refused to accept these bids and withdrew the machines from the auction. The claimant brought an action against the auctioneer for breach of contract.

The Court of Appeal, applying the majority's view in *Warlow v Harrison*, held that the holding of an auction without reserve is an offer by the auctioneer to sell to the highest bidder so that the auctioneer was indeed contractually bound to sell to the claimant (who was entitled to damages of £27,600).

(b) GENERAL OFFERS

An offer need not be made to an ascertained person,[49] but no contract can arise until it has been accepted by an ascertained person.

[43] At that time the Statute of Frauds required such a contract to be evidenced in writing: see below, p 82.

[44] (1858) 1 E & E 309, 317.

[45] See Slade (1952) 68 LQR 238; Gower (1952) 68 LQR 456; Slade (1953) 69 LQR 21; Cox (1982) 132 NLJ 719.

[46] Above, p 32.

[47] See, on tenders, above p 37; *Harvela Investments Ltd v Royal Trust of Canada (CI) Ltd* [1986] AC 207; *Blackpool and Fylde Aero Club Ltd v Blackpool BC* [1990] 1 WLR 1195.

[48] [2000] 1 WLR 1962.

[49] A proposal not addressed to one or more specific persons is presumptively merely an invitation to treat under the Convention on the International Sale of Goods (CISG) art 14(2) but presumptively an offer under the Italian Civil Code, art 1336(1) and also in French law, first by judicial decision and now in the French Civil Code, art 1114: Rowan, *The New French Law of Contact* (2022) 69.

This proposition is best understood by an illustration:

An insurance company offers a reward to any person who finds and returns a valuable diamond brooch insured by them. X who knows of the offer, finds and returns the brooch. She is entitled to claim the reward.[50]

An offer, by way of advertisement, of a reward for the rendering of certain services, addressed to the public at large, prima facie creates a power of acceptance in every person to whom it is made or becomes known. But a contractual obligation to pay the reward only comes into existence when an individual person performs the stipulated services, and not before.[51] A general offer may be susceptible of acceptance either by only one person or by a number of persons.

In some cases, such as the offer of a reward for information or the return of a lost possession, the offer is exhausted once accepted. The offeror clearly does not intend to pay many times over for the same thing. So, where a reward is offered for information and the information asked for reaches the offeror from several sources, it has been held that the person who gave the earliest information is entitled to the reward.[52]

In other cases the nature of the act asked for by the offeror and the circumstances in which the offer is made mean that it remains open for acceptance by any number of persons, such acceptance being signified by performance of its terms. In *Carlill v Carbolic Smoke Ball Co*:[53]

The defendant offered by advertisement to pay £100 to any one 'who contracts the increasing epidemic influenza colds, or any disease caused by taking cold, after having used the ball three times daily for two weeks, according to the printed directions'. It was added that £1,000 was deposited with the Alliance Bank 'showing our sincerity in the matter'. Mrs Carlill used the smoke ball as required by the directions; she afterwards suffered from influenza and sued the company for the promised reward.

The defendant was held liable. Its argument that a notification of acceptance should have been made to it was rejected. The Court held that this was one of the class of cases in which, as in the case of a reward offered for information or for the recovery of lost property, there need be no acceptance of the offer other than performance of the condition.[54] The further argument that the alleged offer was merely an advertisement or puff which no reasonable person would take to be serious was rejected because the statement that £1,000 had been deposited to meet demands was regarded as evidence of the sincerity of the offer. The advertisement was an offer of a unilateral contract[55] which was capable of being accepted by a number of persons, and which had been accepted by Mrs Carlill when she performed the stipulated conditions.

[50] For the position where X does not know of the offer, see below, p 52.

[51] *New Zealand Shipping Co Ltd v AM Satterthwaite & Co Ltd* [1975] AC 154, 168. See also *Williams v Carwardine* (1833) 4 B & Ad 621, below, p 53.

[52] *Lancaster v Walsh* (1838) 4 M & W 16.

[53] [1893] 1 QB 256. See also *Bowerman v ABTA* [1995] 145 NLJR 1815.

[54] Below, p 47.

[55] Mrs Carlill was of course not under any obligation to use the smoke ball, still less to fall ill.

(c) COMMUNICATION OF THE OFFER

In general an offer is effective when, and not until, it is communicated to the offeree. It follows that there can in general be no acceptance in ignorance of an offer, and, despite one somewhat unsatisfactory contrary decision,[56] this seems correct in principle.

(i) Cross-offers

The necessity for the communication of the offer, and for its consequent acceptance, appears to be the reason why two identical cross-offers do not ordinarily make a contract. Two manifestations of a willingness to make the same bargain do not constitute a contract unless one is made with reference to the other.[57] In *Tinn v Hoffman & Co*:[58]

On 28 November 1871, H wrote to T offering to sell him 800 tons of iron at 69*s* per ton, together with a further quantity at the same price. On the same day, T wrote to H offering to buy 800 tons at 69*s*, together with a further quantity at a lower price. The letters crossed in the post. T contended that there was, at all events, a good contract for 800 tons at 69*s* per ton.

A majority of the Court of Exchequer Chamber expressed the opinion that H would not be bound as a result of the simultaneous offers, each being made in ignorance of the other.

(ii) Offer by rendering services must be communicated

Although conduct such as the rendering of services can constitute an offer, where that offer is not communicated to the party to whom it is intended to be made there is no opportunity of rejection and no presumption of acceptance. Thus, if A does work for B without the request or knowledge of B, A can only sue in contract for the value of the work where there is evidence of a recognition or acceptance of the work by B. This is clearly illustrated by *Taylor v Laird*:[59]

T was engaged to command L's ship and to conduct certain explorers on an expedition up the River Niger. He abandoned his command in the course of the expedition, but helped to work the vessel home, though without the knowledge of the defendant. He then claimed to be remunerated for the services thus rendered.

It was held that he could not recover. L never had the option of accepting or refusing the services while they were being rendered; and he repudiated them when he became aware of them. T's offer, being uncommunicated, did not admit of acceptance and could not give him any contractual rights against L. Pollock CB said:[60]

Suppose I clean your property without your knowledge, have I a claim on you for payment? How can you help it? One cleans another's shoes; what can the other do but put them on? Is that evidence of a contract to pay for the cleaning?

[56] *Gibbons v Proctor* (1891) 64 LT 594, 55 JP 616. For criticism and contrary authority, see below, p 52.

[57] If one is made with reference to the other, there is no reason why a contract should not be held to exist, even though it is expressed to be an 'offer' and not an acceptance: but see *Gibson v Manchester City Council* [1979] 1 WLR 294.

[58] (1873) 29 LT 271, 275, 277, 278, 279; ALI *Restatement, Contracts (2d)* para 23.

[59] (1856) 25 LJ Ex 329. See also *Forman & Co Pty Ltd v Ship Liddesdale* [1900] AC 190.

[60] (1856) 25 LJ Ex 329, 332.

In certain circumstances, for instance where the services rendered are necessary services,[61] it may be that there is a liability to make restitution of an unjust enrichment but such liability is not contractual.

3. THE ACCEPTANCE

If a contract is to be made, the offeree must accept the offer. Acceptance of an offer is the expression, by words or conduct,[62] of assent to the terms of the offer in the manner prescribed or indicated by the offeror.

(a) OFFER AND ACCEPTANCE MUST CORRESPOND

The intention of the offeree to accept must be expressed without leaving room for doubt as to the fact of acceptance, or as to the coincidence of the terms of the acceptance with those of the offer. These requirements may be summed up in the general rule, sometimes called the 'mirror image' rule, that the acceptance must be absolute, and must correspond with the terms of the offer.

In determining whether or not an acceptance is conclusive, an alleged acceptance must be distinguished from a counter-offer and rejection; an acceptance with some variation or addition of terms; and an acceptance which is equivocal, or which is qualified by reference to the subsequent arrangement of terms.

(i) Counter-offer and rejection

A counter-offer amounts to a rejection of the offer, and so operates to bring it to an end. In *Hyde v Wrench*,[63] for example:

W offered to sell a farm to H for £1,000. H said that he would give £950. W refused, and H then said he would give £1,000, and, when W declined to adhere to his original offer, H tried to obtain specific performance of the alleged contract.

The Court held that an offer to buy at £950 in response to an offer to sell for £1,000 was a refusal followed by a counter-offer, and that no contract had come into existence. But making express what would otherwise be implied[64] or inquiring whether the offeror will modify his terms does not necessarily amount to a counter-offer. So in *Stevenson, Jacques & Co v McLean*,[65] the offeree could still accept an offer of a certain quantity of iron 'at 40*s*. nett *cash* per ton', even though he had telegraphed to the offeror requesting information as to possible terms of credit. It was held that this was not a counter-offer, but was 'a mere inquiry, which should have been answered and not treated as a rejection of the offer'.[66]

[61] *Jenkins v Tucker* (1788) 1 Hy Bl 90 (burial of the dead); *Re Rhodes* (1890) 44 Ch D 94 (maintenance of a mentally incapable person, although no recovery on the facts because there was no intention to charge).

[62] *Brogden v Metropolitan Railway Co* (1877) 2 App Cas 666, below, p 45; *Day Morris Associates v Voyce* [2003] EWCA Civ 189, [2003] 2 P & CR DG2. See also above, pp 33–4.

[63] (1840) 3 Beav 334.

[64] *Lark v Outhwaite* [1991] 2 Lloyd's Rep 132, 139.

[65] (1880) 5 QBD 346. See also *Gibson v Manchester City Council* [1979] 1 WLR 294, 302.

[66] (1880) 5 QBD 346, 350.

(ii) Change of terms

A purported acceptance of an offer may introduce terms at variance with or not comprised in the offer. In such cases no contract is made,[67] since the offeree in effect rejects the offer and makes a counter-offer.[68]

In *Jones v Daniel*:[69]

A offered £1,450 for a property belonging to B. In a letter accepting the offer B enclosed a contract for the signature of A. This document contained various terms as to payment of deposit, date of completion, and requirement of title which had never been suggested in the offer.

The Court held that there was no contract; B had not accepted A's offer but made a counter-offer of his own, which was never accepted by A.

(iii) 'Battle of the forms'

The problem of the 'battle of the forms' arises where, for example, a firm offers to buy goods from another on a form which contains or refers to its standard conditions of trade. The seller 'accepts' the offer by a confirmation on a form which contains or refers to its (the seller's) standard conditions of trade. These may differ materially from those of the buyer. It may then deliver the goods. Two questions typically arise: is there a contract and, if there is, do the buyer's or the seller's conditions prevail?

In *Butler Machine Tool Co Ltd v Ex-cell-o Corporation (England) Ltd*[70] a majority of the Court of Appeal (Lawton and Bridge LJJ) applied the 'mirror image' rule and stated that the seller's confirmation amounts to a counter-offer. This is capable of acceptance by the buyer. The buyer may indicate that it accepts the counter-offer by some act or performance; for example, the receipt and acceptance of the goods, or the return of an 'acknowledgement' form containing the seller's conditions. This can be called the 'last shot' approach. In our example such an acceptance would conclude a contract subject to the seller's conditions, since it was the seller who fired the 'last shot' in the battle of the forms. Lord Denning MR, while arriving at the same result, advocated a more flexible, but less certain, approach, by which one should look at whether the documents revealed 'an agreement on all material points',[71] but the Court of Appeal in *Tekdata Interconnections Ltd v Amphenol Ltd*[72] confirmed that the majority in *Butler Machine Tool Co Ltd v Ex-cell-o* was correct. Except where there is a long-term clear

[67] Although, exceptionally, the response may be regarded as an acceptance with an offer to enter a further contract: *Monvia Motorship Corp v Keppel Shipyard (Private) Ltd* [1983] 1 Lloyd's Rep 356 (PC).

[68] The position is similar in many European systems; see Lando and Beale, *Principles of European Contract Law Parts I and II* (2000) 179.

[69] [1894] 2 Ch 332. See also *Brogden v Metropolitan Ry Co* (1877) 2 App Cas 666, below, p 45. Cf *Global Tankers Inc v Amercoat Europa NV* [1975] 1 Lloyd's Rep 666, 671.

[70] [1979] 1 WLR 401, 406, 407; Rawlings (1979) 42 MLR 715. See also *British Road Services v Arthur Crutchley Ltd* [1968] 1 All ER 811; *A Davies & Co (Shopfitters) v William Old* (1969) 67 LGR 395; *Tekdata Interconnections Ltd v Amphenol Ltd* [2009] EWCA Civ 1209, [2010] 1 Lloyd's Rep 357.

[71] [1979] 1 WLR 401, 404. Support for similar forms of flexibility can be found in the Uniform Laws on International Sales Act 1967, Sched 2, art 7(2); CISG art 19; von Mehren (1990) 38 Am J Comp Law 265.

[72] [2009] EWCA Civ 1209, [2010] 1 Lloyd's Rep 357.

course of dealing between the parties on particular terms, the normal rules of offer and acceptance must be applied; and the standard result will be that the party which sends its terms last (the party which 'fires the last shot') will win because that will be the offer which is regarded as accepted by the other party's conduct. What this approach lacks in flexibility it gains in terms of certainty.

However, in *Tekdata* the Court of Appeal recognized that the 'last shot' doctrine may be displaced by a contrary intention of the parties[73] and this possibility was applied in *TRW Ltd v Panasonic Industry Europe GmbH*.[74] That case was unusual because the clause in question was carefully drafted such that it was not the 'last shot' which applied but rather the 'first shot': the buyer signed a customer file which included a term that any dealing was to be on the seller's standard terms, and that 'Conditions of the buyer diverging from our terms and conditions shall not be valid even if we effected delivery or rendered services without reservation.' This was done in order to ensure that the seller's standard terms would always apply, which was the 'first shot'. This is a somewhat unusual example,[75] but highlights that the intention of the parties remains of paramount concern.

Courts will generally strive to find that a contract has been concluded,[76] but in some cases it may be impossible to decide that the parties have reached a contractual agreement even though services have been rendered or goods delivered. In such cases, a restitutionary non-contractual obligation in unjust enrichment to pay a reasonable sum may arise.[77] But while restitution may protect the performer by the award of the reasonable value of the performance rendered, a recipient, who may have had certain requirements as to the time of performance or its quality, may be unprotected. This is because, in the absence of a contract, the party rendering the services or delivering the goods will not be liable in damages for delay or for defective performance.[78] However, the better view is that this can be satisfactorily dealt with, within the non-contractual law of unjust enrichment, as going to the relevant enrichment of the recipient.[79]

(iv) Equivocal or qualified acceptance

The acceptance must assent unequivocally and without qualification to the terms of the offer. For example, the reply 'Your order is receiving our attention' is too indefinite to amount to an acceptance.[80] The acceptance may also be qualified by reference to the preparation of a more formal contract or by reference to terms which have still to

[73] eg *ibid*, at [25] (Dyson LJ).

[74] [2021] EWCA Civ 1558.

[75] The 'last shot' doctrine continues to dominate: see eg *Dana UK Axle Ltd v Freudenberg FST GmbH* [2021] EWHC 1751 (TCC) at [84].

[76] *KSY Juice Blends UK Ltd v Citrosuco GmbH* [2025] EWCA Civ 760 at [23], [58].

[77] *Peter Lind & Co v Mersey Docks & Harbour Board* [1972] 2 Lloyd's Rep 234. For the conditions of such liability, see below, pp 66, 70.

[78] McKendrick (1988) 8 OJLS 197, 212–13; Ball (1983) 99 LQR 572.

[79] So, eg, goods delivered late to the defendant may not be as valuable to him as goods delivered on time and this will be reflected in measuring the defendant's enrichment: see Burrows, *The Law of Restitution* (3rd edn, 2011) 375.

[80] *Rees v Warwick* (1818) 2 B & Ald 113; ALI *Restatement, Contracts (2d)* para 57.

be negotiated. In such a case the agreement is incomplete[81] and there is no binding contract.

(b) COMMUNICATION OF THE ACCEPTANCE

(i) Mental assent insufficient

Acceptance means, in general, communicated acceptance, which must be something more than a mere mental assent. A tacit formation of intention is insufficient.

In an old case in the Year Books[82] it was argued that where the produce of a field was offered to a man at a certain price if he was pleased with it on inspection, the contract was made and the property passed when he had seen and approved of the subject of the sale. But Brian CJ said:

It seems to me the plea is not good without showing that he had certified the other of his pleasure; for it is trite learning that the thought of man is not triable, for the devil himself knows not the thought of man; but if you had agreed that if the bargain pleased then you should have signified it to such an one, then I grant you need not have done more, for it is matter of fact.

Lord Blackburn approved this decision in *Brogden v Metropolitan Railway Co*:[83]

B (a supplier of coal) altered a draft coal supply agreement sent to him by M and returned it signed and marked 'approved'. M's agent put it in a drawer. The parties appear to have ordered and supplied coal upon the terms stated but, a dispute having arisen, B contended that he was not bound by the agreement.

It was held that there was a contract between the parties. This had not, however, come into existence at the time M's agent acquiesced in the offer by putting the letter in his drawer but later, either when coal was ordered by M or supplied by B.

(ii) Communication to the offeror

Even if there is some overt act or speech to give evidence of the intention to accept, English law stipulates, in addition, that acceptance is normally not complete *unless and until it is communicated to the offeror*. In the words of Lindley LJ: 'Unquestionably, as a general proposition, when an offer is made, it is necessary in order to make a binding contract, not only that it should be accepted, but that acceptance should be notified.'[84] If an offer is made by telephone, and in the middle of the reply the line goes dead, so that the offeror does not hear the words of acceptance, there is no contract.[85] And if a

[81] See below, p 69.

[82] *Anon* (1477) YB Pasch 17 Edw IV, f 1, pl 2.

[83] (1877) 2 App Cas 666.

[84] *Carlill v Carbolic Smoke Ball Co* [1893] 1 QB 256, 262. See also *Robophone Facilities Ltd v Blank* [1966] 1 WLR 1428; *Allied Marine Transport Ltd v Vale do Rio Doce Navegacao* [1985] 1 WLR 925, 937; CISG art 23. Cf below, p 47 (no need for communication where offer stipulates a prescribed mode of acceptance).

[85] *Entores v Miles Far East Corp* [1955] 2 QB 327, 332 (Denning LJ); Winfield (1939) 55 LQR 499, 514; ALI *Restatement, Contracts (2d)* para 65. But cf below, pp 47–50, for the different rule which applies to acceptance by post.

person shouts to another across a river or courtyard, but the offeror does not hear the reply because it is drowned by an aircraft flying overhead, there is no contract at that moment and the offeree must repeat the acceptance in order that it might be effective.

(iii) Communication other than by offeree

The justification for the rule requiring communication is that the offeror is entitled to know whether a binding contract has been concluded by acceptance. In principle, therefore, there would seem to be no reason (other than one of certainty) why a contract should not come into existence if the offeror is made aware or is informed that the offer has been accepted even though the acceptance is not communicated to the offeror by the offeree.[86] *Powell v Lee*,[87] however, appears to hold that it is necessary that the acceptance be communicated by the offeree or by his duly authorized agent.

The managers of a school resolved to appoint the claimant as its headmaster. One of the managers, acting in his individual capacity, informed the claimant. The claimant received no other communication and subsequently the resolution was rescinded.

It was held that there was no concluded contract: 'the mere fact that the [whole body of] managers did not authorize such a communication, which is the usual course to be adopted, implied that they meant to reserve the power to reconsider the decision at which they had arrived'.[88]

We now turn to the exceptions to the general rule that acceptance must be communicated before it can take effect.

(iv) Waiver of communication

The general rule that an acceptance of an offer made ought to be notified to the offeror is for the benefit of the offeror, who may expressly or impliedly waive the requirement of notification and agree that an uncommunicated acceptance will suffice. But there must be some overt act or conduct on the part of the offeree which is evidence of an intention to accept, and which conforms to the mode of acceptance indicated by the offeror.

In *Carlill v Carbolic Smoke Ball Co*,[89] previously discussed, it will be remembered that Mrs Carlill had performed the condition stipulated by the manufacturers of the smoke balls without communicating to them the acceptance of the offer, and a binding unilateral contract arose. Bowen LJ stated:[90]

The person who makes the offer may dispense with notice to himself if he thinks it desirable to do so, and I suppose there can be no doubt that where a person in an offer made by him to another person, expressly or impliedly intimates a particular method of acceptance as sufficient to make the bargain binding, it is only necessary for the other person to whom such offer is made to follow the indicated mode of acceptance; and if the person making

[86] *Levita's Case* (1867) LR 3 Ch App 36. See also *Dickinson v Dodds* (1876) 2 Ch D 463, below, p 59 (third-party notification of revocation of offer effective).

[87] (1908) 99 LT 284. [88] *Ibid*, 286 (Channell J). [89] [1893] 1 QB 256, above, p 40.

[90] *Ibid*, 269. See also Lindley LJ at 262. See further *Manchester Diocesan Council for Education v Commercial & General Investments Ltd* [1970] 1 WLR 241, 245.

the offer, expressly or impliedly intimates in his offer that it will be sufficient to act on the proposal without communicating acceptance of it to himself, performance of the condition is a sufficient acceptance without notification.

The nature and terms of the offer need to be considered carefully to ascertain whether they entitle the offeree to dispense with notice of acceptance. If A tells B by letter that he will receive and pay for certain goods if B will send them to him, such an offer may be accepted by sending the goods.[91]

(v) Promise for an act

In the case of general offers and other offers which indicate performance as a mode of acceptance so as to create a unilateral contract, as in *Carlill v Carbolic Smoke Ball Co*, it is performance, not notice of acceptance, that is contemplated. An offer of reward for the supply of information, or for the return of a lost dog, does not contemplate an intimation of acceptance from every person who, on becoming aware of the offer, decides to ascertain the information or to search for the dog.[92] Indeed the offeree may already have the information or have found the dog, and can do no more than send it on to the offeror. The question as to whether it is the commencement of performance, or its completion, that constitutes the acceptance of an offer of a unilateral contract is discussed below in the context of revocation of the offer.[93]

(vi) Acceptance by post

A distinction is drawn between acceptance by instantaneous methods such as telephone and e-mail,[94] and acceptance by non-instantaneous methods such as post.[95] Instantaneous methods, where the acceptor will generally know that his communication has not arrived at once and can try again, are subject to the general requirement that acceptance must be communicated to the offeror.[96] Where, however, it is reasonable for the offeree to notify acceptance by post,[97] the acceptance is completed when the letter is posted.[98] The offeror is bound from that time although the acceptance has not been delivered and may never be delivered.

The postal acceptance rule was laid down in *Adams v Lindsell*:[99]

[91] *Harvey v Johnston* (1848) 6 CB 295, 304; *Newcomb v De Roos* (1859) 2 E & E 271. Cf *Kennedy v Thomassen* [1929] 1 Ch 426. But cf *Rust v Abbey Life Assurance Co Ltd* [1978] 1 Lloyd's Rep 386, 392 (offer to invest in property bond accepted by allocation of units; no need to send policy to offeror).

[92] *Carlill v Carbolic Smoke Ball Co* [1893] 1 QB 256, 270.

[93] Below, pp 55–7.

[94] For the view that the same rule should be applied to e-mails as for telex and fax, see Hill (2001) 17 JCL 151; Nolan, in Burrows and Peel (eds), *Contract Formation and Parties* (2010) ch 4.

[95] Before they fell out of use, telegrams were treated legally in the same way as letters.

[96] *Entores v Miles Far East Corp* [1955] 2 QB 327 (telex); *Brinkibon Ltd v Stahag Stahl und Stahlwarenhandelsgesellschaft mbH* [1983] 2 AC 34 (telex); *JSC Zestafoni G Nikoladze Ferralloy Plant v Ronly Holdings Ltd* [2004] EWHC 245 (Comm), [2004] 2 Lloyd's Rep 335 (fax).

[97] *Henthorn v Fraser* [1892] 2 Ch 27, 33.

[98] *Adams v Lindsell* (1818) 1 B & Ald 681; *Dunlop v Higgins* (1848) 1 HLC 381; *Household Fire and Carriage Accident Insurance Co Ltd v Grant* (1879) 4 Ex D 216; *Henthorn v Fraser* [1892] 2 Ch 27; *Port Sudan Cotton Co v Govindaswamy Chettiar & Sons* [1977] 2 Lloyd's Rep 5. For the equivalent rule for telegrams, see *Stevenson, Jacques & Co v McLean* (1880) 5 QBD 346; *Bruner v Moore* [1904] 1 Ch 305, 316.

[99] (1818) 1 B & Ald 681.

On 2 September 1817, L wrote offering to sell to A a certain quantity of wool, and added 'receiving your answer in course of post'. If the letter containing this offer had been properly directed, an answer might have been received by the 7th; but it was misdirected and did not reach A until the 5th so that their acceptance, posted the same day, was not received by L until the 9th. On the 8th—before the acceptance had arrived—L sold the wool to another. A sued for breach of contract.

It was unsuccessfully argued on behalf of L that there was no contract between the parties until the letter of acceptance was actually received. The Court stated:[100]

If that were so, no contract could ever be completed by post. For if [L] were not bound by their offer when accepted by [A] until the answer was received, then [A] ought not to be bound till they had received the notification that [L] had received their answer and assented to it. And so it might go on *ad infinitum*.

The logic of this passage is questionable, but it was undoubtedly necessary for the Court to establish some definite rule as to the time of a postal acceptance.

One of the more obvious consequences of the postal acceptance rule is that the offeror must bear the risk of the letter of acceptance being delayed or lost. In *Household Fire and Carriage Accident Insurance Co Ltd v Grant*:[101]

The defendant offered to buy shares in the claimant company. The claimant sent a letter of acceptance to the defendant but it was lost in the post and never arrived. The liquidator of the company sued the defendant for the money owing for the shares.

The Court of Appeal held that, as an acceptance by post is valid when sent, there was a contract under which the defendant was bound to pay for the shares.

Where, however, the delay or loss is due to the fault of the offeree, as in the case of an acceptance which is improperly addressed or insufficiently stamped, it would seem that it only takes effect if and when it is received by the offeror, provided that this occurs within the time within which a regular acceptance would have been received.[102]

(vii) Place of contracting

Whether the postal acceptance rule applies also determines *where* a contract is made.[103] If the means of communication is by letter, the contract is complete when the letter is posted,[104] and it is there that the contract is made. In other cases the general rule is that the contract is made when and where the acceptance is received.[105]

[100] *Ibid*, 683. The *ratio decidendi* of the case is complicated by the assertion that the delay was caused by the defendants' negligence in misdirecting their offer. The effect of such delay appears to extend the permissible period within which the offer may be accepted (see below, p 61) unless the offeree knows or has reason to know of the delay: ALI *Restatement, Contracts (2d)* para 51.

[101] (1879) 4 Ex D 216.

[102] *Korbetis v Transgrain Shipping BV* [2005] EWHC 1345 (QB). See also *Getreide-Import-Gesellschaft v Contimar SA Compania Commercial y Maritima* [1953] 1 WLR 793; ALI *Restatement, Contracts (2d)* paras 67–8.

[103] Although this was criticized by Lord Sumption in *Brownlie v Four Seasons Holdings Inc* [2017] UKSC 80, [2018] 1 WLR 192 at [16].

[104] *Cowan v O'Connor* (1888) 20 QBD 640.

[105] *Brinkibon Ltd v Stahag Stahl und Stahlwarenhandelsgesellschaft mbH* [1983] 2 AC 34 approving *Entores v Miles Far East Corp* [1955] 2 QB 327 (acceptance by telex from Holland to London held to constitute a contract made in England).

(viii) Rationale of postal rule

Various attempts have been made to justify the postal acceptance rule analytically.[106] One line of reasoning attempts to eliminate any difficulties as to consensus by treating the post office as the agent of the offeror not only for delivering the offer, but for receiving the notification of its acceptance;[107] yet the post office is clearly not an agent to whom acceptance is or could be communicated. Another is based on the fact that posting the acceptance puts it irretrievably out of the offeree's control. The same can, however, be said of other means of communication which are not completed until receipt[108] so this does not explain why posting exceptionally constitutes an acceptance without notification. Difficulties with justifying the postal rule have led to its abolition in Scotland.[109]

Nevertheless, the best explanation for the postal rule would seem to be that the rule is based, not on logic, but on commercial convenience.[110] If hardship is caused, as it obviously may be, by the delay or loss of a letter of acceptance, some rule is necessary, and the rule at which the Courts have arrived is probably as satisfactory as any other would be.[111]

First, it is always open to the offeror to secure protection by requiring actual notification of the acceptance.[112] The nature of the offer or the circumstances in which it was made may indicate that notification is required and Courts may be willing to displace what has been termed an 'artificial concept of communication'.[113] Secondly, the rule is a pragmatic way of limiting the power to revoke an offer before acceptance,[114] even where the offeror has promised not to.[115] It also prevents the offeree from being able to nullify the acceptance while it is in transit and thus from speculating by watching the market and deciding whether to send an overtaking rejection.[116] Further, in the event of delay or loss of the letter of acceptance, it is the offeror who is more likely to be

106 Winfield (1939) 55 LQR 499; Nussbaum (1936) 36 Col L Rev 920.

107 *Household Fire and Carriage Accident Insurance Co Ltd v Grant* (1879) 4 Ex D 216, 221; *Hebb's Case* (1867) LR 4 Eq 9, 12.

108 *Entores v Miles Far East Corp* [1955] 2 QB 327.

109 Contract (Formation and Remedies) (Scotland) Act 2026 s 14.

110 *Re Imperial Land Co of Marseilles (Harris' Case)* (1872) LR 7 Ch App 587, 594; *Brinkibon Ltd v Stahag Stahl und Stahlwarenhandelsgesellschaft mbH* [1983] 2 AC 34, 41, 48.

111 Winfield (1939) 55 LQR 499, 506. Three principal systems seem to be in operation in other countries: (i) *information*: when the offeror is actually informed of the acceptance; (ii) *expedition*: when the offeree despatches the letter of acceptance; and (iii) *reception*: when the acceptance is received at its destination, whether the offeror is actually informed or not. See Evans (1966) 15 ICLQ 553. Under CISG arts 18(2), 24, and 21(2) the acceptance becomes effective at the moment the indication of assent is delivered at the address of the offeror; if the letter is lost, there is no contract, but if it is delayed, there is normally a contract, unless the offeror has promptly informed the offeree that he considers his offer as having lapsed.

112 *Holwell Securities Ltd v Hughes* [1974] 1 WLR 155.

113 *Ibid*, 157, 158, 161; *New Hart Builders Ltd v Brindley* [1975] Ch 342 (rule displaced where contracts required 'notice to . . .' or 'to notify').

114 *Re Imperial Land Co of Marseilles (Harris' Case)* (1872) LR 7 Ch App 587, 594.

115 Below, p 58. Nussbaum (1936) 36 Col L Rev 920, 922–7.

116 Below, p 54.

the first to enquire why no reply has been received to the offer, rather than the offeree to enquire whether the acceptance has been received.

The rule has, however, been criticized.[117] The number of different modes of communication now available[118] has been said to give rise to an increasing number of problems of demarcation and it is argued that the law would be much more coherent if there were only one rule for all means of communication. It has also been said that the law should not, as the postal acceptance rule does, favour the offeree because, while the offeror is in ignorance as to the actions of the offeree, the offeree has full knowledge of what the position is. The offeree knows that the acceptance has been posted and knows or ought to know that mail is not infrequently delayed. Nevertheless, the ability of the offeror to control the method of acceptance, the offeror's ability to revoke even a 'firm' offer before acceptance,[119] and the desirability of preventing speculation by the offeree are, it is suggested, good reasons for the rule.

The rule may in any event not be as anomalous as it appears when compared only with the rules governing instantaneous modes of communication. In a previous edition of this work, it was argued that the principles governing postal acceptance were merely examples of a wider principle that where the offeror either expressly or impliedly indicates the mode of acceptance and this, as a means of communication, proves to be nugatory or insufficient, he does so at his own risk.[120] Suppose that A sends an offer to B by messenger across a lake with a request that B, if she accepts, will at a certain hour communicate her acceptance by firing a gun or lighting a fire. Why, it was asked, should B suffer if a storm renders the gun inaudible or a fog obscures the light of the fire? Although, as we have seen,[121] this 'risk' approach does not apply where instantaneous communication is concerned, it is suggested that it has validity in cases where there is bound to be a substantial interval between the time when the acceptance is sent and the time when it is received.[122]

(ix) Acceptance by silence

In principle, it is difficult to see how the silence or inaction of an offeree who fails to reply to an offer can operate as an acceptance, for there will have been no communication of the acceptance to the offeror. Even if the offeror has waived[123] communication by indicating that acceptance by silence will suffice, it is clear that the offeror cannot confront the offeree with the alternative of either refusing the offer or being subjected to a contractual obligation by reason of the failure to reply. Although a form or time of acceptance may be prescribed, an offeror cannot prescribe the form or time of refusal

[117] eg by Gardner (1992) 12 OJLS 170; Scot Law Com No 144 (1993) paras 4.4–4.7.

[118] Apart from telex, fax, e-mail, and the various types of electronic document interchange, there are also couriers, private messenger delivery, and document exchange services.

[119] Below, p 57.

[120] Anson (20th edn, 1952) 36.

[121] *Entores v Miles Far East Corp* [1955] 2 QB 327; *Brinkibon Ltd v Stahag Stahl und Stahlwarenhandelsgesellschaft mbH* [1983] 2 AC 34, above, p 45.

[122] *Brinkibon Ltd v Stahag Stahl und Stahlwarenhandelsgesellschaft mbH* [1983] 2 AC 34, 48.

[123] See above, p 46.

so as to impose a contract on the other party if the other party does not refuse in some particular way or within some particular time.[124] In *Felthouse v Bindley*, for example:[125]

F offered by letter to buy his nephew's horse for £30 15*s*, adding, 'If I hear no more about him I shall consider the horse mine at £30 15*s*.' No answer was returned to this letter, but the nephew told B, an auctioneer, to keep the horse out of a sale of his farm stock, as he intended to reserve it for his uncle F. B sold the horse by mistake, and F sued him for conversion of his property.

The Court held that as the nephew had never signified to F his acceptance of the offer before the auction sale took place, there was no bargain to pass the property in the horse to F, and therefore he had no right to complain of the sale.[126] Willes J said:[127] 'It is clear that the uncle had no right to impose upon the nephew a sale of his horse for £30 15*s* unless he chose to comply with the condition of writing to repudiate the offer.'

In more modern times this same principle may be illustrated by the practice of sending out unsolicited goods. A publisher may send a book to a prospective customer with a letter saying, in effect, 'If you do not return the book by a certain day, I shall presume that you have bought it.' It is clear that he cannot by these means impose a contract on the unwilling recipient. But persons with no knowledge of the law may well be misled into thinking that they are bound to pay for the book, and the subsequent letters which they receive may frequently be designed to foster this misapprehension. As a result, in 1971, the legislature enacted the Unsolicited Goods and Services Act whereby the recipients of unsolicited goods may, in certain circumstances, treat them as if they were an unconditional gift to themselves, and suppliers may be guilty of a criminal offence if they demand or threaten legal proceedings for payment.[128]

On the other hand, circumstances can arise where acceptance could more legitimately be presumed from silence. Previous dealings between the parties may have been conducted on the basis that orders for goods have been fulfilled by the seller without any notification of acceptance other than the despatch of the goods, and the offeror has thereby been led to believe that the practice will continue.[129] It is even arguable, by analogy with the cases we have noted on waiver by the offeror of the need for communication of acceptance, that, if the offeror stipulates that acceptance may be constituted by silence or inaction, an unequivocal manifestation of an intention to accept on the part of the offeree (or, possibly, detrimental reliance on the offer by the offeree)[130] should bind the offeror. This, however, would run counter to the decision in *Felthouse v Bindley*, where, it

[124] Pollock, *Principles of Contract* (13th edn, 1950) 22.

[125] (1862) 11 CBNS 869, aff'd (1863) 7 LT 835. See also *Allied Marine Transport Ltd v Vale do Rio Doce Navegacao SA* [1985] 1 WLR 925, 937. See further Miller (1972) 35 MLR 489.

[126] In addition, no contract was enforceable on the day of the auction because it was a contract for the sale of goods for a price greater than £10 and there was not in existence a written memorandum of the contract as required by the Statute of Frauds 1677: see pp 78–9.

[127] (1862) 11 CBNS 869, 875.

[128] The Unsolicited Goods and Services Act 1971 has been amended, and partly replaced, by the Consumer Protection (Distance Selling) Regulations 2000 (SI 2000 No 2334).

[129] ALI *Restatement, Contracts (2d)* para 72.

[130] Cf *Fairline Shipping Corp v Adamson* [1975] QB 180; *Schuldenfrei v Hilton (IT)* [1999] STC 821, 831, 833. See also, below, p 121 (promissory estoppel).

will be noted, the nephew made known his intention to accept his uncle's offer. No doubt, in many cases, silence is ambiguous[131] and therefore cannot constitute an acceptance. But if, as in *Felthouse v Bindley* itself, the necessary intention to accept could be proved, there seems to be no convincing reason why a contract should not come into existence, particularly where the offeree has relied on the terms of the offer and it is the offeror who now denies that there is a contract. So, if in a scenario such as *Felthouse v Bindley* the horse had died after the nephew had directed the auctioneer to keep it out of the sale but before the time of that sale, the uncle should not be able to escape paying the price to his nephew on the ground that the nephew had never communicated his acceptance to him. More recent dicta support this. Thus, it has been stated:[132]

[W]here the offeree himself indicates that an offer is to be taken as accepted if he does not indicate to the contrary by an ascertainable time, he is undertaking to speak if he does not want an agreement to be concluded. I see no reason in principle why that should not be an exceptional circumstance such that the offer can be accepted by silence.

(c) ACCEPTOR MUST HAVE KNOWLEDGE OF OFFER

If A offers a promise for an act and B does the act in ignorance of the offer, can B claim performance of the offer on becoming aware of its existence? As illustrated by the case of cross-offers,[133] the answer appears to be that, if B has not heard of the offer before doing the act, it cannot be accepted.[134] In *Gibbons v Proctor*,[135] however, a Divisional Court held that a police officer was entitled to claim a reward for information given to a superintendent of police, although it seems the officer did not know of the reward before giving the information. The decision, as reported, is an unsatisfactory one, for the facts of the case are by no means clear.[136] Accordingly, it cannot be considered a compelling authority, and a New York case, *Fitch v Snedaker*,[137] is sometimes cited to the contrary. It was there laid down that a reward cannot be claimed by one who did not know that it had been offered. The latter decision seems correct in principle. A person who does an act for which a reward has been offered in ignorance of the offer cannot say either that there was a consensus of wills with the offeror, or that the act was done in return for or in reliance on the promise offered. If, however, the acceptor knows of the offer, but is inspired to perform by a motive other than that of claiming the reward, such a motive is

[131] Above, pp 33–4.

[132] *Re Selectmove Ltd* [1995] 1 WLR 474, 478 (Peter Gibson LJ). See also *Vitol SA v Norelf Ltd* [1996] AC 800, 812.

[133] See *Tinn v Hoffman & Co* (1873) 29 LT 271, above, p 41.

[134] *Taylor v Allon* [1966] 1 QB 304, 311; *Tracomin SA v Anton C Nielsen* [1984] 2 Lloyd's Rep 195, 203.

[135] (1891) 64 LT 594, 55 JP 616. Cf *Neville v Kelly* (1862) 12 CBNS 740. See Hudson (1968) 84 LQR 503.

[136] It appears that the officer did know of the offer of reward before the superintendent gave the information to the offeror, and that the officer therefore did know of the offer before the acceptance was complete.

[137] 38 NY 248 (1868). See also *Bloom v American Swiss Watch Co* 1915 AD 100 (South Africa); *R v Clarke* (1927) 40 CLR 227 (Australia); ALI *Restatement, Contracts* (2d) para 51 and Comment a.

immaterial. So in *Williams v Carwardine*[138] where the claimant, with knowledge of the reward, supplied information leading to the conviction of an assailant for murder, but only did this 'to ease her conscience, and in hopes of forgiveness hereafter', she was held entitled to claim the £20 offered. Her acceptance could be referred to the offer.

(d) PRESCRIBED MODE OF ACCEPTANCE

If the terms or the circumstances of the offer do no more than suggest a mode of acceptance, it seems that the offeree would not be bound to this mode so long as the mode used was one which did not cause delay, and which brought the acceptance to the knowledge of the offeror. A departure from the usual or suggested method of communication would probably throw upon the offeree the risk that the acceptance would be delayed, but, subject to this, an offer delivered by hand could be accepted by post, or an offer made by post could be accepted by e-mail. Is, however, an offeror who expressly prescribes the method of communication free to treat any departure from this method as a nullity? In the American case, *Eliason v Henshaw*:[139]

> E offered to buy flour from H, requesting that an answer should be sent to him at Harper's Ferry by the wagon which brought the offer. H sent a letter of acceptance by mail to Georgetown, thinking that this would reach E more speedily. He was wrong, and the letter arrived after the time that the reply might have been expected.

The Supreme Court of the United States held that E was entitled to refuse to purchase:[140]

> It is an undeniable principle of the law of contracts, that an offer of a bargain by one person to another, imposes no obligation upon the former, until it is accepted by the latter, according to the terms in which the offer was made. Any qualification of, or departure from, those terms, invalidates the offer, unless the same be agreed to by the person who made it.

The same rule applies in English law: an offeror, who by the terms of the offer insists upon its acceptance in a particular manner, is entitled to say that he is not bound unless acceptance is effected or communicated in that precise way.[141] Nevertheless, if the stipulation as to the mode of acceptance is inserted at the instance of and for the protection or benefit of the offeror, the offeror may by conduct or otherwise waive strict compliance with it, provided that the offeree is not adversely affected.[142] Moreover, unless as a matter of construction that prescribed mode of acceptance is mandatory, another mode of acceptance which is no less advantageous to the offeror will suffice.[143]

[138] (1833) 4 B & Ad 621; the fact of her knowledge is disclosed by the report in (1833) 5 C & P 566; *Lark v Outhwaite* [1991] 2 Lloyd's Rep 132, 140. Cf *R v Clarke* (1927) 40 CLR 227. See Mitchell and Phillips (2002) 22 OJLS 115.

[139] (1819) 4 Wheaton 225.

[140] *Ibid*, 228 (Washington J).

[141] *Manchester Diocesan Council for Education v Commercial & General Investments Ltd* [1970] 1 WLR 241, 246.

[142] *Ibid*; *Carlyle Finance Ltd v Pallas Industrial Finance Ltd* [1999] All ER (Comm) 659.

[143] *Tinn v Hoffman & Co* (1873) 29 LT 271, 274, 278; *Manchester Diocesan Council for Education v Commercial & General Investments Ltd* [1970] 1 WLR 241, 246; ALI *Restatement, Contracts (2d)* paras 29, 68; Winfield (1939) 55 LQR 499, 516.

(e) REVOCATION OF THE ACCEPTANCE

Since the general rule is that acceptance is not complete until it has been communicated to the offeror, it follows that an acceptance can be revoked at any time before this occurs, provided, of course, that the revocation itself is communicated before the acceptance arrives. But what is the position in relation to postal acceptances? Since the acceptance is complete as soon as the letter of acceptance is posted, a telephone call revoking the acceptance would be inoperative, even though it reached the offeror before the letter. This is both the logical and fair conclusion: otherwise the offeree could blow both hot and cold, having the benefit of certainty in the postal acceptance, and the opportunity to revoke it if the offer turned out suddenly to be disadvantageous.[144] If, for example, shares are offered on a fluctuating market, it would seem unfair if the offeree could bind the offeror by a postal acceptance when the shares advanced in price, but send off a revocation if the market fell. There is no reason why an offeree who chooses to accept by post should have an opportunity of changing his mind which would not have been available if the contract had been made face-to-face.

This solution should not, however, operate to the detriment of the offeror. If the offeror acts on the purported revocation, for example by selling the shares which are the subject-matter of the offer, the offeree would not be permitted once again to change his mind and rely on the postal acceptance rule in order to claim damages for breach of contract.

4. TERMINATION OF THE OFFER

Once the acceptance has been communicated to the offeror, it cannot be recalled or undone. But until an offer is accepted, it creates no legal rights, and it may be terminated at any time. Termination of the offer may come about in a number of ways: it may be revoked before acceptance, or the offeree may reject the offer. Also, an offer may lapse by the passage of time or be determined by the death of the offeror or offeree.

(a) REVOCATION OF THE OFFER

The law relating to the revocation of an offer may be summed up in two rules: (1) an offer may be revoked at any time before acceptance; and (2) an offer is made irrevocable by acceptance.

(i) Revocable before acceptance

The first of these rules may be illustrated by the case of *Offord v Davies*:[145]

[144] In *Countess of Dunmore v Alexander* (1830) 9 S 190 (Scotland), Lord Craigie (dissenting) held that an offeree could not revoke her acceptance, but the majority of the Court treated the case as one of the revocation of an offer. See also *Wenkheim v Arndt* (1873) 1 JR 73 (NZ); *Kinch v Bullard* [1999] 1 WLR 423. Surprisingly, and unpersuasively, in *Household Fire and Carriage Accident Insurance Co Ltd v Grant* (1879) 4 Ex D 216, Bramwell LJ at 255 was of the opinion that the revocation would be effective. See also *Dick v US* 82 Fed Supp 326 (1949); Ellison Kahn (1955) 72 SALJ 246, 257; Hudson (1966) 82 LQR 169.

[145] (1862) 12 CBNS 748; *Scammell v Dicker* [2001] 1 WLR 631.

D made a written offer to O that, if he would discount bills for another firm, D would guarantee the payment of such bills to the extent of £600 during a period of twelve calendar months. Some bills were discounted by O, and duly paid, but before the twelve months had expired D, the guarantor, revoked his offer and notified O that he would guarantee no more bills. O continued to discount bills, some of which were not paid, and then sued D on the guarantee.

It was held that the revocation was a good defence to the action. The alleged guarantee was an offer, for a period of 12 months, of promises for acts, of guarantees for discounts. Each discount turned the offer into a promise, *pro tanto*, but the entire offer could at any time be revoked except as regards discounts made before notice of revocation.

(ii) Irrevocable after acceptance

The rule that an offer is made irrevocable by acceptance is illustrated by *Great Northern Railway Co v Witham*,[146] which, like in *Offord v Davies*, involved a continuing relationship:

The GNR company advertised for tenders for the supply of such iron articles as it might require between 1 November 1871, and 31 October 1872. W sent in a tender to supply the articles required on certain terms and in such quantities as the company 'might order from time to time', and his tender was accepted by the company. Orders were given and executed for some time on the terms of the tender but finally W was given an order which he refused to execute. The company sued him for breach of contract in that he had failed to perform this order.

It is important to note the exact relationship of the parties. The company by advertisement invited all dealers in iron to make tenders, that is, to state the terms of the offers which they were prepared to make. W's tender stated the terms of an offer which might be accepted at any time, or any number of times, in the ensuing 12 months. The acceptance of the tender did not in itself make a contract; it was merely an intimation by the company that it regarded W's tender as a standing offer, which it would be willing to accept as and when it required the articles to be supplied. Each fresh order constituted an acceptance of this standing offer. If W wished to revoke his offer he could have done so, but only as to the future; in the meantime he was bound to perform any order already made. The Court therefore held that he was liable for breach of contract.

(iii) Unilateral contracts

Some difficulty is experienced in the case of 'unilateral' contracts, where an act is done in return for a promise.[147] If one person promises a certain sum to another on performance by that other of a stipulated act, at what point in time is the acceptance of the offer complete? The traditional answer to this question is that the acceptance is complete only when the act has been completely performed. It therefore follows that up to this time the offeror is at liberty to revoke the offer. If, for example, a firm of breakfast food manufacturers were to offer to pay £100 to any person who consumed a certain quantity of their breakfast food within the next three months, they would be able to

[146] (1873) LR 9 CP 16. Contrast *Percival Ltd v LCC Asylums etc Committee* (1918) 87 LJKB 677.

[147] See above, p 32.

revoke their offer after two months had elapsed—to the detriment of those who had almost completed their part of the bargain, and with profit to themselves. Or to use a judicial example,[148] if one man offers another £100 if he will go to York, he can revoke when the other is half-way there.

In order to avoid such an inequitable result,[149] Sir Frederick Pollock argued that a distinction should be drawn between the acceptance of the offer and the performance of the stipulated act: the acceptance is complete once the offeree has unequivocally commenced performance (so that the offeror cannot effectively revoke the offer after this time), but the offeror is not bound to pay the £100 until the act has been completely performed.[150] This view has some judicial support. In *Errington v Errington*,[151] a father promised his son and daughter-in-law that a house in which they were living should belong to them as soon as they had paid off the instalments of a mortgage on the premises. The couple started to pay, at which point Denning LJ considered that the father's promise could not be revoked:[152]

> The father's promise was a unilateral contractual promise of the house in return for their act of paying the instalments. It could not be revoked by him once the couple entered on performance of the act, but it would cease to bind him if they left it incomplete and unperformed.

On this view, the offeror is unable to revoke his offer; but his duty to perform his obligation is conditional upon completed performance of the stipulated act by the offeree.

Denning LJ's statement was approved by the Court of Appeal in *Soulsbury v Soulsbury*:[153]

> The deceased former husband of the claimant promised her that she would receive £100,000 on his death if she did not enforce an order for periodical payments in her favour against him or seek any other order for ancillary relief against him. The question was whether that constituted a binding contract that could be enforced by the claimant against the estate of the deceased.

It was held that there was a binding contract. Although the discussion in the case focused on dismissing policy objections to enforcing this contract (eg that it ousted

[148] *Rogers v Snow* (1573) Dalison 94; *GN Ry v Witham* (1873) LR 9 CP 16, 19.

[149] It has been contended that there is no injustice, since the offeree is not bound to go to York and may give up at any time. The offeror, it is argued, ought to have a similar right to give up his side of the transaction: Wormser (1916) 26 Yale LJ 136. This reasoning is not attractive.

[150] Pollock, *Principles of Contract* (13th edn, 1950) 19; see also *Offord v Davies* (1862) 12 CBNS 748, 753; Law Revision Committee, Sixth Interim Report (Cmd 5449, 1937) para 39; ALI *Restatement, Contracts (2d)* para 45; CISG art 16(2)(b).

[151] [1952] 1 KB 290.

[152] *Ibid*, 295. See also *Daulia Ltd v Four Millbank Nominees Ltd* [1978] Ch 231, 239; *Harvela Investments Ltd v Royal Trust of Canada (CI) Ltd* [1986] AC 207. For a slightly different view, see *Morrison Steamship Co Ltd v The Crown* (1924) 20 Ll LR 283, 297 where Viscount Cave LC suggested that 'when work is done and expense incurred on the faith of a conditional promise, the promisor comes under an obligation not to revoke his promise, and if he does so he may be sued for damages or on a quantum meruit'. On that view, it would appear that the claimant could not insist on completing performance and claiming the promised sum.

[153] [2007] EWCA Civ 969, [2008] Fam 1.

the jurisdiction of the Courts), Longmore LJ, with whom Smith LJ agreed, pointed out that the facts involved a unilateral contract. Citing Denning LJ in *Errington v Errington*, Longmore LJ said that there could be no revocation once the claimant had refrained from suing for maintenance and that this was a stronger case than *Errington* because here the claimant, on the deceased's death, had completed all possible performance of the act required for enforcement of the deceased's promise.

To overcome the objection that the consideration for the promise (ie what the offeror has bargained for) is the completion rather than the starting of the performance, one might argue that there is a subsidiary unilateral contract under which the offeror promises not to revoke the offer of the main unilateral contract once the offeree has started to perform.

It may well be, of course, that the nature of the offer itself, or the circumstances under which it was made, indicate that it was never intended to be irrevocable by the offeror.[154] But otherwise it is submitted that English law will not deny the offeree a remedy if the offer is revoked after the performance requested has been commenced.

(iv) 'Firm' offers

It will be noted that in *Offord v Davies*, discussed above, the mere fact that the defendants promised to guarantee payment for 12 months did not preclude them from revoking before that period had elapsed.[155] It is a rule of English law that a promise to keep an offer open needs consideration[156] to make it binding. The offeree in such a case is said to 'purchase an option': the offeror makes a separate contract not to revoke the offer during a stated period. The position is similar where the offeree expressly or impliedly promises to do or refrain from doing something in exchange for the offeror's promise not to revoke the offer. For example, the offeree may promise not to negotiate with anyone else for a fixed period.[157] Again, a builder tendering for a construction contract may have invited quotations for a fixed period (ie firm offers) from electricity or carpentry subcontractors and expressly or impliedly promised to use the figures contained in those offers in its tender. In these cases the offeror by its promise precludes itself from exercising its right to revoke the offer; but where it receives no consideration for keeping the offer open, it says in effect, 'You may accept within such and such a time, but this limitation is entirely for my benefit, and I make no binding promise not to revoke my offer in the meantime.' The Law Revision Committee recommended reform of the law on firm offers so that 'an agreement to keep an offer open for a definite period of time or until the occurrence of some specified event shall not be unenforceable by reason of the absence of consideration.'[158] This has not been implemented.[159] A firm offer may

[154] *Luxor (Eastbourne) Ltd v Cooper* [1941] AC 108.

[155] Above, p 55. See also *Dickinson v Dodds* (1876) 2 Ch D 463, below, p 59; *Routledge v Grant* (1828) 4 Bing 653.

[156] Which may sometimes be nominal: *Mountford v Scott* [1975] Ch 258. See further, below, pp 103–4.

[157] *Pitt v PHH Asset Management Ltd* [1994] 1 WLR 327, 332, below, p 68 although this is probably better explained as a unilateral contract.

[158] Sixth Interim Report (Cmd 5449, 1937) para 38. See too Law Commission Working Paper No 60 (1975). CISG art 16(2) provides that an offer indicating that it is irrevocable or one that has been relied on by the offeree cannot be revoked.

[159] An offer in a deed is an exception to the general law on firm offers: *Beesly v Hallwood Estates Ltd* [1961] Ch 105; ALI *Restatement, Contracts (2d)* para 25, Comment c.

become irrevocable where the transaction can be characterized as a unilateral contract and the offeree has relied on the offer by embarking on performance of the specified act.[160] English law does not recognize a general principle based on the protection of reliance,[161] so unless a unilateral contract can be found or the action in reliance has been requested by the offeror and amounts to consideration, an offeree who relies on a firm offer will not be protected by the law of contract. Similarly there is unlikely to be a remedy in tort for revoking an offer that has been relied on[162] but, where the offeree's action in reliance consists in the rendering of services or the delivery of goods, unless the offeree can be said to have taken the risk that the offer might be withdrawn, as may well be the case in the context of tendering, the offeror may be obliged by the law of unjust enrichment to pay a reasonable sum in respect of the services or goods.[163]

(v) Revocation must be communicated

Revocation, if it is to be operative, must be communicated. In the case of acceptance we have seen that, in certain circumstances, it is not necessary that the acceptance should have actually come to the notice of the offeror; the posting of a letter, the doing of an act, may constitute an acceptance and make a contract. A revocation of an offer cannot, however, be communicated in the same way, by the posting of a letter of revocation, or by the sale to A of an article offered to B to purchase, but must be brought to the notice of the offeree. The law on this subject was settled by *Byrne* & *Co v Leon Van Tienhoven* & *Co*:[164]

VT, writing from Cardiff on 1 October, made an offer to B in New York asking for a reply by cable. B received the letter on the 11th, and at once accepted in the manner requested. In the meantime, however, VT had, on 8 October, posted a letter revoking the offer. This letter did not reach B until the 20th.

Lindley J held, first, that a revocation was inoperative until communicated, and secondly, that the revocation of an offer was not communicated by the mere posting of a letter; therefore B's acceptance on 11 October could not be affected by the fact that VT's letter of revocation was already on its way. He pointed out the inconvenience which would result from any other conclusion:[165]

If [VT's] contention were to prevail no person who had received an offer by post and had accepted it would know his position until he had waited such a time as to be quite sure that a letter withdrawing the offer had not been posted before his acceptance of it. It appears to me that both legal principles, and practical convenience require that a person who has accepted an offer not known to him to have been revoked, shall be in a position safely to act upon the footing that the offer and acceptance constitute a contract binding on both parties.

[160] Above, pp 55–7.

[161] See below, p 126.

[162] *Holman Construction Ltd v Delta Timber Co Ltd* [1972] NZLR 1081 (negligent pre-contractual statement).

[163] Above, p 44.

[164] (1880) 5 CPD 344. See also *Thomson v James* (1855) 18 D 1 (Scotland); *Stevenson v McLean* (1880) 5 QBD 346; *Henthorn v Fraser* [1892] 2 Ch 27. But in *Shuey v United States* 92 US 73 (1875), where a reward was offered in a newspaper, it was held that this offer could be 'withdrawn through the same channel by which it was made', even though the revocation did not come to the notice of the offeree.

[165] (1880) 5 CPD 344, 348.

It has been stated that a revocation must be 'brought to the mind' of the offeree[166] but it is submitted that where it arrives at its address it will be effective when it would, in the ordinary course of business, have come to the offeree's attention.[167] Where the offeree refrains from opening a letter or neglects to pay attention to an e-mail it should, therefore, be effective on arrival (if received within normal working hours).[168] The requirement that a revocation be communicated means that, in law, an offeror may be bound by an agreement which it does not believe itself to have made; but, again, if one of the two parties must suffer, there would seem no good reason why it should be the offeree rather than the offeror.

The case of *Dickinson v Dodds*[169] establishes that an offeree who knows that an offer has been withdrawn cannot accept it even if the communication has not come from the offeror:

On 10 June 1874, Dodds made a written offer to Dickinson to sell certain premises for £800, and stating that this offer would remain open until 9 a.m. on 12 June. On the 11th, however, he sold the property to a third person without notice to Dickinson. Dickinson had in fact been informed of the sale, though not by anyone acting under the authority of Dodds. Nevertheless before 9 a.m. on the 12th he purported to accept Dodds' offer. He then brought an action for specific performance of the contract.

The Court of Appeal held that there was no contract. James LJ, after stating that a promise to keep the offer open could not be binding, and that at any moment before a completed acceptance of the offer one party was as free as the other, went on to say:[170]

> [I]n this case, *beyond all question, the plaintiff knew* that Dodds was no longer minded to sell the property to him as plainly and clearly as if Dodds had told him in so many words, 'I withdraw the offer'.

Is it then the case that information of the offeror's intention to revoke, from whatever source it reaches the offeree, is good notice of revocation? That could have very harsh consequences. Suppose a company receives an offer of a consignment of goods from a distant correspondent, with liberty to reserve an answer for some days. In the meantime an unauthorized person tells the offeree-company that the offeror has sold or promised the goods to another. What is the offeree to do? The informant may be right, and then, if the offeree accepts, the acceptance may be worthless. Or the informant may be a gossip or mischief-maker and if, because of what the offeree has been told, it refrains from accepting it may lose a bargain. The answer might be that it is open to an offeror, who has revoked an offer without direct communication to the offeree, to show that the offeree knew, *from a trustworthy source*, that the offer had been withdrawn.[171] The Court would

[166] *Henthorn v Fraser* [1892] 2 Ch 27, 32 (Lord Herschell). See also *ibid*, 37 (Kay LJ) ('actual knowledge', 'actually received').

[167] *Tenax SS Co Ltd v The Brimnes (Owners)* [1975] 1 QB 929, 945, 966, 969 (revocation by telex). See also CISG arts 16(1) and 24 (revocation effective if it 'reaches' the offeree's place of business or mailing address before he has dispatched an acceptance).

[168] *Tenax SS Co Ltd v The Brimnes (Owners)* [1975] 1 QB 929, at 970; *Brinkibon Ltd v Stahag Stahl und Stahlwarenhandelsgesellschaft mbH* [1983] 2 AC 34, 42.

[169] (1876) 2 Ch D 463.

[170] *Ibid*, 472; see also 474 (Mellish LJ).

[171] *Cartwright v Hoogstoel* (1911) 105 LT 628; ALI *Restatement, Contracts (2d)* para 42.

have to decide every such case on the facts presented, but the onus should be upon the offeror to establish that the information ought reasonably to have been believed.

(b) REJECTION OF THE OFFER

An offer will be held to have terminated once it has been rejected by the offeree.[172] The rejection need not be express, provided that the offeror is justified in inferring that the offeree does not intend to accept the offer.[173] It would seem, therefore, that a rejection would not operate so as to destroy the power of acceptance until it comes to the notice of the offeror:

Suppose that A makes an offer to B by letter. Immediately on receiving the letter B writes a letter rejecting the offer. Before the rejection arrives, B changes her mind and telephones her acceptance.

There would be a contract between A and B.[174] It should not be supposed, however, that an uncommunicated rejection would always be without effect. It would, in certain circumstances, preclude the operation of the rule that a letter of acceptance is complete when posted:

Suppose that C Ltd makes an offer to D. Immediately on receiving the offer D writes a letter rejecting the offer. Before the rejection arrives, D changes his mind and posts a letter accepting the offer.

Although there is no English authority on this point, it would not seem possible for D to claim that the normal rule as to postal acceptance applied. The letter of acceptance could only possibly create an obligation if received by the offeror before the rejection.[175]

(c) LAPSE OF THE OFFER

An offer may be considered to have lapsed owing to the passing of time.

(i) Offer for a fixed time

The parties may expressly fix a time within which an offer is to remain open. Where the offeror prescribes a specific time limit for acceptance, the offer is conditional upon acceptance within that time.[176] For example, 'This offer to be left open until Friday, 9 a.m. 12 June', allows the offeree to accept the offer, if unrevoked, at any time up to the hour named, after which the offer would lapse.[177] Similarly, an offer to supply goods of a

[172] *Hyde v Wrench* (1840) 3 Beav 334 (counter-offer, constituting a rejection, terminates the offer); *Trollope & Colls Ltd v Atomic Power Constructions Ltd* [1963] 1 WLR 333, 337 (counter-offer 'kills' the original offer). Cf *Stevenson, Jacques & Co v McLean* (1880) 5 QBD 346. See above, p 42.

[173] ALI *Restatement, Contracts (2d)* para 37. The position is similar in many European systems, see, eg, Germany, BGB para 146; Lando and Beale, *Principles of European Contract Law Parts I and II* (2000) 168.

[174] Winfield (1939) 55 LQR 499, 513; ALI *Restatement, Contracts (2d)* para 39.

[175] ALI *Restatement, Contracts (2d)* para 39.

[176] The offeror could nevertheless waive this condition, and treat the late acceptance as valid, provided he did not thereby adversely affect the offeree.

[177] *Dickinson v Dodds* (1876) 2 Ch D 463, above, p 59.

certain sort at a certain price for a year from the present date,[178] or an offer to guarantee the payment of any bills of exchange discounted for a third party for a year from the present date,[179] are offers which may be revoked at any time, except as regards orders already given or bills already discounted, and which will, in any event, lapse at the end of a year from the date of offer.

(ii) No fixed time

In most cases, the offeror will not specify any particular time and it is left to the Court, in the event of litigation, to say what is a reasonable time within which an offer may be accepted. We have already seen that an offer is accepted when acceptance is made in a manner prescribed or indicated by the offeror.[180] If the circumstances of the offer suggest that a reply is required urgently, the offer will be considered to have lapsed if the offeree does not quickly decide whether to accept, or chooses a means of communication which will delay the notification of the acceptance.[181] In other cases, the effluxion of a reasonable time will terminate the offer. An instance of this is provided by *Ramsgate Victoria Hotel Co v Montefiore*:[182]

The defendant, M, offered by letter dated 8 June to purchase shares in the claimant company. No answer was received by him until 23 November, when he was informed that shares were allotted to him. He refused to accept them.

It was held that M's offer had lapsed by reason of the delay of the company in notifying its acceptance, and that he was not bound to accept the shares.

(iii) Express or implied condition

The terms of the offer may expressly indicate that its continuance is conditional upon the existence of circumstances other than time; and a condition of this nature may also be implied. For example, where the contract requires for its performance the existence of a particular thing, and before acceptance the thing is destroyed or substantially damaged, the offer is terminated unless the offeror has assumed the risk of such mischance.[183] Thus, in *Financings Ltd v Stimson*:[184]

S signed an 'agreement' whereby he undertook to buy a car on hire-purchase terms from F company. The agreement contained a clause which stated that it was to become binding only upon acceptance by signature on F's behalf. Before F signed, the car was stolen by thieves. It was subsequently recovered in a damaged condition.

It was clear that the 'agreement' was in fact only an offer by S since it contemplated acceptance by F. The Court of Appeal held that S's offer was only capable of acceptance if the car remained in substantially the same condition as it was when the offer was made. Since this was not the case, the offer had lapsed and there was no binding contract.

[178] *GN Ry v Witham* (1873) LR 9 CP 16.

[179] *Offord v Davies* (1862) 12 CBNS 748.

[180] Above, p 53.

[181] *Quenerduaine v Cole* (1883) 32 WR 185.

[182] (1866) LR 1 Ex 109. See also *Manchester Diocesan Council for Education v Commercial & General Investments Ltd* [1970] 1 WLR 241, 247–9; *Chemco Leasing SpA v Rediffusion Ltd* [1987] 1 FTLR 201.

[183] ALI *Restatement, Contracts (2d)* para 266.

[184] [1962] 1 WLR 1184.

(d) EFFECT OF DEATH

In principle, an offeree cannot accept after being informed of the death of the offeror.[185] An acceptance communicated to the offeror's personal representatives will not bind them, unless the offer is one which could not have been revoked by the offeror during his lifetime.[186] Where the offeree accepts in ignorance of the offeror's death the position is less clear. One view is that the offer is terminated automatically and that knowledge is irrelevant.[187] The alternative, preferable view[188] is that an offeree who does not know of the offeror's death should be entitled to accept the offer, unless the offer on its true construction indicates the contrary,[189] for example where the offer is personal to the offeror.

It would seem that an offer is determined by the death of the offeree;[190] his personal representatives could not accept the offer on behalf of the offeree's estate.

5. UNCERTAIN AND INCOMPLETE AGREEMENTS

Although the parties may have reached agreement in the sense that the requirements of offer and acceptance have been complied with, there may be no contract because the terms of the agreement are uncertain or because the agreement is qualified by reference to the need for a future agreement between them. For 'unless all the material terms of the contract are agreed there is no binding obligation. An agreement to agree in future is not a contract; nor is there a contract if a material term is neither settled nor implied by law and the document contains no machinery for ascertaining it.'[191]

The terms of a contract must provide a basis for determining the existence of a breach and an appropriate remedy.[192] Nevertheless, courts are generally anxious to uphold contracts wherever possible and not be seen as the destroyer of bargains.[193] In addition, where uncertainty or incompleteness prevents an agreement from constituting a contract the factual situation may give rise to liability in tort, for instance for misrepresentation,[194] or in the law of unjust enrichment in respect of benefits received.[195]

185 *Coulthart v Clementson* (1870) 5 QBD 42.

186 *Errington v Errington* [1952] 1 KB 290, 295. Even in this case, death may terminate the offer where it is dependent on the personality of the offeror.

187 *Dickinson v Dodds* (1876) 2 Ch D 463, 475; ALI *Restatement, Contracts (2d)* para 48.

188 *Bradbury v Morgan* (1862) 1 H & C 249, often said to support this, was in fact a case where a contract had been concluded before death.

189 *Harris v Fawcett* (1873) LR 8 Ch App 866, 869; *Coulthart v Clementson* (1870) 5 QBD 42, 46.

190 *Re Cheshire Banking Co (Duff's Executor's Case)* (1886) 32 Ch D 301; *Reynolds v Atherton* (1921) 125 LT 690, 695, but see (1922) 127 LT 189, 191; *Somerville v National Coal Board* 1963 SLT 334 (Scotland).

191 *Foley v Classique Coaches Ltd* [1934] 2 KB 1, 13 (Maugham LJ). For a modern illustration, see *Morris v Swanton Care & Community Ltd* [2018] EWCA Civ 2763 at [27].

192 ALI *Restatement, Contracts (2d)* para 33(2). See also Lando and Beale, *Principles of European Contract Law Parts I and II* (2000) 146, art 2:103.

193 *Hillas v Arcos* (1932) 147 LT 503, 512 (Lord Tomlin).

194 Below, pp 67 and 345–50.

195 Below, pp 66, 70.

(a) CERTAINTY OF TERMS

The law requires the parties to make their own contract; it will not construct a contract for them out of terms which are indefinite or unsettled. A vague or uncertain promise does not give rise to an enforceable contract. Thus:

C agreed to sell land to D. The agreement provided that the price was to be paid by instalments and that on each payment 'a proportionate part' of the land was to be conveyed. It was held that, since the part to be conveyed on each occasion could not be identified, the agreement as a whole was uncertain and unenforceable.[196]

Similarly when a van was to be bought on the understanding that part of the price should be paid on 'hire-purchase' terms,[197] and when woollen goods were to be bought 'subject to war clause',[198] there was no contract in either case, for 'hire-purchase' terms and 'war clauses' may take many forms, and it is for the parties, and not for the Court, to define them.

On the other hand, in many transactions, particularly those for future performance over a period, the parties may not wish or be able to specify all matters. A transaction which at first sight seems to leave some essential term of the bargain undetermined may, by implication, if not expressly, provide some method of determination other than a future agreement between the parties. In that event there will be a good contract, applying the maxim that if something can be made certain then it should be treated as certain.[199] In every case the function of the Court is to put a fair construction on what the parties have said and done, though the task is often a difficult one. As Lord Wright stated:[200]

Business men often record the most important agreements in crude and summary fashion; modes of expression sufficient and clear to them in the course of their business may appear to those unfamiliar with the business far from complete or precise. It is accordingly the duty of the Court to construe such documents fairly and broadly, without being too astute or subtle in finding defects; but, on the contrary, the Court should seek to apply the old maxim of English law, *verba ita sunt intelligenda ut res magis valeat quam pereat*.[201]

[196] *Bushwell Properties Ltd v Vortex Properties Ltd* [1976] 1 WLR 591. See also *Montreal Gas Co v Vasey* [1900] AC 595; *Jacques v Lloyd D George & Partners* [1968] 1 WLR 625; *Stabilad Ltd v Stephens & Carter Ltd (No 2)* [1999] 2 All ER (Comm) 651 (performance left to discretion of promisor); *Blue v Ashley* [2017] EWHC 1928 (Comm) (see below, p 72: in addition to there being no intention to create legal relations there was insufficient certainty not least because no time period was stated for the share price to reach the specified price).

[197] *G Scammell & Nephews Ltd v Ouston* [1941] AC 251.

[198] *Bishop & Baxter v Anglo-Eastern Trading Co and Industrial Ltd* [1944] KB 12; *British Electrical and Associated Industries (Cardiff) Ltd v Patley Pressings Ltd* [1953] 1 WLR 280.

[199] *Id certum est quod certum reddi potest*. See *Scammell v Dicker* [2005] EWCA Civ 405, [2005] 3 All ER 838 distinguishing *Scammell v Ouston* [1941] AC 251. See generally Fridman (1960) 76 LQR 521; Samek (1970) 47 Can Bar Rev 203.

[200] *Hillas & Co v Arcos Ltd* (1932) 147 LT 503, 514.

[201] 'Words are to be interpreted so as to give effect to the subject matter rather than to defeat it.'

The line between discovering the agreement of the parties and imposing an agreement on the basis of what the Court considers the parties ought to have intended can be fine. The Court must be satisfied that the parties have in fact concluded a contract, and not merely expressed willingness to contract in the future. It may have regard to what has been said and done, the context in which it was said or done, the relative importance of the unsettled matter, and whether the parties have provided machinery for settling it.

If the contract contains an indefinite, but subsidiary provision, the Courts have felt at liberty to strike it out as being without significance, and to give effect to the rest of the contract without the meaningless term.[202]

(i) Previous transactions; trade custom

In *Hillas & Co v Arcos Ltd*[203] the terms were ascertained from previous transactions between the same parties and the custom of the particular trade:

In 1930, H agreed to buy from A a quantity of Russian softwood timber 'of fair specification'. The contract contained a clause giving to H an option to purchase further timber in 1931, but the option gave no particulars as to the kind or size or quality of the timber, nor of the manner of shipment. When H sought to exercise the option, A pleaded that the clause was too indeterminate and uncertain to indicate an unequivocal intention to be bound, and that it was merely an agreement to negotiate a future agreement.

The House of Lords held that, given the previous dealings between the parties, there was a sufficient intention to be bound: the terms left uncertain in the option could be ascertained by reference to those contained in the original contract and from the normal practice of the timber trade.[204]

(ii) The standard of reasonableness

Where the intention to buy and to sell is clear, incidents of the transaction may be determined by the standard of reasonableness, or by rules of law. Thus, in *Hillas v Arcos* the phrase 'of fair specification' was held to mean timber distributed over kinds, qualities, and sizes in fair proportions having regard to the season's output, a matter which, if the parties failed to agree, could be ascertained by the Court determining what was reasonable.[205] Similar principles apply to standards provided in the agreement such as 'market value',[206] 'open market value',[207] and that hire shall be 'equitably decreased'.[208]

[202] *Nicolene Ltd v Simmonds* [1953] 1 QB 543. See also *Adamastos Shipping Co Ltd v Anglo-Saxon Petroleum Co Ltd* [1959] AC 133; *Whitlock v Brew* (1968) 118 CLR 445 (Australia).

[203] (1932) 147 LT 503.

[204] On the terms implied by trade custom see further, below, pp 166–8.

[205] (1932) 147 LT 503, 512, 513, 516. See also *Mamidoil-Jetoil Greek Petroleum Co SA v Okta Crude Oil Refinery AD* [2001] 2 Lloyd's Rep 76, 91 (reasonable fees for services); *Durham Tees Valley Airport Ltd v Bmibaby Ltd* [2010] EWCA Civ 485, [2011] 1 Lloyd's Rep 68 (long-term obligation to fly two planes from an airport held to be sufficiently certain). Cf *Baird Textile Holdings Ltd v Marks & Spencer plc* [2001] EWCA Civ 274, [2002] 1 All ER (Comm) 737 (no long-term contract to be supplied with garments because of lack of certainty consequent on there being no objective criteria by which the Court could assess what would be reasonable for the purchaser to acquire either as to quantity or price).

[206] *Brown v Gould* [1972] Ch 53.

[207] *Gillatt v Sky Television Ltd* [2000] 1 All ER (Comm) 46.

[208] *Didymi Corp v Atlantic Lines and Navigation Co Ltd* [1988] 2 Lloyd's Rep 108.

In the case of price, in transactions for the sale of goods or the supply of services the matter is now governed by statute. By section 8 of the Sale of Goods Act 1979:[209]

(1) The price in a contract of sale may be fixed by the contract, or may be left to be fixed in a manner agreed by the contract, or may be determined by the course of dealing between the parties.
(2) Where the price is not determined as mentioned in subsection (1) above the buyer must pay a reasonable price.

In such cases, the Court will allow an action to recover a reasonable sum for what the goods or services are worth.[210]

It has been held that section 8(2) provides for silence as to the price, and will not apply where an agreement states that the parties will subsequently agree the price to be paid.[211]

(iii) Executed transactions

The Court will also have regard to what has been done by the parties. Where a transaction has been wholly or partially performed it will be:

> difficult to submit that the contract is void for vagueness or uncertainty. Specifically, the fact that the transaction is executed makes it easier to imply a term resolving any uncertainty, or, alternatively, it may make it possible to treat a matter not finalised in negotiations as inessential.[212]

In *Wells v Devani*,[213] an estate agent and a seller reached an oral agreement without expressly specifying the event which would trigger the agent's entitlement to a commission. The Supreme Court held that, on a true interpretation of the contract, the commission was payable upon completion of the sale. If that result could not have been reached through interpretation, such a term would have been implied to ensure that the contract did not fail for lack of certainty.[214] Lord Kitchin emphasized that 'the courts are reluctant to find an agreement is too vague or uncertain to be enforced where it is found that the parties had the intention of being contractually bound and have acted on their agreement.'[215]

[209] See also Supply of Goods and Services Act 1982, s 15(1). Cf CISG art 55 ('current trade price').

[210] *British Bank for Foreign Trade Ltd v Novinex* [1949] 1 KB 623; *Powell v Braun* [1954] 1 WLR 401 (executed transactions); *Hondly v M'Laine* (1834) 10 Bing 482 (executory transaction). See too *Barton v Morris* [2023] UKSC 3, [2023] AC 684, discussed below, p 172.

[211] *May & Butcher v R* [1934] 2 KB 17n; *King's Motors (Oxford) Ltd v Lax* [1970] 1 WLR 426; *Smith v Morgan* [1971] 1 WLR 803. For forceful criticism of *May & Butcher v R*, see *Fletcher Challenge Energy Ltd v Electricity Corp of New Zealand Ltd* [2002] 2 NZLR 433, 466–7. See too *KSY Juice Blends UK Ltd v Citrosuco GmbH* [2025] EWCA Civ 760.

[212] *G Percy Trentham Ltd v Archital Luxfer Ltd* [1993] 1 Lloyd's Rep 25, 27 (Steyn LJ). See also *F & G Sykes (Wessex) Ltd v Fine Fare Ltd* [1967] 1 Lloyd's Rep 53, 57–8; *Foley v Classique Coaches Ltd* [1934] 2 KB 1.

[213] [2019] UKSC 4, [2020] AC 129.

[214] See pp 169–74.

[215] [2019] UKSC 4, [2020] AC 129 at [18]. See too *Foley v Classique Coaches Ltd* [1934] 2 KB 1; *Way v Latilla* [1937] 3 All ER 759 (but cf *ibid*, 764–5); *RTS Flexible Systems Ltd v Molkerei Alois Müller GmbH & Co KG* [2010] UKSC 14, [2010] 1 WLR 753 at [45]–[56].

In the case of executed transactions, the basis of liability is not, however, always contractual. As noted in the context of 'the battle of the forms',[216] sometimes no contractual analysis is possible and, where it is held that there is liability, it may be imposed by the Court in the form of an obligation in the law of unjust enrichment to pay a reasonable sum for the work done or the goods received.[217] In determining whether to give a restitutionary remedy, considerations of 'risk' and 'fault' in relation to the reason the transaction fails to come to fruition as a contract are taken into account so that a person who is held to have taken the risk of the transaction failing or to have been responsible for this will not be entitled to recompense for the services rendered.[218]

(iv) Machinery for ascertainment

A contract will not fail for uncertainty even though a material term is to be agreed in future if the contract itself provides machinery for ascertaining it. So, for example, if the contract provides that the parties are to agree a price or quantities for delivery, but also contains an arbitration clause which covers a failure to agree the price or the quantities, the Courts will imply that, in default of agreement, a reasonable price is to be paid, such price to be determined by arbitration.[219] In *KSY Juice Blends UK Ltd v Citrosuco GmbH* the Court of Appeal held that even if the parties intend to fix the price by agreement, that 'does not preclude . . . the implication of a term that in the absence of reaching agreement the price would be a reasonable or market price', despite the absence of a default clause referring to arbitration.[220] This is a bold example of the Courts striving to uphold bargains.

Moreover, in the case of a lease, if premises are let to a tenant for (say) a term of 10 years at a fixed rent for the first five years, but at a rent 'to be agreed' thereafter, the Court will itself determine by inquiry what is a reasonable rent for the premises should the parties fail to agree.[221] Unless the machinery is held to be an essential part of the agreement,[222] the Court will similarly intervene if, for any reason, its operation is stultified, for example, by the refusal of one of the parties to appoint a valuer or an arbitrator.[223]

[216] Above, p 43.

[217] *British Steel Corp v Cleveland Bridge and Engineering Co Ltd* [1984] 1 All ER 504, 511 in the context of goods delivered under a letter of intent, below, pp 69–70. Birks, *An Introduction to the Law of Restitution* (revd edn, 1989) 271–2 explains *Way v Latilla* [1937] 3 All ER 759 in this way and see *ibid*, 764–5. Cf Dietrich [2001] LS 153, Davies [2010] CLJ 467.

[218] *Jennings & Chapman Ltd v Woodman, Matthews & Co* [1952] 2 TLR 409; *William Lacey (Hounslow) Ltd v Davis* [1957] 1 WLR 932; *Regalian Properties plc v London Dockland Development Corp* [1995] 1 WLR 212; *Countrywide Communications Ltd v ICL Pathway* [2000] CLC 324.

[219] *Foley v Classique Coaches Ltd* [1934] 2 KB 1; *F & G Sykes (Wessex) Ltd v Fine Fare Ltd* [1967] 1 Lloyd's Rep 53; *Vosper Thornycroft Ltd v Ministry of Defence* [1976] 1 Lloyd's Rep 58; *Queensland Electricity Generating Board v New Hope Collieries Pty Ltd* [1989] 1 Lloyd's Rep 205, 210.

[220] [2025] EWCA Civ 760 at [53].

[221] *Beer v Bowden* [1981] 1 WLR 522.

[222] As in *Gillatt v Sky Television Ltd* [2000] 1 All ER (Comm) 46.

[223] *Sudbrook Trading Estate Ltd v Eggleton* [1983] 1 AC 444.

(v) Agreements to negotiate and not to negotiate

The position of agreements to negotiate and agreements not to negotiate was considered by the House of Lords in *Walford v Miles*:[224]

On 17 March M agreed that, provided that W's bank confirmed that W had the necessary financial resources to purchase M's photographic processing business for £2 million, they would 'break off any negotiations with any third party and would not consider any other alternative and would not accept a better offer but would deal exclusively with W, with a view to concluding the deal as soon as possible after April 6'. M continued to keep in touch with another interested party and on 27 March withdrew from the negotiations with W. M later sold the business to the third party. W sued for breach of contract and for misrepresentation.

It was found that M had represented that they were not in negotiation with the other interested party and W was awarded tortious damages for misrepresentation.[225] The contractual claims, however, failed.

It was held that an agreement to negotiate (a 'lock-in' agreement) is like an agreement to agree and is unenforceable 'simply because it lacks the necessary certainty'.[226] Two principal reasons have been given for this conclusion. First, in *Walford v Miles*, Lord Ackner asked how the Court is to police such an agreement and questioned whether it is possible to tell whether it has been breached:[227] 'How can a court be expected to decide whether, *subjectively*, a proper reason existed for the termination of negotiations?' The position of parties in negotiations was stated to be adversarial and to entitle them to pursue their own interests so long as they avoided making misrepresentations and, if they so wished, to withdraw from the negotiations at any time and for any reason. It was said not to be possible to cure this uncertainty by asking whether the negotiations have been conducted 'in good faith' because a duty to negotiate in good faith 'is as unworkable in practice as it is inherently inconsistent with the position of a negotiating party'. It has been said that Lord Ackner's reference to an agreement to use 'best endeavours' being different and sufficiently certain must be read as referring to best or reasonable endeavours to achieve a result other than the conclusion of a contract with the other party.[228] However, the distinction between an agreement to use best or reasonable endeavours *to agree* and an agreement to negotiate in good faith is unclear. Secondly, it has been said that 'no court could estimate the damages because no one can tell whether the negotiations would be successful or would fall through: or if successful, what the result would be'.[229]

[224] [1992] 2 AC 128.

[225] These amounted to £700 and were in respect of the expenses of the negotiation and the preparation of the contract documents: [1992] 2 AC 128, 135. On damages for misrepresentation, see below, pp 340–4.

[226] [1992] 2 AC 128, 138. See also *Courtney & Fairbairn Ltd v Tolaini Bros (Hotels) Ltd* [1975] 1 WLR 297; *Mallozzi v Carapelli SpA* [1976] 1 Lloyd's Rep 407. Cf *Hillas v Arcos* (1932) 147 LT 503, 515 (Lord Wright).

[227] [1992] 2 AC 128, 138.

[228] *Little v Courage* (1995) P & CR 469, 475 (Millett LJ). Cf *Jet2.com Ltd v Blackpool Airport Ltd* [2012] EWCA Civ 417, [2012] 2 All ER (Comm) 1053 (obligation to use reasonable endeavours to promote a low-cost airline held sufficiently certain) and *Multiplex Constructions UK Ltd v Cleveland Bridge UK Ltd* [2006] EWHC 1341 (TCC), (2007) 107 Con LR 1 (obligation to use best or reasonable endeavours to negotiate is too uncertain).

[229] *Courtney & Fairbairn Ltd v Tolaini Bros (Hotels) Ltd* [1975] 1 WLR 297, 301 (Lord Denning MR). Cf Leggatt [2019] JBL 104, especially at pp 118–20.

There are, however, difficulties with those reasons and with this aspect of the decision in *Walford v Miles*.[230] First, it is unlikely to give effect to the reasonable expectations of business people, which it is an important object of the law of contract to facilitate.[231] It appears to require a higher degree of certainty and less willingness to use the standard of reasonableness to resolve ambiguity than some of the cases considered above. In *Astor Management AG v Atalaya Mining plc*[232] Leggatt J (albeit without mentioning *Walford v Miles*) held that a term to use reasonable endeavours to make a contract with a third party (ie to secure borrowing from a third party) was sufficiently certain to be enforceable. Leggatt J also cast doubt on there being any 'uncertainty' objection to upholding a term requiring reasonable endeavours to negotiate a contract with the other party or a term requiring negotiation in good faith. Secondly, the objection that it would not be possible to assess damages is also open to question. As will be seen, in other contexts in which the transaction contains a large amount of chance, it has been possible to assess damages and the Court has not held that there is no contract.[233] Lord Wright's dictum in *Hillas v Arcos*,[234] which recognized a contract to negotiate, may perhaps be revisited.

An agreement not to negotiate with any third party, a 'lock-out' agreement, has been held not to be enforceable where, as in *Walford v Miles*, it does not specify a time limit for its duration. This appears to be because it would impose indirectly a duty to negotiate in good faith which, for the reasons given above, could not be a contract.[235] But it was accepted in *Walford v Miles* that such an agreement is sufficiently certain if it is limited to a fixed period.[236] The distinction between these two types of 'lock-out' agreement is difficult to justify. It is submitted that neither indirectly imposes a duty to negotiate in good faith, since the obligation is a negative one and that it should have been possible to resolve the uncertainty of there being no fixed period in *Walford v Miles* by applying the standard of a reasonable period.[237]

[230] For persuasive criticism of *Walford v Miles*, see Neill (1992) 108 LQR 405; Berg (2003) 119 LQR 357; Peel, in Burrows and Peel (eds), *Contract Formation and Parties* (2010) ch 3. In *Petromec Inc v Petroleo Brasileiro SA Petrobas* [2005] EWCA Civ 891, [2006] 1 Lloyd's Rep 161 at [121] Longmore LJ, *obiter*, suggested that it would be a strong thing to declare unenforceable an express clause to negotiate in good faith. In *Emirates Trading Agency LLC v Prime Mineral Exports Pte Ltd* [2014] EWHC 2104 (Comm), [2015] 1 WLR 1145 an express dispute resolution clause in an otherwise binding contract, requiring the parties to seek to resolve a dispute in good faith and within a limited period of time prior to arbitration, was held enforceable.

[231] Pollock (1932) 48 LQR 141; Davenport (1991) 107 LQR 366; Lord Steyn (1997) 113 LQR 433.

[232] [2017] EWHC 425 (Comm), [2018] 1 All ER (Comm) 547 (upheld by the Court of Appeal, without mentioning this point, [2018] EWCA Civ 2407, [2019] 1 All ER (Comm) 885).

[233] *Allied Maples Group v Simmons & Simmons* [1995] 1 WLR 1602, 1620 and below, p 547. Reliance damages may also be available: below, p 554. See generally Leggatt [2019] JBL 104, 118–20.

[234] (1932) 147 LT 503, 515.

[235] *Walford v Miles* [1992] 2 AC 128, 140.

[236] See, eg, *Pitt v PHH Asset Management Ltd* [1994] 1 WLR 327; *Pretoria Energy Co (Chittering) Ltd v Blankney Estates Ltd* [2023] EWCA Civ 482, [2023] L & TR 28.

[237] Neill (1992) 108 LQR 405, 413. Bingham LJ, dissenting in the Court of Appeal, was of this view: (1990) 62 P & CR 410. The agreement provided a standard in stating that the transaction was to be concluded as soon as possible after 6 April: [1990] 1 EGLR 212.

(b) INCOMPLETE AGREEMENT

The parties may agree on certain points, but nevertheless leave other points unresolved. The question then arises whether or not their agreement is complete. Difficulties of interpretation most frequently arise where there have been lengthy negotiations in correspondence. The parties discuss terms, approach, and recede from an agreement; proposals are made and met by the suggestion of fresh terms. Finally there is a difference, and one party asserts that a contract has been made, and the other that matters have never gone beyond the discussion of terms. Where the correspondence appears to result in an agreement at some point, it is necessary to ask whether this agreement amounts to a completed agreement, or whether there are other terms of the intended contract, beyond and besides those expressed in the agreement, which are still in a state of negotiation only, and without the settlement of which the parties have no idea of concluding any contract.[238] Where the correspondence shows that the parties have definitely come to terms, even though certain material points may still be left open, a subsequent revival of negotiations cannot, except with the consent of both parties, affect the contract so made.[239]

(i) Effect of reference to further agreement

The classic statement of the issues involved in cases where the agreement is couched in general terms, but reference is made to a contract in which the intentions of the parties may be more precisely stated, is to be found in the judgment of Parker J in *Von Hatzfeldt-Wildenburg v Alexander*:[240]

> If the documents or letters relied on as constituting a contract contemplate the execution of a further contract between the parties, it is a question of construction whether the execution of the further contract is a condition or term of the bargain or whether it is a mere expression of the desire of the parties as to the manner in which the transaction already agreed to will in fact go through. In the former case there is no enforceable contract either because the condition is unfulfilled or because the law does not recognize a contract to enter into a contract. In the latter case there is a binding contract and the reference to the more formal document may be ignored.

(ii) Letters of intent

Difficulties frequently arise where parties in negotiations reach 'points of agreement' or have a 'memorandum of understanding' or exchange 'letters of intent' or 'letters of comfort', but nevertheless contemplate that a formal document is later to be drawn up.[241] In such situations the question whether or not a binding contract has been concluded is

[238] *Hussey v Horne Payne* (1879) 4 App Cas 311.

[239] *Perry v Suffields Ltd* [1916] 2 Ch 187; *Mitsui Babcock Energy Ltd v John Brown Engineering Ltd* (1996) 51 Con LR 129, 167, 175, 179.

[240] [1912] 1 Ch 284, 288.

[241] See generally Mouzat and Furmston [2008] CLJ 37; Furmston (2009) JCL 95; Furmston, in Burrows and Peel (eds), *Contract Formation and Parties* (2010) ch 2.

a matter of interpretation for the Court. While such a letter can have contractual effect where it contains an express promise as to future conduct,[242] the Court may be unwilling to imply such a promise from a statement of present fact because the language is often vague or equivocal or because the surrounding circumstances, including previous negotiations, indicate that all that is assumed is a moral responsibility.[243]

The position may be even further complicated by the fact that the parties often act on their informal agreement pending the execution of a formal contract. Where a formal contract is eventually concluded, the Court may be prepared to imply a term that, although the informal agreement is not legally binding, the formal contract is to have retrospective effect. It will, in consequence, apply to work done and services rendered before it was made.[244] Where no formal contract is concluded, work done or goods delivered under a letter of intent which is not legally binding may give rise to an obligation in the law of unjust enrichment to pay a reasonable sum for the work or the goods.[245]

(iii) Agreement 'subject to contract'

The initial agreement for the sale or lease of land is usually entered into 'subject to contract' or 'subject to formal contract'. Such an agreement gives rise to no contractual liability.[246] Thus in *Winn v Bull*:[247]

A written agreement was drawn up whereby the defendant agreed to take a lease of a house for a definite period and at a fixed rent, but 'subject to the preparation and approval of a formal contract'.

It was held there was no contract. Jessel MR explained:[248]

It comes, therefore, to this, that where you have a proposal or agreement made in writing expressed to be subject to a formal contract being prepared, it means what it says; it is subject to and is dependent upon a formal contract being prepared.

The insertion of the words 'subject to contract' renders the agreement nugatory in fact, and this is so notwithstanding that a deposit may have been paid.[249] As a normal rule, a binding contract for the sale of land will come into existence only when a formal

[242] *Chemco Leasing SpA v Rediffusion* [1987] 1 FTLR 201 (comfort letter an offer but lapsed before acceptance).

[243] *Kleinwort Benson Ltd v Malaysia Mining Corp Bhd* [1989] 1 WLR 379, 388, 391, 393 (letter of comfort not legally binding because it expressed the present policy of the company rather than containing a promise); *Associated British Ports v Ferryways NV* [2009] EWCA Civ 189, [2009] 1 Lloyd's Rep 595 at [24] (per Maurice Kay LJ: 'I regard a letter of comfort, properly so called, as one that does not give rise to contractual liability'). Cf *Wilson Smithett & Cape (Sugar) Ltd v Bangladesh Sugar Industries Ltd* [1986] 1 Lloyd's Rep 378 (letter of intent for the supply of sugar specifying amount, price, and shipping details held to be an acceptance).

[244] *Trollope & Colls Ltd v Atomic Power Construction Ltd* [1963] 1 WLR 333. See Ball (1983) 99 LQR 572.

[245] *British Steel Corp v Cleveland Bridge & Engineering Co Ltd* [1984] 1 All ER 504. See above, p 66.

[246] See Law Com No 65, *'Subject to Contract' Agreements* (1975) and Law Com No 164, *Formalities for Contracts for Sale etc of Land* (1987) paras 1.4, 4.15.

[247] (1877) 7 Ch D 29. See also *Galliard Homes Ltd v J Jarvis & Sons plc* (1999) 71 Con LR 219, 235–6, 243.

[248] (1877) 7 Ch D 29, 32.

[249] *Coope v Ridout* [1921] 1 Ch 291; *Chillingworth v Esche* [1924] 1 Ch 97; *Eccles v Bryant and Pollock* [1948] Ch 93; *Tiverton Estates Ltd v Wearwell Ltd* [1975] Ch 146.

'exchange of contracts' contained in writing signed by or on behalf of each party[250] has taken place.[251] Up to this time either party is free to renegotiate the price, or even to withdraw entirely from the transaction and to do so because of movements in the value of property. The express use of the words 'subject to contract' has also been held to preclude a claim in the law of unjust enrichment for expenses incurred in respect of the intended contract; the use of those words was said to mean that the parties had in effect expressly agreed that there should be no legal obligation by either party to the other unless and until a formal contract had been entered into.[252] But in other cases, restitutionary remedies for the return of money paid[253] or for the value of work done under anticipated contracts concerning land have been granted.[254]

On the other hand, an agreement for the sale or lease of land will be binding if the terms of the further formal contract are in existence and known to the parties, and not merely in contemplation. For example:

An offer was made to buy land, and 'if offer accepted, to pay deposit and sign contract on the auction particulars'; this was accepted, 'subject to contract as agreed'. The acceptance clearly embodied the terms of the contract mentioned in the offer, and constituted a complete contract.[255]

Further, it has been held that if the parties use the phrase 'a provisional agreement', they then agree to be bound from the beginning, even though they stipulate that a formal document is to be drawn up later on.[256]

In any event, as Lord Clarke pointed out in *RTS Flexible Systems Ltd v Molkerei Alois Müller GmbH and Co KG (UK Production)*,[257] any 'subject to contract' bar may be waived by the parties themselves. In that case, detailed negotiations were said to be 'subject to contract'. Work subsequently began without a formal, signed, written contract in place. The Supreme Court held that even though the 'subject to contract' bar indicated that the detailed terms were not to take effect until the relevant documents were executed and signed,[258] the parties were still free to dictate when and how they enter into contractual obligations; the intention not to be bound before signature could be 'waived'.[259]

[250] Law of Property (Miscellaneous Provisions) Act 1989, s 2, on which see below, pp 85–91.

[251] Cf *Alpenstow Ltd v Regalian Properties Ltd* [1985] 1 WLR 721 (exceptionally, agreement 'subject to contract' drawn up by a lawyer after five months of negotiation containing detailed and mandatory provisions of the approval, amendment, and exchange of contracts held binding). In *A-G of Hong Kong v Humphreys Estates (Queens Gardens) Ltd* [1987] 1 AC 114, 127–8, the possibility (said to be unlikely) of the parties being estopped from refusing to proceed was accepted. See also *Akiens v Saloman* (1992) 65 P & CR 364, 370.

[252] *Regalian Properties plc v London Dockland Development Corp* [1995] 1 WLR 212, 225.

[253] *Chillingworth v Esche* [1924] 1 Ch 97 (restitution of deposit).

[254] *Cobbe v Yeoman's Row Management Ltd* [2008] UKHL 55, [2008] 1 WLR 1752 (quantum meruit for value of work done in obtaining planning permission in respect of an anticipated contract/agreement 'subject to contract').

[255] *Filby v Hounsell* [1896] 2 Ch 737; *Rossiter v Miller* (1878) 3 App Cas 1124.

[256] *Branca v Cobarro* [1947] KB 854. See also *Damon Comp Nav SA v Hapag-Lloyd International SA* [1985] 1 WLR 434, 443, 452; *Global Container Lines Ltd v State Black Sea SS Co* [1999] 1 Lloyd's Rep 127, 156.

[257] [2010] UKSC 14, [2010] 1 WLR 753 at [31].

[258] *Ibid* at [31].

[259] *Ibid* at [86]–[88]. Although any waiver of the 'subject to contract' bar should be unequivocal: *Astra Asset Management UK Ltd v Co-operative Bank Plc* [2019] EWHC 897 (Comm) at [80] citing *Rock Advertising Ltd v MWB Business Exchange Centres Ltd* [2018] UKSC 24, [2019] AC 119 at [29]–[30], discussed further in Chapter 4, especially pp 116–7. See too *Joanne Properties Ltd v Moneything Capital Ltd* [2020] EWCA Civ 1541, [2022] 1 P&CR 1.

Lord Clarke insisted that the parties must have intended to create legal relations through their conduct, and no longer required an executed and signed contract, since '[a]ny other conclusion makes no commercial sense', and that 'the reasonable, honest businessman . . . whether he was an RTS man or a Müller man . . . would have concluded that the work should be carried out for the agreed price on the agreed terms . . . without the necessity for a formal written agreement, which had been overtaken by events'.[260] Of course, it may be difficult to decide exactly when 'the die was cast'[261] and the requirement for a signed contract has been dispensed with, but this is a question to be decided on the facts of any particular case.[262]

As Lord Clarke urged in *RTS v Müller*, '[t]he moral of the story . . . is to agree first and to start work later'.[263] Parties who begin to perform without an agreement in place run substantial risks. Commencing the work contemplated by the parties before any contract is formally concluded does not always give rise to a binding contract.[264]

(iv) Contracts subject to condition

There are situations which at first sight appear to be cases of incomplete agreement, but really turn out to be cases where there is an immediate binding contract, although some of the parties' rights and obligations may be dependent upon the happening of a particular event.[265] For example, the agreement may contain such a term as 'subject to the purchaser's solicitors approving the title'. Until this approval is given, the contract need not be implemented, although neither party is free to withdraw from it unilaterally. Alternatively, the contract may be fully operative at once, but upon the happening of a particular event it is thereby discharged.[266] The insertion of such conditions produces a quite different effect from a reservation like 'subject to contract' which prevents the formation of any contract at all. They are dealt with in Chapter 5.[267]

6. INTENTION TO CREATE LEGAL RELATIONS

Although a separate requirement of intention to create legal relations did not exist until the nineteenth century,[268] it is now established that an agreement will not constitute a binding contract unless it is one which can reasonably be regarded as having been made in contemplation of legal consequences. A mere statement of intention made in the course of conversation will not generally constitute a binding promise, though acted upon by the party to whom it was made,[269] and even negotiated agreements do not

260 *Ibid* at [86]. 261 *Ibid* at [87]. 262 *DAZN Ltd v Coupang Corp* [2025] EWCA Civ 1083.

263 *Ibid* at [1].

264 *SMIT Salvage BV v Luster Maritime SA* [2024] EWCA Civ 260, [2024] 2 All ER (Comm) 504.

265 *Smith v Butler* [1900] 1 QB 694; *Marten v Whale* [1917] 2 KB 480. Cf *Pym v Campbell* (1856) 6 E & B 370, below, p 148.

266 *Head v Tattersall* (1871) LR 7 Ex 7, below, p 149. 267 Below, pp 146–9.

268 Simpson (1975) 91 LQR 247, 263–5; Hedley (1985) 5 OJLS 391.

269 *Weeks v Tybald* (1605) Noy 11; *Guthing v Lynn* (1831) 2 B & Ad 232. But these cases appear to turn on uncertainty and vagueness rather than lack of intent. There is a close link between uncertainty and lack of intention to contract.

necessarily give rise to legal obligations. For example, a collective agreement between employers and trade unions is conclusively presumed not to have been intended by the parties to be legally enforceable unless it is in writing and contains a provision stating that the parties intend it to be a legally enforceable contract.[270]

An entertaining example of the requirement of an intention to create legal relations is provided by *Blue v Ashley*:[271]

> In a conversation in a pub, A said to B that he would pay him £15 million if B could get the price of shares in Sports Direct, which A owned, to £8. B alleged that that was a binding offer of a unilateral contract and that, when the shares did reach £8, A had broken the contract by refusing to pay him the £15 million.

It was held that there was no binding contract. This was essentially because A had had no intention to create legal relations when he made that 'promise'. No one present thought that A had made a serious commitment. What he had said was merely jocular banter. However, in ordinary business matters there is a strong presumption that legal relations are intended, which is even stronger when the parties have acted on their agreement.[272]

(a) SOCIAL ENGAGEMENTS

Sometimes it is clear from the nature of the agreement that there was no intention to enter into a binding contract. A prime example is a social engagement. This is not always because such engagements are not reducible to a money value, since they often may be. The acceptance of an invitation to dinner or to play in a cricket match,[273] of an offer to share the cost of petrol used on a journey,[274] or to take part in a golf club's competition[275] or between friends relating to musical performances by them[276] form agreements in which the promisee may incur expense in reliance on the promise. The damages resulting from breach might be ascertainable, but the Courts would hold that, if no legal consequences could reasonably have been contemplated by the parties, no action will lie.

In *Balfour v Balfour*, Atkin LJ stated:[277]

> It is necessary to remember that there are agreements between parties which do not result in contracts within the meaning of that term in our law. The ordinary example is where

[270] Trade Union and Labour Relations (Consolidation) Act 1992, s 179, see *NCB v NUM* [1986] ICR 736. The position at common law was similar: *Ford Motor Co Ltd v AUEFW* [1969] 1 WLR 339. See Hepple [1970] CLJ 122.

[271] [2017] EWHC 1928 (Comm). Leggatt J also decided that the arrangement was not sufficiently certain to be enforceable: see above, n 196.

[272] eg *Wells v Devani* [2019] UKSC 4, [2020] AC 129 at [17]–[26].

[273] See Atkin LJ in *Balfour v Balfour*, below, n 277.

[274] *Coward v Motor Insurers' Bureau* [1963] 1 QB 259; *Buckpitt v Oates* [1968] 1 All ER 1145. But see now Road Traffic Act 1988, ss 145, 149.

[275] *Lens v Devonshire Club*, The Times, 4 December 1914 (Scrutton J), referred to in *Rose and Frank Co v JR Crompton & Bros Ltd* [1923] 2 KB 261, 288. Cf *Clarke v Earl of Dunraven* [1897] AC 59, above, p 34 (contract between competitors in yacht club regatta).

[276] *Hadley v Kemp* [1999] EMLR 589, 623.

[277] [1919] 2 KB 571, 578. See also *Vaughan v Vaughan* [1953] 1 QB 762, 765; *Gould v Gould* [1970] 1 QB 275.

two parties agree to take a walk together, or where there is an offer and an acceptance of hospitality. Nobody would suggest in ordinary circumstances that those agreements result in what we know as a contract.

(b) FAMILY ARRANGEMENTS

Family arrangements are another category of agreement in which there may be no intention to create legal relations. In *Balfour v Balfour*:

A husband was employed in a government post in Ceylon. He returned with his wife to England on leave, but she was unable to go back to Ceylon with him for medical reasons. He consequently promised orally to make her an allowance of £30 a month until she rejoined him. He failed to make this payment and she sued him.

The Court of Appeal held that, although it was not impossible for a husband and wife to enter into a contract for maintenance, in this case they never intended to make a bargain which could be enforced in law. While that decision has been criticized,[278] agreements between spouses and between parents and children[279] are, as we shall see, presumed not to be enforceable contracts. Thus, it has been said that a parent's promise to pay a child an allowance while at university ordinarily creates only a moral obligation.[280]

(c) DETERMINING INTENTION

The test of an intention to create legal relations is an objective one. It may be that the promisor never anticipated that the promise would give rise to any legal obligation, but if a reasonable person would consider there was an intention so to contract, then the promisor will be bound.[281] It has therefore been contended that the common law does not require any positive intention to create a legal obligation as an element of contract, and that 'a deliberate promise seriously made is enforced irrespective of the promisor's views regarding his legal liability'.[282] This view commands considerable respect, but there are difficulties in the way of its acceptance.

First, parties to a business transaction may deliberately state that they do not intend to enter into any legal obligation, and the Court will then treat their promises as binding in honour only. In *Appleson v Littlewood Ltd*[283] a competitor who claimed to have sent in a successful coupon in a football pool could not rely upon an enforceable contract

[278] Below, pp 75–6.

[279] *Jones v Padavatton* [1969] 1 WLR 328.

[280] *Fleming v Beeves* [1994] 1 NZLR 385, 389 (New Zealand).

[281] *Carlill v Carbolic Smoke Ball Co* [1893] 1 QB 256; *British Airways Board v Taylor* [1976] 1 WLR 13. See above, p 34.

[282] Williston, *Contracts*, vol 1, para 21; Hepple [1970] CLJ 122; Hedley (1985) 5 OJLS 391; ALI *Restatement, Contracts (2d)* para 21B.

[283] [1939] 1 All ER 464. See also *Rose and Frank Co v Crompton & Bros Ltd* [1925] AC 445; *Jones v Vernons' Pools* [1938] 2 All ER 626. Cf *Edwards v Skyways Ltd* [1964] 1 WLR 349 ('*ex gratia*' payment); *Home Insurance Co Ltd v Administratia Asigurarilor* [1983] 2 Lloyd's Rep 674, 677 (agreement to be 'interpreted as an honourable engagement').

since one of the conditions was that the conduct of the pools was not to be 'attended by or give rise to any legal relationship whatsoever'. As regards a 'minister' and his church, there is no longer any presumption of there being no intention to create legal relations but the circumstances may indicate that there was no such intention.[284] Moreover, until recently the Crown and civil servants were held not to be in a contractual relationship because the Civil Service Pay and Conditions Code's statement that 'a civil servant does not have a contract of employment enforceable in the courts' meant that the Crown did not have the requisite intention to contract.[285] What was said when the agreement was made,[286] and the vagueness of the language used[287] may be held to be inconsistent with an intent to contract.

Where the agreement is made in a commercial context, it has been said there that there is a presumption that there is an intention to create legal relations and that the onus on a party who asserts that an agreement was made without the intent is a heavy one.[288] And where a term is introduced into a pre-existing contractual relationship, there is a strong presumption that it is intended to be legally binding.[289] However, the presumption does not apply so strongly in respect of contracts that are wholly or partly implied from conduct, where it is for the party alleging that there is a contract to prove that intention.[290]

Secondly, in contexts where legal contracts are not normally made, exemplified by social engagements or family arrangements, it will be presumed that no intent to create an enforceable contract is present, even though there may have been an exchange of mutual promises and a 'consideration' moving from the promisee.[291] On the other hand, this presumption may be rebutted upon proof of the true intention of the parties, which is to be inferred from the language they use and the circumstances in which they use it. In *Parker v Clark*:[292]

[284] See *Preston v President of the Methodist Conference* [2013] UKSC 29, [2013] 2 AC 163 and *President of the Methodist Conference v Parfitt* [1984] QB 368 (no intention to create legal relations). Cf *Percy v Board of National Mission of the Church of Scotland* [2005] UKHL 73, [2006] 2 AC 28; *New Testament Church of God v Stewart* [2007] EWCA Civ 1004, [2008] ICR 282 (in both of which, an intention to create legal relations was found).

[285] *R v Civil Service Appeal Board, ex p Bruce* [1988] ICR 649, [1989] ICR 171; *McLaren v Home Office* [1990] ICR 84; *R v Lord Chancellor's Department, ex p Nangle* [1991] ICR 743; Trade Union and Labour Relations (Consolidation) Act 1992, ss 62(7) and 245.

[286] *Orion Insurance Co plc v Sphere Drake Insurance plc* [1992] 1 Lloyd's Rep 239.

[287] *Vaughan v Vaughan* [1953] 1 QB 762, 765; *Kleinwort Benson Ltd v Malaysia Mining Corp Bhd* [1988] 1 WLR 799, [1989] 1 WLR 379, above, p 70.

[288] *Edwards v Skyways Ltd* [1964] 1 WLR 349, 355; *Esso Petroleum Co Ltd v Commissioners of Customs and Excise* [1976] 1 WLR 1 (World Cup coins given to purchasers of petrol held to be given under a contractual obligation—because of an intention to create legal relations—and not as a gift); *Orion Insurance Co plc v Sphere Drake Insurance plc* [1992] 1 Lloyd's Rep 239, 263, 292.

[289] *Attrill v Dresdner Kleinwort Ltd* [2013] EWCA Civ 394, [2013] 3 All ER 607.

[290] *Blackpool and Fylde Aero Club v Blackpool BC* [1990] 1 WLR 1195, 1202; *Baird Textile Holdings Ltd v Marks & Spencer plc* [2001] EWCA Civ 274, [2002] 1 All ER (Comm) 737 at [62]; *Assuranceforeningen Gard Gjensidig v The International Oil Pollution Compensation Fund* [2014] EWHC 3369 (Comm) at [89]–[103].

[291] *Balfour v Balfour* [1919] 2 KB 571, 578; *Buckpitt v Oates* [1968] 1 All ER 1145; *Jones v Padavatton* [1969] 1 WLR 328.

[292] [1960] 1 WLR 286. Cf *Re Goodchild* [1997] 1 WLR 1216.

The defendants, an elderly couple, agreed with the claimants, who were 20 years younger, that if the latter would sell their cottage and come to live with the defendants, sharing household expenses, the male defendant would leave them a portion of his estate in his will. The claimants sold their cottage and moved in with the defendants. Difficulties developed between the two couples, and the defendants repudiated the agreement by requiring the claimants to find somewhere else to live. The claimants sought damages for breach of contract.

It was argued that the agreement amounted to no more than a family arrangement of the type considered in *Balfour v Balfour*, but Devlin J held that the circumstances indicated that the parties intended to affect their legal relations and that the defendants were therefore liable. Indeed *Balfour v Balfour* has been said to be an extreme example of this presumption,[293] and there are several cases in which it has been held that a husband's promise to his wife, from whom he was about to separate, that she could have the matrimonial home, was enforceable as a contract.[294] Similarly, in *Radmacher v Granatino*[295] a majority of the Supreme Court took the view, in *obiter dicta*, that pre-nuptial agreements are binding contracts. And an informal family arrangement to share the winnings of a football pool entry was enforceable since the necessary intention was present.[296]

Thirdly, it has been clearly established that the distinction between a warranty, which is a term of a contract, and a 'mere representation' depends upon whether the parties intended the statement to have contractual effect.[297] It would be somewhat curious if contractual intention could be dispensed with in proving the existence of a contract, but not in proving the terms of that contract.

The conclusion is that an intention to create legal relations is essential to the formation of a contract in English law.

FURTHER READING

HUDSON, 'Retractation of Letters of Acceptance' (1966) 82 LQR 169

HUDSON, 'Gibbons v Proctor Revisited' (1968) 84 LQR 503

HEPPLE, 'Intention to Create Legal Relations' [1970] CLJ 122, 127–37

293 *Pettitt v Pettitt* [1970] AC 777, 806, 816.

294 *Ferris v Weaven* [1952] 2 All ER 233; *Merritt v Merritt* [1970] 1 WLR 1121; *Eves v Eves* [1975] 1 WLR 1338 (cohabitation); *Re Windle* [1975] 1 WLR 1628; *Tanner v Tanner* [1975] 1 WLR 1346 (cohabitation). Cf *Vaughan v Vaughan* [1953] 1 QB 762; *Spellman v Spellman* [1961] 1 WLR 921; *Morris v Tarrant* [1971] 2 QB 143; *Horrocks v Forray* [1976] 1 WLR 230 (cohabitation). See generally Freeman, in Halson (ed), *Exploring the Boundaries of Contract* (1996) 68.

295 [2010] UKSC 42, [2011] 1 AC 534 at [52] (Lord Mance and Baroness Hale dissented on this point). But such agreements cannot oust the jurisdiction of the Courts (below, pp 418–9) to make orders about the parties' financial arrangements: see analogously the Matrimonial Causes Act 1973, s 34 (maintenance agreements).

296 *Simkins v Pays* [1955] 1 WLR 975.

297 *Heilbut Symons & Co v Buckleton* [1913] AC 30, 51; *Oscar Chess Ltd v Williams* [1957] 1 WLR 370, 374. See below, pp 143–6.

MILLER, 'Felthouse v Bindley Revisited' (1972) 35 MLR 489

RAWLINGS, 'The Battle of Forms' (1979) 42 MLR 715

HEDLEY, 'Keeping Contract in its Place—*Balfour v Balfour* and the Enforceability of Informal Agreements' (1985) 5 OJLS 391

GARDNER, 'Trashing with Trollope: a Deconstruction of the Postal Rules in Contract' (1992) 12 OJLS 170

SIMPSON, 'Quackery and Contract Law: *Carlill v Carbolic Smoke Ball Company*' in *Leading Cases in the Common Law* (Oxford: Clarendon Press, 1995) 259

NOLAN, 'Offer and Acceptance in the Electronic Age' in BURROWS and PEEL (eds), *Contract Formation and Parties* (Oxford: Oxford University Press, 2010) 61

PEEL, 'The Status of Agreements to Negotiate in Good Faith' in BURROWS and PEEL (eds), *Contract Formation and Parties* (Oxford: Oxford University Press, 2010) 37

LEGGATT, 'Negotiation in Good Faith: Adapting to Changing Circumstances in Contracts and English Contract Law' [2019] JBL 104

3

FORM

1. FORMAL REQUIREMENTS

Sam Goldwyn is reported to have said that 'a verbal contract is not worth the paper it's written on'.[1] Yet valuable agreements involving very substantial sums can be established entirely orally.[2] In *Wells v Devani* Lord Briggs recognized that 'the common law will recognise an enforceable liability to pay as arising from the briefest and most informal exchange between the parties'.[3] And in *Rock Advertising Ltd v MWB Business Exchange Centres Ltd* Lord Sumption acknowledged that '[t]he advantages of the common law's flexibility about formal validity are that it enables agreements to be made quickly, informally and without the intervention of lawyers or legally drafted documents'.[4]

As a general rule, a simple contract need not be made in any special form, but requires the presence of consideration, which broadly means that something must be given in exchange for a promise.[5] The paradigm of the simple contract is therefore a bargain, but because the requirement of consideration can be satisfied by nominal consideration, such as a peppercorn, it has been argued that consideration is really no more than a requirement of form.[6] In some simple contracts, statute imposes (in addition to the requirement of consideration) the necessity of some kind of form, such as writing, either as a condition of their existence or as a requisite of proving the contract.

The other kind of contract recognized by English law is a contract made by deed. This derives its validity neither from the fact of the agreement nor because it is an exchange but solely from the *form* in which it is expressed.

In this chapter, we shall examine (1) contracts by deed and (2) (simple) contracts for which writing is required.[7]

Historically, formal requirements played a large role in the English law of contract because the Statute of Frauds 1677 provided that many important and widely used types of contract were unenforceable unless supported by a note or memorandum in writing,

[1] As recognized by Rares J in *TWW Yachts Sarl v The Yacht 'Loretta' (No 1)* [2021] FCA 240 at [1].

[2] See *Blue v Ashley* [2017] EWHC 1928 (Comm).

[3] [2019] UKSC 4, [2020] AC 129 at [63].

[4] [2018] UKSC 24, [2019] AC 119 at [12].

[5] See Chapter 4.

[6] *Vantage Navigation Corp v Suhail & Saud Bahwan Building Materials Llc, The Alev* [1989] 1 Lloyd's Rep 138, 147 (Hobhouse J); see below, pp 137–9.

[7] See Cartwright, *Formation and Variation of Contracts* (4th edn, 2024) Part II.

in particular contracts for the sale or disposition of an interest in land and, until 1954, contracts for the sale of goods of over £10 in value.[8]

The significance of formal requirements has now diminished, save in sales of land, guarantees, and a limited number of other types of contract, notably to protect parties (such as tenants, consumers, borrowers, and employees) who are in the weaker bargaining position. Nevertheless, although it has been stated that the advantages of requirements of formality are purely negative in nature and consist in the avoidance of various evils,[9] it should not be forgotten that formality serves a number of useful functions.[10]

First, there is an important evidential function.[11] A requirement such as writing facilitates and renders certain the existence of a transaction and its terms as well as identifying the intention of the parties. The particularly significant issues of authenticity and integrity which arise in the case of contracts made by e-mail can, for example, be addressed by a suitable formal requirement for such transactions.[12]

Secondly, there is the paternalistic and cautionary function of helping to ensure that a party deliberately considers whether to contract and to prevent people accidentally binding themselves on impulse or because of improper pressure. For instance, classes of contractors considered to be weaker, such as tenants, employees, borrowers, and consumers, may be protected by requiring a written agreement and clear language.[13] In some such cases, in particular contracts with consumers, there may also be a statutory 'cooling off' period.[14] This is a paternalistic qualification to the substantive requirement of agreement rather than a formal requirement, but the requirement that notice must be given to the protected person of the right to cancel[15] is a requirement of form. The corollary of the evidential and cautionary functions is that formal requirements allow parties to bind themselves with certainty and to know to what they are binding themselves. Formality requirements may also furnish a well-recognized and objective test of enforceability, and provide a 'channel' for the legally effective expression of intention.[16]

As against these useful functions, if the form is complex, it can be inconvenient, mysterious, and inaccessible to ordinary people. Formal requirements may also affront social and commercial attitudes to promises ('my word is my bond') since requiring, for

[8] This requirement was repealed by the Law Reform (Enforcement of Contracts) Act 1954.

[9] Jhering, *Geist des Roemischen Rechts* (4th edn, 1883) vol 2, 480–2.

[10] Law Com No 164, *Formalities for Contracts for Sale etc of Land* (1987) paras 1.4, 2.3–2.11.

[11] *Ibid*, para 2.5. See also Simpson, *A History of the Common Law of Contract* (1975) ch XIII.

[12] Below, pp 93–4.

[13] *Writing*: Consumer Credit Act 1974, s 60. *Notice of specified terms*: Landlord and Tenant Act 1985, s 4; Estate Agents Act 1979, s 18; Employment Rights Act 1996, ss 1–2, 4–6.

[14] eg Consumer Credit Act 1974, ss 67–68; Consumer Contracts (Information, Cancellation and Additional Charges) Regulations 2013 (SI 2013 No 3134); Timeshare, Holiday Products, Resale and Exchange Regulations 2010 (SI 2010 No 2960).

[15] eg Consumer Credit Act 1974, s 64.

[16] This has been described by Fuller as a third 'channeling function' of formalities:(1941) 41 Col L Rev 799, 800–4.

instance, a deed or writing implies mistrust. These factors may mean that the required form is not used, whether deliberately or by accident, and thus the requirement can have the effect of reducing rather than promoting the security of transactions.

Formal requirements can help to prevent impulsiveness, coercion, inadequate evidence, and manufactured evidence, but may undermine security of transactions if their complexity or social or commercial morality mean they are not observed.

2. CONTRACTS BY DEED

(a) HOW A CONTRACT BY DEED IS MADE

At common law it was often said that a contract by deed was executed by being 'signed, sealed and delivered'. But the position is now largely governed by section 1 of the Law of Property (Miscellaneous Provisions) Act 1989.[17] To be a deed an instrument must make it 'clear on its face that it is intended to be a deed by the person making it or, as the case may be, by the parties to it (whether by describing itself as a deed or expressing itself to be executed or signed as a deed or otherwise)'.[18] The 1989 Act does not, however, lay down any prescribed manner of making it clear because to do so 'would invalidate what would otherwise be perfectly acceptable deeds merely for failure to include one vital word'.[19]

(i) Signature and attestation

In the case of deeds executed by an individual the 1989 Act abolished the requirement of sealing.[20] The instrument must either be signed by the person making it in the presence of an attesting witness or, where it is not signed by that person, perhaps because of some physical incapacity, it must be signed at the direction and in the presence of that person and in the presence of two attesting witnesses.[21] In the case of a company incorporated under the Companies Acts either its common seal must be affixed or the instrument must be signed by two 'authorised signatories' (which includes the directors and the company secretary) or by a director of the company in the presence of a witness who attests the signature.[22] The requirement of sealing still applies to corporations sole[23]

[17] Implementing Law Com No 163, *Deeds and Escrows* (1987). Section 1 applies to all deeds, and not just those relating to land, made on or after 31 July 1990; SI 1990 No 1175. The Law Commission has plans to review the law of deeds in its 14th programme of law reform: Law Com No 241 (2025).

[18] Law of Property (Miscellaneous Provisions) Act 1989, s 1(2)(a). For the similar rule for companies, see Companies Act 2006, s 46(1). A document which is executed as a deed but does not meet the requirements of a deed may still take effect as a simple contract as long it is supported by consideration: *Signature Living Hotel Ltd v Sulyok* [2020] EWHC 257 (Ch), [2020] Bus LR 588.

[19] Hansard, HL Deb vol 503, col 599 (24 January 1989) (The Lord Chancellor, Second Reading Debate).

[20] Law of Property (Miscellaneous Provisions) Act 1989, s 1(1)(b).

[21] Law of Property (Miscellaneous Provisions) Act 1989, s 1(3)(a). 'Signature' includes making one's mark: *ibid*, s 1(4). See *Euro Securities & Finance Ltd v Barrett* [2023] EWHC 51 (Ch), [2023] Ch 279.

[22] Companies Act 2006, s 44.

[23] See below, pp 250–1.

and corporations incorporated under other statutes or by royal charter.[24] Today, a seal is often merely an adhesive wafer attached to the document or even a printed circle containing the letters 'LS' (*locus sigilli*).[25] Even a document bearing no indication of a seal at all will suffice, provided that there is evidence (eg attestation) that it was intended to be executed as a deed.[26] Failure to have a signature witnessed and attested or, where this is still required, to have the document sealed, will not be fatal if the signatory is estopped from denying its validity because another has detrimentally relied on it.[27]

(ii) Delivery

The 1989 Act preserves the requirement of 'delivery'.[28] In this context 'delivery' does not signify handing over to the other party, but means an act done or word said so as to make it clear that the person making the deed regards it as binding. Thus, a deed may be 'delivered' even though it is retained in the custody of the grantor.[29]

(iii) Escrow

A deed which is delivered subject to a condition does not take effect until the condition is performed. For example, on a sale of land the vendor does not normally intend the deed to operate until the purchase price has been paid and (where appropriate) the deed has been executed by the purchaser. In such a case, it is termed an *escrow*, but if the condition is fulfilled within a time which is reasonable in all the circumstances,[30] it becomes operative as from the date of its delivery.[31] At one time an escrow could not be handed to one who was a party to it, or else it took effect at once, on the ground that handing it over outweighed oral conditions. But nowadays the intention of the parties prevails if they clearly mean the deed to be delivered conditionally.[32]

(b) WHEN IT IS ESSENTIAL TO CONTRACT BY DEED

Statute sometimes makes it necessary to use an instrument in the form of a deed if the transaction is to be valid. For example, the conveyance of a legal estate in land must normally be made by deed in accordance with the provisions of the Law of Property Act 1925.[33]

[24] Law of Property (Miscellaneous Provisions) Act 1989, s 1(9)–(10).

[25] *First National Securities Ltd v Jones* [1978] Ch 109.

[26] *Ibid*; *Commercial Credit Services v Knowles* [1978] 6 CL 64. Cf *TCB Ltd v Gray* [1986] Ch 621.

[27] *TCB Ltd v Gray* [1986] Ch 621; Law Com No 163, *Deeds and Escrows* (1987) para 2.15; *Shah v Shah* [2001] EWCA Civ 527, [2002] QB 35 (estoppel in relation to the Law of Property (Miscellaneous Provisions) Act 1989, s 1); *Briggs v Gleeds (Head Office)* [2014] EWHC 1178 (Ch), [2015] Ch 212 (distinguishing *Shah v Shah*).

[28] Law of Property (Miscellaneous Provisions) Act 1989, s 1(3)(b). Authority by a party making a deed to an agent to deliver it need not be given by deed: *ibid*, s 1(1)(c).

[29] *Xenos v Wickham* (1867) LR 2 HL 296; *Macedo v Stroud* [1922] AC 330; *Vincent v Premo Enterprises Ltd* [1969] 2 QB 609; *D'Silva v Lister House Development Ltd* [1971] Ch 17.

[30] *Beesly v Hallwood Estates Ltd* [1961] Ch 105; *Kingston v Ambrian Investment Co Ltd* [1975] 1 WLR 161. Cf *Glessing v Green* [1975] 1 WLR 863.

[31] *Alan Estates Ltd v WG Stores Ltd* [1982] Ch 511.

[32] *London Freehold and Leasehold Property Co v Lord Suffield* [1897] 2 Ch 608, 621; *Glessing v Green* [1975] 1 WLR 863.

[33] ss 52, 54.

At common law, a deed need only be used to make a contract if there is no consideration for the promise made on one side and accepted on the other (eg a gratuitous promise). One of the most common uses today of a deed (outside conveyances of land) is that of a promise to make a payment to a charity.

3. CONTRACTS FOR WHICH WRITING IS REQUIRED

(a) STATUTORY REQUIREMENTS OF WRITING

Although there is a popular belief that only contracts in writing are enforceable, this belief is completely illusory and forms no part of the English common law. A simple contract (ie one not made by deed) depends for its validity upon the presence of consideration and is in general valid whether in writing or oral.

In certain exceptional cases, however, the law requires writing, sometimes as a condition of the validity of the contract itself, but sometimes only as evidence without which it cannot be enforced. In these contracts consideration is as necessary as in contracts for which no writing is required: 'If contracts be merely written and not specialties, they are parol, and a consideration must be proved.'[34] The following are examples of contracts which must, by statute, be made in writing:

(1) The Bills of Exchange Act 1882[35] requires that a bill of exchange or promissory note and the acceptance of a bill of exchange must be in writing.
(2) A consumer credit agreement, for example a hire-purchase or loan agreement, must be in writing and be signed by the hirer or debtor and by or on behalf of the owner or creditor. It must also be made in a certain form and contain certain information including prominent notices advising the hirer or debtor of the protection and remedies, including the right to cancel, available under the Act and the annual percentage rate of charge.[36]
(3) A contract for the sale or other disposition of land must be in writing.[37] This is considered in detail below.[38]

Certain other contracts are not required by statute to be made in writing, but merely to be evidenced by writing before they can be enforced. Until 1954 the most frequent examples of such contracts were provided by those specified in the Statute of Frauds 1677, which rendered various contracts unenforceable unless they were supported by a note or memorandum in writing.[39] The object of these statutory requirements was 'for prevention of many fraudulent practices which are commonly endeavoured to be

[34] *Rann v Hughes* (1778) 7 Term R 350n.

[35] ss 3(1), 17(2). See too Electronic Trade Documents Act 2023, s 1.

[36] Consumer Credit Act 1974, ss 60, 64; Consumer Credit (Agreements) Regulations 1983 (SI 1983 No 1553).

[37] Law of Property (Miscellaneous Provisions) Act 1989, s 2(1).

[38] Below, p 87.

[39] See also contracts of marine insurance which, by reason of the Marine Insurance Act 1906, s 22, must be evidenced by a written policy.

upheld by perjury and subornation of perjury'.[40] But almost from its inception, this requirement that a contract be evidenced by writing exhibited a tendency to encourage, rather than to prevent, dishonest dealing. The attempts of the judges consequently to circumvent the Statute of Frauds, and the niceties of legal learning which resulted, rendered its operation both arbitrary and artificial. By the Law Reform (Enforcement of Contracts) Act 1954,[41] most of its provisions, together with their re-enacting statutes,[42] were repealed. The one important type of contract still governed by the Statute of Frauds is a contract of guarantee.

(b) CONTRACTS OF GUARANTEE

By section 4 of the Statute of Frauds 1677:

> No action shall be brought . . . whereby to charge the defendant upon any special promise to answer for the debt, default, or miscarriage of another person . . . unless the agreement upon which such action shall be brought or some memorandum or note thereof shall be in writing, and signed by the party to be charged therewith or some other person thereunto by him lawfully authorized.

A promise 'to answer for the debt, default or miscarriage or another person' is a contract of guarantee or suretyship. It can usually be reduced to this form: 'Deal with X, and if X does not meet his obligations, I will be answerable.'

(i) Guarantees distinguished from contracts of indemnity

A contract of indemnity, unlike a guarantee, is not subject to any statutory requirement of writing. In a contract of guarantee there must always be three parties in contemplation: a principal debtor (whose liability may be actual or prospective), a creditor, and a promisor (the guarantor) who promises to discharge the debtor's liability *if the debtor should fail to do so*. The guarantor's liability is therefore secondary to that of the principal debtor. In a contract of indemnity, however, the promisor is primarily liable, either alone or jointly with the principal debtor, and undertakes to discharge the liability *in any event* whether or not the principal debtor defaults.[43]

For a contract to be a guarantee there must, in fact, be an expectation that another person will perform the obligation undertaken by the promisor. If the promisor is primarily liable the promise is not within the Statute of Frauds, and need not be in writing.[44] The question whether the undertaking is primary or secondary is determined, not merely from the particular words of the promise, but from the general circumstances of the transaction.[45] The borderline is often very artificial and the subject 'has raised

[40] Statutes of the Realm, vol V, p 840.

[41] See the Sixth Interim Report of the Law Revision Committee (Cmd 5449, 1937), and the First Report of the Law Reform Committee (Cmd 8809, 1953).

[42] Sale of Goods Act 1893, s 4 (writing required for contracts for the sale of goods of over £10 in value).

[43] *Guild & Co v Conrad* [1894] 2 QB 885, 896; *Pitts v Jones* [2007] EWCA Civ 1301, [2008] QB 706.

[44] *Birkmyr v Darnell* (1704) 1 Salk 27, 28.

[45] *Keate v Temple* (1797) 1 B & P 158; *Abbhi v Slade* [2019] EWCA Civ 2175, [2019] 2 CLC 949.

many hair-splitting distinctions of exactly that kind which brings the law into hatred, ridicule and contempt by the public'.[46]

(ii) Nature of liability guaranteed

The liability guaranteed may be tortious as well as contractual.[47] It may be prospective at the time the promise is made, as, for example, in consideration of a future advance of money; or it may be past, provided some new consideration is given.[48] Yet there must be a principal debtor at some time; if not, there is no contract of guarantee, and the promise though not in writing will nevertheless be actionable. This is illustrated by *Lakeman v Mountstephen*:[49]

M stated that he would construct certain drains if L, the Chairman of a local Board of Health or the Board, would become responsible for payment. L responded, 'Go on, [M], and do the work, and I will see you paid.' The Board repudiated liability on the ground that it had never entered into any agreement with L. When sued, L pleaded that his statement was a promise to be answerable for the debt of another and, not being in writing, was unenforceable.

The House of Lords held that L's promise was enforceable. The Board had incurred no liability which could be guaranteed, and there could be no contract of guarantee unless there was a principal debtor. L's oral promise to M, when properly construed, indicated that he would be liable, not as guarantor, but as sole debtor.

(iii) A continuing liability

The promise must also not effect a release of the original debtor, whose liability must be a continuing liability. If there is an existing debt for which a third party is liable to the promisee, and the promisor undertakes to be answerable for it, there is no guarantee if the terms of the undertaking are such as to extinguish the original liability. If A says to B, 'Give C Ltd a receipt in full for its debt to you, and I will pay the amount', this promise is not a guarantee within the Statute of Frauds, but a substitution of one debtor for another.[50]

(iv) Exceptions

In two exceptional situations a contract of guarantee has been held to fall outside the Statute of Frauds although it is a promise to answer for the debt, default, or miscarriage of another.

The first is where the guarantee is merely incidental to a larger contract and not the sole object of the parties to the transaction. So in *Sutton & Co v Grey*,[51] where the defendants entered into an oral agreement with a stockbroker to introduce business to him on the terms that they were to receive half the commissions earned and to pay half the losses in the event of a client introduced by them failing to pay, it was held that their

[46] *Yeoman Credit Ltd v Latter* [1961] 1 WLR 828, 892 (Harman LJ).
[47] *Kirkham v Marter* (1819) 2 B & Ald 613.
[48] *Board v Hoey* (1948) 65 TLR 43.
[49] (1874) LR 7 HL 17.
[50] *Goodman v Chase* (1818) 1 B & Ald 297.
[51] [1894] 1 QB 285.

promise to answer for the debt of such a client did not fall within the Statute. It was incidental to a wider transaction and did not have to be evidenced in writing.

Secondly, where the guarantor's main purpose is to acquire or retain property, and the guarantee is given to relieve the property from some charge or incumbrance in favour of a third party, it is not within the Statute of Frauds. Thus if A buys goods from B which are subject to a lien in favour of C, and in order to discharge the lien A promises C to pay B's debt if B does not do so, this promise need not be evidenced in writing.[52] But the interest to be acquired or retained must be substantial and proprietary. An oral promise by a shareholder in a company to guarantee the company's debts in order to prevent an execution being levied on its assets does not come within this exception. The interest of a shareholder in the company's assets is purely personal, and is not a proprietary interest.[53]

(v) Criticism of the scope of the Statute of Frauds

These legal niceties have nothing to commend them. It is a matter for regret that, if special protection is to be afforded by the law to guarantors, it is not embodied in a statute requiring the terms of all contracts of guarantee or indemnity to be set out in a written document,[54] instead of perpetuating subtle distinctions.

(vi) The form required

Until the enactment of the Law Reform (Miscellaneous) Provisions Act 1989 substantially the same form was required for contracts of guarantee and contracts for the disposition of an interest in land. The provisions of the Statute of Frauds 1677, which still govern guarantees, were substantially re-enacted as regards sales of land by section 40(1) of the Law of Property Act 1925. Many of the decisions under section 40(1) concerning contracts for the sale of land remain applicable to guarantees.

Under section 4 of the Statute of Frauds, a guarantee does not have to be signed by both parties, but only by the party to be charged or that person's agent.[55] The signature need not be an actual subscription of the party's name as it may be a mark; nor need it be in handwriting as it may be printed or stamped; nor need it be placed at the end of the document as it may be at the beginning or in the middle.[56]

The parties and the subject-matter of the contract must appear in the note or memorandum. Where the parties are not named they must be so described as to be identified with ease and certainty.[57] All the material terms of the guarantee must be accurately set out in the memorandum, but by section 3 of the Mercantile Law Amendment Act 1856, the consideration need not be stated.

[52] *Fitzgerald v Dressler* (1859) 7 CBNS 374.

[53] *Harburg India Rubber Comb Co v Martin* [1902] 1 KB 778.

[54] As in the case of certain contracts of guarantee and indemnity given in relation to regulated consumer credit agreements: Consumer Credit Act 1974, s 105(1).

[55] Above, pp 80–1.

[56] *Leeman v Stocks* [1951] Ch 941.

[57] *Rossiter v Miller* (1878) 3 App Cas 1124. Cf *Potter v Duffield* (1874) LR 18 Eq 4.

The note or memorandum of a guarantee may consist of various letters and papers, but they must be connected and complete.[58] A sequence of negotiating e-mails may also satisfy the requirements of writing and signature under the 1677 Act.[59]

(vii) The effect of non-compliance

The effect of a failure to comply with the provisions of the Statute of Frauds is not that the contract is void, or voidable, but that it cannot be enforced against a party who has not signed a note or memorandum because it is incapable of proof.[60] No action can be brought until the omission is made good. But, provided the note or memorandum acknowledges the existence of the contract,[61] and is signed by the party or his agent,[62] it may be made at any time before the commencement of the action,[63] and it does not matter that it was never intended to serve as a note or memorandum but was prepared for some entirely different purpose.[64]

The law on claims for restitution of money paid under unenforceable contracts is difficult. Money should be recoverable if the payor can establish that there has been a total failure of consideration.[65] But it is debatable whether the standard ground that a payment made under a mistake of law can be recovered applies where the payor paid money under an unenforceable, but not void, contract mistakenly believing that it could enforce the contract.[66]

(viii) Limited role for estoppel

Estoppel, founded only on the guarantor's promise without any additional encouragement or assurance, cannot be invoked as a means of avoiding section 4 of the Statute of Frauds. In *Actionstrength Ltd v International Glass Engineering SpA*:[67]

An employer in a building project was alleged to have orally promised a sub-contractor to guarantee payments owing to the sub-contractor by the head-contractor in return for the

[58] *Stokes v Whicher* [1920] 1 Ch 411, 418; *Elias v George Saheley & Co (Barbados) Ltd* [1983] 1 AC 646. Cf *Timmins v Moreland Street Property Ltd* [1958] Ch 110; *Moat Financial Services v Wilkinson* [2005] EWCA Civ 1253.

[59] *Golden Ocean Group Ltd v Salgaocar Mining Industries PVT Ltd* [2012] EWCA Civ 265, [2012] 1 WLR 3674.

[60] *Leroux v Brown* (1852) 12 CB 801; *Maddison v Alderson* (1883) 8 App Cas 467, 474.

[61] *Buxton v Rust* (1872) LR 7 Ex 279 (notwithstanding announced intention to repudiate contract). See also *Reuss v Picksley* (1866) LR 1 Ex 342; *Parker v Clark* [1960] 1 WLR 286 (written offer containing all material terms suffices though contract concluded by subsequent oral acceptance). Cf *Tiverton Estates Ltd v Wearwell Ltd* [1975] Ch 146 (agreement 'subject to contract' insufficient).

[62] *Elpis Maritime Co Ltd v Marti Chartering Co Inc* [1992] 1 AC 21, 28.

[63] *Re Hoyle* [1893] 1 Ch 84; *Elpis Maritime Co Ltd v Marti Chartering Co Inc* [1992] 1 AC 21.

[64] *Jones v Victoria Dock Co* (1877) 2 QBD 314 (entry in company's minute book); *Phillips v Butler* [1945] Ch 358 (receipt for deposit).

[65] Cf *Thomas v Brown* (1876) 1 QBD 714; *Monnickendam v Leanse* (1923) 39 TLR 445.

[66] In the leading case on mistake of law, *Kleinwort Benson Ltd v Lincoln CC* [1999] 2 AC 349, the contract in question was void not unenforceable. For a prior case suggesting that money cannot be recovered under an unenforceable contract, see *Boddington v Lawton* [1994] ICR 478 (Nicholls LJ). See further Burrows, *A Restatement of the English Law of Unjust Enrichment* (2012) s 3(6) and pp 32–5.

[67] [2003] UKHL 17, [2003] 2 AC 541. Cf above, n 27 (estoppel in relation to the Law of Property (Miscellaneous Provisions) Act 1989, s 1); below, pp 91–2 (estoppel in relation to the Law of Property (Miscellaneous Provisions) Act 1989, s 2).

sub-contractor not withdrawing its labour. When the sub-contractor sought to enforce the guarantee, the employer argued that it was unenforceable under section 4 of the Statute of Frauds because it was not supported by a written note or memorandum. In answer to this, the sub-contractor sought to rely on estoppel constituted by its reliance on the oral promise.

The House of Lords held that estoppel could not succeed because to allow it to do so would entirely undermine section 4. It would contradict section 4 for relied-upon oral guarantees to be routinely enforceable by means of estoppel.

(c) CONTRACTS FOR THE SALE OR OTHER DISPOSITION OF LAND

(i) Scope of the 1989 Act

The most important class of contracts subject to requirements of form are contracts relating to land. The Law Commission considered and rejected the abolition of all formal requirements for such contracts, primarily because of the need for certainty, but also for protective, paternalistic reasons; time to reflect and, if necessary to seek legal advice 'is especially important in the case of contracts dealing with land because they often involve acceptance of a complexity of rights and duties'.[68] Indeed the Commission's recommendations, substantially enacted by the Law of Property (Miscellaneous Provisions) Act 1989 (the '1989 Act'), are in important respects more rigorous than what had hitherto been required.[69] By section 2(1) of the 1989 Act, contracts for the sale or other disposition of an interest in land:

> can only be made in writing and only by incorporating all the terms which the parties have expressly agreed in one document or, where contracts are exchanged, in each.

The section applies to a contract for a 'disposition'[70] of an interest in land, and 'interest in land' is defined as 'any estate, interest or charge in or over land'.[71] Thus, the section applies to a contract for a lease, a mortgage, a release, and a disclaimer. It applies where neither party has any proprietary interest in the relevant property.[72] Contracts for the grant of a lease for a period not exceeding three years,[73] those made in the course of a public auction, and those regulated under the Financial Services and Markets Act 2000 (for instance unit trusts investing in land) are excluded.[74]

[68] Law Com No 164, *Formalities for the Sale etc of Land* (1987) paras 2.7–2.9. For other advantages of formality, see above, pp 78–80.

[69] Contracts made before the 1989 Act came into force on 27 September 1989 had to comply with Law of Property Act 1925, s 40(1) which substantially re-enacted the relevant portion of the Statute of Frauds, s 4. The principles were therefore substantially the same as those for guarantees.

[70] It has the same meaning as in the Law of Property Act 1925: Law of Property (Miscellaneous Provisions) Act 1989, s 2(6).

[71] Law of Property (Miscellaneous Provisions) Act 1989, s 2(6), as amended.

[72] *Singh v Beggs* (1995) 71 P & CR 120.

[73] Contracts to grant leases not exceeding three years need no formality (Law of Property (Miscellaneous Provisions) Act 1989, s 2(5)) because the grant of such a lease itself needs no formality if it takes effect in possession, but contracts to assign such leases are subject to s 2: see Law Com No 164 (1987) para 4.10.

[74] Law of Property (Miscellaneous Provisions) Act 1989, s 2(5)(b), (c), as amended. See Law Com No 164, paras 4.11–4.12.

Equitable mortgages by deposit of title deeds were previously valid without any writing, but have now been held to be subject to section 2 of the 1989 Act and void if they do not comply with it, because the basis of such equitable mortgage is contract.[75] An option granted by the vendor of land is also a 'contract' within section 2[76] but the subsequent exercise of that option is a unilateral act and not within the section: 'It would destroy the very purpose of the option if the purchaser had to obtain the vendor's countersignature to the notice by which it was exercised.'[77] A 'lock-out' agreement, where the owner of property agrees with a prospective purchaser not to consider any other offers for property for a fixed period, is, however, not subject to section 2 because its negative nature—the vendor cannot sell to a third party but is not committed to a sale to the prospective purchaser—means that there is no disposition of an interest in land.[78] Again, contracts which are preliminary to the acquisition of such an interest, or such as deal with a remote and inappreciable interest, would appear to be outside the section.[79]

In one respect the 1989 Act probably requires a greater degree of formality than the Law Commission recommended. It appears that it is no longer possible to have an enforceable contract by written offer and acceptance in correspondence; there must either be a single document incorporating all the terms agreed and signed by the parties or each party must sign a document incorporating the terms in the expectation that the other has also executed or will execute a corresponding document incorporating the same terms.[80]

Separate supplementary or collateral agreements to contracts relating to land are not within section 2. For instance, in the case of a contract to grant a lease, the agreement by the prospective tenant to carry out certain work on the premises in exchange for payment has been held to be outside it, as long as the non-land elements are independent of the land contract.[81] The line between the contract relating to land and the supplementary

[75] *United Bank of Kuwait v Sahib* [1997] Ch 107, rejecting the argument that such deposits are equitable charges rather than agreements to mortgage. But cf *Target Holdings Ltd v Priestley* (1999) 79 P & CR 305 (writing not needed for agreement which disposed of a mortgage).

[76] *Spiro v Glencrown Properties Ltd* [1991] Ch 537; Law Com No 164, para 4.3.

[77] *Ibid*, 541 (Hoffmann J). See also *Trustees of the Chippenham Golf Club v North Wiltshire DC* (1991) 64 P & CR 527, 530.

[78] *Pitt v PHH Asset Management Ltd* [1994] 1 WLR 327, above, p 68.

[79] eg *Angel v Duke* (1875) LR 10 QB 174 (agreement to repair house for prospective tenant); *Humble v Mitchell* (1839) 11 A & E 205 (agreement to transfer shares in company possessed of land). Cf *Driver v Broad* [1893] 1 QB 744 (contract to sell debentures of company possessed of land is subject to the statute). These decisions concerned the Statute of Frauds.

[80] *Commission for New Towns v Cooper (Great Britain) Ltd* [1995] Ch 259; *Firstpost Homes Ltd v Johnson* [1995] 1 WLR 1567. NB cl 1(1) of the Draft Bill attached to the Report differs from s 2 and see Law Com No 164, para 4.15. But cf *Hooper v Sherman*, 30 November 1994 (CA), which did not refer to the Act's difference from the Law Commission's Draft Bill and relied on para 4.15.

[81] *Tootal Clothing Ltd v Guinea Properties Ltd* (1991) 64 P & CR 452, 455–6 (Scott LJ); cf *Keay v Morris Homes (West Midlands) Ltd* [2012] EWCA Civ 900, [2012] 1 WLR 2855 at [46]–[48]. See also *Record v Bell* [1991] 1 WLR 853; *North Eastern Properties Ltd v Coleman* [2010] EWCA Civ 277, [2010] 1 WLR 2715. For boundary agreements, see *Neilson v Poole* (1969) 20 P & CR 909; *Joyce v Rigolli* [2004] EWCA Civ 79, [2004] 1 P & CR DG22.

or collateral one is, however, not always easy to draw particularly where, as commonly occurs, the contract has been duly signed and is awaiting exchange but a further term is orally agreed immediately prior to exchange. So, in *Record v Bell*:[82]

The vendor of property had not received a copy of the entries from the Land Registry by the day before the contract, which had been drawn up, was to be exchanged. He agreed with the purchaser, who was concerned about undisclosed entries, to warrant his title if the purchaser exchanged contracts and this oral agreement was confirmed by letters. Contracts were exchanged and the title was as warranted but the purchaser, whose financial position had deteriorated, refused to complete and relied *inter alia* on non-compliance with section 2 of the 1989 Act, since all the terms were not in either the contracts exchanged or the exchange of letters.

Although the purchaser seemed to be thinking in terms of amending the main contract rather than a separate contract, the agreement was held to be a collateral contract and outside the section:

It would be unfortunate if common transactions of this nature should nevertheless cause the contracts to be avoided. It may, of course, lead to a greater use of the concept of collateral warranties than has hitherto been necessary.[83]

(ii) The form required

Under section 2(1) of the 1989 Act, contracts for the disposition of an interest in land must now be made in writing and not merely evidenced in writing. Furthermore, section 2(3) of the 1989 Act requires all the parties to a contract for the sale or disposition of an interest in land or their agents[84] to sign the document incorporating the terms. The parties must all be identified by their signature and all the express terms must be incorporated in the document.[85] Section 2 does not require the inclusion of implied terms, such as a landlord's covenant of quiet enjoyment,[86] and, if the parties have reached agreement but fail to record all the terms in writing or record one or more of them wrongly, the Court may order the written document to be rectified, although rectification must not be used to undermine the 1989 Act.[87] Where the written agreement is so rectified, the order does not necessarily have retrospective effect; 'the contract shall come into being . . . at such time as may be specified in the order'.[88] Where contracts

[82] [1991] 1 WLR 853; Smith (1992) 108 LQR 217; Harpum [1991] CLJ 399. Cf *McCausland v Duncan Lawrie Ltd* [1997] 1 WLR 38 (a variation of material term had to comply with s 2).

[83] [1991] 1 WLR 853, 862. This was anticipated by the Law Commission, Law Com No 164, para 5.7. On collateral warranties, see below, p 146.

[84] In *Rabiu v Marlbray Ltd* [2013] EWHC 3272 (Ch) one of the contracts was void as against one of the alleged parties because there had been no authority to sign on behalf of that party (and no ratification). On contracts made by an agent on behalf of an unnamed or undisclosed principal, see below, p 691.

[85] *Francis v F Berndes Ltd* [2011] EWHC 3377 (Ch), [2012] 1 All ER (Comm) 735.

[86] *Markham v Paget* [1908] 1 Ch 697.

[87] *Francis v F Berndes Ltd* [2011] EWHC 3377 (Ch), [2012] 1 All ER (Comm) 735. On rectification see below, pp 284–90.

[88] Law of Property (Miscellaneous Provisions) Act 1989, s 2(4). See Law Com No 164, para 5.6.

are exchanged each document must contain the express terms and each party must sign.[89] The incorporation of the express terms in the document can occur either by their being set out or by reference to some other document or documents. Formerly, implied reference in the signed document sufficed[90] but it may well be that express reference is required under the 1989 Act.[91] Where the document has not been incorporated, it may, as we have seen, nevertheless be effective if it is a separate supplementary or collateral agreement.

(iii) The effect of non-compliance

The fundamental change effected by the 1989 Act is that, whereas the form required under the earlier legislation was merely evidentiary and did not go to the *existence* of the contract, the form required by section 2 of the 1989 Act does. The failure to comply with the requirements as to form thus renders the contract void (ie a nullity) rather than unenforceable.[92] This follows from the wording in section 2(1) that the contract for the disposition of an interest in land 'can only be made in writing and only by incorporating all the [express] terms'.

Thus, whereas a guarantee may be enforceable by having a note or memorandum of the agreement signed at a later date, an oral agreement subject to section 2 of the 1989 Act cannot be subsequently validated in this way. The Law Commission stated that a regime, such as those under the Statute of Frauds 1677 and section 40(1) of the Law of Property Act 1925, which 'allows oral contracts to be binding but unenforceable and which may later become enforceable, but sometimes only against one party, is indefensibly confusing'.[93]

At the heart of the Law Commission's recommendations was the view that the equitable doctrine of part performance should 'no longer have a role to play in contracts concerning land'.[94] Under this doctrine, the Courts, in certain cases, allowed an unenforceable oral contract concerning land to be proved by oral evidence, when the party seeking to enforce the contract had done acts in performance of its obligations under it, provided that the performance was referable to some contract,[95] the acts were performed by the person seeking to enforce the contract,[96] and the contract was one which, if properly evidenced, would have been specifically enforceable.[97]

[89] 1989 Act, s 2(1) and (3).

[90] Law of Property Act 1925, s 40(1); *Timmins v Moreland Street Property Ltd* [1958] Ch 110.

[91] *Record v Bell* [1991] 1 WLR 853, 859–60. See Cartwright, *Formation and Variation of Contracts* (4th edn, 2024) para 5-21.

[92] *United Bank of Kuwait v Sahib* [1997] Ch 107, 122, 136; Law Com No 164, para 6.4.

[93] Law Com No 164, para 4.2.

[94] *Ibid*, para 4.13.

[95] *Rawlinson v Ames* [1925] Ch 96; *Steadman v Steadman* [1976] AC 536 (mere payment of a sum of money could amount to a sufficient act of part performance, but differing views were expressed as to whether the acts performed must be referable to some contract *concerning land*: [1976] AC 536, 542, 547, 554, 562, 568–70, on which see *Re Gonin* [1979] Ch 16; *Sutton v Sutton* [1984] Ch 184). Cf *Maddison v Alderson* (1883) 8 App Cas 467.

[96] *Caton v Caton* (1865) LR 1 Ch App 137, 148, aff'd (1867) LR 2 HL 167.

[97] *Britain v Rossiter* (1882) 11 QBD 123; *McManus v Cooke* (1887) 35 Ch D 681, 697.

This requirement meant the doctrine had no application to contracts of guarantee which equity would not specifically enforce.

Under the new law, although the doctrine of part performance can no longer apply as such, the Commission considered that the parties to an agreement that does not comply with the statutory requirements would not simply be left without a remedy.[98] The use of collateral contracts and the remedy of rectification have been mentioned above.[99] It should also be noted that where the void contract has been performed, for example by the execution of a valid lease or the completion of a conveyance, a property right will have been created and the parties no longer need to rely on the void contract.[100]

The primary tool the Law Commission anticipated would be used, instead of 'part performance', to enable justice to be achieved between the particular parties is the equitable doctrine of proprietary estoppel. Furthermore, although not mentioned by the Law Commission in its Report, its draft Bill excluded from the formalities required by the Act 'implied, resulting and constructive trusts'. This exclusion (which is also found in relation to trusts of land)[101] is embodied in section 2(5) of the 1989 Act.

(iv) Proprietary estoppel and constructive trusts

A party to a transaction who detrimentally relies on the belief (encouraged or acquiesced in by the other party) that he has or will acquire rights in the property of the other may be protected by the equitable doctrine of proprietary estoppel.[102] Acquiescence in improvements to a property has been held to justify the conveyance of the fee simple[103] and non-contractual assurances that a housekeeper could remain in a house have been protected by equitable relief.[104]

Closely akin to proprietary estoppel is a constructive trust based on a common understanding or arrangement relied on by a claimant.[105] Given the explicit exclusion of constructive trusts in section 2(5) of the 1989 Act, it is not surprising that the Courts have sometimes based their decision to give effect to the informal creation of an interest in land by finding a constructive trust rather than by invoking proprietary estoppel.[106] But although the view has been expressed that proprietary estoppel, as opposed to a constructive trust, may unacceptably subvert the policy of section 2,[107] the better view,

[98] Law Com No 164, paras 5.1–5.2.

[99] Above, nn 83, 87.

[100] The completion of the contract will give proprietary effect to the transaction, but does not render (non-land) terms of the void contract enforceable: *Keay v Morris Homes (West Midlands) Ltd* [2012] EWCA Civ 900, [2012] 1 WLR 2855 at [46]–[48], rejecting a contrary interpretation of *Tootal Clothing Ltd v Guinea Properties Ltd* (1991) 64 P & CR 452.

[101] Law of Property Act 1925, s 53(2).

[102] Below, pp 133–4.

[103] *Pascoe v Turner* [1979] 1 WLR 431.

[104] *Greasley v Cooke* [1980] 1 WLR 1306.

[105] *Yaxley v Gotts* [2000] Ch 162.

[106] *Ibid*; *Kinane v Mackie-Conteh* [2005] EWCA Civ 45, [2005] 2 P & CR DG3; *Herbert v Doyle* [2010] EWCA Civ 1095, [2011] 1 EGLR 119.

[107] *Godden v Merthyr Tydfil Housing Association* (1997) 74 P & CR D1 (Simon Brown LJ); *Kinane v Mackie-Conteh* [2005] EWCA Civ 45 (Neuberger LJ, who relied, by analogy, on the guarantee case of *Actionstrength Ltd v International Glass Engineering SpA* [2003] UKHL 17, [2003] 2 AC 541; see above, p 85); *Cobbe v Yeoman's Row Management Ltd* [2008] UKHL 55, [2008] 1 WLR 1952 at [29] (Lord Scott); *Thorner v Major* [2009] UKHL 18, [2009] 1 WLR 776 at [96] (Lord Neuberger).

in line with the Law Commission's intentions, is that, even where there is no finding of a constructive trust, proprietary estoppel can be applied to avoid the formal requirements of section 2.[108]

It is apparent that both proprietary estoppel and constructive trusts may provide what in many cases was hitherto provided by the doctrine of part performance: a remedy in a situation in which a party has acted on the void contract. Indeed, there are significant overlaps. Proprietary estoppel, constructive trusts, and part performance can be seen as manifestations of the equitable principle that a person may not rely on strict legal rights where to do so is unconscionable.[109] It has been suggested[110] that the uncertainties of the Statute of Frauds and section 40(1) of the Law of Property Act 1925 stemmed from the tendency of the judges to prevent technical and unmeritorious circumvention of obligations by relying on non-compliance with the statutory requirements. The indications are of a similar approach to the 1989 Act with its new uncertainties. The Law Commission's recognition that it would be necessary to rely on estoppel and collateral contracts 'to do justice between parties in individual otherwise hard cases',[111] in which the strict application of the statutory requirement would result in injustice, accepted this substantial qualification to its stated aim of increasing certainty.

(v) Restitution of unjust enrichment

The parties to an agreement that does not comply with section 2 may also be entitled to a restitutionary remedy. In principle a purchaser of land who has paid a deposit to the vendor under such an agreement—that is, a void contract—may recover it either for total failure of basis[112] (except where the purchaser has received part of the benefit bargained for in the contract, for example by entering into possession)[113] or for mistake of law.[114]

Where services are rendered under an agreement concerning land in the belief that there was a valid contract, but the contract does not comply with the requirements of section 2, the party conferring the services may be able to recover their reasonable value.[115] For example, restitution should be awarded in respect of alterations to property effected by a lessor or vendor at the request of prospective tenants or purchasers in the belief that

[108] *Kinane v Mackie-Conteh* [2005] EWCA Civ 45 (Arden LJ); *Howe v Gossop* [2021] EWHC 637 (Ch), [2022] 1 P & CR 15; *Thandi v Saggu* [2023] EWHC 2631 (Ch), [2024] WTLR 283.

[109] *Yaxley v Gotts* [2000] Ch 162, 176–7, 180, 181, 188, 193; *Gillett v Holt* [2001] Ch 210, 225.

[110] Above, p 85.

[111] Law Com No 164, para 5.7. See also *ibid*, paras 5.2, 5.4, 5.8.

[112] See *Rover International Ltd v Cannon Film Sales Ltd (No 3)* [1989] 1 WLR 912, 925, 938; *Westdeutsche Landesbank Girozentrale v Islington LBC* [1996] AC 669. Cf *Sharma v Simposh Ltd* [2011] EWCA Civ 1383, [2012] 1 P & CR 12.

[113] *Linz v Electric Wire Co of Palestine* [1948] AC 371, 377. Note that the requirement that the failure of consideration be *total* has been put into question, see below, p 592.

[114] *Kleinwort Benson Ltd v Lincoln CC* [1999] 2 AC 349.

[115] *Rover International Ltd v Cannon Film Sales Ltd (No 3)* [1989] 1 WLR 912, 926–8; *Cobbe v Yeoman's Row Management Ltd* [2008] UKHL 55, [2008] 1 WLR 1752.

there was a valid contract.[116] In principle, restitution should also be awarded in respect of services rendered by the prospective purchaser or lessee, for example improvements to the property and other services rendered at the request of or with the acceptance of the owner of property. As this would be limited to the executed part of the transaction, it would not seem to undermine the policy of section 2, just as restitution in respect of services rendered under contracts unenforceable for non-compliance with the Statute of Frauds and similar provisions has not been held to undermine the policy of those provisions.[117]

(d) ELECTRONIC CONTRACTS

Where contracts are made by e-mail or by trading on a website, any requirement of writing will normally be satisfied. In *Hudson v Hathway* Lewison LJ pointed out that '[g]iven that so much correspondence takes place nowadays by email rather than by letters with a "wet ink" signature, it is . . . entirely appropriate that the law should recognise that technological developments have extended what an ordinary person would understand by a signature'.[118] Provided it satisfies the standard common law test of authenticity, the requirement of a signature can be satisfied by, for example, a digital signature or by typing a name into an electronic document or e-mail.[119] Electronic signatures have readily been recognized by the courts. The Law Commission therefore advised the Government that, with the exception of marine insurance, it would not be necessary to amend statutory requirements of form to enable the use of most current forms of electronic communications in commercial transactions.[120] In line with this, relatively little use has been made of section 8 of the Electronic Communications Act 2000 which, inter alia, empowers the appropriate Minister to modify any enactment for the purpose of authorizing or facilitating the use of electronic communications for the doing of anything which is required to be evidenced in writing or signed or delivered as a deed or witnessed.[121]

In *Pereira Fernandes SA v Mehta*, Judge Pelling QC said:[122]

> I have no doubt that if a party creates and sends an electronically created document then he will be treated as having signed it to the same extent that he would in law be treated as having signed a hard copy of the same document. The fact that the document is created electronically as opposed to as a hard copy can make no difference.

[116] By analogy with *Brewer Street Investments Ltd v Barclays Woollen Co Ltd* [1954] 1 QB 428, above, pp 66, 70 (anticipated contract which failed to materialize).

[117] *Deglman v Guaranty Trust Co of Canada* [1954] 3 DLR 785 (Canada); *Pavey & Matthews Pty Ltd v Paul* (1986–87) 162 CLR 221 (Australia).

[118] [2022] EWCA Civ 1648, [2023] KB 345 at [67].

[119] *Pereira Fernandes SA v Mehta* [2006] EWHC 813 (Ch), [2006] 1 WLR 1543; *Golden Ocean Group Ltd v Salgaocar Mining Industries PVT Ltd* [2012] EWCA Civ 265, [2012] 1 WLR 3674; *Bassano v Toft* [2014] EWHC 377 (QB) at [42]–[45]; *Neocleous v Rees* [2019] EWHC 2462 (Ch).

[120] Law Commission's Advice to Government, *Electronic Commerce: Formal Requirements in Commercial Transactions* (December 2001). See further Law Commission Report No 386, *Electronic Execution of Documents* (2019). And see now Electronic Trade Documents Act 2023.

[121] s 8(1).

[122] [2006] EWHC 813 (Ch), [2006] 1 WLR 1543 at [27]–[29].

In *Mehta*, the judge found that the automatic insertion of an e-mail address in an e-mail did not mean that it was 'intended for signature'. But if the e-mail address had been deliberately inserted in order to provide authenticity the result would likely have been different. Thus in *Golden Ocean Group v Salgaocar Mining Industries*, the requirement for a signature was met when the agent of the guarantor signed off an e-mail with his first name, 'Guy'.[123] The key issue is whether the name was applied with authenticating intent.[124] If it is, then an automatic e-mail footer can mean that the requirement for signature is fulfilled.[125]

4. FORMALITIES AGREED BY THE PARTIES: 'NO ORAL VARIATION CLAUSES'

The Supreme Court has recently decided that the parties can bind themselves to complying with certain formalities for a variation of the contract to be valid. In *MWB Business Exchange Centres Ltd v Rock Advertising Ltd*:[126]

MWB contracted with R to license office space in central London to R for 12 months. The contract contained a 'no oral variation clause' which stated, 'All variations to this Licence must be agreed, set out in writing and signed on behalf of both parties before they take effect.' After R fell into arrears in paying the monthly licence fee, MWB orally agreed that R could stay in the premises if it paid off the arrears in a year under a revised schedule of payments which were initially below the monthly licence fee but above it later in the year. R made the first payment but MWB then locked R the licensee out of the premises.

Two legal issues arose. The first was whether the oral variation was valid even though it was inconsistent with the 'no oral variation' clause.

The Supreme Court held that the oral variation was of no effect because of that clause so that MWB was not in breach of contract. It accepted, however, that estoppel (most obviously promissory estoppel) would be an exception to this in limited circumstances. The decision is controversial[127] because, in principle, parties should be free to change their minds by a new contract or a variation of an existing contract and this includes changing their minds about a term preventing oral variation.[128] The Court considered that such clauses are commercially useful because they avoid an inadvertent variation, but it is hard to see why the Courts should not give effect to a true agreement between both parties to depart from the term requiring formality (which has not been imposed

[123] *Golden Ocean Group Ltd v Salgaocar Mining Industries Pvt Ltd* [2012] EWCA Civ 265, [2012] 1 WLR 3674.

[124] Law Com No 386, *Electronic Execution of Documents* (2019).

[125] *Neocleous v Rees* [2019] EWHC 2462 (Ch), [2020] 2 P & CR 4.

[126] [2018] UKSC 24, [2019] AC 119.

[127] The Singapore Court of Appeal has already expressed its 'reservations': *Charles Lim Teng Siang v Hong Choon Hau* [2021] SGCA 43 at [40], but is has since been supported in the Supreme Court: *Kabab-Ji SAL (Lebanon) v Kout Food Group (Kuwait)* [2021] UKSC 48, [2022] 1 CLC 275 at [55]–[59].

[128] Burrows, in Davies and Raczynska (eds), *The Contents of Commercial Contracts: Terms Affecting Freedoms* (2020).

by statute but by the parties' own choice). Moreover, one can anticipate needless future litigation about the scope of the estoppel exception.[129]

The second legal issue was whether, had it otherwise been valid, the variation was supported by consideration. Unfortunately the Supreme Court considered that that issue should not be decided because it was unnecessary to do so in the light of its decision on the first issue.[130]

FURTHER READING

Fuller, 'Consideration and Form' (1941) 41 Col L Rev 799

McBain, 'Abolishing the Statute of Frauds 1677 section 4' [2010] JBL 420

Phillips, 'Guarantees: Protecting the Bankers' [2012] JBL 248

[129] Raphael (2022) 138 LQR 299.

[130] See below, p 116.

4

CONSIDERATION AND PROMISSORY ESTOPPEL

1. CONSIDERATION

(a) CONSIDERATION DEFINED

Consideration is required in all contracts not made by deed. A bare promise is not enforceable in English law. Consideration is the doctrine designed to establish which promises should be legally enforceable.[1] What, then, is it? In *Currie v Misa*[2] Lush J stated:

> A valuable consideration, in the sense of the law, may consist in some right, interest, profit, or benefit accruing to the one party, or some forbearance, detriment, loss, or responsibility given, suffered, or undertaken by the other.

This brings out the idea of reciprocity as the distinguishing mark; gratuitous promises are unenforceable in English law.

Consideration reflects a variety of policies and serves a number of functions.[3] First, enforceability may depend on the content of the promise or the circumstances in which it was made.[4] Thus, promises to do what one is already obliged to do, particularly where a contract has been renegotiated, have caused difficulties. Secondly, consideration has been said to identify which promises the parties intend to be legally enforceable. They may so intend either where there is a substantive bargain, or where they have put the transaction into the form of an exchange, for instance by providing that the promisee should pay a nominal price to the promisor. Consideration therefore serves an evidential and formal function.[5] Thirdly, consideration is sometimes seen as a requirement which ensures that a promisor has deliberately decided to contract and prevents parties accidentally binding themselves on impulse.[6]

[1] See Atiyah, *Essays on Contract* (1986) ch 8; Treitel (1976) 50 ALJ 439; Cartwright, *Formation and Variation of Contracts* (4th edn, 2024) Part III.

[2] (1875) LR 10 Ex 153, 162. See also *Thomas v Thomas* (1842) 2 QB 851, 859; *Bolton v Madden* (1873) LR 9 QB 55, 56.

[3] Llewellyn (1941) 41 Col L Rev 777, 778, 863; Simpson (1975) 9 LQR 247, 263.

[4] Below, pp 107–13, 377 (pre-existing duties and duress).

[5] Fuller (1941) 41 Col L Rev 799; Cohen (1933) 46 Harv L Rev 553, 582–3; below, pp 137–9.

[6] *Pillans v Van Mierop* (1765) 3 Burr 1663, 1670 (Wilmot J).

(i) Benefit or detriment

The definition in *Currie v Misa* shows that consideration consists either in some benefit to the promisor or some detriment to the promisee; but there is considerable controversy as to the relative importance of these two factors. Although some things cannot count as consideration for reasons of policy,[7] as a general rule anything that the promisor asks for in return for their promise is consideration. As Sir Frederick Pollock succinctly stated, it is 'the price for which the promise of the other is bought'.[8] It is sufficient that the promisor obtained what they asked for—a 'benefit'—and the promisee did or promised something they did not have to do—a 'detriment'.

(ii) Given in return for the promise

The consideration must necessarily be given in return for the promise, and it is almost always[9] given at the request of the promisor. The promisee must, therefore, prove either an exchange of promises (eg a promise to supply goods in return for a promise to pay for them) or some act or forbearance on the part of the promisee in return for the promise made. A benefit conferred or a detriment suffered otherwise than in return for the promise of the other party cannot constitute consideration.[10] There will be no consideration merely because there is detrimental action by the promisee in *reliance* on the promise, but not in *return* for it. Thus, in *Combe v Combe*,[11] where a husband, upon divorce, promised his wife a permanent allowance of £100 a year, the Court of Appeal refused to hold that a consequent forbearance on the part of the wife to apply for maintenance amounted to consideration. The husband had not requested her to forbear, and her action could not be said to have been in return for his promise to pay.

(iii) Consideration and condition

Consideration must also be distinguished from the fulfilment of a condition. If A says to B, 'I will give you £500 if you break your leg', there is no contract, but simply a gratuitous promise subject to a condition.[12] Where the condition consists of the performance of some act by the promisee, the position may be more doubtful. If C says to D, 'You can have my flat if you move in and look after me', there may still be only a conditional gift, unless performance of the stipulation is regarded by the parties as

[7] Below, p 108.

[8] *Principles of Contract* (13th edn, 1950) 133 (and earlier editions), approved in *Dunlop Pneumatic Tyre Co Ltd v Selfridge Ltd* [1915] AC 847, 855, and by the Sixth Interim Report of the Law Revision Committee, *Statute of Frauds and the Doctrine of Consideration* (Cmd 5449, 1937) 12. Cf Atiyah, *Essays on Contract* (1986) 183 (consideration is a 'reason for the recognition of an obligation').

[9] Although see Goodhart (1951) 67 LQR 456, which effectively demonstrates that a request is not essential to a binding obligation provided that the consideration is referable to the promise. Cf Smith (1953) 69 LQR 99. See also *Ball v National and Grindlays Bank Ltd* [1973] Ch 127.

[10] *Wigan v English and Scottish Law Life Assurance Association* [1909] 1 Ch 291.

[11] [1951] 2 KB 215; see below, pp 129–30.

[12] *Shadwell v Shadwell* (1860) 9 CBNS 159, 177 (Byles J).

the price to be paid for the promise.[13] This issue was discussed in *Chappell & Co Ltd v Nestlé Co Ltd*:[14]

C were the owners of the copyright of a tune called 'Rockin' Shoes' and N were manufacturers of chocolate. N offered to the public records of this tune in return for 1*s*/6*d* and the wrappers from three bars of their chocolate. Under the statutory provisions then in force[15] any person had an automatic right to use a copyright tune for a record, provided he paid a certain percentage of the 'ordinary retail selling price' of the record to the copyright owner. C contended that N could not rely on the statute, since it contemplated a price consisting of money alone, whereas in this case the consideration for the record included three chocolate wrappers.

In finding for C, the House of Lords, by a bare majority, held that the wrappers formed part of the selling price (consideration) for the record. The object of selling the record was to increase the sales of chocolate and the stipulated evidence of such sales formed part of the consideration. The acquisition of the wrappers was not simply a condition limiting the class of persons qualified to purchase records.

(b) NECESSITY FOR CONSIDERATION

Consideration is necessary for the formation of every simple contract; a promise (unless in a deed) made without consideration is not actionable as a contract[16] in English law.

Criticisms of the doctrine of consideration are not new. Nearly 300 years ago Lord Mansfield asserted that consideration was only one of several modes of supplying evidence of the promisor's intention to be bound; and that if the terms of a contract were reduced to writing by reason of commercial custom, or in obedience to statutory requirement, such evidence dispensed with the need for consideration.[17] That view was decisively overruled in *Rann v Hughes*.[18] Lord Mansfield also thought that the existence of a previous moral obligation was sufficient to support an express, but gratuitous, promise.[19] That mistake was finally corrected in *Eastwood v Kenyon*:[20]

E had been guardian and agent of Mrs K while she was a minor, and had incurred expenses in the improvement of her property: he did this voluntarily and, in order to do so, was compelled to borrow money, for which he gave a promissory note. When Mrs K came of age she assented to the transaction and after her marriage her husband promised to pay the note. He was sued upon this promise.

[13] *Ellis v Chief Adjudication Officer* [1998] 1 FLR 184 (no intent to contract and condition not performed).

[14] [1960] AC 87.

[15] Copyright Act 1956, s 8. The statutory licence to record was abolished by the Copyright, Designs and Patents Act 1988, s 170 and Sched 1, para 21.

[16] But see Denning (1952) 15 MLR 1, and below, pp 120–1.

[17] *Pillans v Van Mierop* (1765) 3 Burr 1663. This is the position in Scotland: Lord Normand (1939) 55 LQR 358.

[18] (1778) 7 TR 350n. It should be noted, however, that the only report of the actual decision of the House of Lords states that the case was decided on the ground of failure to comply with the Statute of Frauds: (1778) 4 Brown PC 27.

[19] *Lee v Muggeridge* (1813) 5 Taunt 36, 46 (Sir James Mansfield CJ, who was Chief Justice of Common Pleas).

[20] (1840) 11 A & E 438.

It was held that the moral obligation to fulfil such a promise was insufficient where the consideration was wholly past. Lord Denman noted that any other approach 'would annihilate the necessity for any consideration at all, inasmuch as the mere fact of giving a promise creates a moral obligation to perform it'.[21]

However, it is also true that the Courts are reluctant to describe a promise made in a commercial context as gratuitous and it has been said that 'a defence of lack of consideration rarely has merit'[22] since 'businessmen know their own business best even when they appear to grant an indulgence'.[23] The doctrine continues to be the subject of considerable criticism,[24] but it is advisable to reserve a discussion of this until the general rules governing the application of consideration to contracts have been examined.

(c) EXECUTORY AND EXECUTED CONSIDERATION

Consideration may be *executory* (still to be carried out) or it may be *executed* (already performed).

An *executory* consideration consists of a promise to do, forbear, or suffer, given in return for a like promise. Mutual promises are illustrations of executory consideration. The fact that the promise given for a promise may be dependent upon a condition does not affect its validity as consideration. A promises B to do a piece of work for which B promises to pay if the workmanship is approved by a third party. The promise of B is consideration for the promise of A.

A contract arises upon a present or *executed* consideration when one of the two parties has, either in the act which constitutes an offer or in the act which constitutes an acceptance, done all that party is bound to do under the contract, leaving an outstanding liability on one side only. An offer to do work or provide goods might show an obvious expectation that payment be made; the contract arises when the work or goods are accepted by the person to whom they are offered, and that person by accepting them becomes bound to pay a reasonable price. So if a wine merchant sends to a customer a selection of wines, and the customer retains some and returns the rest, the customer will be bound to pay for those retained, since the tender of the wine will be at once the offer and the consideration for the obligation.[25] But sometimes it is not the offeror, but the acceptor, who has performed at the moment when the contract is entered into. If A makes a general offer of reward for information and B supplies the information, A's offer is turned into a binding promise by the act of B, and B simultaneously concludes the contract and furnishes consideration by performance.[26]

21 *Ibid*, 450.

22 *Thoresen Car Ferries Ltd v Weymouth Portland BC* [1977] 2 Lloyd's Rep 614, 619 (Donaldson J).

23 *Woodhouse AC Israel Cocoa Ltd SA v Nigerian Produce Marketing Co Ltd* [1972] AC 741, 757–8 (Lord Hailsham LC). See also *New Zealand Shipping Co Ltd v Satterthwaite* [1975] AC 154, 157.

24 See below, pp 137–9.

25 *Hart v Mills* (1846) 15 M & W 85; cf *Taylor v Laird* (1856) 1 H & N 266; above, p 41.

26 Above, p 40. See *Carlill v Carbolic Smoke Ball Co* [1893] 1 QB 256.

(d) PAST CONSIDERATION

Executed consideration must be distinguished from *past* consideration which is a mere sentiment of gratitude for benefits received. In the case of executed consideration, both the promise and the act which constitutes the consideration are integral and co-related parts of the same transaction.[27] In the case of past consideration, however, the promise is subsequent to the act and independent of it; they are not in substance part of the same transaction. If A saves B from drowning, and B later promises A a reward, A's action cannot be relied on as consideration for B's promise for it is past in point of time. Past consideration is, in effect, no consideration at all; it confers no benefit on the promisor, and involves no detriment to the promisee in return for the promise. It is merely an act or forbearance in time past by which a person has benefited without incurring any legal liability. If afterwards, whether from good feeling or interested motives, the person who has benefited makes a promise to the person whose act or forbearance led to the benefit, and that promise is made upon no other consideration than the past benefit, it is gratuitous and cannot be enforced. In *Roscorla v Thomas*[28] this principle was clearly stated:

> The claimant purchased a horse from the defendant, who afterwards, in consideration of the previous sale, warranted that the horse was sound and free from vice. It was in fact a vicious horse.

The Court held that the sale itself created no implied warranty that the horse was not vicious. The warranty had therefore to be regarded as independent of the sale and as an express promise based upon a previous transaction. It fell 'within the general rule that a consideration past and executed will support no other promise than such as would be implied by law'.

However, this general rule does not apply in certain situations, considered immediately below.

(i) Previous request of the promisor

In *Pao On v Lau Yiu Long*[29] the Judicial Committee of the Privy Council stated that:

> An act done before the giving of a promise to make a payment or to confer some other benefit can sometimes be consideration for the promise. The act must have been done at the promisor's request, the parties must have understood that the act was to be remunerated either by a payment or the conferment of some other benefit, and payment, or the conferment of a benefit, must have been legally enforceable had it been promised in advance.

In that case the defendant had requested the claimant to promise not to sell certain shares for a year and later promised to indemnify the claimant if the shares fell below

[27] *Westminster CC v Duke of Westminster* [1991] 4 All ER 136, 145.

[28] (1842) 3 QB 234. See also *Eastwood v Kenyon* (1840) 11 Ad & E 438, above p 97; *Re McArdle* [1951] Ch 669; *Savage v Uwechia* [1961] 1 WLR 455.

[29] [1980] AC 614, 629. See below, p 111, for the facts.

a certain price. The defendant contended that the consideration for the indemnity was past but it was held that all three conditions mentioned above were satisfied.

However, this is not a real departure from the general doctrine as to past consideration. When a request is made which is in substance an offer of a promise upon terms to be afterwards ascertained, and an act is done in pursuance of that request, a subsequent promise to pay a fixed sum or to confer some other benefit may be regarded as a part of the same transaction, the effect of the promise being merely to render certain that which was uncertain before.[30]

(ii) An antecedent debt

It has sometimes been thought that the existence of an existing debt is sufficient consideration for a subsequent promise to pay that debt.[31] It should not be supposed, however, that the existence of a debt owed by A to B will always be consideration for any subsequent promise which A may make to pay that debt. There must be present consideration in the form of a forbearance to sue by the creditor, or else, if a security is given by the debtor, it must be communicated to the creditor and induce such a forbearance.[32]

(iii) Negotiable instruments

By section 27(1) of the Bills of Exchange Act 1882, valuable consideration for a bill may be constituted by: (a) any consideration sufficient to support a simple contract; or (b) an antecedent debt or liability. So if A, whose account at the bank is overdrawn, negotiates to its banker a cheque drawn by a stranger, the banker becomes a holder for value of the cheque, as the antecedent debt of A is consideration for the instrument.[33] This is a genuine exception to the rule that past consideration does not count, although as the usage of cheques diminishes this exception will become even less significant.

(e) CONSIDERATION MUST MOVE FROM THE PROMISEE

This long-standing maxim is surprisingly ambiguous and confusing.[34] It has three possible meanings.

First, it may mean nothing more than that to be enforceable a promise, not made by deed, must be supported by consideration. If A promises B £1,000, B cannot enforce the promise (unless made by deed) because there is no consideration for A's promise.

[30] This also explains *Lampleigh v Brathwait* (1615) Hob 105 (subsequent promise to pay for requested attempt to obtain pardon held enforceable) and *Re Casey's Patents, Stewart v Casey* [1892] 1 Ch 104 (a subsequent promise to pay for services provided was then an admission of a bargain and fixed the amount of the remuneration on the basis of which the services were originally rendered).

[31] *Slade's Case* (1602) 4 Co Rep 91a, above, pp 15–6. Note that such promises, if in writing, can have the effect of extending the limitation period, below, p 607.

[32] *Wigan v English and Scottish Law Life Assurance Association* [1909] 1 Ch 291.

[33] But see *Oliver v Davis* [1949] 2 KB 727.

[34] Furmston (1960) 23 MLR 373; Law Revision Committee, Sixth Interim Report (1937) para 37; Law Commission, Law Com No 242 (1996) Part VI.

Although B is a promisee, it has not provided consideration and 'consideration must move from the promisee'. In this sense, the maxim merely restates, and adds nothing to, the requirement of consideration.

Secondly, it may mean that, even though the promise is supported by consideration provided by the promisee, the consideration must move *from the claimant*: the person seeking to enforce the contract must itself have provided the consideration for the promise. So if A promises B to pay C £1,000 in return for B doing work for A, C cannot enforce the contract because the consideration has moved from B and not from C. In this sense the maxim overlaps with, and indeed is indistinguishable from, the doctrine of privity of contract according to which only a party to a contract can enforce it. So in the above example, one could explain the result without referring to the consideration maxim by saying that C cannot enforce the contract between A and B because C is not a party to it. Indeed, the early cases which are now regarded as establishing the privity doctrine were ones in which the reasoning used was that the claimant could not enforce the contract because it had not provided the consideration.[35] It follows too that exceptions to privity,[36] in particular the Contracts (Rights of Third Parties) Act 1999, also constitute exceptions to the need for consideration to move from the claimant.

Thirdly, the maxim may mean that a promisee cannot enforce a promise made to it where the consideration for the promise has been provided by someone else. So if A promises B that in return for C doing work for A, A will pay B £1,000, B cannot enforce the promise because, although B is the promisee, C has provided the consideration and 'consideration must move from the promisee'. B has suffered no detriment (unless B impliedly undertook to procure that C would do the work) and, although A has received the benefit, that benefit was conferred by C, and not by B. While used in this sense the maxim has an independent force, separate from the requirement of consideration and the doctrine of privity, the situations where it will apply are extremely rare. So, in the example just considered, unless there is a connection between B and C so that B may itself be providing consideration, it will be very unusual for A to promise to pay B for work that C does for A. More realistic would be a situation where B and C are joint promisees. Say, for example, A promises B and C to pay B £1,000 if C will do certain work desired by A. If C does the work, and A refuses to pay the £1,000 to B, can B sue A? If not, one might say that, even though B is a party to the contract,[37] because the promise is made to B and C, the reason B cannot enforce A's promise is because it has not provided consideration: consideration must move from the promisee. However, while there is no clear English authority, the High Court of Australia in *Coulls v Bagot's Executor & Trustee Co Ltd*[38] indicated that the joint promisee can enforce a contract in

[35] *Tweddle v Atkinson* (1861) 1 B & S 393; *Dunlop Pneumatic Tyre Co Ltd v Selfridge & Co Ltd* [1915] AC 847.

[36] See below, Chapter 21.

[37] This depends on what one means by a 'party' to a simple contract. If one defines a party as someone who has provided consideration, then C would not be a party and would appear to fall foul of the privity doctrine as well as the rule that consideration must move from the promisee.

[38] (1967) 119 CLR 461. See Coote [1978] CLJ 301. Cf *McEvoy v Belfast Banking Co Ltd* [1935] AC 24, 43 (consideration supplied by one of two joint and several promisees).

this situation. It is submitted that that approach ought to be applied in England and, if it were, it would follow that the maxim 'consideration must move from the promisee' in its third independent sense would be rendered inaccurate in relation to its most realistic possible application.

(f) CONSIDERATION NEED NOT BE ADEQUATE

Consideration need not be adequate but it must be of some value in the eye of the law. The Courts will not make bargains for the parties and, if a person gets what has been contracted for, they will not inquire whether it was an equivalent to the promise which was given in return: 'the adequacy of the consideration is for the parties to consider at the time of making the agreement, not for the Court when it is sought to be enforced'.[39] The most trifling detriment or benefit will suffice, and the following cases show that the Courts have been prepared to find a contract where the consideration was virtually non-existent.

We have already seen that in *Chappell & Co Ltd v Nestlé Co Ltd*[40] wrappers from chocolate bars were held to be part of the consideration for the sale of a record. In *Haigh v Brooks*,[41] the consideration of a promise to pay certain bills was the surrender of a document supposed to be a guarantee, which turned out to be of doubtful validity. The worthlessness of the document surrendered was held to be no defence to an action on the promise. The Court was not concerned with the adequacy or inadequacy of the price paid or promised. 'The plaintiffs were induced by the defendant's promise to part with something which they might have kept, and the defendant obtained what he desired by means of that promise.'[42]

The consequence of the rule that the Court is not concerned with the adequacy of consideration is that the requirement can be satisfied by nominal consideration. At common law 'a contracting party can stipulate for what consideration he chooses. A peppercorn does not cease to be good consideration if it is established that the promisee does not like pepper and will throw away the corn.'[43] Statute, however, may make the adequacy of consideration relevant in a particular context. Thus, property legislation distinguishes a transaction for 'nominal' consideration from one for 'valuable'

[39] *Bolton v Madden* (1873) LR 9 QB 55, 57 (Blackburn J).

[40] [1960] AC 87, above, p 98. Cf *Lipkin Gorman v Karpnale Ltd* [1991] 2 AC 548 (gaming chips not consideration, inter alia, because they were 'worthless': but that was in the context not of deciding whether there was an enforceable contract but rather in deciding whether 'value' had been given for the purposes of the defence of being a bona fide purchaser *for value* without notice).

[41] (1839) 10 A & E 309, aff'd *sub nom Brooks v Haigh* (1840) 10 A & E 323, where it was said by Maule J that the delivery of the paper alone would suffice. See also *Bainbridge v Firmstone* (1838) 8 A & E 743, 744; *Veitch v Sinclair* [1975] 1 NZLR 264.

[42] (1839) 10 A & E 309, 320 (Lord Denman CJ). See also *De la Bere v Pearson* [1908] 1 KB 280 (possible benefit to newspaper in publishing letter held to be consideration for offer to give financial advice) although liability today would probably lie in tort: *Hedley Byrne & Co Ltd v Heller & Partners Ltd* [1964] AC 465, 527–8.

[43] *Chappell & Co Ltd v Nestlé Co Ltd*, above, n 40, 114 (Lord Somervell). See also above, p 98.

consideration,[44] and the term 'consideration' in the Local Government Act 1972 only includes elements of commercial or monetary value.[45]

In the Roman law of sale, as in certain modern continental systems, the price had to be a serious one—more than just nominal—otherwise the contract could not be characterized as a contract of sale; and in later Roman law the doctrine of *laesio enormis* was developed under which the seller of land could rescind the contract where the price was less than half the value of the land unless the buyer was willing to come up to the fair price.[46] This doctrine of *laesio enormis* forms no part of the English common law. Even where statute has intervened to protect a class of contractor, such as consumers, it does not always require a 'fair' or 'reasonable' or 'market' price.[47] In equity, inadequacy of consideration is treated as relevant in deciding whether there has been undue influence, or whether the bargain is unconscionable, so as to allow the contract to be rescinded.[48] However, it is arguable that mere inadequacy of consideration is not itself a ground on which the equitable remedy of specific performance of a contract will be refused.[49] Thus specific performance was ordered of an option to purchase a house for £10,000 even though the consideration for the grant of the option was the nominal sum of £1.[50]

(g) CONSIDERATION MUST BE REAL

Though consideration need not be adequate, it must be real. It must be 'something which is of some value in the eye of the law'. Thus, 'it is no consideration to refrain from a course of action which it was never intended to pursue'.[51] This section examines those cases where the reality of consideration has been questioned or defined.

[44] Land Charges Act 1972, s 17(1); Law of Property Act 1925, ss 84(7) and 205(1)(xxi); *Westminster CC v Duke of Westminster* [1991] 4 All ER 136, 146. See also Insolvency Act 1986, s 238 (transactions at undervalue).

[45] *R v Pembrokeshire CC, ex p Coker* [1999] 4 All ER 1007.

[46] Nicholas, *Introduction to Roman Law* (1962) 174–5. For the reception of the Roman doctrines into French law, see Nicholas, *The French Law of Contract* (2nd edn, 1992) 147 (sale at nominal price can be recharacterized as disguised gift), 137–41 (*lésion*) and, for the modern law, Rowan, *The New French Law of Contract* (2022) 135–8, 140. See also Gordley, *Foundations of Private Law* (2006) 364–6.

[47] Consumer Rights Act 2015, which has a core exclusion as regards price: see below, p 229. Cf Rent Act 1977, s 70(1) (fair rent); Agricultural Holdings Act 1986, s 12, Sched 2, para 1(1) (prudent and willing parties).

[48] Below, pp 389, 399.

[49] See, eg, *Coles v Trecothick* (1804) 9 Ves Jun 234, 246 (Lord Eldon). But specific performance will not be ordered of a promise made under deed, and not supported by consideration, applying the maxim that 'equity will not assist a volunteer': *Cannon v Hartley* [1949] Ch 213.

[50] *Mountford v Scott* [1975] Ch 258 (Brightman J). But note that, in contrast to Brightman J, the Court of Appeal in that case regarded the option as having been exercised so that the specific performance related to the contract of sale for £10,000 not the option contract for which the consideration was nominal.

[51] *Arrale v Costain Civil Engineering Ltd* [1976] 1 Lloyd's Rep 98, 106. But an act may be consideration even if it is not solely induced by the promise: *Brikom Investments Ltd v Carr* [1979] QB 467, 490.

(i) Motive and consideration

Motive must be distinguished from consideration. In *Thomas v Thomas*:[52]

A deceased husband's executor promised to allow his widow to occupy a house the deceased had owned in return for her promise to keep it in repair and to pay a ground rent of £1 *per annum*. The executor stated that the agreement was entered into 'in consideration of' the expressed desire of the deceased that his wife should have the use of the house during her lifetime.

It was held that the desire to carry out the wishes of the deceased did not amount to consideration: 'Motive is not the same thing with consideration. Consideration means something which is of some value in the eye of the law, moving from the plaintiff.'[53] So, the desire of one member of a pop group to avoid the danger of internal dissention that might result if he had a larger income than others in the group did not constitute consideration for his promise to make payments to the others.[54]

(ii) Impossibility

Impossibility, either physical or legal, which exists at the time of formation of the contract and is obvious upon the face of it, makes the consideration unreal. The consideration is unreal because 'according to the state of knowledge of the day, [it is] so absurd that the parties could not be supposed to have so contracted'.[55] Thus a covenant in a charterparty that a ship would sail on a date which was already past at the time the contract was executed was held to be void for unreality in the consideration furnished.[56] The old case of *Harvy v Gibbons*,[57] where a bailiff was promised £40 in consideration of a promise made by him that he would release a debt due to his master, is an example of legal impossibility. The Court held that the consideration provided by the bailiff was 'illegal', since a servant could not release a debt due to his master. By 'illegal' it is plain that the Court meant legally impossible. The bailiff's claim therefore failed.

(iii) Uncertainty

A promise which purports to be a consideration may be too vague to be enforced. A promise which leaves performance exclusively in the discretion of the promisor will not be enforceable: the consideration is illusory.[58] *White v Bluett* is instructive:[59]

In proceedings by his father's executors on a promissory note, a son alleged that the father had promised to discharge him from liability in consideration of his promise to cease complaining that he had not enjoyed as many advantages as his brothers.

[52] (1842) 2 QB 851.

[53] *Ibid*, 859 (Patteson J). The issue arose because the executor had argued that the widow's case was procedurally defective because her declaration referred only to her promise to repair and pay rent and omitted to state part of the consideration, ie the desire of her deceased husband. The Court rejected this and found for the widow.

[54] *Hadley v Kemp* [1999] 2 EMLR 589, 625 (Park J).

[55] *Lord Clifford v Watts* (1870) LR 5 CP 577, 588 (Brett J).

[56] *Hall v Cazenove* (1804) 4 East 477.

[57] (1675) 2 Lev 161.

[58] *Stabilad Ltd v Stephens & Carter Ltd (No 2)* [1999] 2 All ER (Comm) 651, 660 (Peter Gibson LJ).

[59] (1853) 23 LJ Ex 36.

It was said that the son's promise was no more than a promise 'not to bore his father', and was too vague to form a consideration for the father's promise to waive his rights on the note. This result is somewhat hard on the son: the father asked his son to stop complaining, and the son agreed to stop doing something he was at liberty to do. The father got what he requested.

It may be that *White v Bluett* should be explained on there being no intention to create legal relations between father and son.[60] Other cases have not been so narrow in finding consideration. For example, in *Ward v Byham* a promise to make a child happy was stated to be part of the consideration,[61] and it has also been held that a promise to cooperate in the recovery from a joint debtor was sufficiently certain to form a consideration for a forbearance.[62]

(iv) Forbearance to sue

There is a clear public interest in encouraging the avoidance of litigation and the resolution of disputes by the parties[63] provided that the settlement or compromise is genuine, and entered into freely without the concealment of essential information, the taking of undue advantage,[64] or the exertion of illegitimate pressure.[65] A forbearance to sue, even for a short time, may be consideration for a promise, although there is no waiver or compromise of the right of action. In *Alliance Bank Ltd v Broom*:[66]

The defendants, Messrs Broom were asked to give security for moneys they owed to the bank. They promised to assign the documents of title to certain goods; they failed to do so, and the bank sued for specific performance of the promise.

The Court held that the bank was entitled to this remedy:

Although there was no promise on the part of the plaintiffs to abstain for any certain time from suing for the debt, the effect was that the plaintiffs did, in effect, give, and the defendant received, the benefit of some degree of forbearance; not, indeed, for any definite time, but, at all events, some extent of forbearance . . . The circumstances necessarily involve the benefit to the debtor of a certain amount of forbearance, which he would not have derived if he had not made the agreement.[67]

The consideration in such a case clearly consists in the benefit received by the promisor in that the promise 'stays the hand of the creditor'.[68]

[60] For other instances of uncertainty in the context of incomplete agreements see above, p 69.

[61] [1956] 1 WLR 496; below, p 108. See also *Dunton v Dunton* (1892) 18 VLR 114 (Australia); *Hamer v Sidway* 27 NE 256 (1891) (USA).

[62] *Bank of Nova Scotia v MacLellan* (1977) 78 DLR (3d) 1 (Canada).

[63] *Mionis v Democratic Press SA* [2017] EWCA Civ 1194, [2018] QB 662 at [89] (Sharp LJ). See generally Davies, in Davies and Tjio (eds) *Fraud and Risk in Commercial Law* (2024).

[64] *Colchester BC v Smith* [1992] Ch 421, 435. Payments made to close a transaction are irrecoverable even if there is no consideration: *Woolwich BS v IRC* [1993] AC 70, 165; Law Com No 227, *Restitution: Mistakes of Law and Ultra Vires Public Authority Receipts and Payments* (1994) paras 2.25–2.38.

[65] *Huyton SA v Peter Cremer GmbH* [1999] 1 Lloyd's Rep 620, 629–30. On duress, see below, Chapter 10.

[66] (1864) 2 Dr & Sm 289.

[67] *Ibid*, 292.

[68] Cf *Cook v Wright* (1861) 1 B & S 559, 569.

In order that the forbearance should be a consideration, some liability should be shown to exist, or to be reasonably supposed to exist, by the parties. If the claim is not only invalid, but is known by the party forbearing to be so, there is no consideration.[69] It would also seem that the claim must be an honest claim and one which the promisee *bona fide* intends to pursue.[70] Where the claim arises out of an illegal agreement, a forbearance to sue on that claim is not sufficient consideration.[71] However, it was recognized in *Simantob v Shavleyan* that there is a strong 'public policy in favour of holding people to their commercial bargains'.[72] In that case it was held that giving up an argument that a clause to pay $1,000 per day in interest was a penalty clause did constitute good consideration, even though that argument had previously been rejected in an application for summary judgment. It did not matter that the claim was probably unlikely to succeed.

(v) Compromise of a dispute

The same public interest in encouraging the avoidance of litigation and the resolution of disputes applies to a compromise of a dispute, for instance by a promise to pay a proportion of a disputed sum claimed, again provided that it is genuine, and entered into freely without the concealment of essential information, the taking of undue advantage, or the exertion of illegitimate pressure.[73] The difference between forbearance and compromise is that in compromise the debtor does not admit the claim and the creditor promises to abandon the claim. So in the case of forbearance, the offer is in effect, 'I admit your claim but will do or promise something if you will stay your hand.' In the case of a compromise the offer is in effect, 'I do not admit your claim but I will do or promise something if you will abandon it.' It has, however, been argued that if the claim compromised is of an insubstantial character the consideration fails. The answer is to be found in the judgment of Cockburn CJ in *Callisher v Bischoffsheim*:[74]

> Every day a compromise is effected on the ground that the party making it has a chance of succeeding in it, and if he *bona fide* believes that he has a fair chance of success, he has a reasonable ground for suing, and his forbearance to sue will constitute a good consideration. When such a person forbears to sue he gives up what he believes to be a right of action, and the other party gets an advantage, and, instead of being annoyed with an action, he escapes from the vexations incident to it . . . It would be another matter if a person made a claim which he knew to be unfounded, and, by a compromise, derived an advantage under it: in that case his conduct would be fraudulent.

In that case, the defendant agreed to deliver to the claimant certain securities in consideration that the claimant would cease to press a claim against the Honduras

[69] *Wade v Simeon* (1846) 2 CB 548, 564.

[70] *Miles v New Zealand Alford Estate Co* (1886) 32 Ch D 266, 284; *Colchester BC v Smith* [1992] Ch 421, 435; *Times Travel (UK) Ltd v Pakistan International Airline Corp* [2021] UKSC 40, [2023] AC 101 at [116]. See also *BCCI SA v Ali* [2001] 1 AC 251 (equitable relief against release procured by concealment of facts).

[71] Cf *Poteliakhoff v Teakle* [1938] 2 KB 816; *Hill v William Hill (Park Lane) Ltd* [1949] AC 530 (gaming contracts, although such contracts are no longer void: Gambling Act 2005, below, p 412). But cf below, n 76.

[72] *Simantob v Shavleyan* [2019] EWCA Civ 1105 at [50].

[73] *Huyton v Cremer* [1999] 1 Lloyd's Rep 620, 629–30.

[74] (1870) LR 5 QB 449, 452.

Government. The claim was worthless, but there was no evidence that the claimant knew this.[75] It was held that there was consideration for the agreement. If, however, one of the parties to the compromise has no case, and knows that there is no case, the agreement to compromise will not be held binding.

As in the case of forbearance, the compromise of a claim arising out of an illegal contract is insufficient as consideration, unless the compromise arises out of a dispute of fact as to whether the contract is in fact illegal.[76]

(h) PERFORMANCE OF, OR PROMISE TO PERFORM, AN EXISTING DUTY

Where what is done, or promised, is no more than that to which the promisee is legally bound, and if nothing is obtained in return for the promise but that to which the promisor is already legally entitled, the consideration seems unreal.[77] This may occur where the promisee is already under an existing duty to do something and then promises to do that thing. If you have to do an act anyway, how can it be to your detriment to reaffirm your obligation? If the act will be done anyway, how does it benefit me to pay you to do it? The law draws a distinction between the performance of, or promise to perform: (i) a public duty; (ii) an existing duty to a third party; and (iii) an existing duty owed to the promisor. In (i) the conventional view is that there is no consideration for the promise. In (ii) the law holds that valuable consideration is present. In (iii) it has been held that only where there is, in the particular circumstances, a 'practical' benefit to the promisee can there be consideration.

(i) Existing public duty

The conventional view is that, where the promisee is already under an existing public duty, an express promise to perform, or performance of, that duty will not amount to consideration.[78] There will be no detriment to the promisee or benefit to the promisor over and above their existing rights and liabilities. In *Collins v Godefroy*:[79]

The claimant received a subpoena to appear at a civil trial as a witness on behalf of the defendant. The defendant promised him a sum of money for his trouble. A person who receives a subpoena is bound to attend and give evidence.

It was held that there was no consideration for the promise, the claimant being under a public duty to attend.

However, where the undertaking of the promisee is to do more than their legal obligation, this may be consideration. In *Glasbrook Brothers Ltd v Glamorgan County*

[75] See also *Wigan v Edwards* (1973) 1 ALR 497 (Australia) (honest claim sufficient).

[76] *Binder v Alachouzos* [1972] 2 QB 151, 158 (Lord Denning MR).

[77] See Davis [1937] CLJ 202; Reynolds and Treitel (1965) 76 Malaya LR 1.

[78] *Thoresen Car Ferries Ltd v Weymouth Portland BC* [1977] 2 Lloyd's Rep 614, 619. Earlier cases tend to suggest that an agreement of this nature is invalid on grounds of public policy: *Wathen v Sandys* (1811) 2 Camp 640; *Bilke v Havelock* (1813) 3 Camp 374.

[79] (1831) 1 B & Ad 950.

Council,[80] a police authority sued for the sum of £2,200 promised to it by a colliery company for whose mine the authority had provided a stronger guard during a strike than was in its opinion necessary. It was held that it was entitled to maintain an action on the promise.[81] Again, in *Ward v Byham* it was held that there was consideration for a promise to pay a weekly sum to the mother of an illegitimate child if the mother proved the child was 'well looked after and happy'.[82] Morris LJ considered the mother had promised more than her statutory duty to maintain the child. Denning LJ's view[83] was that she was only promising to do what she was bound to do but that this sufficed because it was a benefit to the promisor (the child's father).

More recently *Ward v Byham* has been explained as an instance of the recognition that the mother's promise was a 'practical' benefit to the father which thus amounted to consideration for his promise.[84] However, any such recognition of a 'practical' benefit should only be done where 'there is nothing in the transaction which is contrary to the public interest'.[85] For instance, the enforcement of an agreement to make a payment for the performance of a public duty such as the giving of evidence[86] or the renewal of a licence[87] might be thought to be contrary to the public interest in ensuring impartiality in the administration of justice and probity in government and local administration.

(ii) Existing duty owed to a third party

It is now established that consideration which consists in the performance of, or the promise to perform, an existing contract with a third party may be a real consideration. In these cases the promisee obtains the benefit of a direct obligation which can be enforced.[88]

As far as performance of such a duty is concerned, in *Shadwell v Shadwell*:[89]

The claimant was engaged to be married to Ellen Nicholl. His uncle wrote to him stating that he was pleased to hear of the intended marriage and that as he had promised to assist the claimant at starting, would pay him £150 yearly during the uncle's life or until the claimant's income as a Chancery barrister amounted to six hundred guineas. The claimant married Ellen Nicholl. He never earned as much as six hundred guineas. The annuity fell into arrear; the uncle died, and the claimant sued his executors.

80 [1925] AC 270. See also *Leeds United FC Ltd v Chief Constable of West Yorkshire Police* [2013] EWCA Civ 115, [2014] QB 168 (police force not going beyond its public duty to maintain law and order in providing policing for football matches on public land away from the football club's stadium).

81 See also *England v Davidson* (1840) 11 A & E 856; *Neville v Kelly* (1862) 12 CBNS 740 (rewards for police officers) and *Goulden v Wilson Barca* [2000] 1 WLR 167 (payment to expert witness).

82 [1956] 1 WLR 496. See also *Williams v Williams* [1957] 1 WLR 148 (husband's promise to pay weekly sum to wife who had deserted him, and thus forfeited right to maintenance, if she maintained herself and undertook not to pledge his credit held enforceable: Hodson and Morris LJJ, but not Denning LJ, based their decision only on the wife promising more than her legal duty).

83 [1956] 1 WLR 496, 498. See also *Williams v Williams*, above, n 82, 150.

84 *Williams v Roffey Bros & Nicholls (Contractors) Ltd* [1991] 1 QB 1, 13 (Glidewell LJ), below, pp 111–5. Cf Purchas LJ at 20.

85 *Williams v Williams* [1957] 1 WLR 148, 150 (Denning LJ).

86 *Collins v Godefroy* (1831) 1 B & Ad 590. But see now Senior Courts Act (formerly Supreme Court Act) 1981, s 36(4) (tender of expenses).

87 *Morgan v Palmer* (1842) 2 B & C 729, 739.

88 *New Zealand Shipping Co Ltd v AM Satterthwaite & Co Ltd* [1975] AC 154, 168.

89 (1860) 9 CBNS 159.

A majority of the Court thought that there was a benefit to the uncle in that the marriage was 'an object of interest to a near relative', and a detriment to the claimant because 'he might have made a most material change in his position and have induced the object of his affections to do the same, and might have incurred pecuniary liabilities resulting in embarrassments' if the promised income had been withheld. The majority accepted that it was no objection to finding consideration for the uncle's promise that the nephew was already engaged to, and therefore under a contractual duty to marry, Ellen Nicholl, since the uncle had requested that his nephew marry.[90] Byles J dissented, holding that the uncle had made no such request; the claimant had done no more than he was legally bound to do so that his marriage was no consideration for the uncle's promise.

In *Scotson v Pegg*:[91]

S promised to deliver to a third party X, or to his order, a cargo of coal then on board S's ship. X made an order in favour of P. P then made an agreement with S that if S would deliver the coal to him, he would in return unload and discharge the coal at a fixed rate each day from the date when the ship was ready for discharge. When sued for breach, P pleaded that, in delivering the coal to P, S was doing no more than he was bound under his contract with X to do so that there was no consideration for P's promise to unload in the manner specified.

The Court held that P was liable. Wilde B said:[92] 'If a person chooses to promise to pay a sum of money in order to induce another to perform that which he has already contracted with a third person to do, I confess I cannot see why such a promise should not be binding.'

Aspects of these decisions are unsatisfactory. So, in *Shadwell v Shadwell*, as Byles J pointed out, the uncle derived no personal benefit from the marriage; the engagement was in no way induced by his promise, nor was the claimant's subsequent change of position in return for his undertaking. And the promise to deliver to P at a fixed rate in *Scotson v Pegg* may have involved duties more onerous than the existing obligation to deliver to X or there may have been some dispute as to P's right to have the coals.[93] Nevertheless, a majority of the Privy Council in *New Zealand Shipping Co Ltd v AM Satterthwaite & Co Ltd, The Eurymedon*,[94] took them as establishing that actual performance of an existing duty to a third party can be sufficient consideration, even though that performance is no additional detriment to the promisee. In *The Eurymedon* the unloading by stevedores of goods from a ship (which the stevedores were bound by a contract with a third party to do) was held to be consideration for a promise to relieve them of the liability for damaging the goods.

The question then arises whether a distinction should be drawn between cases where the consideration alleged is *executed*, by performance of an existing duty to a third party, and cases where the consideration is *executory*, consisting of a promise

[90] An engagement to marry is no longer a contract: Law Reform (Miscellaneous Provisions) Act 1970, s 1.
[91] (1861) 6 H & N 295. [92] *Ibid*, 300. [93] *Ibid*, 299 (Martin B).
[94] [1975] AC 154. See also *Adams v London Improved Motor Coach Builders Ltd* [1921] 1 KB 495, 501, 504 (trade union's undertaking to pay solicitor the costs of services rendered to a member did not preclude the member from also being liable to the solicitor).

to perform. In principle a promise to perform an existing duty owed to a third party should also constitute consideration because the person making that promise thereby foregoes the liberty to cancel the contract with the third party by mutual agreement and the person to whom that promise is made has the benefit of a direct obligation.[95] The Judicial Committee of the Privy Council so held in *Pao On v Lau Yiu Long*:[96]

The claimants agreed with a company (Fu Chip) to sell certain shares in return for an allotment to them of 4.2 million shares in Fu Chip. If all the newly allotted shares had been immediately sold in the market, this would have depressed the value of the shares. Accordingly the claimants undertook in their agreement with Fu Chip not to sell or transfer for one year 60 per cent of the allotted shares. Subsequently the claimants refused to complete the agreement unless the defendants (who were the majority shareholders in Fu Chip) promised to indemnify them against any fall in value of the allotted shares during the one year period. The defendants gave that indemnity. The allotted shares fell greatly in value, and, in answer to a claim on the indemnity, the defendants pleaded that there was no consideration for their promise to indemnify.

It was held that the consideration for the indemnity was the promise of the claimants to perform their pre-existing contractual obligations to Fu Chip. Lord Scarman did 'not doubt that a promise to perform, or the performance of, a pre-existing contractual obligation to a third party can be a valid consideration'.[97]

(iii) Existing duty owed to the promisor

Where the promisee merely undertakes to fulfil the conditions of an existing contract with the promisor, the perception that it is not detrimental to do what one is obliged to do or beneficial to receive what one is entitled to receive has led to the conclusion that there is no consideration. In this context the need to discourage improper pressure by threatening not to perform one's contract unless the other party offers to pay more has been an important factor, although the pre-existing duty rule was rather a blunt weapon for this since it invalidated non-extortive as well as extortive renegotiations. The regulation of renegotiations was, as we shall see, left to the equitable doctrine of promissory estoppel. Although the development of a concept of economic duress means that the common law now has a more direct and precise method of controlling coercion, that is still a relatively new doctrine, the boundaries of which are not entirely clear.[98] Normally the performance of, or a promise to perform, a duty owed to the promisor will not be consideration.[99] The general position is illustrated by the old case of *Stilk v Myrick*:[100]

95 *De Cicco v Schweizer* 221 NY 431 (1917); Hamson (1938) 54 LQR 233, 237.

96 [1980] AC 614.

97 *Ibid*, 632.

98 Below, Chapter 10.

99 *North Ocean Shipping Co Ltd v Hyundai Construction Co Ltd* [1979] QB 705, 712; *Pao On v Lau Yiu Long* [1980] AC 614, 633; *Vantage Navigation Corp v Suhail & Saud Bahwan Building Materials Llc, The Alev* [1989] 1 Lloyd's Rep 138, 147; *Williams v Roffey Bros & Nicholls (Contractors) Ltd* [1991] 1 QB 1, 16, 19, 20.

100 (1809) 2 Camp 317. But see the report of the same case in 6 Esp 129, and *Harris v Watson* (1791) Peake 102 (promise invalid by reason of public policy). See generally on the two different law reports of *Stilk v Myrick*, Luther (1999) 19 LS 526.

In the course of a voyage from London to the Baltic and back two seamen deserted, and the captain, being unable to replace them, promised the rest of the crew that, if they would work the vessel home, the wages of the two deserters should be divided amongst them.

It was held that:

There was no consideration for the ulterior pay promised to the mariners who remained with the ship. Before they sailed from London they had undertaken to do all they could under all emergencies of the voyage . . . The desertion of a part of the crew is to be considered an emergency of the voyage as much as their death; and those who remain are bound by the terms of their original contract to exert themselves to the utmost to bring the ship in safety to her destined port.[101]

The decision would have been otherwise if the existing contract had been rescinded and a new agreement substituted[102] at a higher rate of pay, or if the promise had been made to compromise a dispute,[103] or if uncontemplated risks had arisen.[104] Then the crew would have provided consideration by entering into the new agreement, or forbearing to exercise what were or were believed to be their legal rights or by undertaking to do more than they were contractually bound to do.

Even where the promise is only to perform the existing contractual obligation, the performance may in fact be detrimental to a performing party whose time or money could have been used to greater advantage elsewhere. It may also be beneficial to the promisor because 'a bird in the hand is worth more than a bird in the bush'[105] and because damages for breach of contract might not compensate fully.[106] In *Williams v Roffey Bros & Nicholls (Contractors) Ltd*:[107]

R & N Ltd contracted to refurbish a block of 27 flats. It sub-contracted the carpentry work to W for an agreed price of £20,000. W completed nine of the flats but ran into financial difficulties because the agreed price was too low and because he failed to supervise his workforce adequately. R & N was concerned about delay because the main contract contained a penalty clause. It offered to pay W an additional £10,300 at the rate of £575 for each flat in which the carpentry work was completed. Eight further flats were completed but R & N made only one further payment of £1,500. W ceased work and sued for the additional sum promised. R & N resisted this claim on the ground that W had given no consideration for their promise to pay the additional sum since he was promising to do no more than he was already bound to do by his subcontract.

This defence failed. In the Court of Appeal Glidewell LJ stated:[108]

(i) If A has entered into a contract with B to do work for, or to supply goods or services to, B in return for payment by B; and (ii) at some stage before A has completely performed

[101] (1809) 2 Camp 317, 319 (Lord Ellenborough CJ).
[102] See below, Chapter 13.
[103] *Wigan v Edwards* (1973) 1 ALR 497; see above, p 107.
[104] *Hartley v Ponsonby* (1857) 7 E & B 872.
[105] *Corbin on Contracts* (1963) para 172. See also *Foakes v Beer* (1884) 9 App Cas 605, 622 (Lord Blackburn).
[106] Below, Chapter 17 (limitations on damages).
[107] [1991] 1 QB 1.
[108] *Ibid*, 15–16. On 'practical benefit', see also *Anangel Atlas Comp Nav SA v Ishikawajima-Harima Heavy Industries Co Ltd (No 2)* [1990] 2 Lloyd's Rep 526, 554–5; *Simon Container Machinery Ltd v Emba Machinery AB* [1998] 2 Lloyd's Rep 429, 435.

his obligations under the contract B has reason to doubt whether A will, or will be able to, complete his side of the bargain; and (iii) B thereupon promises A an additional payment in return for A's promise to perform his contractual obligations on time; and (iv) as a result of giving his promise, B obtains in practice a benefit, or obviates a disbenefit; and (v) B's promise is not given as a result of economic duress or fraud on the part of A;[109] then (vi) the benefit to B is capable of being consideration for B's promise, so that the promise will be legally binding.

The Court identified several 'practical' benefits to R & N. These were: W's continued performance, avoiding a penalty for delay under the main contract, avoiding the trouble and expense of engaging others to complete the carpentry, and replacing a haphazard method of payment by a more formalized scheme which produced more orderly performance by W and thus enabled R & N to direct its other traders to do work in the completed flats which otherwise would have been held up until W completed his work.[110] It is clear that it was the development of economic duress as a method of controlling improper pressure that enabled the Court to take a more flexible approach to the requirement of consideration:[111]

Now that there is a properly developed doctrine of the avoidance of contracts on the grounds of economic duress, there is no warrant for the court to fail to recognize the existence of some consideration even though it may be insignificant and even though there may have been no mutual bargain in any realistic use of that phrase.[112]

The recognition of 'practical' benefit as consideration could be a significant step towards the overt recognition that all promises to pay more (or to accept less) for performing, or promising to perform, a pre-existing contractual duty owed to the promisor made without duress in a commercial context give rise to enforceable contractual obligations. This derives support from the suggestion, in a case involving paying more for performance of a pre-existing duty to the promisor,[113] that *Williams v Roffey* cannot be reconciled with *Stilk v Myrick*; and that the doctrine of consideration no longer needs to be used to protect a participant in such a variation because that role has passed to the law of economic duress which provides a more refined control mechanism.

Several factors, however, make it difficult to assess how radical the impact of *Williams v Roffey* will ultimately prove to be. First, the principle in *Stilk v Myrick*, although refined and limited, was not overruled.[114] It appears from this that, where there is no 'practical' benefit to the promisor, the promise will be 'gratuitous' and unenforceable. Interestingly,

[109] It is hard to see that Glidewell LJ can have been correct to include this as a requirement for establishing consideration. Duress or misrepresentation operate to make a contract, supported by consideration, voidable.

[110] [1991] 1 QB 1, 11, 19, 20.

[111] *Ibid*, 13–14, 21. See also *Pao On v Lau Yiu Long* [1980] AC 614, 624–35, above, p 111.

[112] *Vantage Navigation Corp v Suhail & Saud Bahwan Building Materials Llc, The Alev* [1989] 1 Lloyd's Rep 138, 147 (Hobhouse J). See also *Huyton SA v Peter Cremer GmbH* [1999] 1 Lloyd's Rep 620, 629–30 (Mance J).

[113] *Adam Opel GmbH v Mitras Automotive (UK) Ltd* [2007] EWHC 3481 (QB) at [42] (David Donaldson QC). Cf *South Caribbean Trading Ltd v Trafigura Beheer BV* [2004] EWHC 2676 (Comm), [2005] 1 Lloyd's Rep 128 at [108] where Colman J said, 'But for the fact that *Williams v Roffey Bros* was a decision of the Court of Appeal, I would not have followed it.'

[114] [1991] 1 QB 1, 16, 19, 20.

in *Roffey* the Court of Appeal thought that *Stilk v Myrick* could be explained on the basis of public policy,[115] even though in the most authoritative report of *Stilk v Myrick*, given by Campbell,[116] the public policy ground is doubted by Lord Ellenborough who held that the agreement was void for lack of consideration. Admittedly, a different report of the case does place some weight upon factors of public policy, but that report is given by Espinasse, who was notoriously unreliable,[117] and is more dubious than that of Campbell.[118]

Secondly, on the facts of *Williams v Roffey Bros*, although W did not undertake to do any work additional to that which he had originally undertaken to do, one might argue that the institution of and adherence to the new work scheme constituted a different performance so that, applying the traditional approach, there was consideration since he was not obliged to perform in that way.[119]

Thirdly, as will be seen, in the context of part payment of a money debt, the Court of Appeal has, in some cases since *Williams v Roffey Bros*, declined to have regard to 'practical' benefit.[120]

The notion of 'practical' benefit has been criticized[121] as imprecise, as including the chance of a benefit, as putting into question the adequacy of contract damages, and as undermining the strength of the obligation to perform a contract by recognizing, as Purchas LJ did,[122] that a contracting party can rely upon his own breach to establish consideration. However, we shall see that rigid adherence to the pre-existing duty rule has also been criticized as invalidating many commercially desirable renegotiations and that, before the development of economic duress, it was necessary to have recourse to equitable promissory estoppel to protect the renegotiated transaction. Now that safeguards exist against improper pressure it can be argued that there is no very convincing reason why a promise to perform, or performance of, any existing duty,

[115] See too Gilmore, *The Death of Contract* (1974) 22–8.

[116] (1809) 2 Camp 317.

[117] See eg *Small v Nairne* (1849) 13 QB 840, 844 (Lord Denman CJ): 'I am tempted to remark, for the benefit of the profession, that Espinasse's Reports, in days nearer their own time, when their want of accuracy was better known than it is now, were never quoted without doubt and hesitation; and a special reason was often given as an apology for citing that particular case.'

[118] 6 Esp 129. For further consideration of duress generally, see Chapter 10.

[119] It would appear that this consideration, if valid, would be found in the *performance*; ie the contract was *unilateral*. It is more problematic to argue that there was a new bilateral contract because, although Russell LJ (at 19) considered that 'the terms upon which [W] was to carry out the work were varied', Purchas LJ (at 23) stated that there was 'no obligation added to the contractual duties'. Glidewell LJ did not address the point.

[120] *Re Selectmove Ltd* [1995] 1 WLR 474, 481; *Collier v Wright (Holdings) Ltd* [2007] EWCA Civ 1329, [2008] 1 WLR 643. Cf *MWB Business Exchange Centres Ltd v Rock Advertising Ltd* [2016] EWCA Civ 553, [2017] QB 604 (the issue of consideration was not dealt with on the appeal to the Supreme Court). See below, p 116.

[121] Chen-Wishart, in Beatson and Friedmann (eds), *Good Faith and Fault in Contract Law* (1995) ch 5; Coote (1990–91) 3 JCL 23. But Chen-Wishart now argues, in Burrows and Peel (eds), *Contract Formation and Parties* (2010) ch 5, that performance of a pre-existing duty does constitute valid consideration for a *unilateral* contract because actual performance, rather than a promise to perform, gives the promisor something more than it previously had which was merely the contractual right to performance. The essence of this argument was accepted by Arden LJ (alone) in *MWB Business Exchange Centres Ltd v Rock Advertising Ltd* [2016] EWCA Civ 553, [2017] QB 604.

[122] [1991] 1 QB 1, 23.

including public duties, should not be sufficient consideration provided that it is not contrary to public policy.[123]

An alternative approach to the problem in *Williams v Roffey*, which would have led to the same result, is to say that consideration is not needed for the variation, as opposed to the formation, of a contract. That was the approach adopted in the United States Uniform Commercial Code.[124] It has also been put forward as an alternative to the *Roffey* approach by the New Zealand Court of Appeal.[125]

(i) DISCHARGE OF A DEBT

The principle that the performance of an existing duty owed to the promisor is an unreal consideration has been applied not only to the creation of a new obligation, but also to the discharge of the existing duty. Thus if A owes B a debt of £200, and B agrees to accept £100 in full satisfaction of the debt, B is not bound by the agreement and may subsequently sue for the whole amount. Part payment of a debt is not good consideration for the discharge of that debt. Such payment is no more than the promisee is already bound to do, and is no consideration for a promise, express or implied, to forgo the remainder of the debt.

(i) The general rule

The rule that the payment of a smaller sum in satisfaction of a larger is not a good discharge of a debt is often known as the rule in *Pinnel's Case*,[126] although it was not part of the *ratio decidendi* of that case.

Pinnel brought an action in debt on a bond against Cole for payment of £8 10*s* on 11 November 1600. Cole pleaded that, at the instance of Pinnel, he had paid him the sum of £5 2*s* 2*d* on 1 October, and that Pinnel had accepted this in full satisfaction of the debt.

The Court of Common Pleas stated that the payment of a lesser sum on the day in satisfaction of a greater was no satisfaction of the whole albeit that, on the facts, that rule did not apply because the debt had been paid and accepted in advance of the due date.

The rule was considered and reaffirmed by the House of Lords nearly three centuries later in *Foakes v Beer*:[127]

Dr Foakes was indebted to Mrs Beer on a judgment for the sum of £2,090. Mrs Beer agreed that if Foakes paid her £500 in cash and the balance of £1,590 in instalments she would not take 'any proceedings whatever' on the judgment. Foakes paid the money exactly as required, but Mrs Beer then claimed an additional £360 as interest on the judgment debt. When sued, Foakes pleaded that his duty to pay interest had been discharged by the promise not to sue.

123 *Williams v Williams* [1957] 1 WLR 148, 150 (Denning LJ), above, p 108, n 82; *Huyton SA v Peter Cremer GmbH* [1999] 1 Lloyd's Rep 620, 629–30 (Mance J).

124 Articles 2-209(1) (sale of goods) and 2A-208(1) (lease of goods).

125 *Antons Trawling Co Ltd v Smith* [2003] 2 NZLR 23 (although the court did not need to decide between those alternative approaches). See too *Rosas v Toca* 2018 BCCA 191 (British Columbia). Compare *Ma Hongjin v SCP Holdings Pte Ltd* [2020] SGCA 106, [2021] 1 SLR 304 (Singapore).

126 (1602) 5 Co Rep 117a.

127 (1884) 9 App Cas 605.

Their Lordships differed as to whether, on its true construction, the agreement merely gave Foakes time to pay, or was intended to cover interest as well, but they held that, even on the latter construction, there was no consideration for the promise. Foakes therefore remained bound to pay the additional sum. The Earl of Selborne LC insisted that 'it is not really unreasonable or practically inconvenient that the law should require particular solemnities to give to a gratuitous contract the force of a binding obligation'.[128]

(ii) Irrelevance of 'practical benefit'

Lord Blackburn in particular was minded to dissent in *Foakes v Beer*, but ultimately was persuaded not to do so. Lord Blackburn thought that business people 'do every day recognise and act on the ground that prompt payment of a part of their demand may be more beneficial to them than it would be to insist on their rights',[129] especially where the credit of the debtor is doubtful. Nevertheless, the House of Lords decided that a practical benefit of that nature is not good consideration. In *Re Selectmove Ltd*[130] it was said in *obiter dicta* that the principle that 'practical' benefit may amount to consideration, as found in *Williams v Roffey Bros & Nicholls (Contractors) Ltd*,[131] could not be extended to an obligation to make payment because 'it would in effect leave the principle in *Foakes v Beer* without any application'. *Foakes v Beer* is a decision of the House of Lords, so the Court of Appeal in *Roffey* could not possibly have departed from it. That must be correct due to the rules on precedent. But it creates a strange distinction between obligations to pay money (when *Foakes v Beer* applies) and obligations to render services (when *Roffey* applies).

That distinction was seemingly brushed away by the Court of Appeal in *MWB Business Exchange Centres Ltd v Rock Advertising Ltd*.[132] A landlord's promise, allowing its tenant extra time to pay off the rent owing, was supported by consideration because, applying *Roffey*, it was a practical benefit to the landlord not to have the premises left empty. Unlike in *Roffey*, the Court of Appeal in *MWB* did consider *Pinnel's Case* and *Foakes v Beer*. But both cases were circumvented on the basis that MWB did not *only* receive part payment of a debt, but *further* received a 'practical benefit'. This practical benefit was present because MWB would ultimately be likely to recover a greater sum from Rock, and—most significantly—MWB would avoid the property standing empty for some time, causing further loss. This extension of 'practical benefit' is novel, and controversial because it appears to sideline the superior decision of the House of Lords in *Foakes v Beer*. Unfortunately, the issue of consideration was not dealt with by the Supreme Court on appeal.[133]

In the wake of the Supreme Court decision in *MWB*, at first instance in *Simantob v Shavleyan*, Kerr J reiterated, albeit with some reluctance, the orthodox view that a 'practical benefit' does not constitute good consideration for payment of part of an

[128] *Ibid*, 613.

[129] At *ibid*, 622. See also *ibid*, 630 (Lord Fitzgerald).

[130] [1995] 1 WLR 474, 481 (Peter Gibson LJ). See Peel (1994) 110 LQR 353. See also *Ferguson v Davies* [1997] 1 All ER 315. In *Collier v Wright Holdings Ltd* [2007] EWCA Civ 1329, [2008] 1 WLR 643 the same point was made and was part of the *ratio*.

[131] Above, pp 112–5.

[132] [2016] EWCA Civ 553, [2017] QB 604.

[133] See immediately below.

existing debt, since *Re Selectmove* remains binding.[134] However, Kerr J did not consider the tension between the decisions of the Court of Appeal in *Re Selectmove* and *MWB*. Yet since the Supreme Court in *MWB* did not overturn the Court of Appeal on the issue of consideration, the decision of the Court of Appeal that MWB received a 'practical benefit' is likely to continue to prove troublesome.

(iii) Any difference in performance suffices

If, however, there is a dispute as to the amount due[135] or the thing done or given by the promisee debtor is different from that which the recipient was entitled to demand,[136] however slight the difference,[137] it will be sufficient consideration for the promise to discharge. Even the performance of the identical obligation will be effective if it is to take place at an earlier date or in a different place.

The Court in *Pinnel's Case* recognized that 'the gift of a horse, hawk or robe, etc. in satisfaction is good' because it 'might be more beneficial to the plaintiff than the money . . . or otherwise the plaintiff would not have accepted it in satisfaction'.[138] Judgment was given for the claimant on a technical point of pleading;[139] but the fact that the payment and the acceptance of part of the money had taken place before the due day would otherwise have resulted in judgment for the defendant, for the difference in time would have constituted sufficient consideration for the promise to discharge the debt.

(iv) Appraisal of rule

It has been argued that the rule in *Pinnel's Case* is supportable on the ground that the law should not favour a person who is excused money which they ought to pay any more than a person who is promised money which they have not earned. On the other hand, it is open to the criticism that it not only runs counter to ordinary commercial practice but that, taken in conjunction with the rule that the law will not inquire into the adequacy of consideration, it may lead to absurd results. In *Couldery v Bartrum* Jessel MR said: 'According to English Common Law a creditor may accept anything in satisfaction of his debt except a less amount of money. He might take a horse, or a canary, or a tomtit if he chose, and that was accord and satisfaction; but, by a most extraordinary peculiarity of the English Common Law, he could not take 19*s* 6*d* in the pound.'[140] But that might be justified on the basis that individuals can value goods in

[134] [2018] EWHC 2005 (QB) at [119]–[138]; this point was not considered on appeal: [2019] EWCA Civ 1105 at [53].

[135] Above, p 107.

[136] Even a negotiable instrument (such as a cheque) for the smaller amount would at one time suffice, provided it was accepted by the creditor in discharge of the obligation (*Goddard v O'Brien* (1882) 9 QBD 37), but this is no longer the case (*D & C Builders Ltd v Rees* [1966] 2 QB 617).

[137] eg payment may be in a different currency: cf *RTI Ltd v MUR Shipping BV* [2024] UKSC 18, [2025] AC 675.

[138] (1602) 5 Co Rep 117a. In *Vanbergen v St Edmund's Properties Ltd* [1933] 2 KB 223, however, it was stated that the new element must not have been introduced merely to oblige the debtor and without any independent benefit to the creditor.

[139] See generally Simpson, *A History of the Common Law of Contract* (1975) 105–6.

[140] (1881) 19 Ch D 394, 399.

idiosyncratic ways: in some situations, it is conceivable that a horse with an objective value of £100 might be valued by a particular individual at £500. But money cannot be valued in different ways: it is impossible to say that £100 is worth £500.

In any event, there appears to be a possible distinction between a promise to pay more for the same services, where practical benefit is recognized, and a promise to accept a lesser sum of money owed, where it appears not to be.[141] In principle, this is difficult to justify. The rule in *Pinnel's Case* enables a creditor to go back on an agreement solemnly entered into and intended to affect legal relations; and it has been said that there are no strong policy considerations which would demand the application of the doctrine of consideration to the discharge, as opposed to the formation, of contracts.[142] The impact of the equitable doctrine of promissory estoppel in cases where the debtor's position has been altered in reliance on the promise might further undermine the rule in *Pinnel's Case*.[143] In 1937 the Law Revision Committee recommended the abolition of the rule where the promisee had carried out its side of the agreement,[144] but this reform has never been implemented.

It had been hoped that clarity would be brought to this area of the law by the Supreme Court in *MWB Business Exchange Centres Ltd v Rock Advertising Ltd*[145] However, those hopes were dashed when the Supreme Court decided that case on the basis that the 'no oral variation clause' in the contract meant that the oral variation was not valid whether or not it was supported by consideration. Lord Sumption, giving the majority's judgment, said as follows:

> That makes it unnecessary to deal with consideration. It is also, I think, undesirable to do so. The issue is a difficult one . . . In *Williams v Roffey Bros & Nicholls (Contractors) Ltd*, the Court of Appeal held that an expectation of commercial advantage was good consideration. The problem about this was that practical expectation of benefit was the very thing which the House of Lords held not to be adequate consideration in *Foakes v Beer* . . . There are arguable points of distinction, although the arguments are somewhat forced. A differently constituted Court of Appeal made these points in *In re Selectmove Ltd*, and declined to follow *Williams v Roffey*. The reality is that any decision on this point is likely to involve a re-examination of the decision in *Foakes v Beer*. It is probably ripe for re-examination. But if it is to be overruled or its effect substantially modified, it should be before an enlarged panel of the court and in a case where the decision would be more than obiter dictum.

Such *obiter* comments are somewhat disappointing.[146] The issue had been fully argued, and it is unlikely that the Supreme Court will be presented with a similar opportunity to consider this area in the near future.

[141] Cf O'Sullivan [1996] CLJ 219.

[142] Sir Frederick Pollock, *Principles of Contract* (13th edn, 1950) 150 (extension of the doctrine from formation to discharge was illegitimate). See also Kötz, *European Contract Law* (2nd edn, 2017) 63–6; CISG art 29(1) ('a contract may be modified or terminated by the mere agreement of the parties').

[143] For the view that promissory estoppel outflanks the rule in *Pinnel's Case*, see *Collier v Wright (Holdings) Ltd* [2007] EWCA Civ 1329, [2008] 1 WLR 643, especially at [42]. See below, p 124.

[144] Cmd 5449. In Canada, provincial statutes have now abolished the rule by providing, as the Ontario Mercantile Law Amendment Act RSO 1990, s 16 does, that 'Part performance of an obligation either before or after the breach thereof, when expressly accepted by the creditor in satisfaction or rendered in pursuance of an agreement for that purpose, though without any new consideration, shall be held to extinguish the obligation.'

[145] [2018] UKSC 24, [2019] AC 119 at [18].

[146] Davies [2018] CLJ 464, 466–7.

The equitable doctrine of promissory estoppel is considered in detail below but we shall now consider two common law exceptions to the rule in *Foakes v Beer*. The first is where a debtor makes a composition with creditors; the second is where part payment of a debt is made by a third party to the contract. It will be seen that these two exceptions are based on reasons of policy rather than on logical evasions of the strict doctrine of consideration.

(v) Compositions with creditors

A composition with creditors (apart from the statutory prohibition of preference by debtors who later become bankrupt)[147] is an exception to the rule, inasmuch as each creditor undertakes to accept a lesser sum than is due in satisfaction of a greater. All are bound, both at common law and by virtue of statute.[148] As far as the common law position is concerned, there is no difficulty as to the consideration between the creditors *inter se*; it is the forbearance on the part of each of them to claim the whole amount of their debt so that no one creditor may gain at the expense of the others. But it is difficult to see how the debtor's promise to pay, or the payment of, a portion of the debt can constitute the consideration upon which the creditor renounces the residue.[149]

The consideration must be something other than the payment of a smaller sum in satisfaction of a larger. It has been suggested that it consists in the procuring of a promise from each creditor to accept less than the full amount of the individual debt, thereby conferring a benefit on the creditors generally.[150] This solution is satisfactory so far as it goes, since there is no doubt that such a consideration would be sufficient, but it cannot apply to a case in which the debtor does not in fact procure the creditors' promises.[151] A more acceptable reason for the existence of this exception would seem to be that a party to such an arrangement cannot claim the original debt because to do so would be to commit a fraud on the other creditors.[152]

(vi) Part payment by third party

The second exception to the general rule, that a creditor who accepts, in full satisfaction, part payment of a debt by a third party cannot later recover the balance from the debtor, is also based on the need to prevent fraud on a third party. In *Hirachand Punamchand v Temple*:[153]

A father wrote to the claimants, his son's creditors, offering to pay part of a debt due on a promissory note in satisfaction of the whole, and enclosing a draft for that amount. The claimants cashed the draft, and then sued the son for the balance.

[147] Insolvency Act 1986, s 340.

[148] Insolvency Act 1986, s 260(2). A voluntary arrangement pursuant to the statute is not a contract with the debtor: *Johnson v Davies* [1999] Ch 117.

[149] *Fitch v Sutton* (1804) 5 East 230, 232.

[150] *Good v Cheesman* (1831) 2 B & Ad 328.

[151] Cf *West Yorkshire Darracq Agency Ltd v Coleridge* [1911] 2 KB 326.

[152] *Wood v Roberts* (1818) 2 Stark 417. Another reason (*Corbin on Contracts* (1963) para 190) is that, subject to the statutory prohibition on preferences (Insolvency Act 1986, s 340), the debtor's consideration lies in giving up the opportunity of treating his creditors unequally.

[153] [1911] 2 KB 330. See also *Welby v Drake* (1825) 1 C & P 557.

The Court of Appeal held that the creditors must be deemed to have accepted the draft in full satisfaction, and that the son's debt was extinguished. It approved a dictum of Willes J in *Cook v Lister*:[154] 'If a stranger pays part of the debt in discharge of the whole, the debt is gone, because it would be a fraud on the stranger to proceed.'

(j) LETTERS OF CREDIT

The irrevocable letter of credit has often been said to be an example of an exception to the need for consideration.[155] The purpose of such letters of credit is to finance contracts for the sale of goods between buyers and sellers in different countries, particularly where the delay between despatch from the place of manufacture and arrival at the destination is a considerable one. It enables short-term credit facilities to be made available, guarantees payment to the seller, and safeguards the parties against currency fluctuations.

There are three stages in the transaction. First, a term is inserted in the contract of sale made between the buyer and the seller whereby the buyer undertakes to furnish an irrevocable letter of credit in favour of the seller.[156] Secondly, the buyer approaches its own banker (usually described as the issuing banker) and instructs it to issue an irrevocable letter of credit, giving the banker details of the transaction. This constitutes a contract between the buyer and the banker. Thirdly, the banker advises the seller that an irrevocable letter of credit has been opened in its favour, that is to say, the banker gives an irrevocable undertaking to pay the seller, or to accept bills of exchange drawn on it, provided the seller tenders the required shipping documents in compliance with the terms of the letter of credit.[157] The seller can then ship the goods in the secure knowledge that it will be paid for them. The shipping documents represent the goods themselves,[158] and they are usually retained by the banker as security against its right to be reimbursed by the buyer.

The irrevocable letter of credit does not fit easily into the common law. If the transaction is regarded simply as a contract between the buyer and its banker, the seller is a third party to this contract and technically would be unable to sue should the banker revoke the letter of credit or for some reason fail to make payment.[159] Nevertheless, it has been

[154] (1863) 13 CBNS 543, 594, 595. This is not also an exception to the rule that a non-party to a contract (here the debtor) cannot enforce it (below, Chapter 21) because the transaction between the creditor and the person who pays is best seen as an executed (complete) gift to the debtor of the discharge of the debt: see Birks and Beatson (1976) 92 LQR 188, 193–9.

[155] See generally *The Uniform Customs and Practice for Documentary Credits* (2007 Revision, UCP 600); Jack, *Documentary Credits* (4th edn, 2009).

[156] For the effect of a failure to furnish the letter of credit, see below, p 158.

[157] An irrevocable letter of credit may also be 'confirmed' by a banker operating in the seller's country (known as the correspondent banker) who, by confirming the credit, adds to the promise of the issuing banker its own undertaking to ensure payment.

[158] *Lickbarrow v Mason* (1794) 5 TR 683.

[159] In the Sixth Interim Report of the Law Revision Committee (Cmnd 5449, 1937) para 45, it was pointed out that the liquidator of a bank might be compelled to rely on the defence of privity.

established that the banker is legally under an absolute obligation to pay, irrespective of any dispute there may be between the buyer and seller.[160] It has therefore been argued that the irrevocable letter of credit forms an 'exception' to the doctrine of privity of contract; but it seems better to regard the promise of payment given by the banker to the seller as an autonomous undertaking, independent of any other contract. Thus the irrevocable letter of credit is not an exception to privity of contract but to the doctrine of consideration. It is either an irrevocable offer by the banker to the seller (which is accepted by the seller tendering the shipping documents) or a unilateral contract between the banker and the seller to pay on tender of the shipping documents.[161] But on either analysis the essential theoretical problem is that the banker is bound not to revoke even before the seller has tendered the documents and it is therefore hard to see that the tendering of the documents can constitute the consideration. Nevertheless, in *Taurus Petroleum Ltd v State Oil Marketing Company of the Ministry of Oil, Republic of Iraq* Lord Mance said that it is 'now accepted, realistically, that whatever contractual arrangements are contained in the letters of credit are binding, and that no problem relating to absence of consideration arises'.[162] Letters of credit are best analysed as an example of a promise in the commercial sphere that, for reasons of commercial convenience, is treated as binding despite there being no consideration.

2. PROMISSORY ESTOPPEL

Perhaps the most significant limit to the rule in *Pinnel's Case*[163] is to be found in the equitable principle of estoppel, in this context promissory estoppel. Here we consider the extent to which promissory estoppel operates in effect as an alternative to consideration in the discharge or modification of existing duties and its potential to operate in this way in the formation of contracts.[164]

Before turning to the requirements for the establishment of a promissory estoppel, it should be noted that it is only one form of estoppel. We saw in the last chapter that equity may, by the principle of proprietary estoppel, provide a remedy in respect of an agreement for the sale of land that does not comply with statutory requirements of form. Promissory estoppel is one strand in a broader equitable principle whereby parties to a transaction who have conducted their dealings in reliance on an underlying assumption

[160] *Urquhart, Lindsay & Co Ltd v Eastern Bank Ltd* [1922] 1 KB 318, 321, 322; *Donald H Scott & Co Ltd v Barclays Bank Ltd* [1923] 2 KB 1, 13; *Trans-Trust SPRL v Danubian Trading Co Ltd* [1952] 2 QB 297, 304–5; *Midland Bank Ltd v Seymour* [1955] 2 Lloyd's Rep 147, 166; *Hamzeh Malas & Sons v British Imex Industries Ltd* [1958] 2 QB 127, 129.

[161] Ellinger (1962) 4 Malaya LR 307. In *Urquhart's* case, above, n 160, 321, Rowlatt J thought that the banker's undertaking took effect once the seller acted on it, eg by commencing performance of their contract with the buyer. Cf *Dexters Ltd v Schenker & Co* (1932) 14 Ll LR 586, 588 (when letter of credit received). On either view there appears to be no consideration (because, eg, acting on a promise does not constitute consideration).

[162] [2017] UKSC 64, [2018] AC 690 [100]; see too [95], and [25] (Lord Clarke).

[163] See above, p 114.

[164] See Cartwright, *Formation and Variation of Contracts* (4th edn, 2024) Part IV.

as to a present, past, or future state of affairs, or on a promise or representation by words or conduct, will not be allowed to go back on that assumption, promise or representation when it would be unfair or unjust to do so.[165] The Court will do what is necessary, but not more, to prevent a person who has relied upon such an assumption, promise, or representation from suffering injustice.[166] Promissory estoppel also has similarities to the common law principle of waiver by which the right to performance in accordance with the contract may be lost by a party who in effect promises (albeit without consideration) not to insist on strict adherence to the contract. Common law waiver is considered in Chapter 13.[167]

(a) EMERGENCE OF PROMISSORY ESTOPPEL

Promissory estoppel was invoked in *Central London Property Trust Ltd v High Trees House Ltd*:[168]

In 1937 the claimant leased to the defendant a block of flats for a term of 99 years at a rent of £2,500 a year. In 1940, many of the flats were empty, on account of the war, and the claimant agreed to reduce the rent to £1,250. By 1945 the flats were again full. In September 1945 the receiver of the claimant demanded full rent for the future and some arrears. Subsequently he brought an action against the defendant claiming the full original rent both for the future and also for the last two quarters of 1945.

Denning J held that the action should succeed. The parties intended the reduction of rent to be a temporary expedient while the flats could not be fully let. This had ceased to be the case early in 1945; therefore the full rent was payable for the last two quarters of 1945, which was all that was actually claimed in the action. The importance of the judgment, however, lies in Denning J's contention that, had the claimant sued for the full rent between 1940 and 1945, it would have been *estopped* by its promise from asserting its legal right to demand payment in full. In other words, the promise to accept less rent while wartime conditions prevailed was binding despite the absence of consideration.

Denning J relied on the decision of the House of Lords in *Hughes v Metropolitan Railway Co*:[169]

H served on M a notice to repair, within six months, houses held on lease from him. Failure to comply with this notice would entitle H to forfeit the lease. The parties then negotiated for the purchase by H of M's lease and these negotiations continued for almost the entire period of the notice. Shortly before the notice was due to expire, H broke off the negotiations, and, upon expiry, brought an action for possession claiming to have forfeited the lease.

[165] Below, pp 129–33. For the relationship between promissory estoppel, proprietary estoppel, and estoppel by convention, see *Baird Textiles Holdings Ltd v Marks & Spencer plc* [2001] EWCA Civ 274, [2002] 1 All ER (Comm) 737; below, pp 132–7.

[166] *Crabb v Arun DC* [1976] Ch 179, 198. [167] Below, pp 472–6. [168] [1947] KB 130.

[169] (1877) 2 App Cas 439. See also *Birmingham and District Land Co v L & NW Ry* (1888) 40 Ch D 268. Contrast the view of this case advanced by Gordon [1963] CLJ 222.

The House of Lords held that, by entering into negotiations, H impliedly promised to suspend the notice previously given and that M had acted upon this promise by doing nothing to repair the premises. H was not to be allowed to take advantage of the forfeiture which occurred, and therefore the six months' period was to run only from the breakdown of the negotiations. Lord Cairns described the principle as follows:[170]

> If parties who have entered into definite and distinct terms involving certain legal results—certain penalties or legal forfeiture—afterwards by their own act or with their own consent enter upon a course of negotiation which has the effect of leading one of the parties to suppose that the strict rights arising under the contract will not be enforced, or will be kept in suspense, or held in abeyance, the person who otherwise might have enforced those rights will not be allowed to enforce them where it would be inequitable having regard to the dealings which have thus taken place between the parties.

Denning J stated that the application of this principle led logically to the conclusion that 'a promise to accept a smaller sum in discharge of a larger sum, if acted upon, is binding notwithstanding the absence of consideration.'[171]

The correctness of Denning J's *obiter dicta* has, however, been the subject of considerable controversy.[172] In particular, two criticisms have been levelled against it. First, that the concept of 'promissory' estoppel offends against the rule in *Jorden v Money*[173] in which it was held that only a representation of existing or past fact, and not one relating to future conduct, will ground an estoppel. Estoppel would not therefore apply, as in the *High Trees* case, to a promise as to the future. However, the rule in *Jorden v Money*, is not absolute, and it is qualified by a number of exceptions.[174] One of these exceptions is that principle expressed in *Hughes v Metropolitan Railway Co*, which applies where two parties stand together in a contractual or other similar legal relationship, and one of them makes to the other a promise to forbear from enforcing its strict legal rights. The rule in *Jorden v Money* does not apply in this situation.[175]

Secondly, that the dictum of Denning J is inconsistent with the decision of the House of Lords in *Foakes v Beer*. But the principle upon which he relied in the *High Trees* case was that of estoppel, which must be specially pleaded. A plea of estoppel was never raised in *Foakes v Beer*. Yet it seems unlikely that the House of Lords overlooked the equitable doctrine of estoppel, especially because Lord Selborne and Lord Blackburn heard both

[170] (1877) 2 App Cas 439, 448.

[171] [1947] KB 130, 135.

[172] As well as the articles cited below, see Cheshire and Fifoot (1947) 63 LQR 283; (1948) 64 LQR 28; Wilson (1951) 67 LQR 330; Lord Denning (1952) 15 MLR 1; Sheridan (1952) 15 MLR 338; Bennion (1953) 16 MLR 441; Wilson [1965] CLJ 93; Thompson [1983] CLJ 257; McFarlane, in Burrows and Peel (eds), *Contract Formation and Parties* (2010) ch 6.

[173] (1854) 5 HLC 185, and applied in *Citizen's Bank of Louisiana v First National Bank of New Orleans* (1873) LR 6 HL 352; *Maddison v Alderson* (1883) 8 App Cas 467, 473.

[174] See Jackson (1965) 81 LQR 84, 223.

[175] Denning J further distinguished *Jorden v Money* on the unconvincing basis that the promisor in that case did not intend to be legally bound.

Foakes v Beer and *Hughes v Metropolitan Railway Co*. Nevertheless, in *Collier v Wright (Holdings) Ltd* Arden LJ boldly stated that *High Trees* outflanks *Foakes v Beer*:[176]

> The facts of this case demonstrate that, if (1) a debtor offers to pay part only of the amount he owes; (2) the creditor voluntarily accepts that offer, and (3) in reliance on the creditor's acceptance, the debtor pays that part of the amount he owes in full, the creditor will, by virtue of the doctrine of promissory estoppel, be bound to accept that sum in full and final satisfaction of the whole debt. For him to resile will itself be inequitable. In addition, in these circumstances, the promissory estoppel has the effect of extinguishing the creditor's right to the balance of the debt. This part of our law originated in the brilliant obiter dictum of Denning J, as he was, in the *High Trees* case. To a significant degree it achieves in practical terms the recommendation of the Law Revision Committee chaired by Lord Wright MR in 1937.

It is important to note that these comments were *obiter dicta*, and the Court of Appeal merely had to decide whether there was a genuine triable issue on promissory estoppel. Moreover, Longmore LJ was much more cautious (and Mummery LJ expressed no view). Longmore LJ doubted that the agreement could be construed as a permanent surrender of the right to sue for the balance but also stated that, if Arden LJ was correct about the effect of *High Trees*, it was important to construe agreements which are said to have this effect strictly, and referred to the need for meaningful reliance.[177]

The comments of the Court of Appeal in *MWB Business Exchange Centres Ltd v Rock Advertising Ltd* show similar caution.[178] If there had not been consideration to support the variation in that case, Kitchin LJ, who gave the leading judgment, thought that MWB would not have been estopped from going back on its promise. Even though MWB had received a 'practical benefit', Rock had suffered no detriment, and could readily be restored to its previous position: it was not inequitable for MWB to go back on its representation simply because the representee made a payment in reliance on a representation. This sensible approach seems to undermine some of what was said in *Collier*.[179]

(b) SCOPE OF PROMISSORY ESTOPPEL

The recognition of the principle of promissory estoppel in cases since *High Trees*[180] has led to a more precise definition of its essential elements.

[176] [2007] EWCA Civ 1329, [2008] 1 WLR 643 at [42]. See also Arden LJ's comments on this passage in *MWB Business Exchange Centres Ltd v Rock Advertising Ltd* [2016] EWCA Civ 553, [2017] QB 604 at [92] (the Court of Appeal in *obiter dicta* in that case thought that promissory estoppel could not be established because it was not inequitable for the promisor to revert to its legal rights under the original contract (note that there was no discussion on the appeal to the Supreme Court of the application of promissory estoppel)).

[177] [2007] EWCA Civ 1329, [2008] 1 WLR 643 at [45]–[47].

[178] [2016] EWCA Civ 553, [2017] QB 604 at [92]; see above. This point was not considered in the Supreme Court.

[179] Although Arden LJ, perhaps unsurprisingly, did not see any inconsistency: *MWB Business Exchange Centres Ltd v Rock Advertising Ltd* [2016] EWCA Civ 553 at [92].

[180] *Tool Metal Manufacturing Co Ltd v Tungsten Electric Co Ltd* (1950) 69 RPC 108 and [1955] 1 WLR 761 was the first case. As well as the cases discussed below, see *Bremer Handelsgesellschaft mbH v Vanden Avenne-Izegem* [1977] 1 Lloyd's Rep 133, 165, aff'd [1978] 2 Lloyd's Rep 109, 127; *The Stolt Loyalty* [1993] 2 Lloyd's Rep 281. Cf *Woodhouse AC Israel Cocoa Ltd SA v Nigerian Produce Marketing Co Ltd* [1972] AC 741, 758, 762.

(i) A clear promise

The promise must be clear and unequivocal,[181] although it need not be express and may be implied from words or conduct.[182] No estoppel can arise if the language of the promise is indefinite or imprecise. Silence and inaction, including the absence of protest about a breach, will not normally estop a party from relying on the breach.[183] Where the language is clear, no question arises of any particular knowledge by the promisor.[184]

(ii) Inequitable to go back on promise

It must be inequitable for the promisor to go back on the promise and insist on the strict legal rights under the contract. This will not be so where the promise has been induced by intimidation by the promisee. This is illustrated by *D & C Builders Ltd v Rees*:[185]

Mr and Mrs Rees owed £482 to D & C, a small building company, in respect of work done for them. They delayed payment for several months, and then offered D & C £300, stating in effect that if it did not accept this sum it would get nothing. As D & C was in desperate financial straits, it accepted the £300 in full settlement of the debt. It then sued for the balance.

Lord Denning MR saw the case as turning on promissory estoppel. He considered that it was not inequitable for D & C to go back on its promise; the settlement was not truly voluntary as Mr and Mrs Rees had improperly taken advantage of D & C's weak financial situation.[186] Mr and Mrs Rees were therefore liable for the balance. Although there is little other guidance about the types of conduct by the promisee that will make it 'not inequitable' for a person to go back on a promise, pointers can be found in the developing doctrine of duress.[187] Misrepresentation by the promisee will also presumably rule out the application of promissory estoppel.

(iii) Alteration of position

It has been said that the promisee must have 'altered their position' in reliance on the promise made.[188] There is, however, some doubt as to what is meant by this requirement. Normally, in order to prove an estoppel, it must be shown that the person to whom the representation is made has acted detrimentally in reliance on it. If these ideas are regarded

[181] Woodhouse AC *Israel Cocoa Ltd SA v Nigerian Produce Marketing Co Ltd* [1972] AC 741, 757, 758, 761, 762, 767–8, 771; *Scandinavian Trading Tanker Co AB v Flota Petrolera Ecuatoriana* [1983] QB 549, aff'd [1983] 2 AC 694.

[182] *Hughes v Metropolitan Railway Co*, above, n 169. It is unlikely to arise where the negotiations are 'subject to contract': *Attorney-General for Hong Kong v Humphreys Estates (Queen's Garden)* [1987] 1 AC 114.

[183] *Société Italo-Belge pour le Commerce et l'Industrie v Palm* and *Vegetable Oils (Malaysia) Sdn Bhd* [1982] 1 All ER 19, 25; *Vitol SA v Esso Australia Ltd* [1989] 2 Lloyd's Rep 451, 460.

[184] *Youell v Bland Welch & Co Ltd* [1990] 2 Lloyd's Rep 423, 448–50. (Cf waiver where knowledge of all material facts is required.)

[185] [1966] 2 QB 617. See also *P v P* [1957] NZLR 854.

[186] Cf Danckwerts and Winn LJJ at 626, 632–3, who applied the rule in *Pinnel's Case*.

[187] *Huyton SA v Peter Cremer GmbH* [1999] 1 Lloyd's Rep 620, 629 (Mance J). See also below, Chapter 10.

[188] *Tungsten Electric Co Ltd v Tool Metal Manufacturing Co Ltd* (1950) 69 RPC 108, 112, 115–16; *Tool Metal Manufacturing Co Ltd v Tungsten Electric Co Ltd* [1955] 1 WLR 761, 764, 784; *Ajayi v RT Briscoe (Nigeria) Ltd* [1964] 1 WLR 1326, 1330; *Re Wyvern Developments Ltd* [1974] 1 WLR 1097, 1104.

as fundamentally similar, then the alteration of position which results from the promise must be such that, if the promise is revoked, the promisee will be in a worse position than if the promise had never been made. It is because the position of the promisee has been prejudiced that it is inequitable for the promisor to go back on the promise.

In *Hughes v Metropolitan Railway Co* this requirement was clearly satisfied, since M had refrained from carrying out repairs in reliance on the promise and had thus lost the time which it would have enjoyed had the negotiations never taken place. On the other hand, in the *High Trees* case, no evidence was adduced to show any alteration of position by the tenant company, in the sense that it arranged, or omitted to arrange, its affairs any differently as a result of the promise.[189] It appears that the only thing it did in reliance on the promise was to pay part of the debt which it was contractually bound to pay. If the landlord had gone back on its promise, and claimed the full rent between 1940 and 1945, the tenant would have been in no worse position than if the promise had never been made. As a result, the *High Trees* case cannot be regarded as completely identical to *Hughes v Metropolitan Railway Co.*

In *WJ Alan & Co Ltd v El Nasr Export and Import Co*[190] Lord Denning MR explicitly stated that for the *High Trees* principle to operate (which he here referred to as the principle of 'waiver') detriment to the promisee was not needed. All that was necessary was for the promisee to have 'acted on the belief induced by the other party'.[191] That is, mere reliance was sufficient.

That reliance will suffice is supported by Lord Cairns's statement of principle in the *Hughes* case.[192] He said that the person seeking to enforce his rights will not be allowed to do so 'where it would be inequitable having regard to the dealings which have thus taken place between the parties'. It is therefore arguable that it is for the Court to decide, on the totality of the evidence produced to it, whether the dealings between the parties are such as to render it inequitable for the promisor to go back on the promise. For instance, in *Société Italo-Belge pour le Commerce et l'Industrie v Palm and Vegetable Oils (Malaysia) Sdn Bhd, The Post Chaser*:[193]

The buyers of a cargo of palm oil did not protest about the sellers' failure to make a 'declaration of ship' in writing as soon as possible after sailing and asked the sellers to pass the shipping

[189] It could be suggested that the tenant had 'altered its position' by relying on the informal promise and failing to secure a formal release under seal or by refraining from seeking alternative finance or declaring itself bankrupt.

[190] [1972] 2 QB 189, 213. But cf *ibid*, 221 (Stephenson LJ) for the view that, on the facts, there was detrimental reliance. There was detrimental reliance on the facts in, eg, the following cases: *Combe v Combe* [1951] 2 KB 215, 220, 225; *Tool Metal Manufacturing Co Ltd v Tungsten Electric Co Ltd* [1955] 1 WLR 761, 799 (where, see below, the promisees continued to produce over quota); *Brikom Investments Ltd v Carr* [1979] QB 467, 482; *Youell v Bland Welch & Co Ltd* [1990] 2 Lloyd's Rep 423, 452–4.

[191] These were the words of Lord Cohen in *Tool Metal Manufacturing Co Ltd v Tungsten Electric Co Ltd* [1955] 1 WLR 761, 799.

[192] See above, p 120.

[193] [1982] 1 All ER 19. See also *Scandinavian Trading Tanker Co AB v Flota Petrolera Ecuatoriana* [1983] QB 549, aff'd [1983] 2 AC 694; *Goldsworthy v Brickell* [1987] Ch 378, 411; *Virulite LLC v Virulite Distribution Ltd* [2014] EWHC 366 (QB), [2015] 1 All ER (Comm) 204 at [121]; *MWB Business Exchange Centres Ltd v Rock Advertising Ltd* [2016] EWCA Civ 553, [2017] QB 604 (see above, n 176).

documents to a sub-buyer, a request that was held to be a representation that they were prepared to accept them and a waiver of any defect in them. The sub-buyer rejected the documents within 2 days and the buyers purported to do so as well.

It was stated that to establish inequity within Lord Cairns's principle, 'it is not necessary to show detriment; indeed the representee may have benefited from the representation, and yet it may be inequitable, at least without reasonable notice, for the representor to enforce his legal rights'.[194] However, it does not follow that, in every case where there is non-detrimental reliance by the promisee, it will be inequitable for the promisor to enforce the contract. In *Société Italo-Belge pour le Commerce et l'Industrie v Palm and Vegetable Oils (Malaysia) Sdn Bhd* itself, although the sellers had actively relied on the buyers' representation by presenting the documents, the very short time between the representation and the rejection of the documents meant that, in the absence of evidence that the sellers' position had been prejudiced, it was not inequitable for the buyers to enforce their legal right to reject the documents.

The requirement that the promise be 'acted upon' means that there is, in this respect, a further distinction from contracts supported by consideration which are enforceable even if wholly executory.[195]

(iv) Suspensive or extinctive?

It has been suggested that promissory estoppel only serves to suspend, and not wholly to extinguish, the existing obligation; the promisor may, on giving due notice, resume the right which has been waived and revert to the original terms of the contract.[196] Thus in *Tool Metal Manufacturing Co Ltd v Tungsten Electric Co Ltd*:[197]

In 1938 the appellant granted to the respondent a licence to import, make, use, and sell certain hard metal alloys it had patented. The respondent was to pay royalties, and, if the amount of material made exceeded a named quota, 'compensation'. On the outbreak of war, the appellant agreed to suspend its right to compensation, the parties contemplating that a new agreement would be entered into when the war ended. In 1945, the appellant claimed to have revoked its suspension and to be entitled to compensation from 1 June 1945. This claim failed on the ground that the revocation was premature as no adequate notice had been given to the respondent. In 1950, the appellant brought the present action, claiming compensation from 1 January 1947, at which date the respondent was fully aware that the appellant was determined to revert to the original agreement.

The House of Lords held that the appellant had effectively revoked its promise to suspend its legal rights and that it was entitled to the compensation claimed; the equitable principle

[194] [1982] 1 All ER 19, 27.

[195] See *Waltons Stores (Interstate) Ltd v Maher* (1988) 164 CLR 387, 406 (Mason CJ and Wilson J), below, p 130. Cf Lord Denning, who has contended extra-judicially that the repudiation of a promise solemnly given, and intended to effect legal relations, is in itself inequitable: (1952) 15 MLR 1, 6–8.

[196] *Birmingham and District Land Co v L & NW Ry* (1888) 40 Ch D 268, 286; *Ajayi v RT Briscoe (Nigeria) Ltd* [1964] 1 WLR 1326, 1330. See also Wilson (1951) 67 LQR 330; [1965] CLJ 93.

[197] [1955] 1 WLR 761.

enunciated in *Hughes v Metropolitan Railway Co* was applicable to the situation, but here the promisor, on giving adequate notice to the promisee, could resume its rights under the original agreement. As Bowen LJ had said in an earlier case:[198]

If persons who have contractual rights against others induce by their conduct those against whom they have such rights to believe that such rights will either not be enforced or will be kept in suspense or abeyance for some particular time, those persons will not be allowed by a Court of Equity to enforce the rights until such time has elapsed, without at all events placing the parties in the same position as they were before.

The temporary effect of the estoppel raised is sometimes considered to be characteristic of the doctrine and the reason why it should be considered a 'quasi-estoppel' rather than a true example of estoppel in equity or at common law.

However, that this is not a necessary limitation and there is strong support for the view that promissory estoppel can extinguish, as well as suspend, the promisee's obligations. In *MWB*, Kitchin LJ said that it was 'quite clear . . . that the effect of a promissory estoppel may only be suspensive',[199] but also recognized that 'all will depend on the circumstances' and that 'it may be that it would be inequitable to allow the promisor to go back on his promise at all with the result that the right is extinguished'.[200] For example, it is clear that the promise will become 'final and irrevocable if the promisee cannot resume his position'.[201] More generally, the effect of the estoppel will depend on the terms and intent of the promise. Where the contract imposes an obligation to make periodic payments of money, such as the 'compensation' in the *Tool Metal* case, rent under a lease,[202] or instalments under a hire-purchase agreement,[203] a promise to waive part of these payments will be construed to mean that the promisor reserves the right, on giving reasonable notice, to demand that future payments be made in full.[204] But it has been assumed, although not decided, that the right to claim the balance of past payments is foregone and is thus extinguished,[205] unless the promise is one which simply allows the promisee to postpone payment but does not extinguish the debt.[206] This assumption seems correct. If the promise is such as unequivocally to indicate the intention of the promisor wholly to abandon all right to payment of the money contractually due, whether periodically or as a lump sum, there is no reason why the

198 *Birmingham and District Land Co v L & NW Ry* (1888) 40 Ch D 268, 286.

199 *MWB Business Exchange Centres Ltd v Rock Advertising Ltd* [2016] EWCA Civ 553, [2017] QB 604 at [56].

200 *Ibid* at [61].

201 *Ajayi v RT Briscoe (Nigeria) Ltd* [1964] 1 WLR 1326, 1330. See also *Nippon Yusen Kaisha v Pacifica Navigacion SA* [1980] 2 Lloyd's Rep 245.

202 *Central London Property Trust Ltd v High Trees House Ltd* [1947] KB 130.

203 *Ajayi v RT Briscoe (Nigeria) Ltd*, above, n 201.

204 *Banning v Wright* [1972] 1 WLR 972, 981.

205 *Central London Property Trust Ltd v High Trees House Ltd* [1947] KB 130; *Tungsten Electric Co Ltd v Tool Metal Manufacturing Co Ltd* (1950) 69 RPC 108; *P v P* [1957] NZLR 854; *Collier v Wright Holdings Ltd* [2007] EWCA Civ 1329, [2008] 1 WLR 643.

206 *Ledingham v Bermejo Estancia Co Ltd* [1947] 1 All ER 749.

estoppel should not be held to have permanent effect.[207] Thus promissory estoppel may have an extinctive effect as regards existing obligations, but a suspensory effect as regards future obligations.

(v) Promissory estoppel not a cause of action

It has been seen that the principle of promissory estoppel has been employed to obviate the necessity for consideration in cases where parties are already bound contractually one to the other and one of them promises to waive, modify, or suspend its strict legal rights. The question therefore arises whether the principle might similarly be employed as a supplement or alternative to consideration as a necessary element in the formation of contracts. If it could be so employed, there would be two routes (apart from making the promise by deed) to ensuring that a promise is legally enforceable; first, the furnishing of consideration by the promisee in the form of the incurring of detriment or the conferral of benefit in return for the promise, and secondly, where the promise was intended to affect legal relations and to be acted upon by the promisee, and the promisee's position has been altered in reliance on the promise.[208] This has occurred in some jurisdictions[209] but not (yet?) in England where it is thought illegitimate to outflank the requirement of consideration and where the main doctrinal vehicle for reconciling promissory estoppel and consideration has been the rule that promissory estoppel does not create new causes of action where none existed before; it is 'a shield and not a sword'.[210] It has been said 'that it would be wrong to extend the doctrine of promissory estoppel, whatever its precise limits at the present day, to the extent of abolishing in this backhanded way the doctrine of consideration'.[211] Thus in *Combe v Combe*:[212]

A husband, upon divorce, promised his wife £100 a year as a permanent allowance. In reliance upon this promise, the wife forbore to apply to the Courts for maintenance. The husband failed to make the payments, and the wife sued him on the promise.

The Court of Appeal held that there was no consideration for the promise as the wife's forbearance had not been requested and was not in return for the promise made to her. Nor could the wife rely on promissory estoppel. As Denning LJ explained:[213]

Seeing that the principle [of promissory estoppel] never stands alone as giving a cause of action in itself, it can never do away with the necessity of consideration when that is an essential part of the cause of action. The doctrine of consideration is too firmly fixed to

[207] *Brikom Investments Ltd v Carr* [1979] QB 467, 484–5; *Maharaj v Chand* [1986] AC 898, 908; *Sydenham & Co Ltd v Enichem Elastometers Ltd* [1989] 1 EGLR 257; *Virulite LLC v Virulite Distribution Ltd* [2014] EWHC 366 (QB), [2015] 1 All ER (Comm) 204 at [122]–[125], [141]–[145].

[208] See above, p 123. [209] Below, pp 127–8. [210] *Combe v Combe* [1951] 2 KB 215, 224.

[211] *Brikom Investments Ltd v Carr* [1979] QB 467, 486 (Roskill LJ); *Argy Trading Development Corp Ltd v Lapid Developments Ltd* [1977] 1 WLR 444; *Azov Shipping Co Ltd v Baltic Shipping Co (No 3)* [1999] 2 Lloyd's Rep 159, 175; *Thornton Springer v NEM Insurance Co Ltd* [2000] 2 All ER 489, 516.

[212] [1951] 2 KB 215. See also *Morris v Tarrant* [1971] 2 QB 143, 160; *Argy Trading Development Co Ltd v Lapid Developments Ltd* [1977] 1 WLR 444, 457; *Syros Shipping Co SA v Elaghill Trading Co Ltd* [1980] 2 Lloyd's Rep 390, 393; *Hiscox v Outhwaite (No 3)* [1991] 2 Lloyd's Rep 524, 535.

[213] [1951] 2 KB 215, 220.

be overthrown by a side-wind. Its ill-effects have been largely mitigated of late, but it still remains a cardinal necessity of the formation of a contract, though not of its modification or discharge.

There are similar statements in other cases[214] and, although some decisions are difficult to reconcile with this restriction,[215] the Court of Appeal in *Baird Textile Holdings Ltd v Marks & Spencer plc*[216] has confirmed that promissory, as opposed to proprietary,[217] estoppel cannot create a cause of action. This marks a distinction between the English approach to promissory estoppel and that taken in some other jurisdictions.[218] But it does not mean that promissory estoppel cannot assist a claimant in establishing a cause of action independent of the promise (eg in tort).[219] Nor does it mean that there must be a pre-existing *contractual* relationship: for example, promissory estoppel has been applied to a relationship derived from statute.[220]

If promissory estoppel were to be developed so as to create a cause of action, the question would arise as to the precise 'interest' that the doctrine would be protecting. Contract law has traditionally protected a promisee's expectations of performance. It has sometimes been suggested that, in contrast, promissory estoppel is concerned merely to protect the promisee's reliance. On that approach, traditional contract law with its requirement of consideration and its protection of expectations could happily coexist with promissory estoppel as a cause of action protecting reliance. In *Waltons Stores (Interstate) Ltd v Maher*:[221]

M was in negotiations with W to whom he hoped to lease premises which were to be demolished and redeveloped to W's specifications. Solicitors had been instructed to prepare formal documents and W's solicitors told M's solicitors that 'we believe approval will be forthcoming. Let you know tomorrow if any amendments not agreed to.' Later M submitted a contract and this was sent to W 'by way of exchange'. W did not respond for 2 months because it was privately reconsidering the whole deal and had instructed its solicitors 'to go slow'. Because it believed exchange would take place shortly and because, if the timetable for occupation specified by W was to be met, there was urgency, M started work. Two months later, when he had demolished the old premises and was well advanced with the new premises, W told him it intended to withdraw. M argued *inter alia* that W was estopped from denying that a concluded contract existed.

[214] *Argy Trading Development Co Ltd v Lapid Developments Ltd* [1977] 1 WLR 444, 457; *Syros Shipping Co SA v Elaghill Trading Co* [1981] 3 All ER 189.

[215] *Re Wyvern Developments Ltd* [1974] 1 WLR 1097, 1104, noted by Atiyah (1974) 38 MLR 65; *Pacol Ltd v Trade Lines Ltd, The Henrik Sif* [1982] 1 Lloyd's Rep 456, 466–8.

[216] [2001] EWCA Civ 274, [2002] 1 All ER (Comm) 737.

[217] See *Crabb v Arun* AC [1976] Ch 179, below, p 130.

[218] See especially *Waltons Stores (Interstate) Ltd v Maher* (1988) 164 CLR 387 (Australia).

[219] See Halson [1999] LMCLQ 256.

[220] *Robertson v Minister of Pensions* [1949] 1 KB 227 (soldier and military authorities); *Durham Fancy Goods Ltd v Michael Jackson Fancy Goods Ltd* [1968] 2 QB 839 (statutory liability on director).

[221] (1988) 164 CLR 387. See also ALI *Restatement, Contracts (2d)* para 90; *Harris v Harris* [1989] NZ Conv C 190, 406 (New Zealand). See generally Spence, *Protecting Reliance* (1999).

The majority of the High Court of Australia held that promissory estoppel could found a cause of action and extended to the enforcement of voluntary promises; W was accordingly estopped. The Australian court did not believe this would abolish the doctrine of consideration 'in a backhanded way' because the two protected different interests. The estoppel remedy only seeks to effect the minimum equity needed to avoid the detriment from reliance whereas, where a promise is supported by consideration, the expectations of the promisee are protected even if the promise is entirely executory and there has been no reliance on it.[222]

The step taken in *Walton Stores* has not been taken in England, in part because of the perceived need to protect the doctrine of consideration. For example, in *Johnson v Gore Wood & Co*[223] Lord Goff stated that it was not possible for the test for estoppel by convention—acting on a common assumption—to apply to promises as opposed to existing facts because that would amount to the abandonment of the doctrine of consideration. And in *Baird Textile Holdings Ltd v Marks & Spencer plc*[224] the move to allowing promissory estoppel to be used as a cause of action was not taken even though the claimants confined their claim to damages protecting their reliance interest. However, we have seen that where negotiations have not led to the conclusion of a contract, reliance in the form of the rendering of services or delivery of goods by one party on assumptions created or encouraged by the other may give rise to a restitutionary remedy for the reversal of an unjust enrichment.[225] There are, moreover, examples of reliance generating a contract through unilateral contracts in which promises are rendered legally enforceable by virtue of the performance of an act by the promisee (ie reliance), often where the promisor has not expressly requested the performance of the act[226] and more recently by the recognition that performance of an existing obligation may be a 'practical' benefit.[227] The doctrinal foundations thus exist for it to be held that promissory estoppel is capable itself of creating a cause of action, notwithstanding that the promisee has provided no consideration.[228] It may be that it has not been *necessary* to do so in the cases that have come before the Courts because either a restitutionary remedy could be found or a bargain exchange could be implied. It is, however, arguable that, until this step is taken, it will not be possible to take up the suggestion made by Lord Hailsham LC in 1972 and reduce the sequence of cases based on promissory estoppel to a coherent body of doctrine.[229]

[222] (1988) 164 CLR 387, 406. Cf *Guest v Guest* [2022] UKSC 27, [2024] AC 833 and the split between the majority and minority on the appropriate remedies in proprietary estoppel. See also below, pp 538–41.

[223] [2002] 2 AC 1, 40–1, citing Spencer Bower and Turner, *The Law Relating to Estoppel by Representation* (3rd edn, 1977) 167–8. See also Colman J in *Azov Shipping Co Ltd v Baltic Shipping Co* [1999] 2 Lloyd's Rep 159, 175 and *Thornton Springer v NEM Insurance Co Ltd* [2000] 2 All ER 489, 516.

[224] [2001] EWCA Civ 274, [2002] 1 All ER (Comm) 737.

[225] Above, pp 44, 66, 70 and *Brewer St Investments Ltd v Barclays Woollen Co Ltd* [1954] 1 QB 428.

[226] *Warlow v Harrison* (1858) 1 E & E 309, above, pp 38–9; *Carlill v Carbolic Smoke Ball Co* [1893] 1 QB 256, above, p 40; *Collen v Wright* (1857) 8 E & B 647; *Spiro v Lintern* [1973] 1 WLR 1002; *New Zealand Shipping Co Ltd v Satterthwaite & Co Ltd* [1975] AC 154, 167–8.

[227] Above, pp 111–3.

[228] Thompson [1983] CLJ 257; Lunney [1992] Conv 239.

[229] *Woodhouse AC Israel Cocoa Ltd SA v Nigerian Produce Marketing Co Ltd* [1972] AC 741, 758.

It must be emphasized that the neat division suggested by some[230] between, on the one hand, contract, supported by consideration, protecting expectations and, on the other hand, promissory estoppel protecting reliance does not appear to have been borne out by the promissory estoppel cases. In other words, in several cases the Court has concluded that the minimum equity needed to avoid unconscientiousness will not be satisfied by anything short of enforcing the promise.[231] For instance, the effect of the estoppel in the *High Trees* case would have been to prevent the landlord recovering the full rent between 1940 and 1945, and in *Crabb v Arun DC*[232] (although this is normally viewed as a proprietary estoppel case) the effect of the estoppel was to grant C the right of way the council had undertaken to give him. In *Waltons Stores (Interstate) Ltd v Maher* the effect of the High Court of Australia's ruling that W was estopped from denying that a concluded contract existed appears to have been that M was entitled to damages in lieu of specific performance.[233] In these cases it appears that equitable relief went beyond the protection of reliance.[234]

(c) THREE OTHER TYPES OF ESTOPPEL

Differing views have been expressed by judges as to whether one should regard various similar types of estoppel as underpinned by a single underlying principle. For example, in *Amalgamated Investment & Property Co Ltd v Texas Commerce International Bank Ltd* Lord Denning MR spoke of different estoppels being seen 'to merge into one general principle shorn of limitations'.[235] In contrast, Millett LJ has said, '[the] attempt to demonstrate that all estoppels other than estoppel by record are now subsumed in the single and all-embracing estoppel by representation and that they are all governed by the same requirements has never won general acceptance'.[236] In *Baird Textiles Holdings Ltd v Marks & Spencer plc*[237] the Court of Appeal, while recognizing that estoppel is a flexible concept, accepted that it 'may take different shapes in the context of different fields';[238] and that this made it necessary to continue to distinguish between different estoppels. This has been endorsed by Lord Burrows in *Tinkler v Revenue and Customs Commissioners*: '[a]ttempts have been made over the years to try to unify the various

[230] See, eg, Robertson (1997) 19 Sydney LR 32.

[231] See similarly the judgment of Lord Briggs, for the majority, in *Guest v Guest* [2022] UKSC 27, [2024] AC 833 on proprietary estoppel.

[232] [1976] Ch 179; see below, p 130.

[233] The trial judge's decision to this effect was affirmed by the New South Wales Court of Appeal (1986) 5 NSWLR 407, and the High Court of Australia (1988) 164 CLR 387. Such damages are assessed on the same basis as damages at common law: see below, p 588.

[234] Atiyah, *Essays on Contract* (1986) 239–40; Yorio and Thel (1991) 101 Yale LJ 111. For this debate in the Australian courts, see *Commonwealth of Australia v Verwayen* (1990) 170 CLR 394; *Giumelli v Giumelli* (1999) 196 CLR 101.

[235] [1982] QB 84, 122. More recently, Lewison LJ has said that 'the animating principle of all kinds of estoppel is the prevention of the unconscionable repudiation of promises or assurances': *Morton v Morton* [2023] EWCA Civ 700, [2024] Ch 41 at [44].

[236] *First National Bank v Thompson* [1996] Ch 231, 236.

[237] [2001] EWCA Civ 274, [2002] 1 All ER (Comm) 737.

[238] *Ibid* at [84] (Mance LJ).

estoppels but such unification has proved elusive and the different types of estoppel continue to be seen as having their own particular requirements and effects.'[239]

(i) Proprietary estoppel

Proprietary estoppel arises where a person acts in reasonable reliance and to his or her detriment on the belief that he or she has or will acquire rights in or over the property of another in circumstances in which it is unconscionable for the property owner to deny the rights. Thus, in *Crabb v Arun DC*:[240]

The council built a road along the boundary between its property and C's and gave C a point of access to the road. Later C wished to divide his land and sell off one portion. For this purpose C needed a second point of access and, at a site meeting with officers of the council at which he said he would need access at an additional specified point, he was assured that that would be acceptable to the council. The council subsequently fenced off the boundary and erected gates at the two agreed access points. After C sold the front plot without reserving any right of way from the back plot, the council removed the gates at the access point for the back plot and erected a fence, thus leaving the plot landlocked. It then asked C for £3,000 for a right of access. C sought a declaration claiming that he had a right of way over the second point of access.

The Court of Appeal granted the relief sought. There was no consideration for the council's undertaking and the formality requirements for a contract for the transfer of an interest in land had not been satisfied. But the council, at the meeting and by its conduct in putting up the gates, had led C to believe that he had been or would be granted a right of access at the specified point and it was inequitable for it to insist on its strict title.

Cases on proprietary estoppel have often involved improvements to specific property in the mistaken belief that the improver has or will be given ownership with the owner positively encouraging this detrimental reliance[241] or standing by and acquiescing in it.[242] Not all cases, however, involve such improvements; in some, services were rendered in the belief that ownership would be given.[243] This form of estoppel is narrower than

[239] [2021] UKSC 39, [2022] AC 886 at [28].

[240] [1976] Ch 179, on which see Atiyah (1974) 92 LQR 174; Millett (1974) 92 LQR 342.

[241] *Ramsden v Dyson* (1866) 1 HL 129, 170; *Dillwyn v Llewellyn* (1862) 4 DF & J 517; *Pascoe v Turner* [1979] 1 WLR 431; *Gillett v Holt* [2001] Ch 210. Cf *Blue Haven Enterprises Ltd v Dulcie Ermine Tully* [2006] UKPC 17 (proprietary estoppel not established because the defendant owner did not encourage the claimant's mistaken belief that it would be entitled to the land and hence no unconscionability). See generally Allan (1963) 79 LQR 238; Jackson (1965) 81 LQR 84, 223; Moriarty (1984) 100 LQR 376; Gardner (1999) 115 LQR 353.

[242] *Taylors Fashions Ltd v Liverpool Victoria Trustee Co Ltd* [1982] QB 133, 151–2. See also *A-G of Hong Kong v Humphreys Estates (Queen's Gardens)* [1987] 1 AC 114, 124.

[243] *Tanner v Tanner* [1975] 1 WLR 1346 (property management); *Greasley v Cooke* [1980] 1 WLR 1306 (nursing); *Jennings v Rice* [2002] EWCA Civ 159, [2003] 1 FCR 501 (gardening, shopping, and caring); and *Thorner v Major* [2009] UKHL 18, [2009] 1 WLR 776; *Davies v Davies* [2016] EWCA Civ 463, [2016] 2 P & CR 10; *Habberfield v Habberfield* [2019] EWCA Civ 890 (all work on a farm). Cf *Cobbe v Yeoman's Row Management Ltd* [2008] UKHL 55, [2008] 1 WLR 1752 (obtaining planning permission but proprietary estoppel held not to be made out).

promissory estoppel in requiring detrimental reliance[244] and the belief that a legal right over property[245] has or will be given but broader in not requiring an unequivocal representation and in its ability to create new rights.[246] One reason sometimes given for allowing the creation of new rights is that the legal owner of the property would otherwise be unjustly enriched by getting the benefit of the improved property for nothing. This cannot, however, account for most of the cases. For instance, in *Crabb v Arun DC* the council would not have been unjustly enriched in this way. And even where there has been an unjust enrichment, the remedy for the proprietary estoppel is not concerned to give restitution of the value of that enrichment[247] although there may be a separate claim in the law of restitution.[248] Scarman LJ stated that he did not find the distinction between promissory and proprietary estoppel helpful,[249] but, however tenuous the distinction between the two, they have continued to be treated separately in the subsequent case law.[250]

(ii) Estoppel by convention

When the parties have acted in relation to a transaction upon a shared mistaken[251] assumption (either of fact or law) then, as regards that transaction, each will be estopped against the other from questioning the truth of the facts or of law so assumed where it would be unjust and unconscionable to resile from that shared assumption. In *Amalgamated Investment & Property Co Ltd v Texas Commerce International Bank Ltd*:[252]

AIP negotiated with the TCI bank for a loan to one of its subsidiaries to be secured *inter alia* by a guarantee by AIP. TCI decided to make the loan through Portsoken, a subsidiary company it bought for the purpose, but AIP's guarantee related to *moneys due to you*, ie to loans made by

[244] Detriment is not a narrow or technical concept and need not consist of quantifiable financial detriment so long as it is something substantial: *Gillett v Holt* [2001] Ch 210, 232 (Robert Walker LJ).

[245] *Western Fish Products Ltd v Penwith District Council* [1981] 2 All ER 204, 217. In principle, property should include all forms of property but the cases, while contemplating property in goods, only provide authority for land.

[246] *Baird Textile Holdings Ltd v Marks & Spencer plc* [2001] EWCA Civ 274, [2002] 1 All ER (Comm) 737.

[247] In *Guest v Guest* [2022] UKSC 27 the majority of the Supreme Court held that there is an 'assumption (not presumption) that the simplest way to remedy the unconscionability constituted by the repudiation is to hold the promisor to the promise' (at [75]) whereas the minority thought that the focus should be upon the detriment the representee would suffer if the promise were not kept (eg at [190]).

[248] In *Cobbe v Yeoman's Row Management Ltd* [2008] UKHL 55, [2008] 1 WLR 1752 a quantum meruit for the value of the services in obtaining the planning permission succeeded even though proprietary estoppel was not made out. See Stevens, *The Laws of Restitution* (2023) ch 14.

[249] [1976] Ch 179, 193.

[250] See especially the *Baird Textile* case, above, n 237.

[251] The mistake may be of both parties or of one party acquiesced in by the other: *Republic of India v India Steamship Co Ltd, The Indian Grace (No 2)* [1998] AC 878, 913.

[252] [1982] QB 84, 126, 130; *Lokumal & Sons (London) Ltd v Lotte Shipping Co Pte Ltd* [1985] 2 Lloyd's Rep 28, 34–5 (Kerr LJ); *Hiscox v Outhwaite* [1992] 1 AC 562, 575 (Lord Donaldson MR); *Republic of India v India Steamship Co Ltd, The Indian Grace (No 2)* [1997] 2 WLR 538, 549 (Staughton LJ) and [1998] AC 878, 913 (HL); *The Republic of Serbia v Imagesat International NV* [2009] EWHC 2853 (Comm) at [67]–[71] and [80]–[82]; *Prime Sight Ltd v Lavarello* [2013] UKPC 22, [2014] AC 436 at [29]; *Blindley Heath Investments Ltd v Bass* [2015] EWCA Civ 1023, [2017] Ch 389 at [72]–[102]. The estoppel applies only 'for the period of time and to the extent required by the equity which the estoppel has raised': *Troop v Gibson* (1986) 277 EG 1134, 1144.

TCI. AIP got into financial difficulties and was wound up. TCI had sold property belonging to AIP and applied $750,000 of the proceeds in payment of the outstanding balance of the loan made through Portsoken. AIP's liquidator sought a declaration that AIP was under no liability for loans made by Portsoken, and that TCI had not been entitled to apply the money in this way.

The Court of Appeal held that the guarantee, on its true interpretation, applied to loans by Portsoken, but also stated that even if it did not, AIP was estopped from denying that by an estoppel by convention: both parties had assumed that the guarantee would cover loans by Portsoken. Brandon LJ stated that while a person 'cannot in terms found a cause of action on an estoppel, he may, as a result of being able to rely on an estoppel, succeed on a cause of action on which, without being able to rely on that estoppel, he would necessarily have failed'.[253] In other words, had the TCI bank been suing on the contractual guarantee, the relevant cause of action would have been a standard contractual cause of action: estoppel by convention would have come in not to found the cause of action but to prevent AIP applying an interpretation of the guarantee that was contrary to both parties' understanding and conduct.

The key principles have recently been clarified by the Supreme Court in *Tinkler v Revenue and Customs Commissioners*.[254] That case concerned non-contractual dealings between HMRC and a taxpayer, but Lord Burrows (with whom the other Justices agreed) expressed the view that estoppel by convention did not differ between the contractual and non-contractual contexts.[255] Lord Burrows cited with approval the following influential passage of Briggs J in *Revenue and Customs Commissioners v Benchdollar Ltd*:[256]

> (i) It is not enough that the common assumption upon which the estoppel is based is merely understood by the parties in the same way. It must be expressly shared between them. (ii) The expression of the common assumption by the party alleged to be estopped must be such that he may properly be said to have assumed some element of responsibility for it, in the sense of conveying to the other party an understanding that he expected the other party to rely upon it. (iii) The person alleging the estoppel must in fact have relied upon the common assumption, to a sufficient extent, rather than merely upon his own independent view of the matter. (iv) That reliance must have occurred in connection with some subsequent mutual dealing between the parties. (v) Some detriment must thereby have been suffered by the person alleging the estoppel, or benefit thereby have been conferred upon the person alleged to be estopped, sufficient to make it unjust or unconscionable for the latter to assert the true legal (or factual) position.

It should, however, be borne in mind that, as regards (i), 'something must be shown to have "crossed the line" sufficient to manifest an assent to the assumption'.[257]

253 [1982] QB 84, 132. See also at 122 (Lord Denning MR). Cf at 126 (Eveleigh LJ).
254 [2021] UKSC 39, [2022] AC 886.
255 See too *Musst Holdings Ltd v Astra Asset Management UK Ltd* [2023] EWCA Civ 128 at [61]–[62].
256 [2021] UKSC 39 at [45], citing [2009] EWHC 1310 (Ch), [2010] 1 All ER 174 at [52].
257 *Blindley Heath Investments Ltd v Bass* [2015] EWCA Civ 1023 at [92]; *Tinkler v Revenue and Customs Commissioners* [2021] UKSC 39 at [49]–[50].

(iii) Contractual estoppel

This type of estoppel has been developed in the specific context of the exclusion of liability for misrepresentation by contractual provisions which provide that a party has not made, or the other party has not relied on, a representation.[258] The explanation for why such a 'no reliance' or 'no representation' clause can contradict the truth that the claimant *has relied on a representation* was said by Moore-Bick LJ in *Peekay Intermark Ltd v Australia and New Zealand Banking Group Ltd*[259] to turn on a 'contractual estoppel'. This type of estoppel does not require reliance or detrimental reliance.

It would appear that contractual estoppel can have importance beyond explaining how 'no reliance' or 'no representation' clauses work and can apply more generally to prevent parties denying the existence of a state of affairs which was the basis of their contract. This is most clearly understood from what Moore-Bick LJ said in the *Peekay* case:[260]

> There is no reason in principle why parties to a contract should not agree that a certain state of affairs should form the basis for the transaction, whether it be the case or not. For example, it may be desirable to settle a disagreement as to an existing state of affairs in order to establish a clear basis for the contract itself and its subsequent performance. Where parties express an agreement of that kind in a contractual document neither can subsequently deny the existence of the facts and matters upon which they have agreed, at least so far as concerns those aspects of their relationship to which the agreement was directed. The contract itself gives rise to an estoppel . . .

This makes clear that the scope of contractual estoppel can extend beyond 'no reliance' and 'no representation' clauses and may apply to all situations in which a party has warranted that a certain state of affairs exists. For example, it may be a term of a contract to sell a business that equipment is of a certain age, or that there are no outstanding claims against the business, or that the order books are full. The party providing that warranty cannot then deny that the state of affairs is different than warranted. Indeed one might ask whether there is any need to refer to a contractual estoppel at all since a party denying the state of affairs that it has warranted to be true would be in breach of contract and the other party would be entitled to standard remedies for breach.[261] The fact that one is dealing with breach of a term might explain why, in relation to this type of estoppel, it is irrelevant to consider whether a party relied or detrimentally relied on what was agreed.

If one were seeking to defend the language of estoppel here, one might say that its importance, going beyond the normal consequences of breach of a term, is that it

[258] See below, p 348. See generally Braithwaite (2016) 132 LQR 120; Cockerill [2022] JBL 189.

[259] [2006] EWCA Civ 386, [2006] 2 Lloyd's Rep 511 at [56]–[57]. This was confirmed in *Springwell Navigation Corp v JP Morgan Chase* [2010] EWCA Civ 1221, [2010] 2 CLC 705 at [165]–[169], [177], and in *First Tower Trustees Ltd v CDS (Superstores International) Ltd* [2018] EWCA Civ 1396, [2019] 1 WLR 637 at [47]–[48] (cf at [94]). For a sharp denunciation of the notion of 'contractual estoppel', see McMeel [2011] LMCLQ 185.

[260] [2006] EWCA Civ 386, [2006] 2 Lloyd's Rep 511 at [56].

[261] See the analysis by Andrew Smith J in *Credit Suisse International v Stichting Vestia Groep* [2014] EWHC 3103 (Comm) especially at [309].

explains there being a rule of evidence that the party cannot deny that the state of affairs is different than warranted. The ordinary rules as to breach perhaps cannot explain that rule of evidence. However, a contrary, and probably preferable, view is that the language of estoppel here reflects nothing more than the idea that a party may be prevented by a Court from being in breach of contract and that the concept of a contractual estoppel is unnecessary and unhelpful. Once the court has decided that, as a matter of construction, the relevant term precludes one of the parties from denying the existence of a specified state of facts, then nothing of substance is gained by using the label of 'contractual estoppel'. As Lord Neuberger and Lord Mance observed in *Chen v Ng*:[262]

> ... the description contractual or conventional estoppel may in reality be a confusing misnomer, in circumstances where the parties can (even if there is also reliance on the truth of the agreed proposition) simply be regarded as having committed themselves by contractual term to a particular proposition.

3. APPRAISAL OF CONSIDERATION AND PROMISSORY ESTOPPEL

Attempts have been made to justify the doctrine of consideration on the ground that it is essential both to the form and the substance of a contract. Consideration, it has been argued, is a formal necessity which serves to distinguish those promises by which the promisor intends to be legally bound from those which are not seriously meant: 'buyers intend business where philanthropists may not'.[263] But English law already requires an intent to create legal relations as a distinct element of a contract. Consideration is cogent evidence of the existence of such an intent, but it is by no means conclusive proof that it is present.[264] The abolition of the doctrine would therefore simply mean that the test of contractual intention would assume a greater significance in the law of contract. Few persons would contend that this constituted an insuperable objection to a change in the law,[265] and civil law systems seem to exist quite happily without the need for consideration.[266]

Similarly, aspects of the doctrine, in particular the pre-existing duty rule, have been justified by the need to discourage improper pressure and coercion, a function which might be more directly and effectively served by the recent recognition of economic duress as a ground for avoiding a contract.[267]

It has also been argued that English law has made the choice of enforcing bargains (in the sense of exchanges) rather than promises: 'consideration, offer and acceptance

[262] [2017] UKPC 27 at [30].

[263] Smith and Thomas, *A Casebook on Contract* (2nd edn, 1961) 126.

[264] *Balfour v Balfour* [1919] 2 KB 571; *Coward v Motor Insurers' Bureau* [1963] 1 QB 259; above, pp 72–6.

[265] Cf Atiyah, *Consideration in Contracts: A Fundamental Restatement* (1971).

[266] Lando and Beale, *Principles of European Contract Law Parts I and II* (2000) 140–3; cf Kötz, *European Contract Law* (2nd edn, 2017) ch 4.

[267] Although the law on economic duress is not yet entirely settled: above, pp 113–5; below, Chapter 10.

are an indivisible trinity, facets of one identical notion which is that of bargain'.[268] But this does not explain why it is thought better to enforce bargains.[269] Indeed the opposite appears to be the case. A desire to enforce promises has led the Courts on occasion to find a derisory consideration and to construct a bargain where none in fact was present since there was no real exchange. It has been stated that 'ultimately the question of consideration is a formality as in the use of a seal or the agreement to give a peppercorn'[270] and the recognition that a 'practical' benefit will make a promise enforceable[271] makes it difficult to sustain a purely bargain view of contract. Elsewhere, the absence of consideration may enable one of the parties to 'snap their fingers' at a promise deliberately made, and which the person seeking to enforce it has a legitimate interest to enforce.[272] The perception that this is incompatible with such legitimate interests led to the development of promissory estoppel in the context of the part performance of an existing duty. This development makes it difficult to regard bargain as the fundamental principle of contract. When put together with common law 'waiver',[273] it is arguable that consideration has been effectively confined to the formation of contracts and the error in making it also regulate the discharge of contracts[274] has been substantially corrected.

It has been noted that consideration reflects a variety of policies and serves a number of functions. The doctrine has in the past been the Swiss army knife of the law, performing these functions[275] in an ingenious but imperfect way. Professor Simpson has described the identification and separation of these policies and functions and the development in the last 200 years of new, more targeted doctrines.[276] We now have a doctrine of offer and acceptance, a requirement of intention to create legal relations, a concept of economic duress, and a doctrine of privity of contract. There is considerable force in the conclusion of the Law Revision Committee in 1937,[277] which stated that in many cases consideration was a mere technicality, irreconcilable either with business expediency or common sense. In *Johnson v Gore Wood & Co*[278] Lord Goff stated that although 'the doctrine of consideration may not be very popular nowadays ... [it] still exists as part of our law'. However, it seems likely that the law will slowly develop to confine

[268] Hamson (1938) 54 LQR 233, 234.

[269] It has been said that non-bargain promises are economically sterile (Posner (1977) 6 J Leg Stud 411) and that they should only be enforced if relied upon and only to the extent of the reliance (Eisenberg (1979) 47 U Chi L Rev 1, 3–7).

[270] *Vantage Navigation Corp v Suhail & Saud Bahwan Building Materials Llc, The Alev* [1989] 1 Lloyd's Rep 138, 147 (Hobhouse J).

[271] Above, pp 111–5.

[272] Above, p 107 (pre-existing duty cases) and, albeit in the context of a contract for the benefit of a third party, *Dunlop Pneumatic Tyre Co Ltd v Selfridge & Co Ltd* [1915] AC 847, 855 (Lord Dunedin).

[273] Below, p 472.

[274] Pollock, *Principles of Contract* (12th edn, 1950) 146. See also Kötz, *European Contract Law* (2nd edn, 2017) 63–6.

[275] Above, p 96.

[276] (1975) 91 LQR 247, 263.

[277] Cmd 5449.

[278] [2002] 2 AC 1, 40. See also the wide-ranging judicial examination of consideration (which reads like a law article) by Andrew Phang Boon Leong JA in *obiter dicta* in *Gay Choon Ing v Loh Sze Ti Terence Peter* [2009] SGCA 3, [2009] 2 SLR 332.

the role of consideration to the formation of contracts, supplemented by the principle of promissory estoppel. Promissory estoppel will only come into play where there has been reliance, whereas if there is consideration the expectations of the promisee are protected even if the promise is entirely executory. Although a promissory estoppel can only be raised where there has been reliance, relief may go beyond the protection of that reliance.[279] Such cases are arguably explained as ones in which the Court concluded that unconscientiousness could only be prevented by enforcing the promise or otherwise protecting the promisee's expectations.

FURTHER READING

Atiyah, 'Consideration in Contracts: A Fundamental Restatement' (1971) reprinted (with slight revision) in *Essays on Contract* (Oxford: Clarendon Press, 1986) 179

Atiyah, 'When is an Enforceable Agreement not a Contract? Answer: When it is an Equity' (1976) 92 LQR 174

Millett, 'Crabb v Arun DC—A Riposte' (1976) 92 LQR 342

Treitel, 'Consideration: A Critical Analysis of Professor Atiyah's Fundamental Restatement' (1976) 50 ALJ 439

Burrows, 'Contract, Tort & Restitution—A Satisfactory Division or Not?' (1983) 99 LQR 217, 239–44

Peel, 'Part Payment of a Debt is no Consideration' (1994) 100 LQR 353

O'Sullivan, 'In Defence of Foakes v Beer' [1996] CLJ 219

Cooke, 'Estoppel and the Protection of Expectations' (1997) 17 Legal Studies 258

Halson, 'The Offensive Limits of Promissory Estoppel' [1999] LMCLQ 256

Treitel, *Some Landmarks of Twentieth Century Contract Law* (Oxford: Clarendon Press, 2002) ch 1

Chen-Wishart, 'A Bird in the Hand: Consideration and Promissory Estoppel' in Burrows and Peel (eds), *Contract Formation and Parties* (Oxford: Oxford University Press, 2010) 89

Chen-Wishart, 'In Defence of Consideration' (2013) 13 OUCLJ 209

Chen-Wishart, 'Reforming Consideration: No Greener Pastures' in Degeling, Edelman, and Goudkamp (eds), *Contract in Commercial Law* (Sydney: Thomson Reuters, 2016) 77

[279] Above, p 129.

PART 2

CONTENTS OF THE CONTRACT

5

THE TERMS OF THE CONTRACT

In most cases the contract is composed of a number of contractual terms. This chapter considers the nature and import of those terms. First, terms of a contract will be distinguished from representations, which are statements made by one party to the other that are not intended to be an integral part of the agreement. Similarly, collateral warranties, which are contractually binding although not part of the principal agreement, will be distinguished from representations that are not contractually binding. Secondly, the importance of different types of terms will be examined by reference to the distinction between conditions, warranties, and innominate terms. Thirdly, the chapter will look generally at the interpretation or construction of terms. Finally, the implication of terms into contracts, whether by statute or by the courts, will be explored.

1. TERMS, COLLATERAL WARRANTIES, AND REPRESENTATIONS

(a) TERMS AND REPRESENTATIONS

During the course of negotiations leading to the conclusion of a binding agreement, one or other of the parties may make a statement or give an assurance calculated to produce in the mind of the other party a belief that facts exist which render the proposed bargain advantageous to the interests of the other party. A Court may later have to decide whether this statement or assurance formed part of the contract, or whether it was merely a 'representation', in the sense that the party making it did not undertake to make it good. Although a representation which proves to be false renders the agreement voidable at the suit of the party misled,[1] and may, if made fraudulently or negligently, give rise to a claim for damages, it cannot of itself give rise to an action for breach of contract.[2] Such an action will only lie for breach of a contractual term. The question whether a particular statement is a term of the contract is often difficult.[3]

[1] Below, Chapter 9.
[2] *Behn v Burness* (1863) 3 B & S 751, 753.
[3] Williston (1913) 27 Harv L Rev 1; Atiyah, *Essays on Contract* (1986) 275.

(i) Intention to promise

The primary test is of *contractual intention*: whether there is evidence of an intention by one or both parties that there should be contractual liability in respect of the accuracy of the statement. The key question is: on the totality of evidence, must the person making the statement be taken to have *warranted* its accuracy, that is, promised to make it good?[4] If this intention is shown the Court may construe as a term of the contract a statement or assurance made prior to the final agreement. In *Bannerman v White*:[5]

B offered hops for sale to W. W asked if any sulphur had been used in the treatment of the year's growth, as brewers were refusing hops contaminated with sulphur. B said 'No'. W said that he would not even ask the price if sulphur had been used. They then discussed the price, and W ultimately purchased by sample B's entire growth. After the hops were delivered he repudiated the contract on the ground that the hops contained sulphur. B sued for their price. It was proved that sulphur had been used on five of B's three hundred acres. B had used it for the purpose of trying a new machine, and had either forgotten the matter or thought it unimportant.

Whether W was entitled to reject the hops turned upon whether it was a condition of the agreement that the hops might be rejected if sulphur had been used. It was argued that 'the conversation relating to the sulphur was preliminary to entering on the contract and no part thereof', but the jury found it was understood and intended by the parties to be part of the contract of sale. The Court of Common Pleas upheld this finding, and said that B's assurance was the condition upon which the parties contracted and the breach of it discharged W from liability to take the hops.[6]

That the test is one of the parties' intentions was shown in *Heilbut, Symons & Co v Buckleton*:[7]

B telephoned HS's agent and said 'I understand you are bringing out a rubber company'. The reply was 'We are'. B asked for a prospectus, and was told there were none available. He then asked 'if it was all right', and the agent replied 'We are bringing it out'. On the faith of this, B bought shares which turned out to be of little value. The company was not accurately described as 'a rubber company', although this assurance had not been given in bad faith. B claimed damages for breach of contract.

The House of Lords held that no breach of contract had been committed. There had been merely a representation and no warranty. There was no intention on the part of either or both of the parties that there should be contractual liability in respect of the accuracy of the statement.[8]

[4] *Heilbut, Symons & Co v Buckleton* [1913] AC 30, 50–1.

[5] (1861) 10 CBNS 844. See also *Schawel v Reade* [1913] 2 Ir R 64.

[6] Contrast *Hopkins v Tanqueray* (1854) 15 CB 130, which was probably wrongly decided.

[7] [1913] AC 30, 38, 42, 49–50 (Lord Haldane LC, Lord Atkinson, and Lord Moulton). See also *Independent Broadcasting Authority v EMI Electronics Ltd* (1980) 14 BLR 1, 22–3, 32, 41 (HL) (in respect of a statement made *long* after the contract).

[8] For criticism of the *Heilbut* decision, see Williston (1913) 27 Harv L Rev 1; Greig (1971) 87 LQR 179, Atiyah, *Essays on Contract* (1986) 277–8.

The difficulty of ascertaining intention means that the dividing line between contractual terms and representations is not easy to draw in practice and much turns on the particular facts of a case. For example, in *Oscar Chess Ltd v Williams*,[9] a private seller sold a car to a firm of dealers. He told them that the car was a 1948 model, and the car logbook showed that it had been first registered in 1948. In fact it was a 1939 model. The logbook had been altered by some unknown person. The Court of Appeal held that the seller's statement was not a term of the contract, but merely a representation not giving rise to any action for breach of contract. On the other hand, in *Dick Bentley Productions Ltd v Harold Smith (Motors) Ltd*,[10] a statement made by a motor dealer to a private purchaser, based on a reading of a car's milometer, that the car had done only 20,000 miles, whereas in fact it had done 100,000, was held to be a contractual term. The *Oscar Chess* case was distinguished on the ground that the private seller 'honestly believed on reasonable grounds that [the statement] was true', whereas the motor dealer in *Dick Bentley Productions* 'was in a position to know, or at least to find out the history of the car' but 'stated a fact that should be within his own knowledge. He had jumped to a conclusion and stated it as a fact.'[11]

Courts often take into account a number of factors when ascertaining the parties' intentions, although none is in itself decisive. First, the time between the time of making the statement and the final manifestation of agreement; if the interval is a long one, this points to a representation.[12] Secondly, the importance of the statement in the minds of the parties; a statement which is important is more likely to be classed as a term of the contract.[13] Thirdly, if the statement was followed by the execution of a formal contract in writing, it is more likely to be regarded as merely a representation where it is not incorporated in the written document.[14] Finally, where the maker of the statement is, vis-à-vis the other party, in a better position to ascertain the accuracy of the statement or has the primary responsibility for doing this, the Courts will tend to regard it as a contractual term.[15]

(ii) The influence of wider considerations

The precise place in which the dividing line between representations and terms is drawn may have also been affected by two other factors. The first of these was the distorting effect of the rule that, before the decision of the House of Lords in *Hedley Byrne &*

[9] [1957] 1 WLR 370. Cf *Beale v Taylor* [1967] 1 WLR 1193.

[10] [1965] 1 WLR 623.

[11] [1965] 1 WLR 623, 628, 629.

[12] *Howard Marine and Dredging Co Ltd v A Ogden & Sons (Excavations) Ltd* [1978] QB 574, 591. Cf *Birch v Paramount Estates Ltd* (1956) 167 EG 396.

[13] *Bannerman v White* (1861) 10 CBNS 844. Cf *Oscar Chess Ltd v Williams*, above, n 9.

[14] *Heilbut, Symons & Co v Buckleton* [1913] AC 30, 50. Cf *Miller v Cannon Hill Estates Ltd* [1931] 2 KB 113, and see below, p 142 (collateral warranty).

[15] *Schawel v Reade*, above, n 5; *Dick Bentley Productions Ltd v Harold Smith (Motors) Ltd*, above, n 11. Cf *Heilbut, Symons & Co v Buckleton* [1913] AC 30; *Beale v Taylor* [1967] 1 WLR 1193; *Thake v Maurice* [1986] QB 644 (statement that vasectomy was irreversible not a warranty).

Co Ltd v Heller & Partners Ltd[16] in 1963, damages in tort could not be awarded for negligent misstatement. Parties seeking to escape from this much-criticized feature of English law would often argue that a statement was a warranty.[17] Although damages for negligent misstatement have been available since *Hedley Byrne*, so that the purpose of making the distinction is no longer to determine whether the maker of the statement is liable in damages, there are still differences between damages in tort and contract. Damages for breach of contract do not depend on establishing negligence and the measure of damages for breach of contract differs from that for misrepresentation.[18]

Secondly, in the past it was generally not possible to adduce extrinsic evidence to contradict or vary the terms of a written agreement.[19] This 'parol evidence' rule meant that whatever the intention of the parties and however important the oral statement, it could only exceptionally be held to be a term of the contract. Normally the statement had to be classified as a representation[20] although, as we shall see, it might be classed as a collateral warranty.

(iii) Information provided by a trader to a consumer

The Consumer Rights Act 2015 provides that a consumer contract for the supply of goods, digital content, or services is to be treated as including as a term certain information provided by a trader to a consumer.[21] In practice, this means that most pre-contractual misrepresentations made by a trader to a consumer become terms of the contract between them. For example, in a consumer contract for the supply of services, anything that is said or written to the consumer, by or on behalf of the trader, about the trader or service, which is taken into account by the consumer when deciding to enter into the contract, is to be treated as included as a term of the contract.[22]

(b) COLLATERAL WARRANTIES

Where a preliminary statement or assurance is not a term of the principal agreement the Courts may be prepared to treat it as a contract or 'warranty', collateral to the principal agreement.[23] This device has been used where the principal agreement has been reduced to writing, since the parol evidence rule generally prevented the assurance from constituting a term of that contract. Provided the necessary contractual intention

[16] [1964] AC 465, below, p 343. See also Misrepresentation Act 1967, s 2(1), below, p 344 (non-consumers), and consumers' rights under Part 4 of the Digital Markets, Competition and Consumers Act 2024, below, p 352.

[17] Cf *Heilbut, Symons & Co v Buckleton* [1913] AC 30, 51 and *Esso Petroleum Co Ltd v Mardon* [1976] QB 801, 817.

[18] Below, pp 329–32.

[19] Below, p 148.

[20] For a modern example, see *Lambert v Lewis* [1982] AC 225, 263.

[21] Consumer Rights Act 2015, ss 11–12 (goods contracts), ss 36–37 (digital content contracts), and s 50 (services contracts). The information in question is that specified or mentioned in the Consumer Contracts (Information, Cancellation and Additional Charges) Regulations 2013 (SI 2013 No 3134): see below, p 366.

[22] Consumer Rights Act 2015, s 50.

[23] Wedderburn [1959] CLJ 58.

is present, the assurance can be a collateral contract or warranty conferring a right to damages.[24] Where tenants executed leases upon the oral assurance of the landlord that the drains were in good order,[25] or that the landlord would not enforce a covenant against residing on the premises,[26] the tenant was held entitled to enforce the assurance as a collateral warranty. A statement is more likely to found a warranty where one party refused to enter into a contract unless the other gave it an assurance on a certain point.[27]

In 1913, Lord Moulton said that such collateral warranties are 'viewed with suspicion by the law. They must be proved strictly', and that they 'must from their very nature be rare'.[28] Nevertheless, since that time the Courts have showed themselves much more willing to treat pre-contractual statements as collateral warranties.

In *Esso Petroleum Co Ltd v Mardon*:[29]

Esso found a site on a busy main street which it considered suitable for the erection of a petrol filling station. An experienced employee estimated that the throughput of petrol at the station would reach 200,000 gallons in the third year of operation. But the planning authority refused permission for the forecourt and pumps to be sited on the main street and they had to be sited at the rear of the premises where they were only accessible by side streets. M applied for a tenancy of the filling station. The same experienced employee gave M the same estimate of throughput but failed to take account of the fact that the filling station was now 'back to front'. In reliance on the estimate, M took a 3-year lease of the filling station. Despite his best efforts, the site proved incapable of a throughput of more than 60,000 to 70,000 gallons. In an action by Esso for possession of the station and monies due for petrol supplied, M counterclaimed damages for (inter alia) breach of a collateral warranty.

The Court of Appeal rejected the argument that the estimate could not amount to a warranty because it was a forecast or statement of opinion. It held that the statement as to potential throughput amounted to a collateral warranty—not in the sense that Esso guaranteed that the throughput would reach 200,000 gallons, but a warranty that the forecast had been prepared with reasonable care and skill. Since Esso negligently made 'a fatal error' in the forecast given to M, and on which he took the tenancy, they were liable to him in damages for breach of contract.

This device of a collateral warranty has also been employed where the principal contract is one to which either the person giving, or the person receiving, the assurance is not a party. In *Shanklin Pier Ltd v Detel Products Ltd*:[30]

[24] *Morgan v Griffith* (1871) LR 6 Ex 70; *Frisby v BBC* [1967] Ch 932.

[25] *De Lassalle v Guildford* [1901] 2 KB 215.

[26] *City and Westminster Properties (1934) Ltd v Mudd* [1959] Ch 129.

[27] *Erskine v Adeane* (1873) 8 Ch App 756; *De Lassalle v Guildford* [1901] 2 KB 215; *Couchman v Hill* [1947] KB 554.

[28] *Heilbut, Symons & Co v Buckleton* [1913] AC 30, 47.

[29] [1976] QB 801. Cf *Jonathan Wren & Co Ltd v Microdec plc* (1999) 65 Con LR 157 (Lord Moulton's approach 'applies strongly' where it is sought to make a third party additionally liable for some performance).

[30] [1951] 2 KB 854. See also *Wells (Merstham) Ltd v Buckland Sand & Silica Co Ltd* [1965] 2 QB 170; *Lambert v Lewis* [1982] AC 225, 263.

The owners (B) of Shanklin Pier consulted Detel (A), a firm of paint manufacturers, about painting the pier. Detel told the owners that its paint was suitable for the purpose. Relying on this statement, the owners inserted a term requiring the use of Detel's paint in their agreement with the contractors (C) who were to paint the pier. The paint proved unsuitable and the owners sued Detel for breach of warranty.

The owners were entitled to damages. There was a collateral warranty between the owners (B) and Detel (A), collateral to the purchase of the paint by the contractors (C) from Detel (A). The consideration for A's promise as to the suitability of the paint was B's instruction to C to buy the paint from A. McNair J said:[31]

I see no reason why there may not be an enforceable warranty between A and B supported by the consideration that B should cause C to enter into a contract with A or that B should do some other act for the benefit of A.

This principle is similarly applicable to cases of hire-purchase where a dealer first sells the article to a hire-purchase finance company which then lets it on hire to the hirer. If the dealer gives a warranty, which induces the hirer to enter into the contract of hire, this warranty is enforceable against the dealer by the hirer, even though the actual contract of hire-purchase is not made between them.[32]

(c) EXTRINSIC EVIDENCE

Where an agreement is contained in a written document, the question arises whether extrinsic evidence may be led to establish the existence of a term. It has often been said that 'it is firmly established as a rule of law that parol evidence cannot be admitted to add to, vary or contradict a deed or other written instrument', including a contract,[33] although the 'parol evidence rule' was more favoured in the past than it is now.[34] Its purpose is to promote certainty[35] and to save time in the conduct of litigation;[36] Lord Hobhouse said that the 'rule is one of the great strengths of English commercial law and is one of the main reasons for the international success of English law in preference to laxer systems which do not provide the same certainty'.[37] However, the large number of exceptions to the rule have resulted in uncertainty. We shall see[38] that extrinsic evidence may sometimes be available to assist with the interpretation of a contract. But it is also admissible to prove the existence of a collateral agreement,[39] to establish

[31] [1951] 2 KB 854, 856.

[32] *Andrews v Hopkinson* [1957] 1 QB 229; *Yeoman Credit Ltd v Odgers* [1962] 1 WLR 215.

[33] *Jacobs v Batavia and General Plantations Trust* [4] 1 Ch 287, 295; *Adams v British Airways plc* [1995] IRLR 577, 583.

[34] Law Com No 154, *The Parol Evidence Rule* (1986) paras 2.3–2.4.

[35] *Shore v Wilson* (1842) 9 CL & F 355, 565–6; *Inglis v John Buttery* & Co (1878) 3 App Cas 552, 577.

[36] *Prenn v Simmonds* [1971] 1 WLR 1381, 1384.

[37] *Shogun Finance v Hudson* [2003] UKHL 62, [2004] 1 AC 919 at [49].

[38] Below, pp 162–9.

[39] Above, p 146.

implied terms [40] and, more importantly, if it is shown that the document was not intended to express the entire agreement between the parties.[41] It is also admissible to show that the contract is not operative[42] and to impugn the validity of the contract on the grounds of illegality, misrepresentation,[43] mistake, or duress.

The width of the exceptions led the Law Commission to the view that:

> although a proposition of law can be stated which can be described as the 'parol evidence' rule it is not a rule of law which, correctly applied, could lead to evidence being unjustly excluded. Rather it is a proposition of law which is no more than a circular statement: when it is proved or admitted that the parties to a contract intended that all the express terms in their agreement should be recorded in a particular document or documents, evidence will be inadmissible (because irrelevant) if it is tendered only for the purpose of adding to, varying, subtracting from or contradicting the express terms of that contract.[44]

The Law Commission concluded[45] that there is no *rule of law* precluding the admissibility of evidence solely because a document exists which looks like a complete contract and that there was accordingly no need for legislation to abrogate the supposed rule as it had provisionally recommended in its Working Paper.[46] The presumption that a document which looks like a contract is the whole contract is only a presumption,[47] and, save where the document states that it contains the entire contract,[48] is unlikely to preclude the receipt of evidence of other terms not included expressly or by reference in the document.

Although the traditional description of a parol evidence *rule* may have a lingering influence,[49] the Law Commission's approach has been judicially approved.[50] It is also attractive from a policy point of view. Regarding the issue as governed by a rule of law can have the effect of excluding much evidence of the intentions of the parties without achieving the certainty which the 'rule' aimed to achieve. As Lord Mance has put it, 'the trouble with the parol evidence rule . . . is one is liable to go round in a circle with [it]. If the court finds that . . . all the terms of an agreement have not been reduced to the written document, of course the court is going to let in evidence of other terms.'[51]

40 *Gillespie Bros & Co v Cheney Eggar & Co* [1896] 2 QB 59 (term implied under the Sale of Goods Act 1979); *Hutton v Warren* (1836) 1 M & W 466 (custom).

41 *Mercantile Bank of Sydney v Taylor* [1893] AC 317, 321; *J Evans & Son (Portsmouth) Ltd v Andrea Merzario Ltd* [1976] 1 WLR 1078, 1083.

42 *Pym v Campbell* (1856) 6 E & B 370.

43 *Thomas Witter Ltd v TBP Industries Ltd* [1996] 2 All ER 573, 595.

44 Law Com No 154 (1986), para 2.7. See generally Wedderburn [1959] CLJ 58.

45 Law Com No 154 (1986), para 2.17.

46 Law Com WP No 76 (1976).

47 *Gillespie Bros & Co v Cheney Eggar & Co* [1896] 2 QB 59.

48 Such an entire agreement clause does not operate to exclude a claim for misrepresentation (although it is commonly combined with a separate clause that does exclude misrepresentation): *Axa Sun Life Services Plc v Campbell Martin Ltd* [2011] EWCA Civ 133, [2011] 2 Lloyd's Rep 1. See too below, p 348.

49 eg *AG Securities v Vaughan* [1990] 1 AC 417, 468–9, 475; *Shogun Finance v Hudson* [2003] UKHL 62, [2004] 1 AC 919 (Lord Hobhouse).

50 *Wild v Civil Aviation Authority* (CA, 25 September 1987); *Haryanto (Yani) v ED & F Man (Sugar) Ltd* [1986] 2 Lloyd's Rep 44, 46.

51 *Prince Jefri Bolkiah v State of Brunei Darussalam* [2007] UKPC 63 at [47].

2. CONDITIONS, WARRANTIES, AND INNOMINATE TERMS

(a) INTRODUCTION

In deciding whether a contract can be terminated for breach, or whether the breach merely triggers a right to damages, the Courts have looked at the importance of the term broken as well as the seriousness of the consequences of the breach. This has resulted in the distinction between conditions, warranties, and innominate terms.

One approach, reflected in the Sale of Goods Act 1979,[52] is to classify the term at the time the contract is made as either a condition or a warranty. If the parties regarded the term as essential, it is classified as a *condition*: any breach of a condition gives the innocent party the option of being discharged from further performance of the contract. The innocent party can also claim damages for any loss sustained by the fact that the contract has not been performed. If the parties did not regard the term as essential, but as subsidiary or collateral, it is classified as a *warranty*; its failure gives rise to a claim for such damages as have been sustained by the breach of that particular term, but the innocent party is not given the option of being discharged from further performance. The classification of a term as being either a 'condition' or a 'warranty' will therefore determine the legal remedies available to the innocent party in the event of its breach.

Nevertheless, it is right to observe that the word 'condition' is sometimes used, even in legal documents, to mean simply 'a stipulation, a provision', and does not carry the meaning given to it by lawyers as a term of art. In *LG Schuler AG v Wickman Machine Tool Sales Ltd*:[53]

a contract granted W the sole selling rights of presses manufactured by S. A term of the contract provided that 'it shall be a condition of this agreement' that W send its representative to visit the six largest UK motor manufacturers at least once each week. The majority of the House of Lords held that the term was not a condition and that S was not entitled to terminate the contract when W failed to make the required visits.

No other term in the agreement used the word 'condition', but on an interpretation of the contract as a whole the House of Lords nevertheless found that there was some ambiguity about whether or not 'condition' had been used in its technical sense. This ambiguity was then resolved in favour of W, since the majority[54] thought that it was unlikely that the parties really intended that S should invariably be entitled to terminate the contract if this term was breached. *Schuler* therefore turns on its particular facts. Commercial parties which deliberately chose to use the word 'condition' are generally expected to understand the significance of such language.

[52] See below, p 182.

[53] [1974] AC 235.

[54] Lord Wilberforce forcefully dissented, since he was not prepared to assume 'that both parties to this contract adopted a standard of easygoing tolerance rather than one of aggressive, insistent punctuality and efficiency': *ibid*, 263.

In the context of non-consumer sales, statute has restricted the right of a buyer to reject goods by reason of certain implied conditions if the breach is so slight that it would be unreasonable to reject them.[55] The word 'warranty' is also employed in a variety of senses, and in many of the earlier cases and also in insurance law[56] it is not infrequently used simply to mean a term of the contract, whether a warranty proper or a condition. Whether or not the words 'condition' or 'warranty' are employed in their technical sense must, therefore, depend upon the intention of the parties to be ascertained from their agreement and from the subject-matter to which it relates.

Another approach, often seen as more modern but in fact with older roots,[57] rejects the proposition that every term of a contract can be classified as either a condition or a warranty. On this approach there is a third category of *innominate*[58] (or 'intermediate') terms. The legal consequences of the breach of such a term (ie whether or not the innocent party is entitled to treat itself as discharged) do not follow automatically from a prior classification of the undertaking but depend upon the nature and consequences of the breach.

(b) CONDITIONS

(i) Promissory conditions

A condition may be defined as a promise, as to fact or as to future conduct, which forms an essential term of the contract.[59] If the fact proves untrue, or the promise is not fulfilled, the breach may be treated as a repudiation which entitles the innocent party to be discharged from further performance of the contract.

Behn v Burness[60] is an illustration of a promise as to a fact forming a condition. A ship was stated in the contract to be 'now in the port of Amsterdam'. The fact that the ship was not in the port at the date of the contract discharged the charterer from performance. *Glaholm v Hays*[61] is an example of a promise as to conduct forming a condition:

A charterparty provided that a vessel was to go from England to Trieste and there load a cargo: 'the vessel to sail from England on or before the 4th day of February next'. The vessel did not sail for some days after 4th February. On its arrival at Trieste the charterers refused to load a cargo and treated the contract as repudiated.

[55] Sale of Goods Act 1979, s 15A; below, p 158.

[56] Marine Insurance Act 1906, ss 33–41; *Bank of Nova Scotia v Hellenic Mutual War Risks Association (Bermuda) Ltd* [1992] 1 AC 233.

[57] eg *Freeman v Taylor* (1831) 8 Bing 124, 138. See also *Boone v Eyre* (1779) 1 H Bl 273n; *Davidson v Gwynne* (1810) 12 East 381; *Clipsham v Vertue* (1843) 5 QB 265; *McAndrew v Chapple* (1866) LR 1 CP 643, 648.

[58] So-called because they have 'no name', not being found in the Sale of Goods Act 1893 which codified sales law: see pp 156, 531.

[59] See also below, Chapter 15; English (2021) 137 LQR 630.

[60] (1862) 1 B & S 877, (1863) 3 B & S 751.

[61] (1841) 2 M & G 257. See also *Petrotrade Inc v Stinnes Handel GmbH* [1995] 1 Lloyd's Rep 142, 149.

It was held that the charterers were entitled to be discharged from the contract. The Court of Common Pleas stated:[62]

Whether a particular clause in a charter-party shall be held to be a condition, upon the non-performance of which by the one party, the other is at liberty to abandon the contract, and consider it at an end; or whether it amounts to an agreement only, the breach whereof is to be recompensed by an action for damages, must depend upon the intention of the parties to be collected, in each particular case, from the terms of the agreement itself, and from the subject-matter to which it relates . . . [W]e think the intention of the parties to this contract sufficiently appears to have been, to insure the ship's sailing at the latest by the 4th February, and that the only mode of effecting this is by holding the clause in question to have been a condition precedent; which we consider it to have been.

The idea which underlies the use of the word 'condition' in *Glaholm v Hays* is that the term is so vital to the operation of the contract that its fulfilment by one party is a condition precedent to liability on the part of the other. But a condition also means an essential undertaking in the contract which one party *promises* will be made good. If it is not made good, not only will the other party be entitled to treat itself as discharged, but also *to sue for damages for breach*. A condition is therefore a 'promissory' condition, the breach of which entitles the innocent party to be released from further performance of the contract and to be compensated by damages.

(ii) Non-promissory conditions

It should be stressed that the meaning of condition so far referred to is to be contrasted with another exceptional meaning of condition where the condition is non-promissory. A condition in this sense may be referred to as a 'contingent' condition. For instance, it may be provided that a contract shall not take effect unless or until the condition is fulfilled or that a particular duty under the contract does not become due unless or until the fulfilment of the condition.[63] The existence or enforceability of the contract or the particular obligation is dependent upon the fulfilment of the condition, but there is no guarantee or promise that it will be fulfilled.

The distinction between promissory conditions and the first type of contingent condition was illustrated by Denning LJ in *Trans Trust SPRL v Danubian Trading Co Ltd*[64] when considering a stipulation in a contract of sale of goods which related to the opening by the buyer of a letter of credit[65] in favour of the seller:

What is the legal position of such a stipulation? Sometimes it is a condition precedent to the formation of a contract, that is, it is a condition which must be fulfilled before any contract is concluded at all.[66] In those cases the stipulation 'subject to the opening of a credit' is

[62] (1841) 2 M & G 257, 266, 268.

[63] ALI *Restatement, Contracts (2d)* para 224 provides that a condition is 'an event, not certain to occur, which must occur, unless occurrence is excused, before performance under a contract comes due'.

[64] [1952] 2 QB 297, 304.

[65] See above, pp 120–1.

[66] *Tata Consultancy Services v DBS* [2025] EWCA Civ 380, [2025] 4 WLR 42 at [26].

rather like a stipulation 'subject to contract'.[67] If no credit is provided, there is no contract between the parties. In other cases, a contract is concluded and the stipulation for a credit is a condition which is an essential term of the contract. In those cases the provision of the credit is a condition precedent, not to the formation of a contract, but to the obligation of the seller to deliver the goods. If the buyer fails to provide the credit, the seller can treat himself as discharged from further performance of the contract and can sue the buyer for damages for not providing the credit.[68]

The examples below show that the insertion of a contingent condition may produce one of several effects.[69]

First, it may prevent the formation of any immediately binding contract, as in *Pym v Campbell*[70] where the parties entered into an agreement for the sale and purchase of part of the proceeds of an invention on the express oral understanding that it should not bind them until a third party approved the invention. In such a situation, either party may withdraw from the transaction at any time before the condition is fulfilled.

Secondly, one party may assume an immediate unilateral obligation, say, to sell or to buy from the other, but subject to a condition. In this case, there is a contract from the start imposing a unilateral obligation from which one party cannot withdraw;[71] but no bilateral contract of sale, binding on both parties, comes into existence until the condition is fulfilled.[72] Many options in leases and hire-purchase agreements are of this nature; in such cases the fulfilment of the condition depends on the will of the option holder.

Thirdly, the parties may enter into an immediately binding contract, the operation of which is suspended pending fulfilment of the condition. So, for example, an agreement 'conditional on the seller securing all relevant approvals from the Secretary of State'[73] is a contract from which neither party can resile until it can be definitely ascertained that the condition will not be fulfilled. Alternatively, while the operation of the contract is not suspended, that of a particular obligation under it is. For instance, the obligation of an insurer to pay does not arise until the occurrence of the loss.

In none of these situations does either party render itself liable in damages to the other in the event of non-fulfilment of the condition. Even if, as is often the case, the Court is prepared to imply a term that one of the parties will use all reasonable endeavours to secure fulfilment of the condition, as, for example, where a sale of land is

[67] See above, p 72. The parallel is not an exact one, for in the case of an agreement 'subject to contract' there is no obligation at all, whereas in the case of a contingent condition there may be an implied obligation to facilitate, or not to prevent, the fulfilment of the condition: *Dodd v Churton* [1897] 1 QB 562; *MacKay v Dick* (1881) 6 App Cas 251: *Thompson v ASDA-MFI plc* [1988] Ch 241.

[68] Opening a letter of credit is normally treated as falling within Denning LJ's second category: ie as a promissory, rather than a contingent, condition. See, eg, *UR Power Gmbh v Kuok Oils and Grains Pte Ltd* [2009] EWHC 1940 (Comm), [2009] 2 Lloyd's Rep 495 at [22] (Gross J).

[69] On these effects, see *United Dominions Trust (Commercial) Ltd v Eagle Aircraft Services Ltd* [1968] 1 WLR 74, 82; *LG Schuler AG v Wickman Machine Tool Sales Ltd* [1972] 1 WLR 840, 850–1 (CA), [1974] AC 235 (HL).

[70] (1856) 6 E & B 370. Cf *Haslemere Estates Ltd v Baker* [1982] 1 WLR 1109.

[71] *Smith v Butler* [1900] 1 QB 694.

[72] *United Dominions Trust (Commercial) Ltd v Eagle Aircraft Services Ltd* [1968] 1 WLR 74. Cf *Eastham v Leigh, London & Provincial Properties Ltd* [1971] Ch 871.

[73] *Total Gas Marketing Ltd v Arco British Ltd* [1998] 2 Lloyd's Rep 209, 215, 221.

conditional upon planning permission being obtained,[74] or goods are sold subject to an import or export licence,[75] the fact that the condition is contingent, and not promissory, will prevent any liability from arising if that party's reasonable endeavours prove unavailing. Although non-fulfilment of a contingent condition does not give rise to a claim in damages, non-fulfilment may, when the time has elapsed for its performance, give either party the right to treat the contract as at an end.[76]

The contingent conditions so far considered have been non-promissory conditions precedent; that is, until the condition has been fulfilled the contract is not binding or the contractual duty is not due. Another sense in which the word 'condition' is used is that of a non-promissory condition subsequent. Here the parties agree that the contract is to be immediately binding, but if certain facts are ascertained to exist or upon the happening of a certain event, then either the contract is to cease to bind or one party is to have the option to cancel the contract. In *Brown v Knowsley BC*[77] a contract of employment provided that a temporary teacher's appointment was to last only as long as sufficient funds were provided either by the Manpower Services Commission or other sponsors. It was held that the contract was terminated when such funds ceased to be provided.

(c) WARRANTIES

Breach of a warranty does not entitle the innocent party to treat the contract as repudiated, but only to claim damages. A warranty has been said to be 'an agreement which refers to the subject-matter of a contract, but, not being an essential part of the contract either intrinsically or by agreement, is collateral to the main purpose of such a contract'.[78] The nature of a warranty is illustrated by the case of *Bettini v Gye*:[79]

B contracted with G, the director of the Royal Italian Opera in London, for the exclusive use of his services as a singer in operas and concerts for a period of 3 months. B undertook, inter alia, that he would be in London at least 6 days before the commencement of his engagement, for rehearsals, but only arrived 2 days beforehand. G refused to go on with the contract and was sued by B for breach.

The Court held that, having regard to the length of the contract and the nature of the performances to be given, the rehearsal clause was not vital to the agreement. It was not a condition but merely a warranty. Accordingly its breach did not entitle G to treat the contract as at an end.

[74] *Hargreaves Transport Ltd v Lynch* [1969] 1 WLR 215.

[75] *Re Anglo-Russian Merchant Traders Ltd v John Batt & Co (London) Ltd* [1917] 2 KB 679; *Coloniale Import–Export v Loumidis & Sons* [1978] 2 Lloyd's Rep 560.

[76] *Total Gas Marketing Ltd v Arco British Ltd* [1998] 2 Lloyd's Rep 209, 218, 221, 226. But liabilities which have accrued unconditionally are not discharged: *Kazakstan Wool Processors (Europe) Ltd v Nederlandsche Credietverzekering Maatschappij NV* [2000] 1 All ER (Comm) 708.

[77] [1986] IRLR 102. See also *Gyllenhammer & Partners International Ltd v Sour Brodogradevna Industrija* [1989] 2 Lloyd's Rep 403.

[78] *Dawsons Ltd v Bonnin* [1922] 2 AC 413, 422 (Lord Haldane). See also Sale of Goods Act 1979, s 61(1).

[79] (1876) 1 QBD 183. Cf *Poussard v Spiers* (1876) 1 QBD 410, the condition precedent reasoning in which would surely now be very different following the recognition of innominate terms.

It is reasonable to assume that, in the particular circumstances of *Bettini v Gye*, any breach of the rehearsal clause could have been compensated by damages. But in most cases it would be misleading to conclude that damages would be a sufficient remedy for every breach of even a seemingly unimportant term. The consequences of the breach of such a term might be so serious as to go to the root of the contract. Unless a term has been specifically designated a 'warranty' by statute,[80] or the parties have expressly so provided in their agreement, courts are now unlikely to find that a term is a warranty such that the injured party is only ever entitled to claim damages.

(d) EVALUATION OF THE *AB INITIO* CLASSIFICATION OF TERMS

The dominant approach of the Courts in the 70 years following the enactment of the Sale of Goods Act in 1893 was to classify terms *ab initio* as conditions or warranties. The one clear and obvious advantage in this approach is that of certainty.[81] At least in commercial transactions it is important that parties (or their legal advisers) should be able to know, immediately and unequivocally, what their rights are in the event of a breach by the other party, and to make their decision accordingly. If the term broken is a condition, it will be known with certainty that the breach entitles the innocent party to terminate the contract forthwith.

This certainty is particularly important where the contract is one of a 'string' of contracts under which B buys goods from A and then sells them to C who in turn sells them to D. 'Members of the "string" will have many ongoing contracts simultaneously and they must be able to do business with confidence in the legal results of their actions.'[82] Certainty as to whether there is a right to terminate the contract is also important in cases where it would be difficult for the innocent party to quantify the loss suffered and therefore difficult for the Court to assess damages for a breach of the contract.[83]

On the other hand, the advantage of certainty has to be weighed against the need to reach a fair and just decision in individual cases. Since *any* breach of condition gives rise to a right of termination, the innocent party can refuse to perform the contract even though the breach is trivial in nature, and even though little or no loss has been suffered as a result. For example, it is a condition of a cif contract for the sale of goods that the goods must be shipped within the shipment period specified in the contract. If the goods are shipped one day later—or even earlier[84]—than the specified shipment period, the buyer is entitled to treat the contract as repudiated and to reject the goods, notwithstanding that the breach has caused no loss. A party may seek to rely on such a trivial breach of condition to get out of a contract which has proved unprofitable,

[80] Sale of Goods Act 1979, ss 12(2), (4), (5), and (5A) and 61(1); Supply of Goods (Implied Terms) Act 1973, s 8(1)(b), (2), and (3).

[81] *The Mihalis Angelos* [1971] 1 QB 164, 205; *A/S Awilco of Oslo v Fulvia SpA, The Chikuma* [1981] 1 WLR 314, 322; *Bunge Corp v Tradax Export SA* [1981] 1 WLR 711, 718, 720, 725.

[82] *Bunge Corp v Tradax Export SA* [1981] 1 WLR 711, 720 (Lord Lowry).

[83] *Ibid.*

[84] *Bowes v Shand* (1877) 2 App Cas 455.

perhaps because of changes in the market.[85] It has been said that 'in principle contracts are made to be performed and not to be avoided according to the whims of market fluctuation and where there is a free choice between two possible constructions . . . the Court should tend to prefer that construction which will ensure performance, and not encourage avoidance of contractual obligations'.[86] Moreover, in the context of non-consumer sales, statute has restricted the right of a buyer to reject goods by reason of certain implied conditions if the breach is so slight that it would be unreasonable to reject them.[87]

(e) INNOMINATE TERMS

The distinction between 'conditions' and 'warranties', which placed considerable emphasis on *ab initio* classification of the quality of the term broken, fell out of favour during the 1960s. Greater emphasis has been given to a more flexible test with roots in older authorities which bases the right of termination on the gravity of the consequences of the breach.[88]

In *Hongkong Fir Shipping Co Ltd v Kawasaki Kisen Kaisha Ltd*, Diplock LJ said:[89]

> There are, however, many contractual undertakings of a more complex character which cannot be categorised as being 'conditions' or 'warranties' . . . Of such undertakings all that can be predicated is that some breaches will and others will not give rise to an event which will deprive the party not in default of substantially the whole benefit which it was intended he should obtain from the contract; and the legal consequences of a breach of such undertaking, unless provided for expressly in the contract, depend upon the nature of the event to which the breach gives rise and do not follow automatically from a prior classification of the undertaking, as a 'condition' or a 'warranty'.

The charterers of a ship argued that the shipowners' obligation to provide a seaworthy vessel was a condition, any breach of which entitled them to treat themselves as discharged. The Court of Appeal rejected this contention. The undertaking as to seaworthiness was not a condition, but an *innominate* term. Breach of such a term would not give rise to a right to treat the charterparty as repudiated unless the conduct of the shipowners, and the actual or anticipated consequences of the breach, were so serious as to frustrate the commercial purpose of the venture. As Upjohn LJ explained:[90]

[85] *Arcos Ltd v Ronaasen & Son Ltd* [1933] AC 470.

[86] *Cehave NV v Bremer Handelsgesellschaft mbH* [1976] QB 44, 71 (the rejected goods were later bought by the same buyers at a lower price and used for the same purpose). See also *Reardon Smith Line Ltd v Hansen-Tangen* [1976] 1 WLR 989.

[87] Sale of Goods Act 1979, s 15A, below, p 158.

[88] Above, p 151, n 57.

[89] [1962] 2 QB 26, 70. For the facts of this case, see below, p 519. See also *Hardwick Game Farm v Suffolk Agricultural Poultry Producers' Assn* [1966] 1 WLR 287, 341, aff'd [1969] 2 AC 31. See further Reynolds (1963) 79 LQR 534; Lord Devlin [1966] CLJ 192.

[90] [1962] 2 QB 26, 62.

Why is this apparently basic and underlying condition of seaworthiness not, in fact, treated as a condition? It is for the simple reason that the seaworthiness clause is breached by the slightest failure to be fitted 'in every way' for service . . . If a nail is missing from one of the timbers of a wooden vessel or if proper medical supplies or two anchors are not on board at the time of sailing, the owners are in breach of the seaworthiness stipulation. It is contrary to common sense to suppose that in such circumstances the parties contemplated that the charterer should at once be entitled to treat the contract as at an end for such trifling breaches.

Where a failure of performance is not a breach of condition, but of an innominate term, the right of the innocent party to treat itself as discharged from further performance will depend upon the gravity of the consequences of the breach. Those consequences must be judged at the time of the innocent party's purported termination taking into account what has happened and what is likely to happen.[91] The expressions used to describe the circumstances that justify discharge, are discussed in the chapter on Discharge for Breach.[92] A test frequently applied is whether the failure of performance is such as to deprive the innocent party of substantially the whole benefit which it was intended that it should obtain as the consideration for the performance of its own undertakings.[93] In the *Hongkong Fir* case, which concerned a two-year charterparty, the ship was off hire because of unseaworthiness for all but eight and a half weeks in the first seven months of the charter, but the charterer was held not to be entitled to treat the contract as discharged. Accordingly, in many cases, the innocent party may have to 'wait and see' how serious the consequences of the breach turn out to be.

(f) DISTINGUISHING INNOMINATE TERMS AND CONDITIONS

Whether a term will be classified as a condition depends in part on the Court 'making what is in effect a value judgement about the commercial significance of the term in question.'[94] A term is most likely to be classified as innominate if, as in the *Hongkong Fir* case, it is capable of being broken either in a manner that is trivial and capable of remedy by an award of damages or in a way that is so fundamental as to undermine the whole contract. The modern approach appears to be that any term of a contract will be classified as an innominate term, and not as a condition, unless the Court concludes that it falls within one of the following situations:

(i) Categorization as condition by statute

In non-consumer contracts for the supply of goods,[95] the Sale of Goods Act 1979[96] and the Supply of Goods (Implied Terms) Act 1973[97] expressly define certain implied

[91] *Ampurius Nu Homes Holdings Ltd v Telford Homes (Creekside) Ltd* [2013] EWCA Civ 577, [2013] 4 All ER 377 especially at [44] and [64].

[92] See below, Chapter 15.

[93] *Hongkong Fir Shipping Co Ltd v Kawasaki Kisen Kaisha Ltd* [1962] 2 QB 26, 66; see also below, p 531. Cf CISG art 25.

[94] *State Trading Corp of India Ltd v M Golodetz Ltd* [1989] 2 Lloyd's Rep 277, 283 (Kerr LJ).

[95] In consumer contracts for the supply of goods, the Consumer Rights Act 2015 avoids reference to conditions, warranties, or innominate terms: see below, p 157.

[96] See below, pp 182–8.

[97] See below, p 188.

obligations in contracts of sale of goods or hire-purchase as being 'conditions' or 'warranties'. There can be no doubt that such classification is binding. But in *Cehave NV v Bremer Handelsgesellschaft mbH*[98] the Court of Appeal rejected the argument that the Sale of Goods Act created a statutory dichotomy which divided *all* terms in contracts of sale of goods into conditions and warranties and held that an express term 'shipment to be made in good condition' was an innominate term the breach of which had to be so serious as to go to the root of the contract in order to entitle the buyer to reject the goods.

Section 15A of the Sale of Goods Act provides that, in non-consumer cases, if 'the breach is so slight that it would be unreasonable for [the buyer] to reject [the goods]', then the buyer can only claim damages and cannot reject the goods.[99] In effect, this comes close to treating conditions as innominate terms where the buyer is not dealing as a consumer.

(ii) Categorization as condition by judicial decision

A particular term may have been categorized as a condition by a previous judicial decision. For example, stipulations in a voyage charterparty as to the time at which the chartered vessel is expected to be ready to load,[100] and stipulations in a cif contract for the sale of goods as to the time within which the goods must be shipped[101] or a letter of credit opened,[102] have been held to be conditions, any delay in which entitles the other party to treat itself as discharged.

However, it has been said that a number of previous decisions on such terms are 'excessively technical'[103] and may be open to re-examination. So, for example, although the traditional view is that stipulations in a time charterparty as to the date by which hire is to be paid is a condition,[104] more recently the Court of Appeal has held that a failure to pay the hire of a charterparty punctually was not a breach of a condition,[105] and that a term in a bareboat charterparty requiring the charterer to keep up to date the vessel's classification status and certificates is also an innominate term, not a condition.[106]

(iii) Express designation in contract

The parties may have expressly provided in their contract either that a particular term is to be a condition (in the technical sense)[107] or that the consequences of its non-performance by one party are to be that the other party is to have the right to treat itself as discharged.

98 [1976] QB 44. See also *Tradax International SA v Goldschmidt* [1977] 2 Lloyd's Rep 604.

99 This provision was inserted by the Sale and Supply of Goods Act 1994. The best known case where s 15A would probably now change the result is *Arcos Ltd v Ronaasen & Son* [1933] AC 470 (where a contract was terminated for breach of condition since the timber provided was nine-sixteenths of an inch thick rather than half an inch thick), but much depends on how 'so slight' is interpreted. For the equivalent provisions for contracts of hire-purchase, work and materials, and hire, see the Supply of Goods (Implied Terms) Act 1973, s 11A, and the Supply of Goods and Services Act 1982, ss 5A and 10A.

100 *The Mihalis Angelos* [1971] 1 QB 164.

101 *Bowes v Shand* (1877) 2 App Cas 455.

102 *Ian Stach Ltd v Baker Bosley Ltd* [1958] 2 QB 130.

103 *Reardon Smith Line Ltd v Yngvar Hansen-Tangen* [1976] 1 WLR 989, 998 (Lord Wilberforce).

104 *Mardorf Peach & Co Ltd v Attica Sea Carriers Corp of Liberia* [1977] AC 850.

105 *Spar Shipping AS v Grand China Logistics Holding (Group) Co Ltd* [2016] EWCA Civ 982, [2016] 2 Lloyd's Rep 447. Outside the mercantile context, see *Valilas v Januzaj* [2014] EWCA Civ 436, [2015] 1 All ER (Comm) 1047.

106 *ARK Shipping Co LLC v Silverburn Shipping (IoM) Ltd* [2019] EWCA Civ 1161, [2019] 2 Lloyd's Rep 603.

107 Cf *LG Schuler AG v Wickman Machine Tool Sales Ltd* [1974] AC 235.

A stipulation expressly stating the time of performance is 'of the essence of the contract' is an example of this.[108] Again, stating that a party 'guarantees' to obtain approval within a specified period has been held to indicate that the term is a condition.[109]

(iv) Implication from nature of contract, subject-matter, or circumstances

Finally, if the nature of the contract or the subject-matter or the circumstances of the case lead to the conclusion that the parties must, impliedly, have intended that the innocent party would be discharged from further performance of its obligations in the event that a particular term was not fully and precisely complied with, that term will be held to be a condition.[110] This is more likely to be the case in single-performance contracts and contracts requiring the performance of particular acts at specified times and in sequence. It is less likely to be the case where the contract is for performance over a long term[111] when substantial performance may have been rendered by the contract-breaker before breach and where the term is of a broad and loose nature. A term is also likely to be held to be a condition where adherence to it is fundamental to the transaction in the sense that it cannot proceed without it and where the term is not one which admitted to different types of breach. So, for example, a stipulation in a conditional sale agreement that the seller was at the date of the agreement the owner of the item sold has been held to be a condition.[112] If a term would otherwise be an innominate term, a party cannot (absent an express term permitting it) unilaterally turn it into a condition. For example, serving a written notice to complete in a contract for the sale of land does not make 'time of the essence'.[113]

In *Bremer Handelsgesellschaft mbH v Vanden Avenne-Izegem PVBA*[114] a term in a contract for the sale of United States soya bean meal required the sellers to advise the buyers 'without delay' of impossibility of shipment by reason of a prohibition of export. The House of Lords held it to be an innominate term, since it did not establish any definite time limit within which the advice was to be given. Other provisions in the same contract, which took effect upon a number of events impeding performance and which established a timetable of fixed periods within which the occurrence was to be notified, an extension of time claimed, and the buyer was to have the option of cancelling the contract, were held to be conditions. Punctual compliance with these stipulations was required as part of a 'complete regulatory code'.

In *Bunge Corporation v Tradax Export SA*,[115] another case which concerned a contract for the sale of soya bean meal:

[108] *United Scientific Holdings Ltd v Burnley BC* [1978] AC 904, 923, 937, 944; below, pp 438–9. Cf *Samarenko v Dawn Hill House Ltd* [2011] EWCA Civ 1445, [2013] Ch 36.

[109] *BS & N Ltd v Micado Shipping Ltd (Malta)* [2001] 1 Lloyd's Rep 341, 349–50.

[110] *United Scientific Holdings Ltd v Burnley BC* [1978] AC 904, 937, 941, 944, 950, 958; *Bremer Handelsgesellschaft mbH v Vanden Avenne-Izegem PVBA* [1978] 2 Lloyd's Rep 109, 133; *Bunge Corp v Tradax Export SA* [1981] 1 WLR 711, 716, 717, 720, 729.

[111] *LG Schuler AG v Wickman Machine Tool Sales Ltd* [1974] AC 235; *Decro-Wall SA v Practitioners in Marketing Ltd* [1971] 1 WLR 361.

[112] *Barber v NWS Bank plc* [1996] 1 WLR 641. Such a condition would otherwise be *implied* by the Sale of Goods Act 1979, s 12, below, p 169.

[113] *Urban 1 (Blonk Street) Ltd v Ayres* [2013] EWCA Civ 816, [2014] 1 WLR 756 at [44].

[114] [1978] 2 Lloyd's Rep 109.

[115] [1981] 1 WLR 711. Cf *Universal Bulk Carriers Ltd v Andre et Cie SA* [2001] EWCA Civ 588, [2001] 2 Lloyd's Rep 65 (provision that laydays to be narrowed not a condition).

The sellers were required, by 30 June 1975, to load the goods on board ship at a single United States Gulf port to be nominated by them. The contract further provided that the buyers should give to the sellers 'at least 15 consecutive days' notice of probable readiness of vessel(s) and of the approximate quantity required to be loaded'. The buyers did not give that notice until 17 June, by which time less than 15 days of the loading period remained. The sellers declared the buyers in default and claimed damages for repudiation of the contract on the ground that the term as to notice was a condition.

The House of Lords held that the term, though not expressly stated in the contract to be a condition, was one by implication, so that its breach entitled the sellers to treat themselves as discharged. In general, time was of the essence in mercantile contracts, and in particular in this case where the sellers needed the information to know which loading port they should nominate, so as to ensure that the goods would be available for loading on the ship's arrival at that port before the end of the loading period.

(g) LOSS OF THE RIGHT OF DISCHARGE

(i) Waiver and affirmation

Where one party has been guilty of a breach of condition, the other party need not necessarily treat itself as discharged. Compliance with the condition can be waived by the innocent party[116] and the contract can be enforced as if it had been omitted. Alternatively, if the innocent party has knowledge of the breach, it can elect to affirm the contract and only claim damages, which are available as a remedy in any event.

These general principles of the law of contract were given statutory force in relation to contracts of sale of goods by section 11(2) of the Sale of Goods Act 1979:

> Where a contract of sale is subject to a condition to be fulfilled by the seller, the buyer may waive the condition, or may elect to treat the breach of the condition as a breach of warranty and not as a ground for treating the contract as repudiated.

(ii) 'Acceptance' and substantial benefit

Affirmation is voluntary; but an innocent party may, in certain other circumstances, lose the right to discharge the contract for breach of a condition. For example, an innocent party who has taken a substantial benefit under the contract may sometimes be precluded from opting to be discharged by reason of a breach of condition, and have to sue for damages only.[117] In non-consumer contracts for the sale of goods,[118] the Sale of Goods Act 1979 also provides that a buyer cannot treat the contract as repudiated for breach of condition where the goods which are the subject-matter of the sale have been 'accepted'. By section 11(4) of the Act:[119]

[116] Provided that it is exclusively for its own benefit and not for the benefit of both parties.

[117] *Graves v Legg* (1854) 9 Exch 709, 717; *Pust v Dowie* (1865) 5 B & S 33; *Behn v Burness* (1862) 1 B & S 877; (1863) 3 B & S 751.

[118] Different rules apply to a consumer contract by reason of the Consumer Rights Act 2015, Part 1.

[119] The terms 'condition' and 'warranty' are used in the Act in the senses given above; see Sale of Goods Act 1979, ss 11(3), 61(1).

where a contract of sale is not severable and the buyer has accepted the goods or part of them, the breach of a condition to be fulfilled by the seller can only be treated as a breach of warranty, and not as a ground for rejecting the goods and treating the contract as repudiated, unless there is an express or implied term of the contract to that effect.

Two points require explanation. First, the word 'accept' in the phrase 'and the buyer has accepted the goods' bears a technical meaning. The buyer is deemed to have accepted the goods when he intimates to the seller that he has accepted them, or when the goods have been delivered and the buyer does any act in relation to them which is inconsistent with the ownership of the seller, or when after the lapse of a reasonable time the buyer retains the goods without intimating to the seller that the goods have been rejected.[120] There is no mention of any requirement that the buyer should *know* of the breach of condition before losing the right to reject although, in the case of an intimation of acceptance or an act inconsistent with the seller's ownership, 'acceptance' will not be deemed to have taken place unless and until the buyer has had a reasonable opportunity of examining the goods for the purpose of ascertaining whether they are in conformity with the contract[121] or the buyer has retained the goods during the lapse of a reasonable time without intimating to the seller that he is rejecting them.[122] The availability of a reasonable opportunity of examining goods is a material factor in determining whether a 'reasonable' time has elapsed.[123] Where the buyer has the right to reject goods by reason of a defect that affects all or some of them but accepts some of the goods the right to reject the rest is not lost by that partial acceptance.[124]

Secondly, acceptance does not necessarily have this effect if the contract is severable, for example, if delivery of the goods is to be made by instalments which are to be separately paid for. In such a case section 31(2) of the Sale of Goods Act 1979 provides that where 'the seller makes defective deliveries in respect of one or more instalments, or the buyer neglects or refuses to take delivery of or pay for one or more instalments, it is a question in each case depending on the terms of the contract and the circumstances of the case whether the breach of contract is a repudiation of the whole contract or whether it is a severable breach giving rise to a claim for compensation but not to a right to treat the whole contract as repudiated'.

The right of the innocent party to treat itself as discharged may therefore be lost either voluntarily or as the result of the operation of a rule of law.

(h) PART 1 OF THE CONSUMER RIGHTS ACT 2015

Part 1 of the Consumer Rights Act 2015, applicable to contracts made on or after 1 October 2015, deals with the rights of consumers under consumer contracts for the supply of goods, digital content, or services.[125] The Act does not label certain terms as

120 Sale of Goods Act 1979, s 35, as amended by the Sale and Supply of Goods Act 1994.

121 Sale of Goods Act 1979, s 35(2).

122 Sale of Goods Act 1979, s 35(4). See *Clegg v Olle Andersson* [2003] EWCA Civ 320, [2003] 1 All ER (Comm) 721; *J & H Ritchie Ltd v Lloyd Ltd* [2007] UKHL 9, [2007] 1 WLR 670.

123 Sale of Goods Act 1979, s 35(5).

124 Sale of Goods Act 1979, s 35A(1).

125 For the previous law, which applies to contracts made before 1 October 2015, see the 29th edition of this work at Chapter 5.

conditions or warranties or lay down an innominate term approach. Instead the contract is treated as including certain terms[126] and the right of the consumer to 'discharge' the contract for breach of those terms by the trader is laid down in the Act.[127] Although the practical effect is much the same as if, for example, terms as to the quality of goods were 'conditions', that terminology is not used.

3. INTERPRETATION OF TERMS

This section deals briefly with certain general principles which govern the interpretation (otherwise referred to as the construction) of terms which have been reduced to writing.[128] The interpretation of a written contract is always a matter of law for the Court to determine.[129]

(a) THE OBJECTIVE AND CONTEXTUAL APPROACH

The professed aim of the Court in interpreting a written contract is to discover the mutual intention of the parties.[130] The old approach to construction was that, subject to ambiguity[131] and to some other exceptions (eg the meaning of technical terms, or the avoidance of manifest absurdity[132] or of a very obvious drafting mistake),[133] words were to be interpreted literally—according to their plain meaning—without reference to extrinsic evidence of the background.[134]

In contrast, the modern approach, articulated by Lord Hoffmann in *Investors Compensation Scheme Ltd v West Bromwich Building Society*[135] is that one should always interpret a contract objectively in its context. He said: 'Interpretation is the ascertainment of the meaning which the document would convey to a reasonable person having all the background which would reasonably have been available to the parties in the situation in which they were at the time of the contract.'[136]

126 See below, p 189.

127 See especially Consumer Rights Act 2015, ss 19–20 and 42 which uses the terminology of 'treating the contract as at an end' and not 'discharge'. By s 19(13) 'treating a contract as at end means treating it as repudiated'. In general, by s 42, there is no such right in relation to a consumer contract for digital content.

128 See generally Calnan and Davies, *Principles of Contractual Interpretation* (3rd edn, 2026).

129 The interpretation of oral contracts is a question of fact, which raises different issues; the boundary between interpretation and implication may be more blurred in the context of oral agreements: see, eg, *Wells v Devani* [2019] UKSC 4, [2020] AC 129; Davies [2025] LMCLQ 64.

130 *Pioneer Shipping Ltd v BTP Tioxide* [1982] AC 724, 736; *International Fina Services AG v Katrina Shipping Ltd* [1995] 2 Lloyd's Rep 344, 350.

131 *Shore v Wilson* (1842) 9 Cl & Fin 355, 365 (Tindal CJ).

132 *Abbott v Middleton* (1858) 7 HLC 68, 69; *River Wear Commissioners v Adamson* (1877) 2 App Cas 743, 746–7 (Lord Blackburn).

133 *Homburg Houtimport BV v Agrosin Private Ltd, The Starsin* [2004] 1 AC 715; *Littman v Aspen Oil (Broking) Ltd* [2005] EWCA Civ 1579, [2006] 2 P & CR 2; *Dalkia Utilities Services plc v Celtech International Ltd* [2006] EWHC 63 (Comm), [2006] 1 Lloyd's Rep 599.

134 *Shore v Wilson* (1842) 9 Cl & Fin 355, 365; *Lovell and Christmas Ltd v Wall* (1911) 104 LT 85, 88 (Cozens-Hardy MR).

135 [1998] 1 WLR 896. This contextual approach was heralded by Lord Wilberforce's speeches in *Prenn v Simmonds* [1971] 1 WLR 1381 and *Reardon Smith Line Ltd v Yngvar Hansen-Tangen* [1976] 1 WLR 989.

136 [1998] 1 WLR 896, 912.

He went on to explain that, subject to exceptions (considered below), the background includes 'absolutely anything [relevant] which would have affected the way in which the language of the document would have been understood by a reasonable man';[137] that the literal meaning may be overridden, even though there is no ambiguity, because the background makes clear that 'the parties must ... have used the wrong words or syntax';[138] and that 'the law does not require judges to attribute to the parties an intention which they plainly could not have had'.[139]

This modern objective and contextual approach is thought to be more likely to reflect the parties' intentions than the literal approach. 'The background should be used to elucidate the contract, and not to contradict it.'[140] However, it has been criticized[141] as giving rise to greater uncertainty and as increasing the costs of litigation because more material has to be considered both by the Courts and those advising the parties about their contractual rights and duties. A contextual approach can also produce greater difficulties for third parties who may be assigned the benefit of the contract and yet may be unfamiliar with the background against which the contract was concluded. This concern for third parties lies behind the majority's view in *Cherry Tree Investments Ltd v Landmain Ltd*[142] that the Courts should be more cautious about using background material when interpreting a contract in a public document (in the case itself, a registered legal charge) rather than an ordinary contract.

In the *Investors Compensation Scheme* case:

A number of investors had been given negligent advice and had claims (in tort or for breach of statutory duty) against their financial advisers, building societies and solicitors. A central scheme was set up by the Securities and Investment Board to ensure compensation was paid to the investors. To be entitled to compensation under that scheme, investors concluded a contract of assignment with the Investors Compensation Scheme (the claimant) whereby they assigned to the ICS their claims against their advisers, building societies and solicitors subject to a clause excluding from the assignment 'Any claim (whether sounding in rescission for undue influence or otherwise)' against a building society which would abate sums otherwise owed to that society. In an action by the ICS against the defendant building society, the central question was whether that clause meant that the investors had retained (ie had not assigned) their rights to claim damages, as well as rescission, against the building societies.

The House of Lords held that the right to claim rescission had been retained but that the right to claim damages had been validly assigned. The exclusion from assignment clause, 'Any claim (whether sounding in rescission for undue influence or otherwise)' was interpreted as if it had read, 'Any claim sounding in rescission (whether for undue

[137] *Ibid.* The inclusion of the word 'relevant' reflects the qualification made by Lord Hoffmann in *Bank of Credit & Commerce International v Ali* [2001] UKHL 8, [2001] 1 AC 251 at [39].

[138] [1998] 1 WLR 896, 913.

[139] *Ibid.* Lord Hoffmann here referred to Lord Diplock's reference to 'business commonsense' in *Antaios Compania Naviera SA v Salen Rederierna AB* [1985] AC 191, 201. See also *Lord Napier and Ettrick v R Kershaw Ltd (No 2)* [1999] 1 WLR 756, 763 (Lord Steyn).

[140] *Contra Holdings Ltd v Bamford* [2023] EWCA Civ 374, [2023] 2 All ER (Comm) 683 at [31].

[141] eg Staughton [1999] CLJ 303; Berg (2006) 122 LQR 354; Calnan, in Burrows and Peel (eds), *Contract Terms* (2007) ch 2.

[142] [2012] EWCA Civ 736, [2013] Ch 305 (per Longmore and Lewison LJJ, Arden LJ dissenting).

influence or otherwise).' This construction meant that only claims for rescission, *and not for damages*, against the building societies were excluded from the assignment. Lord Lloyd dissented, insisting that:[143]

> such a construction does violence to the language. I know of no principle of construction ... which would enable the court to take words from within the brackets, where they are clearly intended to underline the width of 'any claim,' and place them outside the brackets where they have the exact opposite effect. As Leggatt LJ said in the Court of Appeal, such a construction is simply not an available meaning of the words used; and it is, after all, from the words used that one must ascertain what the parties meant.

An acceptance of the modern objective and contextual approach leaves open precisely how much weight is to be given to the words used as against other relevant factors including commercial common sense. This balancing exercise is always a matter of judgement, and reasonable people (and judges) regularly differ in the conclusions they reach.[144]

In *Rainy Sky SA v Kookmin Bank*,[145] in applying what Lord Hoffmann had said in *Investors Compensation Scheme*, the Supreme Court indicated that, in a commercial context, where there is more than one plausible meaning, the commercially more sensible meaning is to be preferred. Lord Clarke said: 'if the language is capable of more than one construction, it is not necessary to conclude that a particular construction would produce an absurd or irrational result before having regard to the commercial purpose of the agreement.'[146] And earlier his Lordship said: 'The language used by the parties will often have more than one potential meaning ... If there are two possible constructions, the court is entitled to prefer the construction which is consistent with business common sense and to reject the other.'[147]

However, commercial common sense was downplayed in the leading decision of *Arnold v Britton*:[148]

> Leases of holiday chalets included a term that the lessee pay to the lessor a service charge for 'the yearly sum of Ninety Pounds and value added tax (if any) for the first Year of the term hereby granted increasing thereafter by Ten Pounds per Hundred for every subsequent year'.

At the time of the proceedings, the annual service charge for these chalets was over £2,700—the increase resulting from the effect of 10 per cent annual compound interest over many years. Despite the amount of the service charge increasing exponentially,

[143] [1998] 1 WLR 896, 904. See too the decision of the Court of Appeal: [1997] CLC 348, 368. In *Sara & Hossein Asset Holdings Ltd v Blacks Outdoor Retail Ltd* [2023] UKSC 2, [2023] 1 WLR 575 Lord Briggs similarly dissented on the basis that the contractual language could not bear the majority's interpretation (which, oddly, had been contended for by neither side).

[144] *Al Mana Lifestyle Trading LLC v United Fidelity Insurance Co PSC* [2023] EWCA Civ 61, [2023] 1 CLC 310 at [63].

[145] [2011] UKSC 50, [2011] 1 WLR 2900.

[146] *Ibid* at [43].

[147] *Ibid* at [21].

[148] [2015] UKSC 36, [2015] AC 1619, especially at [14]–[23].

Lord Neuberger was not prepared to invoke broader notions of 'common sense' to depart from the clear meaning of the contractual language.[149]

In *Wood v Capita Insurance Services Ltd*,[150] Lord Hodge, giving the judgment of the Supreme Court, said: 'On the approach to contractual interpretation, the *Rainy Sky* and *Arnold* cases were saying the same thing.'[151] This may be thought a surprising observation given that the focus of the former case was on the importance of the commercial purpose and the emphasis in the latter was on the words used. This was recognized by Lord Sumption, writing extra-judicially after the decision in *Wood v Capita*,[152] who noted a shift in judicial approach: following *Arnold v Britton*, 'the Supreme Court has begun to withdraw from the more advanced positions seized during the Hoffmann offensive'.[153]

On the facts of the *Wood* case:

The seller of a company agreed to indemnify the buyer for compensation the company was required to pay customers who had made 'claims or complaints' about insurance mis-selling prior to the purchase of the company. A scheme agreed by the Financial Services Authority (FSA) included compensation for mis-selling prior to the buyer's purchase of the company.

The Supreme Court held that the indemnity clause did not apply because that compensation did not arise from 'claims or complaints' by customers but from a review instigated by reason of information from 'whistleblowers' employed by the company. This might be considered rather a 'literalist' approach but the Supreme Court regarded it as crucial that there were also time-limited warranties given by the seller to the buyer in the purchase contract and the indemnity had to be interpreted with those warranties in mind.

Lord Hodge adopted a similar approach in *National Commercial Bank Jamaica Ltd v NCB Staff Association (Jamaica)*.[154] He relied upon the prominent trilogy of Supreme Court decisions—*Rainy Sky*, *Arnold v Britton*, and *Wood v Capita*—as having set out the key principles of interpretation, highlighting 'the unitary but iterative task of interpreting a contract'.[155] In summarizing the principles,[156] Lord Hodge emphasized that a court must not depart from the natural meaning of words just because the contractual arrangement has turned out to be a bad bargain for one of the parties, and that it is an important factor whether the contract was professionally drafted. More weight may be put on the contractual language rather than factual matrix when a document has been carefully drafted by sophisticated lawyers, but even in those circumstances there may have been a failure of communication between the parties which could prompt the Court to be place greater weight on background factors.

Perhaps the most controversial aspect of Lord Hoffmann's restatement was his exclusion from the admissible background of evidence of the previous negotiations of the parties.[157] That traditional exclusionary rule was said to rest on 'reasons of practical

[149] Compare the dissent of Lord Carnwath.
[150] [2017] UKSC 24, [2017] AC 1173.
[151] *Ibid* at [14].
[152] [2017] OUCLJ 301.
[153] Sumption [2017] OUCLJ 301, 313.
[154] [2024] UKPC 2.
[155] *Ibid* at [31].
[156] *Ibid* at [32].
[157] [1998] 1 WLR 896, 913. See also *Prenn v Simmonds* [1971] 1 WLR 1381. Less controversially he also excluded 'declarations of subjective intent'.

policy'.[158] Despite powerful criticism by numerous commentators,[159] that exclusion was confirmed, after a detailed examination, by the House of Lords in *Chartbrook Ltd v Persimmon Homes Ltd*:[160]

A dispute arose about how much was payable under a property development agreement by the developers (Persimmon) to the landowners (Chartbrook). This turned on the meaning of the term 'additional residential payment'. The developers argued that, on the true construction of the contract, they owed only £897,051. The owners argued that, on the true construction of the contract, they were owed £4,484,862.

The House of Lords held that the smaller sum was due because, although the owners' construction was 'in accordance with conventional syntax',[161] it made 'no commercial sense'.[162] Applying the approach in *Investors Compensation Scheme*, this was a case where the background made it clear that something must have gone wrong with the language used.

Although finding for the developers, the House of Lords rejected their argument that one should look at the pre-contractual negotiations which, the developers argued, made it plain that the developers' interpretation was the correct one. Lord Hoffmann gave the leading speech. He accepted that to allow such evidence did not contradict the objective theory of interpretation,[163] but considered that evidence of pre-contractual negotiations was usually irrelevant. Even if relevant, admitting it would create greater uncertainty in deciding disputes of interpretation, would add to the cost of advice, litigation, or arbitration, and it would not be easy to distinguish aspiration from provisional agreement. Overall, there was no clearly established case (and no empirical evidence) to justify the House of Lords departing from the long-established rule. He also pointed out that there were two legitimate 'safety nets'—rectification[164] and estoppel by convention—which would in most cases prevent injustice.[165]

Lord Hoffmann further recognized that pre-contractual negotiations may be taken into account in establishing that a background fact was known to the parties.[166] In *Reardon Smith Line v Yngvar Hansen-Tangen* Lord Wilberforce similarly noted that pre-contractual material could be used to establish 'the genesis of the transaction'.[167]

[158] [1998] 1 WLR 896, 913.

[159] McLauchlan (2000) 19 NZULR 147; McMeel (2003) 119 LQR 272; Lord Nicholls (2005) 121 LQR 577. Cf Berg (2006) 122 LQR 354.

[160] [2009] UKHL 38, [2009] 1 AC 1101. [161] *Ibid* at [11]. [162] *Ibid* at [16].

[163] *Ibid* at [33]. He referred, at [40], to the argument that admitting such evidence prejudices third parties who may, eg, take an assignment of the contract. He accepted, however, that while admitting it would increase the risk for third parties, the same point about prejudicing third parties can be made about the admissibility of any form of background material.

[164] The House of Lords, had they not reached the conclusion they did on construction, would have granted rectification to reach the same result: see below, pp 284–90.

[165] [2009] UKHL 38, [2009] 1 AC 1101 at [47].

[166] It will be rare that a dispute on interpretation will turn on whether the parties did or did not know a particular background fact but where pre-contractual negotiations are admissible under this exception they can include even 'without prejudice' pre-contractual negotiations: *Oceanbulk Shipping and Trading SA v TMT Asia Ltd* [2010] UKSC 44, [2011] 1 AC 662.

[167] [1976] 1 WLR 989, 995–6.

Following some equivocation,[168] it appears now to have been established that the focus is on the genesis or purpose of the contract as a whole, rather than one particular provision.[169] However, as Leggatt LJ recognized in *Merthyr (South Wales) Ltd v Merthyr Tydfil CBC*, 'there may be borderline cases in which the line between referring to previous communications to identify the "genesis and aim of the transaction" and relying on such evidence to show what the parties intended a particular provision in a contract to mean may be hard to draw'.[170]

Although not specifically mentioned by Lord Hoffmann in the *Investors Compensation Scheme* case, it is also clearly established that the subsequent conduct of the parties may not be used as an aid to interpretation of a written contract. This has been said to be because subsequent conduct is equally referable to what the parties intended to agree as to the meaning of what they in fact agreed[171] and because 'otherwise one might have the result that a contract meant one thing on the day it was signed, but by reason of subsequent events meant something different a month or a year later'.[172] This exclusion is also controversial.[173] In any event, subsequent conduct may be used to show that a contract exists,[174] that there has been a variation of its terms or an estoppel or a waiver,[175] as well as to construe an oral, rather than a written, contract.[176]

(b) PARTICULAR RULES OF INTERPRETATION

While all 'rules' of interpretation must now be read in the light of the modern objective and contextual approach set out in the *Investors Compensation Scheme* case,[177] there are certain 'rules' that can be usefully set out.

(1) Words susceptible of two meanings should be given the meaning which will make the instrument valid rather than void or ineffective.[178] Where a guarantee was expressed to be given to the claimants 'in consideration of your *being* in advance', it was argued that this showed a past consideration; but the Court held that the words might mean a prospective advance, and be equivalent to 'in consideration of your *becoming* in advance', or '*on condition* of your being

[168] Compare *Investec Bank (Channel Islands) Ltd v Retail Group Plc* [2009] EWHC 476 (Ch) at [76] (Sales J) and *Excelsior Group Productions Ltd v Yorkshire Television Ltd* [2009] EWHC 1751 (Comm) at [25] (Flaux J).

[169] *Merthyr (South Wales) Ltd (FKA Blackstone (South Wales) Ltd) v Merthyr Tydfil County Borough Council* [2019] EWCA Civ 526 at [41]–[61] (Leggatt LJ).

[170] *Ibid* at [55].

[171] *Schuler AG v Wickman Machine Tool Sales Ltd* [1974] AC 235, 261, 263.

[172] *Whitworth Street Estates (Manchester) Ltd v James Miller & Partners Ltd* [1970] AC 583, 603.

[173] The exclusion of such evidence has been rejected in New Zealand: *Wholesale Distributors Ltd v Gibbons Holdings Ltd* [2007] NZSC 37.

[174] *Whitworth Street Estates (Manchester) Ltd v James Miller & Partners Ltd* [1970] AC 583; *Wilson v Maynard Shipbuilding Consultants AG Ltd* [1978] QB 665.

[175] Above, p 122; below, p 472.

[176] *Maggs v Marsh* [2006] EWCA Civ 1058, [2006] BLR 395.

[177] In Lord Hoffmann's words, 'Almost all the old intellectual baggage of "legal" interpretation has been discarded': [1998] 1 WLR 896, 912.

[178] *Verba ita sunt intelligenda ut res magis valeat quam pereat*: Bac Max 3.

in advance'.[179] So strong is this rule in favour of supporting the document that, in suitable cases, the Court is prepared to restrict the written words to those applicable in the agreement, supply obvious omissions, and to transpose or even reject words and phrases if the intention of the parties is clear.

(2) 'An agreement ought to receive that construction which its language will admit, which will best effectuate the intention of the parties, to be collected *from the whole of the agreement*, and greater regard is to be had to the clear intent of the parties than to any particular words which they may have used in the expression of their intent.'[180] The proper mode of interpretation is to take the instrument as a whole, to ascertain the meaning of words and phrases from their general context, and to try and give effect to every part of it.[181]

(3) '[G]reater weight should attach to terms which the particular contracting parties have chosen to include than to pre-printed terms probably devised to cover very many situations to which the particular contracting parties have never addressed their minds.'[182]

(4) Where there is an express mention in the instrument of a certain thing, this will tend to exclude any other thing of a similar nature: *expressio unius est exclusio alterius*.[183] So where a conveyance was made of an iron foundry and two houses, together with the fixtures in the houses, the fixtures in the foundry were held not to pass even though they otherwise would have done so.[184]

(5) The meaning of general words may be narrowed and restrained by specific and particular descriptions of the subject-matter to which they are to apply. Thus in construing a charterparty, where liability to deliver cargo was excluded if through 'war, disturbance, or any other cause' it was not possible to do so, it was held that the words 'any other cause' were restricted to events of the same kind as war and disturbance, and so excluded ice.[185] But this rule (the so-called *ejusdem generis* rule) is again only a canon of construction for the purpose of ascertaining what may be presumed to have been the meaning and intention of the parties to the contract. It is therefore subordinate to the parties' real intention and does not control it. It will have no application if the parties can be shown to have intended a different interpretation to be given to the language which they have used.

[179] *Haigh v Brooks* (1839) 10 A & E 309; *Steele v Hoe* (1849) 14 QB 431.

[180] *Ford v Beech* (1848) 11 QB 852, 866 (Parke B).

[181] *Ex antecedentibus et consequentibus fit optima interpretatio*: 2 Co Inst 317; *Barton v Fitzgerald* (1812) 15 East 529, 541.

[182] *Homburg Houtimport BV v Agrosin Private Ltd, The Starsin* [2003] UKHL 12, [2004] 1 AC 715 at [11] (Lord Bingham).

[183] Co Litt 210a.

[184] *Hare v Horton* (1833) 5 B & Ad 715.

[185] *Tillmanns v SS Knutsford* [1908] 2 KB 385, aff'd [1908] AC 406; *Thorman v Dowgate Steamship Co Ltd* [1910] 1 KB 410.

(6) The words of written documents are interpreted more forcibly against the party putting forward the document.[186] This is based on the ideas that a party putting forward the wording of a proposed agreement may be assumed to have looked after its own interests, is responsible for ambiguities in its own expression, and has no right to induce another to make a contract on the supposition that the words mean one thing, and then to argue for a construction by which they would mean another thing, more to its advantage.[187] However, there is ambiguity as to whether the phrase '*contra proferentem*' means 'against the person who drew it up' or 'against the person relying on it'. Moreover, in the light of the modern approach in the *Investors Compensation Scheme* case, it is unclear whether a '*contra proferentem*' rule is still needed, at least in relation to commercial contracts negotiated between parties of equal bargaining power.[188]

(7) The Court of Appeal has stated that if one is to exclude a condition implied under the Sale of Goods Act 1979, one must use words which expressly (or perhaps necessarily) refer to conditions.[189] This appears to be an application of the 'intellectual baggage' in older cases which Lord Hoffmann stated has been discarded. One would expect that, if given the opportunity, the Supreme Court will depart from this 'rule'.

(8) By section 69 of the Consumer Rights Act 2015, 'if a term in a consumer contract ... could have different meanings, the meaning that is most favourable to the consumer is to prevail'. It is clear that this is a class-protection measure that goes beyond the common law approach to interpretation.[190]

4. IMPLIED TERMS

(a) TERMS IMPLIED BY THE COURTS AND BY STATUTE

Terms which the parties have not themselves inserted may be implied into a contract. In some cases, in particular contracts for the sale and supply of goods and services,[191] contracts of employment, and contracts between landlord and tenant, terms are implied by statute. In the absence of statutory provision the cases in which the Courts will imply

[186] *Verba chartarum fortius accipiuntur contra proferentem*: Bac Max 3. See below, pp 191–2.

[187] *Tan Wing Chuen v Bank of Credit and Commerce Hong Kong Ltd* [1996] 2 BCLC 69, 77 (Lord Mustill).

[188] *Transocean Drilling UK Ltd v Providence Resources plc* [2016] EWCA Civ 372, [2016] 2 All ER (Comm) 606; *Impact Funding Solutions Ltd v Barrington Support Services Ltd* [2016] UKSC 57, [2017] AC 73. Cf McCunn (2019) 39 OJLS 483.

[189] *KG Bominflot Bunkergesellschaft für Mineralöle v Petroplus Marketing AG, The Mercini Lady* [2010] EWCA Civ 1145, [2011] 1 Lloyd's Rep 442. Cf *Air Transworld Ltd v Bombadier Inc* [2012] EWHC 243 (Comm), [2012] 1 Lloyd's Rep 349.

[190] Albeit that, in the past, *contra proferentem* interpretation may have produced the same results.

[191] But in a consumer contract for the supply of goods, digital content, or services, the Consumer Rights Act 2015 does not refer to implied terms. Instead the terminology used is of a term treated as included in the contract.

a term into a contract are strictly limited: it is not their task to make contracts for the parties concerned, but only to interpret the contracts already made.[192] Nevertheless, in certain circumstances the Courts are prepared to imply terms, even into written contracts. After all, 'life is too short to negotiate contract terms designed to cover every contingency that may occur'.[193]

A distinction has developed between two broad categories of case where terms are implied by the Courts. First, terms implied 'in fact' into a particular contract. Such terms are not implied just because it would be reasonable to do so, but only where it is necessary to give business efficacy to the contract or where it is obvious that the term was meant to have been included. Terms implied in fact give effect to the intention of the parties gleaned from the express terms of the agreement and the surrounding circumstances.[194]

Secondly, terms can be implied 'at law' into particular *types* of contract. Common types of contract include sale, carriage, landlord and tenant, and employment, where the parties may have left a lot unsaid. In such cases, when the Court implies a term, it is sometimes laying down a general rule that in all contracts of a defined type some provision is to be implied as an incident of that particular type of contractual relationship unless the parties have expressly excluded it. It is somewhat artificial to attribute such terms to the intention of the parties;[195] terms are implied at law because they are necessary to give effect to broader considerations.[196] A similar process takes place where a term is implied by a trade custom.[197]

(b) TERMS IMPLIED BY THE COURTS

(i) 'Necessary for business efficacy' and the 'officious bystander'

Where the parties do not incorporate into their contract terms which they would certainly have inserted to complete their agreement, the Courts may, in order to give 'business efficacy' to the transaction, imply such terms. But such implication must be necessary to reflect the parties' intention.

In *The Moorcock*,[198] a shipowner and the owner of a jetty contracted to allow a steamship to be discharged, loaded, and moored at the jetty. The ship was grounded and damaged at low tide. The Court of Appeal held that the parties must have intended to contract on the basis that the owner of the jetty had taken reasonable care to ascertain that the riverbed was safe for the vessel at low tide and therefore a term would be implied to that effect. The defendants were liable for breach of this implied term.

[192] *Phillips Electronique Grand Publique SA v BSB Ltd* [1995] EMLR 472, 481 (Sir Thomas Bingham MR).

[193] *Barton v Morris* [2023] UKSC 3, [2023] AC 684 at [127] (Lord Leggatt).

[194] *Luxor (Eastbourne) Ltd v Cooper* [1941] AC 108, 137; *Shell UK Ltd v Lostock Garages Ltd* [1976] 1 WLR 1187, 1196; *Associated Japanese Bank (International) v Crédit du Nord SA* [1989] 1 WLR 255, 263.

[195] *Liverpool City Council v Irwin* [1977] AC 239, 253–4, 257–8; *Shell UK Ltd v Lostock Garages Ltd* [1976] 1 WLR 1187, 1196; *Scally v Southern Health and Social Services Board* [1992] 1 AC 294, 306–7.

[196] Peden (2001) 117 LQR 459.

[197] Below, p 177.

[198] (1889) 14 PD 64.

Bowen LJ said:

Now, an implied warranty, or, as it is called, a covenant in law, as distinguished from an express contract or express warranty, really is in all cases founded on the presumed intention of the parties, and upon reason. The implication which the law draws from what must obviously have been the intention of the parties, the law draws with the object of giving efficacy to the transaction and preventing such a failure of consideration as cannot have been within the contemplation of either side . . . In business transactions such as this, what the law desires to effect by the implication is to give such business efficacy to the transaction as must have been intended to all events by both parties who are business men . . .[199]

The principle in *The Moorcock* is applied where, without the implied term, the contract will not be workable. In *Tesco Stores Ltd v Union of Shop, Distributive and Allied Workers* Lord Leggatt provided the following summary:[200]

Properly understood, Bowen LJ's famous statement of the law describes a more analytical approach. The first step is to identify, from one or more express terms of the contract construed in their factual setting, a relevant contractual purpose. The question then is whether the implication of a term is necessary to give effect to that purpose and prevent it from being defeated. Any term implied must be both strictly necessary and no wider than is necessary [to] give the contract such efficacy. It must also, of course, be consistent with the express terms of the contract.

A term may also be implied if it was so obviously a stipulation in the agreement that it goes without saying that the parties must have intended it to form part of their contract. This test, which often overlaps with the business efficacy test,[201] is applied by asking whether, if an officious bystander were to suggest some express provision for a matter in the agreement, the parties would testily suppress him with a common 'Oh, of course!'[202] Such an implication will only be made if the Court is satisfied that both parties would, as reasonable persons, have agreed to the term had it been suggested to them, so that the differing commercial motives of the parties will often preclude this type of implication.[203] Significantly, the test 'is not concerned with the hypothetical answer of the actual parties, but with that of notional reasonable people in their position at the time of contracting.'[204]

[199] *Ibid*, 68. Cf *Easton v Hitchcock* [1912] 1 KB 535.

[200] [2024] UKSC 28, [2025] ICR 107 at [106].

[201] eg *Ali SS Corp v Shipyard Trogir* [1999] 1 WLR 314, 326 (Potter LJ); *Codelfa Construction Pty Ltd v State Railway Authority of New South Wales* (1982) 149 CLR 337, 347 (High Court of Australia); *Lymington Marina Ltd v MacNamara* [2007] EWCA Civ 151, [2007] 2 All ER (Comm) 825 at [37], [44].

[202] *Shirlaw v Southern Foundries (1926) Ltd* [1939] 2 KB 206, 227 (MacKinnon LJ). See also *Reigate v Union Manufacturing Co (Ramsbottom) Ltd* [1918] 1 KB 592, 605 (Scrutton LJ); *Liverpool City Council v Irwin* [1977] AC 239, 254; *Equitable Life Assurance Society v Hyman* [2002] 1 AC 408 (implication to give effect to reasonable expectations).

[203] *Luxor (Eastbourne) Ltd v Cooper* [1941] AC 108; *Attica Sea Carriers Corp v Ferrostaal Poseidon Bulk Reederei GmbH* [1976] 1 Lloyd's Rep 250; *Liverpool City Council v Irwin* [1977] AC 239, 266; *Hughes v Greenwich LBC* [1994] 1 AC 170, 179.

[204] *Tesco Stores Ltd v Union of Shop, Distributive and Allied Workers* [2024] UKSC 28, [2025] ICR 107 at [102]. As Lord Leggatt pointed out, *ibid*, '[t]his may account for why judges sometimes imagine the officious bystander answering the relevant question rather than posing it to the parties (as the original version of the test envisages)'.

Clearly, however, the Court will be reluctant to make such an implication where the parties have entered into a carefully drafted written contract containing detailed terms agreed between them[205] or where the contract is particularly novel or risky.[206] It must be possible to formulate the term with a sufficient degree of precision, and without over-complication and artificiality,[207] and the term to be implied must not be inconsistent with the express terms of the contract.[208]

A difficult example is provided by the decision of the Supreme Court in *Barton v Morris*:[209]

Barton made two attempts to purchase Nash House from Foxpace, but both transactions fell through. Barton lost £1.2m in forfeited deposits. Barton and Foxpace then agreed that if Barton introduced to Foxpace a purchaser who bought Nash House for £6.5m, Foxpace would pay Barton £1.2m. Barton subsequently found a purchaser who agreed to pay Foxpace £6.5m, but during the conveyancing process potential problems developing the land were discovered. As a result, Foxpace agreed to reduce the price, and sold Nash House for £6 million.

The majority of the Supreme Court held that Foxpace only had to pay Barton anything if the property sold for £6.5m. As a result, Barton could not recover anything. The minority (Lord Leggatt and Lord Burrows) thought that Foxpace only had to pay Barton £1.2m if the property sold for £6.5m—but that would not exclude an obligation to pay an alternative sum if the sale price was lower. On the latter approach, there was scope to imply a term that a reasonable sum must be paid if one party introduces to the other a purchaser and the sale goes through.[210] But this was simply not possible on the majority's approach: such an implied term would have been inconsistent with the express term agreed by the parties.

In any event, the term to be implied must be reasonable.[211] But this does not mean that a term will be implied merely because it would be reasonable to do so,[212] or because it would improve the contract[213] or make its performance more convenient.[214] It must be necessary to imply such a term: 'The touchstone is always necessity and not merely

[205] *Shell UK Ltd v Lostock Garages Ltd* [1976] 1 WLR 1187, 1200. See also *Yorkshire Water Services Ltd v Sun Alliance & London Insurance plc* [1997] 2 Lloyd's Rep 21.

[206] *Phillips Electronique Grand Publique SA v BSB Ltd* [1995] EMLR 472, 482–3 (Sir Thomas Bingham MR).

[207] *Ibid*, 497; *Luxor (Eastbourne) Ltd v Cooper* [1941] AC 108, 117 (Viscount Simon LC); *Ashmore v Corporation of Lloyds (No 2)* [1992] 2 Lloyd's Rep 620, 626–9. But note that the term implied may involve a flexible criterion such as to take 'reasonable' care.

[208] *Duke of Westminster v Guild* [1985] QB 688, 700; *Johnstone v Bloomsbury HA* [1992] 1 QB 333, 347, 350.

[209] [2023] UKSC 3, [2023] AC 684.

[210] This is probably implied at common law, although it is arguable that such a term is implied under s 15 of the Supply of Goods and Services Act 1982: see *ibid* at [42] (Lord Leggatt), cf [41] (Lady Rose), [213] (Lord Burrows). See too *Wells v Devani* [2019] UKSC 4, [2020] AC 129, considered above, p 65.

[211] *Young & Marten v McManus Childs Ltd* [1969] 1 AC 454, 465; *Liverpool City Council v Irwin* [1977] AC 239, 262.

[212] *Reigate v Union Manufacturing Co (Ramsbottom) Ltd* [1918] 1 KB 592, 598; *Liverpool City Council v Irwin* [1977] AC 239.

[213] *Trollope & Colls Ltd v NW Metropolitan Regional Hospital Board* [1973] 1 WLR 601, 609.

[214] *Russell v Duke of Norfolk* [1949] 1 All ER 109.

reasonableness.'[215] For example, where parties to a contract are subject to the rules of a regulatory body there is no need to imply those rules into the contract.[216]

In *AG of Belize v Belize Telecom Ltd*[217] Lord Hoffmann, giving the opinion of the Privy Council, offered a reappraisal of the approach to implying terms.[218] Lord Hoffmann stressed that the implication of a term is an exercise in the construction of the instrument as a whole so that the central question for the Court is whether the implication 'would spell out in express words what the instrument, read against the relevant background, would reasonably be understood to mean'.[219] He considered that what he had said about interpreting a contract in *Investors Compensation Scheme Ltd v West Bromwich Building Society*[220] applied by parity of reasoning to the implication of a term. 'There is only one question: is that what the instrument, read as a whole against the relevant background, would reasonably be understood to mean?'[221] It followed that the tests traditionally put forward of, for example, business efficacy and the 'officious bystander' should be viewed as merely overlapping ways in which the Courts 'have tried to express the central idea that the proposed implied term must spell out what the contract actually means or in which they have explained why they did not think that it did so'.[222] It was dangerous and incorrect to detach those tests from that underlying objective. In Lord Hoffmann's words, 'There are dangers in treating these alternative formulations of the question as if they had a life of their own'.[223]

Lord Hoffmann's recasting of the law was characteristically bold, but must now be read in the light of the Supreme Court's judgment in *Marks and Spencer plc v BNP Paribas Services Trust Company (Jersey) Ltd*.[224] A business tenant had exercised its right to terminate a commercial lease under a 'break clause'. The question was whether a term should be implied into the lease entitling the tenant to repayment of an apportioned part of the rent and charges for the period between the termination of the lease and the end of the quarter for which the rent and charges had been paid. In deciding that no such term should be implied, the majority of the Supreme Court stated that Lord Hoffmann's judgment in *Belize* did not change the law and should not be interpreted as loosening the traditional restrictive approach to implying terms by fact.[225] In particular, a term should not be implied on the basis that it is reasonable to do so. The traditional tests of business necessity and obviousness were reaffirmed. The Supreme Court also stressed that there is a difference between interpreting the express terms and deciding whether

[215] *Liverpool City Council v Irwin* [1977] AC 239, 266 (Lord Edmund-Davies). See also *Equitable Life Assurance Society v Hyman* [2002] 1 AC 408, 459; *Mediterranean Salvage & Towage v Seamar Trading and Commerce Inc* [2009] EWCA Civ 531, [2009] 2 Lloyd's Rep 639 (no implied term that nominated berth was safe); Bryan and Ellinghaus (2000) 22 Syd L Rev 636, 644 ('objective necessity').

[216] *Clarion Ltd v National Provident Institution* [2000] 1 WLR 1899, 1896.

[217] [2009] UKPC 10, [2009] 1 WLR 1988: see McCaughran [2011] CLJ 607; Hooley [2014] CLJ 315.

[218] Although the facts of the case concerned the articles of association of a company, the principles are equally applicable in the law of contract generally.

[219] [2009] UKPC 10, [2009] 1 WLR 1988 at [21].

[220] [1998] 1 WLR 896, 912–13. See above, pp 162–4.

[221] [2009] UKPC 10 at [21]. [222] *Ibid* at [27]. [223] *Ibid* at [22].

[224] [2015] UKSC 72, [2016] AC 742. See also *Wells v Devani* [2019] UKSC 4, [2020] AC 129 at [27]–[29].

[225] See above, p 170.

to imply a term albeit that it accepted that there are factors common to both exercises. In the words of Lord Neuberger (agreed with by Lords Sumption and Hodge):[226]

> [T]he factors to be taken into account on an issue of construction, namely the words used in the contract, the surrounding circumstances known to both parties at the time of the contract, commercial common sense, and the reasonable reader or reasonable parties, are also taken into account on an issue of implication. However, that does not mean that the exercise of implication should be properly classified as part of the exercise of interpretation, let alone that it should be carried out at the same time as interpretation.

Lord Neuberger pointed out that the express terms of a contract must be interpreted before there can be any question of implication,[227] and sidelined the decision in *Belize*. He noted that 'those observations [of Lord Hoffmann in *Belize*] should henceforth be treated as a characteristically inspired discussion rather than authoritative guidance on the law of implied terms'.[228]

The law in this area is still not entirely settled. In recent decisions the UK Supreme Court has quietly rehabilitated *Belize* to some extent. It was cited without disapproval by the majority in *Barton v Morris*,[229] as well as in *Tesco Stores Ltd v Union of Shop, Distributive and Allied Workers*.[230] But in the latter case Lord Leggatt was clear that although *Belize* was correct to highlight that 'the implication of a term does not involve adding something to the parties' agreement: it identifies part of that agreement which is not expressed in the contractual document', he also emphasized that *Belize* 'is misleading in so far as it suggests that the process for deciding whether a term is implied is no different from the process of identifying the meaning of the express terms. That suggestion was decisively rejected by a majority of the Supreme Court in the *Marks and Spencer* case'.[231]

In *Tesco*, the Supreme Court held that a term should be implied into contracts of employment to prevent employers from firing employees only to rehire them on the same terms but with a 'permanent' aspect of their pay removed. Lord Burrows and Lady Simler jointly gave the leading judgment, in which they pointed out that 'the implication of contractual terms by fact involves a distinct exercise from that of contractual interpretation because it involves deciding whether, objectively, the parties would have said something in their contract that they did not in fact say had the point occurred to them'.[232] Whereas all express terms have to be interpreted, it is difficult to interpret words that were never spoken. Silence is inherently ambiguous. It is because there is silence regarding an issue that there is scope to imply a term. No term should be implied unless necessary to do so.[233] And terms which are implied into a contract still need to be interpreted.

[226] [2015] UKSC 72 at [27].

[227] *Ibid* at [28]. See too *Duval v 11–13 Randolph Crescent Ltd* [2020] UKSC 18, [2020] 2 WLR 1167.

[228] *Ibid* at [31].

[229] [2023] UKSC 3, [2023] AC 684, eg at [23] (Lady Rose).

[230] [2024] UKSC 28, [2025] ICR 107.

[231] *Ibid* at[101]; see too Lord Leggatt's doubts (*ibid* at [154]) about some of the reasoning in *Wells v Devani* [2019] UKSC 4.

[232] *Ibid* at [34]. See too *Byron v Eastern Caribbean Amalgamated Bank* [2019] UKPC 16 at [22] (Lady Hale).

[233] *Yoo Design Services Ltd v Iliv Realty Pte Ltd* [2021] EWCA Civ 560 at [47].

(ii) Standardized terms in common relationships

In certain types of contract, terms have become standardized, and they will be implied in all contracts of that type in the absence of any contrary intention. For example, if a builder undertakes to build a house for a purchaser, it is an implied term of the contract that the work will be done in a good and workmanlike manner, that the builder will supply good and proper materials, and that the house will be reasonably fit for human habitation when built or completed.[234] If a travel agent undertakes to arrange for services, such as accommodation and excursions, to be provided by others, it is an implied term of the contract that it would use reasonable care and skill in selecting the service-providers: but, if the travel agent itself undertakes to supply the services, it is an implied term of the contract that the services themselves will be carried out with reasonable care and skill, even where the agent has arranged for its obligation to be performed by others.[235] Some of these standardized terms have subsequently been codified by statute.[236] Others, as will be seen, continue to emerge by a process of common law development.

In these cases concerning a common relationship, for example sale, carriage, landlord and tenant, or employment, the parties may have left a lot unsaid and the process of implication is different. It involves the Court determining, in the light of general considerations of policy, the standard incidents of the particular type of relationship rather than constructing a hypothetical bargain. Although it has usually been said that the criterion for this form of implication is also 'necessity' rather than 'reasonableness',[237] it does appear that a broader approach is taken. The Courts will consider how the proposed implied term will sit with existing law, the effect on the parties to the relationship, and wider issues of fairness.[238] In Dyson LJ's words in *Crossley v Faithful & Gould Holdings Ltd*, '[R]ather than focus on the elusive concept of necessity, it is better to recognise that, to some extent at least, the existence and scope of standardised implied terms raise questions of reasonableness, fairness and the balancing of competing policy considerations'.[239]

While the parties can exclude or modify the standard incidents of the relationship by express words, unless they do so they will form part of the obligation as a legal incident of the particular kind of contractual relationship.[240] Such standardized terms, implied

[234] *Miller v Cannon Hill Estates Ltd* [1931] 2 KB 113; *Lynch v Thorne* [1956] 1 WLR 303; *Hancock v Brazier (Anerley) Ltd* [1966] 1 WLR 1317.

[235] *Wong Mee Wan v Kwan Kin Travel Services Ltd* [1996] 1 WLR 38, 42, 46–7. In the second situation the contractor may be liable despite the absence of personal negligence.

[236] eg Sale of Goods Act 1979, ss 12–15 (below, p 168); Supply of Goods and Services Act 1982, s 13. Those provisions now apply only to non-consumer contracts but there are similar provisions on consumer contracts, which treat terms as included in the contract, under the Consumer Rights Act 2015, Part 1.

[237] *Liverpool City Council v Irwin* [1977] AC 239, 254 (Lord Wilberforce); *Scally v Southern Health and Social Services Board* [1992] 1 AC 294, 307 (Lord Bridge). Cf *Shell UK Ltd v Lostock Garages Ltd* [1976] 1 WLR 1187, 1196 (Lord Denning MR). See also *Lister v Romford Ice & Cold Storage Co Ltd* [1957] AC 555, 576 (Viscount Simonds) and 594 (Lord Tucker).

[238] Peden (2001) 117 LQR 459, 467.

[239] [2004] EWCA Civ 293, [2004] 4 All ER 447 at [36].

[240] *Mears v Safecar Security Ltd* [1983] QB 54, 78.

by law, have been said to 'operate as default rules'.[241] In these cases it has been said[242] that the problem of implication is to be solved by asking:

> [H]as the law already defined the obligation or the extent of it? If so, let it be followed. If not, look to see what would be reasonable in the general run of such cases . . . and then say what the obligation shall be.

In such cases the contract may be partly but not wholly stated in writing and 'in order to complete it, in particular to give it a bilateral character, it is necessary to take account of the parties and the circumstances', that is the nature of the contract and the relationship established by it.[243] In *Liverpool City Council v Irwin*:[244]

> Tenants in a council tower block withheld rent as a protest at conditions in the building. They alleged that the council was in breach of its duty to repair and maintain the lifts, staircases, and rubbish chutes in the common parts of the building which it controlled. There was no formal lease; merely a document entitled 'conditions of tenancy' and the conditions set out only related to the tenants' obligations. They contained nothing about the landlord's obligations.

It was held that the tenants had an implied easement over the common parts for access to their premises and to the rubbish chutes and that the landlord was under an implied obligation to take reasonable care to maintain the common parts in a reasonable state of repair because the contract had not placed the obligation to maintain on the tenants individually or collectively, and the landlord retained control of this essential means of access.

An implied obligation of mutual trust and confidence has been recognized in contracts of employment by which both employer and employee are obliged not to conduct themselves in a manner calculated and likely to destroy or seriously damage the relationship of confidence and trust between them.[245] It has also been suggested that an apparently unrestricted contractual power to terminate a telephone service on a month's notice should be interpreted as subject to an implied term that the power to terminate should not be exercised without demonstrable reason or cause.[246]

The distinction between terms implied as the incidents of a defined relationship and those implied to give business efficacy to a particular transaction was applied in *Scally v Southern Health and Social Services Board*:[247]

> A contract of employment contained a term giving certain employees the right to acquire a valuable additional pension benefit if they took certain action within a certain time. The

[241] *Malik v Bank of Credit & Commerce International SA* [1998] AC 20, 45 (Lord Steyn). See also Rakoff, in Beatson and Friedmann (eds), *Good Faith and Fault in Contract Law* (1995) 191; Riley (2000) 20 OJLS 367.

[242] *Shell UK Ltd v Lostock Garages Ltd* [1976] 1 WLR 1187, 1196 (Lord Denning MR). See also *Liverpool City Council v Irwin* [1977] AC 239, 257–8 (Lord Cross); *Scally v Southern Health and Social Services Board* [1992] 1 AC 294, 307. Cf *Reid v Rush & Tomkins Group plc* [1990] 1 WLR 212 (no such term implied because extent of obligation raised issues of social policy which could only be resolved by the legislature); *Johnson v Unisys Ltd* [2001] UKHL 13, [2003] 1 AC 518 (term not implied where statute provided limited remedy for conduct complained of).

[243] *Liverpool City Council v Irwin* [1977] AC 239; *Lister v Romford Ice & Cold Storage Ltd* [1957] AC 555, 579.

[244] [1977] AC 239.

[245] *Malik v Bank of Credit & Commerce International* [1998] AC 20.

[246] *Timeload Ltd v British Telecommunications plc* (1995) 3 EMLR 459, 467 (Sir Thomas Bingham MR). Some analogical assistance appears to have been derived from the Unfair Contract Terms Act 1977, s 3; below, p 220.

[247] [1992] 1 AC 294. Cf p 215; *University of Nottingham v Eyett (No 1)* [1999] 2 All ER 437.

term derived from a collective bargain negotiated by the employees' representatives and trade unions. The claimants, employees who had not been informed of this right, claimed damages for, inter alia, breach of contract.

It was held that a term obliging the employer to take reasonable steps to inform its employees of this right should be implied into the contract because this term was not the result of individual negotiation but of a collective bargain and, therefore, the employees could not be expected to be aware of the term unless it was drawn to their attention. The implied obligation to inform employees accordingly did not apply to all contracts of employment. If this is an indication that the categories of defined relationships may be subdivided into smaller and more numerous categories with terms that have a less general application, the distinction between implication of terms in cases concerning a common relationship and implication in those concerning a particular contract may be a fragile one.[248] It has, however, been argued that it can be maintained by having recourse to trade usage in identifying what are the defined types of contractual relationship.[249]

(iii) Terms implied by custom

Another situation in which the Courts lay down a general rule that some provision is to be implied in all contracts of a defined type unless the parties have expressly excluded it is where a term is implied by the custom of a locality or by the usage of a particular trade. Such a custom must be strictly proved.[250] It must be as certain as the written contract, notorious, recognized as legally binding, reasonable, and consistent with the express terms of the contract.[251] Furthermore, the custom must not offend against the intention of any legislative enactment.

In *Hutton v Warren*,[252] a term was implied by the custom of the country into an agricultural tenancy giving the outgoing tenant the right to a reasonable allowance for seeds and labour expended on the land even though the lease contained no express term to this effect. Similarly, in *Harley & Co v Nagata*[253] it was held that a custom that the commission of the broker who negotiated a time charterparty should be paid out of the hire that was earned, and should not be payable at all unless hire was in fact earned, should be imported into the brokerage contract.

(a) Certainty. A course of conduct which is said to form a custom must be both identifiable and uniform. It is these qualities that give the course of conduct the required certainty. The requirement of uniformity does not necessarily require total consistency of conduct. The continued adherence of 85 per cent of the Lancashire weaving mills to

[248] See Phang [1993] JBL 242, [1994] JBL 255, and note *Ashmore v Corporation of Lloyd's (No 2)* [1992] 2 Lloyd's Rep 620, 631 (no common relationship in many thousands of contracts between Lloyd's underwriters and the Corporation entered into on the same terms).

[249] Peden (2001) 117 LQR 459, 463.

[250] *Expert Tooling and Automation Ltd v Engie Power Ltd* [2025] EWCA Civ 292 at [155].

[251] *Nelson v Dahl* (1879) 12 Ch D 568, 575; *Cunliffe-Owen v Teather & Greenwood* [1967] 1 WLR 1421, 1438–9 (usage of the Stock Exchange).

[252] (1836) 1 M & W 466.

[253] (1917) 23 Com Cas 121.

a custom was sufficient to maintain it,[254] although a higher degree of uniformity may be required for the creation of a new custom.[255] Once a custom has been proved in a sufficient number of cases, the Court will take judicial notice of it without the need for further evidence.[256]

(b) Notoriety. To be notorious a custom need not be known to all the world, nor even to both parties to the contract.[257] It must, however, be well known in the market to which it applies and readily ascertainable by any person entering into a contract of which it will form a part.[258]

(c) Recognized as Legally Binding. The fact that a course of conduct is uniform, certain, and notorious is not, in itself, enough to give rise to a binding custom. It must also be shown that the course of conduct was intended to have a legally binding effect and that compliance with it was the result of a belief in a legal obligation to do so. A custom must therefore be distinguished from a course of conduct that is frequently, or even habitually, followed in a particular commercial community as a matter of grace or commercial convenience.[259] The clearest way of establishing this is to show that the custom has been 'enforced' but this is not necessary and it is sufficient for it to be established that the custom has been acted upon.[260] Where the conduct is required by the rules of a trade or professional association, that will be good evidence that compliance is the result of belief in an obligation to do so.[261]

(d) Reasonableness. Reasonableness is a question of law and, to qualify, a custom must be 'fair and proper and such as reasonable, honest, and fair-minded men would adopt'.[262] Although evidence of the unreasonableness of a course of conduct may be used to show that it was not generally accepted or known and does not therefore amount to a custom,[263] where a custom has been sufficiently proved, the Courts' tendency to support freedom of bargaining in commercial markets means that it is unlikely to be held to be unreasonable.[264] Where the contracting parties are in a fiduciary relationship, as in the case of an agent or a broker, a stricter approach is taken. The variation, by a trade

[254] *Sagar v H Ridehalgh & Son Ltd* [1931] 1 Ch 310.

[255] *Con-Stan Industries of Australia Pty Ltd v Norwich Insurance (Australia) Ltd* (1985–86) 160 CLR 226 (High Court of Australia), although instances of inconsistency were 'minute': [1981] 2 NSWLR 879, 889–90.

[256] *Universo Insurance Co of Milan v Merchant' s Marine Insurance Co Ltd* [1897] 2 QB 93 (judicial notice taken of a broker's liability for unpaid premium in the marine insurance market). See also *JA Chapman & Co Ltd v Kadirga Denizcilik Ve Ticaret* [1998] Lloyd's Rep IR 377.

[257] *Grissell v Bristowe* (1868) LR 3 CP 112, 128, revs'd on the facts of the case (1868) LR 4 CP 36; *Buckle v Knoop* (1867) LR 2 Exch 125, 129, aff'd *ibid*, 333.

[258] *Strathlorne SS Co Ltd v Hugh Baird & Sons Ltd*, 1916 SC (HL) 134, 136 (Lord Buckmaster LC).

[259] *General Reinsurance Corp v Forsakringsaktiebolaget Fennia Patria* [1983] QB 856, 874 (Slade LJ).

[260] *Cunningham v Fonblanque* (1833) 6 C & P 44, 49; *Hall v Benson* (1836) 7 C & P 711; *Johnson v Clarke* [1908] 1 Ch 303, 309. Cf *Sea Steamship Co Ltd v Price, Walker & Co Ltd* (1903) 8 Com Cas 292, 295.

[261] *Cunliffe-Owen v Teather & Greenwood* [1967] 1 WLR 1421 (Stock Exchange rules); *Shearson Lehman Hutton Inc v MacLaine Watson & Co Ltd* [1989] 2 Lloyd's Rep 570 (London Metal Exchange).

[262] *Produce Brokers Co Ltd v Olympia Oil and Cake Co Ltd* [1916] 2 KB 296, 298.

[263] *Bottomley v Forbes* (1838) 5 Bing (NC) 121, 128.

[264] *Moult v Halliday* [1898] 1 QB 125, 130.

custom, of a fiduciary duty such as the rule that fiduciaries must not place themselves in a position where their own interest conflicts with that of their customer, is less likely to be held to be reasonable,[265] although in some cases it may be so held.[266]

(e) Consistency With Express Terms. A custom or usage which would otherwise become an implied term of the contract may be expressly or impliedly excluded by the parties. In *Les Affréteurs Réunis Société Anonyme v Leopold Walford (London) Ltd*[267] the custom that in a time charter the broker's commission was only payable if the hire was earned was excluded by an express provision that 'a commission of 3 per cent on the estimated gross amount of hire is due (to the broker) *on signing this charter*', regardless of whether any hire was earned or not. In *Exxonmobil Sales and Supply Corp v Texaco Ltd*[268] it was held that an entire agreement clause, which included the wording that there was no other usage or course of dealing affecting the contract, excluded the implying of terms based upon usage or custom.

(iv) Good Faith

English law has traditionally been cautious about wholeheartedly adopting an overriding principle of good faith. As Bingham LJ pointed out in *Interfoto Picture Library Ltd v Stiletto Visual Programmes Ltd*,[269] 'English law has, characteristically, committed itself to no such overriding principle but has developed piecemeal solutions in response to demonstrated problems of unfairness.' Piecemeal solutions include vitiating factors such as misrepresentation[270] and duress,[271] and equitable doctrines which apply when the application of common law rules would be too harsh, such as promissory estoppel[272] and rectification.[273] These piecemeal solutions fit well with the usual approach of the common law: incremental development on a case-by-case basis, gradually building up a corpus of law.

In *Yam Seng Pte Ltd v International Trade Corporation Ltd*, Leggatt J noted a 'traditional English hostility'[274] towards a doctrine of good faith, but implied a term that performance must be carried out in good faith:[275]

The parties entered into a written contract under which the defendant (ITC) granted the claimant (Yam Seng) the exclusive right to distribute certain fragrances bearing the brand

[265] *Robinson v Mollett* (1875) LR 7 HL 802; *Anglo-African Merchants Ltd v Bayley* [1970] 1 QB 311; *North and South Co v Berkeley* [1971] 1 WLR 470.

[266] *Jones v Canavan* [1972] 2 NSWLR 236; *Kelly v Cooper* [1993] AC 205, 214 (although this implication may have been on the ground of business efficacy).

[267] [1919] AC 801, below, p 638.

[268] [2003] EWHC 1964 (Comm), [2004] 1 All ER (Comm) 435.

[269] [1989] QB 433, 439, below, p 196.

[270] Chapter 9.

[271] Chapter 10.

[272] Above, pp 121–37.

[273] Below, pp 281–90.

[274] [2013] EWHC 111 (QB), [2013] 1 All ER (Comm) 1321 at [124]. See eg *Walford v Miles* [1992] 2 AC 128, above, p 67. Part of the hostility stems from the difficulty in defining good faith, which depends heavily upon context. However, it is now clear that express contractual duties of good faith can be enforced (eg *Mid Essex Hospital Services NHS Trust v Compass Group UK and Ireland Ltd (t/a Medirest)* [2013] EWCA Civ 200, [2013] BLR 265; *Re Compound Photonics Group Ltd* [2022] EWCA Civ 1371) and it follows that implied duties of good faith are similarly enforceable.

[275] [2013] EWHC 111 (QB), [2013] 1 Lloyd's Rep 526. See also *Emirates Trading Agency v Prime Mineral Exports Pte Ltd* [2014] EWHC 2104 (Comm), [2015] 1 WLR 1145 at [51].

name 'Manchester United' in parts of the Middle East, Asia, Africa and Australia. After an initially happy relationship, matters deteriorated and Yam Seng terminated the contract for ITC's alleged repudiatory breach and sought damages.

Leggatt J held that ITC was indeed in repudiatory breach in two respects, one of which was that ITC was in breach of an implied term (of fact) to perform in good faith which, more specifically, required ITC not knowingly to give false information, to Yam Seng. The judgment may be regarded as the most wide-ranging and sophisticated analysis by an English judge of why the standard approach to implying terms by fact is likely to lead to there being an implied term imposing a duty to perform in good faith and more specific implied terms built from it.

However, *Yam Seng* has in general been given a rather lukewarm reception, with the Courts tending to stress that the context and type of contract are all-important and that one must not undermine the express terms of the contract.[276] After all, it appears that Leggatt J could have implied the two duties in *Yam Seng* on the basis of the normal principles of implication, without invoking good faith.[277] In *Equitas Insurance Ltd v Municipal Mutual Insurance Ltd*, Males LJ described good faith as 'merely a label';[278] the content of implied duties can be defined more precisely within a broader umbrella of 'good faith'. Nevertheless, in *Sheikh Tahnoon Al Nehayan v Kent*[279] Leggatt LJ built on his approach in *Yam Seng*:

The claimant, a member of the Royal Family of Abu Dhabi, entered into a joint venture with the defendant, a Greek businessman, whereby they agreed jointly to own and develop a hotel business which was subsequently expanded to include an online travel business. The businesses were financially disastrous. The claimant sought to recover some of his huge investment losses by suing the defendant for breach of a framework agreement (restructuring the businesses) and for failure to make payments under a promissory note. The defendant counter-claimed for, inter alia, damages for breach of an implied term of good faith in the joint venture agreement.

Leggatt LJ held that the claimant was in breach of such an implied term by inducing the defendant to enter into the framework agreement and to make payments under a promissory note by means of a threat to use the claimant's position as a co-owner of the business to block a deal which the defendant had negotiated with a third party. The joint venture contract was what he had referred to in *Yam Seng* as a 'relational' contract and Leggatt LJ's reasoning was that the term as to good faith should be implied by fact

[276] eg *Mid Essex Hospital Services NHS Trust v Compass Group UK and Ireland Ltd* [2013] EWCA Civ 200, [2013] BLR 265 (although the issue there was how to construe an *express* term requiring performance in good faith); *Hamsard 3147 Ltd v Boots UK Ltd* [2013] EWHC 3251 (Pat) at [86]; *Greenclose Ltd v National Westminster Bank plc* [2014] EWHC 1156 (Ch), [2014] 2 Lloyd's Rep 169 at [150]–[151]; *UTB LLC v Sheffield United Ltd* [2019] EWHC 2322 (Ch); *Morley (t/a Morley Estates) v Royal Bank of Scotland Plc* [2020] EWHC 88 (Ch) at [148].

[277] Whittaker (2013) 129 LQR 463.

[278] *Equitas Insurance Ltd v Municipal Mutual Insurance Ltd* [2019] EWCA Civ 718, [2020] QB 418 at [116].

[279] [2018] EWHC 333 (Comm), [2018] 1 CLC 216.

because it satisfied the 'business efficacy' test or, and this was a development from his thinking in *Yam Seng*, because such a term should be implied by law into this type of relational contract.[280]

However, it is difficult to accept that there is a defined category of 'relational contracts' into which duties of good faith should be implied at law: the boundaries of this category are very unclear and it remains 'impossible to locate, in the relational-contract literature, a definition that adequately distinguishes relational and non-relational contracts in a legally operational way—that is, in a way that carves out a set of special well-specified contracts for treatment under special well-specified rules'.[281] When implying duties of good faith into contract, the focus should generally be on the usual tests for implication in fact.[282]

A different type of situation where good faith might be implied into a contract arises where one party can exercise contractual powers and make decisions that affect the interests of the counterparty.[283] In *Braganza v BP Shipping Ltd*:[284]

an employee died whilst in the service of the defendant employer. This entitled the employee's widow, the claimant, to compensation unless, in the employer's opinion, the employee's death had been caused by suicide. The employer decided the death had been caused by suicide, and so refused to make the compensation payment.

The claimant argued that the employer had committed a breach of contract. A bare majority of the Supreme Court agreed. All the Justices agreed on the law, and both Lady Hale (in the majority) and Lord Neuberger (in the minority) cited with approval the conclusion of Rix LJ in *Socimer International Bank Ltd v Standard Bank Ltd* that 'a decision-maker's discretion will be limited, as a matter of necessary implication, by concepts of honesty, good faith, and genuineness, and the need for the absence of arbitrariness, capriciousness, perversity and irrationality'.[285] The disagreement between the judges was purely on the facts: the majority thought that the employer's decision had not conformed with the required standards, whereas the minority thought that it had. Significantly, the Supreme Court appeared to consider good faith to play a role alongside other concepts, such as non-arbitrariness and non-capriciousness.

[280] These cases were followed and applied in *Bates v Post Office* [2019] EWHC 606 (QB) in which Fraser J found that such an implied term followed from the contract being a relational contract and stressed that the implied term of good faith went beyond a requirement of honesty. Although understandable on the merits of the case, the reasoning in the case is difficult: Davies and Sales (2024) 140 LQR 106, 122–124. Cf *UTB LLC v Sheffield United Ltd* [2019] EWHC 2322 (Ch); *TAQA Bratani Ltd v Rockrose UKCS8 LLC* [2020] EWHC 58 (Comm), [2020] 2 Lloyd's Rep 64.

[281] Eisenberg, in Beatson and Friedmann (eds), *Good Faith and Fault in Contract Law* (1995). Cf Collins, in Degeling, Edelman, and Goudkamp (eds), *Contract in Commercial Law* (2016).

[282] *Candey Ltd v Bosheh* [2022] EWCA Civ 1103, [2022] 4 WLR 84.

[283] cf Morgan [2008] LMCLQ 230.

[284] [2015] UKSC 17, [2015] 1 WLR 1661.

[285] [2008] EWCA Civ 116 at [66]. See too eg *Paragon Finance Plc v Nash* [2001] EWCA Civ 1466, [2002] 1 WLR 685; *Lymington Marina Ltd v MacNamara* [2007] EWCA Civ 151, [2007] 2 All ER (Comm) 825; *Socimer International Bank Ltd v Standard Bank London Ltd* [2008] EWCA Civ 16, [2008] 1 Lloyd's Rep 558; *British Telecommunications plc v Telefonica O2 UK Ltd* [2014] UKSC 42, [2014] 4 All ER 907 at [37].

However, the influence of good faith in this context should not be overstated. The thrust of the cases on contract discretions seems to be towards a less intrusive measure of control, focusing on whether the power has been exercised for a proper purpose.[286]

(c) TERMS IMPLIED BY STATUTE

(i) Sale of goods

Contracts for the sale of goods are of such everyday occurrence, and are commonly made with so little consideration of the exact legal results which the parties would desire to produce by it, that if their rights and obligations were to be determined only by what they say or do when they make the contract their reasonable expectations would often be defeated. Consequently certain conditions and warranties are *implied* in a contract of sale, originally by common law, but since 1893 pursuant to sections 12–15 of the Sale of Goods Act 1893, now re-enacted (with amendments) in the Sale of Goods Act 1979 and further amended in 1994.[287] The Consumer Rights Act 2015 has further amended the Sale of Goods Act 1979 so that the statutory implied terms are now only implied into non-consumer contracts. For consumer contracts for the supply of goods (and digital content) the equivalent terms (and others) are not implied terms but are rather terms treated as included in the contract.[288]

In principle the statutorily implied terms may be negatived or varied by express agreement, by the course of dealing between the parties, or by a binding usage.[289] This freedom of the parties is, however, made subject to the Unfair Contract Terms Act 1977 which contains significant restrictions so that liability for breach of the statutory implied terms cannot be excluded or restricted or can only be excluded or restricted if the Court is satisfied that doing so is reasonable.[290]

(a) Title. By section 12 of the Sale of Goods Act 1979 the following terms are implied:

(1) a condition[291] 'on the part of the seller that in the case of a sale he has a right to sell the goods, and in the case of an agreement to sell he will have such a right at the time when the property is to pass':

(2) a warranty[292] that

'(a) the goods are free, and will remain free until the time when the property is to pass, from any charge or encumbrance not disclosed or known to the buyer before the contract is made, and

[286] eg *Property Alliance Group Ltd v Royal Bank of Scotland Plc* [2018] EWCA Civ 355, [2018] 1 WLR 3529. See Davies and Sales (2024) 140 LQR 106. It appears that no restrictions should fetter contractual rights to terminate an agreement, since in those circumstances one party seeks to end the relationship rather than continue in a cooperative endeavour (eg *UBS AG v Rose Capital Ventures Ltd and others* [2018] EWHC 3137 (Ch)); different views were expressed on this point, *obiter*, in *Tesco Stores Ltd v Union of Shop, Distributive and Allied Workers* [2024] UKSC 28, [2025] ICR 107 by Lord Leggatt (at [114]–[120]) and Lord Reed (at [149]).

[287] The Sale and Supply of Goods Act 1994 substantially implemented the report of the Law Commission, Law Com No 160, *Sale and Supply of Goods* (1987).

[288] Below, p 189.

[289] Sale of Goods Act 1979, s 55.

[290] Unfair Contract Terms Act 1977, s 6, below, p 214.

[291] Sale of Goods Act 1979, s 12(1), (5A).

[292] Sale of Goods Act 1979, s 12(2), (5A).

(b) the buyer will enjoy quiet possession of the goods except so far as it may be disturbed by the owner or other person entitled to the benefit of any charge or encumbrance so disclosed or known.'

Different and more limited warranties are implied in a contract of sale where 'there appears from the contract or is to be inferred from the circumstances of the contract an intention that the seller should transfer only such title as he or a third person may have'.[293] The seller can, by an express term of the contract, indicate an intention to pass only a limited title and such an intention may also be inferred. Where the goods are sold by an auctioneer[294] the intention of the parties to the contract may be that the buyer should have only such title to the goods, and only such right to take possession of them, as the seller has in fact acquired.[295] But where the seller purports to sell only such title as he or a third person may have, the warranties of freedom from encumbrances and quiet possession are not thereby wholly excluded. The seller must disclose to the buyer, before the contract is made, any known encumbrances, and further warrants that neither he nor anyone claiming under him (or the third person) will disturb the buyer's quiet possession of the goods.[296]

The exclusion or restriction of liability for breach of the terms implied by section 12 is absolutely prohibited[297] and they are accordingly a compulsory part of a contract for the sale of goods.

(b) Sale by description. By section 13 of the Act:

(1) In 'a contract for the sale of goods by description', there is an implied condition[298] that 'the goods will correspond with the description'.

(2) 'If the sale is by sample as well as by description it is not sufficient that the bulk of the goods corresponds with the sample if the goods do not also correspond with the description.'

(3) 'A sale of goods is not prevented from being a sale by description by reason only that, being exposed for sale or hire, they are selected by the buyer.'

A sale of goods by description is a sale in which the buyer contracts in reliance on a description, express or implied,[299] even though the buyer has seen the goods[300] and may have selected the goods. For example, a person who agreed to buy a second-hand reaping machine described as 'new the previous year and only used to cut 50 acres' was entitled to reject the machine on delivery when he found that it was, in fact, a very old

[293] Sale of Goods Act 1979, s 12(3).

[294] *Niblett v Confectioners' Materials Co Ltd* [1921] 3 KB 387, 401; *Rowland v Divall* [1923] 2 KB 500, 505.

[295] *Bagueley v Hawley* (1867) LR 2 CP 625, 629.

[296] Sale of Goods Act 1979, s 12(4), (5).

[297] Unfair Contract Terms Act 1977, s 6(1). But by s 26, UCTA 1977 does not apply to international sale contracts. An express term concerning title will be a condition: *Barber v NWS Bank plc* [1996] 1 WLR 641.

[298] Sale of Goods Act 1979, s 13(1A).

[299] *Wallis, Son & Wells v Pratt & Haynes* [1911] AC 394.

[300] *Grant v Australian Knitting Mills Ltd* [1936] AC 85, 100; *Nicholson & Venn v Smith Marriott* (1947) 177 LT 189.

machine.[301] However, not all descriptive words are conditions; the words must identify the subject-matter of the contract. For instance, words identifying the yard in which a ship that is being sold is to be built are not within section 13.[302]

(c) Satisfactory Quality. Ordinarily there is no implied condition or warranty of the quality of goods sold or of their fitness for any particular purpose: *caveat emptor*. But, where goods are sold in the course of a business,[303] the 1979 Act contains important qualifications of this principle. By section 14:

(2) 'Where the seller sells goods in the course of a business', there is an implied condition[304] that 'the goods supplied under the contract are of satisfactory quality'.

(2C) There is no such condition as regards any matter making the quality of the goods unsatisfactory 'which is specifically drawn to the buyer's attention before the contract is made'; or 'where the buyer examines the goods before the contract is made, which that examination ought to reveal'.

Prior to the 1994 amendment the requirement was that the goods be of 'merchantable' quality, a criterion that was criticized[305] as too open-ended, inappropriate for consumer transactions, and as not expressly requiring reasonable durability.[306] The Law Commission had recommended that the criterion be 'acceptable quality'[307] but this was not accepted, partly due to a concern that a buyer might decide reluctantly that the goods were of 'acceptable' quality even if, by objective standards, the quality was not 'satisfactory'.[308] The new criterion is 'satisfactory quality' and is defined in section 14 of the Sale of Goods Act 1979:[309]

(2A) Goods are of satisfactory quality 'if they meet the standard that a reasonable person would regard as satisfactory, taking account of any description of the goods, the price (if relevant) and all the other relevant circumstances'.

(2B) The quality of goods 'includes their state and condition and the following (among others) are in appropriate cases aspects of the quality of goods—(a) fitness for all the purposes for which goods of the kind in question are commonly supplied (b) appearance and finish (c) freedom from minor defects (d) safety, and (e) durability'.

[301] *Varley v Whipp* [1900] 1 QB 513.

[302] *Reardon Smith Line Ltd v Hansen Tangen* [1976] 1 WLR 989. See also *Ashington Piggeries v Christopher Hill Ltd* [1972] AC 441, 503–4; *Harlingdon & Leinster Enterprises Ltd v Christopher Hull Fine Art Ltd* [1991] 1 QB 564.

[303] This is to be given a broad meaning. There is no restriction that the goods be of a type that the seller deals in: *Stevenson v Rogers* [1999] QB 1028 (fisherman selling boat).

[304] Sale of Goods Act 1979, s 14(6).

[305] *Cehave NV v Bremer Handelsgesellschaft mbH* [1976] QB 44, 80 (Ormrod LJ); Law Com No 162, *Sale and Supply of Goods* (1987), para 2.9 ff.

[306] But see *Mash & Murrell v Joseph I Emmanuel* [1962] 1 WLR 16; *Lambert v Lewis* [1982] AC 225, 276.

[307] Law Com No 162, above, n 305, paras 3.22, 3.27.

[308] Hansard, HC Deb vol 237, col 633 (14 February 1994). See further HC Deb vol 139, col WA 705 (3 November 1988); HC Deb vol 165, col 1225 (26 January 1990).

[309] Inserted by the Sale and Supply of Goods Act 1994, s 1(1).

Recourse to decisions on the old law should only be had in exceptional cases[310] but, in the absence of guidance as to what 'satisfactory quality' means, they provide useful indications of what is likely to be required. In *Rogers v Parish (Scarborough) Ltd*[311] it was said that:

> Starting with the purpose for which ['goods of the kind in question'][312] are commonly bought, one would include in respect of any passenger vehicle not merely the buyer's purpose in driving the car from one place to another but of doing so with the appropriate degree of comfort, ease of handling and reliability and, one might add, of pride in the vehicle's outward and interior appearance. What is the appropriate degree and what relative weight is to be attached to one characteristic of the car rather than another will depend on the market at which the car is aimed.[313]

In that case, a new car had been delivered with substantial defects to its engine, gearbox, and bodywork and attempts to rectify these defects over a six-month period had failed. It was held that the car was not of 'merchantable quality' and the buyer was entitled to reject it, even though the defects did not render it unroadworthy.

In addition to the factors listed in subsection 2B, the Court is likely to consider the consequences of the defect and the ease or otherwise with which it could be remedied. 'In some cases, such as a high-priced quality product, the customer may be entitled to expect that it is free from even minor defects, in other words perfect or nearly so.'[314]

Second-hand goods sold as such and goods sold as 'seconds' or imperfect must still measure up to a reasonable standard, even though not to the standard of a new or perfect article.[315] The price of the goods may frequently be of relevance: a buyer who, for example, buys a cheap carpet cannot expect it to achieve the same quality of resilience or wear as a more expensive one.[316]

The condition as to satisfactory quality extends to 'the goods supplied under the contract' including packaging, containers, and extraneous items mixed with the goods sold. In *Wilson v Rickett, Cockrell & Co Ltd*[317] it was held that a ton of 'Coalite' which contained, unknown to either party, a detonator did not meet the statutory standard. The argument that there was nothing wrong with the 'Coalite' itself was rejected and the defendant was held liable for damage from an explosion caused when a bucketful of the fuel containing the detonator was put on a fire.

[310] *Rogers v Parish (Scarborough) Ltd* [1987] QB 933, 942–3 (Mustill LJ).

[311] [1987] QB 933.

[312] The bracketed words reflect the 1994 amendments. Before those, s 14(6) referred to 'goods of that kind'.

[313] *Rogers v Parish (Scarborough) Ltd* [1987] QB 933, 944.

[314] *Clegg v Andersson* [2003] EWCA Civ 320, [2003] 1 All ER (Comm) 721 at [72] (Hale LJ) (purchase of a yacht). For another post-1994 reform case, holding that goods were not of satisfactory quality, see *Britvic Soft Drinks Ltd v Messer UK Ltd* [2002] EWCA Civ 548, [2002] 2 All ER (Comm) 321 (contaminated carbon dioxide). For post-1994 reform decisions finding that goods were of satisfactory quality, see, eg, *Jewson Ltd v Boyhan* [2003] EWCA Civ 1030, [2004] 1 Lloyd's Rep 505 (boilers); *Bramhill v Edwards* [2004] EWCA Civ 403, [2004] 2 Lloyd's Rep 653 (motor home).

[315] *Bartlett v Sydney Marcus Ltd* [1965] 1 WLR 1013; *Business Appliance Specialists Ltd v Nationwide Credit Corp Ltd* [1988] RTR 332; *Shine v General Guarantee Corp* [1988] 1 All ER 911.

[316] Cf *BS Brown & Son Ltd v Craiks Ltd* [1970] 1 WLR 752.

[317] [1954] 1 QB 598.

However, the condition is excluded if the defects are pointed out to the buyer before the contract is made. Similarly, if, before the contract is made, the buyer examines the goods, then the condition is excluded as regards defects which the examination ought to have revealed.[318]

(d) Fitness for Purpose. Section 14(3) of the 1979 Act deals with the fitness for purpose of the goods sold:

> (3) Where the seller sells goods in the course of a business and the buyer, expressly or by implication, makes known—
>
> (a) to the seller, or
>
> (b) where the purchase price or part of it is payable by instalments and the goods were previously sold by a credit-broker to the seller, to that credit-broker,
>
> any particular purpose for which the goods are being bought, there is an implied [condition][319] that the goods supplied under the contract are reasonably fit for that purpose, whether or not that is a purpose for which such goods are commonly supplied, except where the circumstances show that the buyer does not rely, or that it is unreasonable for him to rely, on the skill or judgment of the seller or credit-broker.

Although no longer applying to consumer contracts (by reason of the Consumer Rights Act 2015), the application of this subsection is illustrated by two cases concerning the purchase of food. In *Wallis v Russell*[320] the claimant bought from a fishmonger 'two nice fresh crabs for tea' and in *Chaproniere v Mason*[321] the claimant bought a bun from the defendant's baker's shop. The crabs were not fresh and the claimant suffered food poisoning after eating them; the bun contained a stone and the claimant broke a tooth when he bit it. In the first case the claimant expressly made it known through her agent[322] that she required the crabs for eating and relied on the fishmonger to select fresh crabs. In the second case, in buying the bun from a baker, the claimant clearly made it known by implication that he required it for the purpose of eating and relied on the baker's skill and judgement. Both defendants were liable in damages for breach of this implied condition.

Where two business people who are equally knowledgeable are dealing with one another, it may still be that the buyer reasonably relies on the seller's skill or judgement.[323]

[318] Sale of Goods Act 1979, s 14(2C); *R & B Customs Brokers Co Ltd v United Dominions Trust Ltd* [1988] 1 WLR 321.

[319] Sale of Goods Act 1979, s 14(6).

[320] [1902] 2 Ir Rep 585.

[321] (1905) 21 TLR 633. See also *Priest v Last* [1903] 2 KB 148 (hot-water bottle bursts); *St Albans City & DC v International Computers Ltd* [1996] 4 All ER 481, 494 (computer disk with defective program); *Britvic Soft Drinks Ltd v Messer UK Ltd* [2002] EWCA Civ 548, [2002] 2 All ER (Comm) 321 (contaminated carbon dioxide). For cases where there was held to be no relevant reliance under s 14(3), see, eg, *Jewson Ltd v Boyhan* [2003] EWCA Civ 1030, [2004] 1 Lloyd's Rep 505 (boilers); *Bramhill v Edwards* [2004] EWCA Civ 403, [2004] 2 Lloyd's Rep 653 (motor home).

[322] The purchase was made by the claimant's granddaughter on her behalf. On agency, see below, Chapter 23.

[323] *Henry Kendall & Sons v William Lillico & Sons Ltd* [1969] 2 AC 31. Cf *Slater & Slater v Finning Ltd* [1997] AC 473 (no reliance because of unusual feature in buyer's machinery).

It is possible, however, that the reliance will be only partial. If, for example, the buyer procures the seller to manufacture goods in accordance with the buyer's formula or specifications, there will be no implied condition that the formula or specifications will produce goods which are reasonably fit for the purpose made known to the seller by the buyer, yet the buyer may rely on the skill or judgement of the seller to ensure that the materials to be compounded in the formula are not toxic or harmful[324] or there may be an area of expertise outside the specifications in respect of which the skill or judgement of the seller is relied on.[325]

(e) Sections 14(2) and 14(3) compared. The two subsections of section 14 overlap to some extent, since both the definition of 'satisfactory quality' and section 14(3) refer to fitness for a purpose for which goods are commonly bought or supplied. However, a buyer who requires the goods for some special or unusual purpose can only recover, if at all, under section 14(3). The special or unusual purpose must be made known to the seller and the buyer must show reliance on the seller's skill and judgement. Under section 14(2) it is not necessary to show such reliance. Where the goods are unfit for a special or unusual purpose, but nevertheless fit for all purposes for which such goods are commonly supplied, they will still be of 'satisfactory quality' and there will be no breach by the seller of section 14(2).

Where the goods are only fit for some of the purposes for which such goods are commonly supplied they will not be of 'satisfactory quality'.[326] As amended in 1994, the subsection places the risk of unfitness for any of the common purposes on the seller. The seller who knows that its goods are not fit for one or more of the purposes for which goods of that kind are commonly supplied can protect itself by ensuring that the description of the goods excludes any common purpose for which they are unfit or by otherwise indicating that the goods are not fit for all their common purposes.[327] The amendment has therefore given the characterization of a purpose as 'common' or 'unusual' a new importance.

(f) Sale by Sample. In a sale by sample there are two implied conditions. First, that the bulk will correspond with the sample in quality. Secondly, that the goods will be free from any defect making their quality unsatisfactory, which would not be apparent on reasonable examination of the sample.[328] The meaning of this last condition, considered in *Godley v Perry*,[329] is still of relevance in non-consumer contracts but as a result of the Consumer Rights Act 2015 it does not now apply to consumer contracts.

324 *Ashington Piggeries Ltd v Christopher Hill Ltd* [1972] AC 441.

325 *Cammell Laird & Co Ltd v Manganese Bronze & Brass Co Ltd* [1934] AC 402.

326 Sale of Goods Act 1979, s 14(2B).

327 See Law Com No 162, *Sale and Supply of Goods* (1987), para 3.36. Prior to 1994 it was not necessary for the goods to be fit for *all* of their common purposes: *Aswan Engineering Establishment Co v Lupine Ltd* [1987] 1 WLR 1, *Henry Kendall & Sons v William Lillico & Sons Ltd* [1969] 2 AC 31, 77.

328 Sale of Goods Act 1979, s 15.

329 [1960] 1 WLR 9.

A 6-year-old boy bought a toy catapult from a shop. It was made of brittle polystyrene which fractured while he was using it, blinding him in one eye. He sued the retailer for damages under section 14(2) and (3) of the Sale of Goods Act. The retailer joined the wholesaler from whom he had bought the catapult by sample as a third party and the wholesaler likewise joined the importer who had supplied him.

The retailer was held liable but it was argued that the wholesaler and importer were not liable for breach of the condition as to satisfactory quality in a contract of sale by sample because a reasonable examination of the catapult would have revealed its fragility. Edmund Davies J said:[330]

Counsel . . . suggested that by holding the toy down with one's foot and then pulling on the elastic its safety could be tested and . . . its inherent fragility would thereby inevitably be discovered. True, the potential customer might have done any of these. He might also, I suppose, have tried biting the catapult, or hitting it with a hammer, or applying a lighted match to ensure its non-inflammability, experiments which, with all respect, are but slightly more bizarre than those suggested by counsel.

The phrase 'reasonable examination' was to be construed by the common-sense standards of everyday life: 'Not extreme ingenuity, but reasonableness, is the statutory yardstick.' The wholesaler and importer were held liable.

(ii) Other statutory implied terms

Certain terms are implied by sections 8–11 of the Supply of Goods (Implied Terms) Act 1973 into non-consumer contracts of hire-purchase. These implied terms resemble very closely those implied in contracts of sale of goods, and relate similarly to title, quality, and fitness for purpose, and correspondence with description or sample. Analogous terms are also implied by the Supply of Goods and Services Act 1982 into non-consumer contracts for the hire of goods,[331] and into non-consumer contracts for work and materials in relation to the materials supplied.[332] By sections 13–15 of the Supply of Goods and Services Act 1982, in a non-consumer contract for the supply of services, there are implied terms that the supplier will carry out the service with reasonable care and skill, that (if no time for completion is fixed) the supplier will carry out the service within a reasonable time, and that (if no price is fixed) the party contracting with the supplier will pay a reasonable charge. Finally, the covenants for title which are implied on a disposition of property are set out in Part I of the Law of Property (Miscellaneous Provisions) Act 1994.

[330] *Ibid*, 15.

[331] Supply of Goods and Services Act 1982, ss 7–10.

[332] Supply of Goods and Services Act 1982, ss 2–5. Food supplied in a restaurant or hotel must be of satisfactory quality applying s 4(2) of the 1982 Act (now replaced, as regards consumer contracts, by the Consumer Rights Act 2015): see *Wood v TUI Travel Ltd* [2017] EWCA Civ 11, [2018] QB 927.

(d) PART 1 OF THE CONSUMER RIGHTS ACT 2015: TERMS TREATED AS INCLUDED

In a consumer contract for the supply of goods, digital content, or services, it is no longer the case that there are statutory implied terms as to title, satisfactory quality, fitness for purpose, and description of the goods or as to the standard of care or timing or price of services. Instead, under the 2015 Act, the contract is to be treated as 'including' terms to that effect.[333] This change of terminology does not in itself effect any real change to the law on the implication of terms so that what has been said above on the statutory implied terms will continue to apply in substance, if not in form, to consumer contracts. As has been noted above, however, the 2015 Act has removed the labelling of the terms as conditions or warranties so that the effect of a breach of those terms on the consumer's right to discharge the contract will now essentially turn on what the statute provides about discharge[334] rather than on the common law.

FURTHER READING

PEDEN, 'Policy Concerns Behind Implication of Terms in Law' (2001) 117 LQR 459

MCMEEL, 'Prior Negotiations and Subsequent Conduct—the Next Step Forward for Contractual Interpretation' (2003) 119 LQR 272

NICHOLLS, 'My Kingdom for a Horse: the Meaning of Words' (2005) 121 LQR 577

CALNAN, 'Construction of Commercial Contracts: a Practitioner's Perspective' in BURROWS and PEEL (eds), *Contract Terms* (Oxford: Oxford University Press, 2007) 17

HOOLEY, 'Controlling Contractual Discretion' [2013] CLJ 65

HOOLEY, 'Implied Terms after *Belize Telecom*' [2014] CLJ 315

LEGGATT, 'Making Sense of Contracts: the Rational Choice Theory' (2015) 131 LQR 454

SUMPTION, 'A Question of Taste: The UK Supreme Court and the Interpretation of Contracts' [2017] OUCLJ 301

HOFFMANN, 'Language and Lawyers' (2018) 134 LQR 553

WILMOT-SMITH, 'Term Limits: What is a Term?' (2019) 39 OJLS 705

ENGLISH, 'The Nature of "Promissory Conditions"' (2021) 137 LQR 630

O'SULLIVAN, 'Implied Terms in Fact and Evidence of Prior Negotiation: An Exploration' (2022) 138 LQR 558

DAVIES and SALES, 'Controlling Contract Discretions: Wednesbury Reasonableness, Good Faith and Proper Purposes' (2024) 140 LQR 106

[333] Consumer Rights Act 2015, ss 9–18 (goods), 34–41 (digital content), 49–53 (services).

[334] Consumer Rights Act 2015, especially ss 19–20 and 42. See below, pp 508–9.

6

EXEMPTION CLAUSES AND UNFAIR TERMS

Written contracts frequently contain clauses excluding or limiting liability.[1] This is particularly so in the case of 'standard form' documents drawn up by one of the parties or a trade association to which one of the parties belongs. At common law there are special rules on the incorporation of exemption clauses (and other onerous terms), special rules of construction applicable to them, and a few miscellaneous other common law rules designed to control them. This chapter considers those common law rules[2] before going on to the legislative control of exemption clauses and unfair terms. That legislative control is now most helpfully understood by separating the control of exemption clauses in non-consumer contracts, in the Unfair Contract Terms Act 1977,[3] from that of exemption clauses and unfair terms in consumer contracts, in the Consumer Rights Act 2015.[4] The 2015 Act, which applies to contracts made on or after 1 October 2015, removed the control of exemption clauses (and indemnity clauses) in consumer contracts that were previously in the Unfair Terms Act 1977 and repealed the Unfair Terms in Consumer Contracts Regulations 1999. In consequence, the controls in consumer contracts are now found in a single Act, the Consumer Rights Act 2015. The thorny issues raised by exemption clauses and third parties are not discussed in this chapter but are dealt with instead in Chapter 21.

1. STANDARD FORMS OF CONTRACT

The idea of contract as an agreement freely negotiated between the parties must be seen in the light of the widespread use of standard form contracts, a uniform set of printed conditions which can be used time and time again, and for a large number of persons,

[1] See Andrews, *Exclusion Clauses and Unfair Contract Terms* (14th edn, 2025).

[2] For the limited non-statutory control of 'unconscionable bargains', see below, Chapter 10.

[3] Clauses in non-consumer contracts excluding or restricting liability for pre-contractual misrepresentation are controlled by the Misrepresentation Act 1967, s 3: see Chapter 9, pp 354–7.

[4] The 2015 Act partly enacted reforms recommended by the Law Commission, Law Com No 292, *Unfair Terms in Contracts* (2005).

and at less cost than an individually negotiated contract. Each time an individual travels by air, bus, or train, buys a car, takes clothes to the dry-cleaner, buys household goods, or even, in some cases, takes the lease of a house or flat, a standard form contract, devised by the supplier, will be provided which the individual must either accept in whole, or, theoretically, go without. In fact, there is little alternative but to accept; the individual does not negotiate, but merely adheres: hence the term contract of adhesion.[5] In some respects, therefore, it would be more correct to regard the relationship which arises not as one of contract at all, but as one of status. The contracting party has the status of a consumer.

The use of standard terms and conditions is not, however, confined to contracts made with consumers. Many contracts between business people—indeed, perhaps the majority of such contracts—are today entered into on the basis of one person's standard form of agreement or on the basis of a standard form of document, such as an order form, confirmation of order, catalogue, or price list, put forward by one party,[6] or which incorporate by reference the standard terms and conditions of trade associations.

The ordinary common law principles of the law of contract may not be capable of providing a just solution for a transaction in which freedom of contract exists on one side only. In particular, the party delivering the document may allocate the risks of non-performance or defective performance to the other party. While such allocation of risks should in principle lead to lower costs, it is only justifiable if at least some of the cost saving is passed on and if the other party is aware of the contractual allocation of risks. In fact, the party delivering the document may seek unfair exemption from certain common law liabilities, and thus seek to deprive the other party of the compensation which that person might reasonably expect to receive for any loss or injury or damage arising out of the transaction. Moreover, standard form contracts with consumers are often contained in some printed ticket, or notice, or receipt, or (in the case of a contract concluded online) a notice which appears only on screen, which is brought to the attention of the consumer at the time the agreement is made and which a prudent consumer would read from beginning to end. In fact, however, the consumer normally has neither the time nor the energy to do this and, even if this was done, it would be of little assistance for the consumer could not vary the terms in any way. It is not until some dispute arises that the consumer realizes how few are the rights in the contract.

Acting within the limitations imposed on them by the contractual framework of these transactions, the Courts have nevertheless endeavoured to alleviate the position of the recipient of the document by imposing certain requirements for the incorporation into the contract of onerous terms, and by construing the document wherever possible in that person's favour. It has been said that 'the judicial creativity, bordering on judicial legislation' which marked the development of these rules was a 'desperate remedy to be invoked only if it is necessary to remedy a widespread injustice'.[7] These rules are still important in determining the efficacy of exemption, or other onerous, clauses, at least where there is in fact inequality between the parties. The measure of protection which they offer against unfair clauses is, however, limited, and the power of the Courts to

[5] See above, p 5.

[6] For the 'battle of the forms', see above, p 43.

[7] *BCCI SA v Ali* [2001] UKHL 8, [2002] 1 AC 251 at [60] (Lord Hoffmann).

control such clauses has been greatly increased since the enactment of legislation, such as the Unfair Contract Terms Act 1977.[8]

2. INCORPORATION

(a) SIGNATURE

A person who *signs*[9] a document which contains contractual terms, or which expressly incorporates terms contained in another document, is normally bound by the terms even though that person has not read them and is ignorant of their precise legal effect.[10] Three exceptions are first, where the party's signature is induced by misrepresentation;[11] secondly, where *non est factum* applies;[12] and thirdly, where the document signed does not purport to have contractual effect as, for example, where the signed document was a time sheet.[13] There have been some suggestions in the cases that, in extreme cases, the signature may not be sufficient to incorporate individual clauses within the signed document or in another document, expressly incorporated by the signature,[14] but the Courts are rightly reluctant to extend the exceptions to the signature rule.[15]

(b) NOTICE

(i) The notice must be contemporaneous with the contract

Where there is no signature, in order that a term should become binding as part of the contract it must be brought to the notice of the contracting party before or at the time that the contract is made. If it is not communicated until afterwards, it will be of no effect unless there is evidence that the parties have entered into a new contract on a different basis.[16] An illustration of the necessity for contemporaneity is provided by *Olley v Marlborough Court Ltd*:[17]

[8] See below, pp 212–26.

[9] Signature includes electronic signatures, such as typing one's name in an e-mail or clicking on a website: see above, p 93; *Hudson v Hathway* [2022] EWCA Civ 1648, [2023] KB 345 at [67].

[10] *Parker v South Eastern Ry* (1877) 2 CPD 416, 421; *L'Estrange v F Graucob Ltd* [1934] 2 KB 394; *Levison v Patent Steam Carpet Cleaning Co Ltd* [1978] QB 69; Spencer [1973] CLJ 104.

[11] *Curtis v Chemical Cleaning and Dyeing Co Ltd* [1951] 1 KB 805: see below, p 211.

[12] Below, pp 282–4.

[13] *Grogan v Robin Meredith Plant Hire* [1996] CLC 1127.

[14] See, eg, *Ocean Chemical Transport Inc v Exnor Craggs Ltd* [2000] 1 Lloyd's Rep 446 at [48]; *Blu-Sky Solutions Ltd v Be Caring Ltd* [2021] EWHC 2619 (Comm), [2022] 2 All ER (Comm) 254 at [99]–[100]; *Parker-Grennan v Camelot UK Lotteries Ltd* [2024] EWCA Civ 185, [2024] ECC 11 at [47] (online contract).

[15] Cf *Peekay Intermark Ltd v Australia and New Zealand Banking Group Ltd* [2006] EWCA Civ 386, [2006] 2 Lloyd's Rep 51 at [43] (the signature rule is 'an important principle of English law which underpins the whole of commercial life': Moore-Bick LJ).

[16] *Levison v Patent Steam Carpet Cleaning Co Ltd* [1978] QB 69.

[17] [1949] 1 KB 532. See also *Hollingworth v Southern Ferries Ltd* [1977] 2 Lloyd's Rep 70 (sailing tickets delivered after booking made).

O and her husband registered at the defendant's hotel, paid for a week's board and lodging in advance, and then went up to their room. There a notice was exhibited stating: 'The proprietors will not hold themselves responsible for articles lost or stolen, unless handed to the manageress for safe custody.' Owing to the negligence of the hotel staff, a thief gained access to the room and stole some of O's property.

The Court of Appeal held that the notice formed no part of the contract since O could not have seen it until after the contract was made; the defendant was accordingly liable for the loss. Similarly, a customer who parked a car in a garage and received at the entrance a ticket from an automatic machine, was held not to be bound by the conditions printed on the ticket; the machine caused the ticket to be issued when the car was driven to the entrance to the garage, and the customer could not be affected by conditions brought to his notice after this time.[18]

(ii) Reasonably sufficient notice

In what circumstances will a party receiving a ticket, receipt, or common form document at the time the contract is made be bound by the conditions contained in it?

Take the example of a railway or cloakroom ticket, which the person receiving it puts into his pocket unread; three general rules have been laid down to determine whether the traveller or depositor will be bound by the terms contained in the ticket:[19]

(1) A person receiving the ticket who did not see or know that there was any writing on the ticket will not be bound by the conditions.
(2) A person who knows there was writing, and knows or believes that the writing contained conditions, is bound by the conditions.
(3) A person who knows that there was writing on the ticket, but does not know or believe that the writing contained conditions, will nevertheless be bound where the delivery of the ticket, in such a manner that the writing on it could be seen, is reasonable notice that the writing contained conditions.

It is the third of these rules which is the most frequently applied and the most difficult in its application.

It means that a person may be bound by an exemption clause in a standard form document, even though subjectively ignorant of its content, if the party seeking to rely on the clause has done what was reasonably sufficient in the circumstances to bring it to the other party's notice. The principles were discussed in *Parker v South Eastern Railway Co*:[20]

P deposited a bag in the defendant's station cloakroom. He received a paper ticket which said on its face 'See back' and on the back were a number of printed conditions, including a condition excluding liability for any bag with a higher value than £10. P admitted that he knew

[18] *Thornton v Shoe Lane Parking Ltd* [1971] 2 QB 163 (only Lord Denning MR found that the contract was concluded at that moment. Megaw LJ and Sir Gordon Willmer reserved their opinions on this point).

[19] *Parker v South Eastern Ry Co* (1877) 2 CPD 416, 421, 423; approved in *Richardson, Spence & Co v Rowntree* [1894] AC 217; *Burnett v Westminster Bank* [1966] 1 QB 742.

[20] (1877) 2 CPD 416; *Hood v Anchor Line (Henderson Bros) Ltd* [1918] AC 837.

there was writing on the ticket but stated that he had not read it and did not know or believe that the writing contained conditions. The bag was lost and P claimed £24 10*s* for its value.

The jury was directed to consider whether P had read or was aware of the special condition upon which the bag was deposited. It answered this question in the negative and accordingly judgment was entered for P. On appeal by the defendant, the Court of Appeal held that the jury had been misdirected. The real question was whether the defendant had done what was reasonably sufficient to give P notice of the condition. A new trial was ordered.

The question whether all that was reasonably sufficient to give notice was done is a question of fact.[21] In answering that question the Courts must look at all the circumstances and the situation of the parties.[22] *Thompson v LM & S Railway Co*[23] represents a very liberal approach to what constitutes reasonable notice. There a passenger travelling on an excursion ticket was injured by the alleged negligence of the defendant railway company. It was held that a clause exempting the company from liability,[24] printed in its timetable, was sufficiently, although circuitously, incorporated into the contract since the ticket referred to the timetables and advertisements (the latter also referred to the timetables). But in *Richardson, Spence & Co v Rowntree*,[25] a term limiting the liability of a steamship company to $100 in a steamship ticket was held not to be incorporated. The ticket had been handed to the claimant folded up, and the conditions were obliterated in part by a stamp in red ink. The jury found that, although the claimant knew there was writing on the ticket, she did not know the writing contained conditions, and that reasonably sufficient notice had not been given. The House of Lords refused to upset this finding.

If the notice is otherwise sufficient, the fact that a particular claimant is under some unknown disability (but not constituting incapacity), for example, unable to speak English[26] or, as in *Thompson v LM & S Railway Co*, illiterate,[27] will be treated as irrelevant.

If there is no reference on the face of a ticket to the fact that there are conditions printed on the back, the Courts have consistently held that such a notification is defective.[28] Strictly, of course, the issue is one of fact in each particular case but this requirement may fairly be said to be one of law.

[21] *Parker v South Eastern Ry Co* (1877) 2 CPD 416; *Richardson, Spence & Co v Rowntree* [1894] AC 217.

[22] *Hood v Anchor Line (Henderson Bros) Ltd* [1918] AC 837, 844 (Lord Haldane).

[23] [1930] 1 KB 41.

[24] The Unfair Contract Terms Act 1977, s 2(1) and the Consumer Rights Act 2015, s 65 now prevent the exclusion or restriction of liability for death or personal injury resulting from negligence.

[25] [1894] AC 217. See also *Union Steamships v Barnes* (1956) 5 DLR (2d) 535 (Canada).

[26] Cf *Geier v Kujawa, Weston and Warne Bros (Transport) Ltd* [1970] 1 Lloyd's Rep 364, 368 (where the plaintiff's ignorance of English was known).

[27] However, the ticket had been bought on the plaintiff's behalf by her niece and it was found that the niece's father had ascertained, before the ticket was taken, that there were conditions for excursion tickets.

[28] *White v Blackmore* [1972] 2 QB 651, 664. See also *Poseidon Freight Forwarding Co Ltd v Davies Turner Southern Ltd* [1996] 2 Lloyd's Rep 388 (reference to terms on back of faxed document but terms not communicated).

(iii) Exhibited notices

Printed notices containing conditions, for example, the notices exhibited at the counter of a left-luggage office at a railway station, have been held to become part of the contract where the ticket or receipt refers to the notice[29] and probably even where it does not, provided the notice is sufficiently prominent and can be plainly seen before or at the time of making the contract.[30] But there is also authority for the view that the terms of the notice must be 'brought home' to the party affected and accepted by that party as part of the contract.[31]

(iv) The notice must be in a contractual document

If the document is one which the person receiving it would scarcely expect to contain conditions, for example, if it consisted of the sort of ticket which a reasonable person would suppose to be merely a voucher or receipt, it cannot be said that the notice given was reasonably sufficient in the circumstances. It would be 'quite reasonable that the party receiving it should assume that the writing contained in it no condition, and should put it in his pocket unread'.[32]

In *Chapelton v Barry UDC*:[33]

C wished to hire a beach deck chair. He took two from a pile belonging to the defendant, paying 2*d* for each and receiving two tickets from an attendant. He set the chairs up firmly, sat on one, went through the canvas, and sued the defendant for personal injuries sustained. The defendant pleaded an exemption clause printed on the back of the ticket: 'The council will not be liable for any accident or damage arising from the hire of the chair.' C had glanced at the ticket but had not realized that it contained conditions.

The Court held that the defendant was not protected. A cheque-book cover[34] and a parking ticket issued by an automatic machine[35] have similarly been held to be non-contractual documents.

(v) Onerous or unusual terms

If the particular condition (whether an exemption clause or not) relied upon by one of the parties is onerous or unusual in that class of contract, special measures may be required fairly to bring it to the notice of the other party. It has even been said that some clauses 'would need to be printed in red ink on the face of the document with a

[29] *Watkins v Rymill* (1883) 10 QBD 178.

[30] *Olley v Marlborough Court Ltd* [1949] 1 KB 532, 549; *Ashdown v Samuel Williams & Sons Ltd* [1957] 1 QB 409; *Parker-Grennan v Camelot UK Lotteries Ltd* [2024] EWCA Civ 185 at [47] (incorporation of terms into online contract).

[31] *Harling v Eddy* [1951] 2 KB 739, 748; *McCutcheon v David Macbrayne Ltd* [1964] 1 WLR 125; *Smith v Taylor* [1966] 2 Lloyd's Rep 231; *Mendelssohn v Normand Ltd* [1970] 1 QB 177, 182.

[32] *Parker v South Eastern Ry Co* (1877) 2 CPD 416, 422 (Mellish LJ).

[33] [1940] 1 KB 532.

[34] *Burnett v Westminster Bank Ltd* [1966] 1 QB 742.

[35] *Thornton v Shoe Lane Parking Ltd* [1971] 2 QB 163.

red hand pointing to it before the notice could be held to be sufficient',[36] giving rise to a so-called 'red hand doctrine', although this is now better referred to as the 'onerous clause' doctrine.[37] This doctrine applies to both consumer and commercial contracts, although it is unlikely to apply in commercial contracts where the parties are of broadly equal bargaining power, and where the challenged clauses are common form or usual terms regularly encountered in the business.[38]

In *Interfoto Picture Library Ltd v Stiletto Visual Programmes Ltd* which, it should be noted, did not concern an exemption clause:[39]

Interfoto hired 47 transparencies to Stiletto. The transparencies were despatched to Stiletto in a bag containing a delivery note containing conditions printed in small but visible lettering on the face of the document, including condition 2, which stated that 'a holding fee of £5 plus VAT per day will be charged for each transparency which is retained . . . longer than . . . 14 days'. The daily rate per transparency was many times greater than was usual but nothing whatever was done by Interfoto to draw Stiletto's attention particularly to condition 2. Stiletto returned the transparencies 4 weeks later and Interfoto claimed £3,783.50.

The Court of Appeal held that the contract was made when, after the receipt of the transparencies, Stiletto accepted them by telephone. Although, to the extent the conditions were common form or usual terms, they were incorporated into the contract, it was held that condition 2 had not been so incorporated.[40] Bingham LJ stated:[41]

[Stiletto] are not to be relieved of . . . liability because they did not read the condition, although doubtless they did not; but in my judgment they are to be relieved because [Interfoto] did not do what was necessary to draw this unreasonable and extortionate clause fairly to their attention.

In Dillon LJ's words:[42]

[I]f one condition in a set of printed conditions is particularly onerous or unusual, the party seeking to enforce it must show that that particular condition was fairly brought to the attention of the other party.

[36] *J Spurling Ltd v Bradshaw* [1956] 1 WLR 461, 466 (Denning LJ); *Thornton v Shoe Lane Parking Ltd* [1971] 2 QB 163, 170. See also *Goodlife Foods Ltd v Hall Fire Protection Ltd* [2018] EWCA Civ 1371, [2018] CTLC 265 at [101] (it is a 'sliding scale'), doubted in *MS Amlin Marine NV v King Trader Ltd* [2025] EWCA Civ 1387, [2026] 2 WLR 163 at [87].

[37] *MS Amlin Marine NV v King Trader Ltd* [2025] EWCA Civ 1387 at [83].

[38] *Ibid* at [84], [101].

[39] [1989] QB 433.

[40] Interfoto could only recover a holding fee assessed on the basis of a quantum meruit, here £3.50 per transparency per week beyond the 14-day period: [1989] QB 433, 439, 445.

[41] [1989] QB 433, 445.

[42] *Ibid*, 439. See also *The Northern Progress* [1996] 2 Lloyd's Rep 321; *AEG (UK) Ltd v Logic Resources Ltd* [1996] CLC 265, 273 (Hirst LJ), but cf Hobhouse LJ *ibid*, 277 who took the view that Courts should lean towards treating clauses as incorporated given that, if unreasonable, they can now be struck down under the Unfair Contract Terms Act 1977; *O'Brien v MGN Ltd* [2001] EWCA Civ 1279, [2002] CLC 33 (rule of a competition held to be neither onerous nor unusual).

(c) COURSE OF DEALING; USUAL TRADE TERMS

An exemption clause will not necessarily be incorporated into a contract by virtue of a previous course of dealing between the same parties on similar terms.[43] But it may be where each party led the other reasonably to believe that it intended that their rights and liabilities should be ascertained by reference to the terms of a document which had been regularly and consistently used by them in previous transactions.[44]

Where the clause is a usual one in the trade, and the parties are of equal bargaining power in the same trade, less will be required in terms of the regularity of the previous course of dealing for it to be included in the contract.[45] Indeed, it may be better to regard such a clause as incorporated not so much because of the course of dealing but rather because of the common understanding of the parties based on the practice of the trade to which they belong.[46]

3. INTERPRETATION OF EXEMPTION CLAUSES

If the terms of a standard form contract have been incorporated, the next issue is the way in which its terms are to be interpreted (construed). The disparity between the bargaining power of consumers and large enterprises (both private and public) means that terms have often been imposed upon consumers which are unfair in their application and which exempt the enterprise putting forward the document, either wholly or in part, from its just liability under the contract. This was one of the reasons why, at common law, the Courts evolved certain canons of construction which normally work in favour of the party seeking to establish liability and against the party seeking to claim the benefit of the exemption. If, however, the clause is appropriately drafted so as to exclude or limit the liability in question, the Courts must (subject to the powers conferred on them by legislation, and in particular the Unfair Contract Terms Act 1977 and the Consumer Rights Act 2015)[47] give effect to it. Moreover, as between businesses, exemption clauses can perform a useful function; for example, anticipating future contingencies which hinder or prevent performance, establishing procedures for the making of claims and allocating of risks between the parties to the contract. In a business transaction, the effect of an exemption clause may simply be to determine which of the parties is to insure against a particular risk. Exemption clauses in business transactions are not necessarily unfair. But even in business transactions the Courts must be satisfied that the clause, on its wording, does

[43] *Hollier v Rambler Motors (AMC) Ltd* [1972] 2 QB 71 (no incorporation where claimant had signed a form containing exemption clauses on three or four occasions over a five-year period). See also *McCutcheon v David MacBrayne Ltd* [1964] 1 WLR 125. See generally Macdonald (1988) 8 LS 48.

[44] *Henry Kendall & Sons v William Lillico & Sons Ltd* [1969] 2 AC 31 (incorporation where parties had contracted three or four times a month over a three-year period). See also *J Spurling Ltd v Bradshaw* [1956] 1 WLR 461, 467; *Gillespie Bros & Co Ltd v Roy Bowles Transport Ltd* [1973] QB 400; *Circle Freight International Ltd v Medeast Gulf Exports Ltd* [1988] 2 Lloyd's Rep 427.

[45] *British Crane Hire Corp Ltd v Ipswich Plant Hire Ltd* [1975] QB 303 (usual term incorporated where only two transactions months before).

[46] *Ibid.*

[47] See below, pp 212–37.

have the effect contended for by the person relying on it, that is, the party seeking to exclude or restrict its liability.

It is a topical question whether the canons of construction for exemption clauses, developed at common law, have been, or should be, loosened not only because of the statutory controls over unfair terms that now exist but also in the light of the modern general approach to construction set out in *Investors Compensation Scheme Ltd v West Bromwich Building Society*.[48] The Courts now generally say that, at least in relation to commercial contracts negotiated between parties of equal bargaining power, the general principles of interpretation are sufficient.[49]

(a) STRICT INTERPRETATION

'If a person is under a legal liability and wishes to get rid of it, he can only do so by using clear words.'[50] The words of the exemption clause must exactly cover the liability which it is sought to exclude. So an exemption clause in a contract excluding liability for 'latent defects' will not exclude the condition as to fitness for purpose implied by the Sale of Goods Act;[51] exclusion of *implied* conditions and warranties will not exclude a term which is actually expressed;[52] and a clause excluding liability for breach of *warranty* will not exclude liability for breach of condition.[53] In *Wallis, Son & Wells v Pratt & Haynes*:[54]

W bought seed from P & H described as 'common English sainfoin' subject to an exemption clause that 'the sellers give no warranty express or implied, as to growth, description, or any other matters'. The seed turned out to be giant sainfoin, indistinguishable in seed, but inferior in quality and of less value. W was forced to compensate those to whom it had subsequently sold the seed, and sued to recover the money lost. P & H pleaded the exemption clause.

The House of Lords held that, even though W had accepted the goods and could therefore only sue for breach of warranty,[55] there was nevertheless originally a breach of the *condition* implied by section 13 of the Sale of Goods Act,[56] and this had not been successfully excluded.

Since the enactment of the Unfair Contract Terms Act 1977, there are indications of a less strict approach to construction, especially in commercial contracts. Although 'the reports are full of cases in which what would appear to be very strained constructions have been placed upon exclusion clauses',[57] mainly in consumer contracts and standard form contracts, it has recently been said that:

48 [1998] 1 WLR 896. See above, pp 162–9.

49 See *Bank of Credit and Commerce International SA v Ali* [2002] 1 AC 251 at [62] (Lord Hoffmann); *Transocean Drilling UK Ltd v Providence Resources plc* [2016] EWCA Civ 372, [2016] 1 CLC 585 at [14] (Moore-Bick LJ); *Triple Point Technology Inc v PTT Public Co Ltd* [2021] UKSC 29, [2021] AC 1148 at [107]–[108] (Lord Leggatt).

50 *Alison (J Gordon) Ltd v Wallsend Shipway and Engineering Co Ltd* (1927) 43 TLR 323, 324 (Scrutton LJ).

51 *Henry Kendall & Sons v William Lillico & Sons Ltd* [1969] 2 AC 31.

52 *Andrews Bros Ltd v Singer & Co Ltd* [1934] 1 KB 17.

53 *Baldry v Marshall* [1925] 1 KB 260.

54 [1911] AC 394.

55 Sale of Goods Act 1893, s 11(1)(c); see now Sale of Goods Act 1979, s 11(2), above, p 160.

56 See above, p 183.

57 *Photo Production Ltd v Securicor Transport Ltd* [1980] AC 826, 851 (Lord Diplock).

in recent years, and especially since the enactment of UCTA, the courts have softened their approach to both indemnity clauses and exemption clauses . . . Exemption clauses are part of the contractual apparatus for distributing risk. There is no need to approach such clauses with horror or with a mindset determined to cut them down. Contractors and consultants who accept large risks will charge for doing so and will no doubt take out appropriate insurance. Contractors and consultants who accept lesser degrees of risk will presumably reflect that in the fees which they agree.[58]

The principle whereby the words of written documents are interpreted more forcibly against the party putting forward the document ('*contra proferentem*') has been considered above.[59] An example of its application is provided by *John Lee & Son (Grantham) Ltd v Railway Executive*:[60]

The lease of a railway warehouse contained a clause exempting the lessors from liability for 'loss damage costs and expenses however caused . . . (whether by act or neglect of the company or their servants or agents or not) which but for the tenancy hereby created . . . would not have arisen'. Goods in the warehouse were damaged by fire owing to the alleged negligence of the lessors in allowing a spark to escape from their railway engines. The lessors claimed that the clause exempted them from liability.

The Court of Appeal held that the operation of the clause was confined by the words 'but for the tenancy hereby created' to liabilities which arose only by reason of the relationship of landlord and tenant created by the lease. Construing the clause against the lessors, they were not protected.

However, the less strict approach to interpretation of exclusion clauses, especially in commercial contracts negotiated between parties of equal bargaining power, along with the ambiguity as to whether the phrase '*contra proferentem*' means 'against the person who drew it up' or 'against the person relying on it', has led to doubts as to whether the *contra proferentem* rule is still needed.[61]

(b) EXCLUSION OF LIABILITY FOR DELIBERATE BREACH

The view that a wilful or deliberate breach necessarily falls outside the scope of an exemption clause has been firmly rejected by the House of Lords. Lord Wilberforce said:[62]

[58] *Persimmon Homes Ltd v Ove Arup and Partners Ltd* [2017] EWCA Civ 373, [2017] 2 CLC 28 at [56]–[57] (Jackson LJ). See also *Triple Point Technology Inc v PTT Public Co Ltd* [2021] UKSC 29 at [107] (Lord Leggatt); *Photo Production Ltd v Securicor Transport Ltd* [1980] AC 826, 843 (Lord Wilberforce), 851 (Lord Diplock).

[59] Above, p 169.

[60] [1949] 2 All ER 581. See also *Adams v Richardson & Starling Ltd* [1969] 1 WLR 1645, 1653 (construction of so-called 'guarantee'); *Tor Line AB v Alltrans Group of Canada Ltd* [1984] 1 WLR 48, 56.

[61] See above, p 169; *K/S Victoria Street v House of Fraser (Stores Management) Ltd* [2011] EWCA Civ 904, [2012] Ch 497 at [68]; *Persimmon Homes Ltd v Ove Arup and Partners Ltd* [2017] EWCA Civ 373 at [52]; *Impact Funding Solutions Ltd v Barrington Support Services Ltd* [2016] UKSC 57, [2017] AC 73 at [6]; *Triple Point Technology Inc v PTT Public Co Ltd* [2021] UKSC 29 at [111].

[62] *Suisse Atlantique Société d'Armement Maritime SA v NV Rotterdamsche Kolen Centrale* [1967] AC 361, 435. See also *ibid*, 394, 414, 415, 429; *Photo Production Ltd v Securicor Transport Ltd* [1980] AC 827; *China Shipbuilding Corp v Nippon Yusen Kabukishi Kaisha* [2000] 1 Lloyd's Rep 367, 376. Cf *Glynn v Margetson & Co* [1893] AC 351; *Sze Hai Tong Bank Ltd v Rambler Cycle Co Ltd* [1959] AC 576 (interpretation of clause so as not to cover deliberate breach which would run counter to the main object of the contract).

Some deliberate breaches ... may be, on construction, within an exceptions clause (for example, a deliberate delay for one day in loading). This is not to say that 'deliberateness' may not be a relevant factor: depending on what the party in breach 'deliberately' intended to do, it may be possible to say that the parties never contemplated that such a breach would be excused or limited ... but to create a special rule for deliberate acts is unnecessary and may lead astray.

(c) EXCLUSION OF LIABILITY FOR FRAUD

For reasons of policy, an exemption clause can never exclude a party's liability for its own fraud in inducing the making of the contract.[63] This is a rule of law, not a rule of construction, and so a clause cannot even by its clear and express terms exclude the contracting party from personal liability for fraud. However, it is not settled whether the rule also covers a purported exclusion of liability for the fraud of an agent or employee in which the contracting party was not personally involved.[64] But even if it is possible as a matter of law for a clause to exclude liability for the agent or employee's fraud, as a matter of construction it will do so only if the clause is clear; general language will not be construed so as to relieve a principal of liability for the fraud of an agent.[65]

(d) EXCLUSION OF LIABILITY FOR NEGLIGENCE

The ability of contracting parties to exclude their liability for negligence has been substantially restricted by legislation.[66] Apart from statutory restrictions, although it is possible to exclude liability in negligence, the Courts have traditionally approached clauses which are said to exclude such liability on the assumption that it is 'inherently improbable' that the innocent party would have agreed to the exclusion of the contract-breaker's negligence.[67] To have this effect the contractual term in question must exclude liability for negligence clearly and unambiguously. In *Rutter v Palmer*:[68]

R left his car at P's garage to be sold. The contract provided that 'customers' cars are driven by your [P's] servants at customers' sole risk'. The car was taken for a trial run by one of P's drivers, there was a collision and the car was damaged.

[63] *HIH Casualty and General Insurance Ltd v Chase Manhattan Bank* [2003] UKHL 6, [2003] 2 Lloyd's Rep 61 at [16] (Lord Bingham); see also at [76], [122]; *S Pearson & Son Ltd v Dublin Corp* [1907] AC 351; *Armitage v Nurse* [1998] Ch 241.

[64] *HIH Casualty and General Insurance Ltd v Chase Manhattan Bank* [2003] UKHL 6 at [16], [76]–[82], [98], [122].

[65] *S Pearson & Son Ltd v Dublin Corp* [1907] AC 351.

[66] Unfair Contract Terms Act 1977, ss 1(1), 2; Consumer Rights Act 2015, ss 57, 62, and 65. 'Gross negligence' and 'negligence' are merely a matter of degree: unlike civil law systems, English law does not equate 'gross negligence' with fraud: *Armitage v Nurse* [1998] Ch 241, 254.

[67] *Gillespie v Bowles (Roy) Transport Ltd* [1973] QB 400, 419 (Buckley LJ); *EE Caledonia Ltd v Orbit Valve Co Europe plc* [1994] 1 WLR 1515, 1523 (Steyn LJ); *Smith v South Wales Switchgear Co Ltd* [1978] 1 WLR 165, 168 (Viscount Dilhorne) (indemnity clause).

[68] [1922] 2 KB 87. See also *Levison v Patent Steam Carpet Cleaning Co Ltd* [1978] QB 69 ('at the owner's risk'); *Thompson v T Lohan (Plant Hire) Ltd* [1987] 1 WLR 649 ('the hirer ... alone shall be responsible for all claims ...').

It was held that the clause placed the risk of negligence on R and so his claim failed. Similarly, such phrases as: 'will not be liable for any damage however caused'[69] 'will not in any circumstances be responsible',[70] 'arising from any cause whatsoever'[71] will ordinarily be construed to cover liability for negligence.

On the other hand, there may be some ground of liability (other than negligence) to which the party seeking exemption is subject in respect of the loss or damage suffered, for example a strict liability for breach of contract.[72] If the alternative ground is not so fanciful or remote that the party cannot be supposed to have desired protection against it,[73] the exemption clause will be construed as extending to that ground alone, even if the words used are prima facie wide enough to cover negligence.[74] In *Canada Steamship Lines Ltd v The King*:[75]

A lease of a freight shed provided that the lessee should 'not have any claim against the lessor for damage to goods' in the shed. Owing to the negligence of the lessor's employees, a fire broke out and the lessee's goods in the shed were destroyed.

The Privy Council held that a strict liability was imposed upon the lessor by the Civil Code of Lower Canada and the exemption clause should be confined to that head of liability. The lessor was accordingly liable for the negligent destruction of the goods. The decision has been applied many times since, including by the House of Lords,[76] and it has been said that:[77]

Commercial contracts are drafted by parties with access to legal advice and in the context of established legal principles as reflected in the decisions of the courts . . . The parties to commercial contracts must be taken to know what those principles are and to have drafted their contract taking them into account; when the suggested result could have been easily obtained by an appropriate use of language but the parties instead only used general language, the result of the general principle is that the parties will not be taken to have intended to include the consequences of a party's negligence.

[69] *Joseph Travers & Sons Ltd v Cooper* [1915] 1 KB 73; *Ashby v Tolhurst* [1937] 2 KB 242; *White v Blackmore* [1972] 2 QB 651. Cf *Bishop v Bonham* [1988] 1 WLR 742.

[70] *Harris Ltd v Continental Express Ltd* [1961] 1 Lloyd's Rep 251; *John Carter (Fine Worsteds) Ltd v Hanson Haulage (Leeds) Ltd* [1965] 2 QB 495.

[71] *AE Farr Ltd v Admiralty* [1953] 1 WLR 965; *Lamport & Holt Lines Ltd v Coubro & Scrutton (M & I) Ltd* [1982] 2 Lloyd's Rep 42.

[72] *White v John Warwick & Co Ltd* [1953] 1 WLR 1285.

[73] *Canada Steamship Lines Ltd v The King* [1952] AC 292; *Smith v South Wales Switchgear Co Ltd* [1978] 1 WLR 165, 178.

[74] *Alderslade v Hendon Laundry Ltd* [1945] KB 189, 192; *Canada Steamship Lines Ltd v The King* [1952] AC 292, 208; *Sonat Offshore SA v Amerada Hess Development Ltd* [1988] 1 Lloyd's Rep 145, 157. Cf *Ailsa Craig Fishing Co Ltd v Malvern Fishing Co Ltd* [1983] 1 WLR 964, 970.

[75] [1952] AC 292.

[76] *Smith v South Wales Switchgear Co Ltd* [1978] 1 WLR 165, 168 (Lord Dilhorne in the context of an indemnity clause).

[77] *EE Caledonia Ltd v Orbit Valve Co Europe plc* [1994] 1 WLR 221, 228, 232 (Hobhouse J). See also *Shell Chemicals UK Ltd v P & O Roadtanks Ltd* [1995] 1 Lloyd's Rep 297, 301.

However, the House of Lords in *HIH Casualty and General Insurance Ltd v Chase Manhattan Bank*[78] has since indicated that the *Canada Steamship* principles, while giving helpful guidance, should not be treated as a rigid code and, more recently, the Court of Appeal has suggested that, at any rate in commercial contracts, the *Canada Steamship* guidelines (insofar as they survive) are now more relevant to indemnity clauses than to exemption clauses.[79] In *HIH Casualty* a generally worded clause excluding all liability of an insured to an insurer for misrepresentation or non-disclosure of its agent was held, on its true construction, not to exclude liability (whether for damages or rescission) for the agent's fraudulent misrepresentation or fraudulent non-disclosure.[80] But as part of the reasoning it was held that the clause did apply to exclude liability for negligent misrepresentation or non-disclosure even though a rigid application of the *Canada Steamship* principles would have led to the contrary result (because liability for innocent misrepresentation or non-disclosure was a realistic possibility).

Where the head of damage in respect of which liability is sought to be imposed by an exemption clause is one which rests on negligence and nothing else, one would expect the clause to be construed as extending to that head of damage, because if it were not so construed 'it would lack subject matter'.[81] However, this conclusion has not always been reached. In *Hollier v Rambler Motors (AMC) Ltd*:[82]

H arranged by telephone to have his car repaired by RM and subsequently sent the car to RM's premises for this purpose. On at least two previous occasions when RM had carried out repairs for him he had signed a form on which appeared the printed words: 'The company is not responsible for damage caused by fire to customer's cars on the premises.' While on the premises, the car was damaged by a fire caused by RM's negligence.

The Court of Appeal held that there was no sufficient previous course of dealing to incorporate the exemption clause into the oral contract;[83] but, in any event, the language of the clause did not exclude liability for negligence. Although the only ground of liability on the part of RM would have been liability in negligence, the clause was not so plain as to indicate that RM was exempting itself in respect of damage caused by fire due to its own negligence. Rather it was a warning to customers as to the legal position where fire was caused without the defendants' negligence.[84] H therefore succeeded in an action against RM for breach of the contract of bailment.

[78] [2003] UKHL 6, [2003] 2 Lloyd's Rep 61, applied in *Lictor Anstalt Mir Steel UK Ltd v Morris* [2012] EWCA Civ 1397, [2013] 2 All ER (Comm) 54 when deciding that an indemnity against 'any claim' in respect of certain machinery covered claims for intentional torts such as inducing breach of contract and conspiracy. See also *Greenwich Millennium Village Ltd v Essex Services Group plc* [2014] EWCA Civ 960, [2014] 1 WLR 3517 at [91], [94].

[79] *Persimmon Homes Ltd v Ove Arup and Partners Ltd* [2017] EWCA Civ 373 at [56]. See also *Triple Point Technology Inc v PTT Public Co Ltd* [2021] UKSC 29 at [111] (Lord Leggatt: the *Canada Steamship* test is an 'old and outmoded formula').

[80] Above, p 200.

[81] *Aldersdale v Hendon Laundry Ltd* [1945] KB 189, 192.

[82] [1972] 2 QB 71.

[83] See above, p 197.

[84] It is arguable (see above, pp 198–9) that, given the protection for particular contractors and types of clause in modern statutes, such a hostile construction would not now be adopted, even in a consumer contract such as this, which would be governed by the Consumer Rights Act 2015.

(e) LIMITATION CLAUSES

It has been held that a less rigorous approach governs clauses that merely limit the compensation payable but do not totally exclude liability. In *Ailsa Craig Fishing Co Ltd v Malvern Fishing Co Ltd and Securicor (Scotland) Ltd*,[85] a case from Scotland:

S undertook to provide continuous security cover in respect of ACF's fishing vessel in Aberdeen harbour but, by reason of negligence and breach of contract, the vessel fouled the boat berthed next to her and sank. The loss of the vessel cost ACF £55,000. S's standard conditions of contract provided inter alia that its liability 'whether under express or implied terms of the contract, or at common law or in any other way' for any loss or damage was limited to £1,000.

The House of Lords held that, although the *contra proferentem* rule applied to limitation clauses, such clauses were not to be construed by the particularly exacting standards applicable to clauses totally excluding liability and indemnity clauses. According to Lord Fraser, this was because there was a higher degree of improbability that a contracting party would agree to a total exclusion of liability than to a limitation of liability particularly where, as in that case, 'the potential losses that might be caused by the negligence of the proferens or its servants are so great in proportion to the sums that can reasonably be charged for the services contracted for'.[86] In Lord Wilberforce's view, the distinction followed because limitation clauses 'must be related to other contractual terms, in particular to the risks to which the defending party may be exposed, the remuneration which he receives, and possibly also the opportunity of the other party to insure'.[87]

It is, however, somewhat difficult to see why such a clear distinction should be drawn between these two types of exemption clause. In particular, it is not clear why only limitation clauses are 'related to other contractual terms' and to 'the opportunity of the other party to insure'. There may also be practical difficulties. Take the example of first, a clause *excluding* all liability, but not until three months after the delivery of goods,[88] and, secondly, a clause *limiting* liability to £100, but from the start.[89] Which is to be construed more generously? It is submitted that '[t]here is no difference in principle between words which save [contracting parties] from having to pay at all and words which save them from paying as much as they would otherwise have had to pay'.[90] It has

[85] [1983] 1 WLR 964.

[86] *Ibid*, 970 (Lord Fraser). This statement was approved by the House of Lords in *George Mitchell (Chesterhall) Ltd v Finney Lock Seeds Ltd* [1983] 2 AC 803, 810, 813, 817.

[87] *Ailsa Craig Fishing Co Ltd v Malvern Fishing Co Ltd* [1983] 1 WLR 964, 966 (Lord Wilberforce).

[88] *Atlantic Shipping & Trading Co Ltd v Louis Dreyfus & Co* [1922] 2 AC 250. See also 'cesser' clauses in charterparties excluding the charterer's liability for breach once a cargo is shipped and replacing it with an alternative remedy by way of lien on the cargo: *Overseas Transportation Co v Mineralimportexport* [1972] 1 Lloyd's Rep 201.

[89] See the combined operation of the package, unit, and weight limitations of Art IV, r 5, of the Hague/Visby Rules and the one-year time bar under Art III, r 6: Carriage of Goods by Sea Act 1971, Sched.

[90] *Atlantic Shipping & Trading Co Ltd v Louis Dreyfus & Co* [1922] 2 AC 250, 260 (Lord Sumner). See also *Darlington Futures Ltd v Delco Australia Pty Ltd* (1986) 161 CLR 500, 510 (High Court of Australia), disapproving the statements in *Ailsa Craig Fishing Co Ltd v Malvern Fishing Co Ltd* [1983] 1 WLR 964.

been suggested that the two types of clause should be characterized by reference to the substance of their provisions rather that the particular wording used, and that the more extreme the consequences are, in terms of excluding or modifying the liability which would otherwise arise, the more stringent the Court's approach should be in requiring that the exclusion or liability be clearly and unambiguously expressed.[91]

(f) 'FUNDAMENTAL' TERMS AND 'FUNDAMENTAL BREACH'

(i) Rule of construction not a rule of law

Previously there was considered to be a common law doctrine which seemed to offer some escape from even the most carefully drafted exemption clauses. This was the doctrine of the 'breach of a fundamental term' or of 'fundamental breach'.[92]

There were, it was said, in every contract certain *terms* which were fundamental, the breach of which amounted to a complete non-performance of the contract. A fundamental term was conceived to be something more basic than a warranty or even a condition. It formed the 'core' of the contract and therefore could not be affected by any exemption clause.[93] For example, 'If a man offers to buy peas of another, and he sends him beans, he does not perform his contract; but that is not a warranty; there is no warranty that he should sell him peas; the contract is to sell peas, and if he sends him anything else in their stead, it is a non-performance of it' against which no exemption clause could prevail.[94]

A closely connected principle was that no party to a contract could exempt himself from responsibility for a fundamental *breach*. Although its limits were never precisely defined, it was said that a party could only claim the protection of an exemption clause 'when he is carrying out his contract, not when he is deviating from it or is guilty of a breach which goes to the root of it'.[95] The two principles were in some cases used interchangeably.[96] They appeared to establish that, however extensive an exemption clause, it could not exclude liability in respect of the breach of a fundamental term or of a fundamental breach. Expressed in this way, the doctrine constituted a substantive rule of law which operated irrespective of the intention of the parties and limited their freedom of contract.

The 'rule of law' approach was rejected in *UGS Finance Ltd v National Mortgage Bank of Greece*.[97] Pearson LJ stated:

[91] *BHP Petroleum Ltd v British Steel plc* [2000] 2 Lloyd's Rep 277, 285.

[92] See Guest (1961) 77 LQR 98; Reynolds (1963) 79 LQR 534; Lord Devlin [1966] CLJ 192; Jenkins [1969] CLJ 251; Legh-Jones and Pickering (1970) 86 LQR 513; Baker (1970) 33 MLR 441; Weir [1970] CLJ 180; Coote [1970] CLJ 221; Dawson (1975) 91 LQR 380; Coote (1977) 40 MLR 31.

[93] *Smeaton Hanscomb & Co Ltd v Sassoon I Setty, Son & Co* [1953] 1 WLR 1468, 1470.

[94] *Chanter v Hopkins* (1838) 4 M & W 399, 404. See also *Bowes v Shand* (1877) 2 App Cas 455, 480.

[95] *J Spurling Ltd v Bradshaw* [1956] 1 WLR 461, 465 (Denning LJ). See also *Alexander v Railway Executive* [1951] 2 KB 882.

[96] Cf Lord Upjohn in the *Suisse Atlantique* case [1967] 1 AC 361, 421.

[97] [1964] 1 Lloyd's Rep 446, 450.

I think there is a rule of construction that normally an exception or exclusion clause or similar provision in a contract should be construed as not applying to a situation created by a fundamental breach of contract. This is not an independent rule of law imposed by the court on the parties willy-nilly in disregard of their contractual intention. On the contrary it is a rule of construction based on the intention of the contracting parties.

Pearson LJ's approach was unanimously endorsed by the House of Lords in *Suisse Atlantique Société d'Armement Maritime SA v NV Rotterdamsche Kolen Centrale*:[98]

SA chartered the *Silvretta* to RKC for a period of 2 years. It was agreed that, in the event of delays in loading or unloading the vessel, RKC would pay to SA $1,000 a day by way of demurrage.[99] Lengthy delays occurred for which SA alleged RKC was responsible, but it nevertheless allowed RKC to continue to have the use of the ship for the remainder of the term. On conclusion of the contract, SA sued RKC for damages, claiming a sum in excess of that stipulated for as demurrage. RKC relied on the demurrage clause as limiting its liability.

The House of Lords rejected the argument that the breaches would have entitled SA to treat the contract as repudiated; that these breaches amounted to a fundamental breach of contract; and that in consequence RKC could not rely upon the clause which limited their liability to $1,000 a day. Their Lordships held that the demurrage clause was not an exemption clause but an 'agreed damages' provision,[100] but considered that, even if it had been considered an exemption clause, as a matter of construction it covered the breaches which had occurred. Assuming that these breaches amounted to a fundamental breach of contract, in the sense that SA would have been entitled to treat itself as discharged from further performance, there was no rule of law which would prevent the application of an exemption clause to such a breach.

Certain statements in the *Suisse Atlantique* case were nevertheless open to the interpretation that in some situations a substantive doctrine of 'fundamental breach' still existed.[101] The heresy that a 'fundamental breach' of contract deprived the party in breach of the benefit of an exemption clause was not finally laid to rest by the House of Lords until *Photo Production Ltd v Securicor Transport Ltd*:[102]

S agreed to provide a visiting patrol service to PP's factory at a charge of approximately 26p per visit. The contract contained an exemption clause, the most relevant part of which stated: 'Under no circumstances shall the company [S] be responsible for any injurious act or default by any employee . . . unless such act or default could have been foreseen and avoided by the exercise of due diligence on the part of the company . . .' An employee of S, while on patrol, deliberately lit a fire in the factory. The fire spread and a large part of the premises was burned down.

98 [1967] 1 AC 361; noted by Treitel (1966) 29 MLR 546.

99 Demurrage is a sum agreed by the charterer to be paid to the owner as liquidated damages for delay beyond a stipulated or reasonable time for loading or unloading.

100 See below, p 583.

101 [1967] 1 AC 361, 398, 427, 432. See *Harbutt's 'Plasticine' Ltd v Wayne Tank and Pump Co Ltd* [1970] 1 QB 447 (exemption clause did not apply where further performance impossible or innocent party accepted breach as terminating contract); *Wathes (Western) Ltd v Austins (Menswear) Ltd* [1976] 1 Lloyd's Rep 14.

102 [1980] AC 827. See also *George Mitchell (Chesterhall) Ltd v Finney Lock Seeds Ltd* [1983] 2 AC 803; *Kenya Railways v Antares Co Pte Ltd* [1987] 1 Lloyd's Rep 424; Unfair Contract Terms Act 1977, s 9 (repealed by the Consumer Rights Act 2015).

The House of Lords reversed the Court of Appeal's decision that, since S had been engaged to safeguard the factory, the deliberate act of their employee in starting a fire was not covered by the exemption clause. It concluded that, on the true construction of the clause in the context of the contract, in particular the limited nature of the contractual task, the modesty of the charge, and the ability of the factory owners to insure against fire more economically, the risk assumed by S was a modest one.[103] Accordingly, S had effectively modified its obligation under the contract to the exercise of due diligence in its capacity as an employer, and there was no evidence of any lack of due diligence on its part to foresee or prevent the fire. S was therefore absolved from liability. Their Lordships once again affirmed their opinion that the question whether or not an exemption clause protected a party to a contract in the event of breach, or in the event of what would (but for the presence of the exemption clause) have been a breach, depended upon the construction of the contract. Even if the breach was so serious as to entitle the injured party to treat the contract as repudiated,[104] or to render further performance impossible, the other party was not prevented from relying on the clause.

Any need for a substantive doctrine of fundamental breach has largely been obviated by the enactment of the Unfair Contract Terms Act 1977.[105] In the *Photo Production* case, Lord Diplock stated[106] that, if the expression 'fundamental breach' was to be retained, it should be confined to the ordinary case of a breach of which the consequences are such as to entitle the innocent party to elect to put an end to all primary obligations of both parties remaining unperformed.[107] Similarly it may be supposed that, if the expression 'fundamental term' is to be retained, it should be employed simply as an alternative method of describing a promissory condition.[108] There does not now exist in English law any special rule or rules applicable to cases of 'fundamental breach' where exemption clauses are concerned. No doubt, in deciding whether an exemption clause is, on its true construction, applicable to a particular breach, the Court may reach the conclusion that the parties never intended the clause to apply to the breach in question because its nature or seriousness is such as not to fall within the contemplated ambit of the clause. The parties are less likely to be taken to have agreed that one of them shall be excused in the case of a total non-performance or a performance which is wholly at variance with the object of the contract as ascertained from its other terms and the circumstances surrounding it. But there is no separate category of 'fundamental breaches' against which exemption clauses cannot prevail; if sufficiently clear, they will do so against even the most serious and deliberate breach. So, for example, the one-year time bar in the Hague-Visby Rules applies to fundamental and deliberate breaches.[109]

[103] [1980] AC 827, 846, 851, 852.

[104] See below, pp 531–3.

[105] See below, p 212. Certain types of contract are wholly or partly excepted from the operation of that Act: see below, p 215.

[106] [1980] AC 827, 849.

[107] See below, pp 531–3.

[108] See *Suisse Atlantique Société d'Armement Maritime SA v NV Rotterdamsche Kolen Centrale* [1967] 1 AC 361, 398, 427, 432–5.

[109] *Kenya Railways v Antares Co Pte Ltd* [1987] 1 Lloyd's Rep 424, 429–30; *Compania Portorafti Commerciale SA v Ultramar Panama Inc* [1990] 1 Lloyd's Rep 310.

Moreover, in Australia it has been held that an exemption clause which stated it applied 'whether or not loss ... is caused by ... fundamental breach of contract' prevailed against a fundamental breach.[110]

Having established that 'fundamental breach' is now a matter of construction, rather than being a rule of law,[111] it is appropriate to consider the construction of exemption clauses for 'fundamental breaches' in certain familiar types of contract.[112]

(ii) Sale of goods

We have seen that, in a contract of sale of goods, by reason of the Sale of Goods Act 1979 and the Consumer Rights Act 2015, certain terms as to title, correspondence with description and sample, fitness for purpose, and satisfactory quality are implied into, or are treated as included in, the contract.[113] The Unfair Contract Terms Act 1977 and the Consumer Rights Act 2015[114] have either absolutely or subject to certain qualifications largely abrogated the power of a seller to exclude these terms.[115] At common law, however, the Courts have refused to apply an exemption clause covering 'defects in quality' to situations where there was a gross disparity between the goods described in the contract of sale and those delivered, or where the goods were so defective that they were completely unfit for the purpose for which they were required.[116] For example, where copra cake contained so great an admixture of castor beans as to render it dangerous to cattle, a clause disclaiming responsibility for 'defects' was held inapplicable, because what was delivered was not truly copra cake at all.[117] As Lord Wilberforce pointed out in the *Suisse Atlantique* case:[118] 'Since the contracting parties could hardly have been supposed to contemplate such a misperformance, or to have provided against it without destroying the whole contractual substratum, there is no difficulty here in holding exemption clauses to be inapplicable.' But this is a matter of construction only and the construction will be affected by the contractual context. So, 'if an anxious hostess is late in the preparation of a meal, she can perfectly well say: "Send me peas or if you haven't got peas, send beans; but for heaven's sake send something". That would be a contract for peas, beans or anything else *ejusdem generis* and it is a perfectly sensible contract to make.'[119]

[110] *Glebe Island Terminals Pty Ltd v Continental Seagram Pty Ltd* [1994] 1 Lloyd's Rep 213 (New South Wales Court of Appeal), cf Handley JA dissenting, at 230.

[111] With the demise of the principle of 'fundamental breach', it can no longer be said that the defendant carries the burden of disproving fundamental breach.

[112] For other types of contract, where the Courts have construed clauses covering very serious breach, see, eg, *A Turtle Offshore SA v Superior Trading Inc* [2008] EWHC 3034 (Admlty), [2009] 1 Lloyd's Rep 177 (towage); *Internet Broadcasting Corp Ltd v MAR LLC* [2009] EWHC 844 (Ch), [2009] 2 Lloyd's Rep 295 (internet broadcasting joint venture); *Mott Macdonald Ltd v Trant Engineering Ltd* [2021] EWHC 754 (TCC), [2021] BLR 440 (engineering consultancy services).

[113] Above, pp 182–8.

[114] See below, pp 217, 227.

[115] The Unfair Contract Terms Act 1977 does not apply to, eg, the international sale of goods.

[116] eg *Munro & Co Ltd v Meyer* [1930] 2 KB 312; *Champanhac & Co Ltd v Waller & Co Ltd* [1948] 2 All ER 724. Cf *George Mitchell (Chesterhall) Ltd v Finney Lock Seeds Ltd* [1983] 2 AC 803.

[117] *Pinnock Brothers v Lewis and Peat Ltd* [1923] 1 KB 690.

[118] [1967] 1 AC 361, 433.

[119] Lord Devlin [1966] CLJ 192, 212. On this example, see above, p 204, n 94.

(iii) Hire-purchase

The exclusion of terms implied, or treated as included, in hire-purchase contracts is also subject to the Unfair Contract Terms Act 1977 and the Consumer Rights Act 2015.[120] At common law it is governed by similar principles to those in sales. A case of this nature arose in *Karsales (Harrow) Ltd v Wallis*:[121]

W was shown a second-hand Buick motor-car in excellent condition and wished to buy it on hire-purchase. His agreement with the finance company contained an exemption clause excluding liability for breach of conditions or warranties of any description. After the contract had been concluded, the car was towed at night to W's premises in a deplorable state. Many detachable parts had been removed; new parts had been replaced by old; and the engine was now so defective that the car would not go. W refused to accept it and was sued by K, the assignee of the finance company.

The Court of Appeal held that the exemption clause was ineffective because what was contracted for had not been delivered: 'a car that would not go was not a car at all'.[122] On the other hand, a similar clause has been held to cover the delivery of a car which, though unroadworthy and unsafe when hired and in a 'lamentable condition', did still function as a car. These defects were covered by the clause.[123]

(iv) Carriage of goods

It is possible that a version of the fundamental breach rule of law lives on in respect of 'deviation' by a carrier, a matter left open by the House of Lords in the *Suisse Atlantic* and *Photo Production* decisions.[124] Most of the cases concern the carriage of goods by sea but the same principles apply to carriage by land.[125] The basic idea is that a carrier, who deviates without justification from the recognized or agreed route, steps outside the 'four corners' of the contract and cannot claim the benefit of a clause designed to protect only when the carrier is acting in pursuance of its provisions.[126] Put another way, if a ship contracted to carry goods from A to B deviates from her ordinary route, the contract voyage comes to an end, and the shipowner cannot thereafter rely upon an exemption clause in the contract even though the loss or damage to the goods is not attributable to the deviation.[127]

[120] See below, pp 217, 227.

[121] [1956] 1 WLR 936. See also *Farnworth Finance Facilities Ltd v Attryde* [1970] 1 WLR 1053, discussing earlier decisions.

[122] [1956] 1 WLR 936, 942 (Birkett LJ). See also Parker LJ at 943.

[123] *Handley v Marston* (1962) 106 SJ 327. See also *Astley Industrial Trust Ltd v Grimley* [1963] 1 WLR 584.

[124] *Suisse Atlantique Société d'Armement Maritime SA v NV Rotterdamsche Kolen Centrale* [1967] 1 AC 361; *Photo Production Ltd v Securicor Transport Ltd* [1980] AC 827, 845.

[125] *London & North Western Ry v Neilson* [1922] 2 AC 263 (disclaimed liability for loss of goods 'in transit' did not cover deviation).

[126] eg *Cunard SS Co Ltd v Buerger* [1927] AC 1; *Stag Line Ltd v Foscolo, Mango & Co Ltd* [1932] AC 328; *Hain Steamship Co v Tate & Lyle* (1936) 41 Com Cas 350. See *Suisse Atlantique Société d'Armement Maritime SA v NV Rotterdamsche Kolen Centrale* [1967] 1 AC 361, 390, 399, 411, 422, 433; Reynolds, 'The Deviation Problem' (Butterworths Lectures 1990–91) 29; Dockray [2000] LMCLQ 76.

[127] *Joseph Thorley Ltd v Orchis Steamship Co Ltd* [1907] 1 KB 660.

Contracts made between businesses for the carriage of goods by ship fall, as respects loss of or damage to the cargo, outside the Unfair Contract Terms Act 1977,[128] so the 'deviation cases' continue to be of considerable importance in this context.

It has been suggested that the deviation cases should be assimilated into the ordinary law of contract,[129] and therefore the non-applicability of an exemption clause where there has been a deviation should be based on its construction, but that such an approach is not open given the authority of an earlier decision of the House of Lords[130] which was not impliedly overruled by the House of Lords' decisions in *Suisse Atlantique* and *Photo Production*.[131] At present, therefore, deviation is a rule of law that applies irrespective of the parties' intentions or the particular wording of the clause in question.

Where a carrier has undertaken to stow cargo below deck but carries it on deck, it has been held to be a question of construction whether an exemption clause applies to such unauthorized deck carriage. Hence a clause limiting liability to a specified sum per package of cargo[132] and a clause requiring all claims to be brought within one year[133] have both been held to apply, as a matter of construction, to unauthorized deck carriage.

Misdelivery of the goods by the carrier may be covered by an appropriately drafted exemption clause.[134] But where the main object and intent of the contract is that delivery should be made to a certain person or persons, the Court may be prepared to limit the operation of the clause to the extent that it is inconsistent with that main object and intent. In *Sze Hai Tong Bank Ltd v Rambler Cycle Co Ltd*:[135]

R despatched goods by sea from England to Singapore. The bill of lading required the goods to be delivered 'unto order or assigns' and stated that 'the responsibility of the carrier shall be deemed to cease absolutely after the goods are discharged from the ship'. After the goods were discharged from the ship, the carrier's agents did not deliver them 'unto order or assigns' but released the goods to the consignees without production of the bill of lading, with the result that R was never paid for the goods.

The Privy Council held that, although the exemption, on the face of it, could hardly have been more comprehensive, it did not permit the shipping company deliberately to disregard its obligations as to delivery.[136] To hold otherwise would defeat the main object and intent of the contract. The carrier was therefore liable.

[128] Sched 1, para 2(c).

[129] *Dera Commercial Estate v Derya Inc, The Sur* [2018] EWHC 1673 (Comm), [2019] 1 All ER 1147 at [107]–[111] (Carr J, agreeing with Lloyd LJ in *Kenya Railways v Antares Co Pte Ltd* [1987] 1 Lloyd's Rep 424, 430 and modern commentaries on maritime law).

[130] *Hain Steamship Co v Tate & Lyle* (1936) 41 Com Cas 350.

[131] *Dera Commercial Estate v Derya Inc, The Sur* [2018] EWHC 1673 (Comm) at [112]–[116].

[132] *Daewoo Heavy Industries Ltd v Klipriver Shipping Ltd, The Kapitan Petko Voivoda* [2003] EWCA Civ 451, [2003] 2 Lloyd's Rep 1. See Hague-Visby Rules, Art III, para 5, contained in the Schedule to the Carriage of Goods by Sea Act 1971.

[133] *Kenya Railways v Antares Co Pte Ltd* [1987] 1 Lloyd's Rep 424 (Hague-Visby Rules, Art III, para 6).

[134] *Chartered Bank v British India Steam Navigation Co Ltd* [1909] AC 369; *FIMBank Plc v KCH Shipping Co Ltd* [2023] EWCA Civ 569, [2023] 1 CLC 732 (Hague-Visby Rules, Art III, para 6).

[135] [1959] AC 576. See also *Motis Exports Ltd v Dampskibsselskabet AF 1912 Akt* [2000] 1 Lloyd's Rep 211, 216–17.

[136] In *Suisse Atlantique Société d'Armement Maritime SA v NV Rotterdamsche Kolen Centrale* [1967] 1 AC 361, the decision in *Sze Hai Tong Bank* was said to be based on construction but the suggestion that a deliberate breach was a fundamental breach which could not be excluded was rejected. See above, p 199.

(v) Bailment

In the *Suisse Atlantique* case Lord Hodson stated:[137]

Under a contract of carriage or bailment if the carrier or bailee uses a place other than that agreed on for storing the goods, or otherwise exposes the goods to risks quite different from those contemplated by the contract, he cannot rely on clauses in the contract designed to protect him against liability within the four corners of the contract . . .

It is first necessary to determine what are the 'four corners' of the contract. If, for instance, a railway company contracts to keep an item in a station cloakroom but keeps it elsewhere in the station and it is stolen or damaged, it will not be able to rely on a clause exempting it from liability in respect of loss or damage. But if, on its true construction, the contract is not to keep the item necessarily in the cloakroom, but to keep it at the station, reliance can be placed on the clause.[138] Again, warehousemen who stored groundnuts in a warehouse otherwise suitable but not rat-proof were able to rely on a term of the contract excluding liability in the absence of 'wilful neglect or default' when sued in respect of damage to and contamination of the nuts by rats.[139] Although the warehousemen's storage had been negligent, the place where the nuts were stored was one permitted by the contract and the risk to which they were exposed was not one which was wholly uncontemplated by the contract. Since no wilful neglect or default had been proved, the warehousemen were not liable.

The Courts are extremely unlikely to allow a bailee who has converted the goods to shelter under the provisions of an exemption clause which simply disclaimed liability for loss or damage to the goods bailed, unless the clause specifically authorized the bailee to do the act in question, for example to sell the goods in the event that they were not claimed.[140] A simple disclaimer of liability cannot have been intended by the parties to permit the bailee 'to give the goods away to some passerby, or to burn them or throw them into the sea'.[141]

On the other hand, an appropriately drafted exemption clause has been held, at common law, to cover an honest, but negligent, redelivery of the goods to the wrong person.[142]

Exemption clauses in consumer contracts of bailment, and in non-consumer contracts where the goods are bailed on the bailee's written standard terms of business or where the goods are lost or damaged by negligence, are subject to the Consumer Rights Act 2015 and the Unfair Contract Terms Act 1977 respectively.[143]

[137] [1967] 1 AC 361, 412.

[138] *Gibaud v Great Eastern Railway Co* [1921] 2 KB 426.

[139] *Kenyon, Son & Craven Ltd v Baxter Hoare & Co Ltd* [1971] 1 WLR 519.

[140] *Alexander v Railway Executive* [1951] 2 KB 882, 889; *Garnham, Harris & Elton Ltd v Alfred W Ellis (Transport) Ltd* [1967] 1 WLR 940, 946.

[141] *Sze Hai Tong Bank Ltd v Rambler Cycle Co Ltd* [1959] AC 576, 587.

[142] *Hollins v J Davy Ltd* [1963] 1 QB 844.

[143] See below, pp 218, 227.

4. OTHER COMMON LAW RULES CONTROLLING EXEMPTION CLAUSES

The operation of exemption clauses may be further limited by the application of certain other rules of the common law.

(a) EXPRESS UNDERTAKINGS

A collateral oral warranty may be enforced even though it runs counter to the terms (including exemption clauses) of the principal agreement.[144] There is a still more general principle, that is, that where an express undertaking is given which is inconsistent with the printed clauses of a standard form document, the latter must be rejected insofar as they are repugnant to the express undertaking. In *J Evans & Son (Portsmouth) Ltd v Andrea Merzario Ltd*:[145]

E, an importer of machines, arranged the carriage of the machines to England under a contract with AM, a forwarding agent. AM orally assured E that machines shipped in containers would be carried under deck. Nevertheless, eight containers carrying E's machines were subsequently loaded on deck. One container fell overboard and was a total loss. AM denied liability, relying on an exemption clause in the contract of carriage.

It was held that AM's oral assurance overrode the exemption clause, and that it was liable for breach of the warranty given.

(b) MISREPRESENTATION OF CONTENT OR OF EFFECT OF CLAUSE

A party who misrepresents (albeit innocently) the content or effect of a clause inserted by it into a contract cannot rely on the clause in the face of the misrepresentation. So in *Curtis v Chemical Cleaning & Dyeing Co*:[146]

C took a dress to the defendant company for cleaning. She signed a receipt containing a clause exempting the defendant from all liability for damage to articles cleaned after the defendant's servant told her that it would not accept liability for certain specified risks, including damage to the beads and sequins on the dress. When it was returned, the dress was badly stained.

It was held that, as C had been induced to believe that the clause only referred to the beads and sequins, the defendant was not entitled to rely on it in respect of damage by staining. Denning LJ, dealing with the question of exemption clauses generally, said:[147]

144 Above, p 146. On the overriding of an exemption clause, see *Webster v Higgin* [1948] 2 All ER 127.

145 [1976] 1 WLR 1078. See also *Couchman v Hill* [1947] KB 544; *Gallagher v British Road Services Ltd* [1970] 2 Lloyd's Rep 440; *Mendelssohn v Normand Ltd* [1970] 1 QB 177.

146 [1951] 1 KB 805. See also *Jacques v Lloyd D George & Partners Ltd* [1968] 1 WLR 625.

147 [1951] 1 KB 805, 808.

Any behaviour, by words or conduct, is sufficient to be a misrepresentation if it is such as to mislead the other party about the existence or extent of the exemption. If it conveys a false impression, that is enough.

(c) REASONABLENESS AT COMMON LAW?

The theory of freedom of contract presupposed that any party to a contract is free to choose whether or not to enter into it, and regarded a party who chose to enter into a contract which is onerous as only having itself to blame.[148] But the bargaining powers of the parties may be so unequal that one can virtually dictate terms to the other. As long ago as 1877 in *Parker v South Eastern Railway Co*,[149] Bramwell LJ asked what the position would be if some unreasonable condition were inserted as, for instance, to forfeit £1,000 if goods in a station cloakroom were not removed within 48 hours. He thought that 'there is an implied understanding that there is no condition unreasonable to the knowledge of the party tendering the document and not insisting on its being read'. Lord Denning MR on numerous occasions[150] maintained that an exemption clause would not be given effect if it was unreasonable, or if it was unreasonable to apply it in the circumstances of the case, for 'there is the vigilance of the common law which, while allowing freedom of contract, watches over to see that it is not abused'.[151] But this approach has not been accepted as part of the common law and it is clear that the Courts have no general power at common law to strike down a contractual term merely because it is unreasonable or unfair.[152] Such a power has, however, been conferred by statute, notably by the Unfair Contract Terms Act 1977 and by the Consumer Rights Act 2015.

5. LEGISLATIVE CONTROL OF EXEMPTION CLAUSES AND UNFAIR TERMS

(a) EXEMPTION CLAUSES IN NON-CONSUMER CONTRACTS: UNFAIR CONTRACT TERMS ACT 1977

The Unfair Contract Terms Act 1977 (UCTA)[153] limits, and, in some cases, takes away entirely, the right to rely on contractual exemption clauses (and non-contractual notices) in certain situations. The Act originally applied to both consumer and

[148] See above, p 4.

[149] (1877) 2 CPD 416, 428.

[150] eg *Gillespie Bros & Co Ltd v Roy Bowles Transport Ltd* [1973] QB 400, 416; *Levison v Patent Steam Carpet Cleaning Co Ltd* [1978] QB 69, 161; *Photo Production Ltd v Securicor Transport Ltd* [1978] 1 WLR 856, 865 (revs'd [1980] AC 827).

[151] *John Lee & Son (Grantham) Ltd v Railway Executive* [1949] 2 All ER 581, 584.

[152] *Suisse Atlantique Société d'Armement Maritime SA v NV Rotterdamsche Kolen Centrale* [1967] 1 AC 361, 406; *Photo Production Ltd v Securicor Transport Ltd* [1980] AC 827, 848.

[153] See Coote (1978) 41 MLR 312; Sealy [1978] CLJ 15; Palmer and Yates [1981] CLJ 108; Adams and Brownsword (1988) 104 LQR 94; Macdonald, in Burrows and Peel (eds), *Contract Terms* (2007) ch 8. The Act derives substantially from recommendations made by the Law Commission: Law Com No 69 (1975); Scot Law Com No 39 (1975). See generally Law Com No 292, *Unfair Terms in Contracts* (2005).

non-consumer contracts and notices, but now applies only to non-consumer contracts and notices.[154]

(i) Scope of the Act

The title of the Act is somewhat misleading. It is not confined to contract terms but also extends to non-contractual notices containing provisions exempting from liability in tort.[155] Secondly, the Act does not give the Courts a general power to strike down any term of a contract on the ground that the term is unfair or oppressive; it applies to terms that 'exclude or restrict liability' (ie exemption clauses). It also does not, in general, purport to affect the basis of liability,[156] so that the first enquiry must normally be whether the person seeking to rely on the term is in fact under any liability (or obligation), for example, in negligence or for breach of contract. Also logically prior to the application of the Act is the question whether the relevant term has become a term of the contract[157] and, if so, whether on its true construction it applies to the liability which it is sought to exclude or restrict.[158] The tests of incorporation and construction, considered earlier in this chapter, must be applied before considering the Act. It has been said that the existence of the statutory controls makes it unnecessary to apply unduly strict tests of incorporation and construction.[159] But, even accepting this, the application of the Act should not be considered until it has been decided that, applying the tests of incorporation and construction, the exclusion or limitation clause in question forms part of the contract and covers the events that have occurred. If it is either not incorporated or does not cover those events, then, however reasonable the clause, it will not apply.

(ii) Pattern of control

Some of the provisions of the 1977 Act overlap, so that, when applying it to a particular situation, it is often necessary to consider whether more than one section is relevant.[160] The pattern of control is also somewhat complicated (see Table 6.1). There are three broad divisions of control: first, control over contract terms that exclude or restrict

[154] The provisions relating to consumer contracts and notices were removed and are now found, together with other protections for consumers, in the Consumer Rights Act 2015, below, pp 226–36. By reason of the 2015 Act, ss 1 and 61, a consumer contract is a contract between a trader and a consumer; and by s 2, a 'trader' means 'a person acting for purposes relating to that person's trade, business, craft or profession' and a 'consumer' means 'an individual acting for purposes that are wholly or mainly outside that individual's trade, business, craft or profession'. The distinction between an 'individual' and a 'person' is that an 'individual' means a natural person whereas a 'person' can include a company. Whether a person is a consumer is determined objectively, in relation to the particular transaction in issue: *Eternity Sky Investments Ltd v Zhang* [2024] EWCA Civ 630, [2024] Bus LR 1550 at [74]. The amendment of UCTA 1977 was effected by the Consumer Rights Act 2015, Sched 4. Cases before 2015 which involved consumer contracts generally remain authoritative, but must be read in their context (eg in their application of the 'reasonableness' test under the 1977 Act, s 11).

[155] Unfair Contract Terms Act 1977, s 2.

[156] But see 1977 Act, s 3(2)(b).

[157] 1977 Act, s 11(2). See above, pp 192–7.

[158] See above, pp 197–210.

[159] *Photo Production v Securicor Transport* [1980] AC 827, 843 (Lord Wilberforce), 851 (Lord Diplock); *AEG (UK) Ltd v Logic Resource Ltd* [1996] CLC 265, 277 (Hobhouse LJ); and see above, pp 198–9.

[160] eg 1977 Act, ss 2, 3, and 7.

Table 6.1 Non-Consumer Contracts: Pattern of Control of UCTA

Types of Contract	Type of Liability Excluded/Restricted	Liability of a Business	Liability of a Non-Business
Any contract	Negligent personal injuries	Unexcludable UCTA, s 2(1)	UCTA does not apply
	Negligent loss or damage	Reasonableness UCTA, ss 2(2) and 11(1)	UCTA does not apply
Standard form contract	Any breach of contract	Reasonableness UCTA, ss 3(2) and 11(1)	UCTA does not apply
Sale of goods*	Breach of Sale of Goods Act 1979, s 12, undertakings as to title	Unexcludable UCTA, s 6(1)	
	Breach of Sale of Goods Act 1979, ss 13 and 15, undertakings as to description or sample	Reasonableness UCTA, ss 6(1A), 11(1)–(2), Sched 2	
	Breach of Sale of Goods Act 1979, s 14, undertakings as to fitness for purpose and satisfactory quality	Reasonableness UCTA, ss 6(1A), 11(1)–(2), Sched 2	Although UCTA on the face of it applies, these terms are implied only where the party relying on the exemption is acting in the course of a business

* Control of terms implied into contracts of hire-purchase follows the same pattern: UCTA, s 6. The control of terms implied into other contracts under which goods pass follows a similar pattern but only for business liability: UCTA, s 7.

liability for 'negligence'[161] (which includes breach of a contractual duty to exercise reasonable care and skill in the performance of a contract); secondly, control over contract terms that exclude or restrict liability for breach of certain terms implied by statute in contracts of sale of goods or hire-purchase, and in other contracts for the supply of goods;[162] thirdly, control in standard form contracts over terms that exclude or restrict liability for breach of contract.[163]

If the contract term is subject to the control of the Act, the control may assume one of two forms: the exclusion or restriction of liability may be rendered absolutely ineffective,[164] or it may be effective only insofar as the term satisfies the requirement of reasonableness.[165]

[161] 1977 Act, s 2. 'Negligence' is defined in s 1(1).
[162] 1977 Act, ss 6, 7.
[163] 1977 Act, s 3.
[164] 1977 Act, ss 2(1), 6(1), 7(3A).
[165] 1977 Act, ss 2(2), 3(2), 6(1A), 7(1A), (4).

(iii) 'Business liability'

The 1977 Act is concerned, for the most part,[166] with terms that exclude or restrict 'business liability', that is, 'liability for breach of obligations or duties arising—(a) from things done or to be done by a person in the course of a business (whether his own business or another's), or (b) from the occupation of premises used for business purposes of the occupier'.[167] The word 'business' has, however, been described as 'an etymological chameleon',[168] and it will not always be easy to determine whether or not there is a business liability, for example, in the case of a university or college, since it does not appear necessary for a business that an activity be carried on with a view to profit.[169]

(iv) Excepted contracts

In addition to consumer contacts,[170] certain very important contracts are wholly or partly excepted from the operation of the 1977 Act. These include contracts of insurance,[171] commercial charterparties,[172] contracts between businesses for the carriage of goods by sea,[173] international supply contracts,[174] contracts of employment (except in favour of an employee)[175] and any contract so far as it relates to[176] the creation or transfer of an interest in land,[177] or of intellectual property,[178] or of securities.[179] In some of these, however, there are specific legislative controls on exemption clauses.[180]

[166] On the face of it, there is a major exception by reason of the 1977 Act, s 6(4) (exclusion of implied terms in contracts of sale of goods or hire-purchase). But the width of that exception is restricted because certain terms will only be implied if the seller or owner sells or hires the goods in the course of a business: see above, pp 184–7. The consequence is that the only application of UCTA to (non-consumer) contracts where the defendant is *not* acting in the course of a business, so that the liability is not business liability, is in a contract for the sale of goods or hire-purchase where there is an exemption of the implied term as to title (non-excludable) or of the implied term as to the goods' conformity with description or sample (only excludable if reasonable).

[167] 1977 Act, s 1(3).

[168] *Town Investments Ltd v Department of the Environment* [1978] AC 359, 383 (Lord Diplock).

[169] See the partial definition in 1977 Act, s 14.

[170] UCTA 1977 now only applies to non-consumer contracts: Consumer Rights Act 2015, Sched 4.

[171] 1977 Act, Sched 1, para 1(a).

[172] 1977 Act, Sched 1, para 2.

[173] 1977 Act, Sched 1, paras 2–3.

[174] 1977 Act, s 26. See *Amiri Flight Authority v BAE Systems plc* [2003] EWCA Civ 1447, [2004] 1 All ER (Comm) 385 (held not to fall within s 26); *Trident Turboprop (Dublin) Ltd v First Flight Couriers Ltd* [2009] EWCA Civ 290, [2010] QB 86 (held to fall within s 26: see also below, p 355).

[175] 1977 Act, Sched 1, para 4.

[176] See *Micklefield v SAC Technology Ltd* [1990] 1 WLR 1002 (share option); *Unchained Growth III plc v Granby Village (Manchester) Management Co Ltd* [2000] 1 WLR 739 (maintenance charge in lease integral to and thus 'relates to' interest in land).

[177] 1977 Act, Sched 1, para 1(b).

[178] 1977 Act, Sched 1, para 1(c); Trade Marks Act 1994, s 106(1) and Sched 4, para 1; *Salvage Association v CAP Financial Services Ltd* [1995] FSR 654.

[179] 1977 Act, Sched 1, para 1(e).

[180] Below, p 236.

(v) Varieties of exemption clause

The 1977 Act applies to contract terms 'excluding or restricting' specific types of liability; but by section 13(1) these are extended to include terms:

(a) making the liability or its enforcement subject to restrictive or onerous conditions;
(b) excluding or restricting any right or remedy in respect of liability, or subjecting a person to any prejudice in consequence of his pursuing any such right or remedy;
(c) excluding or restricting rules of evidence or procedure.

Section 13 also extends to excluding or restricting liability by terms which exclude or restrict the relevant obligation or duty; and section 3(2)(b) applies to a term by which a party claims to be entitled to render a contractual performance substantially different from that which was reasonably expected or no performance at all.[181] The intention is clearly to embrace terms which, though they do not specifically exclude or restrict *liability*, have a similar effect and thus to prevent evasion of the policy of the Act.[182] For example, terms which require one party to make a claim within a certain time limit,[183] which take away the right to reject defective goods or to withhold payment (because of a set-off),[184] which state that an architect's certificate shall be 'conclusive evidence' that building work has been properly carried out, or which declare that the other party does not 'give any warranty or undertaking, express or implied, in respect of the goods supplied' or accept any responsibility with respect to the accuracy of a property valuation it supplies[185]—all of these are subject to control.

The difficulty, however, is to distinguish such terms from provisions which prevent a contractual duty from arising or circumscribe its extent, or which merely allocate the responsibilities under the contract between the parties[186] or which constitute a compromise or settlement or release or waiver of one's rights.[187] A seller's warning that goods should not be used after a specified time and a statement that the seller of a painting had no expertise in paintings of that type have been held to preclude the implication of obligations of fitness for purpose and correspondence with description under the Sale of Goods Act 1979 and not to exclude or restrict them.[188] It has been stated that the

[181] See below, p 219.

[182] Coote, *Exception Clauses* (1964) famously considered that all exclusion clauses are best analysed as merely defining the relevant duty so that there is no breach. But this extreme view has clearly not been accepted in UCTA 1977 which for the most part assumes the validity of the traditional two-stage 'breach and then exemption' analysis.

[183] *RW Green Ltd v Cade Bros* [1978] 1 Lloyd's Rep 602.

[184] *Stewart Gill Ltd v Horatio Myer & Co Ltd* [1992] 1 QB 600; *Skipskredittforeningen v Emperor Navigation* [1998] 1 Lloyd's Rep 66; *Schenkers Ltd v Overland Shoes Ltd* [1998] 1 Lloyd's Rep 498.

[185] *Smith v Eric S Bush* [1990] 1 AC 831.

[186] *Thompson v T Lohan (Plant Hire) Ltd* [1987] 1 WLR 649.

[187] *Tudor Grange Holdings Ltd v Citibank NA* [1992] Ch 53.

[188] *Wormell v RHM Agriculture (East) Ltd* [1987] 1 WLR 1091 (1979 Act, s 14(3)); *Harlingdon & Leinster Enterprises Ltd v Christopher Hull Fine Art Ltd* [1990] 1 All ER 737 (1979 Act, s 13). See above, pp 183–7, on these implied terms.

test is one of substance[189] but also that one has to ask whether 'but for' the clause there would be liability;[190] a formal test. It is submitted that, although it has the attraction of certainty, the latter test is too rigid and that the Courts should determine whether a term in a contract 'excludes or restricts' liability by asking whether it deprives a contracting party of the contractual performance which the parties reasonably expected.[191]

(vi) Liability for negligence

Restrictions are placed by section 2 of the 1977 Act on the power of a party to a contract to secure exemption from business liability for negligence.[192] It is prohibited to exclude or restrict liability for death or personal injury resulting from negligence by reference to any contract term.[193] In the case of other loss or damage, a party to a contract cannot exclude or restrict liability for negligence except insofar as the term satisfies the requirement of reasonableness.[194] Where, in a contract between A and B, a term purports to transfer from A to B responsibility for injury or damage caused to B by A's employees, that term has been held to fall within section 2.[195] But a term requiring B to indemnify A against injury or damage caused to third parties by A's negligence has been held not to fall within section 2 on the ground that it was not an 'exclusion or restriction' of A's liability to the third-party victim but an arrangement by A and B as to the responsibility for compensating the victim.[196]

(vii) Sale of goods and hire-purchase

Section 6 of the 1977 Act restricts the ability of sellers of goods to exempt themselves from liability for breach of the terms implied in contracts of sale by sections 12 to 15 of the Sale of Goods Act 1979. First, it prohibits absolutely the exclusion or restriction of

189 *Phillips Products Ltd v Hyland* [1987] 1 WLR 659, 666; *Johnstone v Bloomsbury Health Authority* [1992] QB 333, 346.

190 *Smith v Eric S Bush* [1990] 1 AC 831, 857 (Lord Griffiths). Note that in the notice there was a non-contractual disclaimer.

191 Macdonald [1992] LS 277. See also Law Com No 69 (1975), para 146.

192 'Negligence' includes breach of a contractual or common law duty to take reasonable care or to exercise reasonable skill, and breach of the common duty of care under the Occupiers' Liability Act 1957.

193 1977 Act, s 2(1); *Johnstone v Bloomsbury HA* [1992] QB 333, 343, 346.

194 1977 Act, s 2(2).

195 *Phillips Products Ltd v Hyland* [1987] 1 WLR 659; *Flamar Interocean Ltd v Denmore Ltd* [1990] 1 Lloyd's Rep 434 ('deemed servant' clauses).

196 *Thompson v T Lohan (Plant Hire) Ltd* [1987] 1 WLR 649; *Hancock Shipping Co Ltd v Deacon & Trysail (Private) Ltd* [1991] 2 Lloyd's Rep 550. See also *Neptune Orient Lines Ltd v JCV (UK) Ltd* [1983] 2 Lloyd's Rep 438, 442 (promise not to sue third party).

liability for breach of the provisions of section 12 of the 1979 Act (terms as to title).[197] Secondly, liability for breach of the provisions of sections 13 to 15 of the 1979 Act (conditions as to satisfactory quality, fitness for purpose, and correspondence with description or sample) cannot be excluded or restricted except insofar as the term satisfies the requirement of reasonableness.[198]

Section 6 of the 1977 Act further contains similar provisions which prohibit, either absolutely or subject to the test of reasonableness, terms excluding or restricting liability for breach of the terms implied in contracts of hire-purchase by the Supply of Goods (Implied Terms) Act 1973.[199]

(viii) Supply contracts

Section 7 of the 1977 Act is concerned with contract terms excluding or restricting business liability for breach of an implied obligation in a contract (other than a contract of sale of goods or hire-purchase) 'where the possession or ownership of goods passes under or in pursuance of' the contract. Examples of such contracts are contracts of hire, and contracts for work and materials, such as building and engineering contracts. The Supply of Goods and Services Act 1982[200] implies into such contracts terms similar to those implied in contracts of sale of goods in respect of the goods' correspondence with description or sample, or their quality or fitness for purpose. The 1977 Act lays down that liability for breach of these implied terms can be excluded or restricted only insofar as the exempting term satisfies the requirement of reasonableness.[201] Terms excluding or restricting liability for breach of implied terms as to title to or quiet possession of the goods are also subject to the test of reasonableness in contracts of hire[202] but are prohibited absolutely in contracts for work and materials.[203]

(ix) Contractual liability under standard terms of business

Section 3 of the 1977 Act effects a more wide-ranging and general control of contractual liability.[204] This section may apply, in addition to sections 6 and 7 mentioned above, to contracts of sale and hire-purchase and supply contracts. But it may also apply to any contract, unless it is of a type expressly excepted by the Act. Thus, it may apply, for example, to a contract to garage a car or store furniture. The section applies as between contracting parties where one of them deals on the other's written standard terms of business,[205] and the liability which it is sought to exclude or restrict is a business liability. Thus, the many contracts between businesses, made by reference to standard terms and conditions printed in order forms, confirmations of order, or in catalogues or price lists are subject to section 3.

The Court of Appeal has recently explained the scope of section 3.[206] A party relying on the section has the burden of showing that the contract term which it challenges

[197] 1977 Act, s 6(1). [198] 1977 Act, s 6(1A). [199] Above, p 188.
[200] Above, p 188. [201] 1977 Act, s 7(1A). [202] 1977 Act, s 7(4).
[203] 1977 Act, s 7(3A).
[204] Where there is the breach of a contractual duty of care, s 2 rather than s 3 (which is narrower) will, in practice, be applied.
[205] 1977 Act, s 3 also originally applied where one party was dealing as a consumer, but the reference to 'as a consumer' was deleted by the Consumer Rights Act 2015, Sched 4, para 5.
[206] *African Export-Import Bank v Shebah Exploration and Production Co Ltd* [2017] EWCA Civ 845, [2018] WLR 487.

is part of the other party's standard terms of business, and that the other is dealing on those standard terms of business.[207] It must be shown that that other party habitually uses those terms of business: it is not enough that it sometimes does and sometimes does not, nor is it enough to show that a model form (drafted by a third party) has, on the particular occasion, been used; the model form must be habitually used by the other party.[208] Secondly, if there have been more than insubstantial variations to the terms which may otherwise have been habitually used by the other party, it is unlikely that the party relying on the Act will be able to show that the contract was made 'on the other's written standard terms of business'.[209] This is a question of fact and degree.[210]

The control imposed by the section is as follows:[211]

As against that party,[212] the other cannot by reference to any contract term—

(a) when himself in breach of contract, exclude or restrict any liability of his in respect of the breach; or
(b) claim to be entitled—
 (i) to render a contractual performance substantially different from that which was reasonably expected of him, or
 (ii) in respect of the whole or any part of his contractual obligation, to render no performance at all,

except in so far as . . . the contract term satisfies the requirement of reasonableness.

The wording of the first limb (a) of this provision, relating to the exclusion or restriction of liability in respect of breach of contract, is relatively easy to interpret. But the second limb (b) is more difficult to construe. It would appear to be the intention of (b) that it should apply in cases where there is *no breach of contract at all*, but one party claims to rely on a term of the contract which purports to entitle it either to render a contractual performance substantially different from that which was reasonably expected at the time of the contract or in respect of the whole or part of the contractual obligation to render no performance at all.[213]

It has been held that the second limb (b) did not apply to a term permitting an employer to dismiss an employee during the first two years of employment without going through the contractual disciplinary procedure.[214] Although expressed in negative terms, it merely set out the employee's entitlement and the limit of his rights.[215]

[207] *Ibid* at [18].

[208] *Ibid* at [20], approving *British Fermentation Products Ltd v Compair Reavell Ltd* [1999] 2 All ER (Comm) 389.

[209] *Ibid* at [25]. The question is not whether the challenged term was varied in the parties' negotiations, but whether the written standard terms as a whole were varied: *ibid* at [36]. See also *Pinewood Technologies Asia Pacific Ltd v Pinewood Technologies Plc* [2023] EWHC 2506 (TCC) at [48]–[49].

[210] *Chester Grosvenor Hotel Co Ltd v Alfred McAlpine Management Ltd* (1991) 56 BLR 115, 131–3; *St Albans City & DC v International Computers Ltd* [1996] 4 All ER 481, 491.

[211] 1977 Act, s 3(2).

[212] ie the person dealing on the other's written standard terms of business.

[213] *Shearson Lehman Hutton Inc v Maclaine, Watson & Co Ltd* [1989] 2 Lloyd's Rep 570, 612.

[214] *Brigden v American Express Bank Ltd* [2000] IRLR 94.

[215] See also *Peninsula Business Services Ltd v Sweeney* [2004] IRLR 49 (clause in employment contract by which an employee forfeited his right to earned commission once the contract has been terminated).

Nor did the exercise by a lender of its contractual right to increase the interest rate payable under a mortgage loan agreement fall within section 3(2)(b): fixing the interest rate was either not 'contractual performance' within section 3(2)(b)(i), or was altering not the lender's performance but the borrower's.[216]

In contrast, examples of the application of the second limb (b) include the following. A holiday cruise line company agrees with a holiday tour operator to provide a certain quality and number of cabins for customers of the tour operator. It nevertheless reserves the right, in certain circumstances, to accommodate the customers in lower quality cabins or to switch the customers to a different cruise-liner, or to cancel the cruise in whole or in part.[217] A telephone company reserves the right to disconnect a telephone service without demonstrable reason or cause.[218] Another possible example is a *force majeure* clause excusing a trader from delivering goods to be supplied under the contract, or to suspend or cancel the contract without any further liability on its part upon the happening of events beyond the trader's control such as strikes, war, civil commotion, inability to obtain supplies, etc. However, while in the cases of the holiday cruise line company and the telephone company, it is likely to be held that such provisions do not satisfy the requirement of reasonableness, it seems unlikely that a *force majeure* clause in a commercial agreement would be held to be unreasonable[219] in the absence of special circumstances.[220]

(x) The 'reasonableness' test

Except in those instances where the 1977 Act prohibits absolutely the exclusion or restriction of liability,[221] the contract terms controlled by the Act are subject to the test of reasonableness.[222] The question to be decided by the Court in all cases where the 'reasonableness' test is applied in relation to a contract term is whether the term is a fair and reasonable one to have been included 'having regard to the circumstances which were, or ought reasonably to have been, known to or in the contemplation of the parties when the contract was made'.[223] It is therefore clear that the crucial time is the time of the making of the contract, and not the time at which liability arises.[224] The reasonableness of a contract term is therefore not affected by the nature or seriousness of the loss or damage sustained, except to the extent that it was or ought to have been

216 *Paragon Finance plc v Nash* [2001] EWCA Civ 1466, [2002] 1 WLR 685 at [71]–[77].

217 Cf *Anglo Continental Holidays Ltd v Typaldos Lines (London) Ltd* [1967] 2 Lloyd's Rep 61.

218 *Timeload Ltd v British Telecommunications plc* (1995) 3 EMLR 459, 468 (Sir Thomas Bingham MR); cf *Paragon Finance plc v Nash* [2001] EWCA Civ 1466 at [73]–[75].

219 *Shearson Lehman Hutton Inc v MacLaine, Watson & Co Ltd* [1989] 2 Lloyd's Rep 570, 612. See also *Brigden v American Express Bank Ltd* [2000] IRLR 94, 96.

220 eg in an exclusive dealing agreement where the supplier is entitled to suspend in the event of *force majeure* but the purchaser is not entitled, during the suspension, to purchase supplies from elsewhere.

221 1977 Act, ss 2(1), 6(1), 7(3A).

222 1977 Act, ss 2(2), 3(2), 6(1A), 7(1A), (4).

223 1977 Act, s 11(1).

224 *Stewart Gill v Horatio Myer & Co* [1992] 1 QB 600, 607, 608. The reasonableness of a non-contractual notice is determined having regard to the circumstances when the liability arose or would have arisen: 1977 Act, s 11(3); *Smith v Eric S Bush* [1990] 1 AC 831, 848, 857.

in contemplation at the time the contract was made. It is also clear that circumstances solely known to one party, that is, the person relying on the exemption clause, such as the experimental nature of the product supplied or the market difficulties involved in procuring it, are to be treated as irrelevant if they were not known, and could not reasonably have been known, to the other party at the time the contract was made.

It has been said that 'it is impossible to draw up an exhaustive list of factors to be taken into account' in assessing the reasonableness of an exemption or limitation clause.[225] In order to assist the Court in determining whether a term satisfies the requirement of reasonableness, the Act sets out five 'guidelines' as to matters to be taken into account.[226] Strictly these guidelines are applicable to the test of reasonableness only in respect of the exclusion or restriction of liability for breach of the implied obligations as to description, sample, quality, and fitness for purpose in contracts of sale of goods and hire-purchase,[227] and supply contracts[228] But 'the considerations there set out are normally regarded as being of general application to the question of reasonableness'.[229] However, even where the guidelines are directly applicable, they are not exhaustive; the Court is required to have regard 'in particular' to those matters, but it can also take account of any other relevant circumstances. The five guidelines are:

(a) the strength of the bargaining positions of the parties relative to each other, taking into account (among other things) alternative means by which the customer's requirements could have been met;
(b) whether the customer received an inducement to agree to the term, or in accepting it had an opportunity of entering into a similar contract with other persons, but without having to accept a similar term;
(c) whether the customer knew or ought reasonably to have known of the existence and extent of the term (having regard, among other things, to any custom of the trade and any previous course of dealing between the parties);
(d) where the term excludes or restricts any relevant liability if some condition is not complied with, whether it was reasonable at the time of the contract to expect that compliance with that condition would be practicable;
(e) whether the goods were manufactured, processed, or adapted to the special order of the customer.

It will be seen that these guidelines could open up quite extensive enquiries, for instance, as to the market position at the time the contract was made. The Court should not, however, be too ready to focus on remote possibilities or to conclude that a clause fails the test by reference to relatively uncommon or unlikely situations.[230]

225 *Smith v Eric S Bush* [1990] 1 AC 831, 858.

226 1977 Act, s 11(2), Sched 2.

227 1977 Act, s 6(1A).

228 1977 Act, s 7(1A). By ss 7(4) and 11(2), they also apply to the implied term as to title or quiet possession in contracts of hire.

229 *Stewart Gill v Horatio Myer & Co* [1992] 1 QB 600, 608 (Stuart-Smith LJ). See also *Flamar Interocean Ltd v Denmore* [1990] 1 Lloyd's Rep 434, 438; *Smith v Eric S Bush* [1990] 1 AC 831, 858 (Lord Griffiths); *Regus (UK) Ltd v Epcot Solutions Ltd* [2008] EWCA Civ 361, [2009] 1 All ER (Comm) 586 at [20] (Rix LJ); *Avrora Fine Arts Investment Ltd v Christie, Manson & Woods Ltd* [2012] EWHC 2198 (Ch), [2012] PNLR 35 at [149] (Newey J).

230 *Skipskredittforeningen v Emperor Navigation* [1998] 1 Lloyd's Rep 66, 75–6.

If a contract term seeks to restrict liability to a specified sum of money (eg a term which limits a seller's total liability for loss or damage arising from defects in the goods to £20,000) and the question arises whether the term satisfies the requirement of reasonableness, the 1977 Act requires that regard is also to be had in particular to (1) the resources which the seller would expect to be available to it for the purpose of meeting the liability should it arise, and (2) how far it was open to it to cover itself by insurance.[231]

The burden of proving that a contract term satisfies the requirement of reasonableness rests upon the party which claims that it is reasonable.[232]

The control of exemption and limitation clauses by a test of reasonableness means that decisions are made on a case by case basis and turn on the type of contract and the precise nature of the relationship between the parties. The consequence is a body of law that is flexible. First instance decisions as to whether a clause is reasonable can be seen as broadly similar to exercises of structured discretion. It has been stated that Courts must entertain a wide 'range of considerations, put them into the scales on one side or the other, and decide at the end of the day on which side the balance comes down'.[233] In such circumstances there will be room for a legitimate difference of judicial opinion as to the correct answer, and for this reason the decision of the judge at first instance will be treated 'with the utmost respect' and appellate Courts will 'refrain from interference with it unless satisfied that it proceeded upon some erroneous principle or was plainly and obviously wrong'.[234] An example of such an error was where the trial judge considered the reasonableness of the part of the exemption clause that was in issue, requiring a purchaser to return defective goods at its own expense, separately from the rest of the clause, which in effect excluded all other warranties and conditions including those implied by the Sale of Goods Act.[235]

In practice the decided cases have indicated that the following factors are the most significant.[236]

(1) The relative bargaining strength of the parties[237] in relation to the clause in question.[238] A clause that has been imposed by one side is less likely to be

[231] 1977 Act, s 11(4). [232] 1977 Act, s 11(5).

[233] *George Mitchell (Chesterhall) Ltd v Finney Lock Seeds Ltd* [1983] 2 AC 803, 816.

[234] *Ibid*, 810 (Lord Bridge). See also *Phillips Products Ltd v Hyland* [1987] 1 WLR 659, 669.

[235] *AEG (UK) Ltd v Logic Resources Ltd* [1996] CLC 265. A rare example of the Court of Appeal overturning the trial judge's assessment of reasonableness is provided by *Watford Electronics Ltd v Sanderson CFL Ltd* [2001] EWCA Civ 317, [2001] 1 All ER (Comm) 696.

[236] As well as decisions on the 1977 Act, guidance is gained from those on the Misrepresentation Act 1967, s 3 (below, p 354, and *Howard Marine and Dredging Co Ltd v A Ogden & Sons (Excavations) Ltd* [1978] QB 574), the Sale of Goods Act 1893, s 55 (as amended by the Supply of Goods (Implied Terms) Act 1973 but now replaced by the Unfair Contract Terms Act 1977, ss 6–7), but see *Rasbora Ltd v JCL Marine Ltd* [1977] 1 Lloyd's Rep 645; *George Mitchell (Chesterhall) Ltd v Finney Lock Seeds Ltd* [1983] 2 AC 803.

[237] *Howard Marine and Dredging Co Ltd v A Ogden & Sons (Excavations) Ltd* [1978] QB 574, 594 (Lord Denning MR); *George Mitchell (Chesterhall) Ltd v Finney Lock Seeds Ltd* [1983] QB 284, 302; *Smith v Eric S Bush* [1990] 1 AC 831, 858; *Singer Co (UK) Ltd v Hartlepool Port Authority* [1988] 2 Lloyd's Rep 164, 169; *St Albans City and District Council v International Computers Ltd* [1995] FSR 686, aff'd [1996] 4 All ER 481; *Regus (UK) Ltd v Epcot Solutions Ltd* [2008] EWCA Civ 361, [2009] 1 All ER (Comm) 586 at [40]. See Guideline (a) in Sched 2 to the 1977 Act.

[238] eg a supplier may be willing to negotiate the price, but will only supply on its standard terms: *Balmoral Group Ltd v Borealis (UK) Ltd* [2006] EWHC 1900 (Comm), [2006] 2 Lloyd's Rep 629 at [407]–[409]; *Last Bus Ltd v Dawsongroup Bus and Coach Ltd* [2023] EWCA Civ 1297, [2023] 4 WLR 80 at [49]–[50].

reasonable than one that was negotiated by the parties, or was the product of negotiations between representative bodies, or had evolved over time as a result of trade practice.[239] The question is not whether the clause is reasonable in the abstract, but in the particular contract between the particular parties.[240] However, the Courts have tended to adopt a 'non-interventionist' approach where the contract has been made between commercial parties of equal bargaining power. In the words of Tuckey LJ, with whom Hart J and Potter LJ agreed, in *Granville Oil and Chemicals Ltd v Davies Turner and Co Ltd*:[241]

> The 1977 Act obviously plays a very important role in protecting vulnerable consumers from the effect of draconian contract terms. But I am less enthusiastic about its intrusion into contracts between commercial parties of equal bargaining strength, who should generally be considered capable of being able to make contracts of their choosing and expect to be bound by their terms.

(2) The question of how far it would have been practicable and convenient to go elsewhere.[242] Similarly, where a party seeking to rely on a clause has given the other party the opportunity to pay more for the contractual performance without the clause, the clause is more likely to be held to be reasonable. For instance, in a number of standard forms governing contracts for the carriage of goods, the liability of the carrier is limited unless the owner of the goods declares their value and pays an increased charge.[243] The size of the limit compared with other limits in widely used standard terms may also be relevant.[244]

(3) The availability of insurance is an important factor, albeit by no means decisive.[245] The statutory requirement that regard is to be had to how far it was open to the party seeking to limit liability to cover itself by insurance[246] seeks to protect the small business, and possibly also professional persons who might not have the resources to meet unlimited liability should it arise, and who might not be able to obtain insurance cover against such liability. In their case, it might well be reasonable to impose a financial limit on liability. The provision

[239] *Howard Marine and Dredging Co Ltd v A Ogden & Sons (Excavations) Ltd* [1978] QB 574, 594 (Lord Denning MR); *George Mitchell (Chesterhall) Ltd v Finney Lock Seeds Ltd* [1983] QB 284, 302, 307, 314; [1983] 2 AC 803, 817; *Schenkers Ltd v Overland Shoes* [1998] 1 Lloyd's Rep 498, 507. Trade practice without negotiation is not a weighty factor.

[240] *Phillips Products Ltd v Hyland* [1987] 1 WLR 659, 668. A clause in a commonly-used standard form contract may still be held to be unreasonable: see, eg, *Walker v Boyle* [1982] 1 WLR 495, 507–8.

[241] [2003] EWCA Civ 570, [2003] 1 All ER (Comm) 819 at [31]. See also *Watford Electronics Ltd v Sanderson CFL Ltd* [2001] EWCA Civ 317; *Goodlife Foods Ltd v Hall Fire Protection Ltd* [2018] EWCA Civ 1371 at [61]–[63], [93], [103]–[104].

[242] *Overseas Medical Supplies Ltd v Orient Transport Services Ltd* [1999] 2 Lloyd's Rep 273, 277.

[243] *Gillespie v Roy Bowles Transport Ltd* [1973] QB 400, 446. See, eg, clause 26(A) and (D) of the British International Freight Association's Standard Trading Conditions (2021 edn). See also Guideline (b) in Sched 2 to the 1977 Act; *Singer Co (UK) Ltd v Hartlepool Port Authority* [1988] 2 Lloyd's Rep 164, 170.

[244] *Overseas Medical Supplies Ltd v Orient Transport Services Ltd* [1999] 2 Lloyd's Rep 273, 277.

[245] *Ibid*; *Balmoral Group Ltd v Borealis (UK) Ltd* [2006] EWHC 1900 (Comm); *Regus (UK) Ltd v Epcot Solutions Ltd* [2008] EWCA Civ 361 at [41]–[42]; *Goodlife Foods Ltd v Hall Fire Protection Ltd* [2018] EWCA Civ 1371 at [64]–[67], [76]–[83].

[246] 1977 Act, s 11(4).

may, however, be held to operate against larger companies with considerable assets, or to render a 'financial limit' clause unreasonable where insurance cover can in fact be obtained. Thus, it has been held that a limitation of liability of £100,000 by a multinational company with insurance cover of £50 million was unreasonable.[247] While the statute makes no reference to the *cost* of such cover, it has been stated that 'the cost of insurance must be a relevant factor when considering which of two parties should be required to bear the risk of a loss'.[248]

(4) Negligence on the part of the party seeking to rely on the clause is also an important factor. The Court will take into account whether there has been such negligence, and, if so, whether it was reasonably practicable for the other party to have done anything to avoid the loss.[249] Excluding or limiting liability for negligence may be reasonable provided it is reasonably practicable for the other party to obtain the service from an alternative source, if the task is very difficult with a high risk of failure, or where it would be impossible to obtain adequate insurance cover against a potential liability that would be ruinous without insurance.[250]

(5) The clarity of the clause has been described as an 'overriding' factor; businesses must take the consequences of the uncertainty which their 'small print' has created; 'uncertainty' involves unfairness to the other side.[251] A clause is also less likely to be reasonable if the innocent party has not had an opportunity of discovering the defect or damage. Thus a term in a bulk sale of seed potatoes requiring claims to be made within three days of delivery was held not to protect the seller when the potatoes were infected by virus, a defect not discoverable by inspection.[252]

(6) The relationship between the potential or actual loss and the extent of the limitation is taken into account. That the clause excludes liability altogether, or limits liability to a small amount, compared to a large potential or actual loss, is a factor which leans towards the clause being judged unreasonable.[253] In contrast, the exclusion of damages for negligence (and for liability under section 2(1) of the Misrepresentation Act 1967) was held reasonable where the claimant

[247] *St Albans City & DC v International Computers Ltd* [1995] FSR 686, aff'd [1996] 4 All ER 481, 491.

[248] *Smith v Eric S Bush* [1990] 1 AC 831, 858 (Lord Griffiths). See also *ibid*, 851–4; *George Mitchell (Chesterhall) Ltd v Finney Lock Seeds Ltd* [1983] 2 AC 803, 817.

[249] *George Mitchell (Chesterhall) Ltd v Finney Lock Seeds Ltd* [1983] QB 284, 307, 313, [1983] 2 AC 803, 817. See also *Smith v Eric S Bush* [1990] 1 AC 831, 858 (non-contractual notice); *Britvic Soft Drinks Ltd v Messer UK Ltd* [2002] EWCA Civ 548, [2002] 2 Lloyd's Rep 368 (exclusion clause failed to pass the reasonableness test in respect of a wholly unexpected manufacturing mishap).

[250] *Smith v Eric S Bush* [1990] 1 AC 831, 858–9.

[251] *George Mitchell (Chesterhall) Ltd v Finney Lock Seeds Ltd* [1983] QB 284, 314 (Kerr LJ); *Monarch Airlines Ltd v London Luton Airport* [1998] 1 Lloyd's Rep 403, 414. Note the overlap with the rules of construction, above, pp 162–9.

[252] *RW Green Ltd v Cade Bros Farms* [1978] 1 Lloyd's Rep 602; *R & B Customs Brokers Co Ltd v United Dominions Trust Ltd* [1988] 1 WLR 321.

[253] *St Albans City and District Council v International Computers Ltd* [1995] FSR 686, aff'd [1996] 4 All ER 481; *Balmoral Group Ltd v Borealis (UK) Ltd* [2006] EWHC 1900 (Comm) at [413] and [424].

was, in any event, entitled by an express term of the contract to the refund of the price paid for a painting that was forged.[254]

(7) The magnitude of the damage in relation to the contract price is also of significance. If the price is small, although the damages are very large, it may favour a finding of reasonableness.[255]

The operation of several of the above factors is well illustrated by *George Mitchell (Chesterhall) Ltd v Finney Lock Seeds Ltd*,[256] although it should be noted that the case concerned the reasonableness test (now repealed) in section 55 of the Sale of Goods Act 1979,[257] which required the Court to consider the reasonableness of *reliance* upon the term and not, as is required by the 1977 Act, whether it is reasonable to include it in the contract. In that case:

GM, a firm of farmers, purchased from F, a seed merchant, a quantity of Dutch winter white cabbage seeds, described as 'Finney's Late Dutch Special' for £201. F negligently supplied seeds of a very inferior variety of autumn cabbage, and as a result the crop failed. GM's loss was £61,513 but F relied on exemption clauses contained in its standard conditions of sale which limited its liability to replacement of the seeds or a refund of the price paid, and excluded any express or implied condition, statutory or otherwise.

The House of Lords held that F could not rely on the clause. Although similar terms were incorporated universally in the terms of trade between seed merchants and farmers, they were never negotiated; the breach was due to negligence for which F was responsible; and seed merchants could insure against crop failure caused by supplying the wrong seeds without materially increasing the price of the seeds. There was also evidence that, in practice, seed merchants always negotiated settlements of claims for damages in excess of the price of seeds if they thought that the claims were 'genuine' and 'justified'. The fact that merchants had not sought to rely on the limitation in the past showed that it would not be reasonable to allow such reliance in this case.[258] Although, under the 1977 Act, reasonableness must be determined at the time of the contract and subsequent reliance is not relevant,[259] it is submitted that it is unlikely to be reasonable to include a term which has never in the past been relied on in a trade, because thought to be unreasonable, and that the absence of such reliance *before* the contract under consideration was made remains relevant under the 1977 Act.

[254] *Avrora Fine Arts Investment Ltd v Christie, Mason & Woods Ltd* [2012] EWHC 2198 (Ch), [2012] PNLR 35.

[255] *George Mitchell (Chesterhall) Ltd v Finney Lock Seeds Ltd* [1983] QB 284, 302 (Lord Denning MR), cf 313–14 (Kerr LJ); [1983] 2 AC 803, 817 (Lord Bridge). See also *Smith v Eric S Bush* [1990] 1 AC 831, 859–60 (non-contractual notice).

[256] [1983] 2 AC 803.

[257] The test was set out in para 11 of Sched 1 to the 1979 Act.

[258] Cf *Schenkers Ltd v Overland Shoes Ltd* [1998] 1 Lloyd's Rep 498 (non-reliance on the clause in the past was not decisive because the past conduct did not indicate that those in the trade thought the clause was unreasonable).

[259] *Stewart Gill Ltd v Horatio Myer & Co Ltd* [1992] QB 600.

(xi) Powers of the Court

As we have seen, the 1977 Act renders some exclusion or limitation clauses absolutely ineffective (ie void) irrespective of the application of a reasonableness test. Where the reasonableness test is to be applied—and even though the Act uses the words 'except in so far as the term satisfies the requirement of reasonableness'—the powers of the Court are limited to declaring the term either to be effective or of no effect (ie void). It cannot re-write the term or, for example, where the term limited liability to a particular sum, render a 'judgment of Solomon' by raising that sum to an amount which it considers reasonable in the circumstances.[260] Moreover, it has been controversially held that a single term must be declared either valid or void as a whole so that the Courts cannot sever the reasonable from the unreasonable parts, even if the defendant is seeking to rely on merely the (alleged) reasonable part.[261]

(b) UNFAIR TERMS IN CONSUMER CONTRACTS: CONSUMER RIGHTS ACT 2015

(i) Legislation on unfair terms in consumer contracts prior to the Consumer Rights Act 2015

By EEC Council Directive 93/13,[262] a term in a contract between a seller or supplier of goods or services and a consumer which has not been individually negotiated is subjected to a requirement of 'fairness'. The Directive was originally implemented in the UK by Regulations[263] which were replaced, for contracts made on or after 1 October 2015, by Part 2 of the Consumer Rights Act 2015. The 2015 Act largely replicates, albeit with some amendments, the 1999 Regulations, which closely followed the language of the Directive.[264] The Consumer Rights Act 2015 also contains provisions which automatically invalidate (ie without applying a test of fairness) certain exemption clauses in consumer contracts, some of which were previously in the Unfair Contract Terms Act 1977. There is therefore no longer an overlap between the application of UCTA 1977 and separate legislation protecting consumers against exemption clauses.

[260] *George Mitchell (Chesterhall) Ltd v Finney Lock Seeds Ltd* [1983] 2 AC 803, 816; *Stewart Gill Ltd v Horatio Myer & Co Ltd* [1992] QB 600.

[261] *Stewart Gill Ltd v Horatio Myer & Co Ltd* [1992] QB 600. But see *RW Green Ltd v Cade Bros Farms* [1978] 1 Lloyd's Rep 602 (three-day time bar invalid, limitation of damages to contract price valid); *Watford Electronics Ltd v Sanderson CFL Ltd* [2001] EWCA Civ 317 (two separate terms, albeit in a single clause); *Regus (UK) Ltd v Epcot Solutions Ltd* [2008] EWCA Civ 361 at [46].

[262] [1993] OJ L95/29, p 29.

[263] The Unfair Terms in Consumer Contracts Regulations 1994 (SI 1994 No 3159), replaced by the Unfair Terms in Consumer Contracts Regulations 1999 (SI 1999 No 2083). See generally, Beale, in Beatson and Friedmann (eds), *Good Faith and Fault in Contract Law* (1995) ch 9; Collins (1994) 14 OJLS 229; Dean (1993) 56 MLR 581; Macdonald [1994] JBL 441; Bright (2000) 20 LS 331; Bright, in Burrows and Peel (eds), *Contract Terms* (2007) ch 9; Law Com No 292, *Unfair Terms in Contracts* (2005).

[264] For the continued influence of EU law, see above, p 21.

(ii) The Consumer Rights Act 2015: overview

Part 1 of the 2015 Act deals with consumer contracts (contracts between traders and consumers)[265] for goods, digital content, and services. It automatically invalidates (without applying a fairness test) certain exemption clauses in such contracts. So, for example, by sections 31 and 47, in a contract for the supply of goods or digital content by a trader to a consumer, a term is not binding on a consumer to the extent that it would exclude or restrict the trader's liability for breach of a term that the goods or digital content are of satisfactory quality, or fit for a particular purpose made known by the consumer to the trader, or as described, or that the trader has the right to supply the goods or digital content. By section 57, in a contract for the supply of services by a trader to a consumer, a term is not binding on the consumer to the extent that it would exclude or restrict the trader's liability for breach of a term that, for example, the trader must perform the service with reasonable care and skill.

Part 2 of the 2015 Act largely replicates, albeit with some amendments, the Unfair Terms in Consumer Contracts Regulations 1999, providing in section 62 a general rule that an unfair term of a consumer contract is not binding on the consumer. By section 65, however, it also automatically invalidates a term by which a trader, in a consumer contract, excludes or restricts liability for death or personal injury resulting from negligence.[266] While it is ultimately for the Courts to interpret and apply the 2015 Act, Part 2 of the Act may also be enforced administratively by the Competition and Markets Authority (CMA) (or other named regulator).[267] The CMA publishes guidance which explains its understanding of the 2015 Act and the tests it contains, including what the Authority considers an unfair term.[268]

(iii) The test of unfairness under Part 2 of the Consumer Rights Act 2015

By section 62(4) of the 2015 Act, a contractual term will be 'unfair' where:

> contrary to the requirement of good faith, it causes a significant imbalance in the parties' rights and obligations under the contract to the detriment of the consumer.

Some guidance is provided by section 62(5) and by the 'indicative and non-exhaustive list' of terms in Schedule 2.[269] Section 62(5) provides:

> Whether a term is fair is to be determined—(a) taking into account the nature of the subject matter of the contract, and (b) by reference to all the circumstances existing when the term

[265] Consumer Rights Act 2015, ss 1(1), 2(2), and 2(3). For the definitions of 'trader' and 'consumer', see above, p 213, n 154.

[266] This provision was previously in UCTA 1977, s 2(1). That provision remains for non-consumer contracts but no longer applies to consumer contracts: see para 4 of Sched 4 to the Consumer Rights Act 2015.

[267] Consumer Rights Act 2015, s 70; below, pp 235–6.

[268] See *Unfair contract terms guidance* (CMA37) (July 2015) and *Unfair contract terms explained* (CMA37(a)) (July 2015). In January 2026 the CMA produced draft revised guidance with a view to replacing CMA37. The Office of Fair Trading fulfilled a similar role under the Unfair Terms in Consumer Contracts Regulations 1999: see, eg, *Unfair contract terms guidance* (OFT311) (September 2008).

[269] See also the factors listed in Recital 16 to Directive 93/13. These were listed in Sched 2 to the 1994 Regulations but were not listed in the 1999 Regulations and are not listed in the Consumer Rights Act 2015.

was agreed and to all the other terms of the contract or of any other contract on which it depends.

A term which, in isolation, might appear to be unfair, might thus not be when looked at in the light of the contract as a whole. So while a term may create an imbalance between the parties' rights and obligations, it might be one that is justified as fair (or reasonable), say in a high risk or speculative contract or where a seller is dependent on a third party who may (because of market strength) supply only on very restrictive terms.

Schedule 2 (Part 1) contains 20 categories of term, which 'may' be unfair. These include terms authorizing or enabling the seller or supplier to dissolve the contract on a discretionary basis where the same facility is not given to the consumer,[270] to terminate a contract of indeterminate duration without reasonable notice except where there are serious grounds for doing so,[271] to alter the terms of the contract unilaterally without a valid reason which is specified in the contract,[272] to determine whether goods, digital content, or services supplied are in conformity with the contract, or giving the trader the exclusive right to interpret any term of the contract,[273] and terms requiring a consumer who decides not to conclude or perform the contract, or fails to fulfil his obligations under the contract, to pay 'a disproportionately high sum in compensation'[274] or to fulfil all the consumer's obligations where the trader does not perform the trader's obligations.[275]

There is a growing body of judicial decisions in English law on the meaning of fairness,[276] and many of the cases the CMA (and, before 2015, the Office of Fair Trading)[277] has considered administratively, as part of its duty to prevent the continued use of unfair terms, have involved 'fairness' and the plainness and intelligibility of the language. For example, following complaints, clauses excluding liability for a failure to supply have either been withdrawn or limited to situations in which the failure is beyond the supplier's reasonable control. Clauses excluding delay have either been withdrawn or limited to delay for a reasonable period. Similarly, suppliers have agreed either to withdraw clauses preventing a consumer from withholding any part of the contractual payment where the goods or services are defective or to amend them to prohibit such withholding in the case of a minor defect beyond a proportionate amount of the contractual sum. Suppliers have also agreed to withdraw clauses excluding liability for damage if concerned with death or personal injury or to limit them to damage which has not been caused negligently.[278] However, it should be noted that the 2015 Act

[270] Consumer Rights Act 2015, Sched 2, para 7.

[271] Consumer Rights Act 2015, Sched 2, para 8.

[272] Consumer Rights Act 2015, Sched 2, para 11.

[273] Consumer Rights Act 2015, Sched 2, para 16.

[274] Consumer Rights Act 2015, Sched 2, paras 5, 6. On para 5, see *Glaser v Atay* [2024] EWCA Civ 1111, [2025] 1 WLR 1627 at [52]–[63]. Such a clause which operates on breach will normally be void as a penalty at common law: below, p 583.

[275] Consumer Rights Act 2015, Sched 2, para 18.

[276] The most important cases have been *Director-General of Fair Trading v First National Bank plc* [2001] UKHL 52, [2002] 1 AC 481 (which concerned the 1994 Regulations) and *ParkingEye Ltd v Beavis* [2015] UKSC 67, [2016] AC 1172 (which concerned the 1999 Regulations).

[277] Above, n 268.

[278] Competition and Markets Authority, *Unfair contract terms guidance* (CMA37) (July 2015), Annex A (historic examples of fair and unfair terms). The CMA publishes on its website reports on consumer outcomes that it has secured in particular cases.

introduced a number of changes and clarifications in the test to be applied to determine whether a contract term is unfair, and earlier decisions and notes of guidance must be read in the light of the current provisions, to which we now turn.

(iv) Exclusion from assessment for fairness: main subject-matter and appropriateness of price, provided transparent and prominent

Section 64 of the 2015 Act contains an important exclusion from the assessment of the fairness of a term. Provided a term is 'transparent and prominent',[279] and not a term listed in Part 1 of Schedule 2,[280] it cannot be assessed for fairness to the extent that '(a) it specifies the main subject matter of the contract, or (b) the assessment is of the appropriateness of the price payable under the contract by comparison with the goods, digital content or services supplied under it'.[281]

Section 64 therefore seeks to make a distinction between terms containing the substance of the bargain and other terms. The similar exclusion from the 1994 and 1999 Regulations,[282] which preceded section 64, has been referred to in shorthand (with some danger of inaccuracy) as excluding the core terms or (and this will here be used) as the 'core exclusion'.[283] The Office of Fair Trading considered that the purpose of the core exclusion was 'to allow freedom of contract to prevail in relation to terms that are genuinely central to the bargain between consumer and supplier' and it saw the core exclusion as 'conditional upon such terms being expressed and presented in such a way as to ensure that they are, or at least are capable of being, at the forefront of the consumer's mind in deciding whether to enter the contract'.[284]

The House of Lords in *Director-General of Fair Trading v First National Bank plc*,[285] applying the 1994 Regulations, held that a provision concerning the rate of interest to be paid on a breach of contract neither defined the main subject of the contract nor realistically concerned the adequacy of the price. To construe such a provision as falling within the core exclusion would mean that almost any provision containing any part of the bargain would be capable of falling within the reach of the core exclusion and would leave 'a gaping hole in the system' of protection.[286] Similarly it has been held that an increase in an estate agent's commission if the sum was not paid within ten days of completion of the sale was not within the core exclusion (which was then contained in regulation 6(2) of the 1999 Regulations) so that it could be struck down by an application of the unfairness test.[287] In Gross J's words, 'Regulation 6(2) must be

[279] Consumer Rights Act 2015, s 64(2).
[280] Consumer Rights Act 2015, s 64(6).
[281] Consumer Rights Act 2015, s 64(1).
[282] The 1994 Regulations, reg 3(2), excluded assessment of a term which '(a) defines the main subject matter of the contract, or (b) concerns the adequacy of the price or remuneration, as against the goods or services sold or supplied'. The 1999 Regulations, reg 6(2), excluded assessment which relates '(a) to the definition of the main subject matter of the contract, or (b) to the adequacy of the price or remuneration, as against the goods or services supplied in exchange'.
[283] *Director-General of Fair Trading v First National Bank plc* [2001] UKHL 52, [2002] 1 AC 481 at [12] (Lord Bingham).
[284] *Unfair Contract Terms Guidance* (OFT311) (September 2008) para 19.13.
[285] [2001] UKHL 52 at [12], [34], [43], [64].
[286] *Ibid* at [34].
[287] *Bairstow Eves London Central Ltd v Smith* [2004] EWHC 263 (QB), [2004] 2 EGLR 25.

given a restrictive interpretation; otherwise a coach and horses could be driven through the Regulations.'[288]

In contrast, the Supreme Court in *Office of Fair Trading v Abbey National plc*[289] held that terms levying bank charges on personal current account customers in respect of unauthorized overdrafts fell within regulation 6(2)(b) of the 1999 Regulations and (assuming 'in plain, intelligible language')[290] could not therefore be assessed for fairness in terms of the appropriateness of the amount of the charges.[291] This was a somewhat surprising decision because one would have expected the Supreme Court to be anxious not to give the core exclusion a wide meaning so a Court could assess the unfairness of the charges. The Supreme Court correctly warned that, especially in the context of regulation 6(2)(b) dealing with price, the shorthand language of 'core terms' was no substitute for construing the words of the regulation directly. But it left the way open to regard the overdraft charges as not part of the price for banking services because most customers do not incur such charges although 'free-in-credit' banking is subsidized by bank charges for unauthorized overdrafts.

It is not absolutely clear what difference, if any, has been made by the differently formulated core exclusion in section 64 of the 2015 Act[292] although it is understood that the intention was to reverse the *Abbey National* decision.[293] Certainly, subsequent to *Abbey National*, the Court of Justice of the European Union (CJEU) has taken a narrow view of the core exclusion.[294] And most recently, the Court of Appeal has followed the decision in *Director-General of Fair Trading v First National Bank* in holding that a clause in a contract between barristers and their client, which provided that the full agreed fee would be payable even if the hearing concluded early or was adjourned, was not within the 'safe harbour' of the core exclusion in section 64(1)(b) of the 2015 Act because it did not concern the adequacy of the fees earned by the barristers, but was designed to ensure that their entitlement to their fees did not come to an end on the hearing being adjourned or otherwise not going ahead: it did not express the substance of the bargain, but was an incidental (even though important) term which surrounded it.[295]

The core exclusion also applies only if the term is 'transparent and prominent'.[296] A term is transparent 'if it is expressed in plain and intelligible language and (in the case of a written term) is legible'.[297] A term is prominent 'if it is brought to the consumer's

[288] *Ibid* at [25].

[289] [2009] UKSC 6, [2010] AC 696.

[290] There was no additional requirement under the 1994 or 1999 Regulations that the term should be prominent as well as transparent.

[291] The Supreme Court stressed that it was consistent with its decision that the fairness of the bank charges could still be challenged for reasons other than the appropriateness of the amount of the charges. But it is very hard to see what room for challenge was realistically being left open.

[292] See above, p 229, nn 281, 282; cf *Glaser v Atay* [2024] EWCA Civ 1111 at [48].

[293] Law Commission, *Unfair Terms in Consumer Contracts: Advice to the Department for Business, Innovation and Skills* (March 2013) paras 2.38–2.43, 3.120–3.121.

[294] C-26/13 *Kásler v OTP Jelzálogbank Zrt* (30 April 2014) [2014] 2 All ER (Comm) 443; C-143/13 *Matei v SC Volksbank România SA* (26 February 2015) [2015] 1 WLR 2385; C-96/14 *Van Hove v CNP Assurances SA* (23 April 2015) [2015] 3 CMLR 31.

[295] *Glaser v Atay* [2024] EWCA Civ 1111 at [47]–[48].

[296] Consumer Rights Act 2015, s 64(2).

[297] Consumer Rights Act 2015, s 64(3).

attention in such a way that an average consumer would be aware of the term'.[298] An 'average consumer' is 'a consumer who is reasonably well-informed, observant and circumspect',[299] which is to be interpreted in context: an average consumer who enters into contracts of the kind which are in issue.[300]

The core exclusion is also inapplicable to a term listed in Part 1 of Schedule 2 to the 2015 Act.[301]

(v) Significant imbalance and good faith: procedural or substantive unfairness?

The basic question whether a term causes a significant imbalance in the parties' rights and obligations is primarily concerned with the substantive fairness of the contract.[302] For instance, a term which gives a significant advantage to the seller or supplier without a countervailing benefit to the consumer (such as a price reduction) might fail to satisfy this part of the test of an unfair term. Despite this, it is submitted that, taking into account also the requirement of good faith, the test of unfairness as a whole will in practice be primarily concerned with procedural fairness, unfair surprise, and the absence of real choice.[303]

(a) Significant Imbalance. The fairness of the term (including whether it causes a 'significant imbalance') is based on an assessment at the date of the contract rather than on what actually happened,[304] and whether there is a significant imbalance depends mainly on whether the consumer is being deprived by the term of an advantage he or she would enjoy under the general law in the absence of the term.[305] The meaning of 'significant imbalance' (under the 1994 Regulations) was considered by the House of Lords in *Director General of Fair Trading v First National Bank plc*. The case concerned the fairness of a term in a bank's loan agreement that, should the borrower default on his repayments, interest would continue to be payable at the contractual rate until any judgment was satisfied. Delegated legislation provided that no statutory interest was payable on a county court judgment given in proceedings to recover money under an agreement regulated by the Consumer Credit Act 1974. It was argued that in these circumstances it was unfair to allow the recovery of contractual interest because that would expose the borrower to further liability after all the instalments the Court ordered him to pay had been paid in full. Lord Bingham stated that:

> the requirement of significant imbalance is met if a term is so weighted in favour of the supplier as to tilt the parties' rights and obligations under the contract significantly in his favour. This may be by the granting to the supplier of a beneficial option or discretion or power, or by the imposing on the consumer of a disadvantageous burden or risk or duty.[306]

[298] Consumer Rights Act 2015, s 64(4). [299] Consumer Rights Act 2015, s 64(5).
[300] *Eternity Sky Investments Ltd v Zhang* [2024] EWCA Civ 630 at [115].
[301] Consumer Rights Act 2015, s 64(6). See above, p 229.
[302] *Director General of Fair Trading v First National Bank plc* [2001] UKHL 52 at [37] (Lord Steyn).
[303] Below, p 234. [304] *Glaser v Atay* [2024] EWCA Civ 1111 at [83].
[305] *ParkingEye Ltd v Beavis* [2015] UKSC 67, [2016] AC 1172 at [105]; *Glaser v Atay* [2024] EWCA Civ 1111 at [79].
[306] [2001] UKHL 52, [2002] 1 AC 481 at [17].

The House of Lords upheld the term. It held that the essential bargain in a bank loan is to make available funds which will be repaid with interest until full repayment. There was nothing unbalanced or detrimental to the consumer in requiring interest to be paid after judgment; indeed the absence of such a term would unbalance the contract to the detriment of the lender.[307] Their Lordships considered that any unfairness in exposing the borrower to further liability after judgment was due to the fact that the judgment did not cover the whole of the indebtedness, not from any inherent unfairness in the contractual term.

(b) Good Faith. The significant imbalance must be contrary to the requirement of good faith. In *Director General of Fair Trading v First National Bank plc* the House of Lords made clear that, since the test derives from a Directive, with the object of harmonizing this area of the law in which the Member States have no common concept of fairness or good faith, the term 'good faith' is to be given an autonomous European interpretation.[308] Lord Bingham stated that good faith looked to good standards of commercial morality and practice; the requirement of 'good faith' sought to promote fair and open dealing, and 'openness requires that the terms should be expressed fully, clearly and legibly, containing no concealed pitfalls or traps'.[309] The Court of Appeal in that case stated that 'terms must be reasonably transparent and must not operate to defeat the reasonable expectations of the consumer' who 'should be put in a position where he can make an informed choice'.[310] These statements were made in the context of the 1994 Regulations, which included a specific provision to the effect that, in making an assessment of good faith, regard should be had in particular to the strength of the bargaining positions of the parties, whether the consumer had an inducement to agree to the term, whether the goods or services were sold or supplied to the special order of the consumer, and the extent to which the seller or supplier has dealt fairly and equitably with the consumer.[311] This list of factors was taken from Recital 16 of the Preamble to the Directive. Although the list was not repeated in the 1999 Regulations, or in the 2015 Act, the interpretation of 'good faith' under the 2015 Act should be the same.[312]

307 *Ibid* at [22]–[24], [38], [55]–[57].

308 *Ibid* at [17], [32], [45]. See also *Glaser v Atay* [2024] EWCA Civ 1111 at [86].

309 *Director General of Fair Trading v First National Bank plc* [2001] UKHL 52 at [17].

310 [2000] QB 672, 687.

311 1994 Regulations (see p 226, n 263), Sched 2. The factors look much like some of the guidelines to the reasonableness test in the 1977 Act: above, p 221.

312 Under EU law, C-106/89 *Marleasing SA v La Commercial* [1992] 1 CMLR 305 permits reference to be made to the Directive and probably also to the preamble (and hence to the recitals) in interpreting national legislation which implement Directives. Although the general principles of EU law are now no longer part of English law (see p 21, n 112), the interpretation by the House of Lords remains authoritative; see also *ParkingEye Ltd v Beavis* [2015] UKSC 67, [2016] AC 1172 at [105], applying EU law in interpreting the 1999 Regulations, followed by *Glaser v Atay* [2024] EWCA Civ 1111 at [87], [92]–[94], interpreting the 2015 Act.

Including in the assessment of fairness of a term the requirement of good faith, and the extent to which the seller or supplier has dealt fairly and equitably with the consumer—or, as Recital 16 of the Directive adds, the consumer 'whose legitimate interests he . . . takes into account'—is in sharp contrast to the common law position. As Lord Ackner's speech in *Walford v Miles*[313] shows, parties to a contractual negotiation are generally considered to be in an adversarial relationship in which they are entitled to pursue their own interests so long as they avoid making misrepresentations.

In an important decision, the CJEU in *Aziz v Caixa d' Estalvis de Catalunya, Tarragona i Manresa*[314] laid down that 'the national court must assess for those purposes [ie assessing good faith] whether the seller or supplier, dealing fairly and equitably with the consumer, could reasonably assume that the consumer would have agreed to such a term in individual contract negotiations'.[315] In applying the test of fairness in the 1999 Regulations, the Supreme Court in *ParkingEye Ltd v Beavis*[316] relied on that decision of the CJEU for guidance. The matter in issue was the fairness of a clearly displayed charge of £85 for car parking beyond a free period of time. The Supreme Court, in deciding that the term was fair,[317] specifically considered how one should apply the approach in *Aziz* of asking whether the supplier could reasonably have assumed that the consumer would have agreed to such a term had it been negotiated. Lords Neuberger and Sumption drew on a number of factors identified in *Aziz*[318]—whether such contractual terms are common (used regularly in similar contracts) or are surprising, whether there is an objective reason for the term, and whether, despite the shift in the contractual balance in favour of the user of the term in relation to the substance of the term in question, the consumer is not left without protection—and concluded as follows: 'a hypothetical reasonable motorist would have agreed to objectively reasonable terms, and these terms are objectively reasonable'.[319] It is noteworthy that much of the more detailed reasoning relied on in deciding that the term imposing the parking charge was fair was similar to that relied on in deciding that the term was not a penalty at common law.[320]

(c) Procedural or substantive fairness? How should the English Courts proceed to put flesh on the bare bones of the elements of 'good faith' and 'significant imbalance', which have been said to overlap substantially?[321] Although good faith is not a concept wholly

[313] [1992] 2 AC 128, 138, above, p 67.
[314] C-415/11 (14 March 2013) [2013] 3 CMLR 5.
[315] *Ibid* at [69].
[316] [2015] UKSC 67 at [105].
[317] *Ibid* at [102]–[114], [200]–[213], [289], [291]. Lord Toulson, at [295]–[315], dissented on this point.
[318] C-415/11 (14 March 2013) [2013] 3 CMLR 5 at AG75 (the Opinion of Advocate General Kokott, on which the CJEU drew), quoted in *ParkingEye Ltd v Beavis* [2015] UKSC 67 at [106] and in *Glaser v Atay* [2024] EWCA Civ 1111 at [92].
[319] [2015] UKSC 67 at [109].
[320] *Ibid* at [104]. See below, pp 584–5.
[321] *Director-General of Fair Trading v First National Bank plc* [2000] QB 672, 687, [2001] UKHL 52 at [37] (Lord Steyn).

unfamiliar to English lawyers, its use in this context is novel, and the Courts might find analogies in the more familiar statutory concept of 'reasonableness' in the Unfair Contract Terms Act 1977,[322] perhaps reinforced by support from the equitable concept of unconscionability considered in Chapter 10 below[323] and the rules on penalty and forfeiture clauses considered in Chapter 17 below.[324] This gains some support from the similarity of the guidelines in Recital 16 of the Preamble to the Directive to those in the 1977 Act.[325] However, we have seen that the Courts favour the view that the term 'good faith', being derived from the Directive, is to be given an autonomous European interpretation.[326]

What then is this autonomous European Union concept of 'good faith'? There is clearly a substantive component in the test and the controlling concept of 'significant imbalance' is primarily a substantive one. The fact that some clauses may cause such a serious imbalance that they should always be treated as being contrary to good faith,[327] also has a substantive flavour. Moreover, Lord Steyn has stated that 'any purely procedural or even predominantly procedural interpretation of the requirement of good faith must be rejected'.[328] Lord Bingham's statement that fair dealing requires that a supplier should not 'deliberately or unconsciously take advantage of the consumer's necessity, indigence, lack of experience, unfamiliarity with the subject matter of the contract, or weak bargaining position'[329] also suggests a substantive concept.

It is, however, submitted that the test as a whole is primarily concerned with procedural fairness. The core exclusion requiring that terms concerning the price and defining the main subject-matter of the contract are left out of account (provided they are transparent and prominent) makes it difficult to regard the test as primarily substantive, because those terms, particularly 'price', are central to substantive fairness.[330] Moreover, the absence of any absolutely prohibited terms and the fact that 'the indicative and non-exhaustive list of the terms which may be regarded as unfair' are couched in an open-textured way also suggest that the test under the 2015 Act is not primarily concerned with substantive fairness but with the prevention of unfair surprise and the absence of real choice. So the Courts are likely to be primarily concerned with the requirements of openness which, as stated by Lord Bingham, are that the terms should be expressed fully, clearly, and legibly, should contain no concealed pitfalls or traps, and should accord appropriate prominence to terms which might operate disadvantageously to

[322] See above, pp 220–5. [323] At pp 406–14. [324] At pp 583–90.
[325] Unfair Contract Terms Act 1977, s 11 and Sched 2. [326] See above, p 232.
[327] Beale, in Beatson and Friedmann (eds), *Good Faith and Fault in Contract Law* (1995) 245. Some of the terms contained in the indicative list of terms which might be regarded as unfair may fall into this category, eg excluding or limiting liability for death or personal injury, making the seller or supplier's duty to perform a matter for its discretion, or giving it the right to determine whether the goods or services are in conformity with the contract or the exclusive right to interpret any term: see Sched 2 to the 2015 Act.
[328] *Director-General of Fair Trading v First National Bank plc* [2001] UKHL 52 at [36].
[329] *Ibid* at [17]. [330] Collins (1994) 14 OJLS 229, 249.

the customer.[331] This is also supported by the decision of the CJEU in *Aziz v Caixa d' Estalvis de Catalunya, Tarragona i Manresa*[332] referred to above.

To this extent, the result achieved is not likely to be very different from that under the 1977 Act albeit in the more limited context of terms excluding or limiting liability.[333] The experience of administrative enforcement by the Office of Fair Trading also suggests that there will not be a sharp difference from that previously taken in English law under the 1977 Act. In part this is because of the similarity of the problems, but in part it is because of an understandable tendency to retreat to familiar ground when confronted by unfamiliar concepts on which there is little guidance.

(vi) Effect of term being held to be unfair

An unfair term 'is not binding on the consumer'.[334] This means that the term is enforceable by, but not against, the consumer. Moreover, 'the contract continues, so far as practicable, to have effect in every other respect'.[335] This gives the Courts a broad discretion to sever the unfair term but presumably this will not be possible where the unfair term is a 'core term' which has failed the requirement of being transparent and prominent.

(vii) Terms must be transparent

We have already seen in our discussion of the 'core exclusion' from the assessment of fairness that the immunity of a term specifying the main subject-matter of the contract or its assessment of the appropriateness of the price will be lost if it is not transparent and prominent. Section 68 of the Consumer Rights Act 2015 separately requires a trader to ensure that any written term of a contract is transparent. This means that it must be expressed in plain, intelligible language and must be legible. Insofar as this is a separate requirement from fairness as assessed by the Courts, it is enforceable by the Competition and Markets Authority (and other regulators). It is to enforcement of the Consumer Rights Act 2015 by regulators that we finally turn.

(viii) Prevention of unfair and non-transparent terms

The Consumer Rights Act 2015 gives the CMA (and other regulators) a role, previously carried out by the Office of Fair Trading, in considering complaints about terms used, or proposed to be used, in consumer contracts, with power to apply for an injunction to prevent a person using, or proposing or recommending the use of, an unfair or non-transparent term in contracts concluded with consumers.[336] Normally, however, cases

331 *Director-General of Fair Trading v First National Bank plc* [2001] UKHL 52 at [17].

332 C-415/11 (14 March 2013), see, p 233.

333 Dean (1994) 56 MLR 581, 585.

334 Consumer Rights Act 2015, s 62(1).

335 Consumer Rights Act 2015, s 67.

336 Consumer Rights Act 2015, s 70 and Sched 3. In *Office of Fair Trading v Foxtons Ltd* [2009] EWCA Civ 288, [2010] 1 WLR 663, it was held (Moore-Bick LJ largely dissenting on this) that, on a general challenge by the Office of Fair Trading under the 1999 Regulations, the Office was entitled to an injunction or declaration against an estate agent in respect of an unfair term in existing, as well as future, contracts; and that the relief did not necessarily preclude a judge deciding that the term was fair as between a consumer and the estate agent in an individual challenge.

are resolved by the regulator accepting informal undertakings to amend the offending terms in lieu of Court proceedings. The regulator applies the same test of fairness as a Court but looks forward rather than backwards and considers the circumstances that are generally likely to obtain, not those attending the conclusion of a particular contract.[337] The regulators have wide powers to obtain documents and information.[338] If the regulator considers a relevant complaint but decides not to make an application for an injunction it must give reasons for its decision to the person who made the complaint[339]

A similar, more general regime was introduced by Part 8 of the Enterprise Act 2002 which gave the CMA and other bodies (eg weights and measures authorities) powers to enforce certain consumer legislation, including the Consumer Rights Act 2015. These provisions of the Enterprise Act were replaced by similar provisions in Part 3 of the Digital Markets, Competition and Consumers Act 2024. The enforcer may apply to the Court for an 'enforcement order'[340] although it is envisaged that compliance will normally be secured by negotiation[341] and undertakings.[342]

(c) OTHER LEGISLATIVE CONTROLS ON EXEMPTION CLAUSES AND UNFAIR TERMS

The exclusion or restriction of liability for pre-contractual misrepresentation is controlled by section 3 of the Misrepresentation Act 1967 in the case of non-consumer contracts. This is dealt with in Chapter 9.[343] Certain other terms by which a party purports to contract out of legislation protecting consumers or others, are invalid. Examples of such legislation include those dealing with consumer credit,[344] product liability,[345] dangerous goods[346] defective premises,[347] package holidays,[348] timeshare contracts,[349] and carriage by land,[350] sea,[351] or air.[352]

As regards unfair terms apart from exemption clauses, perhaps the most important other legislation (ie aside from the Unfair Contract Terms Act 1977 and the Consumer

[337] eg *Unfair Contract Terms*, Office of Fair Trading Bulletin No 4 (December 1997) 21.
[338] Consumer Rights Act 2015, s 77 and Sched 5.
[339] Consumer Rights Act 2015, Sched 3, para 2(3).
[340] Digital Markets, Competition and Consumers Act 2024, ss 153–159.
[341] 2024 Act, s 155.
[342] 2024 Act, s 163.
[343] See below, pp 354–7.
[344] Consumer Credit Act 1974, s 173(1).
[345] Consumer Protection Act 1987, s 7.
[346] Consumer Protection Act 1987, s 41(4).
[347] Defective Premises Act 1972, s 6(3).
[348] Package Travel and Linked Travel Arrangements Regulations 2018 (SI 2018 No 634), reg 30.
[349] Timeshare, Holiday Products, Resale and Exchange Contracts Regulations 2010 (SI 2010 No 2960), reg 19.
[350] Carriage of Goods by Road Act 1965, Sched 1 (Convention on the Contract for the International Carriage of Goods by Road) art 41; Railways (Convention on International Carriage by Rail) Regulations 2005 (SI 2005 No 2092) (art 5 of the Uniform Rules concerning the contract of international carriage of passengers (Appendix A) and goods (Appendix B)).
[351] Carriage of Goods by Sea Act 1971, Sched 1, art III.8; Merchant Shipping Act 1995, Sched 6, art 18.
[352] Carriage by Air Act 1961, Sched 1, art 23; Sched 1B, arts 26, 47.

Rights Act 2015) is the Consumer Credit Act 1974, sections 140A–140C. Those provisions protect against exploitation of the claimant's need for credit by giving the Courts a wide range of remedies to undo credit agreements where the relationship between the creditor and the debtor is unfair to the debtor.[353]

FURTHER READING

ADAMS and BROWNSWORD, 'The Unfair Contract Terms Act: A Decade of Discretion' (1988) 104 LQR 94

BRIGHT, 'Winning the Battle Against Unfair Terms' (2000) 20 LS 331

PEEL, 'Whither Contra Proferentem?' in BURROWS and PEEL (eds), *Contract Terms* (Oxford: Oxford University Press, 2007) 53

BEALE, 'Exclusion and Limitation Clauses in Business Contracts: Transparency' in BURROWS and PEEL (eds), *Contract Terms* (Oxford: Oxford University Press, 2007) 191

BRIGHT, 'Unfairness and the Consumer Contract Regulations' in BURROWS and PEEL (eds), *Contract Terms* (Oxford: Oxford University Press, 2007) 173

GILIKER, 'The Consumer Rights Act 2015—a Bastion of European Consumer Rights?' (2017) 37 LS 78

WHITTAKER, 'Distinctive Features of the New Consumer Contract Law' (2017) 133 LQR 47

MCCUNN, 'The *Contra Proferentem* Rule: Contract Law's Great Survivor' (2019) 39 OJLS 483

FOXTON, 'The Status of the Special Rules of Construction of Exemption Clauses in Commercial Contracts' [2021] JBL 205

MCCUNN, 'Incorporation of Terms: Time for *Blu-Sky* Thinking?' [2022] LMCLQ 189

353 See, eg, *Plevin v Paragon Personal Finance Ltd* [2014] UKSC 61, [2014] 1 WLR 4222; *Smith v Royal Bank of Scotland plc* [2023] UKSC 34, [2024] AC 955 at [12]–[25]; *Hopcraft v Close Bros Ltd* [2025] UKSC 33, [2025] 3 WLR 423 at [317]–[338].

PART 3

FACTORS TENDING TO DEFEAT CONTRACTUAL LIABILITY

7

INCAPACITY

1. GROUNDS OF CONTRACTUAL INCAPACITY

The law limits the capacity of certain persons to bind themselves by contract. These persons are:

(1) the Crown and public authorities;

(2) corporations;

(3) minors;

(4) persons lacking mental capacity and drunken persons.

The consequences of contractual incapacity are not identical. In some cases the contract is void, in others voidable, while in others it is unenforceable at the suit of one or both parties.

The underlying policy of rules limiting contractual capacity is to protect those under the incapacity. In the case of public authorities the policy seeks to protect the public finances and taxpayers, and, in the case of companies, investors and creditors. We shall see that this protective policy can inflict hardship upon those who deal with an incapacitated person in good faith and in ignorance of the lack of capacity. Moreover, before the recognition of independent restitutionary obligations,[1] an incapacitated party to whom money had been paid or property transferred might have been unjustly enriched at the expense of the other. The practical importance of the limitations on contractual capacity has been reduced. In the case of minors this is the result of the reduction in the age of majority from 21 to 18. In the case of local authorities and companies there has been substantial statutory modification of the *ultra vires* doctrine so as to make many contracts enforceable,[2] thus enhancing security of transactions between local authorities and companies and those who deal with them. Moreover, the development of the law of restitution means that, even where the contract is void or unenforceable, money paid and property transferred will, in general, be recoverable, unless this would amount to indirect enforcement of the contract.[3]

[1] *Lipkin Gorman v Karpnale Ltd* [1991] 2 AC 548, above, p 24.

[2] For the principle of the common law that the public authority or company cannot act 'beyond its powers' (*ultra vires*) see below, pp 246, 251.

[3] *Westdeutsche Landesbank Girozentrale v Islington LBC* [1994] 1 WLR 938, aff'd [1996] AC 669, below, pp 250, 254.

2. THE CROWN AND PUBLIC AUTHORITIES

At common law the Crown (acting in its own right or through the agency of others) has unlimited capacity to enter into contracts[4] although, as will be explained below, the peculiar public nature of the Crown affects the scope of obligations undertaken and their enforceability. Other public authorities, however, are created by statute and their capacity to contract depends upon statutory authority, express or implied, while also being subject to special rules of public law.

(a) THE CROWN

(i) Application of public law

Since the passing of the Crown Proceedings Act 1947, actions by or against the Crown or a government department in contract are, for the most part, governed by the same rules of procedure as actions between subjects[5] and the same remedies are available, save that no injunction or order of specific performance can be made against the Crown in 'civil proceedings'.[6] Crown contracts are subject to the procurement procedures imposed on public authorities, which are considered later in this chapter.[7]

Although contracts made with government departments or Crown officers are not subject to the *ultra vires* doctrine,[8] rules which arise from the fact that such bodies have statutory and prerogative powers and duties of a public law nature affect contracts made by them. In both Crown contracts and the contracts of public authorities, it is therefore necessary to consider these public law rules as well as the common law and statutory position.

(ii) Parliamentary funds

In *Churchward v The Queen*[9] the Admiralty undertook to pay £18,000 a year to C for the carriage of cross-channel mails from Dover to Calais and Ostend. Appropriation of funds for this contract was expressly forbidden by Parliament. C sued for the promised sum but failed on the ground that the contract provided for payment to be 'out of

[4] Wade & Forsyth's *Administrative Law* (12th edn, 2023) 38; Turpin, *Government Procurement and Contracts* (1989) 83.

[5] See generally Wade & Forsyth's *Administrative Law* (12th edn, 2023) 663–7; Arrowsmith, *The Law of Public and Utilities Procurement* (3rd edn, 2018; 4th edn due 2026).

[6] Crown Proceedings Act 1947, s 21 (the Court may instead make an order declaratory of the rights of the parties). Although injunctive relief may be given in proceedings for judicial review (*M v Home Office* [1994] 1 AC 377), judicial review is not generally available for disputes concerning contracts: *Mercury Energy Ltd v Electricity Corp of New Zealand Ltd* [1994] 1 WLR 521 (New Zealand); cf *Williams Construction Ltd v Blackman* [1995] 1 WLR 102 (Barbados).

[7] Below, pp 249–50.

[8] But the powers of certain Ministers have been defined by statute (eg Supply Powers Act 1975; Ministers of the Crown Act 1975) which may limit the capacity of the Crown (*Cudgen Rutile (No 2) Pty Ltd v Chalk* [1975] AC 520 (Australia)) or the authority of its agents (below, p 246).

[9] (1865) LR 1 QB 173, 210.

moneys to be provided by parliament' and no such moneys were provided. Shee J went further, stating that 'the providing of funds by parliament is a condition precedent to [the covenant] attaching'. This has been interpreted to mean that all obligations to pay money undertaken by the Crown are subject to the implied condition that funds necessary to satisfy the obligation are appropriated by Parliament,[10] but the better view is that the Crown is under no antecedent incapacity in that respect. The existence of the contract does not depend upon Parliamentary authority. The provision of funds is simply a condition to be fulfilled before actual payment by the Crown, one that is satisfied where there is a fund in existence out of which payment can lawfully be made.[11]

(iii) Fettering future executive action

It is an important principle of public law that public bodies, including the Crown, should preserve the discretionary powers granted to them by statute or the prerogative, and not divest themselves of those powers.[12] This principle may conflict, however, with the principle of sanctity of contracts. In *Rederiaktiebolaget Amphitrite v The King* Rowlatt J stated that 'It is not competent for the Government to fetter its future executive action, which must necessarily be determined by the needs of the community when the question arises. It cannot by contract hamper its freedom of action in matters which concern the welfare of the State.'[13] In that case:

> During the First World War the British legation in Stockholm promised the Swedish owners of the ship *Amphitrite* that, if the ship sailed to England with an approved cargo, she would not be detained. The ship was nevertheless detained and her owners brought a petition of right against the Crown claiming damages for breach of contract.

Rowlatt J held that the guarantee was not a contract for the breach of which damages could be sued for in a court of law; it was merely an expression of intention to act in a particular way in a certain event, because the Crown could not fetter its future executive action by contract.

Rowlatt J's statement has been powerfully criticized on the ground that it is expressed too generally.[14] Three issues must be separated; first, the validity of the contract *ab initio*; secondly, whether, assuming the contract is valid, the Crown is thereafter under a duty to exercise its powers in a manner consistent with it; and thirdly, whether, assuming there is no valid contract, the Crown is nevertheless precluded from exercising its discretion in a particular way by an estoppel or the application of the emerging public law principle of legitimate expectation.[15]

[10] *New South Wales v The Commonwealth (No 1)* (1932) 46 CLR 155, 176 (Australia); *A-G v Great Southern and Western Ry Co of Ireland* [1925] AC 754, 773.

[11] *New South Wales v Bardolph* (1934) 52 CLR 455, 502, 514 (Australia).

[12] See below, pp 247–8, and see generally Wade & Forsyth's *Administrative Law* (12th edn, 2023) 243 ff.

[13] [1921] 3 KB 500, 503.

[14] *Robertson v Minister of Pensions* [1949] 1 KB 227, 230 (Denning J); *Ansett Transport Industries (Operations) Pty Ltd v Commonwealth* (1977) 139 CLR 54, 74, 113–14 (Australia); *A v Hayden (No 2)* (1984) 56 ALR 82, 86 (Australia). But see *Commissioners of Crown Lands v Page* [1960] 2 QB 274, 287–8 (Lord Evershed MR).

[15] Below, p 248.

As far as the first issue is concerned, Rowlatt J acknowledged that the Crown can bind itself by a commercial contract.[16] *The Amphitrite* was not such a case, but the distinction between 'commercial' and 'non-commercial' contracts has been criticized as unworkable in practice because commercial contracts tend to conflict with 'governmental' obligations,[17] and it is difficult to see how, for instance, procurement contracts involving large capital expenditure are to be classified.

Where a Crown contract has been validly entered into, the Crown's freedom to exercise its discretionary powers (whether statutory or prerogative) will not, as a matter of construction, be impliedly excluded by the contract. Even in the case of commercial contracts, the Crown must be free to exercise the discretionary powers conferred upon it for the public good. 'No one can imagine, for example, that when the Crown makes a contract which could not be fulfilled in time of war, it is pledging itself not to declare war for so long as the contract lasts.'[18] Thus, it has been held that an *implied* covenant for quiet enjoyment in a Crown lease did not prevent the Crown from requisitioning the premises.[19] The Crown must be at liberty to detain ships, to requisition property, or to perform other essential acts in time of war, and, although the position of an *express* undertaking is less clear,[20] it is submitted that 'no contract would be enforced in any case where some essential governmental activity would be thereby rendered impossible or seriously impeded'.[21] Furthermore, in such cases, a party is unlikely to be able to invoke the principle of estoppel; it is generally recognized that 'estoppel cannot be allowed to hinder the formation of government policy'.[22] Nor can the principle of legitimate expectation be used to fetter the formation or change of policy.[23] The Crown may, however, be vicariously liable for torts committed by its servants or agents, which will include liability for negligent misstatements, although this does not extend to anything done under the prerogative or statutory powers.[24]

In practice the rule stated in *The Amphitrite* does not often have to be applied since many contracts falling within its scope contain cancellation clauses which usually make provision for compensation.[25]

[16] [1921] 3 KB 500, 503. An estoppel may arise to prevent both parties from refusing to proceed with such a contract: *A–G of Hong Kong v Humphreys Estate (Queen's Gardens) Ltd* [1987] AC 114, 127–8 (Hong Kong).

[17] Mitchell, *The Contracts of Public Authorities* (1954) 62. See also *Ansett Transport Industries (Operations) Pty Ltd v Commonwealth* (1977) 139 CLR 54, 113 (Aickin J).

[18] *Commissioners of Crown Lands v Page* [1960] 2 QB 274, 292 (Devlin LJ).

[19] *Ibid.*

[20] Devlin LJ, *ibid*, 292 thought nothing turned on this and said that even an express covenant 'must by necessary implication be read to exclude those measures affecting the nation as a whole which the Crown takes for the public good', but Evershed MR and Ormrod LJ reserved their position. Devlin LJ's view is inferentially supported in *Ansett Transport Industries (Operations) Pty Ltd v Commonwealth* (above, n 14).

[21] Mitchell, *The Contracts of Public Authorities* (1954) 7. Cf Holdsworth (1929) 45 LQR 166.

[22] *Laker Airways Ltd v Department of Trade* [1977] QB 643, 709 (Roskill LJ), 728 (Lawton LJ); see also at 680–2, 707.

[23] *Hughes v DHSS* [1985] AC 776; Wade & Forsyth's *Administrative Law* (12th edn, 2023) 330–1.

[24] Crown Proceedings Act 1947, ss 2(1)(a), 11.

[25] See generally Turpin, *Government Procurement and Contracts* (1989) 243–6.

(iv) Liability of Crown to employees

The general rule is that persons in Crown employment hold office during the pleasure of the Crown, and at common law Crown servants can be dismissed at any time by the Crown and no action lies for wrongful dismissal.[26] In the older cases the reason given for this rule was that the relationship between the Crown and its servants is not one of contract at all, but of status.[27] But more recently it has been said that 'there is nothing unconstitutional about civil servants being employed by the Crown pursuant to contracts of service'.[28] The modern and better view is that there can be a valid contract of employment, although this is always determinable at the pleasure of the Crown.[29] The older cases may reflect the absence of an intention to contract on the part of the Crown. Although it has been held that the use of language of obligation or even of the word 'contract' did not suffice to indicate an intention by the Crown to enter into a contractual relationship,[30] it has been held that a civil servant had a contract of employment, where his appointment was subject to the Civil Service Pay and Conditions of Service Code which stated that 'a civil servant does not have a contract of employment enforceable in the courts but rather a letter of appointment'. Objectively construed, the appointment created a relationship which the Crown must have intended to constitute a contract of employment.[31]

Whether or not the relation is contractual, the power of the Crown to dismiss at pleasure without payment of compensation is now limited by statute. The remedies available for unfair dismissal now contained in the Employment Rights Act 1996 extend to Crown employees, including members of the military services.[32] The Crown is also liable in tort for breach of the duties normally owed by an employer to its servants or agents.[33]

Although dismissal in breach of the terms of the appointment will not, according to the bulk of the authorities, give rise to a cause of action at common law, it may be susceptible to the public law remedy of judicial review where it is *ultra vires*, an abuse of discretion, or where the principles of procedural fairness have not been observed.[34]

[26] *Shenton v Smith* [1895] AC 229; *Dunn v The Queen* [1896] 1 QB 116; *Terrell v Secretary of State for the Colonies* [1953] 2 QB 482; *Riordan v War Office* [1959] 1 WLR 1046; *A-G for Guyana v Nobrega* [1969] 3 All ER 1064. Cf *Reilly v The King* [1934] AC 176, 179 and *Terrell v Secretary of State for the Colonies* at 498–9 (where the terms of an appointment definitely prescribe a term and expressly provide for a power to determine 'for cause', the implication that the appointment is at pleasure is excluded).

[27] *Shenton v Smith* [1895] AC 229; *Inland Revenue Commissioners v Hambrook* [1956] 2 QB 641.

[28] *R v Civil Service Appeal Board, ex p Bruce* [1988] ICR 649, 660 (May LJ), aff'd [1989] ICR 171.

[29] *Kodeeswaran v A-G of Ceylon* [1970] AC 1111, 1123.

[30] *McClaren v Home Office* [1989] ICR 550 (revs'd on different grounds [1990] ICR 824).

[31] *R v Lord Chancellor's Department, ex p Nangle* [1991] ICR 743, 751–2. On the requirement of intention to create legal relations, see above, pp 72–6.

[32] Employment Rights Act 1996, ss 191, 192. See also Trade Union and Labour Relations (Consolidation) Act 1992, ss 152, 273 (dismissal on grounds of trade union membership, activities, or non-membership).

[33] Crown Proceedings Act 1947, s 2(1)(b).

[34] *R v Secretary of State for the Home Department, ex p Benwell* [1985] QB 554; *Council of Civil Service Unions v Minister for the Civil Service* [1985] AC 374. See also Walsh [1989] PL 131; Fredman and Morris (1991) 107 LQR 298; [1991] PL 485. On estoppel and legitimate expectation, see below, p 248.

(v) Liability of employees to Crown

Where an intention to contract is established, it is submitted that the Crown can sue its employees for breach of contract.[35] Equitable and restitutionary remedies may also be available against the employees in certain circumstances, such as breach of confidence, or where the employee has profited from a breach of duty.[36]

(vi) Crown agents

If a servant or agent of the Crown enters into an unauthorized contract, the Crown will not be bound unless it has held the agent out to have authority.[37] 'The right to act for the Crown in any particular matter must be established by reference to statute or otherwise.'[38] It is only if the act is within the agent's ostensible authority that the Crown may be estopped from going back on a representation which the agent has made.[39] Furthermore, an agent of the Crown who contracts on behalf of the Crown cannot be sued personally, either on the contract or for breach of warranty of authority.[40]

(b) PUBLIC AUTHORITIES

(i) Doctrine of *ultra vires*

Public authorities whose powers are the product of and defined by statute are subject to the doctrine of *ultra vires*, which is a necessary consequence of the statutory nature of the powers of such authorities. The authority's capacity to contract depends on the proper interpretation of the relevant statutes, which cannot be overridden by a statement or promise by the authority that it has the capacity which it lacks.[41] So, at common law the contracts of local authorities will be void unless they relate to functions which the authority is authorized, expressly or impliedly, to perform, or unless the acts are calculated to facilitate, or are incidental to, the discharge of those functions.[42]

The purpose of the *ultra vires* rule is to protect the public funds entrusted to such bodies, in the case of local authorities, by local taxpayers. But it has proved a trap for

[35] Even if there is no contract, the terms are nevertheless deemed to constitute a contract for the purposes of the economic torts: Trade Union and Labour Relations (Consolidation) Act 1992, s 245.

[36] *A-G v Blake* [2001] 1 AC 268; below, p 616.

[37] *A-G for Ceylon v Silva* [1953] AC 461 (Ceylon); *Robertson v Minister of Pensions* [1949] 1 KB 227, 232 (Denning J).

[38] *A-G for Ceylon v Silva* [1953] AC 461, 479.

[39] *Robertson v Minister of Pensions* [1949] 1 KB 227. But contrast *ibid*, 232, and see *Re L (an infant)* [1971] 3 All ER 743; *Laker Airways Ltd v Department of Trade* [1977] QB 643. See also below, p 248.

[40] *Dunn v Macdonald* [1897] 1 QB 555, criticized by Wade & Forsyth's *Administrative Law* (12th edn, 2023) 662. For the position of other agents, see below, pp 709, 711.

[41] *School Facility Management Ltd v Governing Body of Christ the King College* [2020] EWHC 1118 (Comm), [2020] PTSR 1913 at [355]–[358]. Cf Local Government (Contracts) Act 1997, s 2 in relation to local authority contracts, below, p 247.

[42] See, eg, *Hazell v Hammersmith & Fulham LBC* [1992] 2 AC 1; *Crédit Suisse v Allerdale BC* [1997] QB 306; *Crédit Suisse v Waltham Forest LBC* [1997] QB 362. But see Local Government Act 1972, ss 135, 137. See also *School Facility Management Ltd v Governing Body of Christ the King College* [2020] EWHC 1118 (Comm) at [159] (Foxton J (*obiter*): even if a public body has the power to enter into a contract, the contract may still be impugned if the *exercise* of that power was unlawful on public law grounds).

the unwary and can inflict grave hardship on persons who deal in good faith with an authority in ignorance of its lack of capacity. So banks which participated in housing or recreational schemes by local authorities either as a joint venturer or a guarantor, and other banks which entered into interest rate swaps with local authorities, could not sue on their contracts when they were held to be *ultra vires*.[43] The result was uncertainty and concern that private sector companies would be reluctant to enter into transactions with local authorities.

(ii) Statutory modification of *ultra vires* doctrine in relation to local authority contracts

There are two statutory provisions which in substance modify the *ultra vires* doctrine in relation to local authorities. The Localism Act 2011 has the effect of creating a presumption that a local authority has unlimited powers except where there is a specific restriction placed on it by statute.[44] Moreover, in the case of contracts by local authorities for the purposes of or in connection with the discharge of any of their functions which are intended to operate for a period of at least five years, the Local Government (Contracts) Act 1997 provides that where the authority has issued a certificate stating that it has power to enter into the contract and containing information about the statutory provisions conferring the power and the purpose of the contract, the contract has effect 'as if the local authority had had power to enter into it (and had exercised that power properly in entering into it)'.[45] This renders such contracts enforceable, but it is still possible to challenge in judicial review proceedings or in an audit of the authority's activities whether the authority had power to enter into a contract or exercised any power properly in entering into a contract.[46]

(iii) Incompatibility with statutory purpose

Those dealing with public authorities may also encounter the rule considered above that a public authority is not competent to fetter a statutory discretion if this would disable it from fulfilling the primary purpose for which it was created: 'if a person or public body is entrusted by the Legislature with certain powers and duties expressly or impliedly for public purposes, those persons or bodies cannot divest themselves of these powers and duties. They cannot enter into any contract or take any action incompatible with the due exercise of their powers or the discharge of their duties.'[47] Thus in *York Corporation v Henry Leetham & Sons Ltd*:[48]

[43] *Hazell v Hammersmith & Fulham LBC* [1992] 2 AC 1; *Crédit Suisse v Allerdale BC* [1997] QB 306; *Crédit Suisse v Waltham Forest LBC* [1997] QB 362.

[44] Localism Act 2011, s 1 ('A local authority has power to do anything that individuals generally may do'), which is then limited by ss 2–4.

[45] Local Government (Contracts) Act 1997, s 2.

[46] Local Government (Contracts) Act 1997, s 5.

[47] *Birkdale District Electric Supply Co Ltd v Southport Corp* [1926] AC 355, 364 (Lord Birkenhead). But see *Lever (Finance) Ltd v Westminster Corp* [1971] 1 QB 222 (estoppel).

[48] [1924] 1 Ch 557. See also *Ayr Harbour Trustees v Oswald* (1883) 8 App Cas 623; *William Cory & Son Ltd v London Corp* [1951] 2 KB 476; *Dowty Boulton Paul Ltd v Wolverhampton Corp* [1971] 1 WLR 204.

Y entered into a covenant with HL to allow HL to use two rivers which Y maintained and managed under statutory authority in return for an annual payment of £800 in place of the tolls Y that was authorized to charge by the statute.

It was held that this covenant was not one which Y was competent to make because it thereby disabled itself from exercising its statutory powers to increase tolls as necessary in order to perform its statutory duty.

On the other hand, in *Birkdale District Electric Supply Co Ltd v Southport Corporation*:[49]

B, the statutory undertaker for the supply of electricity in Birkdale, was sued by S on an agreement by which B had bound itself not to charge higher prices for electricity than those charged in the borough of Southport. It repudiated this agreement on the ground that it was incompatible with the due discharge of its statutory duties.

The House of Lords held that the agreement was nevertheless binding upon B. It was not wholly incompatible with the fulfilment of the purposes of the statute which empowered B to act as an electricity undertaking. The distinction between this case and the *York Corporation* case is by no means clear but it would seem that a public authority is only incompetent to contract where the contract in question is clearly proved to be incompatible with the full observance of the terms and the full attainment of the purposes for which the statutory powers have been granted. But it possesses contractual capacity where the agreements are mere contracts restricting the undertakers' freedom of action in respect of the business management of their undertaking.[50]

(iv) Estoppel and legitimate expectation

A public authority cannot be estopped by its previous conduct so as to hinder its obligation to carry out its statutory powers or duties. But it has been held that an authority may be estopped in two types of situation. First, where the authority has delegated to its officers the power to determine particular questions, it may be estopped by representations relating to those questions, made by an officer acting within the scope of his ostensible authority, on which another person acts.[51] Secondly, if an authority waives a procedural requirement relating to any application made to it for the exercise of its statutory powers, it may be estopped from relying on lack of formality.[52]

A public authority may also be under a public law duty to act consistently with an arrangement which does not give rise to a contract or an estoppel, under the principle of legitimate expectation. This is because a person who, as a result of the words or conduct of a public authority, has a legitimate expectation that a benefit will be granted or continue to be enjoyed, may be able to argue that later inconsistent action is an abuse of power and reviewable on the ground of unfairness.[53] Inconsistency is, however, not

[49] [1926] AC 355.

[50] *Ibid*, 369, 370 (Lord Sumner).

[51] *Lever (Finance) Ltd v Westminster Corp* [1971] 1 QB 222 (representation that modification to plan was not material and so did not require further planning permission).

[52] *Western Fish Products Ltd v Penwith DC* [1981] 2 All ER 204, 221 (Megaw LJ: 'The extension of the concept of estoppel beyond these two exceptions, in our judgment, would not be justified').

[53] *Council for Civil Service Unions v Minister for the Civil Service* [1985] AC 374, 408; *R v North and East Devon Health Authority, ex p Coughlan* [2001] QB 213; Wade & Forsyth's *Administrative Law* (12th edn, 2023) 331–7.

necessarily unfair, and the Courts will not let an arrangement that has given rise to a legitimate expectation hinder the formation of policy. For example, an authority that has received and resolved to accept a tender from its own workforce might choose to abandon the project or seek fresh tenders.[54]

It has been suggested that, although there is an analogy between a private law estoppel and the public law concept of a legitimate expectation created by a public authority, it is preferable now to rely on the latter, because 'remedies against public authorities also have to take into account the interests of the general public which the authority exists to promote. Public law can also take into account the hierarchy of individual rights which exist under the Human Rights Act 1998.'[55]

(v) Pre-contractual procedures and refusal to contract

Although the general rule, based upon the principle of freedom of contract, is that a person can choose with whom to contract and with whom not to contract,[56] in the case of public authorities this freedom is limited. Both legislation on public sector contracts, and the general principles governing the exercise of discretionary powers, may invalidate refusals to contract at all or only on particular terms. Such refusals may be based on a policy that amounts to an improper fetter on an authority's discretion or be 'unfair' in the light of an individual's legitimate expectations. For instance, a decision not to contract with a company in part motivated by the wish to induce it to cease trading with South Africa during the apartheid era was held to be *ultra vires*.[57]

Under the Local Government Act 1988, local authorities and certain other public authorities are required to exercise their contracting functions (including invitations to tender) without reference to 'non-commercial matters'.[58] Under the Local Government Act 1999 these authorities are required to 'make arrangements to secure continuous improvement in the way in which [their] functions are exercised, having regard to a combination of economy, efficiency and effectiveness'.[59] The Act and any regulations made under it give the government extensive powers to require local and other authorities to achieve 'best value' by a programme of contracting out.[60] The Secretary

[54] *R v Walsall MBC, ex p Yapp* [1994] ICR 528. See also *Hughes v DHSS* [1985] AC 776 (change in local authority's policy about retirement age).

[55] *R (Reprotech (Pebsham) Ltd) v East Sussex CC* [2002] UKHL 8, [2003] 1 WLR 348 at [34] (Lord Hoffmann, in the context of planning law. See also at [35]: 'public law has already absorbed whatever is useful from the moral values which underlie the private law concept of estoppel and the time has come for it to stand upon its own two feet'); *Re Finucane's application for Judicial Review (Northern Ireland)* [2019] UKSC 7, [2019] 3 All ER 191 at [70]–[72], [156]–[160].

[56] But there may be a requirement to conform to specified tendering requirements; *Blackpool and Fylde Aero Club v Blackpool BC* [1990] 1 WLR 1195, above, p 37. See also *R v Lord Chancellor, ex p Hibbit and Saunders* [1993] COD 326.

[57] *R v Lewisham LBC, ex p Shell UK Ltd* [1988] 1 All ER 938. See also *Mercury Energy Ltd v Electricity Corp of New Zealand Ltd* [1994] 1 WLR 521 (New Zealand) (reviewability of termination of contract).

[58] Local Government Act 1988, s 17. See *R v Islington LBC, ex p Building Employers Confederation* [1989] IRLR 383; *R v Enfield LBC, ex p TF Unwin (Roydon) Ltd* (1989) 46 BLR 1. See also Local Government Act 1972, s 135.

[59] Local Government Act 1999, s 3(1).

[60] Local Government Act 1999, s 18.

of State is also empowered[61] to provide that a specified matter cease to be a 'non-commercial matter' for the purposes of section 17 of the Local Government Act 1988.

Under the Procurement Act 2023,[62] public authorities are subject to special rules in awarding major contracts for the supply of goods, services or works, and framework and concession contracts, which require them normally to publicize their intention to seek tenders for the contract. Standard tendering procedures are required; clear, measurable, and specific criteria must be used; and authorities are required to award the contract on the basis of the 'most advantageous' tender. The public authority's duties under the Act are enforceable in civil proceedings in favour of suppliers in the UK or in specified states with which the UK has treaty obligations. The Court has wide powers to remedy breaches of the duties, including setting aside decisions of the public authority, and in many cases the public authority must give notice to tenderers after it has made its decision, but before the contract is entered into, to allow a standstill period for any relevant challenge to be made.

(vi) Restitution of payments made and benefits conferred under void contracts

Payments made under an *ultra vires* contract with a public authority, whether made to or by the incapacitated party, are recoverable in an action for restitution of an unjust enrichment,[63] although where, as in the interest swaps cases, payments have been made both ways, restitution is only available to a party on the basis that credit is given for what has been received.[64] A claim may also be made for the value of benefits conferred under the void contract as long as the claim in unjust enrichment would not stultify the statutory policy by which the public authority lacked power to contract.[65]

3. CORPORATIONS AND UNINCORPORATED ASSOCIATIONS

(a) CORPORATIONS

(i) Different forms of corporation

A corporation is an artificial person recognized by law and therefore having legal capacity. A corporation may consist of an office occupied by a single individual

[61] Local Government Act 1999, s 19.

[62] Replacing earlier regulations which implemented EU Directives on public procurement and utilities contracts.

[63] *Westdeutsche Landesbank Girozentrale v Islington LBC* [1994] 1 WLR 938, aff'd [1996] AC 669; *Guinness Mahon & Co Ltd v Kensington & Chelsea RLBC* [1999] QB 215; *Kleinwort Benson Ltd v Lincoln City Council* [1999] 2 AC 349.

[64] *Westdeutsche Landesbank Girozentrale v Islington LBC*, above, n 63.

[65] *Attorney General of Trinidad and Tobago v Trinsalvage Enterprises Ltd* [2023] UKPC 26, [2023] 1 WLR 4045.

(a 'corporation sole'), such as the Crown, the vicar of a parish, or the Secretary of State; or a collection of several persons who are united into one body (a 'corporation aggregate'), such as the mayor and corporation of a city, a limited liability company incorporated under the Companies Act 2006, or a limited liability partnership under the Limited Liability Partnerships Act 2000. The key feature of every corporation is that it has legal personality distinct from the individual(s) of whom it is formed.

A corporation can be formed only by charter from the Crown under the Royal Prerogative, or by statute.

(ii) Doctrine of *ultra vires*

At common law the capacity of a corporation to enter into a contract depends upon how the corporation was formed. A corporation created by charter from the Crown has the same unlimited capacity to enter into contracts as a private individual.[66] However, any act done by a corporation incorporated by statute outside its statutory powers is *ultra vires* and void.[67] Since the corporation has no existence independent of the statute which creates the corporation or authorizes its creation, it follows that its capacity is limited to the exercise of such powers as are actually conferred by, or may reasonably be deduced from, the language of the statute. Thus at common law a company is bound by the objects, listed in its constitutional documents,[68] for the purposes of which it is incorporated. The company can make no contracts inconsistent with those objects,[69] and, if it does so, a contract so made is, at common law,[70] void and unenforceable as being *ultra vires*.

In *Ashbury Railway Carriage and Iron Co Ltd v Riche*:[71]

A company was incorporated with the object (set out in the memorandum of association) to make, and sell, or to lend on hire, railway wagons and carriages and other rolling stock. The company contracted to assign to another company a concession which it had bought for the construction of a railway in Belgium.

[66] *Baroness Wenlock v River Dee Co* (1883) 36 Ch D 675n, 685. If it exceeds its powers, the effect is not to avoid the contract, but to give cause for forfeiture of the charter: see Gower (1952) 68 LQR 214; *Jenkin v Pharmaceutical Society* [1921] 1 Ch 392, 398. The Crown itself has unlimited contractual capacity, although the public nature of the Crown affects the scope of obligations undertaken and their enforceability: see above, pp 242–6.

[67] Similarly, public authorities created by statute are subject to the *ultra vires* doctrine, although the public nature of their functions gives a special dimension to the operation of that doctrine: see above, pp 246–8.

[68] Before the reforms made by the Companies Act 2006, the objects were contained in the company's memorandum of association. Now, however, the memorandum is a much simpler document; the principal document within a company's 'constitution' is the articles of association; a company's objects are unrestricted unless the articles of association specifically restrict them; and provisions (such as restrictions on objects) which are contained in the memorandum of a company which was incorporated before the coming into force of the 2006 Act are to be treated as provisions of the company's articles: Companies Act 2006, ss 8, 17, 28(1), 31(1).

[69] Matters which are reasonably incidental to, or consequential upon, that which is authorized by the memorandum are not *ultra vires* unless expressly prohibited: *A-G v Great Eastern Ry Co* (1880) 5 App Cas 473, 478.

[70] For statutory modification of the doctrine to provide protection for third parties, see below, p 252.

[71] (1875) LR 7 HL 653.

The House of Lords held that the contract, being related to the actual construction of a railway, as opposed to railway stock, was *ultra vires* the objects in the memorandum and void. Even if the shareholders subsequently ratified the contract, it could not thereby be rendered binding on the company.

The explanation given in this case for the existence of the *ultra vires* rule was not only that it was a necessary consequence of statutory incorporation but also that the rule was required to protect investors in, and creditors of, the company.[72] The rule 'ensured that an investor in a gold mining company did not find himself holding shares in a fried-fish shop, and it gave those who allowed credit to a limited company some assurance that its assets would not be dissipated in unauthorized enterprises'.[73] Nevertheless, the application of the rule not infrequently led to injustice. Persons who entered into an *ultra vires* contract with a company could not enforce it. If they supplied goods to the company or performed services under the contract, they could not obtain payment.[74] If they lent money to the company, and the borrowing was *ultra vires*, then before the recent recognition of independent restitutionary obligations they could not, in general, recover their money.[75] In theory, before entering into the contract with the company, such persons would first scrutinize the memorandum[76] to ascertain the extent of the company's powers. In practice, however, they did not do so, but were nevertheless deemed to have 'constructive notice' of the contents of the memorandum despite the fact that they had no actual knowledge of them. As a result, the doctrine of *ultra vires* proved to be a trap for the unwary and from time to time inflicted grave hardship on persons who dealt in good faith with the company in ignorance of its lack of capacity.[77]

(iii) Statutory modification of *ultra vires* doctrine

The *ultra vires* doctrine was criticized by two committees on the reform of company law,[78] and in 1972, although the doctrine was not abolished, statutory protection[79] was given to those dealing with a company[80] in good faith in respect of transactions decided upon by the directors which were within the capacity of the company, although in fact unauthorized. The Companies Act 1989 took the final step of abolishing the restrictions on capacity of companies formed and registered under the Companies Acts,[81] in a provision which is now found in the Companies Act 2006.

[72] *Ibid*, 667–8 (Lord Cairns).

[73] Gower, *The Principles of Modern Company Law* (4th edn, 1979) 165.

[74] *Re Jon Beauforte (London) Ltd* [1953] Ch 131.

[75] eg *Sinclair v Brougham* [1914] AC 398. But see now *Westdeutsche Landesbank Girozentrale v Islington LBC* [1996] AC 669, above, p 250, below, p 254.

[76] Before the reforms made by the Companies Act 2006, the objects were contained in the company's memorandum of association: above, n 68.

[77] eg *Re Jon Beauforte (London) Ltd* [1953] Ch 131.

[78] Cohen Committee (Cmd 6659, 1945) para 12; Jenkins Committee (Cmnd 1749, 1962) paras 35–42.

[79] European Communities Act 1972, s 9, implementing Art 9 of the first Directive 68/151/EEC on Company Law [1968] OJ L65/7.

[80] The company itself could not enforce an *ultra vires* contract: *Bell Houses Ltd v City Wall Properties Ltd* [1966] 1 QB 207 (revs'd on other grounds, [1966] 2 QB 656). See Furmston (1961) 24 MLR 715.

[81] Companies Act 1989, s 108, amending Companies Act 1985, s 35.

Section 39(1) of the Companies Act 2006 provides that the 'validity of an act done by a company shall not be called into question on the ground of lack of capacity by reason of anything in the company's constitution'. The effect of this section is that a transaction entered into by a company cannot be held invalid merely because it falls within any restriction on the objects listed in the company's articles of association.[82]

(iv) Lack of capacity distinguished from excess or abuse of power

An *ultra vires* contract which is 'beyond the capacity of the company and therefore wholly void'[83] should be distinguished from a contract made by the exercise of a power which the company undoubtedly has but for a *purpose* which is unauthorized. Transactions of the latter sort involve an excess or abuse of power rather than a lack of capacity and will be enforceable against the company unless the other party had notice of the excess or abuse of power. At common law, a contract would not bind the company as against a person who had actual *or constructive* notice of the excess or abuse of power,[84] but by section 40(2)(b)(i) of the Companies Act 2006,[85] a party to a transaction with a company 'is not bound to enquire as to any limitation on the powers of the directors to bind the company or authorise others to do so'. In effect therefore the doctrine of constructive notice is now a dead letter in this context.

Limited liability partnerships have unlimited capacity, and so have never been subject to the *ultra vires* rule.[86]

(v) Powers of directors

At common law similar limitations existed in respect of contracts which, though within the powers of the company, were entered into by the directors of the company and other officers without authority or in breach of its internal constitution.[87] The Companies Act 2006 requires directors to act in accordance with the company's constitution (and therefore to observe any restrictions on the company's objects contained in the articles of association).[88] But section 40(1) protects those dealing with a company in good faith by providing that 'the power of the directors to bind the company, or authorise others to do so, is deemed to be free of any limitation under the company's constitution'.[89]

[82] Before the Companies Act 2006, the objects were set out in the memorandum; under the 2006 Act, however, any restrictions on the company's objects are set out in the articles: above, n 68.

[83] This depends solely upon the true construction of the memorandum of association (now, the articles of association: above, n 68): *Rolled Steel Products (Holdings) Ltd v British Steel Corp* [1986] Ch 246, 303, 306.

[84] *Ibid*, 306–7.

[85] This reform was originally made by Companies Act 1989, s 108 which introduced Companies Act 1985, s 35B.

[86] Limited Liability Partnerships Act 2000, s 1(3).

[87] See *Royal British Bank v Turquand* (1856) 6 E & B 327; Campbell (1959) 75 LQR 469; (1960) 76 LQR 115.

[88] Companies Act 2006, s 171.

[89] See Companies Act 2006, s 40(2) for the meaning of 'deals with' and 'good faith'. Cf *ibid*, s 41 in respect of contracts involving directors of the company. For the circumstances in which a limited liability partnership can be bound by an unauthorized act of one of its members acting as the agent of the partnership, see Limited Liability Partnerships Act 2000, s 6.

(vi) Form of contracts

Since the passing of the Corporate Bodies' Contracts Act 1960 a corporation can, in general, contract in the same manner as any natural person of full age and capacity and is not only bound by contracts made under its corporate seal. The provisions governing contracts made by companies registered under the Companies Acts are contained in the Companies Act 2006.[90]

(vii) Restitution of benefits conferred under an *ultra vires* contract

Payments made to or by a company under an *ultra vires* contract are recoverable in an action for restitution of an unjust enrichment,[91] and a party which has done work under such a contract will be entitled to reasonable remuneration.[92] But the provisions of section 39 of the Companies Act 2006 mean that restitutionary obligations will be of less significance in the context of companies.

(b) UNINCORPORATED ASSOCIATIONS

(i) Contractual capacity

An unincorporated association has no legal personality. It cannot therefore contract, or sue or be sued in its name, unless such a course is authorized by statute or by rules of Court. But a contract which purports to have been entered into by or with an unincorporated association is not necessarily invalid. The person or persons who actually made the contract, for example, the secretary or committee of a club, may be held to have contracted personally and be personally liable on the contract.[93] Further, under the rules of agency, they may be held to have contracted on behalf of the members of the association, and, in certain circumstances, a representative action[94] may be brought by or against one or more of the members, including the trustees of the funds of the association,[95] as representing the others, so as to avoid the necessity of joining numerous persons as parties to the action.

(ii) Partnerships

A partnership can normally sue and be sued in the firm's name,[96] and contracts entered into by one of the partners will, as a general rule, bind the firm since each partner has authority to act for the others in the ordinary course of the partnership business.[97]

90 Companies Act 2006, s 43. On the execution of documents by companies, see *ibid*, s 44, and for the execution of deeds, see *ibid*, s 46. The provisions of the Companies Act apply also in modified form to contracts made by limited partnerships: Limited Liability Partnerships (Application of Companies Act 2006) Regulations 2009 (SI 2009 No 1804), reg 4.

91 *Westdeutsche Landesbank Girozentrale v Islington LBC* [1994] 1 WLR 938, aff'd [1996] AC 669.

92 *Rover International Ltd v Cannon Film Sales Ltd* [1989] 1 WLR 912.

93 *Bradley Egg Farm Ltd v Clifford* [1943] 2 All ER 378. See also *Artistic Upholstery Ltd v Art Forma (Furniture) Ltd* [1999] 4 All ER 277.

94 CPR r 19.8(1).

95 *Ideal Films Ltd v Richards* [1927] 1 KB 374. But see *News Group Newspapers Ltd v SOGAT 1982* [1986] ICR 716.

96 CPR r 7.2A; PD7A, para 7.3.

97 See below, p 703. For a similar application of agency principles to contracts made by a member of a limited liability partnership (which has separate corporate personality but unlimited capacity), see Limited Liability Partnerships Act 2000, s 6.

(iii) Trade unions

A trade union stands juridically in a somewhat anomalous position. Section 10 of the Trade Union and Labour Relations (Consolidation) Act 1992[98] provides that a trade union is not nor is it to be treated as a body corporate, yet it is capable of making contracts,[99] it is capable of suing and being sued in its own name,[100] and a judgment, order, or award made in any proceedings of any description brought against a trade union is enforceable against any property held in trust for it to the same extent and in the same manner as if the union were a body corporate.[101] The same capacity and liability attach to an employers' association which is an unincorporated association.[102]

4. MINORS

On 1 January 1970, the age of majority was lowered from 21 to 18.[103] All persons under that age are known technically as minors (or infants). On attaining their majority they legally become adults. The rights and liabilities of minors under contracts entered into by them during minority rest upon common law rules as altered by the Minors Contracts Act 1987.[104] The desire to protect minors on the one hand, and the wish to safeguard the interests of traders on the other, has led to a complicated body of law.

(a) COMMON LAW: INTRODUCTION

At common law, the only class of contract to which minority did not afford some sort of defence was a contract for 'necessaries' in the sense to be explained below. In all other cases, the common law treated a minor's contracts as being either voidable at the option of the minor, either before or after becoming an adult, or unenforceable against the minor unless he or she ratified them after attaining majority.

Contracts in which the minor acquired an interest of a permanent or continuous nature, such as a contract to acquire an interest in land, were binding until the minor *disclaimed* them, either during minority or within a reasonable time after becoming an adult. They were therefore voidable by the minor.[105] The common law rule for contracts which were neither contracts for necessaries nor continuous in their operation was that they were not binding on a minor unless ratified within a reasonable time after majority. So, for example, a promise by a minor to perform an isolated act, such as to pay for goods supplied other than necessaries, or for work and labour done, required an express ratification after majority before the minor would be bound. Such contracts were also often referred to as 'voidable', although this is not strictly accurate since the

[98] It was already clear that a union is capable of being sued for breach of contract in its own name, and that any damages would be recoverable from its funds: *Bonsor v Musicians' Union* [1956] AC 104.

[99] 1992 Act, s 10(1)(a).

[100] 1992 Act, s 10(1)(b).

[101] 1992 Act, s 12(2).

[102] 1992 Act, s 127.

[103] Family Law Reform Act 1969, s 1.

[104] Implementing the recommendations in Law Com No 134, *Minors' Contracts* (1984).

[105] Above, p 24.

essence of a voidable contract is that it is binding unless rescinded,[106] whereas these contracts were not binding on the minor unless affirmed.

In the case of both these classes of contracts (voidable, and unenforceable unless ratified) there was no objection to the minor enforcing them. But a minor's position differed from that of parties of full contractual capacity in that he or she might recover damages for breach but not obtain specific performance of the contract.[107] Specific performance is granted at the discretion of the Court, which will not grant it where it would not be prepared to enforce the contract at the suit of either party.[108] Since the contract could not be enforced against the minor, equity would not allow the minor to obtain specific performance against the other party.

(b) CONTRACTS FOR NECESSARIES

It has already been stated that, at common law, the only class of contract which was not voidable at the option of a minor was a contract for 'necessaries'.[109] The meaning of the term 'necessaries', however, requires further explanation. We first consider contracts for necessary goods, and then contracts of employment or training, and then other agreements beneficial to the minor.

Part of the common law on this matter has been given statutory form by section 3 of the Sale of Goods Act 1979.[110] This provides:

> (1) Capacity to buy and sell is regulated by the general law concerning capacity to contract and to transfer and acquire property.
> (2) Where necessaries are sold and delivered to a minor or to a person who by reason of drunkenness is incompetent to contract, he must pay a reasonable price for them.
> (3) In subsection (2) above 'necessaries' mean goods suitable to the condition in life of the minor or other person concerned and to his actual requirements at the time of the sale and delivery.

(i) Necessary goods

We must first consider what the word 'necessaries' includes. It has always been held that a minor may be liable for the supply to him or her, not merely of the necessaries of life, but of things suitable to his or her station in life and particular circumstances at the time. Minors are liable for *necessaries*, and not merely for *necessities*.[111] Certain things may be obviously outside the range of possible necessaries. So in *Ryder v Wombwell*:[112]

[106] Above, p 24. [107] *Flight v Bolland* (1828) 4 Russ 298. [108] Cf below, p 597.

[109] But such a contract may be held invalid if the minor was not capable of understanding the nature of the transaction: see *R v Oldham MBC* [1993] 1 FLR 645, 661–2 (Scott LJ. This will vary according to the minor and the nature of the contract: 'at what age a child is able to go to the village shop and enter into an effective contract for the purchase of sweets, I would not wish to guess, but I am sure it would be well under the age of 10 years').

[110] Re-enacting Sale of Goods Act 1893, s 2, and amended by Mental Capacity Act 2005.

[111] The Law Commission did not consider that the narrowing of the category in this way was, on balance, desirable: Law Com No 134, *Minors' Contracts* (1984) paras 5.4–5.6.

[112] (1868) LR 3 Ex 90, aff'd (1869) LR 4 Ex 32.

W, a minor with an income of £500 a year, bought from R a pair of crystal, ruby, and diamond solitaires and an antique goblet in silver gilt.

It was held that neither of these articles could be a necessary, even though W was the son of a deceased baronet and 'moved in the highest society'. Other things may be of a useful character but the quality or quantity supplied may take them out of the character of necessaries. In *Nash v Inman*:[113]

A tailor supplied a Cambridge undergraduate with clothing which included 11 fancy waistcoats at 2 guineas each. It was proved that he had already a sufficient supply of clothing according to his position in life.

The Court of Appeal held that the tailor had failed to prove that the clothing was suitable to the undergraduate's actual requirements at the time of the sale and delivery.

Necessaries also vary according to the minor's station in life or peculiar circumstances at the time of the contract.[114] The Court must take into consideration the character of the goods supplied, the actual circumstances of the minor, and the extent to which the minor was already supplied with them. It is necessary to emphasize the words 'actual circumstances', because a false impression conveyed to the person dealing with the minor as to the station and circumstances of the minor will not affect the minor's liability. A shop which supplies expensive goods to a minor thinking that the minor's circumstances are better than they really are, or which supplies goods of a useful class not knowing that the minor is already sufficiently supplied, does so at its peril.[115]

Section 3 of the Sale of Goods Act 1979 also requires that the goods should be necessary to the minor 'at the time of the sale *and* delivery'. This might seem to indicate that the seller would have to prove them to be necessary at both of these times. But, it is probable that this is simply a reference to the action for goods sold and delivered, which is the normal action for a seller who wishes to recover the purchase price.[116] The seller would have to prove them to be necessary at the time of their delivery alone.

(ii) Loans for necessaries

A loan of money to a minor to pay for necessaries was not recoverable at common law, for 'it may be borrowed for necessaries, but laid out and spent at a tavern'.[117] But in equity it was held that if a minor borrowed money to pay a debt for necessaries, and the debt was actually paid with the money, the lender stood in the place of the person paid and was entitled to recover the money lent.[118] This rule is a branch of the equitable doctrine of subrogation. It is not possible, however, to sue a minor on a negotiable

[113] [1908] 2 KB 1. The clothing was 'of an extravagant and ridiculous style having regard to the position of the boy': Buckley LJ at 11.

[114] *Peters v Fleming* (1840) 6 M & W 42.

[115] The burden of proof is on the supplier: *Nash v Inman* [1908] 2 KB 1, 5.

[116] Below, p 262. See also Winfield (1942) 58 LQR 82, 90.

[117] *Earle v Peale* (1711) 1 Salk 386 (except where necessaries are purchased at minor's request).

[118] *Marlow v Pitfeild* (1719) 1 P Wms 558.

instrument given for the price of necessaries, even though it may have been negotiated to a third party.[119] Also, an account stated with a minor is still void although the items in the account may consist of necessaries.[120]

(iii) Contracts of employment and training

A minor may enter into a contract of employment so as to earn a living or into a contract for the purpose of obtaining instruction or education so as to qualify for a suitable trade or profession whereby he or she may profit himself or herself afterwards.[121] Provided that they are beneficial to the minor, these contracts are binding. In *Clements v London and North Western Railway Company*,[122] a minor entered into a contract of employment with a railway company, promising to accept the terms of an insurance against accidents in lieu of his rights of action under the Employers' Liability Act 1880. It was held that the contract, taken as a whole, was for his benefit and that he was bound by his promise.

On the other hand, a contract of this class which is more onerous than beneficial to the minor will impose no liability. So in *De Francesco v Barnum*:[123]

> B, aged 14 years, agreed to become De F's apprentice in 'the art of choreography' for 7 years. De F was to teach her stage dancing, and during the period of apprenticeship B was not to take any professional engagement without the consent of De F, nor was she to marry. She was to receive certain payments for any performances she might give, but there was no provision for any other remuneration and De F did not undertake to find her any engagements. The effect of the deed was to place B entirely at the disposal of De F.

Fry LJ held that the contract was not beneficial to B and was unenforceable. It should, however, be noted that even though a minor's contract of service contains some terms which are not for the benefit of the minor, the minor cannot necessarily repudiate it, still less select which terms will or will not be followed. 'The Court must look at the whole contract, having regard to the circumstances of the case, and determine . . . whether the contract is or is not beneficial.'[124]

(iv) Other beneficial contracts

The class of contracts for necessaries is not, however, limited to contracts of employment and training. It includes numerous contracts for 'necessaries' other than goods, for example, for medical attendance,[125] or for the hire of a car to fetch a minor's luggage from the railway station.[126] Provided that these are reasonable and beneficial to the minor, the other party can enforce them. Yet the class does not include ordinary trading

[119] *Re Soltykoff, ex p Margrett* [1891] 1 QB 413. Cf Bills of Exchange Act 1882, s 22.

[120] *Williams v Moor* (1843) 11 M & W 256.

[121] Co Litt 172a; *Walter v Everard* [1891] 2 QB 369.

[122] [1894] 2 QB 482.

[123] (1890) 45 Ch D 430. See also *Sir WC Leng & Co Ltd v Andrews* [1909] 1 Ch 763.

[124] *De Francesco v Barnum* (1890) 45 Ch D 430, 439. See also *Slade v Metrodent Ltd* [1953] 2 QB 112.

[125] *Dale v Copping* (1610) 1 Bulst 39. See also *Gillick v West Norfolk and Wisbech AHA* [1986] AC 112, 166–7, 183, 195 (capacity of girl under 16 to consent to medical treatment, including contraception).

[126] *Fawcett v Smethurst* (1914) 84 LJ KB 473.

contracts, such as the hire-purchase of a motor lorry by a haulage contractor who is a minor.[127] Such contracts may be necessary to the minor's business, and so of benefit to the minor, but they are not binding. Thus, in *Cowern v Nield*,[128] a contract to sell a consignment of hay by a hay and straw dealer who was a minor was held not to be a contract for 'necessaries' because it was a trading contract.

The class is therefore a limited one although the limits are not easy to state. In *Doyle v White City Stadium Ltd*,[129] for instance:

A professional boxer, who was a minor, in consideration of his receiving a licence from the British Boxing Board of Control, agreed to be bound by the rules of the Board in all his professional engagements. A purse of £3,000 was withheld from him by the Board, in accordance with its rules, on the ground that he had been disqualified in a contest for hitting below the belt.

It was held that the agreement was binding on him despite his being a minor. The ground of this decision was that the licence was practically essential in order to enable him to become proficient in his profession, and when the conditions attached to the issue of the licence were incorporated in a particular beneficial contract of employment—in this case, an engagement to box for a heavyweight championship—both contracts became binding on the minor, as they were both for his benefit. Also in *Chaplin v Leslie Frewin (Publishers) Ltd*:[130]

C, a minor who was the son of Charlie Chaplin, had been eking out a Bohemian existence in London. In return for an advance of royalties, he assigned to LF publishers the exclusive right to publish an autobiography of himself (entitled *I Couldn't Smoke the Grass on my Father's Lawn*) which was to be written by 'ghost' writers. The completed work, so he alleged, showed him to be 'a depraved creature', and he sought to repudiate the assignment.

The Court of Appeal held that he could not do so. The contract was binding on him since it was one which enabled him to make a start as an author and thus to earn money to keep himself and his wife. It was a beneficial contract, because, as Danckwerts LJ put it,[131] 'The mud may cling but the profits will be secured.'

The judgments in these two cases do not set out to define the contracts which are binding when beneficial to a minor, but they indicate a tendency to enlarge the class by analogy with types of contract which are established as contracts for necessaries. The contracts which the minors had made were arguably merely incidental to the carrying on of a trade or profession and therefore of a kind which had not hitherto been believed to be binding, even when beneficial.

[127] *Mercantile Union Guarantee Corp v Ball* [1937] 2 KB 498.

[128] [1912] 2 KB 419.

[129] [1935] 1 KB 110.

[130] [1966] Ch 71 (Lord Denning MR dissenting). The Court also held that, even if the contract had been voidable by the minor, it could not have been rescinded because it had been executed by the transfer of the copyright.

[131] *Ibid*, 95.

(c) VOIDABLE CONTRACTS

A minor who acquires an interest in permanent property to which obligations attach, or enters into a contract involving continuous rights and duties, benefits and liabilities, and takes some benefit under the contract, will be bound, unless he or she expressly disclaims the contract during the minority or within a reasonable time of coming of age.

Examples of such contracts are the acquisition of an interest in land (such as a lease or tenancy), and of shares in a company. Up to the time that the minor disclaims such a contract he or she will be bound to carry out the obligations under it, provided that these accrue before repudiation. A minor cannot renounce the liabilities until he or she renounces the interest. So a lessee who is a minor is liable for rent until the lease is disclaimed,[132] and if a shareholder, is under a similar liability in respect of calls on the shares until they are expressly repudiated.[133]

(i) Partnership

The position of a member of a partnership who is a minor differs from that of a shareholder. Partnership is a continuous relationship between the partners, but by becoming a partner a minor does not acquire an interest in a subject of a permanent nature to which obligations are attached. During the minority of a partner, the minor is not liable for debts incurred by the partnership; but equally is not entitled to any share of the partnership assets until the firm's debts have been paid.[134] A minor who continues to act as a partner after majority will be liable, equally with the other partners, for the debts subsequently incurred. A minor may also be liable for such debts if, though ceasing to act as a partner, he or she gives no adequate notice of this withdrawal to persons dealing with the firm.[135] The minor's liability in this case, however, merely illustrates a general rule of the law of partnership applicable to any retired partner,[136] and does not depend on any principle peculiar to the law of minors.

(ii) Time of disclaimer

In order that a minor's disclaimer of a permanent interest may take effect, the contract must be repudiated during minority or within a reasonable time of the minor's coming of age. What is a reasonable time will depend upon the circumstances of the case. In *Edwards v Carter*[137] the House of Lords held that a minor who entered into a marriage

[132] *Blake v Concannon* (1870) 4 Ir Rep CL 320. By the Law of Property Act 1925, s 1(6) a minor can no longer hold a legal estate in land; but can have an equitable interest, and so be bound in the same way: *Davies v Benyon-Harris* (1931) 47 TLR 424; and a conveyance to a minor operates as a declaration of trust in his or her favour: Trusts of Land and Appointment of Trustees Act 1996, Sched 1, paras 1, 2; *Hammersmith & Fulham LBC v Alexander-David* [2009] EWCA Civ 259, [2010] Ch 272.

[133] There is some doubt as to whether a minor is bound to pay unpaid calls which accrued due before the repudiation, but the better opinion is that the minor is so bound, provided that he cannot plead total failure of consideration: *Steinberg v Scala (Leeds) Ltd* [1923] 2 Ch 452. See also *Cork & Bandon Ry Co v Cazenove* (1847) 10 QB 935; *North Western Railway Co v M'Michael* (1850) 5 Exch 114; *Newry and Enniskillen Ry Co v Coombe* (1849) 3 Exch 565.

[134] *Lovell and Christmas v Beauchamp* [1894] AC 607.

[135] *Goode v Harrison* (1821) 5 B & Ald 147.

[136] Partnership Act 1890, s 36.

[137] [1893] AC 360. See also *Carnell v Harrison* [1916] 1 Ch 328.

settlement and covenanted to bring into the settlement any property which might come to him under his father's will could not repudiate it nearly five years after coming of age and one year after his father died leaving him property by will.

(iii) Effect of disclaimer

The effect of a valid disclaimer of a contract that binds until repudiated is to release the minor from future obligations under it. A minor who has paid to the other party in the mistaken belief that the contract is enforceable may be able to recover the payment.[138] But in the absence of such a mistake the minor will not be able to recover anything unless there has been a total failure of the consideration for which the money has been paid. Where, for example, shares have been allotted to the minor, money paid for them will be irrecoverable whether or not a dividend has been paid or any other real advantage received.[139] The minor will have received something which had a marketable value and which was the very consideration for which he or she had bargained.

(d) OTHER CONTRACTS: UNENFORCEABLE UNLESS RATIFIED

As explained above, a contract which is not for necessaries, and is not for an interest in permanent property to which obligations attach, nor involves continuous rights and duties, will not bind the minor at common law unless ratified by the minor within a reasonable time after attaining majority. Until the Minors' Contracts Act 1987 came into force this common law rule was displaced by the Infants Relief Act 1874 which made it impossible for a person of full age to be sued on a contract entered into during minority.[140] However, this did not stop the minor enforcing the contract against the other party. The repeal of the 1874 Act means that the common law rule as it existed prior to that legislation has again become the law.

(e) THE NATURE OF THE LIABILITY OF MINORS

Where there is an enforceable obligation against a minor, for example, for necessaries, it remains to characterize that obligation. Two theories have been put forward.

(i) Liability in unjust enrichment

The first is that the liability arises in unjust enrichment rather than contract. The obligation is imposed by the law because the minor has actually received the benefit of performance, and not consensually as a result of entering a valid contract. This was the view taken by Fletcher Moulton LJ in *Nash v Inman*:[141]

[138] *Kleinwort Benson Ltd v Lincoln CC* [1999] 2 AC 349.

[139] *Steinberg v Scala (Leeds) Ltd* [1923] 2 Ch 452. See also *Holmes v Blogg* (1818) 8 Taunt 508 (premium paid by minor for lease not recoverable).

[140] See Infants Relief Act 1874, s 2 (repealed by Minors' Contracts Act 1987, s 4(1)).

[141] [1908] 2 KB 1, 8; *Elkington v Amery* [1936] 2 All ER 86, 88. For the application of this to contracts with those lacking mental capacity, see *Re Rhodes* (1890) 44 Ch D 94, 105; *Re J* [1909] 1 Ch 574, 577.

An infant, like a lunatic, is incapable of making a contract of purchase in the strict sense of the words; but if a man satisfies the needs of the infant or lunatic by supplying to him necessaries, the law will imply an obligation to repay him for the services so rendered, and will enforce that obligation against the estate of the infant or lunatic. The consequence is that the basis of the action is hardly contract. Its real foundation is an obligation which the law imposes on the infant to make a fair payment in respect of needs satisfied.

(ii) Liability in contract

The second theory is that the liability is contractual. The minor can, it is said, enter into a valid contract for necessaries just like any other person. 'The plaintiff', said Buckley LJ in *Nash v Inman*:[142]

> when he sues the defendant for goods supplied during infancy, is suing him in contract on the footing that the contract was such as the infant, notwithstanding infancy, could make. The defendant, although he was an infant, had a limited capacity to contract. In order to maintain his action the plaintiff must prove that the contract sued on is within that limited capacity.

The problem is not academic today since, unless the liability is contractual in nature, the minor will not be liable where the contract is executory. In the case of necessary goods, section 3 of the Sale of Goods Act 1979 indicates that the obligation is restitutionary. It deals only with 'necessaries sold and delivered', and says nothing of necessaries sold to a minor and not delivered, that is to say, of a contract of sale which is still executory.[143] There does not seem to be a single case since the seventeenth century[144] in which a minor has been held liable for the non-acceptance of necessaries or on a contract for necessaries bargained and sold but not delivered. Since the status as 'necessaries' is in part determined at the time of delivery, it is in fact difficult to know whether an executory contract is or is not one for necessaries.[145] Moreover, even if the goods are delivered, the plaintiff will not necessarily recover the contractual price but only 'a reasonable price for them'. This does not suggest a consensual contract.[146]

Contracts of employment, apprenticeship, and the like, provided that they are beneficial to the minor, have, however, always been regarded as merely one variety of contracts for 'necessaries',[147] and there seems to be no authority for regarding the nature of the liability which they create as resting on a different basis from that of contracts for the supply of necessary goods. Nevertheless in *Roberts v Gray*:[148]

[142] [1908] 2 KB 1, 12. See also *Gillick v West Norfolk and Wisbech AHA* [1986] AC 112, 169 (Lord Fraser: child could enter into a 'contract').

[143] Cf the wording of the Infants Relief Act 1874 (repealed by Minors' Contracts Act 1987, s 4(1)), s 1 of which might have suggested the contrary: 'contracts . . . for goods supplied *or to be supplied* (other than contracts for necessaries)'. See generally Winfield (1942) 58 LQR 82.

[144] *Ive v Chester* (1619) Cro Jac 560; *Delavel v Clare* (1652) Latch 156.

[145] *Benjamin's Sale of Goods* (12th edn, 2023) para 2-032.

[146] *Pontypridd Union v Drew* [1927] 1 KB 214, 220 (Scrutton LJ). See also Birks, *An Introduction to Restitution* (1985) 436.

[147] *Walter v Everard* [1891] 2 QB 369; above, p 258.

[148] [1913] 1 KB 520. See also *Hamilton v Bennett* (1930) 94 JPN 136.

G, a minor, entered into a contract by which he agreed to join R, a famous billiard player, in a world tour as 'professional billiardists'. R incurred certain necessary expenses as a result of preparations for the tour, but, before the tour began, G repudiated the contract.

The Court of Appeal held that to play in company with a noted billiard player such as R was instruction of the most valuable kind for a minor who wished to make billiard playing his occupation, and they upheld an award of £1,500 damages for the breach. They rejected the view that a contract for necessaries in this wider sense was not binding on a minor while it was still executory. 'I am unable to appreciate', said Hamilton LJ,[149] 'why a contract which is in itself binding, because it is a contract for necessaries not qualified by unreasonable terms, can cease to be binding merely because it is still executory'. This decision and that in *Doyle v White City Stadium Ltd*,[150] considered above, imply that when the minor is liable the nature of the liability does not differ from that of a contracting party of full capacity; that it is, in fact, a true contractual liability and not restitutionary.

In principle, there is much to be said for the contractual explanation. The law governing minors' contracts is based on the principle of 'qualified unenforceability';[151] the minor has a limited capacity to contract, and within that limited capacity, there is no reason to deny the contractual nature of liability. Moreover, the other party is liable for non-delivery and other non-performance,[152] and it has been argued that section 3 of the Sale of Goods Act 1979 does not exclude the possibility of liability being contractual. This is because a contract for necessaries only binds a minor where it is not, on balance, onerous to the minor. Thus a minor 'will not, in any case, be bound by a contract for necessaries for which more than a reasonable price is charged', a position unaffected by the Sale of Goods Act, the provisions of which 'are consistent with the view that a minor may be liable on an executory contract for necessaries, provided that the terms are not onerous to him'.[153] But in the present state of the authorities it is difficult to state the nature of the minor's liability with certainty.

(iii) Liability for voidable and unenforceable covenants

If the contract is a voidable contract not disclaimed in time, or an unenforceable contract which has been ratified, it is clear that it may be enforced as a contract. The real issue, however, concerns the non-contractual liability of the minor. That is, the tortious or restitutionary liability of the minor in the case where a voidable contract has been disclaimed or an unenforceable contract has not been ratified. On what basis may the minor be liable? This is addressed below.

149 [1913] 1 KB 520, 530.

150 [1935] 1 KB 110; above, p 259.

151 Law Com No 134 (1984) para 1.12.

152 *Farnham v Atkins* (1669) 1 Sid 446; *Bruce v Warwick* (1815) 6 Taunt 118.

153 Mitchell, Mitchell, and Watterson, *Goff & Jones on the Law of Unjust Enrichment* (10th edn, 2022) para 24-16. But note the difficulty of ascertaining this at the executory stage, above, p 262.

(f) LIABILITY OF MINORS IN TORT

Minors are generally liable for torts that they have committed, but a breach of contract may not be treated as a tort so as to make the minor liable. The tort must be more than a misfeasance in the performance of a contract, and must be separate from and independent of it, otherwise the policy of the law of contract to protect the minor could too easily be subverted by switching to a claim in tort.

For instance, in *Fawcett v Smethurst*,[154] it was said that a minor who hired a car to take his luggage from the station would be under no liability in tort if he used the car to drive several miles further than the station, and there met with an accident. Minors who obtain a loan by falsely representing their age cannot be made to repay the amount of the loan in the form of damages for deceit,[155] nor can minors who buy goods on credit be forced to pay for them by charging them with conversion:[156] 'one cannot make an infant liable for the breach of a contract by changing the form of action to one *ex delicto*'.[157]

But this is not to say that every tort of a minor which originates in a contract is not actionable. If the wrongful action is of a kind not contemplated by the contract, the minor may be exposed to tortious liability.[158] In *Ballett v Mingay*,[159] a minor was successfully sued for the non-return of a microphone and amplifier which he had hired and improperly parted with to a friend. The Court of Appeal held that 'the circumstances in which the goods passed from his possession and ultimately disappeared were outside the purview of the contract of bailment altogether',[160] and the minor was liable. In considering the extent of the contract, it seems that the terms of the agreement, the presence or absence of an express prohibition, and the nature of the subject-matter of the contract must all be considered to be relevant, although not necessarily determining, factors.

(g) LIABILITY OF MINORS IN UNJUST ENRICHMENT

(i) Common law

Where, overall, a contract for necessaries is not beneficial to the minor and is not therefore binding, the minor will nevertheless be liable to pay a reasonable price for any necessaries supplied.[161] But a claimant who seeks restitution of money paid or benefits in kind conferred on the minor under a contract cannot simply rely on the normal grounds for restitution of an unjust enrichment, in particular mistake and failure of

[154] (1914) 84 LJ KB 473, although in that case the minor did not, in fact, commit any tort.

[155] *Johnson v Pye* (1665) 1 Sid 258; *Stikeman v Dawson* (1847) De G & Sm 90; *R Leslie Ltd v Sheill* [1914] 3 KB 607.

[156] *Manby v Scott* (1659) 1 Sid 109, 129.

[157] *Burnard v Haggis* (1863) 32 LJ CP 189, 191 (Byles J, cited by Lord Sumner in *R Leslie Ltd v Sheill* [1914] 3 KB 607, 611).

[158] *Ibid*, 190–1 (Willis J); *Fawcett v Smethurst* (1914) 84 LJ KB 473, 475 (Atkin J); *R Leslie Ltd v Sheill* [1914] 3 KB 607, 620 (Kennedy LJ); *Ballett v Mingay* [1943] KB 281, 283 (Lord Greene MR).

[159] [1943] KB 281.

[160] *Ibid*, 283.

[161] Above, p 256.

consideration. This is because the Court will take care not to grant restitution where this would amount to indirectly enforcing the void contract, as it would be if, for example, the minor is ordered to repay a loan. There is authority to the effect that a minor can only be made liable in restitution if it can be shown that a wrong quite independent of the contract has been committed;[162] otherwise minority affords a good defence.[163] Thus in *Cowern v Nield*[164] a hay and straw dealer who was a minor was held entitled to retain money paid to him as the price of a consignment of hay which he had failed to deliver in accordance with his contract. But these decisions reflect the now discredited 'implied contract' theory of liability in such cases, and their reasoning should be rejected now that it has been accepted that the basis of restitutionary liability is the unjust enrichment of the defendant, here the minor.[165] There is force in the argument that a restitutionary claim against a minor should be allowed unless it would contravene the policy underpinning the rule that invalidates the contract.[166]

(ii) Equitable relief against a fraudulent minor

Minors who fraudulently represent themselves to be of full age and thereby induce other persons to enter into contracts, are nevertheless not liable under the contracts despite the fraud. Equity, however, will, in certain circumstances, intervene in order to prevent minors from taking advantage of their own deceit. 'Minors', said Lord Chancellor Hardwicke,[167] 'are not allowed to take advantage of infancy to support a fraud'. This equitable intervention is distinct and separate from the contract. The principle was succinctly stated by Lord Sumner in *R Leslie Ltd v Sheill*:[168]

> When an infant obtained an advantage by falsely stating himself to be of full age, equity required him to restore his ill-gotten gains, or to release the party deceived from obligations or acts in law induced by the fraud, but scrupulously stopped short of enforcing against him a contractual obligation, entered into while he was an infant, even by means of a fraud.

The exact extent of such equitable relief is the subject of some dispute. It is clear that a minor who obtains property, whether consisting of goods or money or any other security, by means of a false representation of full age, can be compelled to restore that property to the person deceived, provided that it is identifiable and still in the minor's possession. It is equally clear that it is impossible to make the minor repay a loan of money which has been borrowed by such a fraud and subsequently spent. In the words of Lord Sumner in *R Leslie Ltd v Sheill*:[169] 'Restitution stops where repayment begins.' In that case:

[162] *Cowern v Nield* [1912] 2 KB 419.

[163] *R Leslie Ltd v Sheill* [1914] 3 KB 607, below, p 259; *Thavorn v Bank of Credit & Commerce International SA* [1985] 1 Lloyd's Rep 259.

[164] [1912] 2 KB 419.

[165] *Lipkin Gorman v Karpnale Ltd* [1991] 2 AC 548.

[166] Mitchell, Mitchell, and Watterson, *Goff & Jones on the Law of Unjust Enrichment* (10th edn, 2022) para 34-04.

[167] *Earl of Buckinghamshire v Drury* (1760) 2 Eden 60, 71.

[168] [1914] 3 KB 607, 618; Atiyah (1959) 22 MLR 273.

[169] [1914] 3 KB 607.

L were a firm of registered moneylenders, and they sued S, to whom they had made two loans of £200 each, to recover £475, being the amount of the loans with interest. At the time of obtaining the loans, S was a minor, but he had falsely represented to L that he was of full age.

The Court of Appeal held that no action could be maintained for the recovery of the money. The loan was rendered void by the Infants Relief Act 1874 then in force[170] and the minor could not be forced to repay:[171]

The money was paid over in order to be used as the defendant's own and he has so used it and, I suppose, spent it. There is no question of tracing it, no possibility of restoring the very thing got by the fraud, nothing but compulsion through a personal judgment to pay an equivalent sum out of his present or future resources, in a word nothing but a judgment in debt to repay the loan. I think this would be nothing but enforcing a void contract.

Once the identity of the property has been lost because it has been dissipated, it is no longer possible to invoke the aid of the equitable doctrine of restitution.

So much is clear; the difficulty arises when the minor has parted with the property obtained by the fraud, but stands possessed of other money or property which represents it. Suppose, for example, that a minor obtains certain goods by the misrepresentation, and then sells the goods and stands possessed of the proceeds of sale. Is it possible to claim that the money represents the goods and so ought to be restored to the person deceived? In *Stocks v Wilson*:[172]

W, a minor, by falsely representing himself to be of full age, induced S to sell and deliver to him certain goods for which he promised to pay £300. The goods were not necessaries. He subsequently sold some of the goods for £30, and granted a bill of sale over the remainder as security for the sum of £100 lent to him by a third party. These goods were later sold by him to the grantee of the bill of sale. S claimed, by way of equitable relief, the value of the goods.

Lush J held that S was not entitled to recover the value of the goods from W as this would be to enforce a void contract. Equity, however, had the power to prevent a minor from retaining the benefit of what had been obtained by reason of his fraud, and since W had obtained the sum of £130 by parting with the goods, he was liable to account to S for this sum. This decision was criticized, but not overruled, by the Court of Appeal in *R Leslie Ltd v Sheill* on the ground that Lush J had proceeded on the false assumption that a minor who had obtained money by a false representation of full age could be compelled to refund it. This may, perhaps, be reconciled with *Stocks v Wilson* on the assumption that it is possible for the party defrauded to 'trace' the value of the goods into the proceeds of their sale.[173] If this is so, then the defrauded party's right is similar

[170] Above, p 261. [171] [1914] 3 KB 607, 619 (Lord Sumner). [172] [1913] 2 KB 235.

[173] *R Leslie Ltd v Sheill* [1914] 3 KB 607, 618. See also *Thavorn v Bank of Credit & Commerce International SA* [1985] 1 Lloyd's Rep 259, 264; Atiyah (1959) 22 MLR 273. *Stocks v Wilson* may fairly be criticized, since it appears that judgment was given *in personam* against the minor and without any proper inquiry as to whether the money had been spent.

to that of a beneficiary in respect of a trust fund in the hands of a trustee.[174] It is possible to trace so long as there is an identifiable fund in existence against which the defrauded party can enforce its claim *in rem*; but, once the fund has been dissipated, it is no longer possible to obtain a judgment *in personam* against the infant for the amount.

Equity will also relieve the deceived party of obligations imposed upon that party by the minor's fraud. Thus it has ordered the setting aside of a lease[175] and the giving up of promissory notes[176] obtained by false representation of age. The Court scrupulously refrained from enforcing the contracts, and merely restored the status quo affected by the minor's fraud. For example, a claim by the lessor for damages for use and occupation of the premises was dismissed as being inconsistent with this relief.

Where a person is induced to lend money by a false misrepresentation of age by the minor, after the minor comes of age the lender is entitled to prove in any bankruptcy proceedings against the minor.[177] The reason seems to be that the lender has a claim, not against the minor personally, but against the minor's assets in competition with the other creditors.[178]

(iii) Minors' Contracts Act 1987

In addition to rights to restitution that may arise at common law and in equity, there is a statutory scheme allowing for restitution. Section 3 of the Minors' Contracts Act 1987[179] provides:

> (1) Where—
>
> (a) a person ('the plaintiff') has after the commencement of this Act entered into a contract with another ('the defendant'), and
>
> (b) the contract is unenforceable against the defendant (or he repudiates it) because he was a minor when the contract was made,
>
> the court may, if it is just and equitable to do so, require the defendant to transfer to the plaintiff any property acquired by the defendant under the contract, or any property representing it.

The provision leaves the issue of restitution to the discretion of the Court. There is no requirement of fault or fraud. It is also only concerned with property acquired under the contract (or property acquired in exchange for property acquired under the contract) and not property gained in any other way. It appears that money is included within this notion of property. The Law Commission's policy was to extend the equitable remedy available against a fraudulent minor to a case where the minor, though not guilty of fraud, had failed to pay for goods obtained on credit.[180] That equitable relief extended, as in *Stocks v Wilson*[181] and as recognized by the Law Commission, to money which was

[174] The representation of full age might be considered to raise an 'equity' in the defrauded party similar to that possessed by a beneficiary of a fiduciary relationship.

[175] *Lemprière v Lange* (1879) 12 Ch D 675.

[176] *Clarke v Cobley* (1789) 2 Cox 173.

[177] *Re King, ex p Unity Joint Stock Mutual Banking Association* (1858) 3 De G & J 63; *Re Jones, ex p Jones* (1881) 18 Ch D 109, 125.

[178] *R Leslie Ltd v Sheill* [1914] 3 KB 607, 616.

[179] See Law Com No 134, *Minors' Contracts* (1984).

[180] *Ibid*, para 4.21.

[181] [1913] 2 KB 235, above, p 266.

the proceeds of the property sold to the minor and resold by him or her. But if property delivered to a minor has been consumed or lost, there will be no remedy under the 1987 Act. The Law Commission considered that to order the minor to pay to the seller a sum equivalent to the purchase price or the value of the property 'would amount to the enforcement of the contract' against the minor.[182]

(h) RESTITUTION IN FAVOUR OF MINORS

In order for the minor to recover money paid to the other party under a contract which does not bind the minor, a ground for restitution making the enrichment unjust must be established, that is, that the money was paid by mistake, under compulsion, or that there has been a failure of consideration. Where the ground of recovery is failure of consideration, in the present state of the authorities it would appear that what is required is a *total* failure of consideration, so that, as noted above,[183] receipt by the minor of any part of the other party's performance will be fatal. But, as will be seen,[184] the indications are that the requirement of totality is being reconsidered, and it is submitted that the authority of the cases requiring it in this context has been fatally undermined. Provided the minor can return what has been received or give recompense for it in a way that does not amount to indirect enforcement of the contract, the minor should, in principle, be able to recover money paid.

(i) THIRD PARTIES

An interesting question arises as to the effect the invalidity of a minor's contract has on third parties. So far, we know that although a minor may enforce a contract the other party to the contract can only enforce it if it is a valid contract for necessaries or if it is a voidable contract that has not been disclaimed or another (unenforceable) contract that has been ratified. If the contract is not enforceable, what is the position of, say, a guarantor of the minor's obligations? Section 2 of the Minors' Contracts Act 1987 provides:

Where—

(a) a guarantee is given in respect of an obligation of a party to a contract made after the commencement of this Act, and
(b) the obligation is unenforceable against him (or he repudiates the contract) because he was a minor when the contract was made,

the guarantee shall not for that reason alone be unenforceable against the guarantor.[185]

[182] Law Com No 134 (1984), para 4.23.

[183] Above, p 261. On the recovery of property, see *Pearce v Brain* [1929] 2 KB 310 but cf *Chaplin v Leslie Frewin (Publishers) Ltd* [1966] Ch 71, above, p 259.

[184] Below, p 609.

[185] Cf the position under the Infants Relief Act 1874, s 1 (repealed by Minors' Contracts Act 1987, s 4(1): above, p 261, n 140) which rendered loans to infants void rather than unenforceable: see *Coutts & Co v Browne-Lecky* [1947] KB 104. See also Law Com No 134 (1984) para 4.15.

5. PERSONS LACKING MENTAL CAPACITY AND DRUNKEN PERSONS

The Mental Capacity Act 2005 set up a new framework within which the Court or other designated persons can take decisions on behalf of a person who lacks capacity, and for the supervision of such a person. A person must be assumed to have capacity unless it is established that he or she lacks capacity;[186] and the lack of capacity is no longer defined as a general disability but as the inability to make a decision in relation to a particular matter, at a particular time, because of permanent or temporary impairment of, or disturbance in the functioning of, the mind or brain.[187] For this purpose a person is unable to make a decision for himself if he is unable: (a) to understand the information relevant to the decision; (b) to retain that information; (c) to use or weigh that information as part of the process of making the decision; or (d) to communicate his decision (whether by talking, using sign language, or any other means).[188]

A person who does not lack capacity within the meaning of the Mental Capacity Act 2005 may, however, still be vulnerable and deprived of the capacity to take relevant decisions, or disabled from making a free choice, or incapacitated or disabled from giving or expressing a real and genuine consent by reason of such things as constraint, coercion, undue influence, or some other vitiating factor.[189] A contract entered into in such circumstances may be voidable on the grounds of duress or undue influence.[190] However, the Court also has a protective inherent jurisdiction to make orders in support of the vulnerable person.[191]

The contract of a person lacking mental capacity or a drunken person is not binding if it can be shown that at the time of making the contract he or she was incapable of understanding the general nature of what was being done, and that the other party was aware[192] of this incapacity. This principle was established by Lord Esher MR in *Imperial Loan Co v Stone*:[193]

When a person enters into a contract, and afterwards alleges that he was so insane at the time that he did not know what he was doing, and proves the allegation, the contract is as binding

[186] 2005 Act, s 1(2).

[187] 2005 Act, s 2(1). Cf *Dunhill v Burgin (Nos 1 and 2)* [2014] UKSC 18, [2014] 1 WLR 933 at [13] (Baroness Hale: 'the general approach of the common law, now confirmed in the Mental Capacity Act 2005, is that capacity is to be judged in relation to the decision or activity in question and not globally'). The law on mental (in)capacity was formerly contained in the Mental Health Act 1983, consolidating major revisions made by the Mental Health Act 1959. The language has changed over the years, and the 2005 Act has abandoned such old terms as 'lunatic' or 'person of unsound mind' (Lunacy Act 1890), 'mentally defective', 'idiot', 'imbecile', or 'feeble-minded person' (Mental Deficiency Act 1913), and 'mentally disordered patient' (1959 and 1983 Acts).

[188] 2005 Act, s 3(1).

[189] *Re L (Vulnerable Adults with Capacity: Court's Jurisdiction) (No 2)* [2012] EWCA Civ 253, [2013] Fam 1 at [10].

[190] Below, Chapter 10.

[191] *Re L (Vulnerable Adults with Capacity: Court's Jurisdiction) (No 2)* [2012] EWCA Civ 253.

[192] But cf Lady Hale's statement in *Dunhill v Burgin (Nos 1 and 2)* [2014] UKSC 18 at [25] that it is 'generally accepted' that it is sufficient if the other party 'ought to have known' of the incapacity; Varney (2017) 37 LS 493.

[193] [1892] 1 QB 599, 601; *York Glass Co Ltd v Jubb* (1925) 134 LT 36; *Hart v O'Connor* [1985] AC 1000. See also Law Com No 231, *Mental Incapacity* (1995) paras 3.5–3.6, 3.16–3.19.

upon him in every respect, whether it is executory or executed, as if he had been sane when he made it, unless he can prove further that the person with whom he contracted knew him to be so insane as not to be capable of understanding what he was about.

Authority for the view that, even if the condition of the person lacking mental capacity was not known to the other party, the contract may be set aside if it was 'unfair' or 'unconscionable' in its terms[194] was disapproved by the Judicial Committee of the Privy Council in *Hart v O'Connor*.[195] Lord Brightman said:[196]

the validity of a contract entered into by a lunatic who is ostensibly sane is to be judged by the same standards as a contract by a person of sound mind, and is not voidable by the lunatic or his representatives by reason of 'unfairness' unless such unfairness amounts to equitable fraud which would have enabled the complaining party to avoid the contract even if he had been sane.

Lack of mental capacity therefore operates differently from minority, where the overriding policy is to protect the minor even if the person dealing with him or her does not know of the minority.[197] A party dealing with the person who lacks mental capacity, by contrast, is protected if he or she did not know of the lack of capacity. The basis on which the contract with a person lacking mental capacity, as also the contract with a drunken person,[198] is voidable is that the other party has improperly taken advantage of the weaker person. Such forms of 'procedural impropriety', 'equitable fraud', or 'unconscionable bargains' are discussed later.[199]

A contract made in such circumstances is voidable at the option of the incapacitated person, who can elect either to avoid the contract, or to affirm it, in which case it is binding. Thus in *Matthews v Baxter*:[200]

B, while drunk, agreed at an auction sale to purchase from M certain houses and land. Afterwards, when sober, B affirmed the contract and then repented of his bargain. When sued on the contract, he pleaded that he was drunk at the time he made it, and to M's knowledge.

The Court held that although B had once an option in the matter and might have avoided the contract, he was now bound by his affirmation of it. 'I think', said Martin B[201] 'that a drunken man when he recovers his senses, might insist on the fulfilment of his bargain, and therefore that he can ratify it, so as to bind himself to a performance of it'. The contract of a mentally disordered or drunken person is thus voidable at the option of the incapacitated person and not completely void. Therefore if property is transferred as the result of such a contract and subsequently passes to a purchaser in good faith for value, it seems that the innocent purchaser would acquire a good title.[202]

194 *Molton v Camroux* (1848) 2 Exch 487, 503, aff'd (1849) 4 Exch 17; *Archer v Cutler* [1980] 1 NZLR 386 (New Zealand). For similar cases in relation to drunkenness, see *Cooke v Clayworth* (1811) 18 Ves 12; *Wiltshire v Marshall* (1866) 14 LT (NS) 396; *Blomley v Ryan* (1956) 99 CLR 362 (Australia).

195 [1985] AC 1000. Cf Hudson [1986] Conv 178.

196 *Ibid*, 1027.

197 Above, p 255.

198 Or a contract with a person incapacitated by drugs: *Irvani v Irvani* [2000] 1 Lloyd's Rep 412.

199 Below, pp 406–9.

200 (1873) LR 8 Ex 132.

201 At 134.

202 Above, p 24.

Section 3 of the Sale of Goods Act 1979, which has already been quoted in respect of minors' contracts for necessaries, provides that 'where necessaries are sold and delivered to a person who by reason of drunkenness is incompetent to contract, he must pay a reasonable price for them'. The Mental Capacity Act 2005 makes a similar provision for contracts for necessary goods or services supplied to a person who lacks capacity to contract for the supply.[203] There is little doubt that the liability arises in restitution[204] and that an executory contract for necessaries, if avoided by the party lacking capacity, would be unenforceable.

FURTHER READING

Hudson, 'Mental Incapacity Revisited' [1986] Conv 178

Watts, 'Contracts Made by Agents on Behalf of Principals with Latent Mental Incapacity: The Common Law Position' [2015] CLJ 140

Häcker, 'Minority and Unjust Enrichment Defences' in Dyson, Goudkamp, and Wilmot-Smith (eds), *Defences in Unjust Enrichment* (Oxford: Hart Publishing, 2016) 195

[203] 2005 Act, s 7, replacing a provision for persons with mental incapacity in Sale of Goods Act 1979, s 3, above, p 256.

[204] *Re Rhodes* (1890) 44 Ch D 94. See also Winfield (1942) 58 LQR 82, 87.

8

MISTAKE

1. INTRODUCTION

A contract may be held to be defective if one or both of the parties enter into it under some misapprehension or misunderstanding but would not have done so had they known the true position.[1] Where one party's misunderstanding was caused by the words or conduct of the other party, the mistaken party will normally challenge the validity of the contract by alleging not his or her own mistake but the other party's *misrepresentation*. The scope of the doctrine of mistake is narrow and rather uncertain, but a claimant may obtain a wider range of remedies for misrepresentation.[2] There are, however, situations in which it is advantageous to a party to seek a remedy based on that party's or both parties' mistake, even where the mistake was induced by misrepresentation, because on the facts an appropriate remedy for misrepresentation is not available.[3] Moreover, a claimant who cannot establish a misrepresentation will be driven to base the claim on mistake.

Mistake is one of the most difficult topics in the English law of contract. The principles have never been precisely settled, the decided cases are open to a number of interpretations, and the position is complicated by changes in the attitude of the Courts to mistake during the last 150 years.[4] A doctrine of mistake was first recognized in the English law of contract in the nineteenth century, under the influence of Roman law and modern civil law.[5] There was a time when, in reliance on the *consensus* theory of contract and influenced by the eighteenth-century French jurist Pothier, the Courts were more readily disposed to hold that, where there was no 'true, full and free' consent, there was no valid contract.[6] Today, however, the Courts are very reluctant to intervene in this manner and the role of mistake is narrower than in many European legal systems.[7]

[1] See Cartwright, *Misrepresentation, Mistake and Non-Disclosure* (7th edn, 2025) Part 2.

[2] Misrepresentation is discussed in Chapter 9.

[3] eg rescission of a contract which is *voidable* for misrepresentation can be barred by delay or intervening third-party rights: below, p 340; but the claimant can assert that it is *void* for mistake: below, p 293.

[4] Cartwright, in Sefton-Green (ed), *Mistake, Fraud and Duties to Inform in European Contract Law* (2005) 65.

[5] Simpson (1975) 91 LQR 247; Ibbetson, *A Historical Introduction to the Law of Obligations* (1999) ch 12; MacMillan, *Mistakes in Contract Law* (2010).

[6] Pothier, *Traité des Obligations* (1761) para 19 (discussing mistake of identity) was cited in *Smith v Wheatcroft* (1878) 9 Ch D 223, 230; *Gordon v Street* [1899] 2 QB 641, 647; *Phillips v Brooks* [1919] 2 KB 243, 248; *Said v Butt* [1920] 3 KB 497, 501; *Lake v Simmons* [1927] AC 487, 501; *Sowler v Potter* [1940] 1 KB 271, 274. Cf *Solle v Butcher* [1950] 1 KB 671, 692 (Denning LJ); *Lewis v Averay* [1972] 1 QB 198, 206 (Lord Denning MR).

[7] Lando and Beale, *Principles of European Contract Law Parts I and II* (2000) 235.

The reasons for this change are first that, at common law, if a contract is entered into under a legally operative mistake, it is void *ab initio*; it has no legal effect whatever. Consequently, if the subject-matter of the contract consists of goods, no property in the goods will pass under the contract. A third party will acquire no title to the goods, even one who takes them in good faith and for value.[8] Secondly, there is a feeling that, once the parties are ostensibly in agreement in the same terms and upon the same subject-matter, they ought to be held to their bargain; they must rely on the terms of the contract for protection from the effect of facts unknown to them.[9] This has led to increased use of the objective test under which matters are judged by the external standard of the reasonable person,[10] a test which tends to protect a third party who relies in good faith on the apparent position. This promotes the certainty and finality of transactions which has been the hallmark of the English law of contract. Thirdly, there is a fear that parties to a contract will plead mistake to get out of a bad bargain or to reallocate the risks and consequently undermine the sanctity of contract.[11] This is coupled with a perception, also used to justify the absence of a general duty of disclosure, that if a person who has acquired expertise in the subject-matter of the contract could be deprived of the benefit of a bargain made with an uninformed counter-party it might imperil the market system.[12] By contrast, where there is no contractual bargain to set aside, the common law recognizes a broader role for mistake. Thus any (non-contractual) payment caused by a mistake is prima facie recoverable,[13] and a voluntary disposition may be rescinded in equity on the basis of mistakes that would be insufficient to render a contract void.[14]

Nevertheless, cases will undoubtedly arise in which it would be unjust to hold the parties strictly to their contract. Such cases will occur quite independently of any warranty or misrepresentation or fraud, and relief must be sought, if at all, on the ground of mistake. The Courts have displayed a mixed response to this problem. In 1932 Lord Atkin took a strict approach, and said that it was each party's responsibility to check the facts which were significant for him in relation to the contract, or at least to ask for confirmation or a warranty from the other party in relation to significant facts.[15] However, taking the lead from an important judgment of Denning LJ in 1949[16] the Courts, alongside their insistence that at common law the doctrine of mistake of facts is extremely narrow (if it exists at all), developed a more flexible doctrine of mistake in

[8] *Cundy v Lindsay* (1878) 3 App Cas 459, below, p 294; cf *Shogun Finance Ltd v Hudson* [2003] UKHL 62, [2004] 1 AC 919, below, p 295, at [13], [35], [60], [82] (Lord Nicholls and Lord Millett (both dissenting)).

[9] *Bell v Lever Brothers Ltd* [1932] AC 161, 224 (Lord Atkin).

[10] *Smith v Hughes* (1871) LR 6 QB 597, below, p 276. See above, p 34.

[11] eg *Tamplin v James* (1880) 15 Ch D 215, 221; *Riverlate Properties Ltd v Paul* [1975] Ch 133, 140–1; *Associated Japanese Bank (International) Ltd v Crédit du Nord SA* [1989] 1 WLR 255, 264.

[12] *Smith v Hughes* (1871) LR 6 QB 597, 604, 606. See generally Kronman (1978) 7 JLS 1. On the absence of a general duty of disclosure, see below, pp 320, 361.

[13] *Kleinwort Benson Ltd v Lincoln CC* [1999] 2 AC 349.

[14] *Pitt v Holt* [2013] UKSC 26, [2013] 2 AC 108 at [114]–[115]; *Van der Merwe v Goldman* [2016] EWHC 790 (Ch), [2016] 4 WLR 71 at [25], [26], [31].

[15] *Bell v Lever Brothers Ltd* [1932] AC 161, 224 (Lord Atkin); below, pp 303, 316.

[16] *Solle v Butcher* [1950] 1 KB 671; below, p 315.

equity which rendered the contract not void *ab initio* but only voidable.[17] Moreover, it appeared that, again under the influence of Lord Denning, the Courts were moving away from the traditional approach under which a mistake made by one party about the identity of the other party can render the contract void, and preferred to find the contract only voidable[18] with the result that, as in the position of a contract vitiated by misrepresentation or duress, the position of third parties who take goods in good faith is protected.[19] However, in 2002 the Court of Appeal rejected Lord Denning's equitable doctrine of mistake and asserted that, in the absence of other vitiating factors such as misrepresentation or statutory protection of the disadvantaged party, only the narrow common law doctrine of mistake can be relied upon to avoid a contract.[20] In addition, the House of Lords has (by a bare majority) reasserted the traditional view that mistake of identity, even though it may occur relatively rarely, renders the contract void.[21] Later in this chapter we shall consider what has been lost in the reversion by the Court of Appeal to the narrower common law doctrine of mistake,[22] and the reassertion by the House of Lords of the traditional common law doctrine of mistake of identity.[23]

2. CATEGORIZING MISTAKES

For the purposes of understanding the law on mistake, the cases can be categorized in different ways. Sometimes it can be helpful to distinguish between a mistake made by only one of the parties ('unilateral') and a mistake shared by both parties (which has been called 'mutual',[24] but is nowadays generally labelled by the Courts as a 'common' mistake).[25] Sometimes the different effects of mistakes on the formation of the contract are distinguished: some mistakes 'negative' the parties' consent, in the sense of preventing there being a sufficient agreement between the parties to bring the contract into existence; other mistakes do not operate to negative the consent but render the contract void by 'nullifying' it.[26] Sometimes we may separate out the effects of operative mistakes under the common law (under which the contract is void) and in equity (which may provide different remedies: rescission of a (voidable) contract, refusal of specific performance even if the contract is valid at common law; rectification of the contract). In this chapter, however, a different categorization is adopted—according to what the mistake is *about*.

[17] *Associated Japanese Bank (International) Ltd v Crédit du Nord SA* [1989] 1 WLR 255, 267–8.

[18] *Solle v Butcher* [1950] 1 KB 671, 692–3 (Denning LJ); *Lewis v Averay* [1972] 1 QB 198, 207 (Lord Denning MR). See also *Ingram v Little* [1961] QB 31, 73–4 (Devlin LJ); *Shogun Finance Ltd v Hudson* [2003] UKHL 62 at [33]–[35] and [61] (Lord Nicholls and Lord Millett, dissenting).

[19] Above, p 24.

[20] *Great Peace Shipping Ltd v Tsavliris Salvage (International) Ltd, The Great Peace* [2002] EWCA Civ 1407, [2003] QB 679; below, p 316. A contract may be *rectified* in equity for mistake: below, p 284.

[21] *Shogun Finance Ltd v Hudson* [2003] UKHL 62; below, p 300.

[22] Below, pp 317–9.

[23] Below, pp 300–1.

[24] eg *Bell v Lever Bros Ltd* [1932] AC 161 and in earlier editions of the present work.

[25] eg *Solle v Butcher* [1950] 1 KB 671, 693; *The Great Peace* [2002] EWCA Civ 1407 at [32].

[26] *Bell v Lever Bros Ltd* [1932] AC 161, 217 (Lord Atkin).

A party may make a mistake about the *terms* of the contract; the *identity* of the other contracting party; or *facts or law* relating to the *subject-matter* of the contract or to the *circumstances* surrounding the formation of the contract. Examining the cases by reference to these different categories helps to understand the approaches of the Courts to mistakes in different circumstances. However, in the course of this examination, we shall also see the relevance of whether the mistake is unilateral or shared; the impact on the formation of the contract; and the range of remedies at both common law and equity.

3. MISTAKES ABOUT THE TERMS OF THE CONTRACT

(a) 'SUBJECTIVE' AND 'OBJECTIVE' AGREEMENT IN THE FORMATION OF A CONTRACT

We here consider the mistake which invalidates a contract because, although to all outward appearances the parties are agreed on the terms of their contract, there is in fact no sufficient agreement between them and the law therefore does not regard a contract as having come into existence. Such cases must be distinguished from cases in which there is not even the outward semblance of agreement because offer and acceptance never coincided in their respective terms.[27] However, these different cases are closely related. It follows from the essential nature of a contract that if there is no agreement between the parties, or, as is commonly said, if the parties are not *ad idem*, there is no contract. This is another way of saying that offer and acceptance must correspond exactly, or no contract will ensue. Therefore, if the offeree thinks that the terms proposed by the offeror are other than those actually proposed, and accepts on that mistaken assumption, there is no real agreement: the offer that was accepted is not the offer that was made.

If the test for the formation of a contract were whether the parties have both actually agreed on the existence and terms of the contract—that is, both parties not only intend to contract with each other but also have in their minds the same terms of the contract—then any mistake by either party about the terms of the contract would prevent the formation of the contract. That would be a *subjective* test for the formation of a contract which would have the merit that a contract would be binding only on a party who genuinely intended to enter into it. But it would also give great scope for a party to avoid being bound by the contract by simply showing a misunderstanding of the terms proposed by the other party, and this could have the effect of undermining the security of contracts. English law has rejected the purely subjective test. It provides that a party may be held to have agreed with the other party if an agreement can reasonably be inferred from objective facts.

We have already seen in the chapters on The Agreement[28] and The Terms of the Contract[29] that, as a general rule, the intentions of the parties must be construed

[27] Above, p 42. [28] Above, pp 34–5. [29] Above, p 162.

objectively. However, the meaning of 'objectivity' varies from one situation to another. Where the question is how to construe a *written* contract, the Courts normally discover the parties' common intentions from the document alone: the words are interpreted as a reasonable reader of the document would have understood them. The actual (subjective) intentions of the parties are in principle irrelevant to the question of construction, although as we shall see they may be relevant to the question of whether the document can be *rectified*.[30] However, where the question is how to construe the communications between parties who are negotiating a contract—the offer, counter-offers, and acceptance—the Courts have generally rejected a test based on 'detached objectivity' and the intentions of each party are interpreted from the perspective of the reasonable person in the position of the other party.[31] This is the general 'objective test' which will be discussed in the following section. Mistakes relating to written contracts will be considered later in this chapter.[32]

(b) THE 'OBJECTIVE TEST'

The general test used to ascertain the intentions of the parties was set out by Blackburn J in *Smith v Hughes*:[33]

> if one of the parties intends to make a contract on one set of terms, and the other intends to make a contract on another set of terms, or, as it is sometimes expressed, if the parties are not ad idem, there is no contract, unless the circumstances are such as to preclude one of the parties from denying that he has agreed to the terms of the other . . . If, whatever a man's real intention may be, he so conducts himself that a reasonable man would believe that he was assenting to the terms proposed by the other party, and that other party upon that belief enters into the contract with him, the man thus conducting himself would be equally bound as if he had intended to agree to the other party's terms.

This makes clear that the fact that the parties are not in real (subjective) agreement does not necessarily prevent the contract being formed, if one party has led the other party reasonably to believe that he was agreeing. In the vast majority of cases the operation of this objective test will exclude the plea that the parties were not in agreement. So the cases in which mistake affects a contract must be considered to be the rare exceptions to this general rule. Parties are bound by agreements to which they have expressed a clear assent. If they exhibit all the outward signs of agreement the law will hold that they have agreed.

Nevertheless it may happen that, although at first sight a contract appears perfectly valid, the law regards it as void because there was no agreement even when the parties'

[30] Below, p 284.

[31] Above, p 34; Spencer [1973] CLJ 104, 106–13; Vorster (1987) 104 LQR 274, criticizing Howarth (1984) 100 LQR 265; Cartwright, *Unequal Bargaining* (1991) 5–24.

[32] Below, p 281.

[33] (1871) LR 6 QB 597, 607. For details of the case, see below, p 280. See also *The Hannah Blumenthal* [1983] 1 AC 854, 914, 915–16, 924; *Centrovincial Estates plc v Merchant Investors Assurance Co Ltd* [1983] Com LR 158; *OT Africa Line Ltd v Vickers plc* [1996] 1 Lloyd's Rep 700.

communications are assessed by reference to the objective test. This may occur in any of four situations:

(1) where, despite outward appearances, there is no coincidence between the terms of the offer and those of the acceptance because when each is tested objectively they conflict;
(2) where there is a mistake about the promise, or terms of the contract, which is known to the other party;
(3) where there is a mistake in relation to a written document;
(4) where there is a mistake about the identity of the person with whom the contract is made.

We shall here consider (1), (2), and (3). Mistakes about the identity of the other party raise particular difficulties and are considered separately in the next section.[34]

(i) Offer and acceptance not coincident

It may happen that, owing to a mistake, an offer may be innocently accepted in a different sense from that in which it was intended by the offeror, and the terms in which the contract is expressed may suffer from such latent ambiguity that it is impossible to say that the conduct of the parties points to one solution rather than another. In such a case each party did not attach the same meaning to the terms as the other party, and it will be impossible to say that their conduct would have induced a reasonable person to make one deduction rather than the other. The contract will be void because the terms of the offer and the acceptance did not coincide.[35]

If, for example, two things have the same name, and A makes an offer to B referring to one of them, which offer B accepts thinking that A is referring to the other, then provided there is nothing in the terms of the contract to identify one or other as its subject-matter, evidence may be given to show that the mind of each party was in fact (and subjectively) directed to a different object: that A offered one thing and B accepted another. Where a reasonable person in each of A and B's positions would also have come to different conclusions about the parties' intentions, there is a (subjective) misunderstanding which cannot be resolved by an application of the objective test. So in *Raffles v Wichelhaus*:[36]

W agreed to buy from R 125 bales of cotton 'to arrive [in Liverpool] *ex Peerless* from Bombay'. There were two ships called *Peerless*, and both sailed from Bombay, but W meant the *Peerless* which sailed in October, and R the *Peerless* which sailed in December.

[34] Below, p 292.

[35] Cited (from Anson, 21st edn, ed Guest (1959) 254–5) with approval in *Alampi v Swartz* (1963) 38 DLR (2d) 300, 302 (Canada).

[36] (1864) 2 H & C 906. See Simpson, *Leading Cases in the Common Law* (1995) ch 6. See also *Falck v Williams* [1900] AC 176.

There was no contract. There was nothing in the agreement which would point to one or other of the vessels as being the one identified in the contract; the offer and acceptance did not coincide.[37]

Similarly, if A makes to B an offer which is ambiguous in its terms, or is rendered ambiguous by the circumstances surrounding it, and B accepts the offer in a different sense from that in which it is meant, then unless an objective construction requires otherwise, B may effectively maintain that there is no binding contract. In *Scriven Bros & Co v Hindley & Co*:[38]

S instructed an auctioneer to sell certain bales of hemp and tow. These bore the same shipping mark and were described in the auction catalogue as so many bales in different lots with no indication of the difference in their contents. H's manager examined samples of the hemp before the sale intending to bid for the hemp alone. At the auction, the tow was put up for sale, and H's buyer, believing it to be hemp, made a bid which was a reasonable one if it had been intended for hemp, but an excessive one for tow. This bid was accepted by the auctioneer, who did not realize the buyer's mistake, but merely thought the bid an extravagant one for tow. S sought to enforce the contract by suing for the price.

Offer and acceptance did not coincide. S intended to sell tow; H's buyer, misled by the auction catalogue, intended to buy hemp. The Court held that there was nothing in H's conduct which would estop it from pleading that the parties were not in agreement as to the subject-matter of the sale—or, to put it in the language of the objective test set out by Blackburn J in *Smith v Hughes*,[39] H had not so conducted itself that a reasonable man would believe that it was assenting to S's terms. Accordingly, no contract had come into existence, and H was not liable.

It has been said that where the objective appearance of agreement is displaced by evidence of (different) subjective intentions, it is not truly a case of mistake rendering the contract void, but rather no agreement, and therefore never a contract at all.[40] This is true, but it is important to see such cases in the context of the application of the objective test to override subjective misunderstandings, since the essential question is whether the offer and acceptance, objectively construed, can be taken to match. They also illustrate the point that proof of a mistake must be adduced before a flaw can be found in an ostensible agreement.

It is also important to realize the limits of these decisions. Where A sues B under an alleged contract but it is shown that there was no subjective agreement between the parties, and A cannot establish that B has so conducted himself as to entitle A reasonably to believe that B was agreeing to A's intended terms, then A's claim against B fails. But that outcome does not necessarily establish whether B could have established that A's conduct had led B reasonably to believe that A was agreeing with B's intended terms.

[37] *Smith v Hughes* (1871) LR 6 QB 597, 609; cf *Van Praagh v Everidge* [1902] 2 Ch 266, 269.

[38] [1913] 3 KB 564.

[39] Above, p 276.

[40] *Statoil ASA v Louis Dreyfus Energy Services LP* [2008] EWHC 2257 (Comm), [2008] 2 Lloyd's Rep 685 at [87] (unilateral mistake as to the terms, known to the other party; see below, p 279).

That is, just because A fails to establish a contract on A's terms does not mean that B could not establish a contract on B's terms. In every case the question is whether the party seeking to establish a contract can do so on the evidence of what the parties intended, and what the defendant's conduct had led the claimant reasonably to believe. If both parties were equally reasonable (or unreasonable) in their different understandings of the agreed terms, then there will be an ambiguity which cannot be resolved, and neither can establish a contract.[41] But if the misunderstanding was a result of the fault of A, which was not known to B, it may often be the case that B can establish a contract on the basis of the terms as B understood them.

(ii) Mistake about the promise, or terms, which is known to the other party

When making contracts people must use their own judgement or, if they cannot rely upon their judgement, must take care that the terms of the contract secure to them what they want. *Caveat emptor* is a general rule of the law of contracts. One party is not bound to disclose to the other all material facts or circumstances which might affect the bargain. Even a party who knows that the other is contracting under a misapprehension about the facts has no general duty to disillusion the mistaken party.[42] The law imposes certain particular duties of disclosure of material facts, where it is required by the particular type of contract[43] or the relationship between the parties (eg a fiduciary relationship).[44] Active concealment may constitute misrepresentation.[45] Save in these cases, however, mere silence will not constitute a misrepresentation, there is no duty of disclosure, and each party must protect itself from the consequences of its own mistake.

Nevertheless a mistake about the terms of the contract is different from a mistake about the facts or the circumstances surrounding the formation of the contract.[46] The law will not allow one party to hold the other to a contract where that party knows that the other does not intend to agree on the same terms—for example, where A purports to accept B's offer knowing that B does not intend it in the sense that A claims to be entitled to interpret it. A cannot 'snap up' B's offer.[47] Moreover, a mistake by one party of which the other ought reasonably to have known will suffice.[48] This follows from the application of the objective test set out in *Smith v Hughes*.[49] Blackburn J said:

> If, whatever a man's real intention may be, he so conducts himself that *a reasonable man would believe* that he was assenting to the terms proposed by the other party, *and that other party upon that belief enters into the contract with him*, the man thus conducting himself would be equally bound as if he had intended to agree to the other party's terms.

[41] Vorster (1987) 103 LQR 274, 286.
[42] Below, pp 361–2.
[43] Below, pp 363–7.
[44] Below, p 368.
[45] Below, p 323.
[46] *Smith v Hughes* (1871) LR 6 QB 597, 606, 607, 610–11; *Bell v Lever Brothers Ltd* [1932] AC 161, 218. On mistakes about facts and circumstances, see below, p 301.
[47] *Tamplin v James* (1880) 15 Ch D 215, 221; *Hartog v Colin & Shields* [1939] 3 All ER 566, 567; *Longley v PPB Entertainment Ltd* [2022] EWHC 977 (QB), [2022] LLR 436 at [92]–[93] (counter-offer).
[48] *Centrovincial Estates plc v Merchant Investors Assurance Co Ltd* [1983] Com LR 158; *OT Africa Line Ltd v Vickers plc* [1996] 1 Lloyd's Rep 700, 703; cf *Longley v PPB Entertainment Ltd* [2022] EWHC 977 (QB) at [94]. Cf the test for rectification in cases of unilateral mistake, below, p 289.
[49] Above, p 276.

The italicized words show that A can hold B to A's offer only if it was *reasonable* for him to believe that B was agreeing with the terms of the offer as A understood them, and only if A *in fact* believed it. So a party can never enforce a contract on terms which he did not in fact himself intend at the time of the formation of the contract.

In *Smith v Hughes*:[50]

S sued H for the price of oats sold and delivered, and for damages for not accepting the oats. S had offered to sell to H, by sample, a parcel of oats at 35s a quarter. According to H, S described the oats as 'good *old* oats', but S denied that the word 'old' had been used. This offer was rejected by H's counter-offer of 34s a quarter, which in turn was accepted by S's delivery of the oats. When they were delivered, they were found to be new oats, and unsuitable for S's purpose.

The trial judge directed the jury to consider:

(1) whether the word 'old' had been used by S or H in making the contract. If so, they were to give a verdict for H;

(2) if the word 'old' had not been used, whether they were of the opinion that S believed H to believe, or to be under the impression, that he was contracting for the purchase of old oats. If so, they were to give a verdict for H.

The jury found for H without stating on which ground they had based their verdict. On a motion for a new trial, the majority of the Court of Queen's Bench were of the opinion that the second of these two directions would not sufficiently bring to the minds of the jury the distinction between agreeing to take the oats under the belief that they were old, and agreeing to take the oats under the belief that S *contracted* that they were old.[51] Hannen J said:[52]

If, therefore, in the present case, [S] knew that [H], in dealing with him for oats, did so on the assumption that [S] was contracting to sell him old oats, he was aware that [H] apprehended the contract in a different sense to that in which he meant it, and he is thereby deprived of the right to insist that [H] shall be bound by that which was only the apparent, and not the real bargain.

But H might merely have been mistaken as to the age of the oats, and not as to the plaintiff's promise. If such were the case, the contract would be valid, and a verdict should have been given for S:[53]

In order to relieve [H], it was necessary that the jury should find not merely that [S] believed [H] to believe that he was buying old oats, but that he believed [H] to believe that he, [S], was contracting to sell old oats.

[50] (1871) LR 6 QB 597. [51] *Ibid*, 608 (Blackburn J). [52] *Ibid*, 610.

[53] *Ibid*, 611 (Hannen J); ie a mere unilateral mistake about the facts relating to the subject-matter is insufficient to render the contract void: below, p 302.

Accordingly, a new trial was ordered.

The same rule was applied in different circumstances in *Hartog v Colin & Shields*:[54]

C & S offered to sell to H 3,000 Argentine hare skins, but by a mistake they offered them at so much per *pound* instead of so much per *piece*. H accepted the offer. It was shown that it was the usual practice of the trade to charge on a per piece basis and that the written and oral negotiations leading up to the sale had proceeded throughout on a price per piece. As a pound contained on average three pieces the price under the agreement was roughly one-third of what it would have been on a per piece basis. H sought to enforce the sale in the terms of the offer, and sued for non-delivery.

Singleton J held that H could not reasonably have supposed that that offer contained C & S's real intention. Indeed, he held that H did in fact know that C & S were under a mistake. The *apparent* agreement (ie so much per pound) was therefore void. However, the Judge did not consider whether C & S could enforce the intended contract (ie so much per piece) but both principle and the analogy of rectification in cases of unilateral mistake[55] suggest that they might have been able to do so.[56]

(c) MISTAKE IN RELATION TO A WRITTEN DOCUMENT

There are two remedies for mistakes about the terms of the contract which are peculiar to written contracts. First, there is the common law defence of *non est factum* which permits one who has signed a written document, which is essentially different from that which he intended to sign, to plead that, notwithstanding his signature, 'it is not his deed'.[57] The term properly applies to a deed but is equally applicable to other written contracts. Secondly, there is the equitable remedy of rectification of the contract, by which the Court can order that the written contract be given effect in terms other than those of the actual document in order to remedy the mistake of one or both parties about the terms of the contract.

Written contracts are different because the parties have taken the step of agreeing a text containing the terms of the contract, and the Courts therefore look for the agreed terms in the document itself. The interpretation of the document, although it takes into account the context of the transaction and the person to whom the document was addressed, is

[54] [1939] 3 All ER 566, followed in *McMaster University v Wilchar Construction Ltd* (1971) 22 DLR (3d) 9 (Canada), aff'd (1973) 69 DLR 3d 410; *Chwee Kin Keong v Digilandmall.com Pte Ltd* [2005] 1 SLR 502 at [80] (Singapore, but drawing a different distinction: actual knowledge of the other party's mistake about a fundamental term renders the contract void at common law; constructive knowledge may render it voidable in equity but only if there is impropriety rendering it unconscionable for the non-mistaken party to insist that the contract be performed).

[55] Below, p 289. See also *Commission for the New Towns v Cooper (Great Britain) Ltd* [1995] Ch 259 (false and misleading statements made to divert mistaken party's attention).

[56] *Chitty on Contracts* (36th edn, 2025) para 5-029, citing *Ulster Bank Ltd v Lambe* [2012] NIQB 31.

[57] *Scriptum predictum non est factum suum*. See *Thoroughgood's Case* (1582) 2 Co Rep 9a; Simpson, *A History of the Common Law of Contract* (1975) 98.

entirely objective.[58] In consequence, the Courts are not easily persuaded that the parties' apparent contract, as set out in the document, should be held to be void or rectified.

(i) Non est factum

The effect of a successful plea of *non est factum* is that the transaction contained in the document is not merely voidable against the person who procured its execution, but is entirely void into whosesoever hands the document may come.

It must be emphasized that *non est factum* is a narrow defence. A party is normally bound by the terms of a document which he has signed,[59] and those too lazy or too busy to read through it before signing it cannot plead *non est factum*. Nor can those who sign a document containing objectionable terms or terms the legal effect of which they are unaware. As Donovan LJ explained in *Muskham Finance Ltd v Howard*:[60]

> Much confusion and uncertainty would result in the field of contract and elsewhere if a man were permitted to try to disown his signature simply by asserting that he did not understand that which he had signed.

The narrowness of *non est factum* is also explained by the fact that it can be invoked against third parties:

> Where a fraudster has tricked, first, the signer of the document, in order to induce the signature, and then some third party, who is induced to rely on the signed document, which of the two victims is the law to prefer? The authorities indicate that the answer is, almost invariably, the latter. The signer of the document has, by signing, enabled the fraud to be carried out, enabled the false document to go into circulation.[61]

(a) Essentially Different Transaction. For the defence to succeed, the person executing the document must show[62] that the transaction which the document purports to effect is essentially different in substance or in kind from the transaction intended. At one time it was thought that the plea of *non est factum* would not succeed if the mistake was as to the contents of a document, as opposed to its essential nature or character.[63] But this distinction between contents and character is not intelligible[64] because a document takes its character from its contents, and it was rejected by the House of Lords in *Saunders v Anglia Building Society*[65] in favour of a more flexible test. There must be

[58] *Investors Compensation Scheme Ltd v West Bromwich Building Society* [1998] 1 WLR 896, 912–13. On interpretation generally, see above, p 162.

[59] Above, p 192.

[60] [1963] 1 QB 904, 912. See also *Blay v Pollard & Morris* [1930] 1 KB 628 (document containing term not in previous oral agreement bound signatory).

[61] *Norwich and Peterborough BS v Steed (No 2)* [1993] Ch 116, 125 (Scott LJ).

[62] The burden of proof lies on the person wishing to establish the defence: *Saunders v Anglia Building Society* [1971] AC 1004, 1016, 1019, 1027, 1038; *Norwich and Peterborough BS v Steed (No 2)* [1993] Ch 116.

[63] *Howatson v Webb* [1907] 1 Ch 537, aff'd [1908] 1 Ch 1.

[64] See Glanville Williams (1945) 61 LQR 179, 194; *Gallie v Lee* [1969] 2 Ch 17, 31, 41, 43; on appeal as *Saunders v Anglia Building Society* [1971] AC 1004, 1017, 1022, 1025, 1039.

[65] [1971] AC 1004, 1017, 1019, 1021, 1026, 1039.

a 'radical' or 'essential' or 'fundamental' or 'serious' or 'very substantial' difference between the document signed and the document which the person signing intended to sign. If, for example, a person signs a guarantee for £10,000 believing it to be a guarantee of a lesser sum, it will depend on the amount of the lesser sum and the surrounding circumstances of the case whether or not the difference between the two transactions is sufficient to satisfy this test. The question is one of degree, and was held not to be satisfied in *Saunders v Anglia Building Society*:

The appellant, an elderly widow, gave the title deeds of her house to her nephew, intending to make a gift to him of the house in order that he could borrow money on the security of the property. It was a condition of the gift that he was to permit her to reside there for the rest of her life. She was subsequently requested by a friend of her nephew, whom she knew to be assisting him to obtain a loan, to sign a document. The friend told her that it was 'to do with the gift by deed to Wally [her nephew] for the house'. As she had broken her spectacles, she signed the document without reading it. The document was in fact a deed conveying the house on sale to the friend. The friend did not pay the appellant or her nephew, but subsequently mortgaged the house to the respondents.

The plea of *non est factum* failed. At first sight there might seem to be an essential difference between a gift of the house to the nephew and a sale of the house to his friend. But, as Russell LJ pointed out in the Court of Appeal,[66] the appellant intended to transfer the house so that the transferee could raise money on it, and she knew that her nephew and his friend were engaged jointly on this project. The 'object of the exercise' might well have been achieved by means of a sale if the friend had been honest and paid the nephew. Although their Lordships were by no means unsympathetic to the appellant's situation,[67] they held that the document which she had executed was not of a fundamentally different nature from the document which she believed she was signing. The building society could therefore enforce the mortgage.

(b) Absence of Negligence of Party Signing. In *Saunders v Anglia Building Society*[68] it was held that, even if the document signed is essentially different from that which the person signing it intended to sign, as against a third party the person will not be entitled to disown the signature without also proving that he or she exercised reasonable care. What is reasonable care will depend on the circumstances of the case and the nature of the document being signed. If one of two innocent parties is to suffer for the fraud of a third, the sufferer should be the one whose negligence has contributed to the loss suffered.

As a normal rule, therefore, if a person of full understanding and capacity forbears, or carelessly omits, to read what he or she signs, the defence of *non est factum* will not be available.[69] However, as Lord Wilberforce pointed out in *Saunders*' case:[70]

[66] *Gallie v Lee* [1969] 2 Ch 17, 40–1.

[67] The building society, in fact, undertook not to evict the appellant during her lifetime.

[68] [1971] AC 1004, 1019, 1023, 1027, 1037–8.

[69] Cf Stone (1972) 88 LQR 190; Spencer [1973] CLJ 104.

[70] [1971] AC 1004, 1025–6.

There remains a residue of difficult cases. There are still illiterate or senile persons who cannot read, or apprehend, a legal document; there are still persons who may be tricked into putting their signature on a piece of paper which has legal consequences totally different from anything they intended . . . Accepting all that has been said by learned judges as to the necessity of confining the plea within narrow limits, to eliminate it altogether would, in my opinion, deprive the courts of what may be, doubtless on sufficiently rare occasions, an instrument of justice.

An example of a case where the defence succeeded is *Foster v Mackinnon*:[71]

Mackinnon, 'a gentleman far advanced in years', was fraudulently induced to indorse a bill of exchange for £3,000 on the assurance that it was a guarantee of a similar nature to one which he had previously signed. Later the bill was indorsed for value to Foster, who took it in good faith.

It was held that the defence of *non est factum* was available to Mackinnon, as he never intended to make such a contract, and had been guilty of no negligence.

It would seem that a person who signs a document in blank, leaving it to another to fill in the terms of the contract in accordance with an oral agreement reached between them, could in theory rely on the defence of *non est factum* if the terms inserted render the transaction essentially different in substance or in kind from the transaction intended. However, unless there are exceptional circumstances, a person who signs a document in blank accepts responsibility for it and takes the risk if, through fraud or error, the document is filled in in some different way,[72] and cannot therefore avoid liability as against an innocent third party.

There is support in other jurisdictions for the view that, where no third party is involved, negligence is irrelevant.[73] But it has also been suggested that in two-party cases remedies for fraud, misrepresentation, or unilateral mistake should be used rather than *non est factum*.[74]

(ii) Rectification of written contracts

(a) Rectification Contrasted with Interpretation. Rectification and interpretation fulfil different purposes. Interpretation discovers the meaning which the law will give to the document as written; rectification changes the document.[75] However, a party who asserts that the written document does not appear by its language to reflect his or her intentions may claim, first, that it should be interpreted so to give effect to those intentions; and secondly, if such an interpretation is not possible, that the document should be rectified to reflect those intentions. In some cases, therefore, a mistake in

[71] (1869) LR 4 CP 704. See also *Petelin v Cullen* (1975) 132 CLR 355 (Australia); *Lloyds Bank plc v Waterhouse* [1993] 2 FLR 97; *Trustees of Beardsley Theobalds Retirement Benefit Scheme v Yardley* [2011] EWHC 1380 (QB) at [53]–[55].

[72] *United Dominions Trust Ltd v Western* [1976] QB 513. Cf *Mercantile Credit Co Ltd v Hamblin* [1965] 2 QB 242. See Allcock (1982) 45 MLR 18.

[73] *Petelin v Cullen* (1975) 132 CLR 355, 360 (Australia); *Bradley West Solicitors Nominee Co Ltd v Keenan* [1994] 2 NZLR 111, 118 (New Zealand).

[74] *Lloyds Bank plc v Waterhouse* [1993] 2 FLR 97, 117, 122–3.

[75] The rules relating to interpretation have been discussed above, p 162.

the document may effectively be remedied by interpretation without the need to have recourse to rectification.[76]

(b) Rectification for Common Mistake. Where a contract has been reduced to writing, or a deed executed, and the writing or deed fails to express the concurrent intentions of the parties at the time of its execution, the Court may rectify the document in accordance with their intentions.

In *Craddock Brothers v Hunt*,[77] for example:

A vendor agreed orally to sell to a purchaser a certain piece of property. By a mistake, the written contract embodying this agreement included an adjoining yard which the parties had excluded from the sale and the subsequent conveyance actually conveyed this land to the purchaser.

The Court ordered the conveyance to be rectified to bring it into line with the parties' oral agreement.

In *Swainland Builders Ltd v Freehold Properties Ltd*[78] Peter Gibson LJ set out the requirements for rectification for common mistake:

The party seeking rectification must show that:

(1) the parties had a common continuing intention, whether or not amounting to an agreement, in respect of a particular matter in the instrument to be rectified;
(2) there was an outward expression of accord;
(3) the intention continued at the time of the execution of the instrument sought to be rectified;
(4) by mistake the instrument did not reflect that common intention.

(1) *Common intention.* The document which it is sought to rectify must fail to express the common intentions and outward accord of the parties. Such accord cannot be shown where there is confusion as to what has been agreed[79] or where a matter is omitted from a document as a result of forgetfulness; an absence of intention does not suffice.[80] The accord need not, however, as some older cases suggested, amount to a complete concluded contract in advance of the execution of the written document.[81] It is now

[76] eg *Chartbrook Ltd v Persimmon Homes Ltd* [2009] UKHL 38, [2009] 1 AC 1101 (decision based on interpretation, so rectification not necessary); cf *KPMG v Network Rail Infrastructure Ltd* [2007] EWCA Civ 363, [2008] 1 P & CR 11 (no ground for rectification, but omission in document corrected by interpretation). See also Burrows, in Burrows and Peel (eds), *Contract Terms* (2007) 77; cf *Cherry Tree Investments Ltd v Landmain Ltd* [2012] EWCA Civ 736, [2013] Ch 305 at [122] (rectification, not interpretation, appropriate where third parties may be affected); Davies [2016] CLJ 62, 68–73 (reasons to prefer rectification over interpretation for correcting mistakes).

[77] [1923] 2 Ch 136. See also *USA v Motor Trucks Ltd* [1924] AC 196, 202.

[78] [2002] EWCA Civ 560, [2002] 2 EGLR 71 at [33], approved in *Chartbrook Ltd v Persimmon Homes Ltd* [2009] UKHL 38 at [48].

[79] *Cambro Contractors Ltd v John Kennelly Sales Ltd*, The Times, 14 April 1994 (CA).

[80] *Olympia Sauna Shipping Co SA v Shinwa Kaiun Kaisha* [1985] 2 Lloyd's Rep 364, 370; *Kemp v Neptune Concrete* (1989) 57 P & CR 369, 377, 379–80.

[81] *Mackenzie v Coulson* (1869) LR 8 Eq 368, 375; *Faraday v Tamworth Union* (1916) 86 LJ Ch 436, 438; *Higgins (W) Ltd v Northampton Corp* [1927] 1 Ch 128, 136; *USA v Motor Trucks Ltd* [1924] AC 196, 200.

clearly established that there is jurisdiction to rectify where the parties have made a mistake in their attempt to embody in the document their concurrent intentions in regard to a particular term which existed at the time it was put into writing or executed.[82] A concluded contract need not be shown. There must, however, be evidence of the parties' 'common intention'. Until recently, when judges referred to the 'intention' of the parties in this context, they were referring to what the parties actually intended: a common *subjective* intention of the parties.[83] However, in *Chartbrook Ltd v Persimmon Homes Ltd*[84] Lord Hoffmann stated that this should be tested objectively by reference to what the reasonable observer would have thought the intentions of the parties to be before the document was executed. This influential *obiter dictum* was followed[85] and sometimes approved,[86] but was heavily criticized.[87]

In *FSHC Group Holdings Ltd v Glas Trust Corp Ltd*:[88]

FSHC was a parent company which entered into a private equity financing transaction in 2012 that required it to provide security over a shareholder loan. In 2016, its lawyers spotted that the relevant security documentation had either never been provided or could not be located. They drafted accession deeds to provide that security, which FSHC entered into with the defendant bank. By mistake, the accession deeds were so drafted that much more onerous obligations were undertaken by FSHC than was required. FSHC sought rectification of the deeds.

The Court of Appeal accepted that, if parties make a binding agreement to execute a document containing particular terms but by mistake execute a document containing different terms, the court may specifically enforce the agreement by rectifying the document; in such a case, the terms of the contract to which the subsequent document is made to conform must be objectively determined in the same way as any other contract.[89] However, the Court affirmed the use of a subjective test as a matter of principle in cases, such as the *FSHC* case, where there is no prior concluded contract

[82] *Crane v Hegemann-Harris Co Inc* [1939] 1 All ER 662, 664, aff'd [1939] 4 All ER 68; *Joscelyne v Nissen* [1970] 2 QB 86, 98; *Chartbrook Ltd v Persimmon Homes Ltd* [2009] UKHL 38 at [59].

[83] *FSHC Group Holdings Ltd v Glas Trust Corp Ltd* [2019] EWCA Civ 1361, [2020] Ch 365 at [52]. See, eg, *Agip SpA v Navigazione Alta Italia SpA* [1984] 1 Lloyd's Rep 353, 359 (the 'true agreement'); *Kemp v Neptune Concrete* (1989) 57 P & CR 369, 377 ('the subjective intention of the party seeking relief').

[84] [2009] UKHL 38 at [60].

[85] *Daventry DC v Daventry & District Housing Ltd* [2011] EWCA Civ 1153, [2012] 1 WLR 1333; *Ahmad v Secret Garden (Cheshire) Ltd* [2013] EWCA Civ 1005, [2013] 3 EGLR 42 at [30]; *Scottish Widows Fund and Life Assurance Society v BGC International* [2012] EWCA Civ 607, (2012) 142 Con LR 27 at [46]. In support of an objective test, see also Smith (2007) 123 LQR 116.

[86] *Daventry DC v Daventry & District Housing Ltd* [2011] EWCA Civ 1153 at [89] (Etherton LJ).

[87] *Ibid* at [176] (Toulson LJ); *Crossco No 4 Unlimited v Jolan Ltd* [2011] EWHC 803 (Ch), [2011] All ER (D) 13 (Apr) at [253]; *Tartsinis v Navona Management Co* [2015] EWHC 57 (Comm), [2015] All ER (D) 110 (Jan) at [90]; *LSREF III Wight Ltd v Millvalley Ltd* [2016] EWHC 466 (Comm), (2016) 165 Con LR 58 at [70]; *AML Global Ltd v Exxonmobil Petroleum & Chemical BVBA* [2018] EWHC 3321 (TCC) at [43]–[44]. See also Davies (2012) 75 MLR 412; Davies [2016] CLJ 62, 73–82.

[88] [2019] EWCA Civ 1361.

[89] *Ibid* at [141]. The 'objective test' for the formation of the prior contract is not (unless it was a written contract) wholly objective, but takes into account the parties' own perspectives and their subjective understandings of each other's intentions: see above, p 276.

and the question is whether the document records the parties' common intentions at the moment the document is executed:[90]

> The justification for rectifying a contractual document to conform to a 'continuing common intention' . . . rests on the equitable doctrine that a party will not be allowed to enforce the terms of a written contract, objectively ascertained, when to do so is against conscience because it is inconsistent with what both parties in fact intended (and mutually understood each other to intend) those terms to be when the document was executed. This basis for rectification is entirely concerned with the parties' subjective states of mind.

On the facts found by the trial judge, the parties had communicated to each other their shared common intention as to the effect of the deeds, which were therefore rectified.[91]

In *Porter v Stokes*[92] the Privy Council reviewed this line of cases, and broadly confirmed the approach taken in the *FSHC* case:

> In the Board's view this distinction between the basis of a rectification claim where there is, or is not, a prior binding contract is well-founded in basic principle. Where there is a prior binding contract, the nature of the claimant's equity is to have their contractual right vindicated by bringing the later implementing document into accordance with the terms of the contract. By contrast, the nature of the equity in a case where there is no prior binding contractual right is to remedy the unconscionability of the enforcement of a binding document which runs counter to the outwardly manifested common intention of the parties making it.

A contract can also be rectified for a unilateral mistake[93] and, as that indisputably rests on the mistaken party's subjective intention, rectification for common mistake and for unilateral mistake both rest on the same underlying principle which was expressed in the *FSHC Group* case as being the equitable principle of good faith,[94] or in *Porter v Stokes* as being unconscionability.[95]

(2) *Outward expression of accord.* The suggestion that the 'outward expression of accord' is a matter of evidence rather than a formal requirement[96] was rejected in *FSHC Group Holdings Ltd v Glas Trust Corp Ltd.*[97] This was because the effect of rectification is not merely to prevent a party from enforcing the written terms of a contract: it is to alter those terms so as to establish legal rights and obligations which differ from those recorded in the original contractual document. It is therefore fundamental that contractual rights and obligations should be based on mutual assent which the parties have manifested to each other and not on uncommunicated intentions which happen, without the parties knowing it, to coincide.

(3) *Continuing intention.* The intention of the parties as expressed in the prior accord must have continued unchanged up to the time of the execution of the written

[90] *Ibid* at [146]. Cf Stevens (2020) 136 LQR 599.
[91] *Ibid* at [177].
[92] [2023] UKPC 11 at [37]–[43]. See also *National Union of Rail, Maritime and Transport Workers v Tyne and Wear Passenger Transport Executive* [2024] UKSC 37, [2025] AC 1222 at [31].
[93] Below, p 289.
[94] [2019] EWCA Civ 1361 at [142].
[95] [2023] UKPC 11 at [43].
[96] eg *Munt v Beasley* [2006] EWCA Civ 370, [2006] All ER (D) 29 (Apr) at [36].
[97] [2019] EWCA Civ 1361 at [76]–[77].

instrument.[98] If there is no clear evidence to this effect, the document (in its different terms) would indicate that the parties had changed their intentions by the time of the execution of the written document.

(4) *Document must fail to represent the common intention.* The party seeking to have a document rectified must adduce convincing evidence that its terms do not accurately record the common intention of the parties at the time.[99]

It has, however, been said that rectification is not an appropriate remedy where the mistake relates to the transaction itself rather than to the document which purports to record it. In *Frederick E Rose (London) Ltd v William H Pim Jnr & Co Ltd*:[100]

Rose received from Middle East associates an order for up to five hundred tons of 'Moroccan horsebeans described here as feveroles'. Rose did not know what feveroles were, and asked Pim. Pim replied that they were simply horsebeans, and so Rose orally contracted to buy from Pim a quantity of horsebeans to meet this order. A subsequent written agreement embodied the same terms. In fact, however, feveroles were quite another type of bean. Rose claimed to have the written agreement rectified to read 'feveroles', intending to claim damages on the agreement if so rectified.

The Court of Appeal refused rectification. Both the oral and the written contracts were for horsebeans. There was no literal disparity between them. Denning LJ stated:[101]

Rectification is concerned with contracts and documents, not with intentions. In order to get rectification it is necessary to show that the parties were in complete agreement on the terms of their contract, but by an error wrote them down wrongly; and in this regard, in order to ascertain the terms of their contract, you do not look into the inner minds of the parties—into their intentions—any more than you do in the formation of any other contract.

This difficult decision has recently been explained as having been decided at a time when the law had not yet clearly recognized that rectification is an available remedy where parties had deliberately chosen words but were mistaken about their meaning.[102] It has been held that, where the parties have expressly agreed the meaning of particular words used in a written contract, the contract can be rectified to make it clear that the words bear the meaning agreed.[103]

[98] *Fowler v Fowler* (1859) 4 De G & J 250.

[99] *Joscelyne v Nissen* [1970] 2 QB 86, 98; *Luk Leamington Ltd v Whitnash plc* [2002] 1 Lloyd's Rep 6. In order to establish the intention, parol evidence is admissible even where the contract is one which is required to be in writing: *Craddock Bros v Hunt* [1923] 2 Ch 136; *USA v Motor Trucks Ltd* [1924] AC 196; or where evidence of the communications between the parties during the negotiations would not be admissible to interpret the written contract: *Chartbrook Ltd v Persimmon Homes Ltd* [2009] UKHL 38; above, pp 165–6.

[100] [1953] 2 QB 450. See also *Ets Georges et Paul Levy v Adderley Navigation Co Panama SA* [1980] 1 Lloyd's Rep 67, 72.

[101] At 461.

[102] *FSHC Group Holdings Ltd v Glas Trust Corp Ltd* [2019] EWCA Civ 1361 at [63]–[71], and concluding at [71] that the best justification for the refusal to grant the remedy of rectification in *Rose v Pim* is that the contract of which rectification was sought was part of a chain of contracts involving third parties: cf below, p 290.

[103] *London Weekend Television Ltd v Paris and Griffith* (1969) 113 SJ 222; *Joscelyne v Nissen* [1970] 2 QB 86, 98; *Re Butlin's Settlement* [1976] Ch 251.

(c) Rectification for Unilateral Mistake. The remedy of rectification was originally granted only in cases of common mistake, to correct the erroneous expression of the common intentions of *both* parties. But it has been extended to cases of unilateral mistake, where the document fails to reflect the intention of only one of the parties at the time of its execution.[104] If, however, the mistake is unilateral, it is more difficult to establish that the document should be rectified because rectification is a 'drastic' remedy[105] which deprives the non-mistaken party of the benefit of the document in the terms which he or she intended and which were apparently agreed by the party who claims to have made a mistake.[106] The knowledge or conduct of the party who was not mistaken must be such as to make it inequitable for that party to object to rectification.

The Court will not order rectification for unilateral mistake unless three conditions are satisfied.[107] First, the other party must have actual knowledge of the mistaken party's intentions and of the mistake.[108] In this context the knowledge of an agent will not suffice[109] but a party who has wilfully shut his or her eyes to the obvious, or wilfully and recklessly failed to make such inquiries as an honest and reasonable person would have made, will be taken to have actual knowledge.[110] Secondly, the party not under a mistake must have failed to draw the mistaken party's attention to the mistake. Thirdly, the mistake must be such that the party not under a mistake would derive a benefit,[111] or the mistaken party would suffer a detriment,[112] if the inaccuracy in the document were to remain uncorrected. Previously there was some authority for the view that the conduct of the party who was not mistaken had to amount to fraud,[113] or at least involve a degree of sharp practice;[114] but this is not required.[115] The question is whether the non-mistaken party's conduct is unconscionable so that he or she cannot insist on

[104] *Roberts & Co Ltd v Leicestershire CC* [1961] Ch 555; *Riverlate Properties Ltd v Paul* [1975] Ch 133, 140; *Thomas Bates & Son Ltd v Wyndham's (Lingerie) Ltd* [1981] 1 WLR 505.

[105] *Agip SpA v Navigazione Alta Italia SpA* [1984] 1 Lloyd's Rep 353, 365 (Slade LJ); *George Wimpey UK Ltd v VI Construction Ltd* [2005] EWCA Civ 77, [2005] BLR 135 at [75]. Cf, however, McLauchlan (2008) 124 LQR 608 (not really 'drastic' at all, but a routine application of the objective principle); McLauchlan (2014) 130 LQR 83; Cartwright, *Unequal Bargaining* (1991) 53–7.

[106] Rectification is more readily available for a voluntary disposition, where what is relevant is the subjective intention of the settlor, rather than (in the case of a contract) the requirement of outward expression of objective communication of that intention: *Day v Day* [2013] EWCA Civ 280, [2014] Ch 114 at [22]. Similarly, for rescission of a voluntary disposition entered into under a unilateral mistake, see *Pitt v Holt* [2013] UKSC 26 at [114]–[115], above, p 273.

[107] *Thomas Bates and Son Ltd v Wyndham's (Lingerie) Ltd* [1981] 1 WLR 505, 515–16, 520–1; *FSHC Group Holdings Ltd v Glas Trust Corp Ltd* [2019] EWCA Civ 1361 at [104] ('the precise scope of this principle remains controversial').

[108] *Riverlate Properties Ltd v Paul* [1975] Ch 133, 140; *Agip SpA v Navigazione Alta Italia SpA* [1984] 1 Lloyd's Rep 353, 365.

[109] *Kemp v Neptune Concrete* (1989) 57 P & CR 369.

[110] *Commission for the New Towns v Cooper (GB) Ltd* [1995] Ch 259.

[111] *Thomas Bates and Son Ltd v Wyndham's (Lingerie) Ltd* [1981] 1 WLR 505, 516.

[112] *Ibid*, 521.

[113] *May v Platt* [1900] 1 Ch 616, 623.

[114] *Riverlate Properties Ltd v Paul* [1975] Ch 133, 140.

[115] *Thomas Bates and Son Ltd v Wyndham's (Lingerie) Ltd* [1981] 1 WLR 505.

performance in accordance to the strict letter of the contract.[116] Nevertheless, it is clear that if a party executes a document in ignorance that the other party is under a mistake, the remedy of rectification will be denied.[117]

(d) Limits on the Remedy of Rectification. The award of the remedy of rectification is within the discretion of the Court. As an equitable remedy, it is barred not only by the mistaken party waiving the claim to the remedy, but also by the equitable doctrine of *laches*—that is, where the other party would be prejudiced by the delay in bringing the claim. Rectification may also not be ordered if it would prejudice the rights of an innocent third party,[118] although the Court may be able to grant the remedy on terms which will avoid such prejudice.[119]

(e) Nature of the Remedy of Rectification. The court order of rectification itself changes the terms of the contract, and the parties do not need to execute a new document.[120] The effect of the court order is normally retrospective to change the terms of the document with effect from the formation of the contract.[121]

(d) EQUITABLE REMEDIES FOR MISTAKES ABOUT THE TERMS

The Courts of Equity developed their own remedies in favour of a party who had made a mistake.[122] In addition to rectification,[123] two other remedies are also relevant: specific performance, which may be refused where there has been a mistake; and rescission.

(i) Refusal of specific performance

In the case of breaches of contracts for the sale or transfer of land, the common law remedy is damages but equity would normally compel the transfer of the land by an order for specific performance.[124] Specific performance is a discretionary remedy[125] and the Court will not order it where it would cause undue hardship. Mistake of a type which is insufficient to render the contract void at law may be a ground for resisting specific

[116] *Commission for the New Towns v Cooper (GB) Ltd* [1995] Ch 259, 280; *Littman v Aspen Oil (Broking) Ltd* [2005] EWCA Civ 1579, [2006] 2 P & CR 2 at [18]–[26]. Cf *FSHC Group Holdings Ltd v Glas Trust Corp Ltd* [2019] EWCA Civ 1361 at [105] (rectification for unilateral mistake gives effect to the same underlying equity as rectification for common mistake); McLauchlan (2008) 124 LQR 608.

[117] *Riverlate Properties Ltd v Paul* [1975] Ch 133; *Agip SpA v Navigazione Alta Italia SpA* [1984] 1 Lloyd's Rep 353, 362.

[118] *FSHC Group Holdings Ltd v Glas Trust Corp Ltd* [2019] EWCA Civ 1361 at [71]. The right to rectification is an 'equity'. For the nature of an equity and the circumstances in which the right to rectify a contract relating to land will bind a purchaser of a legal or equitable interest in the land, see Burn and Cartwright, *Cheshire and Burn's Modern Law of Real Property* (18th edn, 2011) 903–6.

[119] *National Union of Rail, Maritime and Transport Workers v Tyne and Wear Passenger Transport Executive* [2024] UKSC 37 at [35].

[120] *White v White* (1872) LR 15 Eq 247.

[121] *Malmesbury v Malmesbury* (1862) 31 Beav 407, 418. Cf Law of Property (Miscellaneous Provisions) Act 1989, s 2(4) (such time as stated in Court's order).

[122] See also below, p 314.

[123] Above, p 284.

[124] Below, p 597.

[125] Below, p 594.

performance where it would be harsh to enforce performance of a contract against one who has entered into it under a mistake. Specific performance may be refused not only where the mistake is about the facts relating to the land but also where mistake relates to the terms of the contract itself such as the term which identifies the property that the purchaser has agreed to buy. In *Malins v Freeman*[126] where a purchaser bid for and bought one lot of land at an auction in the belief that he was buying a wholly different lot, the Court refused to order specific performance of the contract. The defendant's mistake was due to his own carelessness and to no fault of the claimant, but the Court was prepared to exercise its discretion in his favour, leaving the claimant to claim damages at law. By contrast, in *Tamplin v James*[127] the defendant bid for and bought an inn and outbuildings in the mistaken belief that the lot also included two attached pieces of garden. There was little excuse for this misapprehension as the plans of the property to be sold were exhibited at the sale. The Court made an order for specific performance of the agreement.

(ii) Rescission

It has sometimes been said that, where a contract is binding at law, a party who made a mistake about the terms may be able to obtain rescission in equity;[128] or that, in cases of unilateral mistake in written contracts, equity might give the defendant the option of accepting rectification or having the contract rescinded.[129] However, such statements must now be viewed with caution. There appears not to be any general equitable discretion to grant rescission for mistake about the terms of a contract which is valid at law. On one view, there must be fraud or misrepresentation on the part of the other party before rescission is available.[130] On another, somewhat wider, view, which formed the basis of the decision in *Solle v Butcher*,[131] it is sufficient if the Court 'is of the opinion that it is unconscientious for [the other party] to avail himself of the legal advantage which he has obtained' by the contract.[132] However, the approach in *Solle v Butcher* was rejected in *The Great Peace*.[133] The Court of Appeal held that there is no equitable jurisdiction to rescind a contract for a common mistake of fact where the mistake is not sufficient to render the contract void at common law: 'the premise of equity's intrusion into the effects of the common law is that the common law rule in question is seen in the particular

[126] (1837) 2 Keen 25. The Courts in such cases do not always consider explicitly whether the mistake is about a term of the contract, or only about the facts relating to the subject-matter. See also *Wood v Scarth* (1855) 2 K & J 33; *Denny v Hancock* (1870) LR 6 Ch App 1; *Burrow v Scammell* (1881) 19 Ch D 175, 182. In *Webster v Cecil* (1861) 30 Beav 62 the contract would have been void at common law because the claimant knew or ought to have known about the mistake.

[127] (1880) 15 Ch D 215.

[128] *Solle v Butcher* [1950] 1 KB 671, 692–3; *OT Africa Line Ltd v Vickers plc* [1996] 1 Lloyd's Rep 700, 704.

[129] *Garrard v Frankel* (1862) 30 Beav 445; *Paget v Marshall* (1884) 28 Ch D 255; *Harris v Pepperell* (1867) LR 5 Eq 1; *Bloomer v Spittle* (1872) LR 13 Eq 427; *May v Platt* [1900] 1 Ch 616, 623.

[130] *May v Platt* [1900] 1 Ch 616, 623; *London Borough of Redbridge v Robinson Rentals* (1969) 211 EG 1125; *Riverlate Properties Ltd v Paul* [1975] Ch 133.

[131] [1950] 1 KB 671.

[132] *Torrance v Bolton* (1872) LR Ch App 118, 124.

[133] [2002] EWCA Civ 1407, [2003] QB 679; below, p 316.

case to work injustice, and for some reason the common law cannot cure itself'.[134] A similar argument should apply to a mistake about the terms. The objective test applied by the common law already prevents a party who makes a mistake about the terms of the contract from being bound where the other party knew, or ought to have known, about the mistake.[135] No further role is needed for equity. This also appears to be the approach taken by the Court of Appeal in *Riverlate Properties Ltd v Paul*.[136] The Court of Appeal held that there was no power to grant equitable relief on the grounds of mere unilateral mistake unless the party against whom relief is sought was aware, at the time of the transaction, that the other party was contracting under a mistake. Russell LJ stated:[137]

> Is the lessor entitled to rescission of the lease on the mere ground that it made a serious mistake in the drafting of the lease which it put forward and subsequently executed, when (a) the lessee did not share the mistake, (b) the lessee did not know that the document did not give effect to the lessor's intention, and (c) the mistake of the lessor was in no way attributable to anything said or done by the lessee? . . . If reference be made to principles of equity, it operates on conscience. If conscience be clear at the time of the transaction, why should equity disrupt the transaction? If a man may be said to be fortunate in obtaining a property at a bargain price, or on terms that make it a good bargain, because the other party unknown to him has made a miscalculation or other mistake, some high-minded men might consider it appropriate that he should agree to a fresh bargain to cure the miscalculation or mistake, abandoning his good fortune. But if equity were to enforce the views of those high-minded men, we have no doubt that it would run counter to the attitudes of much the greater part of ordinary mankind (not least the world of commerce), and would be venturing on the field of moral philosophy.

4. MISTAKES ABOUT THE IDENTITY OF THE PERSON WITH WHOM THE CONTRACT IS MADE

Mistakes of this sort can occur only where A contracts with B, believing B to be C: that is, where a party has in contemplation a definite and identifiable person with whom he or she intends to contract. Further, at the time when the contract is made, one party must regard the identity of the other party as a matter of vital importance.[138] One who, for example, accepts a bid at a public auction cannot normally claim to be concerned with the identity of the person who makes the bid.[139]

Mistake about identity has posed particular difficulties because often the issue of its effect on an apparent agreement arises not as between the parties to the agreement but

[134] *Ibid* at [156]; applied to unilateral mistakes of fact in *Statoil ASA v Louis Dreyfus Energy Services LP* [2008] EWHC 2257 (Comm) at [105].

[135] Above, p 279. Cf the different approach in Singapore, where actual knowledge of the other party's mistake about the terms renders the contract void at common law; constructive notice renders it voidable in equity: *Chwee Kin Keong v Digilandmall.com Pte Ltd* [2005] 1 SLR 502; above, p 281, n 54. See also *Taylor v Johnson* (1983) 151 CLR 422 (High Court of Australia).

[136] [1975] Ch 133.

[137] *Ibid*, 140–1.

[138] *Ingram v Little* [1961] 1 QB 31, 57; *Lewis v Averay* [1972] 1 QB 198, 209; *Shogun Finance Ltd v Hudson* [2003] UKHL 62 at [48], [178], [191].

[139] *Dennant v Skinner* [1948] 2 KB 164.

in determining which of two innocent people, defrauded by a third party, is to bear the loss. In many of the decisions A was induced to enter into a contract of sale of goods by a fraudulent misrepresentation by B about B's identity; but by the time A had discovered the truth B had sold and delivered the goods to C. The fraudulent misrepresentation would render the contract between A and B voidable, but rescission is no longer possible once the goods have passed into the hands of an innocent purchaser, C,[140] who can therefore keep the goods and leave A to claim damages against B (if B can be found and is solvent). But if A can show that there was a mistake of identity which rendered the contract void, then B acquired no title to the goods and so could not transfer title to C:[141] C must therefore return the goods or pay damages in the tort of conversion to A.[142] Some of the disagreement between judges in the cases reflects different policies as to the incidence of loss between the innocent parties. Many of the issues have now been settled by the House of Lords in *Shogun Finance Ltd v Hudson*[143] but even there the House was divided as to the proper approach to be taken. The minority (Lord Nicholls and Lord Millett) would have overruled many of the older cases in order to achieve the result that a contract entered into under a mistake of identity is normally only voidable and not void, thus protecting the innocent third-party purchaser.[144] However, the majority affirmed the existing authorities, and held that a contract may be void for mistake of identity. Even under the approach approved by the majority in *Shogun*, however, such an operative mistake will be relatively rare.

(a) AN OFFER CAN BE ACCEPTED ONLY BY THE PERSON TO WHOM IT IS ADDRESSED

A person cannot constitute himself a contracting party with one whom he knows or ought to know has no intention of contracting with him: an offer can be accepted only by the person to whom it is addressed. In *Boulton v Jones*:[145]

B had taken over the business of Brocklehurst, with whom J had been used to deal. J had a running account with Brocklehurst and was entitled to a set-off in respect of sums owed to him by Brocklehurst. J sent an order for goods addressed to Brocklehurst, which B supplied without informing J that the business had changed hands. When J learned that the goods had not come from Brocklehurst, he refused to pay for them, and was sued by B for the price.

[140] Below, p 340.

[141] Above, p 273.

[142] It is the tort of conversion (rather than the law of property) that protects the right to possession of goods; and where the defendant does not return the goods the normal remedy is damages, rather than an order for specific recovery: Goudkamp and Nolan, *Winfield & Jolowicz on Tort* (21st edn, 2025) paras 17-050, 17-057; Bridge, *Personal Property Law* (4th edn, 2015) 120–1.

[143] [2003] UKHL 62. Strictly, the *ratio* relates only to contracts in writing: below, p 297, but there was also significant discussion about the approach to be taken in the case of unwritten contracts: below, p 299.

[144] *Ibid* at [35] and [84], approving the discussion in the 28th edn of this book, p 332.

[145] (1857) 2 H & N 564. Boulton had been Brocklehurst's foreman, and from the report of this case in (1857) 6 WR 107 it appears that Boulton knew of the existence of the set-off. It is, however, an unusual case in that Jones's mistake was not induced by a fraudulent misrepresentation by Boulton.

It was held that he was not liable to pay for the goods. Pollock CB said:[146]

It is a rule of law, that if a person intends to contract with A, B cannot give himself any right under it. Here the order in writing was given to Brocklehurst. Possibly Brocklehurst might have adopted the act of [B] in supplying the goods, and maintained an action for their price. But since [B] had chosen to sue, the only course [J] could take was to plead that there was no contract with him.

Nevertheless it must be remembered that offer and acceptance must here, as elsewhere, be understood in an objective sense. The test is not merely 'Did the offeror intend to contract with the person to whom the offer was made?' but also 'How would a reasonable person in the position of the offeree have interpreted the offer?'[147] So if A makes an offer to B in mistake for C, and B, reasonably believing that the offer is intended for him, accepts, then A is bound even though he can prove that he had made a mistake. An extreme application of this principle can be seen in *Upton-on-Severn RDC v Powell*:[148]

The defendant sent for the Upton fire brigade in mistake for the Pershore fire brigade, in whose area he was, and the call was accepted in good faith by the Upton brigade.

It was held that the defendant was contractually bound to pay for their services despite his mistake and despite the fact that neither party thought they were entering a contract; the defendant thought he was calling the brigade the services of which he was entitled to without charge, and the fire brigade thought they were answering a call within their area for which there would be no charge.[149]

But no contract will be formed if a person accepting an offer believes on reasonable grounds that he is accepting an offer from someone other than the person by whom it has in fact been made, and this fact is known to the offeror. In *Cundy v Lindsay*:[150]

L received an order for goods from Blenkarn, who gave as his address '37 Wood Street, Cheapside'. He imitated the signature of a respectable firm named Blenkiron & Co, who were known by reputation to L and who carried on business at 123 Wood Street. L were thus fraudulently induced to send the goods to Blenkarn's address, which goods he afterwards sold to C. L sued C for conversion of the goods.

If the contract between L and Blenkarn was merely voidable for fraudulent misrepresentation, C would be entitled to retain the goods as they had taken them in good faith and for value. If the contract was void for mistake, Blenkarn had acquired no title to the goods from L, and so could pass no title to C.[151] The House of Lords held that L were entitled to succeed. Lord Cairns said:[152]

Of him [Blenkarn] they knew nothing, and of him they never thought. With him they never intended to deal. Their minds never, even for an instant of time rested upon him, and as between him and them there was no *consensus* of mind which could lead to any agreement or

[146] *Ibid*, 565. [147] *Shogun Finance Ltd v Hudson* [2003] UKHL 62 at [123]–[125] (Lord Phillips MR).

[148] [1942] 1 All ER 220.

[149] It is not clear whether the plaintiff would have been contractually liable if he had cancelled the call before the services were rendered: it is preferable to regard the liability for the services rendered as based on restitution (reasonable recompense for services rendered) rather than on contract. See also above, p 34, n 18.

[150] (1878) 3 App Cas 459. [151] Above, p 293. [152] (1878) 3 App Cas 459, 465.

any contract whatever. As between him and them there was merely the one side to a contract, where, in order to produce a contract, two sides would be required.

When his offer was accepted, Blenkarn knew that L thought they were entering into a contract with Blenkiron & Co. The contract was therefore void *ab initio*. Again, in *Shogun Finance Ltd v Hudson*[153] a finance company agreed to sell a car on hire-purchase terms to a fraudster who then sold it on to the defendant. Under section 27 of the Hire-Purchase Act 1964 a private purchaser of a motor vehicle from the debtor under a hire-purchase agreement can acquire title to the vehicle as long as he purchases in good faith and without notice of the hire-purchase agreement. The defendant's claim to title therefore turned on the validity of the hire-purchase agreement. If the agreement was only voidable for fraud, the defendant would obtain good title. But if it was void for mistake about the fraudster's identity, the fraudster would not be a 'debtor' under a 'hire-purchase agreement' and the defendant would not be protected. As proof of identity the fraudster had produced a genuine but unlawfully-obtained driving licence in the name of a Mr Patel, and the company had checked Mr Patel's credit rating. It was held by the majority of the House of Lords that the hire-purchase agreement was void. It could have been made only between the company and Mr Patel, and this was not possible because Mr Patel knew nothing of it and had not signed the agreement.[154] Accordingly the defendant did not obtain title to the car and the finance company was entitled to it.

(b) THE NEED FOR AN IDENTIFIABLE THIRD PERSON

A mistake regarding the personality of the other party, but not amounting to a mistake about that party's *identity*, will not prevent the formation of a contract. It is sometimes said that mistake as to *attributes* is insufficient.[155] The examples given of mistakes as to 'attributes' include those about the solvency or social position of that person or whether that person holds a driving licence. While the case law draws a distinction between *identity* and *attributes*, there is arguably, in principle, no more intrinsic validity in that distinction than that, as we shall see,[156] between *substance* and *qualities* of the subject-matter of a contract. As Lord Denning MR observed, '[a] man's very name is one of his attributes. It is also the key to his identity.'[157] The law does, however, conveniently distinguish between cases where there are two individuals in the picture (ie A contracts

[153] [2003] UKHL 62.

[154] The majority (Lord Hobhouse, Lord Phillips, and Lord Walker) held that since the contract was in writing, the identity of the parties could be determined only by reference to the written document, but they also considered that the agreement was void because the company intended to contract only with Mr Patel and so there was no consensus. Lord Nicholls and Lord Millett dissented, considering the agreement to be only voidable because a contract is normally entered into between the persons who in fact deal with each other (here, the fraudster and the claimant) even if it may then be voidable for fraud.

[155] *Whittaker v Campbell* [1984] QB 318, 329.

[156] Below, p 311.

[157] *Lewis v Averay* [1972] 1 QB 198, 206. See also the similar view of the minority in *Shogun Finance Ltd v Hudson* [2003] UKHL 62 at [5], [60], [73]–[74].

with B in mistake for C) and cases where there is only one (ie A contracts with B in the belief that B is not B). Glanville Williams stated cogently:[158]

The conclusion is that a so-called 'error of identity' consists in misapprehending (the attributes of) two or more persons. An 'error of attributes' consists in misapprehending (the attributes of) a single person.

In *King's Norton Metal Co Ltd v Edridge, Merrett & Co Ltd*:[159]

KN, a metal manufacturer, received a letter purporting to come from 'Hallam & Co' in Sheffield asking for quotations for metal wire. On the letterhead was a picture of a large factory and a list of overseas depots. KN replied, and Hallam & Co ordered the wire. In fact, the firm of 'Hallam & Co' consisted solely of a fraudulent person named Wallis. The letters had been written, and the writing paper prepared, by him. Wallis subsequently sold the wire to the defendant. KN sued the defendant, contending that the contract with Hallam & Co was void, and that the wire was therefore still its property.

The Court of Appeal held that KN had intended to contract with the writer of the letter. Although it would not have done so if it had known what sort of a person the writer was, and that he was using an alias, a contract had been made which was not void on the ground of mistake, but only voidable for fraud. Consequently the property in the goods delivered had passed under it to Wallis, and an innocent purchaser from him acquired a good title to them. AL Smith LJ put the question as follows:[160]

With whom, upon this evidence, which was all one way, did [KN] contract to sell the goods? Clearly with the writer of the letters. If it could have been shown that there was a separate entity called Hallam & Co and another entity called Wallis then the case might have come within the decision in *Cundy v Lindsay*.

Therefore, in order to establish mistake as to identity, the party contracting must prove not merely that he or she did not intend to contract with the person with whom the apparent contract was concluded, but also that there was a third identifiable person with whom there was an intention to contract.[161]

Where A contracts with B in the belief that B is not B, and B knows of this error, it might be thought that the situation is no different from that where A contracts with B in mistake for C, and B realizes the mistake. There is in fact a considerable difference.[162] In the latter situation the contract is void because B cannot accept an offer knowing that it is not intended for himself but for C. In the former, there is no third person to whom the offer is really addressed: it is addressed to B, even though A mistakenly believes that

158 (1945) 23 Can Bar Rev 278. Cf Wilson (1954) 17 MLR 515, and the reply by Unger (1955) 18 MLR 259.

159 (1897) 14 TLR 98. Cf *Newborne v Sensolid (Great Britain) Ltd* [1954] 1 QB 45.

160 (1897) 14 TLR 98, 99.

161 See also *Citibank NF v Brown Shipley & Co Ltd* [1991] 2 All ER 690, 702 (mistake as to identity of messenger insufficient).

162 This section relies heavily on the convincing argument of Professor Goodhart in (1941) 57 LQR 228, 241 ff.

he is not B. B is not, therefore, prevented from accepting an offer addressed to himself, and the contract will be valid and binding.

In certain circumstances, however, the offer made by A may expressly or impliedly contain a stipulation that excludes B. These are the terms upon which A is prepared to contract, and, as we have seen,[163] it is not possible for an offeree to accept an offer which he knows is made to him in different terms from those which he purports to accept. B cannot, therefore, accept such an offer. For example, the offer may be made to a limited class of persons, such as the members of a club or college, of whom B is not one. B may know, by reason of a previous refusal, that he is a person with whom A is unwilling to contract: a drama critic who is refused a ticket for a theatre performance cannot conclude a contract by going to the box office in disguise, or by employing a friend to buy a ticket for him.[164]

The difficulty is to know in what circumstances such a term is to be *implied* into the offer. In *King's Norton Metal Co Ltd v Edridge, Merrett & Co Ltd*,[165] the mistaken claimant was unable to satisfy the Court that such an implication should be made. This decision does not appear to have been cited in the case of *Sowler v Potter*[166] in which S granted a lease to P, who had formerly been known as Ann Robinson, a person with criminal convictions to whom S claimed she would not have granted the lease had she known of the change of name. It was held that the identity of the tenant was a vital element in a tenancy contract and that therefore *any* mistake with regard to her identity rendered the contract void *ab initio*. But this does not constitute a sound positive test of mistake in English law. The proper approach in such a case as *Sowler v Potter* would be to inquire whether a stipulation could be implied into the offer that the offer excluded the particular person as a tenant, and whether this stipulation was known to the offeree. The answer is clear: no such stipulation could be implied, and the contract should not have been held to be void. The decision in *Sowler v Potter* has incurred almost unanimous disapproval, and must be taken to have been overruled.[167]

(c) WRITTEN CONTRACTS

In the case of a contract wholly in writing, the identity of the parties is established by the names in the written contract. In *Shogun Finance Ltd v Hudson*[168] the majority of the House of Lords based their decision on the fact that the contract was in writing, and therefore the only person who could have been a party to the hire-purchase agreement with Shogun Finance was Mr Patel whose driving licence had been used as

[163] Above, p 279.

[164] *Said v Butt* [1920] 3 KB 497 (this case was primarily concerned with the question of an undisclosed principal and not with mistake).

[165] Above, p 296.

[166] [1940] 1 KB 271.

[167] *Solle v Butcher* [1950] 1 KB 671, 691; *Gallie v Lee* [1969] 2 Ch 17, 33, 41, 45, aff'd [1971] AC 1004; *Lewis v Averay* [1972] 1 QB 198, 206; *Shogun Finance Ltd v Hudson* [2001] EWCA Civ 1000, [2002] QB 834 at [34] (although *Sowler v Potter* was not discussed in the decision of the House of Lords).

[168] [2003] UKHL 62, above, p 295. See also *Hector v Lyons* (1988) 58 P & CR 156.

the basis of the credit check. Because it was not Mr Patel who had signed the agreement, it was void. Lord Hobhouse said:[169]

The agreement is a written agreement with Mr Durlabh Patel. The argument seeks to contradict this and make it an agreement with the rogue. It is argued that other evidence is always admissible to show who the parties to an agreement are. Thus, if the contents of the document are, without more, insufficient unequivocally to identify the actual individual referred to or if the identification of the party is non-specific, evidence can be given to fill any gap. Where the person signing is also acting as the agent of another, evidence can be adduced of that fact . . . But it is different where the party is, as here, specifically identified in the document: oral or other extrinsic evidence is not admissible. Further, the rogue was no one's agent (nor did he ever purport to be). The rule that other evidence may not be adduced to contradict the provisions of a contract contained in a written document is fundamental to the mercantile law of this country; the bargain is the document; the certainty of the contract depends on it.[170]

(d) TRANSACTIONS CONCLUDED IN THE PARTIES' PRESENCE

Where the parties do not conclude their contract in writing, nor through communications at a distance from one another, but deal face to face, there is a presumption that each intended to deal with the other and not with someone else. In *Phillips v Brooks Ltd*:[171]

A man, North, called at P's shop and selected some pearls and a ring. He wrote out a cheque for £3,000, saying 'I am Sir George Bullough' (a person of credit whose name was known to P) and giving Sir George Bullough's address. P, finding on reference to a directory that Sir George lived at that address, allowed North to take away the ring which North then pledged to the defendants for £350. The defendants had no notice of the fraud. P sued for the return of the ring, or its value, alleging that he had never parted with the property in it.

Horridge J held that, although the claimant believed that the person to whom he was handing the ring was Sir George Bullough, he in fact contracted to sell and deliver it to the person who came into his shop. His intention was 'to sell to the person present and identified by sight and hearing'.[172] The contract, therefore, was not void on the ground of mistake, but only voidable on the ground of fraud, and the defendants had acquired a good title to the ring. It does not follow from this decision that there can be no operative mistake as to identity where the parties are in each other's presence, although there is a strong presumption against the mistake being operative.[173]

[169] [2003] UKHL 62 at [94]. See also Lord Phillips at [154], [161], [178] and Lord Walker at [192].

[170] For the general (wholly objective) approach to the interpretation of written contracts, and operation of the parol evidence rule, see above, pp 148–9, 162. For support of the majority decision, see Stevens, in Burrows and Peel (eds), *Contract Terms* (2007) ch 6.

[171] [1919] 2 KB 243, criticized by Goodhart (1941) 57 LQR 228, 241.

[172] Adopting *Edmunds v Merchant Despatch Co* 135 Mass 283, 286 (1883) (Morton CJ).

[173] Viscount Haldane's suggestion in *Lake v Simmons* [1927] AC 487, 500 that a jeweller did not enter into a contract with a customer who was physically present in the shop because he thought that he was dealing with a different person was disapproved in *Shogun Finance Ltd v Hudson* [2003] UKHL 62 at [141]. Cf *Citibank NA v Brown Shipley & Co Ltd* [1991] 2 All ER 690, 700.

Two further cases illustrate the difficulty of deciding whether a contract is void for mistake as to identity, or merely voidable for fraud. In *Ingram v Little*:[174]

Miss Elsie Ingram, Miss Hilda Ingram and Mrs Mary Ann Maud Badger advertised their car for sale. A rogue who called himself Hutchinson visited them and offered to buy the car. When he made as if to pay them by cheque, they refused to accept it and insisted on payment in cash. He then gave his initials and an address, describing himself as a respectable businessman living in Caterham. One of the Ingrams went to the local post office and ascertained from the telephone directory that there was such a person living at that address. They then allowed the rogue to take away the car in return for a worthless cheque and the rogue sold the car to the defendants who took it in good faith.

The Court of Appeal held by a majority that the contract between the ladies and 'Hutchinson' was void for mistake and that the vehicle was still their property. Although in a face-to-face contract there is a presumption that the contract is not void for mistake of identity, the circumstances (particularly the investigation of the telephone directory) indicated that it was with Hutchinson that the claimants intended to deal and not with the rogue who was physically present before them. The presumption was therefore rebutted.

On the other hand, in *Lewis v Averay*:[175]

L, a post-graduate chemistry student, advertised his car for sale. A rogue, posing as the well-known television actor Richard Greene, called on L and offered to buy the car. L accepted the offer, and the rogue wrote out a cheque, signing it 'R.A. Green'. The rogue wished to take away the car at once, but L was not willing for him to have it until the cheque had been cleared. At L's request the rogue produced 'proof' that he was Richard Greene in the form of a special pass of admission to Pinewood studios bearing the name 'Richard A. Green' and an address, a photograph of the rogue and an official stamp. L was satisfied on seeing this pass and allowed the rogue to have the car. The cheque was worthless and the rogue sold the car to A, a music student, who bought it in good faith.

The Court of Appeal held that A intended to contract with the person actually present before him. The contract was therefore merely voidable for fraud, and in consequence A acquired the property in the car as against L.

Although *Shogun Finance Ltd v Hudson*[176] did not involve a contract concluded between parties who were physically present, guidance on the issue was given in two of the majority opinions. Both Lord Phillips and Lord Walker accepted that contracts concluded face to face raise different questions from both contracts concluded at a distance, and written contracts; but they also agreed that in a face-to-face transaction each party is presumed to have intended to deal with the person physically present. This presumption is a 'strong' presumption;[177] perhaps so strong that it can be rebutted only in exceptional cases, such as physical impersonation.[178]

[174] [1961] 1 QB 31 (Devlin LJ dissenting). Cf *Fawcett v Star Car Sales Ltd* [1960] NZLR 406.

[175] [1972] 1 QB 198.

[176] Above, p 295.

[177] [2003] UKHL 62 at [170] (Lord Phillips), [187] (Lord Walker).

[178] *Ibid* at [187] (Lord Walker, who also at [185] thought that the presumption was not rebutted in *Ingram v Little* [1961] 1 QB 31, which was therefore wrongly decided).

(e) THE CURRENT STATE OF THE LAW; CRITIQUE

The decision of the majority in *Shogun Finance Ltd v Hudson*[179] rested on the fact that the contract there was in writing, and the identity of the parties to the contract was therefore to be determined by an objective interpretation of the document itself. All members of the House discussed in general terms the issues raised by mistakes about identity. Lord Nicholls and Lord Millett, in the minority, proposed a radical reconsideration of the law, which would have overruled many of the older cases and would have resulted in a rule by which a mistake of identity would normally render a contract at most voidable, and not void. However, the majority declined to overturn the established authorities. In contracts which are not in writing but formed through offer and acceptance between the parties, such as by an exchange of letters, the intentions of each party as to the person with whom he or she is willing to contract is determined by an objective test of the communications, and a party who knows (for example) that he or she is not the intended recipient of the offer cannot claim to have entered into a contract by accepting it. An apparent contract may therefore still, after *Shogun*, be void for mistake of identity, as it was in *Cundy v Lindsay*.[180] In principle, a contract may even be void for mistake where the parties meet face to face, since it is still said in *Shogun*, following the earlier cases, that there is a presumption that the contract is valid. But it will be very rare that this presumption can in fact be rebutted.

The result of the decision in *Shogun* is, however, unsatisfactory. We have seen that the significance of a contract being void is that it can prejudice an innocent third party who purchases property which was delivered under the contract.[181] Lord Millett considered that, of the two 'innocent' parties—the original owner and the later purchaser—the latter was the more innocent:[182]

> Of course, someone has to bear the loss where there is fraud, but it is surely fairer that the party who was actually swindled and who had an opportunity to uncover the fraud should bear the loss rather than a party who entered the picture only after the swindle had been carried out and who had none.

He went on to point out that in such cases English law is out of step with its continental neighbours, because civilian systems such as Germany provide protection to a purchaser who can acquire good title by purchasing property in good faith from a non-owner.[183] The approach taken in English law is to link the passing of title (and therefore the third

[179] Above, p 295.

[180] (1878) 3 App Cas 459; see [2003] UKHL 62 at [55], [170]. Lord Nicholls and Lord Millett would have departed from *Cundy v Lindsay*: [2003] UKHL 62 at [35], [110]. See also Brodsky [2016] RLR 108, criticizing the analysis of both the majority and the minority in *Shogun*, but preferring an analysis under which the contract will normally be voidable, not void for mistake of identity.

[181] Above, p 293.

[182] *Shogun* [2003] UKHL 62 at [82]. Cf however Lord Walker at [181]–[182]. The difficulties encountered are compounded because of the difficulty, absent a requirement to have an identity card (see Identity Documents Act 2010, ss 1–3), of proving identity, and because a person can freely change his or her name: *Halsbury's Laws*, vol 88 (2025), para 326.

[183] *Shogun* [2003] UKHL 62 at [84]–[85].

party's rights) to the validity of the earlier contract.[184] However it would be preferable if effect were given to a recommendation made by the Law Reform Committee in 1966[185] that, where goods are sold under a mistake as to the buyer's identity, the contract should, so far as third parties are concerned, be considered voidable and not void. In the light of the decision in *Shogun* the Law Commission included this topic in its list of possible projects for reform[186] but later decided not to pursue it.[187]

5. MISTAKES OF FACT OR LAW ABOUT THE SUBJECT-MATTER OF THE CONTRACT OR THE SURROUNDING CIRCUMSTANCES

This section is concerned with the situation where the parties have agreed on the terms of the contract, and neither makes an operative mistake about the other's identity, but one or both of the parties have contracted in the mistaken belief that some fact which lies at the root of the contract is true, either a fact about the subject-matter of the contract, or a fact relating to the circumstances surrounding the formation of the contract, which was relevant to the claimant's decision to enter into the contract. We shall see that it is very rare for such a mistake to satisfy the very narrow test set down by the Courts in this area, but if it does, the mistake renders the contract void. It is sometimes said that this form of mistake invalidates a contract by nullifying consent.[188]

Until recently, for such a mistake to be operative and to invalidate a contract it had to be one of fact and not of law.[189] However, in 1999 the House of Lords held, in the context of claims for the recovery of money paid under a mistake, that a distinction should no longer be made between mistakes of law and mistakes of fact.[190] Similar reasoning has now also been applied to cases of mistake in contract.[191]

It has been argued[192] that there is a close relationship between mistake of fact, which is concerned with misapprehensions or misunderstandings at the time of the formation of

[184] For a robust defence of the English position, however, see Lord Hobhouse in *Shogun* [2003] UKHL 62 at [55]. See also Stevens, in Burrows and Peel (eds), *Contract Terms* (2007) ch 6. The third party is generally protected in English law only where the original possessor's right to claim in the tort of conversion is barred (and his title is extinguished) by the expiry of the six-year period of limitation from the first purchase in good faith: Limitation Act 1980, ss 3, 4.

[185] Twelfth Report of the Law Reform Committee (Cmd 2958, 1966) 15.

[186] Law Commission Ninth Programme of Law Reform, Law Com No 293 (2005) paras 1.16, 3.51–3.57.

[187] Law Commission Eleventh Programme of Law Reform, Law Com No 330 (2011) paras 3.4–3.6.

[188] *Bell v Lever Brothers Ltd* [1932] AC 161, 217.

[189] *British Homophone Ltd v Kunz* (1932) 152 LT 589.

[190] *Kleinwort Benson Ltd v Lincoln CC* [1999] 2 AC 349.

[191] *Brennan v Bolt Burdon* [2004] EWCA Civ 1017, [2005] QB 303. See also below, p 326 (misrepresentations of law).

[192] *Associated Japanese Bank (International) Ltd v Crédit du Nord SA* [1989] 1 WLR 255, 264–5, 268; *William Sindall plc v Cambridgeshire CC* [1994] 1 WLR 1016, 1039–40; *Great Peace Shipping Ltd v Tsavliris Salvage (International) Ltd, The Great Peace* [2002] EWCA Civ 1407 at [61], [73]–[75], [82]–[85]. See generally McKendrick, *Contract Law* (16th edn, 2025) paras 16.1, 16.19; Smith (1994) 110 LQR 400, 403. Cf Peel, *Treitel's Law of Contract* (16th edn, 2025) paras 19-131–19-133.

an apparent contract, and the doctrine of frustration, which concerns uncontemplated events occurring after that time. Both mistake and frustration are concerned with the allocation of risk in which the construction of the contract is central, and the Courts are conscious that both may be pleaded to get out of a bad bargain or to reallocate the risks.[193] Moreover, the two situations may appear factually similar, particularly where it is an accident whether the uncontemplated event occurred before or after the making of the contract.[194] But they are 'different juristic concepts'.[195] Mistake relates to the formation of a contract and, where operative, renders the whole contract void *ab initio*, whereas frustration relates to its termination and only discharges obligations which would have been due to be performed after the time of the frustrating event. Frustration is considered in Chapter 14.

(a) UNILATERAL MISTAKES OF FACT OR LAW

A unilateral mistake of fact or law does not render the contract void. We have already seen that the Court in *Smith v Hughes*[196] drew a clear distinction between a unilateral mistake about the terms of the contract, which may prevent there being a contract unless the objective test can override the absence of subjective agreement, and a unilateral mistake about the facts relating to the subject-matter of the contract, which is irrelevant even if the other party knows about the mistake. The mistaken party will have a remedy if the other party gave a warranty in the contract about the subject-matter, or if the mistake was induced by the other party's misrepresentation.[197] Blackburn J said:[198]

> [O]n the sale of a specific article, unless there be a warranty making it part of the bargain that it possesses some particular quality, the purchaser must take the article he has bought though it does not possess that quality. And I agree that even if the vendor was aware that the purchaser thought that the article possessed that quality, and would not have entered into the contract unless he had so thought, still the purchaser is bound, unless the vendor was guilty of some fraud or deceit upon him, and that a mere abstinence from disabusing the purchaser of that impression is not fraud or deceit; for, whatever may be the case in a court of morals, there is no legal obligation on the vendor to inform the purchaser that he is under a mistake, not induced by the act of the vendor.

More recently it has been said that the correctness of the decision in *Smith v Hughes*, and the analysis in it, has 'never been doubted'.[199] Nor is there a jurisdiction in equity for a Court to set aside a contract on the basis of a unilateral mistake of fact.[200]

[193] *Amalgamated Investment & Property Co Ltd v Walker & Sons Ltd* [1977] 1 WLR 164, 172. See also above, p 273, n 11.

[194] *Ibid.* Compare also the facts of *Griffith v Brymer* (1903) 19 TLR 434 (below, p 314, n 278) and *Krell v Henry* [1903] 2 KB 740 (below, p 484).

[195] *Joseph Constantine Steamship Line Ltd v Imperial Smelting Corp Ltd* [1942] AC 154, 186.

[196] (1871) LR 6 QB 597; above, p 279.

[197] For misrepresentation, see below, Chapter 9.

[198] (1871) LR 6 QB 597, 606–7.

[199] *Statoil ASA v Louis Dreyfus Energy Services LP* [2008] EWHC 2257 (Comm) at [88] (Aikens J). See also *Bell v Lever Bros* [1935] AC 161, 218; *UTB LLC v Sheffield United Ltd* [2019] EWHC 2322 (Ch) at [277]–[280].

[200] *Statoil ASA v Louis Dreyfus Energy Services LP* [2008] EWHC 2257 (Comm) at [105].

(b) COMMON MISTAKES OF FACT OR LAW

Where both parties make the same mistake of fact or law relating to the subject-matter or the facts surrounding the formation of the contract, the contract may be void. However, the Courts have developed a very narrow test for such mistakes, emphasizing that the parties are normally expected to provide in the contract for the allocation of the risk of unknown facts, and that a party should be entitled to rely on the doctrine of mistake only in exceptional cases. There is a clear line of authorities relating to common mistakes which may render a contract void at common law. Between 1949 and 2002 there was also a line of cases in which the Courts held that, even if the common mistake was not sufficient to render the contract void at common law, it might satisfy a less strict test under which the contract would be voidable in equity at the discretion of the Court. However, in *The Great Peace*[201] the Court of Appeal rejected this wider equitable jurisdiction.

(i) Common mistake at common law

The leading case is *Bell v Lever Brothers Ltd*,[202] which was decided by the House of Lords in 1931. The facts of the case are fairly simple, but the opinions are difficult to interpret, which has led to a variety of theories about the scope of the doctrine of common mistake. In 2002 the Court of Appeal sought in *The Great Peace*[203] to give an authoritative interpretation of the doctrine, but this latest decision can be understood only by reference to the decision in *Bell v Lever Brothers Ltd* as well as other cases which had been decided on the basis of common mistakes.

(a) Bell v Lever Brothers Ltd. In this case:

L entered into two agreements with B and with S. The first agreements were service contracts by which B and S were appointed to the Board of the Niger Company, a subsidiary of L, for a period of five years at salaries of £8,000 and £6,000 a year respectively. The second were compensation contracts by which L, in consideration of their retiring within the service period, later promised to pay B £30,000 and S £20,000.

While they were acting under their appointments, both B and S had secretly entered on their own account into speculative transactions in cocoa, conduct which would have given L the right to dismiss them summarily and without compensation. L had entered into the compensation contracts, and paid the sums promised, in ignorance of this fact. L now sought rescission of the compensation contracts and recovery of the money on the ground that it had been paid under a mistake of fact.

The jury found that B and S had been guilty of no fraud and that, at the time they entered into the compensation contracts, they did not have in mind their breaches of duty. The case must therefore be considered as one of *common* mistake,[204] that is, where the parties had both contracted under the same mistaken assumption. L would never

[201] [2002] EWCA Civ 1407.

[202] [1932] AC 161. Cf MacMillan (2003) 119 LQR 625.

[203] [2002] EWCA Civ 1407; below, p 306.

[204] In *Bell v Lever Brothers Ltd* the term used for a shared mistake is 'mutual' mistake, but the more modern term ('common' mistake) is used here; cf above, p 274.

have entered into the contract had it known the true state of affairs, and it therefore alleged that the contract was a nullity from the beginning. Wright J and the Court of Appeal[205] upheld this contention, but the House of Lords, by a bare majority, held that the contract was valid and binding.

There has been considerable discussion as to what this case in fact decided. Lord Blanesburgh, while stating that he was in accord with the other majority opinions, based his own decision mainly on a point of pleading.[206] The other two majority members, Lord Atkin and Lord Thankerton, formulated in the course of their speeches a number of propositions which, although directed to the same end, tend not to be easily reconcilable one with another. The speeches therefore provide support for a variety of conflicting interpretations of the doctrine of common mistake.

First, it has been said that the case establishes that there is no doctrine of mistake, rendering the contract void *ab initio*, in English law.[207] In *Solle v Butcher*, for example, Denning LJ said:[208]

> The correct interpretation of [*Bell v Lever Brothers Ltd*], to my mind, is that, once a contract has been made, that is to say, once the parties, whatever their inmost states of mind, have to all outward appearances agreed with sufficient certainty in the same terms on the same subject matter, then the contract is good unless and until it is set aside for failure of some condition on which the existence of the contract depends, or for fraud, or on some equitable ground. Neither party can rely on his own mistake to say that it was a nullity from the beginning, no matter that it was a mistake which to his mind was fundamental, and no matter that the other party knew that he was under a mistake. A fortiori, if the other party did not know of the mistake but shared it.

Some support for this contention can be found in the speech of Lord Atkin,[209] but both he and other members of the House of Lords assume throughout that certain types of mistake will avoid a contract, although they differ as to the circumstances in which it will do so, and it has been said that Denning LJ's interpretation does not do justice to the speeches of the majority.[210] Nevertheless, it is clear that the effect of the decision in *Bell v Lever Brothers* is to confine the doctrine of common mistake within the most narrow limits; it is only in the most extreme cases that the Court will intervene.

Secondly, it has been said that the case establishes that a contract is void only if some term can be implied in the contract which prevents it from coming into existence if the facts or law are not as the parties assumed. Lord Atkin expressly stated that this is a

[205] [1931] 1 KB 557.

[206] He also pointed out (at 180–1, 183, 197) that the payments made to B and S were, at any rate in part, voluntary payments because their agreement was with the Niger Company not Lever Brothers, and so could not be recovered as money paid under a mistake: see *Morgan v Ashcroft* [1938] 1 KB 49, 66, 71, 77.

[207] Slade (1954) 70 LQR 385; Shatwell (1955) 33 Can Bar Rev 164; Smith (1994) 110 LQR 400; Morgan [2018] CLJ 559; English, *Discharge of Contractual Obligations* (2025) ch 7.

[208] [1950] 1 KB 671, 691, below, p 315. Bucknill and Jenkins LJJ did not mention *Bell v Lever Brothers Ltd.*

[209] *Bell v Lever Brothers Ltd* [1932] AC 161, 224.

[210] *Associated Japanese Bank (International) Ltd v Crédit du Nord SA* [1989] 1 WLR 255, 267 (Steyn J, approved in *The Great Peace* [2002] EWCA Civ 1407 at [92]–[93]). But cf Smith (1994) 110 LQR 400, 412–13.

proposition to which few would demur,[211] but cogently went on to point out that it does not take us very far in the inquiry how to ascertain whether the contract does contain such a term.

An example is provided by *Associated Japanese Bank (International) Ltd v Crédit du Nord SA*:[212]

A fraudulent party purported to sell to AJB, and lease back from it, certain machines which in fact did not exist. CN guaranteed the fraudulent party's obligations under the sale and lease-back. When the fraudulent party was adjudged bankrupt, AJB sued on the guarantee.

It was held that, as the guarantee provided that substitution of the subject of the contract (the machines) could be made only with the guarantor's consent, it was subject to an express condition precedent that the lease related to existing machines. Alternatively, it was stated that the contextual background and the fact that both parties were informed that the machines existed meant that such a condition could be implied.[213]

However, just as the Courts have now rejected as artificial the old view that frustration of a contract depended on the implication of a term into the contract,[214] so it is not possible to base the doctrine of common mistake on implied terms. In *The Great Peace*[215] the Court of Appeal said:

[T]he theory of the implied term is as unrealistic when considering common mistake as when considering frustration. Where a fundamental assumption upon which an agreement is founded proves to be mistaken, it is not realistic to ask whether the parties impliedly agreed that in those circumstances the contract would not be binding.

Thirdly, it has been suggested that the application of the doctrine of common mistake depends upon the true construction of the contract made between the parties.[216] As a general rule, one or other of them will be considered to have assumed the risk of the ordinary uncertainties which exist when an agreement is concluded. Normally, because of the principle *caveat emptor*, the buyer is held to have taken the risk that property sold might prove defective or might be in some way different from that which the parties believed it to be. Alternatively, this risk will have been assumed by the seller if there was an express or implied warranty as to quality or description in the contract. A common misunderstanding will not therefore normally nullify the contract.

The construction of the contract is certainly critical to any claim of mistake. The contract can be held void only where the terms of the contract, construed in the light of the nature of the contract and of the circumstances believed to exist at the time it was made,[217] show that it was never intended to apply to the situation which in reality

211 [1932] AC 161, 225. See also *Whittaker v Campbell* [1984] QB 318, 327; Goldberg and Thomson [1978] JBL 150.

212 [1989] 1 WLR 255.

213 *Ibid*, 263. See also *Financings Ltd v Stimson* [1962] 1 WLR 1184.

214 Below, p 492. For the link between mistake and frustration, see above, pp 301–2.

215 [2002] EWCA Civ 1407 at [73].

216 Atiyah (1957) 73 LQR 340; Atiyah and Bennion (1961) 24 MLR 421; McTurnan (1963) 41 Can Bar Rev 1; Morgan [2018] CLJ 559; English, *Discharge of Contractual Obligations* (2025) ch 7.

217 Extrinsic evidence is admissible to assist for this purpose in the construction of the contract: *Pritchard v Merchants' and Tradesmen's Life Assurance Society* (1858) 3 CB (NS) 622.

existed at that time, and the risk of the relevant mistake has not been allocated to one of the parties.[218] However, it is not sufficient to say that the doctrine of common mistake rests on construction of the contract. If the contract expressly or by implication allocates the risk of the unknown fact to one or other of the parties, then there is no mistake: the contract provides for the situation. But a test is needed for those cases where the unknown fact is not dealt with expressly or impliedly in the contract itself, to determine whether the mistake is sufficient to render the contract void. The Court of Appeal in *The Great Peace*[219] said that the doctrine of mistake:

fills a gap in the contract where it transpires that it is impossible of performance without the fault of either party and the parties have not, expressly or by implication, dealt with their rights and obligations in that eventuality.

(b) The Great Peace. In this case:

The defendant urgently required the use of a vessel in order to carry out salvage services for another ship which was in distress. The defendant was told by a reputable shipping organisation that the claimant's vessel, *The Great Peace*, was in the vicinity, and contacted the claimant's manager in the middle of the night to ask to hire the vessel. A contract was entered into for a minimum five-day hire, both parties believing that *The Great Peace* was 35 miles away from the distressed ship. The information about the location of *The Great Peace* was wrong, however, and she was in fact 410 miles away. After discovering the truth, the defendant waited two hours in order to find another vessel closer to the distressed ship, and then cancelled the contract and argued that it was not required to pay the five days' hire because the contract was void for common mistake about the location of *The Great Peace*.

Toulson J and the Court of Appeal held that the contract was valid, and the defendant was liable to pay the hire charge. They reviewed the authorities, in particularly the decisions in *Bell v Lever Brothers Ltd*[220] and *Associated Japanese Bank (International) Ltd v Crédit du Nord SA*[221] and drew on the related doctrine of frustration of a contract in order to explain the doctrine of mistake, and to articulate it in language which is sometimes also used in relation to frustration.[222] The Court of Appeal suggested that the following elements must be present if common mistake is to avoid a contract:[223]

(i) there must be a common assumption as to the existence of a state of affairs; (ii) there must be no warranty by either party that that state of affairs exists; (iii) the non-existence of the

[218] *Associated Japanese Bank (International) Ltd v Crédit du Nord SA* [1989] 1 WLR 255, 268; *William Sindall plc v Cambridgeshire CC* [1994] 1 WLR 1016, 1035, 1039; *The Great Peace* [2002] EWCA Civ 1407 at [75], [82], [84]; *Amalgamated Investment & Property Co Ltd v John Walker & Sons Ltd* [1977] 1 WLR 164, and below, pp 309–10 and cf *Gamerco SA v ICM/Fair Warning (Agency) Ltd* [1995] 1 WLR 1226.

[219] [2002] EWCA Civ 1407 at [80]. See also *Dana Gas PJSC v Dana Gas Sukuk Ltd* [2017] EWHC 2928 (Comm), [2017] 2 CLC 735 at [62]–[64].

[220] [1932] AC 161; above, p 303.

[221] [1989] 1 WLR 255; above, p 305.

[222] For frustration of the 'contractual adventure', see *Jackson v Union Marine Insurance Co Ltd* (1874) LR 10 CP 125; below, p 482.

[223] [2002] EWCA Civ 1407 at [76]. This was adapted from a test stated by Lord Alverstone CJ in an earlier case relating to frustration: *Blakeley v Muller & Co* (1903) 19 TLR 186.

state of affairs must not be attributable to the fault of either party; (iv) the non-existence of the state of affairs must render performance of the contract impossible; (v) the state of affairs may be the existence, or a vital attribute, of the consideration to be provided or circumstances which must subsist if performance of the contractual adventure is to be possible.

Later cases have generally adopted this as the test to determine whether an alleged common mistake is sufficient to avoid a contract.[224]

The third element listed by the Court of Appeal (absence of fault) was not discussed in *Bell v Lever Brothers Ltd*. However, in the High Court of Australia in *McRae v Commonwealth Disposals Commission* it was said:[225]

> [A] party cannot rely on mutual[226] mistake where the mistake consists of a belief which is, on the one hand, entertained by him without any reasonable ground, and, on the other hand, deliberately induced by him in the mind of the other party.

In *Associated Japanese (International) Bank Ltd v Crédit du Nord SA*[227] Steyn J accepted this qualification of the positive rules regarding mistake, and this was confirmed by the Court of Appeal in *The Great Peace*.[228]

The contract in *The Great Peace* was not void, because performance of the contract—the 'contractual adventure'—was not impossible.[229] *The Great Peace* could still be used for the defendant's salvage operation, even though it would have taken longer to reach the distressed ship and therefore it would have been less useful. Moreover, the fact that the defendant delayed before cancelling the contract showed that *The Great Peace* would have been of some use.[230]

(c) Examples of Situations Considered by the Courts. Relatively few reported cases have been argued, and even fewer have succeeded, on the basis of common mistake. We have already noted that many mistakes will be caused by misrepresentations, and that it will often be better for a claimant to seek a remedy for misrepresentation rather than mistake.[231] The narrow test for common mistake, and the attendant uncertainties of its application, no doubt discourage its use. However, we can see its application by considering a number of factual situations which have been considered by the Courts:

(1) mistake about the existence of the subject-matter of the contract;
(2) mistake about title to property;

[224] See, eg, *Perpetual Trustee Co Ltd v BNY Corporate Trustee Services Ltd* [2009] EWCA Civ 1160, [2010] Ch 347 at [109]; *Acre 1127 Ltd v De Montfort Fine Art Ltd* [2011] EWCA Civ 87, [2011] All ER (D) 111 (Feb) at [38]; *Van der Merwe v Goldman* [2016] EWHC 790 (Ch) at [25]; *Chancery Client Partners Ltd v MRC 957 Ltd* [2016] EWHC 2142 (Ch) at [30]; *Triple Seven MSN 27251 Ltd v Azman Air Services Ltd* [2018] EWHC 1348 (Comm), [2018] 4 WLR 97 at [60]; *John Lobb SAS v John Lobb Ltd* [2022] EWHC 2306 (Ch), [2023] ETMR 1 at [53].

[225] (1950) 84 CLR 377, 408 (Dixon and Fullagar JJ).

[226] ie common mistake: see above, p 274.

[227] [1989] 1 WLR 255, 268. The qualification was said to rest on policy and good sense rather than principles such as estoppel or negligence. Cf also the requirement of absence of fault in the test in equity under *Solle v Butcher* [1950] 1 KB 671, 693; below, pp 315–6.

[228] [2002] EWCA Civ 1407 at [78]–[79].

[229] Cf Reynolds (2003) 119 LQR 177, 178 (doubting whether there was a common mistake at all: 'the owners of the *Great Peace* surely did no more than think, correctly, that the salvors had reason to believe that the *Great Peace* was the nearest ship').

[230] *Great Peace* [2002] EWCA Civ 1407 at [165].

[231] Above, p 272.

(3) mistake about the quality or the substance of the thing contracted for;

(4) a false and fundamental assumption going to the root of the contract, or impossibility of performance of the contract.

The first three are distinct types of situation; the fourth sets out more compendious tests for the doctrine generally.

(1) *Mistake about the existence of the subject-matter of the contract.* If the subject-matter of the contract is what is sometimes called a *res extincta*, that is, at the time of the contract, and unknown to the parties, it has ceased to exist, or if it has never been in existence, then the contract may be void for common mistake.

In a contract for the sale of specific goods, for example, the non-existence of the goods will produce a situation not contemplated by the contract and to which it cannot apply.[232] It is also enacted in section 6 of the Sale of Goods Act 1979[233] that, where there is a contract for the sale of specific goods, and the goods without the knowledge of the seller have perished at the time when the contract is made, the contract is void. As well as physical destruction, 'perishing' includes cases in which the goods are so damaged that they become for business purposes something other than the description under which they were sold.[234]

The leading case is *Couturier v Hastie*:[235]

A contract was made for the sale of a cargo of corn, which the parties believed was being shipped from Salonica to England. Before the date of sale the corn had, in fact, deteriorated and had been unloaded at Tunis and sold. The buyer contended that, since the cargo of corn was not in existence, he was not bound to pay the price. But the seller argued that, on the true construction of the contract, 'this was not a mere contract for the sale of an ascertained cargo, but that the purchaser bought the adventure, and took upon himself all risks from the shipment of the cargo'.

The House of Lords held that the purchaser was not liable to pay for the corn. The contract contemplated a sale of existing goods. Neither Coleridge J, who delivered the judgment of seven judges in the Exchequer Chamber,[236] nor Lord Chancellor Cranworth in the House of Lords, mentioned the word 'mistake': they considered the case purely as one of the construction of the contract. But they intimated that the contract would be void: 'it plainly imports that there was something which was to be sold at the time of the contract, and something to be purchased', whereas the object of the sale had ceased to exist.[237]

[232] *Bell v Lever Brothers Ltd* [1932] AC 161, 217.

[233] See *Barrow, Lane, and Ballard Ltd v Phillip Phillips & Co* [1929] 1 KB 574 (subject-matter of sale stolen prior to it). But cf s 55(1) of the Act which, it has been argued, enables contractual variation of this rule: Atiyah (1957) 73 LQR 340, 348–9; Twigg-Flesner and Ndolo, *Atiyah and Adams' Sale of Goods* (15th edn, 2026) 76–7.

[234] *Asfar & Co v Blundell* [1896] 1 QB 123; *Oilfields Asphalts v Grovedale Coolstores (1994) Ltd* [1998] 3 NZLR 479 (account taken of contemplated use or purpose for goods).

[235] (1856) 5 HLC 673. See also Atiyah (1957) 73 LQR 340.

[236] (1853) 9 Exch 102, reversing the Court of Exchequer at (1852) 8 Exch 40.

[237] (1856) 5 HLC 673, 681. Ibbetson, *A Historical Introduction to the Law of Obligations* (1999) 228 states that the 'reanalysis' of this decision was 'pivotal' to the rooting of mistake in English law.

Similarly, in *Strickland v Turner*,[238] S bought and paid for an annuity on the life of a man who was, unknown to both parties, already dead. He was able to recover the purchase money as the annuity had ceased to exist at the time of sale.

In these cases it is not difficult to see that the non-existence of the subject-matter of the contract gave rise to a total failure of consideration.[239] If a cargo does not exist, it cannot be delivered; if an annuity is purchased on the life of a dead person, the purchaser gets nothing for his money. It does not matter whether the contract is valid or void. In neither case can the seller claim to recover, or retain, the purchase money. The consideration for the contract has totally failed. It is only when the buyer brings an action for *damages* for non-delivery that the crucial question of the validity of the contract will arise. The mere fact that the subject-matter does not exist does not render the contract void: one party may have undertaken in the contract the risk of its existence.[240] So in *McRae v Commonwealth Disposals Commission*:[241]

The Commonwealth Disposals Commission invited tenders for the purchase of a wrecked vessel described as 'an oil tanker lying on Journaund Reef, which is approximately 100 miles North of Samarai' in New Guinea. M's tender was accepted, and he thereupon fitted out a salvage expedition at considerable expense. In fact there was no oil tanker in the locality indicated, nor was there even such a reef as Journaund Reef. M claimed damages against the Commission for the loss sustained by him in the expedition.

The Commission, whose conduct was described by the High Court of Australia as 'reckless and irresponsible', resisted the claim to damages on the ground that the contract was void *ab initio*. It relied on *Couturier v Hastie* for the proposition that common mistake as to the existence of the subject-matter of a contract nullifies consent and avoids the contract. The Court did not, however, accept this argument, considering that the question of the validity of the contract had never arisen in that case; it was merely concerned with the failure of the consideration. If it had arisen, the decision would have depended upon whether the contract was subject to an implied condition precedent that the cargo existed at the time of the contract. No such condition could, in any event, be implied in the case before the Court, for the Commission had clearly contracted that there was a tanker in the position specified, and they must be held liable for breach.

It has been argued that the reasoning of the High Court of Australia in *McRae's* case negatives the existence of any doctrine of common mistake; indeed, it is said that a contract concerning subject-matter which is non-existent is always valid and binding, unless a term can be implied to the contrary.[242] It is submitted, however, that this is not the case. The merit of the decision in *McRae v Commonwealth Disposals Commission* is that it shows that invalidity is not an invariable consequence of such a contract. The question is one of the construction of the agreement.

[238] (1852) 7 Exch 208. See also *Hitchcock v Giddings* (1817) 4 Price 135.

[239] Consideration refers here to *performance* of the contractual promise, and total failure of consideration on one side of the contract gives rise to recovery of money paid (or release from the duty to pay) on the other side: below, pp 607–9. On the terminology, see p 606, n 2.

[240] Above, p 305.

[241] (1951) 84 CLR 377, noted (1952) 15 MLR 229.

[242] Slade (1954) 70 LQR 385. See also Smith (1994) 110 LQR 400, 402.

When properly construed, the contract may indicate that the seller assumed responsibility for the non-existence of the subject-matter. This was so in *McRae's* case, where the seller was held to have guaranteed the existence of the tanker.[243] Alternatively the contract may indicate that the buyer took the risk that the subject-matter might not exist and undertook to pay in any event. This was the point at issue in *Couturier v Hastie*, where the House of Lords was called upon to decide whether or not the buyer had purchased merely the expectation that the cargo would arrive, and the securities (ie the shipping documents) against the contingency of its loss. There is therefore no absolute rule that a contract for the sale of a *res extincta* is necessarily void in English law. But if the true construction of the contract is that the parties entered into it on the footing that the subject-matter was in existence, and neither of them undertook in the contract the risk that this might not be so, then the contract is void for common mistake.[244]

(2) *Mistake about title to property*. Where a person agrees to purchase property which, unknown to both the buyer and the seller, is already owned by the buyer (sometimes called in the older cases *res sua*— 'his own thing'), the contract may be void.

In *Bell v Lever Brothers*, Lord Atkin said:[245]

> Corresponding to mistake as to the existence of the subject-matter is mistake as to title in cases where, unknown to the parties, the buyer is already the owner of that which the seller purports to sell to him. The parties intended to effectuate a transfer of ownership: such a transfer is impossible.

So the contract is void where A agrees to take from B a lease of land of which, contrary to the belief of both parties at the time of the contract, A is already tenant for life;[246] or where A agrees to take from B a life interest in property to which A is already entitled under the terms of a will of which neither party knew.[247]

But this principle must not be applied too widely. For example, a seller is normally taken to warrant title to the property sold;[248] even though the parties both contract under a mistaken belief as to the title of the seller, there is a valid contract, and the seller may be liable in damages. It is only where the buyer happens to purchase his own property, and where no warranty can be implied, that the contract is a nullity from the beginning. For both parties must necessarily have accepted in their minds as an essential and integral element of the subject-matter of the transaction that the seller was, and that the buyer was not, entitled to the property.[249]

[243] (1951) 84 CLR 377, 407. See also *Barr v Gibson* (1838) 3 M & W 390; *Tommey v Finextra* (1962) 106 SJ 1012.

[244] See also *The Great Peace* [2002] EWCA Civ 1407 at [77]–[80].

[245] [1932] AC 161, 218.

[246] *Cooper v Phibbs* (1867) LR 2 HL 149, a case in equity where the contract was rescinded for mistake; but see the views of Lord Atkin in *Bell v Lever Brothers* at 218, and Lord Thankerton at 236, on its validity at common law. Cf Matthews (1989) 105 LQR 599. Cf also *John Lobb SAS v John Lobb Ltd* [2022] EWHC 2306 (Ch) at [148]–[159] (distinguishing *Cooper v Phibbs*).

[247] *British Red Cross v Werry* [2017] EWHC 875 (Ch), [2017] WTLR 441 at [22]–[23]. It was assumed by both parties that B was entitled to the property under the rules governing the distribution of the deceased's supposed intestacy.

[248] For statutory implied terms relating to the seller's title in contracts of sale of goods, see above, pp 182, 189.

[249] [1932] AC 161, 235, 236 (Lord Thankerton).

(3) *Mistake about the quality or the substance of the thing contracted for*. This has proved to be one of the most contentious categories in the law of common mistake. In *Bell v Lever Brothers*, Lord Atkin said:[250]

Mistake as to quality . . . will not affect assent unless it is the mistake of both parties, and is as to the existence of some quality which makes the thing without the quality *essentially different* from the thing as it was believed to be.

In reliance on this statement, it has been suggested that while a mistake as to *quality* (or attributes) will not avoid the contract, a mistake as to *substance* (or essence) will.[251]

Some support may be gained from *Kennedy v Panama, New Zealand, and Australian Royal Mail Co Ltd*:[252]

K was induced to take shares in a further issue of capital by the defendant company by a statement in the prospectus that the new capital was required to carry out a contract recently entered into with the New Zealand government for the carriage of mails. The contract, which the company believed to be valid, had been made with an unauthorized agent of the New Zealand government and the government refused to ratify it. The shares fell greatly in value and K claimed to return the shares and recover back the purchase price.

The Court of Queen's Bench refused to allow K to do so. It held that the shares which he received were far from being of no value, and were not different in substance from those which the company had contracted to deliver. Blackburn J, delivering the judgment of the Court, referred to the Roman Digest of Civil Law[253] which distinguished substance and quality. He considered that the principle of English law was the same as that of Roman law,[254] and that 'the difficulty in every case is to determine whether the mistake or misapprehension is as to the substance of the whole consideration, going, as it were, to the root of the matter, or only to some point, even though a material point, an error as to which does not affect the substance of the whole consideration'.[255]

A mistake as to quality will not generally avoid the contract. We may give some examples, both actual and hypothetical:[256]

A agrees to buy from B a certain parcel of oats which both believe to be old oats. They are in fact new oats, and unsuitable for the purpose for which A wants them. There is a valid contract despite the mistake.[257]

[250] *Ibid*, 218 (emphasis added).

[251] Tylor (1948) 11 MLR 257.

[252] (1867) LR 2 QB 580 (a common law case), expressly approved throughout the opinions in *Bell v Lever Brothers Ltd*. Cf *Emmerson's Case* (1866) LR 1 Ch App 433 (company in liquidation).

[253] (1867) LR 2 QB 580, 588. Digest, 18.1.9, 10, 11.

[254] Cf Lawson (1936) 52 LQR 79.

[255] (1867) LR 2 QB 580, 588. In this case the mistake was induced by a misrepresentation in the prospectus, but there was no fraud and at common law there was no remedy for innocent misrepresentation: below, p 333.

[256] See also *Solle v Butcher* [1959] 1 KB 671 (mistake about whether structural alterations to flat rendered it a 'new' dwelling and therefore not subject to rent control), *Frederick E Rose (London) Ltd v William H Pim Junior & Co Ltd* [1953] 2 QB 450, above, p 288 (parties contracted to buy and sell 'horsebeans', in the belief that they were the same as 'feveroles', an entirely different sort of bean), and *Grist v Bailey* [1967] Ch 532 (mistake as to whether property to be sold was occupied by secure tenant) where the mistakes were said not to be sufficient to make the contract void at common law. However, these were decisions during the period when the Courts applied a wider test for common mistake in equity: below, p 315.

[257] Cf *Smith v Hughes* (1871) LR 6 QB 597 where, however, the mistake was unilateral: above, p 302.

C buys from D a picture which both believe to have been painted by Constable. Several years later, when C tries to sell the picture, he finds that it was not painted by Constable at all. The mistake does not avoid the contract.[258]

E agrees to buy from F '100 bales of Calcutta kapok, Sree brand'. The sale is by sample, but both parties believe that this particular brand of kapok is pure kapok, consisting of tree cotton, whereas it in fact contains an admixture of bush cotton and is a commercially inferior product. The contract is valid.[259]

G buys from H a car which both believe to be a 1948 model. It is actually a 1939 model, and worth very much less. There is no mistake at common law.[260]

It is evident that there is no clear rule that a mistake as to the substance of the thing contracted for will avoid the contract. The distinction between substance and quality is at best an arbitrary one, for there is no metaphysical 'substance' independent of qualities.[261] Moreover, 'the principle enunciated in *Bell v Lever Brothers Ltd* is markedly narrower in scope than the civilian doctrine' and 'it is therefore no longer useful to invoke the civilian distinction'.[262] However, where the mistake is as to 'an essential and integral element in the subject-matter of the bargain'[263] so that it renders the subject-matter 'essentially and radically different from the subject matter which the parties believed to exist'[264] the contract will be void. Accordingly, the following contracts of sale have been held to be void: of a quantity of Georgian table linen erroneously described in the particulars of sale as 'the authentic property' of Charles I and as bearing the arms of that unhappy monarch;[265] of a breeding cow which was mistakenly believed to be a sterile cow and sold by the pound for beef;[266] and of a plot of land, zoned as building land, for which, however, due to the absence of sewage facilities, it was impossible to obtain a building permit.[267]

(4) *A false and fundamental assumption; impossibility of performance of the contract.* A contract may be void where the parties contract under a false and fundamental assumption, going to the root of the contract, and which both parties must be taken

[258] *Leaf v International Galleries* [1950] 2 KB 86; below, p 340, n 118; *Bell v Lever Brothers Ltd* [1932] AC 161, 224.

[259] *Harrison & Jones Ltd v Bunten and Lancaster Ltd* [1953] 1 QB 646.

[260] *Oscar Chess Ltd v Williams* [1957] 1 WLR 370, 373 (Denning LJ); above, p 145.

[261] Glanville Williams (1945) 61 LQR 293. Cf Tylor (1948) 11 MLR 257.

[262] *Associated Japanese Bank (International) Ltd v Crédit du Nord SA* [1989] 1 WLR 255, 268 (Steyn J). The original Roman ('civilian') notion of mistake was developed in some modern continental civilian systems, and particularly in the French Civil Code, where it fits more naturally: above, p 272. For a significantly wider interpretation given to the notions of 'substance' and 'substantial qualities' in modern French Law, see Nicholas, *The French Law of Contract* (2nd edn, 1992) 85–90. Since 2016 the French Civil Code refers to the 'essential qualities': Rowan, *The New French Law of Contract* (2022) 87–91.

[263] *Bell v Lever Brothers Ltd* [1932] AC 161, 236 (Lord Thankerton).

[264] *Associated Japanese Bank (International) Ltd v Crédit du Nord SA* [1989] 1 WLR 255, 264 (Steyn J), approved in *The Great Peace* [2002] EWCA Civ 1407 at [91].

[265] *Nicholson and Venn v Smith Marriott* (1947) 177 LT 189 (the decision was however based on an implied condition as to description under Sale of Goods Act 1893 (now 1979), s 13).

[266] *Sherwood v Walker* 33 NW 919 (1887) (Michigan).

[267] *Alessio v Jovica* (1974) 42 DLR (3d) 242 (Canada). Cf *Amalgamated Investment & Property Co Ltd v John Walker & Sons Ltd* [1977] 1 WLR 164.

to have had in mind at the time they entered into it as the basis of their agreement; or where performance of the contract, as both parties understood it, is impossible. These categories are not separate and distinct from those categories of mistake already mentioned, but rather act as more general tests, which will cover cases of non-existence of the subject-matter, mistakes about title, and mistakes about quality or substance, but will also cover other situations. The test based on a 'fundamental assumption' received approval in *Bell v Lever Brothers Ltd*,[268] although some doubts were expressed as to its value owing to the necessary vagueness of its formulation. It was also referred to by the Court of Appeal in *The Great Peace*, drawing an analogy with similar ideas in the doctrine of frustration.[269] As we have seen, the Court of Appeal in that case suggested that the core of the doctrine of common mistake, like the doctrine of frustration, is that the contract—or the 'contractual adventure'—cannot be performed: a test of impossibility of performance, although this must be interpreted as not limited to physical impossibility but extending to commercial impossibility: the shared purpose of the contract cannot be fulfilled, through no fault of the either party and where neither party has undertaken the risk of non-performance.[270]

However, this test is still narrow, and will not easily be satisfied. It is certainly not sufficient for one party to establish that the mistake was about the effect or commercial consequences of the contract;[271] or that part of the purpose for which the contract was entered into cannot be fulfilled in circumstances where it is not sufficiently important so as to be fundamental to the performance of the contract as a whole;[272] or that, had the true facts been known, that party would never have entered into the bargain. Indeed, there may be assumptions regarded by one or both of the parties as, in some sense, 'fundamental'—for example, that a picture is the work of an old master, or that a flat is free from rent control. Yet the contract will still bind. As Lord Thankerton pointed out:[273]

> The phrase 'underlying assumption by the parties', as applied to the subject-matter of a contract . . . can only properly relate to something which both must have necessarily accepted in their minds as an essential and integral element of the subject-matter.

In *Bell v Lever Brothers Ltd* itself, this requirement was not fulfilled. On its true construction, the agreement to pay compensation applied notwithstanding the fact that the contract of service had been broken:

> The contract released is the identical contract in both cases, and the party paying for release gets exactly what he bargains for. It seems immaterial that he could have got the same result in another way, or that if he had known the true facts he would not have entered into the bargain.[274]

268 [1932] AC 161, 208, 225, 236; cf [1931] 1 KB 557, 564 (Wright J: 'the underlying assumption without which the parties would not have made the contract they did').

269 [2002] EWCA Civ 1407 at [73], [76], [82].

270 *Ibid* at [76]; above, p 306.

271 *Clarion Ltd v National Providential Institution* [2000] 1 WLR 1888, 1899.

272 *Triple Seven Msn 27251 Ltd v Azman Air Services Ltd* [2018] EWHC 1348 (Comm) at [89] (aircraft could not be used for intended purpose for first year of a five-year lease contract).

273 [1932] AC 161, 235.

274 *Ibid*, 223 (Lord Atkin). Cf *Horcal v Gatland* [1984] IRLR 288.

Nor was the test satisfied in *The Great Peace*: because of its distant position, the vessel was much less useful than both parties had expected. But it was not impossible still to use it for the salvage operation.[275]

It is not surprising that the strictness of the test for common mistake has resulted in a dearth of cases on the subject. In *Scott v Coulson*,[276] however, a contract for the assignment of a policy of life insurance was made upon the basis of an erroneous belief, shared by both parties, that the assured was still alive. It was held that the vendor was entitled to the return of the policy and also the moneys payable under it. Similarly the following have been held to be void: a separation deed entered into by a husband and wife on the erroneous assumption that their marriage was valid;[277] a contract for the hire of rooms to watch a coronation procession made in ignorance that the procession had already been cancelled;[278] a contractual licence to cut and manufacture all sisal grown on a particular estate, in return for payment and the delivery of a monthly quantity of sisal which the estate was not in fact capable of producing;[279] and an agreement as to the amount due under two contracts of sale entered into in the erroneous belief that the results in the two certificates of analysis had been transposed.[280]

(ii) Common mistake in equity

The effect of a mistake at common law, if it operates at all, is to render the contract void *ab initio*; but there are circumstances in which equity may be prepared to grant relief where the common law refuses to intervene. For example, we have seen that although a written contract may be valid at common law, equity may grant rectification of the written document, or may refuse to grant specific performance of a contract that is binding at law.[281] In Chapter 9 we shall see that, although the common law allowed rescission of a contract for misrepresentation only in the case of fraud, in equity an innocent misrepresentation sufficed to render the contract voidable. The question here is whether equity will allow rescission of a contract on the basis of common mistake where the mistake is not sufficient to render the contract void under the principles set out in *Bell v Lever Brothers Ltd*[282] and the other cases discussed in the previous section.

275 [2002] EWCA Civ 1407 at [165].

276 [1903] 2 Ch 249.

277 *Galloway v Galloway* (1914) 30 TLR 531.

278 *Griffith v Brymer* (1903) 19 TLR 434, discussed in *The Great Peace* [2002] EWCA Civ 1407 at [67]. Cf *Krell v Henry* [1903] 2 KB 740 (frustration of purpose), below, p 484.

279 *Sheikh Brothers Ltd v Ochsner* [1957] AC 136 (Privy Council, on appeal from Kenya under Indian Contract Act 1872, s 20 which provided: 'Where both the parties to an agreement are under a mistake as to a matter of fact essential to the agreement, the agreement is void'). See also *Clifford v Watts* (1870) LR 5 CP 577; *Associated Japanese Bank (International) Ltd v Crédit du Nord SA* [1989] 1 WLR 255, 269, above, p 305 (guarantee of machine lease agreement said to be void because machines did not exist); cf *Marquis of Bute v Thompson* (1844) 13 M & W 487; *Jefferys v Fairs* (1876) 4 Ch D 448.

280 *Grains & Fourrages SA v Huyton* [1997] 1 Lloyd's Rep 628.

281 Above, pp 284, 290. The equitable remedies in respect of contracts are only one aspect of a much wider equitable jurisdiction to relieve from the consequences of mistake, a jurisdiction which extends to gifts and is less concerned with the nature of the mistake: eg mistake of law was not a bar in equity even before the general recognition of remedies for mistakes of law (above, p 301): *Gibbon v Mitchell* [1990] 1 WLR 1304, 1309.

282 [1932] AC 161; above, p 303.

In *Solle v Butcher*[283] Denning LJ set out an equitable doctrine of common mistake which expanded the range of circumstances in which the Court, in its discretion, could set aside a contract—a doctrine which over a period of 50 years came to be regarded as good law and 'on occasion the passport to a just result'.[284] However, this equitable doctrine was emphatically rejected by the Court of Appeal in *The Great Peace*.[285]

(a) The Equitable Doctrine Set Out in Solle v Butcher. Cases can certainly be found in which the Courts, exercising their equitable jurisdiction, set aside contracts or other instruments on the basis of common mistake,[286] although it is not clear that the mistake would have been insufficient to satisfy the common law test for common mistake.[287] In *Solle v Butcher*,[288] however, such cases were used by Denning LJ as the basis of a new and general doctrine of mistake in equity. He based his doctrine on the proposition that the Court 'had power to set aside the contract whenever it was of opinion that it was unconscientious for the other party to avail himself of the legal advantage which he had obtained',[289] and stated the principle as follows:

> A contract is ... liable in equity to be set aside if the parties were under a common misapprehension either as to facts or as to their relative and respective rights, provided that the misapprehension was fundamental, and that the party seeking to set it aside was not himself at fault.

Denning LJ stated that the Court would grant relief if the mistake was *fundamental*, and the party seeking rescission was *not at fault*. Despite this requirement of 'fundamentality', the cases which applied Denning LJ's principle showed that that the category of operative common mistake was broader in equity than at common law,[290] and there was little guidance on how to apply the requirement that the claimant be not 'at fault'.[291] The approach of the Courts was also open to the criticism that insufficient attention was paid to the question of contractual allocation of risk.[292] As in the case of

[283] [1950] 1 KB 671.

[284] *West Sussex Properties Ltd v Chichester DC* [2000] NPC 74 at [42] (Sir Christopher Staughton).

[285] [2002] EWCA Civ 1407; below, p 316.

[286] eg *Cooper v Phibbs* (1867) LR 2 HL 149, above, p 310 (lease); *Huddersfield Banking Co Ltd v Henry Lister & Son Ltd* [1895] 2 Ch 273 (consent order).

[287] See *Bell v Lever Brothers Ltd* [1932] AC 161, 218 (Lord Atkin: contract in *Cooper v Phibbs* was void); *Huddersfield Banking Co Ltd v Henry Lister & Son Ltd* [1895] 2 Ch 273, 280–1 (Lindley LJ, discussing common law cases with cases decided in equity).

[288] [1950] 1 KB 671. For criticism, see Goodhart (1950) 66 LQR 169; Slade (1954) 70 LQR 385, 407; Atiyah and Bennion (1961) 24 MLR 421, 440–1; Cartwright (1987) 103 LQR 594.

[289] *Torrance v Bolton* (1872) LR 8 Ch App 118, 124, (James LJ), above, p 291.

[290] *Solle v Butcher* [1950] 1 KB 671; *Grist v Bailey* [1967] Ch 532, 541 (mistake as to value of subject-matter); *Magee v Pennine Insurance Co Ltd* [1969] 2 QB 507 (Winn LJ dissenting on the ground that the case was indistinguishable from *Bell v Lever Brothers Ltd*).

[291] *Solle v Butcher* [1950] 1 KB 671, 684, 694; *Grist v Bailey* [1967] Ch 532, 542; *Laurence v Lexcourt Holdings Ltd* [1978] 1 WLR 1128, 1137–8.

[292] *William Sindall plc v Cambridgeshire CC* [1994] 1 WLR 1016, 1035, criticizing the decisions in *Grist v Bailey* [1967] Ch 532 and *Laurence v Lexcourt Holdings Ltd* [1978] 1 WLR 1128. See also *Associated Japanese Bank (International) Ltd v Crédit du Nord SA* [1989] 1 WLR 255, 268.

common law,[293] an express or implied allocation of a particular risk should generally preclude rescission of the contract for mistake.

Two further points should be noted about the doctrine of mistake in equity, as stated by Denning LJ, which made it more attractive than the narrower, common law doctrine. First, the remedy was said to be at the discretion of the Court, and the discretion extended to the imposition of terms for the setting aside of the contract.[294] Secondly, in equity the contract was voidable, rather than void, as a result of the mistake. This not only gave a more nuanced remedy, allowing the mistaken parties to affirm the contract, and allowing the Court to exercise more control over the remedy, but it would also protect third parties since, as we have seen in other contexts, a voidable contract cannot be rescinded if it would prejudice an innocent third party such as the purchaser of property delivered pursuant to the contract.[295]

(b) Rejection of the Equitable Doctrine by The Great Peace. In *The Great Peace*[296] the Court of Appeal roundly rejected Denning LJ's approach and held that *Solle v Butcher* was not good law,[297] on the basis that it was contrary to the binding authority of *Bell v Lever Brothers Ltd*,[298] and was contrary to principle.

We have seen[299] that the Court explained the common law doctrine of mistake, for which *Bell v Lever Brothers Ltd* is the principal authority; but that it also emphasized that mistake was a narrow doctrine, designed for only exceptional cases. As Lord Atkin said in *Bell v Lever Brothers*:[300]

> it is of paramount importance that contracts should be observed, and that if parties honestly comply with the essentials of the formation of contracts—ie, agree in the same terms on the same subject-matter—they are bound, and must rely on the stipulations of the contract for protection from the effect of facts unknown to them . . . Nothing is more dangerous than to allow oneself liberty to construct for the parties contracts which they have not in terms made by importing implications which would appear to make the contract more businesslike or more just.

293 Above, p 310.

294 *Solle v Butcher* [1950] 1 KB 671, 695–6; *Grist v Bailey* [1967] Ch 532, 543. See also *Cooper v Phibbs* (1867) LR 2 HL 149; *Bingham v Bingham* (1748) 1 Ves Sen 126; *Earl Beauchamp v Winn* (1873) LR 6 HL 223.

295 Cf above, pp 293, 300 (mistake of identity).

296 [2002] EWCA Civ 1407; above, p 306.

297 The Court of Appeal held that it had power to depart from its own previous decision: *ibid* at [160], although this has been doubted: Midwinter (2003) 119 LQR 180; Sheehan [2003] RLR 26, 33. However, cases have assumed that *The Great Peace* is authoritative; see, eg, *Islington LBC v Uckac* [2006] EWCA Civ 340, [2006] 1 WLR 1303 at [20]–[21]; *Smithson v Hamilton* [2007] EWHC 2900 (Ch), [2008] 1 WLR 1453 at [118]; *Statoil ASA v Louis Dreyfus Energy Services LP* [2008] EWHC 2257 (Comm) at [105]; *Qayyum v Hameed* [2009] EWCA Civ 352, [2009] 3 FCR 545 at [37]; *Van der Merwe v Goldman* [2016] EWHC 790 (Ch) at [25]. See also *Pitt v Holt* [2013] UKSC 26 at [115]; cf *Test Claimants in the FII Group Litigation v Revenue and Customs Commissioners* [2020] UKSC 47, [2022] AC 1 at [109].

298 [1932] AC 161, above, p 303.

299 Above, pp 306–7.

300 [1932] AC 161, 224, 226, quoted in *The Great Peace* [2002] EWCA Civ 1407, [2003] QB 679 at [48]. See also *Associated Japanese Bank (International) Ltd v Crédit du Nord SA* [1989] 1 WLR 255, 268 (Steyn J: 'The first imperative must be that the law ought to uphold rather than destroy apparent contracts'), approved in *The Great Peace* at [90]–[91].

Before *Solle v Butcher*, there was no evidence in the case law of an equitable jurisdiction to rescind a contract for a common mistake which would not render the contract void under the common law test: Lord Atkin's narrow test for mistake in *Bell v Lever Brothers Ltd* reflected also the circumstances where equity had intervened.[301] The Court of Appeal considered that the test proposed by Denning LJ in *Solle v Butcher* was not only uncertain in its scope and placed too much power into the hands of the Court to exercise its discretion,[302] but also, by allowing a broader test for mistake, had undermined the policy of the common law in setting narrow limits for the doctrine of mistake:[303]

> [T]he premise of equity's intrusion into the effects of the common law is that the common law rule in question is seen in the particular case to work injustice, and for some reason the common law cannot cure itself. But it is difficult to see how that can apply here. Cases of fraud and misrepresentation, and undue influence, are all catered for under other existing and uncontentious equitable rules. We are *only* concerned with the question whether relief might be given for common mistake in circumstances wider than those stipulated in *Bell v Lever Bros Ltd*. But that, surely, is a question as to where the common law should draw the line; not whether, given the common law rule, it needs to be mitigated by application of some other doctrine. The common law has drawn the line in *Bell v Lever Bros Ltd*. The effect of *Solle v Butcher* is not to supplement or mitigate the common law: it is to say that *Bell v Lever Bros Ltd* was wrongly decided.

(c) Critique. The decision of the Court of Appeal in *The Great Peace* was emphatic and uncompromising: there is no place in the law of contract for a broader doctrine of common mistake in equity than the limited common law doctrine; and there is no place for a judicial discretion in remedying mistake because it would undermine the security of contracts. However, it is not obvious that the equitable jurisdiction set out in *Solle v Butcher* would in any event have been exercised in *The Great Peace* to rescind the contract, since the defendants' mistake about the location of the vessel, even though they then shared it with the claimants, surely fell firmly within the scope of risk borne by the defendants under the contract for the hire of the vessel. That risk allocation would be respected not only by the common law, as made clear by the Court in *The Great Peace*, but could also equally be protected by an appropriate application of the equitable test.[304] The Court of Appeal, following the lead of Toulson J at first instance, appeared to be using the case as a vehicle to review this difficult area of jurisprudence.[305]

One ought, however, to reflect on what has been lost by the rejection of the equitable doctrine of common mistake.[306] Other jurisdictions in the common law world have

[301] *The Great Peace* [2002] EWCA Civ 1407 at [118].

[302] *Ibid* at [131], [154] (uncertainty over meaning of 'fundamental' in equity compared with common law test); [138] (application depends on consideration of what is 'fair'). For the strongest criticism, see Toulson J at first instance in *The Great Peace* [2001] All ER (D) 152 (Nov) at [120]: 'Bluntly, the difficulty about this form of the doctrine [ie giving the Court a discretion to decide whether to rescind the contract] is that it puts palm tree justice in place of party autonomy.'

[303] [2002] EWCA Civ 1407 at [156].

[304] Reynolds (2003) 119 LQR 177, 178–9.

[305] Cf *The Great Peace* [2002] EWCA Civ 1407 at [2].

[306] Tettenborn (2011) 27 JCL 91.

adopted it and have applied the approach set out by Denning LJ in *Solle v Butcher*, and some may well be much more reluctant than the English Court of Appeal to wind back the clock in order to restore the law on mistake as it stood before this infusion of equity.[307] The advantages which it appears that Denning LJ sought through the development of his doctrine in *Solle v Butcher* were that a contract would be voidable for mistake (rather than void), thereby protecting the rights of innocent third parties to property delivered pursuant to the contract; and that the Court would have greater control over the remedy, both as to whether rescission should be granted at all, and also as to whether it should be granted only on terms set by the Court. Furthermore, the scope of actionable mistakes in equity could be less restricted than under the common law doctrine. This doctrine therefore moved the Courts closer towards exercising a power over the terms of the contract, particularly in cases where the effect of the mistake was to impose hardship on one of the parties. This was one of the objections raised by the Court of Appeal in *The Great Peace*:[308]

> A common factor in *Solle v Butcher* and the cases which have followed it can be identified. The effect of the mistake has been to make the contract a particularly bad bargain for one of the parties. Is there a principle of equity which justifies the court in rescinding a contract where a common mistake has produced this result?

However, even that Court recognized that there might have been some merit in Denning LJ's endeavour, but considered that any intervention should be by statute, rather than by the common law:[309]

> We can understand why the decision in *Bell v Lever Bros Ltd* did not find favour with Lord Denning MR. An equitable jurisdiction to grant rescission on terms where a common fundamental mistake has induced a contract gives greater flexibility than a doctrine of common law which holds the contract void in such circumstances. Just as the Law Reform (Frustrated Contracts) Act 1943 was needed to temper the effect of the common law doctrine of frustration, so there is scope for legislation to give greater flexibility to our law of mistake than the common law allows.

Relatively few cases were decided in England on the basis of the equitable doctrine of *Solle v Butcher* during the 50 years when it was treated as good authority.[310] There are also relatively few reported cases based on the common law doctrine of common

[307] See, eg, *Chwee Kin Keong v Digilandmall.com Pte Ltd* [2005] 1 SLR 502 at [56] ff, especially at [77] (Singapore: mistake about the terms, but rejecting narrow *Great Peace* approach generally: 'Equity is dynamic. A great attribute, thus an advantage, of equity, is its flexibility to achieve the ends of justice'); *Miller Paving Ltd v B Gottardo Construction Ltd* (2007) 285 DLR (4th) 568 at [26] (Gouge JA in CA Ontario: '*Great Peace* appears not yet to have been adopted in Canada and, in my view, there is good reason for not doing so. The loss of the flexibility needed to correct unjust results in widely diverse circumstances that would come from eliminating the equitable doctrine of common mistake would, I think, be a step backward'); cf *Australia Estates Pty Ltd v Cairns CC* [2005] QCA 328 at [52] (Atkinson J: *Great Peace* should be followed in Queensland in preference to *Solle v Butcher*), although differing views have been expressed amongst the Courts of the States and Territories within Australia.

[308] [2002] EWCA Civ 1407 at [155].

[309] *Ibid* at [161]. For a similar preference of the Courts to rely on statute to deal with exclusion clauses and other unfair terms, see *National Westminster Bank plc v Morgan* [1985] AC 686, 708; below, pp 379, 411–2.

[310] *The Great Peace* [2002] EWCA Civ 1407 at [153].

mistake of fact or law. No doubt this is in part because of the expressly limited scope of the common law doctrine. But it may also be because, although there are many cases involving common mistakes where one of the parties seeks to avoid the contract, they result from misrepresentations made by the other party to the contract. An innocent misrepresentation of fact or law gives rise to a common mistake, since the first party shares the incorrect information with the other, and therefore makes the mistake common. As long as the remedies for misrepresentation are sufficient for the case, the claimant will in practice base the claim not on mistake, but on the defendant's misrepresentation. It is to the remedies available for misrepresentation that we now turn.

FURTHER READING

GOODHART, 'Mistake as to Identity in the Law of Contract' (1941) 57 LQR 228

SLADE, 'The Myth of Mistake in the English Law of Contract' (1954) 70 LQR 385

ATIYAH and BENNION, 'Mistake in the Construction of Contracts' (1961) 24 MLR 412

ATIYAH, 'Judicial Techniques and Contract Law' in *Essays on Contract* (Oxford: Clarendon Press, 1986) 244

CARTWRIGHT, '*Solle v Butcher* and the Doctrine of Mistake in Contract' (1987) 103 LQR 594

SMITH, 'Contracts—Mistake, Frustration and Implied Terms' (1994) 110 LQR 400

MACMILLAN, 'How Temptation Led to Mistake: an Explanation of *Bell v Lever Bros Ltd*' (2003) 119 LQR 625

HARE, 'Identity Mistakes: A Missed Opportunity?' (2004) 67 MLR 993

MACMILLAN, 'Rogues, Swindlers and Cheats: The Development of Mistake of Identity in English Contract Law' [2005] CLJ 711

BURROWS, 'Construction and Rectification' in BURROWS and PEEL (eds), *Contract Terms* (Oxford: Oxford University Press, 2007) 77

STEVENS, 'Objectivity, Mistake and the Parol Evidence Rule' in BURROWS and PEEL (eds), *Contract Terms* (Oxford: Oxford University Press, 2007) 101

MCLAUCHLAN, 'The "Drastic" Remedy of Rectification for Unilateral Mistake' (2008) 124 LQR 608

TETTENBORN, 'Agreements, Common Mistake and the Purpose of Contract' (2011) 27 JCL 91

DAVIES, 'Rectifying the Course of Rectification' (2012) 75 MLR 412

DAVIES, 'Rectification versus Interpretation: the Nature and Scope of the Equitable Jurisdiction' [2016] CLJ 62

MORGAN, 'Common Mistake in Contract: Rare Success and Common Misapprehensions' [2018] CLJ 559

STEVENS, 'What is an Agreement?' (2020) 136 LQR 599

CARTWRIGHT, 'Remedies for Defects in the Formation of a Contract: Learning by Comparing' in Cappelletti, Kennefick, and Leczykiewicz, *Comparative Reflections in Private Law* (Oxford: Oxford University Press, 2026) 66

9

MISREPRESENTATION AND NON-DISCLOSURE

1. INTRODUCTION

This chapter is concerned with relief for misrepresentation and for the exceptional cases in which there may be relief for non-disclosure.[1] Although there is some overlap between these two vitiating factors in cases in which there has been partial disclosure, the rationale for the intervention of the law where a false or misleading statement is made is fundamentally different from that for imposing a duty upon a party to disclose to the other party information about the subject-matter of the proposed contract.

The general rule of the common law is that a person contemplating entering a contract with another is under no duty to disclose information to that other. 'Ordinarily the failure to disclose a material fact which might influence the mind of a prudent contractor does not give the right to avoid the contract.'[2] The parties must look after their own interests and ensure that they acquire the information necessary to avoid a bad bargain. We saw in Chapter 8 that the law is reluctant to allow parties to avoid contracts on the basis of their own mistakes about the facts relating to the subject-matter of the contract or its surrounding circumstances, and the reluctance to impose duties of disclosure is in tune with this. Thus, a person who visits an antiques shop and sees a rare George II table being sold as a nineteenth-century piece need say nothing to the seller before buying it. The seller's mistake does not affect the validity of the contract, and the fact that the buyer realizes that the seller has made a mistake does not impose a duty upon the buyer to disclose information to correct the mistake. Nor does an oil prospector who discovers that there is oil under a given piece of land have to inform the landowner. There are, however, exceptions to the general rule, both at common law and by statute, which impose duties to disclose and where failure to do so makes the contract voidable or may give rise to other remedies.

A misleading statement made during the negotiations leading to a contract—a misrepresentation—is, however, viewed quite differently. The party making the

[1] See Cartwright, *Misrepresentation, Mistake and Non-Disclosure* (7th edn, 2025) Parts 1 and 3; Handley, *Spencer Bower and Handley on Actionable Misrepresentation* (5th edn, 2014); Spencer Bower, Turner, and Sutton, *Actionable Non-Disclosure* (2nd edn, 1990).

[2] *Bell v Lever Bros Ltd* [1932] AC 161, 227 (Lord Atkin).

misrepresentation has induced the other party to enter into the contract on the basis of false information, and this displaces the normal rule that each party takes responsibility for acquiring information relevant to the bargain. The effect of a misrepresentation, subject to certain limitations, is to render the agreement voidable by the misled party. A person who has been induced to enter into a contract by a misrepresentation can refuse to carry out the contract, resist a claim for specific performance, and, if necessary, have the contract set aside by means of the remedy of *rescission*. In addition, the misled party will sometimes be entitled to claim *tortious damages* in respect of loss sustained by reason of the misrepresentation. If the misrepresentation was made fraudulently, damages in the tort of deceit can be recovered. If it was made without reasonable care being taken to ascertain its truth, the misled party may recover damages by virtue of statute, or at common law in the tort of negligence. Where the party making the misrepresentation believed, and had reasonable ground to believe, that the facts represented were true, although the contract is still voidable at the suit of the misled party, tortious damages cannot be claimed but damages may sometimes be awarded in lieu of rescission.

The facts which give rise to a remedy for misrepresentation may also give rise to other remedies. Where the misrepresentation has been incorporated as a term of the contract, the misled party may, instead of relying on the misrepresentation to obtain a remedy, choose to rely on the breach of contract and claim *damages*, or sometimes *discharge of the contract*, *for breach*. The circumstances in which a misrepresentation will be so incorporated were dealt with in Chapter 5.[3] Sometimes a misrepresentation made by a trader which induces a consumer to enter into a contract will also constitute a 'prohibited practice' under Part 4 of the Digital Markets, Competition and Consumers Act 2024, which gives the consumer 'rights of redress' under Regulations to be made under the Act:[4] to 'unwind' the contract, or to a discount or damages.

2. MISREPRESENTATION

(a) PUFFS, REPRESENTATIONS, AND TERMS

A misleading statement made during the negotiations leading to a contract may fall into one of three categories. First, it may be a mere 'puff', a commendatory expression which by virtue of its vagueness or extravagance would not be expected to and does not ground any form of liability. Secondly, the preliminary statement may be intended by neither party to have contractual effect, but nevertheless may affect the inclination of one party to enter into the contract. It is then known as a 'representation'. If it proves false, the misled party will not be entitled to claim damages for breach of contract, because no contractual stipulation has been broken, but will be entitled to claim the relief accorded by the law

[3] See above, pp 143–6.

[4] Replacing the Consumer Protection from Unfair Trading Regulations 2008. The 2008 Regulations continue to apply until new replacement Regulations are made: see below, p 358.

for misrepresentation. Thirdly, the preliminary statement may be a term of the contract, or constitute a warranty collateral to the contract, if the party making the statement undertakes or guarantees that it is true.[5] There is an overlap between the second and third categories because a statement that is a misrepresentation may also become a term of the contract. In such cases there will be a choice of remedy: the misled party will be entitled to claim relief either for misrepresentation or for breach of contract.

(b) REQUIREMENTS FOR RELIEF FOR MISREPRESENTATION

An operative misrepresentation consists in a false statement of existing or past fact or law made by one party (the 'representor') before[6] or at the time of making the contract, which is addressed to the other party (the 'representee') and which induces the other party to enter into the contract.

(i) There must be a false representation

Mere silence does not constitute a misrepresentation.[7] Some positive statement, or some conduct from which a statement can be implied, is required for there to be an operative misrepresentation. In relation to implied representations, the Court of Appeal has said that it is helpful to consider whether a reasonable representee would naturally assume that the true state of facts did not exist and that, if it did, he would necessarily have been informed of it, but this is not to water down the requirement that there must be clear words or clear conduct of the representor from which the relevant representation can be implied.[8] As to conduct, 'a nod or a wink, or a shake of the head, or a smile' may suffice,[9] as may a photograph.[10] The participation by the Spice Girls in the making of a commercial to be shown in the future was held to constitute a representation by conduct that none of the group had an existing declared intention to leave the group before it was shown.[11] And the use of a credit card or cheque implies that such use is authorized by the credit card company or bank and that the state of facts existing when a cheque is handed over is that it will be honoured when presented.[12]

In assessing whether a complex pre-contractual document contains a misrepresentation, it has been suggested that it is preferable to look at the matter broadly and to assess whether overall the statements in the document are substantially

[5] See above, pp 143–8.

[6] *Cramaso LLP v Ogilvie-Grant* [2014] UKSC 9, [2014] AC 1093 at [16], [57].

[7] *Keates v Lord Cadogan* (1851) 10 CB 591.

[8] *Property Alliance Group Ltd v Royal Bank of Scotland plc* [2018] EWCA Civ 355, [2018] 1 WLR 3529 at [132].

[9] *Walters v Morgan* (1861) 3 De GF & J 718, 724 (Lord Campbell). See also *R v Charles* [1977] AC 177; *R v Lambie* [1982] AC 449 (on the meaning of 'deception' in the criminal law).

[10] *Atlantic Estates plc v Ezekiel* [1991] 2 EGLR 202.

[11] *Spice Girls Ltd v Aprilia World Service BV* [2000] EMLR 478, aff'd on this point [2002] EWCA Civ 15, [2002] EMLR 27.

[12] *R v Charles* [1977] AC 177; *R v Gilmartin* [1983] QB 953 (criminal offence of deception).

correct rather than to focus 'more and more microscopically so as to concentrate on each sentence, phrase or word'.[13]

(ii) Partial non-disclosure and active concealment

A partial non-disclosure may constitute a misrepresentation. Suppression of material facts can make what is stated false, as where a seller of land told a purchaser that the land had recently been occupied at a particular rent (which was true) but omitted to inform him that more recently he had failed to find a new tenant except at a lower rent, which created the false impression that the land still had the higher value.[14]

A person may also make a misrepresentation by doing some positive act in order to conceal defects in the subject-matter of the contract, as where a landlord's agents covered up dry rot in a flat.[15]

(iii) Change in facts

To constitute a *mis*representation, the representation must be false. For the purposes of the various remedies for pre-contractual misrepresentation this means that it must be false at the time when the representee enters into the contract in reliance upon it. If the representor makes a representation which is true at the time it is made, but which subsequently becomes false, it constitutes a misrepresentation at least where the representor knows about the change of facts which render it false.[16] In such cases the Courts either treat it as a continuing representation (which is therefore a misrepresentation at the critical time, when the contract is entered into) or state that the representor is bound to disclose the change in circumstances to the other party.[17]

(iv) Representations of opinion normally insufficient

A mere expression of opinion, which turns out to be unfounded, will not invalidate a contract. There is a wide difference between the seller of property saying that it is worth so much, and a statement that the seller gave so much for it. The first is an opinion

[13] *Avon Insurance plc v Swire Fraser Ltd* [2000] 1 All ER (Comm) 573, 632 (Rix J).

[14] *Dimmock v Hallett* (1866) LR 2 Ch App 21. See also *Nottingham Patent Brick and Tile Co v Butler* (1886) 16 QBD 778; *South Western General Property Co v Marton* [1982] 263 EG 1090.

[15] *Gordon v Selico Co Ltd* [1985] 2 EGLR 79, 83. See also *Cottee v Douglas Seaton (Used Cars) Ltd* [1972] 1 WLR 1408, 1417 (plastic filler to cover up rust in car).

[16] Cf Bigwood [2005] CLJ 94 (arguing that unknown change of facts is not tantamount to innocent misrepresentation because 'misrepresentation' is an agency-responsible act).

[17] *Davies v London & Provincial Marine Insurance Co* (1878) 8 Ch D 469, 475 (duty to disclose known change of facts); *With v O'Flanagan* [1936] Ch 575, 582–4 (duty to disclose or continuing representation); *Dietz v Lennig Chemicals Ltd* [1969] 1 AC 170 (innocent misrepresentation on basis of changed facts); *Traill v Baring* (1864) 4 De GJ & S 318 (duty to communicate change of intention); cf *Wales v Wadham* [1977] 1 WLR 199 (where *Traill v Baring* was not cited); *Cramaso LLP v Ogilvie-Grant* [2014] UKSC 9 at [22] (continuing effect of pre-contractual representation). See also Misrepresentation Act 1967, s 2(1) (representor liable 'unless he proves that he had reasonable ground to believe and did believe *up to the time the contract was made* that the facts represented were true').

which the buyer may or may not choose to adopt; the second is an assertion of fact which, if false to the knowledge of the seller, is also a fraudulent misrepresentation.[18] Thus in *Bisset v Wilkinson*:[19]

W agreed to purchase from B certain land in New Zealand, for the purpose of sheep-farming, in reliance on B's statement that his 'idea was that [the land] would carry two thousand sheep'. W was aware that neither B nor another person had at any time carried out sheep-farming on the land in question. When B claimed the balance of the purchase price, W counter-claimed rescission of the contract on the ground of misrepresentation.

The Judicial Committee of the Privy Council held that the statement was merely of an opinion which B honestly held. Accordingly, the claim for rescission failed. Again, *Economides v Commercial Union Assurance Co plc*[20] held that a statement that the cost of replacing the contents of a flat was £16,000, made to an insurance company by a 21-year-old student with no special knowledge, was a statement of opinion. It should not be assumed, however, that what appears to be simply a statement of opinion can never constitute a representation of fact. In one sense it always does so, for it asserts that the opinion is actually held. A statement of opinion which is not in fact held is a fraudulent misrepresentation. Also an opinion will usually be based upon facts; so the person making the representation may impliedly state that facts are known which justify that opinion. This is especially the case where the situation is such that the representor must know the facts much better than the other party. Where the representor had no reasonable grounds for that opinion, or failed to investigate the facts which gave rise to it, there may well be an actionable misrepresentation. For example, in *Smith v Land and House Property Corporation*:[21]

L bought a hotel as an investment at auction from S, who had stated in the auction particulars that it was let to 'a most desirable tenant'. However, the tenant was in significant financial difficulty and had paid his last quarter's rent only 'by driblets under pressure'. S claimed specific performance of the contract, and L counter-claimed for rescission.

It was held that the statement about the tenant was a misrepresentation and L's claim to rescind the contract succeeded. The statement amounted at least to an assertion that nothing had occurred in the relations between the landlords and the tenant which could be considered to make the tenant an unsatisfactory one.

(v) Mere commendatory 'puffs' insufficient

Commendatory expressions, such as advertisements to the effect that a certain brand of beer 'refreshes the parts that other beers cannot reach', or that a perfume

[18] Cf *Lindsay Petroleum Co v Hurd* (1874) LR 5 PC 221, 243–4.

[19] [1927] AC 177. See also *Anderson v Pacific Fire and Marine Insurance Co* (1872) LR 7 CP 65.

[20] [1998] QB 587 (discussing Marine Insurance Act 1906, s 20(3), (4), (5), now repealed and superseded by Consumer Insurance (Disclosure and Representations) Act 2012 and Insurance Act 2015).

[21] (1884) 28 Ch D 7. See also *Brown v Raphael* [1958] Ch 636; *Sirius International Insurance Corp v Oriental Insurance Corp* [1999] 1 All ER (Comm) 699.

will irresistibly attract members of the opposite sex, are not treated in law as representations of fact. Similar latitude is allowed to a seller who wants to gain a purchaser, although the borderline of permissible assertion is not always easily discernible. At an auction sale, land stated to be 'fertile and improvable' was in fact partly abandoned and useless. This was held to be 'a mere flourishing description by an auctioneer'.[22] But, as we have seen, the statement in auction particulars that the property was let to 'a most desirable tenant', was not a mere commendatory puff but a representation.[23]

(vi) Expression of intention or prediction normally insufficient

An expression of the speaker's intention, a promise, and a prediction about the future are not normally misrepresentations. They cannot be regarded as true or false at the time when made, except insofar as a person may misrepresent the state of his or her own mind or power to bring an event to pass.[24] Thus there is a distinction between a promise which the promisor intends to perform and one which the promisor intends to break or knows cannot be performed. In the first case the representation is truly one of an intention that something shall take place in future, and is binding only if it fulfils the requirements of a contractual promise. In the second case there is a misrepresentation of the representor's existing intention: not only is a promise made which is ultimately broken, but when it is made, the representor's ability to perform or state of mind is represented to be something other than it really is. Such a misrepresentation is one of fact. Bowen LJ said:[25]

> the state of a man's mind is as much a fact as the state of his digestion. It is true that it is very difficult to prove what the state of a man's mind at a particular time is, but if it can be ascertained it is as much a fact as anything else. A misrepresentation as to the state of a man's mind is, therefore, a misstatement of fact.

Thus it has been held that a person makes a fraudulent misrepresentation where he buys goods having at the time no means to pay or having formed an intention not to pay for them.[26] There may also be a misrepresentation of fact behind a negligent misprediction. Thus a prediction by a bank manager that the granting of a loan facility would be a formality once supported by insurance from the Export Credit Guarantee Department has been held to contain a statement of fact as to the existing policy of the bank.[27]

22 *Dimmock v Hallett* (1866) LR 2 Ch App 21, 27. See also *Lambert v Lewis* [1982] AC 225, 262–3.

23 *Smith v Land and House Property Corp* (1884) 28 Ch D 7.

24 *R v Sunair Holidays Ltd* [1973] 1 WLR 1105, 1109; *British Airways Board v Taylor* [1976] 1 WLR 13, 17, 21, 23, 27. See also *R v Gilmartin* [1983] QB 953.

25 *Edgington v Fitzmaurice* (1885) 29 Ch D 459, 483. See also *Goff v Gauthier* (1991) 62 P & CR 388.

26 *Ex p Whittaker* (1875) LR 10 Ch App 446; *DPP v Ray* [1974] AC 370. On cheques and credit cards, see above, n 12.

27 *Box v Midland Bank Ltd* [1979] 2 Lloyd's Rep 391, 399; [1981] 1 Lloyd's Rep 434. Cf *Esso Petroleum Co Ltd v Mardon* [1976] QB 801.

(vii) Representation of law

Until 1999, a misrepresentation of law did not give rise to a remedy[28] but the position was unsatisfactory. It is often difficult to distinguish a representation of law from one of fact because many statements of fact contain implicit propositions of law and vice versa. If a house is represented to be a 'new' house for the purposes of the Rent Acts, is this a representation of fact or of law?[29] A misrepresentation that planning permission exists for business use has been treated as a representation of fact,[30] as have misrepresentations as to private rights (as distinct from the general law)[31] or as to the content or effect of documents.[32] A misrepresentation of foreign law has also been treated as a representation of fact.[33] And a *wilful* misrepresentation of law has also sometimes been treated as similar to misrepresentation of an opinion which is not actually held.[34]

In 1999 the House of Lords held, in the context of claims for the recovery of money paid under a mistake, that a distinction should no longer be made between mistakes of law and mistakes of fact.[35] Similar reasoning has also been applied to cases of mistake[36] and misrepresentation[37] in contract and therefore in principle there should be a remedy for misrepresentations of law on the same basis as for misrepresentations of fact.

(viii) The representation must be addressed to the misled party

The representation must have been addressed by the representor (or by someone on his behalf) to the misled party with the intention that the addressee act on it. In *Peek v Gurney*:[38]

The promoters of a company were sued by P who had purchased shares on the faith of false statements contained in a prospectus issued by them. P was not a person to whom shares had been allotted on the first formation of the company; he had merely purchased shares from such allottees.

The House of Lords held that the prospectus was only addressed to the first applicants for shares; that it could not be supposed to extend to others than these; and that on the allotment 'the prospectus had done its work; it was exhausted'.

A statement made directly to the misled party is clearly addressed to that party; but will also be held to have been so addressed where the person is one to whom the representor

[28] Cf *Beattie v Lord Ebury* (1872) LR 7 Ch App 777.
[29] *Solle v Butcher* [1950] 1 KB 671, 695.
[30] *Laurence v Lexcourt Holdings Ltd* [1978] 1 WLR 1128.
[31] *Cooper v Phibbs* (1867) LR 2 HL 149, above, p 310.
[32] *Wauton v Coppard* [1899] 1 Ch 92.
[33] *Andre & Cie SA v Ets Michel Blanc & Fils* [1979] 2 Lloyd's Rep 427.
[34] *West London Commercial Bank v Kitson* (1884) 13 QBD 360, 362; *Beattie v Lord Ebury* (1872) LR 7 Ch App 777, 802.
[35] *Kleinwort Benson Ltd v Lincoln CC* [1999] 2 AC 349.
[36] *Brennan v Bolt Burdon* [2004] EWCA Civ 1017, [2005] QB 303.
[37] *Pankhania v Hackney LBC* [2002] EWHC 2441 (Ch), [2002] All ER (D) 22 (Aug).
[38] (1873) LR 6 HL 377, applied in *Al Nakib Investments Ltd v Longcroft* [1990] 1 WLR 1390.

intended the statement to be passed on.[39] If this fact is established, it is immaterial that the misled party is merely one of a class of persons, even of the public at large.[40]

(ix) The representation must induce the contract

The representation must form a material inducement to the party to whom it is addressed. This means that the representation must have caused the representee to hold a false belief, and that the representee must have acted because of holding that false belief—the representation must have operated on the representee's mind, although this does not logically require the representee to be consciously aware of the representation when acting on it:[41]

> It is an everyday feature of human experience that people form and act on beliefs without any conscious awareness or thought. If someone takes advantage of such unconscious mental processes to deceive another person and cause her to act to her detriment, there is no reason why a claim for damages should not lie. The mischief is no less than in a case involving conscious awareness.

The representee must normally have believed the representation: 'in the paradigm case where A lies to B in the hope of inducing B to do something, B will in fact usually only be induced to do so if he believes A's lie'.[42] However, the Supreme Court has said that it is not necessary to prove that the representee believed that the representation was true if the representee in fact relied on it. In *Hayward v Zurich Insurance Co Plc*:[43]

> Z, the insurers of H's employer, agreed to settle H's claim for damages for personal injury sustained in an accident at work. At the time of the agreement, Z suspected that H had exaggerated the extent of his injuries, but they could not find sufficient evidence to prove their suspicions in court. Z later received such proof, and sued H for damages in deceit, or rescission of the settlement agreement.

The Supreme Court held that the trial judge was entitled to find as a matter of fact that Z was induced to enter into the settlement agreement by H's misrepresentations, although it did not believe them and had carried out its own investigations.[44] It was even suggested that there may be circumstances in which a representee *knows* that the

[39] *Commercial Banking Co of Sydney Ltd v RH Brown & Co* [1972] 2 Lloyd's Rep 360 (Australia); *Smith v Eric S Bush* [1990] 1 AC 831. Cf *Gross v Lewis Hillman Ltd* [1970] Ch 445.

[40] *Andrews v Mockford* [1896] 1 QB 372 (prospectus part of wider scheme of fraud).

[41] *Credit Suisse Life (Bermuda) Ltd v Ivanishvili* [2025] UKPC 53, [2025] 3 WLR 789 at [161]–[162] (deceit). Lord Leggatt rejected suggestions in recent cases, based on a dictum of Bowen LJ in *Edgington v Fitzmaurice* (1885) 29 Ch D 459, 483, that a representation must be 'actively present to [the claimant's] mind': *Raiffeisen Zentralbank Osterreich AG v Royal Bank of Scotland Plc* [2010] EWHC 1392 (Comm), [2011] 1 Lloyd's Rep 123 at [80]; *Marme Inversiones 2007 SL v Natwest Markets plc* [2019] EWHC 366 (Comm) at [288]; *Leeds City Council v Barclays Bank Plc* [2021] EWHC 363 (Comm), [2021] QB 1027 at [102], [146]; *Loreley Financing (Jersey) No 30 Ltd v Credit Suisse Securities (Europe) Ltd* [2023] EWHC 2759 (Comm) at [386], [421], [422].

[42] *Holyoake v Candy* [2017] EWHC 3397 (Ch) at [390] (Nugee J, distinguishing *Hayward v Zurich Insurance* [2016] UKSC 48, below).

[43] [2016] UKSC 48, [2017] AC 142.

[44] *Ibid* at [40].

representation is false but nevertheless may be held to rely upon the misrepresentation.[45] This is, however, controversial, and difficult to support.[46]

The Courts have held that, given the range of factors which motivate a party to agree to enter into a contract, the misrepresentation need not be the sole cause of the representee's decision to contract,[47] although in relation to the test of inducement a distinction is drawn depending on whether or not the misrepresentation was made fraudulently. In cases of innocent or negligent misrepresentation, the representee has the burden of showing that he or she *would have acted differently*—would not have entered into the relevant contract—if the representation had not been made ('but for' causation).[48] Where the defendant's misrepresentation was made fraudulently, however, it is sufficient for the claimant to show that he or she *might have acted differently*—that the decision was influenced, or affected, by it.[49] Thus a person who bought shares in a company on the faith of fraudulent statements contained in a prospectus, but also in the erroneous belief that he would be entitled to the benefit of a charge on the company's assets, was able to claim that he had been materially misled by the statements.[50]

The burden of proving that the representation induced the contract rests upon the misled party.[51] But such inducement may be inferred on the facts. Thus it was said by Lord Blackburn:[52]

> I think that if it is proved that the defendants with a view to induce the plaintiff to enter into a contract made a statement to the plaintiff of such a nature as would be likely to induce a person to enter into a contract, and if it is proved that the plaintiff did enter into the contract, it is a fair inference of fact that he was induced to do so by the statement.

[45] *Ibid* at [44] (Lord Clarke, giving at [45] as a possible case a staged road traffic 'accident' where a party who agrees to a settlement is certain that the other party's statement is a deliberate lie, but still enters into the settlement influenced by the risk that a judge at trial would believe it).

[46] Davies and Day [2019] LMCLQ 390; Loi [2017] JBL 598; Bant [2017] LMCLQ 91. But cf Lee [2017] LMCLQ 150.

[47] *Attwood v Small* (1838) 6 Cl & Fin 232, 502; *Reynell v Sprye* (1852) 1 De GM & G 660, 708.

[48] *BV Nederlandse Industrie Van Eiprodukten v Rembrandt Enterprises Inc* [2019] EWCA Civ 596, [2019] 1 Lloyd's Rep 491 at [15]; *Assicurazioni Generali SpA v Arab Insurance Group* [2002] EWCA Civ 1642, [2003] 1 All ER (Comm) 140 at [59]; *Raiffeisen Zentralbank Osterreich AG v Royal Bank of Scotland Plc* [2010] EWHC 1392 (Comm) at [195]. Legislative remedies for misrepresentation may formulate the test of causation differently: see, eg, Digital Markets, Competition and Consumers Act 2024 (below, p 331), s 232(4) ('significant factor'); Consumer Insurance (Disclosure and Representations) Act 2012, Sched 1, paras 5, 6, 7 (insurer would not have entered into consumer insurance contract on any terms, or would have entered it but on different terms).

[49] *BV Nederlandse Industrie Van Eiprodukten v Rembrandt Enterprises Inc* [2019] EWCA Civ 596 at [34]; *Raiffeisen Zentralbank Osterreich AG v Royal Bank of Scotland Plc* [2010] EWHC 1392 (Comm) at [198]; *Marme Inversiones 2007 SL v Natwest Markets plc* [2019] EWHC 366 (Comm) at [304], [317]. See also *Edgington v Fitzmaurice* (1885) 29 Ch D 459, 483; *Barton v Armstrong* [1976] AC 104, 118–19, below, p 384 (analogy drawn between duress and fraudulent misrepresentation).

[50] *Edgington v Fitzmaurice* (1885) 29 Ch D 459 (deceit).

[51] *Arkwright v Newbold* (1880) 17 Ch D 301, 324. See also *Bristol & West BS v Mothew* [1998] Ch 1.

[52] *Smith v Chadwick* (1884) 9 App Cas 187, 196. See also *Barton v County Natwest Ltd* [1999] Lloyd's Rep (Bank) 408.

The inference of inducement is not easy to rebut, particularly in cases of fraud, where a party who has practised deception which has achieved its object cannot be allowed to deny that the deception actually played a part in inducement.[53]

It will not be inferred that a representation induced the contract where it would not have induced a reasonable person to contract but, in such a case, a representee who proves that he or she was in fact so induced will be entitled to relief.[54]

(x) Opportunities for inspection

The mere fact that the representee has had the opportunity of investigating and ascertaining whether the representation is true or false will not necessarily deprive that person of the right to claim to have been deceived by it,[55] although if the circumstances are suspicious, the representee who has information which ought to put him or her on inquiry may not be able to rely on the misrepresentation to claim a remedy.[56] If, however, the representee does investigate, and consequently relies not upon the misrepresentation but upon the accuracy of those investigations, the action will fail, as it can no longer be said that the representation was a reason for entering the contract.

(c) REMEDIES FOR MISREPRESENTATION: AN OVERVIEW

Once it has been established that there is an operative misrepresentation, the next step is to identify the remedies available to the representee. The circumstances in which the different remedies can be obtained will be explained in more detail below[57] but, in outline, they are as follows.

(i) Rescission of the contract

Misrepresentation renders the contract voidable at the instance of the misled party, and rescission is the remedy by which the representee obtains the retrospective avoidance of the contract. Both parties' obligations under the contract are set aside *ab initio* and the parties must normally return the benefits which they received from each other under the contract. For example, when a contract of sale is rescinded either by the buyer or by the seller, the buyer must return the goods and the seller must repay the price.

[53] *Hayward v Zurich Insurance Co Plc* [2016] UKSC 48 at [36]–[37]; *Sharland v Sharland* [2015] UKSC 60, [2016] AC 871 at [32]; *Smith v Kay* (1859) 7 HL Cas 750, 759.

[54] *Museprime Properties Ltd v Adhill Properties Ltd* (1991) 61 P & CR 111, 124; cf *Goff v Gauthier* (1991) 62 P & CR 388, 397–8.

[55] *Central Ry Co of Venezuela v Kisch* (1867) LR 2 HL 99, 120 (fraudulent misrepresentation); *Redgrave v Hurd* (1881) 20 Ch D 1 (non-fraudulent misrepresentation); *Laurence v Lexcourt Holdings Ltd* [1978] 1 WLR 1128. Contributory negligence is a (partial) defence to a claim for damages in the tort of negligence, but not in the tort of deceit: *Standard Chartered Bank v Pakistan National Shipping Co (Nos 2 and 4)* [2002] UKHL 43, [2003] 1 AC 959.

[56] *Redgrave v Hurd* (1881) 20 Ch D 1, 23; *New Brunswick and Canada Railway Co v Conybeare* (1862) 9 HLC 711, 743.

[57] Below, p 335.

Where a contract is rescinded, the representee may also sometimes be able to obtain an 'indemnity' against obligations which have been incurred in favour of third parties under the terms of the contract. Where the misrepresentation was made otherwise than fraudulently, the Court has a discretion under section 2(2) of the Misrepresentation Act 1967 to refuse rescission and to award damages in lieu.

(ii) Damages in tort

If the representor committed a tort in making the misrepresentation, the representee may sue for damages in tort; in the tort of deceit if the misrepresentation was made fraudulently and in the tort of negligence or in a statutory claim under section 2(1) of the Misrepresentation Act 1967 if it was made negligently—without reasonable care. Deceit and negligence are general torts which are not limited to pre-contractual misrepresentations. The statutory claim was devised specially for pre-contractual misrepresentations, although it does not apply where the representee is a consumer who has a right of redress under Chapter 1 of Part 4 of the Digital Markets, Competition and Consumers Act 2024[58] in respect of the conduct constituting the misrepresentation.[59]

Damages in tort are calculated to compensate the loss which the claimant suffers as a result of the tort. In the context of misrepresentation, this means the amount by which the claimant is worse off as a result of entering into the contract in reliance on the misrepresentation. This may include consequential losses (including loss of profits on other contracts), but not the profits which the claimant hoped to make from the contract induced by the misrepresentation. That would be a claim for 'expectation' measure damages which are available only in a claim for breach of contract.[60]

(iii) Remedies for breach of contract

If the misrepresentation became a term of the contract, or constituted a warranty collateral to the contract, the representee may claim not for the misrepresentation but for breach of contract. Damages are calculated to put the representee into the financial position as if the contract had not been broken (ie the 'expectation' measure). If the representor warranted that the representation was true, this means putting the representee into the position as if it had been true.[61]

If the truth of the representation was a condition of the contract, or if the fact that it is false is a fundamental breach of contract, the representee may also be able to discharge the contract for breach. These remedies for breach of contract are not discussed in detail in this chapter.[62]

[58] Replacing Part 4A of the Consumer Protection from Unfair Trading Regulations 2008, which continue to apply until new replacement Regulations are made: see below, pp 331, 358.

[59] Misrepresentation Act 1967, s 2(4) inserted by SI 2014 No 870 and amended by SI 2025 No 381. An award of damages under s 2(2) is similarly excluded.

[60] An example illustrating the difference between tort and contract measure damages is set out below, p 332.

[61] If the warranty was not that the representation was true, but only that the representor was exercising reasonable case in making it, the measure of damages is similar to damages in the tort of negligence: *Esso Petroleum Co Ltd v Mardon* [1976] QB 801, 820.

[62] See below, Chapter 15 (discharge for breach); Chapter 17 (damages for breach of contract).

(iv) Consumers' rights of redress

If a consumer enters into a contract with a trader, and the trader (or, in certain circumstances, the producer of goods) has made a misrepresentation which constitutes a 'prohibited practice' under Part 4 of the Digital Markets, Competition and Consumers Act 2024 and which is a significant factor in the consumer's decision to enter into the contract, the consumer may have additional rights of redress.[63] The consumer may have a right to 'unwind' the contract, under which the contract comes to an end. The trader must then give a refund to the consumer and the consumer must make any goods which he received under the contract available for collection by the trader. A consumer who transferred goods to the trader under the contract has a right to return of the goods but must repay any amount paid by the trader. A consumer who has not exercised the right to unwind may have the right to a discount in respect of the payments made or due to be made under the contract. And a consumer who has incurred consequential financial loss, or has suffered alarm, distress, or physical inconvenience or discomfort, may have a right to damages.

(v) Defence to a claim under the contract

The representee may also be able to raise the misrepresentation as a defence to a claim by the representor under the contract; for example as a defence to a claim for specific performance of the contract, even in a case where the representee could not obtain rescission of the contract. Specific performance is a discretionary remedy and it will be refused where it would be inequitable for one party to insist on performance of the contract by the other. Thus it will be refused where the party against whom it is sought would not have entered into the contract but for the misrepresentation.[64]

(vi) Choice between remedies

Sometimes the representee can establish a successful claim to more than one remedy. In such a case the representee will make a choice amongst the available remedies based on the benefit which each would give. Some remedies may be obtained simultaneously, whereas other remedies are mutually inconsistent and the representee must choose between them.

For example, the representee may obtain both rescission of the contract and damages in tort (in deceit, negligence, or under section 2(1) of the Misrepresentation Act 1967, as the case may be) because the underlying purpose of these remedies is essentially the same: to restore the position as if the contract had not been entered into, either by setting aside the obligations (rescission) or through a monetary award (damages in tort). Rescission of the contract will reduce much of the loss since it involves each party returning what was received from the other, but if after the rescission the representee

[63] Digital Markets, Competition and Consumers Act 2024, s 232, which will replace Consumer Protection from Unfair Trading Regulations 2008 (SI 2008 No 1277, as amended by SI 2014 No 870) when new replacement Regulations are made: see below, p 358.

[64] *Lamare v Dixon* (1873) LR 6 HL 414.

will still have out-of-pocket losses which fall within a possible tort claim, that claim can also be made.[65] However, the representee cannot obtain both rescission of the contract and damages for breach of contract, since the latter remedy presupposes the continuing existence of the obligations under the contract.

The rights of redress provided by Part 4 of the Digital Markets, Competition and Consumers Act 2024[66] constitute a further route for a consumer to seek a remedy where the misrepresentation constitutes a 'misleading action' under the Act, although the consumer must choose between claims and cannot be compensated both under the Act and under any other rule of law or equity or under any enactment in respect of the conduct.[67]

The representee must choose between damages for breach of contract and damages in tort, since their purpose is different. The measures of damages will often be different, even where the claims arise from the same misrepresentation, and the facts will determine which is better for the representee. Take an example:[68]

A sells a car to B, and makes a misrepresentation, which he also warrants to be true, about the age of the car. The car is really 10 years old, but A says that it is 7 years old. B pays £1,000 for the car. The market value of a 7-year-old car (with, apart from the age, the same characteristics as this car) is £1,200; but the actual value of this 10-year-old car is £700.

If B sues in tort, he claims to be put back into the position in which he would have been if he had not been induced by the misrepresentation to buy the car. He would still have his £1,000. But since he has exchanged that money for a car which is worth only £700, he has lost £300. On the other hand, if he sues for breach of contract, B claims to be put into the position in which he would have been if the representation were true—that is, he would have a seven-year-old car, which would be worth £1,200. So, since the car is in fact worth only £700 his 'loss' is £500. On these facts, the damages in contract are higher than the damages in tort. But this is only because the bargain (apart from the misrepresentation) was good: if the representation had been true, B was getting a good deal in paying only £1,000 for a car which should have been worth £1,200. But if the bargain had been bad, and B was paying too much for the car even if it had been only seven years old, the contract measure would be less generous than the tort measure.

[65] *Archer v Brown* [1985] QB 401, 415.

[66] 2024 Act, ss 232–235. Until new replacement Regulations are made, the Consumer Protection from Unfair Trading Regulations 2008 (SI 2008 No 1277, as amended by SI 2014 No 870) continue in force to provide the detail of the rights of redress: see below, p 358.

[67] 2008 Regulations, reg 27L. There is no choice between claiming damages under Misrepresentation Act 1967, s 2 and a right of redress under the 2024 Act in respect of conduct constituting a misrepresentation, since the consumer who has a right of redress is not entitled to be paid damages under Misrepresentation Act 1967, s 2 in respect of that misrepresentation: Misrepresentation Act, s 2(4), and amended by SI 2025 No 381, below, p 360.

[68] Cartwright, *Unequal Bargaining* (1991) 106. See also *Wemyss v Karim* [2016] EWCA Civ 27 at [23]–[25].

(d) 'FRAUDULENT', 'NEGLIGENT', AND 'INNOCENT' MISREPRESENTATIONS

In the modern law misrepresentations may be categorized as fraudulent, negligent, or innocent. This section outlines the different remedies available in these categories, and the details of each of the remedies is given in the following sections.

(i) Categorization of misrepresentations in the older cases: fraudulent and innocent

Before 1963, the significant difference was between fraudulent misrepresentations for which the contract could be set aside ('rescinded') and for which damages were available in the tort of deceit, and non-fraudulent misrepresentations (known as 'innocent misrepresentations') for which only rescission was available.[69]

The explanation lay in the distinction between common law and equity, and the historical development of the law of tort. In equity a contract could be rescinded for non-fraudulent misrepresentation, but damages, a common law remedy, was not available in the Court of Chancery. By contrast, the common law courts awarded damages for fraud in the tort of deceit, and for the breach of a contractual term, but they gave no remedy for a non-fraudulent misrepresentation.[70] The Judicature Act 1873[71] enabled equitable remedies to be granted in any division of the High Court, but did not affect the substantive rule that damages in addition to rescission cannot be awarded for innocent misrepresentation. The important developments were the decision of the House of Lords in 1963 in *Hedley Byrne & Co Ltd v Heller & Partners Ltd*,[72] which extended the tort of negligence to cover claims for economic loss caused by reliance on a negligent misstatement, and the enactment of the Misrepresentation Act 1967, which created a special remedy for negligent pre-contractual misrepresentations. Since then, it has become usual to use the label 'innocent' (or, sometimes, 'wholly innocent') to refer to misrepresentations which are made neither fraudulently nor negligently. But judges in the cases before 1963 did not make this distinction, and applied the label 'innocent' also to misrepresentations which would now be classified as negligent.

(ii) The remedies available in the modern law for fraudulent, negligent, and innocent misrepresentations

At common law a *fraudulent* misrepresentation not only renders the contract voidable, and therefore allows the representee to obtain rescission of the contract, but also

[69] *Heilbut Symons & Co v Buckleton* [1913] AC 30, 48–9.

[70] *Kennedy v Panama, New Zealand, and Australian Royal Mail Co Ltd* (1867) LR 2 QB 580, 587.

[71] 1873 Act, ss 24(1), (2), and 25(11). See now the Senior Courts Act 1981, s 49.

[72] [1964] AC 465, below, p 349; extended to pre-contractual misrepresentations in *Esso Petroleum Co Ltd v Mardon* [1976] QB 801.

gives rise to an action for damages in tort in respect of the deceit.[73] If, therefore, the misrepresentation was made fraudulently, the injured party will be entitled to choose either to affirm the contract and recover damages in respect of any loss suffered by reason of the fraud, or to rescind the contract and recover damages in respect of any loss which will remain after rescission has been effected.[74]

A person who has been induced to enter into a contract as the result of the other party's *negligent* misrepresentation is entitled to rescind as in the case of fraud, although here the Court has a discretion under section 2(2) of the Misrepresentation Act 1967 to refuse rescission and award damages in lieu of rescission. The representee may also be able to claim damages in the tort of negligence or under section 2(1) of the Misrepresentation Act 1967.[75] Again, the representee has the choice between affirming the contract and claiming damages in negligence or under section 2(1) for all the loss suffered, and rescinding the contract and claiming damages for any loss which will remain following rescission. If the Court refuses rescission and awards damages in lieu under section 2(2) of the 1967 Act, the representee may claim any additional losses in negligence or under section 2(1).[76] A claimant who is a consumer with a right of redress under Chapter 1 of Part 4 of the Digital Markets, Competition and Consumers Act 2024,[77] however, is not entitled to be paid damages under section 2 of the Misrepresentation Act 1967, but may claim the right of redress under the 2024 Act (the rights to unwind, to a discount and/or to damages). The consumer's claim to the general remedies of rescission and/or damages in the tort of negligence are unaffected.

A person who has been induced to enter into a contract as the result of the other party's *innocent* misrepresentation is entitled to the remedy of rescission but, in contrast with cases of fraudulent or negligent misrepresentation, cannot obtain damages in addition to rescission, only an indemnity against obligations incurred in favour of third parties under the terms of the contract. However, the Court has a discretion under section 2(2) of the Misrepresentation Act 1967 to refuse rescission and award damages in lieu of rescission.

[73] A fraudulent misrepresentation may also constitute a criminal offence: eg Fraud Act 2006, s 2; Financial Services Act 2012, Part 7. The Court convicting a defendant for a criminal offence may in some cases also make a compensation order: Sentencing Act 2020, s 133. There are also statutory remedies in respect of certain fraudulent statements: eg Financial Services and Markets Act 2000, s 382 (restitution order where profits made or losses inflicted by contravention of certain requirements, including Financial Services Act 2012, Part 7).

[74] *Archer v Brown* [1985] QB 401.

[75] For the differences between these claims, and between the damages awarded under them, see below, pp 351–3.

[76] 1967 Act, s 2(3).

[77] Replacing Part 4A of the Consumer Protection from Unfair Trading Regulations 2008, which continue to apply until new replacement Regulations are made: see below, p 358.

(e) RESCISSION OF THE CONTRACT

Rescission is, in principle, available for all classes of operative misrepresentation.[78] At common law a contract was voidable for misrepresentation only if it was made fraudulently. But there was no such limitation in equity, and the rules of equity now prevail.[79] When a person has been induced to enter into a contract by a misrepresentation of any description, the effect on the contract is not to make it void, but to give the misled party[80] an option either to avoid it or, alternatively, to affirm it. A party who is misled and elects to avoid the contract may take steps to have it set aside by the Court, or may resist an action for specific performance or for damages brought by the representor, and rescind by way of counterclaim.[81] Rescission, however, is not merely a judicial remedy. Certainly in the case of rescission at common law for fraudulent misrepresentation,[82] but also, it seems, in the case of rescission in equity (extending to negligent and innocent misrepresentation),[83] the misled party can rescind without seeking the assistance of a Court, and any property transferred to the representor under the contract will revest in the party who has so rescinded the contract.[84]

(i) Mode of rescission

Rescission must normally be communicated to the other party.[85] But where a seller of goods has a right to avoid the contract for the buyer's misrepresentation, it suffices

[78] There are, however, special rules for insurance contracts, where the common law remedies for misrepresentation by an insured before the insurance contract is entered into have been replaced for consumer insurance contracts by the Consumer Insurance (Disclosure and Representations) Act 2012, and for non-consumer insurance contracts by the Insurance Act 2015. The insurer may avoid the contract in case of a *deliberate or reckless* misrepresentation (and retain any premiums paid except, in the case of a consumer insurance contract, to the extent (if any) that it would be unfair to the consumer to retain them). Where the misrepresentation was only *careless* (or, in the case of non-consumer insurance contracts, was neither deliberate nor reckless, ie *careless or innocent*) the insurer may avoid the contract only if it would not have entered into the contract on any terms in the absence of the misrepresentation; if it would have entered into the contract but on different terms or would have charged a higher premium, the terms of the contract or the premium may be varied if the insurer so requires: Consumer Insurance (Disclosure and Representations) Act 2012, Sched 1, Part 1; Insurance Act 2015, Sched 1, Part 1. There is no remedy against a consumer insured who exercises reasonable care not to make a misrepresentation to the insurer: 2012 Act, s 2.

[79] *Redgrave v Hurd* (1881) 20 Ch D 1, 12–13; Supreme Court of Judicature Act 1873, s 25(11). See now Senior Courts Act 1981, s 49.

[80] Only the misled contracting party (and not a third party) can obtain rescission: *Flowers v Chief Land Registrar* [2018] UKUT 145 (TCC) at [26].

[81] The setting up of the misrepresentation by way of defence has in some instances been treated as equivalent to rescission: *Clough v London & NW Ry* (1871) LR 7 Ex 26.

[82] *Car and Universal Finance Co Ltd v Caldwell*, below, n 87.

[83] *TSB Bank Plc v Camfield* [1995] 1 WLR 430, 438. Cf, however, O'Sullivan [2000] CLJ 509; *IGE USA Investments Ltd v Revenue and Customs Commissioners* [2021] EWCA Civ 534, [2021] Ch 423 at [91] (Henderson LJ: 'a notoriously difficult subject, on which the authorities are in such a state of disarray that, in my judgment, only the Supreme Court can reconcile them'); *Hopcraft v Close Bros Ltd* [2025] UKSC 33, [2025] 3 WLR 423 at [77] ('equitable rescission is, in sharp contrast to the parallel remedy at common law, neither automatic, nor available by way of self-help': breach of fiduciary duty).

[84] If the nature of the property is such that a particular formality is required to revest the title (eg land or shares), the representor holds the legal title on constructive trust for the representee: *Alati v Kruger* (1955) 94 CLR 216, 224.

[85] *Scarf v Jardine* (1882) 7 App Cas 345, 360, 361.

if the seller, even without the buyer's knowledge, retakes possession of the goods.[86] The Courts have even been prepared to accept that, at least in the case of a fraudulent misrepresentation, it is sufficient for the seller to take all possible steps to regain the goods. In *Car and Universal Finance Co Ltd v Caldwell*:[87]

C was fraudulently induced to sell a motor car to a purchaser in return for a bad cheque. When the cheque was dishonoured, C immediately informed the police and the Automobile Association, but the purchaser had deliberately absconded and could not be found. The purchaser sold the car to a person who had notice of the fraud, but it was later sold on to another person who had no such notice. Eventually, it came into the hands of the claimant who bought it in good faith.

The Court of Appeal held that C had rescinded the contract even though he had not communicated his rescission to the purchaser. The title to the car had revested in the defendant on rescission and so the claimant had no title to the vehicle. It is not, however, clear whether anything less than communication to the purchaser or re-taking the goods would be sufficient to effect rescission in the case of a non-fraudulent misrepresentation.[88]

(ii) No power to award partial rescission

Notwithstanding the flexibility of equity, it was held in *TSB Bank plc v Camfield*[89] that there is no power to order partial rescission. In that case:

as a result of an innocent misrepresentation by her husband,[90] a woman charged her interest in a house to a bank to secure the debts of the husband's business believing that the maximum liability under the charge was £15,000 when it was in fact unlimited.

Despite the wife's willingness at the outset to charge the property for £15,000, the charge was set aside in its entirety. This result has not been followed in Australia[91] and was left open by the Privy Council in an appeal from New Zealand,[92] but is settled law in England unless it is reviewed by the Supreme Court.[93] The approach in the English cases follows from the fact that (apart from the Court's power to award damages in

[86] *Car and Universal Finance Co Ltd v Caldwell* [1961] 1 QB 525, 554–5, 558; *Re Eastgate* [1905] 1 KB 465.

[87] [1961] 1 QB 525. Cf *Newtons of Wembley Ltd v Williams* [1965] 1 QB 560.

[88] *Car and Universal Finance Co Ltd v Caldwell* [1961] 1 QB 525, 551–2, 555, 558–9.

[89] [1995] 1 WLR 430.

[90] For third-party misrepresentations, see below, p 406.

[91] *Vadasz v Pioneer Concrete (SA) Pty Ltd* (1995) 184 CLR 102.

[92] *Far Eastern Shipping Co Public Ltd v Scales Trading Ltd* [2001] 1 All ER (Comm) 319, 326. The New Zealand Court of Appeal had expressed a strong preference for the flexible approach of *Vadasz*'s case (above, n 91).

[93] *De Molestina v Ponton* [2002] 1 Lloyd's Rep 271, 288 (Colman J), on the basis that *Vadasz* is inconsistent with the decision of HL in *Barclays Bank Plc v O'Brien* [1994] 1 AC 180. Cf *Kennedy v Kennedy* [2014] EWHC 4129 (Ch), [2015] BTC 2 at [46] (Etherton C: the rejection of partial rescission makes sense for contract, but does not apply to a self-contained and severable part of a *non-contractual* voluntary transaction). See, however, Poole and Keyser (2005) 121 LQR 273.

lieu of rescission under section 2(2) of the Misrepresentation Act 1967)[94] rescission for misrepresentation is not a discretionary remedy. In this, it is in marked contrast to the approach of equity in analogous situations. Thus, mortgagees' claims have been upheld only to the extent of the other party's understanding of the amount of the mortgage.[95] Again, in rescission for undue influence, the Court is concerned to achieve 'practical justice' for both parties: we shall see that the party seeking rescission may be required to pay the other reasonable remuneration for beneficial services rendered,[96] and, where the market value of property transferred has fallen, to bear a proportionate part of the loss.[97] Where the objectionable parts of a transaction can be severed without rewriting it, setting aside is, moreover, not invariably an 'all or nothing process'.[98] The misled party may also sometimes be able to seek rectification of the contract if (as in *TSB Bank plc v Camfield*) the misrepresentation relates to a term of the contract and the party wishes to enforce the contract on the basis of the terms as he or she believed them to be.[99] But a party who wishes to avoid the whole transaction on the basis of the misrepresentation, may do so, unless the Court exercises its power under section 2(2) of the Misrepresentation Act 1967.[100]

(iii) Indemnity alongside rescission

When a contract is rescinded, each party is entitled to be relieved of the obligations under the contract and to recover any benefit which has been conferred upon the other party. The object of rescission is to restore the position as it was before the contract was entered into, and with this end in view the misled party can claim an indemnity against any obligations which may be incurred, or which have been incurred, under the contract.

In *Newbigging v Adam*:[101]

N entered into a partnership with A and provided £10,000 of new capital. He was induced to enter into the partnership agreement by a material non-fraudulent misrepresentation as to the capacity of certain machinery. The business failed, and N sued for rescission of the agreement, for recovery of his capital, and for an indemnity against all claims which might be made against him by virtue of his having become a partner.

The Court of Appeal agreed that N was entitled to the relief for which he asked, that the right to an indemnity must be less extensive than the right to damages, and that the principle underlying the award of an indemnity is to restore the misled party to his

[94] Below, p 342.

[95] *Bristol & West BS v Henning* [1985] 1 WLR 778 and *Skipton BS v Clayton* (1993) 66 P & CR 233. See Ferguson (1995) 111 LQR 555.

[96] *O'Sullivan v Management Agency and Music Ltd* [1985] 1 QB 428, below, p 400.

[97] *Cheese v Thomas* [1994] 1 WLR 129. See also Jones and Goodhart, *Specific Performance* (2nd edn, 1996) 293 (purchaser's action for specific performance with compensation).

[98] *Barclays Bank plc v Caplan* [1998] 1 FLR 532, 546.

[99] For rectification, see above, pp 284–90.

[100] In *TSB Bank plc v Camfield* the bank conceded that it could not invoke s 2(2) directly and since an award of damages against the husband would have been an empty remedy no Court could have formed the view that it would be equitable to exercise its power under s 2(2).

[101] (1886) 34 Ch D 582, aff'd as *Adam v Newbigging* (1888) 13 App Cas 308.

old position. But they differed in their conclusion as to how the pre-contract position should in general be achieved. Fry LJ was inclined to hold that the misled party 'is entitled to an indemnity in respect of all obligations entered into under the contract when those obligations are within the necessary or reasonable expectation of both of the contracting parties at the time they made the contract'.[102] But an award made on this basis would not differ from damages. A narrower and more satisfactory test was propounded by Bowen LJ when he said the misled party 'is not to be replaced in exactly the same position in all respects, otherwise he would be entitled to recover damages, but he is to be replaced in his position so far as regards the rights and obligations which have been *created by the contract* into which he has been induced to enter'.[103] Cotton LJ similarly said that 'the indemnity to which he is entitled is only an indemnity against the obligations which he has contracted under the contract which is set aside'.[104]

The distinction between damages and an indemnity as it works out in practice may be illustrated by the case of *Whittington v Seale-Hayne*,[105] where the Court adopted the narrower principle suggested by Bowen LJ:

Poultry farmers had been induced to take a lease by the defendant's non-fraudulent misrepresentation that the premises were sanitary. This was not the case, and in consequence of the contamination of the water supply, their manager fell ill and the poultry died. They claimed rescission of the lease, and an indemnity to cover the value of the stock, loss of profit on sales, loss of breeding season, medical expenses of the manager, rates, rent, and money spent on outbuildings, etc. They had also been compelled by the local council to renew the drains, and this item, too, was included.

It was held that the poultry farmers were entitled to have the lease rescinded, and to recover what they had spent on rent, rates, and the renewal of the drains, since these were expenses incurred under the covenants in the lease or arising necessarily out of the occupation of the property, and thus 'obligations created by the contract'. Their claim for payment in respect of the other items of loss was not allowed, since these were damages, there being no obligation to carry on a poultry farm on the leased premises.

In practice, an indemnity is a useful remedy only where the misrepresentation is wholly innocent and the claimant has no claim for damages. In cases of fraudulent or negligent misrepresentation the claimant may claim damages on the tort measure, in addition to rescinding the contract.[106] Damages will be at least as extensive as the indemnity.

(iv) Limitations on the right to rescind

In a number of situations, the misled party may be precluded from rescinding the contract. However, the loss of the remedy of rescission will not prevent a claim for damages in the tort of deceit or the tort of negligence or under section 2(1) of the Misrepresentation Act 1967. The right to damages, where this exists, is independent of

[102] (1886) 34 Ch D 582, 596.
[103] *Ibid*, 592–3 (emphasis added).
[104] *Ibid*, 589.
[105] (1900) 82 LT 49.
[106] Above, p 331.

the claim to rescind and still survives. Nor does the loss of the right to rescind restrict a consumer's rights of redress under Part 4 of the Digital Markets, Competition and Consumers Act 2024,[107] which are also independent of rescission.

There are five limitations on the right to rescind.

(a) Affirmation. If after becoming aware of the misrepresentation the representee affirms the contract either by express words or by an act which shows an intention to affirm it, rescission cannot be obtained. So, for example, if persons who have purchased shares on the faith of a misrepresentation subsequently become aware of its falsity, but act inconsistently with rescission of the contract such as by accepting dividends or attempting to sell the shares,[108] they will not be permitted to avoid the contract. In *Long v Lloyd*:[109]

Long was induced to purchase a lorry by Lloyd's representation that it was in 'exceptional' and 'first class' condition. On the first journey after the sale, the dynamo broke and Long noticed several other serious defects. Lloyd was informed of these and offered to pay half the cost of some of the repairs. On the next long journey, the lorry broke down completely and Long realized that it was in a deplorable condition. He claimed to rescind the contract.

The Court of Appeal held that, although the first journey did not amount to an affirmation of the contract as it had been undertaken merely to test the truth of Lloyd's representation, the second journey did constitute such an affirmation since Long then had knowledge that the representation was untrue.

It has been held that the right to rescind will not be lost by affirmation unless the representee has knowledge both of the facts and that these give rise to the right to rescind.[110] Where there is no such knowledge, the conduct of the representee may, if relied on by the representor, give rise to an estoppel precluding rescission.[111] The position thus differs from that concerning the right to reject for breach of condition in contracts for the sale of goods which may be lost by 'acceptance' without knowledge of the right to reject.[112] In *Long v Lloyd*, where there may not have been such knowledge, the Court may have considered that rescission for misrepresentation should be barred where the right to reject for breach of condition has been lost,[113] although these should be kept separate.[114]

[107] Replacing the Consumer Protection from Unfair Trading Regulations 2008 (SI 2008 No 1277, as amended by SI 2014 No 870) when new replacement Regulations are made: see below p 358.

[108] *Scholey v Central Ry Co of Venezuela* (1867) LR 9 Eq 266; *Re Hop and Malt Exchange and Warehouse Co* (1866) LR 1 Eq 483.

[109] [1958] 1 WLR 753.

[110] *Peyman v Lanjani* [1985] Ch 457, 486–7, 494, 500. See also *Leeds City Council v Barclays Bank Plc* [2021] EWHC 363 (Comm) at [172]–[174] (degree of knowledge required).

[111] *Ibid*, 488, 493, 501; *Motor Oil Hellas (Corinth) Refineries SA v Shipping Corp of India* [1990] 1 Lloyd's Rep 391, 398–9 (Lord Goff).

[112] Sale of Goods Act 1979, s 35 as amended by the Sale and Supply of Goods Act 1994 (which now applies only to non-consumer contracts for the sale of goods by reason of amendment of the 1979 Act by the Consumer Rights Act 2015). See generally above, pp 160–1.

[113] Atiyah (1959) 22 MLR 76; Davies (1959) 75 LQR 32.

[114] Cf *Salt v Stratstone Specialist Ltd* [2015] EWCA Civ 745, [2015] 2 CLC 269 at [49].

(b) Delay. Delay ('lapse of time') in seeking rescission may in certain circumstances bar the right to rescind. It may be treated as evidence of affirmation where the misled party fails to exercise the right to rescind for a considerable time after discovering the representation to be untrue.[115] But, since knowledge is required for affirmation, mere lapse of time does not normally have this effect.[116] Where the misrepresentation was fraudulent, the Court may apply (by analogy) to a claim for equitable rescission the statutory limitation period applicable to a claim in the tort of deceit, although in such a claim time does not run against the representee until he has discovered the fraud (or, at least, should have discovered it).[117] Where the misrepresentation was not fraudulent, however, the passage of time may operate so as to preclude rescission even if the representee has no knowledge of the untruth of the representation.[118] It depends upon whether, on the facts, the representee has failed to rescind within a 'reasonable' time from the contract: such time that it would be inequitable in all the circumstances to grant rescission. In *Salt v Stratstone Specialist Ltd* Roth J said:[119]

> rescission for misrepresentation is an equitable remedy. Absent a statutory bar, an objection to rescission must therefore rest on an equitable basis. Accordingly, it is something of a misnomer to say that rescission may be barred by lapse of time. It is only the lapse of a reasonable time such that it would be inequitable in all the circumstances to grant rescission which constitutes a bar to the remedy. This is in essence the principle of laches, which accordingly requires close attention to the facts of the case.

(c) Rights of Third Parties. Since the contract is not void but voidable, being valid until rescinded, if third parties in good faith ('bona fide') without notice and for value acquire rights in the subject-matter of the contract, those rights are valid against the misled party, provided that the contract has not before that time been rescinded.[120] Thus a shareholder who wishes to rescind a contract to take up shares in a company must do so before winding-up, for once winding-up commences the rights of the creditors become fixed, since they stand in the position of bona fide purchasers for value.[121] Also where goods are obtained by means of a misrepresentation, a third party who, before

115 *Clough v L & NW Ry* (1871) LR 7 Ex 26, 35. Cf *Allen v Robles* [1969] 1 WLR 1193.

116 *Armstrong v Jackson* [1917] 2 KB 822, 830.

117 *Redgrave v Hurd* (1881) 20 Ch D 1, 13; Limitation Act 1980, ss 32(1), 36(1); *IGE USA Investments Ltd v Revenue and Customs Commissioners* [2021] EWCA Civ 534 (but there is no statutory limitation period for the *common law* right to rescind: at [20]); cf Davies [2023] CLJ 402.

118 *Leaf v International Galleries* [1950] 2 KB 86 (rescission of contract for the purchase of a picture, misrepresented to be by Constable, was barred before the purchaser discovered the truth five years later). However, Denning LJ's reasoning in *Leaf*, which linked the test for lapse of time to that for acceptance of goods under the Sale of Goods Act 1893, s 35, has been doubted: *Salt v Stratstone Specialist Ltd* [2015] EWCA Civ 745 at [34], [47]–[48].

119 [2015] EWCA Civ 745 at [43]. In that case, rescission of a contract for the purchase of a car, misrepresented to be 'brand new', was not barred where the purchaser discovered the truth only two years later during the course of disclosure of documents in the purchaser's claim for other defects in the car.

120 *Babcock v Lawson* (1880) 5 QBD 284.

121 *Oakes v Turquand* (1867) LR 2 HL 325.

rescission, acquires the goods in good faith and for value from the fraudulent purchaser cannot be displaced by the representee.[122]

(d) Inability to Make Restitution. It has been said that when a party 'exercises his option to rescind the contract, he must be in a state to rescind; that is, he must be in such a situation to be able to put the parties into their original state before the contract'.[123] Each must give back what has been transferred. But the purpose of this limitation is to prevent the unjust enrichment of the party seeking to rescind[124] and it should not be too strictly construed. The mere fact that the subject-matter of the contract may have deteriorated before the truth is discovered is not sufficient to prevent a party making restitution and so to destroy the right to rescind a contract.[125] In *Adam v Newbigging*[126] rescission was granted of a partnership agreement even though the partnership business was then 'worse than worthless'. It has been suggested that rescission of a contract of sale of quoted shares ought still to be possible even after the specific shares purchased have been sold, since other identical shares can be purchased and the defrauded purchaser can offer substantial restitution,[127] although this idea of making restitution by handing over an equivalent thing, rather than the actual subject-matter of the contract, has not been developed. Nor has English law contemplated the approach taken by some legal systems which allow the misled purchaser, who has sold the goods, to avoid the contract on restoring to the other party not the goods themselves, but the money obtained through the sale.[128]

The Courts have refrained from defining the scope of this equitable remedy by any rigid rules; as a condition of rescission there must be restitution, but at the same time the Court has full power to make all just allowances. It was said by Lord Blackburn in *Erlanger v New Sombrero Phosphate Co*[129] that the practice had always been for a Court of Equity to give relief by way of rescission whenever by the exercise of its powers it can do what is practically just by directing accounts, ordering equitable compensation,[130]

[122] Sale of Goods Act 1979, s 23; *Phillips v Brooks Ltd* [1919] 2 KB 243. This rule is a reason why a misled party may seek to argue that the original contract of sale was void for mistake, rather than only voidable for misrepresentation: *Shogun Finance Ltd v Hudson* [2003] UKHL 62, [2004] 1 AC 919, above, p 293. Cf *Car and Universal Finance Co Ltd v Caldwell* (above, p 336), where the goods were purchased by an innocent third party only after rescission had already been effected; but cf *Newtons of Wembley Ltd v Williams* [1965] 1 QB 560, where Factors Act 1889, s 9 (equivalent to Sale of Goods Act 1979, s 25) protected the innocent third party who bought the goods from the fraudulent purchaser, even after rescission had been effected.

[123] *Clarke v Dickson* (1858) EB & E 148, 154 (Crompton J; see also in argument at 152: 'you cannot both eat your cake and return your cake').

[124] *MacKenzie v Royal Bank of Canada* [1934] AC 468 (Canada); *Bouygues Offshore v Owner of the M/T Tigr Ultisol Transport Contractors Ltd* [1996] 2 Lloyd's Rep 153, 159 (South Africa).

[125] *Armstrong v Jackson* [1917] 2 KB 822, 829; *Lagunas Nitrate Co v Lagunas Syndicate* [1899] 2 Ch 392; *Alati v Kruger* (1955) 94 CLR 216 (Australia).

[126] (1888) 13 App Cas 308, above, p 337.

[127] *Smith New Court Securities Ltd v Citibank NA* [1997] AC 254, 262.

[128] Restitution 'by value' rather than in kind: Lando and Beale, *Principles of European Contract Law Parts I and II* (2000) 277–9; cf Häcker, *Consequences of Impaired Consent Transfers* (2013) 109–13.

[129] (1878) 3 App Cas 1218, 1278–9.

[130] See *Mahoney v Purnell* [1996] 3 All ER 61 (undue influence).

and making allowances, though it cannot restore the parties precisely to the state they were in before the contract.

How this goal of doing 'what is practically just' may be reached depends on the circumstances of the case. For instance, the Court may think that justice requires the making of some allowance for the deterioration, or the improvement, as the case may be, of the subject-matter of the contract. Again, it may require compensation for losses incurred by the representor[131] or recompense for services rendered to the representee.[132] But the Court will be 'less ready to pull a transaction to pieces where the defendant is innocent, whereas in the case of fraud the Court will exercise its jurisdiction to the full in order, if possible, to prevent the defendant from enjoying the benefit of his fraud at the expense of the innocent plaintiff'.[133] Even in a case of fraud, rescission will not be ordered where it is not possible to achieve a broadly just result by orders for monetary adjustment to reflect benefits and detriments which have accrued under the contract, since to do so would unjustly enrich the defrauded party.[134]

(e) Damages in Lieu of Rescission. Except in cases of fraud and cases where the claimant is a consumer with a right of redress under Chapter 1 of Part 4 of the Digital Markets, Competition and Consumers Act 2024,[135] the Court has a discretion to refuse to allow rescission and to award damages in lieu of this remedy. This power is conferred by section 2(2) of the Misrepresentation Act 1967, which states:

> Where a person has entered into a contract after a misrepresentation has been made to him otherwise than fraudulently, and he would be entitled, by reason of the misrepresentation, to rescind the contract, then, if it is claimed, in any proceedings arising out of the contract, that the contract ought to be or has been rescinded, the court or arbitrator may declare the contract subsisting and award damages in lieu of rescission, if of opinion that it would be equitable to do so, having regard to the nature of the misrepresentation and the loss that would be caused by it if the contract were upheld, as well as to the loss that rescission would cause to the other party.

The reason for this provision is that rescission in some situations may be too drastic a remedy; for example, a car might be returned to the seller because of a trifling misrepresentation about the mileage done since the engine was last overhauled.[136] Section 2(2) requires the Court to take into account the relative importance or

[131] *Spence v Crawford* [1939] 3 All ER 271, 283 (Lord Thankerton) (loss to representor from sale by bank of shares held as security conceded to be recoverable). See also *Cheese v Thomas* [1994] 1 WLR 129 (undue influence).

[132] *Atlantic Lines & Navigation Co Inc v Hallam Ltd* [1983] 1 Lloyd's Rep 188, 202 (Mustill J) (services of chartered ship); *O'Sullivan v Management Agency and Music Ltd* [1985] 1 QB 428 (undue influence).

[133] *Spence v Crawford* [1939] 3 All ER 271, 288 (Lord Wright).

[134] *Society of Lloyd's v Wilkinson (No 2)* (1997) 6 Re LR 214, 222, 289, 296.

[135] Misrepresentation Act 1967, s 2(4), inserted by SI 2014 No 870 and amended by SI 2025 No 381. The 2024 Act replaces Part 4A of the Consumer Protection from Unfair Trading Regulations 2008, which continue to apply until new replacement Regulations are made: see below, p 358.

[136] See the Tenth Report of the Law Reform Committee (Cmnd 1782, 1962) para 11.

unimportance of the facts which have been misrepresented, as well as the relationship between the loss caused to the representee by the misrepresentation and the loss which would be caused to the representor if the contract is rescinded. Where the former is significantly less than the latter it is likely that damages in lieu of rescission will be awarded.[137]

(1) *Unavailable where rescission barred.* Is there power to award damages of this nature where the right to rescind, though once in existence, has become barred by reason of affirmation, delay, the intervention of third-party rights, or an inability to make restitution? The subsection and its legislative history are ambiguous,[138] but no such power was proposed by the Law Reform Committee on whose recommendations the 1967 Act was based.[139] Divergent views at first instance in the cases[140] have been resolved by the Court of Appeal deciding that the Court cannot award damages in lieu of rescission if it has become barred:[141]

The words of the statute are 'if it is claimed . . . that the contract ought to be or has been rescinded the court . . . may declare the contract subsisting and award damages in lieu of rescission'. No doubt a claimant can be said to make a claim even if he is subsequently held not to be entitled to do so. But the words 'in lieu of rescission' must, in my view, carry with them the implication that rescission is available (or was available at the time the contract was rescinded). If it is not (or was not available in law) because eg the contract has been affirmed, third party rights have intervened, an excessive time has elapsed or restitution has become impossible, rescission is not available and damages cannot be said to be awarded 'in lieu of rescission'.

(2) *Measure of damages.* The measure of damages to be awarded under this subsection is the loss caused by the misrepresentation as a result of the refusal to allow rescission of the contract, not the loss caused by entering into the contract.[142] In a contract for the sale of land, for example, this would be the difference in value between what the representee was misled into thinking was being bought and the value of what was received. This broadly follows the contractual measure of damages, rather than the tort measure.[143] However, it is not a claim for damages for breach of contract, and it has been stated that the damages under the subsection should never exceed what the claimant

[137] *William Sindall plc v Cambridgeshire CC* [1994] 1 WLR 1016, 1038 (loss to representee £18,000 to divert a sewer; loss to representor some £6 million in return of purchase price and interest for land the value of which had substantially fallen).

[138] Atiyah and Treitel (1967) 30 MLR 369, 375–9. [139] Tenth Report (Cmnd 1782, 1962) para 27.

[140] eg *Atlantic Lines and Navigation Co Inc v Hallam Ltd* [1983] 1 Lloyd's Rep 188, 202; *Government of Zanzibar v British Aerospace (Lancaster House) Ltd* [2000] 1 WLR 2333, 2343 (s 2(2) not available where rescission has become barred); cf *Thomas Witter Ltd v TBP Industries Ltd* [1996] 2 All ER 573, 590 (Jacob J: s 2(2) still available).

[141] *Salt v Stratstone Specialist Ltd* [2015] EWCA Civ 745 at [17] (Longmore LJ). However, on the facts, restitution was not impossible and therefore rescission was not barred.

[142] *William Sindall plc v Cambridgeshire CC* [1994] 1 WLR 1016. See also *UCB Corporate Services Ltd v Thomason* [2005] EWCA Civ 225, [2005] 1 All ER (Comm) 601 at [37] (loss includes financial loss, which may be loss of a chance).

[143] For the difference, see above, p 332.

would have got had the representation been a term. As section 2(2) was enacted because it was thought it might be a hardship to the representor to be deprived of the whole of the benefit of the bargain on account of a minor misrepresentation, 'it could not possibly have been intended the damages in lieu be assessed on a principle which would invariably have the same effect'.[144] Moreover, account is not taken of losses due to a general fall in market values after the contract is made. Where a misrepresentation is made without reasonable ground for belief in its truth, damages can be claimed under section 2(1) of the 1967 Act, and the measure of these damages is that applicable in tort.[145] In certain transactions there may be no difference between the damages recoverable under section 2(1) and section 2(2); but since consequential damage can be recovered under section 2(1)[146] and account may be taken of losses due to a general fall in the market after the contract,[147] damages under that subsection will in many cases be more extensive than those recoverable under section 2(2). Although awards can be made under both section 2(1) and section 2(2), it is not possible to recover damages twice over, for the Act provides that any award under section 2(2) shall be taken into account in assessing the liability of the representor under section 2(1).[148]

Where the Court refuses rescission, the representee is, of course, not entitled to an indemnity in addition to damages under section 2(2). An indemnity is attached to the remedy of rescission and is awarded in order to achieve the restoration of the representee's financial position before the contract.[149] Where, however, the representee would have been entitled to an indemnity had rescission been granted, the Court should, in assessing the damages under section 2(2), take account of any sum recoverable as an indemnity in computing the loss suffered as a result of the refusal of rescission.

(v) Limitations removed by the 1967 Act

Before 1967 it was said that there were two further limitations on the remedy of rescission. These were removed by the Misrepresentation Act 1967.

(a) Executed Contracts. In the case of innocent misrepresentation, there was authority that there could be no rescission of a contract after it had been executed (ie performed) by the transfer of property under it.[150] The extent of this rule was somewhat uncertain and it was the subject of much criticism,[151] for in many cases the falsity of a misrepresentation cannot be discovered until, for example, a lease of a house has been executed and the tenant has moved into occupation of the premises. Section 1(b) of the 1967 Act therefore provides that a contract is to be capable of rescission notwithstanding that it has been performed. This does not affect the other bars to rescission, and a Court

[144] *William Sindall plc v Cambridgeshire CC* [1994] 1 WLR 1016, 1038 (Hoffmann LJ).

[145] See below, p 352.

[146] *Davis & Co (Wines) Ltd v Afa-Minerva (EMI) Ltd* [1974] 2 Lloyd's Rep 27.

[147] Below, pp 347–8, 352.

[148] 1967 Act, s 2(3).

[149] Above, p 337.

[150] *Seddon v NE Salt Co Ltd* [1905] 1 Ch 326; *Angel v Jay* [1911] 1 KB 666.

[151] See, eg, *Lever Bros Ltd v Bell* [1931] 1 KB 557, 588, aff'd [1932] AC 161; *Leaf v International Galleries* [1950] 2 KB 86, 90, 91, 95; Tenth Report of the Law Reform Committee (Cmnd 1782, 1962) paras 6–10.

is more likely to exercise its discretion under section 2(2) of the Act when a contract has been executed than when it is still executory.

(b) Incorporation as Term. If a misrepresentation is also incorporated as a term of the contract, it was previously believed that the right to rescind was lost: the situation was treated simply as involving the breach of a contractual term, for 'the representation becomes merged in the higher contractual right'.[152] This rule was criticized because the representee would be worse off if the misrepresentation were incorporated in the contract as a mere warranty, since the representee would then have no right to rescind the contract but only to claim damages.[153] Section 1(a) of the 1967 Act now provides that rescission is still open notwithstanding that the misrepresentation has become a term of the contract. The present rule is: 'once a misrepresentation, always a misrepresentation'. The representee must choose between the remedies, however, and cannot both rescind the contract for misrepresentation and claim damages for breach of a contractual term, since, by rescinding it, the contract is effectively set aside for all purposes, including the right to claim damages for the breach of it.

(f) DAMAGES FOR FRAUDULENT MISREPRESENTATION: THE TORT OF DECEIT

(i) Elements of the claim in deceit

In order to succeed in a claim in the tort of deceit, the claimant must show that the representor made a misrepresentation; that the representation was made fraudulently; that the representor intended that the claimant (or someone in the claimant's position) should act upon it; and that the claimant did act upon it and suffered loss by so doing.[154]

As with other remedies for misrepresentation, the representation may be by words or conduct, including partial non-disclosure or active concealment which misleads the representee, but it cannot normally be by silence.[155] And we have already discussed the test for inducement in the case of a fraudulent misrepresentation.[156] The remaining elements peculiar to this remedy are the requirement of fraud, and the measure of damages.

[152] *Pennsylvania Shipping Co v Compagnie Nationale de Navigation* [1936] 2 All ER 1167, 1171.

[153] For remedies for breach of warranty (contrasted with breach of a condition of the contract, or a fundamental breach of an innominate term), see above, pp 150–60.

[154] *Bradford Third Equitable Benefit Building Society v Borders* [1941] 2 All ER 205, 211. There is no additional requirement that the claimant was aware of the representation or understood it to have been made, as long as it caused the claimant to act on it: *Credit Suisse Life (Bermuda) Ltd v Ivanishvili* [2025] UKPC 53 at [137], [179]; see above, p 327.

[155] Above, p 322. For cases which allow a claim in the tort of deceit for fraudulent breach of a duty of disclosure, see below, p 371.

[156] Above, p 328.

(ii) The meaning of fraud

The meaning of fraud was laid down by the House of Lords in *Derry v Peek*:[157]

A company obtained a statutory right to run trams by animal power or, if the consent of the Board of Trade was obtained, by steam or mechanical power. The directors believed that the Board would give this consent as a matter of course, as they had already submitted plans to the Board without any objection being made. They therefore issued a prospectus saying that the company had the right to run trams by steam or mechanical power. Peek took up shares in the company on the faith of the representation. The Board of Trade ultimately refused its consent, and the company was wound up.

Peek sued in tort for deceit. Lord Herschell said:[158]

First, in order to sustain an action of deceit, there must be proof of fraud, and nothing short of that will suffice. Secondly, fraud is proved when it is shewn that a false representation has been made (1) knowingly, or (2) without belief in its truth, or (3) recklessly, careless whether it be true or false. Although I have treated the second and third as distinct cases, I think the third is but an instance of the second, for one who makes a statement under such circumstances can have no real belief in the truth of what he states.

Lord Herschell went on to point out that making a false statement through want of care falls far short of fraud; so too does a false representation honestly believed, though on insufficient grounds. However, evidence of the reasonableness of the belief, and of the information available to the representor, will be relevant in the Court's assessment of whether the claimant has established that the representor did not honestly believe his representation.[159] In the present case, there were obviously reasons which had led the directors to make the untrue statement, and they 'honestly believed what they stated to be a true and fair representation of the facts'.[160] Peek's action therefore failed.

Derry v Peek thus established that a negligent misrepresentation will not amount to deceit, however gross the negligence may be.[161] Nothing short of fraud will suffice. On the other hand, it also shows that, to constitute fraud, it is not necessary that there should be a clear knowledge that the statement made was false. What is essential is the absence of an honest belief in its truth. Further, the motive of the person making the representation is irrelevant. It is no justification to show that the representation was made without criminal dishonesty, bad motive, or that there was no intention to cheat or cause loss to another by the deception.[162]

[157] (1990) 14 App Cas 337. [158] *Ibid*, 374. [159] *Ibid*, 375. [160] *Ibid*, 376.

[161] *Angus v Clifford* [1891] 2 Ch 449, 464; *Thomas Witter Ltd v TBP Industries Ltd* [1996] 2 All ER 573, 587–8. The Directors Liability Act 1890 reversed the effect of *Derry v Peek* for misrepresentations in company prospectuses, but there was no general remedy in damages for non-fraudulent but negligent pre-contractual misrepresentation until *Hedley Byrne & Co Ltd v Heller & Partners Ltd* [1964] AC 465 (below, p 349) and Misrepresentation Act 1967, s 2(1) (below, p 350).

[162] *Bradford Third Equitable Benefit Building Society v Borders* [1941] 2 All ER 205, 211; *Brown Jenkinson & Co Ltd v Percy Dalton (London) Ltd* [1957] 2 QB 621.

The elements of the tort of deceit must be established at the moment when the representee acts upon the representation.[163] That is the moment at which the representation must be false, and the representor must be fraudulent. A statement which is believed to be true when made and which is subsequently discovered by the representor to be false, will be considered to be fraudulent if the mistake is not communicated to the other person before that person acts on it.[164]

(iii) Measure of damages

Damages in deceit are designed to compensate the person who is deceived by the misrepresentation, and are assessed in accordance with the tortious measure; that is, in the context of a fraudulent pre-contractual misrepresentation, the amount by which the claimant is worse off as a result of entering into the contract in reliance on the misrepresentation.[165] A wider liability is imposed upon an intentional wrongdoer than a negligent or innocent one in order to deter fraud, and because 'moral considerations militate in favour of requiring the fraudster to bear the risk of misfortunes directly caused by his fraud'.[166] Accordingly, all actual losses directly flowing from the fraud are recoverable even if they could not reasonably have been foreseen[167] and, as contributory negligence is not a defence to fraud, damages will not be reduced on this ground.[168] The defrauded party is, however, required to mitigate the loss once aware of the fraud[169] but where it is claimed that there has been a failure to mitigate, the burden lies on the wrongdoer to show both that the defrauded party has failed to act reasonably and that the failure in fact resulted in an increased loss.[170]

The measure of damages can be illustrated by an example loosely based on the facts in *Smith New Court Securities Ltd v Citibank NA* in which the House of Lords stated the applicable principles.[171]

Suppose a person has been fraudulently induced to buy shares for £24 million. They are in fact worth £12 million at the date of the contract. If the representation had been true they would have been worth £26 million.

The injured party will be entitled to recover the amount by which it is out of pocket (£12 million), but not for the loss of the bargain (£14 million).[172] The injured party must give credit for any benefits received as a result of the transaction, including, as

[163] *Briess v Woolley* [1954] AC 333, 353.

[164] *Davies v London and Provincial Marine Insurance Co* (1878) 8 Ch D 469, 475.

[165] Above, p 332.

[166] *Smith New Court Securities Ltd v Citibank NA* [1997] AC 254, 279–80 (Lord Steyn).

[167] *Doyle v Olby (Ironmongers) Ltd* [1969] 2 QB 158; *Smith New Court Securities Ltd v Citibank NA* [1997] AC 254, 267, 279.

[168] *Standard Chartered Bank v Pakistan National Shipping Co (Nos 2 and 4)* [2002] UKHL 43.

[169] *Smith New Court Securities Ltd v Citibank NA* [1997] AC 254, 266.

[170] *Standard Chartered Bank v Pakistan National Shipping Corp* [2001] EWCA Civ 55, [2001] 1 All ER (Comm) 822.

[171] [1997] AC 254, 267 (Lord Browne-Wilkinson).

[172] See also the illustration of the difference between contract and tort measure damages above, p 332.

a general rule, the market value of the property acquired. Account will not generally be taken of a fall in the market value after the date of the contract unless, as in the case of *Smith New Court Securities Ltd*, the fraudulent misrepresentation continued to operate after that date or the misled party is unable to sell the property because of the fraud.[173] On the other hand, the misled party can undoubtedly recover in respect of damage consequential on entering into the transaction,[174] such as injury to the person or property, or, say, the expense involved in moving into a house which that party has been fraudulently induced to buy,[175] or even intangible losses such as distress caused by the fraud.[176] The misled party may also recover in respect of opportunities foregone as a result of entering the contract. Thus, in *East v Maurer*,[177] the purchasers of a hair salon bought in reliance on a fraudulent representation that the seller had no intention of regularly working at another salon he owned in the same town recovered, inter alia, the profit they would have made if the false representation had not been made, that is, the profit they might have been expected to make in another hairdressing business bought for a similar sum. As Sedley LJ noted in a later case, 'it does not follow that the proper mode of ascertaining damage in certain cases of tort may not mimic reasoning more familiar in contract'.[178]

Damages in tort are calculated principally to compensate the claimant's losses, not to deprive the representor of any profits the representor has made from the fraud. A Court may award punitive or exemplary damages in any tort, including deceit, where the conduct was calculated to make a profit for the defendant which may well exceed the compensation payable to the claimant.[179] A recent trend has been for punitive/exemplary damages to be awarded for insurance fraud.[180] It is doubtful whether an account of profits can be awarded for the tort of deceit to strip profits made by the tortfeasor.[181]

[173] [1997] AC 254, 267 (Lord Browne-Wilkinson).

[174] *Glossop Cartons and Print Ltd v Contact (Print and Packaging) Ltd* [2021] EWCA Civ 639, [2021] 1 WLR 4297 at [43] (it is not necessary to show a causal link between the misrepresentation and the consequential loss).

[175] *Doyle v Olby (Ironmongers) Ltd* [1969] 2 QB 158.

[176] *Shelley v Paddock* [1979] QB 120, aff'd [1980] QB 348; *Archer v Brown* [1985] QB 401 (aggravated damages).

[177] [1991] 1 WLR 461. See also *Smith New Court Securities Ltd v Citibank NA* [1997] AC 254, 282; *Clef Aquitaine SARL v Laporte Ltd* [2001] QB 488 (though transaction not loss-making, a more profitable one would have been entered into but for defendant's deceit).

[178] *Clef Aquitaine SARL v Laporte Materials (Barrow) Ltd* [2001] QB 488, 513.

[179] *Rookes v Barnard* [1964] AC 1129, 1226; *Kuddus v Chief Constable of Leicestershire Constabulary* [2001] UKHL 29, [2002] 2 AC 122. The 'calculation' need not be purely financial: *Hothi v Stokes* [2022] EWHC 2161 (Ch) at [163]. Aggravated damages for distress (above, n 176) are compensatory, not punitive: *Cannell v George* [2024] UKSC 19, [2025] AC 19 at [209].

[180] eg *Axa Insurance UK Plc v Financial Claims Solutions Ltd* [2018] EWCA Civ 1330, [2019] RTR 1. See on this trend, Goudkamp and Katsampouka (2018) 38 OJLS 90, 114.

[181] *Halifax Building Society v Thomas* [1996] Ch 217. Cf *Murad v Al-Saraj* [2005] EWCA Civ 959, [2005] WTLR 1573 (where the award of an account of profits was seen as a conventional award for breach of fiduciary duty).

(g) DAMAGES FOR NEGLIGENT MISREPRESENTATION: THE TORT OF NEGLIGENCE OR SECTION 2(1) OF THE MISREPRESENTATION ACT 1967

(i) Common law: the tort of negligence

Before the passing of the Misrepresentation Act 1967 there was no clear entitlement to claim damages for a non-fraudulent misstatement in the absence of a fiduciary relationship.[182] In 1963, in *Hedley Byrne & Co Ltd v Heller & Partners Ltd*[183] the House of Lords extended liability in damages in tort to negligent misstatement and held that a duty of care could exist where there was an assumption of responsibility creating a 'special relationship' between the person making the statement and the person to whom it was made. The effect of this decision on pre-contractual statements and the law relating to misrepresentation was not directly considered,[184] nor were the tests advanced by their Lordships for determining the existence of this special relationship uniform in their terminology.[185] Nevertheless, it was later made clear that the existence of a contract between the parties does not exclude a parallel or concurrent duty of care in tort.[186] Moreover, it has been held that a negligent misrepresentation made by one party to the other, preparatory to entering into a contract, can give rise to an action for damages in tort for negligent misstatement if the person making it has or professes to have special knowledge or skill in respect of the facts stated[187] or if the representation, in the context in which it is made, is to be regarded as neither casual nor unconsidered, but to be relied on.[188] The burden of proving negligence—both the duty of care and breach of that duty—rests on the party alleging it, that is, on the representee.

The tort measure of damages applies, but for a negligent misstatement the damages extend only to losses of a kind which the representor could reasonably have foreseen. The policy which we have seen in the tort of deceit, that the fraudulent defendant should be made to pay for all the loss caused by the fraud,[189] gives way in the tort of negligence to a policy which holds the defendant liable only for foreseeable losses because the basis of the imposition of the duty of care is that the defendant should, as a reasonable person, have foreseen the consequences of his or her actions.[190] Thus the common law draws distinctions to reflect moral differences between the fraudulent representor and the negligent representor.[191]

182 On the liability and more rigorous duties of a fiduciary, see *Nocton v Lord Ashburton* [1914] AC 932, 954 and below, p 368.

183 [1964] AC 465.

184 But see Lord Pearce, *ibid*, 539.

185 [1964] AC 465, 486, 503, 514, 528, 529.

186 *Henderson v Merrett Syndicates Ltd* [1995] 2 AC 145, 186–91 (Lord Goff).

187 *Esso Petroleum Co Ltd v Mardon* [1976] QB 801; *Cornish v Midland Bank plc* [1985] 3 All ER 513.

188 *Howard Marine and Dredging Co Ltd v A Ogden & Sons (Excavations) Ltd* [1978] QB 574, 592, 600.

189 Above, p 347.

190 *Overseas Tankship (UK) Ltd v Morts Dock & Engineering Co Ltd, The Wagon Mound* [1961] AC 388, 422–3.

191 *Ibid*; *Smith New Court Securities Ltd v Citibank NA* [1997] AC 254, 279–80.

The measure of loss in a claim in the tort of negligence will also depend upon the scope of the duty of care undertaken. If the representor undertakes a general duty to advise the representee about the transaction, the duty may extend to the consequences generally of the representee having entered into the contract, which could include losses flowing from fluctuations in the market in a case where, for example, the advice induces the representee to enter into a contact to purchase property. But where the duty is not to advise but is only to take care that specific information is correct, for example the valuation of a property by a surveyor or information given by a solicitor to a client, it has been held that a valuer is only liable for the foreseeable loss of the information being wrong, so that the damages are the difference between the valuation given and the true value of the property at the time of the breach.[192] However, there is no firm or exhaustive distinction between cases of 'advice' and 'information',[193] and the Supreme Court has more recently preferred a broader general test which focuses on the purpose to be served by the duty of care assumed by the defendant: 'in the case of negligent advice given by a professional adviser one looks to see what risk the duty was supposed to guard against and then looks to see whether the loss suffered represented the fruition of that risk'.[194]

(ii) Misrepresentation Act 1967

Section 2(1) of the Misrepresentation Act 1967[195] establishes a statutory right to damages:

> Where a person has entered into a contract after a misrepresentation has been made to him by another party thereto and as a result thereof he has suffered loss, then, if the person making the misrepresentation would be liable to damages in respect thereof had the misrepresentation been made fraudulently, that person shall be so liable notwithstanding that the misrepresentation was not made fraudulently, unless he proves that he had reasonable ground to believe and did believe up to the time the contract was made that the facts represented were true.

[192] *South Australia Asset Management Corp v York Montague Ltd* [1997] AC 191.

[193] *Hughes-Holland v BPE Solicitors* [2017] UKSC 21, [2018] AC 599 at [39]; *Manchester Building Society v Grant Thornton UK LLP* [2021] UKSC 20, [2022] AC 783 at [18]–[22].

[194] *Manchester Building Society v Grant Thornton UK LLP* [2021] UKSC 20 at [17]. See also *Charles B Lawrence & Associates v Intercommercial Bank Ltd* [2021] UKPC 30, [2022] PNLR 7 at [14]–[17].

[195] Implementing the Tenth Report of the Law Reform Committee (Cmnd 1782, 1962) para 17. The precedent for s 2(1) was in s 43 of the Companies Act 1948 (itself based originally on the Directors Liability Act 1890; above, p 346, n 161). See now Financial Services and Markets Act 2000, s 90, imposing liability in damages in respect of statements in prospectuses and listing particulars issued in support of the public issue of company securities, where those responsible cannot show that they reasonably believed that the statement was true and not misleading (the provisions in s 90 of the 2000 Act concerning prospectuses are replaced by the Public Offers and Admissions to Trading Regulations 2024 (SI 2024 No 105), reg 30). On the Misrepresentation Act, see generally Atiyah and Treitel (1967) 30 MLR 369. In relation to contracts entered into on or after 1 October 2014, s 2(4) (inserted by SI 2014 No 870 and amended by SI 2025 No 381) excludes the entitlement to damages under s 2 where the conduct constituting the misrepresentation gives rise to a right of redress under Part 4 of the Digital Markets, Competition and Consumers Act 2024, replacing Part 4A of the Consumer Protection from Unfair Trading Regulations 2008, which continue to apply until new replacement Regulations are made: see below, p 358.

The words 'reasonable ground to believe' suggest that the duty imposed upon the representor is equivalent to the duty of care in negligence. In general terms, it is appropriate to classify the remedy under section 2(1) as being for 'negligent' misrepresentation,[196] since it does not require proof of fraud, yet does not impose liability if the defendant is able to show 'that he had reasonable ground to believe' his statement (broadly speaking, that he was not negligent).[197] But there are significant differences in the scope of liability under section 2(1) and the tort of negligence. In *Howard Marine and Dredging Co Ltd v A Ogden & Sons (Excavations) Ltd*:[198]

O chartered two barges from HM. During the negotiations leading to the contract, HM's manager represented to O that the barges had a payload of 1,600 tonnes. He based this figure on his recollection of a statement in Lloyd's Register that the deadweight capacity of the barges was 1,800 tonnes. That statement was in fact erroneous. The German shipping documents (which the manager had seen) relating to the barges gave the true deadweight capacity at 1,055 tonnes. O refused to pay the agreed hire charges and HM withdrew the barges and sued for the balance due. O counterclaimed £600,000 on the grounds of misrepresentation, being the loss which it alleged it had sustained because of the low carrying capacity of the barges.

The Court of Appeal was divided as to whether the circumstances were such as to impose a duty of care in negligence at common law.[199] A majority of the Court held[200] that HM was liable under section 2(1), since the subsection goes further than the common law, does not require a special relationship or special skill and does not depend upon the representor being under a duty of care the extent of which may vary according to the circumstances in which the representation is made. The statute imposes an absolute obligation not to state facts[201] which the representor cannot prove it had reasonable ground to believe were true. The burden thus lies on the representor and not, as at common law, on the representee and it may be a heavy one to discharge, particularly since reasonable ground for belief in the truth of the statement must be shown to have existed up to the time the contract was made.

The subsection is narrower, however, than the common law because it is concerned only with representations made by a person who enters into a contract with the representee and with losses arising as a result of entering into that contract.[202] It does not apply to misrepresentations made by a third party. Thus if A enters into a contract

[196] eg *HIH Casualty and General Insurance Ltd v Chase Manhattan Bank* [2003] UKHL 6, [2003] 1 All ER (Comm) 349 at [5] (Lord Bingham).

[197] If the misrepresentation is made by an agent of the contracting party, thus rendering the contracting party liable under s 2(1) (*Resolute Maritime Inc v Nippon Kaiji Kyokai* [1983] 1 WLR 857), it may be that the principal is liable unless both the agent can show that he or she had reasonable ground to believe the statement and the principal had no means of knowledge of facts which would show the representation to be untrue.

[198] [1978] QB 574.

[199] Lord Denning MR and Shaw LJ. Bridge LJ expressed no concluded view on this issue.

[200] Bridge and Shaw LJJ (Lord Denning MR dissenting).

[201] This now includes misrepresentations of law: *Pankhania v Hackney LBC* [2002] EWHC 2441 (Ch); above, p 326.

[202] *Taberna Europe CDO II plc v Selskabet AF1* [2016] EWCA Civ 1262, [2017] QB 633 at [44].

with B as a result of a misrepresentation made to A by C, no action will lie under the subsection unless C is B's agent; nor will C be liable to A under this provision, though C might be liable under a collateral warranty,[203] or in tort for negligent misstatement if a special relationship of care or reliance is shown to exist.[204]

The effect of section 2(1) of the 1967 Act is to confer upon the representee a right to damages for misrepresentation in circumstances in which there would have been such a right had the misrepresentation been fraudulent. It is now clear that the measure of damages is the tortious measure,[205] that is, so as to put the representee into the position as if he or she had never been induced by the misrepresentation to enter into the contract.[206] But the equation with fraud has given rise to certain problems. Most importantly, it appears that under the subsection it is the fraud measure (ie the measure in the tort of deceit) which applies, rather than that for negligent misstatement at common law. This allows the recovery of all losses directly flowing from the misrepresentation even if not foreseeable.[207] In *Royscot Trust Ltd v Rogerson*:[208]

A finance company was induced to advance a greater sum than it would otherwise have done by a car dealer's misrepresentation that a 20 per cent deposit had been paid by a prospective hire-purchaser of a car. The hire-purchaser later ceased to pay the instalments due and dishonestly sold the car. It was held that whether or not the sale by the hire-purchaser was foreseeable, the loss to the finance company of the unpaid instalments was recoverable from the car dealer under section 2(1) of the 1967 Act.

The argument that, as a matter of policy, it was undesirable to adopt the fraud measure for what is basically negligence liability, since fools should not be treated as if they were rogues,[209] was rejected by the Court of Appeal as incompatible with the literal words of the statute. It appears that this literal reading may be what was originally intended by the legislature, because at the time when the proposal for section 2(1) was devised the distinction between the measure of damages in deceit and in negligence was not yet fully developed,[210] and the Law Reform Committee[211] did not think that it was 'in general the function of the civil law to grade the damages which an injured person may recover in accordance with the moral guilt of the defendant'.

[203] Above, p 146.

[204] *Resolute Maritime Inc v Nippon Kaiji Kyokai* [1983] 1 WLR 857.

[205] *Royscot Trust Ltd v Rogerson* [1991] 2 QB 297, 304–5.

[206] Above, p 332.

[207] Above, pp 347 (deceit), 349 (negligence).

[208] [1991] 2 QB 297. See also *William Sindall plc v Cambridgeshire CC* [1994] 1 WLR 1016, 1037; *South Australia Asset Management Corp v York Montague Ltd* [1997] AC 191, 216.

[209] Cf Fairest [1967] CLJ 239, 244; Hooley (1991) 107 LQR 547, 549–51. See also Atiyah and Treitel (1967) 30 MLR 369, 373; Cartwright, *Unequal Bargaining* (1991) 131–2.

[210] The Law Reform Committee (above, n 195) reported in 1962, after the Privy Council in *The Wagon Mound* [1961] AC 388 had laid down the test of remoteness of damage in the tort of negligence, but before the House of Lords in *Hedley Byrne* [1964] AC 465 (above, p 349) extended the tort of negligence to misrepresentations, and long before *Hedley Byrne* was extended to pre-contractual misrepresentations in *Esso Petroleum Co Ltd v Mardon* [1976] QB 801. The natural point of reference for the new statutory liability during the formulation of the proposals was therefore the tort of deceit. See also Cartwright [1987] Conv 423.

[211] Above, n 195, para 22.

However, the law of tort has moved on, and there is now a reluctance to apply the fraud measure for what is in essence only a negligent misrepresentation or, indeed, a misrepresentation which may not even be negligent but where the defendant cannot discharge the burden of proving reasonable ground for his or her belief.[212] The point is, moreover, not beyond argument. First, it was not necessary in *Royscot*'s case to choose between the fraud and negligence measures. This was because the act of disposing of the car by the hire-purchaser was held to be foreseeable, so the unpaid instalments would have been recoverable in any event. Secondly, it is already established that not all the consequences of fraud follow in the case of liability under section 2(1) of the 1967 Act. Damages under section 2(1) may be reduced for contributory negligence where the loss was partly the fault of the representee[213] although, as has been seen,[214] damages for fraudulent misrepresentation in the tort of deceit may not be reduced for contributory negligence. Again, the extended limitation period which applies in an action of deceit[215] will not apply to liability under section 2(1) because the statutory claim is not in fact based on the defendant's fraud. There are, moreover, indications that the Supreme Court would be reluctant to find that what Lord Steyn described as 'the rather loose wording' of the statute 'compels the court to treat a person who was morally innocent as if he was guilty of fraud when it comes to the measure of damages'.[216]

(h) EXCLUSION AND LIMITATION OF LIABILITY

Chapter 6 contains a detailed account of the approach of the common law to the incorporation and interpretation of exclusion and limitation clauses, and the statutory control of such clauses. Here we consider particular issues concerning clauses which seek to exclude or limit a contracting party's liability for misrepresentation—and 'liability' is used here in the broadest sense, including any of the remedies for misrepresentation. Thus a clause may exclude all remedies for misrepresentation; or may exclude or limit damages; or may exclude the right to rescind the contract.

(i) Common law

At common law, a party to a contract is entitled, by means of an appropriately drafted clause, to limit or exclude liability for misrepresentation. We have seen, however, that a

[212] *Howard Marine and Dredging Co Ltd v A Ogden & Sons (Excavations) Ltd* [1978] QB 574, above, p 351. Cf *Avon Insurance plc v Swire Fraser Ltd* [2000] 1 All ER (Comm) 573, 633 (at the margin, 'a misrepresentation should not be too easily found' if the decision in *Royscot*'s case has to be applied).

[213] *Gran Gelato Ltd v Richcliff (Group) Ltd* [1992] Ch 560, 573–4; *Taberna Europe CDO II plc v Selskabet AF1* [2016] EWCA Civ 1262 at [52] (Moore-Bick LJ: 'Section 2(1) of the Misrepresentation Act 1967 creates a form of statutory liability sounding in negligence. In principle, therefore, contributory negligence ought to be available as a defence').

[214] Above, p 347.

[215] Limitation Act 1980, s 32(1)(a): in an action 'based on the fraud of the defendant' the limitation period does not begin to run 'until the plaintiff has discovered the fraud . . . or could with reasonable diligence have discovered it'.

[216] *Smith New Court Securities Ltd v Citibank NA* [1997] AC 254, 283. See also at 267 (Lord Browne-Wilkinson).

clause can never exclude a party's liability for its own fraud in inducing the making of the contract, although it is not settled whether the rule also covers a purported exclusion of liability for the fraud of an agent or employee in which the contracting party was not personally involved.[217]

Two common forms of clause should be noted in particular. First, a party may seek to avoid liability by providing in the contract that no representations were made during the negotiations, or that the other party did not rely on any representations that were made. If there is no representation, or no reliance, there can be no remedy for misrepresentation.[218] It has now been firmly settled by the Court of Appeal that 'no representation' and 'no reliance' clauses can be effective at common law: both parties are estopped by their contract from raising the (mis)representations, which were in fact made, in order to obtain a remedy.[219] However, it is unlikely that a Court would allow such a clause to operate to exclude personal fraud.[220] Even a successful clause of this kind will be subject to the statutory control of section 3 of the Misrepresentation Act 1967 if in substance it constitutes an attempt to exclude or restrict liability for a misrepresentation that was in fact made.[221]

A second common clause is one which provides that a written contract constitutes the 'entire agreement' between the parties. Such a clause does not, however, exclude remedies for pre-contractual misrepresentation: it is interpreted as providing only that the totality of the parties' *contractual* obligations are to be found in the written document and not, for example, in any collateral contract.[222]

(ii) Statute

The Misrepresentation Act 1967, the Unfair Contract Terms Act 1977, and the Consumer Rights Act 2015 restrict the freedom to exclude liability for misrepresentation. The 1967 and 1977 Acts apply only to non-consumer contracts and notices; the 2015 Act applies only to consumer contracts and notices.

(a) Misrepresentation Act 1967. Section 3 of the 1967 Act provides:

> (1) If any contract contains a term which would exclude or restrict:
> (a) any liability to which a party to a contract may be subject by reason of any misrepresentation made by him before the contract was made; or

[217] Above, p 200. [218] Above, p 327.

[219] *First Tower Trustees Ltd v CDS (Superstores International) Ltd* [2018] EWCA Civ 1396, [2019] 1 WLR 637 at [47]. See also *Peekay Intermark Ltd v Australia and New Zealand Banking Group Ltd* [2006] EWCA Civ 386, [2006] 2 Lloyd's Rep 511 at [56]; *Springwell Navigation Corp v JP Morgan Chase* [2010] EWCA Civ 1221, [2010] 2 CLC 705 at [165]–[169], [177]; *Axa Sun Life Services plc v Campbell Martin Ltd* [2011] EWCA Civ 133, [2011] 1 CLC 312 at [93]. On this so-called 'contractual estoppel', see further above, p 136, and Cartwright, in Burrows and Peel (eds), *Contract Terms* (2007) 222–5; Trukhtanov (2009) 125 LQR 648.

[220] *S Pearson & Son Ltd v Dublin Corp* [1907] AC 351, 353–4 (Lord Loreburn LC: 'it seems clear that no one can escape liability for his own fraudulent statements by inserting in a contract a clause that the other party shall not rely upon them'); but cf *Smith v Chadwick* (1882) 20 Ch D 27, 44–5 (Jessel MR).

[221] Below, p 356.

[222] *Deepak Fertilisers and Petrochemicals Corp v ICI Chemicals & Polymers Ltd* [1999] 1 Lloyd's Rep 387, 395.

(b) any remedy available to another party to the contract by reason of such a misrepresentation,

that term shall be of no effect except in so far as it satisfies the requirement of reasonableness as stated in section 11(1) of the Unfair Contract Terms Act 1977; and it is for those claiming that the term satisfies that requirement to show that it does.[223]

(2) This section does not apply to a term in a consumer contract within the meaning of Part 2 of the Consumer Rights Act 2015 (but see the provision made about such contracts in section 62 of that Act).[224]

This provision regulates clauses in contracts, except consumer contracts,[225] which seek to exclude or limit liability or any remedy for pre-contractual misrepresentation: that is, where the misrepresentation is the gist of the claim, such as rescission, or a claim under section 2(1) of the Misrepresentation Act 1967. A non-consumer clause or notice which excludes or limits liability at common law for a negligent misstatement[226] is regulated by section 2 of the Unfair Contract Terms Act 1977,[227] but may also, where the misstatement is made by a party to the contract, be regulated by section 3 of the Misrepresentation Act 1967.[228]

Under the 1967 Act the clause which seeks to exclude or limit liability or any remedy for misrepresentation is prima facie invalid, unless the representor can show that it was a fair and reasonable term to be included in the contract having regard to all the circumstances which were, or ought reasonably to have been, known to or in the contemplation of the parties when the contract was made.[229] A clause purporting to exclude liability for fraudulent misrepresentation, even if it is valid at common law (such as a clause excluding liability for an agent's fraud),[230] will generally not be held to be reasonable.[231] Since a clause which is not proved to be reasonable is ineffective for all

[223] Substituted by the Unfair Contract Terms Act 1977, s 8(1). See also *Trident Turboprop (Dublin) Ltd v First Flight Couriers Ltd* [2009] EWCA Civ 290, [2010] QB 86 at [19] (reference to Unfair Contract Terms Act 1977 renders that Act the controlling instrument, and therefore international supply contracts are excluded from the scope of the Misrepresentation Act, s 3 by the Unfair Contract Terms Act 1977, s 26).

[224] Inserted by Consumer Rights Act 2015, Sched 4, para 1.

[225] For consumer contracts, see below, p 357.

[226] *Hedley Byrne & Co Ltd v Heller & Partners Ltd* [1964] AC 465; above, p 349.

[227] Below, p 357.

[228] Cf Cartwright, *Misrepresentation, Mistake and Non-Disclosure* (7th edn, 2025) para 9-23.

[229] Unfair Contract Terms Act 1977, s 11(1); see above, p 220. For illustrations, see *Walker v Boyle* [1982] 1 WLR 495 (condition 17 of the National Conditions of Sale not reasonable); *First Tower Trustees Ltd v CDS (Superstores International) Ltd* [2018] EWCA Civ 1396 (non-reliance clause in lease and agreement for lease unreasonable; but see Lewison LJ at [67]); cf *McCullagh v Lane Fox & Partners* (1996) 49 Con LR 124 (estate agent's disclaimer about size of plot reasonable); *Cleaver v Schyde Investments Ltd* [2011] EWCA Civ 929, [2011] 2 P & CR 21 at [43] (distinguishing *Walker v Boyle* on the basis that the limitation of the right to rescind in the modern standard conditions of sale are far less draconian); *Lloyd v Browning* [2013] EWCA Civ 1637, [2014] 1 P & CR 11.

[230] Above, p 200.

[231] *Thomas Witter Ltd v TBP Industries* [1996] 2 All ER 573, 598; *South West Water Services Ltd v International Computers Ltd* [1999] BLR 420.

purposes, and the Court has no power to rewrite it so as to limit it to such an exclusion as would have been reasonable,[232] there is a risk that an over-wide exclusion clause which might also have covered fraud will be held ineffective, although the Courts are likely for this reason not to interpret clauses as covering fraud unless they clearly so provide.[233]

The question arises whether it is possible to avoid the application of section 3 of the 1967 Act by means of a contract term which negatives an element of the claim, for example, a clause which provides that statements made are 'not to be construed as assertions of fact', or that they are 'statements of opinion or belief only', or that no representations have been made, or that no representation has been relied on. In *Cremdean Properties Ltd v Nash*,[234] the defendants, by whom it was alleged a misrepresentation had been made, relied on the following clause:

> These particulars are prepared for the convenience of an intending purchaser or tenant and although they are believed to be correct their accuracy is not guaranteed and any error, omission or misdescription shall not annul the sale or the grounds on which compensation may be claimed and neither do they constitute any part of an offer of a contract. Any intending purchaser or tenant must satisfy himself by inspection or otherwise as to the correctness of each of the statements contained in these particulars.

The Court of Appeal rejected the defendants' argument that the effect of this clause was to bring about a situation as if no representation at all had been made. The Court further doubted whether, even if the defendants' argument were correct, it would be possible thus to defeat the application of section 3 of the 1967 Act. This has been confirmed in more recent cases where the Court has accepted that a 'no representation' or 'non-reliance' clause can in principle create a contractual estoppel,[235] but has also indicated that, if a representation has in fact been made, a contract term which purports to deny one or more of the conditions to be fulfilled before a representation is effective will be subject to section 3, and to the test of reasonableness provided for in that section. The question is one of substance rather than form. Section 3 must be interpreted so as to give effect to its evident policy: to prevent contracting parties from escaping from liability for misrepresentation unless it is reasonable for them to do so.[236]

In *Overbrooke Estates Ltd v Glencombe Properties Ltd*,[237] on the other hand:

> An auctioneer sold property belonging to O to G, and in the course of so doing made a misrepresentation as to local authority plans with respect to the property. G refused

[232] *Skipskredittforeningen v Emperor Navigation* [1998] 1 Lloyd's Rep 66, 75; *Stewart Gill Ltd v Horatio Myer & Co Ltd* [1992] QB 600, above, p 226.

[233] *Government of Zanzibar v British Aerospace (Lancaster House) Ltd* [2000] 1 WLR 2333, 2346–7 (disapproving *Thomas Witter Ltd v TBP Industries Ltd* [1996] 2 All ER 573); *HIH Casualty and General Insurance Ltd v Chase Manhattan Bank* [2003] UKHL 6 at [16], [68], [97].

[234] (1977) 244 EG 547.

[235] Above, pp 136, 354.

[236] *First Tower Trustees Ltd v CDS (Superstores International) Ltd* [2018] EWCA Civ 1396 at [51], [67], [99], [107]; see also *Springwell Navigation Corp v JP Morgan Chase Bank* [2010] EWCA Civ 1221 at [181].

[237] [1974] 1 WLR 1355. This decision was accepted as correct by Bridge LJ in *Cremdean Properties Ltd v Nash* (1977) 244 EG 547, 549. See also *Collins v Howell-Jones* (1980) 259 EG 331.

to proceed with the sale because of the misrepresentation and O brought an action for specific performance of the contract. O relied upon a term in the conditions of sale which stated that the auctioneer had no authority to make any representation in relation to the property.

Brightman J held that section 3 of the 1967 Act did not operate to qualify the right of a principal publicly to limit the authority of an agent and was therefore inapplicable. Where, despite a term limiting an agent's actual or ostensible authority, the principal expressly authorizes the agent to make the representation in question, section 3 should apply.[238] The cases permitting the limitation of an agent's authority concern auctioneers and estate agents, and it is not clear whether an employer could rely on a term limiting an employee's actual or ostensible authority in order to avoid the operation of section 3.[239]

(b) Unfair Contract Terms Act 1977. Where a claim for misrepresentation is based on the defendant's breach of a duty of care in the tort of negligence, a non-consumer clause or notice seeking to exclude or limit the defendant's liability will be regulated by section 2 of the Unfair Contract Terms Act 1977.[240] This provides that a person cannot by reference to a contract term or notice exclude or restrict his business[241] liability for death or personal injury resulting from negligence nor (except insofar as the term or notice satisfies the requirement of reasonableness) for any other loss or damage. The operation of section 2 and of other related provisions of the 1977 Act was considered in Chapter 6 above.[242]

(c) Consumer Rights Act 2015. Part 2 of the Consumer Rights Act 2015,[243] which applies to all unfair terms and not only to exclusion or limitation clauses, will also affect clauses excluding or restricting a consumer's remedies for misrepresentation. A term which has the object or effect of limiting the trader's obligation to respect commitments undertaken by his agents is one of those included in the indicative and non-exhaustive list of terms of consumer contract terms which may be regarded as unfair[244] and it therefore appears that clauses such as that in *Overbrooke Estates Ltd v Glencombe Properties Ltd* will be effective only if they satisfy the tests, in the 2015 Act, of good faith and absence of a significant imbalance in the parties' rights to the detriment of the consumer.[245]

[238] *Museprime Properties Ltd v Adhill Properties Ltd* (1991) 61 P & CR 111. Cf *Collins v Howell-Jones* (1980) 259 EG 331, 332; but note Murdoch (1981) 97 LQR 518, 524.

[239] Cf *Mendelssohn v Normand Ltd* [1970] 1 QB 177.

[240] Amended by Consumer Rights Act 2015, Sched 4, para 4.

[241] 1977 Act, s 1(3).

[242] Above, p 212.

[243] Replacing the Unfair Terms in Consumer Contracts Regulations 1999 (SI 1999 No 2083), and reimplementing the Directive on Unfair Terms in Consumer Contracts 93/13/EEC: see above, p 226.

[244] 2015 Act, Sched 2, para 17.

[245] 2015 Act, s 62; above, p 227.

3. CONSUMERS' RIGHTS OF REDRESS UNDER PART 4 OF THE DIGITAL MARKETS, COMPETITION AND CONSUMERS ACT 2024

Part 4 of the Digital Markets, Competition and Consumers Act 2024 replaces the Consumer Protection from Unfair Trading Regulations 2008,[246] which implemented the Unfair Commercial Practices Directive.[247] The 2008 Regulations provided criminal sanctions for unfair commercial practices, and regulatory enforcement, but no private law remedies until a new Part 4A was introduced in 2014[248] to provide 'rights to redress' for consumers in circumstances which include cases where the consumer has entered into the contract in reliance on the other party's misrepresentation. Until new replacement Regulations are made under the 2024 Act,[249] Part 4A of the 2008 Regulations continues in force to provide the detail of the rights of redress for unfair commercial practices as they are now defined under Part 4 of the 2024 Act,[250] and references are therefore given in this section to relevant provisions of the 2008 Regulations as well as the 2024 Act.

If a consumer enters into a contract with a trader, either for the supply by the trader to the consumer of a 'product' (widely defined and including goods, services, and digital content),[251] or for the supply of a product by the consumer to the trader without the trader supplying a product to the consumer,[252] and the trader engages in a 'prohibited practice' (an unfair[253] commercial practice[254] involving a misleading action or an aggressive practice)[255] in relation to the product,[256] and the prohibited practice is a significant factor in the consumer's decision to enter into the contract,[257] the consumer has a right of redress:[258] the right to unwind in respect of the contract or, in certain

[246] SI 2008 No 1277.

[247] Directive 2005/29/EC.

[248] Part 4A was inserted by Consumer Protection (Amendment) Regulations 2014 (SI 2014 No 870) as regards contracts entered into on or after 1 October 2014. For background, see Law Com No 332 (2012).

[249] 2024 Act, s 233.

[250] 2024 Act, s 252(3). The 2008 Regulations also continue to apply to acts or omissions taking place before the commencement date of the 2024 Act: s 252(2).

[251] 2024 Act, ss 248(1), 249; cf 2008 Regulations, reg 2(1). Immoveable property is within the definition of 'product', but for the purposes of the rights to redress under Part 4A of the 2008 Regulations, this includes only certain residential leases: s 27C.

[252] 2024 Act, s 232(2). The 2008 Regulations refer to a contract for the 'sale or supply of a product' by the trader to the consumer, and a contract for the 'sale of goods' to the trader by the consumer: reg 27A(2).

[253] A commercial practice is 'unfair' if it is likely to cause the average consumer to take a transactional decision that the consumer would not have taken otherwise as a result of the practice: 2024 Act, s 225(4).

[254] A 'commercial practice' is 'an act or omission by a trader relating to the promotion or supply of (a) the trader's product to a consumer, (b) another trader's product to a consumer, or (c) a consumer's product to the trader or another person': 2024 Act, s 225(3); cf 2008 Regulations, reg 2(1).

[255] 2024 Act, s 232(7); cf 2008 Regulations, reg 27B.

[256] Or, in the case of a contract for goods or digital content, the *producer* engages in such a practice of which the trader is aware or could reasonably be expected to be aware: 2024 Act, s 232(3)(b); 2008 Regulations, reg 27A(4)(b). The 'producer' is the manufacture, the importer into the United Kingdom, or an 'own-brander' of the goods or digital content: 2024 Act, s 232(6); 2008 Regulations, reg 27A(5).

[257] 2024 Act, s 232(4); 2008 Regulations, reg 27A(6). Cf the (different) test of causation generally adopted in the remedies for misrepresentation: above, p 328.

[258] 2024 Act, s 232; 2008 Regulations, reg 27A.

circumstances, the right to a discount or the right to damages. A misrepresentation will often constitute a 'misleading action',[259] which is defined as including the provision of false or misleading information[260] relating to a product, a trader, or any other matter relevant to a transactional decision, and an overall presentation which is likely to deceive[261] the average consumer about a matter relating to a product, a trader, or any other matter relevant to a transactional decision.[262]

Where the consumer has contracted for the supply of a product by the trader, the consumer has the 'right to unwind' by clearly rejecting the product (by words or conduct) with a period of 90 days from the contract (or sometimes from a later date, such as the delivery of the goods or the first performance of services under the contract), and as long as the product can still be rejected and the consumer has not exercised the right to a discount.[263] The effect of the consumer's exercising this right is that the contract comes to an end so that both parties are released from their obligations under it, the trader must give the consumer a refund and (in the case of contracts for the supply of goods) the consumer must make the goods available for collection by the trader.[264] Where the consumer has contracted to sell goods to the trader, the consumer exercises the right to unwind by indicating clearly to the trader (by words or conduct) that the contract is ended, and the consumer then has a right to the return of the goods (and the duty to repay the price paid by the trader) or, if the goods cannot be returned in the same condition, a right to payment of the amount by which the market value exceeded the price when it was paid by the trader.[265]

The consumer's right to a discount involves the return of a proportion of payments already made (or the reduction of payments due) calculated by reference to the seriousness of the prohibited practice,[266] except where the amount payable for the product under the contract exceeds £5,000 and the market value was less than the contract price at the time of the contract, in which case the discount is based on the difference between the market price and the contract price[267]—in effect, depriving the trader of his profit over the market price.

The consumer's right to damages covers financial loss, and any alarm, distress, or physical inconvenience or discomfort, which would not have occurred if the prohibited practice had not taken place, but does not include the right to be paid damages in respect

[259] Conduct which can be characterized as duress or undue influence may involve an 'aggressive practice': below, p 409.

[260] Including information which, although true, is presented in a misleading way: 2024 Act, s 226(2).

[261] An overall presentation may be deceiving even if the information it contains is true: 2024 Act, s 226(3).

[262] 2024 Act, s 226(1); cf 2008 Regulations, reg 5. For the purposes of the rights to redress under Part 4A of the 2008 Regulations, a 'transactional decision' means the consumer's decision to enter into the contract with a trader: reg 27B(2) (cf the 2024 Act, s 232(8)).

[263] 2008 Regulations, reg 27E.

[264] 2008 Regulations, reg 27F.

[265] 2008 Regulations, reg 27G.

[266] 25 per cent if it is more than minor; 50 per cent if it is significant; 75 per cent if it is serious; 100 per cent if it is very serious. The seriousness is assessed by reference to the behaviour of the person who engaged in the practice, the impact of the practice on the consumer, and the time that has elapsed since the prohibited practice took place: 2008 Regulations, reg 27I(1)–(5).

[267] 2008 Regulations, reg 27I(6), (7).

of the difference between the market price of the product and the contract price[268]—that is, it is not a remedy aimed at covering the core measure of loss covered by an action in tort[269] but other consequential losses. However, the damages are limited to losses that were reasonably foreseeable at the time of the prohibited practice, and there is no right to damages where the trader proves (inter alia) that his misrepresentation was due to a mistake or reliance on information supplied by another person, and he took all reasonable precautions and exercised all due diligence to avoid the occurrence of the prohibited practice.[270]

The rights of redress under Part 4 of the Digital Markets, Competition and Consumers Act 2024 will sometimes arise concurrently with claims under the general law for remedies for misrepresentation discussed earlier in this chapter. With one very significant exception, the 2024 Act is intended to provide additional remedies for consumers, allowing choice between claims under the Regulations and under the general law, and even allowing concurrent claims as long as the consumer does not obtain double compensation.[271] There is therefore no obstacle to the consumer rescinding the contract in equity (rather than exercising the right to unwind under the Regulations) whilst claiming damages for consequential loss under the Regulations. The choice of remedy will no doubt depend on the circumstances, and sometimes one will be more easily available, or more advantageous, than another. For example, the right to unwind under the Regulations is exercisable for a fixed period of 90 days from (normally) the contract,[272] whereas (depending on the circumstances) there may be an earlier bar to rescission based on lapse of time;[273] and a claim in the tort of deceit allows recovery of unforeseeable consequential losses,[274] whereas damages under the Regulations are limited to reasonably foreseeable losses.[275]

The very significant exception, however, is that a consumer who has a right of redress under Chapter 1 of Part 4 of the Digital Markets, Competition and Consumers Act 2024 is not entitled to be paid damages under section 2 of the Misrepresentation Act 1967 in respect of the conduct constituting the misrepresentation.[276] The consumer has no choice: if there is a right of redress under the 2024 Act, section 2 of the 1967 Act is disapplied and so the consumer cannot claim damages on that basis. This has the curious effect of reducing the consumer's protection in relation to unforeseeable consequential losses since, as we have seen, the claimant under section 2(1) may recover the same damages as if there were fraud.[277]

[268] 2008 Regulations, reg 27J(1)–(3).

[269] Above, p 332.

[270] 2008 Regulations, reg 27J(4), (5). Cf the defence to the general claim of damages under Misrepresentation Act 1967, s 2(1), above, pp 350–1; and the fact that the claim for consequential loss under s 2(1) extends to unforeseeable losses: above, p 352.

[271] 2008 Regulations, reg 27L.

[272] 2008 Regulations, reg 27E.

[273] Above, p 340.

[274] Above, p 347.

[275] 2008 Regulations, reg 27J(4).

[276] Misrepresentation Act 1967, s 2(4), inserted by SI 2014 No 870 and amended by SI 2025 No 381.

[277] Above, p 352. The consumer who can prove the trader's fraud may, however, still bring a claim in the tort of deceit.

4. NON-DISCLOSURE

(a) NO GENERAL DUTY TO DISCLOSE

We have noted that silence does not normally amount to a misrepresentation and that at common law there is in general no duty of disclosure of material facts before the contract is made; and that this is consistent with the reluctance of the common law to allow parties to avoid contracts on the basis of their own mistakes.[278] The examples were given of the person who visits an antiques shop and sees a rare George II table being sold as a nineteenth-century piece and the oil prospector who discovers that there is oil under a given piece of land. Neither has to inform the other party. Nor does a bank have to inform its customer that a more attractive rate of interest is available in a different account.[279] There is not even a duty of disclosure where one party realizes that the other is making a mistake about some relevant fact.[280] This reflects a major difference between English law and civil law systems since in most civil law systems not only is a greater place found for mistake as a ground of vitiation of contracts, but also a party who deliberately does not disclose a relevant fact to the other party may be liable for fraud.[281] The justification for the common law rule is said to be the need to give people an incentive to invest in the acquisition of skill and knowledge and consequently to allow 'good deals' to the more intelligent or the hard-working.[282] Even in civil law systems there is no duty to disclose information 'which is the product of one's own efforts in evaluating market conditions or ascertaining the attributes of property that enhance its value'.[283] This economic argument does not apply to information which has been acquired by pure chance or without any investment. Nor can it be conclusive where the information is acquired by a method regarded by the law as illegitimate—for example where it is 'insider' information about the position of a company. There may also be situations where it may be economically efficient to impose a duty of disclosure. In the case of house sales, the absence of a duty of disclosure means that generally it is the intending purchaser who commissions the survey and where several people are interested in a property each will have to invest in the search for information, whereas if sellers were obliged to disclose key elements concerning the state of their houses to all potential buyers, the cost of surveying would in many cases be incurred only once.[284]

[278] Above, p 320. See *Bell v Lever Bros Ltd* [1932] AC 161, 227 (Lord Atkin); *Banque Keyser Ullmann SA v Skandia (UK) Insurance Co Ltd* [1990] 1 QB 665, 798–9, aff'd [1991] 2 AC 249; *Clarion Ltd v National Provident Institution* [2000] 1 WLR 1888, 1905.

[279] *Suriya & Douglas v Midland Bank* [1999] 1 All ER (Comm) 612.

[280] *Smith v Hughes* (1867) LR 6 QB 597, 603–4, 607, 610–11, above, p 302; *Davies v London and Provincial Marine Insurance Co* (1878) 8 Ch D 468, 474.

[281] Lando and Beale, *Principles of European Contract Law Parts I and II* (2000) 256.

[282] See generally Duggan, Bryan, and Hanks, *Contractual Non-Disclosure* (1994); Kronman (1978) 7 JLS 1; Nicholas, in Harris and Tallon (eds), *Contract Law Today* (1989); Fried, *Contract as Promise* (1981) 77 ff; Trebilcock, *The Limits of Freedom of Contract* (1993) 106 ff.

[283] Kötz, *European Contract Law* (2nd edn, 2017) 178.

[284] Fabre-Magnan, in Beatson and Friedmann (eds), *Good Faith and Fault in Contract Law* (1995) 117–18.

Less compellingly, the rule has also been justified by the great difficulty in imposing any sensible limits on a duty of disclosure,[285] because the information which had to be disclosed may be unreliable or doubtful or inconclusive, and because disclosure may expose the informer to criticism or litigation.[286]

As well as the exceptions to the general rule, discussed below, there are situations in which English law affords similar protection by the use of implied terms, such as the implied term that goods should be of satisfactory quality and fit for purpose:[287] even if the seller has no duty to disclose information about the goods, there is an incentive to do so in order to avoid breach of the implied term.[288] Moreover, as we have seen, where A knows that B has misunderstood the *terms* of an offer made by A, no contract will be formed if A does not inform B of its true nature.[289] In this section, we are concerned with the duty to disclose *facts* which are relevant to the other party's decision to enter into the contract.

(b) PARTICULAR DUTIES OF DISCLOSURE

Although there is no general duty to disclose information during the negotiations for a contract, English law recognizes particular duties of disclosure. Two reasons account for most situations where, at common law or in equity, or by statute, parties negotiating a contract have been held to be subject to a duty of disclosure. The first is that, in certain classes of contract, one of the parties is presumed to have means of knowledge which are not accessible to the other, either at all or only by incurring disproportionately high costs. The party who is presumed to have the information is bound to disclose everything which may be supposed likely to affect the judgement of the other party. At common law such contracts have been labelled contracts *uberrimae fidei* (contracts 'of utmost good faith'), although the label is not helpful to identify what has to be disclosed for each of the limited classes of contract which carry duties of disclosure. Moreover, the principal use of this label was in relation to the contract of insurance, which was commonly identified, even by statute, as a contract *uberrimae fidei*;[290] but the rule that

[285] *Laidlaw v Organ* 15 US 178, 194 (1817).

[286] *Banque Financière de la Cité SA v Westgate Insurance Co Ltd* [1991] 2 AC 249, where a narrower range of policy issues relevant to the imposition of a duty of disclosure were addressed in the leading speech by Lord Templeman who concluded at 274 that, 'A professional should wear a halo but need not wear a hair shirt.'

[287] Zimmermann and Whittaker, *Good Faith in European Contract Law* (2000) 194–7, above, p 170.

[288] Cartwright, *Misrepresentation, Mistake and Non-Disclosure* (7th edn, 2025) para 17-46. There are no such wide-ranging statutory terms in contracts for the sale of land, but the seller has a duty to convey the property as contracted which may best be characterized as an implied term that there are no undisclosed latent defects in the title—in effect, a duty of disclosure of defects in the title is imposed indirectly on the seller: see generally Harpum (1992) 108 LQR 280, 320–33; Cartwright, para 17-47.

[289] *Hartog v Colin & Shields* [1939] 3 All ER 566, above, p 281.

[290] Marine Insurance Act 1906, s 17. Cf, however, *Carter v Boehm* (1766) 3 Burr 1905, 1910 where Lord Mansfield referred only to 'good faith'; 'utmost' good faith is a later refinement: *Manifest Shipping Co Ltd v Uni-Polaris Insurance Co Ltd* [2001] UKHL 1, [2003] 1 AC 469 at [44].

a contract of insurance is a contract based on utmost good faith has been, in effect, abolished.[291] The second reason for imposing a duty of disclosure is that, in certain situations, the relationship between the contracting parties during the negotiations is not a pure arm's length commercial relationship but one of trust and confidence or one of dependence which imposes upon the party in whom confidence is reposed a duty to make disclosure. The clearest examples of such situations arise where there is a fiduciary relationship.

The remedies available for breach of duties of disclosure vary, and depend upon the source of the duty to disclose. Rescission is the most generally available remedy; but sometimes damages are available in tort or by statute.

(c) DUTIES OF DISCLOSURE GIVING RISE TO RESCISSION

(i) Contracts of insurance

At common law, before entering into a contract of insurance, the intending insured was under an obligation to disclose to the insurer all material information affecting the risk.[292] This duty to disclose was mutual, based on the fact that the contract of insurance was a contract of 'utmost good faith', and so the insurer was also required to disclose all material information although disclosure by the insurer was in practice rare because the material circumstances are normally known only to the intending insured.[293] The common law duty of disclosure was codified in section 18 of the Marine Insurance Act 1906, one of a group of sections which were held to apply not just to marine insurance but to all classes of insurance because they codified the common law.[294]

If there had been non-disclosure by one party, whether the non-disclosure was fraudulent, negligent or wholly innocent, the other party was entitled to avoid the contract if it had been induced to enter into the policy on the relevant terms,[295] but breach of the duty of disclosure did not of itself give rise to a claim for damages.[296]

In practice, however, insurance companies frequently inserted a 'basis of the contract' clause in the proposal form by which the proposer was made to warrant

[291] Formally it was only modified by Consumer Insurance (Disclosure and Representations) Act 2012, s 2(5) (for consumer insurance contracts) and then by Insurance Act 2015, s 14(2) (for all insurance contracts), but the legal significance of the label *uberrimae fidei* was that non-observance of the utmost good faith allowed the other party to avoid the contract, and, while the label survives, that rule was abolished for insurance contracts by the Insurance Act 2015, s 14(1): see below, p 364.

[292] *Carter v Boehm* (1766) 3 Burr 1905.

[293] *Banque Keyser Ullman SA v Skandia (UK) Insurance Co Ltd* [1990] 1 QB 665, 770, [1991] 2 AC 249, 268, 281.

[294] *PCW Syndicates v PCW Reinsurers* [1996] 1 WLR 1136, 1140; *Pan Atlantic Insurance Co Ltd v Pine Top Insurance Co Ltd* [1995] 1 AC 501, 541.

[295] *Pan Atlantic Insurance Co Ltd v Pine Top Insurance Co Ltd* [1995] 1 AC 501; *St Paul Fire & Marine Insurance Co (UK) Ltd v McConnell Dowell Constructors Ltd* [1996] 1 All ER 96, 112.

[296] *Banque Keyser Ullman SA v Skandia (UK) Insurance Co Ltd* [1990] 1 QB 665, 801.

the accuracy of the information supplied to the company, with a proviso that the company might avoid the contract and forfeit the premium if any part of the information proved untrue. The insured was thus compelled to assume responsibility for the truth of even non-material facts,[297] and of facts which the insured did not know, or did not appreciate, were false.[298] Such provisions could work injustice to the insured by conferring on insurers a discretion to repudiate the policy on technical grounds alone. Lord Greene MR described them as 'particularly vicious' and 'mere traps' which should be construed strictly[299] and the insurance industry's statements of practice provided, inter alia, that insurers should not repudiate liability on grounds of non-disclosure of a fact which the insured could not reasonably be expected to disclose.

The law has now been changed very significantly by two Acts which implement recommendations of the Law Commission.[300] In relation to 'consumer insurance contracts',[301] the consumer's duty of disclosure was removed by the Consumer Insurance (Disclosure and Representations) Act 2012,[302] and replaced with a duty to take reasonable care not to make a misrepresentation to the insurer.[303] In relation to 'non-consumer insurance contracts',[304] the Insurance Act 2015[305] removed the common law duty of disclosure, abolished the associated right for a party to avoid the contract on the ground that the utmost good faith has not been observed by the other party,[306] and repealed section 18 and related provisions of the Marine Insurance Act 1906;[307] but introduced a new duty on the insured to make to the insurer a 'fair presentation of the risk', which still includes a duty of disclosure. Each Act, for its separate area of operation, abolished 'basis of the contract' clauses.[308]

[297] *Thomson v Weems* (1884) 9 App Cas 671, 689; *Dawsons Ltd v Bonnin* [1922] 2 AC 413.

[298] See, eg, *Kumar v Life Insurance Corp of India* [1974] 1 Lloyd's Rep 147 (insurance company entitled to avoid policy of life insurance where applicant declared that she had not had any 'operation' when, in fact, she had given birth to a child by Caesarian section).

[299] *Zurich General Accident and Liability Insurance Co Ltd v Morrison* [1942] 2 KB 53, 58. See also *Joel v Law Union and Crown Insurance Co* [1908] 2 KB 863, 885.

[300] There can still be litigation under the common law in relation to contracts entered into before the Acts came into force: see, eg, *Zurich Insurance Plc v Niramax Group Ltd* [2021] EWCA Civ 590, [2021] 1 CLC 935.

[301] 'a contract of insurance between (a) an individual who enters into the contract wholly or mainly for purposes unrelated to the individual's trade, business or profession, and (b) a person who carries on the business of insurance and who becomes a party to the contract by way of that business (whether or not in accordance with permission for the purposes of the Financial Services and Markets Act 2000)': Consumer Insurance (Disclosure and Representations) Act 2012, s 1.

[302] See Law Com No 319, *Consumer Insurance Law: Pre-Contract Disclosure and Misrepresentation* (2009).

[303] 2012 Act, s 2.

[304] 'a contract of insurance that is not a consumer insurance contract' (within the meaning of the 2012 Act): Insurance Act 2015, s 1.

[305] See Law Com No 353, *Insurance Contract Law: Business Disclosure; Warranties; Insurers' Remedies for Fraudulent Claims and Late Payment* (2014).

[306] 2015 Act, s 14.

[307] 2015 Act, s 21(2).

[308] 2012 Act, s 6 (consumer insurance contracts); 2015 Act, s 9 (non-consumer insurance contracts).

The duty of disclosure which now exists is therefore only on the insured under a non-consumer insurance contract, and its scope (and the remedies for breach of the duty) are defined by the Insurance Act 2015. That Act requires:[309]

(a) disclosure of every material circumstance which the insured knows or ought to know, or

(b) failing that, disclosure which gives the insurer sufficient information to put a prudent insurer on notice that it needs to make further enquiries for the purpose of revealing those material circumstances

in a manner which would be reasonably clear and accessible to a prudent insurer but, in the absence of enquiry, it does not require the insured to disclose a circumstance if it diminishes the risk, the insurer knows it, the insurer ought to know it, the insurer is presumed to know it, or it is something as to which the insurer waives information.

The insurer has a remedy against the insured for breach of the duty of fair presentation only if it shows that, but for the breach, it would not have entered into the insurance contract at all, or would have done so only on different terms.[310] Where the insurer shows that the breach was deliberate (ie the insured knew that it was in breach of the duty of fair presentation) or reckless (ie the insured did not care whether or not it was in breach of the duty)[311] the insurer may avoid the contract and refuse all claims, and need not return any of the premiums paid.[312] In the case of other breaches, however, the remedy depends on whether, in the absence of the breach, the insurer would have entered into the contract not at all, or only on different terms. In the former case, the insurer may avoid the contract and refuse all claims, but must return the premiums paid (ie in effect this is rescission of the contract with restitution as the common law used to provide for breach of the general duty of disclosure). But in the latter case, the insurer's remedy is limited to requiring the contract to be treated as if it had been entered into on the terms which the insured would have accepted (with a proportionate reduction in the payment of claims if the premium would have been higher).[313]

(ii) Partnership contracts

It has long been established that, once a partnership has been formed, each partner is bound to exercise good faith in all that relates to their common business.[314] More recently, however, it has been settled that mutual duties of good faith and disclosure arise also between persons who are negotiating their entry into partnership, so

[309] 2015 Act, s 3. See also ss 4–6 for further definitions of what constitutes 'knowledge' of the insured and of the insurer, and s 7 for what constitutes a 'material circumstance'.

[310] 2015 Act, s 8(1).

[311] 2015 Act, s 8(5).

[312] 2015 Act, Sched 1, para 2.

[313] 2015 Act, Sched 1, paras 3–6.

[314] The duties of partners are, however, for the most part regulated by the provisions of the Partnership Act 1890, ss 28–30. Cf *F & C Alternative Investments (Holdings) Ltd v Barthelemy (No 2)* [2011] EWHC 1731 (Ch), [2012] Ch 613 (no fiduciary duties between members of a limited liability partnership).

that each party owes a duty to the other negotiating parties to disclose all material facts of which that party has knowledge and of which the other parties may not be aware.[315]

(iii) Contracts of suretyship or guarantee

A contract of suretyship (or guarantee) is one under which the surety (or guarantor) undertakes to the creditor to pay the debt, or satisfy some other obligation of the debtor, in the event of the debtor's default. Such contracts are not *uberrimae fidei* and therefore do not carry the same general duty of disclosure of material facts at common law as contracts of insurance or partnership contracts. However, although sureties are expected to inform themselves about the risks they are undertaking in favour of the creditor, the Courts regard surety contracts as different from normal commercial contracts, and the creditor is required to disclose to the surety any unusual feature of the contract between the creditor and the debtor, or between the creditor and other creditors of the debtor, which makes it materially different in a potentially disadvantageous respect from what the surety might naturally expect.[316] Where the creditor is in breach of this duty, and the surety is thereby induced to enter into the surety contract,[317] the surety may rescind (subject to the usual bars to rescission).

Nevertheless it is not always easy in practice to draw the line between contracts of guarantee in the strict sense of contracts to answer for the debt, default, or miscarriage of another, and contracts of insurance taking the form of contracts to indemnify against some risk stated in the contract.[318] It was pointed out by Romer LJ in *Seaton v Heath*[319] that many contracts may with equal propriety be called contracts of insurance or contracts of guarantee, and that whether a contract requires *uberrima fides* or not depends not upon what it is called, but upon its substantial character and how it came to be effected. Generally, in a contract of insurance the person desiring to be insured has means of knowledge of the risk which the insurer does not possess, and puts the risk before the insurer as a business transaction. In a contract of guarantee, on the other hand, the creditor does not as a rule go to the surety, explain the risk, and ask the surety to undertake it. The surety is often a friend or relation of the debtor and knows the risk to be undertaken, or the circumstances indicate that as between the creditor and the surety it is contemplated that the surety will ascertain what the risk is. Only in the exceptional cases when a contract of guarantee has the characteristics which occur normally in a contract of insurance is the former a contract *uberrimae fidei*.

[315] *Conlon v Simms* [2006] EWHC 401 (Ch), [2006] 2 All ER 1024 at [196]–[199], aff'd [2006] EWCA Civ 1749, [2008] 1 WLR 484 at [127] (Jonathan Parker LJ). See also *Bell v Lever Bros Ltd* [1932] AC 161, 227 (Lord Atkin).

[316] *Royal Bank of Scotland Plc v Etridge (No 2)* [2001] UKHL 44, [2002] 2 AC 773 at [81], [114], [186]–[188]; *North Shore Ventures Ltd v Anstead Holdings Inc* [2011] EWCA Civ 230, [2012] Ch 31 at [31].

[317] *North Shore Ventures Ltd v Anstead Holdings Inc* [2011] EWCA Civ 230 at [33].

[318] *Trade Indemnity Co Ltd v Workington Harbour and Dock Board* [1937] AC 1.

[319] [1899] 1 QB 782, 792–3.

Accordingly, it is settled that there is no duty of full disclosure where a surety guarantees to a bank the account of one of the bank's customers.[320] On the other hand, an employer who takes a bond from a surety for the 'fidelity', that is, honesty, of an employee, must disclose to the surety any previous acts of dishonesty of the employee within the employer's knowledge,[321] and even any subsequent acts of dishonesty which would entitle the surety to withdraw the guarantee.[322] And where the relationship between the surety and the principal debtor is non-commercial (such as spouses or cohabitees), putting the creditor on notice of a risk that the surety may be subjected to undue influence or misrepresentation by the debtor, the creditor will be unable to enforce the surety contract if it has not taken reasonable steps to minimize the risk that such a wrong may be committed by satisfying itself that the implications of the proposed transaction have been brought home to the surety in a meaningful way.[323]

(iv) Contracts of compromise and family settlements

Parties who are negotiating the compromise of a disputed claim do not generally owe duties to disclose to each other information relating to the claim or its validity.[324] However, the House of Lords has considered, but not decided, whether there is a duty on one party to disclose the existence of claims which will be covered by a compromise but of which that party knows the other is unaware.[325]

One form of compromise or settlement in which it is, however, established that there is a duty of disclosure is the contract for a family settlement, under which members of a family compromise a dispute such as the division of property. Such a contract requires full disclosure of all material facts within the parties' knowledge. Thus in *Gordon v Gordon*,[326] a family arrangement entered into without a secret marriage being disclosed by one side to the other was set aside under this principle. Parties who are divorcing and make an agreement about the division of the property which is to be embodied in a Court order are under an obligation to make a full and frank disclosure *to the Court which makes the order*. But, although the duty is owed to the Court and not to the other party, it has been held that a party affected by such non-disclosure could rely on it as a ground for setting the order (and therefore the agreement) aside.[327]

320 *National Provincial Bank v Glanusk* [1913] 3 KB 335; *Cooper v National Provincial Bank* [1946] KB 1.

321 *London General Omnibus Co Ltd v Holloway* [1912] 2 KB 72.

322 *Phillips v Foxall* (1872) LR 7 QB 666.

323 *Barclays Bank plc v O'Brien* [1994] 1 AC 180; *Royal Bank of Scotland v Etridge (No 2)* [2001] UKHL 44, [2002] 2 AC 773; *One Savings Bank plc v Waller-Edwards* [2025] UKSC 22, [2026] AC 182 at [40]; see below, pp 404–6.

324 *Turner v Green* [1895] 2 Ch 205.

325 *Bank of Credit and Commerce International SA v Ali* [2001] UKHL 8, [2002] 1 AC 251 at [32]–[33] (Lord Nicholls), [69]–[70] (Lord Hoffmann).

326 (1821) 3 Swan 400.

327 *Livesey v Jenkins* [1985] AC 424, 439–40; *Sharland v Sharland* [2015] UKSC 60 at [29]–[30].

(d) CONTRACTS BETWEEN THOSE IN A FIDUCIARY RELATIONSHIP

A fiduciary relationship imposes a duty on one party to the relationship (or, sometimes, both parties, such as in a partnership) to make full disclosure of all material facts which might be considered likely to affect a transaction with the other to whom the duty is owed. This is a component of wider and rigorous equitable obligations. While not all fiduciaries owe the same duties in all circumstances,[328] they are broadly required to act in good faith, not to place themselves in a position where their duty and their interest may conflict, or to act for their own benefit or the benefit of a third person without the informed consent of those to whom the duty is owed.[329] Breach of these duties is sometimes, rather misleadingly, called 'equitable' or 'constructive' fraud.

(i) Who is a fiduciary?

By contrast to a contractual relationship where, subject to the terms of the contract, the parties may legitimately act for their own interests, albeit sometimes in cooperation with the other party, the key feature of fiduciary relationships is a duty to act in the interests of another.[330] Fiduciary relationships can be divided into two categories, those that are status-based and those that are fact-based.[331] Examples of the former include principal and agent, solicitor and client, guardian and ward, and trustee and beneficiary.

The second category arises where, in the absence of an inherently fiduciary status, the factual situation of the particular relationship between the parties gives rise to a fiduciary relationship.[332] The relationship of the parties may be contractual but a contractual relationship gives rise to particular fiduciary obligations only where specific contractual obligations have been undertaken which place one party in the position in which equity imposes its rigorous duties on that party in addition to the contractual obligations.[333] While fiduciary duties should not be superimposed on common law contractual duties simply to improve the nature or extent of the remedy available,[334] they may arise where one party is in a position of influence over another,[335] is in receipt of information imparted in confidence by the other, or has undertaken to act in the

[328] *Henderson v Merrett Syndicates Ltd* [1995] 2 AC 145, 206 (Lord Browne-Wilkinson).

[329] *Bristol and West BS v Mothew* [1998] 1 Ch 1, 18. See generally Finn, *Fiduciary Obligations* (1977); Glister and Lee, *Hanbury & Martin: Modern Equity* (23rd edn, 2024) paras 22-018–22-026. Fiduciaries are also under a duty to use care and skill: *Nocton v Lord Ashburton* [1914] AC 932, 954.

[330] *Bristol and West BS v Mothew* [1998] 1 Ch 1, 18.

[331] Flannigan (1989) 9 OJLS 285.

[332] *Reading v Attorney-General* [1951] AC 507; *Hospital Products Ltd v United States Surgical Corp* (1984) 156 CLR 41 (High Court of Australia).

[333] *Nottingham University v Fishel* [2000] ICR 1462, 1491 (contract of employment, not otherwise typically fiduciary: see below, p 369).

[334] *Norberg v Wynrib* (1992) 92 DLR (4th) 449, 481.

[335] eg where one reposes trust and confidence in the other so as to give rise to a presumption of undue influence: below, p 393; *Royal Bank of Scotland Plc v Etridge (No 2)* [2001] UKHL 44 at [36] (husband's 'duty of candour and fairness' to wife); *Hewett v First Plus Financial Group plc* [2010] EWCA Civ 312, [2010] 2 P & CR 22.

interests of another or placed himself in a position where he is obliged so to act.[336] In such cases the fiduciary obligation is, however, circumscribed by the contractual terms: equity cannot alter the terms of a contract validly undertaken.[337] Examples of such fact-based fiduciary relationships may be seen in certain joint ventures[338] and employment relationships.[339]

(ii) Examples of duties of disclosure

The duty to disclose all material facts which might be considered likely to affect a transaction can be illustrated by examples. Thus a broker who is employed to buy shares for a client cannot sell his own shares to the client unless a full and accurate disclosure of this fact is made to the client and the client's consent is obtained.[340] Again, the promoters of a company, who stand in a fiduciary relationship with the company, are required to make a full disclosure of their interest either to an independent board of directors or to the intended shareholders.[341] In some situations, all that equity requires is disclosure of material facts. In others, however, where the fiduciary relationship gives rise to a presumption of undue influence[342] disclosure in itself may be insufficient, and it must be shown that the transaction is the result of the act of a free and independent mind of the party to whom the duty is owed.

(iii) Employment

The relationship between an employer and employee is not inherently 'fiduciary' but it may be the foundation for a fiduciary relationship as a result of the terms of the particular contract or where, for example, the employee is in receipt of confidential information. There is an implied term of fidelity, giving rise to duties of loyalty and good faith, in the contract between employee and employer, but this is not to be equated with a fiduciary obligation.[343] Employees are not, however, under a duty to disclose their own misconduct. In *Bell v Lever Brothers Ltd*[344] the respondent, Lever Brothers, had

[336] Millett (1998) 114 LQR 214.

[337] *Nottingham University v Fishel* [2000] ICR 1462, 1491; *Hospital Products Ltd v United States Surgical Corp* (1984) 156 CLR 41, 97.

[338] *Lac Minerals Ltd v International Corona Resources Ltd* [1989] 2 SCR 574 (Supreme Court of Canada). Cf *Yam Seng Pte Ltd v International Trade Corp Ltd* [2013] EWHC 111 (QB), [2013] 1 All ER (Comm) 1321, above, pp 179–80, at [142] (*implied term* of good faith in 'relational contracts' which 'might include some joint venture agreements'); *Al Nehayan v Kent* [2018] EWHC 333 (Comm), [2018] 1 CLC 216, above, p 180, at [153]–[176] (joint venture: no fiduciary duties, but implied duty of good faith).

[339] *Nottingham University v Fishel* [2000] ICR 1462.

[340] *Armstrong v Jackson* [1917] 2 KB 822. For other agents, see *Regier v Campbell-Stuart* [1939] Ch 766; *English v Dedham Vale Properties Ltd* [1978] 1 WLR 93. For contractual modification of fiduciary duty, see *Kelly v Cooper* [1993] AC 205.

[341] *Erlanger v New Sombrero Phosphate Co* (1878) 3 App Cas 1218; *Lagunas Nitrate Co v Lagunas Syndicate* [1899] 2 Ch 392; *Gluckstein v Barnes* [1900] AC 240. See now Financial Services and Markets Act 2000, ss 80–82, 90; Public Offers and Admissions to Trading Regulations 2024 (SI 2024 No 105), below, p 372.

[342] See below, pp 394–5.

[343] *Nottingham University v Fishel* [2000] ICR 1462, 1491; *Customer Systems Plc v Ranson* [2012] EWCA Civ 841, [2012] IRLR 769.

[344] [1932] AC 161, above, p 303.

entered into a contract with two of its employees whereby it promised to pay, and did in fact pay, considerable sums to them in compensation for the premature termination of their contracts of employment. This contract, however, was strictly unnecessary, for during their employment the two men had been guilty of certain breaches of duty which would have entitled Lever Brothers to dismiss them immediately. When Lever Brothers discovered this fact, it claimed to avoid the contract and recover the money paid on the ground, inter alia, that the employees had been bound to disclose these breaches of duty. No member of the House of Lords was prepared to accept this contention,[345] and Lord Atkin said[346] that he was aware of no authority which placed contracts of service within the limited category of contracts *uberrimae fidei*. Nevertheless, it has subsequently been held that in certain circumstances an employee may be under a duty to report to the employer misconduct on the part of fellow employees.[347]

(iv) Special relationships

We have seen that, under the principle enunciated in *Hedley Byrne & Co Ltd v Heller & Partners Ltd*,[348] a special relationship, giving rise to a duty of care in the tort of negligence, may arise between parties negotiating a contract. That duty may be more extensive than merely to refrain from making negligent misstatements, and may impose upon the party in whom confidence is reposed an obligation to disclose to the other party information relevant to the contract[349] or to provide an adequate explanation of the contract into which the other party is about to enter.[350] Prima facie the breach of such a duty would give rise to an action in damages in tort only,[351] and not to rescission of the contract. But, at least in some situations, the facts giving rise to such a duty may also evidence a relationship between the parties imposing a duty of disclosure the breach of which would entitle the party to whom the duty was owed to avoid the contract.

(v) Remedies for breach by a fiduciary of the duty of disclosure

Breach of the fiduciary's duty to make full disclosure will entitle the innocent party to rescind the contract or transaction, to be restored to the pre-contractual position, and to recover any profit made by the other party as a result of the breach. In awarding these remedies, it is well established that equity takes a strict approach, and does not draw a distinction between fraudulent, negligent, and wholly innocent breaches of duty, although there have been some suggestions that the liability to account for profits is too stringent and should not be applied to the fiduciary who acted in good faith.[352]

345 Although it was accepted by the Court of Appeal: [1931] 1 KB 337.

346 [1932] AC 161, 227.

347 *Swain v West (Butchers) Ltd* [1936] 1 All ER 224; *Sybron Corp v Rochem Ltd* [1984] Ch 112.

348 [1964] AC 465, above, p 349.

349 *Al-Kandari v JR Brown & Co* [1988] QB 665, 674; *Banque Keyser Ullman SA v Skandia (UK) Insurance Co Ltd* [1990] 1 QB 665, 790–805, aff'd on other grounds [1991] 2 AC 249. Cf *Dillingham Construction Pty Ltd v Downs* [1972] 2 NSWR 49 (Australia). See also *Horry v Tate & Lyle Refineries Ltd* [1982] 2 Lloyd's Rep 416.

350 *Rust v Abbey Life Assurance Co Ltd* [1982] 2 Lloyd's Rep 386, 391, aff'd [1979] 2 Lloyd's Rep 334.

351 Below, p 371.

352 *Murad v Al-Saraj* [2005] EWCA Civ 959, [2005] WTLR 1573 at [74], [82]–[83].

(e) LIABILITY IN TORT FOR NON-DISCLOSURE

It has generally been said that there is no liability in the tort of deceit for non-disclosure, because deceit requires an active misrepresentation, or at least a partial or fragmentary statement which misleads the representee.[353] Following this approach, the Court of Appeal has also rejected the argument that the tort of deceit applies in the case of an intentional breach of the duty of disclosure in a contract *uberrimae fidei*.[354] However, it has more recently been held that where there is a duty to disclose, and the failure to disclose is fraudulent, there can be an action in deceit on the basis that 'non-disclosure where there is a duty to disclose is tantamount to an implied representation that there is nothing relevant to disclose'.[355] This new approach was adopted without discussion of the older authorities which had assumed that there is no liability for pure non-disclosure, even where there is a duty of disclosure. But if it is confirmed, it may also overturn the existing case-law which has held that section 2(1) of the Misrepresentation Act 1967[356] does not apply in its terms to cases of non-disclosure because it imposes liability only where a 'misrepresentation has been made'.[357]

The tort of negligence can in principle apply to non-disclosure because a claim in negligence does not require a 'misrepresentation', but a breach of a duty of care.[358] To find a duty to take care to provide information requires either some prior conduct by the defendant evidencing an assumption of responsibility towards the claimant in relation to the provision of information, or some pre-existing relationship between the parties giving rise to a duty.[359] However, the Courts are careful not to use the tort of negligence to create duties to provide information or advice which undermine the general principle that there is no duty of disclosure between parties negotiating an ordinary commercial contract;[360] and the mere fact that there is a duty of disclosure for the purpose of the remedy of rescission does not automatically give rise to a concurrent duty of care in tort.[361]

[353] *Peek v Gurney* (1873) LR 6 HL 377, 403; see also Lord Chelmsford at 390–1; *Arkwright v Newbold* (1881) 17 Ch D 301, 318, 320; *Bradford Third Equitable Building Society v Borders* [1941] 2 All ER 205. Cf, however, *Brownlie v Campbell* (1880) 5 App Cas 925, 950.

[354] *Banque Keyser Ullmann SA v Skandia (UK) Insurance Co Ltd* [1990] 1 QB 665, 788.

[355] *Conlon v Simms* [2006] EWCA Civ 1749 at [130]. See also *HIH Casualty and General Insurance Ltd v Chase Manhattan Bank* [2001] EWCA Civ 1250, [2001] 2 Lloyd's Rep 483 at [48], [164], [168] and [2003] UKHL 6 at [21], [75].

[356] Above, p 350.

[357] *Banque Keyser Ullman SA v Skandia (UK) Insurance Co Ltd* [1990] 1 QB 665, 790, aff'd on other grounds [1991] 2 AC 249; *Startwell Ltd v Energie Global Brand Management Ltd* [2015] EWHC 421 (QB) at [81].

[358] *Hedley Byrne & Co Ltd v Heller & Partners Ltd* [1964] AC 465, 511; *Banbury v Bank of Montreal* [1918] AC 626, 713.

[359] *Banque Keyser Ullmann SA v Skandia (UK) Insurance Co Ltd* [1990] 1 QB 665, 794–5; *Al-Kandari v JR Brown & Co* [1988] QB 665; *Hamilton v Allied Domecq plc* [2007] UKHL 33, 2007 SC(HL) 142 at [19]–[23].

[360] *Banque Keyser Ullmann SA v Skandia (UK) Insurance Co Ltd* [1990] 1 QB 665, 798–9.

[361] *Ibid*, 801.

(f) STATUTORY DUTIES OF DISCLOSURE

Certain statutes impose duties of disclosure in relation to particular contracts, and also define the remedy which will be awarded for breach of the duty.

(i) Contracts for the allotment of shares

Promoters and directors of a company have information at their disposal which is not available to the general public, although at common law they have no duty of disclosure akin to parties negotiating a contact of insurance,[362] nor is there any fiduciary relationship between those issuing the prospectus and the public.

Protection to persons applying for shares is, however, afforded by legislation.[363] Those responsible for prospectuses and listing particulars issued in support of the public issue of company securities have a general duty of disclosure of specified information that investors and their advisers would reasonably require and reasonably expect.[364] The statute provides the right to compensation for persons who have acquired securities to which the prospectus or listing particulars apply, and have sustained loss in respect of them as a result of the omission of information required to be included, unless those responsible can show that up to the time of the allotment they had reasonable ground to believe and did believe that the information was properly omitted.[365]

The Financial Services and Markets Act 2000 also established a regulatory regime over those conducting investment business in order to protect the purchasers of the products of the financial services industry, namely insurance policies, investments, and advice. This regime was amended significantly by the Financial Services Act 2012. Detailed treatment of this area would be out of place in the present textbook,[366] but it should be noted that protection is achieved by a licensing system and by close control of the way those licensed conduct their businesses, including statutory 'cooling-off' periods after an agreement has been made. Many financial services practitioners will be in a fiduciary relationship with their clients and therefore equity will sometimes provide a remedy.[367] The 2000 Act replaced specific requirements in the Financial Services Act 1986[368] with a general rule-making power of the Financial Services Authority,[369] which was replaced by the 2012 Act by new general rule-making powers of the Financial Conduct Authority (the renamed Financial Services Authority) and the new Prudential Regulation Authority.[370] Practitioners continue to be obliged to

[362] *Aaron's Reefs Ltd v Twiss* [1896] AC 273, 287.

[363] Financial Services and Markets Act 2000; Public Offers and Admissions to Trading Regulations 2024 (SI 2024 No 105).

[364] Financial Services and Markets Act 2000, ss 80–82 (listing particulars); Public Offers and Admissions to Trading Regulations 2024 (SI 2024 No 105): regs 23–24 (prospectuses).

[365] Financial Services and Markets Act 2000, s 90(1), Sched 10 (listing particulars); Public Offers and Admissions to Trading Regulations 2024 (SI 2024 No 105): reg 30(1), Sched 2 (prospectuses). For the similar liability for untrue or misleading statements in prospectuses and listing particulars, see above, p 350 n 195.

[366] See generally Lomnicka and Powell, *Encyclopedia of Financial Services Law*.

[367] Above, p 368. [368] Sched 8. [369] 2000 Act, ss 138–140.

[370] 2012 Act, s 24, introducing a new Part 9A into the 2000 Act.

subordinate their interests to those of their clients, and to make proper provision for disclosure of interests and facts material to transactions entered into or advice given, and the basis, method, and frequency of payment by the customer and in certain cases termination provisions.[371] Private investors are given a right to damages for contravention of regulatory rules.[372]

(ii) Consumer contracts

In recent years, duties have been imposed on persons who supply goods or services to consumers to provide particular information to consumers before they enter into the contract. These duties have often been imposed in order to implement EU Directives, and the most comprehensive duties are now owed under the Consumer Contracts (Information, Cancellation and Additional Charges) Regulations 2013.[373] The Regulations apply to most 'on-premises', 'off-premises', and 'distance' contracts between a trader and a consumer.[374] The information to be provided is more extensive for off-premises contracts and distance contracts[375] than for on-premises contracts,[376] and the duty does not extend to an on-premises contract which involves a day-to-day transaction and is performed immediately at the time when the contract is entered into. But for all three types of contract, where the duty arises it requires the trader to give information in a clear and comprehensible manner about such things as the main characteristics of the goods, services, or digital content to which the contract relates, and the price. The failure to provide the required information does not give the consumer the right to rescind the contract or claim damages,[377] but in the case of an off-premises or distance contract the consumer has a right to cancel the contract within a period of 14 days from the date of the contract (or, in a contract for the supply of goods, from the date on which the consumer received the goods).[378] Where the trader

[371] See FCA, *Conduct of Business Sourcebook*, chs 2, 4, 6.

[372] 2000 Act, s 138D, introduced by the 2012 Act, s 24 (replacing original provisions in the 2000 Act, s 150).

[373] SI 2013 No 3134, implementing Directive 2011/83/EU, and replacing the Consumer Protection (Distance Selling) Regulations 2000 (SI 2000 No 2334), which implemented Council Directive 97/7/EC. After withdrawal of the UK from the EU the 2013 Regulations remain in force, assimilated into domestic law: see above, p 21.

[374] In essence, an 'off-premises' contract is one formed when, or after, the trader and consumer were physically present together during the negotiations but away from the trader's business premises (sometimes referred to as a 'doorstep contract'); a 'distance' contract is one formed without the parties being physically present together and exclusively through distance communications; and an 'on-premises' contract is one which is neither a distance contract nor an off-premises contract: 2013 Regulations, reg 5. All forms of contracts are therefore, in principle, included; there are some exceptions in regs 6 and 7, such as off-premises contracts under which the payment to be made by the consumer is not more than £42: reg 7(4).

[375] 2013 Regulations, regs 10 and 13 and Sched 2.

[376] 2013 Regulations, reg 9 and Sched 1.

[377] The 'prohibited practices' giving rise to rights of redress under Part 4 of the Digital Markets, Competition and Consumers Act 2024 (above, p 358) do not extend to misleading *omissions* under s 227; see similarly the Consumer Protection from Unfair Trading Regulations 2008, reg 27B(1), to be replaced by the 2024 Act when new Regulations are made under the Act. However, under the 2024 Act the Secretary of State is given the power to add further unfair commercial practices to the list of prohibited practices giving rise to rights of redress: s 242(3).

[378] 2013 Regulations, reg 30.

fails to provide the information required by the regulations the cancellation period is extended, and the right of cancellation is exercisable by the consumer until 14 days after the day on which the trader provides the information or, if the trader fails to provide it for 12 months, the long-stop cancellation period is 12 months and 14 days from the day on which the contract was concluded (or the consumer received the goods).[379] In addition, the contract is treated as including a term that the trader has complied with the regulations requiring information to be provided,[380] therefore providing the consumer with a claim for breach of contract in cases where the information has not in fact been provided.

(g) THE FUTURE

There has been no challenge to the general common law rule of non-disclosure, but questions may be asked about its scope. Should a more liberal approach be taken to the exceptions? Are they too narrow? Take the case of the couple who are divorcing and make an agreement about the division of the property. If the negotiations prior to the agreement proceeded on the basis of the husband's belief, based on the wife's conscientious and religious objections to divorce, that the wife would never remarry, is the agreement vitiated by the failure of the wife to disclose that she had earlier become engaged to be married? On pure common law analysis, on such facts, after considering whether any of the common law and equitable exceptions applied, it has been held that none did and there was no duty to disclose.[381] Although, as we have seen, the common law position has been affected by statute where the property settlement is embodied in a Court order, it was said that this *contractual* aspect of the decision is not open to criticism in any way.[382] But is it right in principle that there should be no duty to disclose in such a case? The economic arguments do not appear applicable, let alone compelling, and it was certainly very difficult and probably impossible for the husband to acquire the information from another source. One commentator who supports the general rule has described the decision as 'repugnant to an ordinary sense of fairness'.[383]

The position might have been different if a broader view had been taken of the concept of 'fiduciary' relationship or if it had been possible to look at the statutory as well as the common law exceptions to the rule and from them find particular analogies or even a general principle which could provide the Courts with a broader,

[379] 2013 Regulations, reg 31.

[380] 2013 Regulations, reg 18.

[381] *Wales v Wadham* [1977] 1 WLR 199.

[382] *Livesey v Jenkins* [1985] AC 424, 439. But in *Wales v Wadham, Traill v Baring* (1864) 4 De GJ & S 318 (duty to communicate change of intention) was not cited; above, p 323.

[383] Smith, *Atiyah's Introduction to the Law of Contract* (6th edn, 2005) 246. The decision, but not the reasoning, may, however, be justified on the merits since the husband had not made a full disclosure of his assets.

principled basis for exceptions to the general rule of non-disclosure. The common law develops by analogy from case to case and sometimes more radically by finding underlying general principles for a whole area of the law.[384] But this approach is taken only for developments of the common law itself; traditionally, statutory provisions have been regarded as isolated irruptions into the body of the common law and have not been seen as expressing a policy from which a principle could be synthesized.[385]

There has, however, been recent significant development by the legislature of duties of disclosure. We have mentioned particular statutory duties of disclosure in the Financial Services and Markets Act 2000 and the rules made under it, and the Consumer Contracts (Information, Cancellation and Additional Charges) Regulations 2013. Other examples are to be found in the Consumer Credit Act 1974,[386] the Hallmarking Act 1973,[387] the Housing Act 1985,[388] the Energy Act 1976,[389] and the Package Travel and Linked Travel Arrangements Regulations 2018.[390] The financial services and consumer credit statutes reflect a legislative decision that consumers buying on credit and the purchasers of the products of the financial services industry require protection. Although there are many differences between the financial services and the consumer credit regimes, they have similar disclosure and 'cooling-off' provisions. Both regimes also exercise close control over the content of advertisements. The fact that the legislative schemes are so detailed means that it is not unreasonable to see them as self-contained codes and that no common law duty should be superimposed on them.[391] However, that part of the regimes which relates to disclosure might arguably be of wider significance. In both contexts the relationship is one of inequality; in financial services (and probably in consumer credit) there is also imbalance of information in the sense that the professional has information that the client cannot acquire from any other source—or cannot do so without incurring considerable expense. We have noted that this imbalance is also

[384] Cartwright, *Contract Law: an Introduction to the English Law of Contract for the Civil Lawyer* (4th edn, 2023) 37–47.

[385] Nicholas, in Harris and Tallon (eds), *Contract Law Today* (1989) 178; Cartwright, above, n 384, 30–37. Cf the different approach in France, in relation in particular to duties of disclosure: Ghestin, in Harris and Tallon (eds), *Contract Law Today* (1989) 153–5; see now Rowan, *The New French Law of Contract* (2022) 63–6.

[386] s 55, and Consumer Credit (Disclosure of Information) Regulations 2004 (SI 2004 No 1481), both amended by SI 2010 No 1010, implementing Directive 2008/48/EC. See also s 60 of the 1974 Act and SI 1983 No 1553, amended by SI 2004 No 1482, which require credit agreements subject to the Act to contain specific information.

[387] s 11 (disclosure by dealer of information explaining hallmarks).

[388] s 125(4A), added by Housing and Planning Act 1986 (disclosure by landlord of known structural defects where secure tenant exercises right to buy landlord's interest).

[389] s 15(3) (disclosure of results of passenger car fuel consumption tests).

[390] SI 2018 No 634, Part 2, implementing Directive (EU) 2015/2302, and replacing Package Travel, Package Holiday and Package Tours Regulations 1992 (SI 1992 No 3288). After withdrawal of the UK from the EU the 2018 Regulations remain in force, assimilated into domestic law: see above, p 21.

[391] *Aldrich v Norwich Union Life Assurance Co Ltd* [1999] 2 All ER (Comm) 707 (Financial Services Act 1986, s 47); *Payne v Barnet LBC* (1998) 30 HLR 295 (Housing and Planning Act 1986, s 125(4A)).

at the root of the duty of disclosure in contracts *uberrimae fidei* and the other non-statutory exceptions. The recent, broader imposition of duties of disclosure in favour of consumers under the Consumer Contracts (Information, Cancellation and Additional Charges) Regulations 2013 reinforces this argument.

It is arguable that the fact that the legislature has imposed a duty of disclosure in the specified cases can be seen, alongside the cases in which a duty exists at common law, as an indication of the underlying rationale and principle of such a duty. If so, such legislative duties could assist a Court which is considering the scope of the exceptions or the extension of the duty to a new fact situation.[392] Such an approach would bring English law closer to its continental neighbours.[393] However, it would not only go beyond the current position, but would also in large measure revert to a general approach which was proposed by Lord Mansfield in 1766, but which was later rejected as a universal proposition and limited to particular classes of contract (notably, insurance contracts):[394]

> The governing principle is applicable to all contracts and dealings.
>
> Good faith forbids either party by concealing what he privately knows, to draw the other into a bargain, from his ignorance of that fact, and his believing the contrary.
>
> But either party may be innocently silent, as to grounds open to both, to exercise their judgment upon.

The objection may be raised that English law does not recognize a general principle of good faith,[395] and so cannot use such a principle to define duties of disclosure in contracts generally. However, as we have seen, the Courts and the legislature have been able to define many particular circumstances in which duties of disclosure arise, and it is submitted that these could serve as analogies for the definition of other particular duties based on a general principle.

[392] See *Timeload Ltd v British Telecommunications plc* (1995) 3 EMLR 459, 468 (Bingham MR); *Malik v Bank of Credit & Commerce International SA* [1998] AC 20, 52–3 (Lord Steyn); Beatson (2001) 117 LQR 247; Burrows, *Thinking About Statutes* (2018) 48–56. Cf the different approach in *Banque Financière de la Cité SA v Westgate Insurance Co Ltd* [1991] 2 AC 249, 273–4 (Lord Templeman).

[393] Study Group on a European Civil Code and Research Group on EC Private Law (Acquis Group), *Principles, Definitions and Model Rules of European Private Law: Draft Common Frame of Reference (DCFR)* (2009), arts II.-3:101–105; II.-7:201, 205; Lando and Beale (eds), *Principles of European Contract Law Parts I and II* (2000) 256; Ghestin, in Harris and Tallon (eds), *Contract Law Today* (1989) 153–5.

[394] *Carter v Boehm* (1766) 3 Burr 1905, 1910; *Manifest Shipping Co Ltd v Uni-Polaris Insurance Co Ltd* [2001] UKHL 1 at [42]–[45]. The common law duties of disclosure in insurance contracts have now been removed by statute (above, p 364) but this is not inconsistent with the argument presented here, since the common law in fact operated against the interests of, especially, the consumer: cf Law Com No 319, *Consumer Insurance Law: Pre-Contract Disclosure and Misrepresentation* (2009); Lowry and Rawlings (2012) 75 MLR 1099.

[395] *Times Travel (UK) Ltd v Pakistan International Airlines Corp* [2021] UKSC 40, [2023] AC 101 at [27]; *Interfoto Picture Library Ltd v Stiletto Visual Programmes Ltd* [1989] QB 433, 439. See also above, pp 67–68, 179–82, 232–5.

FURTHER READING

ATIYAH and TREITEL, 'The Misrepresentation Act 1967' (1967) 30 MLR 369

KRONMAN, 'Mistake, Disclosure, Information and the Law of Contracts' (1978) 7 JLS 1

CARTWRIGHT, 'Damages for Misrepresentation' [1987] Conv 423

BROWN and CHANDLER, 'Deceit, Damages and the Misrepresentation Act 1967, s 2(1)' [1992] LMCLQ 40

O'SULLIVAN, 'Rescission as a Self-Help Remedy: a Critical Analysis' [2000] CLJ 509

CARTWRIGHT, 'Excluding Liability for Misrepresentation' in BURROWS and PEEL (eds), *Contract Terms* (Oxford: Oxford University Press, 2007) 213

HANDLEY, 'Causation in Misrepresentation' (2015) 131 LQR 275

10

DURESS, UNDUE INFLUENCE, AND UNCONSCIONABLE BARGAINS

1. INTRODUCTION

This chapter considers three vitiating factors based on the improper conduct of one party, the vulnerability of the other, or a combination of the two.[1]

Duress and undue influence occur where one party to a contract has coerced the other or exercised such domination that the other's independence of decision was substantially undermined. Although in some respects undue influence is the equitable equivalent of common law duress, in equity relief was granted in cases of pressure or coercion where the common law provided no remedy.[2] Moreover, in some cases the primary concern of equity is to protect certain relationships and it does so by a presumption of influence. Since the Judicature Act 1873, the Courts apply the common law and equitable rules concurrently, and in the event of any conflict or variance between them, the equitable rules are to prevail. The common law and equitable rules have, therefore, now to be treated in the light of their combined effect.[3] Duress, like misrepresentation, is primarily concerned with the process by which the contract was made (procedural unfairness or impropriety) rather than whether the terms of the contract are in fact harsh or unconscionable (substantive unfairness or impropriety). Undue influence, especially in cases of overt acts of improper pressure or coercion, is also said to be primarily concerned with procedural unfairness, but because it also has a role in protecting the excessively vulnerable the position is more complicated, and it has significant substantive aspects.

In the limited category of cases in which the doctrine of unconscionable bargains operates, it is necessary to show not only that the process by which the contract

[1] See Enonchong, *Duress, Undue Influence and Unconscionable Dealings* (4th edn, 2023).

[2] *Royal Bank of Scotland plc v Etridge (No 2)* [2001] UKHL 44, [2002] 2 AC 773 at [6]–[8], [103]. Cf Burrows (2002) 22 OJLS 1, 6.

[3] *United Scientific Holdings Ltd v Burnley BC* [1978] AC 904; *Times Travel (UK) Ltd v Pakistan International Airlines Corp* [2021] UKSC 40, [2023] AC 101 at [2]–[3].

was made was unfair but that there is contractual imbalance, that is, the doctrine extends to the actual substance of the contract and the fairness of its terms. The role of unconscionability was restricted in the nineteenth century by the assumption that parties enjoy freedom of economic decision when entering into contracts which enables them to choose to enter into a contract on whatever terms they may consider advantageous to their interests, or to choose not to,[4] and more recently by the view that the task of limiting such freedom so as to relieve inequality of bargaining power is essentially a legislative task for Parliament.[5] In the case of consumer contracts there has been significant statutory intervention to protect consumers against unfair terms.[6] Employment and landlord and tenant relationships are also regulated by statute so as to protect employees and tenants from unfairness.[7] As in the case of statutory duties of disclosure,[8] it is arguable that to the extent that the statutory regimes can be seen as expressing a policy from which a principle can be derived, they may be of some analogical assistance in developing the common law.[9]

We saw in Chapter 9[10] that a misrepresentation made by a trader which induces a consumer to enter into a contract may also sometimes constitute a 'prohibited practice' under Part 4 of the Digital Markets, Competition and Consumers Act 2024, which gives the consumer 'rights of redress' under Regulations to be made under the Act.[11] Similarly, conduct which constitutes duress or undue influence may constitute an 'aggressive practice' under the 2024 Act, and may offer the consumer an additional choice of remedies.[12]

2. DURESS

(a) NATURE OF DURESS

A contract which has been induced by unlawful or other illegitimate forms of pressure or intimidation is voidable[13] on the ground of duress.[14] It is not necessary to establish that the contract is in addition disadvantageous to the victim of the duress although, if

[4] Above, p 4.

[5] *National Westminster Bank plc v Morgan* [1985] AC 686, 708; *Times Travel (UK) Ltd v Pakistan International Airlines Corp* [2021] UKSC 40 at [26].

[6] Above, pp 226, 236. [7] Above, p 5. [8] Above, p 376.

[9] *Timeload Ltd v British Telecommunications plc* (1995) 3 EMLR 459, 468; *Malik v Bank of Credit & Commerce International SA* [1998] AC 20, 52–3. See generally Beatson (2001) 117 LQR 247; Burrows (2012) 128 LQR 232, *Thinking about Statutes* (2018) 48–56, 74–85.

[10] Above, p 358.

[11] Replacing the Consumer Protection from Unfair Trading Regulations 2008. The 2008 Regulations continue to apply until new replacement Regulations are made: see below, p 409.

[12] Below, p 409.

[13] Coke 2 Inst 483; *Whelpdale's Case* (1605) 5 Co Rep 119a; *North Ocean Shipping Co Ltd v Hyundai Construction Co Ltd* [1979] QB 705; *Pao On v Lau Yiu Long* [1980] AC 614; *Universe Tankships Inc of Monrovia v International Transport Workers Federation, The Universe Sentinel* [1983] 1 AC 366. Cf *Barton v Armstrong* [1976] AC 104, 120 (declaration that the contracts 'are void'; but this may only be describing the contract *after* it has been rescinded). Cf Lanham (1966) 29 MLR 615, contending that duress renders the contract void.

[14] Beatson, *The Use and Abuse of Unjust Enrichment* (1991) ch 5; Cartwright, *Unequal Bargaining* (1991) ch 7; Dawson (1947) 45 Mich L Rev 253; Hale (1943) 43 Col L Rev 603; Halson (1991) 107 LQR 649; Smith [1997] CLJ 343.

the contract conferred a benefit on the victim, an obligation to make restitution might arise.[15] A restitutionary claim also lies for the recovery of money paid under duress, and in many cases the duress will also be tortious and give rise to an action for damages, for example for assault, wrongful interference with property, and, in the case of economic duress, intimidation.[16]

(i) 'Unlawful' pressure and 'illegitimate' pressure

The modern cases generally define the sort of pressure which constitutes duress as 'illegitimate' pressure.[17] This emphasizes that the law must distinguish between pressures to which a contracting party is not expected to submit without having a remedy, and other ('legitimate') pressures which the law does not take into account.

Some forms of pressure which constitute duress are unlawful; but others, though not unlawful, are still illegitimate. Unlawful pressure occurs where the coercive party threatens to do something that is a breach of a common law or statutory duty. The act may be a crime, a tort, or, subject to the qualifications set out below, a breach of contract. Where an unlawful act is threatened, provided it induces the contract, in principle the contract may be set aside by the other party. In the words of Lord Devlin, '[a]ll that matters to the plaintiff is that, metaphorically speaking, a club has been used. It does not matter to the plaintiff what the club is made of—whether it is a physical club or an economic club, a tortious club or an otherwise illegal club.'[18]

The position is different where what is threatened is not an unlawful act. Ordinarily it is not duress to threaten to do that which one has a legal right to do, for instance to refuse to enter into a contract or to terminate a contract lawfully. But exceptionally such a threat may constitute duress when coupled with a demand which is 'illegitimate'.[19]

(ii) Categorization of types of duress

Traditionally, duress has been categorized according to the form of the threat. As we shall see, the Courts first recognized threats to the person, and only later threats to property and finally threats of economic harm. Now that they have unified duress as involving 'illegitimate' pressure one might expect that the different categories of threat could be abandoned. However, there appear still to be differences between them, such

[15] *Law Debenture Trust Corp plc v Ukraine* [2023] UKSC 11, [2024] AC 411 at [182].

[16] *The Universe Sentinel* [1983] 1 AC 366, 385, 400; *Rookes v Barnard* [1964] AC 1129; *Kolmar Group AG v Traxpo Enterprises Pvt Ltd* [2010] EWHC 113 (Comm), [2010] 1 CLC 256. The duress need not constitute a tort: *Dimskal Shipping Co SA v International Transport Workers Federation, The Evia Luck* [1992] 2 AC 152, 169. For further remedies under Part 4 of the Digital Markets, Competition and Consumers Act 2024, see below, p 409.

[17] *The Universe Sentinel* [1983] 1 AC 366, 384, 401; *Times Travel (UK) Ltd v Pakistan International Airlines Corp* [2021] UKSC 40 at [1], [78].

[18] *Rookes v Barnard* [1964] AC 1129, 1209, discussing the tort of intimidation.

[19] *The Universe Sentinel* [1983] 1 AC 366, 401; *Times Travel (UK) Ltd v Pakistan International Airlines Corp* [2021] UKSC 40 at [1], [96]; below, p 385.

as in the rules of causation,[20] and for the purpose of analysis it is also preferable to consider the different types of duress separately.[21]

(iii) Juridical basis of duress

It used to be said that a contract could be set aside for duress only if the will of the victim was coerced so as to vitiate his consent.[22] But this was misleading, because it was interpreted as saying not simply that the victim's consent was defective, but that the entry into the contract was not a voluntary act.[23] The fallacy of this approach was exposed in *The Universe Sentinel*.[24] A person subjected to duress is fully aware of the nature and terms of the contract which is thus entered. The victim still intends to contract, though the freedom to choose whether to enter into the contract is vitiated.[25] 'The classic case of duress is . . . not the lack of will to submit but the victim's intentional submission arising from the realization that there is no other practical choice open to him.'[26] The rationale of duress is thus not lack of knowledge or consent but illegitimate pressure which means that the victim's apparent consent is treated in law as revocable, unless approbated expressly or by implication after the pressure has ceased to operate on the victim's mind.[27]

(b) UNLAWFUL PRESSURE

(i) Types of duress

(a) Duress of the Person. It has long been established that duress can vitiate a contract where it consists of a threat to the person,[28] for example threats to kill the contracting party,[29] although it will suffice if the threat is directed against the contracting party's family or employee, or against a third party, or even, it seems, if A threatens to kill himself unless B consents to a contract.[30] As long as the threats were 'a' reason for the threatened person's entering into the contract, that person is entitled to relief, even

[20] Below, p 384.

[21] Below, pp 381–4; *Law Debenture Trust Corp plc v Ukraine* [2023] UKSC 11 at [148].

[22] *Occidental Worldwide Investment Corp v Skibs A/S Avanti, The Siboen and The Sibotre* [1976] 1 Lloyd's Rep 293, 336; *North Ocean Shipping Co Ltd v Hyundai Construction Co Ltd* [1979] QB 705, 717; *Pao On v Lau Yiu Long* [1980] AC 614, 635. See also *Barton v Armstrong* [1976] AC 1, 121; *Alec Lobb (Garages) Ltd v Total Oil Great Britain Ltd* [1983] 1 WLR 87, 93.

[23] *Pao On v Lau Yiu Long* [1980] AC 614, 636.

[24] [1983] 1 AC 366. See also *Lynch v DPP of Northern Ireland* [1975] AC 653, 670, 675, 680, 690–1, 695, 703, 709 (duress as a defence in criminal law); Atiyah (1982) 98 LQR 197, (1983) 99 LQR 353; Beatson (1976) 92 LQR 496, *The Use and Abuse of Unjust Enrichment* (1991) 113–17; *The Evia Luck* [1992] 2 AC 152, 165–6.

[25] Cartwright, *Unequal Bargaining* (1991) 160–3.

[26] [1983] 1 AC 366, 400 (Lord Scarman).

[27] *Ibid*, 384 (Lord Diplock).

[28] Co 2 Inst 483; Co Litt 253b; 1 Roll Abr 687, pl 5, 6; *Skeate v Beale* (1841) 11 A & E 983.

[29] *Barton v Armstrong* [1976] AC 104.

[30] *Law Debenture Trust Corp plc v Ukraine* [2023] UKSC 11 at [176]–[177]. A threat to the person will normally be unlawful (a crime and/or a tort), but it need not be: *ibid.*

though the contract might well still have been entered into if no threats had been made; indeed, it is for the party who made the threats to establish that they contributed nothing to the victim's decision to sign.[31]

At common law, a threat of lawful imprisonment, for example a criminal prosecution, would not ordinarily amount to duress, but in equity a threat by one party to prosecute the other, or a member of their family, for a criminal offence could constitute a ground on which the contract would be set aside for undue influence.[32] Today, however, such a case can be seen as an example of lawful act duress.[33]

(b) Duress of Goods. It used to be uncertain whether a contract entered into as the result of damage or threatened damage to goods or other property, or their actual or threatened illegal seizure, could be set aside on the ground of duress,[34] but it is now established that it can.[35] Older authority to the contrary can possibly be explained as the voluntary compromise of a claim,[36] or as involving facts in which the degree of coercion applied was insufficient to constitute duress.[37] It was in any event inconsistent with authority granting the recovery of money paid under protest for the release of goods from unlawful detention.[38] In the modern law, duress of goods, like duress of the person, is always considered illegitimate—unlike economic pressure, which has been held to be illegitimate only in limited circumstances.[39]

(c) Economic Duress. It is also now established that, in certain circumstances, a contract can be set aside for economic duress, that is, the threat of such serious financial consequences as give the threatened party no practical choice but to enter into the contract.[40] So it has been held that an unlawful threat by a trade union to

[31] *Barton v Armstrong* [1976] AC 104, 118–19, drawing an analogy with fraudulent misrepresentation (see above, pp 328–9); *Law Debenture Trust Corp plc v Ukraine* [2023] UKSC 11 at [143].

[32] *Williams v Bayley* (1886) LR 1 HL 200; *Mutual Finance Ltd v John Wetton & Sons Ltd* [1937] 2 KB 389.

[33] *Times Travel (UK) Ltd v Pakistan International Airlines Corp* [2021] UKSC 40 at [8]–[9], [89]–[90]; see below, p 387.

[34] There were cases of successful claims for restitution of money paid under duress: *Astley v Reynolds* (1731) 2 Str 915; *Maskell v Horner* [1915] 3 KB 106; but not of avoidance of contracts, for which duress to the person was generally thought to be required: see Guest, *Anson's Law of Contract* (24th edn, 1975) 259–60.

[35] *Vantage Navigation Corp v Suhail & Saud Bahwan Building Materials Llc, The Alev* [1989] 1 Lloyd's Rep 138. See also *Lloyds Bank Ltd v Bundy* [1975] QB 326, 337; *Occidental Worldwide Investment Corp v Skibs A/S Avanti* [1976] 1 Lloyd's Rep 293, 335–6; *North Ocean Shipping Co Ltd v Hyundai Construction Co Ltd* [1979] QB 705, 715; *Pao On v Lau Yiu Long* [1980] AC 614, 635; *The Universe Sentinel* [1983] 1 AC 366.

[36] *Occidental Worldwide Investment Corp v Skibs A/S Avanti* [1976] 1 Lloyd's Rep 293; Beatson, *The Use and Abuse of Unjust Enrichment* (1991) 105–6. On compromises, see above, p 107.

[37] *Skeate v Beale* (1840) 11 A & E 983, 990.

[38] Above, n 34. Cf Burrows, *The Law of Restitution* (3rd edn, 2011) 259–60.

[39] *Law Debenture Trust Corp plc v Ukraine* [2023] UKSC 11 at [148].

[40] *Occidental Worldwide Investment Corp v Skibs A/S Avanti* [1976] 1 Lloyd's Rep 293, 336; *North Ocean Shipping Co Ltd v Hyundai Construction Co Ltd* [1979] QB 705; *Pao On v Lau Yiu Long* [1980] AC 614, 635; *The Universe Sentinel* [1983] 1 AC 366, 383, 391, 397, 400; *Alec Lobb (Garages) Ltd v Total Oil Great Britain Ltd* [1983] 1 WLR 87, 93; *Times Travel (UK) Ltd v Pakistan International Airlines Corp* [2021] UKSC 40 at [62]. Cf *Law Debenture Trust Corp plc v Ukraine* [2023] UKSC 11 at [162] (international law is not a guide to illegitimacy of conduct under English law of duress).

continue the 'boycotting' of a ship[41] and a threat to break an existing contract[42] can be a sufficient ground to render voidable a contract entered into as a result of its pressure. In particular, one party may threaten to break an existing contract unless the contract is renegotiated in its favour,[43] and the other party may accede to this demand in order to avoid the adverse financial consequences which would ensue from the threatened breach. In *Atlas Express Ltd v Kafco (Importers and Distributors) Ltd*:[44]

K contracted to supply basketware to a chain of retail shops and made a contract for its delivery with A, a carrier. A had erroneously estimated that each load would contain over 400 cartons and, on this basis, had agreed a price of £1.10 per carton. The first load was for a smaller number of cartons, and A, believing that carrying such a load at the agreed rate was not financially viable, said that it would not perform unless K agreed to pay a minimum of £440 a load. Because K's commercial survival depended on the contract with the retail chain and it could not find an alternative carrier, it agreed to A's demand but then refused to pay.

It was held that the new terms were agreed under economic duress. In that case there was a direct threat to repudiate the contract, but the threat may be indirect. Thus, in *B & S Contracts and Design Ltd v Victor Green Publications Ltd* an indication by a party to a contract that it was prepared to allow its workers to strike unless the other party agreed to make a payment in addition to the contract price was held to be a veiled threat and to constitute duress because the other party had no other practical choice open to it but to agree to pay.[45] Good faith in the sense that the contractual difficulty is not the fault of the party seeking to renegotiate does not preclude a finding of economic duress.[46]

In the case of variation of an existing contract, there can be difficulties in distinguishing between duress and legitimate renegotiation. Where there is a dispute between the parties and the party seeking to renegotiate honestly believes that in the circumstances it is entitled not to perform, the result will generally be a binding compromise.[47] But the modern development of economic duress makes it important that parties who genuinely face difficulties if they complete performance on the contract terms and wish to renegotiate know what is and what is not permissible conduct. Sometimes it will be clear on the facts that there was no threat (direct or indirect) of a breach of contract, as in *Williams v Roffey Bros & Nicholls (Contractors) Ltd*[48] where R & N, noticing their carpentry subcontractor's difficulties, offered an additional payment which, as we have

[41] *The Universe Sentinel* [1983] 1 AC 366; *The Evia Luck* [1992] 2 AC 152.

[42] *North Ocean Shipping Co Ltd v Hyundai Construction Co Ltd* [1979] QB 705; *Pao On v Lau Yiu Long* [1980] AC 614. See also *Occidental Worldwide Investment Corp v Skibs A/S Avanti* [1976] 1 Lloyd's Rep 293 (threat to put company into liquidation). Cf McKendrick, in Burrows and Rodger (eds), *Mapping the Law: Essays in Memory of Peter Birks* (2006) 181, 188 (threatened breach of contract is always illegitimate).

[43] A renegotiated contract (whether it takes the form of a replacement of the original contract, or a variation of its terms) itself takes effect as a contract (with fresh consideration): see below, pp 471–2.

[44] [1989] QB 833.

[45] [1984] ICR 419, 426, 428.

[46] *Huyton SA v Peter Cremer GmbH & Co* [1999] 1 Lloyd's Rep 620, 629.

[47] Above, p 107. See also the role of promissory estoppel in protecting reasonable renegotiations: above, p 114.

[48] [1991] 1 QB 1, above, p 112. Cf *Adam Opel GmbH v Mitras Automotive (UK) Ltd* [2007] EWHC 3481 (QB) (threat to stop supplies constituted duress and rendered renegotiated contract voidable).

seen, was held binding. But surely the renegotiation would not automatically have been vitiated by duress if it was the subcontractor who had taken the initiative. It should not necessarily be seen as a threat to point out that without renegotiation it will not be possible to continue performance,[49] provided that this is so in fact.

There can, however, also be economic duress in the context of variation of a contract even without a threat to break the contract: such cases of 'lawful act' duress are considered below.[50]

(ii) Causation

There must be a sufficient causal link between the duress and the contract. In duress of the person it needs only be shown that the duress was 'a' reason for entering into the contract, even though the person might well have entered into the contract in the absence of the duress; and the Court may be willing to infer, in the absence of evidence to the contrary, that the duress played a part in inducing the contract.[51] But in cases of economic duress, it is for the party seeking to have the contract set aside to establish that the duress was a significant cause of the contract: 'but for' the illegitimate pressure, the agreement would not have been made either at all or, at least, in the terms in which it was made.[52]

Not every threat to break a contract unless its terms are renegotiated will amount to duress. It is necessary for the threat to induce the renegotiation, and in this context a number of factors will be taken into account. These include the availability of an adequate alternative remedy, whether there has been a compromise or a submission to a claim made in good faith, and whether the victim has protested or taken independent advice. Thus, in *Pao On v Lau Yiu Long*,[53] where one party was coerced into accepting the renegotiation of a business transaction by a threat by the other party to break an existing contract, but did so with legal advice and without protest, and after a considered appraisal of the risk involved, it was held by the Privy Council that the renegotiated agreement would not be set aside on the ground of economic duress.

[49] See, on the difference between a 'threat' and a 'warning' in the context of economic torts, *Conway v Wade* [1909] AC 506, 510; *Rookes v Barnard* [1964] AC 1129, 1166; *Camellia Tanker Ltd SA v International Transport Workers Federation* [1976] ICR 274, 284, 296. See also *Hodges v Webb* [1920] 2 Ch 70; Beatson, *The Use and Abuse of Unjust Enrichment* (1991) 118–20; Smith [1997] CLJ 343, 346–50.

[50] Below, p 385.

[51] *Barton v Armstrong* [1976] AC 104, 118–9, 120. Cf the similar willingness of the Courts to infer reliance on a misrepresentation: above, pp 328–9.

[52] *Huyton SA v Peter Cremer GmbH & Co* [1999] 1 Lloyd's Rep 620, 636, 638–9; *Law Debenture Trust Corp plc v Ukraine* [2023] UKSC 11 at [144]. Cf McKendrick, in Burrows and Rodger, above, n 42, 181, 187. See also above, p 328 (causation tests for fraudulent and non-fraudulent misrepresentations).

[53] [1980] AC 614, above, p 111. See also *Alec Lobb (Garages) Ltd v Total Oil Great Britain Ltd* [1983] 1 WLR 87; *Morley v Royal Bank of Scotland Plc* [2021] EWCA Civ 338, [2022] 1 All ER (Comm) 703 at [54] (agreement was result not of duress but of robust (and even aggressive) negotiation between commercial parties, each with legal advice and well able to look after itself in the negotiation).

(iii) Alternative remedies

A person threatened with duress of goods or a breach of contract can stand up to the threat and, if the other party breaches the contract, sue for damages. In the context of duress of goods the presence of an alternative remedy, such as an action in tort for wrongful interference with goods, is not necessarily a bar to relief; the threatened party might have had 'such an immediate want of his goods that [such an action] would not do'[54] and in any event there is no *right* to recover the goods themselves as opposed to damages in an action in tort.[55]

In the case of duress by threatened breach of contract, although damages and, where available, specific relief may be adequate, there will be situations in which such remedies do not adequately protect the victim, for example where it is imperative that there be no interruption in performance[56] or where, as in *Atlas Express Ltd v Kafco (Importers and Distributors) Ltd*, it is not possible to obtain the contractual services from another source. The existence and adequacy of an alternative remedy is taken into account in such cases. There is some support for treating this as purely evidential and not conclusive, that is, one of the factors (with protest and independent advice) which the Court takes into account in determining whether the victim was in fact coerced by the threat.[57] But it is submitted that, since the basis of the doctrine of duress is the absence of a practical alternative on the part of the victim to submission to the threat, the better view is that the existence of an adequate alternative remedy goes to the essence of and precludes a finding of duress.[58]

(c) THREATS OF LAWFUL ACTION

It is not ordinarily duress to threaten to do that which one has a right to do, for instance to refuse to enter into a contract or to terminate a contract lawfully.[59] In the cut-and-thrust of business relationships various types of pressure may be brought to bear in differing situations. Where there are shortages in goods or services the person who

[54] *Astley v Reynolds* (1731) 2 Str 915, 916; *Maskell v Horner* [1915] 3 KB 106, 122. See also *Kanhaya Lal v National Bank of India* (1913) 29 TLR 314. Cf *Vantage Navigation Corp v Suhail & Saud Bahwan Building Materials Llc, The Alev* [1989] 1 Lloyd's Rep 138, 146–7.

[55] By the Torts (Interference with Goods) Act 1977, ss 3(2)(a), 3(3)(b) an order for delivery of the goods may be made at the discretion of the Court.

[56] *Kolmar Group AG v Traxpo Enterprises Pvt Ptd* [2010] EWHC 113 (Comm).

[57] *Pao On v Lau Yiu Long* [1980] AC 614, 635, 640; *Huyton SA v Peter Cremer GmbH & Co* [1999] 1 Lloyd's Rep 620, 638; *Kolmar Group AG v Traxpo Enterprises Pvt Ptd* [2010] EWHC 113 (Comm) at [92].

[58] *Vantage Navigation Corp v Suhail & Saud Bahwan Building Materials Llc, The Alev* [1989] 1 Lloyd's Rep 138; *Hennessy v Craigmyle & Co Ltd* [1986] ICR 461; *DSND Subsea Ltd v Petroleum Geo Services ASA* [2000] BLR 530 at [131]; *Borrelli v Ting* [2010] UKPC 21, [2010] Bus LR 1718 at [31] ('Put colloquially James Henry Ting had the Liquidators over a barrel'). See also *Times Travel (UK) Ltd v Pakistan International Airlines Corp* [2021] UKSC 40 at [78]–[79] (Lord Burrows: at least in the case of economic duress, the absence of a reasonable alternative to giving in to the threat or pressure is an essential element, separate from causation).

[59] *Leyland DAF Ltd v Automotive Products plc* [1994] 1 BCLC 245, 249–50, 257; *Smith v William Charlick Ltd* (1923) 34 CLR 38, 56, 64–5 (Australia). See also *A-G v R* [2003] UKPC 22, [2003] EMLR 24 (threat to return member of SAS Regiment to his former regiment if he did not sign a lifelong confidentiality agreement was a lawful threat, and the demand supported by the threat was justified).

wishes to acquire them has little choice. Thus a private person or undertaking is generally permitted to refuse to deal with another at all or except on specified terms,[60] and the poor person who has to agree to pay a high rent to get a roof over his head is nevertheless bound. 'No bargain will be upset which is the result of the ordinary interplay of [market] forces'[61] and a contracting party will not be permitted to escape from its contractual obligations merely because it was coerced into making a contract by fear of the financial consequences of refusing to do so.[62] Although this approach leaves many forms of socially objectionable conduct unchecked, as a general rule the determination of when socially objectionable conduct which is not in itself unlawful should be penalized is for the legislature rather than the judiciary.[63]

Duress can exist even where the threat is one of lawful action but in such cases, since the threat is lawful, the illegitimacy of the threat is determined by focusing on the justification of the demand, having regard to, amongst other things, the nature of the behaviour of the threatening party (including the nature of the pressure applied) and the circumstances of the threatened party.[64] Cases of lawful act duress are, however, exceptional:[65]

> a demand motivated by commercial self-interest is, in general, justified. Lawful act economic duress is essentially concerned with identifying rare exceptional cases where a demand, motivated by commercial self-interest, is nevertheless unjustified.

For example, blackmail[66] is often a demand supported by a threat to do what is lawful, for instance to report criminal conduct to the police. The blackmailer typically has no economic interest in the outcome apart from getting what has been demanded, and it is for this reason that the threat is regarded as unwarranted for the purposes of the criminal law—and would be regarded as unjustified and illegitimate for the purposes of a private law claim based on economic duress.[67]

In recent years the existence and scope of the category of 'lawful act' duress has been debated in many common law jurisdictions.[68] In *Times Travel (UK) Ltd v Pakistan International Airlines Corp*[69] the Supreme Court settled authoritatively that there is a such a concept in English law and (by a majority) the circumstances in which it can be found.

[60] For the position of a public body, see *R v Lewisham LBC, ex p Shell UK Ltd* [1988] 1 All ER 938 and the statutory controls discussed above, pp 249–50.

[61] *Lloyds Bank Ltd v Bundy* [1975] QB 326, 336 (Lord Denning MR).

[62] *Hardie and Lane Ltd v Chilton* [1928] 2 KB 306; *Eric Gnapp Ltd v Petroleum Board* [1949] 1 All ER 980.

[63] This paragraph was quoted with approval in *Times Travel (UK) Ltd v Pakistan International Airlines Corp* [2021] UKSC 40 at [29].

[64] *Times Travel (UK) Ltd v Pakistan International Airlines Corp* [2021] UKSC 40 at [1], [96], [136]; *The Universe Sentinel* [1983] 1 AC 366, 401.

[65] *Times Travel (UK) Ltd v Pakistan International Airlines Corp* [2021] UKSC 40 at [136] (Lord Burrows); see also at [30], [97]–[99].

[66] Theft Act 1968, s 21(1) ('A person is guilty of blackmail if, with a view to gain for himself or another or with intent to cause loss to another, he makes any unwarranted demand with menaces').

[67] *Times Travel (UK) Ltd v Pakistan International Airlines Corp* [2021] UKSC 40 at [96]; *The Universe Sentinel* [1983] 1 AC 366, 401.

[68] For discussion of the approach to economic duress in Australia, New Zealand, Singapore, Canada, and the US, see *Times Travel (UK) Ltd v Pakistan International Airlines Corp* [2021] UKSC 40 at [31]–[39].

[69] [2021] UKSC 40. See Day (2022) 138 LQR 194; Branford and Gardner (2023) 139 LQR 629.

Lord Hodge, giving the judgment of the majority in *Times Travel*, emphasized that in the English law of contract there is no doctrine of inequality of bargaining power,[70] nor a principle of good faith in contracting,[71] and that in consequence the scope for lawful act economic duress in contractual negotiations is extremely limited.[72] His Lordship summarized the present state of the law:[73]

> there are to date two circumstances in which the English courts have recognised and provided a remedy for such duress. The first circumstance is where a defendant uses his knowledge of criminal activity by the claimant or a member of the claimant's close family to obtain a personal benefit from the claimant by the express or implicit threat to report the crime or initiate a prosecution. The second circumstance is where the defendant, having exposed himself to a civil claim by the claimant, for example, for damages for breach of contract, deliberately manoeuvres the claimant into a position of vulnerability by means which the law regards as illegitimate and thereby forces the claimant to waive his claim. In both categories of case the defendant has behaved in a highly reprehensible way which the courts have treated as amounting to illegitimate pressure.

The first circumstance (exploitation of knowledge of criminal activity) was illustrated by three cases, all of which predated the development of the common law doctrine of lawful act duress and were decided on the basis of the equitable doctrine of undue influence,[74] but are now seen as examples of lawful act duress:[75]

> the courts have developed the common law doctrine of duress to include lawful act economic duress by drawing on the rules of equity in relation to undue influence and treating as 'illegitimate' conduct which, when the law of duress was less developed, had been identified by equity as giving rise to an agreement which it was unconscionable for the party who had conducted himself or herself in that way to seek to enforce.

However, the circumstances covered by this category of economic duress are limited. It has been said to be doubtful—except perhaps in the extreme case of a particularly terrifying or oppressive threat—whether it extends to a threat of prosecution by due process to obtain agreement from the person liable to prosecution (rather than a family member or other party fearing that prospect), and in respect of sums already due in law from that person.[76]

The second circumstance (using illegitimate means to manoeuvre the claimant into a position of weakness to force him to waive his claim) was illustrated by two cases[77] which found economic duress by reason of the unconscionable conduct of

[70] Below, pp 410–4.

[71] Above, pp 67–8, 179–82, 232–5, 376.

[72] *Times Travel* [2021] UKSC 40 at [26]–[30], agreeing with Beatson, *The Use and Abuse of Unjust Enrichment* (1991) 134.

[73] *Ibid* at [4].

[74] *Williams v Bayley* (1886) LR 1 HL 200; *Kaufman v Gerson* [1904] 1 KB 591; *Mutual Finance Ltd v John Wetton & Sons Ltd* [1937] 2 KB 389. See below, p 390.

[75] *Times Travel* [2021] UKSC 40 at [2].

[76] *Al Saif Group v Cable* [2022] EWHC 271 (QB) at [208]–[209].

[77] *Borrelli v Ting* [2010] UKPC 21 (course of conduct including forgery and the provision of false evidence); *Progress Bulk Carriers Ltd v Tube City IMS LLC, The Cenk Kaptanoglu* [2012] EWHC 273 (Comm), [2012] 1 Lloyd's Rep 501 (repudiatory breach of contract and subsequent misleading activity).

one party, by which it applied pressure on the other, involving bad faith or similar reprehensible behaviour.[78]

Lord Hodge made clear that these two circumstances are not the limit to the doctrine of lawful act duress, the boundaries of which are not fixed and may be developed. However, any such development must be made cautiously, particularly in the context of contractual negotiations between commercial entities, and must take account of analogous equitable remedies, such as undue influence and unconscionable bargains, and the absence in English law of doctrines of good faith in contracting and imbalance of bargaining power.[79]

In the *Times Travel* case:

TT, a small family-owned travel agency, had a contract with PIAC, the sole operator of direct flights from the UK to Pakistan, to sell PIAC tickets. TT's business depended on being able to sell PIAC tickets. A dispute arose between the parties about unpaid commission which TT claimed was due. PIAC gave notice to TT that it would reduce the allocation of tickets for sale by TT and would exercise a termination clause in the contract (both of which it was entitled to do under the contract), but offering a new contract at a lower rate of commission, and including a clause that released PIAC from existing claims to commission. TT reluctantly agreed, but later claimed commission due under the original contract, arguing that the new contract was entered into under economic duress.

The Court of Appeal held that the pressure on TT was lawful and did not amount to duress because PIAC honestly believed itself entitled to make the demand, regardless of whether the belief was reasonable.[80] The Supreme Court agreed that PIAC's pressure did not amount to economic duress, although their reasons were not unanimous. Lord Burrows would have followed the Court of Appeal in holding that in the case of a demand for a waiver by the threatened party of a claim against the threatening party (Lord Hodge's 'second circumstance' of possible lawful act economic duress), 'the "bad faith demand" requirement provides the appropriate certainty that is essential for the recognition of lawful act economic duress'.[81] However, Lord Hodge, speaking for the majority, rejected this on the basis that the focus on whether the demand was made in good or bad faith would carry the risk of extending the doctrine too far, and undermining certainty in commercial transactions:[82]

I . . . do not accept that the lawful act doctrine could be extended to a circumstance in which, without more, a commercial organisation exploits its strong bargaining power or monopoly position to extract a payment from another commercial organisation by an assertion in bad faith of a pre-existing legal entitlement which the other organisation believes or knows to be incorrect.

On the facts of the case, there was no illegitimate demand because 'the reduction of the ticket allocation was a hard-nosed exercise of monopoly power, which, in the absence

[78] *Times Travel* [2021] UKSC 40 at [11]–[16], [22], [56]–[57].
[79] *Ibid* at [3].
[80] [2019] EWCA Civ 828, [2020] Ch 98 at [105].
[81] *Times Travel* [2021] UKSC 40 at [130].
[82] *Ibid* at [52].

of a doctrine of unequal bargaining power, could not by itself amount to illegitimate pressure'. Something more was needed to characterize the behaviour as unconscionable or reprehensible.

Although it is clear that any further development will not readily be made, it is submitted that there is a risk of uncertainty in the scope of the law on lawful act duress. On the basis of the need for certainty, their Lordships rejected the argument that a 'range of factors' approach should be adopted to define lawful act duress,[83] or that a general standard of good faith dealing, or what is commercially unacceptable or unreasonable behaviour, should be applied.[84] Yet the scope of the second circumstance in which lawful act duress can be found, as stated by Lord Hodge, emphasizes the defendant's unconscionable or reprehensible conduct—which may also be open to broad interpretation.[85]

(d) RESCISSION

Duress renders the contract voidable, and the remedy by which the contract is avoided is rescission. Although there are few cases which explore the details of the remedy, in principle it should be no different from rescission for other vitiating factors such as misrepresentation and undue influence.[86] Therefore rescission can be obtained only if restitution can be made to restore both parties to their positions as they were before the contract;[87] and will be barred by affirmation[88] or, presumably, if the subject-matter of the contract has passed into the hands of a purchaser in good faith for value and without notice of the defect in the contract.[89]

3. UNDUE INFLUENCE

We have seen that the term 'fraud' was used in a sense wider and less precise in the Court of Chancery than in the common law courts.[90] It was often used in equity in the sense of unconscientious dealing although, in the words of Lord Haldane, a great equity lawyer, this was unfortunate.[91] One such form of dealing is commonly described as 'undue influence'. The nature and operation of undue influence was considered by

[83] *Ibid* at [1], [94].

[84] *Ibid* at [1], [95]; see also Lord Burrows at [126]–[130].

[85] Morgan [2022] CLJ 17; Day (2020) 138 LQR 194.

[86] *Halpern v Halpern (Nos 1 and 2)* [2007] EWCA Civ 291, [2008] QB 195 at [70]–[76], rejecting the argument that since a contract is voidable for duress at common law (rather than in equity) the nature of the remedy and its limitations are different. For rescission for misrepresentation, see p 335, above; for rescission for undue influence, see p 399, below.

[87] *Ibid.* cf *Borrelli v Ting* [2010] UKPC 21 at [38]–[39] (rejecting the 'unacceptable proposition' that rescission was not available where parties cannot be restored to the position created by the illegitimate means).

[88] *North Ocean Shipping Co Ltd v Hyundai Construction Co Ltd* [1979] QB 705.

[89] Cf *White v Garden* (1851) 10 CBNS 919 (third-party rights were a bar to rescission for fraud at common law).

[90] Above, p 368.

[91] *Nocton v Lord Ashburton* [1914] AC 932, 953.

the House of Lords in eight conjoined appeals in *Royal Bank of Scotland plc v Etridge (No 2)*.[92] Lord Nicholls set out the principles. Although there are some differences of expression and approach, the other members of the Appellate Committee agreed.[93]

(a) NATURE OF UNDUE INFLUENCE

The term 'undue influence' has sometimes been used to describe the equitable doctrine of coercion referred to above,[94] but it also includes, and it would perhaps be more helpful to confine it to, forms of pressure much less direct or substantial than those already discussed. Given that illegitimate threats may nowadays be viewed as falling within the doctrine of duress,[95] undue influence is principally concerned with a situation where, by reason of the relationship between them, one party (B) has such influence over the other (A) that A does not exercise a free judgement, independent of B, in relation to the making of a transaction between A and B (or, in a three-party situation, between A and a third party, C).[96] It is often said that the doctrine of undue influence addresses the unfair exploitation of a relationship of ascendancy or influence,[97] but although undue influence is sometimes described as an 'equitable wrong', the basis of the Court's intervention is not the commission of a dishonest or wrongful act by B against A, but that, as a matter of public policy, B's influence should not operate to A's disadvantage.[98]

A finding of undue influence does not depend upon a conclusion that the victim made no decision of her own, or that her will and intention was overborne: a conscious exercise of will may be vitiated by undue influence.[99] Nor need the claimant show that, but for the influence, the transaction would not have been entered into.[100] 'The question is, not, whether she knew what she was doing, had done, or proposed to do, but how the intention was produced: whether all that care and providence was placed round her, as against those, who advised her, which, from their situation and relation with respect to her, they were bound to exert on her behalf.'[101] The undue influence may consist not only in the positive application of pressure, directly or indirectly, but also in the failure to fulfil

[92] [2001] UKHL 44, [2002] 2 AC 773.

[93] *Ibid* at [3]. See also [91], [100], [192].

[94] *Mutual Finance Ltd v John Wetton & Sons Ltd* [1937] 2 KB 389; *Royal Bank of Scotland plc v Etridge (No 2)* [2001] UKHL 44 at [7]–[8].

[95] Above, pp 380, 385–9.

[96] *Nature Resorts Ltd v First Citizens Bank Ltd* [2022] UKPC 10, [2022] 1 WLR 2788 at [10]. For three-party situations, see below, p 402.

[97] *A-G v R* [2003] UKPC 22 at [21]; *National Commercial Bank (Jamaica) Ltd v Hew* [2003] UKPC 51 at [32]–[33].

[98] *Pesticcio v Huet* [2004] EWCA Civ 372, [2004] WTLR 699 at [20]; *Nature Resorts Ltd v First Citizens Bank Ltd* [2022] UKPC 10 at [15]. See also Birks and Chin, in Beatson and Friedmann (eds), *Good Faith and Fault in Contract Law* (1995) ch 3; Chen-Wishart, in Burrows and Rodger (eds), *Mapping the Law: Essays in Memory of Peter Birks* (2006) 201 and [2006] CLP 231.

[99] *Hewett v First Plus Financial Group plc* [2010] EWCA Civ 312, [2010] 2 P & CR 22 at [25].

[100] *Ibid* at [34]; *UCB Corporate Services Ltd v Williams* [2002] EWCA Civ 555, [2003] 1 P & CR 12 at [86].

[101] *Huguenin v Baseley* (1807) 14 Ves Jun 273, 300 (Lord Eldon).

a duty of candour and fairness arising from the relation of confidence or dependence, involving misrepresentations or the failure to disclose relevant information.[102] There is therefore potential for overlap of claims for undue influence with claims for duress, misrepresentation, or non-disclosure because the facts which justify a finding of undue influence may also give rise to these other claims.

Courts, including the House of Lords in *Etridge*'s case, have been careful not to define precisely the sort of influence which will be regarded as 'undue'.[103] Historically, equity identified broadly two forms of unacceptable conduct, which Lord Nicholls described as follows:[104]

> The first comprises overt acts of improper pressure or coercion such as unlawful threats ... The second form arises out of a relationship between two persons where one has acquired over another a measure of influence, or ascendancy, of which the ascendant person then takes unfair advantage ... In cases of this latter nature the influence one person has over another provides scope for misuse without any specific overt acts of persuasion. The relationship between two individuals may be such that, without more, one of them is disposed to agree a course of action proposed by the other. Typically, this occurs when one person places trust in another to look after his affairs and interests, and the latter betrays this trust by preferring his own interests. He abuses the influence he has acquired.

The first type of case, the direct analogue of common law duress, has been called 'actual' undue influence. The second type of case, where the parties are in a relationship in which duties of care and confidence are imposed on one party towards the other, has been called 'presumed' undue influence. However, as the Privy Council has recently made clear, undue influence is a single concept:[105]

> Ever since *Allcard v Skinner*,[106] it has been commonplace to divide undue influence into two categories: actual and presumed. But in *Etridge* the House of Lords made clear that undue influence is a single concept. It does not have two different forms. The correct analysis of the two categories is that they refer to different ways of *proving* undue influence. Presumed undue influence refers to where the person alleging undue influence relies on an evidential presumption. Actual undue influence refers to where the person alleging undue influence relies on direct proof (of A's conduct, within a relationship with B, which led to B not exercising a free and independent judgment).

The burden of proof of undue influence rests upon the person who claims to have been wronged. The claimant who relies on 'actual' undue influence must discharge the burden of proof that the defendant exerted the improper pressure, coercion, or

[102] *Hewett v First Plus Financial Group plc* [2010] EWCA Civ 312 at [24] (husband's concealment of affair from his wife amounted to exercise of undue influence against her).

[103] *Royal Bank of Scotland plc v Etridge (No 2)* [2001] UKHL 44 at [11]; *National Westminster Bank plc v Morgan* [1985] AC 686, 709; *Allcard v Skinner* (1887) 36 Ch D 145, 183.

[104] *Royal Bank of Scotland plc v Etridge (No 2)* [2001] UKHL 44 at [8]–[9]. See also at [103]–[105] (Lord Hobhouse) and [151]–[158] (Lord Scott). But Lord Clyde at [92] questioned the wisdom of attempting to make classifications of cases of undue influence.

[105] *Nature Resorts Ltd v First Citizens Bank Ltd* [2022] UKPC 10 at [11].

[106] (1887) 36 Ch D 145.

influence alleged. However, the claimant who relies on 'presumed' undue influence must show that the defendant was in a position to exercise influence over the claimant, and that the transaction between the parties calls for explanation; the burden of proof of undue influence may then be discharged unless the defendant adduces sufficient evidence to the contrary.[107]

(b) ACTUAL UNDUE INFLUENCE

Where one party exercised such domination over the mind and will of the other that the latter's independence of decision was substantially undermined, and this domination brought about the transaction, the victim will be entitled to relief on the ground of undue influence:[108]

> It is an equitable wrong committed by the dominant party against the other which makes it unconscionable for the dominant party to enforce his legal rights against the other.

There is no need for any special relationship (of the type mentioned below) to exist between the parties, although, of course, it may do so. The mere fact that domination was exercised is sufficient; no abuse of confidence need be proved. In *Smith v Kay*,[109] for example, a young man, only just of age, incurred liabilities to the appellant by the contrivance of an older man who had acquired a strong influence over him, and who professed to assist him in a career of extravagance and dissipation. It was held that influence of this nature, though in no way 'fiduciary', entitled the young man to the protection of the Court. Similarly, in *Morley v Loughnan*[110] executors sued to recover £140,000 paid by the deceased to a member of the 'Exclusive Brethren' in whose house he had lived for some years, and under whose religious influence he had been. Wright J, in giving judgment for the claimants, said that it was unnecessary to decide whether or not any special relationship existed between the deceased and the defendant, for he 'took possession, so to speak, of the whole life of the deceased, and the gifts were not the result of the deceased's own free will, but the effect of that influence and domination'.[111]

Many older cases on this point have concerned spiritual 'advisers' who have used their expert knowledge of the next world to obtain material advantages in this. In more recent times the cases have often concerned men who have put pressure on their wives or partners to secure business debts by mortgaging the family home.[112] While heavy family pressure will not in itself suffice to constitute domination, in one case wounding and insulting language, and demeaning comparisons between what a husband characterized as his wife's disloyalty and his relations' loyalty, amounted to moral blackmail and coercion.[113] Actual undue influence may also, however, be found in other contexts.[114]

[107] *Royal Bank of Scotland plc v Etridge (No 2)* [2001] UKHL 44 at [13]–[14]; below, p 394.
[108] *Ibid* at [103]. [109] (1859) 7 HLC 750. [110] [1893] 1 Ch 736. [111] *Ibid*, 756.
[112] eg *CIBC Mortgages plc v Pitt* [1994] 1 AC 200.
[113] *Bank of Scotland v Bennett* [1997] 1 FLR 801, 822–7, one of the cases on appeal to HL in *Etridge*'s case: see [2001] UKHL 44 at [312]–[315].
[114] eg *Cissé v Diene* [2024] EWHC 1717 (Ch) at [151] (agent of professional football player took advantage of his ascendency over the player through his superior knowledge, language, and financial proficiency).

Actual undue influence itself suffices for relief. It is not necessary that the transaction induced by it be not readily explicable or be manifestly disadvantageous to the victim:[115]

Actual undue influence is a species of fraud. Like any other victim of fraud, a person who has been induced by undue influence to carry out a transaction which he did not freely and knowingly enter into is entitled to have that transaction set aside as of right . . . A man guilty of fraud is no more entitled to argue that the transaction was beneficial to the person defrauded than is a man who has procured a transaction by misrepresentation. The effect of the wrongdoer's conduct is to prevent the wronged party from bringing a free will and properly informed mind to bear on the proposed transaction which accordingly must be set aside in equity as a matter of justice.

It has been said, however, that in the nature of things questions of undue influence will not usually arise where the transaction is innocuous.[116]

(c) PRESUMED UNDUE INFLUENCE

Even if it cannot be proved that the claimant's mind was a 'mere channel through which the will of the defendant operated,'[117] relief may be given if there existed between the parties some special relationship of confidence which the defendant has abused:

Wherever two persons stand in such a relation that, while it continues, confidence is necessarily reposed by one, and the influence which naturally grows out of that confidence is possessed by the other, and this confidence is abused, or the influence is exerted to obtain an advantage at the expense of the confiding party, the person so availing himself of his position will not be permitted to retain the advantage, although the transaction could not have been impeached if no such confidential relation had existed.[118]

Prior to *Etridge*'s case Slade LJ[119] had divided presumed undue influence into two classes, an approach approved by the House of Lords in *Barclays Bank plc v O'Brien*.[120] The first (class 2A) was where the duties of care and confidence arose as a matter of law by virtue of the relationship between the parties. The second (class 2B) was said to occur where the duties arose in the special circumstances of the parties' association with each other, that is, because on the facts of the particular case the claimant placed trust and confidence in the other party and the transaction between the parties was one calling for an explanation.

In *Etridge*'s case, however, their Lordships considered that it was only in class 2A cases that there is a true presumption of influence, arising from the law's 'sternly protective

[115] *CIBC Mortgages plc v Pitt* [1994] 1 AC 200, 209 (Lord Browne-Wilkinson).

[116] *Royal Bank of Scotland plc v Etridge (No 2)* [2001] UKHL 44 at [12].

[117] *Tufton v Sperni* [1952] 2 TLR 516, 530.

[118] *Tate v Williamson* (1866) LR 2 Ch App 55, 61 (Lord Chelmsford).

[119] *Bank of Credit and Commerce International SA v Aboody* [1990] 1 QB 923, 953.

[120] [1994] 1 AC 180, 189–90.

attitude towards certain types of relationship'. In such cases the claimant 'need not prove he actually reposed trust and confidence in the other party. It is sufficient for him to prove the existence of the relationship.'[121] Even in such cases all that is presumed is the *influence*—that the defendant was in a position to exercise influence over the claimant. It is not automatically presumed that the influence was *undue*—that the defendant abused the relationship—although this may be established on the evidence by the claimant showing that the transaction between the parties called for explanation and no explanation is forthcoming from the defendant.[122]

In class 2B cases, however, although described by generations of equity lawyers as cases in which a presumption of undue influence arises, there is no true presumption but only a shift in the evidential onus. The burden of proving undue influence rests on the claimant, but will normally be discharged by proof that he or she placed trust and confidence in the other party and that the transaction between the parties is one which calls for explanation. Proof of those two facts is prima facie evidence that the defendant abused the influence he or she acquired in the relationship, and it is then for the defendant to counter the inference which should otherwise be drawn. Accordingly, a claimant who succeeds does so because he or she has established a case of undue influence.[123] Analytically, the general burden of proof remains on the claimant, but this can be discharged by establishing a sufficient prima facie case. Despite this difference, since there is a shift in the evidential onus and since the requirement that the transaction must be one calling for explanation is relevant in both categories of case, the two different types of presumption are considered in this section. In both there are two components required for the establishment of a situation in which undue influence will be presumed. The first is the nature of the relationship, and the second is the nature of the transaction, which must be one calling for explanation; that is, not readily explicable by the relationship of the parties, but also, less satisfactorily, sometimes described as one that is 'manifestly disadvantageous' to the victim.

(i) The nature of the relationship

In respect of certain relationships there is what is commonly referred to as an irrebuttable legal presumption (but more appropriately referred to as a legal rule) that the relationship is one of influence.[124] In other situations, proof that on the particular facts trust and confidence has been reposed by one party in the other is necessary.

(a) Presumption Raised as a Matter of Law. Not every fiduciary relationship raises a presumption of undue influence.[125] It must be one of a limited class which the Courts regard as suggesting undue influence. The relations which fall into this category cannot

[121] [2001] UKHL 44 at [18] (Lord Nicholls). See also *ibid* at [107], [161].

[122] *Ibid* at [104].

[123] *Ibid* at [13]–[14].

[124] *Nature Resorts Ltd v First Citizens Bank Ltd* [2022] UKPC 10 at [12].

[125] *Re Coomber* [1911] 1 Ch 723, 726; *Cissé v Diene* [2024] EWHC 1717 (Ch) at [135] (agency; but there was a relationship of trust and confidence on the facts).

be listed exhaustively,[126] but include those between parent (or person *in loco parentis*) and child,[127] solicitor and client,[128] doctor and patient,[129] trustee and beneficiary,[130] and spiritual adviser and any person to whom that person stands in that relationship.[131] It was once the position that the relationship of fiancé and fiancée also raised the presumption,[132] but a different view is now taken of the relationship between an engaged couple, and the existence of influence is no longer assumed automatically, but will depend on the facts.[133] The relationship between a married couple is also certainly not one to which this presumption applies as a matter of law.[134]

As mentioned earlier, it is important to note that the presumption is that one party has acquired influence over the other, it is not a presumption that the influence has been abused. If all that has happened is that a client has left a small bequest to his family solicitor, no inference of abuse or unfair dealing will arise.[135]

(b) Shift in the Evidential Onus as a Result of the Facts of the Particular Case. Where, as in the case of husband and wife, the presumption does not apply as a matter of law, one of the parties may nevertheless be able to demonstrate that on the facts of the particular case he or she placed trust and confidence in the other to a degree that (provided, as discussed below, that the transaction is one that calls for explanation) the Court can infer, in the absence of a satisfactory explanation, that the transaction can only have been procured by undue influence.[136] In such cases there is a rebuttable evidential presumption of undue influence. In the case of wives, it has been stated that 'this special tenderness of treatment' is attributable to the fact that in many cases a wife is able to demonstrate that she placed trust and confidence in her husband in relation to her financial affairs and because 'the sexual and emotional ties between the parties provide a ready weapon for undue influence: a wife's true wishes can easily be overborne because of her fear of destroying or damaging the wider relationship between her and her husband if she opposes his wishes'.[137] Similar principles apply to all other cases where there is an emotional relationship between cohabitees, married or unmarried, heterosexual or homosexual.[138] The trust and confidence may arise generally from the

[126] *Royal Bank of Scotland plc v Etridge (No 2)* [2001] UKHL 44 at [10].

[127] *Bainbrigge v Browne* (1881) 18 Ch D 188; *Lancashire Loans Ltd v Black* [1934] 1 KB 380. But a parent is not presumed without more to be dependent on his or her children: *Enal v Singh* [2022] UKPC 13, [2023] 2 P & CR 5 at [51].

[128] *Wright v Carter* [1980] 1 Ch 27.

[129] *Mitchell v Homfray* (1881) 8 QBD 587.

[130] *Beningfield v Baxter* (1886) 12 App Cas 167.

[131] *Huguenin v Baseley* (1807) 14 Ves Jun 273; *Allcard v Skinner* (1887) 36 Ch D 145. Cf Ridge (2023) 139 LQR 458.

[132] *Re Lloyds Bank Ltd* [1931] 1 Ch 289, 302 (Maugham J).

[133] *Zamet v Hyman* [1961] 1 WLR 1442, 1446. An 'engaged couple' may now be of the same sex: Marriage (Same Sex Couples) Act 2013.

[134] *Barclays Bank plc v O'Brien* [1994] 1 AC 180; *Etridge* [2001] UKHL 44 at [19]. Cf *Backhouse v Backhouse* [1978] 1 WLR 243, 251.

[135] *Etridge* [2001] UKHL 44 at [104].

[136] *Ibid* at [14].

[137] *Barclays Bank plc v O'Brien* [1994] 1 AC 180, 190–1, 196 (Lord Browne-Wilkinson).

[138] *Ibid*, 198. See also *Etridge* [2001] UKHL 44 at [47].

nature of the relationship: for example, trust and confidence by the wife in the husband's conduct of the family's financial affairs, but it may also arise, or be intensified, in the course of the impugned transaction itself.[139]

There is no closed list of situations in which such a relationship exists on the facts of the particular case. The principle applies to every case where influence is acquired and abused, where confidence is reposed and betrayed.[140] It is not confined to cases where trust and confidence is reposed, either financially or generally, but extends to cases where there is evidence of dependence or vulnerability,[141] although it is not enough simply to point to the existence of a vulnerability where there was no resulting relationship of influence.[142] All the circumstances have to be considered to determine whether such a relationship exists.[143] It is not necessary to show that it is one of domination. It suffices that the party in whom trust and confidence is reposed is in a position to exercise influence over the party who reposes it. In *Tate v Williamson*:[144]

An undergraduate, T, aged 23 years, was being pressed to pay his college debts of some £1,000. Being estranged from his father, he asked his great-uncle to advise him how he should find the means to pay. The great-uncle was in ill health and unable to advise, but deputed the defendant, his nephew, to do so. In conversations with the defendant T expressed the desire to sell part of his estate, upon which the defendant offered to buy it for £7,000. Before the sale was completed, the defendant obtained a report from a surveyor on the property, which valued it at £20,000. The defendant did not disclose this fact to T, but proceeded with the purchase. Excessive drinking led to T's death one year later. It was held that the purchase must be set aside. The defendant, having been asked to give advice, stood in a confidential relationship to T, and this prevented him from becoming a purchaser of the property without the fullest communication of all material information which he had obtained as to its value.

139 *Turkey v Awadh* [2005] EWCA Civ 382, [2005] 2 P & CR 29 at [9]–[10]; *Thompson v Foy* [2009] EWHC 1076 (Ch), [2010] 1 P & CR 16 at [100]; *Hewett v First Plus Financial Group plc* [2010] EWCA Civ 312 at [27]–[30].

140 *Smith v Kay* (1859) 7 HLC 750, 779 (Lord Kingsdown).

141 *Sheikh v Malik* [2018] EWHC 973 (Ch), [2018] 4 WLR 86 at [50]; *Birmingham CC v Beech* [2014] EWCA Civ 830, [2015] 1 P & CR 1 at [59].

142 *Azam v Molazam* [2023] EWHC 2202 (Ch) at [81].

143 *Lloyds Bank Ltd v Bundy* [1975] QB 326, 342.

144 (1866) LR 2 Ch App 55. See also *Re Craig* [1971] Ch 95 (secretary-companion and man of 84 years); *Goldsworthy v Brickell* [1987] 1 Ch 378 (85-year-old farmer and farm manager; contrast *Evans v Lloyd* [2013] EWHC 1725 (Ch) at [58] (70-year-old residential ex-farm worker not 'dependent' for purposes of undue influence)); *Lloyds Bank Ltd v Bundy* [1975] QB 326 (banker and customer) but cf *National Westminster Bank plc v Morgan* [1985] 1 AC 686; *Horry v Tate & Lyle Refineries Ltd* [1982] 2 Lloyd's Rep 416 (employer's insurers and injured employee); *O'Sullivan v Management Agency and Music Ltd* [1985] QB 428 (internationally recognized manager and unknown pop musician); *A-G v R* [2003] UKPC 22 at [24] (commanding officer and soldier, in context of military hierarchy and strong regimental pride); *Smith v Cooper* [2010] EWCA Civ 722, [2010] 2 FCR 551 (cohabitees, where man acquired position of ascendancy over the woman because of her mental condition, his awareness of it, and his decision to run her finances). Perhaps the high-water mark is *Credit Lyonnais Bank Nederland NV v Burch* [1997] 1 All ER 144 (employer and employee), recognized in *Etridge* [2001] UKHL 44 at [83], [86], [89] but which may be better regarded (see Chen-Wishart [1997] CLJ 60) as a case of unconscionability, on which see below, p 406.

Similarly, in *Tufton v Sperni*,[145] the situation was such that a confidential relationship arose:

T and S were fellow members of a committee formed to establish a Moslem cultural centre in London, it being understood that T would provide the funds for the centre. S induced T to buy his (S's) own house for the purpose at a price which grossly exceeded its market value.

The Court of Appeal set the contract aside. The situation was not one which was comprehended by the established categories, nor was there any domination of T by S; yet, as Evershed MR pointed out:[146]

If a number of persons join together for the purpose of furthering some charitable or altruistic objective, it would seem not unreasonable to conclude that in regard to all matters related to that objective, each 'necessarily reposes confidence' in the others and each possesses accordingly that 'influence which naturally grows out of confidence'.

(ii) A transaction which is not readily explicable by the relationship and calls for explanation

In *Goldsworthy v Brickell*, drawing on Lindley LJ's classic nineteenth-century formulation in *Allcard v Skinner*,[147] Nourse LJ stated:

[T]he presumption is not perfected and remains inoperative until the party who has ceded the trust and confidence makes a gift so large, or enters a transaction so improvident, as not to be reasonably accounted for on the ground of friendship, relationship, charity or other ordinary motives on which ordinary men act. Although influence might have been presumed beforehand, it is only then that it is presumed to have been undue.[148]

The reason for this requirement is to prevent the presumption applying to obviously innocuous transactions between those in a relationship of trust and confidence, such as a moderate gift as a Christmas present by a child to a parent, an agreement by a client to pay reasonable fees to a solicitor, or a moderate bequest to one's doctor.[149]

In *National Westminster Bank plc v Morgan*[150] Lord Scarman stated that the transaction must be 'manifestly disadvantageous' to the influenced person. This formulation has been widely criticized because its primary focus appears to be financial, that is, the adequacy of the consideration given in exchange for the money paid or property transferred. 'Manifest disadvantage' can generally be shown where a person agrees to guarantee the debts of another and is, of course, an inherent feature of gifts, which have

[145] [1952] 2 TLR 516. See also *Roche v Sherrington* [1982] 1 WLR 599.

[146] [1952] 2 TLR 516, 523. See also *Goldsworthy v Brickell* [1987] 1 Ch 378.

[147] (1887) 36 Ch D 145, 185.

[148] [1987] Ch 378, 401. This requirement does not apply to cases of 'actual' undue influence, above, p 393.

[149] *Royal Bank of Scotland plc v Etridge (No 2)* [2001] UKHL 44 at [24], [104], [156]. See also *Nature Resorts Ltd v First Citizens Bank Ltd* [2022] UKPC 10 at [27] (ordinary commercial transaction entered into on solicitor's advice with third party, rather than with the solicitor, should rarely be regarded as not readily explicable on ordinary motives, even if it is disadvantageous).

[150] [1985] AC 686.

been the subject of many cases of undue influence.[151] It would also exist where a charge over a matrimonial home secured not only money borrowed under the proposed transaction but also any other transaction entered into by the debtor. But in the case of a guarantee of the debts of a business it may be more difficult to determine whether the transaction is 'manifestly disadvantageous'. In the sense that the guarantor undertakes a serious financial obligation with no personal financial return it is disadvantageous. But where the guarantor has an interest in the business, as in the case of a shareholder or a wife where the business is the source of the family income, it may not be.[152] Moreover, the formulation does not readily allow non-financial factors to be taken into account. Where the requisite relationship of trust and confidence exists between two persons, the fact that an offer by one to buy land or a valuable oil painting from the other is for the full or even an enhanced market price should not necessarily prevent the transaction being presumed to be vitiated by undue influence. The person subjected to the influence should not be presumed to wish to sell a family home or business, or an item of particular sentimental value, even for the full market price. A relationship and the influence resulting from it may be abused 'even though the transaction is, on the face of it, one which, in commercial terms, provides reasonably equal benefits for both parties'.[153] In *Etridge*'s case it was accepted that the label 'manifest disadvantage' can give rise to misunderstanding and should be discarded. Lord Nicholls stated that the better approach was to adhere more directly to the classic test which asks whether the transaction can be 'reasonably accounted for on the ground of friendship, relationship, charity or other ordinary motives' as well as whether it is 'improvident'.[154] The core question is whether the nature of the transaction was such as to give rise to an inference that it was obtained by an unfair exploitation of the relationship.[155]

(iii) Rebutting the presumption

Where influence is shown to exist, the presumption of its undue exercise can be rebutted only by proof that the party reposing the confidence has been 'placed in such a position as will enable him to form an entirely free and unfettered judgment, independent altogether of any sort of control'.[156] The most obvious way of establishing this is to show that the party reposing the confidence received independent legal advice and took it. In some (possibly extreme) cases, very cogent evidence has been required to be adduced

[151] eg *Allcard v Skinner* (1887) 36 Ch D 145, below, p 400.

[152] *Royal Bank of Scotland plc v Etridge (No 2)* [2001] UKHL 44 at [28]–[29].

[153] *National Westminster Bank plc v Morgan* [1983] 3 All ER 85, 92 (Slade LJ). Although the House of Lords disagreed ([1985] AC 686, 704), see *Barclays Bank plc v Coleman* [2001] QB 20, 31 (Nourse LJ).

[154] [2001] UKHL 44 at [28]–[29]. See also *ibid* at [104], [156].

[155] *A-G v R* [2003] UKPC 22 at [24] (lifelong confidentiality agreement signed by serving member of SAS was one which anyone who wished to serve could reasonably have been required to sign); *Turkey v Awadh* [2005] EWCA Civ 382 at [22]–[23].

[156] *Archer v Hudson* (1844) 7 Beav 551, 560 (Lord Langdale MR). See also *Re Craig* [1971] Ch 95, 105; *Goldsworthy v Brickell* [1987] 1 Ch 378, 408–9; *Smith v Cooper* [2010] EWCA Civ 722 at [71] (trial judge failed to consider whether presumption rebutted).

by the defendant to prove that the significance of the advice was brought home to the other party. In *Powell v Powell*:[157]

A settlement was executed by a young woman, under the influence of her stepmother, by which she shared her property with the children of the stepmother's second marriage. She received some independent advice from a solicitor, but he was acting for some of the other parties to the settlement as well as for the claimant. It appeared that, although he had expressed disapproval of the transaction, he had not carried his disapproval to the point of withdrawing his services.

It was held that the settlement should be rescinded.

The provision of independent legal advice is not the only way of rebutting the presumption. The essential thing is to show that the transaction was 'the result of the free exercise of independent will'.[158] If this is established, the transaction will be upheld despite the absence of independent advice.[159] On the other hand, such advice will not necessarily rebut the presumption. There must be a full appreciation of the facts. In *Tate v Williamson*, for example, the young man, T, was referred to independent solicitors, but such fair dealing in other respects was, said Lord Chelmsford, 'of no consequence, when once it is established that there was a concealment of a material fact, which the defendant was bound to disclose'.[160]

(d) RESCISSION

The right to rescind contracts and to revoke gifts made under undue influence is similar to the right to rescind contracts induced by misrepresentation. The conditions for and bars to rescission considered in Chapter 9 above in principle apply here.[161]

(i) The need for restitution

If the transaction is to be set aside, the parties must be restored to their original positions.[162] Each must give back what has been received, although here too the flexibility of equity means that the impossibility of restoring the parties precisely to their original position will not bar the remedy.[163] The Court will grant relief whenever, by directing accounts and making allowances, it can do what is practically just. Moreover, since it is restitution that has to be made, not damages paid,[164] when reversing a transaction under which both parties had made a financial contribution to the acquisition of an asset from

[157] [1900] 1 Ch 243.

[158] *Inche Noriah v Shaik Allie Bin Omar* [1929] AC 127, 135.

[159] *Re Brocklehurst* [1978] Ch 14; *A-G v R* [2003] UKPC 22; *Nature Resorts Ltd v First Citizens Bank Ltd* [2022] UKPC 10 at [23].

[160] (1866) LR 2 Ch App 55, 65; see above, p 396.

[161] There is, however, no statutory discretion to refuse rescission for undue influence and award damages in lieu; cf Misrepresentation Act 1967, s 2(2), above, p 342.

[162] *Dunbar Bank plc v Nadeem* [1998] 3 All ER 876 (party setting aside transaction required to restore beneficial interest in lease).

[163] *Cheese v Thomas* [1994] 1 WLR 129. See above, pp 341–2.

[164] *Ibid*, 135 (Nicholls V-C).

which they were both to benefit but the value of which has fallen, if the conduct of the party presumed to have exercised influence was not morally reprehensible, the Court may order the loss in the value of the asset to be borne by the parties in proportion to their contributions to the purchase price.[165] However, the rescission of a property transaction entered into between cohabiting parties in the course of their relationship requires a focus on that transaction, and that the transaction be reversed, in effect and in substance, not that the parties be put back into the position as if they had never had a relationship, nor that all the parties' financial contributions during the course of their relationship be taken into account.[166]

Another example of equity's flexibility where complete restitution is impossible is provided by *O'Sullivan v Management Agency and Music Ltd*.[167] In that case a management agreement between an inexperienced pop musician and an internationally known firm of managers, presumed to have been entered as a result of undue influence, was set aside although the parties could not be restored to their original position, inter alia, because the musician had since achieved considerable fame. The managers were ordered to account for the profit they had made from the agreement, but were also entitled to reasonable remuneration for their skill and work in promoting the musician and making a significant contribution to his success. Where taking an account of profits will not do justice, the defendant may be ordered to pay equitable compensation to the claimant.[168]

(ii) Severance

A finding of undue influence normally vitiates effective consent, so that it will rarely be possible to sever the objectionable parts of the transaction leaving the parts uncontaminated by undue influence enforceable. But, where a person's consent can be regarded as having been freely given in relation to part of the transaction and it is possible to sever that part without rewriting the contract, this will be possible.[169]

(iii) Affirmation of transaction

The right to rescind may be lost by affirmation, and so as soon as the undue influence is withdrawn, the action or inaction of the party influenced may constitute evidence that he or she intended to affirm the transaction. Thus in *Mitchell v Homfray*[170] a jury found as a fact that a patient who had made a gift to her physician determined to abide by her gift after the confidential relationship of physician and patient ceased, and the Court of Appeal held that the gift could not be impeached. Also in *Allcard v Skinner*:[171]

A was introduced by her spiritual adviser and confessor to S who was the lady superior of a Protestant community called 'The Sisters of the Poor'. A subsequently became a professed

165 *Ibid*. See Chen-Wishart (1994) 110 LQR 173.

166 *Smith v Cooper* [2010] EWCA Civ 722 at [101], [110].

167 [1985] QB 428.

168 *Mahoney v Purnell* [1996] 3 All ER 61. See Heydon (1997) 113 LQR 8.

169 *Barclays Bank plc v Caplan* [1998] 1 FLR 532. Cf *Allied Irish Bank plc v Byrne* [1995] 2 FLR 325 and the position concerning rescission for misrepresentation, above, p 336.

170 (1881) 8 QBD 587.

171 (1887) 36 Ch D 145.

member of the community and bound herself to observe rules of poverty, chastity, and obedience. The rule of poverty bound her to relinquish all earthly possessions, and the rule of obedience not to seek the advice of anyone outside the community without permission. In 1872 she came into possession of certain stocks, which she transferred to S as superior of the community; she also made a will in S's favour. In 1879, she left the sisterhood. She immediately revoked the will, but took no steps to retrieve the property which she had conveyed to S until some 6 years had elapsed.

It was held that, by her inactivity after she had been freed from the spiritual influence of S, she had acquiesced in the gift, and her claim was barred by this acquiescence.[172]

Affirmation will not bar the right to rescind unless there is an entire cessation of the undue influence which had brought about the contract or gift. James LJ stated in *Moxon v Payne*:[173]

Frauds or impositions of the kind practised in this case cannot be condoned; the right to property acquired by such means cannot be confirmed in this Court unless there be full knowledge of all the facts, full knowledge of the equitable rights arising out of those facts, and an absolute release from the undue influence by means of which the frauds were practised.

The same principle is applied where someone parts with a valuable interest under pressure of poverty and without proper advice: an 'unconscionable bargain'.[174]

(iv) Delay

Delay ('lapse of time') in seeking rescission may be evidence of affirmation or acquiescence, although acquiescence is not presumed from delay alone; on the contrary, 'it has always been presumed, that the same distress, which pressed him to enter into the contract, prevented him from coming to set it aside'.[175] However, once the complainant is no longer under the defendant's influence, the failure to bring a claim to set aside the transaction within a reasonable time may give rise to the equitable defence of laches.[176]

(v) Rights of third parties

As transactions affected by undue influence are voidable, not void, third parties who acquire some interest in the subject-matter of the contract in good faith without notice and for value cannot be displaced by the person seeking rescission.[177] 'Notice' in this context includes imputed and constructive notice.[178] A transaction into which a person has been induced to enter by the exercise of undue influence may therefore be set

[172] See also *Nicholl v Ryder* [2000] EMLR 632 (acquiescence based on solicitor's knowledge which was imputed to defendant).

[173] (1873) LR 8 Ch App 881, 885. See also *Re Pauling's Settlement Trusts* [1964] Ch 303; *Goldsworthy v Brickell* [1987] 1 Ch 378, 410 (uncertainty whether knowledge of the right to rescind is needed; cf above, p 339 (affirmation as bar to rescission for misrepresentation); below, p 518 (affirmation as bar to termination for breach)).

[174] Below, p 406.

[175] *Fry v Lane* (1888) 40 Ch D 312, 324 (Kay J).

[176] *Humphreys v Humphreys* [2004] EWHC 2201 (Ch), [2005] 1 FCR 712 at [99]; *Evans v Lloyd* [2013] EWHC 1725 (Ch) at [79].

[177] *Bainbrigge v Browne* (1881) 18 Ch D 188.

[178] *Ibid*, 197 (Fry J: 'notice of the circumstances from which the Court infers the equity [ie the right to rescind for undue influence]').

aside, not only as against the person exercising the influence, but also as against a third party having notice of the fact that the compulsion or influence was used. Money or property transferred can be recovered from such a person, and from a person who, even though ignorant of the undue influence, has furnished no consideration: 'Let the hand receiving it be ever so chaste, yet, if it comes through a polluted channel, the obligation of restitution will follow it.'[179]

(e) UNDUE INFLUENCE BY A THIRD PARTY TO THE CONTRACT

The principles discussed so far in this chapter cover the situation where undue influence is exercised over the claimant by the other contracting party. In such cases it is clearly right that the influenced party should have the right to rescind the contract against the party who was responsible for the influence. If, however, it was a third party, rather than the other contracting party, who exercised the influence it is less clear that the contracting party should have a right to rescind. The interference with the freedom to decide, free of undue pressure or influence, whether to enter into the contract, is identical in both situations. However, where the source of the influence is a third party, the other contracting party does not deserve to have its security of contract undermined, unless it is in some way affected by the third party's misconduct. Yet without the right to rescind the contract, the only remedy of the party who has been unduly influenced by a third party will be against the third party personally, such as if the third party's conduct constitutes a tort.

If the third party is acting as the other contracting party's agent, no question arises: the influence of the agent is attributed to the principal.[180] In other circumstances in which a third party might exercise undue influence, the third party will generally have something to gain from the contract being concluded. In recent years, largely as a result of the change in the nature of ownership of the family home,[181] many such cases have involved one co-owner of the property (typically, the husband) putting pressure on the other (typically, the wife) to enter into a contract of guarantee, or a mortgage of the property, in favour of a bank to guarantee a business loan. Such cases are not limited to married couples,[182] nor, within couples, to cases where the woman is the victim,[183] and are not simply a recent phenomenon.[184] But there has been a very significant rise in cases involving guarantees and mortgages relating to the family home where there

[179] *Bridgeman v Green* (1757) Wilmot 58, 65 (Wilmot J).

[180] *Barclays Bank Plc v O'Brien* [1994] 1 AC 180, 191.

[181] *Royal Bank of Scotland plc v Etridge (No 2)* [2001] UKHL 44 at [34].

[182] Guarantors in other relationships include employees (*Credit Lyonnais Bank Nederland NV v Burch* [1997] 1 All ER 144) and friends (*Banco Exterior Internacional SA v Thomas* [1997] 1 WLR 221).

[183] *One Savings Bank plc v Waller-Edwards* [2025] UKSC 22 at [6].

[184] See, eg, *Lancashire Loans Ltd v Black* [1934] 1 KB 380 (mother influencing daughter to sign promissory note and execute charge over property in favour of moneylender).

were claims that one partner had unduly influenced the other to give the guarantee or mortgage,[185] and we have already seen that the law takes notice of the need to protect the weaker party within married or other emotional relationships.[186]

(i) Actual knowledge and constructive notice

In *Royal Bank of Scotland plc v Etridge (No 2)* the House of Lords gave guidance on how to deal with cases involving third parties. Lord Nicholls[187] drew a distinction between the 'traditional view of equity', under which a party who is subjected to undue influence or other misconduct by a third party will be relieved of the bargain only if the other party *knew* of the third party's conduct; and the new principle, introduced by the House of Lords in *Barclays Bank plc v O'Brien*,[188] under which, in certain circumstances, a party to a contract may lose the benefit of it if he *ought to have known* that the other's concurrence had been procured by the misconduct of a third party. That is, in an '*O'Brien* case'—a bank guarantee where the relationship between the surety (guarantor) and the debtor (a third party to the guarantee between the bank and the surety) is non-commercial[189]—constructive notice of the third party's influence is sufficient; in other cases, actual notice is required. This distinction does not however appear to be sound, because although there are cases, some of which were referred to by Lord Nicholls, where the Courts appear to have required 'knowledge' of a third party's wrong,[190] it is not clear that the Courts in using such language had intended to limit such 'knowledge' to actual knowledge of the third party's conduct.[191] It is submitted that the better view is that in any case—not only a non-commercial surety contract—a party to a contract (A) can avoid a contract for undue influence exercised by a third party if the other contracting party (B) knew or ought to have known that A was entering into the contract under that influence.

[185] See, eg, *Barclays Bank plc v O'Brien* [1994] 1 AC 180, 185–6 (Lord Browne-Wilkinson: there had been 11 reported cases in CA in the last eight years); *Royal Bank of Scotland plc v Etridge (No 2)* [2001] UKHL 44 (HL heard appeals in eight separate cases). There have been many further similar cases since *Etridge*'s case. Where the guarantee is voidable, a replacement guarantee will also be voidable, at least if it is taken out as a condition of discharging the earlier guarantee: *Yorkshire Bank plc v Tinsley* [2004] EWCA Civ 816, [2004] 1 WLR 2380 at [19]. Where a joint guarantee or mortgage is voidable by one joint debtor (eg the wife) by reason of undue influence by the other debtor (eg the husband) of which the creditor had notice, the other joint debtor remains liable to the creditor: *Syndicate Bank v Dansingani* [2019] EWHC 3439 (Ch).

[186] Above, p 395. For a sociological analysis of the law and practice relating to surety wives and partners, see Fehlberg, *Sexually Transmitted Debt* (1997). See also *One Savings Bank plc v Waller-Edwards* [2025] UKSC 22 at [38] (Lady Simler, noting that the prevalence of economic abuse between women and their spouses or intimate partners has not reduced in spite of the increased participation of women in the labour market over the decades since *O'Brien* and an increase in their levels of financial and other independence).

[187] [2001] UKHL 44 at [40]–[41].

[188] [1994] 1 AC 180.

[189] *Royal Bank of Scotland plc v Etridge (No 2)* [2001] UKHL 44 at [87].

[190] *Cobbett v Brock* (1855) 20 Beav 524, 528 (fraud and undue influence); *Kempson v Ashbee* (1874) LR 10 Ch App 15, 21. See also *Talbot v Von Boris* [1911] 1 KB 854, 863 (duress); *Lynde v Anglo-Italian Hemp Spinning Co* [1896] 1 Ch 178, 183 (misrepresentation).

[191] Cf *Bainbrigge v Browne* (1881) 18 Ch D 188, 197 (also cited by Lord Nicholls in *Etridge*). See also *Lancashire Loans Ltd v Black* [1934] 1 KB 380, 416–17 (which is, however, in substance an '*O'Brien* case', although it predates *O'Brien* by 60 years).

(ii) Surety cases: putting the lender 'on inquiry'

The Supreme Court in *One Savings Bank plc v Waller-Edwards*[192] has recently made it clear, however, that the non-commercial surety contract is different. The test formulated by the House of Lords in *Barclays Bank plc v O'Brien*[193] and *Royal Bank of Scotland plc v Etridge (No 2)*[194] for such situations was new, and was not a traditional application of the principle of constructive notice: it moved away from a test of actual or constructive notice in fixing the lender with knowledge, and introduced a low threshold for putting the lender on inquiry[195] of the risk of undue influence or similar impropriety by a third party on the surety unless further steps were taken to bring home to the surety the implications of the proposed transaction. *O'Brien* and *Etridge* defined both the circumstances in which a lender, taking a guarantee, is put on inquiry of the risk that the surety is acting under undue influence from the debtor, and the steps that the lender should take in order to avoid being affected by the rights of the surety whose consent may have been procured by the debtor's wrongdoing.

The lender will be put on inquiry whenever, on the face of a three-way transaction,[196] the wife (or other vulnerable partner in the relationship) is offering to stand surety for her husband's debts (or vice versa).[197] Where, however, on the face of the transaction the lending is advanced to husband and wife jointly, the lender is not put on inquiry unless it is aware that the loan is being made for the husband's purposes as distinct from their joint purposes.[198] There can be 'hybrid' transactions, involving non-commercial loans sought by a husband and wife that are, on the face of it, partly for their joint benefit and partly for either the husband or the wife's sole benefit. *One Savings Bank plc v Waller-Edwards* was such a hybrid transaction:[199]

W-E owned a residential property jointly with B, a property developer who had built the property, and with whom she was in a relationship. B exerted undue influence to persuade W-E to apply all her savings to the purchase of the property in 2012, and to enter into a mortgage of the property to OSB (the Bank) in 2013 as security for a loan of £384,000. The Bank knew that the relationship between W-E and B was non-commercial, and that £39,500 of the loan would be used to pay off B's personal debts. It believed that the balance would be

[192] [2025] UKSC 22, [2026] AC 182 at [32], [40].

[193] [1994] 1 AC 180.

[194] [2001] UKHL 44.

[195] Strictly this is a misnomer: the bank is not required to make inquiries, but the terminology has become accepted in this context: *Royal Bank of Scotland plc v Etridge (No 2)* [2001] UKHL 44 at [44].

[196] The burden of proof lies on the party claiming to have been subjected to undue influence by the third party: *Barclays Bank plc v Boulter* [1999] 1 WLR 1919, 1925, but it is the bank's perception of the nature of the transaction that is critical: *One Savings Bank plc v Waller-Edwards* [2025] UKSC 22 at [39].

[197] *One Savings Bank plc v Waller-Edwards* [2025] UKSC 22 at [2]; *Royal Bank of Scotland plc v Etridge (No 2)* [2001] UKHL 44 at [44], [46], [109]–[113], [163]–[165].

[198] *One Savings Bank plc v Waller-Edwards* [2025] UKSC 22 at [2]; *CIBC Mortgages plc v Pitt* [1994] 1 AC 200, 211 (advance to enable parties to purchase shares); *Chater v Mortgage Agency Services Number Two Ltd* [2003] EWCA Civ 490, [2004] 1 P & CR 4 (application for loan by mother and son living in same house, to be secured on house owned by the mother, appeared 'perfectly ordinary', and bank did not know that the money was for son's business).

[199] [2025] UKSC 22.

used for their joint purposes, but it was in fact used by B for his own purposes. After their relationship ended and B moved out of the property, W-E was unable to meet the mortgage payments and the Bank sought possession; W-E argued that the Bank had been put on inquiry of the risk of B's undue influence.

The Supreme Court held in favour of W-E. They emphasized the importance of a 'bright line' test which can be applied easily by banks and other lenders, and rejected the argument that there is a separate, third test for such hybrid cases. A lender is put on inquiry in any non-commercial hybrid transaction where, on the face of the transaction, there is a more than a *de minimis* element of borrowing which serves to discharge the debts of one of the borrowers and so might not be to the financial advantage of the other; such a transaction is regarded as a 'surety' transaction rather than a joint loan. In this case, the surety component of the loan which the bank knew was to be applied for B's sole purposes (£39,500) was not *de minimis* or trivial and therefore the principle set out in *O'Brien* and *Etridge* was engaged.[200]

(iii) Surety cases: steps the lender should take

If the guarantor (in our scenario the wife) shows that the lender was put on inquiry of the risk of undue influence, the burden is then upon the lender to show that it took the steps set out by Lord Nicholls in *Etridge*,[201] which were summarized by the Supreme Court in *One Savings Bank plc v Waller-Edwards*:[202]

> (a) The bank must communicate directly with the wife, informing her that for her own protection it will require written confirmation from a solicitor, acting for her, to the effect that the solicitor has fully explained to her the nature of the transaction and its practical implications for her; and that the purpose of this requirement is that she will not be able to dispute that she is legally bound by the transaction once the surety documents are signed.
> (b) The bank must ask the wife to nominate a solicitor she is willing to instruct to advise her, separately from her husband, and act for her in giving the necessary confirmation to the bank; that solicitor may be the same solicitor who is acting for the husband but if a solicitor is already acting, she should be asked whether she would prefer a different solicitor.
>
> Lord Nicholls made clear that the bank should not proceed with the transaction until it has received an appropriate response directly from the wife. The bank should provide information to the wife about the husband's financial affairs, either directly or through solicitors, and if consent from the husband to do so is not forthcoming, the transaction cannot proceed. In an exceptional case where the bank suspects the wife has been misled (or is not acting of her own free will), the bank must inform the wife's solicitor of the facts giving rise to the suspicion. The bank should obtain written confirmation from the wife's solicitor that the information and necessary advice have been given.

[200] *Ibid* at [55]–[57], [60].

[201] *Royal Bank of Scotland plc v Etridge (No 2)* [2001] UKHL 44 at [79], superseding earlier guidance given in *Barclays Bank plc v O'Brien* [1994] 1 AC 180, 196: see *Etridge* at [51]–[55].

[202] [2025] UKSC 22 at [33]–[34] (the '*Etridge* protocol').

These steps do not eliminate the risk that the wife's consent has been procured by undue influence, but their purpose is rather to reduce the risk to a level which makes it appropriate for the lender to proceed, and to provide certainty in the lending market. The modest requirements placed on lenders are the *quid pro quo* for the low threshold for imposing on them the requirement to take such steps.[203]

(iv) Application of the *O'Brien* and *Etridge* principles to other vitiating factors

The principles discussed in *Barclays Bank plc v O'Brien*, *Royal Bank of Scotland plc v Etridge (No 2)*, and *One Savings Bank plc v Waller-Edwards* in relation to third-party wrongdoing are not limited to claims of undue influence, but also apply to other forms of conduct which render a contract voidable. Many of the cases involving undue influence, including *O'Brien*'s case itself, have also involved misrepresentations, and so it is clear that these decisions of the House of Lords and Supreme Court constitute direct authority for the avoidance of a contract as a result of a third-party misrepresentation of which the other contracting party knows or ought to know, and in a non-commercial surety case, this will extend to the lender being put on inquiry about the risk of misrepresentation.[204] The discussion in *Etridge*'s case is also sufficiently wide to cover duress, and in principle a party to a contract who is subjected to duress by a third party can avoid the contract if, but only if, the other party knows or ought to know of it.[205]

4. UNCONSCIONABLE BARGAINS

There is another class of cases in which equity also throws the burden of justifying the fairness of a bargain on the party who claims the benefit of it. Lord Selborne describes these cases in *Earl of Aylesford v Morris*[206] as cases:

> which, according to the language of Lord Hardwicke,[207] raise, 'from the circumstances or conditions of the parties contracting—weakness on one side, usury on the other, or extortion, or advantage taken of that weakness'—a presumption of fraud. Fraud does not here mean deceit or circumvention, it means an unconscientious use of the power arising out of these circumstances and conditions; and when the relative position of the parties is such as *prima*

[203] *Ibid* at [32], [35], [55], [58].

[204] *One Savings Bank plc v Waller-Edwards* [2025] UKSC 22 at [46] ('a bank is put on inquiry as to undue influence or misrepresentation').

[205] eg *Royal Bank of Scotland plc v Etridge (No 2)* [2001] UKHL 44 at [40] ('misconduct of a third party'). See, eg, *Talbot v Von Boris* [1911] 1 KB 854. Cf Digital Markets, Competition and Consumers Act 2024, above, p 358 (misrepresentation), below, p 409 (duress and undue influence), s 232(3)(b) (which will replace Consumer Protection from Unfair Trading Regulations 2008, reg 27A(4)(b), when new replacement Regulations are made under the 2024 Act) (consumer has right to redress not only where trader engages in prohibited practice but also where trader is aware of, or could reasonably be expected to be aware of, prohibited practice by producer of the product).

[206] (1873) LR 8 Ch App 484, 490. See also *Hart v O'Connor* [1985] AC 1000, 1024.

[207] *Earl of Chesterfield v Janssen* (1751) 2 Ves Sen 125, 157.

facie to raise this presumption, the transaction cannot stand unless the person claiming the benefit of it is able to repel the presumption by contrary evidence, proving it to have been in point of fact fair, just, and reasonable.

Thus although equity will not normally intervene to protect a contracting party against the consequences of his or her own folly, some protection is offered to poor and ignorant persons who are overreached in the absence of independent advice. This ground of relief differs from undue influence in that it is concerned with 'the nature and circumstances of the bargain' whereas undue influence is concerned 'with the prior relationship between the parties and with whether that was the motivation or reason for which the bargain was entered into.'[208]

A particular case of the application of this principle was the protection given by equity to 'expectant heirs', that is, to those persons who have expectations (in the popular sense) of succeeding to property on the death of another.[209] But this is just one illustration, and the principle also applies generally to what have been called 'catching bargains', that is to say, whenever the parties 'meet under such circumstances as, in the particular transaction, to give the stronger party dominion over the weaker.'[210]

In ordinary cases each party to a bargain must take care of his own interest, and it will not be presumed that undue advantage or contrivance has been resorted to on either side; but in the case of the 'expectant heir', or of persons under pressure without adequate protection, and in the case of dealings with uneducated ignorant persons, the burden of shewing the fairness of the transaction is thrown on the person who seeks to obtain the benefit of the contract.[211]

Thus in *Fry v Lane*[212] it was held that when a purchase had been made from a poor and ignorant man at a considerable undervalue, the vendor having had no independent advice, equity would set aside the transaction. At common law, the nearest analogue is to be found in the cases on salvage, in which a refusal to rescue a vessel in distress or those on board save on extortionate terms has led to the resulting contract being set aside.[213]

The cases suggest that three elements are necessary if the Court is to intervene.[214] First, one party must be at a serious disadvantage to the other through, for example poverty, ignorance, or lack of advice. Secondly, this weakness must be exploited by the other party in some morally culpable manner; and thirdly, the resulting transaction must be, not merely harsh or improvident, but overreaching and oppressive. The last

208 *Irvani v Irvani* [2000] 1 Lloyd's Rep 412, 424 (Buxton LJ).

209 By the Law of Property Act 1925, s 174, a bargain with an expectant heir, made in good faith, and without unfair dealing, is not to be set aside merely on the ground of undervalue. But the jurisdiction of the Court to set aside or modify unconscionable bargains is not affected.

210 *Earl of Aylesford v Morris* (1873) LR 8 Ch App 484, 491 (Lord Selborne LC).

211 *O'Rorke v Bolingbroke* (1877) 2 App Cas 814, 823 (Lord Hatherley).

212 (1888) 40 Ch D 312. See also *Cresswell v Potter* [1978] 1 WLR 255n; *Boustany v Piggott* (1993) 69 P & CR 298.

213 *The Port Caledonia* [1903] P 184 ('£1,000 or no rope'; the value of the services was £200).

214 *Alec Lobb (Garages) Ltd v Total Oil (Great Britain) Ltd* [1983] 1 WLR 87, 94–5 (Peter Millett QC). This aspect of his judgment was not varied by the Court of Appeal: see [1985] 1 WLR 173, 182–3.

requirement means that, in the case of a sale by the disadvantaged party, the sale must not merely be at an undervalue, but at a *substantial* undervalue which 'shocks the conscience of the court'.[215] And the second requirement means that a gross disparity in the price does not alone suffice, however serious the disadvantage of the weaker party. In *Hart v O'Connor*[216] the Judicial Committee of the Privy Council held that a contract made with a person who, although apparently of full capacity, was mentally disordered, could not be set aside as unconscionable unless the other party was aware of the mental disorder at the time the contract was made.[217] In *Portman Building Society v Dusangh*[218] the Court of Appeal held that a mortgage entered into by the 72-year-old defendant, who had a low income, was illiterate, and whose understanding of spoken English was poor, where the purpose of the mortgage was to raise money to assist the defendant's son in a business, could not be set aside because 'the building society did not act in a morally reprehensible manner. The transaction, although improvident, was not "overreaching and oppressive". In short, the conscience of the court is not shocked.'[219] So, for relief to be granted, both procedural and substantive unconscionability must be shown.

Although there have been expressions of support for a wider role for this doctrine,[220] particularly by giving a broad meaning to its elements,[221] there has been no fundamental change. The fact that procedural unconscionability must be present means that there will often be an overlap with the doctrines of duress and undue influence, and some cases which would perhaps have been best regarded as cases of unconscionability have been treated as cases of duress or undue influence.[222] This is in contrast to the position

[215] *Alec Lobb (Garages) Ltd v Total Oil (Great Britain) Ltd* [1983] 1 WLR 87, 95.

[216] [1985] AC 1000, 1018 (there must be 'unconscionable dealing').

[217] *Fineland Investments Ltd v Pritchard* [2011] EWHC 113 (Ch) at [77] (the law of unconscionable bargain requires the knowing taking advantage by one party of another).

[218] [2000] 2 All ER (Comm) 221.

[219] *Ibid*, 229 (Simon Brown LJ). The son did not exert undue influence over the father, and therefore the principles set out in *Royal Bank of Scotland plc v Etridge (No 2)*, above, p 403, did not apply. See also *Fineland Investments Ltd v Pritchard* [2011] EWHC 113 (Ch) (no unconscionable bargain because no unfair treatment); *Minder Music Ltd v Sharples* [2015] EWHC 1454 (IPEC), [2016] FSR 2 (settlement agreement not imposed in morally reprehensible manner); *Adare Finance DAC v Yellowstone Capital Management SA* [2020] EWHC 2760 (Comm), [2021] 2 BCLC (deed was product of commercial negotiation); *Azam v Molazam* [2023] EWHC 2202 (Ch) at [90] (defendant's knowledge of claimant's vulnerability insufficient without proof of some further fact by reference to the conduct or behaviour of the defendant which the court regards as unconscionable).

[220] See, eg, *A Schroeder Music Publishing Ltd v Macaulay* [1974] 1 WLR 1308, 1315 (Lord Diplock); *Alec Lobb (Garages) Ltd v Total Oil (Great Britain) Ltd* [1985] 1 WLR 173; Waddams (1976) 39 MLR 369; Bamforth [1995] LMCLQ 538; and for criticism, Trebilcock (1976) 26 U of Tor LJ 359; cf Enonchong (2018) 34 JCL 211.

[221] *Cresswell v Potter* [1978] 1 WLR 255n, 257 (Megarry J: 'the euphemisms of the 20th century may require the word "poor" to be replaced by "a member of the lower income group" or the like, and the word "ignorant" by "less highly educated"'); *Backhouse v Backhouse* [1978] 1 WLR 243; *Watkin v Watson-Smith*, The Times, 3 July 1986 (elderly man, incapacitated in judgement and desirous of a quick sale). Cf, however, *Portman Building Society v Dusangh*, above.

[222] *Credit Lyonnais Bank Nederland NV v Burch* [1997] 1 All ER 144 (undue influence, but see Chen-Wishart [1997] CLJ 60); *CTN Cash and Carry Ltd v Gallaher Ltd* [1994] 4 All ER 714, 720 (Sir Donald Nicholls V-C) (and see Carter and Tolhurst [1996] 9 JCL 220).

in other common law jurisdictions, particularly Australia, the USA, and Canada, where a general doctrine of unconscionability has been developed.[223]

An unconscionable bargain is not void but, as in the case of undue influence, voidable by the weaker party for whose protection equity intervenes. The bars to rescission discussed above in relation to undue influence[224] apply equally here.

5. CONSUMERS' RIGHTS OF REDRESS UNDER PART 4 OF THE DIGITAL MARKETS, COMPETITION AND CONSUMERS ACT 2024

We saw in Chapter 9[225] that Part 4 of the Digital Markets, Competition and Consumers Act 2024[226] provides remedies ('rights to redress') for a consumer who enters into a contract with a trader, either for the supply by the trader to the consumer of a 'product' (widely defined and including goods, services, and digital content),[227] or for the supply of a product by the consumer to the trader without the trader supplying a product to the consumer,[228] and the trader engages in a 'prohibited practice' (an unfair[229] commercial practice[230] involving a misleading action or an aggressive practice)[231] in relation to the product,[232] and the prohibited practice is a significant factor in the consumer's decision to enter into the contract.[233] Conduct which constitutes duress or undue influence,

[223] *Commercial Bank of Australia Ltd v Amadio* (1983) 151 CLR 447; *Louth v Diprose* (1992) 175 CLR 621; *Garcia v National Australia Bank Ltd* (1998) 194 CLR 395; Australian Consumer Law, ss 20–22 (Australia); Uniform Commercial Code section 2-302 (USA); *Bhasin v Hrynew* (2014) 379 DLR (4th) 385 at [42], [43]; *Uber Technologies Inc v Heller* [2020] 2 SCR 118 (Canada); Capper (2010) 126 LQR 403; see also the New Zealand Fair Trading Act 1986, ss 7, 8 (added in 2022). For the approach in continental European jurisdictions to avoidance of the contract on the basis of one party's taking advantage of the other's weakness or necessity, see Lando and Beale, *Principles of European Contract Law Parts I and II* (2000) 261–5; and now in France (following reform in 2016), Rowan, *The New French Law of Contract* (2022) 100–02.

[224] Above, pp 400–2.

[225] Above, pp 358–60.

[226] Supplemented by 4A of the Consumer Protection (Amendment) Regulations 2014 (SI 2014 No 870), until new replacement Regulations are made under the 2024 Act: see 2024 Act, s 233.

[227] 2024 Act, ss 248(1), 249; cf 2008 Regulations, reg 2(1). Immoveable property is within the definition of 'product', but for the purposes of the rights to redress under Part 4A of the 2008 Regulations, this includes only certain residential leases: s 27C.

[228] 2024 Act, s 232(2). The 2008 Regulations refer to a contract for the 'sale or supply of a product' by the trader to the consumer, and a contract for the 'sale of goods' to the trader by the consumer: reg 27A(2).

[229] A commercial practice is 'unfair' if it is likely to cause the average consumer to take a transactional decision that the consumer would not have taken otherwise as a result of the practice: 2024 Act, s 225(4).

[230] A 'commercial practice' is 'an act or omission by a trader relating to the promotion or supply of (a) the trader's product to a consumer, (b) another trader's product to a consumer, or (c) a consumer's product to the trader or another person': 2024 Act, s 225(3); cf 2008 Regulations, reg 2(1).

[231] 2024 Act, s 232(7); cf 2008 Regulations, reg 27B.

[232] Or, in the case of a contract for goods or digital content, the *producer* engages in such a practice of which the trader is aware or could reasonably be expected to be aware: 2024 Act, s 232(3)(b); 2008 Regulations, reg 27A(4)(b). The 'producer' is the manufacture, the importer into the United Kingdom, or an 'own-brander' of the goods or digital content: 2024 Act, s 232(6); 2008 Regulations, reg 27A(5).

[233] 2024 Act, s 232(4); 2008 Regulations, reg 27A(6).

or which gives rise to an application of the equitable rules governing unconscionable bargains, may constitute an 'aggressive practice', defined as a commercial practice which uses harassment, coercion, or undue influence. 'Coercion' includes the use or threat of physical force, and 'undue influence' is defined as exploiting a position of power in relation to the consumer so as to apply pressure in a way which significantly limits the consumer's ability to make an informed decision.[234] In determining whether a commercial practice uses harassment, coercion, or undue influence, account is to be taken of such things as the use of threatening or abusive language or behaviour, any threat to take any action which cannot legally be taken, and the exploitation by the trader of any vulnerability of the consumer.[235]

The consumer's rights of redress are the right to unwind in respect of the contract or, in certain circumstances, the right to a discount or the right to damages.[236] These have been explained above.[237] They constitute additional remedies for consumers who have choice between claims under the 2024 Act and under the general law in respect of conduct constituting duress, undue influence or under the equitable rules governing an unconscionable bargain, including concurrent claims as long as the consumer does not obtain double compensation.[238]

6. INEQUALITY OF BARGAINING POWER?

The intervention of common law and equity in all these cases of coercion, undue influence, and unconscionable bargains, and also in certain other cases such as unfair salvage agreements,[239] was stated by Lord Denning MR in *Lloyds Bank Ltd v Bundy*[240] to be grounded upon the same general principle: 'inequality of bargaining power'. In that case:

B, an elderly farmer, and his only son, had been customers of the bank for many years. The son founded a company which banked at the same bank. In 1966, B guaranteed the company's overdraft for £1,500 and charged his farm to the bank to secure that sum. Subsequently the overdraft was increased and the bank sought further security. In May 1969, B, having taken legal advice, signed a further guarantee in favour of the bank for £5,000 and a further charge for £6,000. In December 1969, the bank manager visited B and indicated to him that continuance of the company's overdraft facility was dependent upon B executing in favour of the bank a further guarantee for £11,000 and a further charge for £3,500. The bank manager

[234] 2024 Act, s 228 (1), (3); cf 2008 Regulations, reg 7(1), (3)(a), (b).

[235] 2024 Act, s 228(2)(c), (d), (e); cf 2008 Regulations, reg 7(2)(b), (c), (e).

[236] 2024 Act, s 232; 2008 Regulations, reg 27A.

[237] Above, pp 358–60.

[238] 2008 Regulations, reg 27L. Cf above, p 360 (claim under Misrepresentation Act 1967, s 2 for damages for *misrepresentation* disapplied where the consumer has a right to redress; in the case of duress, undue influence, and unconscionable bargains, there is a free choice between the remedies under the general common law and under the Regulations).

[239] Above, p 407.

[240] [1975] QB 326, 339.

did not advise B to seek independent advice, and B signed the required guarantee and charge without such advice.

The Court of Appeal held that this last guarantee and charge should be set aside for undue influence, since a special relationship of confidence existed between B and the bank in the particular circumstances of the case. But Lord Denning MR also considered that the guarantee and charge were voidable on the larger ground of inequality of bargaining power:[241]

> There are cases in our books in which the courts will set aside a contract, or a transfer of property, where the parties have not met on equal terms—when the one is so strong in bargaining power and the other so weak—that, as a matter of common fairness, it is not right that the strong should be allowed to push the weak to the wall.

His Lordship nevertheless pointed out that no bargain should be upset which was the result of the ordinary interplay of economic forces, but only 'where there has been inequality of bargaining power, such as to merit the intervention of the court'. He went on to state his principle in the following terms:[242]

> English law gives relief to one who, without independent advice, enters into a contract upon terms which are very unfair or transfers property for a consideration which is grossly inadequate, when his bargaining power is grievously impaired by reason of his own needs or desires, or by his own ignorance or infirmity, coupled with undue influences or pressures brought to bear on him by or for the benefit of the other.

When stated in these terms as a detailed test, however, such a general principle goes too far.[243] It appears to require both substantive unfairness ('terms which are very unfair') and procedural unfairness ('undue influences or pressures'), whereas we have seen that duress and actual undue influence require only procedural impropriety;[244] and the role of substantive unfairness in 'presumed' undue influence is to throw onto the stronger party an evidential burden of justifying the contract, precisely where there is no actual evidence of undue influence or pressure.[245]

Moreover, Lord Denning's principle has not been accepted by the English Courts, which have generally regarded it as involving undue uncertainty. On two occasions Lord Scarman spoke emphatically against it. In *National Westminster Bank plc v Morgan*,[246] he questioned the need for such a general principle on the basis, first, that the doctrine of undue influence was adequate to deal with cases in which remedies are required and, secondly, that the task of restricting freedom of contract was essentially a legislative

[241] *Ibid*, 336–7. See also *Clifford Davis Management Ltd v WEA Records Ltd* [1975] 1 WLR 61, 64–5; *Arrale v Costain Civil Engineering Ltd* [1976] 1 Lloyd's Rep 98, 102; *Backhouse v Backhouse* [1978] 1 WLR 243, 252. Cf *Alec Lobb (Garages) Ltd v Total Oil Great Britain Ltd* [1985] 1 WLR 173, 181–3, 188–9.

[242] *Lloyds Bank Ltd v Bundy* [1975] QB 326, 339.

[243] Cartwright, *Unequal Bargaining* (1991) 216–19.

[244] Above, pp 379, 392.

[245] Above, p 394.

[246] [1985] AC 686, 708. See also *Horry v Tate & Lyle Refineries Ltd* [1982] 2 Lloyd's Rep 416, 423.

rather than a judicial task, and one that Parliament has undertaken in legislation protecting, for example, consumers, employees, tenants, and investors.[247] And in *Pao On v Lau Yiu Long*,[248] giving the opinion of the Privy Council, Lord Scarman rejected the idea that English law should adopt a general rule of public policy to the effect that contracts entered into following the unfair use of a dominant bargaining position are void, on this occasion emphasizing that the doctrine of duress was adequate to deal with cases which called for remedy,[249] and that such a rule would be uncertain and would undermine contractual negotiations between commercial parties:

[W]here businessmen are negotiating at arm's length it is unnecessary for the achievement of justice, and unhelpful in the development of the law, to invoke such a rule of public policy . . . It is unnecessary because justice requires that men, who have negotiated at arm's length, be held to their bargains unless it can be shown that their consent was vitiated by fraud, mistake or duress . . .

Such a rule of public policy as is now being considered would be unhelpful because it would render the law uncertain. It would become a question of fact and degree to determine in each case whether there had been, short of duress, an unfair use of a strong bargaining position.

The Supreme Court has also recently stated that there is in English common law no doctrine of inequality of bargaining power in contract, although such inequality may be a relevant feature in some cases of undue influence.[250] At present, therefore, a contract can be avoided at common law or in equity only if one of the established categories of vitiation can be shown: duress, undue influence, or the rather limited doctrine of unconscionable bargains. Development of the law in this area has rested on two distinct approaches. Rather than generalize a single common law doctrine of inequality of bargaining, the Courts have preferred to develop each of the separate doctrines, such as the significant development in the law of duress to cover economic duress.[251] In other respects, the development of protection of weaker contracting parties has been left to statutory intervention, particularly in the field of consumer contracts, often

[247] He cited as examples Supply of Goods (Implied Terms) Act 1973, Consumer Credit Act 1974, Consumer Safety Act 1978, Supply of Goods and Services Act 1982, and Insurance Companies Act 1982. See now Consumer Protection Act 1987 (repealing Consumer Safety Act 1978), Financial Services and Markets Act 2000 as amended (repealing Insurance Companies Act 1982), Consumer Credit Act 2006, ss 19–21 (replacing Consumer Credit Act 1974, ss 137–140 with new ss 140A–140C). The most general provisions are contained in the Consumer Rights Act 2015, Part 2, above, p 227; and Part 4 of the Digital Markets, Competition and Consumers Act 2024, above, p 409. See also above, pp 4–6.

[248] [1980] AC 614, 634.

[249] *Pao On* is one of the cases which recognized the recent expansion of the doctrine of duress to cover economic duress: above, p 382.

[250] *Times Travel (UK) Ltd v Pakistan International Airlines Corp* [2021] UKSC 40 at [26].

[251] Above, p 382.

(during the period when the United Kingdom was a Member State of the European Union) in response to European Directives,[252] the most significant of which were the Directives on Unfair Terms in Consumer Contracts,[253] on the Sale of Consumer Goods and Associated Guarantees,[254] on Unfair Commercial Practices,[255] and on Consumer Rights.[256] Parliament has not limited intervention to that required by Directives, but has sometimes gone beyond those requirements,[257] or has set its own rules designed to protect consumers.[258] And since the withdrawal from the EU, Parliament has already started to remove a significant number of legislative provisions which derive from EU law, and replace them with new, domestic provisions, such as the replacement of the rules on unfair commercial practices by Part 4 of the Digital Markets, Competition and Consumers Act 2024.[259]

We have seen that, in the context of duress, undue influence, and unconscionable bargains, the most significant of these legislative interventions is the provision of consumers' rights of redress for unfair commercial practices, which, although not defined by reference to the common law and equitable doctrines, in practice overlap significantly with them by the definition in the Regulations of 'aggressive practices'.[260] Whether the Courts might yet be willing themselves to take the step of unifying the doctrine of duress, undue influence, and unconscionable bargains, as Lord Denning sought to do, remains uncertain. We have noted elsewhere that there are examples of statutory regimes, which express a policy from which a principle can be derived, being used analogically in developing the common law.[261] In 1995 Sir Thomas Bingham MR said, in relation to section 3 of the Unfair Contract Terms Act 1977, that it was arguable

[252] For the influence of EU law, see above, pp 20–1.

[253] Directive 93/13/EEC, now implemented in Part 2 of the Consumer Rights Act 2015, replacing earlier implementations in the Unfair Terms in Consumer Contract Regulations 1994 (SI 1994 No 3159) and 1999 (SI 1999 No 2083): see above, p 226.

[254] Directive 1999/44/EC, now implemented in Part 1 of the Consumer Rights Act 2015, replacing earlier implementation in the Sale and Supply of Goods to Consumers Regulations 2002 (SI 2002 No 3045, amending the Sale of Goods Act 1979, the Supply of Goods and Services Act 1982, and the Supply of Goods (Implied Terms) Act 1973).

[255] Directive 2005/29/EC, implemented in (inter alia) the Consumer Protection from Unfair Trading Regulations 2008 (SI 2008 No 1277); the 2008 Regulations have now been replaced by the Digital Markets, Competition and Consumers Act 2024.

[256] Directive 2011/83/EC, replacing Directive 97/7/EC on the protection of consumers in respect of distance contracts and Directive 85/577/EEC to protect consumers in respect of contracts negotiated away from business premises; implemented in (inter alia) the Consumer Contracts (Information, Cancellation and Additional Charges) Regulations 2013 (SI 2013 No 3134), above, p 373.

[257] eg Consumer Rights Act 2015, which goes beyond the Consumer Sales Directive, eg by providing the right not only to repair or replacement of good but also to repeat performance of services (below, pp 596–7); and Part 4A of the Consumer Protection from Unfair Trading Regulations 2008, which went beyond the Unfair Commercial Practices Directive by providing *private* rights to redress (above, pp 358, 409).

[258] eg Unfair Contract Terms Act 1977 (above, p 212); and the Consumer Credit Act 1974, ss 140A–140C (inserted by Consumer Credit Act 2006, ss 19–21), which protect against the claimant's need for credit by giving the Court a wide range of remedies to undo credit agreements where the relationship between the creditor and the debtor is unfair to the debtor.

[259] Above, p 409.

[260] *Ibid.*

[261] Above, p 376; see Beatson (2001) 117 LQR 247.

that 'the common law could, if the letter of the statute does not apply, treat the clear intention of the legislature expressed in the statute as a platform for invalidating or restricting the operation of an oppressive clause'.[262] This has not, however, occurred in the context of duress, undue influence, and unconscionable bargains.

FURTHER READING

ATIYAH, 'Economic Duress and the Overborne Will' (1982) 98 LQR 197

THAL, 'The Inequality of Bargaining Power Doctrine: the Problem of Defining Contractual Unfairness' (1988) 8 OLJS 17

BEATSON, 'Duress, Restitution, and Contract Renegotiation' in *The Use and Abuse of Unjust Enrichment* (Oxford: Clarendon Press, 1991) 95

BAMFORTH, 'Unconscionability as a Vitiating Factor' [1995] LMCLQ 538

BIRKS and CHIN, 'On the Nature of Undue Influence' in BEATSON and FRIEDMANN (eds), *Good Faith and Fault in Contract Law* (Oxford: Clarendon Press, 1995) 57

BIGWOOD, 'Undue Influence: "Impaired Consent" or "Wicked Exploitation"?' (1996) 16 OJLS 503

SMITH, 'Contracting Under Pressure: A Theory of Duress' [1997] CLJ 343

CAPPER, 'Undue Influence and Unconscionability: A Rationalisation' (1998) 114 LQR 479

CHEN-WISHART, 'Undue Influence: Beyond Impaired Consent and Wrongdoing towards a Relational Analysis' in BURROWS and RODGER (eds), *Mapping the Law: Essays in Memory of Peter Birks* (Oxford: Oxford University Press, 2006) 201

MCKENDRICK, 'The Further Travails of Duress' in BURROWS and RODGER (eds), *Mapping the Law: Essays in Memory of Peter Birks* (Oxford: Oxford University Press, 2006) 181

CAPPER, 'The Unconscionable Bargain in the Common Law World' (2010) 126 LQR 403

LOKE, 'Excusable Consent in Duress' (2017) 37 LS 418

ENONCHONG, 'The Modern English Doctrine of Unconscionability' (2018) 34 JCL 211

262 *Timeload Ltd v British Telecommunications plc* (1995) 3 EMLR 459, 468.

11

ILLEGALITY AND RESTRAINT OF TRADE

1. INTRODUCTION

It is not easy to set out in clear terms what the law is on 'illegality' in relation to contracts.[1] This is not only because the law itself has historically been complex and opaque but also because distinctions have been drawn by judges and commentators alike that have tended to confuse rather than illuminate. As a matter of exposition, a central problem has been a failure to recognize that, while there is an initial question as to what counts as 'illegality' for these purposes (ie what types of conduct are covered by 'illegality'), the vast bulk of the law is concerned with the effect of illegality on a contract (ie its enforceability) and on consequential restitution (ie the recovery of benefits conferred under the contract). Asking whether the conduct in question renders a contract unenforceable for illegality already strays into the question of the effect of illegality on the contract. Similarly, asking whether the conduct in question renders a contract illegal involves having in mind, and therefore straying into the question of, the effect of a contract being classed as illegal. Clear exposition dictates that the two questions—what counts as illegality and the effect of illegality—are kept distinct and that the second requires by far the most detailed consideration. This chapter attempts to do that.

The two questions that will therefore be separately addressed are: (i) what counts as illegality and (ii) what is the effect of illegality on a contract and on consequential restitution? The first can be dealt with fairly quickly. The good news on the second question is that (after a period of confusion caused by conflicting approaches in a trilogy of Supreme Court cases)[2] in 2016 the law on the effect of illegality was transformed for the better, and simplified, by the Supreme Court in *Patel v Mirza*.[3] Various difficult rules that previously applied, including distinctions between illegality in formation and illegality in performance, and, especially importantly, the 'reliance rule' (ie the rule that

[1] See Buckley, *Illegality and Public Policy* (6th edn, 2023). This chapter is concerned with illegality at the time the contract is made and not with supervening illegality which is dealt with in Chapter 14, Discharge by Frustration.

[2] *Hounga v Allen* [2014] UKSC 47, [2014] 1 WLR 2889; *Les Laboratoires Servier v Apotex Inc* [2014] UKSC 55, [2015] AC 430; *Bilta (UK) Ltd v Nazir (No 2)* [2015] UKSC 23, [2016] AC 1. None of these concerned illegality in contract as such.

[3] [2016] UKSC 42, [2017] AC 467.

the effect of illegality turned on whether the claimant was relying on the illegality in framing its cause of action), have been replaced by a policy-based approach. Under the new approach, it is also no longer necessary to apply the Latin maxims, which have unhelpfully been given prominence in the past, *ex turpi causa non oritur actio* ('no action arises from a disgraceful cause') and *in pari delicto potior est conditio defendentis* ('where both parties are equally in the wrong the position of the defendant is the stronger').

Contracts in restraint of trade have tended to be treated separately from the rest of the law on illegality[4] and, for that reason, and because of their great importance in practice, they will be afforded separate treatment at the end of this chapter (albeit that some of the cases considered under severance, including the leading case, are restraint of trade cases).

2. WHAT COUNTS AS ILLEGALITY?

We are here considering what types of conduct, whether relevant to the making or performance or purpose of a contract, are covered by illegality.[5] In order to avoid straying into the second question as to the effect of illegality, it is best to try to avoid referring to an 'illegal contract'. Perhaps the most useful neutral and natural terminology is to speak of illegality that 'taints' a contract. The precise effect of that 'tainting' will depend on the issues looked at under the second question.

Illegality can be, and indeed should be, raised by a Court on its own initiative and does not need to be pleaded.[6] This is because it involves matters going to the public interest and beyond the interests merely of the parties.

(a) CRIMES

The most obvious type of illegality is criminal conduct. Crimes are normally created by statute and in the modern world there are very many regulatory offences. Even crimes originally created at common law may have been modified by, or incorporated in, a statute, although the definitions of some crimes (eg murder, manslaughter, assault, and conspiracy to defraud) remain matters of common law. The range of criminal offences is very wide. Some are of the most serious kind (eg murder or rape) whereas others are relatively trivial (eg driving slightly over the speed limit).

[4] *Harcus Sinclair LLP v Your Lawyers Ltd* [2021] UKSC 32, [2022] AC 1271 at [45].

[5] The illegality is tested at the time when the contract is formed, even if the law is later changed to render future similar contracts lawful: *Westlaw Services Ltd v Boddy* [2010] EWCA Civ 929, [2011] PNLR 4 at [47]; see also *Commercial Plastics Ltd v Vincent* [1965] 1 QB 623, 644 (time for assessment of reasonableness of restrictive covenant, below, p 439, is the time of the making of the contract).

[6] See *Cross v Kirkley* [2000] EWCA Civ 426 at [76]; *Bilta (UK) Ltd v Nazir (No 2)* [2015] UKSC 23 at [100]; *Nature Resorts Ltd v First Citizens Bank Ltd* [2022] UKPC 10, [2022] 1 WLR 2788 at [42] (the Court must be satisfied that it has sufficient legal and factual material to deal with the illegality question).

While commentators and judges are fond of hypothetical examples where the relevant illegal conduct is the common law crime of murder (eg A contracts with B, a hitman, to murder C), most of the cases coming before the Courts on illegality in relation to contract have involved crimes that are statutory offences. Without at this stage looking at the effect on the contract, it will be helpful to refer briefly to a few examples.[7]

The criminal illegality in the following two cases comprised a failure to comply with licencing requirements. In *Re Mahmoud and Ispahani*:[8]

The contract was one for the sale of linseed oil. The defendant purchaser (and probably both parties) committed an offence contrary to a wartime statutory order (the Seeds, Oils and Fats Order 1919) because the purchaser did not have the required licence from the Food Controller (albeit that the claimant seller did) for the purchase of the oil.

In *Archbolds (Freightage) Ltd v Spanglett Ltd*:[9]

The contract was for the carriage of cases of whisky by road. The owner of the van (the defendant) that was used (but not the owner of the whisky) was acting contrary to the Road and Rail Traffic Act 1933 because the defendant did not have the correct licence for the van to carry the goods of others for reward.

The criminal illegality in the next two cases comprised an overloading of goods. In *St John Shipping Corp v Joseph Rank Ltd*:[10]

The contract was for the carriage of grain by sea. The owner of the ship had overloaded it and thereby committed an offence under the Merchant Shipping (Safety and Load Line Conventions) Act 1932.

In *Ashmore, Benson Pease & Co Ltd v AV Dawson Ltd*:[11]

The defendant carrier, in performing a contract for the carriage of the claimant's heavy engineering equipment by road, overloaded a lorry (which toppled over and damaged the load) contrary to the Road Traffic Act 1960.

The modern leading case of *Patel v Mirza*[12] also concerned a statutory offence. This was the offence of insider dealing contrary to section 52 of the Criminal Justice Act 1993. Under the contract between them, the claimant had paid the defendant large sums of money for the defendant to bet on the movement of shares using inside information.

(b) CIVIL WRONGS

There is uncertainty as to the extent to which civil wrongs, such as torts, count as 'illegality' which taints a contract. Although there have been some cases in the past that might be interpreted as supporting an approach that civil wrongs always count,[13] the

[7] See also, eg, *Marles v Philip Trant & Sons Ltd* [1954] 1 QB 29 where the seller of some seeds committed a summary offence in not providing written particulars of the seeds to the buyer contrary to the Seeds Act 1920.

[8] [1921] 2 KB 716. See below, p 421.

[9] [1961] 1 QB 374.

[10] [1957] 1 QB 267. See below, p 421.

[11] [1973] 1 WLR 828.

[12] [2016] UKSC 42. See below, p 423.

[13] eg *Clay v Yates* (1856) 1 H & N 73 (contract to publish a libel).

view taken by the Supreme Court in the leading case of *Les Laboratoires Servier v Apotex Inc*,[14] was that, unless dishonesty is an essential element, torts and other civil wrongs do not constitute relevant illegal conduct. This may mean that this type of illegal conduct does not extend very far beyond crimes because it would appear that almost all torts that have dishonesty as an essential element also constitute crimes.[15]

In the *Apotex* case:

> The claim by Apotex was for damages under a cross-undertaking in damages given by Servier, which had been granted an injunction against Apotex, to restrain infringement of a patent. It transpired that Servier should not have been granted that injunction because it had no valid patent in this jurisdiction. The question was whether the breach by Apotex of Servier's valid Canadian patent constituted 'illegality' so as to give Servier a defence to Apotex's claim for damages under the cross-undertaking.

The Supreme Court held that Servier had no defence of illegality because infringement of a patent is only a civil wrong which does not engage the public interest, and does not count as illegality for these purposes.[16] Although not a contract case as such, a cross-undertaking in damages is analogous to a contract to pay damages. The leading judgment was given by Lord Sumption. In his Lordship's terminology, the question that was here at issue was what conduct counts as 'turpitude' for the purposes of the illegality defence. Lord Sumption said:[17]

> [T]he researches of counsel have uncovered no cases in the long and much-litigated history of the illegality defence, in which it has been applied to acts which are neither criminal nor quasi-criminal but merely tortious or in breach of contract. In my opinion the question what constitutes 'turpitude' for the purpose of the defence depends on the legal character of the acts relied on. It means criminal acts, and what I have called quasi-criminal acts. This is because only acts in these categories engage the public interest which is the foundation of the illegality defence. Torts (other than those of which dishonesty is an essential element), breaches of contract, statutory and other civil wrongs, offend against interests which are essentially private, not public.

(c) CONDUCT THAT IS CONTRARY TO PUBLIC POLICY

Even though no legal wrong (criminal or civil) is involved, the Courts have recognized that some other types of conduct should count as 'illegality' that taints a contract. So, for example, sexual immorality,[18] interference with the administration of justice,[19] the committing in a friendly foreign country of what is there (but not here) a criminal act,[20]

[14] [2014] UKSC 55.

[15] But there are exceptions to this: eg the tort of malicious falsehood normally has no criminal counterpart.

[16] [2014] UKSC 55 at [30].

[17] *Ibid* at [28].

[18] eg *Pearce v Brooks* (1866) LR 1 Exch 213 (hire of an ornamental carriage to be used by the lessee for prostitution).

[19] eg *Kearley v Thomson* (1890) 24 QBD 742 (contract not to oppose the discharge of a bankrupt); *Farrar v Miller* [2021] EWHC 1950 (Ch) (champerty).

[20] eg *Foster v Driscoll* [1929] 1 KB 470 (contract to smuggle whisky into the US during prohibition). See also *Magdeev v Tsvetkov* [2020] EWHC 887 (Comm) at [332]; Teo [2021] CLJ 32.

the unacceptable ousting of the jurisdiction of the Courts,[21] the exclusion of liability for a person's own fraudulent misrepresentation,[22] and, most importantly in practice, an unreasonable restraint of trade[23] are all treated as being relevantly contrary to public policy.

Without using the language of the conduct being 'contrary to public policy', Lord Sumption in the *Apotex* case expressed much the same idea when he said that there was:

> a limited category of acts which, while not necessarily criminal, can conveniently be described as 'quasi-criminal' because they engage the public interest in the same way.[24]

He gave as examples (non-criminal) cases of dishonesty, corruption, prostitution, and infringements of competition law triggering penal sanctions.

Three points on this category of conduct that is contrary to public policy should be made. First, the Courts recognize that public policy may change over time[25] so that contracts that in the past were regarded as tainted by conduct that was contrary to public policy may no longer be problematic. A good example is a contract involving cohabitation between unmarried partners including same-sex partners.

Secondly, the notion of conduct that is contrary to public policy is wide and open-ended. But it is clear that it is not intended to cover other established reasons, often concerned with ensuring that the parties have truly consented or that the contract is procedurally or substantively fair, that explain the law's intervention rendering a contract void, voidable, or unenforceable. These include formal requirements (such as writing and signature) for certain types of contract,[26] the striking down of unfair terms under, for example, the Unfair Contract Terms Act 1977 and the Consumer Rights Act 2015,[27] the law on incapacity,[28] the law on misrepresentation, undue influence, and duress,[29] and the law on penalties.[30]

Thirdly, as has already been indicated, the law on restraint of trade is best dealt with separately and is therefore considered at the end of this chapter.

3. THE EFFECT OF ILLEGALITY

(a) INTRODUCTION

Once it has been decided that the type of conduct in question comprises illegality, whether because it is a crime, a civil wrong (where dishonesty is an essential element), or is contrary to public policy, the critical question is then the effect of that illegality

[21] eg *Hyman v Hyman* [1929] AC 601 (wife contracting not to apply to the Courts for maintenance). But note that arbitration and foreign exclusive jurisdiction clauses are not contrary to public policy.

[22] *HIH Casualty Insurance Ltd v Chase Manhattan Bank* [2003] UKHL 6, [2003] 2 Lloyd's Rep 61 at [16], [24], [76], [121]–[122]. See above, p 200.

[23] See below, pp 434–43.

[24] [2014] UKSC 55 at [25].

[25] *Evanturel v Evanturel* (1874) LR 6 PC 1, 29; *Bowman v Secular Society Ltd* [1917] AC 406; cf *Coral Leisure Group Ltd v Barnett* [1981] ICR 503, 507.

[26] See above, Chapter 3.

[27] See above, Chapter 6.

[28] See above, Chapter 7.

[29] See above, Chapters 9 and 10.

[30] See below, Chapter 17.

on the contract and on consequential restitution. When looking at the effect of the illegality 'on the contract', consideration is being given to whether the contract is rendered unenforceable by one or both parties (or is void, which in this context is virtually synonymous with saying that the contract is unenforceable by both parties).[31] In other words, consideration is being given to whether illegality is a defence to what would otherwise be a valid claim for breach of contract (eg for damages for breach or for the payment of the agreed sum). When looking at the effect of the illegality on consequential restitution, the essential issue[32] is whether illegality is a defence to what would otherwise be a valid claim for restitution of an unjust enrichment in relation to benefits conferred under the contract.

This book is about the law of contract but it also covers some aspects of the law of unjust enrichment which deal with the restitution of benefits conferred under contracts that have been terminated or are defective. Our primary focus is therefore on the effect of illegality on the enforceability of a contract, although we also touch on the effect of illegality on consequent restitution. Indeed, while it is important to bear in mind that distinction, the leading case of *Patel v Mirza*[33] has applied the same approach to the effect of illegality at common law both on the enforceability of a contract and on consequent restitution. Moreover, the direct issue in the case concerned restitution of money paid, not contract enforceability.

A further distinction is between the effect of illegality by reason of statute and the effect of illegality at common law.[34] We therefore begin by examining the effect of illegality on contract enforceability by reason of statute before going on to examine the effect of illegality on contract enforceability at common law.

(b) THE EFFECT OF ILLEGALITY ON CONTRACT ENFORCEABILITY (AND CONSEQUENT RESTITUTION) BY REASON OF STATUTE

If a legislative provision has dealt with the effect on a contract of illegality—and that is a matter for ordinary statutory interpretation—then the Courts must apply that. So, for example, if a statute has prohibited a contract, it will be unenforceable by either party.

[31] Cf *Hawkins v Abarbanel Ltd* [2025] UKPC 58, [2026] 1 WLR 115 at [38].

[32] It would appear that in some limited situations, as where the law encourages the claimant to abandon an illegal purpose by giving a right to restitution by withdrawal during the *locus poenitentiae* ('opportunity for repentance'), illegality can operate as an 'unjust factor', founding a claim for restitution in unjust enrichment, rather than as a defence: see below, p 426 and see generally, Burrows, *The Law of Restitution* (3rd edn, 2011) Ch 19.

[33] [2016] UKSC 42; see below, p 423.

[34] These can be, and have been, referred to as 'statutory illegality' and 'common law illegality': see, eg, *Okedina v Chikale* [2019] EWCA Civ 1393, [2019] IRLR 905 at [12]; *Henderson v Dorset Healthcare University NHS Foundation Trust* [2020] UKSC 43, [2021] AC 563 at [74]–[75]. But care must be used in relation to those labels because they are referring to the effect of the illegality and not to the source of the illegality (which will usually be statutory).

A good example is *Re Mahmoud and Ispahani*.[35] The delegated legislation in question prohibited the purchase or sale of linseed oil without a licence from the Food Controller. The claimant (who had a licence) contracted to sell linseed oil to the defendant. The defendant did not have a licence, although he told the claimant that he had one. The defendant refused to accept the oil but the claimant's action for damages for non-acceptance failed because the contract was prohibited by the legislation and was therefore unenforceable by either party.

A modern example of a statute prohibiting a contract is section 32 of the Human Tissue Act 2004. This prohibits commercial dealings in human material for transplantation other than by someone who has been authorized by the Human Tissue Authority. It follows that an unauthorized contract for the sale of human material will be unenforceable by either party.

In contrast, in *St John Shipping Corp v Joseph Rank Ltd*,[36] there was a statute that prohibited the overloading of the ship. However, Devlin J decided that the statute did not prohibit contracts of carriage for overloaded cargo so that the contract was not rendered unenforceable by the statute. The owner of the ship was held entitled to the payment of freight under the contract, including for the excess load, despite the illegal overloading.

A statutory illegality defence also failed in *Okedina v Chikale*:[37]

The claimant employee had been employed by the defendant as a live-in domestic worker for over 18 months after her visa ran out. She had been very poorly paid and made to work seven days a week. When she asked for more money, she was summarily dismissed and ejected from the home. She brought actions for unfair and wrongful dismissal including for significant sums owed by reason, for example, of minimum wage regulations.

Her claims succeeded because there was no statutory illegality defence (nor was there a common law illegality defence).[38] As regards a statutory illegality defence, the Court of Appeal decided that, as a matter of statutory interpretation, the relevant legislative provisions on employing an illegal immigrant (sections 15 and 21 of the Immigration, Asylum and Nationality Act 2006)[39] neither expressly nor impliedly rendered the contract of employment unenforceable by the employee albeit that she did not have a

[35] [1921] 2 KB 716; above, p 417. [36] [1957] 1 QB 267; above, p 417. [37] [2019] EWCA Civ 1393.

[38] At common law, applying the new policy-based approach laid down in *Patel v Mirza*—see below, p 423—it was held in *Okedina* that, for very similar reasons to those discussed in respect of the statutory illegality defence, the contract of employment was enforceable by the employee. In the context of employment contracts, the approach in *Patel v Mirza* was thought to be consistent with the approach at common law in *Hall v Woolston Hall Leisure Ltd* [2001] ICR 99.

[39] At the relevant time, it was not an offence as such for a person without the necessary visa to work in the UK. With effect from 12 July 2016, that is now an offence under the Immigration Act 1971, s 24B. Moreover, the Immigration, Asylum and Nationality Act 2006, s 21 has been amended, with effect from 12 July 2016. The overall effect of these statutory changes is that there may now be a stronger argument that statutory illegality would be a defence (ie that the contract of employment was prohibited and unenforceable by either party) on the facts of *Okedina*.

visa and so was being employed contrary to those provisions.[40] It was significant that she had been falsely led to believe by her employer that a new visa was being arranged for her and she left these matters entirely in her employer's hands.

Apart from prohibiting a contract, legislation may lay down that a contract or a contract term is unenforceable by one or either party or is void. For example, section 4(1) of the Marine Insurance Act 1906 lays down that 'every contract of marine insurance by way of gaming or wagering is void'. That provision remains in force despite the Gambling Act 2005 which has reformed the law on gaming and wagering contracts generally. Another example is section 142(1) of the Equality Act 2010 which provides that 'a term of a contract is unenforceable against a person in so far as it constitutes, promotes or provides for treatment of that or another person that is of a description prohibited by this Act'.

Also of great practical importance are sections 26–30 of the Financial Services and Markets Act 2000 which deal with unauthorized investment business, investment business transacted through unauthorized intermediaries, and investment business resulting from unlawful financial promotion. The provisions lay down that the relevant contract is 'unenforceable against [the customer]' but there is a discretion to enforce the contract if a Court is satisfied that it is 'just and equitable in the circumstances of the case'. There are also provisions dealing with the restitutionary consequences and with the award of compensation.

A good example of a statute that deals with the restitutionary consequences is the Rent Act 1977. Section 125 expressly provides that, where under any agreement a premium (in addition to rent) is paid which could not lawfully be required or received (ie it is a criminal offence under the Act to require or receive that premium) the premium is recoverable by the payor.

There have also been several cases granting restitution where a statute imposed a criminal penalty on one party to protect the class to which the other contracting party belonged.[41] Granting restitution to the party in the protected class may be said to be impliedly provided for by the 'class-protecting' statute as a matter of ordinary statutory interpretation.[42]

In the vast majority of cases the effect of illegality on contract enforceability (or the restitution of benefits conferred under the contract) has not been laid down, whether expressly or impliedly, in a statute (even though, as will usually be the case, the relevant

[40] It was carefully explained that *Hounga v Allen* [2014] UKSC 47 was not directly in point because it did not have to deal with the question of whether an illegal immigrant could enforce a contract of employment (and what was said on that issue, in *obiter dicta*, was difficult to interpret).

[41] See, eg, *Lodge v National Union Insurance Co Ltd* [1907] 1 Ch 300; *Kiriri Cotton Co Ltd v Dewani* [1960] AC 192: cf *Green v Portsmouth Stadium Ltd* [1953] 2 QB 190 (the purpose of the statute was not to protect bookmakers). The 'class-protection' rationale was set out in a classic dictum in *Browning v Morris* (1778) 2 Cowp 790, 792 (Lord Mansfield). It may also be of central importance in allowing severance: see below, p 430.

[42] One can alternatively view these cases as falling within the effect of illegality at common law. Indeed they have traditionally been seen as illustrating the traditional exception to 'no restitution' where the party seeking restitution was *non in pari delicto*. After *Patel v Mirza* [2016] UKSC 42, granting restitution at common law to the party belonging to the protected class would tend to follow straightforwardly because the clear policy of the rule in question would favour granting restitution to the party in the protected class.

illegality is a statutory offence). The effect of illegality on contract enforceability (or restitution) will therefore normally be determined by applying the common law to which we now turn.[43]

(c) THE EFFECT OF ILLEGALITY ON CONTRACT ENFORCEABILITY (AND CONSEQUENT RESTITUTION) AT COMMON LAW

(i) The policy-based approach: *Patel v Mirza*

Although the direct issue in the case concerned restitution of money paid under a contract, rather than contract enforceability, the leading case on the effect of illegality on contract enforceability at common law is *Patel v Mirza*.[44] This decision has transformed the law for the better and has rendered it unnecessary to consider what was previously the effect of illegality at common law. That was governed by rules that were widely viewed—and criticized by, for example, the Law Commission[45]—as being complex and uncertain and as sometimes making it difficult for the Courts to reach decisions that, as a matter of policy, were satisfactory. In *Patel v Mirza*:

Mr Patel, the claimant, paid sums totalling £620,000 to Mr Mirza, the defendant, pursuant to an agreement under which the defendant agreed to use the money to bet on the movement of shares using inside information. The use of inside information to deal in shares (as, for example, by betting on their movement) constituted the offence of insider dealing contrary to s 52 of the Criminal Justice Act 1993. This was therefore a contract for the commission of a crime. In the event, the agreement could not be carried out because the expected inside information was not forthcoming. When that became clear, the claimant sought repayment of the £620,000 as restitution of an unjust enrichment.

At first instance,[46] the judge dismissed the claim as being barred by illegality, holding, first, that the claimant had to rely on the illegality to make out the claim; and, second, that what was known as the doctrine of *locus poenitentiae* ('time for repentance') did not apply on these facts because, as the contractual purpose had been thwarted or frustrated, the claimant had not voluntarily withdrawn from the illegal agreement before it had been performed. The Court of Appeal allowed the claimant's appeal on the basis that the *locus poenitentiae* doctrine applied because no part of the illegal purpose had been carried into effect and it was irrelevant to that doctrine that the claimant had not voluntarily withdrawn.[47]

[43] Another way of expressing the point made in this paragraph is that, where there is no statutory illegality defence, the Courts must go on to consider whether there is a common law illegality defence.

[44] [2016] UKSC 42, [2017] AC 467. This subsection draws heavily on Burrows, in Green and Bogg (eds), *Illegality after* Patel v Mirza (2018) Ch 2. See also Burrows, in Peel and Probert (eds) *Shaping the Law of Obligations* (2023) Ch 4.

[45] Consultation Paper No 154, *Illegal Transactions* (1999); Consultation Paper No 189, *The Illegality Defence* (2009); Report Law Com No 320, *The Illegality Defence* (2010).

[46] [2013] EWHC 1892 (Ch), [2013] 2 P & CR DG23.

[47] [2014] EWCA Civ 1047, [2015] Ch 271.

The Supreme Court unanimously upheld the decision, but not the reasoning, of the Court of Appeal that the claimant was entitled to restitution. There was a clear split in approach between a majority of six (led by Lord Toulson)[48] and a minority of three (Lord Sumption, Lord Mance, and Lord Clarke). The claimant was held entitled to restitution of the money paid because, according to the majority, that was the result reached by applying a flexible, structured approach which considered both the policies involved and proportionality.

Lord Toulson's leading judgment rejected a rule-based approach and, in particular, the 'reliance rule'[49] that, since the decision of the House of Lords in *Tinsley v Milligan*,[50] had become dominant in English law. In its place, and reflecting the views of the Law Commission[51] and a number of judicial views favouring a flexible approach,[52] a Court should consider the policies involved and the need for proportionality. While at a high level of generality a Court should seek to avoid inconsistency in the law (including preventing a person profiting by wrongdoing), thereby maintaining the integrity of the legal system as Justice McLachlin had influentially expressed it in the Supreme Court of Canada in *Hall v Hebert*,[53] a trio of considerations was specified as being relevant in achieving that high level goal. These were, first, the purpose of the illegality in question (ie the purpose of the crime or civil wrong or 'public policy'); second, any conflicting relevant policies; and third, the need to avoid a result that was disproportionate. In deciding on whether denying the claim for illegality was proportionate, a number of factors might be relevant including the seriousness of the illegal conduct, its centrality to the claim (eg to the contract in question), whether the conduct was intentional and whether there was a marked disparity in the blameworthiness of the parties' conduct. Lord Toulson said:

> [O]ne cannot judge whether allowing a claim which is in some way tainted by illegality would be contrary to the public interest, because it would be harmful to the integrity of the legal system, without (a) considering the underlying purpose of the prohibition which has been transgressed, (b) considering conversely any other relevant public policies which may be rendered ineffective or less effective by denial of the claim, and (c) keeping in mind the possibility of overkill unless the law is applied with a due sense of proportionality. . . . That trio of necessary considerations can be found in the case law.[54]

[48] His judgment was agreed with by Lady Hale, Lord Kerr, Lord Wilson, and Lord Hodge. Of these, Lord Kerr additionally gave a separate concurring judgment. Lord Neuberger gave a separate judgment which ultimately agreed with Lord Toulson's approach (although the first part is different in favouring a starting rule of restitution).

[49] See above, pp 415–6.

[50] [1994] 1 AC 340. This applied *Bowmakers Ltd v Barnet Instruments Ltd* [1945] KB 65, CA.

[51] See above, n 45.

[52] See, eg, *Hardy v Motor Insurers Bureau* [1964] 2 QB 745, 768; *ParkingEye Ltd v Somerfield Stores Ltd* [2012] EWCA Civ 1338, [2013] QB 840; *Hounga v Allen* [2014] UKSC 47, [2014] 1 WLR 2889.

[53] [1993] 2 SCR 159. This is the same idea as not 'stultifying the law' which was the language used by Lord Radcliffe in *Boissevain v Weil* [1950] AC 327, HL. Non-stultification has also been emphasized by academics, most influentially by Weinrib (1976) 26 UTLJ 28 (favouring a narrow scope for illegality in relation to tort) and Birks (2000) 1 Theo Inq L 155–204; Birks, *Unjust Enrichment* (2nd edn, 2005) 247–53.

[54] [2016] UKSC 42 at [101]. See also his summary at [120].

While that approach was clearly being put forward as applicable across civil law (whether the claim was in contract, tort, unjust enrichment, or in the law of 'property'),[55] Lord Toulson clarified that, in the law of unjust enrichment, the prima facie position is that illegality should not be a defence. Where the claimant, absent the illegality, would have been entitled to restitution for unjust enrichment, it will be rare to deny that claim because of the illegality. This is no doubt because, far from upholding or enforcing illegality, the claimant is seeking to unwind it.[56] While there might be rare exceptions to that (and Lord Toulson mentioned contracts for murder and drug trafficking), the prima facie position is that the normal law on restitution of an unjust enrichment applies. On the facts of *Patel v Mirza*, and applying the 'trio of necessary considerations' in a situation where one was unwinding illegality, there was no reason to depart from the standard law on restitution of an unjust enrichment. Here the claimant, absent the illegality, would have been entitled to restitution of the money paid for a consideration that had totally failed in the sense that no part of the promised performance had been carried out (ie there had been no bets placed). This was not an exceptional case in which the illegality involved overrode that prima facie position.

Two additional points about Lord Toulson's judgment are noteworthy. First, there was no attempt to apply separately the *locus poenitentiae* doctrine. It is tempting to think that that doctrine has been rendered superfluous, as having been swallowed up by the new policy-based approach. That is largely correct. Where illegality is being used as a defence, there is now no need to agonize, as previously, about the requirements of the *locus poenitentiae* doctrine (eg the point of time at which the claimant loses the opportunity to repent; and whether the doctrine applies where the claimant has not genuinely repented but has been forced to do so by the thwarting of the illegal purpose).[57] However, to treat the doctrine as completely redundant after *Patel v Mirza* goes too far. Although a full explanation of this would require a detailed examination of the law of unjust enrichment, which would be inappropriate for a book on the law of contract, the essential point is that there can be situations where the *locus poenitentiae* doctrine has to be invoked in order to establish that there has been an unjust enrichment.[58] Put another way, it may not always be possible to treat illegality as a defence rather than as providing a ground in itself for withdrawal and restitution. But in the usual case where illegality is being used as a defence, it is submitted that the *locus poenitentiae* doctrine has been swallowed up by the policy-based approach laid down in *Patel v Mirza*.

[55] For an example of *Patel v Mirza* being applied to a claim for damages for professional negligence for the tort of negligence and breach of contract, see *Grondona v Stoffel & Co* [2020] UKSC 42, [2021] AC 540; below, p 427.

[56] One can argue that, analogously, the same should apply to compensation claims in tort (eg where, in fleeing from a crime, a person is injured by a co-criminal's negligence).

[57] Leading cases applying the *locus poenitentiae* doctrine include *Taylor v Bowers* (1876) 1 QBD 291; *Kearley v Thomson* (1890) 24 QBD 742; *Bigos v Bousted* [1951] 1 All ER 92; *Tribe v Tribe* [1996] Ch 107. For academic analysis of the limits of the doctrine, see, eg, Grodecki (1955) 71 LQR 254; Beatson (1975) 91 LQR 313; Merkin (1981) 97 LQR 420; Burrows, *The Law of Restitution* (3rd edn, 2011) 495–6.

[58] See above, n 32.

Secondly, Lord Toulson left open whether *Parkinson v College of Ambulance Ltd*[59] remains good law. There, C had entered into an agreement with D for D to secure a knighthood for C in return for payment. It was held that C was not entitled to restitution of the bribe paid to D when the knighthood was not forthcoming. Although there was a total failure of consideration, it was held that illegality was a defence. One might have thought that this was similar to the facts of *Patel v Mirza* and that, applying the reasoning of the majority in *Patel v Mirza*, restitution should have been granted in *Parkinson*. But, while suggesting that that was probably so, the correctness of *Parkinson* was left open. Lord Toulson said:

> Bribes of all kinds are odious and corrupting, but it does not follow that it is in the public interest to prevent their repayment. There are two sides to the equation. If today it transpired that a bribe had been paid to a political party, a charity or a holder of public office, it might be regarded as more repugnant to the public interest that the recipient should keep it than that it should be returned. We are not directly concerned with such a case . . .[60]

In other words, although the force favouring restitution of an unjust enrichment means that it will be rare for illegality to be a defence, insider trading cannot simply be equated with bribery. Nevertheless, the clear steer is that, as it will be rare for illegality to succeed as a defence to an otherwise successful claim for restitution of an unjust enrichment, we should tend towards the view that *Parkinson* was incorrectly decided.

The minority in *Patel v Mirza* came to the same decision as the majority but by a very different route. The leading minority judgment was given by Lord Sumption,[61] who held that the so-called 'reliance rule'[62] remained the correct approach to illegality, although he said that the leading case of *Tinsley v Milligan*[63] had incorrectly applied it.[64] The details of his argument, and the problems to which it would give rise, need not concern us here,[65] given that the decision of the majority in *Patel v Mirza*, which rejected the reliance rule, has now been firmly established as the law.

(ii) Four further observations on *Patel v Mirza*

The first observation is that, although *Patel v Mirza* concerned illegality in respect of restitution for unjust enrichment, it is clear that the majority saw itself as laying down a new approach to illegality across civil law. So the new approach is plainly applicable to the enforcement of a contract (or a tort claim or a claim based on property law).[66] It is an important point to stress that, because the variables involved in respect of a contract claim are so great, the majority's approach is even more obviously to be

[59] [1925] 2 KB 1.
[60] [2016] UKSC 42 at [118].
[61] Lord Clarke agreed with Lord Sumption albeit that he gave a separate judgment. Lord Mance, although he too gave a separate judgment, also essentially agreed with Lord Sumption.
[62] See above, pp 415–6.
[63] [1994] 1 AC 340.
[64] [2016] UKSC 42 at [236].
[65] For a powerful argument that 'Lord Sumption's approach does not stand up to scrutiny. If it were the law, it would produce, on the face of it, results that no legal system would tolerate', see Burrows, in Green and Bogg (eds), *Illegality after* Patel v Mirza (2018) 30–3.
[66] *Henderson v Dorset Healthcare University NHS Foundation Trust* [2020] UKSC 43 at [76].

welcomed in respect of enforcement of a contract than in respect of restitution of an unjust enrichment. The idea that the application of a rigid reliance rule deals properly with the illegality defence in relation to contract claims is fanciful.[67]

Secondly, Lord Toulson's 'trio of considerations' may appear to involve a structured discretion, balancing a range of factors. It is a structured approach, but it does not simply involve the Court engaging with an open and unsettled range of factors.[68] And in *Grondona v Stoffel & Co*[69] Lord Lloyd-Jones, with whom the other members of the Supreme Court agreed, emphasized that Lord Toulson's 'trio of necessary considerations' is directed specifically at determining whether to allow the claim in question would damage the integrity of the law by permitting incoherent contradictions; and that such an evaluation of policy considerations, while necessarily structured, must not be permitted to become a mechanistic process.

Thirdly, one can expect that the evaluation of policy considerations required by *Patel v Mirza* will in time lead to rules, albeit flexible rules, that will guide that process. Indeed, we now know from the case itself that, in general but not always—and it is the exceptions that will emerge over time—illegality is not a defence to restitution of an unjust enrichment.

The fourth observation is that all past cases on illegality must now be viewed through the lens of the approach in *Patel v Mirza*. As a matter of precedent, the Supreme Court did not say that any past case had been wrongly decided in the sense of reaching the wrong result. Indeed, although the reliance rule reasoning in *Tinsley v Milligan* was rejected, Lord Toulson indicated that the same result would be justified applying the new approach.[70] It follows that, while much of the reasoning in past cases on the effect of illegality can no longer stand, Courts should look at the results of past cases and, so far as possible, seek to ensure that the same results would be reached applying the approach laid down in *Patel v Mirza*. As Underhill LJ said in *Okedina v Chikale*:[71]

In his judgment in *Patel v Mirza* Lord Toulson was attempting to identify the broad principles underlying the illegality rule. His judgment does not require a reconsideration of how the rule has been applied in the previous case-law except where such an application is inconsistent with those principles.

(iii) Application of the new approach of *Patel v Mirza*

In *Grondona v Stoffel & Co*[72] Lord Lloyd-Jones explained how Lord Toulson's 'trio of necessary considerations' in *Patel v Mirza* should be applied:

In the application of stages (a) and (b) of this trio a court will be concerned to identify the relevant policy considerations at a relatively high level of generality before considering their

[67] Burrows, *A Restatement of the English Law of Contract* (2016) 225–35, which sets out many examples.

[68] *Patel v Mirza* [2016] UKSC 42 at [123] (Lord Kerr). Cf Burrows, in Peel and Probert (eds) *Shaping the Law of Obligations* (2023) 66 ('lingering concerns' whether the courts should be allowed 'more freely to consider and articulate a range of factors').

[69] [2020] UKSC 42 at [22]–[26].

[70] [2016] UKSC 42 at [112].

[71] [2019] EWCA Civ 1393, [2019] IRLR 905 at [62]. See also *Henderson v Dorset Healthcare University NHS Foundation Trust* [2020] UKSC 43 at [77] (*Patel* does not represent 'year zero').

[72] [2020] UKSC 42 at [26].

application to the situation before the court. In particular, I would not normally expect a court to admit or to address evidence on matters such as the effectiveness of the criminal law in particular situations or the likely social consequences of permitting a claim in specified circumstances. The essential question is whether to allow the claim would damage the integrity of the legal system. The answer will depend on whether it would be inconsistent with the policies to which the legal system gives effect. The court is not concerned here to evaluate the policies in play or to carry out a policy-based evaluation of the relevant laws. It is simply seeking to identify the policies to which the law gives effect which are engaged by the question whether to allow the claim, to ascertain whether to allow it would be inconsistent with those policies or, where the policies compete, where the overall balance lies. In considering proportionality at stage (c), by contrast, it is likely that the court will have to give close scrutiny to the detail of the case in hand. Finally, in this regard, since the overriding consideration is the damage that might be done to the integrity of the legal system by its adopting contradictory positions, it may not be necessary in every case to complete an exhaustive examination of all stages of the trio of considerations. If, on an examination of the relevant policy considerations, the clear conclusion emerges that the defence should not be allowed, there will be no need to go on to consider proportionality, because there is no risk of disproportionate harm to the claimant by refusing relief to which he or she would otherwise be entitled. If, on the other hand, a balancing of the policy considerations suggests a denial of the claim, it will be necessary to go on to consider proportionality.

In that case:

G agreed to purchase a leasehold property from M, the purchase to be financed by a mortgage from a high street lender whose interest would be secured by a charge over the property to be registered at the Land Registry. The mortgage advance was procured by fraudulent misrepresentations made by G to the lender: the purpose was for G to use her good credit history to raise capital finance for M which he would not otherwise have been able to obtain. S, a firm of solicitors acting for G, M and the lender, negligently failed to register both the transfer of the property to G and the charge in favour of the lender. When mortgage payments fell into arrears, the lender was unable to enforce its security over the property and brought proceedings against G for a money judgment. G brought a claim against S for negligence and breach of contract. S admitted its breach of duty but contended that damages were not recoverable by the respondent because the purpose of putting the property into her name and obtaining the mortgage was illegal;[73] that the purpose of instructing S could only have been to further that fraud and that, accordingly, they were entitled to rely on the defence of illegality.

The Supreme Court rejected the illegality defence. Lord Lloyd-Jones held that this decision could be taken on the basis of just the first two of Lord Toulson's 'trio of necessary considerations':[74]

To permit the respondent's claim in the particular circumstances of this case would not undermine the public policies underlying the criminalisation of mortgage fraud and could, indeed, operate in a way which would protect the interests of the victim of the fraud, ie

[73] At the time, this constituted an offence contrary to the Theft Act 1968, s 15 (repealed and replaced by the Fraud Act 2006).

[74] [2020] UKSC 42 at [35].

the mortgagee.[75] Furthermore, to deny the respondent's claim would run counter to other important public policies. It would be inconsistent with the policy that the victims of solicitors' negligence should be compensated for their loss. It would be a disincentive to the diligent performance by solicitors of their duties. It would also result in an incoherent contradiction given the law's acknowledgment[76] that an equitable property right vested in the respondent.

Although it was not strictly necessary to go on to consider the third of the trio of considerations, Lord Lloyd-Jones did so, and concluded that denial of the claim would not be a proportionate response to the illegality. The illegality was not central to the breach of duty of which G complained, because by the time S was required to register the transaction the fraud had already been achieved and equitable property had already passed to G. Moreover, the Court was not being asked to lend its processes to recovery of an award calculated by reference to the profits which would have been obtained had the illegal scheme succeeded, but to a claim for compensation for property lost by the negligence of S.[77] His Lordship noted, however, that since *Patel v Mirza* it is clear that the notion that persons should not be permitted to profit from their own wrongdoing is unsatisfactory as a rationale of the illegality defence: the true rationale is that recovery should not be permitted where to do so would result in an incoherent contradiction damaging to the integrity of the legal system, and to allow G's claim to proceed would not involve any such contradiction.[78]

(iv) Collateral transactions

There was no mention of collateral transactions in *Patel v Mirza*. But in considering the effects of illegality, it has long been accepted at common law that, if one contract will not be enforced by reason of illegality, the same may apply to a second contract that is linked to that first contract. For example, in *Fisher v Bridges*[79] a deed executed to secure the payment of the price for land conveyed to the defendant for an illegal purpose was held to be unenforceable. Jervis CJ said that the deed:[80]

> springs from, and is a creature of, the illegal agreement; and, as the law would not enforce the original illegal contract, so neither will it allow the parties to enforce a security for the purchase money, which by the original bargain was tainted with illegality.

Similarly, it was held in *Spector v Ageda*[81] that a loan, knowingly made to finance a contract that was unenforceable for illegality, was itself tainted and therefore unenforceable.

[75] If G could recover compensation against S, it could be applied to meet or reduce her liability to the lender on her personal covenant: at [31].

[76] On the facts, the illegality did not prevent an equitable interest in the property being passed to G, and 'she should have available to her as the holder of that interest the remedies provided by law for its protection': at [34].

[77] [2020] UKSC 42 at [40], [45].

[78] *Ibid* at [46].

[79] (1854) 3 E & B 642.

[80] *Ibid*, 649.

[81] [1973] Ch 30. See also *Cannon v Bryce* (1819) 3 B & Ald 179.

Not all collateral transactions are tainted. For example, an innocent party may have an action for breach of a collateral warranty. So in *Strongman (1945) Ltd v Sincock*[82] a builder recovered damages for the breach of a collateral assurance by his client that he would obtain the necessary licences to enable the work to be carried out, even though a contract to build without a licence was absolutely prohibited by statute.

After *Patel v Mirza*, the question will be whether, applying the trio of considerations and the various factors relevant to deciding whether denying the claim is proportionate, the linked contract, as well as the main contract, should be unenforceable because of the illegality.

(v) Severance

There was also no mention in *Patel v Mirza* of the long-established doctrine of severance. By this doctrine, if a contract would otherwise be unenforceable for illegality, the contract may be severed so that the objectionable part of the contract is disregarded and the rest of the contract is enforceable.[83] It should be noted at the outset that several of the cases on severance, including the leading case, deal with the restraint of trade doctrine, the details of which are dealt with at the end of this chapter.

An initial condition to be met before severance will be permitted is that the severance is in accordance with public policy. After *Patel v Mirza*, this preliminary condition will be naturally determined by applying the new policy-based approach. In other words, severance should only be made if Lord Toulson's trio of considerations—and in particular the assessment of proportionality—favour it.

So if the illegal conduct involves a serious element of moral turpitude—as, for example, one which has as its object the deliberate commission of a serious criminal offence—it is likely that the whole of the contract will be infected and that the Courts will refuse to give any effect to the agreement, at least at the suit of one who knew of or participated in the illegality.[84] Thus in *Napier v National Business Agency Ltd*:[85]

The defendant agreed to employ N at a salary of £13 a week, with a further £6 a week for 'expenses'. In fact, N's expenses were nowhere near that sum, and this further provision was merely a device to defraud the income tax authorities. N brought an action to recover his salary, abandoning his claim to the expense allowance.

[82] [1955] 2 QB 525. See also *Gregory v Ford* [1951] 1 All ER 121. The claimant may also have a tort claim for misrepresentation inducing the contract that is unenforceable for illegality: see, eg, *Burrows v Rhodes* [1899] 1 QB 816; *Road Transport & General Insurance Co v Adams* [1955] CLY 2455; *Shelley v Paddock* [1980] QB 348; *Saunders v Edwards* [1987] 1 WLR 1116. Rescission on the ground of fraud may also be available: see *Hughes v Clewley, The Siben (No 2)* [1996] 1 Lloyd's Rep 35 (not available in that case).

[83] It is through this common law doctrine of severance that a particular term may be isolated as unenforceable or void for illegality while leaving the rest of the contract intact. It is noteworthy that an analogy can be drawn between this doctrine and a statute which, as we have seen (see above, p 422), may explicitly target a particular contract term only (so that, depending on how central a term is, the rest of the contract may be left intact).

[84] *Bennett v Bennett* [1952] 1 KB 249, 254.

[85] [1951] 2 All ER 264. See also *Kenyon v Darwen Manufacturing Co Ltd* [1936] 2 KB 193; *Miller v Karlinski* (1945) 62 TLR 85; and *Hyland v JH Barker (North West) Ltd* [1985] ICR 861.

The Court of Appeal held that the provision as to expenses infected the whole agreement and no severance could be allowed.

On the other hand, if, for example, the conduct in question is illegal by virtue of a statute passed for the protection of a class of persons, it is likely that a Court will sever the objectionable provision and give effect to the remainder of the contract in an action brought by a member of the protected class.[86]

If the preliminary public policy condition for severance is satisfied, past cases establish that there are then three requirements for severance.[87] First, that it is possible to separate the objectionable part of the contract from the rest of the contract without rewriting (the 'blue pencil' test). Secondly, that the objectionable part of the contract does not form the main consideration under the contract. Thirdly, that severance would not entirely alter the nature of the agreement. After *Patel v Mirza*, those requirements remain (as confirmed by the Supreme Court in *Tillman v Egon Zehnder Ltd*)[88] but it may be that they will be flexibly, rather than rigidly, applied. We shall now examine each in turn.

(a) The 'Blue Pencil' Test. Severance is only permissible where one can simply strike out the offending words without rewriting. This is generally known as the 'blue pencil' test, so that 'severance can be effected when the part severed can be removed by running a blue pencil through it'[89] without affecting the meaning of the part remaining. The rule in practice can be seen in *Goldsoll v Goldman*:[90]

A sold his imitation jeweller's business to B and covenanted that for a period of two years he would 'not carry on the business of a vendor or dealer in real or imitation jewellery in the United Kingdom or any other country in the world'. Shortly afterwards, A joined a rival firm of jewellers in the same street. B sought an injunction to restrain the breach of contract.

Although the restrictive covenant was unenforceable as it stood (because it was contrary to public policy as an unreasonable restraint of trade), the objectionable parts could be 'blue pencilled' (by deleting the words 'real or' and 'or any other country in the world'). The injunction was granted.

(b) The Objectionable Part of the Contract Does Not Form the Main Consideration. Normally severance is not appropriate where it would remove the main consideration. For example, in *Bennett v Bennett*:[91]

[86] *Ailion v Spiekermann* [1976] 1 Ch 158. See above, p 422, n 41.

[87] See, eg, *Beckett Investment Management Group Ltd v Hall* [2007] EWCA Civ 613, [2007] ICR 1539.

[88] [2019] UKSC 32, [2000] AC 154. However, disappointingly, there was no reference at all by the Supreme Court to *Patel v Mirza*.

[89] *Attwood v Lamont* [1920] 3 KB 571, 578 (Lord Sterndale MR). See also *Business Seating (Renovations) Ltd v Broad* [1989] ICR 729, 734 and *Ginsberg v Parker* [1988] IRLR 483.

[90] [1915] 1 Ch 292. See also *Putsman v Taylor* [1927] 1 KB 637; *Ronbar Enterprises Ltd v Green* [1954] 1 WLR 815.

[91] [1952] 1 KB 249. But the Matrimonial Causes Act 1973, s 34 effectively allows severance in this situation, ie it lays down that a clause ousting the jurisdiction of the Courts to make an order for financial provision is void but the financial arrangements made in the contract are not thereby rendered void or unenforceable.

A entered into a contract with his wife B. Under the contract, A promised to pay B an annuity in return for B promising (i) not to apply to the Court for maintenance (ii) to maintain the children herself and (iii) to indemnify A against any legal expenses arising out of the contract. A failed to pay and was sued by B.

It was held that the objectionable part of the contract (that requiring B not to apply for maintenance thereby ousting the jurisdiction of the Courts and being contrary to public policy) could not be severed from the rest because it was the main consideration provided by B under the contract.

On the other hand, in *Goodinson v Goodinson*:[92]

A contracted with his wife B to pay her a weekly sum in return for her promise (i) to indemnify him against any debts incurred by her using his account (ii) not to pledge A's credit and (iii) not to divorce him. B sued A for not paying the agreed weekly sum.

The objectionable part of the contract (the promise not to divorce A which was contrary to public policy) could be severed from the rest because it was not the main consideration provided by B. In other words, there was ample consideration to support the agreement apart from the covenant not to sue for divorce, and so A was liable.

(c) Severance Must Not Constitute a Major Change in the Overall Effect of the Agreement. The Court will not permit severance where the offending provisions are 'inextricably interwoven with the other promises in the agreement'[93] so that severance would 'alter entirely the scope and intention of the agreement'.[94] This is not easy to apply. It has now been decided by the Supreme Court in *Tillman v Egon Zehnder Ltd*[95] that *Attwood v Lamont*,[96] the previously leading case on the application of this third requirement, was incorrectly reasoned and decided, and should be overruled. In the *Attwood* case:

A owned a clothing department store selling off-the-peg and made-to-measure clothes and hats for men, women and children. B was a tailor, employed by A. B covenanted that, after termination of his employment, he would not be concerned in the trade or business of a tailor, dressmaker, general draper, milliner, hatter, haberdasher, gentlemen's, ladies', or children's outfitter within ten miles of A's place of business in Kidderminster.

The restrictive covenant was unenforceable because it was contrary to public policy as an unreasonable restraint of trade; and the Court of Appeal held that it could not be severed, so as to leave the covenant as applying only to work as a tailor, because the contract was concerned to protect A's whole business and not merely a part of it so that severance would alter entirely the nature of the agreement. In reaching this decision the Court of Appeal applied the opaque reasoning that severance was permissible only where the covenant to be severed was 'not really a single covenant but was in effect a combination of several distinct covenants'.[97] The Supreme Court in

[92] [1954] 2 QB 118.

[93] *Kuenigl v Donnersmarck* [1955] 1 QB 515, 538.

[94] *Attwood v Lamont* [1920] 3 KB 571, 580 (Lord Sterndale MR). See also *Routh v Jones* [1947] 1 All ER 179, 758; *Marshall v NM Financial Management Ltd* [1995] 1 WLR 1461; *Crehan v Courage (No 1)* [1999] Eu LR 834.

[95] [2019] UKSC 32.

[96] [1920] 3 KB 571.

[97] *Ibid*, 593.

the *Tillman* case rejected that reasoning. According to the Supreme Court, the clause in *Attwood v Lamont* should have been severed, so as to leave the covenant as applying only to work as a tailor, rather than holding the whole post-employment restraint to be unenforceable.

In *Tillman v Egon Zehnder Ltd*:[98]

The defendant held a senior position in a recruitment company (the claimant). By her employment contract, if she left the claimant company, she was required for 6 months not to 'directly or indirectly engage or be concerned or interested in any business carried on in competition' with the claimant without its prior written consent. The defendant informed the claimant that she was leaving and her contract was terminated. The defendant then informed the claimant that she was going to work for a competitor and submitted that the above clause was unenforceable as an unreasonable restraint of trade. The claimant sought an interim injunction to stop her breaking that clause.

In granting the injunction in favour of the employer, the Supreme Court held that, first, the clause was an unreasonable restraint of trade because the words 'or interested in' were too wide and would prevent the defendant even holding a small number of shares in a rival company (although she herself did not own such shares and had no intention of acquiring any). Secondly, and crucially, the clause should be severed so as to remove the words 'or interested'. Each of the three requirements for severance was held to be satisfied. The 'blue pencil' test was satisfied because 'or interested' could simply be deleted without further rewriting. Severance would not remove the main consideration. And, according to the Supreme Court, severance would not produce a major change in the overall effect of the post-employment restraints in the contract.

Although one might interpret this decision as opening the way, through severance, to employers more readily being granted injunctions against employees to restrain the breach of post-termination restrictive covenants, it should be stressed that the Supreme Court did not say that the traditionally narrow approach to severance in post-termination covenants should now be abandoned. Lord Wilson, giving the leading judgment, said this:[99]

It is clearly common practice for an employer to present a prospective employee with a substantial written contract, many terms of which, including those imposing post-employment restraints, are derived from books of precedent. It is as valid in 2019 as it was in 1913[100] to infer that most prospective employees will not be able, even if minded, to decline to accept such terms, still less, following the end of their employment, to defend a claim that they are in breach of them. The courts must continue to adopt a cautious approach to the severance of post-employment restraints.

[98] [2019] UKSC 32.

[99] *Ibid* at [82].

[100] This was the date of *Mason v Provident Clothing and Supply Co Ltd* [1913] AC 724.

4. CONTRACTS IN RESTRAINT OF TRADE

(a) INTRODUCTION

One of the very well-established and, in practice, very important heads of illegality, in the sense of being contrary to public policy, is an unreasonable restraint of trade. The common law does not favour agreements that prohibit or restrain a person in the exercise of a lawful trade, employment, or profession: the restraint of trade doctrine protects the right of individuals to work and prevents them from disabling themselves from earning a living by an unreasonable restriction. Contracts in restraint of trade are part of the wider specialized area of the law commonly referred to as competition law or, in the United States, anti-trust law.

The Supreme Court has said that restraint of trade should be treated separately from the rest of the law on illegality in relation to contracts:[101]

> the principles governing contracts in restraint of trade are well-established and (with the exception of the rules on severance)[102] self-contained and already reflect the type of flexibility that *Patel v Mirza*[103] has brought to the law on contracts affected by illegality. It seems preferable, therefore, to treat the law on the enforceability of contracts in restraint of trade as being separate from, albeit similar to, the law on the enforceability of contracts affected by illegality as laid down in *Patel v Mirza*.

We have followed that approach in this chapter.

We must first examine what is meant by a restraint of trade before going on to explore the all-important concept of reasonableness. Not all restraints of trade are contrary to public policy, but an agreement in restraint of trade is enforceable only if it is established that the restrictions in it are reasonable in the interests of the parties and of the public.

(b) RESTRAINT OF TRADE DEFINED

The first question is whether the contract engages the doctrine of restraint of trade at all. Some instances are clear, but the boundaries of the doctrine are not easy to draw. In one sense, all commercial contracts restrain trade; for when one person binds another by contract, say to sell a rare Sheraton writing table or a particular cargo of oil, the seller's future liberty to deal lawfully in that subject-matter with persons not parties to the contract is restricted. Yet ordinary commercial contracts are clearly not unenforceable

[101] *Harcus Sinclair LLP v Your Lawyers Ltd* [2021] UKSC 32 at [45].

[102] Above, p 430. It may be that *Patel v Mirza* will lead to the doctrine of severance being more flexibly applied than previously: see above, p 431; this would apply equally in its application to cases of contracts in restraint of trade.

[103] Above, p 423.

for being in restraint of trade. The issue is how to determine which agreements are 'in restraint of trade'.[104]

Two categories of agreement have long been recognized as 'in restraint of trade'. First, agreements between employers and employees, whereby the employees covenant not to set up business on their own account on leaving the employers' service or to enter into employment with a rival firm. Lord Wilson's statement in *Tillman v Egon Zehnder Ltd*,[105] set out above, is a modern illustration of the sensitivity of the Courts to the potential inequality of bargaining power in such contracts. Secondly, agreements between the buyer and seller of a business together with its goodwill, whereby the seller covenants not to carry on a business which will compete with that of the buyer.

Apart from these types of agreement, there is no definitive way of determining whether or not an agreement is in restraint of trade. Lord Wilberforce has said:[106]

> [I]t would be mistaken, even if it were possible, to try to crystallise the rules of this, or any, aspect of public policy into neat propositions. The doctrine of restraint of trade is one to be applied to factual situations with a broad and flexible rule of reason.

The factual situations which invite the application of the doctrine will change with prevailing economic and social conditions,[107] and it is important to bear in mind that 'the classification must remain fluid and the categories can never be closed'.[108] In *Esso Petroleum Co Ltd v Harper's Garage (Stourport) Ltd*[109] the House of Lords held (by a majority) that, in determining whether a covenant restricting the use of land was within the doctrine of restraint of trade, the question was whether, by agreeing to the covenant, the person was giving up a previous right to trade on the land. However, the focus on whether the person has agreed to give up some freedom which he or she otherwise had is not a satisfactory test; if applied too literally it could include most commercial contracts. In *Peninsula Securities Ltd v Dunnes Stores (Bangor) Ltd*[110] the Supreme Court rejected the reasoning of the majority in *Esso*, and departed from the decision in

[104] In *obiter dicta* in *Tillman v Egon Zehnder Ltd* [2019] UKSC 32 at [28]–[30], the Supreme Court considered the 'outer reaches of the doctrine' but did not need to form a view as to the scope of the doctrine in order to decide the case at hand which concerned the classic situation of a restrictive covenant operating post-termination in an employment contract. In *Peninsula Securities Ltd v Dunnes Stores (Bangor) Ltd* [2020] UKSC 36, [2021] AC 1014, however, the Court had no choice but to examine the boundaries of the doctrine more closely.

[105] See above, p 433.

[106] *Esso Petroleum Co Ltd v Harper's Garage (Stourport) Ltd* [1968] AC 269, 331.

[107] Lord Wilson, giving the judgment of the Supreme Court in *Tillman v Egon Zehnder Ltd* [2019] UKSC 32 at [26], said, 'Based as it is on public policy, the doctrine has regularly had to adjust to social change.' See also *Peninsula Securities Ltd v Dunnes Stores (Bangor) Ltd* [2020] UKSC 36 at [46].

[108] *Esso Petroleum Co Ltd v Harper's Garage (Stourport) Ltd* [1968] AC 269, 337. See also *Proactive Sports Management Ltd v Rooney* [2011] EWCA Civ 1444, [2012] FSR 16 at [93] (contract restricting footballer's exploitation of his image rights subject to restraint of trade doctrine, although ancillary to his primary activity as footballer).

[109] [1968] AC 269. Lord Wilberforce's reasoning was different.

[110] [2020] UKSC 36. Cf Stevens, in Fox-Decent, Goldberg, and Smith (eds), *Understanding Private Law: Essays in Honour of Stephen A Smith* (2025) 167.

that case. The Court preferred, and applied, the reasoning of Lord Wilberforce in the *Esso* case, who said:[111]

the development of the law does seem to show that judges have been able to dispense from the necessity of justification under a public policy test of reasonableness such contracts or provisions of contracts as, under contemporary conditions, may be found to have passed into the accepted and normal currency of commercial or contractual or conveyancing relations. That such contracts have done so may be taken to show with at least strong prima force that, moulded under the pressures of negotiation, competition and public opinion, they have assumed a form which satisfies the test of public policy as understood by the courts at the time.

This has become known as the 'trading society' test. Accepting it as the test for covenants restricting the use of land, Lord Wilson said in the *Peninsula* case:[112]

In these circumstances the common law is inevitably a patchwork; and in it we will search in vain for perfect congruity. This is a truth which Lord Wilberforce's pragmatic test recognises. Although criticised, the phrase 'trading society' aptly describes the test. For it reflects the importance attached on the one hand to freedom to trade and on the other to the enforceability of contracts in the interests of trade. It is the former which generates the doctrine and the latter which keeps it within bounds.

This does not mean, however, that the 'trading society' test is now to be seen as 'the' test for all purposes. The Court of Appeal[113] has noted that Lord Wilson in *Peninsula* endorsed Lord Wilberforce's statement in *Esso*, quoted above,[114] that the doctrine cannot be crystallized into neat propositions. Considering the application of the doctrine of restraint of trade in the novel case of a bespoke services agreement entered into by commercial parties, Carr LJ said:[115]

The search is for one or more features of the Services Agreement which, in all the circumstances, can be said to be such a cause for concern (or apparently oppressive) as to justify (as a matter of public policy) requiring the covenantee to prove reasonableness.

Being based on public policy, the law concerning restraint of trade has changed from time to time, both in form and in spirit, in response to changes in conditions of trade.[116] It should be noted, however, that in the modern law the operation of the common law doctrine, particularly concerning agreements for exclusive dealing and market-sharing, has been significantly overtaken by legislative provisions which seek to control

111 [1968] AC 269, 332–3.

112 [2020] UKSC 36 at [45].

113 *Quantum Actuarial LLP v Quantum Advisory Ltd* [2021] EWCA Civ 227, [2022] 1 All ER (Comm) 473 at [72].

114 Above, p 436; see *Peninsula Securities Ltd v Dunnes Stores (Bangor) Ltd* [2020] UKSC 36 at [26].

115 *Quantum Actuarial LLP v Quantum Advisory Ltd* [2021] EWCA Civ 227 at [80].

116 Above, n 107.

anti-competitive practices, which are of wider application than the common law doctrine and which are primarily administered by regulatory authorities.[117]

(c) 'REASONABLENESS' OF THE RESTRAINT

If the contract engages the doctrine of restraint of trade, the restraints are prima facie unenforceable unless they are reasonable. The foundation of the modern law on restraint of trade is contained in the speech of Lord Macnaghten in *Nordenfelt v Maxim Nordenfelt Guns and Ammunition Co Ltd*:[118]

N was a maker and inventor of guns and ammunition. He sold his business to the MN company for £287,500 and entered into a covenant (later to be repeated in a contract of service) that he would not for 25 years 'engage . . . either directly or indirectly in the trade or business of a manufacturer of guns, gun mountings or carriages, gunpowder explosives or ammunition, or in any business competing or liable to compete in any way with that for the time being carried on by the company', but expressly reserved the right to deal in explosives other than gunpowder, in torpedoes or submarine boats, and in metal castings or forgings. After some years N entered into a business with a rival company dealing with guns and ammunition, and MN sought an injunction to restrain him from so doing.

The House of Lords was of the opinion that the covenant not to compete with the company 'in *any* business competing or liable to compete in any way with that for the time being carried on by the company' was unreasonable, as it attempted to protect not only the business as it was when sold, but any future activities of the company. It was therefore void; but this clause was distinct and severable from the rest of the agreement.[119] As for the remainder of the restraint, insofar as it protected the business actually sold, it was reasonable between the parties, because N not only received a large sum of money, but also by his reservation retained scope for the exercise of his inventive and manufacturing skill. Moreover, the wide area over which the business extended necessitated a restraint co-extensive with that area for the protection of the respondents. Finally it could not be said to be contrary to the public interest since it transferred to an English company the making of guns and ammunition for foreign lands. The restraint was therefore valid.

[117] For domestic legislation, see in particular the Competition Act 1998, the Enterprise Act 2002, and the Enterprise and Regulatory Reform Act 2013. Very significant European Union legislation applied directly in English law during the period when the UK was an EU Member State: see the TFEU, arts 101 and 102 (formerly EEC Treaty, arts 85 and 86, later EC Treaty, arts 81 and 82). The domestic legislation was amended to take account of the UK's withdrawal from the EU (see SI 2019 No 93 and SI 2020 No 1343), and there are provisions relating to competition law in a Trade and Cooperation Agreement between the EU, Euratom, and the UK (2021): see Whish and Bailey, *Competition Law* (11th edn, 2024), 60–1, 370–4, 419–22.

[118] [1894] AC 535.

[119] For severance, see above, p 430.

As a result of this decision and later cases in which it has been elucidated, certain propositions of law can be stated:

(1) All restraints of trade, in the absence of special justifying circumstances, are contrary to public policy and unenforceable[120] or void.[121] If the parties confer benefits on each other under the contract, there were past cases indicating that the Courts will not allow them restitution[122] but these will now require re-analysis in the light of *Patel v Mirza*.[123]

(2) It is a question of law for the decision of the Court whether the special circumstances adduced do or do not justify the restraint; and if a restraint is not justified, the Court will, if necessary, take the point, since it relates to a matter of public policy, and the Court does not enforce agreements which are contrary to public policy.[124]

(3) A restraint can only be justified if it is reasonable (a) in the interests of the contracting parties, and (b) in the interests of the public.[125]

(4) The onus of showing that the restraint is reasonable between the parties rests upon the person alleging that it is so, that is to say, upon the covenantee.[126] To satisfy this burden, the covenantee must show that the restraint protects legitimate interests of the covenantee and that it goes no further than is reasonably necessary to protect those interests. The restriction must also be commensurate with the benefits secured to the covenantor under the contract.[127]

(5) The onus of showing that, notwithstanding that a covenant is reasonable between the parties, it is nevertheless injurious to the public interest and therefore unenforceable, rests upon the party alleging it to be so, that is to say, usually upon the covenantor.[128] But once the agreement is before the Court it is open to scrutiny in all its surrounding circumstances as a question of law.[129]

[120] *Joseph Evans & Co Ltd v Heathcote* [1918] 1 KB 418, 431 (Bankes LJ).

[121] *Mason v Provident Clothing & Supply Co Ltd* [1913] AC 724.

[122] *Boddington v Lawton* [1994] ICR 478, 491–3 (Nicholls V-C). See also *Joseph Evans & Co Ltd v Heathcote* [1918] 1 KB 418; *Esso Petroleum Co Ltd v Harper's Garage (Stourport) Ltd* [1968] AC 269, 297; *A Schroeder Music Publishing Co Ltd v Macaulay* [1974] 1 All ER 174, 181, aff'd [1974] 1 WLR 1308.

[123] Above, p 423.

[124] *Wyatt v Kreglinger and Fernau* [1933] 1 KB 793, 806; *North Western Salt Co Ltd v Electrolytic Alkali Co Ltd* [1914] AC 461, 470. See also above, p 418.

[125] *Proactive Sports Management Ltd v Rooney* [2011] EWCA Civ 1444 at [93] (Arden LJ: 'Public policy is concerned with the manner in which a person may properly realise his potential, not only for the good of that individual but for the economic benefit of society generally').

[126] *Mason v Provident Clothing & Supply Co Ltd* [1913] AC 724, 733; *Herbert Morris Ltd v Saxelby* [1916] 1 AC 688, 700; *Attwood v Lamont* [1920] 3 KB 571, 587.

[127] *Harcus Sinclair LLP v Your Lawyers Ltd* [2021] UKSC 32 at [48]. Such benefits can extend beyond the contractual consideration: *ibid* at [79].

[128] *Herbert Morris Ltd v Saxelby* [1916] 1 AC 688, 700, 708; *A-G of Commonwealth of Australia v Adelaide Steamship Co Ltd* [1913] AC 781, 795; *Harcus Sinclair LLP v Your Lawyers Ltd* [2021] UKSC 32 at [49].

[129] *Esso Petroleum Co Ltd v Harper's Garage (Stourport) Ltd* [1968] AC 269, 319.

(6) Covenants in restraint of trade are construed (a) with reference to the object sought to be obtained, that is the protection of one of the parties against competition in trade, and (b) in their context and in the light of the factual matrix when the agreement was made.[130] Where there are two equally realistic constructions of the covenant, one of which would render the restraint of trade reasonable, the other unreasonable, the Court should lean in favour of the former, thus upholding the covenant.[131]

Reasonableness as a test for the validity of a restraint requires further consideration.

(d) REASONABLENESS IN THE INTERESTS OF THE PARTIES

The application of this test will depend on the answers to two questions: what is it that the covenantee is entitled to protect, and how far can such protection extend? A covenant cannot be considered reasonable unless it is designed to protect the legitimate interests of the covenantee.[132] The issue of whether a covenant in restraint of trade is reasonable ultimately falls to be decided by reference to the legitimate interests that are sought to be protected and not by a classification of the relationship between the parties.[133] But the nature of the interests recognized as legitimate by the law will vary according to the subject-matter and nature of the contract. Moreover, in determining the legitimate interests of the covenantee one can take into account what the parties (objectively) intended or contemplated, consequent on the contract, at the time the contract was made as well as the contract terms.[134]

The different approaches of the Courts can be illustrated by comparing restraints on the seller of a business and those on former employees.[135] The buyer of a business with its goodwill is entitled to prevent the seller from competing with the business sold. The buyer has acquired a business which, inevitably, has been immune from competition by the person who has sold it, and the goodwill of that business is an interest which

[130] *Clarke v Newland* [1991] 1 All ER 397, 402; *Commercial Plastics Ltd v Vincent* [1965] 1 QB 623, 644.

[131] *Tillman v Egon Zehnder Ltd* [2019] UKSC 32 at [42]; *Boydell v NZP Ltd* [2023] EWCA Civ 373, [2023] IRLR 572 at [24]–[26].

[132] The restraint must be reasonable for *both* parties: *Herbert Morris Ltd v Saxelby* [1916] 1 AC 688, 707 (Lord Parker), and the reasonableness is assessed at the time when the covenant is entered into; cf, however, *Shell UK Ltd v Lostock Garage Ltd* [1976] 1 WLR 1187 (Lord Denning MR, not supported by Ormrod and Bridge LJJ).

[133] *Bridge v Deacons* [1984] 1 AC 705, 714.

[134] *Harcus Sinclair LLP v Your Lawyers Ltd* [2021] UKSC 32 at [70] (although it will be rare for this question to arise and to be critical in the determination of the case: *ibid* at [64]).

[135] For other contexts, see *Esso Petroleum Co Ltd v Harper's Garage (Stourport) Ltd* [1968] AC 269 ('solus tie' for purchase of petrol; the majority reasoning in the case was departed from in *Peninsula Securities Ltd v Dunnes Stores (Bangor) Ltd*: see above, p 435); *A Schroeder Music Publishing Co Ltd v Macaulay* [1974] 1 WLR 1308 ('exclusive services' agreement between young and unknown song-writer and music publishing company); *Credico Marketing Ltd v Lambert* [2022] EWCA Civ 864 (exclusive services agreement between two commercial parties); *Harcus Sinclair LLP v Your Lawyers Ltd* [2021] UKSC 32 at [47] (a 'novel situation': a non-compete undertaking given by one law firm to another in relation to a group litigation claim).

the buyer is legitimately entitled to protect.[136] A different set of considerations comes into play in the case of restraints upon former employees. An employer cannot prevent competition by a former employee, or restrict the use by the employee of personal skill and knowledge acquired in the course of the employment. The employer is entitled only to protect its trade secrets, and to prevent the use by the employee of influence acquired over its clients or customers.[137]

Where the covenantee has a legitimate interest which it is entitled to protect, the restriction must not be longer in point of time, or wider in area, or otherwise be more extensive in scope than is necessary to protect that interest.[138] The assessment of reasonableness in any individual case, however, must necessarily depend upon a range of factors, including the character of the business, inequality of bargaining power between the parties, standard forms of contract, whether the restraints operate during or post-contract, and the surrounding circumstances, including the factual and contractual background.[139]

The quantum of the consideration which the covenantor has received in exchange for the restraint is relevant to the determination of the reasonableness of the contract.[140]

(e) REASONABLENESS IN THE INTERESTS OF THE PUBLIC

Cases in which a restraint has been held unenforceable as not being reasonable in the interests of the public are not common. Indeed, in 1913, the Privy Council observed that 'their Lordships are not aware of any case in which a restraint though reasonable in the interests of the parties has been held unenforceable because it involved some injury to the public',[141] and it was further said that 'if once the Court is satisfied that the restraint is reasonable as between the parties this onus [of proving injury to the public] will be no light one'.[142] More recently, however, in relation to certain types of restrictive trading agreements there has been a distinct shift of emphasis in favour of recognizing the importance of the interests of the public.[143] Such agreements are, as a

[136] *Herbert Morris Ltd v Saxelby* [1916] 1 AC 688, 713.

[137] *Faccenda Chicken Ltd v Fowler* [1987] Ch 117, 137.

[138] eg *Esso Petroleum Co Ltd v Harper's Garage (Stourport) Ltd* [1968] AC 269 (covenant for four years and five months was reasonable; covenant for 21 years was unreasonable); *Mason v Provident Clothing & Supply Co* [1913] AC 724 (covenant for three years within 25 miles of London was unreasonable); cf *Foster & Sons Ltd v Suggett* (1918) 35 TLR 87 (covenant extending to the whole of the UK was reasonable); *Bromley v Smith* [1909] 2 KB 235 (restriction on baker from opening restaurant was unreasonable).

[139] *Quantum Actuarial LLP v Quantum Advisory Ltd* [2021] EWCA Civ 227 at [65].

[140] *Nordenfelt v Maxim Nordenfelt Guns and Ammunition Co Ltd* [1894] AC 535, 565; *Esso Petroleum Co Ltd v Harper's Garage (Stourport) Ltd* [1968] AC 269, 300, 318, 323; *Allied Dunbar (Frank Weisinger) Ltd v Weisinger* [1988] IRLR 60.

[141] *A-G of Commonwealth of Australia v Adelaide Steamship Co* [1913] AC 781, 795.

[142] *Ibid*, 797.

[143] *Esso Petroleum Co Ltd v Harper's Garage (Stourport) Ltd* [1968] AC 269, 300–1, 318–19, 321, 324, 330, 340–1. See also *Pharmaceutical Society of Great Britain v Dickson* [1970] AC 403, 441. But cf the more cautious approach adopted by Ungoed-Thomas J in *Texaco Ltd v Mulberry Filling Station Ltd* [1972] 1 WLR 814, 826–9. See also *Alec Lobb (Garages) Ltd v Total Oil (Great Britain) Ltd* [1985] 1 WLR 173, 191.

general rule, freely entered into between traders who are perfectly capable of deciding for themselves what is reasonable in their own interests. So the real point at issue is whether the maintenance of the restraint is detrimental to the interests of the public.

Even where cases are decided on the basis of reasonableness between the parties, it is *ultimately* on the ground of public policy that the Court will decline to enforce an unreasonable restraint. As Lord Pearce has said: 'There is not, as some cases seem to suggest, a separation between what is reasonable on grounds of public policy and what is reasonable as between the parties. There is one broad question: is it in the interests of the community that this restraint should, as between the parties, be held to be reasonable and enforceable?'[144]

(f) CARTEL AGREEMENTS

Business organizations frequently enter into cartels, that is to say, agreements to regulate the production and marketing of the commodities manufactured by them, and to maintain prices and standards in relation to those commodities. Similarly, employers may enter into agreements attempting to regulate labour and to impose mutual restrictions upon the re-employment of former employees. The rules of professional organizations also restrict professionals such as lawyers or doctors as to how they may work, for instance, by restricting advertising or controlling the charges for services. Cartel agreements are, like all other agreements in restraint of trade, prima facie unenforceable at common law and must be justified as being reasonable in the interests of the parties and of the public.

In this type of agreement, which is generally freely negotiated, the parties can be regarded 'as the best judges of what is reasonable between themselves'.[145] They are entered into for the purpose of avoiding undue competition and carrying on trade without excessive fluctuations or uncertainty. As a result, it is difficult for a Court to say that they are unreasonable between the parties, and in fact the Courts have only done so if an agreement contains no provision, or virtually no provision, for voluntary withdrawal.[146]

The position adopted by the common law has been to regard many cartels at least as being not injurious to the public,[147] and in some cases even as positively beneficial.[148] Indeed, the Courts virtually excluded the possibility that a cartel should be held contrary to the public interest by requiring it to be one which was calculated to produce 'a pernicious monopoly, that is to say, a monopoly calculated to enhance prices to an

144 *Esso Petroleum Co Ltd v Harper's Garage (Stourport) Ltd* [1968] AC 269, 324.

145 *North Western Salt Co v Electrolytic Alkali Co Ltd* [1914] AC 461, 471 (Viscount Haldane LC); *English Hop Growers v Dering* [1928] 2 KB 174, 180.

146 *McEllistrim v Ballymacelligott Co-operative Agriculture and Dairy Society Ltd* [1919] AC 548; *Joseph Evans & Co v Heathcote* [1918] 1 KB 418; *Bellshill and Mossend Co-operative Society v Dalziel Co-operative Society* [1960] AC 832.

147 *A-G of Commonwealth of Australia v Adelaide Steamship Co* [1913] AC 781.

148 *North Western Salt Co Ltd v Electrolytic Alkali Co Ltd* [1914] AC 461.

unreasonable extent'.[149] The effect was that in this context the common law did not promote competition. Even if the Courts had, in fact, adopted a different economic attitude, the doctrine of restraint of trade could not have been employed to any real effect in the suppression of cartels, since, save in exceptional circumstances, a cartel agreement would only have come before the Courts if one of the parties failed to perform it and was sued for the breach.

The exception concerns agreements between employers which attempt to regulate labour and to impose mutual restrictions upon the re-employment of former employees. These may be struck down as being employer–employee covenants in disguise or as being contrary to the public interest.[150] So, in *Eastham v Newcastle United Football Club Ltd*[151] a professional football player, who could be debarred by rules in an agreement between his club and the Football Association from playing for any other club, was entitled to a declaration that the rules were invalid. Wilberforce J accepted that some restriction was required for the proper and stable organization of the game of football in England, but concluded the rules were more restrictive on the player's liberty of employment than was necessary to protect this interest. He therefore granted a declaration that the system was invalid, not only against the defendant club, but also in respect of the rules of the Football Association. Although these rules constituted an agreement between employers only, they were calculated to affect the employees' freedom of employment and so could be challenged by the player on the same grounds as if they had been contained in an agreement between him and his employer. Similarly, in *Greig v Insole*[152] Slade J held unenforceable as being in unreasonable restraint of trade resolutions of the International Cricket Conference and the Test and County Cricket Board disqualifying from playing in test and county matches any player who took part in a match arranged by a private promoter (Mr Kerry Packer) during a certain period.

The common law doctrine of restraint of trade also extends to cover the rules of professional bodies. Thus the Court of Appeal refused to strike out a claim that a rule of the Jockey Club preventing a woman from holding a trainer's licence was invalid,[153] and a rule of the Pharmaceutical Society restricting the types of goods in which their members might deal has been held invalid.[154] The doctrine may even apply to the rules of professional bodies the members of which do not technically engage in 'trade',[155] though

[149] *A-G of Commonwealth of Australia v Adelaide Steamship Co* [1913] AC 781, 796.

[150] *Mineral Water Bottle Exchange and Trade Protection Soc v Booth* (1887) 36 Ch D 465; *Kores Manufacturing Co Ltd v Kolok Manufacturing Co Ltd* [1959] Ch 108; *Esso Petroleum Co Ltd v Harper's Garage (Stourport) Ltd* [1968] AC 269, 300, 319. But see Trade Union and Labour Relations (Consolidation) Act 1992, s 128 (purposes of employers' associations, defined in s 122, not unlawful or unenforceable by reason only that they are in restraint of trade).

[151] [1964] Ch 413, 432. See also *Buckley v Tutty* (1971) 46 ALJR 23; *Hall v Victorian Football League* [1982] VR 64 (Australia).

[152] [1978] 1 WLR 302.

[153] *Nagle v Feilden* [1966] 2 QB 633. See also *Greig v Insole* [1978] 1 WLR 302; *Adamson v NSW Rugby League Ltd* (1991) 103 ALR 319.

[154] *Pharmaceutical Society of Great Britain v Dickson* [1970] AC 403.

[155] *Ibid*, 420, 427, 430, 436, 441.

possibly not to those rules which are related solely to the maintenance of professional honour or standards.[156] But the basis upon which a person who is not a member of the relevant professional body, and thus a party to the restrictive agreement, can challenge it, has been put into question[157] and in practice the field has largely been left to modern legislation promoting competition or proscribing certain forms of discrimination.[158]

FURTHER READING

Winfield, 'Public Policy in the English Common Law' (1928) 42 Harv LR 76

Burrows, 'A New Dawn for the Law of Illegality' in Green and Bogg (eds), *Illegality after* Patel v Mirza (Oxford: Hart Publishing, 2018) 23

Burrows, 'The Illegality Defence in the Courts Today' in Peel and Probert (eds), *Shaping the Law of Obligations* (Oxford: Oxford University Press, 2023) 59

Stevens, 'The Scope of Restraint of Trade' in Fox-Decent, Goldberg, and Smith (eds), *Understanding Private Law: Essays in Honour of Stephen A Smith* (Oxford: Hart Publishing, 2025) 167

156 *Ibid*, 421, 436.

157 Privity of contract precludes an action in contract at common law (see below, Chapter 21), and in *R v Disciplinary Committee of the Jockey Club, ex p Aga Khan* [1993] 1 WLR 909 it was said by Hoffmann LJ at 933 that gaps in private law remedies should not be filled by subjecting them to public law and the judicial review procedure. Where there is unlawful discrimination or the restriction seeks to prevent those subject to the rules from dealing with a non-party, there may be a remedy: *Cutsforth v Mansfield Inns Ltd* [1986] 1 WLR 558.

158 Above, n 117.

PART 4

PERFORMANCE AND DISCHARGE

12

PERFORMANCE

1. PERFORMANCE MUST BE PRECISE AND EXACT

(a) STANDARDS OF CONTRACTUAL DUTY

The general rule is that performance of a contract must be precise and exact. That is, a party performing an obligation under a contract must perform that obligation exactly within the time frame set by the contract and exactly to the standard required by the contract. Sometimes that standard will be strict. This is so in the case of many common law obligations such as a seller's obligation to load cargo,[1] not to ship dangerous cargo,[2] and to obtain an export licence.[3] It is also so in the case of the statutory implied terms of title and quality in contracts for the sale and supply of goods.[4] Sometimes, as in the case of contracts for services, it will only require the exercise of reasonable care[5] or due diligence.[6] Whether the alleged performance satisfies this criterion is to be answered by construing the contract in accordance with the objective and contextual approach described in Chapter 5, to see what the parties meant by performance, and then by applying the ascertained *facts* to that construction, to see whether what has been done corresponds to what was promised.

[1] *Kurt A Becher GmbH & Co KG v Roplak Enterprises SA, The World Navigator* [1991] 2 Lloyd's Rep 23.

[2] *The Anathasia Cominos* [1990] 1 Lloyd's Rep 277, 282.

[3] *Pagnan SpA v Tradax Ocean Transportation SA* [1987] 3 All ER 565.

[4] Non-consumer goods contracts: Sale of Goods Act 1979, ss 12, 14 (as amended), above, pp 182–8; Supply of Goods and Services Act 1982, ss 2, 4, 7, and 9; Supply of Goods (Implied Terms) Act 1973, ss 8, 10 (hire-purchase); consumer goods contracts: Consumer Rights Act 2015, ss 9, 17, above, p 189. See also Consumer Rights Act 2015, ss 34, 41 (consumer contracts to supply digital content).

[5] eg *Lister v Romford Ice and Cold Storage Co Ltd* [1957] AC 555 (driving lorry); *Thake v Maurice* [1986] QB 644, 684–7, cf 677–8 (medical treatment); *Smith v Eric S Bush* [1990] 1 AC 831, 843 (surveying house); *Henderson v Merrett Syndicates Ltd* [1995] 2 AC 145, 176 (managing agents of Lloyd's underwriters). See also Supply of Goods and Services Act 1982, s 13 (non-consumer services contracts); Consumer Rights Act 2015, s 49 (consumer services contracts). Cf *Samuels v Davis* [1943] 1 KB 526 (contract to supply services and materials in finished product).

[6] Carriage of Goods by Sea Act 1971, s 3 (seaworthiness); *Union of India v NV Reederij Amsterdam* [1963] 2 Lloyd's Rep 233 (HL).

(b) DEVIATION FROM CONTRACTUAL TERMS

If there is the slightest deviation from the terms of the contract, the party not in default will be entitled to say that the contract has not been performed, and will be entitled to sue for damages for breach and, in certain cases, to elect to be discharged. Thus in *Re Moore & Co and Landauer & Co*:[7]

D agreed to buy from P 3,000 tins of canned fruit from Australia to be packed in cases containing 30 tins. When the goods were tendered it was found that a substantial part of the consignment was packed in cases containing 24 tins.

D was entitled to reject the whole consignment. Even if the performance effected is commercially no less valuable than that which was promised, there is a default in performance. So a contract to ship goods direct from Singapore to New York was held not to have been performed by shipping them to the American Pacific Seaboard and thence to New York by train.[8]

Only if the deviation is 'microscopic' will the contract be taken to have been correctly performed.[9] A party who does not render precise and exact performance of a contract is nevertheless exceptionally treated as having performed to some extent where that party has attempted (tendered) performance but the other party has prevented that performance, and in certain cases where there has been partial performance of an entire obligation.

2. TIME OF PERFORMANCE

(a) STIPULATIONS AS TO TIME AT COMMON LAW

Where a time was fixed for the performance of an undertaking by one of the parties to the contract, the common law as a general rule held this to be 'of the essence of the contract'. This phrase is often used but is capable of causing confusion because the question relates not to the contract as a whole but to the particular term which has been breached.[10] If the condition as to time was not fulfilled, the other party might treat the contract as broken and elect to terminate it.[11] For instance, in a contract for the sale of a flat where time was stated to be of the essence, the vendor was entitled to terminate when the purchaser tendered the price 10 minutes late.[12]

[7] [1921] 2 KB 519.

[8] *Re L Sutro & Co and Heilbut Symons & Co* [1917] 2 KB 348.

[9] *Arcos Ltd v EA Ronaasen & Son* [1933] AC 470, 479, 480 (Lord Atkin).

[10] *British and Commonwealth Holdings plc v Quadrex Holdings Inc* [1989] QB 842, 857 (Browne-Wilkinson V-C).

[11] *United Scientific Holdings Ltd v Burnley BC* [1978] AC 904, 940–1 (Lord Simon). Cf *ibid*, 927–8 (Lord Diplock). See further, above, pp 151, 157–9 (conditions).

[12] *Union Eagle Ltd v Golden Achievement Ltd* [1997] AC 514 (express termination and forfeiture clause). See also *Compagnie Commerciale Sucres et Denrées v C Czarnikow Ltd* [1990] 1 WLR 1337, 1347. But cf Sale of Goods Act 1979, s 10(1), below, p 450.

(b) STIPULATIONS AS TO TIME IN EQUITY

Equity did not regard a condition as to time as of the essence. Where it could do so without injustice to the contracting parties it decreed specific performance notwithstanding failure to observe the time fixed by the contract for completion, and as an incident of specific performance relieved the party in default by restraining proceedings at law based on such failure.[13]

(c) LAW OF PROPERTY ACT 1925, SECTION 41

Since the passing of the Judicature Acts, the rules of common law and equity have been fused,[14] and section 41 of the Law of Property Act 1925[15] provides:

Stipulations in a contract, as to time or otherwise, which according to rules of equity are not deemed to be or to have become of the essence of the contract, are also construed and have effect at law in accordance with the same rules.

But this relief is not available in three instances:

(1) where the agreement expressly states that time is of the essence of the contract;[16]

(2) where time was not of the essence of the contract, but upon a breach by one party,[17] the other has given notice requiring performance of the contract within a reasonable time.[18] This has often been referred to incorrectly as the service of a notice 'making time of the essence' of the contract, although strictly one party cannot unilaterally transform an innominate term into a condition;[19]

(3) where from the nature of the contract, its subject-matter, or the circumstances of the transaction, time must be taken to be of the essence of the agreement. The most common examples of this are provided by mercantile contracts, considered below, but, although time is prima facie not of the essence in sales of land,[20] or provisions in leases, such as rent review clauses,[21] in certain cases it will be. Thus, in the case of the sale of a public house as a going concern,[22] or of a leasehold

[13] *United Scientific Holdings Ltd v Burnley BC* [1978] AC 904, 942. See also *Stickney v Keeble* [1915] AC 386, 415.

[14] *United Scientific Holdings Ltd v Burnley BC* [1978] AC 904, 924–5, 926–7, 940, 956–7, 964.

[15] Re-enacting the Judicature Act 1873, s 25(7). Cf *Raineri v Miles* [1981] AC 1050 (damages available).

[16] *Steedman v Drinkle* [1916] 1 AC 275; *Union Eagle Ltd v Golden Achievement Ltd* [1916] 1 AC 688.

[17] *Behzadi v Shaftesbury Hotels Ltd* [1992] Ch 1; *British and Commonwealth Holdings plc v Quadrex Holdings Inc* [1989] 1 QB 842, 857–8; *Ramlal v Chaitlal* [2003] UKPC 12, [2004] 1 P & CR 1 (party giving notice must not be in default).

[18] *Stickney v Keeble* [1915] AC 386; *Behzadi v Shaftesbury Hotels Ltd* [1992] Ch 1; *Finkielkraut v Monohan* [1949] 2 All ER 234. See also Stannard (2004) 120 LQR 137. On 'reasonableness', see also *Oakdown Ltd v Bernstein and Co* (1985) 49 P & CR 282.

[19] *Urban 1 (Blonk Street) Ltd v Ayres* [2013] EWCA Civ 816, [2014] 1 WLR 756 at [44].

[20] *Webb v Hughes* (1870) LR 10 Eq 281; *Chancery Lane Developments Ltd v Wade's Department Stores Ltd* (1986) 53 P & CR 306, 312.

[21] *United Scientific Holdings Ltd v Burnley BC* [1978] AC 904.

[22] *Tadcaster Tower Brewery Co v Wilson* [1897] 1 Ch 705.

house required for immediate occupation,[23] or of an option to acquire property,[24] or the power under a 'break' clause in a lease to determine the lease prematurely,[25] time may well be of the essence and, if so, no relief is permitted. Similarly, failure to make timely payment of a deposit normally constitutes a repudiatory breach and any presumption that time is not of the essence is rebutted.[26]

(d) MERCANTILE CONTRACTS

Mercantile contracts are commercial agreements for the sale of goods, services, or other transactions between individuals, businesses, or other entities. In such contracts, time will readily be assumed to be of the essence of the contract. For example, if a contract to purchase shares provides for payment by a fixed date, payment must be made on or before that date, and in default the seller can treat the contract as discharged.[27] Similarly, time is of the essence for payment under a time charterparty of a ship if the owner is given the right to withdraw the vessel in default of 'punctual payment' of hire.[28] However, section 10(1) of the Sale of Goods Act 1979 provides that, unless a different intention appears from the terms of the contract, stipulations as to time of *payment* are not of the essence of a contract of sale of goods. Where the goods are perishable, or where the unpaid seller gives notice of his intention to re-sell the goods, if payment is not tendered within a reasonable time the seller may re-sell and recover damages for any loss.[29] Whether or not any other stipulation as to time is of the essence of a contract of sale of goods depends upon the terms of the contract;[30] but it is very often held to be so.[31]

Where a person is required to perform on or before a particular date, the performance may normally be carried out during the whole of that day.[32] Thus if payment of hire under a time charterparty is due on 14 June, the charterer has (regardless of banking hours) until midnight on 14/15 June to make the payment, and the shipowner cannot withdraw the ship for non-payment before that time.[33] Where no time is fixed by the contract for performance, it must normally be performed within a reasonable time.[34]

[23] *Tilley v Thomas* (1867) LR 3 Ch App 61.

[24] *Hare v Nicoll* [1966] 2 QB 130.

[25] *United Scientific Holdings Ltd v Burnley BC* [1978] AC 904, 929; *Coventry City Council v J Hepworth & Sons Ltd* (1982) 46 P & CR 170. But cf *Metrolands Investments Ltd v JH Dewhurst Ltd* [1986] 3 All ER 659.

[26] *Samarenko v Dawn Hill House Ltd* [2011] EWCA Civ 1445, [2013] Ch 36.

[27] *Hare v Nicoll* [1966] 2 QB 130. See also *Union Eagle Ltd v Golden Achievement Ltd* [1997] AC.

[28] *Scandinavian Trading Tanker Co AB v Flota Petrolera Ecuatoriana, The Scaptrade* [1983] 2 AC 694.

[29] Sale of Goods Act 1979, s 48(3).

[30] Sale of Goods Act 1979, s 10(2). But see *Hartley v Hymans* [1920] 3 KB 475, 483.

[31] *Reuter v Sala* (1879) 4 CPD 239, 246, 249; *Hartley v Hymans* [1920] 3 KB 475, 484; *Finagrain SA Geneva v P Kruse Hamburg* [1976] 2 Lloyd's Rep 508; *United Scientific Holdings Ltd v Burnley BC* [1978] AC 904, 924, 937, 944, 950, 958; *Bunge Corp v Tradax Export SA* [1981] 1 WLR 711, above, p 159; *Compagnie Commerciale Sucres et Denrées v C Czarnikow Ltd* [1990] 1 WLR 1337, 1347.

[32] Cf Sale of Goods Act 1979, s 29(5) (demand or tender of delivery may be treated as ineffectual unless made at a reasonable hour).

[33] *Afovos Shipping Co SA v Pagnan* [1983] 1 WLR 195.

[34] *Postlethwaite v Freeland* (1880) 5 App Cas 599; Sale of Goods Act 1979, s 29(3) (non-consumer sales contracts); cf Consumer Rights Act 2015, s 28(3) (consumer sales contract: unless time or period agreed, trader must deliver goods without undue delay, and in any event not more than 30 days after day of contract).

3. PLACE OF PERFORMANCE

The place of performance depends upon the express or implied intentions of the parties, judged from the nature of the contract and the surrounding circumstances. If no place of performance is specified even by implication, then in a non-consumer contract for the sale of goods it is the duty of the buyer to collect the goods rather than the seller to send them,[35] although in a consumer sales contract it is the trader's duty to deliver the goods to the consumer buyer;[36] and in contracts to pay money it is the debtor's duty to pay the creditor at the creditor's place of business or residence.[37]

4. ORDER OF PERFORMANCE

Where the contract makes no express provision, the order of performance depends on whether the obligation of one party to perform is interdependent on or independent of the other's obligation. The obligations may be interdependent in one of two ways. The obligation of one to perform may either be conditional upon performance by the other or concurrent with the obligation of the other. The determination of this is a matter of intention, and thus of the construction of the contract. The distinction between interdependent obligations (ie conditions precedent and concurrent obligations), and independent promises is discussed in Chapters 5 and 15.[38] In a contract of sale, unless the contract provides otherwise, payment and delivery are treated as due simultaneously and as concurrent,[39] but in a contract of employment the general rule is that the performance of the work is a condition precedent to the obligation to pay. The order of performance determines whether one party has to extend credit to the other and whether failure to perform is a breach of contract,[40] and, if so, whether the innocent party is entitled to be discharged from its obligations. The position differs from that in many civil law countries where a party may withhold performance until the other party performs, not only in cases of concurrent obligations but also where the other party has to perform first.[41]

5. PAYMENT

(a) INTRODUCTION

One mode of complete performance of an obligation is by payment of a money obligation. No request or demand for payment is normally necessary[42] unless the contract so provides.[43]

[35] Sale of Goods Act 1979, s 29(1), (2). See also CISG art 31.

[36] Consumer Rights Act 2015, s 28.

[37] *Charles Duval & Co Ltd v Gans* [1904] 2 KB 685; *Fowler v Midland Electricity Corporation for Power Distribution Ltd* [1917] 1 Ch 656 (debenture). On payment through the banking system, see below, p 452.

[38] Above, p 152; below, p 529.

[39] Sale of Goods Act 1979, s 28.

[40] Below, Chapter 15.

[41] Lando and Beale, *Principles of European Contract Law Parts I and II* (2000) 407. Cf Tettenborn, in Barker, Fairweather, and Grantham, *Private Law in the 21st Century* (2017) ch 16 (arguing that there is a general principle allowing suspension of performance in the common law).

[42] *Bell & Co v Antwerp, London & Brazil Line* [1891] 1 QB 103, 107 (Lord Esher MR); *Carne v Debono* [1988] 1 WLR 1107, 1112.

[43] *Libyan Arab Foreign Bank Co v Bankers Trust Co* [1989] 1 QB 728, 748–9. On the need for notice by a tenant of want of repair before the landlord's obligation to repair is due, see *Calabar Properties Ltd v Stitcher* [1984] 1 WLR 287, 298; *British Telecommunications plc v Sun Life Assurance Society plc* [1996] Ch 69.

There is a common, but mistaken, belief that payment of a debt can be proved only by the production of a written receipt. But payment may be proved by any evidence,[44] and a receipt is only prima facie evidence that a debt has been paid.[45]

Payment normally means payment in cash. The parties may, however, agree, expressly or impliedly, that payment may be made in some other manner, and, in the absence of any express stipulation, the method of payment may be determined by the course of dealing between the parties or by trade custom. If the parties are dealing together on a regular basis, it may be agreed that, at periodic intervals, sums due from one party shall be set off against sums due to that party by the other, and such set-off is then equivalent to an actual cash payment.[46]

(b) INTERBANK TRANSFERS

Nowadays payment is frequently made by use of the banking system. The debtor instructs its bank to pay a specified sum to the account of the creditor at another bank. The transfer may be effected by letter, telex, or nowadays generally electronically from the one bank to the other.[47] Such payment, when made, 'is the equivalent of cash, or as good as cash' for the purposes of a contract that requires payment in cash.[48] But difficulties can arise. If payment has to be made by a certain date, does the receipt of the payment order by the creditor's bank constitute payment? Or is payment only made when the order has been processed and the amount credited to the creditor's account? In *Mardorf Peach & Co Ltd v Attica Sea Carriers Corporation of Liberia*,[49] where the evidence was that the system of processing might take up to 24 hours before the account was credited, members of the House of Lords expressed differing opinions. Lord Salmon[50] and Lord Russell[51] were inclined to the view that, since a payment order was as between banks the equivalent of cash, it should suffice for punctual payment that such cash equivalent was tendered in due time to the creditor's bank to be credited to its account.[52] But Lord Fraser[53] was of the opinion that payment would not take place until the creditor's bank acted on the request in the order and credited the amount to the creditor's account. However, in *A/S Awilco of Oslo v Fulvia SpA di Navigazione of Cagliari, The Chikuma*:[54]

R chartered A's vessel *Chikuma*. Failing punctual payment of hire in cash in American currency monthly in advance, A was entitled to withdraw the vessel from service. Payment of one instalment of hire fell due on 22 January. On 21 January R instructed its Norwegian bank

[44] *Eyles v Ellis* (1827) 4 Bing 112. See also Cheques Act 1957, s 3.

[45] *Wilson v Keating* (1859) 27 Beav 121.

[46] *Larocque v Beauchemin* [1897] AC 358, 365–6.

[47] *K v A* [2019] EWHC 1118 (Comm), [2020] 1 Lloyd's Rep 28 at [26] ('any commercially recognised method of transferring funds, providing it is equivalent to cash'), allowing therefore for developments in banking practice.

[48] *A/S Awilco of Oslo v Fulvia SpA di Navigazione of Cagliari, The Chikuma* [1981] 1 WLR 314, 320.

[49] [1977] AC 850.

[50] *Ibid*, 880.

[51] *Ibid*, 889.

[52] In the case of a transfer between branches of the same bank, *Momm v Barclays Bank International Ltd* [1977] QB 79 held that payment was effected when the staff of the bank received the debtor's instructions and set in motion the bank's internal procedures for crediting the creditor's account.

[53] [1977] AC 850, 885.

[54] [1981] 1 WLR 314 (criticized by Mann (1981) 97 LQR 379).

to make the required payment by credit transfer. By a telex message before noon on the 22nd there was a credit transfer to A's bank in Italy of the sum due. The bank credited this on the same day to A's account. By Italian banking law, however, although A would have immediate access to the money, interest would not start to be paid by the bank until 26 January, and if A had withdrawn the sum credited it would probably have incurred liability to the bank to pay interest for those 4 days. A withdrew the vessel for default in punctual payment.

The House of Lords upheld their right to do so. The payment on 22 January was not equivalent to cash for it could not be used to earn interest, for example by immediate transfer to a deposit account. The fact that A could withdraw the money, but subject to payment of interest, did not make the payment equivalent to cash, since the arrangement amounted in substance to an overdraft facility.

(c) PAYMENT BY NEGOTIABLE INSTRUMENT OR DOCUMENTARY CREDIT

A negotiable instrument such as a bill of exchange, cheque, or promissory note may, by agreement, be given and accepted in payment. But the presumption where a negotiable instrument is taken in lieu of a money payment is that the parties intend it to be a conditional discharge only:[55]

Suppose that A, being owed a sum of money by B, agrees to take a cheque in payment of the sum due.

So far, B has satisfied the debt.[56] But if the cheque is dishonoured when presented for payment, A's right to sue on the debt revives and A's original rights are restored.[57] Exceptionally, however, a negotiable instrument may be given and accepted as absolute payment. In such a case, in the example given above, B's debt would then be wholly discharged. A would have to rely upon the rights conferred by the cheque, and, if the cheque is dishonoured, A must sue on it, and cannot revert to the original claim for the debt.[58] Similar principles apply to payment by documentary credit.[59]

(d) PAYMENT BY CREDIT OR CHARGE CARD

By contrast, payment by a credit or charge card is an unconditional and absolute payment unless the contract provides otherwise. So, the liability of a cardholder who has paid for goods or services in this way is discharged and the cardholder will not be

[55] *Re Romer and Haslam* [1893] 2 QB 286, 296, 300, 303.

[56] *Sayer v Wagstaff* (1844) 5 Beav 415, 423; *Hadley & Co Ltd v Hadley* [1898] 2 Ch 680; *Bolt & Nut Co (Tipton) Ltd v Rowlands, Nicholls & Co Ltd* [1964] 2 QB 10.

[57] *Sayer v Wagstaff* (1844) 5 Beav 415; *Re Romer and Haslam* [1893] 2 QB 286.

[58] *Sard v Rhodes* (1836) 1 M & W 153; *Sibree v Tripp* (1846) 15 M & W 23; *Re Romer and Haslam* [1893] 2 QB 286, 296, 300.

[59] *WJ Alan & Co Ltd v El Nasr Export and Import Co* [1972] 2 QB 189, 209–12; *Re Charge Card Services Ltd* [1989] Ch 497, 511.

liable to the seller or supplier if the credit or charge card company fails to pay the seller or supplier the amount charged to the card.[60]

6. VICARIOUS PERFORMANCE

There may be circumstances which make it permissible for contracting parties to perform their sides of the contract by getting someone else to do in a satisfactory fashion the work for which the contract provides.[61] A contract may be vicariously performed where this is expressly permitted by the contract,[62] or where it may properly be inferred from the terms of the contract, its subject-matter, and surrounding circumstances that it is a matter of indifference whether the performance is that of the contracting party or that party's nominee. Thus it has been held that a contract to let out railway wagons and keep them in repair could be vicariously performed.[63] The repairs were 'a rough description of work which ordinary workmen conversant with the business would be perfectly able to execute'.[64] If, however, the person employed has been selected with reference to their individual skill, competence, or other personal qualification, that person is not entitled to sub-contract the performance of the contract to another. Thus it has been held that personal care and skill is an ingredient in contracts by a warehouseman for the storage of furniture,[65] by a publishing firm for the publication of a book,[66] and by an architect in the design of a building.[67] Such contracts cannot be vicariously performed without the consent of the promisee. Contracts of service are normally personal to the contracting parties.[68] Furthermore, payment of a debt which is made by a person other than the debtor or the debtor's agent will not be effective to discharge the debt.[69]

Even where the contract may not, in principle, be vicariously performed, if the promisee in fact agrees to it being performed by a non-party and accepts such performance, the contract will be discharged.[70]

[60] *Re Charge Card Services Ltd* [1989] Ch 497; *Customs & Excise Commissioners v Diners Club Ltd* [1989] 1 WLR 1196.

[61] See below, p 693, for the distinction between vicarious performance and assignment.

[62] eg *Société Commerciale de Réassurance v ERAS International Ltd* [1992] 1 Lloyd's Rep 570, 596.

[63] *British Waggon Co v Lea & Co* (1880) 5 QBD 149.

[64] *Ibid*, 153 (Cockburn CJ).

[65] *Edwards v Newland & Co* [1950] 2 KB 534.

[66] *Griffith v Tower Publishing Co Ltd* [1897] 1 Ch 21.

[67] *Moresk Cleaners Ltd v Hicks* [1966] 2 Lloyd's Rep 338.

[68] *Nokes v Doncaster Amalgamated Collieries Ltd* [1940] AC 1014 (rights). But note the Transfer of Undertakings (Protection of Employment) Regulations 2006 (SI 2006 No 246), reg 4(1), below, p 692.

[69] See *Belshaw v Bush* (1851) 11 CB 191; *Walter v James* (1871) LR 6 Ex 124; *Owen v Tate* [1976] 1 QB 402. See generally Beatson and Birks (1976) 91 LQR 188; Beatson, *The Use and Abuse of Unjust Enrichment* (1991) ch 7; Friedmann (1983) 99 LQR 534.

[70] *Belshaw v Bush* (1851) 11 CB 191; *Hirachand Punamchand v Temple* [1911] 2 KB 483, above, p 119.

7. ALTERNATIVE MODES OF PERFORMANCE

A contract can provide for alternative modes of performance in one of two ways.[71] First, it may provide for performance in a particular way, for instance a shipper's obligation to load a cargo of wheat, but give that party the option to perform in an alternative way, for instance, to change to a cargo of barley. Secondly, it may permit one party to choose[72] between alternative modes of performance without specifying one as the primary mode, for instance, a shipper's obligation to load a full cargo in the month of September or October.

(a) CONTRACT OPTION

In the first situation, once the option is exercised, the contractual obligation is varied; in the example above, the contract ceases to be one to load wheat and becomes one to load barley. The option must be exercised within a reasonable time and this must be communicated to the other party;[73] if it is not exercised it is lost. But, in considering whether to exercise the option, the promisee is not generally bound to consider the interests of the other party.[74] For example, if the primary mode of performance becomes impossible, the option-holder is not obliged to exercise it in order to avoid the contract being frustrated.[75] But, in the case of a non-consumer contract, an attempt to rely on the exercise of such an option to render a contractual performance substantially different from that which was reasonably expected may be ineffective against a party dealing on the other's written standard terms of business,[76] and in a consumer contract such an option may be an unfair term and therefore not binding on the consumer.[77]

(b) PERFORMANCE OPTION

In the second situation there is a truly alternative obligation. The promisor is obliged to perform in any of the authorized modes. If, prior to a choice being made, one mode ceases to be available, that simply narrows the scope of contractually authorized performance.[78] So, in the example given above, if access to the loading port is impossible

[71] See generally Peel, *Frustration and Force Majeure* (4th edn, 2021) ch 10.

[72] If the contract does not specify which party has the option, it will be the one who has to do the first act: *Reed v Kilburn Co-operative Society* (1875) LR 10 QBD 264.

[73] *Reardon Smith Line Ltd v Ministry of Agriculture, Fisheries & Food* [1963] AC 691, 731.

[74] *Ibid*, 719–20, 730. See also *Thompson v ASDA-MFI Group Plc* [1988] Ch 241, 251, 266–7 (no general principle that a party cannot take advantage of own acts to avoid obligations under the contract).

[75] On frustration, see below, Chapter 14.

[76] Unfair Contract Terms Act 1977, s 3(2)(b). See generally above, p 219.

[77] Consumer Rights Act 2015, ss 62, 63 and Sched 2, Part 1, paras 2, 3, 11, 13, 15. See generally above, pp 227–8.

[78] *Reardon Smith Line Ltd v Ministry of Agriculture, Fisheries & Food* [1963] AC 691, 717, 720, 730; *Atlantic Lines & Navigation Co Ltd v Didymi Corp, The Didymi* [1984] 1 Lloyd's Rep 583, 587; *Libyan Arab Foreign Bank v Bankers Trust Co* [1989] QB 728, 766; *J Lauritzen AS v Wijsmuller BV, The Super Servant Two* [1990] 1 Lloyd's Rep 1, 9.

due to strikes or bad weather during September, that does not affect the obligation to ship a full cargo; the shipper remains liable to load a full cargo in October, even if the shipper had planned to do so in September. But once a party chooses the alternative to be performed, that choice binds.[79]

8. RIGHT OF PARTY IN BREACH TO CURE BAD OR INCOMPLETE PERFORMANCE

We have seen that English law treats a serious misperformance such as incomplete delivery, or breach of a condition such as delivery of goods that are not of satisfactory quality, as the standard examples of breach entitling the innocent party to treat the contract as discharged.[80] Unlike the position in some other systems, the innocent party is not required to serve notice requiring the other party to perform in a stated time[81] and there is only a limited right to cure defective performance.[82] If, however, a bad or incomplete performance is tendered before the time of performance has arrived, the promisor is not generally prevented from making another tender of performance within time that does comply. The promisee must accept this fresh tender unless the first amounted to a repudiation which the promisee had already acted upon and terminated the contract.[83] One situation in which the defective performance will be treated as a repudiation is where it has destroyed the confidence of the promisee.[84]

9. TENDER

Tender is attempted performance; and the word is applied to attempted performance of two kinds, dissimilar in their results: performance of a promise to do something, and of a promise to pay money. In each case the performance may be prevented by the act of the party for whose benefit it is to take place.

[79] *Schneider v Foster* (1857) 2 H & N 4; *Gath v Lees* (1865) 3 H & C 558. Authority (*Brown v Royal Insurance Co* (1859) 1 E & E 853) suggesting the party remains bound even where it is no longer possible to perform the contract in that way is doubtful since it predates the development of the doctrine of frustration, on which see below, Chapter 14.

[80] Above, pp 150–1, 156–7 (conditions and innominate terms). See further Chapter 15.

[81] Treitel, *Remedies for Breach of Contract* (1988) 327–34 (*Nachfrist* in German law, *délai de grâce* in French law).

[82] *Ibid*, 371–4; CISG art 48; ALI *Restatement, Contracts (2d)* para 237 (serious breach initially only justifies suspension of performance by innocent party).

[83] *Borrowman, Phillips & Co v Free & Hollins* (1878) 4 QBD 500; *Motor Oil Hellas (Corinth) Refineries SA v Shipping Corporation of India, The Kanchenjunga* [1990] 1 Lloyd's Rep 391, 399.

[84] On repudiation, see further Chapter 15.

(a) TENDER OF ACTS

Where one party is obliged by the contract to perform a promise to do something, but the other party refuses to accept the performance when tendered,[85] the promisor is discharged from performing that obligation and may sue for damages. In addition, if the promisee commences an action against the promisor for failure to perform the obligation, the promisor is entitled to set up the refusal to accept the tender as a defence.[86] The promisor will not, however, be treated as having performed the obligation. If the refusal to accept the tender amounts to a repudiation of the contract the promisor can elect to terminate the contract and sue for damages.[87] Although such a refusal does not always have this effect,[88] if it is absolute and unqualified it entitles the promisor to elect to be discharged. For example, section 37 of the Sale of Goods Act 1979 provides that when the seller is ready and willing to deliver the goods and requests the buyer to take delivery, the buyer must do so within a reasonable time or become liable for any loss occasioned to the seller by the buyer's neglect. But this does not affect the rights of the seller where the non-acceptance amounts to a repudiation of the contract.

(b) TENDER OF PAYMENT

Where, however, the performance due consists of the payment of a sum of money, a tender by the debtor, though refused by the creditor, does not discharge the debtor from the obligation to pay the debt. The debtor is bound in the first instance 'to find out the creditor and pay him the debt when due';[89] if the creditor will not take payment when tendered, the debtor must nevertheless continue to be ready and willing to pay the debt. Then, the debtor, if sued, can plead that a tender had been made, but must pay the money into Court.[90] If the debtor proves this plea, the creditor gets nothing but the money originally tendered, that is, no interest or damages, while the debtor gets judgment for the costs of the action, and so is placed in as good a position as at the time of the tender. Tender of payment, to be a valid performance to this extent, must observe exactly any special terms in the contract as to time, place, and mode of payment. The nineteenth-century authorities further prescribed extremely strict requirements for a valid tender: it must be unconditional and it must be in legal currency;[91] there must be an offer of money produced and accessible to the creditor, not necessarily of the exact sum, but of such a sum as will allow the creditor to take exactly what is due without

[85] Tender must be in strict accordance with the terms of the contract. In the absence of express terms a tender of goods must be made at a reasonable hour: Sale of Goods Act 1979, s 29(5).

[86] *Startup v Macdonald* (1843) 6 M & G 593.

[87] *Ibid.*

[88] See, eg, Sale of Goods Act 1979, s 31(2) (non-consumer sales contracts); Consumer Rights Act 2015, s 26(3), (4) (consumer goods contracts); above, p 161.

[89] *Walton v Mascall* (1844) 13 M & W 452, 458 (Parke B).

[90] CPR r 37.2.

[91] The Currency and Bank Notes Act 1954, the Coinage Act 1971, and the Currency Act 1983 define legal tender.

being called upon to give change;[92] and the cash must be produced to the creditor in person. 'Great importance', it was said,[93] 'was attached to the production of money, as the sight of it might tempt the creditor to yield'. But these requirements may be dispensed with expressly or impliedly by the creditor,[94] and the requirement of payment in cash must be interpreted against the background of modern commercial practice. In commercial transactions, it would appear that any commercially recognized method of transferring funds, the result of which is to give the transferee the immediate use of the funds transferred, will nowadays suffice.[95]

(c) EARLY TENDER

A promisee need not, moreover, accept an early tender, but, as we have seen, if a bad tender is made before the time of performance has arrived, it does not generally prevent the promisor making another tender within time that does comply with the contract.[96]

10. PARTIAL PERFORMANCE

(a) ENTIRE AND DIVISIBLE OBLIGATIONS

Since the performance of a contractual obligation must be precise and exact, where one party's performance is made conditional on complete and entire performance by the other party,[97] at common law[98] the general rule is that the other can recover nothing for incomplete performance. It is immaterial how the failure to effect complete performance comes about. It may be due to a deliberate abandonment of the contract, to a negligent act or omission, or to a simple misfortune occurring without any fault. In *Cutter v Powell*,[99] for example:

A seaman was engaged to act as second mate on a voyage from Jamaica to Liverpool. He was to be paid 30 guineas, almost four times the going rate, in a single payment upon completion of the voyage. Nineteen days out from Liverpool, when the voyage was nearly completed, he died. His widow sued to recover a proportion of the agreed sum.

[92] *Betterbee v Davis* (1811) 3 Camp 70.
[93] *Finch v Brook* (1834) 1 Bing NC 253, 257 (Vaughan J).
[94] *Farquharson v Pearl Assurance Co Ltd* [1937] 3 All ER 124.
[95] *Tenax Steamship Co Ltd v The Brimnes (Owners)* [1975] 1 QB 929, 963; *Mardorf Peach & Co Ltd v Attica Sea Carriers Corp of Liberia* [1977] AC 850, 880, 885, 889; see above, p 452; *Libyan Arab Foreign Bank Co v Bankers Trust Co* [1989] 1 QB 728, 749–50; *K v A* [2019] EWHC 1118 (Comm) at [26].
[96] Above, p 456.
[97] See Williams (1941) 57 LQR 373; Treitel (1967) 30 MLR 139, 141 ff; Law Com No 121, *Pecuniary Restitution on Breach of Contract* (1983). Mr Brian Davenport QC dissented and the government rejected the report: 19th Annual Report (1983–84) Law Com No 140, para 2.11.
[98] For statutory exceptions, see Apportionment Act 1870, s 2 (rents, annuities, dividends, and other periodic payments in the nature of income prima facie considered as accruing from day to day); Law Reform (Frustrated Contracts) Act 1943, below, p 507.
[99] (1795) 6 Term R 320; Stoljar (1956) 34 Can Bar Rev 288. But the effect of this decision has been alleviated by statute: see the Law Reform (Frustrated Contracts) Act 1943, below, p 507, and what is now the Merchant Shipping Act 1995, s 38.

Her action failed. The seaman's obligation was construed as an entire contract or, more accurately, an entire obligation, that is to say, if the voyage was completed he was to receive the stipulated sum, but, if it was not, he was to receive nothing. As Sir George Jessel MR said: 'if a shoemaker agrees to make a pair of shoes, he cannot offer you one shoe, and ask you to pay one half the price'.[100]

It is inaccurate to refer to 'entire contracts'[101] because it is very unlikely that complete performance of each and every obligation in a contract by one party is a condition precedent to the liability of the other. The contract may, for example, be a complex one, composed of a number of undertakings differing in character or importance; or it may be a promise to do a number of successive acts; or to do a single act which can be partly or defectively performed.[102] Very often a contract may be entire as to one aspect but 'divisible' or 'severable' (in the sense that the right to payment accrues incrementally as the performance is rendered) as to another. For example, in *Cutter v Powell*, although the seaman's obligation to complete the voyage was entire, his obligation to exercise reasonable care in the performance of his duty was unlikely to be entire, so that, had he completed the voyage, but had performed his duty badly, it seems he would have been able to recover his wages, subject to a claim against him for poor work.[103] Again, in contracts for the carriage of goods by sea, whereas the obligation to deliver the cargo to the stipulated port is entire, so that no freight at all is payable if delivery is made at an intermediate port,[104] the obligations with respect to the quantity or condition of the cargo are not, so that, if half the cargo is delivered, half the freight is payable,[105] and if all the cargo arrives damaged (but still of the same commercial description), freight will be payable subject to a counterclaim against the carrier for damages.[106]

Because the consequences can be draconian, Courts are reluctant to construe an obligation as 'entire'.[107] But where the payment for the performance was to be a lump sum to be paid after completion they have generally done so, so that the promisee cannot recover anything until the work is completely executed.[108] Thus, apart from *Cutter v Powell*, this construction has been put on obligations by a builder to build two houses and stables for a client,[109] and by a plumber to supply and install a combined central heating and hot water system in a private house.[110]

[100] *Re Hall & Barker* (1878) 9 Ch D 538, 545.

[101] An 'entire agreement' clause within a written contract serves a different purpose: see above, p 149.

[102] See the discussion in *Baltic Shipping Co v Dillon* (1993) 176 CLR 344, 350, 384 (High Court of Australia).

[103] Law Com No 121, above, n 97, para 2.12, citing Somervell LJ in *Hoenig v Isaacs* [1952] 2 All ER 176, 178.

[104] *St Enoch Shipping Co Ltd v Phosphate Mining Co* [1916] 2 KB 624; *Metcalfe v Britannia Iron Works Co* (1877) 2 QBD 423.

[105] *Ritchie v Atkinson* (1808) 10 East 295, 530. But where there is a stipulation for lump freight or freight to be computed on loading, the carrier will be entitled to full freight: *Aries Tanker Corp v Total Transport Ltd, The Aries* [1977] 1 WLR 185; *Colonial Bank v European Grain & Shipping Ltd, The Dominique* [1989] AC 1056. See further *Scrutton on Charterparties* (25th edn, 2024) ch 16.

[106] *Dakin v Oxley* (1864) 15 CB(NS) 646, 667. See further *Scrutton on Charterparties*, above, n 105.

[107] *Button v Thompson* (1869) LR 4 CP 330, 342.

[108] *Appleby v Myers* (1867) LR 2 CP 651, 660–1; *The Madras* [1898] P 90; and *Sumpter v Hedges* [1898] 1 QB 190, below, p 463, appear to adopt this as a general rule. For criticism, see below.

[109] *Sumpter v Hedges* [1898] 1 QB 190.

[110] *Bolton v Mahadeva* [1972] 1 WLR 1009.

(i) Rationale of rule

The general rule has been justified in a number of ways.[111] First, the recipient of the performance has not contracted to buy part of the performance for a proportionate part of the price and should not be compelled to pay for performance different from that agreed and, in some cases, insisted upon.[112] Where, like the seaman in *Cutter v Powell*, the performer is to be paid significantly more than the going rate for the job, it can also be said that he has accepted the risk of incomplete or defective performance.[113] Secondly, the rule holds people to their contracts and gives them a strong incentive to complete.[114] It is particularly important where there is inequality of bargaining power or scope for opportunistic behaviour, as there often is in contracts for small building works on private houses. It is all too common for a builder not to complete one job before moving on to the next, and the rule enables the householder to withhold all payment unless the job is finished.[115] Thirdly, the losses the innocent party suffers may be ones for which the law finds it difficult to compensate.[116]

(ii) Critique of rule

The principle precluding recovery, however, if rigorously applied, could lead to great injustice. It is hard to contend, for example, that even the most trivial defect of workmanship in the decoration of a flat,[117] or some momentary slip or inefficiency on the part of an employee,[118] should entitle the 'injured' party to refuse all payment save where the injured party has made it absolutely clear that the trivial defect or breach will have this effect.[119] It should not, accordingly, be inferred, as it has been,[120] that such penal consequences follow from the mere postponement of payment of a lump sum by one party until after the other party has completely performed.[121] Such postponement may be prompted by a number of other reasons, including easing the 'cash-flow' of the party who will have to pay, and protecting that party from the risk that the other may become insolvent. Moreover, the application of the principle would often result

[111] See generally, Waddams, in Reiter and Swan (eds), *Studies in Contract Law* (1980) 163 ff; Law Com No 121, above, n 97, paras 2.24–2.26.

[112] *Wiluszynski v Tower Hamlets LBC* [1989] ICR 493; *Miles v Wakefield MBC* [1987] AC 539, below, p 463, n 132; *British Telecommunications plc v Ticehurst* [1992] ICR 383.

[113] See also *Barton v Morris* [2023] UKSC 3, [2023] AC 684 at [35] (Lady Rose); cf Lord Leggatt at [180].

[114] *Munro v Butt* (1858) 8 E & B 738, 754; Law Com No 121, above, n 97, para 2.25.

[115] Law Com No 121, above, n 97, 37 (Mr BJ Davenport QC's dissent). A builder may protect itself by requiring payments before the completion of performance, which (below, pp 607, 611) will generally be irrecoverable. In contracts for the sale of goods, consumers have wider power of rejection than non-consumers: Sale of Goods Act 1979, ss 15A(1), 30(2A), below, n 130.

[116] eg non-pecuniary loss (*Vigers v Cook* [1919] 2 KB 475; and see below, pp 549–51) or loss to a third party (below, pp 631, 633).

[117] *Hoenig v Isaacs* [1952] 2 All ER 176 (contract price £750, defects remedied for £55).

[118] *Ibid*, 178.

[119] *Miles v Wakefield MBC* [1987] AC 539, 551, 561, 568; *Wiluszynski v Tower Hamlets LBC* [1989] ICR 493, 500, 503.

[120] Above, n 108.

[121] Law Com No 121, above, n 97, paras 2.11, 2.27, and 2.67; Williams (1941) 57 LQR 373, 389 ff.

in the unjust enrichment of the injured party if that party could retain the benefit of the incomplete performance without having to pay for it. A general acceptance of the risk of incomplete performance by the part performer may not extend to a situation where the other party is incontrovertibly benefited, and a restitutionary remedy does not necessarily constitute a redistribution of risks allocated by the contract.[122]

The unpalatable consequences that can follow have led Courts to seek to avoid construing an obligation as entire. Broadly speaking this can properly be done in two situations; where the injured party has *accepted* the partial performance, and, although this is not so clearly established, where the part performer can establish that the services rendered or the work done has *incontrovertibly benefited* the other party so as to give rise to a claim for restitution of the unjust enrichment. The underdevelopment until recently of the law of restitution for unjust enrichment, and the tendency to construe an obligation as 'entire' simply because the contract provides for a lump sum has, however, also led to authority favouring a remedy in a third situation; where the part performer has *substantially performed* the 'entire' obligation.

(b) DOCTRINE OF 'SUBSTANTIAL PERFORMANCE'

Where the contract is *substantially* performed, there is authority that the injured party is not discharged from the obligation to pay, but is protected by a counterclaim or set-off for any loss which may have been sustained by reason of the incomplete or defective performance.[123] A Court will hold a contract to have been substantially performed if the actual performance falls not far short of the required performance, and if the cost of remedying the defects is not too great in comparison with the contract price.[124] In *H Dakin & Co Ltd v Lee*:[125]

D were builders who had contracted to execute certain repairs to L's premises for £1,500. They carried out a substantial part of the contract, but failed to perform it exactly in three unimportant respects (which could have been rectified at a cost of £80). The official referee appointed by the parties held that D were consequently not entitled to recover any part of the contract price.

[122] Although it *might* do so; see Beatson, *The Use and Abuse of Unjust Enrichment* (1991) ch 4, and *Wiluszynski v Tower Hamlets LBC* [1989] ICR 493, below, p 463. Cf McFarlane and Stevens (2002) 118 LQR 569, supporting the decision in *Sumpter v Hedges* [1898] 1 QB 673, below, p 463, on the basis that a party in breach should have no claim for value of services rendered or goods supplied unless he has an accrued *contractual* right to payment.

[123] *Boone v Eyre* (1779) 1 H Bl 273; *Broom v Davis* (1794) 7 East 480n; *Bolton v Mahadeva* [1972] 1 WLR 1009, 1015; *Sim v Rotherham Metropolitan Borough Council* [1987] Ch 216, 253; *Wiluszynski v Tower Hamlets LBC* [1989] ICR 493, 499; *Williams v Roffey Bros & Nicholls (Contractors) Ltd* [1991] 1 QB 1, 8–10, 17.

[124] Compare *Hoenig v Isaacs* [1952] 2 All ER 176 (cost of remedying defects was 7.3 per cent of contract price) and *Bolton v Mahadeva* [1972] 1 WLR 1009 (no substantial performance where cost of remedying defects was 31 per cent of contract price).

[125] [1916] 1 KB 566, 579. Note Greer LJ's criticism in *Eshelby v Federated European Bank Ltd* [1932] 1 KB 423, 431 and cf *Vigers v Cook* [1919] 2 KB 475; *Bolton v Mahadeva* [1972] 1 WLR 1009.

On appeal, it was held that this finding was erroneous. The contract had been substantially, if not precisely, performed. Pickford LJ stated that the fact that the work was done badly did not mean that it had not been performed at all.[126] D was accordingly entitled to recover the price less a reduction for the breach. In the USA a more flexible approach has been taken whereby the Court may look at the quality of performance so that, even if the cost of compliance is great, there may still be substantial performance if the work that is done is of the same quality as that contracted for. In *Jacob & Youngs Inc v Kent*[127] the New York Court of Appeals held that a builder who failed to use galvanized piping of 'Reading manufacture' for the plumbing in a building had substantially performed the contract; the pipes in fact used were of the same quality as those specified and the defect could only be remedied by demolishing a substantial part of the building. There are indications that this approach may also be taken in English law.[128]

Since the basis of the rules governing entire obligations is that the parties have made *complete* and *precise* performance by one party a condition to entitlement to performance by the other, it is submitted that it is logically difficult to justify applying a principle of substantial performance to such obligations. To do so is to set aside the contractual allocation of risks. But the cases which have construed an obligation as entire simply because the contract provided for a lump sum to be paid after the completion of performance provide some pragmatic justification, since this fact alone may not truly indicate that the risks of any trivial incompleteness in performance are to lie with the part performer. On principle, however, the correct approach is greater caution in the categorization of an obligation as entire, and development of the emerging restitutionary principles to which we now turn.

(c) ACCEPTANCE OF PARTIAL PERFORMANCE BY INNOCENT PARTY

A party who renders incomplete performance of an entire contract may nevertheless claim remuneration where the other party has freely accepted such partial performance or otherwise waived the need for complete performance. So, if the customer of Sir George Jessel's shoemaker had accepted one shoe he would have been obliged to pay for the shoe he accepted.[129] In the case of the sale of goods, where the seller delivers to the buyer a quantity of goods less than he contracted to sell, the buyer may reject them, but if the buyer accepts the goods so delivered he must pay for them at the contract rate.[130]

[126] This suggests that on a true analysis the obligation concerning the *quality* of the work may not have been entire. See Williams (1941) 57 LQR 373, 386–7, and see above, p 459.

[127] 129 NE 889 (1921).

[128] In *Ruxley Electronics Ltd v Forsyth* [1996] 1 AC 344 (below, p 553, but not involving an entire obligation), *Jacob & Youngs Inc v Kent*, was approved at 363 in a slightly different context.

[129] Above, p 459. See also *Baltic Shipping Co v Dillon* (1993) 176 CLR 344, 378.

[130] Sale of Goods Act 1979, s 30(1) (non-consumer sale of goods contracts); Consumer Rights Act 2015, s 25(1) (consumer goods contracts). But a non-consumer may not reject where the shortfall, or the breach of the conditions implied by ss 13–15 of the 1979 Act, is so slight that it would be unreasonable for him to do so: 1979 Act, ss 30(2A), and 15A, inserted by the Sale and Supply of Goods Act 1994.

In most cases, such a claim will arise upon a quantum meruit, that is to say, for a reasonable sum in respect of the services rendered or the work done by the partial performance. But it will do so only if the party not in default has the option whether to accept or to refuse the partial performance. Thus in *Sumpter v Hedges*:[131]

S agreed to erect two houses and stables on H's land for £565. He failed to complete the contract. H thereupon completed the buildings himself, using the materials left on the site by S. S brought an action to recover the value of the work done before he abandoned the contract, and also claimed in respect of the building materials used.

It was held that S was entitled to recover the value of the materials left which H used, for H had the choice whether or not to use these to complete the building. But S could not recover for the work he had done, for H had no option but to accept the partly erected building which was on his land. Similarly, an employer who told employees working 'to rule' and not carrying out part of their contractual services not to come to work at all unless they were prepared to work normally, was not held to have 'accepted' the partial performance simply because it did not send them home; 'a person is not treated by the law as having chosen to accept that which is forced down his throat despite his objections'.[132]

Originally the basis of this liability was said to be that acceptance of partial performance implies a fresh agreement between the parties to pay for the work already done or goods supplied[133] but the implication of such a contract can be fictional, and, in such cases, it is better to regard the obligation to pay as restitutionary arising from the operation of the principle of unjust enrichment.[134]

(d) INCONTROVERTIBLE BENEFIT

The failure of the claim in respect of the partially erected building in *Sumpter v Hedges* shows that the mere fact that a person appears to have benefited from the part performance of an entire obligation, does not suffice to ground a claim for restitution.[135] This is because in the law of unjust enrichment, objective benefits may be 'subjectively devalued' by the defendant.[136] But, where it can be shown that the recipient of the

[131] [1898] 1 QB 673. See also *Munro v Butt* (1858) 8 E & B 738; *Forman & Co Proprietary Ltd v Ship 'Liddesdale'* [1900] AC 190; McFarlane and Stevens (2002) 118 LQR 569.

[132] *Wiluszynski v Tower Hamlets LBC* [1989] ICR 493, 504 (Nicholls LJ), but see Mead (1990) 106 LQR 192. In *Miles v Wakefield MBC* [1987] AC 539, 553, 561, Lord Brightman and Lord Templeman suggested that, if the employer has not made it clear that reduced or inefficient work will not be accepted, the employee will be entitled to a reasonable sum for that reduced work. But, as the contract had not been discharged, there are formidable difficulties with any restitutionary claim: below, p 614. Cf Lord Bridge's doubts, *ibid*, 552. Lord Brandon and Lord Oliver reserved their opinions.

[133] *Sumpter v Hedges* [1898] 1 QB 673; *Steele v Tardiani* (1946) 72 CLR 386, 394, 402 (High Court of Australia).

[134] *Baltic Shipping Co v Dillon* (1993) 176 CLR 344, 374, 385 (High Court of Australia). For the recognition of unjust enrichment in England, see *Lipkin Gorman v Karpnale* [1991] AC 548, above, p 24.

[135] See also *Bolton v Mahadeva*.

[136] *Benedetti v Sawiris* [2013] UKSC 50, [2014] AC 938; Birks, *Unjust Enrichment* (2nd edn, 2005) ch 3; Burrows, *The Law of Restitution* (3rd edn, 2011) ch 3.

part performance has gained a readily realizable financial benefit or has been saved expense which must have been incurred, there is some support for the view that the part performer would be entitled to restitution[137] save where the parties have made it clear that the risk of non-completion is to be borne by the part performer even where there is such a benefit.[138]

FURTHER READING

McFarlane and Stevens, 'In Defence of *Sumpter v Hedges*' (2002) 118 LQR 569

Tettenborn, '"I'll Perform If and When You Do": Non-Performance and the Suspension of Contractual Duties' in Barker, Fairweather, and Grantham (eds), *Private Law in the 21st Century* (Oxford: Hart Publishing, 2017) ch 16

[137] *Hain SS Co Ltd v Tate & Lyle Ltd* (1936) 41 Com Cas 350, 358 (Lord Atkin), 367–8 (Lord Wright MR), and 373 (Lord Maugham); *Procter & Gamble Philippine Manufacturing Corp v Peter Cremer GmbH & Co, The Manila* [1988] 3 All ER 843, 855; *Miles v Wakefield MBC* [1987] AC 539, 553, 561. See also *Britton v Turner* 6 NH 481 (1834) (New Hampshire). Cf Beatson (1981) 98 LQR 389, 411, 413.

[138] Law Com No 121, above, n 97, paras 2.66–2.69, 2.73, and see above, n 132.

13

DISCHARGE BY AGREEMENT

1. INTRODUCTION

Contract rests on the agreement of the parties: as it is their agreement which binds them, so by their agreement they may be discharged. This mode of discharge may occur by release under seal; by accord and satisfaction; by rescission or variation; or by the operation of some provision contained in the contract itself.

Two difficulties, however, render the topic of discharge by agreement one of considerable artificiality and refinement.

(a) CONSIDERATION APPLIES TO DISCHARGE

The first is that the doctrine of consideration applies to the discharge as well as to the formation of a contract.[1] As a result, a distinction has to be drawn between those situations where the contract is still *executory* on both sides, and those where the contract has been *executed* on one side. In the case of an executory contract, the consideration for the discharge by agreement is found in the relinquishment by each promisee of its right to performance. Where, however, the contract has been wholly executed by one party, leaving the other party still to perform its side of the obligation, as, for example, where A has sold and delivered goods to B, but B has not yet paid for them, any release of B would be purely gratuitous since A would not receive any benefit, nor would B suffer any detriment, by this action. This distinction was emphasized by Parke B in *Foster v Dawber*:[2]

> It is competent for both parties to an executory contract, by mutual agreement, without any satisfaction, to discharge the obligation of that contract. But an executed contract cannot be discharged except by release under seal,[3] or by performance of the obligation, as by payment, where the obligation is to be performed by payment.

The agreement to discharge must therefore be by deed, or be supported by some other consideration ('accord and satisfaction') on the part of the person seeking to be released.

[1] See above, p 115. [2] (1851) 6 Exch 839, 851. [3] ie by deed: see above, p 80.

(b) CONTRACTS EVIDENCED BY WRITING

The second difficulty is that certain contracts are required by law to be in writing, or to be evidenced by writing,[4] and any subsequent variation of such a contract must also be in writing, or proved by writing.[5] But writing is not required for the rescission (or discharge) by agreement of such a contract,[6] nor for the waiver of a term contained in it.[7] The distinction between rescission, variation, and waiver is, as we shall see, a fine one, and there is much artificiality in the lines to be drawn between almost identical cases. This difficulty has lessened with the reduction in the types of contract required to be in writing.[8] But writing is still required for contracts for the sale or other disposition of land and contracts of guarantee, so the difficulties have not entirely disappeared.

2. FORMS OF DISCHARGE BY AGREEMENT

(a) RELEASE

The right to performance of a contract can be abandoned by release contained in a deed;[9] it is then immaterial that the contract has been executed on one side, for the deed dispenses with the need for consideration. A release not contained in a deed requires consideration: the agreement is then discharged by accord and satisfaction. A release is construed in the same way as any other contract. It has been held that a general release could not be interpreted as covering rights which the parties had no idea existed.[10]

An agreement not to sue in perpetuity amounts to a release[11] but, at common law, an agreement not to sue for a limited period merely gave rise to a cross-action for damages.[12] Equity, however, would restrain the promisor from suing within that time,[13] and today the equitable rule prevails[14] so that the agreement acts as a bar to the original action.

[4] See above, Chapter 3.

[5] eg *McCausland v Duncan Lawrie Ltd* [1997] 1 WLR 38 (variation of material term in a contract for sale or other disposition of an interest in land must comply with Law of Property (Miscellaneous Provisions) Act 1989, s 2).

[6] *Morris v Baron & Co* [1918] AC 1, below, p 469; *McCausland v Duncan Lawrie Ltd* [1997] 1 WLR 38, 48; *Kilcarne Holdings Ltd v Targetfollow (Birmingham) Ltd* [2004] EWHC 2547 (Ch), [2005] 2 P & CR 8 at [208].

[7] *Courtney v Corp Ltd* [2006] EWCA Civ 518 at [14].

[8] See above, Chapter 3.

[9] For the requirements of a deed, see above, pp 80–1.

[10] *BCCI SA v Ali* [2001] UKHL 8, [2002] 1 AC 251 (Lord Hoffmann dissenting). It did not release rights to stigma damages (below, p 551) which the law did not recognize at the time of the release.

[11] *Hodges v Smith* (1599) Cro Eliz 623. See, however, *Cutler v McPhail* [1962] 2 QB 292, 298.

[12] *Ford v Beech* (1848) 11 QB 852.

[13] *Beech v Ford* (1848) 7 Hare 208.

[14] Senior Courts Act 1981, s 49.

(b) ACCORD AND SATISFACTION

Discharge of a contract in return for a consideration which consists in some satisfaction other than the performance of the original obligation is termed 'accord and satisfaction':

Accord and satisfaction is the purchase of a release from an obligation whether arising under contract or tort by means of any valuable consideration, not being the actual performance of the obligation itself. The accord is the agreement by which the obligation is discharged. The satisfaction is the consideration which makes the agreement operative.[15]

It is effective to discharge any contract, whether executory or executed, and even if the original contract was contained in a deed.[16]

(i) Executory satisfaction

Formerly, a contractual obligation, or cause of action arising from the breach of a contract, was not discharged so long as the satisfaction remained executory, that is, so long as the agreement to furnish new consideration had not been carried out.[17] As it was said in an old case:[18] 'Accord executed is satisfaction; accord executory is only substituting one cause of action in the room of another, which might go on to any extent.' But now the question is one of the construction of the agreement; the promise only, as distinct from the actual performance of it, may be a good satisfaction and discharge the original obligation, if it clearly appears that the parties so intended.[19] The original obligation or claim is then discharged from the date the promise is accepted. If the promisor fails to perform its promise, the promisee's only remedy is to sue for breach of the promise, and it cannot return to the original obligation or claim.[20]

Under the rule in *Pinnel's Case*,[21] however, the payment of a smaller sum in satisfaction of a larger is not a good discharge of a debt. So if B owes A £50 for goods sold and delivered, and A agrees to excuse him £45 out of this amount, the debt is not discharged by the payment of £5. But the acceptance by A of some satisfaction different in kind, or of a fixed sum instead of an uncertain sum, or of a lesser sum at an earlier date or in a different place than that required by the contract, is sufficient. Compromises of a disputed claim,[22] compositions with creditors,[23] and payments by a third party,[24] also afford exceptions to this rule.

[15] *British Russian Gazette and Trade Outlook Ltd v Associated Newspapers Ltd* [1933] 2 KB 616, 643–4 (Scrutton LJ).

[16] *Steeds v Steeds* (1889) 22 QBD 537.

[17] *Peytoe's Case* (1612) 9 Co Rep 79b.

[18] *Lynn v Bruce* (1794) 2 H Bl 317, 319 (Eyre LCJ).

[19] *Good v Cheesman* (1831) 2 B & Ad 328; *Morris v Baron & Co* [1918] AC 1, 35; *British Russian Gazette and Trade Outlook Ltd v Associated Newspapers Ltd* [1933] 2 KB 616, 650, 654–5; *Jameson v Central Electricity Generating Board* [1998] QB 323, 335.

[20] *British Russian Gazette and Trade Outlook Ltd v Associated Newspapers Ltd* [1933] 2 KB 616, 644, 654; *Green v Rozen* [1955] 1 WLR 741.

[21] (1602) 5 Co Rep 117a; above, p 115; *Ferguson v Davies* [1997] 1 All ER 315.

[22] Above, p 107, and see *Kitchen Design & Advance Ltd v Lea Valley Water Co* [1989] 2 Lloyd's Rep 221.

[23] Above, p 119.

[24] Above, p 119.

(ii) Promissory estoppel

Accord without satisfaction is not contractually binding, and it is still not certain whether the principle of promissory estoppel considered above in Chapter 4 could be successfully relied upon to obviate the necessity for consideration where the accord involves the permanent abandonment by one party of the right to performance by the other. It has been said that promissory estoppel serves only to suspend, and not totally to extinguish, existing rights,[25] although this is probably not a necessary limitation on the doctrine. As we have seen, there is in particular an unresolved question about whether a debt can be extinguished through the operation of promissory estoppel.[26]

(iii) Bills of exchange

One important exception does, however, exist. It was a rule of the law merchant, imported into the common law, that no satisfaction was required for the discharge of a bill of exchange or promissory note. Section 62 of the Bills of Exchange Act 1882 gives statutory force to this rule, but subject to the provision that the discharge must be in writing, or the bill delivered up to the acceptor.

(c) RESCISSION

(i) By agreement

A contract which is executory on both sides may be discharged by agreement between the parties that it shall no longer bind them. This is commonly referred to as a rescission of the contract, although whether it rescinds the obligations under the contract *ab initio* or merely discharges the parties from their outstanding obligations will depend on the parties' agreement. Such an agreement is formed of mutual promises, and the consideration for each promise of each party is the abandonment by the other of its rights under the contract.

(ii) Abandonment

The Court can infer from a long period of delay or inactivity that the parties have agreed to abandon their contract. It must be shown that one party conducted itself in such a way that the other party reasonably assumed that it was agreed that the contract was abandoned.[27] Courts have come close to inferring an offer to abandon a contract from mere silence, although some overt act is almost always likely to be required.[28] In the case of arbitration, legislation now gives arbitrators the power to dismiss a claim where there has been inordinate and inexcusable delay on the part of the claimant in pursuing its claim, irrespective of whether the arbitration contract has been abandoned.[29]

[25] Above, p 127. [26] Above, p 128.

[27] *Paal Wilson & Co A/S v Partenreederei Hannah Blumenthal, The Hannah Blumenthal* [1983] 1 AC 854, 865, 885, 914, 916, 924.

[28] On landlord and tenant, see *Collin v Duke of Westminster* [1985] 1 QB 581.

[29] Arbitration Act 1996, s 41(3).

(iii) Substituted contract

Rescission of a contract may also take place by such an alteration in its terms as substitutes a new contract for the old one. The old contract may be expressly discharged in the new one, or discharge may be implied by the introduction of new terms or new parties. This method of discharge is therefore a form of rescission with a new contract superadded.

An example of the discharge of a contract by the substitution of new terms is provided by *Morris v Baron & Co*:[30]

A dispute had arisen out of a contract for the sale of cloth and an action had been begun. Before the case came on for trial the parties made an oral arrangement of which the chief terms were that the action and counterclaim were to be withdrawn, an extension of credit was to be given to the buyer for a sum admittedly due from him under the old contract, and, as regards the balance of goods contracted for but undelivered, there was to be substituted for a firm contract of sale an option for the buyer to take them if he pleased.

The House of Lords held that in these circumstances it must be concluded that the parties had agreed to abrogate the old contract and substitute a new one for it.

Similarly, the introduction of new parties[31] may impliedly rescind an existing contract and substitute a new one for it:

Suppose A has entered into a contract with B and C, and that B and C agree among themselves that C shall retire from the contract and cease to be liable upon it.

A may of course insist upon the continued liability of C; but if A continues to deal with B after becoming aware of the retirement of C, A's conduct will probably justify the inference that a new contract to accept the sole liability of B has been made, and A cannot then hold C to the original contract. 'If one partner goes out of a firm, and another comes in, the debts of the old firm may, by the consent of all three parties—the creditor, the old firm, and the new firm—be transferred to the new firm',[32] and this consent may be implied by conduct, if not expressed in words or writing.

(iv) Form of discharge by agreement

As regards the form needed for the expression of an agreement which purports to rescind an existing contract, the old rule of the common law was that a contract under seal could only be discharged by agreement expressed under seal. But, in equity, an agreement to rescind which was not under seal afforded a defence to an action on the deed. Since the Judicature Acts the rule of equity prevails, and a contract contained in a deed may be rescinded by a parol contract (a simple contract, oral or in writing) as well as by deed.[33]

30 [1918] AC 1.

31 See also 'novation', below, p 693.

32 *Hart v Alexander* (1837) 2 M & W 484, 493 (Parke B). In the case of partnership, these rules are substantially embodied in the Partnership Act 1890, s 17(3).

33 *Berry v Berry* [1929] 2 KB 316; Senior Courts Act 1981, s 49.

A parol or simple contract, whether in writing or not, may be discharged by a subsequent agreement, either written or oral. Even when the original agreement is one required by statute to be in or evidenced by writing, as in the case of contracts for the sale or other disposition of land, or contracts of guarantee,[34] there is no need for a written discharge since there is no requirement that they shall be dissolved in writing. In *Morris v Baron & Co*,[35] for example, the original contract for the sale of cloth was required by section 4 of the Sale of Goods Act 1893 (now repealed) to be evidenced by writing. The substituted contract was itself unenforceable because it did not comply with that section. Nevertheless, it operated as a discharge of the old contract with the result that the buyer, who claimed damages for non-delivery of the goods alternatively under the original and under the substituted agreement, was unable to succeed on either ground.

Rescission of an agreement by substitution of new terms must, however, be distinguished in form and in effect from (i) variation, and (ii) forbearance or waiver.

(d) VARIATION

The parties to a contract may effect a variation of the contract by modifying or altering its terms by mutual agreement, but without intending to rescind it and to substitute a wholly new contract for it.[36] A contract may also give one of the parties the power unilaterally to vary the obligations, for example by a price variation clause, as long as it is clear.[37] In the case of consumer contracts, however, this power has been restricted by legislation.[38]

(i) Form of variation

A deed may be varied, as it may be rescinded, by a parol contract.[39] A simple contract, again, whether in writing or not, may be varied by a subsequent agreement either written or oral.[40] This does not conflict with the rule that extrinsic evidence is not admissible to vary or add to the contents of a written document, which refers to the ascertainment of the *original* intention of the parties and has no application to the case of a *subsequent* variation.[41] But a contract required by law to be in writing, or to be evidenced by writing, must be varied in writing. In *Goss v Lord Nugent*:[42]

[34] See above, Chapter 3.

[35] [1918] AC 1, above, p 469.

[36] *British and Beningtons Ltd v North Western Cachar Tea Co Ltd* [1923] AC 48; Stoljar (1957) 35 Can Bar Rev 485; Dugdale and Yates (1976) 39 MLR 680.

[37] *Lombard Tricity Finance Ltd v Paton* [1989] 1 All ER 918; *Amberley (UK) Ltd v West Sussex CC* [2011] EWCA Civ 11.

[38] Consumer Rights Act 2015, ss 62, 63, and Sched 2, above, p 227, replacing similar provisions in Unfair Terms in Consumer Contracts Regulations 1999 (SI 1999 No 2083).

[39] *Berry v Berry* [1929] 2 KB 316.

[40] Cf *MWB Business Exchange Centres Ltd v Rock Advertising Ltd* [2018] UKSC 24, [2019] AC 119 (the parties may in a contract bind *themselves* to complying with certain formalities for the variation of the contract); see above, p 94.

[41] *Goss v Lord Nugent*, below, n 42, 64–65.

[42] (1833) 5 B & Ad 58. See also *Noble v Ward* (1867) LR 2 Ex 135; *United Dominions Corp (Jamaica) Ltd v Shoucair* [1969] 1 AC 340.

By an agreement in writing G had contracted to sell to N several lots of land and to make good title to them. It was afterwards discovered that a good title could not be made to one of the lots, and N orally agreed not to insist on a good title to that lot. N later, relying on the defective title, refused to pay the purchase money.

The contract, being one for the sale of land, was at that time required to be evidenced in writing.[43] The promise to accept the defect in title would operate to vary that contract. But the Court held that G could not rely on this variation as it was merely oral, and N was therefore entitled to succeed on the ground that a good title had not been made.

Whether there has been a mere variation of terms or a rescission must depend upon the intention of the parties in each particular case[44] and the question is often not easy to determine; but the following test has been suggested by Lord Dunedin:[45]

In the first case [variation] there are no such executory clauses in the second arrangement as would enable you to sue upon that alone if the first did not exist; in the second [rescission] you could sue on the second arrangement alone, and the first contract is got rid of either by express words to that effect, or because, the second dealing with the same subject-matter as the first but in a different way, it is impossible that the two should be both performed. When I say you could sue on the second alone, that does not exclude cases where the first is used for mere reference, in the same way as you may fix a price by a price list, but where the contractual force is to be found in the second by itself.

The changes must go to the 'very root' of the original agreement,[46] and 'there should have been made manifest the intention in any event of a complete extinction of the first contract, and not merely the desire of an alteration, however sweeping, in terms which leave it still subsisting'.[47]

(ii) Consideration for variation

A variation involves a definite alteration, *as a matter of contract*, of contractual obligations by the mutual agreement of both parties.[48] It must be supported by consideration. In most cases, consideration for the variation can be found in a mutual abandonment of existing rights or the conferment of new benefits by each party on the other.[49] Alternatively, consideration may be found in the assumption of additional obligations

[43] See now Law of Property (Miscellaneous Provisions) Act 1989, s 2, above, p 87 (contract must be *in writing*); *McCausland v Duncan Lawrie Ltd* [1997] 1 WLR 38.

[44] *Cobalt Data Centre 2 LLP v Revenue and Customs Commissioners* [2024] UKSC 40, [2024] 1 WLR 5213 at [139], applying *Morris v Baron & Co* [1918] AC 1 (see above, p 469), *British and Beningtons Ltd v North Western Cachar Tea Co Ltd* [1923] AC 48, and *Stead v Dawber* (1839) 10 A & E 57. However, the parties' agreement will not be given effect if their characterization of the transaction is 'utterly absurd' and brings the law into disrepute: *Cobalt Data Centre 2 LLP* at [139], [147].

[45] *Morris v Baron & Co* [1918] AC 1, 26.

[46] *British and Beningtons Ltd v North Western Cachar Tea Co Ltd* [1923] AC 48, 68 (Lord Sumner).

[47] *Morris v Baron & Co* [1918] AC 1, 19 (Lord Haldane).

[48] *Besseler Waechter Glover & Co v South Derwent Coal Co* [1938] 1 KB 408, 416 (Goddard J).

[49] *Re William Porter & Co Ltd* [1937] 2 All ER 361; *WJ Alan & Co Ltd v El Nasr Export and Import Co* [1972] 2 QB 189.

or the incurring of liability to an increased detriment.[50] Although an agreement whereby one party undertakes an additional obligation, but the other party is merely bound to perform its existing obligations, will, as a general rule, not be effective to vary a contract, as no consideration is present,[51] it has been held that the contract may exceptionally be varied where the Court can identify a 'practical' benefit to the party undertaking the additional obligation.[52] And if one party merely agrees not to enforce one of the terms of the contract to be performed by the other, this does not constitute a variation. Such an agreement may, however, be binding as a (common law) waiver or in equity by reason of promissory estoppel.[53]

(e) WAIVER

A party who voluntarily agrees to forbear from insisting on the mode of performance or time of performance fixed by the contract, or forbears from so insisting, will be held to have waived the right to require that the contract be performed by the other party in accordance with its terms.[54] But 'waiver' is a term which bears many meanings, has been criticized as a 'slippery word worn smooth with overuse',[55] and is also used to refer to an election between inconsistent rights.[56] We shall here confine ourselves to the common law doctrine of waiver. This is relevant where difficulties of form or absence of consideration mean that there is no variation of the contract. Waiver was developed by the common law mainly as a device for evading the formal requirements of the Statute of Frauds, but because, as we have noted, formal requirements are much less important in the modern law, this aspect is now of less importance, although still relevant for certain types of contract, such as contracts for the sale of land and guarantees.[57]

(i) Form of waiver

Where a contract has to be in, or evidenced by, writing, an oral agreement to forbear, for example by acceding to a request to extend the time of performance, might be met by the plea that the contract had been discharged by an alteration of the time of performance, that a new contract was thereby created, and that the new contract was

[50] *North Ocean Shipping Co Ltd v Hyundai Construction Co Ltd* [1979] QB 705.

[51] *Stilk v Myrick* (1809) 2 Camp 317; *Syros Shipping Co SA v Elaghill Trading Co* [1980] 2 Lloyd's Rep 390; see above, pp 111–5.

[52] *Williams v Roffey Bros & Nicholls (Contractors) Ltd* [1991] 1 QB 1, above, p 112; *Anangel Atlas Compania Naviera SA v Ishikawajima-Harima Heavy Industries Co Ltd (No 2)* [1990] 2 Lloyd's Rep 526; *MWB Business Exchange Centres Ltd v Rock Advertising Ltd* [2016] EWCA Civ 553, [2017] QB 604 (but cf [2018] UKSC 24, [2019] AC 119 at [18], above, p 118).

[53] See above, p 121; below, pp 474–6.

[54] See Phipps (2007) 123 LQR 286 for a valuable discussion of waiver and forbearance at common law.

[55] Roscoe Pound's forward to Ewart, *Waiver Distributed* (1917) vi. See also Carter (1991) 4 JCL 59.

[56] eg the right of one party to treat itself as discharged by reason of a repudiatory breach by the other, below, pp 517–8; or to terminate a contract for breach under an express contractual provision to that effect, below, p 534.

[57] Above, pp 466, 470, and see generally Chapter 3.

not binding or was unenforceable for non-compliance with the statutory requirements as to form.[58] Alternatively, the party which agreed to extend the time for performance, if sued by the other party, might plead that the other party was never ready and willing to perform within the time originally fixed for performance. A party could therefore not rely on the other's assent to more time for performance, as this constituted a variation of the contract which was nugatory since it was not in writing.[59]

(ii) Variation and waiver distinguished

In order to overcome these difficulties, and so that statutory requirements of formality might not become a cloak for fraud, the Courts drew a distinction between variation on the one hand and mere waiver or forbearance on the other. Whereas a variation might, in the cases previously mentioned, be required to be in writing, an oral waiver would be effective although not in the statutory form. In *Levey & Co v Goldberg*,[60] for example:

G agreed in writing to buy from L certain cloth over £10 in value, delivery to be made within a specified time. At the request of G, L orally consented to withhold delivery during that period. Subsequently, however, before delivery was made, G sought to terminate the contract claiming that L had repudiated the contract by not being ready and willing to deliver the cloth within the contract time or within a reasonable time, and pleading the Sale of Goods Act 1893, section 4,[61] as a defence to L's subsequent action for non-acceptance of the goods.

It was held that the forbearance by L at the request of G to deliver within the defined period did not constitute a variation but was a valid and effective waiver although not in writing. G was therefore liable for his failure to accept the cloth. The distinction between variation and waiver has been said to depend upon the intention of the parties;[62] for there to be a variation the parties must intend permanently to alter the contractual obligation; if the party forbearing wishes to preserve the possibility of reverting to the contract, it is at most a waiver. The distinction is difficult to apply in practice,[63] and, although now much less important in respect of formal requirements, it is still important in commercial transactions.

(iii) Waiver does not require consideration

Waiver is important because it is a very common occurrence in commercial transactions. It is, however, open to the technical objection that it ought to have no binding force since it is gratuitous and made without consideration. As it benefits only the promisor,

[58] *Stead v Dawber* (1839) 10 A & E 57.

[59] *Plevins v Downing* (1876) 1 CPD 220, 225.

[60] [1922] 1 KB 688.

[61] Sale of Goods Act 1893, s 4, required the contract to be evidenced by writing. Cf Sale of Goods Act 1979, s 4 (contract of sale may be made in writing, with or without seal, or by word of mouth, or partly in writing and partly by word of mouth, or may be implied from the parties' conduct).

[62] *Stead v Dawber* (1839) 10 A & E 57; *Tallerman & Co Pty Co Ltd v Nathan's Merchandise (Vic) Pty Ltd* (1954) 91 CLR 288, 297 (High Court of Australia). Dugdale and Yates (1976) 39 MLR 680 distinguish pre-breach statements which are likely to be variations from post-breach ones, which are not.

[63] Compare, eg, *Goss v Lord Nugent* (1833) 5 B & Ad 58 with *Hickman v Haynes* (1875) LR 10 CP 598.

without any corresponding benefit to the promisee, the element of consideration is lacking. It should therefore be without legal effect. But the Courts have not hesitated to hold that the waiver of a contractual stipulation is valid and binding even though there is no consideration. The party granting the indulgence cannot go back on the promise and require strict adherence to the contract.[64] However, in cases of postponement of performance, if no period of postponement is fixed, that party may give reasonable notice to the other party requiring the contract to be performed within a certain time, and the contract must then be performed within that time.[65] Similarly, in cases of the waiver of other types of contractual term, the party granting the indulgence may as a general rule, upon reasonable notice, require the other party to comply with the original contractual stipulation; but cannot treat the forbearance as of no effect. In *Panoutsos v Raymond Hadley Corporation of New York*:[66]

P contracted to buy from RH 4,000 tons of flour which RH was to ship to Greece, by means of separate shipments. The contract required payment to be effected by P opening a bankers' confirmed letter of credit in RH's favour. P did open a letter of credit, but it was not 'confirmed'. RH made some shipments and received payment for these by this letter of credit. Subsequently, however, RH summarily terminated the remainder of the contract on the ground that the letter of credit was not in accordance with the contractual stipulation. P sued for breach.

It was held that RH, by its acceptance of payment by means of the unconfirmed letter of credit, had impliedly waived this condition in the contract. This, however, did not mean that it was consequently bound to accept that letter of credit until the end of the contract; it might, by giving reasonable notice, insist on the strict contractual terms. But it was not entitled to cancel the contract summarily.

(iv) Risk borne by party requesting forbearance

The party to whom the forbearance is granted is also bound by its terms.[67] Moreover, if that party asks to have the performance of the contract postponed, it does so at its own risk. If that party subsequently refuses to accept the goods, and the market value of the goods which it should have accepted at the earlier date has altered at the later date, the measure of damages may be increased by the addition of damages consequent on the delay.[68]

(v) Promissory estoppel and waiver distinguished

In developing waiver mainly as a common law device for evading the formalities required by the Statute of Frauds, little attempt was made to explain why a gratuitous promise

[64] *Leather Cloth Co v Hieronimus* (1875) LR 10 QB 140; *Besseler Waechter Glover & Co v South Derwent Coal Co* [1938] 1 KB 408; *Tankexpress A/S v Compagnie Financière Belge des Petroles SA* [1949] AC 76.

[65] *Charles Rickards Ltd v Oppenhaim* [1950] 1 KB 616.

[66] [1917] 2 KB 473.

[67] *Hickman v Haynes* (1875) LR 10 CP 598; *Levey & Co v Goldberg* [1922] 1 KB 688.

[68] *Levey & Co v Goldberg* [1922] 1 KB 688.

should thus be binding. If it is to be justified analytically, it may be more satisfactory to regard waiver as a species of (common law) estoppel. It will be remembered that equity, by use of the principle of promissory estoppel,[69] is also prepared to give effect to a promise made in similar circumstances:

If persons who have contractual rights against others induce by their conduct those against whom they have such rights to believe that such rights will either not be enforced or will be kept in suspense or abeyance for some particular time, those persons will not be allowed by a Court of Equity to enforce the rights until such time has elapsed, without at all events placing the parties in the same position as they were before.[70]

The party who has waived strict performance may be said to be estopped from going back on the promise or representation to do so, at any rate without giving fair and adequate notice to the promisee.

The similarity between waiver and estoppel was noted by Denning LJ in *Charles Rickards Ltd v Oppenhaim*:[71]

CR contracted with O to build a body on a Rolls Royce car chassis, and to deliver the completed car to O by 20 March 1948 at the latest. On that day it was still not completed, but O continued to press for delivery. On 29 June, however, he wrote to CR stating he would not take delivery after 25 July. CR still having failed to deliver the car, O treated the contract as repudiated.

The Court of Appeal held that he was entitled to do so. Although by his conduct he had impliedly waived the original stipulation as to time, he had given reasonable notice of his intention to reimpose a new time limit. CR having failed even then to perform, the contract was clearly discharged by its breach. Denning LJ said of O's consent to postponement:[72]

Whether it be called waiver or forbearance on his part, or an agreed variation or substituted performance, does not matter. It is a kind of estoppel. By his conduct he evinced an intention to affect their legal relations. He made, in effect, a promise not to insist on his strict legal rights. That promise was intended to be acted on, and was in fact acted on. He cannot afterwards go back on it.

The analogy, however, is not exact: promissory estoppel may be more limited than waiver. For promissory estoppel, it has been said that the promisee must alter its position in reliance on the promise,[73] but the requirement of reliance has not been strictly enforced

[69] See above, p 121.

[70] *Birmingham and District Land Co v London and North Western Railway Co* (1888) 40 Ch D 268, 286 (Bowen LJ).

[71] [1950] 1 KB 616; cf Stoljar (1957) 35 Can Bar Rev 485. For more recent discussion on waiver in the sense of estoppel, see *Motor Oil Hellas (Corinth) Refineries SA v Shipping Corp of India, The Kanchenjunga* [1990] 1 Lloyd's Rep 391; *Commonwealth of Australia v Verwayen* (1990) 170 CLR 394.

[72] [1950] 1 KB 616, 623. Cf Phipps (2007) 123 LQR 286, 298–9.

[73] Above, p 125.

for waiver,[74] although in cases of waiver of a time fixed for performance (but not in the case of waiver of other types of stipulation) it will usually be satisfied.

(f) PROVISIONS FOR DISCHARGE CONTAINED IN THE CONTRACT ITSELF

A contract may contain within itself the elements of its own discharge, in the form of provisions, express or implied, for its termination in certain circumstances. Apart from the statutory protection given to non-consumers dealing on the other party's written standard terms of business[75] and to consumers,[76] and the power of the Court to give equitable relief against forfeiture,[77] there is no general requirement that a party act reasonably when deciding to exercise a contractual right to terminate.[78]

The parties may expressly provide that, upon the happening of a certain event, either the contract shall automatically determine,[79] or one party is to have the option to cancel the contract.[80]

(i) Automatic termination

Where the event is one over which the parties have no control and cannot bring about themselves, then effect will generally be given to a provision that the contract is automatically to cease to bind.[81] But if the relevant event is a breach of contract the Courts are likely to interpret the contract as nevertheless requiring an election by the

[74] *WJ Alan & Co Ltd v El Nasr Export and Import Co Ltd* [1972] 2 QB 189, 213; but cf *ibid*, 221; *Finagrain SA Geneva v P Kruse Hamburg* [1976] 2 Lloyd's Rep 508, 535, 542.

[75] Unfair Contract Terms Act 1977, s 3(2)(b)(ii); above, p 219.

[76] Consumer Rights Act 2015, ss 62, 63, and Sched 2, Pt 1, especially paras 7, 8, replacing similar provisions in Unfair Terms in Consumer Contracts Regulations 1999 (SI 1999 No 2083); Consumer Credit Act 1974, ss 76, 86B, 86D, 86E, 87, 88, 98 (amended by Consumer Credit Act 2006).

[77] Below, pp 611–3. See also Law of Property Act 1925, s 146 (forfeiture of lease).

[78] In some legal systems, a party is required to exercise its rights and remedies, including the right to terminate, in good faith: Lando and Beale, *Principles of European Contract Law Parts I and II* (2000) 117–19 or (in particular) to give notice requiring the other party to perform before terminating the contract: above, p 456, n 81. Cf *Union Eagle Ltd v Golden Achievement Ltd* [1997] AC 514, 519 (Lord Hoffmann: 'The existence of an undefined discretion to refuse to enforce the contract on the ground that this would be "unconscionable" is sufficient to create uncertainty'). A duty to perform in good faith is not generally implied into contracts in English law. If, however, the contract gives the party the discretionary power to determine whether circumstances have arisen to entitle the termination right to be exercised, the discretion must be exercised in good faith, and not arbitrarily, capriciously, or irrationally: see *Braganza v BP Shipping Ltd* [2015] UKSC 17, [2015] 1 WLR 1661; above, pp 181–2. Cf *Tesco Stores Ltd v Union of Shop, Distributive and Allied Workers* [2024] UKSC 28, [2025] ICR 107 at [114]–[120], [127] (Lord Leggatt, arguing that termination rights, like discretionary powers, are in general circumscribed by an implied qualification that they be exercised in good faith), rejected by Lord Reed at [149].

[79] *Continental Grain Export Corp v STM Grain Ltd* [1979] 2 Lloyd's Rep 460.

[80] *Head v Tattersall* (1871) LR 7 Ex 7; *Brown v Knowsley BC* [1986] IRLR 102, above, p 154. For the contractual right of a party to terminate for the other party's breach, see below, p 534.

[81] *New Zealand Shipping Co v Société des Ateliers et Chantiers* [1919] AC 1, 15 (Lord Wrenbury); *Gyllenhammar & Partners International Ltd v Sour Brodogradevna Industrija* [1989] 2 Lloyd's Rep 403, 413 (Hirst J).

innocent party before holding that the contract is terminated. This is an application of the principle that a party may not rely on its own breach to bring the contract to an end;[82] that is, a party may not take advantage of its own wrong.[83] The better view is that this is not an independent rule of law,[84] but a principle of construction reflecting the presumed intention of the parties, and which may be rebutted by the express terms of the contract.[85] Moreover, even if the event triggering the automatic termination provision is not a breach of contract, a party will not be able to take advantage of that provision if its wrongful action gave rise to the event upon which the automatic termination provision is based.[86]

(ii) Termination on notice

More often, a provision is inserted making the contract terminable at the option of one or both of the parties upon notice. This right of termination may be exercisable upon a breach of the contract by one party (whether or not the breach would amount to a repudiation of the contract),[87] or upon the occurrence or non-occurrence of a specified event other than breach,[88] or simply at the will of the party upon whom the right is conferred. For example, the contract may be terminable 'by three months' notice in writing on either side'. A similar provision may be incorporated by implication, or by the usage of trade. At common law[89] a contract of employment may be terminated by reasonable notice by either party, the length of the notice depending upon the nature of the employment and the intervals at which remuneration is to be paid. Moreover, even where the duration of a written contract is on the face of the instrument indefinite and unlimited, such a provision may sometimes be implied from the nature of the contract,[90]

[82] The principle does not apply if breach is of a duty owed to a person who is not a party to the contract: *Cheall v Association of Professional Executive Clerical and Computer Staff* [1983] 2 AC 180, 189 (Lord Diplock) and *Thompson v ASDA-MFI Group plc* [1988] 1 Ch 241, 266.

[83] *Alghussein Establishment v Eton College* [1988] 1 WLR 587; *Cheall v Association of Professional Executive Clerical and Computer Staff* [1983] 2 AC 180; *Brown v Knowsley BC* [1986] IRLR 102.

[84] *New Zealand Shipping Co v Société des Ateliers et Chantiers* [1919] AC 1; *Alghussein Establishment v Eton College* [1988] 1 WLR 587; *Cheall v Association of Professional Executive Clerical and Computer Staff* [1983] 2 AC 180.

[85] See, eg, *Gyllenhammar & Partners International Ltd v Sour Brodogradevna Industrija* [1989] 2 Lloyd's Rep 403, 416 (Hirst J).

[86] See *Cheall v Association of Professional Executive Clerical and Computer Staff* [1983] 2 AC 180, 189 (Lord Diplock). This principle means that even where such a provision declares that the contract is to be 'void', it is not absolutely so: *New Zealand Shipping Co v Société des Ateliers et Chantiers* [1919] AC 1, 15 (Lord Wrenbury). See also below, p 500 (self-induced frustration).

[87] But cf *Laing Management Ltd v Aegon Insurance Co (UK) Ltd* (1998) 86 BLR 70 (reliance on contractual right to terminate did not constitute acceptance of repudiatory breach, although this may be questioned).

[88] *Mannai Investment Co Ltd v Eagle Star Life Assurance Co Ltd* [1997] AC 749 ('break' clause in lease). See also *Head v Tattersall* (1871) LR 7 Ex 7 and above, p 154 (condition subsequent).

[89] But see now Employment Rights Act 1996, s 86 (minimum periods of notice by employer).

[90] *Crediton Gas Co v Crediton UDC* [1928] 1 Ch 447; *Winter Garden Theatre (London) Ltd v Millennium Productions Ltd* [1948] AC 173; *Re Spenborough UDC's Agreement* [1968] Ch 139. Cf *Kirklees Metropolitan BC v Yorkshire Woollen District Transport Co* (1978) 77 LGR 448 (fixed-term agreement could not be terminated by notice). See also Carnegie (1969) 85 LQR 392.

particularly where the contract is for a fixed price[91] or is a commercial contract.[92] Thus a partnership for no fixed time is terminable by notice.[93]

Any notice given must be clear and unambiguous in its terms, and if it is to be given in a certain form, for example in writing, or within a certain time, or if a specified period of notice must be given, these requirements must normally be strictly complied with, otherwise the notice will be of no effect.[94] In interpreting a clause in a contract which lays down a procedure for the termination of the contract, the Court will have regard to the commercial purpose served by the clause,[95] although even in a commercial context, if the requirements for the exercise of the termination clause are clear, the Court will require full compliance.[96]

FURTHER READING

PHIPPS, 'Resurrecting the Doctrine of Common Law Forbearance' (2007) 123 LQR 286

[91] *Staffordshire Area Health Authority v South Staffs Waterworks Co* [1978] 1 WLR 1387 (see below, p 499). Where there are price variation provisions, such an implied term is unlikely: *The Queensland Electricity Generating Board v New Hope Collieries Pty Ltd* [1989] 1 Lloyd's Rep 205; *Watford Borough Council v Watford Rural Parish* (1987) 86 LGR 524, 528.

[92] *Martin-Baker Aircraft Co Ltd v Canada Flight Equipment Ltd* [1955] 2 QB 556, 577; *Re Spenborough UDC's Agreement* [1968] Ch 139; *Watford Borough Council v Watford Rural Parish* (1987) 86 LGR 524, 532.

[93] Partnership Act 1890, s 26.

[94] *Afovos Shipping Co SA v Pagnan* [1983] 1 WLR 195. Cf *Bremer Handelsgesellschaft mbH v Vanden Avenne-Izegem PVBA* [1978] 2 Lloyd's Rep 109, above, p 159.

[95] *Mannai Investment Co Ltd v Eagle Star Life Assurance Co Ltd* [1997] AC 749 (minor misdescription did not preclude notice from being effective where, construed in its contractual setting, it would unambiguously inform a reasonable recipient how and when it was to operate); *Ellis Tylin Ltd v Co-operative Retail Services Ltd* [1999] BLR 205.

[96] *Friends Life Ltd v Siemens Hearing Instruments Ltd* [2014] EWCA Civ 382, [2015] 1 All ER (Comm) 1068 at [66].

14

DISCHARGE BY FRUSTRATION

1. INTRODUCTION

Some legal systems accept that changes of circumstances may justify modifying a contract if maintaining the original contract would produce intolerable results incompatible with justice.[1] But many, including English law, concerned that modification would undermine certainty and alter the risks allocated by the contract, make provision for the discharge of a contract only where, after its formation, a change of circumstances makes contractual performance illegal or impossible. In English law, such a situation is provided for by the doctrine of frustration.[2] Originally, this term was confined to the discharge of maritime contracts by the 'frustration of the adventure', but it has now been extended to cover all cases where an agreement has been terminated by supervening events beyond the control of either party.[3] But the doctrine is not simply one of supervening impossibility. Impossibility may in some circumstances not discharge the contract at all, while 'impossibility' does not accurately describe the cases of frustration of a commercial purpose where the fundamentally different situation which has unexpectedly occurred means that performance would be, as a matter of business, radically different from the contractually stipulated performance.[4] In these cases the contract is discharged although performance is not literally impossible.

[1] Lando and Beale, *Principles of European Contract Law Parts I and II* (2000) 328; and now in France (following reform in 2016), Rowan, *The New French Law of Contract* (2022) 181–7.

[2] See Peel, *Frustration and Force Majeure* (4th edn, 2022). Cf McKendrick [2024] LMCLQ 34 (discussing whether the English law of change of circumstances needs reform, in the light of the COVID-19 pandemic and comparative law).

[3] Initial impossibility and misunderstandings that exist at the time of the formation of the contract, sometimes referred to as 'pre-contractual frustration', are considered in Chapter 8. Care should be taken not to treat such cases as frustration; cf *Gamerco SA v ICM/Fair Warning (Agency) Ltd* [1995] 1 WLR 1226, where it may have been wrongly so treated; see Carter and Tolhurst (1996) 10 JCL 264, 265–6. For discussion of the relationship between frustration and common mistake, see above, pp 301–2, 313.

[4] *Joseph Constantine Steamship Line Ltd v Imperial Smelting Corp Ltd* [1942] AC 154, 164 (Viscount Simon). See also *Jackson v Union Marine Insurance Co Ltd* (below, p 482) and *Krell v Henry* (below, p 484). In the US common law, 'impossibility' (or 'impracticability' of performance) and 'frustration of purpose' are separate doctrines: Farnsworth and Wolfe, *Farnsworth on Contracts* (4th edn, looseleaf) §§9.08, 9.09.

The defining characteristics of the doctrine of frustration that have emerged from the case law were summarized by Bingham LJ[5] in the following terms:

> The doctrine of frustration was evolved to mitigate the rigour of the common law's insistence on literal performance of absolute promises . . . The object of the doctrine was to give effect to the demands of justice, to achieve a just and reasonable result, to do what is reasonable and fair, as an expedient to escape from injustice where such would result from enforcement of a contract in its literal terms after a significant change in circumstances . . . Since the effect of frustration is to kill the contract and discharge the parties from further liability under it, the doctrine is not to be lightly invoked, must be kept within narrow limits and ought not to be extended . . . Frustration brings the contract to an end forthwith, without more and automatically . . . The essence of frustration is that it should not be due to the act or election of the party seeking to rely on it . . . A frustrating event must be some outside event or extraneous change of situation . . . A frustrating event must take place without blame or fault on the side of the party seeking to rely on it.

This chapter traces the history of the doctrine and examines the scope of its present application. It should, however, be noted that as the doctrine has developed, so too has the use, particularly in standard form contracts and negotiated commercial contracts, of so-called *force majeure* clauses, which entitle one or both of the parties to be excused (in whole or in part) from performance of the contract. Such clauses may cover non-frustrating events and may provide for more flexible remedies than total discharge. For instance they may entitle a party to suspend performance, to claim an extension of time for performance, or to be compensated for performance which will be more onerous.[6] Some *force majeure* clauses may impose on the parties a duty to renegotiate the terms of the contract in the light of changed circumstances, but (unless the basis of the variation of the contract is defined with sufficient certainty) it is not certain that such a duty will be enforceable because the duty to renegotiate, like the duty to negotiate, has been held to be too uncertain to be enforced in English law.[7] *Force majeure* clauses are generally interpreted as applicable only if the party invoking the clause can show that the event or state of affairs was beyond its reasonable control and could not be avoided by the taking of reasonable steps; and the requirement to take reasonable steps does not (in the absence of clear words in the clause) extend to a duty to accept a variation in the terms of the contract.[8]

[5] *J Lauritzen AS v Wijsmuller BV, The Super Servant Two* [1990] 1 Lloyd's Rep 1, 8. For the facts, see below, p 501.

[6] On such clauses, which fall outside the scope of this book, see generally, *Channel Island Ferries Ltd v Sealink UK Ltd* [1988] 1 Lloyd's Rep 323; *RTI Ltd v MUR Shipping BV* [2024] UKSC 18, [2025] AC 675 at [92]; McKendrick, *Force Majeure and Frustration of Contract* (2nd edn, 1995), especially chs 1 and 3. '*Force majeure*' is a term of art in French and Belgian law. It has no clear meaning in English law: *Matsoukis v Priestman & Co* [1915] 1 KB 681, 685–6; *Thomas Borthwick (Glasgow) Ltd v Faure Fairclough Ltd* [1968] 1 Lloyd's Rep 16, 28, but is generally interpreted as requiring legal or physical impossibility: *Channel Island Ferries Ltd v Sealink UK Ltd* [1988] 1 Lloyd's Rep 323, 327. It is, however, normal for the clause to make detailed provision for the circumstances in which it may be invoked, and the consequences.

[7] *Walford v Miles* [1992] 2 AC 128, 138; above, p 67. Cf *Petromec Inc v Petroleo Brasilieiro SA* [2005] EWCA Civ 891, [2006] 1 Lloyd's Rep 121 at [121]; Peel, in Burrows and Peel (eds), *Contract Formation and Parties* (2010) ch 3; Cartwright, in Peel and Probert (eds), *Shaping the Law of Obligations* (2023) 33–4; Foxton [2025] JBL 161, 173–5.

[8] *RTI Ltd v MUR Shipping BV* [2024] UKSC 18 at [25], [42], [46].

2. EMERGENCE OF THE DOCTRINE

Before 1863 it was a general rule of the law of contract that a person was absolutely bound to perform any obligation which had been undertaken. A person could not claim to be excused by the mere fact that performance had subsequently become impossible; for 'where there is a positive contract to do a thing, not in itself unlawful, the contractor must perform it or pay damages for not doing it, although in consequence of unforeseen accidents, the performance of his contract has become unexpectedly burdensome or even impossible'.[9] So in *Paradine v Jane* in 1647:[10]

P sued J for rent due upon a lease. J pleaded 'that a certain German Prince, by name Prince Rupert, an alien born, enemy to the King and kingdom, had invaded the realm with an hostile army of men; and with the same force did enter upon the defendant's possession, and him expelled, and held out of possession . . . whereby he could not take the profits'. This plea was in substance a plea that the rent was not due because the lessee had been deprived, by events beyond his control, of the profits from which the rent should have come.

The Court held that this was no excuse:[11]

When the party by his own contract creates a duty or charge upon himself, he is bound to make it good, if he may, notwithstanding any accident by inevitable necessity, because he might have provided against it by his contract. And therefore if the lessee covenant to repair a house, though it be burnt by lightning, or thrown down by enemies, yet he ought to repair it.

It has always, however, been open to the parties to provide expressly that the fulfilment of a condition or the occurrence of an event should discharge one or both of them from some or all of their obligations under their agreement.[12] Moreover, there are cases in which a contract, though containing no express provision, will be interpreted by the Courts as containing such a provision by implication. An implication of this nature would, it might be thought, readily be made where, without the fault of either party, an event occurs which renders the contract not merely more onerous, but completely impossible of performance.

This was the device[13] used by the Court of Queen's Bench in 1863 in *Taylor v Caldwell*[14] to introduce an exception into the existing law:

C agreed with T to hire to him a music-hall and gardens for the purpose of entertainment. Before the day of performance arrived, the music-hall was destroyed by fire. T sued C for damages for breach of the contract which C, through no fault of his own, was unable to perform.

C was held not liable to pay, for 'the contract is not to be construed as a positive contract, but as subject to an implied condition that the parties shall be excused in case, before

[9] *Taylor v Caldwell* (1863) 3 B & S 826, 833 (Blackburn J).

[10] (1647) Aleyn 26 and Style 47. On the antecedents of this decision, see Ibbetson, in Rose (ed), *Consensus ad Idem* (1996) ch 1.

[11] (1647) Aleyn 26, 27.

[12] See above, p 154.

[13] See Trakman (1983) 46 MLR 39.

[14] (1863) 3 B & S 826.

breach, performance becomes impossible from the perishing of the thing without default of the contractor'.[15] Blackburn J said:[16]

The principle seems to us to be that, in contracts in which the performance depends on the continued existence of a given person or thing, a condition is implied that the impossibility of performance arising from the perishing of the person or thing shall excuse the performance. In none of these cases is the promise in words other than positive, nor is there any express stipulation that the destruction of the person or thing shall excuse the performance; but that excuse is by law implied, because from the nature of the contract it is apparent that the parties contracted on the basis of the continued existence of the particular person or chattel.

Following this decision the Courts have been prepared to hold that, unless a contrary intention appears, the continuance of a contract was conditional upon the possibility of its performance.

The new doctrine was soon extended beyond the sphere of literal impossibility to situations where there had been a 'frustration of the adventure'. Most of the early frustration cases arose out of delay, attributable to the fault of neither party, in the carrying out of charterparties; and they seem at first to have been treated as raising a question which was regarded as connected, rather than identical, with that raised by the cases of impossibility.

In *Jackson v Union Marine Insurance Co Ltd*:[17]

J's ship had been chartered to proceed in January to Newport to load a cargo of iron rails for San Francisco. On the way to Newport she ran aground and it took over a month to refloat her. She was then taken into Liverpool and underwent lengthy repairs lasting until August. In the meantime the charterers had chartered another ship. J claimed from the defendant insurance company for a total loss, by perils of the sea, of the freight to be earned under the charterparty.

Whether there had been such a loss depended on whether the charterers had been justified in throwing up their contract with J instead of waiting until the ship was repaired and then loading her. The jury found that the time necessary to get the ship off, and to repair her so that she might become a cargo-carrying ship, had been so long as to put an end in a commercial sense to the speculation entered into by J and the charterers; and on this finding the Court held that a voyage undertaken after the ship had been repaired would have been an adventure different from that which both parties had contemplated at the time of the contract. It was, they said, an implied term of the contract that the ship should arrive at Newport within a reasonable time, and her inability to arrive put an end to it. 'The adventure', said Bramwell B,[18] 'was frustrated by perils of the seas, both parties were discharged, and a loading of cargo in August would have been a new adventure, a new agreement'.

The dislocation of business caused by the 1914 to 1918 war brought a large number of frustration cases into the Courts, and it soon became clear that they raised the same questions as those raised by cases previously considered under the head of impossibility.

[15] *Ibid*, 833. [16] *Ibid*, 839. [17] (1874) LR 10 CP 125. [18] *Ibid*, 148.

'When this question arises in regard to commercial contracts', said Lord Loreburn,[19] 'the principle is the same, and the language used as to "frustration of the adventure" merely adapts it to the class of cases in hand'. 'The doctrine of frustration is only a special case of the discharge of contract by an impossibility of performance arising after the contract was made.'[20] The modern practice is to use the term 'frustration' to cover cases of both classes.

3. INSTANCES OF FRUSTRATION

Before turning to the theoretical basis of the doctrine of frustration, we consider examples of factual situations in which the Courts have been ready to infer, from the nature of the contract and from the circumstances surrounding it, that it has been frustrated by the happening of a subsequent event. While the reasoning in some of these examples is based on the 'implied term' theory of frustration, which, as we shall see, is now discredited, they remain useful illustrations of situations in which a contract may be frustrated.

(a) DESTRUCTION OF SUBJECT-MATTER OF CONTRACT

The simplest case is probably that where the performance of the contract is made impossible by the destruction of a specific thing *essential* to that performance, for example, the destruction of the music-hall in *Taylor v Caldwell*. So if A agrees with B to supply and install certain machinery in B's factory premises, and the premises are destroyed by fire, the contract will be frustrated.[21] But if only the machinery is destroyed, leaving the premises untouched, then it is still possible to obtain other machinery and A must do the work over again: the contract will not be discharged.[22] Where an agreement for the sale of specific goods has been made and, before the risk passes to the buyer, without any fault on the part of the seller or buyer, the goods perish, the agreement is avoided.[23]

(b) NON-OCCURRENCE OF A PARTICULAR EVENT

The principle of frustration has also been held to apply to cases concerning the cancellation of an expected event. In the so-called 'Coronation cases', which arose out of the postponement of the coronation of King Edward VII owing to his sudden illness,

[19] *FA Tamplin Steamship Co Ltd v Anglo-Mexican Petroleum Products Ltd* [1916] 2 AC 397, 404.

[20] *Joseph Constantine Steamship Line Ltd v Imperial Smelting Corporation Ltd* [1942] AC 154, 168 (Viscount Maugham).

[21] *Appleby v Myers* (1867) LR 2 CP 651; below, p 506.

[22] *Ibid*, 660.

[23] Sale of Goods Act 1979, s 7. See further below, pp 512–4 (effect of frustration and partial perishing of goods).

it was applied to contracts the performance of which depended on the existence or occurrence of a particular state of things forming the basis on which the contract had been made. In *Krell v Henry*,[24] for instance:

H agreed to hire a flat from K during the daytime of 26 and 27 June 1902; the contract itself contained no express reference to the coronation processions, but K had advertised that the windows of the flat were to be let to view the processions which would pass the flat on those days, and H had entered into the contract after reading the advertisement. The processions were cancelled.

Only one-third of the agreed sum had been paid as a deposit when the processions were abandoned and the Court of Appeal held that K could not recover the balance. The Court considered that the processions and the relative position of the flat lay at the foundation of the agreement. The contract was therefore discharged.

Failure, before performance, of the factor which induced the parties to enter into the agreement will not, however, necessarily discharge the contract: 'it may be that the parties contracted in the expectation that a particular event would happen, each taking his chance, but that the actual happening of the event was not made the basis of the contract'.[25] In *Herne Bay Steamboat Co v Hutton*:[26]

The defendant chartered from the claimant the SS *Cynthia* for 28 and 29 June 1902, for the express purpose of taking paying passengers to see the Coronation naval review at Spithead and to tour the fleet. The review was cancelled, but the fleet remained.

The Court of Appeal, composed of the same judges as in *Krell v Henry*, refused to hold the defendant discharged. They did so, partly on the ground that a tour of the fleet was still possible, but mainly because they considered that it was the defendant's own venture and it was at his risk. The Court pointed out that if the existence of a particular state of things was merely the motive or inducement to one party to enter into the contract, as distinct from the basis on which both contracted, the principle cannot be applied. In both *Krell v Henry*[27] and *Herne Bay Steamboat Co v Hutton*[28] the example was given of the hire of a vehicle to take the hirer to Epsom to view the races on Derby day; the hirer will not be discharged if the races are cancelled, for the hirer's purpose is not the common foundation of the contract to hire the vehicle, even if the hirer was charging an enhanced rate.

[24] [1903] 2 KB 740. See also *Chandler v Webster* [1904] 1 KB 493 (below, p 506). Cf *Griffith v Brymer* (1903) 19 TLR 434 (mistake, rather than frustration, because the parties made the contract in ignorance of the fact that the coronation had already been cancelled; above, p 314). See also *Salam Air SAOC v Latam Airlines Groups SA* [2020] EWHC 2414 (Comm), [2021] 1 CLC 795 at [49]–[50] (six-year lease of aircraft which could not be flown during the period of COVID-19 regulations: the use of the aircraft was not a shared purpose, so no 'frustration of purpose', 'a doctrine which has seldom been applied since it first emerged in the Coronation cases at the start of the last century, and in particular in *Krell v Henry*': Foxton J).

[25] *Larrinaga & Co Ltd v Société Franco-Américaine des Phosphates de Medulla, Paris* (1923) 39 TLR 316, 318 (Lord Finlay); *Maritime National Fish Ltd v Ocean Trawlers Ltd* [1935] AC 524, 529 (Lord Wright: *Krell* 'is certainly not . . . to be extended').

[26] [1903] 2 KB 683.

[27] [1903] 2 KB 740, 750–1.

[28] [1903] 2 KB 683, 689.

(c) DEATH, OR INCAPACITY FOR PERSONAL SERVICE

Where performance of obligations under a contract for personal services is rendered impossible or radically different by the death or incapacitating illness of the promisor, the contract will be frustrated. In *Stubbs v Holywell Railway Co*[29] it was held that a contract for personal services was put an end to by the death of the party by whom the services were to be rendered. And in *Robinson v Davison*:[30]

D's wife, an eminent piano player, promised to perform at a concert, but was prevented from doing so by a dangerous illness. An action was brought against D claiming damages for breach of contract.

It was held that the contract was discharged by D's wife's illness, and it was not therefore broken by her failure to perform, nor, on the other hand, could she have insisted on performing when she was unfit to do so as frustration is not brought about by an act of election.[31] These are examples of cases where performance by the relevant party is personal and cannot be carried out by anyone else so that death or illness gives rise to frustration.[32] Similar decisions have been reached in the case of the discharge of a seaman's contract of service by his internment,[33] and of that of a music-hall artist by his call-up for service in the army.[34] However, absence—even prolonged absence—through illness will not necessarily determine a contract of employment. In *Marshall v Harland & Wolff Ltd*[35] it was stated that a number of factors must be considered: the terms of the contract (including any sick pay provisions), the nature and the expected duration of the employment, the period of past employment, and the nature and duration of the illness and the prospects for recovery.[36] Donaldson J formulated the test for frustration of a contract of employment as follows, 'Was the employee's incapacity … of such a nature, or did it appear likely to continue for such a period, that further performance of his obligations in the future would either be impossible or would be a thing radically different from that undertaken by him and agreed to be accepted by the employer under the agreed terms of his employment?'[37] The application of the doctrine of frustration to employment contracts can give rise to results that may appear harsh. In *Notcutt v Universal Equipment Co (London) Ltd*[38] frustration was held to have occurred when it became apparent to the parties that an employee who had suffered a heart attack would never work again. This had the effect of automatically terminating the contract of employment and thereby releasing the employer from the contractual provisions which required that notice be given before terminating the contract and the statutory obligation to pay the employee during the period of notice.

29 (1867) LR 2 Ex 311.
30 (1871) LR 6 Ex 269.
31 Below, p 505.
32 If performance is not of a personal character then the contract is not necessarily frustrated by death or incapacity: *Phillips v Alhambra Palace Co* [1901] 1 QB 59.
33 *Horlock v Beal* [1916] 1 AC 486.
34 *Morgan v Manser* [1948] 1 KB 184.
35 [1972] 1 WLR 899, 903.
36 *Ibid*, 903–5. An employee who is suspended from work on medical grounds is entitled to be paid by the employer for up to 26 weeks: Employment Rights Act 1996, s 64.
37 [1972] 1 WLR 899, 903 but see *Egg Stores (Stamford Hill) Ltd v Leibovici* [1977] ICR 260, 264 ('has the time arrived when the employer can no longer reasonably be expected to keep the absent employee's post open for him?'). See also *FC Shepherd & Co Ltd v Jerrom* [1987] 1 QB 301 (imprisonment of employee).
38 [1986] 1 WLR 641.

(d) REQUISITIONING OF SHIPS AND INTERFERENCES WITH CHARTERPARTIES

Cases concerning charterparties provide some of the most important instances of the application of the doctrine.

In wartime, ships are often requisitioned for such time and for such purposes as the Government may require them. If the ship is under charterparty the question will arise whether the requisitioning operates so as to frustrate the rights of the shipowners and charterers under the agreement. In *FA Tamplin Steamship Co Ltd v Anglo-Mexican Petroleum Products Co Ltd*:[39]

The steamship *FA Tamplin* was chartered by a time charterparty for 5 years from 4 December 1912, to 4 December 1917. In February 1915 the Government requisitioned the ship for use as a troopship and made certain structural alterations to her for this purpose. The charterers were willing to go on paying the agreed freight under the charterparty, but the owners claimed that the contract had been frustrated by the requisition as they wished to obtain a larger amount of compensation from the Crown.

The House of Lords, by a bare majority, held that the contract still continued. The interruption was not of sufficient duration to make it unreasonable for the parties to go on. There might be many months during which the ship would be available for commercial purposes before the five years expired.

In *Bank Line Ltd v Arthur Capel & Co*,[40] on the other hand:

In February 1915, BL chartered the steamship *Quito* to C for 12 months from the time the vessel should be delivered. The charterparty provided that (i) if the steamer had not been delivered by 30 April 1915, C, the charterers, were to have the option to cancel the contract or to proceed with it, and (ii) 'Charterers to have option of cancelling this charterparty should steamer be commandeered by Government during this Charter.' The steamer was not delivered by 30 April, and, on 11 May, before delivery, she was commandeered by the Government and not released until September. She was then sold by BL. C sued for non-delivery, having never exercised their options to cancel.

The House of Lords held that the contract had been frustrated. The clauses in the charterparty were not intended to place the shipowners indefinitely at the charterers' mercy, to oblige them to deliver however long the delay. They merely gave to the charterers the option to cancel the contract without the necessity of proving frustration:

A contingency may be provided for, but not in such terms as to show that the provision is meant to be all the provision for it. A contingency may be provided for, but in such a way as shows that it is provided for only for the purpose of dealing with one of its effects and not with all.[41]

Lord Haldane, who dissented, was of the opinion that there was no frustration: the requisition was not of such a permanent character as to make the terms of the charterparty wholly inapplicable.

[39] [1916] 2 AC 397. [40] [1919] AC 435. [41] *Ibid*, 456 (Lord Sumner).

These differences of opinion within the highest tribunal show that cases of frustration raise most difficult questions of fact and principle. In the *Bank Line* case Lord Loreburn stated[42] that 'the main thing to be considered is the probable length of the total deprivation of the use of the chartered ship compared with the unexpired duration of the charterparty'. On this basis, the two decisions can perhaps be reconciled without undue difficulty, since the *Bank Line* charter was of one year's duration only, whereas that in the *Tamplin* case had still nearly three years to run at the time the requisitioning took place. But it is not certain that Lord Loreburn's test is the correct one to apply.[43]

Events other than the seizure or requisitioning of the ship may also frustrate a charterparty. It has already been seen that, in *Jackson v Union Marine Insurance Co Ltd*,[44] the charterparty was frustrated by the stranding of and damage to the ship. In a number of cases a charterparty has been held to have been frustrated by the inability of the ship to leave port, due, for example, to the refusal of a foreign government to allow the ship to depart,[45] or to the outbreak of hostilities, as happened in 1980 when some 60 ships were trapped in the Shatt-el-Arab river upon the outbreak of war between Iran and Iraq,[46] or to the arrest of the ship.[47] More difficulty, however, arises where strikes prevent the loading or unloading of the ship. The charterer usually undertakes in the contract to load and unload the cargo within a specified number of days, and, in default, to pay a certain sum of money to the shipowner by way of 'demurrage'. If strikes occur at the port of loading or discharge, this does not (in the absence of any express provision to the contrary) absolve the charterer from its liability to pay demurrage in respect of the delay.[48] However, a prolonged strike may in exceptional circumstances frustrate a charterparty, that is if the delay is such as to make further performance something radically different from that which was undertaken in the contract.[49] Prolongation of a voyage by interruption of the contemplated route might also bring about frustration, but did not do so, for example, where the blocking of the Suez Canal necessitated a voyage round the Cape, since the alternative route was not fundamentally different, but merely longer and more expensive.[50]

[42] *Ibid*, 454. See also the *Tamplin* case [1916] 2 AC 397, 405.

[43] *International Sea Tankers Inc v Hemisphere Shipping Co Ltd* [1982] 1 Lloyd's Rep 128, 131, 133, 135. The alternative tests were discussed by Diplock J in *Port Line Ltd v Ben Line Steamers Ltd* [1958] 2 QB 146. Cf also *Edwinton Commercial Corp v Tsavliris Russ, Worldwide Salvage & Towage Ltd, The Sea Angel* [2007] EWCA Civ 547, [2007] 2 Lloyd's Rep 517 at [117]–[120]. See also below, p 494.

[44] (1874) LR 10 CP 125, above, p 482.

[45] *Embiricos v Sydney Reid & Co* [1914] 3 KB 45; *Scottish Navigation Co v Souter* [1917] 1 KB 222; *Lloyd Royal Belge v Stathatos* (1917) 34 TLR 70.

[46] *International Sea Tankers Inc v Hemisphere Shipping Co Ltd* [1983] 1 Lloyd's Rep 400; *Kodros Shipping Corp of Monrovia v Empresa Cubana de Fletes* [1983] 1 AC 736; *Finelvet AG v Vinava Shipping Co Ltd* [1983] 1 WLR 1469.

[47] See *Adelfamar SA v Silos E Mangimi Martini SpA, The Adelfa* [1988] 2 Lloyd's Rep 466.

[48] *Budgett & Co v Binnington & Co* [1891] 1 QB 35.

[49] *The Penelope* [1982] P 180; *Pioneer Shipping Ltd v BTP Tioxide Ltd* [1982] AC 724.

[50] *Ocean Tramp Tankers Corp v V/O Sovfracht, The Eugenia* [1964] 2 QB 226, overruling *Société Franco Tunisienne D'Armement v Sidermar SpA* [1961] 2 QB 278.

(e) SALE AND CARRIAGE OF GOODS

Similar principles have been applied to contracts for the sale of goods to be carried by sea. In *Nickoll v Ashton Edridge & Co*,[51] for example, a cargo sold by the defendants to the claimants was to be shipped 'per steamship *Orlando* . . . during the month of January'. Without default on the defendant's part the ship was so damaged by stranding as to be unable to load in January. It was held that in these circumstances the contract must be treated as at an end.

The Anglo-French invasion of Egypt in 1956 and the consequent closure of the Suez Canal led to a number of cases concerning the frustration of cif contracts[52] for the sale of goods. Among these was *Tsakiroglou & Co Ltd v Noblee Thorl GmbH*:[53]

T agreed to sell to NT a quantity of groundnuts to be shipped from the Sudan to Hamburg during November or December 1956. On 2 November, the Suez Canal was closed and remained closed for the next 5 months. The price of the groundnuts cif Hamburg was clearly calculated on the basis of shipment via the canal, but the contract contained no term to this effect. T refused to perform the contract, claiming that it had been frustrated by the closure of the canal.

The House of Lords held there was no frustration, since it would still be possible to ship the nuts to Hamburg around the Cape of Good Hope. Such a journey would not be commercially or fundamentally different from that by the canal, but merely more expensive. Their Lordships also pointed out that the contract was one of sale of goods, the transport of which is normally of no direct concern to the buyer. Nevertheless, they indicated that, if the goods had been perishable or if a definite date had been fixed for delivery, the contract might possibly have then been frustrated by the necessity for the longer Cape route.

(f) BUILDING CONTRACTS

Further instances of the doctrine of frustration are provided by cases concerning building or construction contracts. Events may occur which hold up completion of the works. Such delays inevitably increase the contractor's costs. If the contract is a fixed-price contract, the contractor may lose the profit which it expected to gain, or even be forced into loss. In *Davis Contractors Ltd v Fareham UDC*:[54]

In July 1946, D entered into a contract with Fareham UDC to build 78 houses for a fixed sum of £94,424 within eight months. Owing to the unexpected shortage of skilled labour and of certain materials the contract took 22 months to complete, and cost some £115,000. D contended that the contract had been frustrated and that they were entitled to claim on a quantum meruit for the cost actually incurred.

[51] [1901] 2 KB 126.

[52] 'Cif' stands for cost, insurance, and freight. In a cif contract the price will be agreed on the basis that it includes insurance of the goods while in transit and the expenses of carriage (freight) to the port of destination.

[53] [1962] AC 93, overruling *Carapanayoti & Co Ltd v ET Green Ltd* [1959] 1 QB 131.

[54] [1956] AC 696.

The House of Lords refused to accept this contention. The mere fact that unforeseen circumstances had delayed the performance of the contract, and rendered it more onerous to the appellants, did not discharge the agreement. The ultimate situation was still within the scope of the contract; the thing undertaken was not, when performed, different from that contracted for.

These strict requirements were, however, fulfilled in the case of *Metropolitan Water Board v Dick, Kerr & Co Ltd*:[55]

DK & Co contracted with the MWB to construct a reservoir within 6 years. Two years elapsed when the Minister of Munitions, acting under statutory powers, required them to cease work on their contract and to remove and sell their plant. The MWB brought an action claiming that the contract still continued.

The House of Lords held that the interruption created by the prohibition was of such a character and duration as to make the contract, if resumed, in effect a different contract, and that the original contract was therefore discharged.

(g) CHANGE IN THE LAW

The performance of a contract may be made legally impossible either by a change in the law or by a change in the operation of the law by reason of new facts supervening. The law may actually forbid the doing of some act undertaken in the contract;[56] or it may take from the control of the promisor something in respect of which it has contracted to act or not to act in a certain way, as, for example, where a piece of land subject to a restrictive covenant against building is compulsorily acquired and built upon by Act of Parliament.[57] Such cases are explained by policy and 'the elementary proposition that if further performance of a contract becomes impossible by legislation having that effect the contract is discharged'.[58]

For there to be frustration, the change in the law must be such as to strike at the root of the agreement, and not merely to suspend or hinder its operation in part. So it has been held that a nine-year building lease was not frustrated by Government restrictions on building for only a small part of the term,[59] and that the rights of a payee of a cheque drawn on a bank in Holland were not discharged by an enemy invasion

[55] [1918] AC 119.

[56] *Denny, Mott & Dickson Ltd v James B Fraser & Co Ltd* [1944] AC 265.

[57] *Baily v De Crespigny* (1869) LR 4 QB 180. See also *Studholme v South Western Gas Board* [1954] 1 WLR 313; *Hildron Finance Ltd v Sunley Holdings Ltd* [2010] EWHC 1681 (Ch), [2010] 3 EGLR 1.

[58] *Reilly v The King* [1934] AC 176, 180 (Lord Atkin). On the implications for the theoretical basis of the doctrine, see below, pp 490–6. Supervening illegality, for the purposes of the doctrine of frustration, is not limited to 'public policy' grounds considered in *Patel v Mirza* [2016] UKSC 42, [2017] AC 467 (above, Chapter 11): *Canary Wharf (BP4) T1 Ltd v European Medicines Agency* [2019] EWHC 335 (Ch), [2019] L & TR 14 at [170].

[59] *Cricklewood Property and Investment Trust Ltd v Leighton's Investment Trust Ltd* [1945] AC 221; below, p 503. See also *Libyan Arab Foreign Bank v Bankers Trust Co* [1989] QB 728, 772 (Staughton J); *Wilmington Trust SP Services (Dublin) Ltd v Spicejet Ltd* [2021] EWHC 1117 (Comm) at [65] (use of leased aircraft suspended for (so far) only 10 per cent of the term of lease, by reason of Indian Government restrictions which were expected to be temporary).

and occupation of that country rendering presentation for payment illegal there but not elsewhere.[60] Lesser interruptions may, however, be covered by provisions in the contract, for instance clauses providing a seller with an excuse for non-performance in the event of 'prohibition of export . . . preventing fulfilment',[61] although, as will be seen, the presence of such a clause may preclude the application of the doctrine of frustration.

The outbreak of war is another event which, by changing the operation of the law, may have the effect of abrogating obligations outstanding under a contract by reason of supervening illegality, if one of the parties resides in this country and the other in enemy or enemy-occupied territory, and the contract is one which involves commercial dealings with the enemy.[62] So strong are the public policy considerations in this situation that the contract will be wholly frustrated, even though the parties themselves provide that their obligations shall be merely postponed.[63]

(h) PERFORMANCE OF ONLY ONE PARTY AFFECTED

The illustrations above show that, save in cases of supervening illegality, a frustrating event often affects the ability of only one of the parties to perform, while the other party, who usually has to pay money, is still capable of performing. So, in the requisitioning cases considered above, the charterers were able to pay the hire, and may have been willing to do so notwithstanding the non-availability of the ship, since the rate paid by the Government for requisitioned ships was higher than that payable under the charter.[64] Nevertheless, if the event is a frustrating one, it excuses both parties even where this may be to the advantage of the party who is unable to perform.

4. THE THEORETICAL BASIS OF FRUSTRATION

Considerable judicial attention has been paid to the theoretical basis of the doctrine of discharge of a contract by frustration, perhaps because of a perceived need to explain why a finding of frustration does not constitute a reallocation of risks nor permit an escape from a bad bargain.[65]

Successive pronouncements of the House of Lords have set out a number of learned, but often contradictory, opinions concerning this issue and a number of theories

[60] *Cornelius v Banque Franco-Serbe* [1942] 1 KB 29.

[61] On such clauses, see *Bremer Handelsgesellschaft mbH v Vanden Avenne-Izegem PVBA* [1978] 2 Lloyd's Rep 109; *Bremer Handelsgesellschaft mbH v C Mackprang Jr* [1979] 1 Lloyd's Rep 221; *Bremer Handelsgesellschaft mbH v Westzucker GmbH (No 3)* [1989] 1 Lloyd's Rep 198, and Peel, *Frustration and Force Majeure* (4th edn, 2022) para 12-025 ff.

[62] *Ertel Bieber & Co v Rio Tinto Co Ltd* [1918] AC 260; *Fibrosa Spolka Akcyjna v Fairbairn Lawson Combe Barbour Ltd* [1943] AC 32 (below, p 507); McNair and Watts, *The Legal Effects of War* (4th edn, 1966) ch 3.

[63] *Ertel Bieber & Co v Rio Tinto Co Ltd* [1918] AC 260.

[64] *FA Tamplin Steamship Co Ltd v Anglo-Mexican Petroleum Products Co Ltd* [1916] 2 AC 397, 405, 410, 422; *Bank Line Ltd v Arthur Capel & Co* [1919] AC 435, above, p 486.

[65] *Pacific Phosphates Co Ltd v Empire Transport* (1920) 4 LLR 189, 190.

have been put forward at various times. Since there is now general agreement on the appropriate test to be applied, it is necessary to refer only briefly to the four principal tests or 'theories' which have been advanced.[66]

(a) IMPLIED TERM

At one time the preponderance of judicial opinion favoured the view that frustration of a contract depended upon the implication of a term although this did not explain discharge where the performance of the contract is made *legally* impossible by a change in the law or its operation.[67] Lord Loreburn's speech in *FA Tamplin Steamship Co Ltd v Anglo-Mexican Petroleum Products Co Ltd*[68] contains the classic exposition of the reasons on which the implied term theory of frustration was based:

> [A] Court can and ought to examine the contract and the circumstances in which it was made, not of course to vary, but only to explain it, in order to see whether or not from the nature of it the parties must have made their bargain on the footing that a particular thing or state of things would continue to exist. And if they must have done so, then a term to that effect will be implied, though it be not expressed in the contract . . . Sometimes it is put that performance has become impossible and that the party concerned did not promise to perform an impossibility. Sometimes it is put that the parties contemplated a certain state of things which fell out otherwise. In most of the cases it is said that there was an implied condition in the contract which operated to release the parties from performing it, and in all of them I think that was at bottom the principle upon which the Court proceeded. It is in my opinion the true principle, for no Court has an absolving power, but it can infer from the nature of the contract and the surrounding circumstances that a condition which was not expressed was a foundation on which the parties contracted . . . Were the altered conditions such that, had they thought of them, they would have taken their chance of them, or such that as sensible men they would have said, 'If that happens, of course, it is all over between us'?

A contract would therefore be frustrated if a term could be implied that, in the events that subsequently happened, the contract would come to an end. The expression 'an implied term' is, however, ambiguous. It may be used in a subjective sense, that is to say, it may mean a term which the Court reads into the contract in order to give effect to what it regards as the parties' real intention at the time of contracting. As was said in a later case[69] 'the law is only doing what the parties really (though subconsciously) meant

[66] In *National Carriers Ltd v Panalpina (Northern) Ltd* [1981] AC 675, 687, Lord Hailsham LC stated there were at least five theories; in addition to those considered below, he referred to and rejected one based on total failure of consideration. For a failed attempt to argue failure of consideration or failure of basis (rather than frustration) to justify non-payment of rent during the COVID-19 pandemic, see *Bank of New York Mellon (International) Ltd v Cine-UK Ltd* [2022] EWCA Civ 1021, [2023] L & TR 2. See also English, *Discharge of Contractual Obligations* (2025) ch 6 (frustration as failure of an implied condition).

[67] In the heyday of the implied contract theory, legal impossibility was sometimes said to differ from other categories of frustration: *Joseph Constantine SS Line Ltd v Imperial Smelting Corp Ltd* [1942] AC 154, 163.

[68] [1916] 2 AC 397, 403–4; see above, p 486, for the facts. For more recent support for this theory, see Smith (1994) 110 LQR 400, 403.

[69] *Hirji Mulji v Cheong Yue SS Co Ltd* [1926] AC 497, 504.

to do for themselves'. To such an implied term a number of objections may be raised. The general test for implication of terms on the facts is not subjective but objective.[70] In any event, it is difficult to see how the parties could be taken, even impliedly, to have provided for something which never occurred to them.[71] Moreover, had it occurred to them, it is unlikely that they would have agreed that the contract was to come to an end. Lord Wright said:[72]

It is not possible, to my mind, to say that if they had thought of it, they would have said: 'Well, if that happens, all is over between us'. On the contrary, they would almost certainly on the one side or the other have sought to introduce reservations or qualifications or compensations.

That this is so is shown by the widespread use of so-called *force majeure* clauses which specify what is to happen on the occurrence of an event which affects one or both parties' performance.[73]

On the other hand, the implied term may be formulated more objectively. It may mean a term which, in the light of the events which have actually arisen, the parties *as reasonable people* would have imported into the contract to deal with that possibility.[74] When used in this sense, the implied term is betrayed by a similar artificiality. The 'reasonable person' has no real existence and represents 'no more than the anthropomorphic conception of justice'; an opinion ascribed to such a person is, in fact, that of the Court, which is and must be the spokesman of the fair and reasonable person.[75] An implied term of this sort is no more than a fiction, something added to the contract by the law.

(b) 'JUST AND REASONABLE RESULT'

The discharge of a contract by frustration occurs, not because of the actual or imputed will of the parties, but by operation of law. The doctrine of frustration is, as Lord Sumner pointed out, 'a device, by which the rules as to absolute contracts are reconciled with a special exception which justice demands'.[76] In declaring a contract to have been frustrated, the Court exercises a positive function: it releases the parties from further performance of the obligations which they would otherwise be bound to perform.

Recognition of these facts led certain of the judges (and notably Lord Wright and Lord Denning) to the conclusion that the basis of the doctrine of frustration was the

[70] Above, pp 170–9.

[71] *Davis Contractors Ltd v Fareham UDC* [1956] AC 696, 728. Also see the example given by Lord Sands in *James Scott & Sons Ltd v Del Sel* 1922 SC 592, 597: 'A tiger has escaped from a travelling menagerie. The milkgirl fails to deliver the milk. Possibly the milkman may be exonerated from any breach of contract: but, even so, it would seem hardly reasonable to base that exoneration on the ground that "tiger days excepted" must be held as if written into the milk contract.' See further, *FC Shepherd & Co Ltd v Jerrom* [1987] 1 QB 301, 322.

[72] *Denny, Mott & Dickson Ltd v James B Fraser & Co Ltd* [1944] AC 265, 275.

[73] On '*force majeure*' clauses, see above, p 480, n 6.

[74] *Dahl v Nelson, Donkin & Co* (1881) 6 App Cas 38, 59.

[75] *Davis Contractors Ltd v Fareham UDC* [1956] AC 696, 728 (Lord Radcliffe).

[76] *Hirji Mulji v Cheong Yue SS Co Ltd* [1926] AC 497, 510.

desire of the Courts to reach a just and reasonable result.[77] 'The truth is', Lord Wright said,[78] 'that the Court or jury as a judge of fact decides the question in accordance with what seems just and reasonable in its eyes'. This view might be taken to suggest that a Court had the power to release the parties from their obligations whenever it was just and reasonable to do so,[79] even, for example, where the only effect of the subsequent event had been to render the contract financially more onerous than the parties had anticipated. But it is clear that the circumstances in which a contract will be held to have been frustrated are far more limited in scope.[80]

(c) FOUNDATION OF THE CONTRACT

Some test was, therefore, required which would recognize that frustration did not depend on the intentions of the parties, but which would not permit contracts to be too easily discharged. The first such test to be formulated was that of the 'disappearance of the foundation of the contract'. The question to be asked was whether the events that had occurred were of a character and extent so sweeping as to cause the foundation of the contract to disappear.[81] It was adopted, for example, by Goddard J in *WJ Tatem Ltd v Gamboa*:[82]

During the Spanish Civil War, T chartered to G, acting on behalf of the Republican Government of Spain, a steamship, for 30 days from 1 July 1937. The ship was to be used for the evacuation of refugees from Northern Spain to French ports. The hire was to be at the rate of £250 a day and was payable until the ship was returned to T. On 14 July, the ship was seized by the Nationalists and detained in the port of Bilbao until 11 September. In answer to T's claim for hire, G pleaded that the contract had been frustrated.

Goddard J was prepared to assume that the circumstances of the contract (including the very high rate of hire) showed that the parties contemplated that seizure and detention of the vessel might occur. He nevertheless held that the contract was frustrated: the foundation of the contract was destroyed by the seizure, as G thereafter no longer had the use of the vessel. The expression 'foundation' of the contract is, however, imprecise, and it leaves open the question what is the foundation of the contract in a particular case. Moreover, the test is difficult to apply to situations other than those in which the subject-matter of the contract ceases to be available. It has, therefore, been rejected by the House of Lords.[83]

[77] *Joseph Constantine Steamship Line Ltd v Imperial Shipping Corp Ltd* [1942] AC 154, 186.

[78] *Legal Essays and Addresses* (1939) 259. See also *Denny, Mott & Dickson Ltd v James B Fraser & Co Ltd* [1944] AC 265, 274–6.

[79] *British Movietonews Ltd v London and District Cinemas Ltd* [1951] 1 KB 190, 201–2 (Denning LJ, disapproved on appeal: [1952] AC 166, 185, 188).

[80] See *Notcutt v Universal Equipment Co (London) Ltd* [1986] 1 WLR 641, 646–7, where the Court of Appeal rejected an argument to the effect that, before a Court could determine that a contract was frustrated, it must be shown that it would be unjust to hold the parties to the contract.

[81] *FA Tamplin Steamship Co Ltd v Anglo-Mexican Petroleum Products Co Ltd* [1916] 2 AC 397, 406.

[82] [1939] 1 KB 132.

[83] *National Carriers Ltd v Panalpina (Northern) Ltd* [1981] AC 675.

(d) RADICAL CHANGE IN THE OBLIGATION

There is now general agreement that the appropriate test to apply to determine whether a contract has been frustrated is that of a 'radical change in the obligation'. In *Davis Contractors Ltd v Fareham UDC*, Lord Radcliffe said:

[F]rustration occurs whenever the law recognizes that without default of either party a contractual obligation has become incapable of being performed because the circumstances in which performance is called for would render it a thing radically different from that which was undertaken by the contract. Non haec in foedera veni. It was not this that I promised to do.[84]

This test has been adopted by the House of Lords in several cases,[85] and was reformulated by Lord Simon in *National Carriers Ltd v Panalpina (Northern) Ltd*:[86]

Frustration of a contract takes place when there supervenes an event (without default of either party and for which the contract makes no sufficient provision) which so significantly changes the nature (not merely the expense or onerousness) of the outstanding contractual rights and/or obligations from what the parties could reasonably have contemplated at the time of its execution that it would be unjust to hold them to the literal sense of its stipulations in the new circumstances; in such a case the law declares both parties to be discharged from further performance.

This approach has sometimes been called the 'construction' theory, because it requires the Court first to construe the terms of contract in the light of its nature and the relevant surrounding circumstances when it was made. The original obligation undertaken by the parties can thus be determined. The Court must then consider whether there would be a radical change in that obligation if performance were enforced in the circumstances which have subsequently arisen. A mere rise in cost or expense will not suffice. 'It is not hardship or inconvenience or material loss itself which calls the principle of frustration into play. There must be as well such a change in the significance of the obligation that the thing undertaken would, if performed, be a different thing from that contracted for.'[87] However, the Court of Appeal has emphasized that the application of this test

[84] [1956] AC 696, 729; for the facts, see above, p 488. The Latin phrase is said to be drawn from Virgil's *Aeneid*, Book 4, lines 338–9: see Sir John Megaw, letter to *The Times*, 20 December 1980 and *Edwinton Commercial Corp v Tsavliris Russ (Worldwide Salvage & Towage) Ltd, The Sea Angel* [2007] EWCA Civ 547 at [84] n 1 (Rix LJ: 'It is ironic that Aeneas's shabby excuse to Dido has become the watchword of the modern doctrine of frustration'). But whether the relationship between Aeneas and Queen Dido was affected by a supervening event (Mercury's intervention) or an initial mistake (as to the nature of the relationship) is not entirely clear. Neither is it clear that Aeneas's 'excuses' for his planned desertion of Queen Dido, were as shabby as many (from Ovid to Sir John Megaw) consider them to be; see Williams, *Tradition and Originality in Roman Poetry* (1968) 378–6 and John Sparrow, Jackson Knight Memorial Lecture, *Dido v Aeneas: The Case for the Defence* (1973).

[85] *Tsakiroglou & Co Ltd v Noblee Thorl GmbH* [1962] AC 93, 131; *Pioneer Shipping Ltd v BTP Tioxide Ltd* [1982] AC 724, 744, 745, 751; *Paal Wilson & Co A/S v Partenreederei Hannah Blumenthal* [1983] 1 AC 854, 909, 918. See also *William Sindall plc v Cambridgeshire County Council* [1994] 1 WLR 1016, 1039.

[86] [1981] AC 675, 700. See also *ibid*, 688, 717. For the facts, see below, p 504.

[87] *Davis Contractors Ltd v Fareham UDC* [1956] AC 696, 729 (Lord Radcliffe). See also *British Movietonews Ltd v London and District Cinemas Ltd* [1952] AC 166, 185; *Tsakiroglou & Co Ltd v Noblee Thorl GmbH* [1962] AC 93.

cannot safely be performed without the consequences of the decision being measured against the demands of justice since, among other considerations, the frustration of a contract may well mean that the contractual allocation of risk is reversed.[88]

(i) Application of test

The test is clearly meant to be difficult to satisfy. It is, moreover, easier to state than to apply. 'The data for decision are, on the one hand, the terms and construction of the contract, read in the light of the then existing circumstances, and on the other hand the events which have occurred.'[89] If the parties have themselves provided for the situation that has arisen the contract governs and there is no frustration. If they have not provided for it then the new situation must be compared with the situation for which they did provide to see how different it is.[90] The comparison is between the rights and obligations of the parties after the event, assuming the contract still binds them, and what their rights and obligations would have been had the event not occurred. We have noted the factors taken into account in contracts of employment.[91] In contracts for the carriage of goods by sea and charterparties, account may be taken of the extent to which the goods carried or to be carried are liable to damage or to deterioration,[92] or are subject to a seasonal market,[93] and the extent to which the vessel and crew are fit to proceed in the new circumstances. To constitute frustration, the event or events must make performance of the contract a thing 'radically' or 'fundamentally' different in a commercial sense from that undertaken by the contract. These concepts are elusive and the Courts recognize that it is often difficult to draw the line[94] and that the question is one of degree.[95] It has been said that application of the doctrine of frustration requires a 'multi-factorial approach':[96]

> Among the factors which have to be considered are the terms of the contract itself, its matrix or context, the parties' knowledge, expectations, assumptions and contemplations, in particular as to risk, as at the time of contract, at any rate so far as these can be ascribed mutually and objectively, and then the nature of the supervening event, and the parties' reasonable and objectively ascertainable calculations as to the possibilities of future performance in the new circumstances.

[88] *Edwinton Commercial Corp v Tsavliris Russ (Worldwide Salvage & Towage) Ltd, The Sea Angel* [2007] EWCA Civ 547 at [112].

[89] *Denny, Mott & Dickson Ltd v James B Fraser & Co Ltd* [1944] AC 265, 274–5 (Lord Wright).

[90] *The Eugenia* [1964] 2 QB 226, 239.

[91] Above, p 485.

[92] *Tsakiroglou & Co Ltd v Noblee Thorl GmbH* [1962] AC 93, 115, 118, 123. See also *Jackson v Union Marine Insurance* (1874) LR 10 CP 125, 146 (carriage of ice would be frustrated by shorter delay than carriage of iron rails).

[93] *Jackson v Union Marine Insurance* (1874) LR 10 CP 125, 115. See also *ibid*, 146.

[94] *The Eugenia* [1964] 2 QB 226, 239.

[95] *National Carriers Ltd v Panalpina (Northern) Ltd* [1981] AC 675, 688; *Pioneer Shipping v BTP Tioxide* [1982] AC 724, 744.

[96] *Edwinton Commercial Corp v Tsavliris Russ (Worldwide Salvage & Towage) Ltd, The Sea Angel* [2007] EWCA Civ 547 at [111] (Rix LJ), applied frequently; see eg *Canary Wharf (BP4) T1 Ltd v European Medicines Agency* [2019] EWHC 335 (Ch) at [30]–[40]; *Iris Helicopter Leasing Ltd v Elitaliana SRL* [2021] EWHC 2459 (Comm) at [21] (Rix LJ's judgment 'might be regarded as the currently leading judgment').

However, long-term contracts are in general less easily frustrated than short-term contracts.[97]

(ii) Similarity to test for discharge for breach

The terms 'radical' and 'fundamental' are also used to determine whether a contract may be discharged for breach of an innominate term.[98] In *Hongkong Fir Shipping Co Ltd v Kawasaki Kisen Kaisha Ltd*[99] Diplock LJ stated that *Jackson v Union Marine Insurance Co Ltd*[100] was seeking to apply to frustrating events the same standard as if they had arisen by a breach by one of the parties. For the purpose of determining whether a contract may be discharged, it is the happening of the event and not whether the event was the result of a breach that is crucial.[101] Despite this, in practice it is more likely than not that there will be differences between cases of frustration and cases of breach because in the context of breach, factors other than the ratio of failure to the performance undertaken are relevant to the question of whether the breach is fundamental.

(iii) Question of law

The application of the 'radical change in the obligation' test is a matter of law; but once it is shown that a judge or arbitrator has correctly applied the test to the facts found by him, an appellate Court should be slow to differ from their conclusion.[102]

5. INCIDENCE OF RISK

The doctrine of frustration is principally concerned with the incidence of risk—who must take the risk of the happening of the supervening event? The Courts have therefore to determine whether the contract, on its true construction, has made provision for that risk. We have noted that increased expense, even if caused by wholly abnormal fluctuations in prices, does not frustrate.[103] In this connection, the cases show that a number of difficult questions may arise.

[97] *National Carriers Ltd v Panalpina (Northern) Ltd* [1981] AC 675, 691 (Lord Hailsham LC); see also *Lord Strathcona Shipping Co Ltd v Dominion Coal Co Ltd* [1926] AC 108, 114.

[98] Below, p 531. See also above, pp 156–7.

[99] [1962] 2 QB 26, on which see below, p 531.

[100] Above, p 482.

[101] [1962] 2 QB 26, 49, 68. See also, in the same context, *The Hermosa* [1980] 1 Lloyd's Rep 638, 649 (delay by a variety of events, some the consequences of breach and some not).

[102] *Pioneer Shipping Ltd v BTP Tioxide Ltd* [1982] AC 724, 738, 752–3.

[103] Above, p 489: *Davis Contractors Ltd v Fareham UDC* [1956] AC 696, 724 (Lord Reid) and *Tsakiroglou & Co Ltd v Noblee Thorl GmbH* [1962] AC 93. But note that in the latter case at 118 Lord Reid reserved his position on an increase which reached a wholly astronomical figure, and cf *William Cory v LCC* [1951] 1 KB 8, 13, aff'd [1951] 2 KB 476.

(a) EXPRESS PROVISION

Except in certain cases of illegality[104] there is little doubt that it is open to the parties to provide that the contract shall continue, or be merely suspended, and not discharged, upon the occurrence of a particular event, or to allocate the risks attendant upon that event. Where the contract makes provision (ie full and complete provision, so intended) for a given contingency, this will preclude the Court from holding that the contract is frustrated.[105] But the parties may fail to make complete provision, as happened in the *Bank Line* case,[106] where the option given to the charterers to cancel or continue with the charterparty if the ship should be requisitioned, was held not to be intended to apply to requisitioning of so long a duration as to make the charter, as a matter of business, a wholly different thing. And a provision in a building contract, for example, that the contractor is to be allowed an extension of time in the event of 'delays', may be construed as inapplicable to a situation where the delay which occurs is such as to bring about a radical change in the obligation.[107] In this type of case, the contract can still be frustrated.

It is also open to the parties to provide that the contract is to be suspended or discharged by a non-frustrating event.[108] There are, for example, difficulties in determining whether a given delay or prospective delay frustrates a contract.[109] As a matter of interpretation the Court may conclude that the parties preferred the certainty of termination after a specified period of delay, pursuant to a contractual term, to the uncertainty of possible discharge under the doctrine of frustration.[110]

(b) FORESEEN EVENTS

The second question is whether events which were foreseen by the parties at the time of contracting can be relied upon to establish frustration. In many of the cases reference is made to the occurrence of an 'unforeseen' or 'unexpected' or 'uncontemplated' event, and it may be argued that the parties must be taken to have assumed the risk of an event which was present in their minds at the time the contract was made. It is, however, a question of construction of the contract whether it was intended to continue to be binding in that event,[111] or whether, in the absence of any express

[104] See above, p 489.

[105] *Bank Line Ltd v Arthur Capel & Co* [1919] AC 435, 455; *Joseph Constantine Steamship Line Ltd v Imperial Smelting Corporation Ltd* [1942] AC 154, 163. See also *Salam Air SAOC v Latam Airlines Groups SA* [2020] EWHC 2414 (Comm) (risk assumed on 'hell or highwater' basis); *Barclays Bank Plc v VEB.RF* [2024] EWHC 1074 (Comm) at [53]–[54] (objective construction of the agreement).

[106] [1919] AC 435, above, p 486. See also *Jackson v Union Marine Insurance Co Ltd* (1874) LR 10 CP 125 (clause excusing one party only from liability in a given contingency).

[107] *Metropolitan Water Board v Dick, Kerr & Co Ltd* [1918] AC 119, above, p 489.

[108] Above, pp 476, 480.

[109] Below, p 498.

[110] *Total Gas Marketing Ltd v Arco British Ltd* [1998] 2 Lloyd's Rep 209, 222 (Lord Steyn).

[111] *Larrinaga & Co v Société Franco Américaine des Phosphates de Medulla* (1923) 39 TLR 316; *Maritime National Fish Ltd v Ocean Trawlers Ltd* [1935] AC 524; *Chandler Bros Ltd v Boswell* [1936] 3 All ER 179.

provision, the issue has been left open,[112] so as to allow the incidence of risk to be determined by the law relating to frustration. In *WJ Tatem Ltd v Gamboa*,[113] for example, the fact that seizure of the ship was within the contemplation of the parties did not preclude the operation of frustration since the contract made no express provision for the contingency.

(c) PREVENTION OF PERFORMANCE IN MANNER INTENDED BY ONE PARTY

The third question is whether a contract will be frustrated by an event which prevents performance in a manner intended by one party alone. In *Blackburn Bobbin Co Ltd v TW Allen & Sons Ltd*:[114]

A agreed to sell and deliver to BB at Hull a quantity of Finnish birch timber. A found it impossible to fulfil this contract because the outbreak of war cut off its source of supply from Finland. BB was unaware that timber from Finland was normally shipped direct from a Finnish port to England, and that timber merchants did not, in practice, hold stocks of it in England.

The Court of Appeal held that there was no frustration. What had happened was merely that an event had occurred which rendered it practically impossible for the defendants to deliver: that event might have been, but was not, provided for in the contract. To free A from liability, it would have to be shown that the continuance of the normal mode of shipping the timber from Finland was a matter which *both* parties contemplated as necessary for the fulfilment of the contracts. Since this was not the case, A bore the risk.

(d) DELAY

Frequently, as we have seen, a subsequent event causes delay[115] in the performance of the contract, bringing financial loss to one of the parties. But the risk of delay is one which has to be accepted in commercial transactions. Lord Sumner said:[116]

Delay even of considerable length and of wholly uncertain duration is an incident of maritime adventure, which is clearly within the contemplation of the parties . . . so much so as to be often the subject of express provisions. Delays such as these may very seriously affect the

[112] *WJ Tatem Ltd v Gamboa* [1939] 1 KB 132, 138; *The Eugenia* [1964] 2 QB 226, 239; *The Nile Co for the Export of Agricultural Crops v H & JM Bennett (Commodities) Ltd* [1986] 1 Lloyd's Rep 555, 582. See also *Edwinton Commercial Corp v Tsavliris Russ (Worldwide Salvage & Towage) Ltd, The Sea Angel* [2007] EWCA Civ 547 at [99]–[103].

[113] [1939] 1 KB 132; see above, p 493.

[114] [1918] 2 KB 467. It was also said in this case that there could never be frustration of a contract for the sale of unascertained goods, but this is probably too wide: see *Re Badische Co Ltd* [1921] 2 Ch 331; *Tsakiroglou & Co Ltd v Noblee Thorl GmbH* [1962] AC 93; above, p 488; *CTI Group Inc v Transclear SA, The Mary Nour* [2008] EWCA Civ 856, [2008] 2 Lloyd's Rep 526.

[115] See Stannard (1983) 46 MLR 738.

[116] *Bank Line Ltd v Arthur Capel & Co* [1919] AC 435, 458–9.

commercial object of the adventure, for the ship's expenses and overhead charges are running on . . . None the less this is not frustration.

The delay must be such as 'to render the adventure absolutely nugatory',[117] 'to make it unreasonable to require the parties to go on',[118] 'to destroy the identity of the work or service when resumed with the work or service when interrupted',[119] 'to put an end in a commercial sense to the undertaking'.[120] It may, however, be difficult for the parties to determine whether, at any particular point of time, the delay is of this nature. On this point, Lord Roskill, in *Pioneer Shipping Ltd v BTP Tioxide Ltd*,[121] provided guidance:

> [I]t is often necessary to wait upon events in order to see whether the delay already suffered and the prospects of further delay from that cause, will make any ultimate performance of the relevant contractual obligations 'radically different'. . . from that which was undertaken by the contract. But, as has often been said, business men must not be required to await events too long. They are entitled to know where they stand. Whether or not the delay is such as to bring about frustration must be a question to be determined by an informed judgment based upon all the evidence of what has occurred and what is likely thereafter to occur.

While, therefore, it is for the tribunal to which the issue has been referred to decide as a question of law whether or not the contract has been frustrated, 'that conclusion is almost completely determined by what is ascertained as to mercantile usage and the understanding of mercantile men'[122] about 'the significance of the commercial differences between what was promised and what in the changed circumstances would now fall to be performed'.[123]

Even where the delay is prima facie sufficient, where one or both parties are responsible for it, the rule that reliance cannot be placed on a self-induced frustration will preclude discharge.[124]

(e) INFLATION

In *Staffordshire Area Health Authority v South Staffordshire Waterworks Co*[125] a contract was entered into in 1929 under which the defendants agreed 'at all times hereafter' to supply water to a hospital at a fixed price of seven (old) pence per 1,000 gallons. By 1978 the equivalent cost of supplying the water was some 20 times the contract price. The Court of Appeal held that the contract was, on its true construction, terminable by the

[117] *Bensaude & Co v Thames and Mersey Marine Insurance Co* [1897] 1 QB 29, 31 (Lord Esher), [1897] AC 609, 611, 612, 614.

[118] *Metropolitan Water Board v Dick, Kerr & Co Ltd* [1918] AC 199, 131 (Lord Atkinson); *FA Tamplin Steamship Co Ltd v Anglo-Mexican Petroleum Products Co Ltd* [1916] 2 AC 397, 405 (Lord Loreburn).

[119] *Metropolitan Water Board v Dick, Kerr & Co Ltd* [1918] AC 199, 128 (Lord Dunedin); *Bank Line Ltd v Arthur Capel & Co* [1919] AC 435, 460 (Lord Sumner).

[120] *Jackson v Union Marine Insurance Co Ltd* (1874) LR 10 CP 125.

[121] [1982] AC 724, 752.

[122] *Tsakiroglou & Co Ltd v Noblee Thorl GmbH* [1962] AC 93, 124.

[123] *Pioneer Shipping Ltd v BTP Tioxide Ltd* [1982] AC 724.

[124] *Paal Wilson & Co A/S v Partenreederei Hannah Blumenthal* [1983] 1 AC 854. See below, p 500.

[125] [1978] 1 WLR 1387.

defendants upon reasonable notice.[126] But Lord Denning MR expressed the opinion[127] that, by reason of 50 years of continuing inflation, a fundamentally different situation had emerged in which the contract had ceased to bind. His reasoning was not, however, accepted by the other members of the Court of Appeal, and the orthodox view is that any depreciation in the purchasing power of sterling,[128] or the devaluation of a foreign currency in which a debt is expressed,[129] is a risk which must be borne by the creditor. If the creditor does not wish to bear this risk, provision may be made in the contract. In certain contexts, for example leases, it is not unusual for the terms of the contract to provide for modification of the price to take account of inflation.

6. SELF-INDUCED FRUSTRATION

It is well established that a party whose act or election has given rise to the event which is alleged to have frustrated the contract cannot invoke the doctrine of frustration; reliance cannot be placed upon a self-induced frustration.[130] In *Maritime National Fish Ltd v Ocean Trawlers Ltd*:[131]

OT chartered to MNF a steam trawler fitted with an otter trawl. Both parties knew at the time of the contract that it was illegal to use an otter trawl without a licence from the Canadian Government. Some months later MNF applied for licences for five trawlers which it was operating, including OT's trawler and three trawlers owned directly or indirectly by MNF. It was informed that only three licences would be granted, and was requested to state for which of the three trawlers it desired to have licences. It named two trawlers that it owned directly or indirectly and a third chartered from a person other than OT, and then claimed that it was no longer bound by the charterparty as its object had been frustrated.

The Privy Council held that the failure of the contract was the result of MNF's own election, and that since 'reliance cannot be placed upon a self-induced frustration' there was no frustration. Similar conclusions have been reached where, in breach of contract,

[126] On the implication of a term to this effect (less likely where there is a price variation clause), see above, p 477.

[127] [1978] 1 WLR 1387, 1397–8. He did not, however, hold that the contract was terminated automatically (see below, p 505), but only on reasonable notice.

[128] *Wates Ltd v GLC* (1987) 25 BLR 1, 35.

[129] *British Bank for Foreign Trade Ltd v Russian Commercial and Industrial Bank* (1921) 38 TLR 65; *Re Chesterman's Trusts* [1923] 2 Ch 466.

[130] *J Lauritzen AS v Wijsmuller BV, The Super Servant Two* [1990] 1 Lloyd's Rep 1, 8; *Canary Wharf (BP4) T1 Ltd v European Medicines Agency* [2019] EWHC 335 (Ch) at [201]–[207]. A party cannot rely on its own self-induced frustration to say that the contract is not frustrated: *FC Shepherd & Co Ltd v Jerrom* [1987] 1 QB 301, below, p 506. But where the relevant act is caused by a third party for whose action the party claiming frustration is not responsible the result is not considered to be self-induced frustration: *Adelfamar SA v Silos E Mangimi SpA, The Adelfa* [1988] 2 Lloyd's Rep 466, 471.

[131] [1935] AC 524 (see [1934] 1 DLR 621, especially at 623 and [1934] 4 DLR 288, especially at 299 for a full statement of the facts). See also *Bank Line Ltd v Arthur Capel & Co* [1919] AC 435, 452; *The Eugenia* [1964] 2 QB 226, 237; *Denmark Productions Ltd v Boscobel Productions Ltd* [1969] 1 QB 699, 725, 736–7; *Paal Wilson & Co A/S v Partenreederei Hannah Blumenthal* [1983] 1 AC 854.

a charterer of a ship allowed the ship to enter a war-zone, where she was trapped,[132] and where parties to arbitration proceedings were in breach of their mutual contractual obligations to apply to the arbitral tribunal for directions to prevent delay in the conduct of the arbitration.[133]

(a) CHOOSING BETWEEN DIFFERENT CONTRACTS

The position is more complicated where a party enters into a number of contracts and the supervening event means that, while it is possible to perform one or more of the contracts, it is not possible to perform them all. This was the position in *J Lauritzen AS v Wijsmuller BV, The Super Servant Two*:[134]

In July 1980 W contracted with L to carry a drilling rig from Japan to a location off Rotterdam using, at its option, either the *Super Servant One* or the *Super Servant Two*. It also entered into two contracts with third parties containing similar substitution clauses, one before the contract with L and one afterwards. In its internal schedules W planned to use the *Super Servant Two* for L's contract and the *Super Servant One* for the other two contracts, but, prior to the time set for performance, the *Super Servant Two* sank. W informed L that it would not transport the rig with either the *Super Servant One* or the *Super Servant Two*, but the parties agreed, without prejudice to their rights under the contract, that the drilling rig would be transported by another, more expensive, method. In answer to L's claim for the losses suffered, W counterclaimed *inter alia* that the sinking of the *Super Servant Two* frustrated the contract.

The Court of Appeal held that the contract was not frustrated. Even if the sinking of the *Super Servant Two* occurred without any fault on the part of W, it was not the cause of the inability to perform. The real cause was said to be W's election not to use the *Super Servant One*, something which it would have been physically possible for it to do. It was said that that exercise of choice meant that W had accepted the risk of the *Super Servant Two* being unable to perform with the result that its unavailability gave rise to a breach not a frustrating event. Moreover, to allow W to rely on the unavailability of the *Super Servant One* as a frustrating event would allow it to rely on its own act of election whereas frustration in theory occurs automatically.

The reasoning in this case has been criticized[135] for not taking sufficient account of the fact that, in the *Maritime National Fish* case, it was possible for OT to perform all

[132] *The Eugenia* [1964] 2 QB 226.

[133] *Paal Wilson & Co A/S v Partenreederei Hannah Blumenthal* [1983] 1 AC 854. The problem of stale arbitrations has now been addressed by legislation empowering the arbitrator to dismiss a claim in the case of inexcusable and inordinate delay where the delay results in a substantial risk that it would not be possible to have a fair resolution of the issues or of serious prejudice to the respondent: Arbitration Act 1996, s 41; see also above, p 468.

[134] [1990] 1 Lloyd's Rep 1, affirming [1989] 1 Lloyd's Rep 149.

[135] Peel, *Frustration and Force Majeure* (4th edn, 2022) para 14-032. Treitel's earlier arguments on the issue were considered and rejected by the Court: [1989] 1 Lloyd's Rep 148, 152–3, 154, 158; [1990] 1 Lloyd's Rep 1, 9, 13–14.

contracts made with third parties, and because the rule that frustration is automatic is not an absolute one.[136] W's 'election' was only as to which contract it was not going to perform and it is submitted that the decision is likely to lead to practical difficulties. It would appear to mean, for instance, that where a farmer agrees to sell to A 250 tons of a crop to be grown on specific land which normally yields over 500 tons, and 250 tons to B, but there is a poor harvest and the yield is only 250 tons, neither contract would be frustrated. But this result is difficult to reconcile with cases, apparently not considered in *The Super Servant Two*, in which neither party to a contract for the sale of a specific crop was held to be liable if the crops failed to materialize.[137] It is also difficult to reconcile with cases in which a seller who, following a partial failure of supply, delivered to other customers or delivered the available supply to all customers on a *pro rata* basis, was held entitled to rely on a *force majeure* clause.[138] In the present state of the law, however, a promisor who wishes protection in the case of a partial failure of supply 'must bargain for the inclusion of a suitable *force majeure* clause in the contract'.[139]

(b) NEGLIGENT ACTS

Where the act of the party pleading frustration was inadvertent and merely negligent the position is not altogether clear. Although there have been frequent statements to the effect that the frustrating event must occur without the 'default' of either party, this point has never been expressly decided. It was discussed by the House of Lords in *Joseph Constantine Steamship Line Ltd v Imperial Smelting Corporation Ltd*, where Lord Russell, commenting on the kind or degree of fault which might debar a party from relying on a self-induced frustration, said:[140]

> The possible varieties are infinite, and can range from the criminality of the scuttler who opens the sea-cocks and sinks his ship, to the thoughtlessness of the prima donna who sits in a draught and loses her voice. I wish to guard against the supposition that every destruction of corpus for which a contractor can be said, to some extent or in some sense, to be responsible, necessarily involves that the resultant frustration is self-induced within the meaning of the phrase.

136 See below, p 506.

137 eg *Howell v Coupland* (1876) 1 QBD 258; *HR & S Sainsbury Ltd v Street* [1972] 1 WLR 834; see below, p 514.

138 *Intertradex SA v Lesieur Tourteaux SARL* [1978] 2 Lloyd's Rep 509, 513; *Bremer Handelsgesellschaft mbH v Mackprang Jr (No 2)* [1979] 1 Lloyd's Rep 221; *Bremer Handelsgesellschaft mbH v Continental Grain Co* [1983] 1 Lloyd's Rep 169, 292; *Bremer Handelsgesellschaft mbH v Vanden Avenne-Izegem PVBA* [1978] 2 Lloyd's Rep 109. In *The Super Servant Two* the *force majeure* cases were said to be of no assistance in the context of frustration: [1989] 1 Lloyd's Rep 148, 158; [1990] 1 Lloyd's Rep 1, 9. For a different view, see Hudson (1968) 31 MLR 535.

139 *J Lauritzen AS v Wijsmuller BV, The Super Servant Two* [1989] 1 Lloyd's Rep 148, 158 (Hobhouse J), although the distinction from frustration may be put into question since his Lordship also accepted that protection might be afforded by an implied term. On '*force majeure*' clauses, see above, p 480, n 6.

140 [1942] AC 154, 179.

In that case:

JC chartered to ISC its steamship *Kingswood* to proceed to Australia and load a cargo there. Before this could be done, a violent explosion occurred in the boiler of the ship which resulted in such a delay as would discharge the contract. The cause of the explosion was never ascertained, but ISC alleged that JC had first to establish that it occurred without its fault before it could rely on the doctrine of frustration and so not be liable for breach of contract.

It was not necessary for the House of Lords to decide whether mere negligence would suffice, for it held that the burden of proving that the event which causes the frustration is due to the act or default of a party lies on the party alleging it to be so. Since ISC failed to satisfy the Court on this point, the contract was discharged. It would appear logical, however, for a finding of negligence to prevent a party claiming that the contract was frustrated where that negligent act caused the alleged frustrating event.[141]

7. LEASES AND CONTRACTS FOR THE SALE OF LAND

There was at one time considerable doubt as to whether the doctrine of frustration applied to leases of land.[142] In 1945, in *Cricklewood Property and Investment Trust Ltd v Leighton's Investment Trust Ltd*[143] the House of Lords held unanimously that, since wartime restrictions preventing the performance of a building lease covered only a small part of the 90 years remaining on the lease, it had not been frustrated. But on the question whether a lease could in any circumstances be terminated by frustration the House was evenly divided. Viscount Simon and Lord Wright considered that, on very rare occasions, frustration could occur, giving as illustrations some vast convulsion of nature which might sweep the property into the sea, or the frustration of a building lease by a perpetual statutory prohibition on building for the remainder of the term. Lord Russell and Lord Goddard took the contrary view. A lease was more than a contract: it vested an estate in land in the lessee, and the contractual obligations which it contained were merely incidental to the relationship of landlord and tenant. If all or some of these should become impossible of performance, the lease would remain.[144] The estate in the land would still be vested in the tenant. Lord Porter, the fifth member of the House, refused to express an opinion.

[141] See *J Lauritzen AS v Wijsmuller BV, The Super Servant Two* [1990] 1 Lloyd's Rep 1, 10.

[142] Leases of chattels do not raise the same policy questions, but the terms of such leases will often preclude the operation of the doctrine of frustration: see, eg, *Salam Air SAOC v Latam Airlines Groups SA* [2020] EWHC 2414 (Comm), and *Wilmington Trust SP Services (Dublin) Ltd v Spicejet Ltd* [2021] EWHC 1117 (Comm) (aircraft leases).

[143] [1945] AC 221.

[144] But there may be excuses for non-performance of covenants short of frustration: *ibid*, 233–4 (Lord Russell); *John Lewis Properties plc v Viscount Chelsea* [1993] 2 EGLR 77, 82.

In 1981, this question was reconsidered by the House of Lords in *National Carriers Ltd v Panalpina (Northern) Ltd*:[145]

P let a warehouse to NC for 10 years from 1 January 1974. NC covenanted that it would not without P's consent use the premises for any purpose other than that of warehousing in connection with its business, or assign, underlet, or part with possession. In May 1979, the local authority temporarily closed the street which provided the only vehicular access to the warehouse. The closure lasted for 20 months and during this period the warehouse could not be used for the purpose contemplated by the lease. In answer to a claim for rent, NC counterclaimed that the lease had been frustrated.

Their Lordships unanimously held that there was no frustration. A majority,[146] however, agreed with Viscount Simon and Lord Wright in the *Cricklewood* case that, in principle, the doctrine of frustration was applicable to leases. 'Coastal erosion as well as the "vast convulsion of nature" . . . can . . . cause houses, gardens, even villages and their churches, to fall into the North Sea.'[147] However, it was said[148] that in practice the doctrine would 'hardly ever' apply. In the present case, having regard to the nature and length of the interruption, and in particular to the fact that the lease would still have some three years to run after the interruption came to an end, it could not be said that the lease had been frustrated.

There appears to be no reported English case in which it has been held that a lease has been frustrated.[149] One reason for this may be the relative indestructibility of land. But the absence of cases of frustration is more likely to be due to the fact that the events which are most likely to occur, for example, fire,[150] are normally expressly provided for in the lease, and the incidence of the risk of less common events (such as requisitioning or war damage)[151] may be held to have been assumed by the tenant and not by the landlord.[152] It is also very improbable that some personal incapacity which prevents

[145] [1981] AC 675. For criticism, see Price (1989) 10 J Leg Hist 90, 101–3.

[146] Lord Russell of Killowen dissenting.

[147] [1981] AC 675, 691 (Lord Hailsham LC). See also *Holbeck Hall Hotel Ltd v Scarborough BC* (1998) 57 Con LR 113, 152–3 (point not considered by CA: [2000] QB 836).

[148] [1981] AC 675, 692, 697, 717.

[149] Cf *Rom Securities Ltd v Rogers (Holdings) Ltd* (1967) 205 EG 427 (agreement for a lease; *obiter*). Contrast *Tay Salmon Fisheries Co Ltd v Speedie* 1929 SC 593 (Scotland). See also *Ramsbury Properties Ltd v Ocean View Construction Ltd* [2024] UKPC 40, [2025] 1 WLR 924 (repudiatory breach of lease; PC drew on the frustration cases at [33]).

[150] Cf *National Carriers Ltd v Panalpina (Northern) Ltd* [1981] AC 675, 690.

[151] *Matthey v Curling* [1922] 2 AC 180; *Swift v Macbean* [1942] 1 KB 375; *Redmond v Dainton* [1920] 2 KB 256.

[152] *Bank of New York Mellon (International) Ltd v Cine-UK Ltd* [2021] EWHC 1013 (QB), [2022] Lloyd's Rep IR 141 (enforced closure of commercial premises during COVID-19 pandemic did not frustrate leases so as to relieve tenants of duty to pay rent); on appeal the frustration claim was not pursued, but CA held that the terms of the leases regarding payment of rent allocated the risk to the tenants: [2022] EWCA Civ 1021, [2023] L & TR 2.

the tenant from using the premises would be sufficient to terminate the lease,[153] at least if the tenant's personal occupation was not the common basis of the venture.[154] But if commercial premises are let (particularly for a short term) for one principal purpose, known to the lessor, which gives to the premises a large part of its rental value, the failure of that purpose by legal prohibition or otherwise might be sufficient to bring about the radical change in the obligation required to frustrate the lease.

Similar problems arise in relation to contracts for the sale of land where a change of circumstances occurs after exchange of contracts but before completion. The risk that the premises may be destroyed or damaged, for example, by fire, is one which must be borne by the purchaser, and in respect of which it is usual to insure.[155] It has further been held that such a contract was not frustrated when the land agreed to be sold was made the subject of a compulsory purchase order[156] and where a building intended for development was listed as being of historic or architectural interest.[157] The position is in doubt, but the answer to the question whether a contract of sale of land can be frustrated would again appear to be 'hardly ever' rather than 'never'.[158]

8. EFFECTS OF FRUSTRATION

(a) COMMON LAW

(i) Contract generally determined automatically

Generally, the contract is not merely dischargeable at the option of one or other of the parties; it is brought to an end forthwith and automatically. In *Hirji Mulji v Cheong Yue Steamship Co Ltd*:[159]

In November 1916 CY chartered its ship, the *Singaporean*, agreeing that it should be placed at HM's disposal on 1 March 1917, for 10 months. Shortly before this date the ship was requisitioned by the Government. Believing that she would soon be released, CY asked if HM would be willing to take up the charter. HM said that they would. The ship was, however, not released until February 1919, and HM then refused to accept her.

[153] *London and Northern Estates Co v Schlesinger* [1916] 1 KB 20 (internment of tenant). See also *Youngmin v Heath* [1974] 1 WLR 135 (death); *Canary Wharf (BP4) T1 Ltd v European Medicines Agency* [2019] EWHC 335 (Ch) at [226] (UK's withdrawal from the EU would not frustrate a 25-year lease of premises in London held by the European Medicines Agency as its headquarters, because the terms of the lease contemplated that the Agency might need to leave the premises involuntarily for some reason).

[154] See *Sumnall v Statt* (1984) 49 P & CR 367, and above, p 484.

[155] Cheshire and Burn's *Modern Law of Real Property* (18th edn, 2011) 979–81; *PJP (NE) Ltd v Taylor* [2022] EWHC 709 (Ch) at [65].

[156] *Hillingdon Estates Co v Stonefield Estates Ltd* [1952] Ch 627; *E Johnson & Co (Barbados) Ltd v NSR Ltd* [1997] AC 400.

[157] *Amalgamated Investment & Property Co Ltd v John Walker & Sons Ltd* [1977] 1 WLR 164.

[158] See also *Denny, Mott & Dickson Ltd v James B Fraser & Co Ltd* [1944] AC 265 (option to purchase land was part of transaction which was frustrated as a whole).

[159] [1926] AC 497. See also *J Lauritzen AS v Wijsmuller BV, The Super Servant Two* [1990] 1 Lloyd's Rep 1, 8.

The shipowners contended that HM had so conducted themselves as to oust the doctrine of frustration. But the House of Lords held that frustration, unlike breach, brings the contract to an end automatically, and could not be waived in this manner.[160]

The rule precluding a party relying on a self-induced frustration, considered above, shows that the rule that discharge is automatic is not absolute. We have seen that the party whose act or default has caused the frustrating event is not entitled to treat himself as discharged. But *FC Shepherd & Co Ltd v Jerrom*[161] shows that this will not affect the position of the other party, for whom the event is not 'self'-induced. In that case:

An employee was sentenced to a term of detention, and his employer stated that it would not take him back on his release. Once released, he instituted proceedings for unfair dismissal, which the employer defended inter alia on the ground that the contract had been frustrated by the imposition of the sentence of imprisonment.

Although it was clear that the employee could not rely on his detention as frustrating the contract of employment, it was held that the employer could.

(ii) All future obligations discharged

The effect of frustration is to release both parties from any further performance of the contract. There is no such thing as 'temporary frustration', by which the contract would be suspended during a period of time.[162] All obligations falling due for performance after the frustrating event occurred are discharged. In *Appleby v Myers*,[163] for example:

A undertook to erect certain machinery upon M's premises, the agreement providing that the work was to be paid for on completion. While the work was in progress, and before it was completed, the premises and the machinery already erected were wholly destroyed by fire.

The contract was frustrated, but since it had been agreed that payment was to be made only on completion, A could recover nothing for the work already done.

(iii) Accrued obligations remain

Legal rights or obligations already accrued and due, before the frustrating event occurred, are left undisturbed. In *Chandler v Webster*:[164]

C agreed to hire from W a room in Pall Mall to watch the Coronation procession. The price was £141, payable immediately. C paid £100 of this sum, but before he paid the balance, the procession was cancelled. He claimed to recover back the money paid.

160 [1926] AC 497, 509 (Lord Sumner). See also *BP Exploration (Libya) Co Ltd v Hunt (No 2)* [1979] 1 WLR 783, 810 (waiver or estoppel could not prevent reliance on frustration).

161 [1987] 1 QB 301. See also *Joseph Constantine Steamship Line Ltd v Imperial Smelting Corp Ltd* [1942] AC 154, 199–200 (Lord Porter); *Notcutt v Universal Equipment Co (London) Ltd* [1986] 1 WLR 641.

162 *Bank of New York Mellon (International) Ltd v Cine-UK Ltd* [2021] EWHC 1013 (QB) at [211] (the point was not raised on appeal: [2022] EWCA Civ 1021). Cf Bridge (2021) 137 LQR 580.

163 (1867) LR 2 CP 651. See also *Compania Naviera General SA v Kerametal Ltd* [1983] 1 Lloyd's Rep 373.

164 [1904] 1 KB 493.

It was held not only that he could not recover the £100 already paid, but that he was also liable to pay the other £41 as this obligation had fallen due before the frustrating event occurred. In part because of the underdevelopment of restitutionary principles at that time, the Court of Appeal rejected C's argument that he was entitled to recover the £100 in restitution as money paid under a consideration which had totally failed. The effect of the frustration was regarded as not wiping out the contract altogether but only releasing the parties from further performance, so it could not be said that the 'consideration' had failed completely.

(iv) Development of a restitutionary response

The harshness of the decision in *Chandler v Webster*, which allocated all the risks of the frustrating event on to C, excited considerable criticism,[165] and in 1942 it was overruled by the House of Lords in *Fibrosa Spolka Akcyjna v Fairbairn Lawson Combe Barbour Ltd*:[166]

The respondent contracted with the appellant, a Polish company, to manufacture certain machinery and deliver it to Gdynia. Part of the price was to be paid in advance, and the appellant accordingly paid £1,000. The contract was frustrated by the occupation of Gdynia by hostile German forces in September 1939. The appellant thereupon requested the return of the £1,000. This request was refused on the ground that considerable work had been done, and expense incurred, under the contract.

Under the rule in *Chandler v Webster* this money would have been irrecoverable, as it had already been paid at the time the frustrating event occurred. The House of Lords, however, allowed the appellants to recover. It was pointed out that an action for the recovery of the sum paid was not an action on the contract, which *ex hypothesi* had ceased to exist, but an action in restitution to recover money paid on a consideration which had totally failed.[167] The House held that, in the context of a claim to recover money paid, the term 'consideration' should be understood not in the sense of the consideration which is necessary to the formation of a contract, but rather in the sense of the performance of an obligation already incurred. A party who has paid money but has received no part of the bargained-for performance, is entitled to recover it, for the consideration has totally failed.

(b) LAW REFORM (FRUSTRATED CONTRACTS) ACT 1943

(i) Underlying principle

The law as the *Fibrosa* case left it was still not satisfactory, for the party who had to return the pre-payment might have incurred expenses for the purpose of the performance of the contract, or might be left with goods which were made valueless by

[165] *Cantiare San Roco SA v Clyde Shipbuilding & Engineering Co Ltd* [1924] AC 226, 257.

[166] [1943] AC 32.

[167] See below, p 607 (total failure of basis, now the preferred term: see p 606, n 2).

the failure of the contract.[168] Moreover, the insistence that the failure of consideration be total[169] meant that if the party seeking recovery of the money had received any part, however small, of the performance of the contract, the *Fibrosa* case did not apply, and the money was irrecoverable. It was to remedy this situation that the Law Reform (Frustrated Contracts) Act 1943 was passed.[170]

It has been stated that the 'fundamental principle underlying the Act . . . is prevention of the unjust enrichment of either party to the contract at the other's expense' and not the apportionment of the loss caused by the frustrating event between the parties.[171] Although it has been argued that the law is defective in not providing for such loss-apportionment,[172] especially since the line between action in reliance on a contract which results in a benefit, and action which does not, can be very fine,[173] the case for a financial adjustment is stronger where such pre-frustration action has resulted in a benefit to one of the parties. But it is important not to allow an over-wide interpretation of 'enrichment' or 'benefit' to operate as loss-apportionment by subsuming virtually all action taken by a contracting party in reliance on the contract. The Act does not apply insofar as there is a contrary provision in the contract.[174]

(ii) Money paid or payable

By section 1(2) of the 1943 Act:

All sums paid or payable to any party in pursuance of the contract before the time when the parties were so discharged (in this Act referred to as 'the time of discharge') shall, in the case of sums so paid, be recoverable from him as money received by him for the use of the party by whom the sums were paid, and, in the case of sums so payable, cease to be payable:

Provided that, if the party to whom the sums were so paid or payable incurred expenses before the time of the discharge in, or for the purpose of, the performance of the contract, the court may, if it considers it just to do so having regard to all the circumstances of the case, allow him to retain or, as the case may be, recover the whole or any part of the sums so paid or payable, not being an amount in excess of the expenses so incurred.

[168] This was probably not a problem in *Fibrosa* since, although the sellers had done a considerable amount of work in manufacturing the machines ([1942] 1 KB 12, 14), it was accepted that they could be resold without loss: [1943] AC 32, 49.

[169] See below, p 607.

[170] See Williams, *Law Reform (Frustrated Contracts) Act 1943* (1944); Mitchell, Mitchell, and Watterson, *Goff and Jones on the Law of Unjust Enrichment* (10th edn, 2022) ch 15; Peel, *Frustration and Force Majeure* (4th edn, 2022) para 15-058 ff.

[171] *BP Exploration (Libya) Co Ltd v Hunt (No 2)* [1979] 1 WLR 783, 799–800 (Robert Goff J). Cf Lawton LJ in CA at [1981] 1 WLR 232.

[172] Williams, *Law Reform (Frustrated Contracts) Act 1943* (1944) 35; McKendrick, in Burrows (ed), *Essays on the Law of Restitution* (1991) 147; cf Posner and Rosenfield (1977) 6 JLS 83, 112 ff (part-performer can generally evaluate the risk better and insure more cheaply than the other party); Stewart and Carter [1992] CLJ 66, 86–9, 109–10; Burrows, *The Law of Restitution* (3rd edn, 2011) ch 15; Stevens, in Peel and Probert (eds), *Shaping the Law of Obligations* (2023) 125.

[173] Below, pp 608–9.

[174] 1943 Act, s 2(3). Cf *BP Exploration (Libya) Ltd v Hunt (No 2)* [1983] 2 AC 352, 372, 373.

The first paragraph of this subsection embodies the rule in the *Fibrosa* case, although it is now no longer necessary to prove a total failure of consideration. So if A agrees to manufacture and deliver to B certain machinery, B promising to pay £10,000 down and the balance on completion, then even if A has delivered part of the machinery to B before the frustrating event occurs, B can recover the £10,000, if paid, and, if not paid, it ceases to be payable.[175]

(iii) Expenses incurred by payee

Section 1(2) of the Act goes further than the *Fibrosa* case, however, in that it gives to the Court a discretionary power to allow the payee to set off against the sum so paid or payable a sum not exceeding the value of any expenses which the payee has incurred in or for the purpose of performing the contract before the frustration.[176] So if, in the above example, A has incurred expenses totalling, say, £6,000, then the Court has power to permit A to recover or retain the whole or part of this sum from the £10,000 due from B under the contract. But expenses can only be set off against 'the sums so paid or payable', that is, those due before frustration, so that if the expenses amounted to, say, £12,000, it would not be possible to charge the £2,000 in excess of £10,000 against the unpaid balance due after the frustrating event occurred.

In *Gamerco SA v ICM/Fair Warning (Agency) Ltd*[177] Garland J considered three methods by which the Court should exercise its discretion; allowing the payee to retain all the expenses incurred[178] as a statutory recognition of the defence of change of position,[179] equal division of the loss caused by the frustrating event,[180] and a broad discretion to do what the Court considers just, 'having regard to all the circumstances of the case'.[181] His Lordship favoured the third, concluding that the task of the Court 'is to do justice in a situation which the parties neither contemplated nor provided for, and to mitigate the possible harshness of allowing all loss to lie where it has fallen'.[182] In *Gamerco*'s case:

$775,000 was payable by the promoters of a pop concert to the defendant group, Guns N' Roses, at the time the contract was frustrated, $412,500 of which had been paid. Both parties had incurred expenses before the date of frustration which were wholly wasted: the defendant $50,000, and the promoters $450,000. Neither party was left with any residual benefit or advantage.

[175] A's position may be protected by s 1(3), on which see below.

[176] 'Expenses' include a reasonable sum in respect of overhead expenses: s 1(4), and the onus of proof lies on the payee: *Gamerco SA v ICM/Fair Warning (Agency) Ltd* [1995] 1 WLR 1226, 1235. See also *Lobb v Vasey Housing Auxiliary (War Widows Guild)* [1963] VR 239 (Victoria, Australia).

[177] [1995] 1 WLR 1226.

[178] This was favoured by the Law Revision Committee (Cmd 6009, 1939) 7.

[179] As suggested in *BP Exploration Co (Libya) Ltd v Hunt (No 2)* [1979] 1 WLR 783, 800. This decision was substantially approved by the House of Lords: [1983] 2 AC 352.

[180] Williams, *Law Reform (Frustrated Contracts) Act 1943* (1944) 35–6.

[181] cf Peel, *Frustration and Force Majeure* (4th edn, 2022) para 15-088.

[182] [1995] 1 WLR 1226, 1237.

In these circumstances, and having particular regard to the promoters' loss, and his view that there was no question of any change of position by the defendant as a result of the promoters' advance payment,[183] his Lordship made no deduction under the proviso and ordered repayment of the $412,500.

(iv) Obligations other than to pay money

Section 1(3) of the 1943 Act provides for the adjustment of the financial relations of the parties:

> Where any party to the contract has, by reason of anything done by any other party thereto in, or for the purpose of, the performance of the contract, obtained a valuable benefit (other than a payment of money to which the last foregoing subsection applies) before the time of discharge, there shall be recoverable from him by the said other party such sum (if any) not exceeding the value of the said benefit to the party obtaining it, as the court considers just, having regard to all the circumstances of the case and, in particular—
>
> (a) the amount of any expenses incurred before the time of discharge by the benefited party in, or for the purpose of the performance of the contract, including any sums paid or payable by him to any other party in pursuance of the contract and retained or recoverable by that party under the last foregoing subsection, and
> (b) the effect, in relation to the said benefit, of the circumstances giving rise to frustration of the contract.

The result is that recompense may be awarded in respect of a valuable benefit conferred by either party upon the other party in pursuance of the contract. In *BP Exploration Co (Libya) Ltd v Hunt (No 2)*[184] Robert Goff J pointed out that the subsection must be applied in two distinct stages. The first is the identification and valuation of the benefit. The second stage is for the Court to assess what sum (not exceeding the value of the benefit) it considers just to award to the party by whom the benefit has been conferred.

With regard to the identification and valuation of the benefit, there are three situations to be considered. The first is where the performance rendered results in the delivery of an item which is unaffected by the frustrating event. If, for example, in the illustration set out above, A has delivered to B some of the machinery, the machinery so delivered could constitute a benefit to B. The value of that benefit will ordinarily be its value to B at the date of frustration. This may be more or less than the expenses incurred by A in manufacturing and delivering that machinery. It was stated by Robert Goff J that as a matter of construction 'benefit' in the subsection normally meant the end product of services rather than the services themselves.[185]

The second is where, although the performance results in the delivery of an item or an end product, in our example the machinery, the event which frustrates the contract (as in *Appleby v Myers*),[186] destroys it or renders it useless and of no value to B without

[183] The decision may be questioned: see *Lipkin Gorman v Karpnale Ltd* [1991] 2 AC 548; Carter and Tolhurst (1996) 10 JCL 265.

[184] [1979] 1 WLR 783. For the facts, see below, pp 511–2.

[185] *Ibid*, 801–2.

[186] (1867) LR 2 CP 651, above, p 506. See also *Parsons Bros Ltd v Shea* (1965) 53 DLR (2d) 86 (Canada).

delivery of the remainder. Under paragraph (b) of the subsection regard is to be had to 'the effect, in relation to the ... benefit, of the circumstances giving rise to the frustration of the contract'. The interpretation of this provision is problematic. Robert Goff J stated[187] that 'benefit' in section 1(3)(b) clearly refers to the end product of the services, rather than the services themselves, and that the subsection 'makes it plain that the plaintiff [the party conferring the benefit] is to take the risk of depreciation or destruction by the frustrating event'. If this view is correct,[188] then the value of the benefit in such a case will be nil, and no award could be made in favour of A under the subsection.

The third situation is where the performance rendered is a 'pure' service, without any end product, such as gardening, surveying, or transporting goods.[189] Here, Robert Goff J stated that the 'benefit' in the subsection was the services themselves,[190] and it is these that must be valued. In such cases, however, care must be taken not to cross the line between restitution in respect of a benefit conferred, which is permitted by the subsection, and recompense for action taken by one party in reliance on the contract without conferring a benefit on the other.[191]

The second stage is for the Court to assess what sum (not exceeding the value of the benefit) it considers just to award to the party by whom the benefit has been conferred. This has been termed the 'just sum'. The purpose of the award has been said to be to prevent the unjust enrichment of the defendant at the claimant's expense.[192] In the example given above, if the machinery delivered remained of value to B after the frustrating event, the just sum would probably be assessed as the reasonable value of that machinery,[193] or a rateable part of the contract price.

The principles were applied in *BP Exploration Co (Libya) Ltd v Hunt (No 2)*:[194]

BP entered into a contract to explore and develop an oil concession in Libya owned by H. BP was to make initial payments and a transfer of oil to Hunt, and in return was to get a 50 per cent share in the concession and 'reimbursement oil' calculated by a formula. A significant oil field was discovered and oil was produced and transferred under the contract for four and a

[187] *BP Exploration Co (Libya) Ltd v Hunt (No 2)* [1979] 1 WLR 783, 803. Contrast Williams, *Law Reform (Frustrated Contracts) Act 1943* (1944) 48–51.

[188] Cf Peel, *Frustration and Force Majeure* (4th edn, 2022) para 15-078 (s 1(3) applies where a valuable benefit has been obtained 'before the time of discharge' and subparas (a) and (b) are relevant to the assessment of the just sum, not the identification of the benefit); Birks, *An Introduction to the Law of Restitution* (revd edn, 1989) 253.

[189] See, eg, *Angus v Scully* 57 NE 674 (1900) (Massachusetts) and the facts of *Cutter v Powell* (1795) 6 TR 320, above, p 458.

[190] *BP Exploration Co (Libya) Ltd v Hunt (No 2)* [1979] 1 WLR 783, 803.

[191] cf *Coleman Engineering v North American Aviation* 420 P 2d 713 (1966) (California) 729 (Traynor CJ: 'if in fact the performance of services has conferred no benefit on the person requesting them, it is pure fiction to base restitution on a benefit conferred'); Mitchell, Mitchell, and Watterson, *Goff & Jones on the Law of Unjust Enrichment* (10th edn, 2022) para 16-19.

[192] *BP Exploration Co (Libya) Ltd v Hunt (No 2)* [1979] 1 WLR 783, 805.

[193] *Ibid*, 805–6.

[194] [1979] 1 WLR 783 (aff'd by the Court of Appeal [1981] 1 WLR 232, and by the House of Lords [1983] 2 AC 352).

half years, but the contract was then frustrated when both parties' interests were expropriated by the Libyan Government, which paid some compensation to H. BP claimed under section 1(3) of the 1943 Act.

It was held that, under section 1(3), the 'valuable benefit' had to be not the work exploring and extracting oil but the end product of that work, the enhancement of the value of H's concession. But the effect of the frustrating event was to make this valueless and unrealizable by H, and subparagraph (b) required this to be reflected in the valuation of the benefit. But H had received considerable amounts of oil produced prior to the expropriation, and compensation thereafter, and half the value of this ($85 million) was held to be the benefit obtained from BP's exploration and development, and the upper limit of any award.[195] The 'just sum' was determined by taking account of the cost to BP of the work done for H and the oil it initially transferred to H reduced by the amount of the 'reimbursement oil' it had received. This amounted to just under $35 million. Since this was in effect the value of 'reimbursement oil' due to BP but not transferred at the date of frustration, the remedy given approximately corresponded to a scaled-down contract price, that percentage of the contract price which the part-performer had 'earned' by performance before the frustrating event.

Neither under subsection (2) nor under subsection (3) can any allowance be made for the time-value of money, that is to say, for the fact that money may have been paid, or expenses incurred, long before the date of frustration.[196]

(v) Carriage of goods by sea and voyage charters

The Act does not apply to contracts for the carriage of goods by sea or a charterparty (other than a time charterparty or a charterparty by way of demise).[197] This recognizes a well-established custom, which has become part of the business practice of shipowners and insurers, that freight paid or payable in advance under such contracts is not recoverable even though the completion of the voyage is frustrated.[198]

(vi) Sale of goods and insurance

The Act is also not applicable to contracts of insurance[199] and certain contracts for the sale of goods.

The exclusion of contracts for the sale of goods is complex in its drafting,[200] but its effect is to exclude all contracts for the sale of specific goods, where the frustration

[195] The other half was attributed to Hunt's ownership of the concession prior to the exploration and development under the contract.

[196] *BP Exploration Co (Libya) Ltd v Hunt (No 2)* [1979] 1 WLR 783, 800, 804. The court may, however, order statutory interest to be paid on sums due under the Act calculated from a date on or after the accrual of the cause of action (the frustrating event): *ibid*, 845–7; [1983] 2 AC 352, 373–4.

[197] 1943 Act, s 2(5)(a).

[198] *Compania Naviera General SA v Kerametal Ltd* [1983] 1 Lloyd's Rep 373.

[199] 1943 Act, s 2(5)(b).

[200] See Jayathilaka (2025) 88 MLR 433 for discussion and criticism of law on supervening impossibility in contracts for the sale of goods.

occurs by reason of the perishing of the goods. By section 2(5)(c) the Act does not apply to:

> any contract to which section 7 of the Sale of Goods Act 1979 (which avoids contracts for the sale of specific goods which perish before the risk has passed to the buyer) applies or to any other contract for the sale, or for the sale and delivery, of specific goods, where the contract is frustrated by reason of the fact that the goods have perished.

The first part of this subsection (exclusion by reference to section 7 of the 1979 Act) covers contracts where the goods perish before the risk has passed to the buyer. If the goods then perish without the fault of either party, the contract is *avoided* by section 7 of the Sale of Goods Act 1979 and the 1943 Act does not apply. The general rule in the case of the non-consumer sale of goods is that they are at the risk of the person whose property they are: *res perit domino*.[201] Where there is a sale of *specific* goods property in the goods normally passes to the buyer at the time the contract is made,[202] and so it follows that they are also at the buyer's risk. In the case, however, of a consumer sale, the goods remain at the trader's risk until they come into the physical possession of the consumer or the consumer's agent.[203] But the second part of the subsection quoted above also exempts cases where there is a contract for the sale, or sale and delivery, of specific goods and the goods perish but which are not covered by section 7 of the 1979 Act. This will apply to cases where the risk has passed to the buyer. In such circumstances the buyer will bear the loss resulting from the perishing of the goods.

These exclusions relate only to contracts for specific goods, which are defined by section 61(1) of the Sale of Goods Act 1979 as 'goods identified and agreed on at the time a contract of sale is made'. Goods which are unascertained at this time do not therefore come within the exclusion, although it must be noted that the doctrine of frustration rarely then applies. If A agrees to sell to B 'six hundred tons of coal', there can normally be no frustration of this contract. Even though A may have had in mind a particular source, this assumption is not common to both parties. The contract can be fulfilled at any time and A must obtain sufficient coal from another source or be liable for breach.[204] On the other hand, if the goods, though unascertained, are to come from a source which is specifically defined, for example, 'six hundred tons of coal from the ship *Rose Marie* now in dock', and subsequently the ship and cargo are destroyed by fire, this contract is clearly capable of frustration, but there is some doubt as to whether it falls outside the 1943 Act. In one case,[205] goods of this nature were held not to be specific goods for the purposes of section 52 of the Sale of Goods Act 1979 (specific performance), and it is submitted that, for the purposes of frustration, the goods are likewise not specific goods and so are subject to the provisions of the 1943 Act.[206]

[201] Sale of Goods Act 1979, s 20.

[202] Sale of Goods Act 1979, s 18, Rule 1.

[203] Consumer Rights Act 2015, s 29.

[204] *Blackburn Bobbin Co Ltd v TW Allen & Sons Ltd* [1918] 2 KB 467, above, p 498; *CTI Group Inc v Transclear SA, The Mary Nour* [2008] EWCA Civ 856, [2008] 2 Lloyd's Rep 526 at [23]. Cf *Re Badische Co Ltd* [1921] 2 Ch 331; see above, p 498.

[205] *Re Wait* [1927] 1 Ch 606.

[206] See also Hudson (1968) 31 MLR 535.

A similar problem may arise in the type of situation exemplified by *Howell v Coupland*:[207]

C agreed to sell to H 200 tons of potatoes to be grown on a particular field. The crop failed, so that C was able to deliver only 80 tons. In answer to H's claim for non-delivery of the other 120 tons, C pleaded that he had duly delivered all that it was possible for him to deliver and that he was excused from delivering the remainder.

It was held that C was not liable. Mellish LJ said:[208]

This is not like the case of a contract to deliver so many goods of a particular kind, where no specific goods are to be sold. Here there was an agreement to sell and buy 200 tons of a crop to be grown on specific land, so that it is an agreement to sell what will be and may be called specific things; therefore neither party is liable if the performance becomes impossible.

Despite the use by Mellish LJ of the word 'specific' in this case, it is clear that the potatoes were not 'specific goods' within the meaning of the Sale of Goods Act. Nevertheless this is not a situation to which the provisions of the 1943 Act would appear to apply. It has been held[209] that a contract of sale of this nature is subject to a condition. Depending on the intention of the parties, the condition which will be implied may be one that neither party shall be liable if any part of the promised goods fails to materialize;[210] alternatively, it may, as in *Howell v Coupland*, be a condition that the buyer can require such performance as remains possible, but the seller is excused from delivering the remainder of the goods.[211]

Then exclusion of contracts for the sale of goods from the operation of the 1943 Act only applies where the frustration occurs by reason of the perishing of the goods. Other grounds of frustration, such as the performance of the contract becoming illegal, are not covered and the 1943 Act would then apply.

FURTHER READING

POSNER and ROSENFIELD, 'Impossibility and Related Doctrines in Contract Law: An Economic Analysis' (1977) 6 JLS 83

MCKENDRICK, 'Frustration, Restitution and Loss Apportionment' in BURROWS (ed), *Essays on the Law of Restitution* (Oxford: Clarendon Press, 1991) 147

SMITH, 'Contracts—Mistake, Frustration and Implied Terms' (1994) 110 LQR 400

MCKENDRICK, '*Force Majeure* Clauses: the Gap Between Doctrine and Practice' in BURROWS and PEEL (eds), *Contract Terms* (Oxford: Oxford University Press, 2007) 233

MCMEEL, 'The Juridical Basis of Frustration Revisited' [2020] LMCLQ 297

BRIDGE, 'Frustration and Excused Non-Performance' (2021) 137 LQR 580

MCKENDRICK, 'Covid, Contracts and Change of Circumstances' [2024] LMCLQ 34

207 (1876) 1 QBD 258.

208 *Ibid*, 262.

209 *HR & S Sainsbury Ltd v Street* [1972] 1 WLR 834. See also *Re Wait* [1927] 1 Ch 606, 631.

210 See the Sale of Goods Act 1979, s 5(2) (condition precedent). The sale might also be subject to a condition subsequent: above, pp 154, 476–8.

211 *HR & S Sainsbury Ltd v Street* [1972] 1 WLR 834.

15

DISCHARGE FOR BREACH

A party who breaches an obligation which the contract imposes is in breach of contract. The breach may consist in the non-performance of the obligation, or its performance in a manner or at a time which fails to comply with the requirements of the contract. English law does not generally distinguish between these different forms of breach of contract, but applies the same remedial regime to them all, and as soon as the party is in breach a new obligation will arise by operation of law—an obligation to pay damages to the other party in respect of any loss or damage sustained by the breach. However, the duty to perform the contractual obligation normally remains unchanged, although there are circumstances under which the breach not only gives rise to a right of action for damages but also gives the innocent party the right to decide to discharge both parties from their obligations under the contract—that is, to terminate the contract.[1] The remedy of damages is discussed in detail in Chapter 17. Here we consider the circumstances in which the contract may be discharged following a breach of contract, and we shall see that this is only if the breach is sufficiently serious in its effects (it 'goes to the root of the contract', or is a 'repudiation' of the contract) or if it is a breach of a sufficiently serious term of the contract (breach of 'condition'). These rules were devised by the common law to provide the innocent party with a general remedy for serious breaches, or breaches of serious terms, of the contract. Under the Consumer Rights Act 2015, however, the consumer's common law right to treat a contract to supply goods or digital content as at an end for breach is substantially modified.[2]

1. DISCHARGE AT THE OPTION OF THE INJURED PARTY

It is common to speak of the contract as having been 'discharged by the breach'. This is not strictly accurate. A breach does not, of itself, effect discharge;[3] what it may do is to give the innocent party the option either to treat the contract as still continuing

[1] *Photo Production Ltd v Securicor Transport Ltd* [1980] AC 827, 849–50 (Lord Diplock, who labels the obligations contained in the contract, express or implied, 'primary' obligations, and the obligation to pay damages for the loss or damage caused by the breach or by the termination of the contract 'secondary' obligations); see also *Moschi v Lep Air Services Ltd* [1973] AC 331, 350 (Lord Diplock), below, p 519. On the terminology of 'discharge', 'termination', and 'rescission' for breach, see below, p 535.

[2] See below, p 521.

[3] See below, pp 516, 517–8, 534–5.

or to accept the breach and treat the contract as discharged by reason of the breach. An acceptance of a breach, in order to discharge the contract, must be clear and unequivocal,[4] although the innocent party has a reasonable period to decide what to do, and 'if he does nothing for too long there may come a time when the law will treat him as having affirmed'.[5] Once the option is exercised either to keep the contract on foot or terminate it, the decision is irrevocable.[6] A fresh option may arise, however, if the breach continues, or there is another separate breach, sufficient to justify the innocent party terminating the contract.

(a) EFFECT OF UNACCEPTED REPUDIATION

In principle, an innocent party who does not 'accept' a repudiation[7] is entitled to continue to insist on performance because the contract remains in full effect. Thus in *White and Carter (Councils) Ltd v McGregor*:[8]

W & C, an advertising contractor, agreed with McG, a garage proprietor, to display advertisements for his garage for 3 years. On the same day, McG refused to perform the agreement and requested W & C to cancel the contract. W & C refused to do so, and elected to treat the contract as still continuing. It made no effort to relet the space, displayed advertisements as agreed, and sued for the full amount due for the 3-year term. Under the terms of an acceleration clause in the contract, the full amount became payable if any instalment remained unpaid for 4 weeks.

McG argued that, since he had renounced the agreement before anything had been done under it, W & C was not entitled to carry out the agreement and sue for the price: its remedy, if any, lay in damages. A bare majority of the House of Lords rejected this contention and held that W & C was entitled to the full contract sum.

The decision has been criticized as encouraging wasteful and unwanted performance. The criticisms are considered in the context of specific remedies.[9] It is in any event clear from the speeches of the majority in this case that the party not in breach will not always be entitled to complete the contract and sue for the contract price. In the first place, if the contract cannot be carried out without the cooperation of the party who has refused to perform, and such cooperation is withheld, the innocent party's only remedy is to sue for damages and not for the price.[10] So an employee who is wrongfully dismissed

[4] *Vitol SA v Norelf Ltd* [1996] AC 800, 810–11 (Lord Steyn). See also *Heyman v Darwins Ltd* [1942] AC 356, 361; *Bliss v South East Thames Regional Health Authority* [1987] ICR 700, 716–17; *State Trading Corp of India Ltd v M Golodetz Ltd* [1989] 2 Lloyd's Rep 277, 286 (silence not unequivocal); *Geys v Société Générale, London Branch* [2012] UKSC 63, [2013] 1 AC 523 at [17].

[5] *Stocznia Gdanska SA v Latvian Shipping Co (No 2)* [2002] EWCA Civ 889, [2003] 1 CLC 282 at [87]; *White Rosebay Shipping SA v Hong Kong Chain Glory Shipping Ltd* [2013] EWHC 1355 (Comm), [2013] 2 CLC 884.

[6] *Motor Oil Hellas (Corinth) Refineries SA v Shipping Corp of India, The Kanchenjunga* [1990] 1 Lloyd's Rep 391, 398 (Lord Goff); *Peyman v Lanjani* [1985] Ch 457.

[7] See below, p 522.

[8] [1962] AC 413; on the facts, see Rodger (1977) 93 LQR 168. See also Liu (2011) 74 MLR 171.

[9] See below, pp 593–4.

[10] [1962] AC 413, 430, 432, 439.

from employment can only claim damages. The employee cannot claim the salary payable after dismissal on the ground that he is ready, able, and willing to serve the employer if only the employer would allow him to do so.[11] Secondly, the rule in *White and Carter (Councils) Ltd v McGregor* does not apply 'if it can be shown that a person has no legitimate interest, financial or otherwise, in performing the contract rather than claiming damages',[12] in which case a claimant may be compelled to resort to the remedy of damages, provided the damages are an adequate remedy for any loss suffered.

The need for acceptance of a repudiation for the contract to be discharged led to Asquith LJ's famous and influential aphorism that 'an unaccepted repudiation is a thing writ in water'.[13] But an unaccepted repudiation is not altogether without effect. An innocent party who remains ready and willing to perform[14] can rely on the unaccepted repudiation as a defence in an action brought by the guilty party.[15] Again, while the suggestion that contracts of employment are an exception to the normal rule and are discharged by a unilateral repudiation by the employer, without the need for acceptance by the employee, has been rejected,[16] it has been held that an employee's right to damages following an unlawful dismissal does not continue beyond the time at which the employer could have lawfully brought the contract to an end.[17]

(b) FAILURE OF PERFORMANCE

In cases of a failure of performance by one party which goes to the root of the contract,[18] the contract is likewise not determined by the breach,[19] and it is open to the innocent party to treat the contract as continuing or to accept the defective performance when tendered. An innocent party who adopts this course is sometimes said to have elected

[11] *Denmark Productions Ltd v Boscobel Productions Ltd* [1969] 1 QB 699, 726, 737; *Hill v CA Parsons & Co Ltd* [1972] Ch 305, 314; *Gunton v Richmond LBC* [1981] Ch 448; *Geys v Société Générale, London Branch* [2012] UKSC 63 at [79].

[12] *White and Carter (Councils) Ltd v McGregor* [1962] AC 413, 431 (Lord Reid); *Attica Sea Carriers Corp v Ferrostaal Poseidon Bulk Reederei GmbH, The Puerto Buitrago* [1976] 1 Lloyd's Rep 250; *Gator Shipping Corp v Trans-Asiatic Oil Ltd SA* [1978] 2 Lloyd's Rep 357, 372–4; *Stocznia Gdanska SA v Latvian SS Co* [1996] 2 Lloyd's Rep 132, 138–9 (cf [1998] 1 WLR 574, 581, 602); *Reichman v Beveridge* [2006] EWCA Civ 1659, [2007] 1 P & CR 20; *MSC Mediterranean Shipping Co SA v Cottonex Anstalt* [2016] EWCA Civ 789, [2017] 1 All ER (Comm) 483 at [32]–[40] (Moore-Bick LJ, reviewing the cases). On the action for the agreed sum, and its contrast with a claim for damages, see further pp 591–4, below.

[13] *Howard v Pickford Tool Co Ltd* [1951] 1 KB 417, 421. See also *Fercometal SARL v Mediterranean Shipping Co SA, The Simona* [1989] AC 788, 800; *State Trading Corp of India Ltd v M Golodetz Ltd* [1989] 2 Lloyd's Rep 277, 285.

[14] *Fercometal SARL v Mediterranean Shipping Co SA, The Simona* [1989] AC 788.

[15] *Peter Turnbull & Co Pty Ltd v Mundus Trading Co (Australasia) Pty Ltd* (1954) 90 CLR 235, 245, 251; *Foran v Wight* (1989) 168 CLR 385, 438 (Australia). See further *Carter's Breach of Contract* (3rd edn, 2024) 316–21.

[16] *Geys v Société Générale, London Branch* [2012] UKSC 63, approving *Gunton v Richmond LBC* [1981] Ch 448. Cf Lord Sumption (dissenting) at [139].

[17] *Boyo v Lambeth LBC* [1994] ICR 727.

[18] See below, p 531.

[19] *Photo Productions Ltd v Securicor Transport Ltd* [1980] AC 827 (overruling *Harbutt's 'Plasticine' Ltd v Wayne Tank and Pump Co Ltd* [1970] 1 QB 447).

to *affirm* the contract, that is, to have waived the right to be treated as discharged, although the right to claim damages for the breach is still retained.[20] Affirmation may be express or implied. Affirmation will be implied if, to the knowledge of the party in default, the innocent party does some unequivocal[21] act which shows an intention to go on with the contract regardless of the breach or from which it may be inferred that the right to be treated as discharged will not be exercised.[22] And affirmation must be total. A contracting party cannot affirm part of the contract and disaffirm the rest, for that would be to make a new contract.[23]

(c) AFFIRMATION OF CONTRACT

Affirmation is a voluntary act, and requires knowledge. Although old authorities to the contrary can be found, the traditional position was that a party need only have knowledge of the facts which give rise to the right to affirm or terminate.[24] Recent cases go further and suggest that a party cannot be called upon to make an election or be held to have made an election, unless, in addition to knowledge of the relevant facts, that party has knowledge of the right to elect.[25] Despite this debate, as we have seen,[26] there are circumstances where the innocent party will be deprived of the right to be treated as discharged even though that party has no knowledge of the breach. There may also be cases where an innocent party who has led the party in default to believe that it will not exercise that right will be estopped from exercising it.[27]

(d) EFFECT OF ELECTION TO ACCEPT BREACH

If the innocent party decides to accept the breach, this discharges all the future contractual obligations of that party which have not already been performed. At the same time, the primary obligations of the party in default to perform any of that party's

[20] See below, p 545.

[21] *China National Foreign Trade Transportation Corp v Evlogia Shipping Co SA of Panama* [1979] 1 WLR 1018; *Yukong Line Ltd of Korea v Rendsburg Investments Corp of Liberia* [1996] 2 Lloyd's Rep 604 (very clear evidence required).

[22] *Bentsen v Taylor, Sons & Co* [1893] 2 QB 274; *Hain SS Co Ltd v Tate & Lyle Ltd* (1936) 41 Com Cas 350, 355, 363; *Suisse Atlantique Société d'Armement Maritime SA v NV Rotterdamsche Kolen Centrale* [1967] 1 AC 361; *Delta Petroleum (Caribbean) Ltd v British Virgin Islands Electricity Corp* [2020] UKPC 23, [2021] 1 WLR 5741 at [21] (affirmation only capable of applying where a choice must be made between two alternative and inconsistent (mutually exclusive) courses of action).

[23] *Suisse Atlantique Société d'Armement Maritime SA v NV Rotterdamsche Kolen Centrale* [1967] 1 AC 361, 398.

[24] *Matthews v Smallwood* [1910] 1 Ch 777, 786; *Kammins Ballrooms Co Ltd v Zenith Investments (Torquay) Ltd* [1971] AC 850, 877–8, 883.

[25] *Peyman v Lanjani* [1985] Ch 457; *Sea Calm Shipping Co SA v Chantiers Navals de L'Esterel* [1986] 2 Lloyd's Rep 294. Cf *The Kanchenjunga* [1990] 1 Lloyd's Rep 391, 398; *URE Energy Ltd v Notting Hill Genesis* [2025] EWCA Civ 1407 at [88] (express termination right).

[26] See above, p 475 (waiver).

[27] The incidence of estoppel in this situation depends upon interpretation of the difficult case of *Panchaud Frères SA v Établissements General Grain Co* [1970] 1 Lloyd's Rep 53 (especially at 57–8) and cases consequent thereon.

contractual promises which remain unperformed are likewise discharged.[28] However, in the case of the party in default, in place of the primary obligations imposed by the contract there arises a secondary obligation to pay damages for the breach. In *Moschi v Lep Air Services Ltd*:[29]

R Ltd was indebted to L Ltd, the respondent, in the sum of £40,000, which it agreed to pay to L Ltd at the rate of not less than £6,000 per week. M, the appellant, guaranteed to L Ltd the performance by R Ltd of its obligation to make these payments. R Ltd defaulted from the outset and, after 3 weeks, paid only some £10,000 of the £18,000 then due. L Ltd elected to treat this default as a repudiation of the contract which it accepted. R Ltd went into liquidation and L Ltd sued M in respect of both the accrued and future instalments unpaid.

M argued that, since the repudiation had been accepted, the obligation of the company to pay the outstanding instalments due after that time came to an end, and in consequence his obligation as guarantor also came to an end. The House of Lords found little difficulty in disposing of this argument and held that he was liable on the guarantee. In the first place, upon acceptance of the repudiation, although the company's primary obligation to pay the future instalments came to an end, it was replaced, by operation of law, by a secondary obligation to pay damages for the breach. This secondary obligation was just as much an obligation arising from the contract as were the primary obligations it replaced. Secondly, M had undertaken that R Ltd would perform its contract and so was in breach of his contract of guarantee. The damages which R Ltd had not paid constituted the loss flowing from M's breach of contract for which M was liable.

(e) NO REASON OR BAD REASON FOR CLAIMING TO BE DISCHARGED

Where one party refuses to go on with the contract, giving no reason for this refusal or the wrong or an inadequate reason, the action can still be justified if (even if this is unknown to that party) the other party had at the time committed a breach of contract which would have provided a good reason.[30] So, for example, if an employer dismisses an employee without giving any reason at all, the employer can justify the dismissal should it subsequently be discovered that, prior to the dismissal, the employee had been guilty of dishonesty which would have entitled the employer to dismiss the

[28] For the terminology of 'primary' and 'secondary' obligations, see above, p 515, n 1. It may, however, be the intention of the parties that certain primary obligations, eg, an arbitration or jurisdiction clause, should continue notwithstanding that their other primary obligations have come to an end: see *Heyman v Darwins Ltd* [1942] AC 356; *Moschi v Lep Air Services Ltd* [1973] AC 331, 350. See also above, pp 205–6 (exemption clauses); below, pp 535–6.

[29] [1973] AC 331. See also *Photo Production Ltd v Securicor Transport Ltd* [1980] AC 827, 849.

[30] *Taylor v Oakes Roncoroni & Co* (1922) 127 LT 267, 269; *British & Beningtons Ltd v NW Cachar Tea Co* [1923] AC 48, 71; *The Mihalis Angelos* [1971] 1 QB 164, 195, 200, 204; *Scandinavian Trading Co A/B v Zodiac Petroleum SA* [1981] 1 Lloyd's Rep 81, 90.

employee.[31] Similarly if a buyer of goods rejects the goods on the erroneous ground that they are defective in quality, that rejection will still be lawful should the goods turn out not to have been in conformity with the contract description—a breach of contract which would have justified rejection. This rule, though well established, could be criticized on the ground that it allows a party to a contract to 'blow hot and cold', first alleging one reason then in fact relying on another. There is some authority[32] for the view that a party will be estopped from relying on a ground which was not specified at the time of the refusal to perform if that party has thereby led the other party to believe that no reliance would be placed on that ground and it would be unfair or unjust now to allow such reliance.

Where, however, a party purports to terminate by accepting a breach which does not in law justify termination, it risks being itself in repudiatory breach of contract, although the Courts are reluctant so to hold as long as the purported termination was done in good faith, honestly (if mistakenly) believing that there was a right to terminate.[33]

(f) CONSUMER SALE AND SUPPLY CONTRACTS: INTERACTION WITH OTHER REMEDIES

Until 1 October 2015 the common law remedy of termination of the contract, set out above and in the following sections of this chapter, applied equally to consumer and non-consumer sale contracts, although in the case of contracts for the sale or supply of goods to consumers there was a special additional remedial regime for non-conforming goods, giving the consumer in certain circumstances the right to repair or replacement of the goods, reduction of the price, or rescission of the contract.[34] These remedies, introduced in order to implement the Consumer Sales Directive,[35] were in addition to the right to reject the goods for breach of a condition as to description, quality, or conformity with sample implied by sections 13 to 15 of the Sale of Goods Act 1979.[36]

The complex overlap of remedies in this area was reviewed by the Law Commission,[37] and Part 1 of the Consumer Rights Act 2015 amends significantly the special remedial

[31] *Ridgway v Hungerford Market Co* (1835) 3 A & E 171, 177, 178, 180; *Boston Deep Sea Fishing & Ice Co v Ansell* (1888) 39 Ch D 339, 352, 364; *Cyril Leonard & Co v Simo Securities Trust* [1972] 1 WLR 80, 85, 87, 89. But the rule does not apply to cases of unfair dismissal under statute: *W Devis & Co v Atkins* [1977] AC 931.

[32] *Panchaud Frères SA v Établissements General Grain Co* [1970] 1 Lloyd's Rep 53, 57–8. See also *Heisler v Anglo-Dal Ltd* [1954] 1 WLR 1273, 1278.

[33] *Woodar Investment Development Ltd v Wimpey Construction UK Ltd* [1980] 1 WLR 277, where HL was divided on this issue; but see Lord Wilberforce at 283, followed in *Vaswani v Italian Motors (Sales and Services) Ltd* [1996] 1 WLR 270, 276 (Privy Council held that conduct of seller of Ferrari car who acted bona fide in demanding higher price than due under contract was not a repudiatory breach).

[34] Sale and Supply of Goods to Consumers Regulations 2002 (SI 2002 No 3045), introducing new provisions into Sale of Goods Act 1979 (Part 5A); Supply of Goods and Services Act 1982 (Part 1B) which have now been removed and replaced by provisions of the Consumer Rights Act 2015, below.

[35] Directive 1999/44/EC.

[36] For the terms implied by the Sale of Goods Act 1979 and their classification as conditions, see above, pp 182–8.

[37] Law Com No 317, *Consumer Remedies for Faulty Goods* (2009).

regime for consumer contracts, replacing the earlier implementation of the Consumer Sales Directive and in certain respects going beyond its provisions, in relation to contracts between a trader and a consumer for the trader to supply goods, digital content, or services.[38]

A particularly significant change is that the consumer no longer has the common law right to treat a contract to supply goods as at an end where the breach is of a term required by the 2015 Act to be treated as included in the contract,[39] but instead the consumer has new statutory remedies to reject the goods and to treat the contract as at an end for breach of the statutory terms as to quality, fitness for purpose, description, and matching a sample or model.[40] There is a *short-term right to reject* (and to treat the contract as at an end) which may generally be exercised during the 30 days after the later of the transfer of ownership or possession of the goods to the consumer, delivery of the goods, and installation of the goods;[41] and a *final right to reject* (and to treat the contract as at an end) which may be exercised if the consumer has instead claimed the right to repair or replacement of the non-conforming goods and after one repair or one replacement the goods still do not conform to the contract, or the trader has failed to repair or replace the goods within a reasonable time and without significant inconvenience to the consumer, or if the consumer cannot require repair or replacement because it is impossible or disproportionate.[42] In all cases the right to reject is exercised by the consumer clearly indicating (by words or conduct) to the trader that he or she is rejecting the goods and treating the contract as at an end,[43] and the trader then generally has a duty to give the consumer a refund and the consumer has a duty to make the goods available for collection by the trader, at the trader's cost.[44]

In the case of consumer contracts to supply digital content, the common law remedy of termination is similarly excluded in the case of non-conformity with the terms treated as included in the contract, but in this case there is no statutory right of rejection but there are rights to repair or replacement, or price reduction, as well as other common law remedies such as damages and specific performance.[45] In the case of contracts for the supply of services, the common law remedy of termination is unchanged.[46]

[38] Consumer Rights Act 2015, s 1(1). For the influence of EU law after withdrawal of the UK from the EU, see above, p 21.

[39] Consumer Rights Act 2015, s 19(12), also excluding the case where the goods do not conform to the contract by reason of defective installation (s 15) or non-conforming digital content (s 16). Cf s 28 (non-exclusive right to treat the contract as at an end for late delivery of goods).

[40] Consumer Rights Act 2015, s 19(3). For these statutory terms, see above, p 189.

[41] Consumer Rights Act 2015, ss 20, 22.

[42] Consumer Rights Act 2015, ss 20, 24. In such circumstances the consumer may claim either the final right to reject or reduction of the price, but not both: *ibid*, s 24.

[43] Consumer Rights Act 2015, s 20(5), (6). For rejection of part of the goods under a severable contract, see s 20(20), (21); and for partial rejection of non-conforming goods, see s 21.

[44] Consumer Rights Act 2015, s 20(7), (8).

[45] Consumer Rights Act 2015, s 42.

[46] Consumer Rights Act 2015, s 54(7)(f).

2. FORMS OF BREACH WHICH JUSTIFY DISCHARGE

The right of a party to be treated as discharged from further performance may arise in any one of three ways: the other party to the contract (a) may renounce its liabilities under it, (b) may by its own act make it impossible to fulfil them, (c) may fail to perform what it has promised.[47] Of these forms of breach the first two may take place not only in the course of performance but also while the contract is still wholly executory, that is, before either party is entitled to demand a performance by the other of the other's promise. In such a case the breach is usually termed an 'anticipatory breach'.[48] The last can only take place at or during the time for performance of the contract.

(a) RENUNCIATION

Renunciation (often termed 'repudiation') occurs where one of the parties makes clear that it is not going to perform at all or that it is not going to perform a condition[49] or that it is not going to perform an innominate term where the breach will go to the root of the contract,[50] such that the other party would have a right to terminate.[51] If there is an express and unqualified refusal to perform, this intention will, of course, be clear and obvious.[52] But renunciation can also be evinced by conduct.

(i) By conduct

The test of whether an intention to renounce a contract is evinced by conduct is 'whether the party renunciating has acted in such a way as to lead a reasonable person to the conclusion that he does not intend to fulfil his part of the contract'.[53] Acts or omissions from which renunciation can be inferred may also entitle the injured party to be treated as discharged on one or both of the two other grounds previously mentioned.[54] But if the injured party relies upon renunciation as a ground for discharge, they must be such as to lead to the conclusion that the other party no longer intends to be bound by the contract. Whether or not there has been a repudiatory breach is, however, highly fact-sensitive: the test is not easy to apply, and comparison with other cases is of limited value.[55]

[47] This statement of the law was approved by Lord Porter in *Heyman v Darwins Ltd* [1942] AC 356, 397 and by Devlin J in *Universal Cargo Carriers Corp v Citati* [1957] 2 QB 401, 436, aff'd in part [1957] 1 WLR 979 and revs'd in part [1958] 2 QB 254.

[48] Below, pp 524–6; Dawson [1981] CLJ 83. [49] Below, p 530. [50] Below, p 531.

[51] Burrows, *A Restatement of the English Law of Contract* (2nd edn, 2020) 121–2; *Spar Shipping AS v Grand China Logistics Holding (Group) Co Ltd* [2016] EWCA Civ 982, [2017] 2 All ER (Comm) 701 at [21].

[52] A party who makes its performance dependent on a discretion to be exercised by a third party is not *ipso facto* deemed to be evincing an intention not to perform: *Geden Operations Ltd v Dry Bulk Handy Holdings Inc, The Bulk Uruguay* [2014] EWHC 885 (Comm), [2014] 2 All ER (Comm) 196.

[53] *Universal Cargo Carriers Corp v Citati* [1957] 2 QB 401, 436 (Devlin J). See also *Nottingham Building Society v Eurodynamics plc* [1995] FSR 605, 611–12; *Eminence Property Developments Ltd v Heaney* [2010] EWCA Civ 1168, [2011] 2 All ER (Comm) 223 at [61].

[54] *Mersey Steel and Iron Co v Naylor, Benzon & Co* (1884) 9 App Cas 434, 441 (renunciation) and 444 (failure of performance).

[55] *Eminence Property Developments Ltd v Heaney* [2010] EWCA Civ 1168 at [62], [64].

(ii) Intention to renounce

The importance of this intention was emphasized in *Freeth v Burr*,[56] where there was a failure on the part of the buyer to pay for one instalment of several deliveries of iron, under an erroneous impression that he was entitled to withhold payment as a set-off against damages for non-delivery of an earlier instalment. The seller was not discharged. Keating J said:[57] 'It is not a mere refusal or omission of one of the contracting parties to do something which he ought to do, that will justify the other in repudiating the contract; but there must be an absolute refusal to perform his part of the contract.'

Also in *Mersey Steel and Iron Co v Naylor, Benzon & Co*:[58]

NB bought from MS 5,000 tons of steel, to be delivered at the rate of 1,000 tons each month commencing in January 1881, payment to be made within 3 days of the receipt of the shipping documents. MS delivered part only of the first instalment in January, but delivered another in February. Shortly before payment for these was due, a petition was presented for the winding up of MS, whereupon NB refused to pay as it had been erroneously advised not to do so unless MS obtained the leave of the Court. MS informed NB that it would treat this refusal as breach, but NB continued to express its willingness to take delivery and to make the payments if possible.

The House of Lords held that MS was not entitled to treat itself as discharged. The Earl of Selborne LC said:[59]

I cannot ascribe to their [NB's] conduct, under these circumstances, the character of a renunciation of the contract, a repudiation of the contract, a refusal to fulfil the contract. It is just the reverse; the purchasers were desirous of fulfilling the contract; they were advised that there was a difficulty in the way, and they expressed anxiety that that difficulty should be as soon as possible removed.

In neither of these two cases did the breach, in the particular circumstances in which it had been committed, indicate an intention in the party in default to throw up the contract altogether, so as to set the other party free.

The contract-breaker's intention is assessed objectively, not subjectively; but motive may be relevant if it is something, or it reflects something, of which the innocent party was, or a reasonable person in his or her position would have been, aware and throws light on the way the alleged repudiatory conduct would be viewed by such a reasonable person.[60] Moreover, a Court may be reluctant to find that there has been a renunciation where a party insists on performing the contract in a particular way which, although

[56] (1874) LR 9 CP 208, 214, applied in *Aktion Maritime Corp of Liberia v S Kasmas & Brothers Ltd* [1987] 1 Lloyd's Rep 283, 306. See also *Mitsubishi Heavy Industries Ltd v Gulf Bank KSC* [1997] 1 Lloyd's Rep 343, 350, 354.

[57] (1874) LR 9 CP 208, 214. Note here that the word 'repudiating' is used in the sense of an election to discharge the contract. It is more normal to describe the guilty party as repudiating the contract: the innocent party discharges the contract by 'accepting the repudiation'.

[58] (1884) 9 App Cas 434. See also *Sweet & Maxwell Ltd v Universal News Services Ltd* [1964] 2 QB 699.

[59] (1884) 9 App Cas 434, 441.

[60] *Eminence Property Developments Ltd v Heaney* [2010] EWCA Civ 1168 at [63].

ultimately held to be a breach of contract, arose from a bona fide belief as to the construction of the contract which is also consistent with its continuance.[61] On the other hand, an unequivocal refusal, by words or conduct, to perform the contract will entitle the other party to be discharged from any further performance of its obligations even where the party who has failed to perform acted in good faith.[62] So, for example, if a buyer contracts to buy goods by instalments and agrees to pay cash for them, but then demands credit in respect of all future deliveries of the goods, the seller may refuse to make any further deliveries.[63] Similarly if, in breach of a contract of employment, a gardener insolently refuses to carry out instructions,[64] or a school teacher refuses to supervise school meals when required to do so,[65] the employer is justified in dismissing that person, that is, terminating the contract of employment.

Renunciation may take place either before performance is due or during performance itself.

(iii) Renunciation before performance is due: 'anticipatory breach'

The parties to a contract which is wholly executory have a right to something more than the performance when the time arrives. They have a right to the maintenance of the contractual relation right up to that time, as well as to a performance of the contract when due.

The renunciation of a contract by one of the parties before the time for performance has come does not, of itself, put an end to the contract, but the 'anticipatory breach' entitles the other to choose to be discharged and to sue at once for damages. A leading case is *Hochster v De la Tour*:[66]

T engaged H on 12 April to enter into his service as a courier and to accompany him upon a tour; the employment was to commence on 1 June. On 11 May T wrote to H to inform him that his services would no longer be required. H at once brought an action, although the time for performance had not yet arrived.

The Court held that he was entitled to do so.

The rule has also been applied to situations where the performance is not absolute as in *Hochster v De la Tour*, but contingent. In that case a time was fixed for performance, and before it arrived T renounced the contract, but in *Frost v Knight*,[67] performance was contingent upon an event which might not happen within the lifetime of the parties:

K, a bachelor, promised to marry F upon his father's death; but during his father's lifetime he renounced the contract.

[61] *Vaswani v Italian Motors (Sales and Services) Ltd* [1996] 1 WLR 270. See also *Woodar Investment Development Ltd v Wimpey Construction UK Ltd* [1980] 1 WLR 277; see p 520, n 33.

[62] *Federal Commerce & Navigation Co Ltd v Molena Alpha Inc* [1979] AC 757.

[63] *Withers v Reynolds* (1831) 2 B & Ad 882.

[64] *Pepper v Webb* [1969] 1 WLR 514.

[65] *Gorse v Durham CC* [1971] 1 WLR 775.

[66] (1853) 2 E & B 678.

[67] (1872) LR 7 Ex 111.

F was held entitled to sue. The principle of anticipatory breach was justified by Cockburn CJ as follows:[68]

The promisee has an inchoate right to the performance of the bargain, which becomes complete when the time for performance has arrived. *In the mean time he has a right to have the contract kept open as a subsisting and effective contract.* Its unimpaired and unimpeached efficacy may be essential to his interests.

The principle enables the innocent party to assert its rights speedily and so to minimize the damage which may be suffered from the breach.[69] Nevertheless, a party who has been guilty of an anticipatory breach by renunciation may not withdraw that renunciation once it has been accepted by the other party,[70] even though the guilty party tenders performance within the time originally fixed by the contract and even though the position of the other party has not changed as a result of the renunciation.

The promisee, however, has the right to continue to insist on the performance of the promise and to refuse to accept the renunciation. If this is done, the promisee loses the right to rely on the anticipatory breach and the contract remains in existence for the benefit and at the risk of both parties. Should anything occur subsequently to discharge the contract from other causes, the promisor, whose renunciation has been refused, may take advantage of such discharge. In *Avery v Bowden*:[71]

A chartered his ship to B. It was agreed that the ship would sail to Odessa, and there take a cargo from B's agent, which was to be loaded within a certain number of days. The vessel reached Odessa, and her master demanded a cargo, but B's agent was unable to supply one. Nevertheless, the master of the ship continued to demand a cargo, but before the specified number of days had elapsed the Crimean War broke out between England and Russia and the performance of the contract became legally impossible. A afterwards sued for breach of the charterparty.

His action failed. If B's agent had positively informed the master that no cargo would be provided, and that there was no use in his remaining there any longer, the master might have treated this as an anticipatory breach and sailed away. A would then have had the right to sue at once upon the contract. But the Court found that as the conduct of B's agent was not such as to constitute a renunciation of the contract there was therefore no breach committed by B before the contract was frustrated. Even if there had been a renunciation, however, the Court considered that it could not be treated as a cause of action after the master still continued to insist upon having a cargo in fulfilment of the charterparty. Again, it has been held by the House of Lords[72] that where, following an anticipatory breach by charterers which was not accepted by the shipowners, the

[68] *Ibid*, 114 (emphasis added). But see Vold (1928) 41 Harv LR 340.

[69] *Bunge SA v Nidera BV* [2015] UKSC 43, [2015] 3 All ER 1082 at [12].

[70] *Xenos v Danube, etc, Ry* (1863) 13 CBNS 824. Cf *Aegnoussiotis Shipping Corp of Monrovia v A/S Kristian Jebsens Rederi of Bergen* [1977] 1 Lloyd's Rep 268, 276 (resumption of performance by both parties after termination may constitute new contract).

[71] (1855) 5 E & B 714, (1856) 6 E & B 953. See also *Michael v Hart & Co* [1902] 1 KB 482.

[72] *Fercometal SARL v Mediterranean Shipping Co SA, The Simona* [1989] AC 788.

owners later failed to tender the vessel ready to load on time, the charterers were entitled to cancel the charterparty.

Despite the utility of the principle of 'anticipatory breach', the term itself is somewhat misleading. It suggests that the cause of action lies in the future breach that will occur on the date fixed for performance, which the innocent party is, in some sense, permitted to anticipate. But it is clear that, at any rate where the anticipatory breach consists of a renunciation of the contract, the breach is constituted by the renunciation itself, and, if this is accepted, the innocent party is immediately entitled to recover by way of damages the true value of the contractual rights which have been lost, subject to the innocent party's duty to mitigate.[73]

(iv) **Renunciation during performance**

If during the performance of a contract one of the parties by words or conduct unconditionally refuses to perform its side of the contract, the other party is forthwith entitled to be released from any further performance of its obligations, and to sue.

In *Cort v Ambergate etc Railway Co*:[74]

C contracted with the defendant to supply it with 3,900 tons of railway chairs, at a certain price, to be delivered in certain quantities at specified dates. After 1,787 tons had been delivered, the defendant requested C to deliver no more, as they would not be wanted. C brought an action upon the contract, averring that he was always ready and willing to perform his part, but had been prevented from doing so by the action of the defendant.

C obtained a verdict, and the Court rejected the defendant's motion for a new trial which claimed that C should have proved not merely that he was ready and willing to deliver, but an actual delivery. Since the contract had been renounced, C could maintain an action without manufacturing and tendering the rest of the goods.

(b) IMPOSSIBILITY CREATED BY ONE PARTY

If by the act or default of one party further performance of the contract is made impossible,[75] although that party has not, by words or conduct, renounced the intention to fulfil it, the other party will be discharged.

Renunciation is usually easier to establish because the innocent party need only show that the conduct of the promisor was such as to lead a reasonable person to believe that the promisor did not intend to perform the promise, whereas if reliance is placed on impossibility the innocent party must show that the contract was in fact impossible of performance due to the default of the promisor. But it is an independent ground for discharge, as shown by *Universal Cargo Carriers Corp v Citati*:[76]

UCC chartered a ship to C who agreed to nominate a berth and a shipper, and to provide a cargo, all before a certain day. Three days before the due date C had done none of these

[73] *The Mihalis Angelos* [1971] 1 QB 164.

[74] (1851) 17 QB 127.

[75] If the impossibility arises through the occurrence of some external event, which radically changes the obligation, the contract may be discharged by frustration: see above, Chapter 14.

[76] [1957] 2 QB 401, aff'd in part [1957] 1 WLR 979 and revs'd in part [1958] 2 QB 254. See also *Sanko Steamship Co Ltd v Eacom Timber Sales Ltd* [1987] 1 Lloyd's Rep 487, 492.

things. Although C was willing to perform the contract if he could, UCC cancelled it and found another charterer.

Devlin J held that C had not renounced the contract, but, since he could not have performed before the delay became so long as to frustrate the commercial purpose of the contract, UCC was entitled to treat this inability to perform as discharging its obligations.

Here also the impossibility may be created either before performance is due or in the course of performance.

(i) Impossibility created before performance is due: anticipatory breach

If the act or default of a promisor which makes performance impossible occurs before the time for performance arrives, the effect is the same as though the promisor had renounced the contract at that time. Such impossibility need not be deliberately created: 'Anticipatory breach was not devised as a whip to be used for the chastisement of deliberate contract-breakers, but from which the shiftless, the dilatory, or the unfortunate are to be spared. It is not confined to any particular class of breach, deliberate or blameworthy or otherwise; it covers all breaches that are bound to happen.'[77]

The aggrieved party may sue at once. In *Lovelock v Franklyn*:[78]

F promised to assign to L within 7 years from the date of his promise, all his interest in a lease for the sum of £140. Before the end of 7 years he assigned his interest to another person.

It was held that L need not wait until the end of the seven years to bring an action. Lord Denman CJ stated:[79]

[L] has a right to say to [F]: 'You have placed yourself in a situation in which you cannot perform what you have promised; you promised to be ready during the period of seven years; and, during that period, I may at any time tender you the money and call for an assignment, and expect that you should keep yourself ready; but, if I now were to tender you the money, you would not be ready'. That is a breach of the contract.

Similarly, in *Universal Cargo Carriers Corp v Citati*,[80] the shipowners' cancellation of the contract was not premature. They were permitted to anticipate a breach which was in fact inevitable.

(ii) Impossibility created during performance

The rule is similar where the complete performance of the contract is made impossible by the act or default of one party. This is illustrated by *O'Neil v Armstrong*:[81]

O'N, a British subject, was engaged by A, the captain of a warship owned by the Japanese Government, to act as a fireman on a voyage from the Tyne to Yokohama. In the course of the voyage the Japanese Government declared war on China. O'N was informed that

[77] *Universal Cargo Carriers Corp v Citati* [1957] 2 QB 401, 438 (Devlin J).
[78] (1846) 8 QB 371.
[79] *Ibid*, 378. See also *Omnium D'Enterprises v Sutherland* [1919] 1 KB 618.
[80] [1957] 2 QB 401.
[81] [1895] 2 QB 418.

performance of the contract would bring him under the penalties of the Foreign Enlistment Act 1870. He consequently left the ship, and sued A for the wages agreed upon.

It was held that he was entitled to succeed in his action because the act of A's principal, the Japanese Government, had made his performance of the contract legally impossible.

It will be seen from this case that discharge by breach may occur, not only where one party disables itself from performing the contract, but also where it prevents completion of the contract by the other party.[82] The Courts may imply a term that the parties cooperate to ensure performance. A duty to cooperate cannot be imposed so as to compel a party to do something which the contract on its true construction relieved that party from doing, and cannot be used to compel a party to do something which that party is in fact unable to do.[83] But the Courts are often ready to imply a term that each party undertakes to do all that is necessary to secure performance of the contract.[84] Thus if a licence is required for the export of goods, and the buyer fails to provide the seller with the information necessary to obtain the licence, no action will lie against the seller for non-delivery.[85]

There has been debate over whether there is a principle that, where a party wrongfully prevents the fulfilment of a condition precedent to that party's debt obligation (eg the duty to pay for goods being bought), the condition is treated as being fulfilled, thus entitling the other party to sue for the debt—a principle said to be based on the decision of the House of Lords in the (Scottish) case of *Mackay v Dick*.[86] However, the Supreme Court has now made clear that this is not a principle of English law. Subject to contrary provision in the contract, where a condition precedent has not been fulfilled because of the debtor's breach of contract, that breach is appropriately and adequately dealt with through the claimant's remedy in damages.[87]

(c) FAILURE OF PERFORMANCE

Failure of performance, whether total or partial, is the most common ground for the discharge of a party by breach. But it is not every failure of performance by one party which entitles the other to be discharged from its own liabilities under it. In order to determine if this is so, it is necessary to ask a number of questions.

[82] See also *Ogdens Ltd v Nelson* [1905] AC 109. Cf *Bremer Vulkan v South India Shipping Co* [1981] AC 909 (both parties in breach).

[83] *North Sea Energy Holdings NV v Petroleum Authority of Thailand* [1999] 1 Lloyd's Rep 483, 492.

[84] *Stirling v Maitland* (1864) 5 B & S 840, 852; *Southern Foundries (1936) Ltd v Shirlaw* [1940] AC 701; *The Unique Mariner (No 2)* [1979] 1 Lloyd's Rep 37. Cf *Rhodes v Forwood* (1876) 1 App Cas 256; *Luxor (Eastbourne) Ltd v Cooper* [1941] AC 108. See Bateson [1960] JBL 187; Burrows (1968) 31 MLR 390.

[85] *Kyprianou v Cyprus Textiles Ltd* [1958] 2 Lloyd's Rep 60.

[86] (1881) 6 App Cas 251.

[87] *King Crude Carriers SA v Ridgebury November LLC* [2025] UKSC 39, [2025] 3 WLR 707 at [61]–[68].

(i) Are the promises independent?

In certain circumstances, the obligations entered into by each party may be independent of each other in the sense that neither party can claim to be released from its promise by the failure of the other to perform its part. Put in another way, each party can enforce the obligations undertaken by the other even though it has not performed its own. For example, in the case of leases, a tenant's covenant to pay rent is independent of a landlord's covenant to repair; the tenant cannot withhold payment on the ground that the landlord has failed to repair the premises.[88] Again, a covenant by a husband in a separation deed to pay his wife maintenance has been said to be independent of any covenant on her part, for example not to molest him.[89] And, because of the involvement of third parties in documentary sales, the obligation of a buyer to pay when the shipping documents are tendered has been held to be independent of the seller's obligation to supply goods conforming to the contract.[90] But the tendency of the Courts is against construing a contract in this way unless the parties clearly intend to do so because such a construction means that both parties are inadequately protected from the risk of non-performance by the other.[91] Thus, in a contract for work or services, the obligation to pay would fall due although the work had not been done.

Normally, however, the obligations of each party will be regarded as *interdependent*. For example, an employee who has been wrongfully dismissed is not bound to observe a covenant in restraint of trade.[92] The clearest example of obligations which are dependent on each other arises if the parties agree that the performance of their respective promises shall be simultaneous, or at least that each shall be ready and willing to perform its promise at the same time. Then the obligation to perform each promise is dependent or conditional on this concurrence of readiness and willingness to perform the other; their mutual promises are *concurrent conditions*. Thus section 28 of the Sale of Goods Act 1979 provides that in a contract for the sale of goods:

> Unless otherwise agreed, delivery of the goods and payment of the price are concurrent conditions, that is to say, the seller must be ready and willing to give possession of the goods to the buyer in exchange for the price and the buyer must be ready and willing to pay the price in exchange for possession of the goods.

Failure to tender the goods discharges the buyer from its obligation to pay the price; failure to tender the price discharges the seller from its obligation to deliver the goods.

[88] *Taylor v Webb* [1937] 2 KB 283.

[89] *Fearon v Earl of Aylesford* (1884) 14 QBD 792, 800. See also *Winstone v Linn* (1823) 1 B & C 460 (contract of apprenticeship); cf *Ellen v Topp* (1851) 6 Exch 424.

[90] *Gill & Duffus SA v Berger & Co* [1984] AC 382 (cif sale). See also *Vagres Compania Maritima SA v Nissho-Iwai America Corp, The Karin Vatis* [1988] 2 Lloyd's Rep 330 (terms of contract rendered obligation to pay freight when cargo loaded independent of charterer's obligations).

[91] See also above, pp 458–64.

[92] *General Billposting Co Ltd v Atkinson* [1909] AC 118. See doubts of Phillips LJ in *Rock Refrigeration Ltd v Jones* [1997] 1 All ER 1, 18–19 but cf *Brown v Neon Management Services Ltd* [2018] EWHC 2137 (QB), [2019] IRLR 30 at [170]–[174]. Some primary obligations do continue after discharge, above, p 519, n 28; below, pp 535–6.

(ii) Is the obligation 'entire' or 'divisible'?

We saw earlier[93] that certain obligations are 'entire' in the sense that the liability of one party is dependent upon the complete performance of the obligation by the other. Subject to the doctrine of substantial performance,[94] if A agrees to make a dress for B in return for a promise to pay for the dress on completion, anything less than complete performance by A will release B from her obligation to pay. It is immaterial how the failure to effect complete performance comes about. It may be due to a deliberate abandonment of the contract, to a negligent act or omission, or, as in *Cutter v Powell*,[95] to a simple misfortune occurring without any fault.

Entire obligations are, however, the exception rather than the rule. The obligations in most bilateral contracts are 'divisible' in the sense that the breach of any one or more of them will not necessarily constitute a ground of discharge. The contract may, for example, be a complex one, composed of a number of undertakings differing in character or importance; or it may be a promise to do a number of successive acts; or to do a single act which can be partly or defectively performed. A failure by one party precisely to perform its obligations under the contract will give a right of action in damages to the other; but it will not necessarily discharge the innocent party from the performance of its own obligations under the contract.

(iii) Is the term broken a condition?

Assuming that the obligations in the contract are divisible, and not entire, the question then arises whether the particular term which has been broken is a condition of the contract. From an historical point of view, the right of the innocent party to choose to be treated as discharged was said to turn upon the non-performance of a 'condition precedent' in the contract.[96] Performance by one party of that party's promise or 'covenant' was regarded as a condition precedent to the liability of the other. The classification of contractual terms is dealt with in Chapter 5.[97] It was there noted that, today, a term will only be classified as a condition if it has been so categorized by statute (eg by the Sale of Goods Act 1979) or by judicial decision, or if the parties have so agreed in their contract, either expressly or by implication.[98] Any breach of a condition will entitle the innocent party to choose to be treated as discharged.[99] It was also noted, however, that there has now emerged a category of 'innominate terms', the breach of which will not necessarily produce that effect.[100]

[93] Above, pp 458–9. [94] Above, p 461. [95] (1795) 6 Term R 320, above, p 458.

[96] *Pordage v Cole* (1669) 1 Wms Saund 319; *Kingston v Preston* (1773) 2 Doug 689, 691. The history of the expression is expounded in *Cehave NV v Bremer Handelsgesellschaft* [1976] QB 44, 57, 72; *United Scientific Holdings Ltd v Burnley BC* [1978] AC 904, 927. See also *Hurst v Bryk* [2002] 1 AC 185, 193 (Lord Millett); Dawson [1981] CLJ 83, 87.

[97] Above, pp 150–60. [98] Above, pp 157–60.

[99] Above, p 151. See, eg, *Union Eagle Ltd v Golden Achievement Ltd* [1997] AC 514 (vendor entitled to terminate where purchaser tendered price 10 minutes late). In the case of a contract for the sale of goods a non-consumer buyer may not reject goods by reason of a breach of the statutory implied conditions by the seller as to description, quality, or conformity with sample, where the breach is so slight that it would be unreasonable for him to reject them: Sale of Goods Act 1979, s 15A. See also Supply of Goods and Services Act 1982, ss 5A (non-consumer transfer of goods), 10A (non-consumer hire of goods).

[100] Above, p 156.

(iv) Does the breach go to 'the root of the contract'?

If the term broken is not a condition, but an innominate term, the right of the innocent party to choose to be treated as discharged from further performance will depend upon the nature and consequences of the breach. Differing terminology has been used by the Courts to describe the test to be applied, the most common being that the breach must go to 'the root of the contract'.[101] It has also been said that the breach must be 'fundamental',[102] that it must 'affect the very substance of the contract'[103] or 'frustrate the commercial purpose of the venture'.[104] The use of these and similar expressions emphasizes that the breach must be far-reaching in its effect in order to justify discharge, taking as the starting-point the benefit the injured party was intended to obtain from performance of the contract.[105] A test which is frequently applied is that stated by Diplock LJ in *Hongkong Fir Shipping Co Ltd v Kawasaki Kisen Kaisha Ltd*:[106] 'Does the occurrence of the event deprive the party who has further undertakings to perform of substantially the whole benefit which it was the intention of the parties as expressed in the contract that he should obtain as the consideration for performing those undertakings?' In that case:

H chartered to K the *Hongkong Fir* for a period of 24 months, on terms that she was 'in every way fitted for ordinary cargo service'. The vessel was an old one, and by reason of its age needed to be maintained by an experienced, competent, careful, and adequate engine room staff. This H did not provide. The chief engineer was addicted to drink and inefficient, and the engine room complement inadequate, with the result that there were many serious breakdowns in machinery. In the first 7 months of the charter the ship was only eight and a half weeks at sea, the rest of the time being spent in breakdowns and repair to make the ship seaworthy; but this was eventually achieved. K refused to continue with the charterparty.

It was argued on behalf of K that the term as to seaworthiness was a condition of the contract, and that it was therefore entitled as of right to treat itself as discharged. This argument was not accepted by the Court of Appeal.[107] The Court then went on to hold, on the facts, that the delays which had already occurred, and the delay which was likely to occur, as a result of the vessel's unseaworthiness, and the conduct of H in taking steps to remedy these, were not, when taken together, such as to deprive K of substantially

[101] *Mersey Steel & Iron Co v Naylor, Benzon & Co* (1884) 9 App Cas 434, 444; *Heyman v Darwins Ltd* [1942] AC 356, 397; *Suisse Atlantique Société d'Armement SA v NV Kolen Centrale* [1967] 1 AC 361, 422; *Cehave NV v Bremer Handelsgesellschaft* [1976] QB 44, 60, 73; *Federal Commerce & Navigation Co Ltd v Molena Alpha Inc* [1979] AC 757, 779; *Ramsbury Properties Ltd v Ocean View Construction Ltd* [2024] UKPC 40, [2025] 1 WLR 924 at [45] (repudiatory breach of lease).

[102] *Suisse Atlantique Société d'Armement SA v NV Kolen Centrale* [1967] 1 AC 361, 397, 409–10, 421–2, 431; *Photo Production Ltd v Securicor Transport Ltd* [1980] AC 827, 849.

[103] *Wallis, Son and Wells v Pratt and Haynes* [1910] 2 KB 1003, 1012.

[104] *MacAndrew v Chapple* (1866) LR 1 CP 643, 647, 648; *Jackson v Union Marine Insurance Co* (1874) LR 10 CP 125, 145, 147, 148; *Trade and Transport Inc v Iino Kaiun Kaisha Ltd* [1973] 1 WLR 210, 223.

[105] *Ampurius Nu Homes Holdings Ltd v Telford Homes (Creekside) Ltd* [2013] EWCA Civ 577, [2013] 4 All ER 377 at [51].

[106] [1962] 2 QB 26, 66; above, p 156. See also *Photo Production Ltd v Securicor Transport Ltd* [1980] AC 827, 849 (Lord Diplock).

[107] See above, p 156.

the whole benefit which it was the intention of the parties K should obtain from further use of the ship under charterparty. K had therefore unjustifiably treated the contract as repudiated. It is to be noted that the Court considers the position as at the date of purported termination of the contract, but taking into account any steps taken by the guilty party to remedy the accrued breach of contract, as well as likely future events, judged by reference to objective facts as at the date of purported termination.[108]

It has been said that Diplock LJ's test 'sets the bar high',[109] and that other cases adopt a view more favourable to the injured party.[110] However, whichever expression of the test one takes, a number of factors have to be addressed on the facts of the case:[111]

> the starting point must be to consider what benefit the injured party was intended to obtain from performance of the contract. . . .
>
> The next thing to consider is the effect of the breach on the injured party. What financial loss has it caused? How much of the intended benefit under the contract has the injured party already received? Can the injured party be adequately compensated by an award of damages? Is the breach likely to be repeated? Will the guilty party resume compliance with his obligations? Has the breach fundamentally changed the value of future performance of the guilty party's outstanding obligations?

The same general approach has been adopted with respect to contracts to deliver and pay for goods by instalments. If the seller makes defective deliveries in respect of one or more instalments, or the buyer neglects or refuses to take delivery of or pay for one or more instalments, this will not necessarily permit the innocent party to choose to be treated as discharged. The question will arise whether the breach is a repudiation of the whole contract or whether it is a severable breach giving rise to a claim for damages but not to a right to treat the whole contract as repudiated.[112] The breach or breaches may, of course, amount to an express or implied renunciation of the contract.[113] But if they amount only to a failure of performance, they must go to the root of the contract in order to justify discharge. Thus in *Simpson v Crippin*:[114]

> C agreed to deliver 6,000 to 8,000 tons of coal to S in equal monthly instalments during a period of 12 months, the buyer to send wagons to receive the coal. S sent wagons for only 158 tons in the first month.

[108] *Ampurius Nu Homes Holdings Ltd v Telford Homes (Creekside) Ltd* [2013] EWCA Civ 577 at [44] (delay of some months in construction of properties not sufficient to justify termination bearing in mind the ultimate objective was to grant 999-year leases).

[109] *Ampurius Nu Homes Holdings Ltd v Telford Homes (Creekside) Ltd* [2013] EWCA Civ 577 at [48] (Lewison LJ).

[110] eg *Decro-Wall International SA v Practitioners in Marketing Ltd* [1971] 1 WLR 361, 380 ('substantial part of the benefit', rather than 'substantially the whole benefit').

[111] *Ampurius Nu Homes Holdings Ltd v Telford Homes (Creekside) Ltd* [2013] EWCA Civ 577 at [51]–[52]; see also *Galtrade Ltd v BP Oil International Ltd* [2021] EWHC 1796 (Comm), [2021] 2 CLC 408 at [86]–[90] (it is a 'multi-factorial test').

[112] Sale of Goods Act 1979, s 31 (non-consumer contracts); see also Consumer Rights Act 2015, s 26 (similar provisions relating to consumer's entitlement to exercise right to reject for defective instalment deliveries).

[113] See above, p 522.

[114] (1872) LR 8 QB 14.

The Court rejected the argument that the breach went 'to the whole root and consideration of the agreement' and held that C could not cancel the contract. On the other hand, in *Honck v Muller*:[115]

H, in October 1879, bought from M 2,000 tons of pig iron to be delivered 'in November, 1879, or equally over November, December and January next at 6*d* per ton extra'. H failed to take delivery of any iron in November, but claimed to have delivery of one-third of the iron in December and one-third in January. M refused, and gave notice that he considered the contract discharged.

H brought an action for breach and failed, as a majority of the Court considered that his failure of performance was so substantial as to discharge M from further liability.

In contracts for the sale and delivery of goods by instalments, the most relevant factors have been said to be, 'first, the ratio quantitatively which the breach bears to the contract as a whole, and secondly the degree of probability or improbability that such a breach will be repeated'.[116] The importance of the second factor was emphasized by Bigham J in *Millar's Karri and Jarrah Co v Weddel*:[117]

If the breach is of such a kind, or takes place in such circumstances as reasonably to lead to the inference that similar breaches will be committed in relation to subsequent deliveries, the whole contract may there and then be regarded as repudiated and may be rescinded. If, for instance, a buyer fails to pay for one delivery in such circumstances as to lead to the inference that he will not be able to pay for subsequent deliveries; or if a seller delivers goods differing from the requirements of the contract, and does so in such circumstances as to lead to the inference that he cannot, or will not, deliver any other kind of goods in the future, the other contracting party will be under no obligation to wait to see what may happen; he can at once cancel the contract and rid himself of the difficulty.

It follows that, the further the parties have proceeded with the due performance of a contract, the less likely it is that one party will be able to claim that it has been discharged by a single breach.[118] However, a series of non-repudiatory breaches in a continuing contract may cumulatively amount to a repudiation of the contract.[119]

The right of discharge therefore depends on the answer to this question: Does the breach go so far to the root of the contract as to entitle the injured party to say, 'I have lost all that I cared to obtain under this contract; further performance cannot make good the prior default'?[120]

[115] (1881) 7 QBD 92. See also *Munro & Co Ltd v Meyer* [1930] 2 KB 312 (nearly half of goods seriously adulterated).

[116] *Maple Flock Co Ltd v Universal Furniture Products (Wembley) Ltd* [1934] 1 KB 148, 157 (Lord Hewart CJ).

[117] (1909) 100 LT 128, 129.

[118] *Cornwall v Henson* [1900] 2 Ch 298, 304.

[119] *Force India Formula One Team Ltd v Etihad Airways PJSC* [2010] EWCA Civ 1051, [2011] ETMR 10 at [87]; *SK Shipping Europe Plc v Capital VLCC 3 Corp* [2020] EWHC 3448 (Comm), [2020] 2 CLC 816 at [305].

[120] Cited with approval in *Alkok v Grymek* (1966) 56 DLR (2d) 393 (Canada).

(v) Termination clauses

A contract may contain a clause setting out the circumstances and conditions upon which one party shall have the right to terminate by reason of the other party's breach. Such a clause may make clear that a particular term is a condition of the contract so that the rules of termination for breach of condition, discussed above, will then apply.[121] But the clause may be drafted more generally to provide a remedial regime (including the right for the innocent party to terminate the contract) for breach of contract in specified circumstances,[122] and it may refer to a standard of breach which is different from that which gives rise to the right to terminate at common law—such as where the breach is 'material', which has been held to cover breaches which are less than 'fundamental', but where it is more than trivial or minimal.[123] The party seeking to rely on such a clause must establish strictly that the clause entitles it to terminate in relation to the breach which has occurred,[124] and the Courts will not hold that the common law right to terminate for repudiatory breach has been excluded by an express termination clause without clear words showing such an intention.[125] Where the clause provides a right to terminate which corresponds to a right under the general law (eg for breach which goes to the root of the contract), the injured party need not elect between the two termination rights, and notification that it treats the contract as discharged will not preclude the (common law) claim to damages following the termination.[126] Where, however, the clause provides different rights from the general law (eg termination independent of any breach), if the notification of termination is made under the clause, the claim for damages (consequential on termination at common law) cannot run.[127]

3. CONSEQUENCES OF DISCHARGE

(a) RELEASE FROM FUTURE OBLIGATIONS

An innocent party who is entitled to, and does, choose to be treated as discharged by the other party's breach, is thereby released from further performance of those future obligations which remain still to be performed.[128] After such discharge the innocent

[121] *Union Eagle Ltd v Golden Achievement Ltd* [1997] AC 514; above, p 530, n 99.

[122] *Lombard North Central plc v Butterworth* [1987] QB 527;

[123] *Dalkia Utilities Services plc v Celtech International Ltd* [2006] EWHC 63 (Comm), [2006] 1 Lloyd's Rep 599; *Mid Essex Hospital Services NHS Trust v Compass Group UK and Ireland Ltd* [2013] EWCA Civ 200, [2013] BLR 265 at [124]–[126].

[124] Cf *Rice v Great Yarmouth BC* (2001) 3 LGLR 4 (clause in long-term contract involving substantial investment, which allowed the defendant to terminate for 'a breach of any of the [claimant's] obligations' was construed as applying only to repudiatory breach), criticized by Whittaker, in Burrows and Peel (eds), *Contract Terms* (2007) 253; *Mears Ltd v Costplan Services (South East) Ltd* [2019] EWCA Civ 502, [2019] 4 WLR 55 at [37]–[42].

[125] *Dalkia Utilities Services plc v Celtech International Ltd* [2006] EWHC 63 (Comm); *Stocznia Gdynia SA v Gearbulk Holdings Ltd* [2009] EWCA Civ 75, [2010] QB 27 at [23].

[126] *Stocznia Gdynia SA v Gearbulk Holdings Ltd* [2009] EWCA Civ 75 at [44].

[127] *Shell Egypt West Manzala GmbH v Dana Gas Egypt Ltd* [2010] EWHC 465 (Comm); *Phones 4U Ltd v EE Ltd* [2018] EWHC 49 (Comm), [2018] 2 All ER (Comm) 315.

[128] See Shea (1979) 42 MLR 623; Beatson (1981) 97 LQR 389; Rose (1981) 34 CLP 235; Law Com No 121, *Pecuniary Restitution on Breach of Contract* (1983).

party is not bound to accept, or pay for, any further performance by the party in breach. The duty of the party in default to perform future unperformed obligations likewise comes to an end, as does that party's right to perform them.

(b) CONTRACT NOT RESCINDED *AB INITIO*

In the terminology employed in many of the cases, these consequences are often described as a 'rescission' of the contract; or it is stated that the contract is 'terminated' or 'put an end to' by the breach. But these expressions are somewhat misleading:

> To say that the contract is rescinded or has come to an end or has ceased to exist may in individual cases convey the truth with sufficient accuracy, but the fuller expression that the injured party is thereby absolved from future performance of his obligations under the contract is a more exact description of the position. Strictly speaking, to say that on acceptance of the renunciation of the contract the contract is rescinded is incorrect.[129]

Certainly, this so-called rescission is quite different from rescission *ab initio*, such as may arise, for example, in cases of misrepresentation.[130] The contract is not set aside as from the beginning.

(c) ACCRUED OBLIGATIONS REMAIN

Although both parties are discharged from further performance of their obligations, rights are not divested which have already been unconditionally acquired. Rights and obligations which arise from the partial execution of the contract and causes of action which have accrued from its breach alike continue unaffected.[131] So, for instance, if a time charterparty of a ship is repudiated by the charterer, the shipowner can recover arrears of hire charges due but unpaid up to the date of the shipowner's acceptance of the repudiation.[132] Again, if building work is to be paid for by instalments, the builder can sue for any instalment due but unpaid at the time of discharge.[133]

It makes no difference in this respect whether the accrued obligation is in favour of the innocent or the guilty party. An employee who repudiates a contract of employment can nevertheless sue for wages earned before that time[134] and, following termination of a partnership agreement, it seems that the innocent partner remains liable for the

[129] *Heyman v Darwins Ltd* [1942] AC 356, 399 (Lord Porter). This statement was unanimously approved by the House of Lords in *Johnson v Agnew* [1980] AC 367. See also *Bank of Boston Connecticut v European Grain and Shipping Ltd* [1989] AC 1056, 1098–9 and *State Trading Corp of India Ltd v M Golodetz Ltd* [1989] 2 Lloyd's Rep 277, 286; *Howard-Jones v Tate* [2011] EWCA Civ 1330, [2012] 1 P & CR 11 at [15], [29].

[130] *Johnson v Agnew* [1980] AC 367, 393.

[131] *McDonald v Dennys Lascelles Ltd* (1933) 48 CLR 457, 476–7 (Dixon J) (Australia); *Photo Production Ltd v Securicor Transport Ltd* [1980] AC 827, 844, 850. But, once the contract has been discharged, equitable relief, eg an injunction, cannot be granted: *Walker v Standard Chartered Bank plc* [1992] BCLC 535.

[132] *Leslie Shipping Co v Welstead* [1921] 3 KB 420. See also *Chatterton v Maclean* [1951] 1 All ER 761 (hire-purchase).

[133] *Hyundai Heavy Industries Co Ltd v Papadopoulos* [1980] 1 WLR 1129 (HL).

[134] *Taylor v Laird* (1856) 25 LJ Ex 29. Cf Apportionment Act 1870, s 2.

accrued liabilities of the partnership, provided these were incurred when the innocent party was a partner.[135]

Admittedly, if money has been paid by one party to the other under the contract, and the basis for the payment has wholly failed, the money may be recoverable in unjust enrichment by an action for money had and received.[136] But, in principle, accrued liabilities remain enforceable despite the discharge. Moreover, as we have seen,[137] only the primary obligations of the parties as a general rule come to an end. The primary obligations of the party in default are then replaced by a secondary obligation to pay compensation to the injured party for the breach. Note, however, certain primary obligations will survive discharge and continue to be enforceable. The continued enforcement of such obligations simply reflects the presumed intention of the parties. The best examples of obligations that survive are arbitration clauses and dispute resolution mechanisms,[138] and exclusion and limitation clauses.[139] In addition, there are clauses that may only come into operation upon discharge such as certain liquidated damages clauses. It has also been held that an obligation to pay a retainer for a specified period[140] and an agent's duty to provide records to its principal survive discharge.[141]

(d) RESTITUTIONARY CLAIMS

With respect to payments not yet due at the time of discharge, for example, for goods supplied or for services rendered under the contract, the innocent party can sue in unjust enrichment for restitution in the form of a reasonable price for the goods supplied (quantum valebat) or reasonable remuneration for the services rendered (quantum meruit),[142] or include them in the claim for damages for breach. Whether the guilty party has any claim will depend on whether the contract is entire or divisible. If it is entire, in principle no claim is possible.[143] But if it is divisible, the guilty party may be entitled to claim in respect of performance completed, subject to a counterclaim for damages by the innocent party in respect of loss suffered by the breach.

4. LOSS OF THE RIGHT OF DISCHARGE

The right of discharge may be lost by waiver, affirmation, acceptance, and operation of law. In addition, a party may be estopped from claiming to be entitled to treat a contract as discharged. This has been dealt with earlier.[144]

[135] *Hurst v Bryk* [2002] 1 AC 185. See also Partnership Act 1890, s 9.

[136] See below, p 607.

[137] See above, pp 534–5.

[138] *Heyman v Darwins Ltd* [1942] AC 356.

[139] *Photo Production Ltd v Securicor Transport Ltd* [1980] AC 827, 850.

[140] *Duffen v Frabo SpA* [2000] 1 Lloyd's Rep 180.

[141] *Yasuda Fire & Marine Insurance Co of Europe Ltd v Orion Marine Insurance Underwriting Agency Ltd* [1995] QB 174.

[142] See below, p 613.

[143] See above, pp 458–9. But see below, p 609.

[144] See above, pp 160–1, 472–6.

FURTHER READING

SMITH, 'Anticipatory Breach of Contract' in LOMNICKA and MORSE (eds), *Contemporary Issues in Commercial Law* (London: Sweet & Maxwell, 1997) 175

WHITTAKER, 'Termination Clauses' in BURROWS and PEEL (eds), *Contract Terms* (Oxford: Oxford University Press, 2007) 253

LIU, 'The *White & Carter* Principle: A Restatement' (2011) 74 MLR 171

WILMOT-SMITH, 'Termination after Breach' (2018) 134 LQR 307

16

DISCHARGE BY OPERATION OF LAW

There are rules of law which, in certain circumstances, will bring about the discharge of a contract.

1. MERGER

(a) ACCEPTANCE OF HIGHER SECURITY

If a higher security is accepted in place of a lower, the security which in the eye of the law is inferior in operative power,[1] in the absence of a contrary intention manifested by the parties, merges and is extinguished in the higher.

Thus, if two parties to a simple contract embody its contents in a deed which they both execute, the simple contract is thereby discharged. This most often happens in the case of a contract for the sale of land, the written agreement being merged and extinguished in the subsequent conveyance or transfer of the land which is executed as a deed.[2]

The rules governing this process may thus be summarized:

1. The later security must be of higher efficacy than that which it is sought to replace. A negotiable instrument is not a higher security for the purposes of this rule,[3] although the giving of a negotiable instrument may constitute payment of a debt.[4]
2. The subject-matter of the two securities must be the same, that is, they must secure the same obligation and be made between the same parties.[5]

[1] *Price v Moulton* (1851) 10 CB 561.

[2] *Knight Sugar Co Ltd v Alberta Ry and Irrigation Co* [1938] 1 All ER 266, 269–70. Cf *Tito v Waddell (No 2)* [1977] Ch 106, 284 (contrary intention).

[3] *Drake v Mitchell* (1803) 3 East 251.

[4] See above, p 453.

[5] *Twopenny v Young* (1824) 3 B & C 208; *Holmes v Bell* (1841) 3 M & G 213; *Hissett v Reading Roofing Co Ltd* [1969] 1 WLR 1757.

(b) RIGHTS VESTING IN SAME PERSON

The rights and liabilities under a contract are also extinguished if they become vested by assignment or otherwise in the same person and in the same right, for it is not possible to contract with oneself. So where a tenant for a term of years acquires the reversion, at common law the lease merges in the reversion and is destroyed.[6] Similarly, a bill of exchange is discharged if the acceptor is or becomes the holder of it at or after its maturity in his own right.[7]

2. DISCHARGE BY JUDGMENT OF A COURT

A right of action arising from breach of contract is discharged by the coercive[8] judgment of a court of record[9] in the claimant's favour for the same demand. The right is thereby merged in the more solemn form of obligation sometimes referred to as a contract of record.[10] The result of legal proceedings taken upon a broken contract may be summarized as follows:

(a) EFFECT OF BRINGING ACTION

The bringing of an action does not itself discharge the right to bring the action. Another action may be brought for the same cause, although proceedings in such an action would, if they were merely vexatious, be struck out or stayed upon application to the summary jurisdiction of the Court.[11]

(b) EFFECT OF JUDGMENT FOR CLAIMANT

When judgment is given in the claimant's favour, the cause of action is merged into matter of record, and only the judgment can be enforced.[12] Further, 'damages resulting from one and the same cause of action must be assessed and recovered once for all',[13]

[6] In equity, however, the intentions of the parties may operate to prevent such merger, and under the Law of Property Act 1925, s 185 (replacing Judicature Act 1873, s 25(4)) the equitable rule now prevails: *Capital and Counties Bank Ltd v Rhodes* [1903] 1 Ch 631. See generally Burn and Cartwright, *Cheshire and Burn's Modern Law of Real Property* (18th edn, 2011) 1124–5.

[7] Bills of Exchange Act 1882, s 61.

[8] That is, a judgment for the payment of a sum of money or to enforce a right of property by ordering the return of property. It does not include a purely declaratory judgment, which itself imposes no obligation but only confirms the obligation which already exists: *Zavarco plc v Nasir* [2025] UKSC 5, [2025] AC 738 at [39], [50] (Lord Hodge, reserving judgment on whether the doctrine of merger extends to final injunctions, or to a declaration of the Crown under the Crown Proceedings Act 1947, s 21: *ibid* at [49], [57]).

[9] The county court is a court of record: County Courts Act 1984, s A1(2), added by Crime and Courts Act 2013, s 17(1).

[10] *Isaacs & Sons v Salbstein* [1916] 2 KB 139, 143.

[11] CPR rr 3.4(2), and 3.1(2)(f); cf County Courts Act 1984, s 35.

[12] *Kendall v Hamilton* (1879) 4 App Cas 504; *Director General of Fair Trading v First National Bank plc* [2001] UKHL 52, [2002] 1 AC 481 at [3]; *Zavarco plc v Nasir* [2025] UKSC 5 at [28].

[13] *Brunsden v Humphrey* (1884) 14 QBD 141, 147 (Bowen LJ); *Furness, Withy & Co Ltd v Hall Ltd* (1909) 25 TLR 233.

so that successive judgments cannot be obtained for different breaches of a single undertaking.[14]

(c) EFFECT OF JUDGMENT FOR DEFENDANT

A person may be estopped from re-litigating in subsequent proceedings a cause of action in respect of which judgment was given against that person in earlier proceedings, or an issue raised and determined against him or her in such proceedings.[15] But, for such an estoppel to arise, certain conditions must be satisfied:[16] first, there must have been a final judgment on the merits[17] in the earlier proceedings by a Court of competent jurisdiction;[18] secondly, there must be identity of parties in the two sets of proceedings;[19] thirdly, there must be identity of subject-matter in the two proceedings.[20] Cause of action and issue estoppel, together with the doctrine of merger, are based upon the public interest in finality of litigation.[21]

3. ALTERATION OR CANCELLATION OF A WRITTEN INSTRUMENT

(a) RULE AS TO ALTERATION

If a deed or contract in writing is altered by addition or erasure, it is discharged, except as against a party making or assenting to the alteration, for 'no man shall be permitted to take the chance of committing a fraud, without running any risk of losing by the event, when it is detected'.[22]

[14] *Conquer v Boot* [1928] 2 KB 336; *Zavarco plc v Nasir* [2025] UKSC 5 at [29]. Cf *Overstone Ltd v Shipway* [1962] 1 WLR 117 (separate causes of action).

[15] *Palmer v Temple* (1839) 9 A & E 508. Both cause of action estoppel and issue estoppel are included (together with the doctrine of merger) under the 'portmanteau term' *res judicata*: *Virgin Atlantic Airways Ltd v Premium Aircraft Interiors UK Ltd* [2013] UKSC 46, [2014] AC 160 at [17]; *Zavarco plc v Nasir* [2025] UKSC 5 at [29]–[30].

[16] *Carl Zeiss Stiftung v Rayner & Keeler Ltd (No 2)* [1967] 1 AC 853, 909, 910.

[17] *Hines v Birkbeck College (No 2)* [1992] Ch 33.

[18] *Midland Bank Trust Co Ltd v Green* [1980] Ch 590; *Hines v Birkbeck College (No 2)* [1992] Ch 33; *The European Gateway* [1987] QB 206.

[19] *Gleeson v J Wippell & Co Ltd* [1977] 1 WLR 510; *North West Water Ltd v Binnie & Partners* [1990] 3 All ER 547; *House of Spring Gardens Ltd v Waite* [1991] 1 QB 241, 252; *Talbot v Berkshire CC* [1994] QB 290, 296–7. Cf *Marginson v Blackburn BC* [1939] 2 KB 426; *C (a minor) v Hackney LBC* [1996] 1 WLR 789.

[20] *Haystead v Commissioner of Taxation* [1926] AC 155.

[21] *Republic of India v India Steamship Co Ltd* [1993] AC 410, 415; *ibid (No 2)* [1998] AC 878, 912; *Thrasyvoulou v Secretary of State for the Environment* [1990] 2 AC 273, 289; *Zavarco plc v Nasir* [2025] UKSC 5 at [31]. While a foreign coercive judgment does not operate as a merger, under the Civil Jurisdiction and Judgments Act 1982, s 34, further proceedings are barred unless waived: [1993] AC 410, 423–4; *Zavarco plc v Nasir* at [55].

[22] *Master v Miller* (1791) 4 Term Rep 320, 329 (Lord Kenyon CJ).

This principle is subject to the following rules:

1. The alteration must be made deliberately by the promisee or by one acting with the promisee's consent;[23] and even an alteration by a stranger while the instrument is in the custody of the promisee will have the same effect.[24] Earlier editions of this book stated that this responsibility for the acts of officious burglars could not be supported, but although described as 'a harsh and ancient common law doctrine', it is good law.[25]
2. The alteration must be made without the consent of the other party; otherwise, it would operate as a new agreement.
3. The alteration must be made in a material part. What amounts to a material alteration necessarily depends upon the character of the instrument, and it is possible for the character of an instrument to be affected by an alteration which does not touch the contractual rights set forth in it. In most cases, a material alteration will be one which imposes a greater liability on the promisor.[26]
4. If the alteration is made not in the instrument which itself creates obligations, but in another written instrument designed to carry out the contract, or some aspect of it, the alteration does not automatically render the underlying transaction void. However, making a material alteration to such an instrument may itself amount to conduct which entitles the other party to treat it as discharged.[27]

(b) BILLS OF EXCHANGE

Section 64 of the Bills of Exchange Act 1882 provides that a bill shall not be avoided as against a holder in due course, though it has been materially altered, if the alteration is not apparent, and the holder may enforce payment of it according to its original tenor.

(c) CANCELLATION AND LOSS

Intentional cancellation of a written instrument by the promisee also discharges the obligation, but the loss of the instrument only affects the rights of the parties insofar as it may occasion a difficulty of proof. In the case of bills of exchange and promissory

[23] *Pattinson v Luckley* (1875) LR 10 Ex 330; *Hongkong & Shanghai Banking Corporation v Lo Lee Shi* [1928] AC 181. Cf *Co-operative Bank v Tipper* [1996] 4 All ER 366, 371 (pencilled alteration insufficient).

[24] *Pigot's Case* (1614) 11 Co Rep 26b; *Davidson v Cooper* (1844) 13 M & W 343.

[25] *Co-operative Bank v Tipper* [1996] 4 All ER 366, 369; *Goss v Chilcott* [1996] AC 788. But the nullifying operation is confined to cases falling strictly within its ambit: *Farrow Mortgage Services Pty Ltd v Slade* (1996) 38 NSWLR 636, 640 (Australia).

[26] On the different position of alterations to bank notes, see *Suffell v Bank of England* (1882) 9 QBD 555.

[27] *Habibsons Bank Ltd v Standard Chartered Bank (Hong Kong) Ltd* [2010] EWCA Civ 1335, [2011] QB 943 at [34].

notes, the holder of the instrument who loses it may require the drawer to give him another bill upon giving an indemnity against possible claims.[28]

4. BANKRUPTCY

A contract is not discharged by bankruptcy of one of the parties to it;[29] but where the bankrupt has obtained from the Court an order of discharge, this effects a statutory release of the bankrupt from debts and liabilities provable under the bankruptcy.[30]

5. DEATH

As a rule, a contract is not discharged by the death of one of the parties to it;[31] the rights and liabilities of the deceased under the contract pass to his or her personal representatives.[32] However, where the contract is of a personal character, the contract will be discharged by frustration,[33] although the personal representatives may enforce rights (and the estate will be liable for claims) already accrued under the contract before the death.

[28] Bills of Exchange Act 1882, s 69.

[29] *Re Edwards, ex p Chalmers* (1873) LR 8 Ch App 289.

[30] Insolvency Act 1986, s 281(1). On bankruptcy, see below, p 694.

[31] *Phillips v Alhambra Palace Co* [1901] 1 QB 59.

[32] See below, p 694.

[33] See above, p 485.

PART 5

REMEDIES FOR BREACH OF CONTRACT

17

DAMAGES

1. DAMAGES AND OTHER REMEDIES FOR BREACH OF CONTRACT

Where a party performing a contract does not do so to the standard required by the contract[1] or within the time frame set, that party will breach the contract. Chapter 15 sets out the rules which govern the discharge of a contract for breach, and it now remains to consider the various remedies which are available apart from the entitlement of the innocent party in an appropriate case to be treated as discharged from further performance.

These remedies fall under three heads:[2]

(1) Every breach of contract entitles the injured party to damages. Damages are primarily concerned to compensate the injured party for the loss suffered.

(2) In certain circumstances the injured party may obtain the enforcement of the promise by an order for specific performance of the contract, an injunction to restrain its breach or for the payment of the sum due under it.

(3) In certain circumstances the parties to a contract that has been broken may be entitled to the return of money paid or restitution of the value of services rendered or goods transferred. These are restitutionary remedies for the independent cause of action of unjust enrichment. They are not remedies for the breach of contract. Exceptionally an injured party may be granted an award reflecting the gain made by the contract-breaker from the breach of contract. This is a restitutionary remedy for the breach of contract.

This and the following two chapters consider each of these remedies in turn, and a further chapter examines how they may be barred by lapse of time.

The development of the law has been marked by a broadening approach to the concept of loss and the law's ability to protect the claimant's interest in the performance by the other party of the contractual obligations. Except in the case of a debt, the repayment of which may be enforced at common law by an award of the agreed sum, the common law remedy for breach of a contractual promise is that of damages. There

[1] The standard may be strict or may require only the exercise of reasonable care, above p 447.

[2] See Burrows, *Remedies for Torts, Breach of Contract, and Equitable Wrongs* (4th edn, 2019); Rowan, *Remedies for Breach of Contract* (2012).

has been increased sophistication in identifying and calculating economic interests and in recognizing intangible interests of no economic value but for which a contractor has paid, and in reflecting these in awards of damages. Where the claimant's interest in the performance of the contractual obligations cannot adequately be protected by an award of damages, there has been greater willingness to order that the contract be specifically performed where this is possible and practicable.

In certain cases, for example professional negligence cases, there are overlapping claims for damages in contract and in tort. The rules discussed in this section only apply to contractual damages. However, it should be borne in mind that in cases of overlap damages within the law of tort may present an alternative, and sometimes preferable, remedy.[3]

2. COMPENSATORY NATURE OF DAMAGES

(a) COMPENSATION FOR LOSS

Damages for breach of contract are normally designed to compensate for the damage, loss, or injury the claimant has suffered through that breach. A claimant who has not suffered any loss by reason of the breach is nevertheless entitled to a verdict, but the damages recoverable will be purely nominal (usually £2–£10).

Whereas physical losses are the most frequent subject of actions in tort, commercial (ie financial) losses are the most frequent subject of actions for breach of contract. However, damages for breach of contract are not necessarily limited to compensation of financial loss alone. Damages may also be awarded in contract to compensate for physical damage to the person or property, for the loss of an attribute of property (such as comfort or privacy) even where this has not affected its value, for inconvenience, and, in certain circumstances, for disappointment.

(b) DAMAGES ARE NOT PUNITIVE

Damages for breach of contract are given to compensate for loss suffered by the innocent party and not to punish the contract-breaker. 'Punitive' or 'exemplary' damages have no place in the law of contract.[4] Contractual damages cannot be used to punish, however outrageous the defendant's conduct.[5] In *Addis v Gramophone Co Ltd*:[6]

[3] Above, p 25. See, eg, *Henderson v Merrett Syndicates Ltd* [1995] 2 AC 145; *Midland Bank Trust Co Ltd v Hett Stubbs & Kemp* [1979] Ch 384 (limitation). For a recent example of a claim framed in tort rather than contract in the context of claims regarding unsafe buildings, see *URS Corp Ltd v BDW Trading Ltd* [2025] UKSC 21, [2025] 2 WLR 1095.

[4] They may be recoverable in certain circumstances in tort: see *Rookes v Barnard* [1964] AC 1129, 1221; *Broome v Cassell & Co Ltd* [1972] AC 1027; *Kuddus v Chief Constable of Leicestershire Constabulary* [2001] UKHL 29, [2002] 2 AC 122. For discussion of an account of profits in cases of 'cynical' breach, see below, pp 616–8.

[5] *Devenish Nutrition Ltd v Sanofi-Aventis SA* [2008] EWCA Civ 1086, [2009] Ch 390 at [143]. For the very different approach taken in Canada, see *Whiten v Pilot Insurance Co* 2002 SCC 18, [2002] 1 SCR 595.

[6] [1909] AC 488, followed on this point but not others by *Malik v Bank of Credit & Commerce International SA* [1998] 1 AC 20, 50–1. See also *Co-operative Insurance Society Ltd v Argyll Stores (Holdings) Ltd* [1998] 1 AC 1, 15. Cf McBride (1995) 24 Anglo-American L Rev 369 and Cunnington (2006) 26 LS 369 for arguments that punitive damages should be available for breach of contract.

A was employed by G as manager of their business in Calcutta at a salary together with a commission on trade done. G wrongfully dismissed A without giving him the required 6 months' notice.

The House of Lords held that, although A might recover a sum representing his salary for the period of notice and the commission he would have earned during that period, his employers were not to be penalized in damages for the humiliating and oppressive manner in which they had dismissed him.[7]

(c) DIFFICULTY OF ASSESSMENT NO BAR

Difficulty in assessing damages does not disentitle a claimant from having an attempt made to assess them, unless they depend on entirely speculative possibilities. It has been said that '[t]he restoration by way of compensation is therefore accomplished to a large extent by the exercise of a sound imagination and the practice of the broad axe'.[8] In *Simpson v London and North Western Railway Company*,[9] S was deprived of the opportunity of exhibiting his products at an agricultural show. Although the ascertainment of damages was difficult, it was held that this was no reason for not giving any damages at all. And in *Chaplin v Hicks*,[10] a candidate in a beauty competition, who had successfully passed the earlier stages of the competition, was, in breach of contract, not allowed to compete in the later stages with 49 others from whom 12 winners were to be chosen. She was awarded substantial damages for the loss of the chance of being successful of which she had been wrongfully deprived. Similar considerations may affect the measure of damages in the cases where an offer to consider all conforming tenders is held to give rise to an enforceable obligation.[11] The value of the chance depends upon the number and type of contingencies upon which it depends.[12]

(d) THE DATE FOR ASSESSMENT

This is normally thought to be the date when the cause of action arose: that is, the date of the breach of contract.[13] This may be thought desirable for reasons of commercial certainty: it enables the parties to assess at the date of breach how much is likely to be

[7] See also *Malik v Bank of Credit & Commerce International SA* [1998] 1 AC 20, 51; *Johnson v Unisys Ltd* [1999] 1 All ER 854, 861, but note that the manner and circumstances of a dismissal may increase the claimant's financial loss: see below, p 551.

[8] *Watson, Laidlaw, & Co Ltd v Pott, Cassels & Williamson* 1914 SC (HL) 18, 29–30; *Sainsbury's Supermarkets Ltd v Visa Europe Services LLC* [2020] UKSC 24, [2020] 4 All ER 807 at [175]–[226].

[9] (1876) 1 QBD 274.

[10] [1911] 2 KB 786. See also *Allied Maples Group v Simmons & Simmons* [1995] 1 WLR 1602; *Flame SA v Glory Wealth Shipping PTE Ltd, The Glory Wealth* [2013] EWHC 3153 (Comm), [2014] QB 1080 (both cases illustrating, in very different contexts, that uncertainty as to what the claimant, as opposed to a third party, would have done should be decided in an all-or-nothing way by applying a balance of probabilities test): this approach was confirmed, in the context of a professional negligence claim in tort, in *Perry v Raleys Solicitors* [2019] UKSC 5, [2020] AC 352.

[11] *Blackpool and Fylde Aero Club Ltd v Blackpool BC* [1990] 1 WLR 1195, above, p 39, where the measure of damages was not considered.

[12] *Ministry of Defence v Wheeler* [1998] 1 WLR 637.

[13] See, eg, *Dodd Properties (Kent) v Canterbury City Council* [1980] AC 174.

payable in damages, and then seek to settle their disputes accordingly.[14] However, a more flexible approach has been adopted by courts, in which a later date for assessment has been taken so as to enable compensation to be more accurately calculated (subject to not infringing the mitigation principle).[15] In *Golden Strait Corporation v Nippon Yusen Kubishika Kaisha, The Golden Victory*:[16]

After three years of a seven-year charterparty the charterers committed a repudiatory breach. Fifteen months later, the Iraq war broke out which, under a war clause, would have entitled the charterers to terminate the contract in any event. It was assumed that, had the contract still been on foot, they would have done so.

Were damages to be assessed as at the date of breach on the basis of the value of a four-year remaining charterparty ignoring the outbreak of war, or as at the date of trial taking into account the known outbreak of war and hence on the basis of only a fifteen-month remaining charterparty? A bare majority held that damages should be assessed on the second basis. This is justified as more precisely measuring the claimant's known loss in a situation where the mitigation principle was essentially irrelevant because the claimant had not attempted to mitigate its loss by concluding a substitute charterparty for the four-year period.

In *Bunge SA v Nidera BV* the Supreme Court emphatically upheld the majority in *The Golden Victory*. Lord Sumption explained:

The real difference between the majority and the minority [in *The Golden Victory*] turned on the question what was being valued for the purpose of assessing damages. The majority were valuing the chartered service that would actually have been performed if the charterparty had not been wrongfully brought to a premature end. On that footing, the notional substitute contract, whenever it was made and at whatever market rate, would have made no difference because it would have been subject to the same war clause as the original contract . . . The minority on the other hand considered that one should value not the chartered service which would actually have been performed, but the charterparty itself, assessed at the time that it was terminated, by reference to the terms of a notional substitute concluded as soon as possible after the termination of the original. That would vary, not according to the actual outcome, but according to the outcomes which were perceived as possible or probable at the time that the notional substitute contract was made. The possibility or probability of war would then be factored into the price agreed in the substitute contract . . .

The Supreme Court in *Bunge* insisted that the reasoning in *The Golden Victory* applied to contracts of sale of a single cargo, and was not limited to instalment contracts. However, the Court of Appeal has since held that it is important that both *The Golden Victory* and

[14] See the minority judgments of Lord Bingham and Lord Walker in *Golden Strait Corporation v Nippon Yusen Kubishika Kaisha, The Golden Victory* [2007] UKHL 12, [2007] 2 AC 353.

[15] See below, pp 554–6. If the claimant could only reasonably have been expected to take reasonable steps in mitigation at a date subsequent to the breach, damages should be assessed at such later date: *Radford v De Froberville* [1977] 1 WLR 1262, 1285–6; *Hooper v Oates* [2013] EWCA Civ 91, [2014] Ch 287; *Stanford International Bank Ltd v HSBC Bank Plc* [2022] UKSC 34, [2023] AC 761 at [43].

[16] [2007] UKHL 12, [2007] 2 AC 353. See also *Johnson v Agnew* [1980] AC 367; Stevens, in Neyers, Bronaugh, and Pitel (eds), *Exploring Contract Law* (2009); Dyson and Kramer (2014) 130 LQR 259.

Bunge involved anticipatory breach,[17] where it is appropriate to consider subsequent events, but that the same approach should not necessarily be adopted in cases of 'actual' breaches of contract.[18]

(e) COMPENSATION FOR INCONVENIENCE OR MENTAL DISTRESS

Contractual damages may be recovered for substantial physical inconvenience or discomfort arising from a breach. Examples include where a family was transported by a railway company to the wrong station, with the result that they had to walk several miles home on a drizzling wet night,[19] and where a man, with his wife and child, was forced to live for two years in discomfort with his wife's parents owing to the failure of a solicitor to take any effective steps to obtain possession of a house.[20]

Damages are not generally recoverable for 'any distress, frustration, anxiety, displeasure, vexation, tension or aggravation' caused by the breach even where it was in the contemplation of the parties that the breach would expose the parties to distress.[21] The reparation of such non-pecuniary, non-physical harm poses problems of incommensurability and subjectivity, and difficulties of proof.

There are two exceptions to this general rule. Damages for mental distress can be awarded where the claimant's distress is directly consequential on physical inconvenience caused by the breach of contract.[22] They can also be awarded where an important purpose of the contract is to provide enjoyment or peace of mind, or to prevent distress.[23] In *Jarvis v Swans Tours Ltd*:[24]

J, a solicitor, entitled to two weeks' paid holiday a year, booked with S Tours a 15-day Christmas winter sports holiday at a hotel in Switzerland. He did so on the faith of S's brochure which

[17] Which is dubious on the facts of *The Golden Victory*: see Reynolds (2008) 38 HKLJ 333. On anticipatory breach, see p 524.

[18] *Classic Maritime Inc v Limbungan Makmur Sdn Bhd* [2019] EWCA Civ 1102, [2019] 4 All ER 1145 at [80]–[89]; *MDW Holdings Ltd v Norvill* [2022] EWCA Civ 883, [2023] 4 WLR 33 at [49].

[19] *Hobbs v L & SW Ry* (1875) LR 10 QB 111.

[20] *Bailey v Bullock* [1950] 2 All ER 1167. Noise can amount to physical inconvenience: *Farley v Skinner* [2001] UKHL 49, [2002] 2 AC 732 at [30], [60].

[21] *Watts v Morrow* [1991] 1 WLR 1421, 1445 (Bingham LJ). See also *Johnson v Gore Wood & Co* [2002] 2 AC 1 (claim for professional negligence against solicitor) in which Lord Cooke remarked (at 108) that '[c]ontract-breaking is treated as an incident of commercial life which players in the game are expected to meet with mental fortitude'.

[22] *Perry v Sidney Phillips & Son* [1982] 1 WLR 1297 (anxiety and distress of living in a house in poor condition which had been bought in reliance on negligence in breach of contract in a surveyor's report). But such damages should be 'modest': *Watts v Morrow* [1991] 1 WLR 1421, 1443, 1445. Cf Lord Cooke (dissenting) in *Johnson v Gore Wood & Co* [2002] 2 AC 1, 49 (distress due to poverty and changed way of life akin to that due to physical loss).

[23] *Ruxley Electronics & Constructions Ltd v Forsyth* [1996] AC 344, 374 (Lord Lloyd) (cf Lord Mustill, *ibid*, 360–1); *Farley v Skinner* [2001] UKHL 49, [2002] 2 AC 732 at [28]; *Johnson v Gore Wood & Co* [2002] 2 AC 1, 37 (Lord Bingham). Lord Cooke, *ibid*, 49, considered that contracts for status such as membership of a trade union or club are also included.

[24] [1973] QB 233. See also *Jackson v Horizon Holidays Ltd* [1975] 1 WLR 1468. For the quantum of mental distress damages, see *Milner v Carnival plc* [2010] EWCA Civ 389, [2010] 3 All ER 701.

described the holiday as a 'house-party', and promised a variety of entertainments including excellent skiing, a yodeller evening, a bar, and afternoon tea and cakes. In the first week there were only 13 people at the hotel and in the second week he was entirely alone. The promised entertainments proved to be wholly inferior in quality in comparison with the description in the brochure.

The Court of Appeal held that J was entitled to damages consisting of the amount which he had paid for the holiday and an additional sum of £60 as compensation for the disappointment he had suffered. Similarly, damages were awarded for anxiety and distress suffered by a woman whose solicitors failed to take prompt and effective measures against a man who was pestering her,[25] by a woman whose solicitors had failed to obtain proper financial relief in matrimonial proceedings,[26] by a bride when a photographer failed to keep his promise to be present and take photographs at her wedding,[27] and by children when a cemetery owner broke its contract to grant exclusive burial rights in a plot adjacent to that in which their parents were buried.[28] Such damages are compensatory in nature. They are not designed to inflict retribution on the defendant for inflicting the harm.

Originally this exception only applied if 'the sole' object of the contract was to provide enjoyment or peace of mind, or to prevent distress.[29] Accordingly, a contract with an architect to design a house for a couple who contemplated that it would be their 'dream home' did not qualify.[30] This meant that the non-economic purposes of a party to a contract would be protected where they were the only purposes but would not be where there were also economic purposes. To that extent part of the purposes of the contract were unenforceable.[31] But *Farley v Skinner* held that it suffices that the provision of peace of mind, or the prevention of distress, is 'an important object' of the contract.[32] In that case:

F, a prospective purchaser of a house who wanted peace and quiet, employed a surveyor to report on the property and specifically requested him to advise whether the house might be affected by aircraft noise. The surveyor advised that it was unlikely that the property would suffer greatly from aircraft noise and F bought the house.[33] In fact, the house was near a navigation beacon used by aircraft waiting to land at Gatwick Airport and was substantially affected by noise.

[25] *Heywood v Wellers* [1976] QB 446; *McLeish v Amoo-Gottfried & Co*, The Times, 13 October 1995 (solicitor's negligence led to wrongful conviction). Cf *Cook v Swinfen* [1967] 1 WLR 457, 461; *Hayes v James & Charles Dodd* [1990] 2 All ER 815.

[26] *Dickinson v James Alexander & Co* (1990) 20 FLR 137.

[27] *Diesen v Samson* 1971 SLT (Sh Ct) 49.

[28] *Reed v Madon* [1989] Ch 408.

[29] *Watts v Morrow* [1991] 1 WLR 1421, 1445 (Bingham LJ).

[30] *Knott v Bolton* (1995) 45 Con LR 127 (overruled by *Farley v Skinner*).

[31] Capper (2000) 116 LQR 553, approved in *Farley v Skinner* [2001] UKHL 49, [2002] 2 AC 732 at [24], [51].

[32] *Farley v Skinner* [2001] UKHL 49, [2002] 2 AC 732. See also *Hamilton Jones v David & Snape* [2003] EWHC 3147 (Ch), [2004] 1 All ER 657 (mental distress damages awarded for loss of custody of claimant's children consequent on defendant solicitor's negligent failure to renew 'agency notifications' of the risk of the children being taken out of the jurisdiction by the claimant's former husband).

[33] The price F paid coincided with the house's market value with the aircraft noise, so he had no claim for diminution of value.

The House of Lords held that F was entitled to damages for the significant interference with his enjoyment of the property caused by the noise but made it clear that a contract for an ordinary survey report on a house would not fall within the exception. What made this case different was the specific request relating to the noise.

(f) LOSS OF REPUTATION

Although damages cannot be recovered in a contractual action for injury to reputation *per se*,[34] they may be where the loss of reputation caused by the breach of contract causes financial loss. In *Malik v Bank of Credit & Commerce International SA*:[35]

M and other relatively senior employees of BCCI, were made redundant following the bank's insolvency. They claimed that they were unable thereafter to obtain employment in the financial services industry because of the stigma attached to former employees of BCCI, and sought substantial compensation for this handicap in the labour market. For the purposes of the proceedings it was assumed that BCCI had carried on its business in a corrupt and dishonest manner, that this had become widely known, that M and the other employees were innocent of any involvement, were at a handicap in the labour market because of the stigma, and had suffered financial loss as a result.

The House of Lords held that contracts of employment contained an implied term of mutual trust and confidence so that the defendant was under an implied obligation not to carry on a dishonest or corrupt business, and that, in principle, financial loss in respect of damage to reputation caused by breach of this term is recoverable in a contractual action. However, it will often be difficult to prove a handicap on the labour market.

The effect of this decision is to establish that financial loss resulting from a loss of reputation caused by a breach of contract is recoverable subject to standard contractual principles. *Malik*'s case explained the contrary statements in *Addis v Gramophone Co Ltd*[36] on the basis that the earlier case was decided before the development of the implied obligation of mutual trust and confidence so that the loss of reputation there had not been caused by a relevant breach of contract.[37] Having said that, it has been established that a claim for wrongful dismissal will still not trigger damages for loss of reputation.[38] This is not because *Addis* is regarded as correctly reasoned but because the Courts are anxious not to undermine the statutory regime—and the levels of compensation laid down—for unfair dismissal.

Cases previously regarded as exceptional can now be seen as examples of the general rule. So, where a bank refuses to pay a customer's cheque when the customer is in credit, it will be liable for any loss to the customer's trade reputation or credit-rating caused by the breach.[39] In view of the assumed facts in *Malik*'s case, there was no need

[34] *Addis v Gramophone Co Ltd* [1909] AC 488.

[35] [1998] 1 AC 20.

[36] [1909] AC 488, eg at 491 (Lord Loreburn).

[37] [1998] 1 AC 20, 38 (Lord Nicholls) and 51 (Lord Steyn).

[38] *Johnson v Unisys Ltd* [2001] UKHL 13, [2003] 1 AC 518; *Eastwood v Magnox Electric plc* [2004] UKHL 35, [2005] 1 AC 503; *Edwards v Chesterfield Royal Hospital NHS Foundation Trust* [2011] UKSC 58, [2012] 2 AC 22.

[39] *Kpoharor v Woolwich Building Society* [1996] 4 All ER 119, suggesting that a distinction between trade and personal transactions should no longer be made.

to deal with a breach of contract that causes non-financial loss, for instance distress and injured feelings resulting from loss of reputation, but the increased willingness to award contractual damages for such losses[40] suggests that this aspect of *Addis*'s case may also be ripe for reconsideration.

3. BASIS OF ASSESSMENT OF DAMAGES

The general principle that damages are compensatory in nature is only a starting point and one must go on to ask how exactly that principle is to be effected.

(a) THE 'PERFORMANCE' OR 'EXPECTATION' MEASURE

The object of an award of damages for breach of contract is to place the claimant, so far as money can do it, in the same situation, with respect to damages, as if the contract had been performed.[41] Claimants can therefore recover damages in respect of the loss of gains suffered as a result of the breach. For example, if machinery is not delivered to a person in breach of contract, that person will have a claim for loss of profits for being deprived of its use. A claim for loss of profits is not peculiar to an action in contract, since a similar claim would lie if the machinery were damaged or destroyed by a tort. But the law of contract goes further and entitles claimants to damages for the loss of the bargained-for performance, that is to say, for the loss of the particular benefit which it was expected would be received by the contract which has been broken: an art dealer contracts to purchase a painting which is worth far more than the agreed price; a record company obtains for a relatively modest sum the sole right to distribute the records of what proves to be a highly successful pop-group; a caterer obtains an extremely lucrative contract to cater for a banquet. In each case, if the contract is broken by the other party, the damages will be assessed by reference to the claimant's 'performance' or 'expectation' loss, consisting of what would have been received had the contract been duly performed.[42]

(i) Assessment by reference to contract terms

Damages must be assessed by reference to the terms of the contract sued upon. The Court cannot take account of 'the expectations, however reasonable, of one contractor that the other will do something that it has assumed no legal obligation to do'.[43] Thus an employee who is wrongfully dismissed and sues the employer for breach of contract may be unable to recover contractual damages for the loss of 'fringe benefits' from the employment unless the employer has assumed a contractual obligation to

[40] For the conditions under which such an award will be made, see above, pp 549–51.

[41] *Robinson v Harman* (1848) 1 Exch 850, 855.

[42] See Fuller and Perdue (1936–37) 46 Yale LJ 52, 573; Burrows (1983) 99 LQR 217; Friedmann (1995) 111 LQR 628; Coote [1997] CLJ 537. Cf Atiyah (1978) 94 LQR 193.

[43] *Lavarack v Woods of Colchester Ltd* [1967] 1 QB 278, 294. Cf *Horkulak v Cantor Fitzgerald International* [2004] EWCA Civ 1287, [2005] ICR 402.

provide those benefits.[44] Also, where the defendant has a choice of two methods of performance, damages will be assessed on the basis of the minimum legal obligation, on the assumption that the contract would have been performed by the method least onerous to the defendant and least beneficial to the claimant.[45]

(ii) 'Difference in value' or 'cost of cure'

In many cases the assessment of the claimant's loss of bargain will be the 'difference in value' between the performance received and that promised in the contract.[46] However, in appropriate circumstances, damages may be assessed on the basis of the 'cost of cure': what it has cost or will cost the claimant to have the contract performed by a third party.[47] So if work contracted for is not performed or is performed badly, the claimant is entitled to the cost of substitute or remedial work to be carried out by a third party where it is possible to do so.[48] An exception arises where, in all the circumstances, this is unreasonable, such as where the cost of cure is wholly disproportionate to any resulting benefit[49] or, even more controversially, where the claimant does not intend to have the work carried out.[50] In *Ruxley Electronics & Constructions Ltd v Forsyth*:[51]

F contracted with R for the construction of a swimming pool in his garden with a diving area 7 feet 6 inches deep at a price of £17,797. In breach of contract the diving area was only 6 feet 9 inches deep but was suitable for diving and there was no adverse effect on the market value of the pool. The estimated cost of rebuilding the pool to the specified depth was £21,560.

[44] *Lavarack v Woods of Colchester Ltd*, above, n 43.

[45] *Re Thornett & Fehr and Yuills Ltd* [1921] 1 KB 219; *Abraham v Herbert Reiach Ltd* [1922] 1 KB 477; *Bunge Corp v Tradax Export SA* [1981] 1 WLR 711; *AA Ltd v MacKenzie* [2022] EWCA Civ 901, [2022] ICR 1362. Cf *Paula Lee Ltd v Robert Zehil & Co Ltd* [1983] 2 All ER 390; *Lion Nathan Ltd v C-C Bottlers Ltd* [1996] 1 WLR 1438; *Durham Tees Valley Airport Ltd v BmiBaby Ltd* [2010] EWCA Civ 485, [2011] 1 Lloyd's Rep 68. For critique of the minimum performance rule, see Pearce (2016) 36 OJLS 781. See generally Burrows, *Remedies for Torts, Breach of Contract, and Equitable Wrongs* (4th edn, 2019) 68–73.

[46] See below, p 556; Landlord and Tenant Act 1927, s 18; Sale of Goods Act 1979, ss 50(3), 51(3), 53(3).

[47] *East Ham Corp v Bernard Sunley & Sons Ltd* [1966] AC 406, 434; *Tito v Waddell (No 2)* [1977] Ch 106, 329; *Radford v de Froberville* [1977] 1 WLR 1262, 1269–70; *Ruxley Electronics & Constructions Ltd v Forsyth* [1996] 1 AC 344. Where the 'cost of cure' is less than the reduction in value, the mitigation principle, below, p 569, will restrict the claimant to the former.

[48] Cf *Ward v Cannock Chase DC* [1985] 3 All ER 537 (a tort case where cost of cure was awarded subject to planning permission). Note that where a surveyor in breach of contract fails to identify defects in the property surveyed the prima facie measure is the diminution in the value of the property, not the cost of repairing it: *Phillips v Ward* [1956] 1 WLR 491; *Watts v Morrow* [1991] 1 WLR 1421; *Patel v Hooper & Jackson* [1999] 1 WLR 1792, 1801.

[49] *Ruxley Electronics & Constructions Ltd v Forsyth* [1996] 1 AC 344, 354, 361. In principle 'benefit' should include non-monetary benefits such as bathroom tiles matching an existing colour scheme. For Australia, see *Tabcorp Holdings Ltd v Bowen Investments Pty Ltd* [2009] HCA 8, (2009) 236 CLR 272.

[50] *Ruxley Electronics & Constructions Ltd v Forsyth* [1996] 1 AC 344, 354, 359 (Lord Jauncey) and 372–3 (Lord Lloyd). See also *Tito v Waddell (No 2)* [1977] Ch 106, 317; *Radford v de Froberville* [1977] 1 WLR 1262, 1248; *Dean v Ainley* [1987] 1 WLR 1729. However, courts are not generally concerned with the uses to which claimants put an award of damages: *Endurance Corporate Capital Ltd v Sartex Quilts & Textiles Ltd* [2020] EWCA Civ 308, [2020] Bus LR 1729 at [45], [60]–[68]. See too *Terrenus Energy SL2 Pte Ltd v Attika Interior + MEP Pte Ltd* [2025] SGHC(A) 4; [2025] 1 SLR 306.

[51] [1996] 1 AC 344, on which, see Coote [1997] CLJ 537; O'Sullivan, in Rose (ed), *Failure of Contracts* (1997) ch 1. See also *Harbutt's 'Plasticine' Ltd v Wayne Tank and Pump Co Ltd* [1970] 1 QB 447, 473.

The House of Lords held that F was not entitled to the 'cost of cure'. In this case, the trial judge had found that F did not intend to rebuild the pool even if awarded the cost of so doing. It would also have been unreasonable to do so given the large disparity between the cost of so doing and the nil difference in value. However, it was held that as F had lost his personal preference for a deeper pool he was entitled to £2,500 for loss of amenity. This is best regarded as compensation for mental distress (ie loss of pleasure) as in the ruined holiday cases. Economists see this as a recognition of F's non-monetary 'consumer surplus'.[52] The decision has been said to be an example of the Courts taking steps to recognize and remedy a deficiency in the remedial regime for breach of contract where the claimant's loss is non-financial by giving fuller recognition to the performance interest as the basis of contractual damages.[53] In cases where there was never any question of being able to 'cure' the breach, for example where a carrier provided a low grade delivery service rather than the 'enhanced' service that was promised and paid for, it should, in principle, also be possible to put a figure to any non-monetary loss suffered.[54]

The increased willingness to award damages in such cases is a reflection of recognition that 'the principle of pacta sunt servanda would be eroded if the law did not take account of the fact that the consumer often demands specifications which, although not of economic value, have value to him'.[55]

(b) THE RELIANCE MEASURE

At first sight an alternative *basis* for the assessment of damages is that the claimant should recover its 'reliance loss', that is to say, expenses which it has incurred in preparing to perform or in part performance of the contract and which have been rendered futile by the breach. Even expenses incurred prior to, and in anticipation of, the making of the contract are recoverable, provided it was reasonably in the contemplation of the parties that they would be wasted if the contract was broken. In *Anglia Television Ltd v Reed*,[56] the television company obtained damages in respect of expenses of £2,750 which had been thrown away by reason of the defendant's refusal, in breach of contract, to play the leading part in a television play, even though the expenses had been incurred before the contract was made. A claimant may be compelled to claim damages for wasted

[52] Harris, Ogus, and Phillips (1979) 95 LQR 58; Muris (1983) 12 JLS 379; Lord Bridge and Lord Mustill in *Ruxley* at 354, 360–1; Lord Lloyd, at 374, reserving his position but regarding it as compensation for F's disappointment. See also *Morris-Garner v One Step (Support) Ltd* [2018] UKSC 20, [2019] AC 649 at [39].

[53] O'Sullivan, in Johnston and Zimmermann (eds), *Unjustified Enrichment: Key Issues in Comparative Perspective* (2002) adopted in this context by Lord Goff and Lord Millett (dissenting) in *Alfred McAlpine Construction Ltd v Panatown Ltd* [2001] 1 AC 518, 548, 587.

[54] See Beale (1996) 112 LQR 205, discussing *White Arrow Express Ltd v Lamey's Distribution Ltd* (1995) 15 Tr LR 69.

[55] *Farley v Skinner* [2001] UKHL 49, [2002] 2 AC 732 at [21] (Lord Steyn); see also at [79]; *Ruxley Electronics & Constructions Ltd v Forsyth* [1996] 1 AC 344, 360 (Lord Mustill).

[56] [1972] 1 QB 60. See also *Lloyd v Stanbury* [1971] 1 WLR 535.

expenses rather than for the loss of its bargain by reason of its inability to prove that financial benefit would have accrued to it had the contract been performed.[57]

If, however, the defendant can prove that the claimant would not have benefited financially had the contract been performed, the claimant will not be permitted to escape from a bad bargain by recovering as damages sums spent in reliance on the contract instead of loss of expectancy.[58] In such a case the reliance losses are considered to flow from entering into a losing contract and not from the defendant's breach.[59] A claimant who recovers for the loss of bargain cannot, as a general rule, combine a claim for reliance loss with one for loss of expectation so as to recover twice in respect of the same loss.[60] Damages for expenses rendered futile by the breach cannot be sought at the same time as damages for loss of profit, since such expenses would have had to be incurred in order to earn the profit claimed.

Although traditionally the reliance measure has been seen as an alternative basis to the expectation measure, the 'no escape from a bad bargain' and the recovery of pre-contractual expenses suggests that the reliance measure is better viewed as merely a *method* of assessing the claimant's expectation measure. Where the claimant has incurred reliance expenses it is given the benefit of a rebuttable presumption that, if the contract had been performed, it would at the very least have made financial gains to cover its reliance expenses or, in a non-commercial contract, would have enjoyed non-financial benefits (eg mental pleasure) so that those expenses would not have been wasted.[61] This analysis of the reliance measure was adopted in *Omak Maritime Ltd v Mamola Challenger Co, The Mamola Challenger*:[62]

Charterers, under a long-term charterparty, repudiated that contract even though the contract was a good one for them, since the charter rate was below the market rate (by about $7,500 per day). The owners accepted that repudiatory breach and thereby became able to trade the ship at the higher market rate. The owners nevertheless claimed substantial damages based on the expenses they had incurred in preparing to perform the charterparty.

The owners' argument was that they were entitled to the expenses incurred as reliance damages and that it was irrelevant to those damages that they had entirely mitigated the loss of hire because reliance damages were not concerned with the owners'

[57] *Anglia Television Ltd v Reed* [1972] 1 QB 60 (inability to prove what profits from TV play would have been); *McRae v Commonwealth Disposals Commission* (1950) 84 CLR 377 (value of ship to be salvaged too speculative; price paid and cost of salvage expedition recovered).

[58] *C & P Haulage v Middleton* [1983] 1 WLR 1461; *CCC (London) Films Ltd v Impact Quadrant Films Ltd* [1985] QB 16.

[59] Cf below, Chapter 19 (restitutionary remedies can 'save' a claimant from a bad bargain).

[60] See *Cullinane v British 'Rema' Manufacturing Co Ltd* [1954] 1 QB 292, below, p 560.

[61] See the decisions of the High Court of Australia in *Commonwealth of Australia v Amann Aviation Pty Ltd* (1991) 174 CLR 64 and *Cessnock City Council v 123 259 932 Pty Ltd* [2024] HCA 17. See also McLauchlan [2007] NZLR 417; Burrows, *Remedies for Torts, Breach of Contract, and Equitable Wrongs* (4th edn, 2019) ch 6. Cf *Liu Shu Ming v Koh Chew Chee* [2023] SGHC(A) 15, [2023] 1 SLR 1477 (Singapore); *Soteria Insurance Ltd (formerly CIS General Insurance Ltd) v IBM United Kingdom Ltd* [2022] EWCA Civ 440, [2022] 2 All ER (Comm) 1082.

[62] [2010] EWHC 2026, [2011] 1 Lloyd's Rep 47, noted by McLauchlan (2011) 127 LQR 23.

position had the contract been performed. That argument of the owners was firmly rejected by Teare J.[63] He made clear that reliance damages are not based on a separate principle from the expectation measure laid down by *Robinson v Harman*.[64] The expectation measure is the one and only compensatory measure to be applied so that, as the owners' loss assessed according to that measure had been entirely mitigated, there was no other loss to be compensated. The recovery of wasted reliance expense is merely an indirect method, supported by a reverse burden of proof, of applying that expectation measure.

4. CAUSATION

The claimant must show that the breach of contract caused the loss. It is not enough to show 'but for' causation (ie that but for the breach of contract, the loss would not have been suffered). The breach of contract must be the 'effective' cause of the loss, as opposed to an event which merely gives the opportunity for the claimant to sustain the loss.[65] The Courts have treated the determination of whether a breach was the cause of the loss in a broad way, in the end turning to their 'common sense'[66] in interpreting the facts. Accordingly, it is not easy to articulate the relevant rules of law.

Where another event has also affected the fact situation, it will generally not be held to break the chain of causation if that other event was *likely* to happen once the breach of contract had occurred. In *Monarch Steamship Co Ltd v Karlshamns Oljefabriker (A/B)*[67] a voyage was delayed by the unseaworthiness of the vessel so that it arrived in European waters after the outbreak of the Second World War and was diverted by the Admiralty to Glasgow. It was held that the outbreak of war and the Admiralty's action did not break the chain of causation; the cause of the cargo-owners' loss was the defendant's breach of contract in failing to provide a seaworthy ship. But where the other event was *not likely* to happen once the breach of contract has occurred, the chain of causation may well be held to have been broken. A breach of contract by a solicitor in wrongfully ceasing to act for a client gave rise to the opportunity for the client to sustain loss by acting without alternative legal advice and lodging a defective application, but was not the cause of such loss.[68]

[63] In *Yam Seng Pte Ltd v International Trade Corp Ltd* [2013] EWHC 111 (QB), [2013] 1 Lloyd's Rep 526, at [186], Leggatt J praised Teare J's 'masterly judgment'.

[64] (1848) 1 Exch 850, 855.

[65] *Weld-Blundell v Stephens* [1920] AC 956; *Banco de Portugal v Waterlow & Sons Ltd* [1932] AC 452; *Compania Naviera Maropan S/A v Bowaters Lloyd Pulp & Paper Mills Ltd* [1955] 2 QB 68; *Quinn v Burch Bros (Builders) Ltd* [1966] 2 QB 370; *Galoo Ltd v Bright Grahame Murray* [1994] 1 WLR 1360; *Borealis AB v Geogas Trading SA* [2010] EWHC 2789 (Comm), [2011] 1 Lloyd's Rep 482.

[66] *Galoo Ltd v Bright Grahame Murray* [1994] 1 WLR 1360, 1374–5.

[67] [1949] AC 196. On the question of reducing damages for contributory negligence where the other event is the act of the claimant, see below, pp 577–8.

[68] *Young v Purdy* [1997] PNLR 130; *Galoo Ltd v Bright Grahame Murray* [1994] 1 WLR 1360.

5. REMOTENESS

Even where the test of causation is satisfied, the defendant is not liable for all the loss which the claimant may have suffered as a consequence of the breach. Certain losses may be too 'remote', and for these the claimant is not entitled to compensation.[69]

(a) THE BASIC TWO-BRANCHED RULE

The foundation of the law on remoteness is contained in the judgment of Alderson B in the Court of Exchequer in *Hadley v Baxendale*. Drawing on the civilian principle of foreseeability and the French Civil Code, he stated that where the parties have made a contract which one of them has broken damages are recoverable: (1) when they are 'such as may fairly and reasonably be considered arising naturally, ie, according to the usual course of things' from the breach, or (2) when they are 'such as may reasonably be supposed to have been in the contemplation of both parties, at the time they made the contract, as the probable result of the breach of it'.[70] Alderson B explained the effect of the second branch of the rule as follows:[71]

[I]f the special circumstances under which the contract was actually made were communicated by the plaintiffs to the defendants, and thus known to both parties, the damages resulting from the breach of such a contract, which they would reasonably contemplate, would be the amount of injury which would ordinarily follow from a breach of contract under these special circumstances so known and communicated. But, on the other hand, if these special circumstances were wholly unknown to the party breaking the contract, he, at the most, could only be supposed to have had in his contemplation the amount of injury which would arise generally, and in the great multitude of cases not affected by any special circumstances, from such a breach of contract. For, had the special circumstances been known, the parties might have specially provided for the breach of contract by special terms as to the damages in that case; and of this advantage it would be very unjust to deprive them.

One can see, therefore, that liability under the second branch of the rule depends upon the special circumstances made known to the party in default at the time the contract was made. In *Hadley v Baxendale*:

H's mill was stopped by the breakage of a crankshaft, and it was necessary to send the crankshaft to the makers as a pattern for a new one. The defendants, who were carriers, undertook to deliver the shaft to the makers, but the only information given to them was 'that the article to be carried was the broken shaft of a mill, and that H was the owner of the mill'.[72] By some neglect on their part the delivery of the shaft was delayed, and in consequence the

[69] Although the burden of establishing remoteness lies on the contract-breaker: *Armstead v Royal & Sun Alliance Insurance Company Ltd* [2024] UKSC 6, [2025] AC 406 at [62].

[70] (1854) 9 Exch 341, 354. The French Civil Code, however, allows unforeseeable losses to be recovered where the breach is deliberate. *Hadley v Baxendale* and the English cases which have followed it do not distinguish between deliberate and non-deliberate breach.

[71] *Ibid*, 354, 355.

[72] *Ibid*, 355 (Alderson B). It was stated by Asquith LJ in *Victoria Laundry (Windsor) Ltd v Newman Industries Ltd* [1949] 2 KB 528, 537, that the headnote is misleading in that it wrongly ascribes to the defendants knowledge that the mill was stopped for want of the shaft.

mill could not be restarted until some time after it could otherwise have been. H lost profits which he would otherwise have made.

The question was whether this loss of profits was recoverable. Applying the principles quoted above, the Court stated that the circumstances communicated to the defendants did not show that a delay in the delivery of the shaft would entail loss of profits of the mill; H might have had another shaft, or there might have been some other defect in the machinery to cause the stoppage. Accordingly, H could not recover for this loss because:

[I]n the great multitude of cases of millers sending off broken shafts to third persons by a carrier under ordinary circumstances, such consequences would not, in all probability, have occurred; and these special circumstances were here never communicated by [H] to the defendants.[73]

The rule was further considered in *Victoria Laundry (Windsor) Ltd v Newman Industries Ltd*:[74]

V, a launderer and dyer, wished to expand its business, and for this purpose entered into a contract with the defendant to purchase from it a new boiler. It was agreed that the boiler was to be delivered on 5 June, but it was not delivered until November. Due to this delay, V lost the profits which it would have earned during between June and November, and, in particular, certain highly lucrative dyeing contracts which it could have obtained with the Ministry of Supply. V sued to recover these losses.

Streatfeild J's decision, that V was not entitled to recover the loss of any business profits during the period of delay, was reversed. Asquith LJ, delivering the judgment of the Court of Appeal, stated that the defendant knew before, and at the time of the contract, that V was a launderer and dyer and required the boiler for immediate use in its business. From the defendant's own technical experience, and from the business relations existing between the parties, the defendant must be presumed to have anticipated that some loss of profits would occur by reason of its delay. But in the absence of special knowledge on its part, the defendant could not reasonably foresee the additional losses suffered by V's inability to accept the highly lucrative dyeing contracts.

Although there are two branches to the rule in *Hadley v Baxendale*, in essence they both form a part of a single general principle. This was made clear by Asquith LJ in the *Victoria Laundry* case[75] who used the terminology of the loss being reasonably foreseeable rather than reasonably contemplated. According to Asquith LJ, the general principle which governs both branches of the rule is that the aggrieved party is only entitled to recover such part of the loss actually resulting from the breach as was at the time of the contract reasonably foreseeable as liable to result from the breach. What was at that time reasonably so foreseeable depends on the knowledge then possessed by the

[73] (1854) 9 Exch 341, 356 (Alderson B).

[74] [1949] 2 KB 528.

[75] Ibid, 539. See also *The Heron II* [1969] 1 AC 350, 385, 415; *The Pegase* [1981] 1 Lloyd's Rep 175, 182; *Khophraror v Woolwich Building Society* [1996] 4 All ER 119.

parties or, at all events, by the party who later commits the breach. For this purpose, knowledge 'possessed' is of two kinds: one imputed, the other actual. Everyone, as a reasonable person, is taken to know the 'ordinary course of things' and consequently what loss is liable to result from a breach of contract in that ordinary course. This is the subject-matter of the first branch of the rule. But to this knowledge, which a contract-breaker is assumed to possess whether it is actually possessed or not, there may have to be added in a particular case knowledge which the claimant actually possesses, of special circumstances outside the 'ordinary course of things', of such a kind that a breach in those special circumstances would be liable to cause more loss.[76] Such a situation attracts the operation of the second branch of the rule and makes this additional loss recoverable. Under neither branch is it necessary that the contract-breaker should actually have asked what loss is liable to result from a breach. It suffices that, if the issue had been considered, the contract-breaker would as a reasonable person have concluded that the loss in question was liable to result.

The *Victoria Laundry* case was considered in *Koufos v C Czarnikow Ltd, The Heron II*:[77]

The respondent, a sugar merchant, chartered the ship *Heron II* from the appellant to carry a cargo of sugar from Constanza to Basrah. The ship deviated without authority from the agreed voyage, with the result that the cargo was delayed. Owing to a fall in the market for sugar at Basrah, the respondent obtained £3,800 less for the sugar than the price obtainable when it should have been delivered.

The appellant contended that he was not liable for this sum as he had no special knowledge of the seasonal and other fluctuations of the sugar market. But the House of Lords held that a shipowner must be presumed to know that prices in a commodity market were liable to fluctuate, and judgment was given against him.

Asquith LJ's judgment in the *Victoria Laundry* case was described as 'a justifiable and valuable clarification of the principles which *Hadley v Baxendale* was intending to express' particularly in explaining that the phrase used by Alderson B—'in the contemplation of the parties ... as the probable result'—did not mean an odds-on probability.[78] Nevertheless, there was some criticism of the way in which Asquith LJ formulated the general principle in terms of 'reasonable foresight' of the loss 'liable to result'. This, it was said, may engender confusion with the rule regarding remoteness of damage in tort,[79] where a defendant will be held responsible for damage which is

[76] Knowledge of special circumstances may, however, in some situations be such as to lead the parties to believe that the loss will be reduced: see *Biggin & Co Ltd v Permanite Ltd* [1951] 1 KB 422, 436; *The Heron II* [1969] 1 AC 350, 416.

[77] [1969] 1 AC 350.

[78] *Ibid*, 417. See also at 399, but contrast at 389, 390, 410–11, 424–5. In *R & H Hall Ltd v WH Pim (Junior) & Co Ltd* (1927) 33 Com Cas 324, 330 Lord Dunedin stated that 'probable' did not mean more than an even chance.

[79] *Overseas Tankship (UK) v Morts Dock and Engineering Co, The Wagon Mound* [1961] AC 388.

reasonably foreseeable as liable to happen even if the risk is very small,[80] because it is said that normally in tort, unlike in contract, there is no opportunity for the injured party to protect itself against an unusual risk by informing the defendant.[81] Lord Reid and Lord Morris interpreted Alderson B's phrase as meaning the contemplation of a result which was 'not unlikely' to happen rather than an odds on probability;[82] and a majority of their Lordships distinguished the tort rule by requiring that the loss must be 'not very unusual and easily foreseeable',[83] or that there must be 'a real danger' or 'a serious possibility'[84] of its occurrence.

In *Jackson v Royal Bank of Scotland plc*[85] it was again stressed by the House of Lords that the contract remoteness test looks at the defendant's knowledge at the date the contract was made and not at the date of the breach of contract; and, as in *The Heron II*, it was explained that this is because it is at that date that the parties have the opportunity to draw attention to special circumstances outside the ordinary course of things, affording their counterparties the opportunity to limit their liability, or demand a higher price, or refuse to contract, and so on.

(b) TYPE OF DAMAGE

In the context of physical injury it is established that the word 'damage' refers to the type or kind of damage in question; it is not necessary for a claimant to go further and show contemplation of the exact nature of the damage that has arisen, or the amount of damage of the type or kind.[86] In principle the same should apply to cases of loss of profit,[87] but this is not easy to reconcile with the decision of the Court of Appeal in the *Victoria Laundry* case in which the 'ordinary' loss of profits were recovered but not that from the highly lucrative Ministry of Supply contracts.[88] In *Brown v KMR Services Ltd* Stuart-Smith LJ stated that, although categorization into types is difficult in the case of financial loss, loss of ordinary business profits is different *in type or kind* from loss flowing from a particular contract which gives rise to very high profits, whereas underwriting losses of a far larger magnitude than any contemplated were of the same *type* as those foreseeable.[89]

[80] *The Heron II* [1969] 1 AC 350, 385–6, 389.

[81] *Ibid*, 385–6, 411, 422–3. See also *Jackson v Royal Bank of Scotland plc* [2005] UKHL 3, [2005] 1 WLR 377 at [36] (Lord Hope). But this suggests that where the parties to a tort claim are in a contractual or similar relationship there should be no difference in the remoteness tests. See below, pp 567–9.

[82] *The Heron II*, above, n 80, 388, 406. See also at 416–17 (Lord Pearce), 424 (Lord Upjohn).

[83] *Ibid*, 383.

[84] *Ibid*, 414–15, 425.

[85] [2005] UKHL 3, [2005] 1 WLR 377.

[86] *Koufos v C Czarnikow Ltd* [1969] 1 AC 350, 382, 383, 385–6, 417.

[87] *H Parsons (Livestock) Ltd v Uttley Ingham & Co Ltd* [1978] QB 791, 804, 813; *Wroth v Tyler* [1974] Ch 30, 60–2; *Transworld Oil Ltd v North Bay SS Corp* [1987] 2 Lloyd's Rep 173, 175 (relying on cases of physical injury); *Homsy v Murphy* (1997) 73 P & CR 26, 36, 45.

[88] Above, p 558. See also *Islamic Republic of Iran SS Lines v Ierax SS Co of Panama* [1991] 1 Lloyd's Rep 81, 85–6.

[89] [1995] 4 All ER 598, 620–1.

(c) DAMAGE ARISING IN THE USUAL COURSE OF THINGS

Although the two branches of the rule in *Hadley v Baxendale* are not rigidly separate, it is helpful to examine the operation of each branch. Each may be regarded as covering a different degree of knowledge possessed by the contracting parties. The first branch deals with such damage as may fairly and reasonably be considered to flow naturally from the breach of contract, as the probable result of the breach in the usual course of things. It depends, as we have seen, on the knowledge which the parties are presumed to possess.

(i) Normal business position of parties

Damages will not be too remote if they flow from the normal business position of the parties, for the Court will assume that this is known to both of them. In *Monarch Steamship Co Ltd v Karlshamns Oljefabriker (A/B)*,[90] the facts of which are summarized above,[91] as a result of the diversion of the delayed vessel to Glasgow the purchasers of the cargo of soya incurred expenses in having them forwarded to the contractual destination in Sweden.

The purchasers were held to be entitled to recover this cost. Lord Wright pointed out that the question must always be 'what reasonable business men must be taken to have contemplated as the natural or probable result if the contract was broken. As reasonable business men each must be taken to understand the ordinary practices and exigencies of the other's trade or business.'[92] In that case, the possibility of war must have been present in the minds of the parties, and experienced business people would know that one of the risks that would be consequent upon prolongation of the voyage at that time would be the diversion of the vessel by the order of the Admiralty. The cost of transhipment was therefore not too remote a consequence of the unseaworthiness of the ship.

(ii) Non-delivery or late delivery

The Sale of Goods Act 1979 contains provisions for the standard assessment of damages for breach of a contract of sale founded on the first branch of the rule in *Hadley v Baxendale*. These are considered later in this chapter.[93] But the first branch of the rule also applies where a seller fails to deliver or is late in delivering what is on the face of it obviously a profit-earning chattel, for instance, a merchant or passenger ship, or some essential part of that ship.[94] In such cases the party injured will be entitled to recover the loss of profit which might reasonably be expected to arise if the contract were broken.[95]

90 [1949] AC 196, above, p 542. Cf *Diamond v Campbell-Jones* [1961] Ch 22.

91 p 556.

92 [1949] AC 196, 224. See also *Bulk Oil v Sun International* [1984] 1 Lloyd's Rep 531, 544.

93 Below, p 571.

94 *Victoria Laundry (Windsor) Ltd v Newman Industries Ltd* [1949] 2 KB 528, 536 (Asquith LJ). See also *Fletcher v Tayleur* (1855) 17 CB 21; *Saint Lines v Richardsons Westgarth & Co* [1940] 2 KB 99.

95 *Cory v Thames Ironworks & SS Co* (1868) LR 3 QB 181 (use of hull as coal store); *Fyffes Group Ltd v Reefer Express Lines Pty Ltd* [1996] 2 Lloyd's Rep 171, 203 (sub-charter of vessel on three-year time charter).

In contracts for the carriage of goods, if the carrier's default results in the loss or delay in transit of the goods which it has contracted to deliver, certain loss will ordinarily be assumed to have been suffered by the consignee as the natural and probable result of the breach. In the case of loss, the normal measure of damages is the market value of the goods at the time when they ought to have arrived, less the freight payable on safe delivery.[96] In the case of delay in delivering the goods, it is the difference between the market value of the goods on the day on which they ought to have arrived and their market value on the day on which they did arrive.[97]

(iii) Exceptional loss not covered

On the other hand, the first branch of the rule in *Hadley v Baxendale* does not cover losses which are the consequence of special facts not known to the party in default at the time the agreement was made. In *Hadley v Baxendale* itself, H was unable to recover damages arising from the fact that they had only one shaft, and in *Victoria Laundry* V was unable to recover in respect of the exceptionally lucrative Ministry of Supply contracts because information about those facts had not been conveyed to the defendants. Again in *British Columbia Saw-Mill Co Ltd v Nettleship*:[98]

A number of cases of machinery intended for the erection of a sawmill at Vancouver were shipped on the defendant's vessel. The defendant failed to deliver one of the cases, but was unaware of the fact that it contained a material part without which the sawmill could not be erected at all. BC Saw-Mill claimed the cost of replacing the lost parts, and the loss incurred by the stoppage of its works during the time that the rest of the machinery remained useless owing to the absence of the lost parts.

It was held that the measure of damages was the cost of replacing the lost machinery at Vancouver only. The Court said:[99]

> The defendant is a carrier, and not a manufacturer of goods supplied for a particular purpose . . . He is not to be made liable for damages beyond what may fairly be presumed to have been contemplated by the parties at the time of entering into the contract. It must be something which could have been foreseen and reasonably expected, and to which he assented expressly or impliedly by entering into the contract.

This principle will exclude the recovery of damages in respect of loss of profit on actual or contemplated forward contracts where the carrier has no actual or imputed knowledge of these at the time of the contract. The loss of profit on such sales is too remote. An illustration is provided by *Horne v Midland Railway Company*:[100]

H being under contract to deliver military shoes in London for the French army at an unusually high price by a particular day, delivered them to the defendant to be carried,

[96] *Rodocanachi v Milburn* (1886) 18 QBD 67, 76.
[97] *Wilson v Lancs & Yorks Ry* (1861) 9 CBNS 632; *Koufos v C Czarnikow Ltd* [1969] 1 AC 350.
[98] (1868) LR 3 CP 499.
[99] *Ibid*, 505 (Bovill CJ).
[100] (1873) LR 8 CP 131. Although this case was one of an exceptionally lucrative contract, the same principle applies to ordinary loss of profit: *Heskell v Continental Express* [1950] 1 All ER 1033.

with notice of the contract only as to the date of delivery. The shoes were delayed in carriage, and were consequently rejected by the intending purchasers. H sought to recover, in addition to the ordinary loss for delay, the difference between the price at which the shoes were actually sold and the high price at which they would have been sold if they had been punctually delivered.

It was held that this damage was not recoverable unless it could be proved that the company was informed of the exceptional loss which H might suffer from an unpunctual delivery. Similarly, it has been held that a person who contracts to purchase land intending to resell it to an identified sub-purchaser at a profit will not be able to recover in respect of the loss of the sub-sale where the seller does not know of the purchaser's intention and purpose and the consequent exposure of the seller to the risk of such damage in the event of breach.[101]

(iv) Immaterial that breach not contemplated

In *Banco de Portugal v Waterlow & Sons Ltd*:[102]

W & Sons agreed to print for the Bank of Portugal a quantity of Portuguese banknotes of a particular type. They negligently delivered to M, the head of an international band of criminals, 580,000 of these notes, which were subsequently put into circulation in Portugal. Upon discovery of the fraud, the Bank issued notices withdrawing from circulation all notes of that type, and undertook to exchange them for other notes. The Bank then brought an action against W & Sons claiming as damages for breach of contract the value of the notes exchanged, and the cost of printing the genuine notes withdrawn.

It was held by a majority of the House of Lords that these losses were recoverable. The damage suffered, although the result of a breach which could scarcely be said to have been in the contemplation of the parties at the time they made the contract, was nevertheless to be considered as flowing from the business positions of the parties and arising naturally from the breach.

(d) DAMAGE REASONABLY SUPPOSED TO BE IN THE CONTEMPLATION OF THE PARTIES

The application of this second branch of the rule depends upon the knowledge which the contract-breaker possesses at the time of the contract of special circumstances outside the 'ordinary course of things', of such a kind that a breach in those circumstances will cause more loss. The question is whether the damage is such as may reasonably be supposed to have been in the contemplation of both parties, at the time they made

[101] *Seven Seas Properties v Al Essa (No 2)* [1993] 1 WLR 1083 (purchaser concealed purpose). See also *Seven Seas Properties v Al Essa* [1988] 1 WLR 1272, 1276.

[102] [1932] AC 452. See *The Portuguese Bank-note Case* (1932) by Sir Cecil Kisch for an exciting account of this case.

the contract, as the probable result of the breach of it. In *Simpson v London and North Western Railway Company*:[103]

S, a manufacturer, was in the habit of sending specimens of his goods for exhibition to agricultural shows. After exhibiting in a show at Bedford, he entrusted some of his samples to an agent of the defendant company for carriage to a show-ground at Newcastle. On the consignment note he wrote: 'Must be at Newcastle Monday certain.' Owing to a default on the part of the company, the samples arrived late for the Newcastle show. S therefore claimed damages for his loss of profits at the show.

The company was held liable. Its agent had knowledge of the special circumstances, that the goods were to be exhibited at the Newcastle show, and so should have contemplated that a delay in delivery might result in this loss.

It is usually said that 'bare knowledge' of the special circumstances surrounding the contract is sufficient to make the contract-breaker liable.[104] But there is some authority for the view that, in addition, the contract-breaker should either expressly or impliedly have contracted to assume liability for the exceptional loss. On this view, the mere communication to a party of the existence of special circumstances is not enough: there must be something to show that the contract was made *on the terms* that the defendant was to be liable for that loss.[105]

This view cannot be supported. No doubt a casual intimation would not suffice, for the special circumstances must be disclosed in such a manner as to render it a fair inference of fact that both parties contemplated the exceptional loss as a probable result of the breach. Thus in *Kemp v Intasun Holidays Ltd*:[106]

While booking a holiday Mrs K remarked to the travel agent that her husband was not present because he was suffering, as he sometimes did, from an asthma attack. In breach of contract Mr and Mrs K were accommodated for the first 30 hours of their holiday in a filthy and dusty room in an inferior hotel and Mr K had an asthma attack throughout the period.

The trial judge awarded Mr K inter alia £800 for the consequences of having suffered an asthma attack due to the state of the alternative accommodation. But the Court of Appeal held that this casual remark was insufficient to give the defendant the necessary degree of knowledge of special circumstances to make the defendant responsible for the consequences of the asthma attack he had suffered. What is necessary to enlarge the area of contemplation is that the special circumstances should be brought home to the party.[107] But, although one might interpret the reasoning of Lord Hoffmann and Lord

[103] (1876) 1 QBD 274.
[104] *Patrick v Russo-British Grain Export Co Ltd* [1972] 2 KB 535, 540 (Salter J).
[105] *British Columbia Saw-Mill Co Ltd v Nettleship* (1868) LR 3 CP 499, 509; *Horne v Midland Ry* (1873) LR 8 CP 131, 141. See also *Victoria Laundry (Windsor) Ltd v Newman Industries Ltd* [1949] 2 KB 528, 538; *Seven Seas Properties v Al Essa (No 2)* [1993] 1 WLR 1083, 1088 (a party should not be exposed to risks of liability going beyond the first branch of *Hadley v Baxendale* without the opportunity of making an informed decision whether to accept such risk and whether to negotiate some exclusion from liability).
[106] [1987] 2 FTLR 234.
[107] See *Heywood v Wellers* [1976] 1 QB 446, 459 (Lord Denning MR) (tort). A much-discussed hypothetical example is of A booking a taxi for £50 with B, a taxi-driver. A explains to B when booking that it is essential for him to reach his specified destination on time as he is meeting a business client there to clinch a highly lucrative deal. In breach of contract, B takes the wrong route so that A arrives late at his destination. As a consequence A loses the lucrative deal (worth an estimated £10m net profit). Is A entitled to damages of £10m from B?

Hope in *The Achilleas* (considered immediately below) as offering some support for this, the Courts have expressly denied that it is necessary for there to be a term of the contract that the defendant is to be liable for that loss.[108]

(e) THE IMPACT OF *THE ACHILLEAS*

The law on remoteness, as so far set out, has arguably been altered by the House of Lords in *Transfield Shipping Inc v Mercator Shipping Inc, The Achilleas*.[109]

Under a time charter, the defendant charterers should have redelivered the ship to the claimant owners by 2 May 2004. In breach of contract, they did not redeliver to the owners until 11 May. The owners had entered into a follow-on time charter (referred to as a follow-on 'fixture') under which they were bound to deliver the ship to the new charterers by 8 May. When they were unable to do so as a result of the defendants' breach, the owners renegotiated the follow-on fixture and, because rates had fallen, they agreed to reduce the rate of hire on that follow-on fixture from $39,500 to $31,500, a loss of $8,000 a day.

The defendants accepted that they were liable for damages of the difference between the market rate and the charter rate for the nine-day overrun period between 2 May and 11 May. That came to $158,301. However, the owners sought damages to cover the loss of $8,000 a day for the whole period of the follow-on fixture. That came to $1,364,584. It was held by the House of Lords that the owners' damages were limited to $158,301. The rest of the loss was too remote.

Lord Rodger and Baroness Hale applied the conventional remoteness test that has been set out above. The question they were therefore asking was whether it was reasonably contemplatable as a serious possibility at the time of contracting that, in the event of breach by late redelivery, a follow-on fixture might be lost. One would have thought that, on the facts, the answer to that would have been 'yes' so that the loss on the follow-on fixture would not have been too remote. However, the answer given was 'no' so that that loss was held to be too remote.

Lord Hoffmann and Lord Hope arrived at the same result by significantly different reasoning. In effect they departed from the conventional test for remoteness by adding to it a requirement that the defendant must have accepted liability or responsibility for the loss. Lord Hoffmann reasoned that the charterers had not accepted liability for the loss because the understanding of the shipping industry was that charterers were only liable for loss during the overrun period. Lord Hope thought that the charterers had not accepted liability for the loss because it was out of their control and unquantifiable.

The additional requirement insisted on by Lord Hoffmann and Lord Hope is very controversial. As we have seen, the Courts have previously rejected the view that loss should be regarded as too remote unless the defendant has accepted liability for it as

[108] *The Heron II* [1969] 1 AC 350, 422; *GKN Centrax Gears Ltd v Matbro Ltd* [1976] 2 Lloyd's Rep 555.

[109] [2008] UKHL 48, [2009] 1 AC 61. For criticism, see Peel (2009) 125 LQR 6; Wee [2010] LMCLQ 150; Stiggelbout [2012] LMCLQ 97; Burrows, in Davies and Pila (eds), *The Jurisprudence of Lord Hoffmann* (2015) ch 14. For support, see Kramer (2009) 125 LQR 408; Hoffmann (2010) 14 Edin LR 47.

a term of the contract[110] and yet that appears to be very close to the reasoning of Lord Hoffmann and Lord Hope. It also seems doubtful whether leading decisions, such as *The Heron II*,[111] can be reconciled with their approach. Admittedly, there have long been doubts about whether merely informing the claimant of the special risks involved is sufficient in all circumstances to make a defendant liable for the loss under the second branch of the rule in *Hadley v Baxendale*.[112] But that was not the issue in *The Achilleas*. Although their Lordships did not sharply distinguish between the two branches of the rule, the facts clearly concerned the first branch and not the second.[113] A further problem with Lord Hoffmann's reasoning is that it is far from clear that he should have paid such deference to the apparent views of the shipping industry on a matter that had never previously been litigated and which, applying the previously accepted law on remoteness, was based on a mistaken understanding of the law.

Lord Hoffmann saw remoteness as an aspect of construing the contract. He also invoked his approach in *South Australia Asset Management Corp v York Montague Ltd*[114] to determining the scope of the duty of care. The counter-argument to his approach is that rules of remoteness are policy default rules of fairness set by the Courts although they can be departed from by the contracting parties by express or implied terms. To treat the rules of remoteness as 'agreement-centred' is to put the matter the wrong way round[115] and leads to 'construction' of the contract becoming a fictional mask for a decision that in reality is imposed on the parties.[116]

That the law of remoteness has been rendered less certain, and that *The Achilleas* is not to be confined to its own narrow sphere of shipping, is well illustrated by *Supershield Ltd v Siemens Building Technologies FE Ltd*.[117] The Court of Appeal, in the context of deciding that a settlement reached by the parties was reasonable, stated that, while *Hadley v Baxendale* remains the standard rule and is grounded on policy, it can be displaced if, on examining the contract and the commercial background, the loss in

[110] Above, p 565, especially n 108. [111] Above, p 559. [112] Above, p 563.

[113] See [2008] UKHL 48 at [6] (Lord Hoffmann) and at [93] (Baroness Hale). That the change in market rates was very extreme should not affect the *type* of loss suffered: see above, p 560.

[114] [1997] AC 191. It was controversially held in *SAAMCO* that, where there had been a fall in property prices, valuers who had negligently undervalued property were not liable to lenders, who had relied on that negligent undervaluation in lending money on the security of those properties, for losses greater than the difference between the represented value of the property and its actual value at the date of valuation. *The Achilleas* suggests that Lord Hoffmann would regard *SAAMCO* as correct because the market fall loss was too remote as being outside the scope of the duty assumed by the valuer. For criticism of *SAAMCO*, see Burrows, *Remedies for Torts, Breach of Contract, and Equitable Wrongs* (4th edn, 2019) 117–27. But for confirmation and clarification of the *SAAMCO* principle, see *BPE Solicitors v Hughes-Holland* [2017] UKSC 21, [2018] AC 599.

[115] And also drives a distinction between contract and tort: see below, p 567.

[116] Robertson (2008) 28 LS 172 criticizes the agreement-centred approach of Kramer, in Cohen and McKendrick (eds), *Comparative Remedies for Breach of Contract* (2004) 249. For the latter type of approach, see also Tettenborn (2007) 23 JCL 120. These three articles were cited by Lord Hoffmann in *The Achilleas*.

[117] [2010] EWCA Civ 7, [2010] 1 Lloyd's Rep 349. See also *Sylvia Shipping Co Ltd v Progress Bulk Carriers Ltd* [2010] EWHC 542 (Comm), [2010] 2 Lloyd's Rep 8 (the 'assumption of responsibility' approach in *The Achilleas* to be confined to exceptional cases where the orthodox approach would result in unquantifiable, unpredictable, disproportionate liability or a result contrary to clear market understanding and expectations).

question was within or outside the scope of the contractual duty. Thus, the approach in *The Achilleas* might displace the standard rule by making loss that would be recoverable under *Hadley v Baxendale* too remote (an 'exclusionary effect') or by making loss that would be non-recoverable under *Hadley v Baxendale* not too remote (an 'inclusionary effect'). On the facts, although it was unlikely that loss by flooding would occur as a consequence of the defendant's breach in failing properly to install a float valve in a fire-sprinkler water storage system—because normally the drains would have taken the overflow water but here the drains were blocked—that loss was thought not to be too remote because it was within the scope of the installer's duty. Although this is helpful in clarifying that *Hadley v Baxendale* remains good law and is the standard rule, it does show that it is far from clear what triggers the displacement of that standard rule.

Hadley v Baxendale must remain good law since it is one of the *ratios* of *The Achilleas*: Lord Walker supported the approach based upon *Hadley v Baxendale* favoured by Lord Rodger and Baroness Hale. However, Lord Walker also agreed with the new approach adopted by Lord Hoffmann and Lord Hope. As a result, a majority of the House of Lords endorsed *Hadley v Baxendale*. And a majority of the House of Lords also endorsed the 'assumption of responsibility' view.

In *Attorney General of the Virgin Islands v Global Water Associates Ltd*:[118]

> GWA entered into two contracts with the Government of the British Virgin Islands. The first was to design and build a water reclamation plant. The second was to manage, operate, and maintain that plant for 12 years. The Government failed to provide a site for the plant, breaching the first contract. Overturning the decision of the court below, the Privy Council held that GWA was able to recover profits lost from not being able to perform the second contract: both contracts were entered into at the same time, and the Government contemplated as a serious possibility that failure to perform the first contract would lead to loss of profits on the second contract.

Lord Hodge relied exclusively on *Hadley v Baxendale*[119] and explicitly stated that there was no need to consider what Lord Hoffmann and Lord Hope had said in *The Achilleas* since the case did not concern 'the recoverability of damages caused by unusual volatility in the market or questions of market understanding'.[120] *Hadley v Baxendale* will be sufficient in most cases; only in unusual circumstances might the Court go on to consider whether the result would be any different under the 'assumption of responsibility' test.

(f) SHOULD THERE BE A DIFFERENCE BETWEEN THE TESTS OF REMOTENESS IN CONTRACT AND TORT?

The reasoning of the House of Lords in *The Heron II* shows that, in the usual case where a tort claim is brought but the parties are not in a contractual relationship, the *Wagon Mound* tort remoteness test is applied which is less strict than the contract remoteness test.[121] The interrelation of the tests for remoteness in contract and tort was further

[118] [2020] UKPC 18, [2021] AC 23. [119] *Ibid*, [30]–[35]. [120] *Ibid*, [26]. [121] Above, p 559.

considered by the Court of Appeal in the context of physical damage in *H Parsons (Livestock) Ltd v Uttley Ingham & Co Ltd*.[122]

UI agreed to supply and erect on P's pig farm a bulk food storage hopper for the purpose of storing pig nuts for P's top grade pig herd. When the hopper was installed, UI failed to ensure that a ventilator at the top of the hopper was open, with the result that the pig nuts stored in it became mouldy. P fed the mouldy nuts to their pigs believing (as would normally be the case) that no harm could result. But the pigs suffered an attack of E coli, an intestinal infection triggered by feeding on the mouldy nuts, and 254 pigs died.

At first instance, Swanwick J held that the damage caused was not within the reasonable contemplation of the parties as a result of UI's breach of contract. The Court of Appeal reversed that decision. Lord Denning MR expressed the opinion[123] that the observations in *The Heron II* were limited to cases where the claim was for loss of profit or, at any rate, for economic loss. In his view, where the claim was for damages for personal injury or damage to property, or for resulting expenses to which the claimant had been put, the rule in contract was the same as that in tort, so that a defendant would be liable for any loss or damage which ought reasonably to have been foreseen at the time of the breach as a possible consequence, even if it was only a slight possibility.

Distinguishing between loss of profit and physical damage might be justified on the ground that a person is unlikely to consider the possibility of physical injury in advance and thus to disclose unusual risks.[124] However, Orr and Scarman LJJ, who held that the parties could have contemplated as 'a serious possibility' that the pigs might become ill as a result of the breach, considered that neither authority[125] nor principle supported a distinction in remoteness tests between loss of profit and physical damage. Nevertheless, Scarman LJ stated[126] that although the formulation of the remoteness test is not the same in tort and contract because the relationship of the parties in a contractual situation differs from that in tort, it would be absurd if the amount of damages recoverable were to depend upon whether the claimant's cause of action was in contract or in tort. In his opinion the difference between 'reasonably foreseeable' (the test in tort) and 'reasonably contemplated' (the test in contract) was semantic, not substantial. This suggests that where there is a contractual relationship between the parties and concurrent liability in contract and tort there should, in principle, be no difference between the remoteness tests in contract and tort. Moreover, in *Wellesley Partners LLP v Withers LLP*[127] the Court of Appeal, after a full and enlightened consideration of the issues, held that,

[122] [1978] QB 791.

[123] *Ibid*, 803–4.

[124] This may not be the case for all types of contracts, eg a contract for medical services or for instruction in a sporting activity.

[125] The authority relied on by Lord Denning, *Ashington Piggeries Ltd v Christopher Hill Ltd* [1972] AC 441 and *Henry Kendall & Sons v William Lillico & Sons Ltd* [1969] 2 AC 31, in fact applied *The Heron II* [1969] 1 AC 350, as, subsequently to *Parsons*, did *Kemp v Intasun Holidays Ltd* [1987] 2 FTLR 234 (asthmatic attack caused by dirty hotel room too remote).

[126] [1978] QB 791, 806–7. See also *Archer v Brown* [1985] QB 401, 418.

[127] [2015] EWCA Civ 1146, [2016] Ch 529. See also *Brown v KMR Services Ltd* [1995] 4 All ER 598. See generally Burrows, *Remedies for Torts, Breach of Contract, and Equitable Wrongs* (4th edn, 2019) 105–6.

where the defendant assumed responsibility to the claimant under the contract or, put another way, the relevant risks were allocated in the contract, the stricter 'contractual' remoteness test applies to a concurrent claim in the tort of negligence for pure economic loss by a client against a solicitor. Because the parties have the opportunity to bring special risks to each other's attention, the contractual rules should apply even where the claim is brought in tort. This approach has been approved by the Supreme Court in *URS Corp Ltd v BDW Trading Ltd*.[128]

6. MITIGATION

A person who has suffered loss from a breach of contract must take any reasonable steps that are available to mitigate the extent of the damage caused by the breach.[129] The innocent party cannot claim to be compensated by the party in default for loss which is really due not to the breach but to its own failure to behave reasonably after the breach.[130] The underlying policy is the desirability of avoiding waste, in this context a loss which could have been avoided by reasonable action. It is often said that the law imposes 'a duty' on claimants to mitigate their loss. But this expression is misleading. The claimant cannot itself be sued for failure to comply with its duty: the consequence is simply that no damages are given for the avoidable loss. 'Damages are assessed as if the claimant acted reasonably, if in fact it did not act reasonably.'[131]

(a) ACTING REASONABLY

An employee who is wrongfully dismissed must make reasonable efforts to obtain, and must accept an offer of, suitable alternative employment. Failure to do so may mean that the employee is entitled to nominal damages only.[132] Similarly, where a seller wrongfully refuses to deliver goods due under a contract for the sale of goods, a buyer who fails to buy substitute goods which are available will be debarred from claiming any part of the damage which is due to the failure to do so.[133] A claimant may even be required to accept a reasonable offer from the defendant which would make good the loss or part of it.[134] But there is no obligation to do anything other than in the 'ordinary

[128] [2025] UKSC 21, [2025] 2 WLR 1095 at [33].

[129] Bridge (1989) 105 LQR 398. See generally Summers, *Mitigation in the Law of Damages* (2024).

[130] *British Westinghouse Electric Co Ltd v Underground Electric Rys Co of London Ltd* [1912] AC 673, 689.

[131] Dyson and Kramer (2014) 130 LQR 259, 26, cited in *Sharp Corporation v Viterra BV* [2024] UKSC 14, [2024] 4 All ER 273 at [85].

[132] *Beckham v Drake* (1847–49) 2 HLC 579; *Shindler v Northern Raincoat Co Ltd* [1960] 1 WLR 1038; *Brace v Calder* [1895] 2 QB 253.

[133] *Kaines (UK) v Osterreichische Warenhandelsgesellschaft Austrowaren Gesellschaft mbH* [1993] 2 Lloyd's Rep 1 (in volatile market buyer must act quickly); *Coastal (Bermuda) Petroleum Ltd v VTT Vulcab Petroleum (No 2)* [1994] 2 Lloyd's Rep 629, 635.

[134] *Brace v Calder* [1895] 2 QB 253; *Payzu Ltd v Saunders* [1919] 2 KB 581; *Sotiros Shipping Inc v Sameiet Solholt* [1983] 1 Lloyd's Rep 605. Cf Bridge (1989) 105 LQR 398, 411 ff.

course of business'[135] and it is a question of fact in each case whether the claimant has acted as a reasonable person might have been expected to act. There is no compulsion to accept goods of inferior quality[136] or to risk one's commercial reputation[137] or to embark upon complicated litigation[138] or to undergo an operation with the risk of surgical complications[139] in order to mitigate loss. The claimant need not take steps which it cannot financially afford: impecuniosity is an excuse for failure to mitigate.[140] In cases of wrongful dismissal, an employee is not compelled to accept re-employment if it involves lower status, if relations are irretrievably affected by the circumstances of dismissal (as where there has been a public charge of misconduct), or if it is likely to be less permanent than alternatives.[141]

A claimant who has taken unreasonable steps cannot hold the defendant liable for loss which has been suffered as a result.[142] Again, the question of reasonableness is a question of fact. For example, it has been held reasonable to incur hire-purchase charges to replace a damaged rotor,[143] legal expenses in proceedings with a third party,[144] advertising to safeguard one's commercial reputation,[145] and voluntary expenses to meet the claimant's commercial (but legally unenforceable) obligations to the public.[146]

(b) COMPENSATING ADVANTAGES MAY REDUCE DAMAGES

Where a person mitigates loss and obtains a compensating advantage, the advantage will be deducted from the damages provided it arose directly from the breach and the act of mitigation and is not merely an 'indirect' or collateral benefit.[147] So, where turbines which were less efficient than the contract specification and used more coal were replaced by turbines which resulted in an overall saving of coal over the whole period, the damages had to be reduced by the savings achieved.[148] But, where the benefit

[135] *Dunkirk Colliery Co v Lever* (1878) 9 Ch D 20, 25.

[136] *Heaven & Kesterton Ltd v Et Francois Albiac & Cie* [1956] 2 Lloyd's Rep 316. See also *Strutt v Whitnell* [1975] 1 WLR 870.

[137] *James Finlay & Co Ltd v NV Kwik Hoo Tong HM* [1929] 1 KB 400; *London & South of England Building Society v Stone* [1983] 1 WLR 1242.

[138] *Pilkington v Wood* [1953] Ch 770.

[139] *Selvanayagam v University of West Indies* [1983] 1 WLR 585.

[140] *Clippens Oil Co Ltd v Edinburgh & District Water Trustees* [1907] AC 291, 303. See generally *Lagden v O'Connor* [2003] UKHL 64, [2004] 1 AC 1067.

[141] *Yetton v Eastwoods Froy Ltd* [1967] 1 WLR 104. Cf *Brace v Calder* [1895] 2 QB 253.

[142] *Sotiros Shipping Inc v Sameiet Solholt* [1983] 1 Lloyd's Rep 605, 608.

[143] *Bacon v Cooper (Metals) Ltd* [1982] 1 All ER 397.

[144] *The Antaios* [1981] 2 Lloyd's Rep 284, 299.

[145] *Holden Ltd v Bostock & Co Ltd* (1902) 18 TLR 317.

[146] *Banco de Portugal v Waterlow & Sons Ltd* [1932] AC 452, the facts of which are set out above, p 563.

[147] *British Westinghouse Co v Underground Electric Rys Co of London* [1912] AC 673; *Lavarack v Woods of Colchester* [1967] 1 QB 278; *Dimond v Lovell* [2002] 1 AC 384; *Thai Airways International Public Co Ltd v KI Holdings Co Ltd* [2015] EWHC 1250 (Comm), [2016] 1 All ER (Comm) 675 at [46]–[62]; *Fulton Shipping Inc of Panama v Globalia Business Travel SAU of Spain, The New Flamenco* [2017] UKSC 43, [2017] 1 WLR 2581 (noted at [2018] LMCLQ 171); *Barrowfen Properties Ltd v Patel* [2025] EWCA Civ 39.

[148] *British Westinghouse Co v Underground Electric Rys Co of London* [1912] AC 673. See Dyson [2012] LMCLQ 412.

is independent of the act of mitigation, damages will not be reduced. Benefits from wholly independent transactions, for example sums due under an insurance policy, will not lead to a deduction.[149] The fact that replacement property bought is better than the original property, which was damaged as a consequence of the breach of contract, will not in itself reduce damages;[150] rather it must be shown that the claimant will derive a real pecuniary advantage from the better property.[151]

7. ASSESSMENT OF DAMAGES IN CONTRACTS FOR THE SALE OF GOODS

Useful illustrations of the application of the principles discussed are provided by the manner of assessment of damages in contracts for the sale of goods. For example, sections 50 and 51 of the Sale of Goods Act 1979 (the latter now applies only to non-consumer contracts for the sale of goods)[152] state that the measure of damages for non-acceptance or non-delivery of the goods is 'the estimated loss directly and naturally resulting, in the ordinary course of events, from the buyer's or seller's breach of contract'; and where there is an available market for the goods in question, this is prima facie to be ascertained by the difference between the contract price and the market or current price at the time when the goods ought to have been accepted or delivered, as the case may be, or, if no time was fixed, then at the time of the refusal to accept or deliver. The reason for this prima facie 'breach-date' rule[153] is that in a case of non-delivery by the seller the buyer may go into the market and buy alternative goods at the current price and, in a case of the buyer's failure to accept goods, the seller may take his goods into the market and obtain the current price for them.[154] These may be viewed as steps the innocent party should reasonably take to mitigate its loss.[155]

(a) NON-DELIVERY

Suppose that A promises to sell and deliver to B 1,000 tonnes of coal at £112 per tonne on 8 February. A fails to carry out its contract. On 8 February the market price of coal of that quality is £120 per tonne. B can recover as damages for non-delivery the difference between the contract price and the market price on that day, that is, £8 per tonne.[156]

[149] *Bradburn v GW Ry* (1874) LR 10 Ex 1; *Arab Bank plc v John D Wood Commercial Ltd* [2000] 1 WLR 857.

[150] *Bacon v Cooper (Metals) Ltd* [1982] 1 All ER 397. See also *Harbutt's Plasticine Ltd v Wayne Tank and Pump Co Ltd* [1970] 1 QB 447.

[151] *Voaden v Champion, The Baltic Surveyor* [2002] EWCA Civ 89, [2002] 1 Lloyd's Rep 623.

[152] See the amendment of the 1979 Act by the Consumer Rights Act 2015.

[153] ss 50(3) and 51(3). For examples of its displacement, see *Van den Hurk v R Martens & Co Ltd* [1920] 1 KB 850 (sale of goods); *Johnson v Agnew* [1980] AC 367, 400–1 (sale of land). See generally Waddams (1981) 97 LQR 445 and above, pp 533–4.

[154] *Barrow v Arnaud* (1846) 8 QB 604, 609 (Tindal CJ); *Kaines (UK) Ltd v Osterreichische Warenhandelsgesellschaft Austrowaren Gesellschaft mbH* [1993] 2 Lloyd's Rep 1 (in a volatile market this must be done at the first practical opportunity).

[155] Above, p 569.

[156] s 51(3).

Uncontemplated forward or sub-sales must ordinarily be disregarded. If, for instance, in the expectation of receiving the coal, B has contracted to sell a similar quantity to C at £117 per tonne, its damages will still be £8 (and not £5) per tonne, since it must normally go into the market in order to fulfil its contract with C.[157] And the same is true where the sub-sale is at a price higher than the market price at the date when delivery should be made.[158]

(b) LATE DELIVERY

Where the seller is late in delivering the goods, the damage is normally the difference between the market value at the time they ought to have been delivered and the market value at the time when they actually were delivered.[159] Difficulties have arisen where the goods have been resold for more than their market value. In *Wertheim v Chicoutimi Pulp Co Ltd*:[160]

The seller was late in delivering the goods. The market price of the goods at the time when they ought to have been delivered was 70*s* per ton, and, at the time they were delivered, 42*s* 6*d* per ton. The normal measure of damages would therefore have been 27*s* 6*d* per ton, and this was the sum claimed by the buyer. But proof was adduced that he had actually sold the goods for 65*s* per ton.

The Privy Council held that the seller could rely on this sale to reduce the damages to 5*s* per ton. Lord Atkinson considered that the prima facie market value rule was displaced where the sub-sale proves that the value of the goods to the buyer was more than their market value at the time of delivery and that to assess damages by reference to market value would allow the buyer to be 'compensated for a loss he never suffered'.[161] A possible counter-argument is that the buyer was not obliged to fulfil the subcontract by delivering the specific goods received.[162] The buyer would have been free to resell the goods at the time they ought to have been delivered at their then market price (70*s* per ton) and to procure other goods for the subcontract. In a falling market a buyer is likely to do this and, on the facts of *Wertheim*'s case, to sell one lot at 70*s* per ton and to fulfil the 65*s* per ton sub-sale by buying in at the market price of 42*s* 6*d* per ton. The late delivery therefore deprived the buyer in that case of the opportunity to sell at the due date, a fact that was unaffected by the sub-sale.

157 Cf *Williams Bros v ET Agius Ltd* [1914] AC 510.

158 *Great Western Ry v Redmayne* (1866) LR 1 CP 329. But contrast *Hall Ltd v Pim Junr & Co* (1928) 139 LT 50 and *Coastal International Trading Ltd v Maroil AG* [1988] 1 Lloyd's Rep 92 where it was contemplated that the buyer might resell the particular goods purchased.

159 *Elbinger Aktiengesellschaft v Armstrong* (1874) LR 9 QB 473; Sale of Goods Act 1979, s 53(3).

160 [1911] AC 301 approved in *Williams Bros v ET Agius Ltd* [1914] AC 510, 522.

161 [1911] AC 301, 307–8.

162 *Slater v Hoyle & Smith Ltd* [1920] 2 KB 11, 23 (Scrutton LJ). See also *Campbell Mostyn (Provisions) Ltd v Barnett Trading Co* [1954] 1 Lloyd's Rep 65. But in *Bence Graphics Ltd v Fasson UK Ltd* [1998] QB 87, *Slater's* case was not followed, it was stated that it 'should be reconsidered', and Auld LJ approved of *Wertheim*'s case. For the *Bence Graphics* case, see below, p 575.

(c) NON-ACCEPTANCE

Although the normal rule, as set out in section 50(3) of the Sale of Goods Act 1979 is that the measure of damages is the difference between the contract price and the market price on the day fixed for acceptance, in modern trading conditions the retail price is frequently that recommended by the manufacturers, so that there is no difference between the contract and the market price. The question then arises whether a seller who is a dealer can recover its loss of profit on the sale. In *WL Thompson Ltd v Robinson (Gunmakers) Ltd*:[163]

R contracted to buy a new Vanguard car from T, a car dealer. The price of the car was that fixed by the manufacturers, which T was unable to vary in any way. R refused to accept the car, but T managed to persuade its wholesale suppliers to take the car back. T nevertheless claimed from R the loss of its profit on the sale.

R claimed that T was entitled to nominal damages only, there being no difference between the market price of the car and the contract price. Upjohn J refused to accept this contention. He held that section 50(3) of the Sale of Goods Act 1979 laid down only a prima facie rule, and that it was displaced by proof in this case that the supply of Vanguard cars currently exceeded demand. T therefore acted reasonably in returning the car to its suppliers, but it had sold one less Vanguard car than it would otherwise and so was entitled to claim its loss of profit on the transaction. It had therefore suffered a loss in the volume of its sales.[164]

On the other hand, in *Charter v Sullivan*,[165] the Court of Appeal held that a car dealer could recover only nominal damages for non-acceptance of a car when the state of the motor trade was such that he could sell all the cars he could get, and he in fact sold the vehicle in question within ten days of the failure to accept; here the breach did not result in loss in the volume of sales. Jenkins LJ went so far as to doubt whether it could be said that there was an 'available market' for the operation of the market price rule when goods could only be sold at a fixed retail price. But the Court was agreed that the dealer in this case could not be held to have made 'only one sale instead of two', since he was limited in the number of sales he could make by the fact that demand exceeded supply. The dealer had therefore suffered no loss of profit by the breach. The conclusion seems to be that loss of profit is not recoverable where demand exceeds supply, but can be recovered where supply equals or exceeds demand.[166]

A buyer who delays in accepting delivery is liable to the seller for any loss occasioned by the delay including for a reasonable charge for the care and custody of the goods.[167]

[163] [1955] Ch 177. Contrast *Lazenby Garages Ltd v Wright* [1976] 1 WLR 459 (second-hand BMW 'unique').

[164] On 'lost volume sellers', see Harris (1962) 60 Mich L Rev 577, 600–1; (1964) 18 Stan L Rev 66; Childres and Burgess (1973) 48 NYU L Rev 833. Cf economists' scepticism about an *assumption* of lost volume in the case of retail sales, Goetz and Scott (1979) 31 Stan L Rev 323, 355; Goldberg (1984) 57 S Cal Rev 283.

[165] [1957] 2 QB 117.

[166] See also *Re Vic Mill Ltd* [1913] 1 Ch 465.

[167] Sale of Goods Act 1979, s 37. Also under s 48(3) of the Act, an unpaid seller has the right to sell perishable goods, or any goods after notice, and to recover from the original buyer damages for any loss occasioned by the breach.

(d) BREACH OF WARRANTY

Where goods are delivered in breach of warranty, section 53 of the Sale of Goods Act 1979 (which now applies only to non-consumer contracts for the sale of goods)[168] provides a prima facie rule that the buyer is entitled to the difference between the value of the goods at the time of delivery to the buyer and the value which they would have had if they had fulfilled the warranty.

(i) Sub-sales

If it was within the reasonable contemplation of the parties at the time they made the contract that the goods would probably be re-sold to sub-purchasers on the same or substantially similar terms, either as they were or after manufacturing them into another product, the Court may have regard to the sub-sale. The buyer will, for example, be able to recover from the seller any damages which it has been forced to pay to those sub-purchasers together with any costs reasonably incurred in defending an action against him by them. In *Hammond & Co v Bussey*:[169]

H, a shipping agent, contracted with B, a coal merchant, for the supply of a quantity of 'steam-coal' to be used in steamships. B knew at the time of the contract that H was buying the coal for resale as fit for this purpose. H resold the coal, which was not fit for the purpose of steamships and they reasonably, but unsuccessfully, defended an action brought against them by their sub-purchaser.

It was held that H might recover not only the damages paid by it to its sub-purchaser, but the costs incurred in defending the action: this damage came within the second branch of the rule in *Hadley v Baxendale*, since B had special knowledge of the probability of the subcontracts.

Where the buyer has not been faced with claims by the sub-purchasers, it remains somewhat unclear whether the buyer should be able to recover from the seller for the difference between the value of the goods delivered and the value which they would have had if they had fulfilled the warranty. In *Slater v Hoyle & Smith Ltd*[170] the claimant bought cotton from the defendant. The claimant had contracted to sell the cotton on to the third party. The cotton which was delivered was of inferior quality than warranted. However, the claimant suffered no financial loss because the sub-purchasers paid the contract price in full. Nevertheless, the Court of Appeal awarded the claimant a substantial sum based upon the difference in market value at the time of delivery between the defective cotton and cotton conforming to the quality requirements of the contract. Scrutton LJ said:

If the goods are delivered damaged, [the buyer] has got goods and has paid the contract price; what he has not got is sound goods, and his loss is therefore the difference between

[168] By reason of the amendment of the 1979 Act by the Consumer Rights Act 2015.

[169] (1887) 20 QBD 79. *Biggin & Co Ltd v Permanite Ltd* [1951] 2 KB 314. Cf *Coastal International Trading Ltd v Maroil AG* [1988] 1 Lloyd's Rep 92 (terms of sub-sale unusual so loss of profit irrecoverable).

[170] [1920] 2 KB 11. See too *Clark v Macourt* [2013] HCA 56.

the market value of sound goods and the market value of these damaged goods. Again, sub-contracts do not come into account, for the buyer is under no obligation to use these goods for his sub-contract . . .

On the other hand, in *Bence Graphics Ltd v Fasson UK Ltd*:[171]

B bought vinyl film from the defendant for £564,300, and used it to manufacture decals which it then sold to companies to be used to identify bulk containers. It was a term of the contract that the decals should have a 'guaranteed minimum five year life'. Due to a latent defect the vinyl film degraded prematurely and many of the decals became illegible. There were many complaints but only one claim, for which the defendant had compensated B. B returned defective decals worth £22,000 to the defendant, and the defendant conceded that B was entitled to be reimbursed for this. The lack of durability was found by the trial judge to render the vinyl film worthless, and he awarded B £564,300, being the difference between the value of the product had it fulfilled the warranty and its actual value. By the date of the trial, there was no possibility of further claims against B by its customers because the limitation period for such claims had expired.

A majority of the Court of Appeal allowed an appeal by the defendant, and held that since the parties contemplated that the vinyl film would be manufactured and sold on, they contemplated that the measure of damages would be the claimant's liability to the ultimate users, thus displacing the prima facie measure of damages in section 53 of the Sale of Goods Act 1979. The majority cast doubt on the ignoring of the sub-sales in *Slater v Hoyle & Smith Ltd.*[172] This greater willingness shown in *Bence* to depart from the statutory prima facie rule has been criticized.[173] For example, it has been said that, had B's customers brought claims against B, the defendant would have undoubtedly been liable for the cost of meeting them so that the effect of the decision gave a defendant who delivered worthless goods a windfall gain, namely the benefit of the forbearance of a person's customers from claiming. However, it might be thought that this criticism sits uneasily with the rule, considered above, that in general a claimant may not recover for loss that has been avoided.[174]

The *Bence* and *Slater* cases may perhaps be reconciled on the basis that in *Slater* the claimant knew the cotton was defective *before* it employed it in the sub-sale, whereas in *Bence* the defect was discovered *after* the vinyl films had been delivered to the sub-buyers.[175] Only in the former case could the claimant have gone to the market before the sub-sale, which explains why the difference in market value was awarded. The fact that he did not do that and yet still managed to sell the cotton was '*res inter alios acta*:

[171] [1998] QB 87.

[172] [1920] 2 KB 11.

[173] Treitel (1997) 113 LQR 188 prefers the reasoning in *Slater v Hoyle & Smith Ltd* [1920] 2 KB 11, which the Court of Appeal refused to follow. But cf Burrows, *Remedies for Torts, Breach of Contract, and Equitable Wrongs* (4th edn, 2019) 193–4.

[174] Above, p 570. The position may have been different if the limitation period for claims by B's customers had not expired, since it would have still been at risk of such a claim.

[175] See Dyson and Kramer (2014) 130 LQR 259, 274–5.

"circumstances peculiar to the plaintiff" which cannot affect his claim one way or the other'.[176] By contrast, in *Bence* the claimant had no choice whether to resort to the market, and it had not acted unreasonably or unforeseeably in selling on the goods in ignorance of the defect. Any difference in value was irrelevant. Admittedly, such a reconciliation of the cases is not to be found in the decisions themselves.

More tellingly, perhaps, Auld LJ in *Bence* simply refused to follow *Slater*.[177] This might be welcomed on the basis that there is no reason why a claimant should be able to recover more than its actual financial loss. As Lord Sumption observed in *Bunge SA v Nidera BV*, concerns of certainty 'can rarely be thought to justify an award of substantial damages to someone who has not suffered any'.[178]

In *Euro-Asian Oil SA v Credit Suisse AG*,[179] the claimant entered into a contract to purchase oil from the defendant, and further contracted to sell oil to a third party.[180] When the defendant breached its contract, the Court held that the claimant was not simply entitled to the market measure of damages. Rather, the price agreed on the sub-sale contract could be taken into account to reduce the award of damages. The award therefore focused on the claimant's actual loss, and therefore aligns well with the decision in *Bence Graphics*, and sits uneasily with *Slater v Hoyle & Smith*.[181] The Court of Appeal thought damages should be awarded based upon financial loss rather than as a substitute for a right to performance regardless of the financial consequences suffered.

(ii) Loss of profit

If, at the time of making the contract, the seller knew or may be presumed to have known that goods were to be used to produce a profit, and the breach of warranty precludes or reduces the profit likely to have been made, the buyer may recover damages for the loss of profit caused by the breach.[182] Such a buyer who brings an action for breach of warranty in respect of the quality or performance of goods sold to it cannot recover both the whole capital loss in the value of the goods and also the whole of the profit which it would have made by its use of them for this would be to allow the recovery of damages twice over. In *Cullinane v British 'Rema' Manufacturing Co Ltd*:[183]

C purchased from the defendants a clay pulverizing plant, warranted to be capable of pulverizing clay at the rate of six tons per hour. This warranty was not fulfilled, and C claimed

[176] *Slater v Hoyle & Smith Ltd* [1920] 2 KB 11, 23 (Scrutton LJ).

[177] Otton LJ preferred to distinguish it because in that case, in contrast to *Bence*, the same goods were sub-sold without any manufacturing process. However, as Auld LJ pointed out, this distinction is unconvincing on the facts of the two cases.

[178] *Bunge SA v Nidera BV* [2015] UKSC 43 at [23].

[179] [2018] EWCA Civ 1720, [2019] 1 All ER (Comm) 706.

[180] The defendant and third party were linked, but separate entities, and the contracts were not, strictly, string contracts either: *ibid* [73].

[181] Although contrast *Skyros Maritime Corp v Hapag-Lloyd AG* [2025] EWCA Civ 1529, where the Court of Appeal held that the owners of ships could claim damages at market rates for the late redelivery of their ships, even though the owners had made contractual promises to third parties not to charter their ships again: Males LJ held that such promises were '*res inter alios acta*'.

[182] *Richard Holden Ltd v Bostock & Co Ltd* (1902) 18 TLR 317.

[183] [1954] 1 QB 292. Cf *TC Industrial Plant Pty Ltd v Robert's (Queensland) Pty Ltd* [1964] ALR 1083 (Australia).

as damages (a) the difference between the purchase price of the plant and its residual value, and (b) his loss of profits from the date of installation to the date of trial of the action.

The Court of Appeal held that these claims could not be cumulative but must be alternative because the profits would only have been made if the capital expenditure had been incurred. C could claim one or other, but not both.

8. CLAIMANT'S CONTRIBUTORY NEGLIGENCE

(a) NO APPORTIONMENT AT COMMON LAW

As a general rule, where the claimant's loss has been caused partly by the defendant's breach of contract and partly by the claimant's own blameworthy conduct, the damages are not reduced[184] unless the claimant's conduct breaks the chain of causation[185] or constitutes a failure in the claimant's duty to mitigate its loss[186] or itself amounts to a breach of contract.[187]

(b) LAW REFORM (CONTRIBUTORY NEGLIGENCE) ACT 1945

The 1945 Act applies to reduce damages, where the claimant has been at fault in relation to his or her own damage. Damages are reduced proportionately taking into account both the causal potency and comparative blameworthiness of the parties' conduct.[188] The Act plainly applies to claims brought in tort. As regards breach of contract, the interpretation of the definition of 'fault' in the 1945 Act has led to a tripartite classification of claims.[189] The Act does not apply to the breach of a strict contractual duty (category one)[190] nor does it apply to the breach of a duty of care imposed by the contract which does not give rise to a liability in tort (category two).[191] However, the Act does apply to the breach of a duty of care imposed by the contract where there is concurrent liability in the tort of negligence,

[184] See generally Law Com No 219, *Contributory Negligence as a Defence in Contract* (1993).

[185] *Quinn v Burch Bros (Builders) Ltd* [1966] 2 QB 370; *Lambert v Lewis* [1982] AC 225; *Schering Agrochemicals Ltd v Reisbel NV SA* (1992, CA), noted by Burrows (1993) 109 LQR 175; *Borealis AB v Geogas Trading SA* [2010] EWHC 2789 (Comm), [2011] 1 Lloyd's Rep 482. See above, p 556.

[186] See above, pp 569–71.

[187] *Tennant Radiant Heat Ltd v Warrington Development Corp* [1988] 1 EGLR 41; *Harper v Ashton's Circus Pty Ltd* [1972] 2 NSWLR 395.

[188] See, eg, *Davies v Swan Motor Co (Swansea) Ltd* [1949] 2 KB 291, 326.

[189] This classification was first put forward by Hobhouse J, and confirmed by the Court of Appeal in *Forsikringsaktieselskapet Vesta v Butcher* [1986] 2 All ER 488, [1989] AC 852, aff'd on a different point [1989] AC 880, HL.

[190] *Schering Agrochemicals Ltd v Reisbel NVSA* (1992, CA), noted by Burrows (1993) 109 LQR 175; *Barclays Bank plc v Fairclough Building Ltd* [1995] QB 214.

[191] *Forsikringsaktieselskapet Vesta v Butcher* [1989] AC 852, 866; *Raflatac Ltd v Eade* [1999] 1 Lloyd's Rep 506. Cf *Clark Boyce v Mouat* [1992] 2 NZLR 559, 564, revs'd on other grounds [1994] 1 AC 428.

as where services are negligently rendered to a client by lawyers, builders, or carriers (category three).[192]

While this position is not entirely logical, particularly in respect of breaches of contractual obligations to exercise reasonable care where the defendant's liability exists solely in contract,[193] it has been argued that permitting apportionment in contract cases would allow Courts to vary an agreed allocation of risks. It has also been said that existing contract doctrines, in particular implied terms obliging claimants to take care for their own interests, mitigation, and causation, recognize and give effect to the principle that account should be taken of the fact that it is the claimant who is part author of the loss suffered. Those who take this view, while recognizing that these doctrines operate in an 'all or nothing' manner either allowing full recovery or no recovery, believe that apportionment would unduly undermine the certainty which is important in the English law of contract. The Law Commission accepted that this would be so in the (category one) case of a breach of a strict contractual duty but recommended that apportionment should be available in (category two) cases where the defendant is in breach of a purely contractual obligation to exercise reasonable care.[194] However, since the authoritative acceptance of concurrent liability in contract and tort,[195] it will be very rare for a case to fall within category two rather than category three so that the Law Commission's recommendation would, in practice, make very little difference to the law and has no prospect of being implemented.

9. THE TAX ELEMENT IN DAMAGES

Since damages are designed to compensate the claimant for the actual loss suffered and no more, any liability to pay tax may have to be taken into account. In *British Transport Commission v Gourley*,[196] where G claimed for loss of earnings arising out of personal injuries caused by negligence, the House of Lords held that damages awarded to G on the basis of his gross earnings before deduction of income tax and surtax (£37,720) should be reduced by the amount which he would have had to pay in tax. G was therefore left

[192] *Forsikringsaktieselskapet Vesta v Butcher* [1989] AC 852, which was held to be 'correctly decided and has a sound basis in principle' by the Privy Council in *Primeo Fund v Bank of Bermuda (Cayman) Ltd* [2023] UKPC 40, [2024] AC 727 at [353]. Cf the different conclusion of the High Court of Australia in *Astley v Austrust Ltd* (1999) 197 CLR 1 which was rejected in *Primeo*: see generally [2023] UKPC 40 at [288]–[353]. It is not settled whether the 1945 Act applies where the claimant has a right of action in tort which is not coextensive with the one it has in contract. The Law Commission concluded that the Act does not apply: Law Com No 219 (1993) para 3.29. Cf *Vacwell Engineering Co Ltd v BDH Chemicals Ltd* [1971] 1 QB 88 and *Bank of Nova Scotia v Hellenic Mutual War Risks Association (Bermuda) Ltd* [1988] 1 Lloyd's Rep 514, 555, [1990] 1 QB 818, revs'd on other grounds [1992] 1 AC 233, 266.

[193] In those circumstances there is an odd incentive for the *defendant* to argue that it did not just breach a strict contractual duty, but was also at fault and committed a tort, in order to avail itself of the defence of contributory negligence: see *Barclays Bank Plc v Fairclough Building Ltd (No 3)* (1995) 44 Con LR 35.

[194] Law Com No 219 (1993) Parts III and IV.

[195] *Henderson v Merrett Syndicates Ltd* [1995] 2 AC 145. See above, p 25.

[196] [1956] AC 185.

with a *net* sum of £6,695. This principle has subsequently been applied to contractual claims arising out of the wrongful dismissal of an employee[197] and to a claim for loss of profits on a contract for the purchase of goods.[198] Before it can be applied, however, two conditions must be satisfied: first, the earnings or profits in respect of which the claim is made must be subject to tax; secondly, the sum awarded as damages must either not be subject to tax in the claimant's hands or, if it is, the tax payable on the damages must be taken into account in assessing the damages.

The first requirement means that the principle in *Gourley*'s case does not apply to a claim in respect of the loss of a capital asset, for this would not have been subject to income tax.[199] The second excludes from its operation most claims for loss of profit, for sums awarded as damages for loss of profit are normally subject to tax (at the same rate) in the claimant's hands as part of the profits of his or her business.[200] The *Gourley* case itself has been the subject of considerable criticism. It is said, for example, that it has added needless complexity to the assessment of damages; and that the Courts treat damages for loss of earnings arising out of personal injuries as taxable income, whereas the Legislature exempts them, in part, from tax as being compensation for the loss of what may be called 'natural capital equipment'.[201] Nevertheless, the *Gourley* case is fully in accord with the avowed compensatory aim of damages and should remain good law.[202]

10. INTEREST

Until recently, the position at common law was that the general loss of use of money (ie interest) could not be awarded as damages for the late payment of money.[203] In general,[204] therefore, parties to a contract would have to rely either on a term of the contract, express or implied,[205] requiring the payment of interest or on the statutory power to award interest on debts and damages conferred by section 35A of the Senior

[197] *Beach v Reed Corrugated Cases Ltd* [1956] 1 WLR 807; *Re Houghton Main Colliery Co Ltd* [1959] 1 WLR 1219; *Phipps v Orthodox Unit Trusts Ltd* [1958] 1 QB 314. But under the Income Tax (Earnings and Pensions) Act 2003, ss 401–403, damages for wrongful dismissal are made taxable in the claimant's hands, save that tax is not chargeable on the first £30,000 of such payment. It has been held that the rule in *Gourley*'s case nevertheless continues to apply to the exempted amount: *Parsons v BNM Laboratories Ltd* [1964] 1 QB 95; *Bold v Brough, Nicholson & Hall Ltd* [1964] 1 WLR 201; *Lyndale Fashion Manufacturers v Rich* [1973] 1 WLR 73; *Shove v Downs Surgical plc* [1984] ICR 582.

[198] *Amstrad plc v Seagate Technology Inc* (1998) 86 BLR 34.

[199] *Hull & Co Ltd v Pearlberg* [1956] 1 WLR 244. Capital gains tax is to be disregarded.

[200] *Diamond v Campbell-Jones* [1961] Ch 22; *Dickinson v Jones Alexander* [1993] 2 FLR 521.

[201] See Baxter (1956) 19 MLR 373; Hall (1957) 73 LQR 212; Jolowicz [1959] CLJ 85; Tucker, *ibid*, 185; Bishop and Kay (1987) 103 LQR 211; Kerridge (1992) 108 LQR 433, 442–5.

[202] This was also the view of the Law Reform Committee in its 7th Report (Cmd 501, 1958).

[203] *London, Chatham and Dover Railway Co v South Eastern Railway Co* [1893] AC 429; *President of India v La Pintada Co Nav* [1985] AC 104.

[204] Specific losses caused by not receiving money or receiving it late, eg interest charges paid on taking out a loan, have been recovered as 'special damages' where not too remote within the second rule in *Hadley v Baxendale* (1854) 9 Ex 341: *Wadsworth v Lydall* [1981] 1 WLR 598. Cf *President of India v Lips Maritime Corp, The Lips* [1988] AC 395 (currency exchange losses).

[205] *Re Marquis of Angelsey* [1901] 2 Ch 548.

Courts Act 1981. That section enables the High Court[206] to include in any sum for which judgment is given simple (but not compound) interest at such rate as the Court thinks fit or as rules of Court may provide, on all or any part of the debt or damages for which judgment is given for all or any part of the period between the date when the cause of action arose and the date of the judgment. Further, if the debtor pays the debt after the institution of proceedings but before judgment, the Court has a similar power to award interest in respect of the period between the date when the cause of action arose and the date of payment.

However, the common law rule barring interest as damages was swept aside by the House of Lords, albeit arguably in *obiter dicta*, in *Sempra Metals Ltd v IRC*.[207] Interest, including compound interest, can now be awarded as damages where the loss of use, at the rate claimed, is proved and subject to the normal limitations, such as remoteness and the duty to mitigate.

The Late Payment of Commercial Debts (Interest) Act 1998 provides that it is an implied term in contracts for the supply of goods or services (other than consumer credit agreements or contracts intended to operate by way of security) where both parties are acting in the course of a business,[208] that any 'qualifying debt' created by the contract carries simple interest from the day after 'the relevant day'[209] at a rate prescribed by the Secretary of State.[210] The interest may be remitted, wholly or in part, because of the creditor's conduct.[211] Where the contract provides a 'substantial remedy' for late payment of the debt, the parties are permitted to oust or vary the right to statutory interest.[212] A remedy is to be regarded as 'substantial' unless it is insufficient for the purpose of compensating for or for deterring late payment, and it would not be 'fair or reasonable' to allow it to be relied on to oust or vary the right to statutory interest.[213]

Where the relationship between the creditor and the debtor is not purely contractual but also gives rise to equitable duties, such as where the parties are in a fiduciary

[206] For the county court, see analogously the County Courts Act 1984, s 69.

[207] [2007] UKHL 34, [2008] 1 AC 561. The actual award of compound interest in the case was an award of restitution in the law of unjust enrichment and was not an award of compensatory damages for a wrong. Without affecting what was said on damages, the decision in the law of unjust enrichment was overruled in *Prudential Assurance Co v HMRC* [2018] UKSC 39, [2019] AC 929.

[208] This includes a profession and the activities of government: s 2(7).

[209] The period from when the statutory interest runs—which turns on the definition of the 'relevant day'—is extremely complex. It is principally laid down in s 4 (and for advance payments in s 11) of the 1998 Act but complexity has been added by the amendments to s 4 by the Late Payment of Commercial Debts Regulations 2013 (SI 2013 No 395) and the Late Payment of Commercial Debts (Amendment) Regulations 2015 (SI 2015 No 1336). By s 4 it appears that where no date for payment has been agreed, the interest normally runs from 30 days after the date (which, for shorthand, may be referred to as the 'performance/notice date') on which the creditor performed or on which the debtor had notice of the amount of the debt, whichever is the later: but if the parties have agreed a date for payment, interest runs from the day after that date or, if earlier than the agreed payment date, 60 days from the performance/notice date (or if the debtor is a public authority 30 days from the performance/notice date). By reason of s 3(2) interest under this Act does not run after there is a judgment debt because then the Judgments Act 1838, s 17 applies.

[210] The rate of interest has been fixed at the base rate plus 8 per cent: SI 2002 No 1675.

[211] s 5.

[212] ss 1(3) and 7–10.

[213] s 9. For an application of this, see *Yuanda (UK) Co Ltd v WW Gear Construction Ltd* [2010] EWHC 720 (TCC), [2011] 1 All ER (Comm) 550.

relationship, then interest, including not only simple interest but also compound interest, has long been recoverable in certain circumstances even in the absence of any agreement or custom to that effect.[214]

11. NEGOTIATING DAMAGES

We have seen that compensation for breach of contract is assessed using the expectation measure; and that the reliance measure is best viewed as merely a method of assessing that expectation measure. However, in some cases the Courts have adopted a different approach which, instead of thinking about what the claimant has lost by reason of the non-performance, looks instead at the price that the claimant could reasonably have charged the defendant, had the defendant approached the claimant prior to breach, to release the defendant from the contractual duty that has been broken. These damages have been referred to by several different labels, such as '*Wrotham Park* damages' (named after the case examined below), 'hypothetical release damages', or, as the Supreme Court now prefers, 'negotiating damages'.[215]

In *Wrotham Park Estate Ltd v Parkside Homes Ltd*,[216] houses had been built in breach of a restrictive covenant. Brightman J refused to grant a mandatory injunction ordering the houses to be pulled down given the social waste that would have involved. But he did make an award of substantial damages. The important point is that the diminution in value of the claimant's land caused by the breach of covenant was zero. Assessing compensatory damages in the normal way, by considering what the claimant's position would have been had there been no breach of covenant and the houses not been built, would have led to a nominal award only. Nevertheless, substantial damages were awarded by Brightman J: he assessed damages by the price which the claimant could reasonably have demanded for releasing the defendant from the restrictive covenant had the defendant approached the claimant prior to building the houses.

The damages were actually given in substitution for the mandatory injunction under what was Lord Cairns' Act 1858 and is now section 50 of the Senior Courts Act 1981 so that they were 'equitable damages', not standard common law damages. But there have been several subsequent cases where negotiating damages have been awarded at common law where no injunction was sought or denied.

There have been two main uncertainties about 'negotiating damages' (which have been awarded for torts and equitable wrongs as well as breach of contract). First, what is the purpose of negotiating damages? Are they compensatory (ie covering the claimant's loss)? Or are they restitutionary (ie reversing gains made by the defendant)? Secondly, when can such damages be awarded (ie what is their availability)?

[214] *Wallersteiner v Moir (No 2)* [1975] QB 373, 388; *Re Fox, Walker & Co* (1880) 15 Ch D 400 (surety). For a wider view of the equitable jurisdiction, see *Westdeutsche Landesbank Girozentrale v Islington LBC* [1996] AC 669, 695–6 (Lord Goff, dissenting) and 719–21, 735–6 (Lord Woolf, dissenting). Cf the majority, *ibid*, 717, 718–19, 737–41.

[215] See generally Burrows, *Remedies for Torts, Breach of Contract, and Equitable Wrongs* (4th edn, 2019) ch 18.

[216] [1974] 1 WLR 798.

In *Morris-Garner v One Step (Support) Ltd*[217] the Supreme Court sought to answer both those questions in the context of a claim for breach of contract.

The claimant, One Step (Support) Ltd, was in the business of providing support for young people leaving care. Karen Morris-Garner, the first defendant, was a 50% shareholder and director of that company and the second defendant, Andrea Morris-Garner, was manager of that company. When both left the company, and the first defendant sold her shares in it, each entered into three-year covenants with the company promising not to compete with it or solicit the company's clients and to keep certain information about the company confidential. The defendants had in fact already set up a competing company (Positive Living Ltd) of which they were the sole shareholders and, after the defendants left One Step, Positive Living started to trade in competition with One Step. Through that trading, the defendants were acting in breach of their non-competition and non-solicitation covenants, and the first defendant was acting in breach of the confidentiality clause. Positive Living was very successful and was sold by the defendants, some three years after starting trading, for £12.8m. One Step, meanwhile, suffered a significant downturn in its business.

In the claimant's action for breach of contract, it was estimated by the claimant's expert that the loss to the claimant's business (ie the loss of profits) caused by the defendants' breach of the non-competition covenant (and, incidentally, the other covenants) was between £3.4 million and £4.6 million. But the claimant argued that it was entitled to '*Wrotham Park* damages' with the hypothetical release fee from the covenants being estimated by the claimant's expert as being between £5.6 million and £6.3 million.

While at first instance and in the Court of Appeal the claimant succeeded in its argument that it was entitled to elect for negotiating damages, rather than normal compensatory damages, that argument was unanimously rejected by the Supreme Court. In remitting the assessment of damages back to the trial judge, it was held that negotiating damages were not here available as an alternative measure of damages (albeit that a hypothetical release fee might be used as evidence in calculating ordinary compensatory damages for the claimant's loss of business). The leading judgment was given by Lord Reed, who held as follows. The purpose of negotiating damages is to compensate the claimant for a loss.[218] They are not restitutionary. As regards availability, there are two categories of case in which negotiating damages can be awarded. First, where the damages are being given (for a future or anticipated wrong) in substitution for an injunction (or specific performance) under section 50 of the Senior Courts Act; and secondly, where the wrong in question constitutes the infringement of a property right or a closely analogous right. On the facts, neither category was in play. Hence negotiating damages could not here be awarded.

[217] [2018] UKSC 20, [2019] AC 649.

[218] The best-known compensatory analysis is by Sharpe and Waddams (1982) 2 OJLS 290. But this has been criticized as sometimes being fictional: see, eg, Burrows, in Saidov and Cunnington (eds), *Contract Damages* (2008) 165 and Rotherham [2008] LMCLQ 25.

That reasoning is controversial. In particular, it is not clear which rights count as closely analogous to proprietary rights. Lord Reed said that such damages were appropriate provided 'the breach of contract results in the loss of a valuable asset created or protected by the right which was infringed'.[219] However, it is not clear what precisely is meant by this and, in particular, it is not clear why the facts of the *One Step* case did not fall within those words.[220] Why could one not say that the purpose of the non-competition covenant was to protect the claimant against the loss of a valuable asset namely business profit, including goodwill?

12. AGREED DAMAGES CLAUSES

(a) LIQUIDATED DAMAGES AND PENALTIES

The parties to a contract not infrequently make provision in the contract for the damages to be paid on a breach of contract.[221] Such provision does not exclude the application of the general rule that damages for breach are intended to compensate for the actual loss sustained by the claimant. It is a question of the proper construction of the contract to decide whether a sum fixed by the parties, however they may have described it, is a 'penalty', in which case it cannot be recovered, or a genuine attempt to 'liquidate', that is to say, to reduce to certainty, prospective damages of an uncertain amount, in which case the sum will be recoverable.

The rule against penalties originated in equity which would relieve against penalties, cutting them down to the actual loss suffered, but was taken up and applied by the common law, and reinforced by statute.[222] Under the traditional test, enunciated in 1915 by Lord Dunedin in *Dunlop Pneumatic Tyre Co Ltd v New Garage and Motor Co Ltd*,[223] the Court will accept as liquidated damages the sum fixed by the parties if it is a genuine pre-estimate of the loss which seems likely to be caused if the breach provided for should occur. The question is one of construction, to be decided upon the terms and inherent circumstances of each particular contract, judged as at the time of making the contract, not as at the time of breach.[224] If, although it is not an estimate of the probable loss, the parties had fixed that sum because they were agreed in limiting the damages recoverable to an amount less than that which a breach would probably cause, it will similarly be accepted by the Court.[225]

219 [2018] UKSC 20, [2019] AC 649 at [92]. For further judicial analysis of this category, see *Priyanka Shipping Ltd v Glory Bulk Carriers Pte Ltd* [2019] EWHC 2804 (Comm) (no negotiating damages for breach of a promise not to trade with a vessel being bought).

220 Cf *Experience Hendrix LLC v PPX Enterprises Inc* [2003] EWCA Civ 323, [2003] 1 All ER (Comm) 830, which Lord Reed (at [89]) thought was rightly decided. See Davies [2018] LMCLQ 433.

221 *Triple Point Technology Inc v PTT Public Company Ltd* [2021] UKSC 29, [2021] AC 1148 at [35] (Lady Arden), [74] (Lord Leggatt).

222 8 & 9 Will III, c 11 (an Act for the better preventing frivolous and vexatious Suits), s 8. For history, see *Wall v Rederiaktiebolaget Luggude* [1915] 3 KB 66, 72–3; Simpson (1966) 82 LQR 392.

223 [1915] AC 79.

224 *Ibid*; *Phillips Hong Kong Ltd v A-G of Hong Kong* (1993) 61 BLR 41 (PC).

225 *Cellulose Acetate Silk Co Ltd v Widnes Foundry (1925) Ltd* [1933] AC 20.

The Supreme Court reconsidered the law on penalties in *Cavendish Square Holding BV v Talal El Makdessi* ('*Makdessi*') and *ParkingEye Ltd v Beavis* ('*ParkingEye*').[226] It was made clear that, although a stipulated sum is not a genuine pre-estimate of loss, it is not a penalty if it protects a legitimate interest of the claimant in the performance of the contract and is not out of all proportion in doing so. In other words, the traditional focus on (non-excessive) compensation is only one of the legitimate interests that the claimant may protect. Lord Neuberger and Lord Sumption stated that 'The true test is whether the impugned provision is a secondary obligation which imposes a detriment on the contract-breaker out of all proportion to any legitimate interest of the innocent party in the enforcement of the primary obligation.'[227]

In the *Makdessi* case:

M agreed to sell to C a majority interest in a company. A large part of the price reflected goodwill. A clause in the contract stated that if M became a defaulting shareholder, he would not receive any further payment in respect of the price (Clause 5.1). Various restrictive covenants which set out when a shareholder would be in default. A further clause granted C a right to buy M's remaining shareholding if M became a defaulting shareholder; the price was to be calculated by reference to the net asset value of the company, without incorporating the goodwill value (Clause 5.6).

All the judges agreed that if the rule against penalties was engaged[228] these clauses were not penal. Clause 5.1 had no relationship with the measure of loss attributable to the breach of contract, but this was not crucial, and the contrary suggestion of Lord Dunedin in the *Dunlop* case was criticized. Their Lordships found that C had a legitimate interest in ensuring that the restrictive covenants were respected, and the goodwill of the business was of critical value to C. The loyalty of M was crucial to the goodwill, and the clause was not extravagant or unconscionable in seeking to achieve the legitimate aim of ensuring that M's loyalty and the goodwill were properly maintained. The same conclusion was reached as regards Clause 5.6 for similar reasons. It was commercially legitimate for C not to pay for the value of goodwill if M defaulted such that his efforts and connections were no longer available for the benefit of the company. The purpose of both Clauses 5.6 and 5.1 may have been to deter breach, but this did not make the clauses penal since they were not extravagant or unconscionable.

In the *ParkingEye* case:

P ran a car park at a retail park. Customers who parked at the car park had a contract with ParkingEye. The terms of the contract stated that there was a '2 hour max stay', and that parking was free during that 2-hour period. Staying longer than 2 hours would lead to a

[226] [2015] UKSC 67, [2016] AC 1172. See generally Burrows, *Remedies for Torts, Breach of Contract, and Equitable Wrongs* (4th edn, 2019) 388–97.

[227] [2015] UKSC 67, [2016] AC 1172 at [32]. See also the similar formulations of Lord Mance at [152]; and Lord Hodge at [255] supported by Lord Toulson at [293].

[228] Lord Neuberger and Lord Sumption (with whom Lord Carnwath agreed) thought that the clauses were in any event primary, not secondary, obligations so that they fell outside the penalty jurisdiction (see below, p 572). But a majority (Lords Mance, Hodge, Clarke, and Toulson) took a different view on this point.

'Parking Charge' of £85. B left his car in the car park for nearly 3 hours, and P sued for the Parking Charge of £85.

The Supreme Court held that the parking charge was not a penalty but was justified by two legitimate objectives. The first was to manage the efficient use of the parking spaces by deterring commuters or other long-stay motorists from parking for long periods of time, which would reduce the space available to other members of the public. The second was to provide an income stream to P. Both objectives meant that P had a legitimate interest in charging motorists who stayed longer than 2 hours. Lord Neuberger and Lord Sumption emphasized that 'deterrence is not penal if there is a legitimate interest in influencing the conduct of the contracting party which is not satisfied by the mere right to recover damages for breach of contract'.[229] The detriment imposed on B was not out of all proportion to those legitimate interests.

In clarifying the law in this way, the Supreme Court may be regarded as having built on the approach articulated in *Lordsvale Finance plc v Bank of Zambia*,[230] and followed in a number of subsequent cases.[231] In *Lordsvale*, Colman J said that a clause would be upheld if it was 'commercially justifiable, provided always that its dominant purpose was not to deter the other party from breach'. However, the Supreme Court stressed that it is unhelpful to regard deterrence as objectionable. It has replaced the notion of 'commercial justification' with an emphasis on protecting a legitimate interest and doing so proportionately.

Lord Dunedin's traditional 'genuine pre-estimate of loss' test will no doubt continue to be the usual means of determining whether a clause is a penalty or not, particularly in simple damages clauses in standard contracts.[232] But the important step taken by the Supreme Court is to make it clear that the underpinning and wider principle is one of legitimate interest and proportionality. The general trend appears to be one of upholding all but the most extreme clauses in commercial contracts.[233]

In construing the terms 'penalty' and 'liquidated damages' when inserted in a contract, the Courts will not be bound by the phraseology used, but will look to the substance rather than to the form. The parties may call the sum specified 'liquidated damages' if they wish, but if the Court finds it to be a penalty, it will be treated as such. Conversely, if the parties had described the sum fixed as a 'penalty', but it turns out to be a genuine pre-estimate of the loss, it will be treated as liquidated damages.[234]

229 [2015] UKSC 67, [2016] AC 1172 at [99].

230 [1996] QB 752, 764.

231 eg *Murray v Leisureplay plc* [2005] EWCA Civ 963, [2005] IRLR 946; *Lansat Shipping Co Ltd v Glencore Grain BV, The Paragon* [2009] EWCA Civ 855, [2009] 2 Lloyd's Rep 688.

232 [2015] UKSC 67, [2016] AC 1172 at [22]. See also *Triple Point Technology Inc v PTT Public Co Ltd* [2019] EWCA Civ 230 at [68]–[71]; *Armstead v Royal & Sun Alliance Insurance Company Ltd* [2024] UKSC 6, [2025] AC 406 at [49].

233 *Houssein v London Credit Ltd* [2024] EWCA Civ 721. Cf *Vivienne Westwood Ltd v Conduit Street Development Ltd* [2017] EWHC 350 (Ch). For the advantages of such clauses, including avoiding difficulties of measuring loss and the inability of the penalty rule accurately to identify unfairness, leading to the argument that such clauses should be upheld subject to standard factors invalidating a contract or contract terms, see Goetz and Scott (1977) 77 Col L Rev 554; Rea (1984) 13 JLS 147; Downes, in Birks (ed), *Wrongs and Remedies in the Twenty-First Century* (1996) ch 11; Chen-Wishart, in the same publication, ch 12. But cf Fenton (1975/6) 51 Ind L Rev 189, 191–2.

234 *Cellulose Acetate Silk Co Ltd v Widnes Foundry (1925) Ltd* [1933] AC 20. See also *Union Eagle Ltd v Golden Achievement Ltd* [1997] AC 514; *Britvic Soft Drinks Ltd v Messer UK Ltd* [2002] 1 Lloyd's Rep 20.

Alongside the common law rules, in consumer contracts Part 2 of the Consumer Rights Act 2015[235] allows the Courts to protect consumers against unfair terms by, for example, holding that such terms are not binding on the consumer. One of the examples given of a term that may be unfair is one requiring any consumer who fails to fulfil his obligation to pay a disproportionately high sum in compensation.[236] In respect of sums payable on breach, it is likely that the 2015 Act will be construed so as to be consistent with the common law on liquidated damages and penalties. This is borne out by *ParkingEye*[237] in which, for much the same reasons as relied on in deciding that the parking charge was not a penalty, it was decided that the term was fair (applying the now repealed Unfair Terms in Consumer Contracts Regulations 1999).

(b) APPLICATION OF THE TRADITIONAL TEST

The leading case on the traditional test[238] is *Dunlop Pneumatic Tyre Co Ltd v New Garage and Motor Co Ltd*:[239]

The appellant sold motor tyre-covers, tyres, and tubes to the respondent which contracted not to resell them, or offer them for sale, at a price below the appellant's list prices and to pay the sum of £5 by way of liquidated damages for every breach of this agreement. The respondent sold a tyre-cover at less than the list price, and was sued by the appellant for liquidated damages for breach.

The House of Lords held that the sum fixed by the parties was a genuine pre-estimate of the loss which might ensue and not a penalty. In the course of his speech Lord Dunedin laid down the following rules:[240]

(i) 'It will be held to be a penalty if the sum stipulated for is extravagant and unconscionable in amount in comparison with the greatest loss that could conceivably be proved to have followed from the breach.'

An illustration was provided by the Earl of Halsbury in an earlier case, where he said:[241]

For instance, if you agreed to build a house in a year, and agreed that if you did not build the house for £50, you were to pay a million of money as penalty, the extravagance of that would be at once apparent.

The question is one of fact in each particular case.[242]

(ii) 'It will be held to be a penalty if the breach consists only in not paying a sum of money, and the sum stipulated is a sum greater than the sum which ought to have been paid.'

[235] See above, pp 226–36. [236] Sched 2, para 5. [237] [2015] UKSC 67, [2016] AC 1172.
[238] For the continued relevance of this, see above, n 232. [239] [1915] AC 79. [240] *Ibid*, 87.
[241] *Clydebank Engineering and Shipbuilding Co Ltd v Don Jose Ramos Yzquierdo y Castaneda* [1905] AC 6, 10.
[242] In *Jeancharm Ltd v Barnet Football Club Ltd* [2003] EWCA Civ 58 (2003) 92 Con LR 26 a clause requiring the contract-breaker to pay interest that amounted to a rate of 260 per cent was struck down as a penalty.

In *Kemble v Farren*:[243]

The defendant agreed to perform at the Covent Garden Theatre for four seasons at £3 6*s* 8*d* a night. The contract provided that if either party refused to fulfil the agreement or any part thereof, such party should pay to the other the sum of £1,000 as 'liquidated damages'. The defendant refused to perform during the second season.

It was held that the stipulation was penal. The obligation to pay £1,000 might have arisen upon a failure to pay £3 6*s* 8*d* and was therefore a penalty. The most obvious example of this presumption is where a borrower of money promises to pay the lender an additional sum (over and above interest) if the money is not repaid by a fixed day. In contrast, 'accelerated payment' clauses, which are common in sales by instalments and leasing arrangements and which accelerate an *existing* liability to pay on default, are not invalid as penalties.[244]

(iii) 'There is a presumption (but no more) that it is a penalty when a single lump sum is made payable by way of compensation, on the occurrence of one or more of all of several events, some of which may occasion serious and others but trifling damage.'

An illustration is offered by *Ford Motor Co v Armstrong*:[245]

A retailer of motor-cars agreed with a manufacturer inter alia not to sell any one of the manufacturer's cars, or any part, below the listed price. For every breach of this agreement he was to pay £250, as 'agreed damages'.

A majority of the Court of Appeal held that this was a penalty. The defendant might have become bound to pay the sum of £250 for the breach of a term which would cause only trifling damage. Similarly, in *Kemble v Farren*, the same factor provided an additional reason for the Court to hold that the £1,000 was a penalty because that very large sum was to become immediately payable if 'the defendant had refused to conform to any usual regulation of the theatre, however minute or unimportant'.[246]

A single sum, as opposed to a sum proportioned to the seriousness of the breach (eg per week for delay or per item for items sold in breach of covenant), is presumed to be penal because one tests it against the least serious breach possible. The presumption does not apply where the sum is payable for breach of a single obligation which can be broken in a number of ways, for example non-completion of a building contract.[247] Where it is difficult to estimate the loss and it is therefore uncertain that losses from one breach would be greater than those from another, a Court may hold that the presumption is rebutted. It may also be rebutted where it is clear that the contractual provision has sought to average out the probable losses from all the breaches provided, however, that the disparity is not too great.[248]

[243] (1829) 6 Bing 141.

[244] *Protector Loan Co v Grice* (1880) 5 QBD 529; *O'Dea v All States Leasing System Pty Ltd* (1983) 152 CLR 359; *The Angelic Star* [1988] 1 Lloyd's Rep 122.

[245] (1915) 31 TLR 267.

[246] (1829) 6 Bing 141, 148.

[247] *Law v Local Board of Redditch* [1892] 1 QB 127.

[248] *Dunlop Pneumatic Tyre Co Ltd v New Garage and Motor Co Ltd* [1915] AC 79, 99; *English Hop Growers v Dering* [1928] 2 KB 174.

On the other hand:

(iv) 'It is no obstacle to the sum stipulated being a genuine pre-estimate of damage, that the consequences of the breach are such as to make precise pre-estimation almost an impossibility.'

For example, in the *Dunlop Tyre* case itself, the stipulated sum of £5 could only, at the most, be a very rough and ready estimate of the possible damage which might be suffered if a trader undercut the manufacturer's listed price. In public works contracts, such as those for the construction of roads or tunnels, the nature of the loss may in part be non-financial and therefore be particularly difficult to evaluate: in *Phillips Hong Kong Ltd v Attorney-General of Hong Kong* a clause using a formula based on estimates, of the loss of return on the capital at a daily rate, the effect of the delay on related contracts, and increased costs, was said to be sensible.[249]

Applying the traditional test, all these rules were no more than presumptions as to the intention of the parties; they could be rebutted by evidence of a contrary intention, appearing from a consideration of the contract as a whole.[250]

(c) NECESSITY FOR BREACH

At common law the question whether the sum of money or other performance[251] stipulated for is a penalty or liquidated damages can only arise when the event upon which it becomes payable is a *breach of the contract between the parties*.[252] It does not therefore arise where the obligation is a true alternative mode of performing the contract.[253] However, it has been held that a 'take or pay' clause, whereby a buyer agreed to pay for a minimum quantity of goods per month whether it had ordered that minimum quantity or not, does fall within the scope of the rule against penalties although on the facts the clause in question was not a penalty.[254]

The distinction between clauses within and outside the penalty jurisdiction has given rise to litigation in the context of hire-purchase agreements. Finance companies sometimes provide that, in the event of termination of the agreement, not only shall they be entitled to take possession of the goods hired and to forfeit instalments already

[249] (1993) 61 BLR 41 (PC).

[250] *Pye v British Automobile Commercial Syndicate Ltd* [1906] 1 KB 425.

[251] *Jobson v Johnson* [1989] 1 WLR 1026 (transfer of shares); *Cavendish Square Holdings BV v El Makdessi* [2015] UKSC 67 at [16], [157]–[159], [170], [230]–[233] (transfer of property), [69]–[73], [154], [170], [226]–[228] (withholding a sum otherwise due). For the forfeiture of money paid, see below, pp 611–3.

[252] *Export Credits Guarantee Department v Universal Oil Products Co* [1983] 1 WLR 399; *Cavendish Square Holdings BV v El Makdessi* [2015] UKSC 65 at [12]–[13], [40]–[43], [239]–[241] (firmly rejecting the contrary view taken by the High Court of Australia in *Andrews v Australia and New Zealand Banking Group Ltd* [2012] HCA 30, (2012) 247 CLR 205, as has the Singapore Court of Appeal: *Denka Advantech Pte Ltd* v. *Seraya Energy Pte Ltd* [2020] SGCA 119, [2021] 1 SLR 631). See also *Office of Fair Trading v Abbey National plc* [2008] EWHC 875 (Comm), [2008] 2 All ER (Comm) 625 at [295]–[323] (bank charges not payable on breach and therefore could not be penalties).

[253] *Alder v Moore* [1961] 2 QB 57. See also *Golden Bay Realty v Orchard Investment* [1991] 1 WLR 981 (penalty rules not applicable to contract in statutory form).

[254] *M & J Polymers Ltd v Imerys Minerals Ltd* [2008] EWHC 344 (Comm), [2008] 1 Lloyd's Rep 541.

paid, but that the hirer shall also pay a certain sum as compensation for 'loss of profit on the transaction'. If the hiring is terminated as a result of a breach of the agreement by the hirer, the Courts may hold this payment to be a penalty.[255] But if it is terminated voluntarily by the hirer, or by his death or bankruptcy, so that there is no breach of the agreement, the question of a penalty or liquidated damages cannot arise.[256] At common law,[257] this may mean that it is more expensive for a hirer to terminate the agreement voluntarily than to repudiate and break the contract.

(d) AMOUNTS RECOVERABLE

Where the clause is a liquidated damages clause the claimant will recover the stipulated sum without being required to prove damage and irrespective of any actual damage, even where this is demonstrably smaller than the stipulated sum.[258] However, where the actual loss is greater, the claimant is limited to the stipulated sum. In *Cellulose Acetate Silk Co Ltd v Widnes Foundry (1925) Ltd*:

The appellant agreed to pay 'by way of penalty the sum of £20 per week for every week we exceed 18 weeks' in the completion of the delivery and erection of an acetone recovery plant. The work was completed 30 weeks late. Calculated on the agreed basis, the damages recoverable by the respondent on breach amounted to some £600, but its actual loss amounted to £5,850. It therefore claimed that it was entitled to disregard the penalty and to sue for the damages actually suffered.

It was, however, clear from the circumstances that the parties must have known that the damage which would be incurred might greatly exceed the stipulated sum. The House of Lords therefore held that the sum was not a penalty, but was liquidated damages and that damages must be limited to this agreed amount.[259]

Where a clause is held to be penal, the damages recoverable must be assessed in the usual way. Normally this will produce a lower award than the penalty. But it is possible for the claimant to recover a sum, equivalent to normal damages, that is greater than the stipulated penal sum.[260] It cannot be said that the clause has a penal effect in such

[255] *Bridge v Campbell Discount Co Ltd* [1962] AC 600; *Cooden Engineering Co Ltd v Stanford* [1953] 1 QB 86; *Financings Ltd v Baldock* [1963] 1 QB 887; *Lombard North Central plc v Butterworth* [1987] QB 527.

[256] *Bridge v Campbell Discount Co Ltd*, above, n 255, 613, 614, 625; cf Lord Denning at 631; *Goulston Discount Co v Harman* (1962) 106 SJ 369. See also *Alder v Moore* [1961] 2 QB 57; *Richco v AC Toepfer* [1991] 1 Lloyd's Rep 136.

[257] Contrast the Consumer Rights Act 2015, Sched 2, para 5. See also the Consumer Credit Act 1974, s 100 dealing with regulated hire-purchase and conditional sale agreements: where a debtor exercises its statutory right to terminate, its maximum liability, despite a higher agreed sum payable on termination (assuming it has taken reasonable care of the goods) is to pay what is needed to bring its payments up to half the purchase price, and the Court can further reduce this if the creditor's loss is less.

[258] *Wallis v Smith* (1882) 20 Ch D 243, 267.

[259] [1933] AC 20. See also *Diestal v Stevenson* [1906] 2 KB 345. Cf *AKT Reidar v Arcos* [1927] 1 KB 352 (unliquidated damages available in respect of breaches outside ambit of clause).

[260] *Wall v Rederiaktiebolaget Luggude* [1915] 3 KB 66; *Watts, Watts & Co v Mitsui* [1917] AC 227; *AMEV-UDC Finance Ltd v Austin* (1986) 162 CLR 344 (Australia). For criticism, see *Robophone Facilities v Blank* [1966] 1 WLR 1428, 1446; Law Com WP No 61 (1975) paras 46–8; Hudson (1974) 90 LQR 25, (1985) 101 LQR 480; Gordon (1974) 90 LQR 25.

circumstances and invalidating the penalty also means that a claimant who has acted unfairly by inserting a penal clause is treated more favourably than one whose clause is a genuine attempt to 'liquidate' prospective damages. However, this result can be seen as following from the principle that the validity of a clause is determined by reference to the time at which the contract is made.

FURTHER READING

Fuller and Perdue, 'The Reliance Interest in Contract Damages' (1936–37) 46 Yale LJ 52, 373

Ogus, Harris, and Phillips, 'Contract Remedies and the Consumer Surplus' (1979) 95 LQR 581

Sharpe and Waddams, 'Damages for the Lost Opportunity to Bargain' (1982) 2 OJLS 290

Friedmann, 'The Performance Interest in Contract Damages' (1995) 111 LQR 628

Cartwright, 'Remoteness of Damage in Contract and Tort: a Reconsideration' [1996] CLJ 488

Coote, 'Contract Damages, *Ruxley* and the Performance Interest' [1997] CLJ 537

Burrows, 'Limitations on Compensation' in Burrows and Peel (eds), *Commercial Remedies* (Oxford: Oxford University Press, 2003) 27–43

Kramer, 'An Agreement-Centred Approach to Remoteness and Contract Damages' in Cohen and McKendrick (eds), *Comparative Remedies for Breach of Contract* (Oxford: Hart Publishing, 2004) 249

Cunnington, 'Should Punitive Damages be Part of the Judicial Arsenal in Contract Cases?' (2006) 26 LS 369

Burrows, 'Are "Damages on the Wrotham Park Basis" Compensatory, Restitutionary or Neither?' in Saidov and Cunnington (eds), *Contract Damages* (Oxford: Hart Publishing, 2008) ch 7

Robertson, 'The Basis of the Remoteness Rule in Contract' (2008) 28 LS 172

Wee, 'Contractual Interpretation and Remoteness' [2010] LMCLQ 150

Hoffmann, '*The Achilleas*: Custom and Practice or Foreseeability?' (2010) Edin LR 47

Dyson and Kramer, 'There is No "Breach Date Rule": Mitigation, Difference in Value and Date of Assessment' (2014) 130 LQR 259

Burrows, 'Lord Hoffmann and Remoteness in Contract' in Davies and Pila (eds), *The Jurisprudence of Lord Hoffmann* (Oxford: Hart Publishing, 2015) 251–67

Mullan, 'Damages for Breach of Contract: Quantifying the Lost Consumer Surplus' (2016) 36 OJLS 83

Rowan, 'Cost of Cure Damages and the Relevance of the Injured Promisee's Intention to Cure' [2017] CLJ 616

Peel, 'Negotiating Damages After One Step' (2019) 35 JCL 216

Rowan, 'The "Legitimate Interest in Performance" in the Law on Penalties' [2019] CLJ 148

18

SPECIFIC REMEDIES

Under certain circumstances, a contractual promise may be enforced directly. This may be by an action for the agreed sum, by an order for specific performance of the obligation, or by an injunction to restrain the breach of a negative stipulation or to require the defendant to take positive steps to undo a breach of contract. These remedies have different historical roots: the claim for an agreed sum is a common law remedy whereas specific performance and injunctions are equitable remedies.

1. ACTIONS FOR THE AGREED SUM

Where it is agreed to sell goods for a certain price, for example, the seller may seek payment of the agreed price.[1] The claim, a liquidated claim for the precise sum, is for the payment of a debt. Although the award of an agreed sum orders the defendant to perform its positive contractual obligation to pay money, and in that sense is similar to specific performance, it is distinct from specific performance and does not attract the same bars.[2] The law of contract also draws a clear distinction between a claim for the agreed sum and a claim for damages for breach of contract. The claimant need prove no loss where the claim is for the payment of an agreed sum and rules, such as remoteness of damage and mitigation of loss, are irrelevant. However, a seller who suffers loss over and above the sum due may recover both the agreed sum and damages.[3]

An action for an agreed sum will not be available until the contractual duty to pay has arisen, whether expressly or impliedly.[4] Subject to any provision in the contract, in sale of goods, by section 49(1) and (2) of the Sale of Goods Act 1979, the seller is not entitled to the price unless the property in the goods has passed to the buyer or payment is due

1 Burrows, *Remedies for Torts, Breach of Contract, and Equitable Wrongs* (4th edn, 2019) ch 21.

2 But this remedy was incorrectly treated as if it were specific performance and hence subject to, eg, a want of mutuality bar in *Ministry of Sound (Ireland) Ltd v World Online Ltd* [2003] EWHC 2178 (Ch), [2003] 2 All ER (Comm) 823.

3 *Overstone Ltd v Shipway* [1962] 1 WLR 117. For interest on the agreed sum, including damages as interest, see above, pp 563–5.

4 *Mount v Oldham Corporation* [1973] QB 309 (implied term that school fees be paid in advance).

'on a day certain irrespective of delivery'.[5] In *PST Energy 7 Shipping LLC v OW Bunker Malta Ltd, The Res Cogitans*,[6] the dispute concerned the non-payment of the price by defendant shipowners for fuel bunkers acquired from the claimant. Under the contract, the claimant retained title to the bunkers until payment, although the defendant was permitted as bailee to 'consume' the fuel bunkers, and had done so, for the purposes of propulsion of the ship. The central question was whether the claimant's action for the price failed because, applying section 49 of the Sale of Goods Act 1979, title in the bunkers had not passed to the defendant and the price was not otherwise payable on a day certain. The Supreme Court held that this was not a contract for the sale of goods (rather it was a *sui generis* contract)[7] so that section 49 of the Sale of Goods Act 1979 did not apply. However, in *obiter dicta*, the Supreme Court took the view contrary to the Court of Appeal's decision in *Caterpillar (NI) Ltd v John Holt & Co (Liverpool) Ltd*[8] that, even if this had been a contract for the sale of goods, section 49 was not an exclusive regime for when the action for the price was payable. Rather the common law continued to exist outside section 49 and, under the common law, the price would here have been payable even though title in the bunkers had not passed. But such *obiter* comments are not binding on lower courts, which (with understandable reluctance) continue to apply the *Caterpillar* decision.[9]

The contractual duty to pay and the correlative right to payment may arise on entering the contract, as in the case of the deposits required in contracts for the sale of land,[10] or during the course of performance, as in the case of hire in charterparties[11] or progress payments in building contracts.[12] By the Apportionment Act 1870, all rents, annuities (including salaries and pensions), dividends, and other periodic payments in the nature of income shall be considered as accruing from day to day and are, subject to express contrary stipulation, apportionable in respect of time.[13]

Where the sum due is simply an advance payment of the price and was not required as security for due performance, the right to it is conditional upon subsequent completion of the contract. Where the contract is discharged before completion, the payment ceases to be due and the innocent party is relegated to its claim for damages.[14] Where the sum

[5] *Stein Forbes & Co Ltd v County Tailoring & Co Ltd* (1916) 86 LJKB 448 (provision for payment in cash 'against documents on arrival of steamer' means an action for the price can be brought before delivery of the goods).

[6] [2016] UKSC 23, [2016] AC 1034.

[7] For criticism see, eg, Goode, *Fundamental Concepts of Commercial Law* (2018) ch 14.

[8] [2013] EWCA Civ 1232, [2014] 1 WLR 2365.

[9] See, eg, *CE Energy DMCC v Bashar* [2025] EWHC 297 (Comm), [2025] 1 WLR 2810 at [65]. For a thorough review of the case law on s 49(2), see Appendix B to the judgment of Andrew Baker J in *Trans Trade RK SA v State Food and Grain Corp of Ukraine* [2025] EWHC 1803 (Comm).

[10] *Howe v Smith* (1884) 27 Ch D 89.

[11] *Leslie Shipping Co v Welstead* [1921] 3 KB 420.

[12] *Hyundai Heavy Industries Co Ltd v Papadopoulos* [1980] 1 WLR 1129; *Stocznia Gdanska SA v Latvian Shipping Co* [1998] 1 WLR 574 (ship-building contracts).

[13] Apportionment Act 1870, ss 2, 7.

[14] *Dies v British and International Mining and Finance Co Ltd* [1939] 1 KB 724; *McDonald v Dennys Lascelles* (1933) 48 CLR 457, 477; *Chinery v Viall* (1860) 5 H & N 288. On the position where the payment has been made, see below, pp 607–13.

due is a deposit or other sum required as security for due performance of the contract, as a general rule it remains payable where the contract has been discharged.[15] It makes no difference whether the accrued obligation is one in favour of the innocent or the guilty party, although a claim by the guilty party may be off-set by the innocent party's claim for damages. An employee who repudiates a contract of employment can nevertheless sue for wages earned before that time.[16]

The effect of a repudiatory breach by the party who will become liable to pay the agreed sum but before the agreed sum has fallen due has been considered in the context of discharge.[17] *White and Carter (Councils) Ltd v McGregor*[18] established that an injured party who can perform without the cooperation of the contract-breaker[19] has an almost unfettered option to hold the contract open, to perform, and to recover the sum once it becomes due. Admittedly Lord Reid indicated that that option is not available where it can be shown that the innocent party had 'no legitimate interest'[20] in performing the contract rather than claiming damages; and Kerr J subsequently expressed the same idea by saying that the innocent party could not hold the contract open to claim an agreed sum 'where damages would be an adequate remedy and where an election to keep the contract alive would be wholly unreasonable'.[21] However, this fetter or qualification on the innocent party's right to perform and create an entitlement to an agreed sum applies only in extreme cases.[22] After all, Lord Reid, who formulated the 'legitimate interest' exception in *White & Carter*, must have thought the pursuers in that case did have a legitimate interest, since otherwise he would have decided it differently. Yet *White &*

[15] *Dies v British and International Mining and Finance Co Ltd* [1939] 1 KB 724. See also *Hinton v Sparkes* (1868) LR 3 CP 161, 166; *Damon Compania Naveria v Hapag Lloyd* [1985] 1 WLR 435, 451; *Rover International Ltd v Cannon Film Sales Ltd (No 3)* [1989] 1 WLR 912, 924–5; *Griffon Shipping LLC v Firodi Shipping Ltd, The Griffon* [2013] EWCA Civ 1567, [2014] 1 Lloyd's Rep 471. See further, above, pp 534–6.

[16] *Taylor v Laird* (1856) 25 LJ Ex 329, above, p 41; Apportionment Act 1870, s 2. Cf *Boston Deep Sea Fishing and Ice Co v Ansell* (1888) 39 Ch D 339. Note the difference of opinion in *Moriarty v Regent's Garage & Engineering Co* [1921] 1 KB 423. Cf *ibid*, 434 (Lush J) and 448–9 (McCardie J).

[17] Above, Chapter 15.

[18] [1962] AC 413; above, p 516.

[19] This can include passive cooperation: *Hounslow London BC v Twickenham Garden Developments Ltd* [1971] Ch 233; *Ministry of Sound (Ireland) Ltd v World Online Ltd* [2003] EWHC (Ch) 2178, [2003] 2 All ER (Comm) 823.

[20] [1962] AC 413, 431.

[21] *Gator Shipping Corp v Trans-Asiatic Oil Ltd SA, The Odenfeld* [1978] 2 Lloyd's Rep 357, 374.

[22] *Ibid*; *Reichman v Beveridge* [2006] EWCA Civ 1659, [2007] 1 P & CR 20 at [41]; *Isabella Shipowner SA v Shagang Shipping Co Ltd, The Aquafaith* [2012] EWHC 1077 (Comm), [2012] 2 Lloyd's Rep 61 at [56]. For three cases where the qualification was held to apply, see *Attica Sea Carriers Corp v Ferrostaal Poseidon Bulk Reederei GmbH, The Puerto Buitrago* [1976] 1 Lloyd's Rep 250 (interest not legitimate where cost of repairing ship exceeded the value of the ship when repaired); *Clea Shipping Corp v Bulk Oil International Ltd, The Alaskan Trader* [1984] 1 All ER 129 (which is controversial because the facts were not extreme); *MSC Mediterranean Shipping Co SA v Cottonex Anstalt* [2016] EWCA Civ 789, [2016] 2 Lloyd's Rep 494 (where the Court of Appeal muddled matters by taking the view that the contract had been automatically terminated rather than saying that the 'no legitimate interest' or 'wholly unreasonable' qualification applied: more conventionally the Court of Appeal disagreed with Leggatt J's reasoning at first instance, [2015] EWHC 283 (Comm), [2015] 1 Lloyd's Rep 359, that it was helpful to view the qualification as an aspect of good faith in contractual dealings).

Carter itself may be thought to be an extreme case: it would not have been very difficult for the defenders to find another company to pay for the advertising space and thereby mitigate any loss that might be suffered. It may be that the 'acceleration clause', which meant that the entire amount for the three-year contract period became payable at a much earlier date than the end of the contract, was important in *White & Carter*, such that it could be distinguishable on its facts, but their Lordships did not seem to have placed much emphasis on the existence of that clause. The interest of the pursuers was essentially financial: they would obtain more money through the action for the agreed sum than they would have obtained had they been limited to a claim in damages, with the concomitant duty to mitigate their loss. Yet on that basis any claimant will be able to point to a similar 'legitimate interest'. In *The Aquafaith*, Cooke J rightly thought that it would need to be 'an extreme or unusual case' before the 'legitimate interest' exception would apply.[23]

The almost unfettered option established by *White* & *Carter* may be said to uphold directly what the parties agreed in their contract and is consistent with the rejection in English law of a rule that contract remedies must be exercised reasonably. As Lord Reid put it, 'it never has been the law that a person is only entitled to enforce his contractual rights in a reasonable way, and that a court will not support an attempt to enforce them in an unreasonable way'.[24] But it can be, and has been, criticized[25] as encouraging wasteful performance, as being inconsistent with the mitigation rule (which it is said should apply to actions for an agreed sum), and as giving what amounts to indirect specific performance of contracts which are not specifically enforceable.

2. SPECIFIC PERFORMANCE

An order for specific performance is one by which the Courts direct the defendant to perform the contract in accordance with its terms. By contrast to civil law systems, which generally regard the innocent party's primary recourse as, in principle, to have the contract performed,[26] the equitable jurisdiction to order specific performance is supplementary to the common law remedy of damages. Specific performance will therefore not be granted where damages are adequate. Even if damages are inadequate, there are other grounds upon which specific performance may be refused. A party who fails to comply with an order of specific performance, or an injunction, will be in contempt of court, and exposed to fines and even imprisonment. The sanctions for

[23] [2012] EWHC 1077 (Comm), [2012] 2 Lloyd's Rep 61 at [56].

[24] [1963] AC 413, 430.

[25] Nienabar [1962] CLJ 213; Goodhart (1962) 78 LQR 263; Morgan [2015] LMCLQ 575. But cf (1962–66) 2 Adelaide LR 103; Tabachnik [1972] CLP 149, 164 ff.

[26] Lando and Beale, *Principles of European Contract Law Parts I and II* (2000) 399–402. Although civil law systems may refuse specific performance on a variety of grounds which appear to be similar to those on which English Courts would also refuse the remedy, in practice civil law judges will order specific performance in a wider range of circumstances than the English Courts. Cf *Co-operative Insurance Society Ltd v Argyll Stores (Holdings) Ltd* [1998] AC 1, 11–12.

failure to comply with equitable orders are therefore much more onerous than those for breaches of contract, which is one reason why specific performance is sometimes considered to be an exceptional remedy in contract law.

(a) ADEQUACY OF DAMAGES

The main reason why damages are considered inadequate is because no substitute for the failed performance can be bought. But damages may also be inadequate where the contract provided for a series of regular payments but damages could only be sought as each payment fell due,[27] or, as discussed in Chapter 21, where the loss is suffered by a person who is not a party to the contract.[28] Sometimes the Courts have preferred to use different terminology than adequacy to explain the relationship between specific performance and damages. For example, it has been said that specific performance will be ordered if that remedy will 'do more perfect and complete justice than an award of damages'.[29] However, while some of the other bars to specific performance have been weakened in the modern law, so that an order of specific performance has become easier to obtain, it seems clear that no different underlying approach to the relationship between the two remedies has been heralded merely by such a change of terminology.

Should the inadequacy of damages requirement remain? Put another way, should specific performance remain a secondary remedy to damages? Two factors suggest that it should.[30] First, specific performance, unlike damages, does not take account of the desirability of a claimant taking reasonable steps to mitigate its loss and granting specific performance avoids the policy of the mitigation rule. Secondly, there have been many improvements in the techniques for identifying and quantifying loss recoverable by damages.

(i) Sale of goods in general

Where there has been a failure to supply goods, substitute goods can usually be bought so that damages are adequate. Specific performance has therefore only been awarded where the goods sold were in some sense unique, such as where they have special beauty, rarity, or interest,[31] so that substitutes cannot (easily) be bought. In contrast, specific performance has been refused where the chattel is 'an ordinary article of

[27] *Beswick v Beswick* [1968] AC 58.

[28] *Ibid*, below, p 634. But not always, see *Co-operative Insurance Society Ltd v Argyll Stores (Holdings) Ltd* [1998] AC 1, 18, below, p 600 (wrongful closure of 'anchor' supermarket in shopping centre caused losses to other tenants).

[29] *Tito v Waddell (No 2)* [1977] Ch 106, 322 (Megarry V-C). See also *Beswick v Beswick* [1968] AC 58, 77, 83, 88; *The Stena Nautica (No 2)* [1982] 2 Lloyd's Rep 336, 346–7. In *Tesco Stores Ltd v Union of Shop, Distributive and Allied Workers* [2024] UKSC 28, [2025] ICR 107, considered below, p 598, the Supreme Court recognized (at [78]) that viewing damages as inadequate in that case might be 'regarded as, to some extent, side-stepping *Addis v Gramophone Co Ltd*' (discussed above, pp 546–7).

[30] Burrows, *Remedies for Torts, Breach of Contract, and Equitable Wrongs* (4th edn, 2019) 412–15.

[31] *Holroyd v Marshall* (1862) 10 HL Cas 191, 209; *Falcke v Gray* (1859) 4 Drew 651, 658; *Gregor Fisken Ltd v Carl* [2021] EWCA Civ 792, [2021] 4 WLR 91.

commerce' such as a piano or even a set of Hepplewhite chairs, as substitute goods can be obtained.[32]

Section 52 of the Sale of Goods Act 1979 (which now applies only to non-consumer contracts for the sale of goods)[33] provides that, in any action for breach of contract to deliver specific or ascertained goods, the Court may, if it thinks fit, direct that the contract shall be performed specifically, without giving the defendant the option of retaining the goods on payment of damages. This section has not, however, affected the law on specific performance. In particular, it does not mean that specific performance should be ordered simply because goods are specific or ascertained. And even in the case of a contract falling outside section 52 for the sale of generic goods, such as petrol or steel, specific performance may, in exceptional cases, be ordered where scarcity of supplies means that substitutes are not available.[34]

(ii) Consumer contracts for the supply of goods, digital content, or services

There are special remedies provided for a consumer in Part 1 of the Consumer Rights Act 2015. By sections 19 and 23 and sections 42–43 of the Consumer Rights Act 2015 these include that a consumer, who has a contract for the supply of goods or digital content by a trader, has a right to the repair or replacement, within a reasonable time, of goods or digital content which do not conform to the contract terms (as defined in sections 19(1)–(2) and 42(1)) unless repair or replacement is impossible or disproportionate (compared to the other of those two rights). Similarly, by sections 54–55 of the 2015 Act, a consumer who has a contract for the supply of a service by a trader, has a right to require repeat performance, within a reasonable time and unless impossible, where the performance has not been in conformity with the contract terms (as defined in section 54(2)). By section 58 (which is headed 'powers of the courts'), the Courts are expressly given the power to enforce these special remedies—the right to repair or replacement, or the right to repeat performance—by an order of specific performance.

It is important to appreciate that section 58 on specific performance, enforcing a consumer's statutory right to repair or replacement, or the right to repeat performance, represents a move away from the normal requirement for specific performance that damages must be inadequate.[35] This is because section 58 appears to militate against the Courts applying the normal common law approach of denying specific performance unless damages are inadequate. Since the origin of the regime of consumer remedies

[32] *Whiteley Ltd v Hilt* [1918] 2 KB 808, 819; *Cohen v Roche* [1927] 1 KB 169. Cf *The Oro Chief* [1983] 2 Lloyd's Rep 509 (ship); *Record v Bell* [1991] 1 WLR 853, 862 (furniture in house separately sold to claimant).

[33] By reason of amendment of the 1979 Act by the Consumer Rights Act 2015.

[34] *Sky Petroleum Ltd v VIP Petroleum Ltd* [1974] 1 WLR 576 (scarcity due to oil embargo); *Howard E Perry v British Railways Board* [1980] 1 WLR 1375 (steel strike). Cf *Société des Industries Metallurgiques v Bronx Engineering Co Ltd* [1975] 1 Lloyd's Rep 465; *Watson's Dairies Ltd v AG Lambert and Partners* [2020] EWHC 2825 (Ch).

[35] See Harris (2003) 119 LQR 541 (referring to the original introduction of these provisions in relation to contracts for the supply of goods by the Sale and Supply of Goods to Consumers Regulations 2002 (SI 2002 No 3045)); Whittaker (2017) 133 LQR 47, 64–6.

in the 2015 Act is found in the implementation of an EC Directive it is perhaps not surprising that, in the primacy apparently afforded to specific performance, it reflects a civilian rather than a common law approach. It appears that (subject to the Court's discretion to decide that the exercise of another right is appropriate)[36] a Court should only refuse specific performance (ordering repair or replacement of goods or digital content or ordering the repeat performance of services) if impossible or, as between repair and replacement, disproportionate to the other.[37] One may therefore regard the law on specific performance under the 2015 Act as departing not only from the adequacy of damages requirement but also, on the face of it, from several other bars which are discussed below (eg the bars concerning personal services, mutuality, constant supervision, and severe hardship to the defendant).

(iii) Sale of land

As a general rule, either party to a contract for the sale of land is entitled to sue for specific performance of the agreement.[38] As regards the vendor's obligation, the reason traditionally given for this is that each piece of land is unique and cannot readily be replaced in the market. And, as regards the purchaser's obligation to pay the price, the reasoning appears to be that the vendor should be entitled to a reciprocal remedy (not least because, by reason of the availability of specific performance, the purchaser acquires under the contract an immediate equitable interest in the land).[39] The power of the Court to grant specific performance is not limited to those situations in which at law damages would be recoverable. Thus specific performance may be ordered in respect of an anticipatory breach of a contract for the sale of land in circumstances where the claimant, having elected to affirm the agreement, would have no immediate right of action for damages.[40]

(b) WANT OF MUTUALITY

In considering whether or not to entertain a claim for specific performance, it has been said that the Court will take into account whether 'mutuality' exists between the parties. If one party were compelled to perform its obligations in accordance with the terms of the contract while the obligations of the other party under the contract, or some of them, remained unperformed, it might be unfair that the former party should be left to its remedy in damages if the latter party failed to perform any of its unperformed

[36] Consumer Rights Act 2015, s 58(3).

[37] Consumer Rights Act 2015, ss 23(3), 43(3), 55(3).

[38] *Sudbrook Trading Estate Ltd v Eggleton* [1983] 1 AC 444 478. In cases of misdescription by a vendor of land, eg where the area of the land is less than that stated in the contract, the purchaser may claim specific performance with an abatement of the purchase price to compensate for the misdescription: see Harpum [1981] CLJ 108.

[39] This is also of great practical importance, given that one property transaction often forms part of a longer chain of transactions: see generally Davies [2018] Conv 324. Contrast the decision of the Canadian Supreme Court in *Paramadevan v Semelhago* [1996] 2 SCR 415.

[40] *Hasham v Zenab* [1960] AC 316.

obligations.[41] At one time it was supposed that the Court would not grant specific performance to one party unless, at the time the contract was entered into, it could have been specifically enforced against that party by the other.[42] But this supposed rule was subject to a number of exceptions[43] and has since been exploded.[44] Lack of mutuality is now only relevant if, at the date of the hearing, the claimant has not performed its obligations under the contract and could not be compelled for some reason to perform its unperformed obligations specifically.[45] Even where mutuality in this sense does not exist, the Court may possibly, in the exercise of its discretion, order specific performance if damages would be an adequate remedy to the defendant for any default on the claimant's part.[46]

In *Tesco Stores Ltd v Union of Shop, Distributive and Allied Workers*:[47]

Tesco embarked on an expansion programme which involved closing certain distribution centres and opening new sites elsewhere, making some workers redundant. In order to ensure that it did not lose all its experienced employees, Tesco offered a 'permanent feature' of 'retained pay' as an incentive to staff to relocate to another site. Some years later, Tesco wanted to bring retained pay to an end. Tesco offered affected workers an advance payment of 18 months of retained pay to agree to a termination of their retained pay rights. If the workers did not agree, Tesco intended to fire them, and then offer to re-hire them on the same terms, but without the retained pay element. This approach of 'fire and re-hire' was rejected by the claimants who, backed by their union, resisted Tesco's plan.

The Supreme Court held that Tesco was not able to terminate its employees' contracts of employment in order to eliminate retained pay. A term was implied into the contract to make that impossible: any other conclusion would render the word 'permanent' in the retained pay clause irrelevant.[48] The Justices further held that the appropriate remedy for the employees was an injunction, which was tantamount to an order of specific performance against Tesco. The Supreme Court was unconcerned that a similar order would not be granted in favour of Tesco against the employees to force them to work.[49] Lord Burrows and Lady Simler said: 'Nor do we think there is any "want of mutuality" objection to indirect specific performance at least on the facts of this case.'[50] This bar, if it even continues to exist, is now of very little substance.

(c) CONTRACTS OF PERSONAL SERVICE

The Court will not, in general, compel the performance of contracts which involve personal service.[51] In the case of contracts of employment, and as regards enforcing an employee's obligations, this principle is now embodied in legislation which provides

[41] *Price v Strange* [1978] Ch 337, 361.
[42] Fry, *Specific Performance* (6th edn, 1921) 219.
[43] Ames, *Lectures on Legal History* (1913) 370.
[44] *Price v Strange* [1978] Ch 337.
[45] *Ibid*; *Sutton v Sutton* [1984] Ch 184.
[46] *Price v Strange* [1978] Ch 337, 368.
[47] [2024] UKSC 28, [2025] ICR 107.
[48] See above, p 171.
[49] For fears of modern slavery: see below, p 599.
[50] [2024] UKSC 28 at [82].
[51] *Rigby v Connol* (1880) 14 Ch D 482, 487; *Scott v Rayment* (1868) LR 7 Eq 112 (partnership). But see above, pp 596–7, for specific performance being ordered under the Consumer Rights Act 2015, s 58, to enforce a consumer's right to repeat performance by a trader in a consumer contract for the supply of a service.

that an employee shall not be compelled to perform a contract of employment.[52] The basis of this approach seems to be that to make one person serve another against his or her will would be improper and could 'turn contracts of service into contracts of slavery'.[53] But this does not explain why specific performance should not be ordered in favour of an employee against an employer and, on this side of the relationship, there have been departures from the general rule. So, for example, by declaration, a public official[54] and a university lecturer[55] may in effect be reinstated; an employment tribunal may make an order for re-engagement or reinstatement of an employee who has been unfairly dismissed;[56] and, in exceptional circumstances, especially where there is no breakdown in mutual confidence, an injunction may be granted to restrain an employer from dismissing an employee even though this amounts to specific enforcement of the contract of employment. The *Tesco* case is a good illustration of this: Tesco clearly still had confidence in the employees since it was willing to re-hire them, albeit on different terms (without the element of retained pay).[57]

(d) UNCERTAINTY

The obligations in an agreement which it is sought to enforce may be so ill-defined, or what has to be done in order to comply with the order of the Court may not be capable of sufficient definition, that specific performance would in the circumstances be an unsuitable remedy. A covenant to 'lay out £1,000 in building'[58] and a contract to construct 'a railway station' with nothing to indicate the nature, materials, style, dimensions, or anything else[59] have been held not to be specifically enforceable.

(e) CONSTANT SUPERVISION BY THE COURT

At one time it was said that an order for specific performance would not be granted if the Court would be required constantly to supervise the execution of the contract. In *Ryan v Mutual Tontine Westminster Chambers Association*[60] the Court held that it could not grant specific performance of a covenant to maintain a resident porter in

[52] Trade Union and Labour Relations (Consolidation) Act 1992, s 236. Cf *Stevenson v United Road Transport Union* [1977] ICR 893.

[53] *De Francesco v Barnum* (1890) 45 Ch D 430, 438.

[54] *Ridge v Baldwin* [1964] AC 40; *R v BBC, ex p Lavelle* [1983] 1 WLR 23. But cf *Chief Constable of North Wales Police v Evans* [1982] 1 WLR 1155, 1175–6; *R v East Berkshire HA, ex p Walsh* [1985] QB 152; *McLaren v Home Office* [1990] ICR 808.

[55] *Thomas v University of Bradford* [1987] AC 795, 824; *Pearce v University of Aston (No 2)* [1991] 2 All ER 469.

[56] Employment Rights Act 1996, ss 114–115, 130.

[57] See above, p 598. See too *Hill v CA Parsons & Co Ltd* [1972] Ch 305; *Irani v Southampton and SW Hampshire Health Authority* [1985] ICR 590; *Powell v Brent LBC* [1988] ICR 176. Cf *Chappell v Times Newspapers Ltd* [1975] 1 WLR 482; *Ashworth v Royal National Theatre* [2014] EWHC 1176 (QB), [2014] 4 All ER 238.

[58] *Moseley v Virgin* (1796) 3 Ves 184.

[59] *Wilson v Northampton and Banbury Ry Co* (1874) 9 Ch App 279.

[60] [1893] 1 Ch 116.

constant attendance at a block of flats for the benefit of the tenants as it was a contract which would require such supervision as the Court was not prepared to undertake. However, the impossibility for the Court to supervise the doing of the work has since been rejected as a ground for denying relief[61] and in *Posner v Scott-Lewis*[62] a covenant to employ a resident porter was specifically enforced. In the case of contracts which involve continuing or complex obligations, difficulties may arise in formulating with sufficient precision (having regard to the terms of the contract) what it is that the defendant must do to comply with the order for specific performance, any breach of which is punishable as a contempt of court. If those difficulties can be overcome, there is no reason why such a contract cannot be specifically enforced if damages would be an inadequate remedy.

However, a narrower approach was taken by the House of Lords in *Co-operative Insurance Society Ltd v Argyll Stores (Holdings) Ltd.*[63] Their Lordships refused to order the specific performance of an undertaking in a lease (which had 19 years to run) to keep a supermarket 'open for retail trade during the usual hours of business'. A distinction was drawn between cases in which the order would require the party to achieve a result, for instance building or repairing a house, and those in which it would require the party to carry on an activity, such as to run a business over an extended period of time. The more liberal approach was said to apply only to the first type of case[64] since, in the second type of case, there was a greater possibility of repeated applications to the Court to rule on whether the order would be breached. In the *Co-operative Insurance Society Ltd* case it was also said to be contrary to the long-standing and settled practice of the Court to order a person specifically to perform a contract to run a business,[65] and that the contract in that case did not define the obligation sufficiently precisely to make it capable of specific performance because it said nothing about the level of trade, the areas of trade, or the kind of trade.[66]

(f) CONDUCT AND HARDSHIP

Specific performance is a discretionary remedy. The Court has a choice in the matter and, although this does not mean that the choice will be exercised in an arbitrary or capricious manner, the Court can consider whether it would be fair to grant the remedy[67] and refuse it in circumstances which would not justify a refusal of the common

[61] *Shiloh Spinners Ltd v Harding* [1973] AC 691, 724 (Lord Wilberforce). See also the statements of Megarry V-C cited below, n 64.

[62] [1987] Ch 25. See also *Rainbow Estates v Tokenhold Ltd* [1999] Ch 64 (repairing covenant).

[63] [1998] AC 1. For criticism, see Burrows, *Remedies for Torts, Breach of Contract, and Equitable Wrongs* (4th edn, 2019) 418–19.

[64] [1998] AC 1, 13–15. Lord Wilberforce's rejection of the nineteenth-century authorities in *Shiloh Spinners Ltd v Harding* [1973] AC 691, 724, was made in that context and Megarry V-C's statements in *CH Giles & Co Ltd v Morris* [1972] 1 WLR 307, 318 and *Tito v Waddell (No 2)* [1977] Ch 106, 321 were said to be based on incomplete analysis.

[65] [1998] AC 1, 13–15. See also below, n 71.

[66] *Ibid*, 16–17.

[67] *Shell UK Ltd v Lostock Garages Ltd* [1976] 1 WLR 1187.

law remedy of damages. 'He who comes to Equity must come with clean hands.' Thus the Court can take into account the fact that the claimant's conduct has been tricky or unfair,[68] or that the claimant has tried to take advantage of a mistake on the part of the defendant.[69] It can also take account of the conduct of the defendant,[70] and it can refuse specific performance if great hardship would otherwise be caused to the defendant.[71] The defendant's bad conduct may also induce the Court to grant the remedy where there has been a gross breach of personal faith or an attempt to use the threat of non-performance as blackmail.[72] But where the parties' interests are purely financial, acting 'with gross commercial cynicism' will not suffice.[73] These considerations are, of course, generally considered to be irrelevant at common law.[74]

(g) MISCELLANEOUS

In addition to the above bars, the Court will also refuse specific performance where the interest to be transferred is merely transitory,[75] or where an entire obligation is specifically enforceable in part only.[76] Contracts to appoint an arbitrator,[77] to convey the goodwill of a business without the business premises,[78] and to exercise a testamentary power of appointment[79] will also not be specifically enforced.

3. INJUNCTIONS

Injunctions are either prohibitory or mandatory.[80] A prohibitory injunction may be granted to restrain the breach of a negative contract or of a negative stipulation in a contract. A mandatory injunction compels the positive performance of an act and may be used to restore the situation to what it was before the breach of contract.

[68] *Mortlock v Buller* (1804) 10 Ves 292; *Walters v Morgan* (1861) 3 De GF & J 718; *Sang Lee Investment Co v Wing Kwai Investment Co* (1983) 127 SJ 410.

[69] *Webster v Cecil* (1861) 30 Beav 62; above, p 291.

[70] *Sang Lee Investment Co v Wing Kwai Investment Co* (1983) 127 SJ 410.

[71] *Malins v Freeman* (1837) 2 Keen 25; *Denne v Light* (1857) 8 De GM & G 774; *Patel v Ali* [1984] Ch 283. But cf *Mountford v Scott* [1975] Ch 258; *Howard E Perry & Co v British Railways Board* [1980] 1 WLR 1375.

[72] *Co-operative Insurance Society Ltd v Argyll Stores (Holdings) Ltd* [1998] AC 1, 18 (Lord Hoffmann).

[73] *Ibid.*

[74] But see Friedmann, in Beatson and Friedmann (eds), *Good Faith and Fault in Contract Law* (1995) ch 16, and below, pp 616–8.

[75] *Lavery v Pursell* (1888) 39 Ch D 508, 519 (tenancy for a year).

[76] *Ryan v Mutual Tontine Westminster Chambers Association* [1893] 1 Ch 116. Cf *Rainbow Estates Ltd v Tokenhold Ltd* [1999] Ch 64, 73.

[77] *Re Smith & Service and Nelson & Sons* (1890) 25 QBD 545.

[78] *Baxter v Connelly* (1820) 1 J & W 576. But see *Beswick v Beswick* [1968] AC 58, 89, 97.

[79] *Re Parkin* [1892] 3 Ch 510.

[80] The Senior Courts Act 1981, s 37(1) gives the High Court the power to grant an injunction 'whenever just and convenient to do so'. See also the County Courts Act 1984, s 38. On damages in lieu of an injunction, see below, p 605. On *interim* injunctions, see generally *American Cyanamid Co v Ethicon Ltd* [1975] AC 396.

(a) PROHIBITORY INJUNCTIONS

(i) General

Although the grant of an injunction is discretionary, an injunction will normally be granted to restrain the breach of a negative contract or stipulation.[81] A negative contract or stipulation is one whereby a promisor covenants not to do something, for example, not to carry on a certain trade,[82] or not to build on land,[83] or not to ring church bells early in the morning,[84] or not to ride a rival horse in 'The Derby'.[85] A negative stipulation, though not express, may be implied, for example in the case of an exclusive dealing agreement relating to a particular product,[86] or an agreement to charter a ship to a particular person,[87] the injunction being granted to restrain the promisor from buying (or selling) the product elsewhere or chartering the ship to another.

(ii) Indirect specific performance?

An injunction may be granted to restrain the breach of a negative stipulation in a contract even though the Court would not order specific performance of the positive stipulations contained in the same contract.[88] Also, it has been granted in cases where its practical effect may be to enforce performance of the contract, even though the contract is one which the Court might not normally specifically enforce. In *Metropolitan Electric Supply Co Ltd v Ginder*,[89] an express promise by the defendant to take the whole of his supply of electricity from the Company was held to import a negative promise that he would take none from elsewhere, and an injunction was granted.

The question of whether a prohibitory injunction should be refused because it amounts to indirect specific performance of a contract that cannot be directly specifically enforced has been particularly raised in the context of contracts of personal service. As we have seen, contracts of personal service cannot generally be specifically enforced.[90] But the Courts have traditionally accepted that it is possible by means of an injunction to encourage performance in an oblique manner. In *Lumley v Wagner*,[91] for instance:

The defendant agreed to sing at the claimant's theatre, and during that season to sing nowhere else. She then made a contract with another person to sing at another theatre, and refused to perform her contract with the claimant.

[81] *Doherty v Allman* (1878) 3 App Cas 709, 720; *Araci v Fallon* [2011] EWCA Civ 668; *AB v CD* [2014] EWCA Civ 229, [2015] 1 WLR 771.

[82] *Nordenfelt v Maxim Nordenfelt Guns and Ammunition Co Ltd* [1894] AC 535.

[83] *Wrotham Park Estate Co v Parkside Homes Ltd* [1974] 1 WLR 798 (in relation to building that had been undertaken before the decision, see above, p 581).

[84] *Martin v Nutkin* (1724) 2 Peere Wms 266.

[85] *Araci v Fallon* [2011] EWCA Civ 668.

[86] *Catt v Tourle* (1869) LR 4 Ch App 654; *Evans Marshall & Co Ltd v Bertola SA* [1973] 1 WLR 349.

[87] *Lord Strathcona SS Co v Dominion Coal Co* [1926] AC 108; *Associated Portland Cement Manufacturers Ltd v Teigland Shipping A/S* [1975] 1 Lloyd's Rep 581.

[88] *Lumley v Wagner* (1852) De GM & G 604; *Sky Petroleum Ltd v VIP Petroleum Ltd* [1974] 1 WLR 576; *Hill v CA Parsons & Co Ltd* [1972] Ch 305.

[89] [1901] 2 Ch 799.

[90] Above, pp 598–9.

[91] (1852) 1 De GM & G 604.

The Court refused to order specific performance of her positive engagement to sing at the claimant's theatre, but granted an injunction to restrain the breach of her promise not to sing elsewhere.

In *Lumley v Wagner* the contract was of very short duration (only three months) and Miss Wagner was not prevented from plying her trade for very long. However, an injunction will not be granted if its effect will be to compel the defendant to fulfil a contract for personal service or to abstain from any business whatsoever, for this would be to compel a contract-breaker to choose between specific performance and starvation. In *Ehrman v Bartholomew*,[92] therefore, where a traveller promised that he would serve a firm for ten years and would not, during that period, 'engage or employ himself in any other business', an injunction was refused, among other grounds, because to have granted it would have given him no real choice but to work for the firm. But if the employment is of a special kind, an injunction may be granted to restrain the defendant from doing similar work of that kind. So in *Warner Brothers Pictures Incorporated v Nelson*:[93]

A film actress, Mrs Nelson (professionally known as Bette Davis), agreed that she would render her exclusive services as an actress to the claimants for a three-year period, and would not during that period render any similar services to any other person *or engage in any other occupation*. In breach of these stipulations, she entered into an agreement to appear for another film company. The claimants sought an injunction to restrain her.

Branson J held that, although it was impossible to grant an injunction to prevent her from engaging in any other occupation as this would amount to specific performance, an injunction should be granted to restrain her from working as an actress for any other person for a period of up to three years. There were other spheres of activity which, even if not so remunerative, would still be open to her. As a result, she would not be forced to perform the contract.[94] This has been criticized as implying that nothing short of idleness or starvation is compulsive, since Branson J's view that 'an actress of her then youth and soaring talent' might employ herself usefully and remuneratively in other spheres of activity for a period of up to three years appeared 'extraordinarily unrealistic'.[95] More recent cases have examined the practical realities of granting an injunction and have been more willing to infer compulsion where a longer term injunction was being sought. So in *Warren v Mendy*:[96]

There was a dispute over the management of the boxer, Nigel Benn. The case differed from the usual restrictive covenant case in that the injunction being sought by the claimant (Warren) was not against Benn for breach of contract but against another manager (Mendy) in a tort action for inducing breach of Benn's contract with the claimant. But as the claimant would have sought an injunction against anyone who arranged to manage Benn, the same principles were applicable as if the injunction had been sought against Benn for breach of contract.

92 [1898] 1 Ch 671.
93 [1937] 1 KB 209.
94 *Ibid*, 217.
95 *Warren v Mendy* [1989] 1 WLR 853, 865 (Nourse LJ).
96 [1989] 1 WLR 853. See also *Page One Records Ltd v Britton* [1968] 1 WLR 157 (injunction not granted to restrain breach of management contract by pop group); *Young v Robson Rhodes* [1998] 3 All ER 524, 534–5.

The Court of Appeal refused the injunction on the ground that to grant it would constitute indirect specific performance of Benn's contract to be exclusively managed by the claimant for the three-year contract period.

On the other hand, *Warren v Mendy* was distinguished in *LauritzenCool AB v Lady Navigation Ltd*:[97]

In 1998 the defendant owners chartered two ships to the claimant charterers under a time charter that was due to run until 2010. The ships were part of a 'pool' managed by the claimants. Following a dispute the owners informed the charterers that they wished to withdraw the two ships from the pool: that is, they wished to pull out of the charterparty in respect of the two ships. Pending final arbitration, the charterers sought an interim injunction to restrain that alleged breach.

That injunction was granted. Although a time charter is a contract for personal services (the owner being required to provide the ship and services of the crew),[98] the Court of Appeal reasoned that it was acceptable to grant the injunction even though its practical effect would be to compel performance of the contract. *Warren v Mendy* was distinguished because the personal services in that case required very special skills and talents. But while that distinction may explain a greater willingness to order specific performance, it does not satisfactorily explain why the injunction granted did not indirectly amount to specific performance.[99]

It has been assumed in the above discussion that the claimant wants the defendant to perform his or her positive contractual obligations. Where this is not so, for example where there is a restrictive covenant to take effect after termination of the defendant's employment[100] or where the claimant undertakes to pay the defendant and to give him his other contractual benefits even though the defendant does no work for him,[101] there is no question of an injunction amounting to indirect specific performance.

(b) MANDATORY INJUNCTIONS

An injunction may also be granted to restore the situation which would have prevailed but for the defendant's breach of contract, for example to put back a tenant wrongfully evicted by a landlord.[102] Such mandatory injunctions are not as readily granted as prohibitory injunctions[103] but the Court will intervene in this way where it is shown that

[97] [2005] EWCA Civ 579, [2005] 1 WLR 3686.

[98] It was accepted in *The Scaptrade* [1983] 2 AC 694, per Lord Diplock, that specific performance will not be ordered of a time charter because it is a contract for personal services.

[99] For further discussion, see Davies, in Virgo and Worthington (eds), *Commercial Remedies: Resolving Controversies* (2017) 144–150.

[100] As in, eg, *General Billposting Co Ltd v Atkinson* [1909] AC 118; *Credit Suisse Asset Management Ltd v Armstrong* [1996] ICR 882; *Rock Refrigeration Ltd v Jones* [1997] ICR 938.

[101] *Evening Standard Co Ltd v Henderson* [1987] IRLR 64; *Provident Financial Group plc v Hayward* [1989] 3 All ER 298. The defendant under such an arrangement is described as being on 'garden leave'.

[102] *Luganda v Service Hotels Ltd* [1969] 2 Ch 209.

[103] *Sharp v Harrison* [1922] 1 Ch 502, 512; *Shepherd Homes Ltd v Sandham* [1971] Ch 340.

the defendant has deliberately ridden roughshod over the claimant's rights[104] or that the claimant would be gravely prejudiced if the remedy were withheld.[105] At trial, specific performance, rather than a mandatory injunction, orders a defendant to perform its positive contractual obligations.[106]

4. EQUITABLE DAMAGES

Since Lord Cairns' Act 1858 there has been jurisdiction to grant damages either in addition to or in substitution for specific performance or an injunction.[107] Such damages—often referred to as equitable damages—are governed by the same principles as are damages at common law.[108] But in contrast to common law damages, damages in substitution for an injunction or specific performance may compensate for an anticipated, rather than just an accrued, cause of action.[109] They can also be awarded where an order for specific performance has been made and not complied with.[110] In *Morris-Garner v One Step (Support) Ltd*[111] Lord Reed thought, *obiter*, that damages in lieu of an injunction should only be awarded if an application for an injunction was before the court. This contrasts with the advice of Lord Walker in *Pell Frischmann Engineering Ltd v Bow Valley Iran Ltd*, who held that there was no need for the claimant to make an application for an injunction for damages to be claimed in lieu.[112]

FURTHER READING

Kronman, 'Specific Performance' (1978) 45 U Chi L Rev 351

Schwartz, 'The Case for Specific Performance' (1979) 89 Yale LJ 271

Davies, 'Being Specific About Specific Performance' [2018] Conv 324

104 *Luganda v Service Hotels Ltd*, above, n 102; *Mortimer v Bailey* [2004] EWCA Civ 1514, [2005] 2 P & CR 9.

105 *Durell v Pritchard* (1865) LR 1 Ch App 244, 250; *Shepherd Homes Ltd v Sandham* [1971] Ch 340; *Wrotham Park Estate Co v Parkside Homes Ltd* [1974] 1 WLR 798.

106 For *interim* mandatory injunctions enforcing positive contractual obligations, see *Nottingham Building Society v Eurodynamics Systems* [1993] FSR 468; *Zockoll Group Ltd v Mercury Communications Ltd* [1998] FSR 354.

107 See now the Senior Courts Act 1981, ss 49, 50.

108 *Johnson v Agnew* [1980] AC 367, 400 overruling *Wroth v Tyler* [1974] Ch 30. Cf *Morris-Garner v One Step (Support) Ltd* [2018] UKSC 20, [2019] AC 649 at [47]. In *One Step* Lord Reed also said (at [63]) that 'the cases did not purport to lay down a general rule as to how damages under Lord Cairns' Act should be quantified, regardless of the circumstances' leaving it to judges to decide the appropriate method of quantification. But it is not clear why negotiating damages should not always be awarded under Lord Cairns' Act; different bargains may encompass different levels of gains and loss depending on what sort of bargain reasonable parties would have struck.

109 *Oakacre Ltd v Claire Cleaners (Holdings) Ltd* [1982] Ch 197; *Jaggard v Sawyer* [1995] 1 WLR 269.

110 *Biggin v Minton* [1977] 1 WLR 701; *Johnson v Agnew* [1980] AC 367.

111 [2018] UKSC 20.

112 [2009] UKPC 45, [2011] 1 WLR 2370.

19

RESTITUTIONARY AWARDS

A person who pays money or renders services or supplies goods to the defendant pursuant to a contract which is discharged by breach may be entitled to restitution of the money paid or to restitution in the form of a reasonable remuneration for the services rendered (quantum meruit) or a reasonable price for the goods supplied (quantum valebat). These restitutionary remedies may be available not only to an innocent party but also, in certain situations, to a contract-breaker. These remedies may also be available in respect of money paid or non-money benefits rendered under other ineffective agreements including those that are void, tainted by illegality, discharged for frustration, or too uncertain to amount to contracts: such claims, which are outside the scope of this part of the book, since they do not follow a breach of contract, have been briefly considered in the chapters on ineffective contracts.[1] It should also be stressed that, even where the innocent party is seeking these remedies where the contract has been discharged for breach, the cause of action is not breach of contract but rather unjust enrichment with the relevant ground of unjust enrichment being, for example, total failure of basis.[2] A major advantage to an innocent party in seeking restitution after breach, rather than compensatory damages for the breach, is that restitution may enable the innocent party to escape from a bad bargain.[3]

In very rare circumstances, the claimant may, by way of exception to the normal compensatory measure, be able to claim a restitutionary remedy (ie an account of profits) *for* the breach of contract (ie the cause of action is breach of contract) to strip the profits the contract-breaker made from the breach.

[1] Above, pp 66, 70–1, 241, 250, 254, 264–8, 419–29, 505–14.

[2] This ground of unjust enrichment was traditionally known as 'total failure of consideration' or 'total failure of condition', but both 'consideration' and 'condition' have different meanings and courts now prefer the language of 'failure of basis': *Barnes v Eastenders Cash and Carry Plc* [2014] UKSC 26, [2015] AC 1 at [105] (Lord Toulson); *Dargamo Holdings Ltd v Avonwick Holdings Ltd* [2021] EWCA Civ 1149, [2022] 1 All ER (Comm) 1244 at [78] (Carr LJ); *Barton v Morris* [2023] UKSC, [2023] AC 684 at [231] (Lord Burrows). However, nothing of substance turns on the label used.

[3] *BP Exploration Co (Libya) Ltd v Hunt (No 2)* [1979] 1 WLR 783, 800, aff'd [1983] 2 AC 352; *Bush v Canfield* 2 Conn 485 (1818) (Connecticut). The limitation period may also be more favourable: see below, p 619.

1. THE RECOVERY OF MONEY PAID

(a) RECOVERY BY THE INNOCENT PARTY

If one party is entitled to be treated as discharged from further performance of the contract by reason of the other party's breach, and does so, any money paid by that party to the other party under the contract can be recovered provided that the basis for the payment has failed.[4] Strictly, the rule requires that the failure be *total*,[5] but several factors indicate that the requirement of totality may be 'on the turn'. We shall first consider total failure, and then the recent developments.

(i) Total failure of basis

In *Kwei Tek Chao v British Traders and Shippers Ltd*,[6] a case concerned with a cif contract for the sale of goods, Devlin J said:

> If goods have been properly rejected, and the price has already been paid in advance, the proper way of recovering the money back is by an action for money paid on a consideration which has wholly failed, i.e. money had and received.

As well as the requirement that the failure of consideration, or basis, be total, the party seeking repayment must have elected to accept the breach as discharging the contract.[7]

The need for a total failure of basis is illustrated by *Hunt v Silk*:[8]

> The claimant paid £10 to the defendant in return for a promise by the defendant to give him immediate possession of certain premises, to put them into repair, and to execute a lease of them in his favour within 10 days. The claimant obtained possession, but left soon afterwards when the defendant failed to carry out the rest of his promise; he also sued to recover the £10.

His action failed. It was held that, the contract having been in part performed, no money could be recovered.

The common law has required the failure of basis to be total for two main reasons.[9] First, the common law has set its face against apportionment, partly because one cannot assume that all parts of the payee's performance are equally valuable and that the contract price is earned incrementally. For example, in a contract to build a house, the preparation of the ground and the foundations on a difficult site may involve greater expense in either time or labour than the completion of the brickwork, the roof, and the interior. Secondly, in many cases the benefit the payer has received from the payee's part performance cannot easily be valued in money. This is particularly so where it consists of services. So, where a builder who has agreed to modernize a bathroom, abandons the contract after disconnecting the old fittings and removing some of them, it is not

[4] See generally Wilmot-Smith [2013] CLJ 414.

[5] See recently *HEB Enterprises Ltd v Richards* [2023] UKPC 7 at [58]–[64].

[6] [1954] 2 QB 459, 475.

[7] *Ibid.*

[8] (1804) 5 East 449.

[9] *Whincup v Hughes* (1871) LR 6 CP 78, 81 (Bovill CJ). Birks, *An Introduction to the Law of Restitution* (revd edn, 1989) 242–4. For other justifications, see Law Com No 121, *Pecuniary Restitution on Breach of Contract* (1983) paras 3.8–3.10.

obvious what the benefit of such part performance is to the owner of the house,[10] who will have to pay another person to clear the room as well as having the trouble of finding another builder to complete the task.

Total failure of basis occurs where none of the promised performance has been rendered.[11] Basis in this context refers to performance by the payee of the (contractual) promise.[12] This means that any performance of the actual thing promised, as determined by the contract, is fatal to recovery. But in practice the concept of total failure of basis has been applied somewhat arbitrarily, and has ignored real benefits received by the payer and significant detrimental reliance by the payee. For instance, in the case of a contract for the sale of goods,[13] or of hire-purchase,[14] a failure by the seller to convey a good title to the goods in breach of the condition implied by statute[15] will constitute a total failure of basis. In *Rowland v Divall*:

R bought a motor-car from D for £334, repainted it and sold it on to a third party. It then turned out that the car had been stolen, although D had dealt with it in good faith. The police took possession of it on behalf of the true owner and R brought an action to recover from D the £334.

The Court of Appeal held that, since R 'had not received any part of that which he had contracted to receive—namely, the property and right to possession' of the car, there had been a total failure of basis. He was entitled to recover the whole purchase price, notwithstanding that he and his sub-purchaser had had four months' use and enjoyment of the vehicle and that he could not restore the car to D.[16] Similarly, in *Butterworth v Kingsway Motors*[17] the hire-purchase price of a car (£1,275) was recovered although by the time the car, which had been used by the hire-purchaser for nearly a year, was returned it was worth only £800. In an action for damages, account would be taken of the benefit received by purchasers in these cases.[18] Similarly, there will be a total failure

[10] *Sumpter v Hedges* [1898] 1 QB 673, 514.

[11] *Fibrosa Spolka Akcyjna v Fairbairn Lawson Combe Barbour Ltd* [1943] AC 32; *Rover International v Cannon Film Sales Ltd (No 3)* [1989] 1 WLR 912; *Stocznia Gdanska SA v Latvian SS Co* [1998] 1 WLR 574.

[12] *Fibrosa Spolka Akcyjna v Fairbairn Lawson Combe Barbur Ltd* [1943] AC 32, 48. There is a wider meaning of failure of basis that extends beyond non-performance of a contractual obligation to a failure of purpose or condition, whether promissory or not. That wider meaning was stressed by the High Court of Australia in *Roxborough v Rothmans of Pall Mall Ltd* (2001) 208 CLR 516 in which restitution was granted of money paid under a contract that had not been discharged.

[13] *Hudson v Robinson* (1816) 4 M & S 475; *Rowland v Divall* [1923] 2 KB 500.

[14] *Karflex Ltd v Poole* [1933] 2 KB 251; *Warman v Southern Counties Car Finance Corp Ltd* [1949] 2 KB 576.

[15] Above, p 182.

[16] [1923] 2 KB 500, 504, 506–7. The principle has been both criticized and defended; see Law Reform Committee, Twelfth Report (Cmnd 2958, 1966); Law Com No 24, *Exemption Clauses in Contracts* (1969); Law Com No 160, *Sale and Supply of Goods* (1987) paras 6.1–6.5 (recommending no reform of the rule by requiring a buyer seeking to recover the price to make a money allowance in favour of the seller in respect of the use). Cf Torts (Interference with Goods) Act 1977, s 6(3).

[17] [1954] 1 WLR 1286.

[18] *Harling v Eddy* [1951] 2 KB 739. But where a buyer has spent money on the goods while they are in its possession, damages may be the preferable remedy because this can be recovered in such an action but not in an action for the return of the price: *Mason v Burningham* [1949] 2 KB 545.

of basis even though a buyer or hirer has incurred substantial reliance expenditure for the purpose of the contract[19] or where, although there has been partial performance by the payee, the Court is able to divide the contract and hold that there has been a total failure in relation to the parts not performed,[20] or can find that the parties have impliedly acknowledged that the basis can be 'broken up' or apportioned.[21]

(ii) Partial failure of basis

The willingness of the Court so to divide the contract may indicate dissatisfaction with the requirement of totality. We have seen that the requirement of totality can produce fine and sometimes arbitrary distinctions. In the case of frustrated contracts, dealt with in Chapter 14, the requirement of a total failure has been removed by statute so that money paid can be recovered even though there has only been a partial failure of basis.[22] We shall also see that where a quantum meruit claim is made in respect of services rendered, the difficulty of valuing the work done is not regarded as an insurmountable bar to relief.

It may be difficult to maintain the requirement that the failure be *total* now that the principle of unjust enrichment and the defence of change of position have been recognized in English law.[23] It has been said that 'if counter-restitution is relatively simple . . . insistence on total failure of consideration can be misleading and confusing',[24] and in *Goss v Chilcott*,[25] the Privy Council relaxed the requirement that the failure be total by the use of apportionment. It was held that a loan could be apportioned between the principal sum lent and the interest, so that the receipt by the lender of interest did not prevent the lender recovering the principal sum lent, and the Court indicated that it would have been willing to apportion the principal sum itself so that partial repayment of the principal sum would not have prevented a restitutionary claim but would have merely reduced such a claim to the balance of the loan. Moreover, support has been expressed in the House of Lords for the reformulation of the total failure of basis rule.[26] Although these cases all concerned loans or other transactions in which

19 *Fibrosa Spolka Akcyjna v Fairbairn Lawson Combe Barbour Ltd* [1943] AC 32, above, p 495 (work done by payees in manufacturing machines); *Rover International v Cannon Film Sales Ltd (No 3)* [1989] 1 WLR 912, 932, 936, 937 (expenditure in buying back films to fulfil terms of distributorship contract).

20 *DO Ferguson v Sohl* (1992) 62 BLR 92 (building contract; total failure of basis in respect of sum paid in excess of value of work done); *White Arrow Express Ltd v Lamey's Distribution Ltd* (1995) 15 Tr LR 69, noted Beale (1996) 112 LQR 205; *Baltic Shipping Co v Dillon* (1993) 176 CLR 344, 375 (High Court of Australia).

21 *David Securities Pty Ltd v Commonwealth Bank of Australia* (1992) 175 CLR 353, 383.

22 Above, p 496 (Law Reform (Frustrated Contracts) Act 1943, s 1(2)).

23 *Lipkin Gorman v Karpnale Ltd* [1991] 2 AC 548.

24 *David Securities Pty Ltd v Commonwealth Bank of Australia* (1992) 175 CLR 353, 383 (High Court of Australia). 'Counter-restitution' means restitution *to the defendant* of any benefits received *by the claimant.*

25 [1996] AC 788, 798.

26 *Westdeutsche Landesbank Girozentrale v Islington LBC* [1996] AC 669, 682–3. See also Birks, *An Introduction to the Law of Restitution* (revd edn, 1989) 259–64; but cf Law Com No 121, *Pecuniary Restitution on Breach of Contract* (1983) paras 3.8–3.9 and *Stocznia Gdanska SA v Latvian SS Co* [1998] 1 WLR 574, 590.

the part performance received by the payer consisted of money so that the problems of valuing non-monetary performance did not arise, it is submitted that, in principle, restitution should be available in all cases of a failure of basis subject to giving counter-restitution.

(b) RECOVERY BY THE PARTY IN BREACH

It is similarly possible for the party who has broken the contract to recover from the innocent party money pre-paid by it. The recoverability of such payments partly depends on the construction of the contract and the purpose for which the payment is required. A distinction is drawn between deposits and other payments required as security for due performance on the one hand and advance payments of the price on the other.

(i) Advance payments of the contract price

Where the payment was not a deposit or otherwise required as security for due performance and where recovery was not otherwise expressly or impliedly precluded by the terms of the agreement (eg by express provision that it be forfeited) it may be recoverable. In *Dies v British and International Mining and Finance Corporation Ltd*:[27]

The defendant contracted to sell rifles and ammunition to Quintana at a total price of £270,000 of which £100,000 was paid before the agreed delivery date. Subsequently, in breach of contract, Quintana failed to take delivery or to pay the balance. The defendant elected to treat the contract as discharged but refused to return the £100,000. Quintana assigned his rights to the claimant, who brought an action to recover the money.

Stable J held that the claimant might recover £100,000, less the amount of any damages suffered by the defendant through Quintana's breach of contract. It might seem strange, at first sight, that the party in breach should have succeeded. But as the judge pointed out, the defendant was 'amply protected', since it could set off its claim for damages against the sum sought to be recovered. However, the basis for the payment must have totally failed. So if the party in default has received a benefit from the subject-matter of the sale before the discharge, it cannot, subject to any equitable relief,[28] recover any part payment made. Where a contract for work and materials provides for payment of the purchase price by instalments, a contractor, who is bound to incur expense as the work proceeds, will be entitled to retain any instalment paid if the other party repudiates the contract before completion of the work. This is because, subject to a *de minimis* rule, the services rendered by the innocent party are to be regarded as part of the bargained-for

[27] [1939] 1 KB 724. See also *McDonald v Dennys Lascelles Ltd* (1933) 48 CLR 457 (sale of land); *Rover International Ltd v Cannon Film Sales Ltd (No 3)* [1989] 1 WLR 912; Beatson, *The Use and Abuse of Unjust Enrichment* (1991) ch 3 (updating (1981) 97 LQR 389).

[28] See below, pp 612–3.

performance and there is therefore no total failure of basis in such a contract once performance has commenced.[29]

(ii) Deposits and other payments as security for due performance

It is settled law that a sum paid by way of 'deposit' for the purchase of goods or land is security for completion of the contract by the buyer and cannot as a general rule be recovered if the buyer fails to perform its side of the contract.[30] Similarly, where the contract provides that on default instalments of the price already paid shall be forfeited, there will generally be no recovery.

The general rule that deposits and other payments required as security or subject to forfeiture clauses are irrecoverable is, however, subject to statutory and equitable exceptions. By section 49(2) of the Law of Property Act 1925 the Court has an unqualified discretion to order repayment of a deposit paid under a contract for the sale of land where the justice of the case requires it.[31] Another legislative exception can be found in the Consumer Rights Act 2015 which provides that a term which permits the trader 'to retain sums paid by the consumer where the consumer decides not to conclude or perform the contract, without providing for the consumer to receive compensation of an equivalent amount from the trader where the trader is the party cancelling the contract' may be unfair.[32] Secondly, where the provision for the forfeiture of the sum paid is penal and it is unconscionable for the payee to retain the money, equitable relief may be available.[33] Thus a person who purchases goods or land by instalments, or who hires goods in return for payment of rent, may be entitled to equitable relief against forfeiture of the property or purchase money if he defaults in prompt payment of the instalments or rent when due.[34] The principle is similar to that governing penalty clauses[35] but the law has treated the two situations as separate.[36] Plainly the 'genuine

[29] *Hyundai Heavy Industries Co Ltd v Papadopoulos* [1980] 1 WLR 1129; *Stocznia Gdanska SA v Latvian Shipping Co* [1998] 1 WLR 574. The case for relaxing the rule requiring that the failure of basis be *total* is much weaker where the person seeking recovery is a contract-breaker: see above, p 458, in the context of the rule precluding recovery for part performance of an entire obligation.

[30] *Howe v Smith* (1884) 27 Ch D 89. See generally Harpum [1984] CLJ 134; Beatson, *The Use and Abuse of Unjust Enrichment* (1991) 46–50, 76–7, 90–4.

[31] *Universal Corporation v Five Ways Properties Ltd* [1979] 1 All ER 552. Cf *James Macara Ltd v Barclay* [1945] 1 KB 148; *Midill (97PL) Ltd v Park Lane Estates Ltd* [2008] EWCA Civ 1227, [2009] 1 WLR 2460 (both cases indicating a somewhat narrow approach to the discretion).

[32] Consumer Rights Act 2015, Sched 2, para 4. See generally above, pp 226–36.

[33] See *Workers Trust & Merchant Bank Ltd v Dojap Investments Ltd* [1993] AC 573, where it was stated that the amount of the deposit has to be reasonable and that, as long usage established the reasonableness of a 10 per cent deposit in sales of land, a larger deposit would, unless justified, be penal.

[34] *Stockloser v Johnson* [1954] 1 QB 476; *Shiloh Spinners Ltd v Harding* [1973] AC 691, 726–7 (Lord Simon). Cf Lord Wilberforce, *ibid*, 723–4.

[35] Above, pp 583–90. See *Public Works Commissioners v Hills* [1906] AC 368.

[36] *Linggi Plantations Ltd v Jagatheesan* (1972) 1 MLJ 89, 91 (Lord Hailsham LC); *Workers Trust & Merchant Bank Ltd v Dojap Investments Ltd* [1993] AC 573. It may sometimes be hard to say whether a contract is providing for forfeiture of money paid absolutely or for a penal liability: *Else (1982) Ltd v Parkland Holdings Ltd* [1994] 1 BCLC 130, 146.

pre-estimate of loss' test does not apply to stipulations for security for due performance; 'the forfeiture rule looks at the position after the breach when the innocent party is enforcing the forfeiture'.[37] But in the light of its clarification that the underpinning principle for determining whether a clause is a penalty is one combining legitimate interest and proportionality, the Supreme Court in *Cavendish Square Holding BV v Talal El Makdessi* ('*Makdessi*') and *ParkingEye Ltd v Beavis*[38] has opened the way for clauses allowing the innocent party to retain pre-payments by the contract-breaker to be treated as penalties. *Obiter dicta* of the Supreme Court Justices also indicated that both the law on penalties and on relief against forfeiture may be applied to the same clause.[39]

The scope of the jurisdiction to relieve against forfeiture is somewhat uncertain.[40] It probably does not apply to those commercial contracts where speed and certainty are of paramount importance.[41] The Courts may also only relieve against the forfeiture of proprietary or possessory interests as opposed to the forfeiture of 'mere contractual rights'.[42] This may, however, leave open the possibility of seeking relief where a contract is specifically enforceable and thus creates equitable rights, although in the case of breach of an essential condition as to time relief by way of specific performance is less likely to be given than relief by way of restitution, for example by repayment of retained money.[43] Apart from the uncertainty as to the scope of the equitable jurisdiction it is also possible, though unlikely, that the only form of relief available is to give the contract-breaker more time to perform the contract so that there will be no relief if it is clear that the contract-breaker will not be able to pay after such extension of time.[44]

In the exercise of the equitable jurisdiction account has been taken of whether the sum to be forfeited is much greater than the damage caused by the breach,[45] whether the party seeking relief had received a substantial part of the consideration for the

[37] *Else (1982) Ltd v Parkland Holdings Ltd* [1994] 1 BCLC 130, 144 (Hoffmann LJ).

[38] [2015] UKSC 67, [2016] AC 1172 at [16]–[18], [156], [234]–[238]. See above, pp 584–5.

[39] *Ibid* at [16]–[18], [156], [160]–[161], [230], [291].

[40] See generally Smith [2001] CLJ 178; Gullifer, in Burrows and Peel (eds), *Commercial Remedies* (2003) 191, 205–19.

[41] *The Laconia* [1977] AC 850; *Scandinavian Trading Tanker Co AB v Flota Petrolera Ecuatoriana, The Scaptrade* [1983] 2 AC 694; *Union Eagle Ltd v Golden Achievement Ltd* [1997] AC 514. Cf the broader approach of the High Court of Australia: *Legione v Hateley* (1983) 152 CLR 406; *Stern v McArthur* (1988) 165 CLR 489.

[42] *Scandinavian Trading Tanker Co AB v Flota Petrolera Ecuatoriana, The Scaptrade* [1983] 2 AC 694; *BICC plc v Burndy Corporation* [1985] Ch 232, 251–2; *Nutting v Baldwin* [1995] 1 WLR 201. See also *The Manchester Ship Canal Co Ltd v Vauxhall Motors Ltd* [2019] UKSC 46 (relief against forfeiture of possessory rights under a perpetual licence over land).

[43] *Union Eagle Ltd v Golden Achievement Ltd* [1997] AC 514; *Steedman v Drinkle* [1916] 1 AC 275. Cf *Re Dagenham (Thames) Dock Co, ex p Hulse* (1873) LR 8 Ch App 1022 and the broader Australian approach: *Legione v Hateley* (1983) 152 CLR 406; *Stern v McArthur* (1988) 165 CLR 489.

[44] *Stockloser v Johnson* [1954] 1 QB 476 (Romer LJ; cf Denning and Somervell LJJ); *Galbraith v Mitchenall Estates Ltd* [1965] 2 QB 473; *Workers Trust and Merchant Bank Ltd v Dojap Investments Ltd* [1993] AC 573. See also *Jobson v Johnson* [1989] 1 All ER 621.

[45] *Stockloser v Johnson* [1954] 1 QB 476, 484, 490; *Transag Haulage Ltd v Leyland DAF Finance plc* [1994] 2 BCLC 88, 101–2.

payment,[46] whether there has been any fraud or sharp practice,[47] whether it is reasonable to require the party who is prima facie entitled to forfeiture to accept an alternative to the property it is sought to forfeit,[48] and whether relief would permit the evasion of a contractual obligation simply because the contract has turned out to be an unwise one.[49]

2. RESTITUTION IN RESPECT OF SERVICES OR GOODS

(a) INTRODUCTION

Sometimes a quantum meruit (or quantum valebat) claim is genuinely contractual:[50] the remedy is awarded where there is a promise to pay for services (or goods) but no particular remuneration has been specified. The party performing the services is entitled at common law to a quantum meruit, that is, as much as the services are worth or, as it is generally described, a 'reasonable' sum.[51] The principle is statutorily embraced in section 8(2) of the Sale of Goods Act 1979, section 15(1) of the Supply of Goods and Services Act 1982, and section 51 of the Consumer Rights Act 2015, which provide that the buyer and the recipient of services must pay a reasonable price or charge.[52]

However, in many situations a quantum meruit (or quantum valebat) is a non-contractual remedy awarded to effect restitution of an unjust enrichment.[53] There is no promise to pay, express or implied, and the obligation is imposed. We are here concerned with this non-contractual quantum meruit.

(b) RESTITUTIONARY CLAIMS BY THE INNOCENT PARTY

Where a contract has been broken in such a way as to entitle the innocent party to be treated as discharged, and it has elected to be so treated, it may sue on a quantum meruit for the value of the work done under the contract, as an alternative to bringing an action on the contract for damages. In such a case the quantum meruit claim arises in the

[46] *Stockloser v Johnson* [1954] 1 QB 476, 484, 492.

[47] *Ibid*, 495–6 (Romer LJ).

[48] *Shiloh Spinners Ltd v Harding* [1973] AC 691, 726–7; *Transag Haulage Ltd v Leyland DAF Finance plc* [1994] 2 BCLC 88, 101–2.

[49] *Galbraith v Mitchenall Estates Ltd* [1965] 2 QB 473; *Hyundai Ship Building and Heavy Industries Co Ltd v Pournaras* [1978] 2 Lloyd's Rep 502, 508–9.

[50] Winfield, *The Province of the Law of Tort* (1931) 157; (1947) 63 LQR 35; Birks, *An Introduction to the Law of Restitution* (revd edn, 1989) 275; Mitchell and Mitchell [2020] LMCLQ 498.

[51] *Steven v Bromley and Son* [1919] 2 KB 722; *Sir Lindsay Parkinson & Co Ltd v Commissioners of Works* [1949] 2 KB 632; *The 'Batis'* [1990] 1 Lloyd's Rep 345, 352.

[52] See above, pp 65, 189.

[53] Birks, *An Introduction to the Law of Restitution* (revd edn, 1989) 265–76. Cf Beatson, *The Use and Abuse of Unjust Enrichment* (1991) ch 2.

law of restitution. Two cases provide possible illustrations of this remedy. In *Planché v Colburn*:[54]

The claimant had contracted to write a book on custom and ancient armour for a periodical publication, called the *Juvenile Library* to be published by the defendant. For this he was to receive the sum of £100 on completion. When he had completed half, but not the whole, of his volume, the defendant abandoned the publication.

The claimant was held entitled to retain a verdict for £50 which the jury had awarded him. Tindal CJ said:[55]

I agree that when a special contract is in existence and open, the plaintiff cannot sue on a quantum meruit: part of the question here, therefore, was whether the contract did exist or not. It distinctly appeared that the work was finally abandoned; and the jury found that no new contract had been entered into. Under these circumstances, the plaintiff ought not to lose the fruit of his labour.

Again, in *De Bernardy v Harding*:[56]

The defendant appointed the claimant his agent to advertise and sell tickets for seats to view the funeral of the Duke of Wellington, the claimant to receive a commission on the tickets sold. The defendant wrongfully revoked the claimant's authority after he had already incurred expenses in carrying out the contract.

It was held that the claimant was entitled to a quantum meruit for the work done.

(c) QUANTUM MERUIT COMPARED WITH DAMAGES

If the contract has not been discharged, the innocent party cannot use the quantum meruit remedy, but can only sue for damages.[57] However, if the restitutionary remedy is available and the injured party chooses to sue on a quantum meruit, the principle of assessment differs from that which is applied in assessing damages for breach of contract and the sum which the innocent party is entitled to recover may differ from that which is recoverable as damages:[58]

Suppose that by the terms of a contract A plc is to pave one mile of road for B plc for £100,000, payable on its completion. B repudiates the contract when A has done half of the work and A accepts that repudiation as discharging it from further performance of its obligations under the contract.

[54] (1831) 8 Bing 14.

[55] *Ibid*, 16. As no part of the book had been handed over, there is controversy as to whether the services were a benefit to the defendant and hence whether the case concerned *restitution* of an unjust *enrichment*.

[56] (1853) 8 Ex Ch 822. See also *Prickett v Badger* (1856) 1 CBNS 296; *Chandler Bros Ltd v Boswell* [1936] 3 All ER 179.

[57] *Barton v Morris* [2023] UKSC, especially [189]–[193] (Lord Leggatt) and [103], [107] (Lady Rose); cf [237]–[240] (Lord Burrows). See too *Dargamo Holdings Ltd v Avonwick Holdings Ltd* [2021] EWCA Civ 1149 at [121]–[133]; *Bank of New York Mellon (International) Ltd v Cine-UK Ltd* [2022] EWCA Civ 1021, [2023] 2 P & CR 19 at [147].

[58] *Heyman v Darwins Ltd* [1942] AC 356, 398 (Lord Porter). See also *The Batis* [1990] 1 Lloyd's Rep 345, 353.

It is clear that A cannot claim the stipulated sum since the work has not been completed.[59] Should it claim damages, it will receive £100,000 less any saving on labour and materials. If a quantum meruit is sought, A will be paid the reasonable value of the work done, as restitution of the unjust enrichment. Ordinarily, damages will be the more favourable remedy since the profit element in the transaction can then be recovered. But there might be special circumstances where the contract price had been underestimated, or the costs of doing the work had risen considerably since the contract was made, for example. In these circumstances it is arguable that a claimant may secure a higher measure by suing on a quantum meruit instead of for damages. It has generally been held that relief by way of quantum meruit is not limited to a proration of the contract price (in our example £50,000) or the contract price itself (in our example, £100,000).[60] Although this can be criticized as inconsistent with the contract and as reallocating contractual risks, proration is difficult in a complex contract and may be unfair because it takes no account of fixed costs which may be incurred at the early stages of a contract or of economies of scale which may have affected the determination of the contract price but be lost on part performance.

Restriction to the contract price, while having some attractions on pragmatic grounds, would give the contract-breaker a proportion of the profits expected under the contract even though the contract has been discharged. It would also produce disequilibrium between the position of an innocent party who has only done a small proportion of the work before the contract is discharged, where the contract price limit would rarely apply, and a person who has done the bulk of the work, where the limit would be more likely to apply. So, in the example above, if the market value of half the work is in fact £200,000, the limit would not apply, and A would recover the true value of the work, £100,000, but if A has completed three-quarters of the job, the limit would apply and A would only recover £100,000 as the quantum meruit. On the other hand, it may be that some reference to the contract price ought to be applied as part of the standard exercise in the law of unjust enrichment of determining whether the particular defendant has been benefited. In other words, it is the value of the work to the particular defendant that one ought to be awarding and in determining that one would have expected the price under the contract to be relevant if lower than the market price.

[59] See above, pp 458, 591.

[60] *Lodder v Slowey* (1900) 20 NZLR 321, 358, [1904] AC 442; *Boomer v Muir* 24 P 2d 570 (1933); *Newton Woodhouse v Trevor Toys Ltd*, 20 December 1991, CA. The contrary view was taken in *Taylor v Motability Finance Ltd* [2004] EWHC 2619 (QB) in which it was also held that restitution for work done could not be granted where the claimant had substantially performed the contract because then there was a claim for the agreed sum under the contract. See also the decision of the High Court of Australia in *Mann v Paterson Constructions Pty Ltd* [2019] HCA 32 in which all seven of the judges agreed that there could be no award of a restitutionary quantum meruit where the claimant builder had an accrued right to payment of the agreed sum for work done. By a 4–3 majority it was accepted that, where there was no accrued right and the contract had been terminated for breach, a restitutionary quantum meruit, as opposed to damages for breach, could be awarded to the innocent party and three of those four (Nettle, Gordon, and Edelman JJ) held that, albeit exceptionally, the restitutionary award could exceed the (pro rata) contract price.

(d) RESTITUTIONARY CLAIMS BY THE PARTY IN BREACH

Where the contractual obligations are entire the party in breach will have no entitlement to a restitutionary quantum meruit for past performance unless, perhaps, the other party freely accepted the work.[61] In *Sumpter v Hedges*[62] the party in breach was held entitled to recover the value of materials left on the building site and used by the defendant who had a choice whether or not to use them to complete the building but not in respect of the partially completed building. This rule can work harshly where substantial benefits are conferred on an innocent party who has suffered no loss whatsoever from the breach of contract.[63] In one case it was suggested that a shipowner who deviated but delivered the goods at the port of discharge without injury or substantial delay would be entitled to reasonable remuneration.[64] Perhaps the best explanation is that the case was not really one of part performance but one in which the goods' owner, in the end, got everything he had contracted for. Where the innocent party has made it clear that anything other than full and precise performance is not wanted a quantum meruit will clearly not be awarded.[65]

3. AN ACCOUNT OF PROFITS

A defendant may make a gain from a breach of contract as where a financier broke his contract to invest £15,000 in the claimant's timber business but instead invested it in a distillery which proved much more profitable;[66] or where a developer built more houses on a site than was permitted by the contract and thereby made extra profit.[67] Alternatively, a defendant may gain by saving expense from its breach as where remedial work, for instance replacing soil or planting trees on the claimant's land, is not done.[68] The traditional approach, which remains the general rule, is that the gain to a defendant from a breach of contract is irrelevant.[69]

However, the possibility of making a contract-breaker account for gains made from breach of contract was accepted by the House of Lords in *Attorney-General v Blake*.[70] B, a former member of the intelligence services, undertook not to divulge any

[61] Although free acceptance was rejected as a ground of restitution by Lord Burrows in *Barton v Morris* [2023] UKSC 3, [2023] AC 684 at [229]–[230].

[62] [1898] 1 QB 673 (for facts, see above, p 463); *Bolton v Mahadeva* [1972] 1 WLR 1009. See generally McFarlane and Stevens (2002) 118 LQR 569.

[63] Law Com No 121, *Pecuniary Restitution on Breach of Contract* (1983) proposed reform but this was rejected by the Lord Chancellor; Law Com No 140, *19th Annual Report*, para 2.11.

[64] *Hain SS Co Ltd v Tate and Lyle Ltd* (1936) 41 Com Cas 350 (HL).

[65] *Wilusznynski v Tower Hamlets LBC* [1989] ICR 493. See also *British Telecommunications plc v Ticehurst* [1992] ICR 383. Cf *Miles v Wakefield MBC* [1987] AC 539. See also above, pp 458–61.

[66] *Teacher v Calder* (1899) 1 F 39.

[67] *Surrey CC v Bredero Homes Ltd* [1993] 1 WLR 1361.

[68] *Tito v Waddell (No 2)* [1977] Ch 106.

[69] *A-G v Blake* [2001] 1 AC 268. See also *The Siboen* [1976] 1 Lloyd's Rep 293, 337; *Tito v Waddell (No 2)* [1977] Ch 106, 332; *Surrey CC v Bredero Homes Ltd* [1993] 1 WLR 1361.

[70] [2001] 1 AC 268.

official information gained as a result of his employment and broke the undertaking by publishing an autobiography. The Crown sought to recover the royalties he was to be paid by his publishers. Their Lordships confirmed that, in general, damages are measured by the claimant's loss, but held that in an exceptional case, where compensatory damages, specific enforcement, and injunction are inadequate or are not available, the Court can require the defendant to account to the claimant for profits received from a breach of contract even where the breach of contract does not involve the use of or interference with the claimant's property.

In determining whether to order an account of profits, Lord Nicholls of Birkenhead (with whom Lord Goff and Lord Browne-Wilkinson agreed) stated that 'a useful general guide, although not exhaustive, is whether the plaintiff had a legitimate interest in preventing the defendant's profit-making activity and, hence, in depriving him of his profit'.[71] The Crown was held to have such an interest in preventing B from profiting from breaches of the undertaking in an autobiography. B was therefore liable to account to the Crown for the royalties.

Their Lordships declined to give more specific guidance as to when an account of profits might be awarded for breach of contract. But they indicated that it would not in itself suffice that (a) the breach was cynical and deliberate;[72] (b) the breach enabled the defendant to enter into a more profitable contract elsewhere; and (c) by entering into a new and more profitable contract the defendant put it out of his power to perform the contract with the claimant.[73] Their Lordships also did not consider the two categories that had been suggested by the Court of Appeal in the *Blake* case for 'restitutionary damages'[74] were satisfactory. The first was the case of 'skimped' performance, where defendants fail to provide the full extent of the contracted services, as where a security firm which has agreed to guard premises using a stipulated number of guards uses a much smaller number and saves a considerable sum.[75] This was said not to fall within the scope of an account of profits as ordinarily understood and in any event, an account of profits was not needed in this context. Suppliers of inferior goods have to refund the difference in price as damages for breach of contract, and a similar approach should apply in cases where the defendant provided inferior and cheaper services than those contracted for.[76] The second category suggested by the Court of Appeal—where, as in

[71] *Ibid*, 285. See also Lord Steyn at 292 (defendant's position closely analogous to that of a fiduciary).

[72] Cf Birks [1987] LMCLQ 421 who suggested that gains should be recovered in all cases of cynical exploitation of breach for the purpose of making a gain so as to deter breaches of contract. This, however, would revolutionize contract remedies since in many cases, particularly commercial cases, the breach is in fact deliberate in the sense that it is knowingly done for commercial reasons. Eg a seller of goods may choose to breach its contract and sell to a third party who is willing to pay a premium over and above the market price. See, eg, *AB Corpn v CD Company, The Sine Nomine* [2002] 1 Lloyd's Rep 805 in which an account of profits was refused by arbitrators for the withdrawal, and use, of a ship in breach of a charterparty.

[73] [2001] 1 AC 268, 286, 290, 293. See [1998] Ch 439, 457, 458 (CA).

[74] Lord Nicholls preferred (at 284) to avoid this term, although it does not seem problematic.

[75] See *City of New Orleans v Firemen's Charitable Association* 9 So 486 (1891). See also *White Arrow Express Ltd v Lamey's Distribution Ltd* (1995) 15 Tr LR 69; Beale (1996) 112 LQR 205.

[76] [2001] 1 AC 268, 286, 290, 291.

Blake's case, defendants profited by doing the very thing that they contracted not to do—was considered to be too widely defined because it embraced all express negative obligations.[77]

If an account of profits is to be awarded for breach of contract, it is the net profits from the breach that must be given up although, by analogy to cases awarding an account of profits for breach of fiduciary duty,[78] the Courts may give an allowance to the defendant for the skill and labour provided.

The decision in *Blake* is very controversial. Lord Hobhouse powerfully dissented, insisting that compensation is invariably the proper monetary remedy for breach of contract. Only once has *Blake* been applied to disgorge a contract-breaker of their gains; but that was a first instance decision in the immediate aftermath of *Blake* and would be decided differently today.[79]

Blake is an outlier in English law. The result is perhaps understandable on its unusual facts: the majority was not prepared to allow a traitor, who used to be a fiduciary, to retain the profits he made. However, unless the same, improbable circumstances as *Blake* were to reoccur, it is very unlikely that an English court will disgorge a defendant of the profits made from a breach of contract. In *Morris-Garner v One Step*, discussed in detail in Chapter 17, Lord Reed emphasized that it does not matter whether the breach was deliberate.[80] Perhaps pointedly, his Lordship observed that '[t]he soundness of [*Blake*] is not an issue in this appeal'.[81] If it had been, it may be that *Blake* would not have survived: the dissent of Lord Hobhouse of Woodborough in *Blake* chimes much better with the approach taken by Lord Reed in *One Step*.

FURTHER READING

McKendrick, 'Breach of Contract, Restitution for Wrongs and Punishment' in Burrows and Peel (eds), *Commercial Remedies* (Oxford: Oxford University Press, 2003) 93

Mitchell and Mitchell, 'Recurring Issues in Failure of Basis' [2020] LMCLQ 498

[77] *Ibid*, 286, 291.
[78] See, eg, *Boardman v Phipps* [1967] 2 AC 46.
[79] *Esso Petroleum Co Ltd v Niad* [2001] All ER (D) 324.
[80] [2018] UKSC 20, [2019] AC 649 at [35], [90], [97].
[81] *Ibid* at [82].

20

LIMITATION OF ACTIONS

At common law, lapse of time does not affect contractual rights. But it is the policy of the law to discourage stale claims, because after a long period a defendant may not have the evidence to rebut such claims and should be in a position to know that after a given time an incident which might have led to a claim is finally closed. Accordingly, in the Limitation Act 1980, the Legislature has laid down certain periods of limitation after the expiry of which no action can be maintained.[1] Equity has developed a doctrine of laches, under which a claimant who has not shown reasonable diligence in prosecuting the claim may be barred from equitable relief.

1. LIMITATION ACT 1980

(a) THE GENERAL RULE

The Act provides that an action founded on a simple contract must be commenced within six years, and one created or secured by a deed, within 12 years, from the date on which the cause of action accrued.[2] In contract, the cause of action accrues, not, as in the tort of negligence, when the damage is suffered, but when the breach of contract takes place[3] or, in the case of an anticipatory breach, when the innocent party elects to treat the contract as terminated.[4] In the case of certain loans, however, the six-year period does not start to run unless and until a demand in writing for the repayment of the debt is made by or on behalf of the creditor.[5]

[1] For proposals for reform, see Law Com Report No 270, *Limitation of Actions* (2001); Law Com No 316, Annual Report 2008–09 (2009) 60.

[2] Limitation Act 1980, ss 5, 8. But in the case of personal injuries arising from a breach of contract, ss 11 and 14 of the Act provide that the limitation period is to be three years from the date on which the cause of action accrued or the date of the claimant's knowledge (if later) of certain relevant facts: and that period may be disapplied at the Court's discretion under s 33. See also ss 12, 13, 14 (fatal accidents).

[3] *Battley v Faulkner* (1820) 3 B & Ald 288; *Short v M'Carthy* (1820) 3 B & Ald 626; *Howell v Young* (1826) 5 B & C 259. For accrual at the date of damage of a concurrent action in the tort of negligence, see, eg, *Midland Bank Trust Co Ltd v Hett, Stubbs & Kemp* [1979] Ch 384; *Forster v Outred & Co* [1982] 1 WLR 86; *Pirelli General Cable Works Ltd v Oscar Faber & Partners* [1983] 2 AC 1; *Henderson v Merrett Syndicates Ltd* [1995] 2 AC 145. In *URS Corp Ltd v BDW Trading Ltd* [2025] UKSC 21, [2025] 2 WLR 1095 at [70]–[77] the Supreme Court acknowledged that *Pirelli* raises 'difficult issues' which did not need to be decided in that case.

[4] *Reeves v Butcher* [1891] 2 QB 509.

[5] Limitation Act 1980, s 6; *Boot v Boot* [1996] 2 FCR 713.

A distinction is drawn between a 'once and for all' breach and a 'continuing' breach. In the case of a continuing breach, such as of an obligation to repair a building, the promisor's duty is considered as persisting and as being forever renewed until that which has been promised has been done; 'a further breach arises in every successive moment of time during which the state or condition is not as promised, during which ... the building is out of repair'.[6] In cases of continuing breaches the claimant will be able to recover in respect of that part of the breach which occurred within the six or, in the case of an obligation created or secured by a deed, 12 years before the action was brought.

It is no answer to a plea of limitation that the claimant was unaware or could not have been aware of the existence of the cause of action for breach of contract until after the expiry of the limitation period. The 'discoverability' rule for economic loss claims in the tort of negligence[7] does not apply to breach of contract.[8]

Where the action is for restitution of an unjust enrichment, the limitation period is normally six years from the accrual of the claimant's cause of action which normally accrues when the defendant is unjustly enriched whether by the receipt of money or otherwise.[9]

(b) PERSONS UNDER A DISABILITY

If on the date on which the cause of action accrued the person to whom it accrued was under a disability, that is, was a minor or lacked capacity within the meaning of the Mental Capacity Act 2005 to conduct legal proceedings,[10] the action may be brought within six years from the date when he or she ceased to be under the disability, or dies.[11] This enlargement of time does not apply when the disability supervenes after the right of action has already accrued, or where the same person is afflicted by successive disabilities (eg minority followed by insanity) separated by an interval in which he or she is under no disability.[12] Again, no extension is allowed when the right of action first accrues to a person not under a disability through whom the person under a disability claims.[13]

[6] *Larking v Great Western (Nepean) Gravel Ltd* (1940) 64 CLR 221, 236 (Dixon J) (High Court of Australia). See also the facts of *Midland Bank Trust Co Ltd v Hett, Stubbs & Kemp* [1979] Ch 384.

[7] Limitation Act 1980, ss 14A–14B.

[8] *Iron Trades Mutual Insurance Co Ltd v JK Buckenham Ltd* [1990] 1 All ER 808; *Société Commerciale de Réassurance v Eras International Ltd* [1992] 1 Lloyd's Rep 570.

[9] *Kleinwort Benson v South Tyneside MBC* [1994] 4 All ER 972, 978; *Aspect Contracts (Asbestos) Ltd v Higgins Construction Plc* [2015] UKSC 38, [2015] 1 WLR 2961 at [25]. See generally McLean [1989] CLJ 472; Burrows, *The Law of Restitution* (3rd edn, 2011) ch 22; Burrows, *A Restatement of the English Law of Unjust Enrichment* (2012) 143–9; Virgo, *The Principles of the Law of Restitution* (4th edn, 2024) ch 29.

[10] Limitation Act 1980, s 38(2) (as amended).

[11] Limitation Act 1980, s 28.

[12] *Purnell v Roche* [1927] 2 Ch 142.

[13] Limitation Act 1980, s 28(2).

(c) EFFECT OF FRAUD, CONCEALMENT, AND MISTAKE

Where an action is based on the fraud of the defendant,[14] or where any fact relevant to the right of action has been deliberately concealed from the claimant by the defendant,[15] whether before or after the cause of action has accrued,[16] or where an action is for relief from the consequences of a mistake,[17] the period does not begin to run until the claimant has discovered the fraud, concealment, or mistake, or could with reasonable diligence have discovered it.[18] The 1980 Act further provides that a deliberate breach of duty in circumstances in which it is unlikely to be discovered for some time amounts to deliberate concealment of the facts involved in that breach of duty.[19] So, for example, if a builder fails to disclose the deliberate breach of a building contract by using defective bricks[20] or putting in inadequate foundations,[21] or if the vendors of a house knowingly fail to warn the purchaser of the risk of subsidence, when they are aware that the house has been built on a disused rubbish tip,[22] the running of the limitation period will be postponed until such time as the claimant discovers the concealment or could with reasonable diligence discover it.[23]

(d) ACKNOWLEDGEMENT AND PART PAYMENT

An acknowledgement or part payment of 'any debt or other liquidated pecuniary claim'[24] may extend the period of limitation. The 1980 Act provides[25] that in such a case the right shall be treated as having accrued on, and not before, the date of the acknowledgement or payment. Thus where A owes B the sum of £500, say, as the price of goods sold and delivered, B's remedy is barred after the passing of six years from the date on which

[14] *Beaman v ARTS Ltd* [1949] 1 KB 550; *Clef Aquitaine SARL v Laporte Materials (Barrow) Ltd* [2001] 1 QB 488; *Seedo v El Gamal* [2023] EWCA Civ 330, [2023] Ch 473. An action under the Misrepresentation Act 1967, s 2(1) does not fall within s 32(1)(a) of the 1980 Act despite the statutory fiction of fraud: above, p 353.

[15] *Cave v Robinson Jarvis & Rolf* [2002] UKHL 18, [2003] 1 AC 384; *Canada Square Operations v Potter* [2023] UKSC 41, [2024] AC 679.

[16] *Sheldon v RHM Outhwaite (Underwriting Agencies) Ltd* [1996] AC 102.

[17] This has been interpreted to mean that the mistake must be an element of the cause of action: *Phillips-Higgins v Harper* [1954] 1 QB 411; *Claimants in the Franked Investment Group Litigation v Revenue and Customs Commissioners* [2012] UKSC 19, [2012] 2 AC 337. The mistake can be a mistake of law resulting from a 'change' in the law: *Kleinwort Benson Ltd v Lincoln City Council* [1999] 2 AC 349.

[18] Limitation Act 1980, s 32. But this provision is not to affect the rights of third parties taking bona fide and for value.

[19] Limitation Act 1980, s 32(2).

[20] *Clark v Woor* [1965] 1 WLR 650.

[21] *Applegate v Moss* [1971] 1 QB 406.

[22] *King v Victor Parsons & Co* [1973] 1 WLR 29.

[23] Note, however, these cases were decided on the wording of the Limitation Act 1939, s 26(b), now repealed. But the same approach still generally applies: see *Cave v Robinson, Jarvis and Rolf* [2002] UKHL 18, [2003] 1 AC 384; *Test Claimants in the FII Litigation v Revenue and Customs Commissioners* [2020] UKSC 47, [2022] AC 1; *OT Computers v Infineon Technologies AG* [2021] EWCA Civ 501, [2021] QB 1183; *Gemalto Holding BV v Infineon Technologies AG* [2022] EWCA Civ 782, [2023] Ch 169.

[24] This includes a claim for a quantum meruit: *Phillips & Co v Bath Housing Co-operative Ltd* [2012] EWCA Civ 1591, [2013] 1 WLR 1479.

[25] s 29(5).

payment became due. But if A, during that period, either acknowledges the debt and its legal liability to pay it[26] or makes a part payment on account of the debt, time begins to run afresh from the date of the acknowledgement or part payment. The limitation period may thus be repeatedly extended. Once it has expired, the right of action cannot subsequently be revived.[27] To be effective, an acknowledgement must be in writing and signed by the person making it or that person's agent, and either an acknowledgement or part payment must be made to the person or to the agent of the person whose claim is acknowledged or in respect of whose claim the payment is made.[28]

(e) STATUTE BARS REMEDY NOT RIGHT

The Act operates merely to bar the contractual remedy, but not to extinguish the right.[29] It is procedural and not substantive. Accordingly, a debtor who pays a statute-barred debt cannot recover the money as money not due.[30] And if the debtor owes to the creditor certain debts some of which are, and some of which are not, statute-barred, the creditor is entitled to appropriate any payment made by the debtor to those debts which are statute-barred, unless the debtor at the time expressly indicates that he is discharging a debt which is still actionable.[31]

2. BARS TO EQUITABLE RELIEF: LACHES

(a) THE STATUTE APPLIED BY ANALOGY

The statutory periods of limitation for contract do not apply to claims for 'specific performance of a contract or for an injunction or for other equitable relief' except insofar as the Court may apply them by analogy.[32] The situations to which the statute will be applied by analogy include those situations in which there is 'correspondence' between the remedies available at law and in equity, and equity is providing a remedy analogous to that which would have been available at law. For example, it would appear that the statute will be applied by analogy to a claim for equitable compensation for dishonest assistance

[26] *Surrendra Overseas Ltd v Government of Sri Lanka* [1977] 1 WLR 565; *Kamouh v Associated Electrical Industries International Ltd* [1980] QB 199; *Bradford and Bingley plc v Rashid* [2006] UKHL 37, [2006] 1 WLR 2066; *Habib Bank Ltd v Central Bank of Sudan* [2006] EWHC 1767 (Comm), [2007] 1 All ER (Comm) 53; *Lia Oil SA v ERG Petroli SpA* [2007] EWHC 505 (Comm), [2007] 2 Lloyd's Rep 509; *Ofulue v Bossert* [2009] UKHL 16, [2009] 1 AC 990.

[27] Limitation Act 1980, s 29(7).

[28] Limitation Act 1980, s 30.

[29] *Royal Norwegian Government v Constant & Constant and Calcutta Marine Engineering Co Ltd* [1960] 2 Lloyd's Rep 431, 442; *Ronex Properties Ltd v John Laing Construction Ltd* [1982] 3 WLR 875, 879. But exceptionally delay may extinguish title to goods (Limitation Act 1980, s 3(2)) and unregistered land (Limitation Act 1980, s 17); and the right to damages for product liability under Part I of the Consumer Protection Act 1980 is extinguished by a ten-year long-stop (Limitation Act 1980, s 11A(3)).

[30] *Bize v Dickason* (1786) 1 Term R 286, 287.

[31] *Mills v Fowkes* (1830) 5 Bing NC 455.

[32] Limitation Act 1980, s 36(1).

of a breach of fiduciary duty;[33] and the right to a final injunction will not be barred so long as the substantive legal right which it seeks to protect has not become barred (ie so long as the claimant could still recover damages for infringement of the right).[34]

However, '[i]t is symptomatic of the incoherent development of the statutes concerning limitation that under section 36 equitable remedies are only subject to limitation periods by analogy' and the law in this area is very unclear.[35] The reasoning and results of three decisions of the Court of Appeal illustrate the difficulties faced. In *P & O Nedlloyd BV v Arab Metals Co, The UB Tiger*[36] it was held that the usual contractual limitation period of six years does not apply by analogy under section 36(1) to a claim for specific performance.[37] This was apparently because there is no directly equivalent remedy at common law to specific performance, since it is not even a requirement for specific performance that there be an existing breach of contract.[38] By contrast, a much broader approach, resting on 'similarity of relief', was adopted in *IGE USA Investments Ltd v Revenue and Customs Commissioners*, which held that the six-year limitation period under section 2 of the Limitation Act 1980 for claims founded on the tort of deceit applies by analogy to claims for equitable rescission of a contract for fraudulent misrepresentation.[39] In *Claimants in the Royal Mail Group Litigation v Royal Mail Group Ltd* the Court held that it was bound by *The UB Tiger* to conclude that, for the purpose of section 36, an injunction to compel the defendant to perform its statutory duty was not analogous to a claim in tort for breach of that same statutory duty, although the Court expressed its 'reservations' about *The UB Tiger*[40] and the *IGE* case was not cited to it. It is suggested that only a decision of the Supreme Court or legislative reform can now achieve coherence in this area.[41]

(b) LACHES

Equitable claims or remedies to which the statute does not apply expressly or by analogy are subject to the equitable doctrine of laches.[42] Equity has always refused its aid to stale claims. Delay which is sufficient to deprive a person of the right to claim

[33] *Cattley v Pollard* [2006] EWHC 3130 (Ch), [2007] Ch 353. For the contrary (less persuasive) view, see *Statek Corp v Alford* [2008] EWHC 32 (Ch), [2008] BCC 266.

[34] *Fullwood v Fullwood* (1878) 9 Ch D 176. This was a tort case. There appears to be no example of this principle being applied where a final injunction is being sought for a breach of contract.

[35] Davies [2023] CLJ 402, quoted in *THG Plc v Zedra Trust Company (Jersey) Ltd* [2024] EWCA Civ 158, [2024] Ch 318 at [16].

[36] [2006] EWCA Civ 1717, [2007] 1 WLR 2288.

[37] See Beatson, in Lomnicka and Morse (eds), *Contemporary Issues in Commercial Law* (1997) 9–23.

[38] As shown in *Hasham v Zenab* [1960] AC 316.

[39] [2021] EWCA Civ 534, [2021] Ch 423.

[40] [2021] EWCA Civ 1173 at [182].

[41] Davies [2023] CLJ 402.

[42] It is not clear whether laches can apply to bar an equitable remedy even where a statutory limitation period does apply. It may be that the best answer to this turns on whether the laches in question comprises mere delay or delay plus prejudice to the defendant. As regards the latter, there seems no reason why laches should not apply even within a statutory limitation period given that 'acquiescence' can so apply (as laid down in the Limitation Act 1980, s 36(2)). For this distinction as to the nature of the laches, see *obiter dicta* of Moore-Bick LJ in *The UB Tiger* [2006] EWCA Civ 1717 at [61].

specific performance or injunction is known technically as 'laches'. This doctrine has been described in a well-known passage in the advice of the Privy Council in *Lindsay Petroleum Co v Hurd*,[43] as follows:

> The doctrine of laches in Courts of Equity is not an arbitrary or a technical doctrine. Where it would be practically unjust to give a remedy, either because the party has, by his conduct, done that which might fairly be regarded as equivalent to a waiver of it, or where by his conduct and neglect he has, though perhaps not waiving that remedy, yet put the other party in a situation in which it would not be reasonable to place him if the remedy were afterwards to be asserted, in either of these cases lapse of time and delay are most material. But in every case, if an argument against relief, which otherwise would be just, is founded upon mere delay, that delay of course not amounting to a bar by any statute of limitations, the validity of that defence must be tried upon principles substantially equitable. Two circumstances, always important in such cases, are, the length of the delay and the nature of the acts done during the interval.

Delay may therefore bar equitable remedies such as claims for rescission,[44] rectification,[45] specific performance,[46] or for an interim injunction.[47] It has traditionally been said that the claimant must show himself to be 'ready, desirous, prompt and eager'[48] to assert his rights, and even a short lapse of time may, in certain circumstances,[49] be fatal. But in exceptional circumstances, as where the parties have been negotiating, a long lapse of time will not be fatal.[50]

FURTHER READING

Beatson, 'Limitation Periods and Specific Performance' in Lomnicka and Morse (eds), *Contemporary Issues in Commercial Law* (London: Sweet & Maxwell, 1997)

Davies, 'Section 36 of the Limitation Act 1980' [2023] CLJ 402

[43] (1874) LR 5 PC 221, 239 (Lord Selborne). This was applied in *Fisher v Brooker* [2009] UKHL 41, [2009] 1 WLR 1764: it was not 'practically unjust' to grant a declaration of copyright despite 38 years' delay because there was no prejudice to the defendant (and, in any event, the relief sought was not 'equitable'). See also *Legends Live Ltd v Harrison* [2016] EWHC 1938 (QB) at [81]–[110] (injunction to restrain breach of restrictive covenant refused because of laches).

[44] *Lindsay Petroleum Co v Hurd*, above, n 43; *Salt v Stratstone Specialist Ltd* [2015] EWCA Civ 745, [2015] 2 CLC 269.

[45] *Beale v Kyte* [1907] 1 Ch 564.

[46] *Mills v Haywood* (1877) 6 Ch D 196; *P & O Nedlloyd BV v Arab Metals Co, The UB Tiger* [2006] EWCA Civ 1717, [2007] 1 WLR 2288. But delay does not bar specific performance ordering mere transfer of the legal estate where a party has taken possession of the property in reliance on that interest: *Williams v Greatrex* [1957] 1 WLR 31 (specific performance despite ten-year delay).

[47] *Great Western Ry v Oxford, Worcester and Wolverhampton Ry* (1853) 3 De GM & G 341; *Shepherd Homes Ltd v Sandham* [1971] Ch 340 (four-month delay).

[48] *Milward v Earl of Thanet* (1801) 5 Ves 720n. Contrast *Lazard Bros & Co Ltd v Fairfield Properties Co (Mayfair) Ltd* (1977) 121 SJ 793.

[49] *Lehmann v McArthur* (1868) LR 3 Ch App 496 (short leasehold interest); *First National Reinsurance Co. Ltd v Greenfield* [1921] 2 KB 260 (shares). Cf *Jones v Jones* [1999] 1 WLR 1739 (mere delay in seeking relief does not signify acquiescence).

[50] *Southcomb v Bishop of Exeter* (1847) 6 Hare 213. See also *Tito v Waddell* [1977] Ch 106, 244–52 (specific performance refused 17 years after the breach of contract not because of delay but because of futility).

PART 6

LIMITS OF THE CONTRACTUAL OBLIGATION

21

THIRD PARTIES

1. INTRODUCTION

This chapter deals with the scope of a valid contract when formed, and the question, to whom does the obligation extend? This question must be considered under two separate headings: (1) the acquisition of rights by a third party, and (2) the imposition of liabilities upon a third party. At common law the general rule is that no one but the parties to a contract can be entitled under it, or bound by it. This principle is known as that of *privity of contract*.

Both aspects of this principle have long been subject to common law and statutory exceptions. But the first aspect, which prevented parties to a contract from enabling a third party to acquire rights under it, was subject to widespread criticism by judges, law reform bodies, and scholars.[1] Despite these criticisms it was reaffirmed on several occasions by the House of Lords in the late twentieth century. However, the criticisms were eventually heeded by the legislature. The Contracts (Rights of Third Parties) Act 1999, largely implementing a Law Commission report,[2] enables a third party to enforce a contract where the parties so intend.

While the 1999 Act creates a potentially 'general and wide-ranging exception'[3] to the first aspect of the privity principle, it does not abolish it and leaves it intact for cases not covered by the Act. It also preserves the statutory and common law exceptions to the rule.[4] A third party who is able to invoke one of these may be in a better position than one who relies on the 1999 Act.[5] The statutory and common law exceptions to the rule will also continue to be of importance because of the tendency of commercial contracts drafted since its enactment to exclude the Act. Moreover, the Act does not enable a contract term to be directly enforced against a third party and thus does not change the second aspect of the principle under which a burden cannot be imposed on a third party.[6] Accordingly, it remains necessary to consider the common law principle and the exceptions to and circumventions of it.

[1] Below, pp 638–9.

[2] Law Commission No 242, *Privity of Contract: Contracts for the Benefit of Third Parties* (1996), hereinafter 'Law Com No 242'.

[3] Law Com No 242, paras 5.16, 13.2.

[4] s 7(1).

[5] Below, pp 639–52.

[6] Hansard, HL Deb vol 596, col 21 (11 January 1999) (Lord Irvine LC).

2. THE ACQUISITION OF CONTRACTUAL RIGHTS BY THIRD PARTIES

(a) THE DEVELOPMENT OF THE COMMON LAW RULE

If A and B make a contract in which A promises to do something or to refrain from doing something for the benefit of C, all three may be willing that C should have all the rights of an actual contracting party.[7] Thus A may promise to pay a sum of money to,[8] or perform a service for,[9] C. Alternatively, A may promise not to sue C, either at all[10] or in circumstances covered by an exclusion or limitation clause in the contract between A and B.[11] Many systems of law give effect to the intentions of those concerned but the rule of the English common law, now modified by the Contracts (Rights of Third Parties) Act 1999, is that a person who is not a party to a contract can neither sue on nor rely on defences based on that contract.

(i) A relative latecomer

This rule was not clearly established until the middle of the nineteenth century. There are earlier decisions permitting the third party, often a relative of the promisee[12] but not always,[13] to enforce the promise. The development of the rule of privity of contract was linked with that of the doctrine of consideration and the early cases used both strands of reasoning. In *Price v Easton*:[14]

WP owed Price £13. WP promised to work for E, and in return E undertook to discharge the debt to Price. The work was done by WP, but E did not pay the money to Price. Price sued E.

It was held that Price could not recover because he was not a party to the contract. However, the reasoning of the judges differed. Lord Denman CJ said that the claimant did not 'shew any consideration for the promise moving from him to the defendant',[15] while Littledale J said, 'No privity is shewn between the plaintiff and the defendant';[16] and Patteson J that there was 'no promise to the plaintiff alleged'.[17]

In *Tweddle v Atkinson*,[18] it was also held that no action could be brought by a non-party:

H and W married. After the marriage, X and Y, their respective fathers, made a contract by which they undertook that each should pay a sum of money to H, and that H should have power to sue for such sums. After the death of X and Y, H sued the executors of Y for the money promised to him.

[7] Dowrick (1956) 19 MLR 374.
[8] *Beswick v Beswick* [1968] AC 58, below, p 615.
[9] *Jackson v Horizon Holidays Ltd* [1975] 1 WLR 1548, below, pp 631–2 (provision of holiday accommodation).
[10] *Snelling v John Snelling Ltd* [1973] QB 87, below, p 636.
[11] *Scruttons v Midlands Silicones Ltd* [1962] AC 446, below, p 662.
[12] *Bourne v Mason* (1699) 1 Ventr 6; *Dutton v Poole* (1672) 2 Lev 210.
[13] *Marchington v Vernon* (1787) 1 Bos & P 101n (doubted in *Phillips v Bateman* (1812) 16 East 356); *Carnegie v Waugh* (1823) 1 LJ (OS) 89.
[14] (1833) 4 B & Ad 433.
[15] *Ibid*, 434.
[16] *Ibid.*
[17] *Ibid*, 435.
[18] (1861) 1 B & S 393.

Wightman J said:[19]

Some of the old decisions appear to support the proposition that a stranger to the consideration of a contract may maintain an action upon it, . . . But there is no modern case in which the proposition has been supported. On the contrary, it is now established *that no stranger to the consideration can take advantage of a contract, although made for his benefit.*

The modern rule is based on Lord Haldane's formulation in *Dunlop Pneumatic Tyre Co Ltd v Selfridge & Co Ltd*:[20]

[I]n the law of England certain principles are fundamental. One is that only a person who is a party to a contract can sue on it. Our law knows nothing of a *jus quaesitum tertio* arising by way of contract. Such a right may be conferred by way of property, as for example, under a trust, but it cannot be conferred on a stranger to a contract as a right to enforce the contract *in personam*.

The House of Lords reaffirmed the rule in several cases, notably in 1968 in *Beswick v Beswick*:[21]

B, a coal merchant, agreed to transfer the business to his nephew in return for a promise by the nephew to employ him as 'consultant' during his lifetime, and, after his death, to pay an annuity of £5 a week to his widow. On B's death, the nephew failed to pay the money to the widow. She brought an action against him in her personal capacity as the beneficiary of the contract, and also in her capacity as administratrix of her deceased husband's estate.

The House of Lords, applying the doctrine of privity, held that she was not entitled to enforce the obligation in her personal capacity because she was not a party to the contract (although she was able to sue as administratrix of the estate, that is, as her deceased husband's personal representative, being in that capacity a party to the contract).

(ii) Relationship with doctrine of consideration

Price v Easton and *Tweddle v Atkinson* might seem to rest solely on the rule that consideration must move from the promisee and it has been argued, therefore, that the privity rule is really no more than an application of the doctrine of consideration.[22] However, in *Dunlop Pneumatic Tyre Co Ltd v Selfridge & Co Ltd* Lord Haldane[23] distinguished the two and there is support for this in other cases.[24] Certainly in a broad

[19] *Ibid*, 397–8, emphasis added.

[20] [1915] AC 847, 853.

[21] [1968] AC 58, 72, 78, 83, 92, 95, 105. See also *Scruttons Ltd v Midland Silicones Ltd* [1962] AC 446; *The Eurymedon* [1975] AC 154; *Woodar Investment Development Ltd v Wimpey Construction (UK) Ltd* [1980] 1 WLR 277, 284, 291, 297, 300; *JH Rayner (Mincing Lane) Ltd v DTI* [1990] 2 AC 418, 479, 506; *White v Jones* [1995] 2 AC 207, 262–3, 266.

[22] Furmston (1960) 23 MLR 373.

[23] [1915] AC 847, 853.

[24] *Vandepitte v Preferred Accident Insurance Corp of New York* [1933] AC 70, 79; *Scruttons Ltd v Midland Silicones Ltd* [1962] AC 446; *Kepong Prospecting Ltd v Schmidt* [1968] AC 810, 826. See also Atiyah, *Essays on Contract* (1986) 220; *KH Enterprise v Pioneer Container* [1994] 2 AC 324, 355; *White v Jones* [1995] 2 AC 207, 262–3; *Coulls v Bagot' s Executor and Trustee Co Ltd* (1967) 119 CLR 460, 478, 486, 493; *Trident General Insurance Co Ltd v McNiece Bros Pty Ltd* (1988) 165 CLR 107, 164 (High Court of Australia); *London Drugs Ltd v Kuehene & Nagel International Ltd* [1992] 3 SCR 299, 417 (Supreme Court of Canada).

sense privity and consideration may be said to reflect two logically separate issues of policy.[25] The first, primarily associated with the privity doctrine, relates to who can enforce a contract. The second, primarily associated with consideration, concerns the types of promises that can be enforced. Having said that, the closeness of the link between the two depends on the precise sense in which one is using the maxim 'consideration must move from the promisee'. This has been discussed in Chapter 4 above.[26] Suffice it to say here that, insofar as one means by that maxim that consideration must move *from the claimant*, the maxim overlaps with, and is indistinguishable from, the doctrine of privity according to which only a party to a contract can enforce it.

(b) REMEDIES OF THE PROMISEE

Notwithstanding the fact that the third party cannot enforce the contract, the contract is binding between the parties to it. The remedies that may be available to the promisee if the promisor fails to perform the promise are only relevant where the promisee is able and willing to enforce the contract for the benefit of the third party. The widow in *Beswick v Beswick*[27] would not have been able to obtain her annuity had Peter Beswick appointed his nephew the executor of his estate instead of the widow. There is no procedure by which an unwilling or uncooperative promisee can be compelled to institute proceedings on behalf of the third party.[28] The existence of a right of action in the promisee does not, in consequence, necessarily ensure that the third party will obtain damages or the performance promised in the contract. Even where the promisee seeks a remedy there are certain difficulties.

(i) Damages for loss sustained by the promisee

The general rule is that damages are for loss suffered by the claimant. Therefore, where the breach of contract consists of failure to perform in favour of the third party, the damages will, in principle, be nominal only.[29] Thus in *Beswick v Beswick*[30] the promisee's estate suffered no loss because the promise was to benefit the widow and not Peter Beswick (or his estate).[31] In some situations, however, including many commercial transactions, the promisee will suffer loss by reason of the breach, either because an obligation it owes to the third party is not discharged, as in *Price v Easton*,[32] or where

[25] Law Revision Committee, Sixth Interim Report (Cmnd 5449, 1937) para 37; Law Com CP No 121, *Privity of Contract: Contracts for the Benefit of Third Parties* (1991) para 2.9 and see (albeit more equivocally) Law Com No 242, Part VI.

[26] Above, pp 101–3.

[27] Above, p 629.

[28] But see the suggestion that the third party be joined as a party to the action made by Lord Denning in *Beswick v Beswick* [1966] Ch 538, 554, and (in a different context) *Snelling v John Snelling Ltd* [1973] QB 87, below, p 621. Contrast *Gurtner v Circuit* [1968] 2 QB 587, 599, 606; *White v Jones* [1995] 2 AC 207, 267.

[29] See Coote's argument ([1997] CLJ 537, 549 ff) that Courts have confused loss of the enjoyment of the fruits of performance (which the promisee *has not* lost) and loss of the bargained-for contractual rights (which the promisee *has* lost).

[30] [1968] AC 58.

[31] *Ibid*, 102 (Lord Upjohn). See also at 72, 78, 101. Cf Lord Pearce, at 88.

[32] (1833) 4 B & Ad 433, above, p 628.

the consequence is that the promisee comes under a legal obligation to the third party. In such cases substantial damages will, in principle,[33] be recoverable.

In principle, the promisee should also be able to recover substantial damages if, by reason of the breach of contract, the promisee (a) comes under a moral obligation to compensate the third party, though under no legal obligation to do so,[34] or (b) voluntarily incurs expense in making good the default.[35] Thus if a vicar hires a coach for an outing for the choir, and the coach operator leaves the choir stranded half way, the vicar might recover substantial damages in respect of the taxi fares incurred in getting the choir home, whether the choir paid their own fares (in which case the vicar would recompense the choir from the damages recovered) or the vicar paid their fares for them.[36]

There may also be certain cases of contracts for the benefit of a third party where what might at first sight appear to be the third party's loss can in fact be analysed as the promisee's. One example, discussed below, is where the promisee contracts for a family holiday.[37]

(ii) Damages for loss sustained by the third party rejected as a general rule

The principle that as a general rule substantial damages can only be given for loss suffered by the claimant, applied by the House of Lords in *Beswick v Beswick*,[38] has been affirmed on several occasions since then. In *Woodar Investment Development Ltd v Wimpey Construction UK Ltd*:[39]

The defendants contracted to buy land from the claimants for £850,000. It was agreed that on completion £150,000 was to be paid by the defendants to a third party. The claimants sought damages for a repudiatory breach of the contract by the defendants.

A majority of the House of Lords held that the defendants had not repudiated the contract. But their Lordships agreed that, if the contract had been repudiated, the claimants could not, without showing that they had themselves suffered loss or were agents or trustees for the third party, have recovered damages for non-payment of the £150,000.

In *Jackson v Horizon Holidays Ltd*[40] Lord Denning MR, with whom Orr LJ agreed, had stated that whenever a contract was made for the benefit of a third party and the

[33] ie subject to the ordinary rules, including those concerning remoteness and mitigation on which see above, Chapter 17.

[34] *Jackson v Watson* [1909] 2 KB 193; *Radford v de Froberville* [1977] 1 WLR 1262.

[35] It may be reasonable to make a voluntary payment: *URS Corp Ltd v BDW Trading Ltd* [2025] UKSC 21, [2025] 2 WLR 1095 at [53], [61], [191] (no 'bright-line' rule precluding recovery for voluntarily incurred losses); *Banco de Portugal v Waterlow & Sons Ltd* [1932] AC 452, above, p 563 (mitigation of damages). See also *Admiralty Commissioners v SS Amerika* [1917] AC 38, 61.

[36] An example given by Lord Denning MR in *Jackson v Horizon Holidays Ltd* [1975] 1 WLR 1468, 1472–3.

[37] Below, pp 631–2.

[38] [1968] AC 58, 72, 78, 101.

[39] [1980] 1 WLR 277, 283–4, 291, 293, 297, 300.

[40] *Jackson v Horizon Holidays Ltd* [1975] 1 WLR 1468. Cf in tort, where voluntary services by the victim's carer are analysed as the carer's loss and damages are held on trust by the victim for the carer: *Cunningham v Harrison* [1973] QB 454; *Donnelly v Joyce* [1974] QB 454; *Housecroft v Burnett* [1986] 1 All ER 332, 343; *Hunt v Severs* [1994] AC 350, 363.

third party suffered loss as a result of the failure of the promisor to perform the contract, the promisee could recover damages in respect of the loss sustained by the third party, holding the damages as money had and received to the use of the third party and paying them over. In that case:

J contracted with a travel company for the provision by the company of holiday accommodation for himself, his wife and two children. The accommodation provided fell below the standard required by the contract and the whole family suffered discomfort, vexation, inconvenience and distress. The trial judge awarded J £1,100 damages including £500 for his mental distress.

The Court of Appeal upheld the award. James LJ appeared to agree with the trial judge. Lord Denning MR said that, if regarded as only for the distress of the claimant himself, the award was excessive but held that the claimant could recover both for his loss and that of his family.

In *Woodar*'s case the House of Lords disapproved of this view[41] but it was said that the decision in *Jackson*'s case could be supported either on the ground that the claimant there was recovering damages in consequence of the loss which he had himself sustained[42] or as a case which called for 'special treatment'.[43] In view of its decision on the repudiation point it was not necessary for the House to make a decision on the damages point and it did not state any rule of law regarding the recovery of damages for the benefit of third parties. Nevertheless certain members of the House of Lords were strongly critical of the result produced by the combined effect of these two aspects of the privity of contract principle; neither the third party for whom the benefit was intended nor the promisee who contracted for it could recover damages for that which the promisor had agreed, but failed, to provide.

The hope was expressed that the House of Lords would soon have the opportunity of reconsidering this matter[44] but when the question again came before the House in *Linden Gardens Trust Ltd v Lenesta Sludge Disposals Ltd* and *St Martins Property Corporation Ltd v Sir Robert McAlpine Ltd*[45] and again in *Alfred McAlpine Construction Ltd v Panatown Ltd*,[46] the opportunity was not taken. In the *Linden Gardens* case the decision was that the case fell within the rationale of the exceptions to the general rule[47] and in *Alfred McAlpine Construction Ltd v Panatown Ltd* it was held that the exceptions did not apply where the third party has a direct contractual right against the promisor.[48]

[41] Lord Denning had relied on a statement of Lush LJ in *Lloyd's v Harper* (1880) 16 Ch D 290, 321 which was made in the context of the 'trust of a promise' exception to the general rule; see below, pp 637–8 and *Beswick v Beswick* [1968] AC 58, 101; *Woodar Investment Development Ltd v Wimpey Construction UK Ltd* [1980] 1 WLR 277, 283, 293–4, 297. The Package Travel and Linked Travel Arrangements Regulations 2018 (SI 2018 No 634, implementing Directive (EU) 2015/2302), below, p 658 now give the beneficiaries of package holidays a direct right of action.

[42] [1980] 1 WLR 277, 293, 297; *Jackson v Horizon Holidays Ltd* [1975] 1 WLR 1468, 1474 (James LJ).

[43] [1980] 1 WLR 277, 283, 291, 293. See also *Calabar Properties Ltd v Sticher* [1984] 1 WLR 287, 290 (tenant's damages included sum in respect of spouse's ill-health).

[44] [1980] 1 WLR 277, 291, 297–8, 300–1.

[45] [1994] AC 85, varying (1992) 57 BLR 57.

[46] [2001] 1 AC 518.

[47] [1994] AC 84, 114.

[48] [2001] 1 AC 518. It appears that such a contractual right may arise under the 1999 Act: see below, pp 639–52.

(iii) Exceptionally third party's loss recoverable

What then are the exceptions to the general rule? A trustee-promisee may recover in respect of the beneficiary's loss,[49] an agent may recover in respect of the undisclosed principal's loss,[50] and a person with a limited interest in property who has taken out full insurance may recover the full amount of loss or damage.[51]

Again, in a contract for the carriage of goods by sea, a consignor may recover substantial damages even where it has sold the goods and they are not at its risk provided it is not contemplated that the carrier would also be put into a direct contractual relationship with whomsoever might become the owner of the goods.[52] This exception (commonly referred to as the '*Albazero* exception') concerns a commercial contract about goods where the parties contemplate that the proprietary interest in the goods may be transferred after the contract has been entered into but before the breach which causes loss or damage to the goods. This exception has been held to apply also to a contract for the development of land where the land was owned or occupied, or it was contemplated that the land was going to be owned or occupied, by third parties.[53] In such a case, where the third-party owner or occupier has no direct right to sue for breach of contract,[54] the contracting party can recover substantial damages as representing the third party's loss. In *obiter dicta* in *Swynson Ltd v Lowick Rose LLP*[55] the Supreme Court referred to the *Albazero* exception as the 'transferred loss' principle. In Lord Sumption's words:

> It is . . . an essential feature of the principle that the recognition of a right in the contracting party to recover the third party's loss should be necessary to give effect to the object of the transaction and to avoid a 'legal black hole', in which in the anticipated course of events the only party entitled to recover would be different from the only party which could be treated as suffering loss . . . That is why, as the House of Lords held in [*Alfred McAlpine v Panatown*], it is not available if the third party has a direct right of action for the same loss, on whatever basis.

However, Lord Sumption also said that 'the principle of transferred loss, whether in its broader or narrower form, is an exception to a fundamental principle of the law of obligations and not an alternative to that principle'.[56] This statement is confusing. The

[49] *Lloyd' s v Harper* (1880) 16 Ch D 290, 331. See also *St Albans City and District Council v International Computers Ltd* [1996] 4 All ER 481, 489 (local authority recovered in respect of chargepayer's loss).

[50] *Allen v F O' Hearn & Co* [1937] AC 213, 218.

[51] *Hepburn v A Tomlinson (Hauliers) Ltd* [1966] AC 451; Marine Insurance Act 1906, s 26(3). See also the right of the bailee, albeit in tort, in *The Winkfield* [1902] P 42 and the analogous fact situation in *Bovis International Inc v The Circle Limited Partnership* (1995) 49 Con LR 12.

[52] *Dunlop v Lambert* (1839) 6 Cl & F 600; *The Albazero* [1977] AC 774, 846–7. The direct contractual relationship, rendering the exception unnecessary, might be by the operation of the Carriage of Goods by Sea Act 1992 or by making a separate contract.

[53] *Linden Gardens Trust Ltd v Lenesta Sludge Disposals Ltd* and *St Martins Property Corporation Ltd v Sir Robert McAlpine Ltd* [1994] AC 85, 114–15 (contracting party owner of land); *Darlington BC v Wiltshier Northern Ltd* [1995] 1 WLR 68 (contracting party had no proprietary interest).

[54] *Alfred McAlpine Construction Ltd v Panatown Ltd* [2001] 1 AC 518 (exception did not apply because third party had direct contractual right).

[55] [2017] UKSC 32, [2018] AC 313 at [14]–[17], [52]–[54], [101]–[108].

[56] [2017] UKSC 32 at [16].

idea of transferred loss is consistent with what has been called the 'narrow ground' of damages: the third party's loss is transferred to the promisee, such that damages are awarded to reflect the third party's loss.[57] But the so-called 'broad ground' of damages is very different: damages are awarded to reflect the promisee's 'loss'.[58] In that sense, the broad ground is not an exception to the fundamental principle Lord Sumption was discussing, namely that damages are awarded to compensate a party for its own loss.

The confusion displayed in *Swynson* was replicated by the Court of Appeal in *BV Nederlandse Industrie Van Eiprodukten v Rembrandt Entreprises Inc.*[59] Coulson LJ discussed 'a successful claim for transferred loss that seeks to rely on the so-called broader ground'.[60] This makes the same mistake as Lord Sumption in *Swynson*: the narrow ground and broad ground are distinct and must be separated, and transferred loss is not relevant to the broader ground. This was perceptively noted in *Dr Jones Yeovil Ltd v Stepping Stone Group Ltd* by HHJ Russen QC, who observed that 'the analysis of the broader ground is perhaps not so much about a loss transferred (with real or personal property) but an interest retained'.[61]

(iv) Specific performance

The promisee may be able to obtain an order for specific performance against the promisor to compel him to carry out the promise in favour of the third party. Thus in *Beswick v Beswick*[62] the House of Lords held that the widow, in her capacity as personal representative of Peter Beswick (the promisee), could obtain specific performance of the promise in favour of herself as third party. As Lord Pearce explained: 'The estate (though not the widow personally) can enforce it.'[63]

Specific performance is, as has been seen, a discretionary equitable remedy which is not available as a matter of course. As a general rule, an order for specific performance will not be made against a defendant in any case where damages are an adequate remedy,[64] where, had the positions been reversed, the claimant's undertaking could not have been specifically enforced, so 'mutuality' was lacking,[65] or where the contract has been discharged and is no longer in existence.[66] Contracts of personal service are normally not specifically enforceable;[67] and not all contractual undertakings are sufficiently precisely defined to be enforced specifically.[68]

[57] See the speeches of Lord Clyde and Lord Jauncey in *Alfred McAlpine Construction Ltd v Panatown Ltd* [2001] 1 AC 518.

[58] See the speeches of Lord Millett and Lord Goff in *Panatown* [2001] 1 AC 518. Lord Browne-Wilkinson was prepared to 'assume that the broader ground is sound in law' (at 577) but was somewhat more equivocal his approach. In *Panatown* at 584 Lord Millett deprecated the 'unduly narrow approach which the courts have adopted towards the concept of loss'. See Webb, in Virgo and Worthington (eds), *Commercial Remedies: Resolving Controversies* (2017).

[59] [2019] EWCA Civ 596, [2020] QB 551.

[60] *Ibid* at [73].

[61] [2020] EWHC 2308 (TCC) at [137]. See further Davies [2022] LMCLQ 92.

[62] [1968] AC 58.

[63] *Ibid*, 89.

[64] See above, p 595.

[65] See above, p 597.

[66] *Woodar Investment Development Ltd v Wimpey Construction UK Ltd* [1980] 1 WLR 277, 300.

[67] See above, p 598.

[68] See above, p 600.

In *Beswick v Beswick* an award of damages was considered inadequate and specific performance appropriate for a number of reasons. First, damages would not have taken account of the loss to the third party and would have been purely nominal.[69] Secondly, the defaulting promisor had received the full benefit of the contract by the completed transfer of the business.[70] Thirdly, had the business not been transferred, the defaulting promisor could have obtained specific performance of the promise.[71] Fourthly, specific performance was more appropriate for a promise to make a series of regular payments than a succession of actions for damages which would have had to have been brought as each payment fell due. It does not therefore follow that specific performance will necessarily be ordered in all cases where performance is to be made to a third party.

(v) Action for the agreed sum

Where money is promised to be paid to a third party, the contracting party to whom the promise is made has normally no claim whatsoever to the money which is properly due to the third party. It follows that the promisee cannot by means of an action for the agreed sum require the promisor to pay the agreed sum to the promisee.[72] However, although there is no clear support for this in the authorities,[73] it would seem that in principle the promisee should be able to bring an action for the agreed sum to enforce payment to the third party. This is simply to enforce the promise made.

(vi) Recovery of money paid

Where a contract is made for the benefit of a third party and the promisee has paid money to the promisor in consideration of a promise which the promisor has totally failed to perform, the promisee will be entitled to recover the money as paid on a consideration which has totally failed. This remedy for restitution of an unjust enrichment, which might be less advantageous than damages or specific performance, would not be available in the present state of the law if the promisor had partly performed the promise, as there would not be a total failure of basis.[74]

(vii) Injunction

Where the promisor, either expressly or by necessary implication, promises not to sue a third party, the third party, as a stranger to the contract, cannot rely directly on the terms of the contract as a defence to any action brought by the promisor.[75] But the promisee may obtain an injunction enforcing the negative promise or a declaration that

[69] Above, p 630. [70] [1968] AC 58, 83, 89, 97. [71] *Ibid*, 89 (Lord Pearce).

[72] *Re Stapleton-Bretherton* [1941] Ch 482; *Re Schebsman* [1944] Ch 83; *Coulls v Bagot's Executor and Trustee Co Ltd* (1967) 119 CLR 460, 502; *Beswick v Beswick* [1968] AC 58, 94, 96. Cf *Re Sinclair's Life Policy* [1938] Ch 799.

[73] Passages in *Beswick v Beswick* [1968] AC 58, 81, 88, 97 may be thought to suggest that the administratrix could sue for arrears to be paid *to the widow* in her personal capacity.

[74] See above, p 607. [75] See below, p 661 (exemption clauses).

the promise is binding on the promisor thereby effectively preventing the promisor from suing the third party. In *Snelling v John Snelling Ltd*:[76]

Three brothers were shareholders and directors of a family company which owed each of them considerable sums of money. Differences arose between them, and, as part of an effort to settle these, they made a contract, agreeing, *inter alia*, that, in the event of any director resigning, he would immediately forfeit all moneys due to him from the company. Subsequently, one brother (Brian) resigned his directorship and brought an action against the company for payment of the money owed to him. His two brothers applied to be, and were, joined as co-defendants to the action, and they counterclaimed for a declaration that the sums due to Brian from the company had been forfeited.

The question arose whether the company, which was not a party to the agreement, could rely on it. In principle, it could not do so, and so Brian would be entitled to judgment on his claim. The two brothers would, however, also be entitled to a declaration that the provisions of the agreement were binding on Brian. In the view of Ormrod J the resulting situation was absurd, and he held that the proper order to make was to dismiss Brian's claim. The reality of the situation was that Brian's claim had failed since his two brothers had succeeded in their counterclaim, and the order of the Court should reflect that fact. It would therefore seem that, where all parties are before the Court, the Court may stay[77] or dismiss a claim brought by a contracting party against a third party whom the other contracting party has promised not to sue.

It has been said that for the Court to exercise its power to stay or dismiss a claim, the promisee must have a sufficient interest,[78] such as a legal or equitable right to protect,[79] and must be able to show a real possibility of prejudice to himself, for example by being exposed to an action by the third party.[80] In *Snelling*'s case the promisees were not subject to this kind of 'legal' prejudice since they would not have been exposed to an action by the company. However, they would have been commercially and financially prejudiced by any deterioration in the company's financial position, as would have occurred had Brian's action succeeded.

(c) RATIONALE AND APPRAISAL OF THE COMMON LAW RULE

(i) Justification of rule

The case for the common law rule that a third party cannot enforce a contract rests on a number of factors. First, although consideration has been provided for the promise, it has not been provided by the third party. Secondly, it would be unjust if a person could

[76] [1973] QB 87.

[77] This power is now in Senior Courts Act 1981, s 49(2). But contrast *Gore v Van der Lann* [1967] 2 QB 31.

[78] *Gore v Van der Lann* [1967] 2 QB 31.

[79] *European Asian Bank v Punjab & Sind Bank* [1982] 2 Lloyd's Rep 356, 369.

[80] *The Elbe Maru* [1978] 1 Lloyd's Rep 206. Cf *The Chevalier Roze* [1983] 2 Lloyd's Rep 438, 443; *The Starsin* [2001] 1 Lloyd's Rep 437, 461–2.

sue on a contract but not be sued upon the contract.[81] Thirdly, if third parties could enforce contracts made for their benefit, the rights of the contracting parties to vary or terminate such contracts would be affected. Fourthly, it is undesirable for the promisor to be liable to two actions from both the promisor and the third party, and the privity rule limits the potential liability of a contracting party to a wide range of possible third-party claimants.[82] The Law Commission did not regard any of these explanations as convincing justifications of the rule.[83]

Those who favour the common law rule[84] also point out that it is not absolute. The Courts and the Legislature have created exceptions and circumventions to avoid perceived injustice. These are considered below.[85] In some, particularly those based on statute, the third-party rule is simply overridden. In others the third-party claimant does not need to rely on the contract but is able to have recourse to other areas of the law and to rely on a property right, a possessory right, or is able to sue in tort.[86] Alternatively, the third party may be able to establish a collateral contract with the promisor.[87] Other exceptions to and circumventions of the rule may be seen in assignment,[88] agency (including the doctrine of the undisclosed principal),[89] transfer on death,[90] and bankruptcy.[91]

(ii) Criticism of rule

The considerable criticism of the principle that a third party cannot acquire rights under a contract has been noted. Its desirability as a matter of policy has been questioned by judges,[92] law reform bodies,[93] and commentators.[94] Its pedigree has also been criticized on the ground that it was doubtful that the nineteenth-century cases on which it is based in fact established its existence and that it was only a rule of procedure.[95] It is said that it serves only to defeat the intentions of the contracting parties and the legitimate

[81] *Tweddle v Atkinson* (1861) 1 B & S 393, 398; *London Drugs Ltd v Kuehne & Nagel International Ltd* [1992] 3 SCR 299, 418, 440 (Canada). But see above, p 32 for the position in the case of unilateral contracts.

[82] *Trident General Insurance Co Ltd v McNiece Bros Pt Ltd* (1988) 165 CLR 107, 121–2 (Australia).

[83] Law Com CP No 121, *Privity of Contract: Contracts for the Benefit of Third Parties* (1991) para 4.4; Law Com No 242, para 3.1.

[84] Kincaid (1994) 8 JCL 51, (1999) 12 JCL 47, (2000) 116 LQR 43; Smith (1997) 17 OJLS 643; Stevens (2004) 120 LQR 292.

[85] See below, pp 639–52, 657–8.

[86] See below, pp 660 (tort), 653, 659 (property).

[87] See generally, above, p 146 and, on exemption clauses and third parties, below, p 667.

[88] See below, Chapter 22.

[89] See below, Chapter 23.

[90] See below, p 694.

[91] See below, p 694.

[92] *Scruttons Ltd v Midland Silicones Ltd* [1962] AC 446, 467–8; *Beswick v Beswick* [1968] AC 58, 72; *Woodar Investment Development Ltd v Wimpey Construction UK Ltd* [1980] 1 WLR 277, 291, 297–8, 300; *Forster v Silvermere Gold and Equestrian Centre* (1981) 125 SJ 397; *Swain v The Law Society* [1983] 1 AC 598, 611; *Darlington BC v Wiltshier Northern Ltd* [1995] 1 WLR 68, 73, 76.

[93] Law Revision Committee Sixth Interim Report (Cmnd 5449, 1937); Law Com No 242.

[94] Corbin (1930) 46 LQR 12; Furmston (1960) 23 MLR 373; Flannigan (1987) 103 LQR 564; Andrews (1988) 8 LS 14; Adams and Brownsword (1990) 10 LS 12. Cf Kincaid [1989] CLJ 243, (1994) 8 JCL 51, (2000) 116 LQR 43; Smith (1997) 17 OJLS 643; Stevens (2004) 120 LQR 292.

[95] *Drive Yourself Hire Co (London) Ltd v Strutt* [1954] 1 QB 250, 273; *Beswick v Beswick* [1968] Ch 538, 553–4, 557 (Lord Denning MR, a particularly vigorous critic).

expectations of the third party, who may have organized its affairs on the faith of the contract; that it undermines the social interest of the community in the security of bargains; and that it is commercially inconvenient.[96] In the standard situation the person who has suffered the loss cannot sue, while the person who has suffered no loss can sue but may be able to obtain only nominal damages.[97] Where the object of the contract is to benefit the third party, the effect of this is tantamount to ruling that the object of the contract is unenforceable. The exceptions and circumventions are complicated and not always available, particularly to those who do not have access to sophisticated legal advice. Moreover, their technicality has led to artificiality and uncertainty.

(iii) Reform

The right of a third party to sue on a contract made for its benefit is recognized by the law of Scotland and the legal systems of the United States. It has also been introduced by statute in several Commonwealth jurisdictions[98] while in others the privity doctrine has been modified judicially.[99] In England, the Courts, while criticizing the principle that a third party cannot acquire rights under a contract, indicated that a radical change in the common law, such as abrogation of the principle, should be introduced by legislation.[100] This reluctance stemmed from the nature of the third-party rule itself, which some saw as a 'fundamental' rule and which, in Anson's words, 'seems to flow from the very conception we form of contract'.[101] As such, it fixed 'a reference point for the development of subsidiary rules', here the rules of trust, agency, and estoppel. Those who took this view considered that it was not possible to abrogate the rule without leaving open major issues of policy, which it was not appropriate for Courts to decide.[102]

As long ago as 1937 the Law Revision Committee recommended that where a contract by its express terms purports to confer a benefit directly on a third party, the third party should be entitled to enforce the provision in its own name.[103] Although widely supported, the recommendation was not implemented because of the outbreak of the Second World War.[104] In 1991 the Law Commission returned to the subject and in 1996 it recommended that the rule should be reformed so as to enable contracting parties

[96] For difficulties in construction and insurance contracts, see Law Com No 242, paras 3.10–3.27.

[97] Above, p 630.

[98] Western Australia, Queensland, and New Zealand. For a summary of this legislation, see Law Com No 242, Appendix B, and for a summary of the position in other legal systems, including Scotland, the United States, France, and Germany, see the Appendix to Law Com CP No 121 (1991).

[99] *London Drugs Ltd v Kuehne & Nagel International Ltd* [1992] 3 SCR 299 (Canada), below, p 666 (exemption clauses); *Trident General Insurance Co Ltd v NcNiece Bros Pty Ltd* (1988) 165 CLR 107 (Australia).

[100] *Scruttons Ltd v Midland Silicones Ltd* [1962] AC 446, 467–8; *Beswick v Beswick* [1968] AC 58, 72; *Woodar Investment Development Ltd v Wimpey Construction UK Ltd* [1980] 1 WLR 277, 291, 297–8, 300. But cf *KH Enterprise v Pioneer Container* [1994] 2 AC 324, 335; *Darlington BC v Wiltshier Northern Ltd* [1995] 1 WLR 68. Cf *The Mahkutai* [1996] AC 650, 665.

[101] *Principles of the Law of Contract* (1879) 195.

[102] See Brennan and Deane JJ's minority judgments in *Trident General Insurance Co Ltd v NcNiece Bros Pty Ltd* (1988) 165 CLR 107, 128, 131–2, 134, 140–1, 142–5 and Beatson (1992) 44 CLP 1.

[103] Sixth Interim Report (Cmnd 5449, 1937) para 48.

[104] See further Beatson (1992) 44 CLP 1, 10–15.

to confer a right to enforce the contract on a third party.[105] The Law Commission saw its proposals 'as achieving at a stroke and with certainty and clarity what a progressive House of Lords might well itself have brought about over the course of time', and as not cutting across the underpinning principles of the common law.[106]

While the simple recognition of some form of third-party right might be uncontroversial, the determination of its precise extent is not. The most important difficulties concern the test of enforceable benefit, the validity of defences that would have been available had the promisee sued, and whether the contracting parties should have power to vary or cancel the contract. The way that these issues are dealt with by the Contracts (Rights of Third Parties) Act 1999, which substantially implemented the Law Commission's Report,[107] is considered in the next section.

(d) THE CONTRACTS (RIGHTS OF THIRD PARTIES) ACT 1999

(i) Introduction

The Contracts (Rights of Third Parties) Act 1999 enables the parties to a contract to make it enforceable by a third party.[108] It enables a third party both to sue to enforce a positive provision in the contract, such as a promise to pay money, and to rely on an exemption or limitation clause in its favour as a defence.[109] The Act thus removes the limit on the autonomy of the parties represented by the first rule of the privity principle. It is fundamental to the scheme of the Act that the parties to the contract control both whether a third party has an enforceable right and, if so, the extent of such right.[110] The third party's rights are thus derived from the parties' intentions as embodied in the contract. But they are distinct from, and additional to, the rights of the promisee, which the promisee retains.[111] The existing statutory and common law exceptions, by which the third party has rights, are preserved.[112] These are considered later in this chapter.[113] It will be seen that some of the common law and statutory exceptions give third parties more secure rights than those given by the 1999 Act.

105 Law Com No 242, paras 3.29, 3.32, including (see now s 1(6) of the 1999 Act) the right to rely on clauses limiting or excluding the third party's liability to a contracting party. See Adams, Beyleveld, and Brownsword (1997) 60 MLR 238.

106 Law Com No 242, para 1.10.

107 s 6(2)–(4), exempting contracts of employment and the contract contained in a company's articles from the Act, is not based on recommendations of the Law Commission and s 8, on arbitration clauses, differs from the Draft Bill attached to the Commission's Report.

108 For contemporary commentary on the Act, see Andrews [2001] CLJ 353; Bridge (2001) 5 Edin LR 85; Burrows [2000] LMCLQ 540; MacMillan (2000) 63 MLR 721; Roe (2000) 63 MLR 887; Merkin, *Privity of Contract* (2000) ch 5 (usefully containing the Law Commission consultation paper, report, and the Parliamentary debates on the bill in appendices). For criticism of the Act, see Stevens (2004) 120 LQR 292. For an assessment of the Act 25 years on from its enactment, see generally O'Sullivan, Merrett, and Day (eds), *The Contracts (Rights of Third Parties) Act 1999 at 25* (2025).

109 1999 Act, s 1(6).

110 1999 Act, s 1(4).

111 1999 Act, s 4.

112 1999 Act, s 7(1). See Law Com No 242, paras 12.1–12.2. But note the position of negotiable instruments and certain contracts of carriage, below, p 640.

113 Below, pp 653–67.

(ii) The scope of the Act

Although it is general, certain types of contract are not affected by the Act. The common law position for contracts in the constitution of a company, binding on the company and its members under section 33 of the Companies Act 2006, is preserved by section 6(2) of the 1999 Act. Moreover, section 6(3) prevents third parties from relying on the 1999 Act to enforce terms in contracts of employment and similar contracts purporting to enable them to sue an employee, a worker, or an agency worker.[114]

A second category of contracts is excluded from the 1999 Act because they are subject to an alternative legislative regime recognizing and regulating third-party rights which might otherwise be undermined. Bills of exchange, promissory notes, and negotiable instruments are excluded by section 6(1). Contracts of carriage subject either to the Carriage of Goods by Sea Act 1992 or international conventions governing carriage by road, air, and rail to which the United Kingdom is party are, subject to one qualification, excluded by section 6(5). The qualification is that a third party may avail itself of an exclusion or limitation of liability in such a contract.[115] Contracts by way of charterparties are not excluded.[116]

In the case of negotiable instruments, only third parties who are 'holders' of the instrument can sue[117] whereas, if the 1999 Act applied, this would have opened up the possibility of others suing. In the case of contracts of carriage, where third parties are given the right to enforce the contract under the Carriage of Goods by Sea Act 1992 they also take some or all of the burdens, whereas under the 1999 Act the third party takes only the benefits.[118] Moreover, under section 2(1) of the 1992 Act, 'all rights of suit' are transferred to the third party[119] so that, unlike under the 1999 Act, the promisee is left with no rights of enforcement.

(iii) The tests of enforceability

The 1999 Act contains two tests of enforceability. By section 1:

> (1) Subject to the provisions of this Act, a person who is not a party to a contract (a 'third party') may in his own right enforce a term of the contract if—
> (a) the contract expressly provides that he may, or
> (b) subject to subsection (2), the term purports to confer a benefit on him.
> (2) Subsection (1)(b) does not apply if on a proper construction of the contract it appears that the parties did not intend the term to be enforceable by the third party.
> (3) The third party must be expressly identified in the contract by name, as a member of a class or as answering a particular description, but need not be in existence when the contract is entered into.

Each of the two tests will be considered in turn.

114 As defined by the National Minimum Wage Act 1998, ss 54 and 34–35. See Hansard, HL Deb vol 596, coll 21 (11 January 1999) (Lord Irvine LC)

115 1999 Act, s 6(5).

116 See the definitions in 1999 Act, s 6(6) and (7).

117 Bills of Exchange Act 1882.

118 See Law Com No 242, paras 12.7–12.16.

119 See below, p 658.

(a) Express Provision. Section 1(1)(a) of the 1999 Act provides a simple and certain test: a third party acquires an enforceable right where the contract contains an express provision to that effect. Section 1(3) provides that the third party must be expressly identified in the contract by name, class, or description.[120] Identification in the course of negotiations does not suffice. But the third party need not be in existence when the contract is made. Accordingly, a contracting party's present and future employees and subcontractors may qualify, as may unborn children.[121] Third parties who qualify under section 1(1)(a) may enforce a contractual term (including an exclusion or limitation clause) even if they are not intended to be the beneficiaries of the term, as where they are trustees[122] or security agents.[123]

The Law Revision Committee had recommended that this should be the only way that a third party could acquire an enforceable right.[124] But, while a requirement of express contractual provision is conducive to certainty, it means that the intentions of contracting parties (including those reflected in trade practice or by the principles governing implied terms)[125] will not always be recognized. Nor would it cover the facts of many of the cases where the privity doctrine caused a problem, such as *Beswick v Beswick*.[126] For these reasons, and because requiring express contractual provision would 'operate to the disadvantage of those who do not have the benefit of (good) legal advice',[127] the Law Commission concluded that there should also be a second test of enforceability to cover situations where the parties do not expressly contract to confer a legal right on the third party.

(b) Term Purporting to Confer a Benefit on En expressly Identified Third Party. The effect of section 1(1)(b) and section 1(2) is in general terms to provide for what the Law Commission and the Lord Chancellor described as a rebuttable presumption in favour of there being a third-party right where a contractual term purports to confer a benefit on a third party expressly identified by name, class, or description.[128] This will be rebutted where, on the proper construction of the contract as a whole, that is, including the surrounding circumstances,[129] the parties do not intend the third party to have a right to enforce it.

[120] In the similarly worded New Zealand legislation, the words 'or nominee' may not sufficiently identify the third party (*Karangahape Road International Village Ltd v Holloway* [1989] 1 NZLR 83) and may be insufficient to indicate an intention to create an enforceable right in the nominee (*Field v Filton* [1988] 1 NZLR 482). But cf *Rattrays Wholesale Ltd v Meredyth Young and A'Court Ltd* [1997] 2 NZLR 363.

[121] Law Com No 242, paras 8.1–8.16.

[122] Law Com No 242, para 7.12 ff.

[123] *HNW Lending Ltd v Lawrence* [2025] EWHC 908 (Ch), [2025] 1 WLR 4145 (Andrew Lenon KC), disagreeing with the earlier decision of HHJ Dight in *HNW Lending Ltd v Mark* (unreported, Central London County Court, 7 August 2024). Both decisions are currently the subject of appeal.

[124] Law Com No 242, paras 8.1–8.16.

[125] Sixth Interim Report (Cmnd 5449, 1937).

[126] [1968] AC 58. See Law Com No 242, para 7.11.

[127] Law Com No 242, para 7.11.

[128] Law Com No 242, para 7.17; Hansard, HL Deb vol 596 col 1425 (2 February 1999). The identification requirement in s 1(3), above, p 640, also applies to s 1(1)(b).

[129] See above, p 162.

It has been suggested that the words 'purport to confer a benefit' mean that the presumption in section 1(1)(b) is triggered only where the third party is to receive a benefit directly from the promisor,[130] but this is not entirely clear from the words of the Act or the Law Commission's report.[131]

The approach of the 1999 Act should avoid a problem which has arisen in the United States where an 'intention to benefit' test has been used. That test has led to difficult distinctions between the 'intended beneficiary' and the 'incidental beneficiary': the latter is the third party who benefits *incidentally* by the performance of a contract by others.[132] Where A contracts with B to construct a new road on B's land, C, whose adjoining land would be enhanced in value by the building of the road, is merely an incidental beneficiary of the performance of the contract between A and B, the primary benefit of which is conferred upon B. Moreover, while the road may be intended for the benefit of all road-users, it is unlikely that the parties intend that road-users should have a right of action in the event of a delay in construction.

It is clear that the 1999 Act does not enable either C or other road-users to enforce the terms of the contract between A and B. Again, a standard liability insurance policy indemnifying the assured against liability to third parties is plainly for the benefit of those who may make claims against the assured. But, in general, payment is to be made to the assured and the term so providing purports to confer a benefit on the assured. It is accordingly difficult to say that the term purports to confer a benefit on a person with a claim against the assured.[133]

The Law Commission illustrated the application of the test now contained in section 1(1)(b) by reference to a number of hypothetical situations and some of the celebrated cases in which the first aspect of the privity principle has caused difficulty.[134] A selection is set out below. First, there are cases or situations in which the Commission considered the third party would be able to enforce the term on the basis of what is now section 1(1)(b).

(1) In *Beswick v Beswick*[135] the contract gave Mrs Beswick, who was expressly named, a presumed right of enforceability because the nephew promised to confer the benefit (the annuity payments) on her. As there was no indication in the contract that the parties did not intend her to enforce the term, she would have been able to enforce it under section 1(1)(b).

(2) B takes out a policy of insurance with A Ltd to cover her employees against medical expenses. The policy provides that payments under it will be made directly to ill employees or, at the discretion of A Ltd, to the provider of the

[130] Burrows [2000] LMCLQ 540, 544.

[131] Cf the example in Law Com No 242, paras 7.33, 7.51, based on the facts of *Green v Russell* [1959] 2 QB 226, below, pp 628–9.

[132] ALI *Restatement, Contracts* (1932) paras 133(1) and 147; ALI *Restatement, Contracts (2d)* (1981) para 302. See Prince (1985) 25 Boston College L Rev 919, 934–7, 979.

[133] Merkin, *Privity of Contract* (2000) 105; Burrows [2000] LMCLQ 540, 544–5.

[134] Law Com No 242, paras 7.28–7.51. For other examples, see Burrows [2000] LMCLQ 540, 552–3.

[135] [1968] AC 58, above, p 629. See Law Com No 242, para 7.46.

medical services in discharge of an employee's liability. C, an employee, becomes ill and requires hospitalization. Meanwhile B disappears. C seeks to sue as a beneficiary of B's contract of insurance with A Ltd In the absence of some contrary indication in the contract triggering section 1(2), C would be able to do so. A Ltd has promised to confer a benefit (direct payment or the discharge of C's liability) on C, who is expressly identified by class.[136]

(3) B Ltd, the owner of land, takes out a liability insurance policy with A Ltd, an insurance company, whereby A Ltd agrees to indemnify B Ltd and B's subsidiary companies, contractors, and subcontractors. C, one of B Ltd's contractors, incurs liability while carrying out work for B Ltd C seeks to sue as a beneficiary of B's contract of insurance with A Ltd In the absence of some contrary indication in the contract triggering section 1(2), C would be able to do so. The contract purported to confer a benefit on C, who is expressly identified by class.[137]

(4) B Ltd takes out a personal accident insurance policy with A Ltd to cover its employees against accidents. By the terms of the policy, payments are to be made to B Ltd C, an employee, is injured and B Ltd is insolvent. The Commission considered this a difficult case because it is arguable that, since payment is to be made to B Ltd, it is difficult to say that under the contract A purports to confer a benefit on C so as to bring section 1(1)(b) into operation. But it concluded that, once received by B Ltd, the money is held on trust for C, so that the contract does purport to confer a benefit on C and the provision that the money be paid to B Ltd would not show that the parties did not intend C to be able to enforce the term because channelling the money in this way is a matter of administrative convenience.[138]

Secondly, there are those cases or situations in which the Commission considered that the third party would not be able to rely on section 1(1)(b). The first is the clear case where the parties expressly provide that the third party is to have no rights, or where the intention to benefit the third party is not known to one of the parties (illustration (5)). It is also likely to be the case where the third party is an incidental beneficiary of the contract (illustration (6)), or where the transaction is part of a customary chain of contracts which gives the third party a contractual claim against someone else (illustrations (7) and (8)).

(5) On Mr and Mrs C's marriage, their wealthy relative B buys an expensive set of china dishes as a wedding gift from A Ltd, a well-known department store. The china is delivered to B, who sends it to Mr and Mrs C. The glazing is defective and after two weeks of use the pattern is fading badly. Mr and Mrs C could not

[136] Law Com No 242, para 7.32.

[137] Law Com No 242, para 7.50, broadly the facts of *Trident General Insurance Co Ltd v McNiece Bros Pty Ltd* (1988) 165 CLR 107 (High Court of Australia).

[138] Law Com No 242, paras 7.33, 7.51, broadly the facts of *Green v Russell* [1959] 2 QB 226. See Pearce LJ, *ibid*, 246–7.

sue A Ltd under the 1999 Act since the contract between A Ltd and B does not purport to confer a benefit on them and they are not identified in the contract.[139] The position would be different if B had made it clear to A Ltd when purchasing the china that it was a gift and A Ltd agreed to deliver it to Mr and Mrs C's home. In such circumstances the Commission concluded that A Ltd would have promised to confer a benefit (china of satisfactory quality) on Mr and Mrs C, who have been expressly identified by name.[140]

(6) In *White v Jones*[141] a firm of solicitors, A, contracted with B to draw up a will benefiting C but, as a result of the solicitors' negligence, the will was never drawn up. Although the intended legatee is expressly designated as a beneficiary, the contract is not one in which the solicitor promises the testator to confer a benefit on the third party, the intended legatee, but one by which the solicitor is to enable the testator to do so. The relevant contractual beneficiary is the testator who intends to confer on the third party the benefit of his assets after death and not the benefit of the solicitor's promise to draft the will. Accordingly, the contract does not fall within section 1(1)(b) of the 1999 Act. The intended legatee, however, has a claim in tort against the solicitors.[142]

(7) C, the owner of property, contracted with B Ltd for the erection of a factory. The contract entitled C to nominate subcontractors and B Ltd made a contract with A, a nominated flooring subcontractor. The floor was defective. The Commission considered that in such a case, even if A's obligations, including the obligation to use reasonable care in laying the floor, purported to benefit C, who was expressly identified, C would not be able to sue A under section 1(1)(b). It considered that the presumption of an enforceable right would be rebutted because A's subcontract was part of a wider chain of contracts, under which C's rights for breach of A's obligations, were to lie against B Ltd, the head contractor.[143]

(8) A person who purchases goods from a retailer against whom he has a claim under the contract of sale is, in general, unlikely to be able to rely on section 1(1)(b) to sue the manufacturer of the goods for breach of the manufacturer's contract with the retailer.[144]

[139] Based on the example in Law Com No 242, para 7.42. On the rejection of a special test for consumers, see Law Com No 242, para 7.54.

[140] Based on the example in Law Com No 242, para 7.41.

[141] [1995] 2 AC 207.

[142] See Law Com No 242, paras 7.19–7.27, 7.48. Because there was a claim in tort (on which see below, p 645), the Commission was content (Law Com No 242, para 7.25) to leave these cases outside its proposed third-party right although 'at a theoretical level' it preferred the view that the right of the prospective beneficiaries more properly belongs within the realm of contract than tort: Law Com No 242, para 7.27.

[143] Law Com No 242, para 7.47, the facts of *Junior Books Co Ltd v Veitchi Co Ltd* [1983] 1 AC 520. The owner successfully sued the subcontractor in tort in respect of the economic loss suffered. Macmillan (2000) 63 MLR 721, 725 considers the view that the presumption of enforceability was rebutted to involve a certain circularity.

[144] See Law Com No 242, para 7.54.

As regards cases in which the 1999 Act has been considered, we shall consider a number of cases, concluding with the recent decision of the Supreme Court in *Secretary of State for the Department of Environment, Food and Rural Affairs v Public and Commercial Services Union*,[145] which is the first case concerning the Act to reach our apex court.

In *Nisshin Shipping Co Ltd v Cleaves & Co Ltd*:[146]

A chartering broker (Cleaves) had negotiated a number of charterparties on behalf of the shipowners (Nisshin). In each of the charterparties, Nisshin agreed with the charterers to pay Cleaves its commission. In each charterparty, there was also an arbitration clause by which the parties agreed to refer all disputes arising out of the contract to arbitration.

Colman J held that, applying the second test of enforceability, Cleaves had the right as a third party under the 1999 Act, to enforce Nisshin's promise to pay it commission; and that it was entitled, and indeed bound (as a condition of enforcement), to enforce that right by arbitration. The most difficult argument facing Colman J was that, as the contract had not provided for arbitration by the third party, so the parties could not have intended the third party to have a right of enforceability. The contracting parties could only have intended either a right of enforceability by arbitration (which they had not provided for) or no right of enforceability at all. Colman J rejected that argument by accepting that the parties could have intended the third party to have a right of enforceability by court action. In any event, he went on to hold that the third party, by reason of the elaborate provisions on arbitration in section 8 of the 1999 Act, *did* have the right to enforce payment of the commission by arbitration (and indeed was bound to do so, applying a 'conditional benefit' analysis).[147]

In *Laemthong International Lines Company Ltd v Artis, The Laemthong Glory (No 2)*:[148]

By a contractual letter of indemnity given by the receivers (ie buyers) of sugar to the charterers of the ship carrying the sugar, the receivers promised to indemnify the charterers against loss sustained by them. Under clause 1 of the letter of indemnity, the promise was to indemnify the charterers and their 'servants and agents' against loss caused by releasing the goods without the bill of lading. Under clause 3 the promise was to provide security for the ship's release, and to indemnify the charterers against loss caused, if the ship was arrested in connection with the delivery of the cargo. The ship was arrested by a bank for non-payment to it in relation to the cargo.

145 [2024] UKSC 41, [2025] ICR 291.

146 [2003] EWHC 2602 (Comm), [2004] 1 Lloyd's Rep 38.

147 For further analysis of s 8, see *AES Ust-Kamenogvok Hydropower Plant v Ust-K* [2010] EWHC 772 (Comm), [2010] 2 Lloyd's Rep 493 at [26]–[32] (aff'd without discussing this point at [2013] UKSC 35, [2013] 1 WLR 1889); *Fortress Value Recovery Fund v Blue Skye Special Opportunities Fund* [2013] EWCA Civ 367, [2013] 1 WLR 3466.

148 [2005] EWCA Civ 519, [2005] 1 Lloyd's Rep 688. See also *Starlight Shipping Co v Allianz Marine & Aviation Versicherungs AG* [2014] EWHC 3068 (Comm), [2014] 2 Lloyd's Rep 579 (in which Flaux J controversially held that the word 'underwriters' in a settlement agreement between underwriters and the owners of a ship constituted express identification by class of the servants and agents of the underwriters, including their solicitor and loss adjuster).

The question at issue was whether the third-party shipowners could enforce clause 3 of the letter of indemnity given by the receivers to the charterers. The Court of Appeal held that, applying the second test of enforceability, they could. In deciding that the letter of indemnity purported to confer a benefit upon the shipowners, the term 'agents' in clause 1 was construed as referring to the shipowners and as applying equally to clause 3. Moreover, although the charterers had also given a direct letter of indemnity to the shipowners, so that there was a chain of contracts, this was thought on the facts not to rebut the presumption under section 1(1)(b). In contrast to the chain of contracts in the context of construction or sales, the third-party right would not here cut across a legal framework that has customarily been employed.[149]

Chudley v Clydesdale Bank plc[150] concerned a very short contract. The claimant was one of a number of investors who had been defrauded in relation to a purported development of the Paradise Beach Resort in the Cape Verde Islands. The defendant bank was in breach of a contract with a company called Arck LLP, whereby the bank was bound to open a bank account, to be named 'ARCK LLP—Segregated Client Account', for the sole purpose of holding and dealing with money provided by investors for the Paradise Beach Resort development. In breach of contract, that account was not opened and investors' money instead went into an ordinary account with Arck and was lost to the investors. The Court of Appeal held that the investors were entitled to damages for breach of contract from the bank under the Contracts (Rights of Third Parties) Act 1999. The term requiring the opening of the specified account was held to purport to confer a benefit on the investors.

This illustrates that the presumption raised under section 1(1)(b) of the Act does not invariably give effect to the parties' intentions: it is improbable that the Bank intended to expose itself to claims brought by parties it did not know and to whom it made no promise. And it is just as unlikely that Arck intended to confer enforceable rights against the Bank upon the investors. Moreover, the investors had no idea about the terms of the contract between Arck and the Bank until after they instructed lawyers.[151] Flaux LJ observed that '[i]t may be said that it is somewhat serendipitous that the appellants can take the benefit of the contract . . . given that they were unaware of its existence at the time of their investment and when they first sought to recover that investment in 2010'.[152] Their ability to rely upon the 1999 Act was probably as surprising to the investors as it was to Arck and the Bank. But there was nothing in the contract to rebut the presumption of enforceability once the court had held that section 1(1)(b) was satisfied.

Chudley also raised a difficult issue concerning section 1(3). The Court of Appeal decided that the words 'segregated client account' constituted their express identification by class. This appears to take a very broad view of 'express identification', effectively encompassing implication. This is inconsistent with the approach favoured by the

[149] Similarly, in *Secretary of State for the Department of Environment, Food and Rural Affairs v Public and Commercial Services Union* [2024] UKSC 41 at [49] Lord Sales and Lady Rose preferred to leave open the difficult question of whether a presumption of enforceability could be rebutted under s 1(2) simply because it is one contract in a chain of contracts. This appears to be a question of interpretation: see the discussion below.

[150] [2019] EWCA Civ 344, [2020] QB 284.

[151] *Ibid* at [24].

[152] *Ibid* at [80].

Law Commission,[153] and has been described by Lord Burrows as a 'problem with the reasoning of the Court of Appeal in *Chudley*'.[154]

On this point, *Chudley* can usefully be contrasted with *Avraamides v Colwill*:[155]

On the takeover of a company (B) by a partnership (A), A agreed to 'pay any liabilities properly incurred' by B. B had a liability to C. On B's insolvency, C sought to enforce that liabilities clause against A.

It was held that the second test of enforceability was not satisfied not least because C had not been expressly identified in the liabilities clause so that the requirement of section 1(3) was not met.

In *Dolphin Maritime & Aviation Services Ltd v Sveriges Angfartygs Assurans Forening*:[156]

A cargo of scrap steel was damaged in a collision at sea. The insurers of the cargo paid the cargo-owners for the damage and hence took over their rights to recover compensation from the relevant ship. The insurers instructed the claimant (Dolphin) as their agent to recover the compensation. The interests of the ship were represented by the defendant P & I Club. The defendant gave a letter of undertaking (LOU) to the insurers promising that, in return for the non-arrest of the ship, the defendant would pay the claimant, on the cargo-interest's behalf, such sums as might be held, or agreed, to be owing by the owners of the ship for the damage. Subsequently the defendant paid the insurers $8.5 million directly.

The claimant argued that, by reason of the Contracts (Rights of Third Parties) Act 1999, it was entitled to be paid the $8.5 million under the terms of the LOU and that it could then deduct its commission from that before accounting for it to the insurers. That argument failed. The LOU did not 'purport to benefit' the claimant under section 1(1)(b). Payment to the claimant was merely the means by which the defendant's obligation to the insurers was to be discharged and the intended beneficiaries were the insurers not their agent. In any event, under section 1(2), on a proper construction of the contract, the parties to the LOU did not intend the term to be enforceable by the claimant.

The decision of the Supreme Court in *Secretary of State for the Department of Environment, Food and Rural Affairs v Public and Commercial Services Union*[157] is the first decision on the 1999 Act to reach the highest level.

Collective agreements originally reached between the government and trade unions in the 1960s provided for 'check-off' arrangements, under which a civil servant could authorize the deduction of union subscriptions from their wages and the money was paid directly to the union. These arrangements also constituted a term of an individual civil servant's contract of employment. In 2014 and 2015, such check-off arrangements were withdrawn by some government departments. This was a breach of individuals' contracts of employment. The question for the Supreme Court was whether the trade union, PCSU, could also bring a claim to enforce the check-off arrangements. The Justices held that they could.

153 Law Com No 242, para 8.1.

154 *Secretary of State for the Department of Environment, Food and Rural Affairs v Public and Commercial Services Union* [2024] UKSC 41 at [152].

155 [2006] EWCA Civ 1533, [2007] BLR 76.

156 [2009] EWHC 716 (Comm), [2009] 2 Lloyd's Rep 123.

157 [2024] UKSC 41, [2025] ICR 291.

By the time the case reached the Supreme Court it was accepted by the parties that the check-off terms did purport to confer a benefit on the unions as third parties (under section 1(1)(b)) and that the unions were expressly identified in the employment contracts as a member of a class (under section 1(3)). The key issue in the case was whether the presumption of enforceability could be rebutted under section 1(2). Since the contracts were silent as to their enforceability by third parties, the Supreme Court unanimously held that there was nothing to rebut the presumption of enforceability. The majority of the Court of Appeal had reached the contrary conclusion, on the basis that the collective agreements themselves were not legally enforceable, and considered this to mean that the parties did not intend the unions to acquire legally enforceable rights. Such reasoning was rejected by the Supreme Court. Whether the collective agreement was enforceable or not is irrelevant under the statutory regime. The focus is squarely upon the contracts of employment, the terms of which—including the check-off terms—clearly were enforceable.

The above cases—particularly *Chudley* and *Public and Commercial Services Union*—show that the 1999 Act has been interpreted in a broad manner, and can sometimes have surprising results. It is therefore understandable why commercial parties regularly exclude the operation of the 1999 Act through an express contractual term.[158] Ironically, the fact that the Act is excluded so frequently may drive the Courts towards an expansive interpretation of the legislation. In *Chudley*, Longmore LJ emphasized that the parties could have excluded the third party's right to enforce the contract but did not do so. Where commercial parties do not make the most of this option, Courts might feel emboldened to interpret the Act broadly in favour of third parties.

(iv) The nature of the rights under the Act

(a) The Third Party's Rights. The third party's rights are derived from the parties' intentions as embodied in the contract and are supplementary to rights the third party has under the common law or other statutes. But, as will be seen in the discussion of defences and variation and cancellation below, the third party entitled to sue under the 1999 Act does not specifically step into the shoes of the promisee and is not treated as a party to the contract.[159]

By section 1(5), a third party who has a right to enforce a contractual provision under the 1999 Act will be able to claim any remedy for breach of contract given by the Courts that would have been available if he had been a party to the contract. Accordingly, while the third party may claim damages for its own loss, an award of an agreed sum, specific performance, and an injunction, the Act does not permit him or her to terminate the contract since termination is a self-help remedy, or to claim restitution of money paid or a restitutionary quantum meruit, since those are not remedies for breach of contract.[160] Where the third party seeks damages, it would appear that rules,

[158] Davies (2021) 137 LQR 101.

[159] Save for the limited purposes set out in ss 1(5) and 3(4), see the next paragraph and below, p 650.

[160] Law Com No 242, para 3.33.

such as those concerning remoteness and mitigation, will be applied by reference to the position of the third party rather than the contracting party, so that, for example, it would be the third party's loss that had to be contemplated.[161]

Section 1(4) contains an important limitation on the third party's rights. A third party has no right to enforce a term 'otherwise than subject to and in accordance with any other relevant terms of the contract'. In this way, although the Act does not change the rule whereby parties to a contract cannot generally impose an obligation upon a third party, if the benefit conferred is qualified or subject to a condition, the third party cannot ignore the qualification or condition.[162]

The distinction between the imposition of a burden and the conferral of a conditional benefit is easy to draw where the condition does not require any performance by the third party, for example where the contract states that the benefit is conditional on the third party reaching a certain age or where the contract contains a clause exempting or limiting the promisor's liability to the third party. Where, however, the condition requires performance by the third party, for example the grant of a right of way over a path subject to a condition that the third party keeps the path in repair, the distinction may be less easy to draw. In order to avoid the possibility of the third party being overall worse off by being given the right to enforce, the Commission considered that in such a case the third party should be bound by the condition in the limited sense that the promisor can use the condition as the basis of a defence or set-off to a claim by the third party to enforce the contract.[163]

(b) The Promisee's Rights. The third party's rights are distinct from the rights of the promisee, which are preserved by the provision in section 4 that section 1 'does not affect any right of the promisee to enforce any term of the contract'.[164]

(c) Avoidance of Double Liability Since, unless otherwise agreed between the contracting parties, both the promisee and the third party have independent and concurrent rights to sue, the Law Commission was concerned to protect the promisor against double liability. This is not a problem where the promisee either recovers nominal damages or is granted specific performance of the obligation to benefit the third party. The Commission considered that it is also not a problem where the third party first recovers damages because then the promisee will be left with no corresponding loss outstanding. In the occasional cases in which the promisee has suffered personal loss which is independent of the third party's loss, the promisee should be entitled to sue for that loss in its own name.[165] That leaves the situation in which the promisee has recovered substantial damages and the third party then brings an action in reliance on

[161] An amendment to make this clear was rejected as unnecessary: Hansard, HL Deb vol 601, col 1052 (27 May 1999).

[162] Including jurisdiction clauses: *Campeau v Gottex Real Asset Fund 1 (OE) Waste SARL* [2025] EWHC 2322 (Comm).

[163] Law Com No 242, para 10.27.

[164] On damages in such cases, see above, pp 630–5.

[165] Andrews [2001] CLJ 353, 371.

section 1.[166] Section 5 of the 1999 Act provides that in any such action by the third party the Court or arbitral tribunal shall reduce any award to the third party to such extent as it thinks appropriate to take account of the sum recovered by the promisee.

(v) Defences

(a) Defences That Would Have Been Available Against the Promisee. Section 3(2) of the Act provides that the rights of the third party are subject to the entitlement of the promisor to raise any defence or set-off which arise out of or in connection with the contract and which would have been available against the promisee.[167] Counterclaims are excluded because a counterclaim may exceed the value of the third party's claim and thus impose a burden on the third party.[168] 'Defences' include matters which render the contract void (such as mistake), voidable (such as misrepresentation), or which have led to the contract being discharged (such as serious breach or frustration). But the Law Commission did not consider that personal bars on the promisee, such as inequitable conduct by the promisee which would bar a claim by him for specific performance or a failure to mitigate his loss, should automatically bar or restrict the third party's remedy.[169]

That is the default position. The Act enables the parties to the contract by an express term either to enlarge the defences available to the promisor to include all defences available against the promisee whether or not they arise out of or are connected with the contract,[170] or to preclude the promisor from raising any defence available against the promisee.[171]

(b) Defences That Would Have Been Available Had the Third Party Been a Party to the Contract. By section 3(4) the third party's claim is also subject to the defences, set-offs, and counterclaims (not arising from the contract) that would have been available to the promisor had the third party been a party to the contract. Again, the parties may expressly contract out of this. Section 3(5) enables the parties to provide that such defences, set-offs, and counterclaims are not to be available in a claim by the third party.

(vi) Variation and rescission

Perhaps the most difficult question in deciding on the precise extent of a third-party right is when the contracting parties should have power to vary or cancel the contract by agreement. A balance has to be struck between preserving the freedom of the contracting parties to implement their intentions at any particular time and allowing the creation of effective third-party rights so that a third party can arrange its affairs with some certainty.[172]

[166] But of the two situations envisaged in s 5, that in s 5(a) no longer raises the 'double liability' problem because, according to *Alfred McAlpine Construction Ltd v Panatown Ltd* [2001] 1 AC 518, a promisee cannot recover a third party's loss where the third party has its own contractual right against the promisor. Such a contractual right is precisely what is given to the third party under the 1999 Act.

[167] Law Com No 242, para 10.12. Cf Law Revision Committee (Cmnd 5449, 1937) para 47.

[168] Law Com No 242, para 10.10.

[169] Law Com No 242, para 10.2.

[170] 1999 Act, s 3(3).

[171] 1999 Act, s 3(5).

[172] Law Com No 242, para 9.8.

(a) The Range of Solutions. The matter has not been satisfactorily solved in certain jurisdictions which recognize third-party rights.[173] The Law Revision Committee considered that third-party rights should be subject to cancellation of the contract by the contracting parties at any time before the third party had adopted the contract either expressly or by conduct. But this notion lacks precision and may lead to Courts presuming that there has been acceptance.[174] In New Zealand, variation is allowed until the third party has materially altered his position in reliance on the contract.[175] In certain cases, such as contracts of insurance[176] and possibly other contracts which expressly name a third party, it is even arguable that the third party's rights should not be subject to cancellation unless the contract expressly provides for this.

The Law Commission sought to balance the freedom of the contracting parties to implement their intentions with the need to create effective third-party rights by having a statutory scheme as the 'default' arrangement but allowing the parties to vary it by express provision in the contract. The Commission considered that reliance should be the primary test for the crystallization of the third party's rights but that there should also be an alternative test of acceptance to enable a third party who has successfully communicated its assent to the promisor to be secure in its entitlement without having to show reliance.

(b) Section 2(1) of the 1999 Act. Section 2(1) of the 1999 Act gives effect to the Law Commission's recommendations. It provides that the contracting parties' right to vary or rescind the contract by agreement should be lost in two situations. First, where the third party has relied on the term and the promisor is aware of such reliance or could reasonably have foreseen that the third party would rely on it.[177] The third party will have to prove that it has relied on the term, but such reliance does not need to be to the third party's detriment. Secondly, the right to rescind is lost where the third party has communicated its assent to the term by words or conduct[178] to the promisor.[179] Communication of the acceptance to the promisee will not suffice and by section 2(2)(b) if sent by post the acceptance shall not be regarded as communicated to the promisor until received by him; the Law Commission considered that it would be inappropriate to apply the postal acceptance rule.[180]

(c) Contractual Provision. The Commission's recognition of the autonomy of the parties resulted in it recommending that the contracting parties be able expressly to reserve the right to vary or rescind the third party's right without the third party's

[173] In Scotland, while *Carmichael v Carmichael's Executrix* 1920 SC (HL) 195 suggests the right becomes irrevocable when brought to the notice of the third party, the position is unclear; McCormick [1970] Jur Rev 228, 236; Scot Law Com Memorandum No 38 (1977).

[174] Law Com CP No 121 (1991), paras 4.32, 5.31; Law Com No 242, para 9.17.

[175] Contract and Commercial Law Act 2017, s 14. See also ALI *Restatement, Contracts (2d)* para 311.

[176] As in the case of the Married Women's Property Act 1882, s 11, below, p 658.

[177] 1999 Act, s 2(1)(b) and (c). See Law Com No 242, paras 9.26–9.30.

[178] 1999 Act, s 2(2)(a).

[179] 1999 Act, s 2(1)(a). See Law Com No 242, paras 9.20, 9.26.

[180] Law Com No 242, para 9.20. On postal acceptance, see above, p 47.

consent irrespective of reliance or acceptance by the third party; or to provide that, for rescission or variation, the third party's consent is needed in specified circumstances (including that the third party's consent is *always* needed)[181] instead of, and irrespective of, whether there has been reliance or acceptance.[182] These are enacted in section 2(3) (a) and (b) of the 1999 Act.

(d) Discretion to Dispense With the Third Party's Consent. Where the consent of a third party is, or may be, required for any variation or rescission of the term by agreement, a Court or arbitral tribunal has power to dispense with such consent in three limited situations. First, where consent cannot be obtained because the third party's whereabouts cannot reasonably be ascertained.[183] Secondly, where the third party is mentally incapable of giving his consent.[184] Thirdly, where it cannot reasonably be ascertained whether or not the third party has in fact relied on the term.[185] This limited conferral of discretion is designed to allow the contracting parties to escape from being unreasonably 'locked in' to a contract that confers a right on a third party.

(vii) The relationship with the Unfair Contract Terms Act 1977

Say a third party is given a right under the 1999 Act but there is an exclusion or limitation clause in the contract (valid as between the promisor and promisee) which excludes or limits the promisor's contractual liability to the third party. Might that exclusion or limitation clause be struck down as unreasonable under the Unfair Contract Terms Act 1977? To ensure that the answer to this question is 'no'—which the Law Commission thought important in reassuring contracting parties that their intentions do govern[186]—section 7(2) of the 1999 Act lays down that section 2(2) of UCTA 1977 does not apply in this situation. It was thought unnecessary to curtail the operation of any other section of UCTA or of the Unfair Terms in Consumer Contracts Regulations 1999 (now Part 2 of the Consumer Rights Act 2015) because they could not apply in any event where a third party is seeking to enforce its rights.[187]

(viii) The meaning of 'contract' under the 1999 Act

The term 'contract' was not defined in the 1999 Act. The better view is that, in accordance with our general understanding of what a contract is,[188] it includes both simple contracts (contracts supported by consideration) and contracts made by deed.[189]

[181] Law Com No 242, paras 9.45–9.47, are unclear on this point. But the broad wording of s 2(3) of the 1999 Act clearly allows for this.

[182] Law Com No 242, paras 9.37–9.42.

[183] 1999 Act, s 2(4)(a). [184] 1999 Act, s 2(4)(b). [185] 1999 Act, s 2(5).

[186] Law Com No 242, para 13.10, point (viii).

[187] Law Com No 242, para 13.10, point (x) and para 13.12. [188] Above, p 78.

[189] This is supported by s 7(3) of the 1999 Act in the references made to the Limitation Act 1980.

(e) ASSIGNMENT AND AGENCY

Assignment and agency (especially the doctrine of the undisclosed principal), may be viewed as exceptions to the benefit or *rights* side of privity (and are also, with the exception of voluntary assignment, exceptions to the burden side of privity). They are dealt with in Chapters 22 and 23 and will not be discussed further in this chapter.

(f) TRUSTS OF CONTRACTUAL RIGHTS

(i) Rights based on equitable property not contract

Equity allows a third party to enforce a contract where it can be construed as creating a completely constituted trust of the contractual right, also known as a trust of the promise. However, as Lord Haldane stated in *Dunlop v Selfridge*,[190] the rights do not arise by way of contract but are based on the third party's equitable proprietary interest in the subject-matter of the contract and the right of the equitable owner to enforce the trust in his favour. Property may be tangible or intangible[191] and certain rights under a contract, 'choses in action', constitute an important example of intangible property.[192]

Thus a promisee under a contract, either at the time when the contract is made or thereafter, may constitute a trust of the right to which the promisee is entitled in favour of a third party which is enforceable in equity.[193] The subject of the trust, the contractual right to money or property,[194] is at law vested in the trustee, that is to say, in the promisee under the contract.

As with the enforcement of equitable rights in general, the person having the legal right in the thing demanded, in this case the promisee who has thus become a trustee, must in general be a party to the action. 'The trustee then can take steps to enforce performance to the beneficiary by the other contracting party as in the case of other equitable rights. The action should be in the name of the trustee. If, however, the trustee refuses to sue, the beneficiary can sue, joining the trustee as defendant.'[195] A trustee who sues on behalf of the third party may recover not merely nominal damages representing the trustee's own meagre interest in the performance of the contract, but the whole loss suffered by the beneficiary.[196]

Although this equitable principle was first enunciated in the eighteenth century by Lord Hardwicke,[197] the important developments occurred in the nineteenth century. Thus in *Lloyd's v Harper*:[198]

190 [1915] AC 847, 853.
191 Lawson and Rudden, *The Law of Property* (3rd edn, 2003) ch 2.
192 *Ibid*, 26–8.
193 Williston (1902) 15 Harv L Rev 767; Corbin (1930) 46 LQR 12; Glanville Williams (1944) 7 MLR 123; Barton (1975) 91 LQR 236; Rickett (1979) 32 CLP 1; Law Com No 242, paras 2.8–2.9.
194 Cf *Southern Water Authority v Carey* [1985] 2 All ER 1077, 1083 (no trust of the benefit of an exemption clause).
195 *Vandepitte v Preferred Accident Insurance Corporation of New York* [1933] AC 70, 79.
196 *Lloyd's v Harper* (1880) 16 Ch D 290.
197 *Tomlinson v Gill* (1756) Amb 330.
198 (1880) 16 Ch D 290. See also *Fletcher v Fletcher* (1844) 4 Hare 67.

H, whose son was about to be elected a member of Lloyd's, wrote to the committee guaranteeing his son's solvency. When the son became insolvent, Lloyd's claimed against the father on behalf of members who had suffered thereby, and also on behalf of some outsiders.

It was held that the creditors were entitled to the benefit of the contract made, since the committee had entered into it as trustee for all those who had suffered by the insolvency of the son.

The principle was applied by the House of Lords in *Les Affréteurs Réunis Société Anonyme v Leopold Walford (London) Ltd*:[199]

In a charterparty made between the appellant, the owner of a steamship, and a firm of charterers, the appellant promised to pay a commission of 3 per cent on the gross amount of hire to the respondent, the broker who had negotiated the contract of charterparty. It failed to pay, and the respondent sued to obtain its commission.

The respondent was not a party to the contract. Although it would not normally be entitled to any rights under it, it was the practice for a charterer, if necessary, to sue the shipowner for the amount of a broker's commission *as trustee for the broker*. Here the action had been brought by the broker, but by consent it was treated as brought by the charterers as trustees for the broker. The House of Lords recognized the practice and gave judgment in the broker's favour.

(ii) Intention to create trust

To establish a trust of the promise it is necessary to establish that the promisee intended to enter the contract as trustee but, in the absence of express words,[200] there is no satisfactory test to determine whether the requisite intention exists. The consequence is uncertainty.[201]

The different judicial approaches to the question at different stages of the doctrine have led to a complicated body of case law which is not possible to reconcile. *Lloyds v Harper* and *Walford*'s case may suggest that it is possible to infer an intention to create a trust solely from the intention to benefit the third party and, as such, the device of a trust could be fictionally employed as a way round the privity rule.[202] However, the approach of the Courts in more recent times has been stricter. It is said that the intention to constitute the trust must be affirmatively proved by substantial evidence,[203] in part because the presence of a trust renders the contract immutable where the parties might otherwise wish to be free to vary it.[204] Thus it will be more difficult to establish a trust where the intention to benefit the third party is not irrevocable,[205] where the contract

[199] [1919] AC 801. For the approach to this situation under the Contracts (Rights of Third Parties) Act 1999, see *Nisshin Shipping Co Ltd v Cleaves & Co Ltd* [2003] EWHC 2602, [2004] 1 Lloyd's Rep 38; above, p 645 and below, pp 656–7.

[200] *Fletcher v Fletcher* (1844) 4 Hare 67.

[201] Glanville Williams (1944) 7 MLR 123.

[202] Corbin (1930) 46 LQR 12, 17; Lord Wright (1939) 55 LQR 189, 208 (a 'cumbrous fiction').

[203] *Vandepitte v Preferred Accident Insurance Corp of New York* [1933] AC 70, 80.

[204] *Re Schebsman* [1944] Ch 83, 104; *Green v Russell* [1959] 2 QB 226, 241.

[205] *Re Sinclair's Life Policy* [1938] Ch 799.

consists of a complex package of benefits and burdens,[206] or where the third party may not need the benefit.[207]

An example of the differences of approach is provided by the contrast between *Re Flavell*[208] and *Re Schebsman*.[209] In *Re Flavell*:

Partnership articles provided that, in the event of the death of one of the partners, an annuity out of the firm's net profits each year was to be paid to his widow or children as he should appoint and, in default of appointment, to his widow.

It was held that the executors of the deceased partner were trustees for the widow under this contract, and that she was entitled to be paid the promised sums. But in *Re Schebsman*:

In 1940 S's employment was terminated, and, in consideration of his retirement, the company agreed to pay him the sum of £5,500 by instalments. If he died before the completion of the payments to him they were to be paid to his widow and daughter. S later became bankrupt, and then died. His trustee in bankruptcy claimed to intercept the sums being paid to his widow, on the ground that S himself could have intercepted them, and so they were available for his creditors.

The Court refused to hold that the contract created a trust in favour of the widow and daughter; they had therefore no enforceable right to the money. But the company was free to perform its obligation if it so wished, and, if it did so, neither S nor his trustee in bankruptcy could intercept the money and put it in his own pocket. Accordingly, the claim failed. Du Parcq LJ said:[210]

It is true that, by the use possibly of unguarded language, a person may create a trust, as Monsieur Jourdain talked prose, without knowing it, but unless an intention to create a trust is clearly to be collected from the language used and the circumstances of the case, I think that the Court ought not to be astute to discover indications of such an intention. I have little doubt that in the present case both parties (and certainly the debtor) intended to keep alive their common law right to vary consensually the terms of the obligation undertaken by the company, and if circumstances had changed in the debtor's life-time injustice might have been done by holding that a trust had been created and that those terms were accordingly unalterable.

Similar contrasts can be found in the approach of the Courts to contracts of insurance. Thus while in some cases such contracts have been held to create a trust in favour of third parties,[211] in others they have not.[212] In this context too it would appear that English

[206] *Vandepitte v Preferred Accident Insurance Corp of New York* [1933] AC 70, 81; *Swain v The Law Society* [1983] 1 AC 598, 612; *Southern Water Authority v Carey* [1985] 2 All ER 1077, 1083.

[207] *Vandepitte v Preferred Accident Insurance Corp of New York* [1933] AC 70, 80 (contracting party liable for infant third party's torts); *Swain v The Law Society* [1983] 1 AC 598, 612, 621 (third-party beneficiary accorded direct action against promisor by statute).

[208] (1883) 25 Ch D 89.

[209] [1944] Ch 83.

[210] *Ibid*, 104.

[211] *Royal Exchange Assurance v Hope* [1928] Ch 179; *Re Webb* [1941] Ch 225; *Re Foster's Policy* [1966] 1 WLR 222. See also *Williams v Baltic Insurance Association of London Ltd* [1924] 2 KB 282.

[212] *Re Englebach's Estate* [1924] 2 Ch 348; *Clay's Policy of Assurance* [1937] 2 All ER 548; *Re Sinclair's Life Policy* [1938] Ch 799; *Green v Russell* [1959] 2 QB 226; *Swain v The Law Society* [1983] 1 AC 598; *McCamley v Cammell Laird Shipbuilders Ltd* [1990] 1 WLR 963, 969.

Courts no longer favour the device of a trust of a contractual right. It has been stated in Australian decisions that this may be too cautious and that there is 'considerable scope for the development of trusts' particularly in the context of insurance policies for the benefit of third persons.[213] One recent English case also indicates less hostility.[214] However, the dominant approach is exemplified by the decision of the Privy Council in *Vandepitte v Preferred Accident Insurance Corporation of New York*[215] on appeal from British Columbia:

B insured his car with the respondent. The contract of insurance was stated to cover not only B himself, but all persons driving the car with his consent. B's daughter, while driving it with his consent, knocked down and injured the appellant, V. She was successfully sued in negligence by V, but the judgment was unsatisfied. By the British Columbia Insurance Act, an injured person could, in such circumstances, avail himself of any rights possessed by the driver of the vehicle against the insurance company. V therefore brought an action against the respondent under this Act.

In order to succeed, he had to establish that the daughter had some rights against the company under the policy, and he could only do this by showing that a trust had been created for her benefit. The Privy Council was not satisfied that this was B's intention. First, as British Columbia law provided that a father was liable for the torts of his minor children living with the family, B would 'naturally expect' any claim to be against him.[216] Secondly, a trust was not appropriate for a contract, such as insurance which imposes 'serious duties and obligations . . . on any person claiming to be insured, which necessarily involve consent and privity of contract'.[217]

The strict approach to the requirement of intention means that, other than where a trust of the promise is expressly created by the draftsman, or where the finding of a trust is established by binding authority, it will now be rare for the Courts to find that a contract for the benefit of a third party creates a trust of the promise.[218]

(iii) Relationship to rights under the 1999 Act

Any incentive to strain to find the necessary intention to create a trust in this context has been weakened still further by the Contract (Rights of Third Parties) Act 1999, which provides a straightforward non-fictional way of upholding the rights of third parties. In *Nisshin Shipping Co Ltd v Cleaves & Co Ltd*,[219] Colman J held that the finding of a trust of the promise, in line with the binding authority of the *Les Affréteurs Réunis*

[213] *Trident General Insurance Co Ltd v NcNiece Bros Pty Ltd* (1988) 165 CLR 107, 166 (Toohey J). See also *ibid*, 120–1, 146–51, 156; *Wilson v Darling Island Stevedoring and Lighterage Co* (1956) 95 CLR 43, 67.

[214] *Darlington BC v Wiltshier (Northern) Ltd* [1995] 1 WLR 68, 75, 81 (a constructive trust). Cf Law Com No 242, para 2.9.

[215] [1933] AC 70. Cf *Williams v Baltic Insurance Association of London Ltd* [1924] 2 KB 282; Road Traffic Act 1988, s 148(7).

[216] [1933] AC 70, 80.

[217] *Ibid*, 81.

[218] For a rare example, see *Burton v FX Music Ltd* [1999] EMLR 826, 840–1 (trust of promise to pay royalties due under a music distribution agreement).

[219] [2003] EWHC 2602 (Comm), [2004] 1 Lloyd's Rep 38; above, p 645.

Société Anonyme v Leopold Walford (London) Ltd,[220] did not preclude the conferral of rights on the third-party broker under the 1999 Act; and that the Act provided a more natural and direct approach to enforcement of the broker's right to commission than the 'cumbrous fiction'[221] of the trust of the promise. He particularly had in mind the procedural disadvantage that it is necessary in an action based on a trust of the promise for the promisee to be joined in the action, whereas under the 1999 Act this is unnecessary.[222] This indicates that, in time, the trust of the promise may wither away as an exception to privity.

Having said that, and while it is clearly more difficult for a third party to establish a trust of a contractual promise for the third party's benefit than to establish a right to enforce the promise under the 1999 Act, the third party's rights under the 1999 Act may be more limited because, subject to section 2, they can be altered or extinguished by the agreement of the contracting parties whereas the third party's rights under a trust of a promise are irrevocable.

(g) MISCELLANEOUS STATUTORY EXCEPTIONS TO PRIVITY

We have seen that the Contracts (Rights of Third Parties) Act 1999 is a wide-ranging statutory exception to privity on its benefit side. But there have been many statutes conferring rights on third rights to enforce specific types of contract (particularly insurance contracts). We here refer to a few of them as illustrations.

(i) Road traffic insurance

Under section 148(7) of the Road Traffic Act 1988, the person issuing a policy of insurance against death or bodily injury to third parties in accordance with the requirements of the Act is made liable to indemnify not only the persons taking out the policy, but 'the person or classes of persons specified in the policy in respect of any liability which the policy purports to cover'. This means that the driver of a motor vehicle is entitled to the benefit of an insurance policy made with an insurance company by the owner of the vehicle and which purports to cover the driver.[223] The Act also permits an injured third party to proceed directly against the insurance company on obtaining judgment against the assured.[224] It precludes the insurer relying on various defences which would have been available in a claim by the assured.[225] Victims of road accidents are also protected by agreements entered into between the Secretary of State and the Motor Insurers' Bureau.[226] These are designed to compensate those injured by untraced ('hit and run') drivers and by uninsured drivers. Where the victim claims against the Bureau in respect of injuries sustained, as it is the policy of the Bureau not to raise the

220 [1919] 1 AC 801; above, p 654.

221 Citing at [31] Lord Wright, above, n 202.

222 Although, applying the normal approach in CPR r 19.2, the Court has a discretion to join other parties where desirable to do so.

223 *Tattersall v Drysdale* [1935] 2 KB 174.

224 Road Traffic Act 1988, ss 151–3.

225 Road Traffic Act 1988, ss 148, 152. Cf 1999 Act, s 3 above, p 650.

226 For interpretation of the 1998 agreement, see *White v White* [2001] UKHL 99, [2001] 1 WLR 481.

defence that the victim is not a party to the agreement between it and the Secretary of State,[227] the victim may proceed and even obtain judgment.[228]

(ii) Third Parties (Rights Against Insurers) Act 2010

Under the Third Parties (Rights against Insurers) Act 2010[229] a third party, who has a claim against a defendant who has taken out insurance against liability to third parties, can claim against the insurer where the defendant has become, inter alia, insolvent either before or after incurring the liability to the third party.

(iii) Life assurance

Under section 11 of the Married Women's Property Act 1882 a husband may effect an insurance on his life for the benefit of his wife and children; and a wife may effect an insurance on her life for the benefit of her husband and children. By section 11, such an insurance creates a trust in favour of the objects of the policy, and does not form part of the assured's estate. The Law Revision Committee proposed that this be extended to all life, endowment, and education policies which name a beneficiary[230] but the Law Commission considered that this would only be sensible as part of a general review of insurance.[231] Nevertheless, those named as beneficiaries under such policies may have a right to enforce them by virtue of the 1999 Act, albeit subject to the limits set out in it, in particular those in sections 2 and 3.

(iv) Carriage of goods by sea

Under the Carriage of Goods by Sea Act 1992, a person may have transferred to him rights under a contract for the carriage of goods by sea to which he was not an original party. So, for example, the lawful holder of a bill of lading has transferred to him the rights under the contract which is contained in, or evidenced by, that bill of lading.[232] Such a person may also be subject to the liabilities under the original contract: for example, if he takes or demands delivery of the goods.[233] But as regards the liabilities, the original party remains liable so that there is no transfer of liability as such.[234]

(v) Package holidays

Where a consumer makes a contract for the provision of a package holiday, the beneficiaries of that contract (eg family members and others who go on the holiday) are given direct contractual rights against the 'organiser' (eg the trader who sells the travel service package) even where they are not parties to the contract.[235]

[227] *Hardy v Motor Insurers' Bureau* [1964] 2 QB 745, 757; *Gurtner v Circuit* [1968] 2 QB 587, 599.

[228] But see the criticism voiced by Lord Dilhorne in *Albert v Motor Insurers' Bureau* [1972] AC 301, 320.

[229] The 2010 Act is based on Law Commission Report No 272, *Third Parties—Rights against Insurers* (2001). There are amendments to the 2010 Act contained in the Insurance Act 2015.

[230] Sixth Interim Report (Cmnd 5449, 1937) para 49.

[231] Law Com No 242, para 12.26.

[232] s 2(1)(a). By s 2(5), the rights of the original party are extinguished by the transfer so that the effect is the same as an assignment.

[233] s 3(1)(a).

[234] s 3(3).

[235] Package Travel and Linked Travel Arrangements Regulations 2018 (SI 2018 No 634) as amended by the Package Travel and Linked Travel Arrangements (Amendment) (EU Exit) Regulations 2018 (SI 2018 No 1367), implementing Directive (EU) 2015/2302. See also *Jackson v Horizon Holidays Ltd* [1975] 1 WLR 1468, above, pp 631–2.

(h) CONTRACTS CONCERNING LAND

(i) Covenants

The benefit (and burden) of the landlord's and the tenant's covenants in a lease, as long as they are not personal, will run upon an assignment of the lease or of the reversion.[236] Also, under the rule in *Tulk v Moxhay*,[237] a vendor of freehold land may attach to the land sold restrictive covenants as to its future use (eg that no buildings shall be erected on the land). Provided that the covenant was imposed for the benefit of neighbouring land, any subsequent owner of that land may enforce the covenant if he shows that the benefit of the covenant has become annexed to the land,[238] has been assigned to him, or that its benefit has passed to him under a building scheme.[239] Third parties may thus acquire rights under a covenant to which they were not privy. These rules, however, are simply rules applicable to rights over land.[240]

(ii) Law of Property Act 1925, section 56(1)

A more controversial exception is provided by section 56(1) of the Law of Property Act 1925, which states:

> A person may take an immediate or other interest in land or other property, or the benefit of any condition, right of entry, covenant or agreement over or respecting land or other property, although he may not be named as a party to the conveyance or other instrument.

The word 'property' is defined in the Act, unless the context otherwise requires, as including 'any thing in action, and any interest in real or personal property'.[241]

The scope of this subsection has long been debated.[242] In the view of some it is merely a conveyancing provision and applies only to land; but others, in particular Lord Denning, interpreted it much more widely.[243] There has also been considerable doubt as to who can properly rely on it. In its terms the subsection is wide enough to permit any person who might conceive it of 'benefit' to take advantage of a covenant or agreement made by others, but such could scarcely have been the intention of the legislature. Accordingly, the Courts have construed it in a more limited fashion. In *White v Bijou*

236 Landlord and Tenant (Covenants) Act 1995, s 3 (covenants in post-1995 leases). For pre-1996 leases, the covenant must 'touch and concern the land': *Spencer's Case* (1583) 5 Co Rep 16a; Law of Property Act 1925, ss 141, 142.

237 (1848) 2 Ph 774; see below, pp 669–70.

238 In *Federated Homes Ltd v Mill Lodge Properties Ltd* [1980] 1 WLR 594 Brightman LJ indicated this could take place automatically without express words.

239 See the Law of Property Act 1925, s 78(1) and also *Smith and Snipes Hall Farm Ltd v River Douglas Catchment Board* [1949] 2 KB 500.

240 See generally Dixon, Bignell, and Hopkins, *Megarry & Wade: The Law of Real Property* (10th edn, 2024) ch 31.

241 s 205(1)(xx).

242 See Elliott (1956) 20 Conv (NS) 43, 114; Andrews (1959) 23 Conv (NS) 179; Furmston (1960) 23 MLR 373, 380–5; Ellinger (1963) 26 MLR 396; Wade [1964] CLJ 66.

243 See *Smith and Snipes Hall Farm Ltd v River Douglas Catchment Board* [1949] 2 KB 500, 517; *Drive Yourself Hire Co (London) Ltd v Strutt* [1954] 1 QB 250, 274; *Beswick v Beswick* [1966] Ch 538.

Mansions Ltd Simonds J said that the only person who could rely on section 56 is one who, although not expressly named, the instrument purports to grant something to, or covenant with.[244]

This, which we may call the orthodox meaning, however, does not assist a person who is not a party to a contract but wishes to sue on that contract. The agreement is not 'made with him', nor does it 'grant something to him' since the subsection does not give to the non-party a right to the performance of a contract if, apart from the subsection, that person has no such right.[245] The subsection did not create any fresh rights to sue under a contract, but only assisted the protection of rights shown to exist.

In *Beswick v Beswick*[246] the House of Lords held unanimously that the context of section 56(1) required that a limited interpretation should be given to the word 'property', but there was no agreement as to what that interpretation should be. Lord Guest thought that it meant land,[247] but Lord Upjohn did not accept that the word was limited to an interest in real property.[248] There was similar disagreement about the orthodox meaning of the scope of the subsection.[249] And Lord Upjohn expressed the view, based on historical grounds, that the words 'conveyance or other instrument' were confined to documents *inter partes* and under seal.[250] These differences of opinion have yet to be resolved,[251] and the enactment of the 1999 Act with its wider scope for third-party enforcement may mean that they will not be. It is, however, clear that section 56(1) does not apply to a simple promise by A to B to pay a sum of money to C.

(i) CONTRACTS GIVING RISE TO TORTIOUS DUTIES OF CARE TO THIRD PARTIES

The tort of negligence sometimes entitles a claimant, who has suffered injury or loss, to sue a defendant who was performing a contract with another party. So, for example, in *Donoghue v Stevenson*[252] the claimant was held to be owed a duty of care by a manufacturer in relation to injury caused by a defective product supplied by the manufacturer under a contract with the distributor or retailer. In that very general sense, the standard application of the tort of negligence evades the doctrine of privity of contract.

[244] [1937] Ch 610, 625. See also (on appeal) [1938] Ch 351, 365; *Re Ecclesiastical Commissioners for England's Conveyance* [1936] Ch 430; *Amsprop Trading Ltd v Harris Distribution Ltd* [1997] 1 WLR 1025. Contrast *Stromdale and Ball Ltd v Burden* [1952] Ch 223.

[245] *Re Miller's Agreement* [1947] Ch 615. See also *Re Foster* [1938] 3 All ER 357; *Re Sinclair's Life Policy* [1938] Ch 799; *Green v Russell* [1959] 2 QB 226; *Scruttons Ltd v Midland Silicones Ltd* [1962] AC 446.

[246] [1968] AC 58.

[247] *Ibid*, 87.

[248] *Ibid*, 105, with whom Lord Pearce agreed (at 94).

[249] *Ibid*, 74–5, 81, 87, 94, 106.

[250] *Ibid*, 107, with whom Lord Pearce agreed (at 94). See also Lord Reid at 76–7.

[251] In *Lyus v Prowsa* [1982] 1 WLR 1044, 1049 and *Amsprop Trading Ltd v Harris Distribution Ltd* [1997] 1 WLR 1025 the orthodox meaning was considered correct.

[252] [1932] AC 562.

However, in some more limited situations, liability for pure economic loss in the tort of negligence more obviously represents an exception to privity in that, arguably, it is tantamount to enforcement of a contract by a third-party beneficiary. For example, in *Ross v Caunters*[253] and *White v Jones*[254] solicitors, who had contracted with a testator to draw up wills benefiting third parties, were held liable in tort to the third parties where, as a result of their negligence, in the first case the will was executed in such a way as to invalidate the gift, and in the second case it was never drawn up. In these cases the relationship created by the contract gave rise to a duty of care to a third party who was thus able to sue the contracting party in tort in a situation where no loss was suffered by the testator's estate.[255]

It has been noted[256] that these cases do not fall within section 1(1)(b) of the 1999 Act. Although the intended legatee is expressly designated as a beneficiary, the contract is not one in which the solicitor promises the testator to confer a benefit on the third party, the intended legatee, but one by which the solicitor is to enable the testator to do so.[257] The direct contractual beneficiary is the testator who intended to confer on the third party the benefit of his assets after death and not the benefit of the solicitor's promise to draft the will. Given that the legatees were incidental beneficiaries, a solution through the tort of negligence seems appropriate.

(j) THIRD PARTIES TAKING THE BENEFIT OF EXEMPTION CLAUSES

(i) Introduction

Say a contracting party (A) has sought to exempt persons who are not parties to the contract, for example, its employees or subcontractors who participate in the performance of the contract from liability to the other party to the contract (B).[258] A's employees and subcontractors, although not in a contractual relationship with B, may nevertheless be under duties to B imposed by the law of tort. If the employees or independent contractors are not able to rely on the exemption clause as a defence to a tort action by B, they in turn may have a right to be indemnified by A. Even where there is no right to be indemnified, A may, particularly in the case of employees, nevertheless agree to meet the damages awarded to B.[259] In both cases the risk is ultimately borne by A, thus defeating the purpose of the exemption clause. Whether or not it is A who ends up paying, permitting B to succeed against the employees or independent contractors will in many cases upset the allocation of risks and consequent pattern of insurance in the

253 [1980] Ch 287.

254 [1995] 2 AC 207. See Weir (1995) 111 LQR 357. See further *Hill v Van Erp* (1997) 142 ALR 687 (Australia). See generally Barker (1994) 14 OJLS 137; Markesinis (1987) 103 LQR 354; Macmillan (2000) 63 MLR 721, 724.

255 *Carr-Glynn v Frearsons* [1997] 2 All ER 614, 623–4, 628.

256 Above, pp 643–4.

257 *White v Jones* [1995] 2 AC 207, 262–3, 273; *Gartside v Sheffield, Young & Ellis* [1983] NZLR 37, 42, 49.

258 See Law Com No 242, paras 2.19–2.35.

259 *Adler v Dickson* [1955] 1 QB 158.

transaction, since A and its employees and independent contractors will have expected B to insure against the relevant loss and not done so themselves.[260]

Despite this, prior to the Contracts (Rights of Third Parties) Act 1999, such attempts by third parties to rely on exemption clauses encountered great difficulties, primarily because A's employees or subcontractors were not parties to the contract. The tension between the doctrine of privity of contract and the commercial expectations of those who take part in multiparty transactions produced a very complicated body of law. At times the Courts applied the doctrine and prevented a defendant from relying on an exemption clause. At other times, and particularly more recently, they have been willing to circumvent the doctrine and even to contemplate some form of modification or exception to it with regard to exemption clauses.

(ii) Privity applied

The operation of the doctrine of privity in such cases will first be considered. In *Scruttons Ltd v Midland Silicones Ltd*:[261]

A drum of chemicals was shipped from New York to London and consigned to the respondents upon the terms of a bill of lading which exempted the carriers from liability in excess of $500 (£179) per package. The drum was damaged by the negligence of the appellants, a firm of stevedores employed by the carriers, and the damage amounted to £593. The consignees sued the stevedores in the tort of negligence for that damage. Although the stevedores were not a party to the bill of lading, nor expressly mentioned therein, they claimed to be entitled to the benefit of the clause limiting liability.

In the House of Lords, Lord Denning (dissenting) considered that the stevedores were protected by an accepted principle of the law of tort, that of voluntary assumption of risk, since the consignees had assented to the limitation of liability. But the majority of their Lordships unequivocally reasserted the doctrine of privity of contract. They held that the stevedores could not claim the benefit of an exemption clause in a contract to which they were not a party.[262]

At one time the proposition was advanced that where a contract contained an exemption clause, any employee or agent while performing the contract was entitled to the same immunity from liability as the employer or principal.[263] But this principle of 'vicarious immunity' was rejected by the House of Lords in *Scruttons Ltd v Midland Silicones*.[264]

[260] eg where there is a limitation clause, the non-party performer would be expected to insure up to the limit and the contracting party (B) beyond that: see *Scruttons Ltd v Midland Silicones Ltd* [1962] AC 446, where the non-party stevedores only agreed to take out insurance in excess of a $500 limitation where that limitation did not apply: Lord Denning at 481–2. See also *The Mahkutai* [1996] AC 650; *London Drugs Ltd v Kuehne & Nagel International Ltd* [1992] 3 SCR 299, 423 (Iacobucci J) (Canada); *Fraser River Pile & Dredge Ltd v Can-Dive Services Ltd* [2000] 1 Lloyd's Rep 199 (third party able to enforce waiver of subrogation clause).

[261] [1962] AC 446.

[262] Article IV *bis* (2) of the Hague-Visby Rules, contained in the Schedule to the Carriage of Goods by Sea Act 1971, now extends protection to the servants and agents (but not independent contractors) of the carrier in respect of loss or damage to goods covered by a contract of carriage of goods by sea to which the Rules apply.

[263] *Elder Dempster & Co Ltd v Peterson, Zochonis & Co Ltd* [1924] AC 522, 534 (Viscount Cave). See also at 548 (Viscount Finlay) and [1923] 1 KB 436, 441 (Scrutton LJ).

[264] [1962] AC 446.

(iii) Privity avoided

Exemption clauses are unambiguously brought within the 1999 Act[265] so that effect can now be given to the commercial expectations of those who take part in multiparty transactions. The Act thus sweeps 'away the technicalities applying to the enforcement by expressly designated third parties of exclusion clauses'.[266]

Nevertheless, discussion of the complex common law position remains necessary. There may be cases in which the 1999 Act does not apply or in which, if it does, it will be advantageous for a person to rely on the common law.

There are a number of ways in which the doctrine of privity may be avoided at common law. The willingness of the Courts to do so has varied. The application of the doctrine in some cases can be seen as part of the process by which Courts sought to alleviate the position of those affected by onerous terms,[267] for instance clauses seeking to exclude liability for personal injury resulting from negligence, now prohibited by statute.[268] The reluctance to save negligent people from the normal consequences of their fault, however, extended beyond such cases and may have influenced the decision in *Scruttons Ltd v Midland Silicones Ltd*.[269] Since that decision, the perceived need to support established commercial practice and to avoid redistributing the risks of transactions has led to greater judicial dissatisfaction with the operation of privity in such situations and a greater willingness to avoid the operation of the doctrine.

There are two methods of avoiding the privity doctrine at common law; these may be termed the 'direct contractual relationship' route and the 'negating the tortious duty' route. The contractual route involves the identification of a second contract between the claimant (B) and the person wishing to rely on the exemption clause. The second route is based on the exemption clause showing that the claimant (B), in its contract with A, assumed the risk of damage or loss resulting from the negligence of the defendant so as to qualify or negate the defendant's tortious duty of care to it. In its wider form this was not favoured by the majority in *Scruttons Ltd v Midland Silicones Ltd* but has since attracted some support.[270] One should also not forget that the promisee may be willing to intervene in the proceedings to protect the defendant. So, where the contract containing the exemption clause can be construed as a promise by the claimant not to sue the third-party defendant, if the promisee intervenes in the proceedings to protect the defendant, the Court may stay or dismiss the claim.[271]

[265] 1999 Act, s 1(6). This includes such clauses in contracts of carriage which are otherwise excluded from the 1999 Act by s 6(5).

[266] Law Com No 242, paras 2.35, 3.32.

[267] Above, Chapter 6.

[268] *Cosgrove v Horsfall* (1945) 62 TLR 140; *Adler v Dickson* [1955] 1 QB 158; and *Genys v Matthews* [1966] 1 WLR 758 concerned such clauses. See now the Unfair Contract Terms Act 1977, s 2 and the Consumer Rights Act 2015, s 65.

[269] See [1962] AC 446, 472 (Viscount Simonds), relying on *Wilson v Darling Island Stevedoring & Lighterage Co Ltd* (1956) 95 CLR 43, 78 (Fullagar J). See also *The Mahkutai* [1996] AC 650, 660 (Lord Goff).

[270] See *Pacific Associates v Baxter* [1990] 1 QB 933, 1011 (Purchas LJ); *Norwich CC v Harvey* [1989] 1 WLR 828; *Marc Rich & Co AG v Bishop Rock Marine Co Ltd, The Nicholas H* [1996] AC 211, 239–40 (Lord Steyn).

[271] See above, pp 635–6.

(a) Finding a Direct Contractual Relationship. The Courts may be able to imply that a party (A) to a contract containing an exemption clause which is intended to benefit third parties such as its employees or subcontractors was either acting as agent for the third parties or as agent for the other party to the contract (B) so as to create a direct contractual relationship (in particular by means of a unilateral contract) between B and the employees or subcontractors.

This device was first employed during the nineteenth century, when England was (as it is again) covered by a network of small railway companies and a contract made with one might entitle the holder of a ticket to travel on one or more of them. In such circumstances, the passenger was not allowed to say that only the company which was a party to the primary agreement was protected by the exemption clauses contained in it. The Courts were ready to find either that the contracting company was acting as agent for the other companies,[272] or that it was acting as agent for the passenger.[273] The passenger was thus brought into a direct contractual relationship with the other companies. In reliance on the principle of agency many enterprises have framed contractual clauses designed to protect their employees and subcontractors from liability.

In *Scruttons Ltd v Midland Silicones Ltd*,[274] the House of Lords left open the question whether the stevedores could have been protected if the carriers had contracted as agents on their behalf. Lord Reid said:[275]

> I can see a possibility of success of the agency argument if (first) the bill of lading makes it clear that the stevedore is intended to be protected by the provisions in it which limit liability, (secondly) the bill of lading makes it clear that the carrier, in addition to contracting for these provisions on his own behalf, is also contracting as agent for the stevedore that these provisions should apply to the stevedore, (thirdly) the carrier has authority to do that, or perhaps later ratification by the stevedore would suffice, and (fourthly) that any difficulties about consideration moving from the stevedore were overcome.

These conditions set out in *Scruttons Ltd v Midland Silicones Ltd* were held to have been satisfied in *New Zealand Shipping Co Ltd v AM Satterthwaite & Co Ltd, The Eurymedon*,[276] where the bill of lading contained a clause by which the carrier, as agent of the stevedore, stipulated that both he and the stevedore should be entitled to the limitation of liability contained in the bill. The Privy Council held that the stevedore had furnished consideration by unloading the goods under its contract with the carrier.[277] The contract was, however, only established by somewhat artificially[278] identifying an offer to the stevedore in the contract between the carrier and the shipper.[279] That is, the offer was treated as being the offer of a unilateral contract under which the owner

[272] *Hall v NE Ry* (1875) LR 10 QB 437, 442. [273] *Ibid*, 443. [274] [1962] AC 446; above, p 662.
[275] *Ibid*, 474. [276] [1975] AC 154. [277] See above, p 110.
[278] See Reynolds (1974) 90 LQR 301; Coote (1974) 37 MLR 453; Battersby (1978) 28 U of Tor LJ 75.
[279] The claimant was in fact the consignee not the shipper. It would be party to the offer made by the shipper to the stevedore either by statute (then the Bills of Lading Act 1855, now the Carriage of Goods by Sea Act 1992, s 2) or by presenting the bill of lading to the ship and requesting delivery of the goods thereunder: *Brandt v Liverpool Brazil & River Plate Navigation Co Ltd* [1924] 1 KB 575.

excluded or limited the liability of the stevedore in return for the stevedore unloading the goods. This technical approach will not be possible in all cases. The carrier may not have authority to act as agent of the stevedore and, although in the majority of cases this may be solved by recourse to the principle of ratification,[280] this may not always be possible.[281] Again, the company seeking the benefit of the exemption clause will only be held to have furnished consideration where it is performing the contract containing the exemption clause.[282] More fundamentally, the exclusion clause may not refer to the employee or subcontractor.[283]

Although, in cases of the carriage of goods by sea, it has been said that stevedores and others performing the contract would normally be protected and that Courts should not search for 'fine distinctions' which would diminish this general position,[284] this approach has not been applied in other contexts.[285] It is in such contexts that the 1999 Act is likely to make a real difference. It is, moreover, inevitable, even in carriage of goods by sea, 'so long as the principle continues to be understood to rest upon an enforceable contract as between the cargo owners and the stevedores entered into through the agency of the shipowner . . . that technical points of contract and agency law will continue to be invoked'.[286]

The approach in *The Eurymedon* was approved by the House of Lords in *Homburg Houtimport BV v Agrosin Private Ltd, The Starsin*:[287]

The claimants were owners of a cargo of timber who had entered into a contract of carriage with the charterers of a ship. Under that contract, they excluded liability for negligent stowage. In their action in the tort of negligence against the shipowners, who were the actual performing carriers, one question was whether the shipowners could take the benefit of that exclusion.

While approving *The Eurymedon*,[288] the House of Lords held that it was inapplicable to these facts. This was because to allow the actual performing carriers to take the benefit of the exclusion clause would undermine the Hague-Visby Rules (given legislative force by the Carriage of Goods Act 1971) which, in a contract of carriage, invalidate the exclusion clause in question.

280 *The Mahkutai* [1996] AC 650.

281 *The Suleyman Stalskiy* [1976] 2 Lloyd's Rep 609 (Sup Ct of British Columbia); *Lummus Co Ltd v East African Harbours Corp* [1978] 1 Lloyd's Rep 317, 322–3 (High Ct of Kenya).

282 *Raymond Burke Motors Ltd v The Mersey Docks and Harbour Co* [1986] 1 Lloyd's Rep 155 (goods damaged while they were being stored and not during loading or unloading).

283 eg in *London Drugs Ltd v Kuehne & Nagel International Ltd* [1992] 3 SCR 299 the clause did not refer to warehouseman's employees. Cf Contracts (Rights of Third Parties) Act 1999, s 1(3).

284 *Port Jackson Stevedoring Pty Ltd v Salmond and Spraggon (Australia) Pty Ltd* [1981] 1 WLR 138, 144 (Lord Wilberforce). See Reynolds (1979) 95 LQR 183; Coote [1981] CLJ 13.

285 *Southern Water Authority v Carey* [1985] 2 All ER 1077, 1084 (construction); *Kendall v Morgan*, The Times, 2 December 1980 (employment).

286 *The Mahkutai* [1996] AC 650, 664 (Lord Goff).

287 [2003] UKHL 12, [2004] 1 AC 715.

288 There are clear analyses by Lord Hoffmann at [93], by Lord Hobhouse at [149]–[153] and, especially helpful, by Lord Millett at [196]–[197]. Cf Lord Bingham at [34] who talks of a bilateral contract.

(b) Negating the Tortious Duty. The majority in *Scruttons Ltd v Midland Silicones Ltd*[289] rejected Lord Denning's powerful reasoning based on the general defence to actions in tort where a claimant has voluntarily consented to take the risk of a loss or injury. But a defendant who is sued in tort may rely on an exclusion clause in a contract to which the claimant but not the defendant is a party as restricting or excluding the duty of care that it would otherwise owe to the claimant. Where this is so the defendant is taking the benefit of an exemption clause in a contract to which it is not a party.

So, in *Pacific Associates Inc v Baxter*[290] a consultant engineer successfully defended a claim for negligence by the contractor by relying on a term of the contract between the employer and the contractor which provided that neither the engineer nor any of his staff 'shall be in any way personally liable for the acts or obligations under the Contract . . . .' Purchas LJ said:

> The presence of such an exclusion clause, while not directly binding between the parties, cannot be excluded from a general consideration of the contractual structure against which the contractor demonstrates reliance on, and the engineer accepts responsibility for, a duty in tort, if any, arising out of the proximity established between them by the existence of that very contract.[291]

The contractual structure may be relevant even where there is no express provision seeking to exempt the third party.

In *Norwich CC v Harvey*:[292]

> A building was damaged by fire as a result of the negligence of a roofing subcontractor. The main contract provided that the building owner was to bear the risk of damage by fire and the subcontractor contracted on the same terms and conditions as in the main contract. The owner of the building brought an action against the subcontractor.

It was held that, although there was no direct contractual relationship between the owner and the subcontractor, nevertheless they had both contracted with the main contractor on the basis that the owner had assumed the risk of damage by fire and the subcontractor owed no duty in respect of the damage which occurred. It is not, however, necessary for the defendant's contract to contain the exemption clause; what is important is whether the recognition of a duty of care by the defendant would outflank the contractual structure governing dealings between the claimant and others.[293]

[289] [1962] AC 446. See also *Leigh & Sillavan Ltd v Aliakmon SS Co Ltd* [1986] AC 785, 817 (Lord Brandon) but cf Robert Goff LJ [1985] QB 350, 399. Cf also the cases considered below.

[290] [1990] 1 QB 993. See also *Southern Water Authority v Carey* [1985] 2 All ER 1077.

[291] [1990] 1 QB 993, 1022–3.

[292] [1989] 1 WLR 828.

[293] *Marc Rich & Co AG v Bishop Rock Marine Co Ltd, The Nicholas H* [1996] AC 211, 239–40 (Lord Steyn) (if the cargo owner recovered from the defendant, a classification society, the cost of insuring against such claims would be passed on to shipowners and the contractual structure governing dealings between shipowners and cargo owners and the limitation of shipowners' liability would be destroyed). See also *Henderson v Merrett Syndicates Ltd* [1995] 2 AC 145, 197.

(c) A General Common Law Exception for the Benefit of Exemption Clauses? The commercial inconvenience that results from the application of the doctrine of privity in the context of exemption clauses has led to the recognition by the Supreme Court of Canada of a wide exception whereby employees and subcontractors acting in the course of their employment and performing the services provided for in the main contract can rely on an exemption clause in that contract which is intended to protect them.[294]

Prior to the enactment of the 1999 Act there were indications that the artificiality and technical nature of the approach based on *New Zealand Shipping Co Ltd v AM Satterthwaite, The Eurymedon*[295] inclined senior judges to regard the development started in that decision as not yet complete. They appeared to be prepared to recognize a fully fledged exception to the doctrine of privity where a contract clearly provides that (for example) independent contractors such as stevedores are to have the benefit of exceptions and limitations contained in that contract.[296] The case for such recognition is that the reasons for and justifications of the privity doctrine do not apply where a third party seeks to rely on a contractual provision as a defence; there is an identity of interest between the contracting party and the third party as far as the performance of the contracting party's contractual obligations is concerned, and it is commercially undesirable to allow a person to circumvent a contractual exclusion clause and thus redistribute the contractual allocation of risk by suing the employee or subcontractor of the other party to the contract.[297]

It is important to realize, however, that the wide Canadian common law exception goes further in the context to which it applies than the 1999 Act. This is because, contrary to the 1999 Act, the Canadian exception does not require the third party to be expressly identified by name, class, or description.[298] In the light of that, the English Courts may consider it inappropriate to adopt the Canadian exception.[299] On the other hand, the Law Commission, as we shall now see, indicated that it did not want its reform to curtail further development of the common law.

294 *London Drugs Ltd v Kuehne & Nagel International Ltd* [1992] 3 SCR 299. It may be more problematic to establish a clear intention to extend the protection of an exemption clause to an independent contractor than to an employee; *ibid*, 441. See also *Fraser River Pile & Dredge Ltd v Can-Dive Services Ltd* [2000] 1 Lloyd's Rep 199 (third party able to enforce waiver of subrogation clause).

295 [1975] AC 154, above, pp 664–5.

296 *The Mahkutai* [1996] AC 650, 665 (but the exclusive jurisdiction clause was held not to be intended to benefit third parties). See also *Dresser UK Ltd v Falcongate Freight Management Ltd* [1992] 1 QB 502, 511 (Bingham LJ) (describing the principle of bailment on terms as 'a pragmatic legal recognition of commercial reality'); Law Com CP No 121 (1991) paras 4.8–4.12; Law Com No 242, para 2.19 ff.

297 *London Drugs Ltd v Kuehne & Nagel International Ltd* [1992] 3 SCR 299, 440–7. For these reasons and justifications, see above, pp 644–5 and Law Com CP No 121, *Privity of Contract: Contracts for the Benefit of Third Parties* (1991) para 4.3; Law Com No 242, paras 2.33–2.35.

298 s 1(3), above, p 640.

299 Cf *Alfred McAlpine Construction Ltd v Panatown Ltd* [2001] 1 AC 518, 535 (Lord Clyde).

(k) FURTHER DEVELOPMENT OF THE COMMON LAW

The traditional reluctance of English Courts to reform the third party rule has been noted.[300] What is the effect of the enactment of the Contracts (Rights of Third Parties) Act 1999 on further development of the common law?[301]

The Law Commission stated that it intended that legislation based on its recommendations, which it described as 'relatively conservative and moderate' should not hamper the judicial development of third-party rights where the Courts decide that in a particular sphere the reform did not go far enough.[302] It is submitted that this cannot mean that, in situations in which the 'intention that the third party should enforce the contract' test is not satisfied, Courts should have no regard to the existence of the 1999 Act and its policy and should continue to develop the common law in the same way as they would have done without the 1999 Act. So, for example, it would seem inappropriate to build on the suggestion, based on dicta in *Darlington BC v Wilshier (Northern) Ltd*[303] that, despite an unpromising history, the trust of a promise should be deployed as a way of granting a right of action to a third party.

In contrast, it may be appropriate for the Courts in a particular context to identify some common law principle other than the intention of the parties upon which to rest third-party rights of suit, for instance 'reasonable reliance'. Moreover, there seems no good reason why the 1999 Act should prevent Courts, after careful consideration, accepting the Canadian exception adopted in the *London Drugs* case,[304] albeit that that exception applies a wider intention test than that under the 1999 Act.[305] It may also be appropriate for there to be judicial development where, as in the case of the promisee's remedies in contracts for the benefit of third parties, this has expressly been left to the common law.[306]

3. THE IMPOSITION OF CONTRACTUAL LIABILITIES UPON THIRD PARTIES

(a) INTRODUCTION

As a general rule, two persons cannot, by any contract into which they may enter, thereby impose contractual liabilities upon a third party.

This principle may be illustrated by reference to building contracts, where a person (the employer) engages a contractor to carry out certain building work. The contractor

300 Above, p 638.

301 See Beatson (2001) 117 LQR 106.

302 Law Com No 242, para 5.11. See also paras 5.15, 12.1. See, eg, the exception for exemption clauses developed by the Supreme Court of Canada in *London Drugs Ltd v Kuehne & Nagel International Ltd* [1992] 3 SCR 299.

303 [1995] 1 WLR 68, 75, 81.

304 [1992] 3 SCR 299.

305 See above, n 298.

306 Law Com No 242, paras 5.12–5.17. See *Alfred McAlpine Construction Ltd v Panatown Ltd* [2001] 1 AC 518, 551–2 (Lord Goff), 590 (Lord Millett) (both dissenting). Cf Lord Clyde at 535.

frequently subcontracts parts of the work to subcontractors. A subcontractor has no cause of action against the employer for the price of work done or materials supplied under the subcontract, since the employer is not a party to that contract.[307] Even if the employer has nominated the subcontractor and taken the benefit of the subcontractor's work, the employer will not be liable to the subcontractor for the price, as there is no privity of contract between them. Conversely, the employer has no claim in contract[308] against the subcontractor,[309] since the subcontractor is not a party to the main contract between the employer and the contractor.

Further, the principle of privity of contract normally prevents a person from being bound by an exemption clause contained in a contract to which it is not a party.

This is not to deny that third parties may be legally affected by contracts to which they are not parties. For example, a person who intentionally induces a breach of contract may be liable for an 'economic tort'; the contractual creation of *proprietary* rights (in land or personal property) bind most third parties who deal with the property; and a contractual obligation to keep information confidential can sometimes render a third party liable for the equitable wrong of breach of confidence.

There are also a few exceptions where a third party is liable *in contract* for breach of the duty created by a contract to which it is not a party. Agency is considered in Chapter 23 and transfer by death and bankruptcy in Chapter 22. In this chapter, we consider covenants concerning land and the controversial issue as to whether a similar approach applies to contracts concerning chattels. We also look at situations where exemption clauses have been held to bind third parties.

(b) COVENANTS CONCERNING LAND

Certain kinds of covenants concerning land are enforceable against third parties whether or not there is notice. If A leases land to B, there is privity of contract between them. But covenants in a lease which have reference to the subject-matter of the lease will be enforceable, not only between A and B, but against assignees of the lease or of the reversion.[310]

Also, under the rule in *Tulk v Moxhay*,[311] the burden of covenants restricting the use to which land may be put can 'run with the land'. In that case:

T, who owned houses in Leicester Square, sold the garden in the centre of the square to E. E covenanted to maintain the land sold as a garden and not to build on it. The land was sold several times before being purchased by the defendant with notice of the covenant. The defendant proposed to build on the land and T sought an injunction to restrain him.

[307] *Hampton v Glamorgan CC* [1917] AC 13. See also *Schmaling v Tomlinson* (1815) 6 Taunt 147 (principal and sub-agent).

[308] But a claim may lie in tort.

[309] Unless there is a collateral warranty: see above, p 146.

[310] See above, n 236.

[311] (1848) 2 Ph 774.

The injunction was granted. The defendant was not permitted to use the land in a manner inconsistent with the covenant entered into by E. The ground for the decision was the defendant's *notice* of the covenant at the time of the purchase.[312] But in subsequent cases the principle in *Tulk v Moxhay* has undergone a considerable change. It must now be shown that the covenant was imposed for the benefit of neighbouring land owned by the person seeking to enforce it and that the benefit of the covenant has passed to that person.[313] The right of a person entitled to the benefit of the covenant to prevent the inconsistent use has taken on a proprietary quality, an 'equitable interest'[314] in the land burdened by the covenant. A subsequent purchaser of that land buys it subject to the equitable interest and with the burden of the interest attached.[315]

(c) CONTRACTS CONCERNING CHATTELS

The question arises as to whether an analogous approach applies to contracts concerning chattels.

In *De Mattos v Gibson* Knight Bruce LJ said:

> Reason and justice seem to prescribe that, at least as a general rule, where a man, by gift or purchase, acquires property from another, with knowledge of a previous contract, lawfully and for valuable consideration made by him with a third person, to use and employ the property for a particular purpose in a specified manner, the acquirer shall not, to the material damage of the third person, in opposition to the contract and inconsistently with it, use and employ the property in a manner not allowable to the giver or seller.[316]

In *Lord Strathcona Steamship Co Ltd v Dominion Coal Co Ltd*:[317]

> The D Co had a long-term time charterparty of a ship. The owners sold the ship, which eventually came into the possession of the LS Co, who took it with notice of the charterparty and on the understanding that the agreement should be honoured. They did not honour the agreement, and, when sued by the charterers, D Co pleaded that they were not bound by the charterparty as there was no privity of contract between them.

The Privy Council upheld the decision of the Courts in Nova Scotia granting the charterers an injunction restraining the LS Co from using the ship inconsistently with the charterparty. The Board relied upon the dictum of Knight Bruce LJ in *De Mattos v Gibson* quoted above.[318] The case was said to fall under the rule in *Tulk v Moxhay* relating to the use of land: whether the subject-matter was land or a chattel, the principle is the

[312] The doctrine of notice no longer applies to such covenants, which must now be protected by registration if they are to bind a purchaser of the land: Land Charges Act 1972, ss 2(5), 4(6) (unregistered land); Land Registration Act 2002, ss 28, 29 (registered land).

[313] *London CC v Allen* [1914] 3 KB 642; see above, p 659.

[314] *Re Nisbet and Potts' Contract* [1905] 1 Ch 391, 398, [1906] 1 Ch 386, 403, 405.

[315] *Rogers v Hosegood* [1900] 2 Ch 388, 407.

[316] (1858) 4 De G & J 276, 282.

[317] [1926] AC 108.

[318] Above, n 316.

same: 'the remedy is a remedy in equity by way of injunction against acts inconsistent with the covenant, with notice of which the land was acquired'.[319]

This reasoning has, however, been the subject of considerable criticism,[320] and it has been said that the case was wrongly decided.[321] In the first place, it is argued that reliance should not have been placed on the dictum of Knight Bruce LJ. In *De Mattos v Gibson* an interim injunction was granted to restrain the mortgagee of a ship, who had acquired his mortgage with knowledge of an existing voyage charterparty, from interfering with the performance of the charter. Knight Bruce LJ's reasoning did not, however, form part of the concurring judgment of Turner LJ and has been doubted.[322] When the case came before Lord Chelmsford LC,[323] a final injunction was refused.[324] Although the Lord Chancellor expressed the opinion that the mortgagee was bound to abstain from any act which would have the immediate effect of preventing performance of the charter, he appeared to do so on the ground that any right to an injunction was based on an extension of the principle whereby a person who knowingly induces one party to break his contract with another is liable to that other in tort in respect of any loss which may have been suffered by the breach.[325]

Secondly, insofar as the Privy Council in the *Strathcona* case drew an analogy with the rule in *Tulk v Moxhay*, this too will not bear examination. We have seen that the *Tulk v Moxhay* rule is now dependent upon the ownership of neighbouring land for the benefit of which the covenant was imposed: the person seeking to enforce the covenant must have a continuing proprietary interest in its enforcement.[326] But a charterer under a voyage or time charterparty (even if of long duration) only has a personal right that the shipowner should continue to use the ship to perform the services which he has covenanted to perform. The charterer has no proprietary interest in the subject-matter of the contract, the ship.[327]

Although the principle stated by Knight Bruce LJ in *De Mattos v Gibson* was subsequently applied in cases of the mortgage of ships subject to a charterparty,[328] these are open to the same criticisms. The better view is that any right of the charterer to an injunction to restrain a use of the ship inconsistent with his charterparty arises if, but

319 [1926] AC 108, 119.

320 *Greenhalgh v Mallard* [1943] 2 All ER 234, 239.

321 *Port Line Ltd v Ben Line Steamers Ltd* [1958] 2 QB 146, 168.

322 *London CC v Allen* [1914] 3 KB 642, 658; *Barker v Stickney* [1919] 1 KB 121, 132.

323 (1859) 4 De G & J 288.

324 On the ground that the mortgagee had not interfered with performance of the charter until it was evident that the shipowner was wholly unable to perform it (at *ibid*, 299–300).

325 *Lumley v Gye* (1853) 3 E & B 216. See also Wade (1926) 42 LQR 139; *The Lord Strathcona* [1925] P 143; below, n 329.

326 See above, p 659.

327 *Port Line Ltd v Ben Line Steamers Ltd* [1958] 2 QB 146, 166 (Diplock J). Unless it is a charterparty by demise, when the charter could be said to acquire a 'possessory interest' in the vessel: see *Baumwoll Manufacturer Von Carl Scheibler v Furness* [1893] AC 8. See also *Lorentzen v White Shipping Co Ltd* (1943) 74 Ll LR 161.

328 *Messageries Imperiales v Baines* (1863) 7 LT 763; *The Celtic King* [1894] P 175.

only if, the conduct of the purchaser is such as to constitute the tort of intentionally inducing a breach of the charterer's contractual rights.[329]

There may, moreover, be alternative explanations for the decision in the *Strathcona* case. One is that there was an implied contract between the third party and the charterers, or a 'novation' of the original agreement,[330] for the Board pointed out: 'This is not a mere case of notice of the existence of a covenant affecting the use of the property sold, but it is the case of the acceptance of their property expressly *sub conditione*.'[331] Alternatively, there may be some ground for saying that the third party was in the position of a 'constructive trustee'[332] with obligations which a Court of Equity would not permit it to violate.[333]

With these reservations in mind, we have now to consider the scope of the decision. This was considered in *Port Line Ltd v Ben Line Steamers Ltd*:[334]

The ship *Port Stephens* was chartered to Port Line by its owner, Silver Line Ltd, on a time charter for 30 months from March 1955. In February 1956, Silver Line sold the ship to the defendant, it being agreed that the defendant should immediately charter the ship back to Silver Line by demise in order that it might fulfil its contract with Port Line. Unfortunately, this second charterparty contained the term that 'If the ship be requisitioned this charter shall thereupon cease', although no such clause appeared in the original time charterparty. The defendant was unaware of this disparity. In August 1956 the ship was requisitioned by the Crown, and as a result Port Line lost the use of the ship. Its claim against Silver Line was settled, but it then brought an action against the defendant to recover the whole or part of the compensation received by the defendant from the Crown in respect of the period of requisition.

Diplock J stated that the *Strathcona* case was wrongly decided but held that, even if it was correct, Port Line could not bring its claim within its principles, as the defendant had no knowledge at the time of its purchase of Port Line's rights under the time charter. The principle in the *Strathcona* case thus only applies where there is actual knowledge by the subsequent purchaser at the time of the purchase of the charterer's rights.[335] Constructive notice is insufficient.[336] Moreover, Diplock J considered that, even if notice had been shown, (a) the defendant was not in breach of duty to Port Line since it was not by its act that the vessel during the period of requisition was used inconsistently with the terms of Port Line's charter—it was by act of the Crown by title paramount—and (b) Port Line

[329] *Lumley v Wagner* (1852) 1 De GM & G 604. See also *Torquay Hotel Co Ltd v Cousins* [1969] 2 Ch 106; *Acrow Ltd v Rex Chainbelt Inc* [1971] 1 WLR 1676; *Law Debenture Trust Corp v Ural Caspian Oil Corp Ltd* [1995] Ch 152. In *Swiss Bank Corp v Lloyd's Bank Ltd* [1979] Ch 548, 573 (revs'd [1982] AC 584), Browne-Wilkinson J stated that the principle of Knight Bruce LJ represented 'the counterpart in equity of the tort of knowing interference with contractual rights'. But although they may cover the same ground they are doctrinally distinct and subject to different requirements: see Cohen-Grabelsky (1982) 45 MLR 241, 265–7; Gardner (1982) 98 LQR 279, 289–93; Tettenborn [1982] CLJ 58, 82.

[330] See below, p 694.

[331] [1926] AC 108, 116.

[332] Cf above, p 653.

[333] [1926] AC 108, 125. See also *Swiss Bank Corp v Lloyd' s Bank Ltd* [1979] Ch 548, 573 (revs'd [1982] AC 584).

[334] [1958] 2 QB 146.

[335] *Ibid*, 168.

[336] The doctrine of constructive notice does not apply to chattels (*Joseph v Lyons* (1884) 15 QBD 280, 287) nor to the contents of documents in commercial transactions (*Manchester Trust v Furness* [1895] 2 QB 539, 545).

was not entitled to any remedy against the defendant except an injunction to restrain the defendant from using the vessel in a manner inconsistent with the terms of the charter.[337]

The charterer cannot obtain specific performance of the contract,[338] nor, it seems, damages or monetary compensation.[339] It would also seem that the Court will not be prepared to grant an injunction if the situation is such that, in any case, the vendor was incapable of further performing the charterparty,[340] or if, in the case of the mortgage of a vessel, the charter is such as substantially to impair the security.[341]

There is even more doubt as to whether the principle stated by Knight Bruce LJ in *De Mattos v Gibson*, and the decision in the *Strathcona* case, would apply to contracts under which the owner of a particular chattel, other than a ship, undertakes to use the chattel to perform its obligations to the other contracting party: for example, where the owner of a costly machine[342] agrees to use the machine to manufacture goods for the other party over a certain period. In *De Mattos v Gibson* Lord Chelmsford LC stressed that 'a vessel engaged under a charterparty ought to be regarded as a chattel of peculiar value to the charterer',[343] and it has been said that the *Strathcona* decision may be confined to 'the very special case of a ship under charterparty'.[344] Nevertheless, there would seem to be no reason why the immediate purchaser of a chattel should not be restrained by injunction if it commits or threatens to commit the tort of knowingly participating in a breach of such a contract.[345] The same would probably apply to any covenant by the owner of a chattel to use[346] or not to use[347] the chattel in a particular manner. But the relief granted against the third-party purchaser would depend upon the commission of a distinct tort, and not upon notice of any 'interest' in the chattel.

Moreover, it is highly unlikely that any covenant affecting the use of a chattel would be held to 'run with the goods', so as to bind all persons who subsequently purchased the chattel with notice of the covenant.[348] There are good reasons why landowners should be entitled to prevent neighbouring land from being put to a use that would be prejudicial to their property. But no such reasons would justify the imposition of incumbrances on chattels.[349]

337 *Port Line Ltd v Ben Line Steamers Ltd* [1958] 2 QB 146, 167.

338 *De Mattos v Gibson* (1859) 4 De G & J 277, 297.

339 Although the form of the order made in the *Strathcona* case would seem to indicate that damages could be awarded, cf *Port Line Ltd v Ben Line Steamers Ltd* [1958] 2 QB 146, 169; *Law Debenture Trust Corp v Ural Caspian Oil Corp Ltd* [1993] 1 WLR 138, 144; revs'd on another ground [1995] Ch 152.

340 *Lord Strathcona* [1925] P 143. See also above, n 324.

341 *The Celtic King* [1894] P 175.

342 *De Mattos v Gibson* (1858) 4 De G & J 276, 283 (Knight Bruce LJ).

343 (1859) 4 De G & J 288, 299.

344 *Clore v Theatrical Properties Ltd* [1936] 3 All ER 483, 490 (Lord Wright MR).

345 See Cohen-Grabelsky (1982) 45 MLR 241; Gardner (1982) 98 LQR 279; Tettenborn [1982] CLJ 58.

346 *Sefton v Tophams Ltd* [1965] Ch 1140 (land). But see *Clarke v Price* (1819) 2 Wils Ch 157; *Haywood v Brunswick Permanent Benefit Building Soc* (1876) 3 Ch D 694.

347 *British Motor Trade Association v Salvadori* [1949] Ch 556 (covenant not to resell chattel). See also *Esso Petroleum Co Ltd v Kingswood Motors (Addlestone) Ltd* [1974] QB 142 (land); *Law Debenture Trust Corp v Ural Caspian Oil Corp Ltd* [1995] Ch 152 (shares).

348 *Taddy v Sterious & Co* [1904] 1 Ch 354; *McGruther v Pitcher* [1904] 2 Ch 306; above, p 669.

349 The position is different where there are competing 'proprietary' claims to the same goods. The starting point in resolving such title conflicts is *nemo dat quod non habet* ('one cannot give what one does not have'). But there are numerous exceptions to that which often protect a bona fide purchaser for value without notice.

(d) EXEMPTION CLAUSES BINDING THIRD PARTIES

An exemption clause will, as a general rule, only operate so as to take away the rights of the contracting parties, and not those of third parties who suffer injury or damage. In *Haseldine v CA Daw & Son Ltd*:[350]

The owners of a block of flats employed the defendant engineers to repair a lift in the building. Owing to their negligence, the lift was badly repaired and H, a visitor to the premises, was injured when the lift fell to the bottom of the lift-shaft.

The defendant was held liable in tort for negligence. Goddard LJ said:[351]

It is, however, argued that it is not right that a repairer who, as in the present case, has stipulated with the person who employs him that he shall not be liable for accidents, should none the less be made liable to a third person. The answer to this argument is that the duty to the third party does not arise out of the contract, but independently of it.

Nevertheless it has been held that a third party may be bound by an exemption clause where that clause relates to goods that have been bailed by the third party.

Bailment involves the transfer of possession (or an agreement to transfer possession) of goods to a person (the 'bailee') who holds (or agrees to hold) the goods either for or at the direction of the bailor, to whom they will be returned.[352] The hirer of a car is a bailee as is the dry cleaning firm which takes in a customer's clothes for cleaning. In many situations there will be a series of bailments and the question is whether, if the ultimate sub-bailee loses or damages the goods and is sued by the bailor either in tort or for breach of duties arising from the bailment,[353] it can rely on the terms of the contract it made with its immediate bailor as a defence. In *Morris v CW Martin & Sons Ltd*:[354]

Morris sent a mink stole to a furrier to be cleaned. The furrier did not clean furs himself, so, with Morris's consent, he delivered it for cleaning to the defendant, one of whose servants later stole it. The contract between the furrier and the defendant contained an exemption clause, on which the defendant sought to rely when sued by Morris.

On the facts the exemption clause was held, as a matter of construction, not to apply but Lord Denning MR said that, had it applied, in principle the defendant could have relied on it. Morris would be bound by the conditions if she had expressly or impliedly consented to the furrier making a sub-bailment containing those conditions. Since she had agreed that the furrier should send the stole to the defendant, she impliedly consented to his making a contract for cleaning on the terms current in the trade.[355]

350 [1941] 2 KB 343. By the Occupiers' Liability Act 1957, s 3(1), a contract made by an occupier of premises may increase its liability to non-parties beyond the common duty of care but may not reduce it below that duty. Cf, at common law, *Fosbroke-Hobbes v Airwork Ltd* [1937] 1 All ER 108, 112.

351 [1941] 2 KB 343, 379.

352 *Palmer on Bailment* (3rd edn, 2009).

353 eg only to deal with the goods in the manner authorized.

354 [1966] 1 QB 716.

355 *Ibid*, 729. See also Salmon LJ at 741. See also *Singer Co (UK) Ltd v Tees and Hartlepool Port Authority* [1988] 2 Lloyd's Rep 164; *The Captain Gregos (No 2)* [1990] 2 Lloyd's Rep 395, 405.

In *KH Enterprise v Pioneer Container*[356] this principle was applied to a contract for the carriage of goods by sea:

KHE contracted for the carriage of goods from Taiwan to Hong Kong. The carrier was permitted to sub-contract 'on any terms' and did so to the defendant who took possession of the goods under bills of lading providing that any dispute was exclusively to be determined in Taiwan. The goods were lost and KHE sued in Hong Kong, contending that it was not bound by the exclusive jurisdiction clause because there was no contract between it and the defendants.

The Privy Council stated that a person who voluntarily takes another person's goods into its custody holds them as bailee of that person (the owner) even if it does so without the owner's consent, but can only invoke the terms of the sub-bailment under which it received the goods from an intermediate bailee (the carrier) as qualifying its responsibility if the owner consented to them.[357] It held that consent to subcontract and therefore to sub-bail 'on any terms' was wide enough to constitute express consent to the clause and KHE was bound by it.

Privity questions may also be avoided by the implication of a contract between the claimant and the third party. In *Pyrene Co Ltd v Scindia Navigation Co Ltd*:[358]

P sold to ISD in India certain fire-tenders 'fob London'. The defendant agreed with ISD to carry the tenders to India. The contract of carriage contained a clause limiting the liability of the defendant to £200. Owing to the negligence of the defendant, a tender was damaged while being loaded. But since it had not yet crossed the ship's side, it was still at P's risk. P made good the damage and sued the defendant for the loss, which amounted to more than £900.

Devlin J held that P was bound by the exemption clause. Although it was not a party to the contract of carriage, it was entitled to the benefits of the contract and had in consequence also to accept its liabilities. But this approach would constitute a wide-ranging exception to privity and has not subsequently found favour. In the *Midland Silicones* case it was stated that this decision could be supported 'only upon the facts of the case, which may well have justified the implication of a contract between the parties'.[359] It may therefore be an example of an implied contract, that is to say, all three parties intended P to participate in the contract of affreightment.

356 [1994] 2 AC 324.

357 *Ibid*, 342, disapproving *Johnson Matthey & Co Ltd v Constantine Terminals Ltd* [1976] 2 Lloyd's Rep 215. The principles in *The Pioneer Container* were applied in *Sonicare International Ltd v East Anglia Freight Terminal Ltd* [1997] 2 Lloyd's Rep 48 and *Spectra International plc v Hayesoak Ltd* [1997] 1 Lloyd's Rep 153.

358 [1954] 2 QB 402.

359 [1962] AC 466, 471 (Viscount Simonds), and see at 470 where *Elder Dempster & Co Ltd v Paterson, Zochonis & Co Ltd* [1924] AC 522 was similarly explained. See also *Hispanica de Petroleos SA v Vencedora Oceanica SA, The Kapetan Markos NL (No 2)* [1987] 2 Lloyd's Rep 321, 331; *Comp Portorafti Comm SA v Ultramar Panama Inc, The Captain Gregos (No 2)* [1990] 2 Lloyd's Rep 395, 401–3.

(e) THE CONTRACTS (RIGHTS OF THIRD PARTIES) ACT 1999

The Contracts (Rights of Third Parties) Act 1999 Act does not affect the principle that a third party to a contract cannot be subjected to a liability, or the burden of an exemption clause, in that contract.[360] This must be distinguished from the clarification in the Act that a benefit being enforced may be conditional. So, by section 1(4), a third party who wishes to enforce a term conferring a benefit on him or her can only do so subject to and in accordance with any other terms of the contract. Those other terms may impose burdens and conditions upon the enjoyment of any benefit.

FURTHER READING

Coote, 'Consideration and the Joint Promisee' [1978] CLJ 301

Flannigan, 'Privity—The End of an Era (Error)' (1987) 103 LQR 564

Smith, 'Contracts for the Benefit of Third Parties: in Defence of the Third Party Rule' (1997) 17 OJLS 643

Burrows, 'Contracts (Rights of Third Parties) Act 1999 and Its Implications for Commercial Contracts' [2000] LMCLQ 540

MacMillan, 'A Birthday Present for Lord Denning: The Contracts (Rights of Third Parties) Act 1999' (2000) 63 MLR 721

Burrows, 'No Damages for a Third Party's Loss' (2001) 1 Ox Univ Commonwealth LJ 107

Coote, 'The Performance Interest, Panatown and the Problem of Loss' (2001) 117 LQR 81

Treitel, *Some Landmarks of Twentieth Century Contract Law* (Oxford: Clarendon Press, 2002) ch 2

Stevens, 'The Contracts (Rights of Third Parties) Act 1999' (2004) 120 LQR 292

Beale, 'A Review of the Contracts (Rights of Third Parties) Act 1999' in Burrows and Peel (eds), *Contract Formation and Parties* (Oxford: Oxford University Press, 2010) 225

Davies, 'Excluding the Contracts (Rights of Third Parties) Act 1999' (2021) 137 LQR 101

[360] Hansard, HL Deb vol 596, col 21 (11 January 1999) (Lord Irvine LC).

22

ASSIGNMENT

The benefit of a contract may, in certain circumstances, pass to a third party. B's contractual rights against A may be assigned to C by means of an agreement between B (the assignor) and C (the assignee) irrespective of A's (the debtor's) consent.[1] After examining assignment, we will distinguish it from several similar concepts: vicarious performance, novation, and the transfer of rights and liabilities by operation of law on death and bankruptcy.

1. ASSIGNMENT

(a) NO ASSIGNMENT AT COMMON LAW

At common law the benefit of a contract could not be assigned so as to enable the assignee to bring an action upon it in its own name. This rule was sometimes expressed by the phrase 'a chose in action is not assignable'.

'"Choses in action" is a . . . legal expression used to describe all personal rights of property which can only be claimed or enforced by action, and not by taking physical possession.'[2] A chose in action is intangible personal property, which does not physically exist and cannot be physically possessed. It is contrasted with 'choses in possession', which refers to tangible personal property (goods). A chose in action includes not only debts and all other contractual rights but rights to tort damages, intellectual property rights, shares, and equitable rights in a trust fund.[3] Our focus is on the assignment of contractual rights.

The only exceptions to the no assignment at common law rule were assignments by or to the Crown.[4] The common law also recognized the law merchant by which rights to payment of a sum of money embodied in a negotiable instrument could be transferred by transfer of the instrument to a holder for value. The reason for the

[1] See generally Smith and Leslie, *The Law of Assignment* (3rd edn, 2018).

[2] *Torkington v Magee* [1902] 2 KB 427, 430 (Channell J); revs'd [1903] 1 KB 644.

[3] In *Investors Compensation Scheme Ltd v West Bromwich Building Society* [1998] 1 WLR 896 the House of Lords clarified that a right to rescind a mortgage is not a chose in action or part of a chose in action (and an owner cannot therefore assign a right to rescission separately from his property).

[4] *Master v Miller* (1791) 4 Term Rep 320, 340.

non-recognition of assignments of choses in action seems to have been that common law judges feared that to permit assignments would both undermine the doctrine of privity of contract and encourage unnecessary litigation and maintenance and champerty.[5] But even at common law it was (and still is) possible for the right to sue on a contract to be transferred to a third party by other, albeit cumbrous and unsatisfactory, means.

First, the contracting party could give the third party a power of attorney and thus enable the third party to sue the debtor as the contracting party's representative.[6]

Secondly, the contracting party could allow the third party to sue the debtor in the contracting party's name, taking from the third party an indemnity against costs.

Thirdly, with the consent and cooperation of the debtor, the contracting party could effect a transfer by means of a substituted agreement, or 'novation'.[7]

(b) ASSIGNMENT IN EQUITY: THE HISTORICAL BACKGROUND

In contrast to the common law's approach, equity would permit the assignment of a chose in action, including debts and other contractual rights, regardless of whether such chose was equitable or legal.

(i) Equitable choses

An *equitable* chose is one which, before 1875, could only be enforced in the Court of Chancery, such as a share in a trust fund, a legacy, or a reversionary interest under a will. Where there was an assignment of an equitable chose, the assignee was allowed to proceed in its own name, and only an assignor who retained an interest in the action (eg if the assignment was not absolute but conditional) had to be made a party to it.[8] The reason for this was that, since there was no claim that might be asserted by an action at law, the Court of Chancery had exclusive jurisdiction over the whole transaction; there was therefore no risk that the trustees of the fund (ie the debtors) would be exposed to a second action at law by the assignor.

(ii) Legal choses

A *legal* chose in action is one which, before 1875, could be enforced by an action at law, for example, a right under a contract, such as a debt or a claim under a policy of insurance. Equity would recognize the assignment of a legal chose in action, but had here to proceed more carefully. If equity itself enforced the claim of the assignee, that would not prevent the assignor from bringing an action at law; and the debtor would have been put to the inconvenience of resorting to equity to restrain the assignor from enforcing the judgment on the ground that the assignee had already recovered in equity. Consequently, the Court of Chancery did not in the ordinary case enforce the assignee's

[5] *Lampert's Case* (1612) 10 Co Rep 46b, 48a; *Fitzroy v Cave* [1905] 2 KB 364, 372.

[6] *Re Bowden* [1936] Ch 71, 74.

[7] See below, p 694.

[8] *Goodson v Ellisson* (1827) 3 Russ 583; *Cator v Croydon Canal Co* (1841) 4 Y & C Ex 593; *Donaldson v Donaldson* (1854) Kay 711.

claim. What it did was infer from the assignment a duty on the assignor to exercise the right for the benefit of the assignee. On receiving a proper indemnity against costs, the assignor's duty was to permit the assignee to use the assignor's name so that the assignee might bring an action at law. If necessary, it would enforce this duty.[9] So whenever a legal chose in action was assigned in equity—and it could not be assigned otherwise—the action in a Court of law was brought in the assignor's name.[10] This was primarily in the interests of the party liable, so that it was not susceptible to more than one action; and partly in the interests of the assignor, who might dispute the assignment.

Since 1875, when the Judicature Act 1873 came into force, an assignment in equity will be recognized by all divisions of the High Courts of Justice, whether it be of a legal or equitable chose in action. But the rules relating to such assignments (including the use of the assignor's name) are based on those in operation before the passing of the Act. These rules are examined in detail below, but it is first necessary to examine section 136(1) of the Law of Property Act 1925[11] which provides a form of statutory assignment.

(c) ASSIGNMENT UNDER THE LAW OF PROPERTY ACT 1925

By section 136(1) of the Law of Property Act 1925:

> Any absolute assignment by writing under the hand of the assignor (not purporting to be by way of charge only) of any debt or other legal thing in action, of which express notice in writing has been given to the debtor, trustee or other person from whom the assignor would have been able to claim such debt or thing in action, is effectual in law (subject to equities having priority over the right of the assignee) to pass and transfer from the date of such notice—
>
> (a) the legal right to such debt or thing in action;
> (b) all legal and other remedies for the same; and
> (c) the power to give a good discharge for the same without the concurrence of the assignor.

The effect of this section, provided the conditions laid down in it are fulfilled, is to allow the assignee to sue the debtor in its own name.[12]

[9] *Hammond v Messenger* (1838) 9 Sim 327.

[10] See, however, the statement of practice by Buller J in *Master v Miller* (1791) 4 Term Rep 320, 341, which shows that a Court of law did not always insist on the rule.

[11] This replaced and substantially re-enacted the Judicature Act 1873, s 25(6). Other statutes have created specific further exceptions to the rule that there can be no assignment at law. Eg by the Policies of Assurance Act 1867, s 1 and by the Marine Insurance Act 1906, s 50(2), policies of life and marine insurance can be assigned, but the former Act requires notice to be given by the assignee to the insurance company. Stock and shares in a company are transferable under the Companies Act 2006, s 544 and the Stock Transfer Act 1963, and assignments of patents and copyright are regulated by the Patents Act 1977, ss 30 and 32 and the Copyright, Designs and Patents Act 1988, ss 90 and 94.

[12] *Warner Bros Records Inc v Rollgreen Ltd* [1976] QB 430. The assignee's right is subject to the right of a debtor who receives notice of a disputed assignment to call upon the persons giving notice to interplead.

This sub-section is merely machinery; it enables an action to be brought by the assignee in his own name in cases where previously he would have sued in the assignor's name, but only where he could so sue.[13]

It is necessary to examine the words of the section in some detail.

(i) 'Absolute' and not a charge

The Act requires the assignment to be 'absolute', that is, unconditional. This means that it must be an assignment of a sum due or about to become due, not of an amount which is dependent on any question as to the state of accounts between assignor and assignee. An assignment by way of charge is one which merely gives a right to payment out of a particular fund, and does not transfer the fund to the assignee.

If the assignment is to take effect or to cease upon the happening of a future uncertain event, so that the original debtor is uncertain as to the person in whom the right to receive the money is vested, it is not absolute. Thus in *Durham Brothers v Robertson*:[14]

A building contractor wrote to the claimants in the following terms: '*Re* Building Contract, South Lambert Road. In consideration of money advanced from time to time we hereby charge the sum of £1,080, being the price . . . due to us from [the defendant] on the completion of the above buildings as security for advances, and we hereby assign our interest in the above-mentioned sum until the money with added interest be repaid to you'.

It was held that the assignment was not within the section. It purported to be by way of charge and so did not transfer the whole debt to the claimants unconditionally, but only until the advances were repaid. The defendant could not be sure that he was paying his debt to the right person without knowing the state of accounts between the assignor and assignee.

A further illustration is furnished by *Jones v Humphreys*:[15]

A schoolmaster, in consideration of a loan to him of £15, assigned to the claimant so much and such part of his income, salary and other emoluments from his employers as should be necessary and requisite for repayment of the sum borrowed (with interest) or of any further or other sums in which he might thereafter become indebted to the claimant.

It was held that this was not an absolute assignment, but was a mere security purporting to be by way of a charge. Even the assignment of a definite part of an existing debt, for example part of a sum deposited in a bank account,[16] is not absolute, but merely a charge upon the whole debt;[17] for otherwise it would be in the power of the original creditor

[13] *Torkington v Magee* [1902] 2 KB 427, 435 (Channell J); *Marchant v Morton, Down & Co* [1901] 2 KB 829, 832.

[14] [1898] 1 QB 765. See also *Raiffeisen Zentralbank Österreich AG v Five Star General Trading LLC* [2001] EWCA Civ 68, [2001] QB 825.

[15] [1902] 1 KB 10. See also *Court Line Ltd v Akt Gøtaverken* [1984] 1 Lloyd's Rep 283.

[16] *Deposit Protection Board v Dalia* [1994] 2 AC 367.

[17] *Williams v Atlantic Assurance Co* [1933] 1 KB 81.

'to split up the single legal cause of action for the debt into as many separate legal causes of action as he might think fit',[18] thus obviously prejudicing the position of the debtor. But it must be remembered that an assignment which is not within the section because it is not absolute may nevertheless be a valid equitable assignment.[19] An assignment which passes the entire interest of the assignor in the debt (ie it is a mortgage rather than a charge) is absolute despite the fact that it contains a proviso for redemption and reassignment on repayment.[20] The assignment cannot prejudice the debtor, who will receive notice first of the assignment, and then of the reassignment, if one is made. The debtor will always know to whom the debt is owed. There may, too, be an absolute assignment of a debt arising out of an existing contract, even though it does not become payable until a date later than the assignment.[21] All contracted rights are vested from the moment the contract is made, even if they are not presently enforceable.[22]

(ii) 'Writing'

The assignment must be in writing and signed by the assignor; signature by an agent is insufficient.[23]

(iii) 'Notice'

The Act requires that notice in writing should be given to the debtor (although it does not specify which party must give the notice). This requirement has been strictly construed so that in a case where the debtor was unable to read and it was therefore thought useless to give him written notice, there was held to be no legal assignment even though the assignment was read over to him and understood by him.[24] The written notice need not be in any particular form, provided that it sufficiently indicates the fact of the assignment.[25] The notice takes effect when it is received by the debtor.[26]

(iv) Consideration

An assignment under the Act does not require the assignee to have furnished consideration.[27]

[18] *Durham Brothers v Robertson* [1898] 1 QB 765, 774 (Chitty LJ); *Forster v Baker* [1910] 2 KB 636. See Hall [1959] CLJ 99.

[19] *National Bank of Abu Dhabi PJSC v BP Oil Int Ltd* [2016] EWHC 2892 (Comm) at [24] (revs'd, but not on this point: *First Abu Dhabi Bank PJSC v BP Oil International Ltd* [2018] EWCA Civ 14).

[20] *Tancred v Delagoa Bay and East Africa Ry* (1889) 23 QBD 239. See also, eg, *Bexhill UK Ltd v Razzaq* [2012] EWCA Civ 1376 at [42]–[56].

[21] *G & T Earle Ltd v Hemsworth RDC* (1928) 44 TLR 758; *Care SS Corp v Latin American SS Corp* [1983] QB 1005.

[22] *Marathon Electrical Mfg Corp v Mashreqbank PSC* [1997] CLC 1090, approving Oditah, *Legal Aspects of Receivables Financing* (1991) 28–9.

[23] *Wilson v Wallani* (1880) 5 Ex D 155; *Frischmann v Vaxeal Holdings SA* [2023] EWHC 2698 (Ch) at [56]–[61].

[24] *Hockley v Goldstein* (1922) 90 LJ KB 111.

[25] *Van Lynn Developments Ltd v Pelias Construction Co Ltd* [1969] 1 QB 607; *Promontoria (Oak) Ltd v Emanuel* [2021] EWCA Civ 1682, [2022] 1 WLR 2004.

[26] *Holt v Heatherfield Trust Ltd* [1942] 2 KB 1.

[27] *Re Westerton* [1919] 2 Ch 104.

(v) Rights assignable

The Act refers to 'any debt or other legal thing in action'.[28] This expression is not, as might appear at first sight, confined to legal choses in action, which were enforceable only in a Court of Common Law, but extends to choses in equity as well; that is, rights which a Court of Equity would have dealt with as being assignable.[29]

A 'legal thing in action' may therefore be defined as any right the assignment of which a Court of law or equity would, before the Judicature Act, have recognized or enforced.

(d) EQUITABLE ASSIGNMENT

We have seen that assignment was possible in equity but not at common law.[30] An assignment which does not comply with one or more of the requirements of section 136(1) of the Law of Property Act 1925 (eg because it is by way of charge or because no written notice has been given to the debtor) may still be a perfectly good and valid equitable assignment. 'The statute does not forbid or destroy equitable assignments or impair their efficacy in the slightest degree.'[31] But whereas a statutory assignee acquires a legal title to the chose assigned, an assignee in equity does not do so.[32] Thus a statutory assignee is entitled to bring an action without the necessity of joining the assignor as a party to the action, but an assignee in equity will not always enjoy this right.

(i) Joinder of the assignor

If the chose in action is *equitable*, the assignee is entitled to sue without joining the assignor as a party unless the assignor still has some interest in the suit.[33] This may arise where there is still some question of accounts outstanding between the assignor and the assignee, or where the assignment consists of a charge upon a trust fund. In such a case the parties interested must be made parties to the action so that the Court may make a final adjudication binding them all.

If the chose in action is *legal*, the assignee cannot normally recover damages or other relief without joining the assignor as a party to the action, if the assignor is willing as co-claimant, if not, as co-defendant.[34] Moreover the *assignor* of part of a debt cannot recover the balance in excess of the sum assigned without joining the assignee.[35] Attempts have been made to justify these requirements on the ground that they serve to protect the debtor who might otherwise pay the debt to the wrong person,[36] and that they allow an assignor who wishes

[28] See, eg, *King v Victoria Insurance Co Ltd* [1896] AC 250; *Investors Compensation Scheme v West Bromwich BS* [1998] 1 WLR 896.

[29] *Re Pain* [1919] 1 Ch 38; *Torkington v Magee* [1902] 2 KB 427, 430, revs'd on other grounds [1903] 1 KB 646.

[30] See above, pp 677–9.

[31] *Brandt's Sons & Co v Dunlop Rubber Co Ltd* [1905] AC 454, 461 (Lord Macnaghten). See also *Raiffeisen Zentralbank Österreich AG v Five Star General Trading LLC* [2001] EWCA Civ 68, [2001] QB 825.

[32] *Warner Bros. Records Inc v Rollgreen Ltd* [1976] QB 430.

[33] See above, p 678.

[34] *Brandt's Sons & Co v Dunlop Rubber Co Ltd* [1905] AC 454; *Performing Right Society Ltd v London Theatre of Varieties Ltd* [1924] AC 1; *Roberts v Gill & Co* [2010] UKSC 22, [2011] 1 AC 240 at [62]–[71].

[35] *Walter & Sullivan Ltd v J Murphy & Sons Ltd* [1955] 1 QB 584.

[36] *Ibid*, 588 (Parker LJ).

to dispute the assignment to do so.[37] But the first reason is only relevant where the assignor retains an interest in the chose, and the second would apply even in the case of a statutory assignment, where the assignee is entitled to sue alone. Where the assignor retains no interest in the chose in action and the assignment only fails to be statutory because it was not in writing or because no notice has been given, for example, a requirement that the assignor be made a party to the proceedings would seem to serve no useful purpose.[38]

(ii) Form

No particular form is necessary for an equitable assignment, and, except where the interest assigned is an equitable interest or trust within section 53(1) of the Law of Property Act 1925,[39] it need not even be in writing. It may be addressed to the debtor or to the assignee. If it is addressed to the debtor:

It may be couched in the language of command. It may be a courteous request. It may assume the form of mere permission. The language is immaterial if the meaning is plain. All that is necessary is that the debtor should be given to understand that the debt has been made over by the creditor to some third person.[40]

In *Thomas v Harris*,[41] it was addressed to the assignee:

A father handed to his son certain insurance policies on his life with the request that the son should erect a tombstone in his memory, using the policy monies for this purpose. No notice was given to the insurance company.

It was held that, by this informal act, the father had assigned the policies to his son by way of charge for the cost of the tombstone. There was a valid equitable assignment.

While no formalities are required, it has been said in recent cases that there must be 'an outward expression by the assignor of his intention to make an immediate disposition of the subject matter of the assignment'.[42]

(iii) Notice

No notice to the debtor is necessary; the assignment is effective as between assignor and assignee from the moment it is made.[43] Notice is nevertheless *advisable* for several reasons.[44] First, the assignment will not bind the debtor until it has notice of the assignment.

37 *Durham Brothers v Robertson* [1898] 1 QB 765, 770 (Chitty LJ).

38 *The Aiolos* [1983] 2 Lloyd's Rep 25, 33–4; *Raiffeisen Zentralbank Österreich AG v Five Star General Trading LLC* [2001] EWCA Civ 68, [2001] QB 825 at [60].

39 *Grey v IRC* [1960] AC 1; *Oughtred v IRC* [1960] AC 206. Cf *Vandervell v IRC* [1967] 2 AC 291; *Neville v Wilson* [1997] Ch 144; *Frenkel v La Micro Group (UK) Ltd* [2024] UKSC 42, [2025] 2 WLR 1.

40 *Brandt's Sons & Co v Dunlop Rubber Co Ltd* [1905] AC 454, 462 (Lord Macnaghten). See also *Allied Carpets Group Plc v MacFarlane* [2002] EWHC 1155 (TCC), [2002] PNLR 38; *Burridge v MPH Soccer Management Ltd* [2011] EWCA Civ 835. But the assignment must either have been made by prior arrangement with, or be communicated to, the assignee: *Re Hamilton* (1921) 124 LT 737.

41 [1947] 1 All ER 444.

42 *Phelps v Spon-Smith & Co* [2001] BPIR 326 at [33]; *Coulter v Chief of Dorset Police* [2003] EWHC 3391 (Ch), [2004] 1 WLR 1425; *Finlan v Eyton Morris Winfield* [2007] EWHC 914 (Ch), [2007] 4 All ER 143.

43 *Brandt's Sons & Co v Dunlop Rubber Co Ltd* [1905] AC 454, 462.

44 *Phoenix Group Foundation v Harbour Fund II LP* [2023] EWCA Civ 36 at [91].

So, if, before notice, the debtor pays the assignor, that is a good discharge of the debt;[45] but if the debtor pays the assignor after notice that is no answer to a claim by the assignee.[46] Secondly, notice to the debtor is necessary to establish priority under the rule in *Dearle v Hall*, which we shall deal with later.[47] Thirdly, notice to the debtor will prevent the debtor from setting up new equities which may mature after receipt of the notice.

(iv) Consideration

The question whether consideration between assignor and assignee is necessary in an equitable assignment is a difficult one.[48] Equity will not assist a volunteer, and it has been said that 'for every equitable assignment . . . there must be consideration. If there be no consideration, there can be no equitable assignment'.[49] However, this statement is much too wide, since value is not required in every case.

Valuable consideration for this purpose may consist in any consideration sufficient to support a simple contract.[50] If A assigns to B the benefit of a contract in satisfaction of a debt owed by A to B, this is good consideration for the assignment. Similarly, if the assignment is by way of security for an existing debt in such circumstances that a forbearance to sue will be implied on the part of the assignee, this is sufficient to give the assignee a right to sue the debtor.[51] If consideration has been furnished by the assignee, no problem will arise; it is where the assignment is gratuitous that some doubt exists.

It is well established that a mere *agreement* to assign a chose in action must, like other contracts, have consideration to support it; if it is gratuitous, it is unenforceable.[52] An assignment of a future chose in action therefore requires consideration.[53] A future chose in action is a mere expectancy which may or may not materialize, such as a share of a trust fund which will be received only if an uncertain event occurs,[54] damages in an action which is still pending,[55] or the right to payments falling due under contracts not yet made.[56] Such an assignment can only operate as a contract to assign when the subject-matter comes into existence, since 'nothing passes even in equity until the property comes into present existence';[57] it is therefore unenforceable unless value has been given.[58]

[45] *Stocks v Dobson* (1853) 4 De GM & G 15.

[46] *Deposit Protection Board v Dalia* [1994] 2 AC 367, 387 (CA), revs'd on other grounds, *ibid*.

[47] Below, pp 688–9.

[48] For a discussion of this subject, see Megarry (1943) 59 LQR 58; Hollond (1943) 59 LQR 129; Sheridan (1955) 33 Can Bar Rev 284; Hall [1959] CLJ 99; Marshall, *The Assignment of Choses in Action* (1950) 109; Smith and Leslie, *The Law of Assignment* (3rd edn, 2018) paras 7.78–7.83.

[49] *Glegg v Bromley* [1912] 3 KB 474, 491 (Parker J).

[50] *Currie v Misa* (1875) LR 10 Ex 153; *Leask v Scott* (1877) 2 QBD 376, (1943) 59 LQR 208.

[51] *Glegg v Bromley* [1912] 3 KB 474.

[52] *Re McArdle* [1951] Ch 669.

[53] *Tailby v Official Receiver* (1888) 13 App Cas 523.

[54] *Re Ellenborough* [1903] 1 Ch 697. See also *Norman v Federal Commissioner of Taxation* (1963) 109 CLR 9 (future interest and dividends).

[55] *Glegg v Bromley* [1912] 3 KB 474.

[56] *E Pfeiffer Weinkellerei-Weineinkauf GmbH & Co v Arbuthnot Factors Ltd* [1988] 1 WLR 150; *Annangel Glory Comp Nav SA v M Golodetz, Middle East Marketing Corp Ltd* [1988] 1 Lloyd's Rep 45.

[57] *Glegg v Bromley* [1912] 3 KB 474, 490 (Parker J).

[58] *Phoenix Group Foundation v Harbour Fund II LP* [2023] EWCA Civ 36 at [73].

But just as it is possible to make a gift of a chattel, it is also possible to make a gift of a chose in action, provided that the transfer is effected in whatever manner is necessary for a transfer of that particular chose. Such a transfer must be 'complete and perfect', for if anything remains to be done by the donor in order to give effect to the donor's intention, the gift will fail. Equity will not intervene to perfect an imperfect gift.[59] The question of consideration in equitable assignments turns on whether any act remains to be done by the assignor in order to perfect the assignment; the assignor must have made every effort to complete the transaction.[60]

If the subject-matter assigned is an equitable chose in action, the assignment is complete when the assignor has unequivocally, even though informally, expressed an intention that the chose should henceforth belong to the assignee.[61] The assignee is then, as we have seen, in a position to enforce the right to the chose without more ado: 'such an assignment without any valuable consideration is not a mere agreement but is an actual transfer of the equitable right'.[62] But if the subject of the assignment is a legal chose in action, can a merely equitable assignment of it be said to be complete and perfect given that a statutory assignment could have been made which would have entitled the assignee to sue in its own name? The answer to this question is still not entirely clear. But, as noted above,[63] it is not now necessary for the assignee to ask the Court to compel the assignor to join as co-claimant, since an unwilling assignor can be made a defendant. An equitable assignee of a legal chose in action is able to enforce the rights under the contract against the debtor without seeking the aid either of the assignor or of the Court. In that sense the assignor has done all those things which it and only it could do[64] and there seems no reason why the assignment should not be regarded as complete and perfect without consideration.[65]

There may, of course, be other reasons why a particular equitable assignment is not complete and perfect, for example because the assignor fails to complete the transfer of shares or stock in the sole recognized form,[66] or because the necessary consent of a third party to the transfer has not been obtained.[67] But the better view is that, as between assignor and assignee, an equitable assignment of an existing chose in action, whether legal or equitable, is not rendered ineffective merely because there is no consideration.

[59] A similar principle is that in *Milroy v Lord* (1862) 4 De GF & J 264, 274. See also *Pennington v Waine* [2002] EWCA Civ 227, [2002] 1 WLR 2075.

[60] *Fortescue v Barnett* (1834) 3 My & K 36, (1943) 59 LQR 58, 61, 129; *Kekewich v Manning* (1851) 1 De FM & G 176, [1959] CLJ 99.

[61] *Voyle v Hughes* (1954) 2 Sm & G 18; *Re Wale* [1956] 1 WLR 1346; cf *Re Earl of Lucan* (1890) 45 Ch D 470 where an assignment which failed to create a complete and perfect charge on a reversionary interest was held to be unenforceable for want of consideration.

[62] *Voyle v Hughes* (1954) 2 Sm & G 18; *Letts v IRC* [1957] 1 WLR 201.

[63] Above, p 682.

[64] *Corin v Patton* (1990) 169 CLR 540 (High Court of Australia). Cf *Olsson v Dyson* (1969) 120 CLR 365.

[65] *Holt v Heatherfield Trust Ltd* [1942] 2 KB 1; *Harding v Harding* (1886) 17 QBD 442; *Re Patrick* [1891] 1 Ch 82; *Re Griffin* [1899] 1 Ch 408; *German v Yates* (1915) 32 TLR 52; *Re Rose* [1952] Ch 499; *Pulley v Public Trustee* [1956] NZLR 771; *Mascall v Mascall* (1984) 50 P & CR 119.

[66] *Milroy v Lord* (1862) 4 De GF & J 264.

[67] *Re Fry* [1946] 312.

(v) Transfer of rights?

The traditional view is that an equitable assignment, like a statutory assignment, involves a transfer of rights from the assignor to the assignee. However, this has recently been challenged.[68] It has been argued that equitable assignment, as distinct from statutory assignment, does not involve any *transfer* of rights. Rather the assignee in equity is given new rights by the assignor in respect of the rights of the assignor which are still retained by the assignor: the assignee's rights encumber the assignor's rights but the assignor's rights are not transferred. In effect, the assignor holds its rights on trust for the assignee.[69] Although this theory runs counter to the long-standing view that all assignments involve a transfer and that an assignment in equity and a trust are different concepts, it does have the merit of providing a substantive reason, rather than a somewhat vague procedural explanation, for why the assignor must (at least normally) be joined to the assignee's action: since the assignor retains the relevant rights it follows that the assignee's action must be brought in the assignor's name.

(e) ASSIGNEE TAKES 'SUBJECT TO EQUITIES'

Whether the assignment of a chose in action is statutory[70] or equitable,[71] the assignee takes 'subject to equities', that is, subject to all such defences as might have prevailed against the assignor. An assignee of contractual rights must therefore take care to ascertain the exact nature and extent of those rights; an assignee cannot be exempt from the effect of transactions by which the assignor may have lessened or invalidated the rights assigned.

(i) Claims arising out of contract assigned

The debtor is entitled to raise, by way of defence to an action brought by the assignee, all claims that directly arise out of the contract or transaction which forms the subject-matter of the assignment, whether such claims accrue before or after notice of the assignment is received. So, for example, despite the fact that the assignee is wholly innocent and has given value for the contractual rights assigned, the debtor can rescind the contract on the ground that it was induced to enter into it by the fraud of the assignor[72] or set off a claim for unliquidated damages for breach of the contract by

[68] Edelman and Elliott (2015) 131 LQR 228.

[69] For a similar view, emphasizing also agency aspects of the relationship, see Tham, *Understanding the Law of Assignment* (2019).

[70] The wording of the Law of Property Act 1925, s 136 is 'subject to equities having priority over the right of the assignee': see above, p 663.

[71] *Mangles v Dixon* (1852) 3 HLC 702, 731; *Crouch v Crédit Foncier of England Ltd* (1873) LR 8 QB 374, 380.

[72] *Graham v Johnson* (1869) LR 8 Eq 36; *Banco Santander SA v Bayfern Ltd* [2000] 1 All ER (Comm) 776 (letter of credit).

the assignor,[73] or obtain a stay where the assignor's action would have been stayed for failure to pay the costs of an earlier action.[74]

But a debtor with a tort claim against the assignor cannot set that claim up against an innocent assignee. The debtor is restricted to claims which arise out of the contract itself and do not exist independently of it. For instance, while, as we have seen, the debtor can assert a right to rescind a contract because of the fraud of the assignor, a claim for damages for fraud cannot be asserted by the debtor in proceedings by the assignee. In *Stoddart v Union Trust*:[75]

The Union Trust were fraudulently induced by one Price to buy a newspaper called 'Football Chat' for the sum of £1,000, of which £200 was to be paid immediately, and the balance of £800 by instalments. Price assigned this £800 to the claimant, Stoddart, who took in good faith without knowledge of the fraud. When sued by Stoddart, the Union Trust pleaded that they had sustained damage exceeding £800 and that therefore no money was owed by them.

The Court of Appeal rejected this contention and held that the Union Trust could not set off their claim for damages against the assignee. Kennedy LJ said:[76]

> The defendants are claiming damages for the fraud which induced them to enter into the contract on the footing that they are liable under it, and at the same time seeking to repudiate their obligation under it. The claim for damages is a personal claim against the wrong-doer; it is something dehors the contract.

The debtor may also not recover from the assignee hire paid to the assignee, even though the hire was to be repaid by the assignor to the debtor if unearned.[77]

(ii) Claims arising out of other transactions

Where a claim arises out of a contract or transaction other than the one which forms the subject-matter of the assignment, the debtor can set off such a claim against the assignee if but only if the claim accrues[78] *before the debtor has notice of the assignment*. An example is where money on deposit with a bank is assigned, but the bank has a claim against the assignor for taking up and paying bills of exchange.[79] The effect of notice is to prevent the debtor from setting up against the assignee any fresh equities which may mature. 'After notice of assignment of a chose in action the debtor cannot by payment or otherwise do anything to take away or diminish the rights of the assignee as they stood at the time of the notice.'[80]

73 *Young v Kitchin* (1878) 3 Ex D 127; *Newfoundland Government v Newfoundland Ry* (1888) 13 App Cas 199. See also *Bank of Boston Connecticut v European Grain and Shipping Ltd* [1989] AC 1056 (if debtor's claim against assignor could not be set off against debt, it cannot be set off against assignee).

74 *Sinclair v British Telecommunications plc* [2000] 2 All ER 461, 469.

75 [1912] 1 KB 181.

76 *Ibid*, 194.

77 *Pan Ocean Shipping Co Ltd v Creditcorp Ltd* [1994] 1 WLR 161.

78 *Business Computers Ltd v Anglo-African Leasing Ltd* [1977] 1 WLR 578; *Bibby Factors Northwest Ltd v HFD Ltd* [2015] EWCA Civ 1908, [2016] 1 Lloyd's Rep 517.

79 *Re Pinto Leite and Nephews* [1929] 1 Ch 221.

80 *Roxburghe v Cox* (1881) 17 Ch D 520, 526 (James LJ).

(iii) Assignee cannot recover more than assignor

A further aspect of the idea that an assignee takes an assignment 'subject to equities' is the principle that an assignee cannot recover more from the debtor than the assignor could have done had there been no assignment.[81] The principle has given rise to particular difficulties where damaged or defective buildings have been sold along with the assignment of claims in contract or tort relating to the building. But the problem of damages disappearing into some 'legal black hole' has now been solved by the Court of Appeal's clarification in *Offer-Hoar v Larkstore Ltd* that, in applying in this context the principle that the assignee cannot recover more than the assignor, one should be asking what damages the assignor could itself have recovered had there been no assignment and *had there been no transfer of the land* to the assignee.[82] Substantial damages were therefore recoverable by the assignee where an assignor had sold its land to an assignee along with, or prior to, the assignment of the relevant cause of action relating to the land.

The problem has, in any event, normally been circumvented because of the Courts' recognition that, where a third party is, or will become, owner of the defective or damaged property, there is an exception to the general rule that a contracting party can recover damages only for its own loss and not the loss of the third party.[83] Where the exception applies, the contracting party (the assignor) is entitled to substantial damages for the loss suffered by the third party (the assignee): by the same token, there is no question of an award of substantial damages to the assignee infringing the principle that the assignee cannot recover more than the assignor.

(f) PRIORITIES

It may happen that an assignor makes two or more assignments of the same chose in action (whether statutory or equitable) to different assignees. If the fund is insufficient to meet all the claims, a problem of their respective priorities will arise. The rule is that *assignments have priority according to the priority of notice*.[84] Successive assignees of an obligation rank in priority according to the dates when notice was given to the party to be charged, rather than the dates when the creditor assigned the contractual rights to each assignee. This rule is generally known as the rule in *Dearle v Hall*.[85] Its justification

[81] *Dawson v Great Northern & City Railway Co* [1905] 1 KB 260.

[82] [2006] EWCA Civ 1079, [2006] 1 WLR 2926; the assessment of damages is subject to the usual rules on causation and remoteness: *Orchard Plaza Management Company Ltd v Balfour Beatty Regional Construction Ltd* [2022] EWHC 1490 (TCC).

[83] *Linden Gardens Trust Ltd v Lenesta Sludge Disposals Ltd* [1994] 1 AC 85; *Darlington BC v Wiltshier Northern Ltd* [1995] 1 WLR 68; *Alfred McAlpine Construction Ltd v Panatown Ltd* [2001] 1 AC 518. The exception is based on *Dunlop v Lambert* (1839) 6 Cl & F 600 and *The Albazero* [1977] AC 774. See above, p 633.

[84] *Marchant v Morton, Down & Co* [1901] 2 KB 829.

[85] (1823) 3 Russ 1. See generally *E Pfeiffer Weinkellerei-Weineinkauf GmbH & Co v Arbuthnot Factors Ltd* [1988] 1 WLR 150; Bridge, Gullifer, and Lomnicka, *The Law of Security and Title-Based Financing* (4th edn, 2024) paras 14.09–14.20; Smith and Leslie, *The Law of Assignment* (3rd edn, 2018) paras 27.48–27.105; Oditah (1989) 9 OJLS 513.

seems to be that, by failing to give notice to the debtor, the first assignee has enabled the assignor to make a second, and possibly fraudulent, assignment to the subsequent assignee. Accordingly, even though the first assignee's assignment was first in time, it ought to be postponed to the later assignment.

But the first assignee will only be postponed to a subsequent assignment of which prior notice has been given, if, at the time of the first assignment, the second assignee had no knowledge of the previous assignment.[86] A second assignee who had such knowledge could scarcely claim to have been misled.

Except where the interest assigned is an equitable interest in land or in personalty, when the notice must be in writing,[87] no special form is required for a notice to gain priority. Provided it is clear and unequivocal, and brought home to the party charged, oral notice is sufficient. Even a notice in a newspaper read by the debtor has been held to suffice.[88] If the interest assigned is an equitable interest in a trust fund, it is advisable to give notice to all the trustees in order to be perfectly safe; otherwise notice given to one trustee alone may determine with his death or resignation.[89]

(g) RIGHTS NOT ASSIGNABLE

Some choses in action are not assignable, and not every right which arises under or out of a contract can be assigned. These restrictions apply to both statutory and equitable assignments.[90]

(i) Assignment prohibited by contract

The contract may expressly provide that the rights arising under it, or some of them, shall not be assignable.[91] In such a case, a purported assignment of those rights will be invalid as against the debtor,[92] although it may be effective as between assignor and assignee[93] and enable the assignee to sue the assignor for breach of contract.[94]

86 *Re Holmes* (1885) 29 Ch D 786.

87 Law of Property Act 1925, s 137(3).

88 *Lloyd v Banks* (1868) LR 3 Ch App 488.

89 *Re Phillips' Trusts* [1903] 1 Ch 183.

90 See generally MacMahon [2020] CLJ 288.

91 The usual principles of contractual interpretation apply: *Dassault Aviation SA v Mitsui Sumitomo Insurance Co Ltd* [2024] EWCA Civ 5, [2024] KB 421.

92 *Helstan Securities Ltd v Hertfordshire CC* [1978] 3 All ER 262; *Linden Gardens Trust Ltd v Lenesta Sludge Disposals Ltd* [1994] 1 AC 85, 103; *First Abu Dhabi Bank PJSC v BP Oil International Ltd* [2018] EWCA Civ 14; Turner [2008] LMCLQ 306; Goode [2009] LMCLQ 330; Tolhurst and Carter [2014] CLJ 405; Beale, Gullifer, and Paterson [2016] JBL 203. The validity of 'no-assignment clauses' at common law has been thought to be inconvenient, especially for small businesses, in the context of 'receivables financing': this has led to the Small Business, Enterprise and Employment Act 2015, s 1, which empowered the relevant Minister to make Regulations rendering ineffective some 'no-assignment clauses', and the Business Contract Terms (Assignment of Receivables) Regulations 2018 (SI 2018 No 1254), which have been made in exercise of that power.

93 *Re Turcan* (1888) 40 Ch D 5; *Re Westerton* [1919] 2 Ch 104. Contrast *Spellman v Spellman* [1961] 1 WLR 921, 928, but cf at 925.

94 *R v Chester & North Wales Legal Aid Office, ex p Queensferry Ltd* [1998] 2 BCLC 436; *Bawejem Ltd v MC Fabrications Ltd* [1999] 1 All ER (Comm) 377.

It has also been held that a clause prohibiting assignment does not necessarily prohibit a declaration of trust in favour of a third party.[95]

(ii) Bare right of action

Due to the rules against champerty and maintenance, a mere right to sue for damages (a 'bare right of action') cannot be assigned.[96] However, rights of action arising out of or incidental to rights of property can be assigned with the property transferred. Thus the purchaser of an estate was permitted to sue for damages for breaches of covenant committed by the vendor's tenants before the sale,[97] and the purchaser of land injuriously affected by a railway was permitted to claim compensation in respect of damages already sustained.[98] Again, a debt, as opposed to a mere right to sue for damages, is assignable:[99] the practice of 'selling' debts to debt-collecting agencies ('factoring') could not be carried on if the law were otherwise. Further, in *Trendtex Trading Corporation v Crédit Suisse*,[100] the House of Lords made it clear that even an assignment of a bare right of action may be upheld if the assignee has a 'genuine commercial interest' in taking the assignment. An assignment of the insured's right of action to an insurer, who has indemnified the insured under a policy of insurance, has been held valid on the ground that the insurer has a legitimate interest in recouping the loss sustained by paying out on the policy.[101] Likewise, an assignee who has financed the transaction giving rise to the right of action assigned will have a legitimate commercial interest in taking the assignment if its sole object is to enable the assignee to recoup its loss on the transaction.[102]

On the other hand, in the *Trendtex* case, the purchase of a right of action arising out of the breach and repudiation of a letter of credit, purely with a view to profit, was held to be invalid in English law as 'savouring of maintenance', since it involved trafficking in litigation.[103] Similarly, an assignment by a client of their cause of action to their solicitor has been held to be void.[104] But where the assignee has a genuine commercial interest then an assignment by a party unable to fund litigation to recover damages for breach of

[95] *Don King Productions Inc v Warren* [2000] Ch 291; *Barbados Trust Co Ltd v Bank of Zambia* [2007] EWCA Civ 148, [2007] 1 Lloyd's Rep 495, noted by Smith (2008) 124 LQR 517; *First Abu Dhabi Bank PJSC v BP Oil International Ltd* [2018] EWCA Civ 14 at [26]–[28], noted by Turner (2018) 134 LQR 532.

[96] *De Hoghton v Money* (1866) LR 2 Ch App 164; *May v Lane* (1894) 64 LJ QB 236; *Torkington v McGee* [1902] 2 KB 427, 433 (decision revs'd [1903] 1 KB 644); *Defries v Milne* [1913] 1 Ch 98. Cf *Glegg v Bromley* [1912] 3 KB 474 (fruits of action).

[97] *Defries v Milne* [1913] 1 Ch 98; *Ellis v Torrington* [1920] 1 KB 399.

[98] *Dawson v GN & City Ry* [1905] 1 KB 260.

[99] *Ellis v Torrington* [1920] 1 KB 399, 411; *Camdex International Ltd v Bank of Zambia* [1998] QB 22.

[100] [1982] AC 679, 694, 696, 697, 703. For criticism of the *Trendtex* test and a call for a reconsideration of this area of the law so that assignments of rights to compensation are recognized as valid, subject to a few specific exceptions, see Tettenborn [2007] LMCLQ 392.

[101] *Compania Colombiana de Seguros v Pacific Steam Navigation Co* [1965] 1 QB 101.

[102] *Trendtex Trading Cpn v Crédit Suisse*, above, n 100, 694, 696, 697, 703 (but not if the object is to sell on to and divide the 'spoils' with a subsequent assignee).

[103] See also *Re Trepca Mines Ltd (No 2)* [1963] Ch 199; *Laurent v Sale & Co* [1963] 1 WLR 829; *Re Oasis Merchandising Services Ltd* [1998] Ch 170.

[104] *Farrar v Miller* [2022] EWCA Civ 295.

contract to a person who can, where the object and effect of the assignment is to enable the litigation to be funded, is not contrary to public policy or unlawful[105] unless there is an obvious disproportion between the assignee's true interest and what it bargained to receive under the assignment.[106] In *Simpson v Norfolk & Norwich University Hospital NHS Trust*[107] it was held, after a detailed consideration of the issue, that while an action for damages for personal injury is capable of being assigned, the claimant in the case had no legitimate interest in the claim (applying the *Trendtex* test) and the assignment plainly savoured of champerty. The assignment was therefore void.

(iii) Personal relationship

Where there is a relationship of personal confidence between the parties, or their personal qualifications are of the essence of a contract, one party cannot assign the right to the performance of the obligations of the other, since to do so would be to alter the nature of the contract without the other's consent.

So, for example, a cake manufacturer was held not to be able to assign the right to be supplied with 'all the eggs he should require for manufacturing purposes for one year' to a new company on the amalgamation of the business.[108] What the supplier had undertaken to do was to supply all the eggs that the manufacturer, and not all that any other person or company, should require. Moreover, the manufacturer had undertaken not to buy eggs elsewhere and this introduced a personal element which was material to the contract. This undertaking would not be binding on the assignee, so the supplier would be deprived of its benefit. For a similar reason, a motor insurance policy cannot be assigned to the purchaser if the car is sold, unless the insurance company consents to the assignment, for that would be to 'thrust a new assured upon a company against its will'.[109] On the other hand, where it appears from the nature of the contract that no special personal considerations are involved, so that it can make no difference to the obligor whether the performance is rendered for the original contracting party or another, then the right to the performance of an obligation may be assigned.[110] Moreover, the fact that a contract is non-assignable has been held not to preclude the making of a declaration of trust of the benefit of the contract for a third party.[111]

The paradigm example of a personal contract is a contract of employment. Although at common law an employer could not assign its rights under contracts of employment with employees if it transferred the business without consent,[112] the position has been altered by legislation. On transfers of a business by sale, other disposition or by operation of law (eg on

[105] *Norglen Ltd v Reeds Rains Prudential Ltd* [1999] 2 AC 1; *Circuit Systems Ltd v Zuken-Redac (UK) Ltd* [1997] 1 WLR 721.

[106] *Advanced Technology Structures Ltd v Cray Valley Products Ltd* [1993] BCLC 723.

[107] [2011] EWCA Civ 904, [2012] QB 640.

[108] *Kemp v Baerselman* [1906] 2 KB 604.

[109] *Peters v General Accident and Life Assurance Corp Ltd* [1937] 4 All ER 628, 633 (Goddard J).

[110] *Tolhurst v Associated Portland Cement Manufacturers (1900) Ltd* [1903] AC 414; *Shayler v Woolf* [1946] Ch 320.

[111] *Don King Productions Inc v Warren* [2000] Ch 291.

[112] *Nokes v Doncaster Amalgamated Collieries Ltd* [1940] AC 1014, 1026; *Newns v British Airways* (1992) 21 IRLR 575, 576.

insolvency), there is a statutory novation by which all rights, powers, duties, and liabilities under a contract of employment operate between the employee and the transferee[113] unless the employee gives notice that he or she objects to being employed by the transferee.

(iv) Miscellaneous

For reasons of public policy, no assignment may be made of the salary of a public officer paid out of national funds (eg of a civil servant's pay),[114] of maintenance granted to a wife,[115] or of benefits under social security legislation.[116]

(h) LIABILITIES CANNOT BE ASSIGNED

The burden of a contract can never be assigned without the consent of the other party to the contract.[117] A promisee should not be compelled, by reason of an agreement between the promisor and a third party, to accept anyone but the promisor as the person liable on the promise.

The rule is illustrated by the case of *Robson and Sharpe v Drummond*:[118]

S hired a carriage to D for 5 years, undertaking to paint it every year and to keep it in repair. R was the partner of S, but the contract was made with S alone. After 3 years S retired from business, and D was informed that R was thenceforth answerable for the painting and repair of the carriage and would receive the payments. D refused to deal with R, and returned the carriage.

It was held that he was entitled to do so. Lord Tenterden stated:[119]

[T]he defendant may have been induced to enter into this contract by reason of the personal confidence which he reposed in [S], and therefore have agreed to pay money in advance. The . . . defendant had a right to object to its being performed by any other person, and to say that he contracted with [S] alone, and not with any other person.

Parke J stated that D 'had a right to have the benefit of the judgment and taste of [S] to the end of the contract'.[120]

Although liabilities cannot be assigned, the 'conditional benefit' principle means that rights assigned may themselves be qualified or conditional, the condition being that certain restrictions be observed or certain obligations assumed.[121] In such situations, an assignee who takes the benefit of the contract must also bear the burden.[122] The question whether a contract creates a conditional benefit is one of construction.[123]

[113] Transfer of Undertakings (Protection of Employment) Regulations 2006 (SI 2006 No 246).

[114] *Wells v Foster* (1841) 8 M & W 149, 151. See also *Roberts v Roberts* [1986] 1 WLR 437 (statutory prohibition of assignment of soldiers' pay and benefits). Cf *Re Mirams* [1891] 1 QB 594.

[115] *Re Robinson* (1884) 27 Ch D 160.

[116] eg Social Security Administration Act 1992, s 187.

[117] *Linden Gardens Trust Ltd v Lenesta Sludge Disposals Ltd* [1994] 1 AC 85, 103.

[118] (1831) 2 B & Ad 303.

[119] *Ibid*, 307.

[120] *Ibid*, 308.

[121] *Tolhurst v Associated Portland Cement Manufacturers Ltd* [1903] AC 414; *Tito v Waddell (No 2)* [1977] Ch 106, 290–307. See also *Pan Ocean Shipping Co Ltd v Creditcorp Ltd, The Trident Beauty* [1994] 1 WLR 161, 171.

[122] For doubt cast on a wide 'pure principle of benefit and burden', see *Rhone v Stephens* [1994] 2 AC 130.

[123] *Tito v Waddell (No 2)* [1997] Ch 106, 302.

2. VICARIOUS PERFORMANCE

At first sight, an exception to the rule that there can be no assignment of liabilities is that there may be circumstances which make it permissible for a contracting party to perform its side of the contract by getting someone else to do the stipulated work. If A undertakes to do work for B which needs no special skill, and it does not appear that A has been selected with reference to any personal qualification, B cannot complain if A sub-contracts the work to an equally competent subcontractor. Such cases are sometimes loosely referred to as assignments of a contractual liability, but they are really instances of the *vicarious performance* of a contract. This is because the original contracting party remains liable on the contract and, as a rule, is the only person entitled to sue for payment. This is clearly stated by Lord Greene MR in *Davies v Collins*:[124]

> In many contracts all that is stipulated for is that the work shall be done and the actual hand to do it need not be that of the contracting party himself; the other party will be bound to accept performance carried out by somebody else. The contracting party, of course, is the only party who remains liable. He cannot assign his liability to a subcontractor, but his liability in those cases is to see that the work is done, and if it is not properly done he is liable. It is quite a mistake to regard that as an assignment of the contract; it is not.

The circumstances in which a contract may be vicariously performed, which are similar to those which determine whether a contractual right is assignable, are discussed in Chapter 12.

3. NOVATION

Another way by which the benefit or burden of a contract may be transferred to a third party is through the cooperation of all the parties.

> If A owes M £100, and M owes X £100, it may be agreed between all three that A shall pay X instead of M, which terminates M's legal relationship with either party. In such a case the consideration for A's promise to pay X is the discharge by X of M's debt; for M's discharge of A, the promise of A to pay X; for X's discharge of M, the discharge by M of A's debt to M.

This is in effect the rescission of one contract and the substitution of a new one in which the same acts are to be performed by different parties. This is called a novation and it can only take place by an agreement between all the parties.[125] Novation is not, therefore, 'compulsory';[126] and precisely because it involves the consent of all three parties it cannot properly be regarded as an assignment.

124 [1945] 1 All ER 247, 249. See also *Stewart v Reavell's Garage* [1952] 2 QB 545.

125 Novation can be created and evidenced by conduct: *Musst Holdings Ltd v Astra Asset Management UK Ltd* [2023] EWCA Civ 128 at [54]–[60].

126 Approved in *Re United Railways of the Havana and Regla Warehouses Ltd* [1960] Ch 52, 84, revs'd in part on other grounds *sub nom Tomkinson v First Pennsylvania Banking and Trust Co* [1961] AC 1007.

As novation is different from assignment, it follows that the rule that assignment is 'subject to equities' does not apply to novation. Say, for example, a contract was induced by a misrepresentation and there has then been an assignment by the person making the misrepresentation: the debtor can rely on the misrepresentation vis-à-vis the assignee. In contrast, it is irrelevant to a novation that the original contract was induced by a misrepresentation. Once there has been a novation, the original contract has been extinguished and with it the power to rescind for the original misrepresentation.

4. ASSIGNMENT BY OPERATION OF LAW

So far we have dealt with the voluntary assignment by parties to a contract of the benefit of the contract. But rules of law may also operate to transfer these rights, or contractual liabilities, from one to another. Two areas are here considered: death and bankruptcy.

(a) THE EFFECT OF DEATH

The general rule is that rights and liabilities under a contract pass, on the death of a party to the contract, to his or her personal representatives. They can, therefore, both sue, and be sued,[127] on the contract made by the deceased.

But performance of contracts which require the personal service or skill of the deceased cannot be demanded of personal representatives, nor can they insist upon offering such performance, though they can sue for money earned by the deceased which is unpaid at the time of death.[128] Contracts of agency and of personal service expire with the death of either of the parties to them; for instance, an apprenticeship contract is terminated by the death of the master, and no claim to the services of the apprentice survives to the executor or administrator.[129]

(b) BANKRUPTCY

Where the Court makes a bankruptcy order, the Official Receiver becomes, or another person may be appointed to be, the trustee of the bankrupt's estate.[130] The estate comprises 'all property belonging to or vested in the bankrupt at the commencement of the bankruptcy'[131] and this passes to the trustee[132] as may property which has been acquired by or has devolved upon the bankrupt since the commencement of the

[127] But only to the extent of the assets of the estate.
[128] *Stubbs v Holywell Railway Co* (1867) LR 2 Ex 311.
[129] *Baxter v Burfield* (1746) 2 Stra 1266.
[130] Insolvency Act 1986, ss 291A, 296.
[131] Insolvency Act 1986, s 283(1). 'Property' includes 'things in action': *ibid*, s 436.
[132] Insolvency Act 1986, s 306.

bankruptcy.[133] The object of the laws of bankruptcy is that 'every beneficial interest which the bankrupt has shall be disposed of for the benefit of his creditors'.[134] It suffices to note that:

(1) Where any part of the property of the bankrupt consists of a chose in action, it is deemed to have been assigned to the trustee.[135]

(2) The trustee may disclaim, and so discharge, unprofitable contracts.[136]

(3) The trustee is excluded from suing for personal losses arising out of breaches of contract, such as injuries to reputation or credit.[137]

(4) Executory contracts personal to the bankrupt do not pass.[138]

The trustee, as statutory assignee of the bankrupt's choses in action, is in one respect in a more favourable position than an ordinary assignee. If a chose in action has been assigned by the bankrupt *before* the bankruptcy took place, the assignment will be void as against the trustee if (i) it is of a future chose in action for which the consideration is not supplied until after the commencement of the bankruptcy[139] or (ii) it is a general assignment of book debts by a trader and has not been registered under the Bills of Sale Act 1878.[140]

FURTHER READING

Edelman and Elliott, 'Two Conceptions of Equitable Assignment' (2015) 131 LQR 228

Bridge, 'The Nature of Assignment and Non-Assignment Clauses' (2016) 132 LQR 47

MacMahon, 'Rethinking Assignability' [2020] CLJ 288

133 Insolvency Act 1986, s 307.

134 *Smith v Coffin* (1795) 2 H Bl 444, 461.

135 Insolvency Act 1986, s 311(4). Where there is a cross-claim what is assigned is a claim to the net balance: *ibid*, s 323; *Stein v Blake* [1996] AC 243.

136 Insolvency Act 1986, s 315. An administrative receiver of a company becomes liable on any contract of employment 'adopted' by him: *ibid*, s 44; *Powdrill v Watson* [1995] 2 All ER 65.

137 *Wilson v United Counties Bank* [1920] AC 102 (credit); *Re Kavanagh* [1949] 2 All ER 264, aff'd [1950] 1 All ER 39n (reputation). Cf *Beckham v Drake* (1849) 2 HLC 579 (wrongful dismissal). See *Heath v Tang* [1993] 1 WLR 1421.

138 *Gibson v Carruthers* (1841) 8 M & W 321 (contract to marry); *Lucas v Moncrieff* (1905) 21 TLR 683 (contract to publish book).

139 *Wilmot v Alton* [1897] 1 QB 17; *Re Collins* [1925] Ch 556; *Re de Marney* [1943] Ch 126. Cf *Re Davis & Co* (1888) 22 QBD 193; *Re Trytel* [1952] 2 TLR 32.

140 Insolvency Act 1986, s 344.

23

AGENCY

Agency is the relationship which exists where one person (the principal) authorizes another (the agent) to act on its behalf and the agent agrees to do so.[1] Although agency can be relevant in various areas of the law (eg tort and unjust enrichment), this chapter is solely concerned with the agent making contracts with others for a principal.

For an agent to act on behalf of its principal in making contracts with other parties, the agent must have the principal's authority. Where a (bilateral) contract is concluded by an agent for its principal, the principal can both sue and be sued on the contract (although, if the agent's authority is merely ostensible, rather than actual, the principal cannot sue unless it has ratified the contract). So, one *could* argue that the whole law of agency in contract is an exception to, or a way round, the doctrine of privity.[2] The principal, albeit in one sense a stranger to the contract concluded by its agent, is able to sue and be sued on that contract.

However, in most circumstances, one can say without any fiction that the principal, not the agent, is the party to the contract concluded by the agent. Indeed in most circumstances the agent will not be named in the contract and will 'drop out'[3] of the picture once the contract has been concluded. But that is generally not the case where one has an undisclosed principal: that is, where the other party has not been informed, and hence does not know, that it is dealing with an agent rather than with a principal.[4] Where the principal is undisclosed, the agent usually does not drop out of the picture: in general, the agent, as well as the principal, can sue and be sued on the contract. Therefore, it is artificial to say that the principal, not the agent, is the party to the contract. Where the principal is undisclosed, the other party has no knowledge of the principal's existence and may find that it is in a contractual relationship with someone of whom it has never heard and with whom it never intended to contract.

It follows that, whatever one says about agency where there is a disclosed principal, agency where the principal is undisclosed is clearly an exception to, or way of avoiding,

[1] The leading textbook on this subject is Watts and Reynolds (eds), *Bowstead and Reynolds on Agency* (23rd edn, 2024). See generally Dowrick (1954) 17 MLR 24; McMeel (2000) 116 LQR 387.

[2] See above, p 653.

[3] This language is convenient and often used, but can be misleading: the reason why the agent cannot sue, or be sued by, the third party is that, on an objective interpretation of the circumstances, the contract is between principal and third party only. See too Stevens [2005] LMCLQ 101.

[4] See below, pp 705–7.

the doctrine of privity. It avoids not only the benefit side of privity but also the burden side: the undisclosed principal can both sue, and be sued by, the other party.

Even when confined to contracts, this chapter is not concerned with all the relevant law on agency which includes, for example, the fiduciary duties owed by the agent to the principal and how one terminates an agency. Instead, the focus is on understanding how agency may be regarded as an exception to, or a way round, the privity doctrine. The relevant material will be divided into two parts: first, the creation of agency; and, secondly, the effects of agency in respect of the contractual relations between the principal and the third party and between the agent and the third party.

1. MODES OF CREATION

Agency may be created in any one of three main ways:[5]

(1) by an actual authority to contract given by the principal to the agent;

(2) by the principal's ratification of a contract entered into by the agent on the principal's behalf but without its authority (ie the authority is retrospectively conferred);

(3) by an ostensible authority conferred by the principal on the agent even though no actual authority has been given.

In the first two cases, the principal can sue and be sued by the third party and rights and duties also arise between the principal and the agent. In the last case, the principal can be sued but cannot always sue. We shall deal with each of these in turn.

(a) ACTUAL AUTHORITY

Actual authority to contract may be express or implied.

Normally the authority given by a principal to its agent is an express authority enabling the latter to bind the former by acts done within the scope of that authority. Such authority may, in general, be given orally. But in some cases it is necessary that the authority should be given in a special form. First, in order that an agent may make a binding contract by deed, it is necessary that authority should normally be given in a deed.[6] Certain transactions, for example, conveyances of land, must still be made by deed.[7] Secondly, the Law of Property Act 1925,[8] which requires the creation or

[5] This chapter does not consider the law on 'agency of necessity': see *Bowstead and Reynolds on Agency* (23rd edn, 2024) ch 4.

[6] Watts and Reynolds (eds), *Bowstead and Reynolds on Agency* (23rd edn, 2024) Art 10.

[7] See above, p 80. On formalities for the creation of powers of attorney, see Powers of Attorney Act 1971, s 1; Mental Capacity Act 2005, s 9.

[8] ss 53(1)(a), (c), 54. This is to be contrasted with a contract for the disposition of an interest in land: *McLaughlin v Duffill* [2008] EWCA Civ 1627, [2010] Ch 1.

disposition of any equitable interest, or interest in land, to be in writing, signed by the grantor or the grantor's agent, lays down that in such case the agent shall be authorized in writing.[9]

The authority of an agent may also be implied.[10] But such implied authority can be negatived by an express limitation. In most cases implied authority is said to be *incidental* to an express authority or *required* due to the circumstances of the case. The category of implied authority also includes *usual* and *customary* authority. Generally, agents have the authority *usually* possessed by agents in their position. Therefore if an agent is authorized to conduct a particular trade or business, or to perform certain duties, that agent has implied authority to do such acts as are usual in the trade or business, or ordinarily incidental to the due performance of the duties. In addition, every agent has implied authority to act in accordance with the reasonable customs and usages of the particular place, trade, or market where the agent is employed, for example, the London Stock Exchange.[11]

(b) RATIFICATION

Even if the agent enters into a contract without the authority of the principal, the principal may subsequently ratify, that is to say, adopt the benefit and liabilities of a contract made on the principal's behalf.

This may occur in one of two ways. First, when A, though contracting as P's agent, and having P in contemplation as the principal, was not at the time of the contract P's agent in fact, as no precedent authority had been received. Secondly, when A was in fact P's agent at the time of making the contract, but exceeded the authority which P had given. In either case a ratification duly made places the parties in exactly the same position in which they would have been if A had P's authority at the time the contract was made. It is said to 'relate back' to the time of contracting and to have a retrospective effect.[12] An unauthorized acceptance may therefore be ratified even though the offer has in the meantime been withdrawn. So in *Bolton Partners v Lambert*:[13]

The managing director of a company, purporting to act as agent on the company's behalf, but without its authority, accepted an offer by the defendant for the purchase of some sugar works belonging to them. The defendant then withdrew his offer, but the company ratified the manager's acceptance.

It was held that the defendant was bound. The ratification related back to the time of the agent's acceptance and so prevented the defendant subsequently revoking the offer.

[9] However, s 53(1)(b) does not include the language of agents, such that an agent cannot provide the signed writing required to evidence a declaration of trust over land: *National Iranian Oil Co v Crescent Gas Corp Ltd* [2025] EWCA Civ 1211.

[10] *Freeman & Lockyer v Buckhurst Park Properties (Mangal) Ltd* [1964] 2 QB 480, 502; *Hely-Hutchinson v Brayhead Ltd* [1968] 1 QB 549.

[11] *Pollock v Stables* (1848) 12 QB 765.

[12] *Wilson v Tumman* (1843) 6 M & G 236, 242 (Tindal CJ).

[13] (1888) 41 Ch D 295.

But there can be no true ratification where an agent purports to accept an offer 'subject to ratification'. In such a case the so-called ratification would itself be an acceptance of the offer of the other party, which may be withdrawn at any time before the so-called ratification takes place.[14]

The following rules govern ratification:

(i) The agent must purport to act as an agent for a disclosed principal

An individual may not conclude a contract on its own behalf and then transfer it to someone else under colour of ratification. The individual must contract as agent at the time of the contract. An undisclosed principal, who is not disclosed by the agent to the third party at the time of contracting, may not step in and ratify acts done by the agent in excess of what had previously been authorized.[15] In *Keighley, Maxsted & Co v Durant*:[16]

A corn merchant was authorised to buy wheat at a certain price on a joint account for himself and KM. Acting in excess of his authority, he purchased wheat at a higher price from D, but in his own name. KM next day ratified the transaction, but later failed to take delivery of the wheat. D brought an action against KM for breach.

The action failed. The corn merchant had contracted in his own name without mentioning that KM was his principal. Any purported ratification by KM was therefore ineffective, and KM was consequently under no contractual obligation to D.

On the other hand, if this requirement is satisfied, it makes no difference that the agent's act was a fraud on the principal. So where an agent, without authority, and fraudulently, entered into a contract for the sale of wheat in the principal's name, but intending to take the benefit of it, the principal could nevertheless ratify and adopt the contract and hold the buyers to their bargain.[17] But a forged signature cannot be ratified, for one who forges the signature of another is not an agent. The forger does not act for another; but rather personates the person whose signature has been forged.[18]

(ii) The principal must be in existence

To ratify the contract, the intended principal must have been in existence, and ascertainable, at the time that the contract was made. It is not necessary for the principal to be named as long as it is ascertainable.[19]

[14] *Watson v Davies* [1931] 1 Ch 455; *Warehousing & Forwarding Co of East Africa Ltd v Jafferali & Sons Ltd* [1964] AC 1.

[15] Cf *Welsh Development Agency v Export Finance Co Ltd* [1992] BCLC 148, 159, 173, 182 (this principle is qualified by the maxim *id certum est quod certum reddi potest*, ie that which is capable of being made certain is to be treated as certain).

[16] [1901] AC 240.

[17] *Re Tiedemann and Ledermann Frères* [1899] 2 QB 66.

[18] *Brook v Hook* (1871) LR 6 Ex 89.

[19] *National Oilwell (UK) Ltd v Davy Offshore Ltd* [1993] 2 Lloyd's Rep 582, 592–7.

This rule is important in its bearing on the liabilities of companies for the contracts made by promoters on their behalf before they are formed. In *Kelner v Baxter*:[20]

The promoters of an unformed company entered into a contract on its behalf, which the company, when duly incorporated, ratified. It went into liquidation and the promoters, who had contracted as agents, were sued upon the contract. They pleaded that the liability had passed, by ratification, to the company, and no longer attached to them.

The Court rejected this argument. Willes J said:[21]

Could the company become liable by a mere ratification? Clearly not. Ratification can only be by a person ascertained at the time of the act done,—by a person in existence either actually or in contemplation of law; as in the case of assignees of bankrupts and administrators, whose title, for the protection of the estate, vests by relation.

This limitation might work hardship to solicitors and others who are called in to do the preliminary work leading to the formation of a company as they will have no right of action against the company when formed. But as the above case shows, and as embodied in statute,[22] they will normally be able to assert a right of action against the agent (the promoter) in such cases, since the agent will be considered to have incurred personal liability on the contract.

(iii) Capacity of the principal to contract

'At the time the act was done the agent must have had a competent principal.'[23] Thus, if an agent enters into a contract on behalf of a principal who is, at the time, incapable of making it, no ratification is possible.[24]

(iv) Manner of ratification

The principal who accepts the contract made by a person whom the principal thereby undertakes to regard as its agent, may accept by words or conduct. The principal may avow responsibility for the act of the agent, or take the benefit of the contract, or by acquiescence in what is done create a presumption of authority. In the absence of an express avowal, however, the ratification must be founded on full knowledge of the facts,[25] and the principal must have had the option to accept or to refuse the contract.[26]

[20] (1866) LR 2 CP 174. See also *Natal Land and Colonization Co Ltd v Pauline Colliery and Development Syndicate Ltd* [1904] AC 120.

[21] (1866) LR 2 CP 174, 184.

[22] Companies Act 2006, s 51(1). See below, p 710. In *Braymist Ltd v Wise Finance Co Ltd* [2002] EWCA Civ 127, [2002] Ch 273 it was held that this statutory provision meant that the agent was not only liable on the contract but entitled to enforce it.

[23] *Firth v Staines* [1897] 2 QB 70, 75 (Wright J).

[24] *Ashbury Railway Carriage and Iron Co v Riche* (1875) LR 7 HL 653 (*ultra vires* contract); *Boston Deep Sea Fishing and Ice Co Ltd v Farnham* [1957] 1 WLR 1051 (alien enemy).

[25] *La Banque Jacques-Cartier v La Banque d'Epargne de Montréal* (1887) 13 App Cas 111.

[26] *Forman & Co Pty Ltd v Ship 'Liddesdale'* [1900] AC 190, above, p 463.

Otherwise it will be unenforceable against the principal. It is not, however, necessary for the ratification to be communicated to the third party.[27]

(v) Time and retrospectivity of ratification

The general rule is that the effect of ratification is retrospective so that the agent is treated as having had the relevant authority at the time it purported to make the contract. So an offer accepted without authority by an agent can be later ratified by a principal even though at that later time the other party, to the principal's knowledge, has withdrawn its offer.[28]

An exception to that general rule is that 'an estate once vested cannot be divested, nor can an act lawful at the time of its performance be rendered unlawful by the doctrine of ratification'.[29] Similarly the traditional rule for non-marine insurance, albeit controversial, is that a contract of insurance made by an agent without the principal's authority cannot be ratified after the principal has become aware that the event insured against has in fact occurred.[30]

Subject to any express time limit for ratification fixed by the parties, and assuming that a time fixed for performance by the other party has not expired, the principal has a reasonable time to ratify after acquiring notice of the unauthorized act.[31]

(c) OSTENSIBLE AUTHORITY

The principal may, by words or conduct, create an inference that an agent has authority to act on behalf of the principal even though no authority exists in fact. In such a case, if the agent contracts within the limits of the apparent authority, although without any actual authority, the principal will be bound to third parties by the agent's acts.

(i) Requirements

This doctrine of apparent authority, or ostensible authority as it is often called, is really an application of the principle of estoppel, since estoppel means that a person is not permitted to resist an inference which can reasonably be drawn from that person's

[27] *Shell Co of Australia Ltd v Nat Shipping Bagging Services Ltd, The Kilmun* [1988] 2 Lloyd's Rep 1, 11. See also *Pagnan SpA v Feed Products Ltd* [1987] 2 Lloyd's Rep 601.

[28] *Bolton Partners v Lambert* (1881) 41 Ch D 295: see above, p 698. See also *Presentaciones Musicales SA v Secunda* [1994] Ch 271 (the unauthorized commencement of legal proceedings within the limitation period by an agent could be ratified by the principal outside the limitation period); *The Borvigilant* [2002] EWHC 1759 (Admlty), [2002] 2 Lloyd's Rep 631.

[29] *Bolton Partners v Lambert* (1881) 41 Ch D 295, 307 (Cotton LJ).

[30] *Grover & Grover v Matthews* [1910] 2 KB 401. The contrary rule applies to marine insurance (see Marine Insurance Act 1906, s 86; *Williams v North China Insurance Co* (1876) 1 CPD 757): in *obiter dicta* in *National Oilwell (UK) Ltd v Davy Offshore Ltd* [1983] 2 Lloyd's Rep 582, 607–8, Colman J expressed the strong view that the rule in marine insurance should be extended to non-marine insurance.

[31] *Re Portuguese Consolidated Copper Mines* (1890) 45 Ch D 16; *Bedford Insurance Co Ltd v Instituto de Resseguros do Brasil* [1985] QB 966, 987.

words or conduct.[32] Where one person expressly or impliedly represents another to have authority to act as agent, so that a third party reasonably believes the person who is so held out to possess that authority and deals with that person in reliance on the representation made, the person making the representation will be bound to the same extent as if actual authority had in fact been conferred.[33] The person making the representation is estopped from denying the ostensible authority it created.

It is important to note three things. First, the representation must be made by *the principal*. Ostensible authority cannot be created simply by a representation by the agent.[34] Secondly, subject to certain exceptions discussed below,[35] the third party must rely on a representation of the agent's authority to act *as agent*. The doctrine cannot apply where the third party does not know or believe that person to be an agent, for example, if the existence of the principal is unknown to the third party.[36] Thirdly, the agent's want of authority must be *unknown* to the third party.[37]

(ii) Never any authority

These requirements mean that there will seldom be ostensible authority where a person has never at any time had authority to contract. But that there can be an exceptional case is exemplified by *Freeman & Lockyer v Buckhurst Park Properties (Mangal) Ltd*:[38]

The articles of a company contained the power to appoint a managing director. With the knowledge and approval of the board of directors, K acted as managing director, although he was never appointed to this post. K instructed the claimants, a firm of architects, to do certain work for the company. The company disclaimed liability for payment for this work on the ground that K had no authority to contract on the company's behalf.

[32] For a different view, based on a model of offer and acceptance, see Krebs, in Burrows and Peel (eds) *Contract Formation and Parties* (2010).

[33] For a clear general statement of the law, see *Freeman & Lockyer v Buckhurst Park Properties (Mangal) Ltd* [1964] 2 QB 480, 503–4 (Diplock LJ). For examples of factual situations in which ostensible authority may exist, see *Egyptian Intl Foreign Trade Co v Soplex Wholesale Supplies Ltd, The Raffaella* [1985] 2 Lloyd's Rep 36; *Shearson Lehman Hutton Inc v MacLaine, Watson & Co Ltd (No 2)* [1988] 1 WLR 16; *Polish SS Co v AJ Williams Fuels (Overseas Sales) Ltd, The Suwalki* [1989] 1 Lloyd's Rep 511. A person negotiating a contract on behalf of a company but known not to have authority to bind the company may, nevertheless, have ostensible authority to communicate that those with authority to bind the company have approved the contract in question: *First Energy (UK) Ltd v Hungarian International Bank Ltd* [1993] 2 Lloyd's Rep 194 distinguishing *Armagas Ltd v Mundogas SA, The Ocean Frost* [1986] AC 717.

[34] *A-G for Ceylon v Silva* [1953] AC 461, 479; *Freeman & Lockyer v Buckhurst Park Properties (Mangal) Ltd* [1964] 2 QB 480, 505; *British Bank of the Middle East v Sun Life Assurance Co of Canada (UK) Ltd* [1983] 2 Lloyd's Rep 9; *First Sport Ltd v Barclays Bank plc* [1993] 1 WLR 1229; *First Energy (UK) Ltd v Hungarian Int'l Bank Ltd* [1993] 2 Lloyd's Rep 194. See too *Kelly v Fraser* [2012] UKPC 25, [2013] 1 AC 450; *East Asia Co Ltd v PT Satria Tirtatama Energindo (Bermuda)* [2019] UKPC 30, [2020] 2 All ER 294.

[35] See below, p 704.

[36] *Farquharson Bros v King & Co* [1902] AC 325; *Freeman & Lockyer v Buckhurst Park Properties (Mangal) Ltd* [1964] 2 QB 480, 503.

[37] See *Armagas Ltd v Mundogas SA* [1986] 1 AC 717, 777–9.

[38] [1964] 2 QB 480. But see now Companies Act 2006, s 39(1), and above, p 239 (*ultra vires* contracts).

The Court of Appeal held that, although K had no actual authority to employ the claimants, the company had created an ostensible authority by its conduct in permitting him to act as managing director to the knowledge of the board. Any act done within the usual ambit of that ostensible authority was therefore binding on the company.

(iii) Limited or revoked authority

The doctrine of ostensible authority is more likely to apply where an authorized agent goes beyond the limits of its actual authority, yet acts within an authority which it is made to appear to possess.[39] In particular, where a principal has publicly allowed the agent to assume an authority, that authority cannot be revoked privately. The principal will be bound by the acts of the agent if the principal has given other persons reason to suppose that they are done with authority.

So, an employer who habitually allows employees to purchase goods on credit[40] or a husband who takes upon himself the liability in respect of his wife's past dealings with suppliers of goods or services[41] 'holds out' the employees or wife as agent. They will be liable on such contracts unless and until they actually make known to the supplier the fact that the agency has ended.

(iv) Partnership

Every partner is an agent of the firm and of the other partners for the business of the partnership; this is simply a case of implied authority. But any act done by a partner for carrying on in the usual way business of a kind carried on by the firm binds the firm and the other partners, even if the partner so acting has in fact no authority to act for the firm in the particular matter, unless the person with whom the partner is dealing either knows that person has no authority, or does not know or believe that person to be a partner.[42] Moreover, a partner who retires from a firm may still be liable for partnership debts contracted after retirement. A person dealing with a firm after a change in its constitution is entitled to treat all apparent members of the old firm as still being members of the firm until that person has notice of the change.[43] The retiring partner will be estopped from denying the continuation of that authority,[44] except where he was not known to be a partner by the person dealing with the firm.[45]

39 *Todd v Robinson* (1825) 1 Ry & M 217; *Summers v Solomon* (1857) 7 E & B 879; *Manchester Trust v Furness* [1895] 2 QB 539; *AMB Generali Holding AG v SEB Trygg Liv Holding AB* [2005] EWCA Civ 1237, [2006] 1 WLR 2276.

40 *Summers v Solomon*, above, n 39.

41 *Drew v Nunn* (1879) 4 QBD 661; *Jetley v Hill* (1884) Cab & El 239. See also *Ryan v Sams* (1848) 12 QB 460 (mistress).

42 Partnership Act 1890, s 5. See also *ibid*, s 8. See further, *United Bank of Kuwait Ltd v Hammoud* [1988] 1 WLR 1051.

43 Partnership Act 1890, s 36(1). Under s 36(2), notice in the *London Gazette* is sufficient notice as to persons who had no dealings with the firm before the change; otherwise express notice is required.

44 *Scarf v Jardine* (1882) 7 App Cas 345, 349.

45 Partnership Act 1890, s 36(3).

(d) USUAL AUTHORITY?

There are a number of cases which appear to establish that, in certain circumstances, a principal may be liable for the unauthorized acts of an agent, even though the third party did not rely upon any representation by the principal of the agent's authority to act as agent. In these cases, the existence of the principal was unknown to the third party, so it could not be said that the principal held out the agent to have authority to act as agent and was estopped. The apparent rule to be extracted from them is as follows: an undisclosed principal who employs an agent to conduct business is liable for any act of the agent which is incidental to or usual in that business, even though such act may have been forbidden by the principal. The leading example is *Watteau v Fenwick*:[46]

F, a firm of brewers, bought a pub from H, but kept him on as manager, and his name appeared above the door. They instructed H not to buy cigars although it was usual for such a business to deal in cigars. H bought some cigars on credit from W, who thought H was the owner of the business and gave credit to him personally. On discovering that he was employed by F, W sued F for the price of the cigars.

It was held that F was liable. Wills J rejected the argument that a principal could only be bound where there had been a holding out of authority—which could not be said of this case where the person supplying the goods knew nothing of the existence of the principal: 'The principal is liable for all the acts of the agent which are within the authority usually confided to an agent of that character, notwithstanding limitations as between the principal and the agent, put upon that authority.'[47]

This case is anomalous, and has been criticized as such.[48] One attempt made to explain it and similar cases is that they are cases of 'usual authority'. But, as noted above,[49] the usual authority of an agent is normally merely an example of implied authority, which could be negatived by an express limitation. If this and similar cases[50] are rightly decided, which seems unlikely, they are perhaps best regarded as examples of the operation of a quasi-tortious principle whereby an employer is rendered vicariously liable for the acts of an agent if done in the course of the agent's employment.

2. EFFECTS OF AGENCY

As has been explained, this chapter is focused upon the effects of agency in respect of the contractual relations between the principal and the third party[51] and between the agent and the third party.[52]

[46] [1893] 1 QB 346.

[47] *Ibid*, 348.

[48] *Rhodian River Shipping SA v Halla Maritime Corporation* [1984] 1 Lloyd's Rep 373, 378–9 (Bingham LJ); *Sign-o-Lite Plastics Ltd v Metropolitan Life Insurance Co* (1990) 73 DLR (4th) 541 (British Columbian CA). See also Hornby [1961] CLJ 239; Fridman (1991) 70 Can Bar Rev 329; Tettenborn [1998] CLJ 274.

[49] Above, p 698.

[50] See, eg, *Edmunds v Bushell and Jones* (1865) LR 1 QB 97.

[51] For a principal's liability in tort for the misrepresentation of its agent, see *Bowstead and Reynolds on Agency* (23rd edn, 2024) Arts 90 and 91.

[52] For the relations between the principal and the agent, see *Bowstead and Reynolds on Agency* (23rd edn, 2024) chs 6 and 7.

(a) THE CONTRACTUAL RELATIONS BETWEEN THE PRINCIPAL AND THE THIRD PARTY

(i) The general position

When a principal endows an agent with actual authority to contract, the principal is bound, as regards third parties, by all acts of the agent which are done within the limits of that authority. This rule is often expressed in the maxim, *Qui facit per alium, facit per se*, a person who acts through another acts in person.

The same rule applies where the agent is acting within its ostensible authority.[53] The principal will be liable to third parties even though the agent has acted for its own benefit and in fraud of the principal.[54] However, where the third party dealing with the agent is aware that the agent is acting for its own benefit, or where the circumstances of the transaction are such as to put the third party on enquiry, the principal is not bound.[55]

A principal also acquires rights against a third party under a contract entered into by an agent on its behalf where the agent has acted within the limits of its actual authority.[56] But a principal does not acquire rights (as opposed to liabilities) against the third party by reason of ostensible authority because that doctrine is based on a representation by the principal. In other words, a principal must ratify a contract entered into without authority before it can acquire rights (as opposed to liabilities) against the third party.

(ii) Undisclosed principal

Normally, where an agent acts on behalf of a principal whose existence, at the time the contract is made, is not disclosed, that 'undisclosed principal' can sue and be sued under the contract; and the agent does not 'drop out'[57] so that there is a contract between the undisclosed principal and agent on the one hand and the third party on the other.[58] This doctrine of the undisclosed principal is peculiar to English law,[59] and has sometimes been criticized as an anomaly, since it runs counter to the principles of privity of contract.[60] But it serves a useful commercial purpose.[61] Moreover, it is subject to the qualification that the authority must have been in existence at the time the contract was

[53] Above, p 701.

[54] *Hambro v Burnand* [1904] 2 KB 10. See also Watts (2001) 117 LQR 300.

[55] *Reckitt v Burnett, Pembroke & Slater Ltd* [1929] AC 176; *East Asia Co Ltd v PT Satria Tirtatama Energindo (Bermuda)* [2019] UKPC 30, [2020] 2 All ER 294 at [84]–[89]; *Philipp v Barclays Bank UK plc* [2023] UKSC 25, [2024] AC 346 at [81]–[89].

[56] This might be excluded by the terms of the contract, but 'there is a heavy burden of persuasion on a party who seeks to argue that a known and identified principal is to be excluded from a contract': *Filatona Trading Ltd v Navigator Equities Ltd* [2020] EWCA Civ 109, [2020] 2 All ER (Comm) 851 at [101].

[57] Watts and Reynolds (eds), *Bowstead and Reynolds on Agency* (23rd edn, 2024) para 9-012. See below, pp 705, 711.

[58] *Welsh Development Agency v Export Finance Co* [1992] BCLC 148, 173, 182.

[59] Lando and Beale, *Principles of European Contract Law Parts I and II* (2000) 221.

[60] Pollock (1888) 3 LQR 359; Ames, *Lectures on Legal History* (1913) 453. Cf Goodhart and Harrison [1932] CLJ 320; Tan Cheng-Han (2004) 120 LQR 480. See too *Magellan Spirit ApS v Vitol SA* [2016] EWHC 454 (Comm), [2017] 1 All ER (Comm) 241 at [15] (Leggatt J). In continental systems the absence of the doctrine of privity of contract makes such a principle commercially unnecessary. Cf Müller-Freienfels (1953) 16 MLR 299.

[61] See *Siu Yin Kwan v Eastern Insurance Co Ltd* [1994] 2 AC 199, 207.

made: it is not possible to ratify a contract unless the principal is named therein, or is at any rate identifiable. Otherwise it would be open to any stranger to intervene and sue.[62]

But the right of the undisclosed principal to intervene as a contracting party is subject to certain limitations.

First, intervention is excluded if the contract is in terms which import that the agent is the real and only principal, for then the idea of agency is incompatible with the terms of the contract. In *Humble v Hunter*,[63] where an agent in making a charterparty described himself as 'owner' of the ship, it was held that evidence was not admissible to prove that another person was the real owner and that he was merely acting as agent on his behalf. His principal could not intervene, nor could he be sued. On the other hand, where the agent was described as 'charterer',[64] 'landlord',[65] 'tenant',[66] 'disponent owner',[67] and 'employer'[68] evidence has been admitted to show who the real principal was. It appears that the principal will now only be excluded by descriptive words where such intervention would clearly be inconsistent with the object and intent of the contract.[69]

Secondly, where the personality of the agent is of such importance that the contract must be taken to have been made with that person alone, no one else can interpose and adopt the contract.[70] For example, in the case where there is an agreement to write a book,[71] or to underwrite shares in a company,[72] or to purchase goods subject to a right of set-off,[73] if the agent contracts in its own name without disclosure of the agency, the principal cannot intervene. Of course, if the third party subsequently discovers the identity of the principal, and elects to affirm the contract rather than reject it (eg by retaining goods purchased), the third party will be bound to the principal, but not otherwise.[74]

In any case, a person who contracts with an agent, honestly and reasonably believing the agent to be the principal party to the transaction, is entitled to set up against the principal, when discovered, any set-off which is available against the agent, and which accrued before the person knew that the party with whom the contract was made was

[62] *Keighley, Maxsted & Co v Durant* [1901] AC 240; above, p 683.

[63] (1848) 12 QB 310. See also *Formby v Formby* (1910) 102 LT 116 ('proprietor'); *Asty Maritime Co Ltd and Panagiotis Stravelakis v Rocco Guiseppe & Figli, SNC, The Astyanax* [1985] 2 Lloyd's Rep 109 ('disponent owner'); *Magellan Spirit ApS v Vitol SA* [2016] EWHC 454 (Comm) at [28] (Leggatt J).

[64] *Fred Drughorn Ltd v Rederiaktiebolaget Transatlantic* [1919] AC 203.

[65] *Epps v Rothnie* [1945] KB 562.

[66] *Danziger v Thompson* [1944] KB 654.

[67] *O/Y Wasa SS Co v Newspaper Pulp and Wood Exports* (1949) 82 Ll LR 936. Cf *Asty Maritime Co Ltd and Panagiotis Stravelakis v Rocco Guiseppe & Figli, SNC, The Astyanax* [1985] 2 Lloyd's Rep 109.

[68] *Ferryways NV v Associated British Ports, The Humber Way* [2008] EWHC 225 (Comm), [2008] 2 All ER (Comm) 504.

[69] See, eg, *JH Rayner (Mincing Lane) Ltd v Department of Trade and Industry* [1989] Ch 72, 190–1; *Welsh Development Agency v Export Finance Co* [1992] BCLC 148, 159; *Siu Yin Kwan v Eastern Insurance Co Ltd* [1994] 2 AC 199, 209.

[70] *Said v Butt* [1920] 3 KB 497, above, p 290. Cf *Dyster v Randall & Sons* [1926] Ch 932.

[71] *Boulton v Jones* (1857) 2 H & N 564, 566 (Bramwell B).

[72] *Collins v Associated Greyhound Racecourses Ltd* [1930] 1 Ch 1.

[73] *Boulton v Jones* (1857) 2 H & N 564, above, p 286; *Greer v Downs Supply Co* [1927] 2 KB 28.

[74] *Greer v Downs Supply Co* [1927] 2 KB 28, 33.

in fact an agent.[75] This rule rests upon the doctrine of estoppel.[76] But a person who has not been misled cannot claim such a set-off. So in a case where a man dealt with brokers whom he knew to be in the habit of selling, sometimes as brokers for principals, and sometimes on their own account, he could not set off his indebtedness to the brokers against his debt to the principal.[77]

Upon discovering the principal, the other contracting party may elect to sue either the agent or the principal. Any act which unequivocally indicates the adoption of either principal or agent as the party liable determines the election, and the contracting party cannot afterwards sue the other.[78]

A contract for the sale or other disposition of land must be in writing 'signed *by or on behalf* of each party to the contract'.[79] Although, as we have noted, the contract to which the undisclosed principal is a party is considered not to be separate from the contract between the agent and the other party,[80] the subsection would seem to preclude an undisclosed or an unnamed principal from suing or being sued on contracts signed by their agents.[81] But the Law Commission's Working Paper stated that 'plainly agents should be permitted to sign on behalf of the parties' and that it was intended to 'let the ordinary principles of agency operate',[82] and the Commission's Report indicates that its recommendations were made on this basis.[83] So, it is arguable that, as was the case before the enactment of the 1989 Act,[84] an agent signs 'on behalf of' the principal whenever the contract is signed with authority and the agent intends to act on behalf of the principal.

(iii) Settlement with the agent

It often happens that either the principal or the third party incurs a debt to the other under a contract made through an agent and the principal or the third party thereupon settles with the agent, intending that the agent should pay across the money and so discharge the debt. Sometimes, however, the agent fails to do so, and makes away with the money or becomes bankrupt. Is the debtor then liable to pay over again? The answer will depend on whether it is the principal or the third party who is making the payment.

Where the principal pays the agent, the general rule is that the principal is not discharged.[85] But where there are indications that the third party looks to the agent alone for payment and in consequence the principal settles with the agent,[86] or where

75 *Isberg v Bowden* (1853) 8 Exch 852, 859; *Montagu v Forwood* [1893] 2 QB 350.

76 *Cooke v Eshelby* (1887) 12 App Cas 271, 278 (Lord Watson).

77 *Cooke v Eshelby* (1887) 12 App Cas 271.

78 *Scarf v Jardine* (1882) 7 App Cas 345. Cf *Clarkson Booker Ltd v Andjel* [1964] 2 QB 775; *Pyxis Special Shipping Co Ltd v Dritsas & Kaglis Bros Ltd* [1978] 2 Lloyd's Rep 380 (institution of legal proceedings not conclusive). See Reynolds (1970) 86 LQR 318.

79 Law of Property (Miscellaneous Provisions) Act 1989, s 2(3), above, pp 87–8.

80 *Welsh Development Agency v Export Finance Co* [1992] BCLC 148.

81 See Watts and Reynolds (eds), *Bowstead and Reynolds on Agency* (23rd edn, 2024) para 8-004.

82 Law Com WP No 92 (1985) para 5.16.

83 Law Com No 164 (1987) para 4.8.

84 *Basma v Weekes* [1950] AC 441, 454, on the Law of Property Act 1925, s 40.

85 *Irvine & Co v Watson & Sons* (1880) 5 QBD 414.

86 *Smith v Ferrand* (1827) 7 B & C 191.

the third party's conduct leads the principal to suppose that the debt has already been paid,[87] the third party is estopped from claiming to be paid over again. Normally, however, this is not the case. Where the third party knows that the agent is contracting on behalf of a principal, this indicates that the third party did not look exclusively to the agent for payment.[88] It is necessary to show conduct by the third party which would estop it from proceeding against the principal, or a custom of the trade to this effect.

It was laid down in *Armstrong v Stokes*[89] that, if an undisclosed principal pays the agent for the price of goods sold to it, and the existence of the undisclosed principal is then discovered, the seller cannot sue the undisclosed principal. This decision proceeded on the ground that a demand for payment could not be made from 'those who were only discovered to be principals after they had fairly paid the price to those whom the vendor believed to be the principals, and to whom alone the vendor gave credit'.[90] But this case is contrary to earlier authority,[91] and it was subsequently criticized by the Court of Appeal.[92] No estoppel could legitimately arise since the seller was unaware of the undisclosed principal's existence, and thus could not have induced it to settle with the agent. It may therefore be that it does not represent the law.

If it is the third party who settles with the agent, again the general rule is that the third party is not discharged. The reason for this is that an agent who is authorized to sell is not necessarily authorized to accept the purchase money.[93] However, payment to an agent who has such authority, either from an express mandate of the principal or in the ordinary course of business, will constitute a good discharge.[94] It would also seem that where the principal is undisclosed, payment to the agent before disclosure would be effective, for the principal has led the third party to believe that the agent is dealing on its own account.[95]

(b) THE CONTRACTUAL RELATIONS BETWEEN THE AGENT AND THE THIRD PARTY

An agent who is employed to establish privity of contract between the principal and a third party will usually acquire no rights and incur no liabilities in respect of the contract which is entered in the capacity of agent. But 'it is not the law that, if a principal is liable, his agent cannot be',[96] and the agent may be found to have undertaken personal liability.[97] It is therefore our first task to discover the circumstances in which an agent may be under a personal contractual liability.

87 *Wyatt v Marquis of Hertford* (1802) 3 East 147.
88 *Irvine & Co v Watson & Sons* (1880) 5 QBD 414.
89 (1872) LR 7 QB 598.
90 *Ibid*, 610.
91 *Heald v Kenworthy* (1855) 10 Exch 739, 745.
92 *Irvine & Co v Watson & Sons* (1880) 5 QBD 414, 417 (Bramwell LJ).
93 *Butwick v Grant* [1924] 2 KB 483.
94 *Howard v Chapman* (1831) 4 C & P 508; *International Sponge Importers v Watt* [1911] AC 279.
95 *Curlewis v Birkbeck* (1863) 3 F & F 894. Cf *Drakeford v Piercy* (1866) 7 B & S 515.
96 *Yeung Kai Yung v Hong Kong and Shanghai Banking Corp* [1981] AC 787, 795 (Lord Scarman).
97 See Reynolds (1969) 85 LQR 92.

(i) Personal contractual liability of the agent

Where an agent contracts, as agent, for a disclosed principal, so that the other party to the contract looks through the agent to a principal, it may be laid down, as a general rule, that the agent drops out of the transaction as soon as the contract is made. The agent acquires neither rights nor liabilities. But there are several situations in which the agent is personally liable.

(a) Agent Undertakes Liability. Whether the agent has undertaken personal liability depends on the proper construction to be put upon the conduct of the parties where the contract is oral, or upon the wording of the document and the surrounding circumstances if it is written.[98] There is nothing to prevent both principal and agent being severally liable on, and entitled to enforce, a contract which the agent has made on behalf of the principal, if that was the intention of the parties.[99] The agent may, for example, expressly or impliedly undertake liability for payment,[100] or may be considered to have done so by trade usage.[101] Or the document in which the contract is written may give no indication that the agent was acting as such, although both parties knew this to be the case: 'Where a person signs a contract in his own name, without qualification, he is prima facie to be deemed to be a person contracting personally: and, in order to prevent this liability from attaching, it must be apparent from the other portions of the document that he did not intend to bind himself as principal.'[102]

(b) Agent Party to a Deed. An agent who is party to a deed is bound thereby even though described as agent,[103] except possibly where the agent is acting under a power of attorney.[104]

(c) Negotiable Instruments. An agent who signs as party to a negotiable instrument, such as a bill of exchange or promissory note, either as drawer, indorser, or acceptor, will be personally liable even though words which describe the agent as such, or as filling a representative character, are added to the signature.[105] The agent must go

[98] *Chapman v Smith* [1907] 2 Ch 97, 103. See also *Elpis Maritime Co Ltd v Marti Chartering Co Inc, The Maria D* [1992] 1 AC 21; *Punjab National Bank v De Boinville* [1992] 1 WLR 1138, 1155.

[99] *The Swan* [1968] 1 Lloyd's Rep 5, 13–14.

[100] *Hall v Ashurst* (1833) 1 C & M 714; *Rusholme & Bolton, etc Ltd v SG Read & Co* [1955] 1 WLR 146; *Format International Security Printers Ltd v Mosden* [1975] 1 Lloyd's Rep 37; *Fraser v Equitorial Shipping Co Ltd* [1979] 1 Lloyd's Rep 103.

[101] *Fleet v Murton* (1871) LR 7 QB 126; *Perishables Transport Co v Spyropoulos* [1964] 2 Lloyd's Rep 379.

[102] 2 *Smith's Leading Cases* (12th edn, 1915) 379; *HO Brandt & Co v HN Morris & Co Ltd* [1917] 2 KB 784; *Hichens Harrison Woolston & Co v Jackson* [1943] AC 266, 273; *Tudor Marine Ltd v Tradax Export SA* [1976] 2 Lloyd's Rep 134. Cf *The Santa Carina* [1977] 1 Lloyd's Rep 478 (oral contract); *Seatrade Groningen BV v Geest Industries Ltd* [1996] 2 Lloyd's Rep 375 (signature had to be read in conjunction with other parts of document).

[103] *Appleton v Binks* (1804) 5 East 148.

[104] Powers of Attorney Act 1971, s 7(1), as amended by the Law of Property (Miscellaneous Provisions) Act 1989 and SI 2005 No 1906. This exception probably only applies where the principal is named in the deed: *Harmer v Armstrong* [1934] Ch 65.

[105] Bills of Exchange Act 1882, s 26. Cf *ibid*, s 17. See also Companies Act 2006, s 83. Cf *Bondina v Rollaway Shower Blinds Ltd* [1986] 1 WLR 517.

even further and indicate clearly that the signature is only on the principal's behalf. The addition of the words 'receiver',[106] 'executor',[107] or 'director'[108] will not necessarily relieve the agent of liability; but such expressions as 'for and on behalf of X as agent', or '*per pro*' will do so.[109]

(d) Foreign Principal. Although there is no rule of law to the effect that an agent who contracts on behalf of a foreign principal will be personally liable, the fact that a principal is a foreigner may be of some weight in determining whether the mutual intention of the third party and the agent was that the agent should be personally liable to be sued as well as the principal, particularly if credit has been extended by the third party.[110]

(e) Principal Not in Existence. An agent who contracts on behalf of a non-existent principal (eg a company before it has been incorporated) risks incurring personal liability on the contract so made.[111] At common law this was a question of construction. While the Court may assume that the agent making the contract would be personally liable,[112] there was no rule of law that an agent is automatically a party whenever there is no principal capable of being bound by the agreement.[113] The construction of the particular contract, and the signature on the contract may show that it was made with the principal alone, so that the agent acquires neither rights[114] nor liabilities[115] under the contract. However, section 51(1) of the Companies Act 2006 provides that a contract which purports to be made by or on behalf of a company at a time when the company has not been formed has effect, subject to any agreement to the contrary, as one made with the person purporting to act for the company or as agent for it, and that person is personally liable on the contract accordingly. This provision applies whatever the form of the signature, that is, whether the agent signs on behalf of the company or as the company itself.[116] Moreover, the agent can sue as well as be sued.[117]

(f) Unnamed Principal. An agent who contracts as agent, but does *not* disclose the name of the principal, is also, as a rule, not personally liable on the contract which is made. Yet here too, as where the name of the principal is disclosed, the matter is one of construction.[118] But, although there is a prima facie rule that the agent drops out of the transaction, the terms of the contract or trade usage may again indicate a contrary intention.[119]

[106] *Kettle v Dunster and Wakefield* (1927) 43 TLR 770.
[107] *Liverpool Bank v Walker* (1859) 4 De G & J 24.
[108] *Elliott v Bax-Ironside* [1925] 2 KB 301.
[109] *Ibid*, 307 (Scrutton LJ); Bills of Exchange Act 1882, ss 25, 31(5).
[110] *Teheran-Europe Co Ltd v ST Belton (Tractors) Ltd* [1968] 2 QB 545, 558.
[111] *Kelner v Baxter* (1866) LR 2 CP 174, above, p 683.
[112] *Ibid*, 185 (Willes J).
[113] *Black v Smallwood* (1966) 117 CLR 52 (Australia).
[114] *Newborne v Sensolid (Great Britain) Ltd* [1954] 1 QB 45.
[115] *Hollman v Pullin* (1884) 1 Cab & El 254.
[116] *Phonogram Ltd v Lane* [1982] QB 938.
[117] *Braymist Ltd v Wise Finance Co Ltd* [2002] EWCA Civ 127, [2002] Ch 273.
[118] *Fleet v Murton* (1871) LR 7 QB 126, 131.
[119] *Southwell v Bowditch* (1876) 1 CPD 374, 376; *Hichens, Harrison Woolston & Co v Jackson & Sons* [1943] AC 266; *Perishables Transport Co v N Spyropoulos (London) Ltd* [1964] 2 Lloyd's Rep 379.

(ii) 'Agent' acting as principal

Is it possible for a person who has purported to contract as agent for an unnamed principal, to state that he or she is in fact the real principal? The answer is Yes, since if the other party to the contract was willing to take the liability of an unknown person, it is hard to suppose that the agent was the one person in the world with whom the other party was unwilling to contract. The character or the solvency of the unnamed principal could not have induced the contract. In *Schmaltz v Avery*:[120]

S entered into a contract of charterparty with D. S described themselves as 'agents of the freighter', and it was provided in the contract that, since they were contracting 'on behalf of another party', all personal liability on their part should cease when the cargo was shipped. They then revealed themselves as principals and sought to enforce the charterparty.

It was held that they were entitled to do so. In this case, the 'agent' was allowed to sue on the contract, and by the same token ought similarly to incur liability under it.

(iii) Undisclosed principal

If the agent acts on behalf of a principal whose existence is not at the time disclosed (the 'undisclosed principal'),[121] the other contracting party, when discovering the true facts, is entitled to elect whether to treat the principal or the agent as liable.

The reason for this rule is plain. If T enters into a contract with A, T is entitled at all events to treat A, the party with whom T supposed the contract was made, as liable. If T subsequently discovers that A is in fact the representative of P, T is entitled to choose whether to accept the actual state of things, and treat P as liable, or whether to adhere to the supposed state of things upon which the contract was entered, and continue to treat A as liable.

The liability of the agent continues until the other contracting party has done some act which unequivocally indicates that it regards the principal as the party solely liable.[122]

(iv) Unauthorized acts of the agent: breach of warranty of authority

Where a person purports to act as agent for a disclosed principal but without any authority to do so, the party who was induced to enter into a contract has a contractual action against the agent for breach of warranty of authority (as well as possible claims for the tort of deceit[123] or negligence[124]). A warranty of authority is an implied promise on the part of the professed agent that, in consideration of the other party entering into the contract, the professed agent warrants the existence of a principal and that the contract is within the authority conferred by that principal.[125]

This rule applies not only to transactions or representations which would result in contract, but also to any representation of authority whereby one induces another

[120] (1851) 16 QB 655. See also *Harper & Co v Vigers* [1909] 2 KB 549. Cf *Sharman v Brandt* (1871) LR 6 QB 720.

[121] See above, p 705.

[122] See above, p 707.

[123] *Polhill v Walter* (1832) 3 B & Ad 114.

[124] *Hedley Byrne & Co Ltd v Heller & Partners Ltd* [1964] AC 465, 532.

[125] *Collen v Wright* (1857) 8 E & B 647; *Penn v Bristol and West Building Society* [1997] 1 WLR 1356; *AMB Generali Holding AG v SEB Trygg Liv Holding AB* [2005] EWCA Civ 1237, [2006] 1 WLR 2276 at [60].

to act detrimentally.[126] It is immaterial that the agent had no knowledge or means of knowledge that it was acting without authority, for 'moral innocence, so far as the person who has been induced to contract is concerned, in no way aids that person or alleviates the inconvenience and damage which he sustains'.[127] The warranty is, moreover, a continuing warranty, and therefore the agent is liable even though the authority, though valid at the time of the contract, has, unknown to the agent, been determined, as by the death or mental incapacity of the principal.

FURTHER READING

McMeel, 'Philosophical Foundations of the Law of Agency' (2000) 16 LQR 387

Krebs, 'Agency Law for Muggles: Why There is No Magic in Agency' in Burrows and Peel (eds), *Contract Formation and Parties* (Oxford: Oxford University Press, 2010)

[126] *Starkey v Bank of England* [1903] AC 114.

[127] *Collen v Wright* (1857) 8 E & B 647, 657 (Willes J). See also *Suart v Haigh* (1893) 9 TLR 488; *Yonge v Toynbee* [1910] 1 KB 215.

INDEX